# 19th EDITION

# GUNS
## ILLUSTRATED®

# 1987

## Edited by Harold A. Murtz
and the Editors of Gun Digest

MEMBER OF THE
NATIONAL
SHOOTING SPORTS
FOUNDATION
INC.

# DBI BOOKS, INC.

## About Our Covers

Redfield has been doing things right for many years, and 1987 is no exception. In their line for '87 (and seen on our front cover) is the superb Golden Five Star 3-9x variable-power scope mounted on a Parker-Hale in 270 Winchester. The Golden Five Star series is extensive. You can get a variable Five Star in 3-9x, 2-7x, 4-12x or 6-18x. Of interest to shooters who like fixed-power scopes, the Golden Five Star is also available in either 4x or 6x. Features? Lots of 'em: Multi-coated lenses, ¼-minute click adjustments, one-piece tube construction, a no-cost set of Bulter Creek lens covers and Redfield's written lifetime guarantee.

Also here is the new Redfield All-Sports Widefield binocular. Shown is the 10x50 model, with others in 7x35, 8x20, 8x24 or 6-15x24 (Electric Zoom) also available. The All-Sports binoculars are all of the roof-prism design which makes a compact package for the outdoorsman. Other features include coated optics throughout and a black rubber-armor coating that sheds water, provides a non-slip grip and is quiet should it bump against gun or gear.

On our back cover is the Redfield Magnum-Proof pistol scope in 2½x (4x available, too), mounted on a T/C Contender with Redfield's new 2- or 3-ring (your choice) base. That base, with 3 rings installed, will tame the toughest magnum.

What's next? It's the icing on the cake—Redfield's new Regal VI spotting scope. It has a 60mm objective lens that's U.V. coated, 45° prismatic head that can be rotated a full 180°, center (objective barrel) focusing, 25x eyepiece, 20-60x zoom eyepiece, tripod and rugged foam-padded aluminum case.

*Photos by John Hanusin*

## GUNS ILLUSTRATED STAFF

### EDITOR
Harold A. Murtz

### ASSOCIATE EDITOR
Robert S.L. Anderson

### ASSISTANT EDITOR
Lilo Anderson

### GRAPHIC DESIGN
James P. Billy

### MANAGING EDITOR
Pamela J. Johnson

### PUBLISHER
Sheldon L. Factor

## DBI BOOKS, INC.

### PRESIDENT
Charles T. Hartigan

### VICE PRESIDENT & PUBLISHER
Sheldon L. Factor

### VICE PRESIDENT—SALES
John G. Strauss

### TREASURER
Frank R. Serpone

# CONTENTS

## FEATURES

## DEPARTMENTS

# John T. Amber
# A Look Back

by HAROLD A. MURTZ

Some notes and thoughts on the man who was the guiding light of Gun Digest.

A favorite shot of John in 1981. By this time he had ''mellowed'' considerably (his temper less volatile) but was still ''sharp as a tack'' (pardon the pun, John) and could keep up with the crowd.

"HELLO JOHN," I said into the phone, as I'd done so many times over the past 14 years, "this is Harold. How the hell are you?"

Long pause. "Who?"

"Harold—you know, your able-bodied servant, your slave, the one who writes all of your copy!"

"Oh, yea, yea, yea! Murtz—whaddya know, kid?"

So it went with nearly every call to John, and I was never *really* sure if he was (1) simply trying to be cute, (2) just couldn't hear me (a distinct possibility because all those years of shooting had taken their toll on his audi-

tory functions), or (3) he was just incredibly dense, even after all the years of our working together. You could never be sure what kind of a re-action you'd get from John on the phone.

For those gun-types who came in late, John T. Amber was the editor and guiding light of *Gun Digest* from 1949 through 1979, a 30-year reign (at times of terror!) that saw many gun writers come and go, new devel-opments in the firearms field, and in-numerable rounds fired by him through a dizzying array of guns of all types. John Amber *was Gun Digest*.

The gun fraternity lost a lot of ro-mance and polish when John passed away at the age of 82 at his beloved Creedmoor Farm on January 1, 1986. He shall be missed by generations of shooters, hunters and, in general, gun buffs, who are all indebted to him for bringing us so many years of fine gun-related material.

When John took the helm of *Gun Digest* in 1949 (he started with the 5th Edition), it was a 224-page book chock-full of the kind of information hunters, collectors and shooters thirsted for. In his first year of publi-cation, John was able to include the

A young, clean-shaven John Amber in the mid-1950s with one of his treasures — a Police Model Gatling with six 12-inch barrels in 45-70, serial number 1! The 1883-patent Accles cartridge drum holds 65 rounds. John paid $400 for the gun and five drums.

John was a regular visitor at the annual NRA meetings and loved to handle the high-grade guns on display. His favorite people there seemed to be the custom gunsmakers, with whom he spent hours talking about the finer points of making fine guns. 1973 photo by Ken Warner.

Col. Jim Crossman and John Amber shared the gun scene for many years. Both are/were recognized experts in the field of firearms. Photo taken 1975, Houston, Texas.

Amber was a tough editor and a stickler for accuracy. He was able to bring out the best in a writer and made many not—so—good authors read like Hemingway while still preserving their original style and flavor. John and me discussing a manuscript in his Marengo office, about 1981.

writings of such now-famous names as Maj. Gen. Julian S. Hatcher, Jack O'Connor, Roy Weatherby, Elmer Keith, Col. Townsend Whelen, Phil Sharpe, Charles Askins, and others. With that book John was off and running on a career, a life-long labor of love, that lasted 30 years.

That love of firearms began when John was a boy, when a fond uncle gave him a 22 rifle. Born in 1903, in Freeport, Illinois, John was about 4 years old when the family moved to Chicago where he attended public schools. He was an alumnus of the Illinois Institute of Technology, majoring in Civil Engineering.

John's insatiable curiosity about things historical, mechanical, people and places laid the groundwork for his long tenure at *Gun Digest*. One of his earliest jobs was as a police reporter for the City News Bureau in Chicago. Following that was a spate of different jobs all around the country, for Amber was a restless, moving type—a young man on the go, never content to stay in one place very long what with so much of the world to see and "do." He worked as a dishwasher, section hand, highway laborer, cabin boy (he signed on as a "3rd assistant steward" on a 'round-the-world-bound freighter out of San Francisco), clerk, and, believe it or not, dance instructor. To boot, after a season's work as a Chicago distillery representative the first year of Repeal, he became a roving representative for the old R. F. Sedgeley Company of Philadelphia, makers

of sporting firearms. In 1935 John went to work in Marshall Field and Company's famous Gun Shop. It was there that he made many good contacts in the gun business, a number of great deals, and a name for himself.

Throughout his wanderings, John amassed a couple of good gun collections, both disposed of before coming to *Gun Digest*—one in the Depression days, the other before joining the U.S. Navy for WW II service in the Pacific. His last collection, the one I remember, I was told (by John and others), was his largest and best.

When I first met John at his Marengo, Illinois, office in 1972, I was awe-struck by what I saw there. The office was on the second floor of a bank of stores in the "downtown" section of that sleepy little farm community, the building three-quarters of a century old even at that time. John's "domain" was much like a mini-museum with little semblance of order. Dark and dusty, it measured something like 30 feet by 50 feet, just one big room with a 14-foot ceiling, filled with books, old trophy game heads of past world-wide hunts, reloading tools that hadn't been used in years, ammunition, and guns—lots and lots of guns. Some were leaning against whatever would hold them up, some lying on table or desk, others partially disassembled as if ready to be cleaned. In one corner a 3-foot stack of rifles lay on the floor, neatly piled in layers with blankets separating each tier. When John was busying himself with

Bob Brownell got to know Amber well over the years. An appreciation of good craftsmanship, tools and guns kept them close together. This pow-wow in 1975 undoubtedly had something to do with one of the above.

some matter or another and wasn't looking, I took a quick peek at the guns. From what I could see, they were mostly Trapdoor Springfields, but there was a smattering of other types—a few Remington rolling blocks (high-grade, of course, with tang rear sights, spirit-level fronts, etc.), a couple of Sharps, and others

Right—John and Gun Digest Associate Editor Bob Anderson talking guns after we'd finished test firing one of John's double rifles on his Creedmoor Farm range.

Amber had a number of ''favorite'' guns, one of which was this Wm. Billinghurst buggy rifle which he fairly coveted. It is a caplock muzzleloader with underhammer ignition and detachable buttstock. It came to him complete with a beautifully-figured rosewood veneer case with all accessories, full-length telescope sight and several gold inlays and appliques. It cost John the tidy sum of $150.

Another of John's treasures and what he considered the best (and most valuable) single shot rifle in his collection, was this George Gibbs-Farquharson-Metford he bought in 1951. The gun was brought back from Japan after the war and it's believed to have been owned by someone in the Royal Japanese household. John appears justifiably proud and smug here.

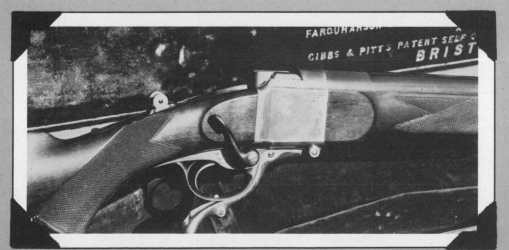

Close-up of Amber's ''Tokyo Treasure'' Gibbs rifle shows the Farquharson action of a scarce form that included a cocking lever in addition to the normal underlever. Gun came with short and long Vernier tang sights, an even 20 front sight apertures, false muzzle, tools, etc. Barrel length is 36 inches!

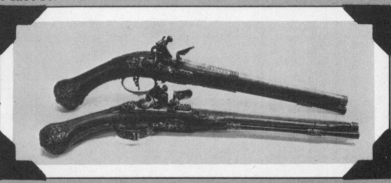

While visiting Amber one day in 1981, I noticed an engraved, gold-inlaid Winchester Model 21 Skeet shotgun standing in a corner of his barn. I don't remember the story behind it now, but it was a beautiful gun. I don't think John ever shot it.

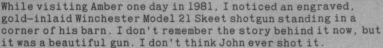

One of John Amber's admitted triumphs in gun collecting was owning this pair of Pietro Manani flintlock pistols of the late Renaissance period. They are 17th century, with barrels by Nicolas Bis, Spanish royal gunmaker.

which I couldn't see clearly. All of them were in *beautiful* condition, lightly oiled.

In the ensuing years I got to see the rest of the collection scattered among the office, the house (Creedmoor Farm, named after the famed Long Island rifle range of long ago), and "the barn," a large outbuilding about 100 yards from the main house.

On many of my all-too-infrequent trips to visit or work with John, I spent more than a few hours with an oily rag wiping down almost every piece in the collection and loved every minute of it. When I'd finish one gun and pick up another, John would tell me the history of it, and how it shot. It took a *lot* of time, but I didn't care. It was an education, and I only wish I could recall half of what I'd been told.

The core of that collection was mostly fine old single shot rifles of every description, and I don't think there was one piece in anything but NRA Excellent or better condition.

Guns were John Amber's life, his passion—his avocation and vocation

rolled into one. When he wasn't shooting or handling them, John read about them. He was a voracious reader and gained most of his knowledge about them in that way. His library exceeded a thousand titles and included many highly valuable old volumes. One piece of advice John passed on to many budding collectors was that for each new gun added to their collection, a new book should be acquired—and read.

Because of his truly tireless research in the lore and history of firearms, it is no exaggeration to say that his combined knowledge of guns, shooting and hunting was second to none in the U.S. However, *he* never considered himself an "expert" in any particular segment—only a "general practitioner" of his craft.

When John retired in 1979, it was not to sit in a rocker on the front porch. Of course, he no longer was in the mainstream of publishing and guns, but he kept quite busy with writing, trips here and there, dealing in collector-type guns, and was even

hawking single-shot rifles and actions for a small-volume European armsmaker. No moss grew under John's feet.

I learned much about guns and shooting from John Amber, and though he had a pretty short fuse and was tough to be around at times, we did manage to spend a fair amount of time together and became good friends. Over the years I was to become a confidant, a sounding board for new whims and ideas, companion, errand boy, co-worker, and student. Some of those roles were pretty demanding, others I relished, but above all, I feel privileged to have known him well.

It would be easy to go on for quite some time about John's accomplishments, his irascible personality, his possessions, but that would simply belabor the point that he was what he was—the best at what he did.

Rather, I think it best now to show a few photos of John T. Amber during his years with *Gun Digest*.

So long, John—see ya kid!  ●

Left—Amber's study was filled
with memorabilia from his many
trips all over the world, and
held a small part of his large
arms library. I took this shot
of him rummaging through his
desk in 1983. He would
constantly forget where he put
things and even ''lost'' a
couple of guns for a month or so
before they mysteriously
reappeared. He was not as neat
and orderly as his copy!

John lived about 70 miles from
Chicago outside the small town of
Marengo, Illinois, and named his
spread after the famed Creedmoor
rifle range on Long Island. He had his
own rifle range (100 and 300 yards)
such as most shooters dream of
owning. The weather vane atop his
garage was a complete Remington
rolling block carbine.

John was nearly always armed as he went about
his chores or walks around Creedmoor Farm,
and this was a familiar sight to visitors as
he bid them *adieu*. So long, John—see ya, kid!

After 75 years, the Government Model auto has been retired. Like the Colt Single Action Army, however, the G.M. will be around long after its military usefulness is history.

# Who Needs The 45?

## by RICK FINES

**Yes, the U.S. military has a new sidearm, and it's a dandy, but there's a lot of whining going on about the virtues of the ol' 45 Warhorse. Here are some well thought-out facts and opinions about both guns that make good sense.**

WE HAVE A NEW service pistol. Finally.

Some 35 years after the 1911-A1 Government Model 45 was judged obsolescent for military issue, we have a new G.I. sidearm that holds its own against any design.

"Standard issue" or not, several U.S. service branches decided years ago that the 1911-A1 was overdue for honorable discharge. The thousands of Smith & Wesson and Ruger revolvers in current military use document

that observation. Those revolvers also debunk the myth that the Government Model has been the "standard U.S. military sidearm" since George Patton was a lieutenant. The 1911 has been an issue pistol, but it has

hardly been the "standard" sidearm. World War I brought the Colt and S&W Model 1917 revolvers. World War II, Korea and Viet Nam saw enormous quantities of 38 Special revolvers issued to combat personnel. A

Compared to a World War II vintage 1911-A1, there's little size difference, but the alloy-framed Beretta has a slight weight advantage. Dimensions of the fatter grip, necessary to handle the double-column magazine, measure no more than ¹⁄₁₀-inch greater than the G.M.

Below—The G.I. Beretta has a business-like matte black finish. Magazine release is aft of the trigger guard in the Colt-Browning position, and is reversible for right- or left-hand use. Grips are molded black composition.

few years back, those tired Colts and Smiths were supplemented by thousands of new Ruger 38s.

I feel a bit odd making these comments, after 20-odd years of shooting, carrying and collecting just about every 1911 variation. The point is not to suggest that the Government Model is a bad design. The pistol was—and is—a superb piece of equipment. But it's time to wake up and admit that engineering has advanced in the 75 years since the first 1911 left Col. Colt's armory.

Until recently, American shooters had little serious interest in auto pistols, except rimfire plinkers, low-powered pocket types and war souvenirs. Until the inconclusive 1953 service pistol trials, the Colt Government Model was the only locked-breech auto regularly produced here. No U.S.-made 9mm pistol was offered until, following the '53 trials, S&W introduced the Model 39 and Colt offered Government Model 9mm variants.

The situation changed in the 1970s, when the 45 Government Model became an overnight civilian success after 60-plus years on the market.

At the same time American shooters discovered auto pistols, the World War II generation of military autos was being retired around the world and replaced with new designs from a host of European manufacturers.

With a few exceptions, the new pistols have features in common, including double-action lock work, 9mm Parabellum chambering, double-column magazine capacity and ambidextrous safety levers.

Interest peaked with the announcement that new service pistol trials would be held to finally replace the old 1911. Interest turned to argument when the Beretta 92 won the trials. Some debates in favor of designs other than Beretta's are persuasive, but the least convincing arguments insist that the 1911 single-action auto is superior to any of the new D.A. pistols,

and that the U.S. should remain the only major power on the planet to cling to the 45 ACP cartridge.

The trials subjected the Beretta to tests far more challenging than any writer might hope to match, so the object of this exercise is to put the most vocal and illogical arguments into perspective—not to rehash the tests.

Yes, I, along with a great many people, am disappointed that the new pistol is not an American design. Neither, for that matter, was the Model 1903 Springfield service rifle, which is considered as American as Sgt. York (who didn't use one) and apple pie. Shooters and collectors have long forgotten that the '03 combined Mauser design, for which we paid a $200,000 license fee, with minor changes to suit American preferences. I suspect that our new Italian-designed Beretta service pistol will soon be considered as American as Lee Iacocca.

Elements of Beretta's engineering composition are original, spiced with touches of Walther and Browning. Appearance is distinctly Beretta, while the locked-breech system is similar to Walther's P-38. The double-action mechanism resembles the P-38, but contains fewer, stronger parts. The recoil spring and business-end of the slide are familiar to anyone who has field-stripped a Browning P35. The safety is reminiscent of Walther practice, but is less prone to malfunction, breakage and accidental discharge than most adaptations of the circa-1920s Ulm design. Unlike some hammer-drop safety systems, which dump the hammer on a potentially breakable safety bar, the Beretta design drops the hammer on a beefy steel web in the slide.

Distinctive Beretta touches include

the thumb-actuated magazine release that is readily reversible for right or left-hand operation, and the standard ambidextrous safety lever. Some writers have commented that the both-ways safety is redundant. A generation ago, sporting arms makers noticed that some shooters are left-handed. Going beyond the sport shooter's question of preference, an injured soldier or police officer might find that his only choice is to shoot with his weak hand. That morbid observation means that ambidextrous operation is more than just a neat idea.

Take-down of the new Beretta is a joy to anyone who has suffered the duty to teach non-shooting types how to hold their mouths correctly when aligning the slide stop with the illusive barrel link of the old Government Model. With the Beretta, it is necessary only to depress a spring-loaded plunger, rotate a captive latch, and pull the upper half of the pistol forward and free of the frame assembly. Reassembly amounts to reversing the drill. There is no barrel bushing to bind and no recoil spring plunger to launch itself across the room.

The stripped Beretta shows mixed lineage. The locking system, with hinged block, is similar to Walther practice, while the recoil spring resembles a Browning. Stripping and assembly are simpler than with the old 1911 auto.

The loaded chamber indicator is another nice touch. A chambered round causes the extractor to protrude slightly from the slide and expose a red marked portion. Pistol condition can be determined by feel or sight, rather than jacking the slide back, as with the 1911.

One quality can't be reduced to numbers. The Beretta feels as though all the parts belong together. The slide cycles to and fro as though it were mounted on ball bearings. The moving parts have a velvet-smooth, precise feel about them. Contrasted to some D.A. autos that feel like wet sand was the factory assembly lubricant, the Beretta action is a refreshing change.

As has been Beretta practice since the 1940s, the bore is hard chromed. External finish is matte black on the steel parts as well as the alloy frame. Grips on the military model Beretta are checkered black composition.

Double-action trigger pull is a quality shooters check first when looking at a new D.A. auto. The sample Beretta's D.A. trigger pull is butter smooth, and scales at 13 pounds; single-action pull breaks at just under 5 pounds.

Another writer pointed out that

part of the double-action lock work is partially exposed, and suggested that an accidental discharge hazard exists. A portion of the Beretta's trigger bar is visible in much the same way as on the P-38. I fiddled and fooled with the exposed part of the trigger bar in an attempt to make the hammer fall, but short of using a mallet and chisel, I could not convince the hammer to drop. If there's fault there, I can't find it.

The greater bulk that comes with a frame large enough to accommodate the 15-round magazine has caused some to question whether small soldiers—particularly women—could handle the pistol. Handing the Beretta to several women of average or below average size and weight caused me to conclude that there should be little trouble. Measuring the frame showed that most dimensions exceed those of the 1911 by little more than $\frac{1}{10}$-inch.

The fixed sights are a luminous two-dot system. The rear dot is larger than the front dot, which is the opposite of my preference. The fact that the top of the test pistol's front sight blade was not perfectly square was a distraction.

Along with the realization that the 45 auto has finally been ordered to the old soldier's home, it's time to address a string of myths that have assumed the stature of "Great Pistol Shooting Truths." Most of these ballistic fairy tales surfaced during the 1970s, and have been repeated so often that we no longer take the time to think when we read them.

Myth Number One questions the need for the double-action auto. Some of the oft-repeated nonsense suggests that the D.A. auto is an answer to a question no one asked. That's a cute turn of phrase, but absolute rubbish. For nearly 50 years, successful new military/police auto pistol designs have featured D.A. lock work. The double-action feature is there for the same reason it is present on modern police and military revolvers—because the pistols are easier for most people to use, quicker to deliver a first shot and safer to handle.

The next fantasy insists that the shooter must "shift his grip" between the first and second shot when firing a double-action auto. That one is difficult to understand. The fingers that wrap around the D.A. pistol frame remain in the same position from first

In the hands of an inexperienced female shooter, the Beretta is a handful, but hardly too big for this 5-ft., 4-in woman to shoot. She hasn't yet read articles written by large men that suggest that small women can't handle the "great big Beretta."

The Beretta was the first pistol this shooter ever held—a situation similar to that which will be experienced by many military trainees. He found the Beretta "easier to hit the target with" than a 1911-A1 45 he shot during the same session.

shot to empty magazine. The tip of the index finger does not move from the trigger. Reality is that the index finger moves the trigger farther in the D.A. fire mode than in S.A. shooting. The "feel" of the double-action auto therefore changes slightly between the first shot, squeezed off with a long pull of the trigger, and subsequent single-action shots. The shooter's grip does not "shift." Adjusting to that nuance of D.A. shooting involves some training, just as all shooting skills demand. If time permits, the D.A. auto may be thumb-cocked in precisely the same manner as older S.A. pistols. A fast first shot, without fumbling with safety levers or quick-draw thumb cocking the hammer, is the obvious advantage of the D.A. auto.

Some brave souls suggest that carrying the double-action auto with the hammer cocked over a loaded chamber is a viable option. Why anyone would want or need to do this is unclear. I would suggest the habit only to people I don't like.

Carrying a single-action auto for defense use complicates the task. Drawing the S.A. auto cocked-and-locked means that the manual safety must be unlatched before firing,

which is a distraction in a stress situation.

One alternative is to carry the S.A. pistol with the hammer down on a loaded chamber, and to cock the hammer as the pistol is drawn, in the style of a cowboy in a TV gun fight. Others suggest that it is preferable to carry the S.A. auto with an empty chamber, and to cycle the slide as the pistol is drawn. Considering that pistols carried for defense use are drawn because they are needed *now,* the thought of pulling what amounts to an empty pistol, then betting that a round will chamber with no hang up, seems a bit chancy.

Interestingly, current Colt advertising for the new compact Officer's ACP endorses empty-chamber carry, with the caution " . . . never chamber a round until you are ready to shoot."

An accidental discharge is a light squeeze away with a cocked S.A. auto, compared to the deliberate action required to trigger a D.A. shot. The danger—and frequency—of accidental discharges has caused a number of police departments (Los Angeles comes to mind) to remove the S.A. fire capability from their issue revolvers. The concern regarding accidental dis-

charge is one good reason why single-action auto pistols, including the Government Model, are about as common among uniformed police as Edsel patrol cars.

Lowering the hammer on a live round is also a problem with the S.A. auto. A combination of perspiration and adrenalin is a good formula for helping that hammer spur to slip away, with a loud "bang" being the predictable result. The Beretta hammer-drop safety, like most modern D.A. designs, allows the pistol to be rendered "safe" with little risk.

Concealed carry with S.A. auto pistols offers a few more hazards. It is easy to inadvertently snag a manual safety from the "safe" to the "fire" position, or even to lose track of the position of the safety. Considering that the victim of an accidental discharge is likely to be the owner of the pistol, I greatly prefer a D.A. auto for concealed carry.

Another odd contention insists that the 9mm Parabellum round is somehow a "minor" caliber; whatever that means. While the 45 ACP uses a heavy, slow bullet, the 9mm pushes a lighter projectile at higher velocity. The result is that the muzzle energy

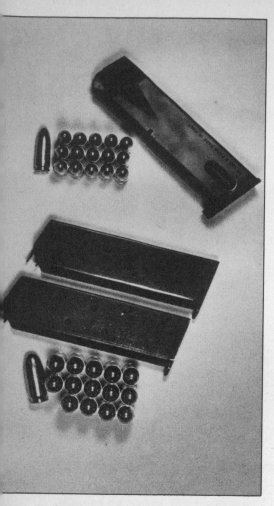

Assuming a round in the chamber, two loaded 1911-A1 magazines still miss—by one round—the firepower available from one loaded 15-round Beretta 92 magazine. Those who spend hours practicing high-speed 45 magazine changes may feel cheated. Unlike the old Colt magazine, the Beretta unit may be stripped for cleaning.

figures of both rounds are comparable.

The fact that light, fast bullets are as effective as slow, heavy bullets was realized by rifle shooters back in the 1890s, who couldn't wait to swap their 45-70s for new 30-30s. Yet, we persist in contriving rating scales that suggest that the only effective handgun rounds are either duplicates of black powder loads, or really heavy numbers that are hardly suited to police or military use.

The late Gen. Julian Hatcher devised a scale that sought to objectively compare cartridge performance. At first glance, the Hatcher Scale appears useful. A closer look leads one to wonder. For example, a 45 ACP load, pushing a 245-grain semi-wadcutter bullet at a leisurely 612 fps is a squib in most anyone's estimation. That pipsqueak 45 load rates 62.5 on the

Hatcher scale. A 357 Magnum load that moves a 158-grain SWC bullet at 1410 fps rates a slightly *lower* 61.8 on the General's scale. The scale also contains some other questionable numbers. The 30 Luger, moving a 93-grain round-nose jacketed bullet at 1220 fps rates lower than the 380 ACP pushing a similar 95-grain bullet moving 265 fps slower. If the object of the scale was to "prove" that slow, fat bullets are more "effective" than small, fast bullets, it worked to the extent that many shooters still buy the conclusion.

This sort of thinking is one of the reasons that so much ink has been devoted to moaning about the "lack of stopping power" of the 9mm. As a matter of perspective, note that the 9mm Parabellum has become the most-used military pistol round in the free world, and is rapidly gaining popularity for police issue. The 45 ACP, in use for about the same length of time, was adopted by the U.S., as well as the great military powers of Argentina and Norway. The latter two nations dumped the round decades ago. Other than in countries to whom we gave the guns and the ammo, or in areas where the standard is "any gun," the 45 ACP has been something of an orphan.

Another factor that figures in suspicion about the 9mm is that no commercial American pistols were chambered for the round until 1953(!), when the earlier military pistol trials were held. While Colt offered the Government Model and the then-new Commander in 9mm and S&W introduced the Model 39, it took a good many years for sales to amount to much.

It's also interesting to note that Browning's earliest locked-breech Colt pistols were chambered for a 38-caliber round that virtually duplicated 9mm Parabellum performance. Military insistence on a 45 led to the Model 1905 and the later M1911.

The story behind that original preference for the 45 suggested that the lousy performance of the 38 Colt revolver in the Philippine Insurrection was responsible for a return to the 45. Writers often suggest that the old Colt round was roughly comparable to the 38 Special. The dimensions might have been similar, but the 38 military round was ballistically closer to the 38 S&W than the 38 Special. While there's no doubt that the Colt 38 military load was weak, we persist in the thought that anything with a similar bore diameter lacks "stopping power," regardless of the power of the round.

When logic and math fail, the best

of the fairy tales comes out of the closet. It goes like this: The (pick one: generic foreign adversary, Viet Cong, burglar) was shot at point-blank range with (pick one: 38 Special, 5.56mm NATO, other) and didn't flinch. The war story concludes with the statement that if the adversary had only been hit by one shot of the narrator's pet caliber, the bad guy would have been picked up bodily and dropped as though hit by a train.

The favorite caliber to pick on, in the absence of anything original to talk about, used to be the 5.56mm NATO rifle round. Now that the 5.56mm is a free-world standard, and even the Soviets have adopted a similar round, the grumbling has died down. Our adoption of the 9mm will surely inspire new variations of this entertaining yarn.

These stories flourish because the study of small arms terminal ballistics is imprecise at best. If the target happens to be wood, metal or paper, empirical data is simple to generate. The question is vastly and unpredictably complicated if the target happens to be human. The variables are such that a single hit from a 22 rimfire may or may not produce an instant stop, while a hit from a 45 ACP or a 30-06 also may or may not produce a "one-shot stop." Those who question that statement should talk with a coroner. None of the fairy tales or pseudo-technical mutterings about "shocking power" change the facts, no matter how often the stories are told.

The final argument in favor of the big, slow bullet makes sense—but is flawed. The 45 fans point out that light, fast bullets may go in one side of the target and out the other, expending much of their energy in whatever they eventually hit. Slow, heavy bullets with less ability to penetrate, as the story goes, expend all their energy in the target, rather than in a wall perhaps a half-block away. Blocks of gelatin, clay or Duxseal are used to illustrate the point. The evidence is compelling, as long as the target does not wear heavy clothing, does not hide behind car doors or walls and contains no heavy bone or vital organs. Since soldiers and cops shoot at targets that do all the above, penetration is important.

The 9mm vs. 45 argument won't end here, nor will the double-action vs. single-action auto debate. The point to remember is that the rest of the world settled those tired questions and got on with business decades ago. American shooters might at least consider doing the same.  ●

# The 270 Winchester

by CLAY HARVEY

Jack O'Connor hunted nearly everything with his beloved 270 Winchester and is shown here with a black bear he bagged in Alaska. A properly placed 130-gr. bullet did the job well.

## O'Connor's Cartridge

A lot of game has fallen to the 270 Winchester over the years, but since 1925 the late Jack O'Connor of *Outdoor Life* fame probably did more to popularize it than anyone. It's one of the most accurate and effective all-round American big game cartridges made.

THE MULE DEER BUCK was nervous. Not scared, apprehensive. He was trotting along a juniper-choked hillside, perhaps 200 yards away from an equally excited hunter who had just plopped his fanny in the sage to prepare for a shot. The buck disappeared behind a juniper; when he popped out on the far side, still pacing a good clip, the nimrod swung the bead front sight of his Winchester three or four feet ahead of the animal's chest and touched off. As the

hollow "whomp" of a gut shot assailed the shooter's ears, he saw the deer sag at the hindquarters. It sagged, but it did not go down.

The hunter felt nauseous. Either his buck had run behind a juniper and toppled over, or it had used the tree as cover, and run off downhill out of sight. Moving to his right and downwind, the hunter climbed the hill until he was above the juniper where he had last seen the buck, then pussyfooted along as quietly as possible so

as not to alert the deer if it were still alive.

The buck was lying beside the juniper, swiveling its head from side to side. Aiming just behind the shoulder, the hunter closed the book. The buck sported a fine non-typical head, eight points on one side, seven on the other. The year was 1925. The hunter was Jack O'Connor. The buck was probably the first ever killed with the spanking new 270 Winchester Center Fire, certainly the first in Arizona.

O'Connor was amazed at the damage done to the deer's abdominal cavity and lung area. That fall, he lent his rifle—a Winchester Model 54, forerunner of the famous Model 70—to a couple of other hunters who slew deer with it. He said it really smacked them down.

Unsatisfied with the stock on that original Model 54, O'Connor had it restocked by R. D. Tait of Dunsmuir, California, and dressed it up with a Lyman 48 receiver sight. Then he used it for several years to knock off some more mule deer and a couple of antelope. He noted that it more often stopped a deer in its tracks than a 30-06 with 150 grain bullets, and shot a bit flatter in the bargain. Additionally, it seemed to massage his shoulder with a less heavy hand than did his 'ought-six. He was sold.

But along came the Depression and away went that 270—for eatin' money. Several years hence, O'Connor bought a barrel from Bill Sukalle of Phoenix, Arizona, had it mated to a flat-bolt Mauser action and chambered to 270. Al Linden, the famous stockmaker from Bryant, Wisconsin, carved out a handle from straight-

Harvey's friend Jimmy Michael shooting the Winchester Model 70 Featherweight in 270. He says the straight stock made the recoil seem inconsequential.

Below—Remington's Model 700 Classic *averaged* 1.36 inches with Winchester 110-gr. PSP varmint ammo. None of the handloads would beat the best factory stuff. Bottom left—This 1.42-inch group with the Classic is representative of what the gun would do. Load noted on the target.

130 SIERRA SP
54.7/IMR 4350
REM 9½M
WIN CASE

1.42"

grained Bosnian walnut, checkered it, and billed O'Connor for 75 bucks. (For that tidy sum, Linden furnished the walnut and a trap buttplate!) Frank Pachmayr mounted a 2½-power Noske scope in Noske mounts fitted to his own form-fitting bases.

O'Connor hied off to the Cucurpi Mountains of Sonora and bumped off a whitetail with his new 270. The buck was about 150 yards away; Jack nailed him with a 130-grain spitzer and the deer never knew what hit him.

With that same rifle, O'Connor shot a trainload of coyotes and jackrabbits. He also took his best desert mule deer with that 270, a monster that he guessed weighed from 230 to 240 pounds on the hoof.

A list of game O'Connor took with various 270s over the years would fill the rest of my space, but it includes black bear, elk, sheep, goat, moose, caribou, grizzly, and a host of African game. He hunted with the 270 all over the world, from Sonora to the Yukon, from Chad to Botswana. No centerfire rifle cartridge has ever been so inexorably linked with one man as were the 270 and Jack O'Connor.

But Jack O'Connor was not the only user of the 270 Winchester, just the most celebrated. Despite the fact that the 270s birth stirred scarcely a ripple on the surface of the shooting press way back in 1925, the new load did manage to sink a few roots. Lt. Townsend Whelen was sent a Model 54 from the Winchester factory about the same time Jack O'Connor bought his. Whelen stuck a Zeiss Zielklein scope on the bridge, with a dial graduated by Griffin & Howe. He found it to be more accurate with the factory 130-grain soft points than any factory hunting load he'd ever tried in a 30-06, something O'Connor had also not-

ed. The flatter trajectory provided by the zippy 270 and its welterweight slugs enabled Lt. Whelen to connect reliably at longer ranges than he'd been able to with any other cartridge before that time. Whelen wrote up the new load in the shooting journals.

Hardly anyone else did. The incumbent gun editor of *Outdoor Life* never got around to reviewing the 270; Captain Paul Curtis of *Field & Stream* took a look at it, decided it wasn't as good as the 30-06, and dismissed it. The *American Rifleman*, journalistic factotum for the NRA, finally got around to publishing some dope on the 270 two or three years after it

came out. The 270 was not off to a hot start.

Then in the '30s, Monroe Goode of *Sports Afield* printed some kind words about the 270. Townsend Whelen was writing it up. When O'Connor was signed by *Outdoor Life* in the early '40s, the 270 took off. It has scarcely slowed down since.

Not for lack of trying! Remington took aim at the 270 with their 280 Remington back in 1957; scarcely a dent in 270 sales did it make. Winchester went after its own offspring with the 284 Winchester in 1963; if you had all the 284 rifles ever built stuck in your shoe, you probably wouldn't limp. The hot 6.5s were around, Remington with the 6.5 Remington Magnum and Olin with the 264 Winchester Magnum. One is dead, the other moribund.

Only the 7mm Remington Magnum has attained much popularity, and I'm not so sure the Big Seven is actually competition for the 270. To my way of thinking, the Seven Mag is a bit more specialized than either the 270 or the 30-06, or the 308 Winches-

Above—The Model 70 Featherweight shoots as good as it looks. With Federal Premium 150-gr. SPBT ammo, this rifle *averaged* 1.27 inches at 100 yards. Right—The average of the three groups on the left of the target shows the 1.27 inches.

ter for that matter. The latter loads are all-rounders for game *up to* elk and moose; I feel that the 7mm mags are all-rounders for game from elk and moose *up*. Sure, the Big Seven can be used on 100-lb. pronghorn; the 270 can and has been used on 1200-lb. Alaskan brown bear. Let's just say that neither is ideal for either application and let it go at that.

Most of the 270s reputation was established with the 130-grain pointed soft point bullet. Not all. Jack O'Connor often used a 120-grain Barnes handloaded to about 3200 fps. He wrote that when he shot a deer with one of those wicked little bullets, the animal seemed to disappear it collapsed so fast. For elk and moose,

Jack felt that 130-grain controlled-expansion bullets—such as the Winchester Silvertip—were just right.

Townsend Whelen used the now-defunct 140-grain Modern Gun Shop two-diameter spire point bullet. Loaded over 57.0 grains of IMR-4350 (which seems a tad warm to me), he quoted a muzzle speed of about 3100 fps. Five-shot strings ran under three inches with this bullet, at 200 yards! That was more than 30 years ago!

Interestingly, of the dozen bull moose killed by Jack O'Connor with a 270, not one was dumped with a single shot. Furthermore, he wrote that he had never seen a moose dropped with one shot from any cartridge. Townsend Whelen's first kill with the 270 was a big bull moose. He decked it from 75 yards. With one shot. Whelen subsequently shot another moose, a caribou, and several deer with his Model 54 in. 270. All were one-shot kills.

Enough hunting exploits; let's go back to accuracy. O'Connor wrote many years ago something that I have reread many times. It can be found on page 220 of *The Rifle Book*, and goes: "It has been my experience that the average factory-produced .270 will outshoot the average factory-produced .30-06 with standard factory ammunition." For years I held that passage sacrosanct, unquestioned.

Loaded with Lyman dies, these bullets all gave good results. The Sierra 130-gr. SP turned in the best over-all accuracy.

These two powders are excellent for the venerable 270, and provided good results.

Hodgdon's H4831 is a traditional performer in the 270, and the newer H4350 is nearly as good.

Among other loads, Winchester offers a 100-gr. varmint load (left) and a 150-gr. big game loading.

Hornady offers these three big game loads, including the only factory-loaded 140-gr. bullet popular with some hunters.

But over the years I worked with several 30-06 sporters, factory guns, and found them to group very well. Very well, indeed. I began to doubt. After a while I became convinced: O'Connor was wrong. The average 30-06 is fully as accurate as the average 270. Maybe more so.

The most accurate 270 I've ever shot was a Ruger No. 1 I owned in the late '60's. I have misplaced the targets but if memory serves, that Ruger 270 would group some load or other around an inch for five shots, on the average, at 100 yards. For years it was to remain the most accurate sporter I'd tested.

However, upon reflecting I was not certain just how many loads I'd tried in that rifle, how many groups were included in that one-inch average. Since that time I have worked with very few 270 rifles, and those few with factory loads only. I tested one lot of factory ammo in a couple of 270s back in 1977; one averaged just under 1¾ inches, the other just under 2¼ inches. Didn't seem remarkably accurate to me.

Of the 30-06 rifles I've tested, every turnbolt would group under 1½ inches for an average of five shots with select handloads. Some would do as well or better with factory ammo. My three most recent 30-06s—a Smith & Wesson Model 1500, a Kleinguenther K15, and a Savage Model 111—all averaged under 1¼ inches for five shots with their favorite handloads.

To be fair to the 270, I decided to acquire a pair of them, subject them to a strict testing regimen using both handloads of known accuracy and factory loads of good reputation. I called U.S. Repeating Arms and nabbed a new Featherweight Model 70 on loan, then I went to Phipps' hardware and bought a Remington 700 Classic over

the counter. (That was in case US-RAC had slipped me a hand-selected wringer for a writer's sample.)

On the Featherweight Model 70 I mounted a 2-7x Redfield Low-Profile in Redfield rings and bases. The Classic carries a 4x Weaver Wider-View in Bushnell mounts. Both glasses are excellent, with superb resolution and a flat field. Made the group-squeezin' easier.

I fired three to five five-shot groups from each rifle, benchrest at 100 yards, using three handloads and five factory. A load table is nearby, but I'll hit the high spots. The Featherweight was the more accurate of the two with its best load, by a slight margin; it grouped 1.27 inches with Federal's 150-grain Premium Soft Point Boat-

tail. The Remington was only a hair behind the 1.36 average using Winchester's 100-grain soft point factory stuff.

Aha! Neither gun would equal any of the three 30-06 rifles mentioned above, using the pet handload in each. O'Connor *was* wrong! Rue the day.

But something was nagging at my mind. I reread the passage in *The Rifle Book*. And there it was, the fat fly in the porridge, in black and white, as Jack had written it and I had read but not absorbed it: ". . . average factory-produced .270 will outshoot the average factory-produced .30-06 *with standard factory ammunition*." (Italics mine.) Back to the target files.

Only one of the 30-06s would go under 1½ inches with a factory load, the Savage 111; it grouped into 1.47 inches with 180-grain Federal factory soft points. The Smith & Wesson printed 1.54 inches with 165-grain Frontier SPBT factory loads; no other load would stay under two inches. The Kleinguenther is too new to have been tested extensively with factory ammo. It's best showing was one five-shot string in 1.38 inches with Remington Accelerators, of all things.

Both 270s had fired many groups under two inches. In fact, each rifle would average under two inches with six of the eight loads! Over-all average for the Classic was 1.81 inches for all loads tried; for the Featherweight the average was 1.90 inches.

O'Connor wasn't wrong—Harvey was.　　●

## 270 Winchester Data

| Bullet | Charge/ Powder | *Group Avg. M700 | M70 | MV fps | ME fp | ES | Sd | Remarks |
|---|---|---|---|---|---|---|---|---|
| 100 Remington PSP | 58.0/WW 760 | 2.62 | 2.40 | 3293 | 2404 | 37 | 18 | Fastest load tested; not very accurate |
| 100 Speer HP | 59.9/IMR 4350 | 1.64 | 1.85 | 3268 | 2367 | 108 | 54 | Accurate in M700 |
| 130 Sierra SP | 54.7/IMR 4350 | 1.75 | 1.55 | 2943 | 2501 | 48 | 24 | Shot well in both rifles |
| 100 Winchester PSP (Factory) | | 1.36 | 1.84 | 3277 | 2617 | 123 | 47 | Most accurate in M700 |
| 130 Federal SPBT Premium (Factory) | | 2.07 | 1.82 | 2962 | 2532 | 54 | 28 | Acceptable load in both rifles |
| 130 Winchester PSP (Factory) | | 1.54 | 2.71 | 2964 | 2536 | 147 | 58 | Accurate in M700, poor in M70 |
| 150 Federal Partition Premium (Factory) | | 1.91 | 1.77 | 2771 | 2559 | 31 | 13 | Uses Nosler Partition bullet |
| 150 Federal SPBT Premium (Factory) | | 1.62 | 1.27 | 2819 | 2647 | 15 | 7 | Most accurate in M70; excellent in M700 |

*Average for several five-shot groups, fired from 100 yards, bench rest.

Loads chronographed in M70 Featherweight (22-inch barrel) using Oehler M33 Chronotach/Skyscreen system. Average temperature 65°.

ES-Extreme Spread　　Sd-Standard Deviation

Handloads listed were safe in both test guns, and are listed for reference only. If used as a guide, start below and work up carefully.

# Bucks, Krico, and Bucks

TWO MULE DEEER STEPPED out of cover on the snowy hillside about a ½-mile from where we were standing. Even before giving them a closer look with my binoculars, I knew that they both had to be bucks. We were in scrub cover, had the wind on the deer, and were motionless. As a result, those bucks had no idea they were being looked over. My companions, guide and outfitter Jerry Martin and Todd Smith, Feature Editor of *Petersen's Hunting* magazine, both had their binoculars out and were also taking a close look.

It was the fourth day of a five day mule deer hunt in Montana. The second annual Buck Knives buck hunt was rapidly drawing to a close. Fellow gun scribe and close friend Jim Woods had organized the hunt as one of the series of Buck Knives buck hunts, on behalf of Chuck T. Buck, President of the giant knifemaking

Turpin (right) with guide-outfitter Jerry Martin and the very determined buck.

## by TOM TURPIN

**All is not as it appears, as you'll read here. The author goes forth into the field with a scope that *looked* okay but wasn't. It could have cost him a nice deer, but it all worked out in the end.**

firm. Both Chuck and his son, Chuck B., Jr. (not really a junior, but using Sr. and Jr. was a convenient way to distinguish between them) were in camp with us.

Jim had booked a five day trophy mule deer hunt with Buckhorn Mountain Guide and Outfitting Service, (P.O. Box 9, Dayton, Wyoming 82836). Six hunters would make the trip: the Buck duo, Jim and I, Steve Comus, Gun and Hunting Editor of *Western Outdoors* magazine and Todd

Smith of *Petersen's Hunting.* Dave Romano and Jerry Martin, owners and operators of Buckhorn, along with guide Ed Gouine, cook Dennis Conger and Cowboy, a big black Lab belonging to Dennis, made up our camp.

When Jim invited me on this hunt several months earlier, I contacted GUNS ILLUSTRATED editor Harold Murtz to see if he had a suitable rifle lying around the office that needed a workout. As it turned out, he had a Krico Model 600, chambered for one of my favorite calibers, the 270 Winchester. The only drawback was that the rifle was sans scope. A quick call to Dietrich Apel, president of Paul Jaeger, Inc., fixed that dilemma. Shortly, a Schmidt and Bender 1.5x6 variable scope and a set of EAW mounts for the Krico were on their way to Arizona to be married up with the rifle.

For my money, the 270 caliber is pretty close to ideal for mule deer

any role, in the design process. I must, of course, admit that function is far more important than looks in a using rifle. Being the glutton that I am, however, I want both attributes in my own rifles.

When I managed to get the package open, I found about what I had expected. To be brutally frank, for my taste in rifles, the Krico was not very attractive. I must here add that the Krico I received was a pre-Beeman import. The Krico Model 600 currently being imported and marketed in the country by Bob Beeman is a far more handsome rifle and no comparison cosmetically to the earlier version. Functionally, however, they are the same. As later events were to prove, that is a big plus.

This Krico was really a plain Jane. The walnut stock was finished in the typical Germanic fashion, using pure linseed oil. I have nothing against

instead of being rounded. On the plus side though, the checkering is hand cut and runs about 18 lines per inch. The wood to metal fit was quite good and the stock fit me well.

The metal work, as opposed to the stock, was beautifully done. I found no flaws in the fit and finish of the metal. The action itself was smooth as glass and the trigger had a crisp, clean break at about 4 pounds. As later events on the range and in the field demonstrated, the Krico functioned flawlessly. There were no failures of any kind, nor did I expect any.

Again, I would like to emphasize that the rifle is a pre-Beeman import and the currently imported version has eliminated the majority of my objections. I also add that all of my objections were cosmetic in nature, and no two tastes are alike. What I personally find to be aesthetically pleasing might very well bore another to

A model of function, if not cosmetic beauty, the Krico Model 600 in 270 Win. did its job perfectly. Right—The Schmidt and Bender 1½-6x variable scope in EAW quick-detachable mount looks right at home on the gun.

hunting. Just for the record, Steve Comus selected a Browning single-shot rifle in 7mm Rem. Mag., Todd Smith chose an old but immaculate Remington Model 725 in 284, Jim Woods a new Heym SR-20 Classic in 270, Chuck Sr. a Ranger Arms custom 270 and Chuck Jr. a Weatherby Fibermark in 270 Weatherby. As you can see from the list, I was not alone in caliber selection.

In due time, a package arrived from Editor Murtz. As I began unpacking the box, I did so with some reservations. I was familiar with the Krico product, and was well aware that Krico made a high quality rifle. However, cosmetically, the Teutonic taste of most of the German firearms manufacturers and my own are at least 180 degrees apart. German manufacturers are primarily concerned with function and innovation in rifle design, with cosmetics playing little, if

pure oil finishes—in fact, I prefer them. The way it is done in Germany however, leaves the wood almost black. Any figure or color that might have been present in the blank is effectively disguised by the oil. I assume the oil is heated and the stock dunked into it until it has soaked up as much as the wood will absorb. In addition, the stock design was typical of German rifles, a Monte Carlo comb and fairly skimpy and boxy fore-end. The fore-end itself is almost square

tears. My taste in women, cars, whiskey and rifles is particularly personal and I would not expect agreement from anyone else.

As the late Elmer Keith so often said, "The proof of the whiskey is in the drinking and the proof of the rifle is in the shooting." I don't think anyone can seriously disagree with that philosophy. With that in mind, I headed to the range with the Krico. I didn't put a sling on the rifle before the range session as all my slings are equipped with quick-detachable swivels and the Krico had non-detachable swivels. I was later to regret this move.

I drove out to Jim Woods' spread and we gave the Krico and his Heym a workout. As both rifles were chambered for 270, we took an assortment of factory ammunition to try in the rifles. When all the smoke had cleared, Jim settled on Federal 130-grain loads and I on the Frontier Hornady 130-grain number. Both rifles were giving three-shot groups that were hovering around 1 inch center-to-center, striking 3 inches high at the 100-yard range. The Krico even produced one 3-shot group of just ½-inch. That is outstanding accuracy from any rifle. Both Jim and I felt that our rifles were ready for the trek to Montana.

In the afternoon, after returning from the range, all that remained to be done was to mount the sling and pack the rifle for the trip. Although I have mounted hundreds of slings previously, I did something differently that day. Like an idiot, while mounting the sling, I dropped the rifle! It hit hard on my shop floor, landing on the objective lens portion of the scope tube. A thorough visual inspection, however, showed no apparent damage. At dawn the next morning though, I was enroute back to the range to check it out.

My first shot was some 18 inches high at 100 yards. A few shots and scope adjustments later, my shot printed again exactly 3 inches high. I was beginning to run low on ammunition and proceeded to make my next mistake. I didn't shoot a 3-shot group, but was content with the one shot printing where I wanted it. I took the rifle back home, packed it up and awaited D-day.

Our group assembled at Stapelton Airport in Denver and then flew on together to Sheridan. We were met at the Sheridan airport by Dave Romano, one of the partners in Buckhorn Mountain.

We had a lazy morning next day as we weren't scheduled to depart for camp until 1:30 in the afternoon. At the appointed hour, Dave, Jerry and Ed rolled up in their 4WD pickups and we headed for Montana. Enroute, we stopped off at the local rifle range to check out our rifles. Most of the group required just one shot to ensure that their rifles were still on. On the other hand, my rifle was again 18 inches high. Even a total dummy should have expected something was amiss, but not me. I attributed it to rough baggage handling. More rounds and more adjustments, and my final shot was 3

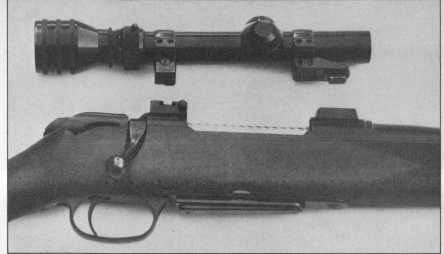

One of the advantages of using the EAW mount system is that different scopes can be used on the same rifle, each with its own rings and zeroed separately. The mount returns to zero each time the scope is replaced. The safety, just behind the bolt handle, is a rather long, curved and checkered affair that's easy to find even while wearing gloves. Rifle has a detachable box magazine.

While preparing for his Montana trek, Turpin zeroed the Krico 270 using Frontier 140-gr. loads. The best target shot was this ½-inch, three-shot group at 100 yards.

inches high. I stopped shooting.

Dave and Jerry lease hunting rights on several private ranches in Southeastern Montana, north of Sheridan, Wyoming. For a campsite, they had selected an old abandoned homestead. A couple of existing structures were rebuilt to provide a kitchen and dining area, as well as a shed for hanging the deer. It also provided an outdoor privy. All sleeping however, was done in tents. I shared a large wall tent with the Bucks, and Jim,

Steve and Todd shared the other. Each tent had its own wood burning stove, as well as mattresses laid out on the floor. This eliminated the need for bringing our own cot or air mattress. It was a very comfortable and efficient camp. After dinner and a couple sundowners that first evening, the snow started falling in earnest.

During dinner that first evening, we paired up for the hunt. I would hunt with Chuck Sr., guided by Dave. Todd and Chuck Jr. would hunt to-

Four tired but happy hunters, left to right: Todd Smith, Jim Woods, Steve Comus, and Turpin. The racks on the tent behind them include those taken by the Bucks.

The author (left) and writer Jim Woods pose with their very respectable racks taken during the snowy hunt that wasn't without its frustrations and anxious moments.

gether guided by Jerry, and Jim and Steve would go out with Ed. Chuck Sr. and I flipped a coin to determine who would get the first shot and Chuck won. After all the formalities of deciding who would hunt with who, and which would get the first shot, we called it an early evening and turned in.

My down bag hardly seemed to have gotten warm when I heard Jerry building a fire in the tent stove and rousting us out for breakfast. The time had arrived. During the night, it had snowed a fair bit and we had some 4 inches of the white stuff on the ground. The thermometer stood in the mid-teens, ideal weather for hunting mulies.

After a hearty breakfast, we headed off in different directions. Each of the three groups would be hunting on a different ranch, separated by several miles. Using the 4WD vehicles, we could cover a lot of territory. We would drive to a particular area that Dave wanted to check out, and once there, scout it on foot. The first area we checked out was a ridge overlooking a large valley. It wasn't even full daylight when, directly below our vantage point, out pranced a nice four-pointer with his harem of three does. When we first spotted him, he wasn't more than 70 to 80 yards away, but was intent on putting some distance between us. Though a very nice buck, he wasn't quite good enough to be a super trophy. He needed to live for another year or two before reaching that category. Chuck passed on him and so did I. It was, however, a super beginning for our hunt.

Steve Comus drew the first blood. When we got back into camp that first day, Steve had a nice four-pointer hanging in the shed. The second day, both Chuck Jr. and Todd scored. Each took a beautiful four-pointer with nice spreads and heavy beams. Chuck Jr.'s buck turned out to be the best

one taken by our party, with Todd's not far behind. At this point, we changed partners. I went with Jerry, Jim with Ed, and Chuck Sr. remained with Dave.

Chuck Sr. filled on the third day, taking a very nice three-pointer. He was a very high and wide buck, and quite large bodied. Four down and two to go. By the end of the third day, only Jim and I had not taken our deer. Both of us had seen numerous bucks, but were holding out for a grandfather. At times, the hillsides were literally full of deer but, so far, neither of us had spotted the one we wanted.

As the hunt proceeded, the weather continued to deteriorate. The temperatures were steadily dropping and the snow continued to fall. The final days of the hunt, the highs were in the teens and the lows hovering around zero. The winds also drifted the snow, making it quite deep in some areas and leaving the ground almost bare in others.

On the fourth day of our hunt, Todd Smith decided to tag along with Jerry and I to observe and take pictures. I was very lucky that he did. We had parked the truck and hiked a ½-mile or so when we spotted the two bucks mentioned earlier.

When I got the glasses on them, the first buck was an enormous fork-horn, the biggest I have ever seen. He was being chased by a beautiful 5 x 4. Although one heck of a nice buck, the 5 x 4 was smaller than the fork-horn. At any rate, I hadn't come all the way to Montana for a fork-horn so Jerry and I decided to go after the 5 x 4.

When the two deer dropped over the ridgeline out of sight, Jerry and I left Todd behind and started our stalk. We reached the point where the deer had been with no difficulty. The country dropped off sharply on the other side of the ridge and we carefully inched our way along the ridgeline, trying to spot the buck below us. Their tracks

in the snow showed clearly the direction they had taken. After what seemed to be an hour, but was probably closer to 10 minutes, Jerry spotted him.

He was straight down the hill at a range of perhaps 250 yards, give or take a yard or two. I don't think he'd spotted us, but he was jittery. Nothing was available to use as a rifle rest, so I dropped into a sitting position and started my aim. The buck was standing with his rear end toward me, offering no other shot. My rifle was (I thought) zeroed to be 3" high at 100 yards, so it should be dead on at about 275 yards, and only slightly low at 300. Both Jerry and I had estimated the range at 250, but shooting downhill as I was, one will always shoot low. Keeping all this in mind, I held the crosshair at the root of the tail and squeezed the trigger. The buck didn't fall! Neither Jerry nor I heard the bullet smack, but neither did we see an impact on the ground. Had I missed the deer completely, we should have seen the bullet strike the snow, but we didn't.

Naturally, the deer was off and running after the shot. Jerry headed down the hill like a billy goat, with me slipping and sliding through the snow behind him. We managed to remain in cover and made it to a small

way of apparent damage. I did see one shot that broke the deer's leg, but couldn't see any other damage. I had very few rounds of ammo with me, and in short order, I was out. Jerry took off after the deer while I back-tracked, as fast as I could go, to pick up a spare rifle from the truck. That was about the only smart thing that I had done.

I finally was able to labor back to the ridge line, going almost straight up through the snow, to where I could see Todd. Through a judicious appli-cation of hand signals, I got the mes-sage across to Todd to head back to the truck and pick up the spare rifle.

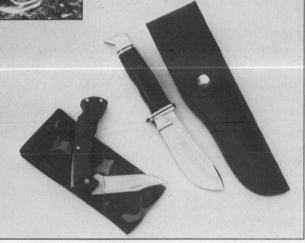

Left—Chuck Buck, Sr. (right) and guide/out-fitter Dave Romano give Buck knives a work-out on Chuck's buck. Below—The Bucklight folder (left) and Buck "Skinner" models lived up to everyone's expectations.

in a fine trophy for me. Without their assistance however, there is no way I would have gotten him.

When we field dressed the buck, we found a wound through the ham and into the intestines. I believe that was the result of the first shot as that was the only shot I had from the rear. If that is true however, it's mighty strange that he stopped on the hillside to chase does. At any rate, I had my buck but not in the style I wanted.

Jim took his buck on the fifth and final day of the hunt. A very nice three pointer, this one turned out to be the heaviest one taken. Field dressed and weighed on a reasonably accurate scale, he weighed 175 pounds. The others ran between 153 and 160 pounds, field dressed.

With Jim filled out, the head caped, carcass skinned, etc., we packed up camp and headed back to Sheridan, ending a fine hunt. Our hosts, Chuck Buck and his son, were fine hunting companions, great sports, and all around good guys. The knives Chuck brought with him for us to use really got a workout, and they did the job they were designed to do extremely well indeed. I used one of his new Bucklight folders (Model 422) for ev-erything except skinning, and his skinner (Model 103) for that chore. Although I own and use a number of custom knives, no knife could have performed better than the two I used on the hunt.

Chuck's eyes really lit up when we arrived in camp and he saw that Jer-ry was carrying a Buck personal mod-el as his working knife, and had been doing so for more than 20 years! Chuck even gave us all a lesson on sharpening knives. That little chore is something that everyone does from time to time, but that very few are able to do well.

The Krico Model 600 functioned flawlessly, and the Schmidt & Bender scope is one of the very best scopes I have ever used. It was the fault of nei-ther that I banged up the scope through my careless act. I would be delighted to take either or both on a hunt again. The best equipment in the world won't overcome dumb ac-tions on the part of the user.

One of the first things I did upon re-turning from the hunt was to take the rifle to the range again. You can guess where the first shot went—yep, 18 inches high again! The scope is back in Germany now, in Hans Bend-er's capable hands, for repair of the er-rant reticule. I am sure that Hans' let-ter back to me will contain a few terse words of reinforcement. I can hardly wait. ●

scrub-covered knoll where we had a good view of the side hill in the direc-tion the buck had gone. I must admit, I didn't have much hope as, generally, once shot at an old buck will put as much distance as he can between you and him. Lo and behold however, the buck went about 1000 yards or so from where he was standing at my shot, and took a *lively* interest in the several does on the hillside. He finally offered me a broadside shot at about 250 yards. I assumed a good solid sit-ting position once again and shot. Once again, it was as if I were loaded with blanks.

Well, to spare the reader the not too admirable details, I shot several times at the buck without much in the

He did so and joined me on the ridge.

We then set out in pursuit of Jerry. To make a very long story somewhat shorter, we finally caught up and fin-ished off the buck. He was a beauty, as the photo nearby shows. However, without the help of Todd and Jerry, he would have been lost. By the time I got to him, I was so tuckered out that I was not at all sure that I would be able to make it back to the truck. The combination of snow, uphill and side-hill climbing, too many cigarettes and too much time behind a desk really took its toll on me. Todd and Jerry on the other hand, seemed to be just warming up. The combination of Jer-ry doggedly tracking the buck, and Todd bringing the spare rifle resulted

# The Model 1886.

LEVERGUNS. They're special in many sportsmens minds. I have a personal fondness for carbines, levers, repeaters, saddleguns or whatever others might call them. I'm sure that growing up watching westerns at my hometown movie theater or on television had a lot to do with my love for levers. John Wayne, Chuck Connors and a few other western heroes made their rise to fame with Winchesters in hand.

If you have a use for levers in the practical sense or you are simply a history buff or collector, the Winchester Model 1886 or, simply, '86 as it's affectionately known, will or should have special meaning to you. At the time of its introduction, it was one of the biggest breakthroughs in modern gun design.

In the mid- to late 1800s, other Winchesters were doing their share to aid in settling the West. Leverguns like the Winchester Model 1866, the Models 1873 and 1876 were popular among those who needed firepower with reasonable accuracy.

If you're somewhat familiar with the Model 1886, you certainly recognize it as a Winchester and probably as one of the all-time best levers to ever make the American scene. But, did you realize this gun was actually the brainchild of John M. Browning? A bit confusing you might say. Let's turn back the clock a hundred years or so and see how this Browning/Winchester came about.

To begin with, you should know a little about John M. Browning. He was born in 1855 in the small town of Ogden, Utah, where his father, Jonathan Browning, had settled just a few years before. He was one of the original Mormon pioneers who were driven out of Illinois because of his religious beliefs and forced to move West.

Many of the Mormons settled in what is now Salt Lake City, Utah, but there were smaller communities such as Ogden (which is about 30 miles north of Salt Lake City) where Mormon families settled as well. Jonathan Browning was a well known gunmaker in Illinois and in Utah. He actually made most of the firearms the Mormon pioneers carried when they moved West.

When he settled in Ogden, he built a small shop where he made guns and tools for the settlers. He also served his community as a mechanic and an engineer. Realizing the importance that Jonathan's shop played in his family's survival, it's not hard to picture John M. Browning and his younger brother Matt growing up alongside their father while he worked and tinkered in his shop. Gun parts, scraps of iron and metal became the toys of their childhood. John M.'s mechanical aptitude was incredible as-

John M. and Mathew Browning's first shop and arms factory in downtown Ogden, Utah. Left to right: Sam Browning, George Browning, John M. Browning, Mathew (Matt) Browning, Ed Browning and one of their gunsmiths (name unknown). Photo courtesy Browning.

# Then . . .

# And Now

Following close on the heels of success with its recreation of the Model 1895 rifle, Browning has brought forth another lever-action winner that was designed by John M. Browning—the big Model 1886 chambered for 45-70.

## by REX THOMAS

suming his limited education, and soon manifested itself as he designed and manufactured his first firearms long before the age of 20. His creative genius soon surpassed the ingenuity of his father.

Before long, John M. Browning and his younger brother Matt set up their own gunmaking business. From his early teens and throughout the remainder of his life, his mind was always busy developing new and better firearms. He was never satisfied, with what had been and was being used, and strived for improvement constantly.

It is known that many of the Winchester lever rifles available at that time left something to be desired for those who wanted firepower and a rifle that could handle the 45 and 50 caliber black powder cartridges of that era. John Browning was very aware of what sportsmen wanted and demanded and it seems that he used earlier vintage Winchesters as models for improvement. It was during 1882 and 1883 that John tinkered with the idea of a new gun that could handle the larger calibers. Until that time, there simply was no lever gun available that was built to withstand the pressures of 45 and 50 caliber cartridges.

Sometime during 1883, John and Matt were visited by Winchester's T.G. Bennett. He was authorized to buy the manufacturing rights to one of Browning's single-shot rifles. Through verbal agreement, John agreed to accept $8,000 for the patent and the rights to manufacture what later became known as the Winches-

This interior shot of Browning's first shop shows John M.'s workbench. Hardly a model of neatness and order, it's interesting nonetheless.

The Brownings aparently had an early-day sporting goods store as well as a machine shop. This ad appeared regularly in the late 1800's.

One of the many variations of the Model 1886 Winchester was this half-mgazine style with round barrel. The options were nearly limitless and allowed the buyer to tailor the gun to his own tastes (or pocketbook).

ter High-Wall. But, while Bennett was in Utah, John showed him a handmade wooden model of a lever-action rifle that would, in theory, handle the large caliber rounds. Bennett quickly realized the possibilities and demanded that when the first working model was ready that he have first chance to buy the patent for Winchester.

In late 1884, John and Matt made their first trip east to visit Winchester and present the first Model 1886. The main difference in Browning's new gun was a pair of vertical locking lugs and elimination of the toggle-link system that was then being used in the Winchester Models 1873 and 1876. What John had done was to combine the best qualities of the lever action repeaters of earlier Winchesters with the camming and bolt locking methods of then popular single shot rifles. It was a step that would forever change the course of modern gun design.

After a short visit with Bennett in New Haven, John and Matt returned home minus their prototype and very wealthy men. Although the exact amount is not known, Winchester his-

torians seem to agree that Browning received about $50,000 for the patent and manufacturing rights to the new gun.

The first Winchester Model 1886 levers were available in 1886—the model designation assuming the year of introduction.

From that time forward, Winchester had total control and the new gun was an instant success. It was the only lever-action repeater that could handle the internal pressures of 45 and 50 caliber cartridges. Before long, it was available in an array of calibers including 45-70 U.S. Government, 40-82 W.C.F., and 45-90 W.C.F. in the year of its introduction. One year later, it was also available in 40-65 W.C.F., 38-56 W.C.F. and 50-110 Express. During later years it was available in 40-70 W.C.F., 38-70 W.C.F., 50-100-450 and 33 W.C.F.

With so many caliber options, the Model '86 was obviously being used for many different purposes and Winchester found that sportsmen wanted various options for their new rifles. As a result, numerous model variations came about. These included field-grade rifles, fancy sporters and high grade rifles, lightweight versions, carbines and muskets. There were also full-stock and half-stock versions, full magazine and half maga-

zine models, as well as take-down models and some with extra sets of barrels. Other variations or options included double set triggers, Lyman windgauge tang sights, peep sights, Sheard sights, receiver sights, octagon barrels, round barrels, half-round barrels, sling swivels, "Winchester slings," straight stocks or pistol-grip stocks. Barrels could be special ordered in lengths from 22 to 36 inches and some models were sold with a take-down cleaning rod that stored out of sight right in the buttstock of the rifle. You could actually order practically any combination of features you so desired.

Record books will tell you that the reign of the Model 1886 Winchester drew to a close in 1932 when production ceased. By that time some 159,994 rifles had been produced. Many of these rifles are still in use today by Winchester lovers who refuse to retire them under lock and key. There are many more, though, in the hands of collectors who recognize true collector value. All they want is to handle and admire these old Winchesters and wonder what stories the guns might tell of days long since gone.

There is no denying the popularity of the Model '86 or the significant roll it played in changing lever-action gun design. It is and probably always will be one of the most popular rifles in the eyes of serious gun collectors. Considering total production to be less than 200,000, it's easy to assume there are just not enough to go around. For those of us who aren't fortunate enough to own our own original Winchester Model '86 there is new hope, thanks to Browning of Morgan, Utah. This fine arms company is reintroducing the *Browning* Model 1886. The Model '86 has, in a sense, come home. It's sheer coincidence that just 100 years later Browning is now producing the famous rifle originally designed by the founder of the company. A limited number are available and are expected to be of high interest to collectors. They are chambered only for 45-70 Government and are available in Grade One (field grade) or High Grade versions. The latter has a

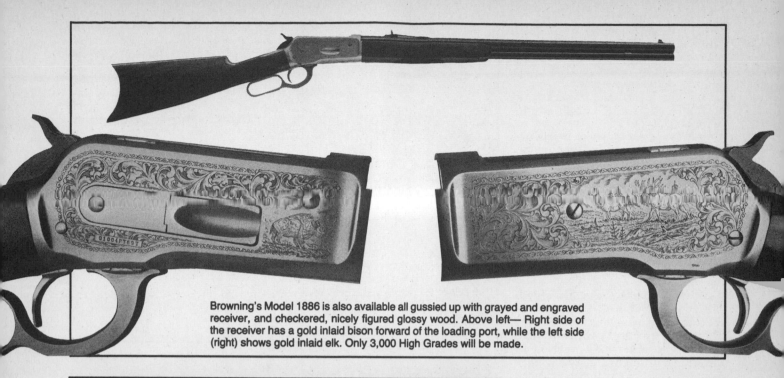

Browning's Model 1886 is also available all gussied up with grayed and engraved receiver, and checkered, nicely figured glossy wood. Above left— Right side of the receiver has a gold inlaid bison forward of the loading port, while the left side (right) shows gold inlaid elk. Only 3,000 High Grades will be made.

Top left— The top tang of the Browning '86 is stamped with the model designation, as was the Winchester. Above— Rear sight is a semi-buckhorn style with ramp elevation adjustment; it's drift-adjustable for windage. Left— The front sight is a post with gold bead dovetailed into the barrel and, therefore, drift adjustable.

grayed steel receiver, scroll engraving and gold inlayed elk on one side of the receiver and bison on the other. There will be only 7,000 Grade One rifles and but 3,000 High Grades.

You may recall that in 1984 Browning also sold a limited number of Browning Model 1895s. They were also produced in two grades and in the same quantities. Obviously, the new '86 Brownings are meant to be sold to those who purchased the Model 95s. And although this seems to imply the beginning of a continuous set, there is nothing concrete to go on at this time. There are strong rumors, though, that 1987 may be the year for a Browning Model 1871. Knowing this may determine whether or not you want to buy one of the few Browning Model '86 leverguns.

Of special interest here is an additional 2,000 Model 1886 rifles that will be available in Montana as a special Montana Centennial edition. Montana's centennial is not until 1989, but this special edition will be ready for sportsmen in late 1986. These rifles will have the Montana State Seal, a grizzly and a bison on the receiver but more on that rifle, and how to locate one, later.

I had the opportunity to work with both a Grade 1 and a High Grade Browning Model 1886. They are, in almost every sense, exact reproductions of the original, full-magazine Winchester Model 1886. The main difference is an inertia firing pin in Browning's new version. The Grade 1 is a beautiful rifle with well executed wood-to-metal fit. The two-piece, straight grip stock is select walnut with very little figure, no checkering and a satin finish. I was personally disappointed in the plain-Jane look of the wood.

All metal parts are richly blued. The gun has a 26-inch octagonal barrel with an adjustable, semi-buckhorn rear sight and an open, gold bead front sight. Over-all length is 45 inches and it weighs a hefty 9 pounds 5 ounces. It takes a man to carry such a heavy rifle very far. I later found the over-all weight to be a definite advantage in reducing the effects of recoil and minimizing muzzle jump. It also has a crescent metal buttplate and a full length tubular magazine that holds 8 rounds.

The High Grade '86 is basically the same rifle dressed to kill. It has a high grade walnut buttstock and fore-end with beautiful figure, glossy finish, and cut checkering running 14 lines to the inch. The lever and receiver are grayed steel and the trigger is gold. Both sides of the receiver have scroll engraving that surrounds two wildlife scenes. The right side has a bison set off handsomely by a unique gold plating and hand engraving process. The left side features a cow and bull elk, also in gold. The actual game scenes were original works of art by Leon Parson, the famous artist from Rexburg, Idaho, who does much of the artwork for *Outdoor Life* magazine and who sells his highly sought works throughout the U.S.

I did my test firing with the Grade 1 Model '86 and used both Federal 300 grain hollow-point ammunition and Remington 405 grain soft point ammunition. I used only open sights and shot from a solid bench at ranges of 50 and 100 yards. Numerous five-shot groups were recorded at these distances to give an over-all view of accuracy, loading, feeding and extraction.

I want to mention that I was expecting very uncomfortable recoil because of the crescent buttstock, large caliber cartridges and the amount of lead I'd be throwing at each squeeze of the trigger. I was very surprised to find that the recoil wasn't unpleasant at all. In fact, it was only about half of what I was expecting. I would say that the amount of recoil I felt at the shoulder was even less than a standard 30-06 bolt-action rifle. Even the 405 grain Remington ammo was not uncomfortable. I also noted that there was very little muzzle jump. I'm sure this was due to the weight and length of the barrel, and weight of the rifle.

I began five-shot groups at 50 yards using both Federal and Remington ammunition. After several groups, I found that both brands were grouping well and there seemed to be no prefer-

With the action open, it's easy to see the locking bolts as well as their recesses in the breech bolt. This feature is part of what made the gun as popular as it was because of the strength it offered for the large caliber chamberings. Browning stamps the serial number on the right side of the receiver.

The author was able to print this five-shot 1⅝-inch group at 50 yards using Federal 300-gr. hollow point bullets.

Because of the '86s weight, Thomas found the recoil of the new 1886 not at all unpleasant—about like that of a 30-06, maybe a bit less.

ence for either load. Groups with Remington ammunition measured 2⅛, 2¼, and 1¾ inches. Federal ammo grouped at 2¼, 1⅝ and 1⅞ inches.

At 100 yards, Remington ammunition averaged groups of just slightly over 4 inches. Federal ammo did slightly better, averaging 3⅞ inches.

During testing, I had no trouble with misfires, extraction or ejection but did note that when the lever is cycled down and another cartridge is fed onto the cartridge carrier and lifted up into the loading position, that it takes a little extra effort or push to complete this part of the loading cycle. I can't say if this will be a long term problem or if it will eventually work itself out as moving parts wear together.

I was pleased with the accuracy test results and felt like the Browning Model 1886 performed somewhat better than expected. I intend to do some more testing with handloads and if the gods are willing, I hope to put the iron sights on the ribcage of a big bull elk next fall in the Bob Marshall Wilderness of Montana. But, that re-

minds me . . . I was going to tell you more about the limited edition Montana Centennial 1886.

This unique Model 1886 is actually the brainchild of Robert (Bob) Bradford of The Powder Horn in Bozeman, Montana. After several years insistence, he managed to talk Browning into supplying some 2,000 Model 1886 rifles to be engraved as he specified. They will be similar in design and quality (but with different serial numbers) to the Browning High Grade 1886, but the scenes on the receiver will include a bison designed by Scott Huntsman—an artist from Bozeman, Montana; the Montana State Seal; a gold ribbon that says, "Montana 1889-1989;" and a grizzly bear.

These rifles are to commemorate Montana's Centennial which takes place in 1989. Rifles should be available in late 1986. The going rate for these is $999.50. However, if you get your order in early and provide a $500 down payment, the total price will be reduced to only $899.50.

If you would like to know more about the Montana edition, Bob Bradford is your best source of information. You can write him at The Powder Horn, P.O. Box 849, Bozeman, MT 59715, phone 406/587-7373.

As you can see, 1986 is a very big year for the Winchester Model 1886. What was the best levergun 100 years ago is this year of high interest to levergun lovers and collectors alike.

If you are a hunter with a fondness for levers, buy yourself a Grade 1. If you desire something fancy, go for the High Grade or the Montana Centennial edition. And, if you are a firearms collector, you should have noticed by now that Browning seems to have started a series of limited production, Winchester reproductions. First, there was the Model 1895 and now the Model 1886 produced in the same quantities. Rumblings from within the walls at Browning (although they're officially unconfirmed rumors) lead me to believe 1987 could be the year for reintroduction of the Winchester Model 1871. After reviewing Browning's past ten year history of various limited edition guns, it wouldn't surprise me in the least to see the Model '71 as the next in a series of Browning-made vintage Winchesters. ●

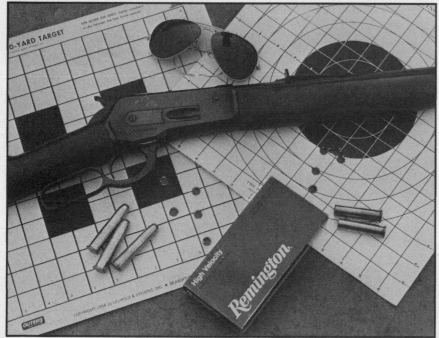

Remington 405-gr. soft point loads gave this five-shot 100-yd. group of 3⅜ inches (left target), and at 50 yards the same load went into 2⅛ inches (right target).

Thomas shooting his 1885 Winchester chambered for 32-20. Though it's 90 years old, the rifle is very accurate. It has little recoil, is relatively quiet and is powerful enough to take small game—all fun gun attributes.

# Loafin' Totin' Fun Guns

Four of the author's handguns which fit the fun gun requirements, top to bottom: S&W Model 15, 38 Spec.; Ruger Super Blackhawk, 44 Mag./44 Spec.; Ruger Blackhawk, 45 Colt; S&W Model 25-5, 45 Colt. All have adjustable sights.

FEW OF US TODAY depend on a firearm in the same sense that our ancestors did. We don't daily fire a gun to ward off attackers and neither do we use a firearm to provide supple fare for the dinner table on a regular basis. Nor do we fashion clothing or other items from the hides of animals that we might down in the woods during a survivalistic sojourn. Clearly, the situation is markedly different today compared to what it was decades or centuries ago. We no longer *need* guns as a means of perpetuating our existence (save the rare instances of warfare or for the protection of lives and property). Our forefathers used firearms as working tools, not as objects of leisure, as we now employ them, for the most part.

I am of the opinion that all guns are to be shot, at least occasionally. Many other enthusiasts are of the same

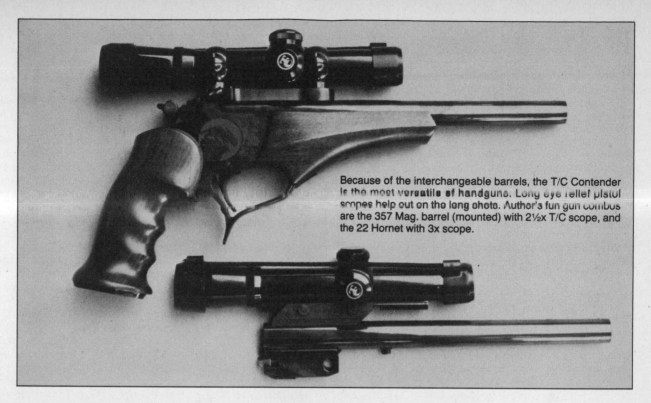

Because of the interchangeable barrels, the T/C Contender is the most versatile of handguns. Long eye relief pistol scopes help out on the long shot. Author's fun gun combos are the 357 Mag. barrel (mounted) with 2½x T/C scope, and the 22 Hornet with 3x scope.

This shooting sport is serious business, of course, but that doesn't mean you can't have fun at the same time. Here's one man's thoughts on guns that can be used for shooting at less than serious targets—varmints, small game and the beastly tin can.

## by MIKE THOMAS

mind, and would never buy a gun strictly for use as a wallhanger. We feel that a fine firearm was designed, manufactured, and sold to be fired. Many collectors may not share our philosophy, but we can easily and pragmatically justify our line of reasoning. A firearms enthusiast may meticulously care for a new gun, but combating nature's elements (rocks, tree limbs, rain, snow, and mud) will eventually prove nature the winner. As they say, "The first scratch is the worst." It all boils down to "use that gun."

We all have a favorite rifle or handgun. If we are fortunate enough to have a large personal inventory of firearms, we may have even three or four guns or more that we like to shoot better than the rest. Our reasons for such favoritism may be varied, but the reasons are unimportant.

A "fun gun" may not give benchrest accuracy, its appearance may leave something to be desired, and it may not be of custom quality. But de-

spite all this, we have confidence in it. Such assuredness is worth a great deal more than cosmetic appeal. We are familiar with the trajectory of a bullet fired from the gun and we know the limitations of the cartridge for which the gun is chambered. At 25 yards, we can make consistent head shots on rabbits and squirrels. At the same distance, we can "kill" ten out of ten beer cans. At 50 yards, or even 100, we can drop "big game" like an occasional turkey or a coyote.

What are the requirements for a "fun gun?" Obviously, there are no rigid guidelines. I have done no formal research in this area, but hopefully my years of experience with a variety of fun guns make up for a lack of in-depth technical study. Consequently, I have come up with some flexible qualifications which are practical ones and have proven effective for me in the selection of fun guns, be they rifles or handguns. They are as follows: reasonably light weight, chambered for a cartridge which provides non-ex-

istent or very light recoil and low muzzle report, reasonably good accuracy (100-yard groups of less than 4 inches), sights (iron or glass) of sufficient quality to take advantage of the gun's accuracy potential, and the capability of firing a bullet that provides sufficient killing power on animals to the size of coyotes, yet is not overly destructive to the carcasses of small, edible game.

When talking about fun guns, the 22 Long Rifle almost immediately comes to mind. The 22 rimfire is probably the king cartridge of the fun guns. However, in spite of its usefulness for plinking and small game hunting, it cannot be classified as the perfect "all-round" fun gun cartridge. In a particular area where turkey, fox, coyote, javelina, or similar size game and varmints abound, the 22 proves to be lacking in killing power. If such animals are not likely to be encountered, then the 22 is quite satisfactory. Most guns chambered for the cartridge are capable of good to excellent accuracy. It goes without saying that such ammo is the cheapest available. The 22 Winchester Magnum Rimfire betters the performance of the Long Rifle, but it, too, is still a cartridge that minimally fits into the list of fun gun cartridges. The ammunition is also rather expensive.

A number of centerfire cartridges sufficiently fill the bill in terms of accuracy, power, low or minimal recoil, and light muzzle report. They are more flexible in their adaptability to specific situations than the rimfires. For the handloader, this flexibility allows the performance of these cartridges to be enhanced, and, quite naturally, the cost of ammunition, compared to factory ammo, is considerably decreased. The list includes (but is not limited to) the following cartridges: 22 Hornet, 22 Jet, 218 Bee, 25-20 Winchester, 32-20 Winchester, 38 Special, 44 Special, and the 45 Colt. Most of these have been around for a long time but are just as useful today as they ever were. Because of the age of these various cartridges, there are lots of old but very serviceable guns available on the used market that fit the fun gun parameters.

As I've said, the cartridge list is not necessarily complete. For the sake of brevity, however, no real need exists to go on endlessly by mentioning such candidates as the down-loaded 44 Magnum or a reduced lead-bullet load for the 30-06. These *are* suitable fun gun cartridges, but I think you get the picture.

Loafin', totin' fun guns are in plentiful supply and can often be had for quite reasonable cash outlays. Possibly this is because fun guns may be a fad that hasn't caught on yet.

The list of rifles and handguns (new and used) that readily adapt to fun gun utilization defies any sort of orderly tabulation. However, some treatment must be given to a random sampling of what is available.

For the handgun enthusiast, calibers such as the 38 Special, 44 Special, and 45 Colt are available in a multitude of revolvers, some very old, some very new. Many old Colt and Smith Wesson revolvers are still around in 32-20 caliber. Ruger and Harrington & Richardson have both recently introduced revolvers chambered for the new 32 H&R Magnum (more or less in the same ballistic category as the 32-20). The Thompson/Center Contender single shot, with its interchangeable barrel system, is available, and different barrels can be had in just about any of the fun gun calibers. With proper loads, a fairly accurate semi-automatic pistol, such as a 9mm or 38 Super, can also qualify as a fun gun, providing the user can shoot it well.

Although there is a large selection of handguns in various chamberings that can be classified as fun guns, this in no way compares with the assortment of usable rifles and carbines. Lever actions, bolt actions, and single shots dominate the field. The numerous Winchester and Marlin lever actions are naturals as fun guns. Likewise, for today's reproductions of the old Winchesters—the Rossi Model 92 Saddle Ring Carbine in 38 Special/357 Magnum or 44 Special/44 Magnum, or the newer Marlin lever actions in the same calibers. There also are bolt action rifles in 22 Hornet caliber. Many older rifles are often discovered in 218 Bee, which slightly improves the performance level of the Hornet. Thompson/Center and custom barrel makers make rifle and carbine barrels (and stocks) to transform the Contender into a longarm. Barrels in many different fun gun chamberings can be ordered, and at reasonable cost. Many old Winchester low wall single shots are still in good shooting condition and can often be picked up for much less than many would imagine.

My personal preferences? I'll name a few handguns and rifles I consider to be fun guns. With handguns, I find the Smith & Wesson Model 15 in 38 Special with a 4″ barrel to be excellent. It has adjustable sights, a decided advantage for any fun gun. Power is adequate, ammo cheap, and the noise and recoil aren't objectionable. The T/C Contender with a 10″ barrel in 357 Magnum and a 2½x scope allow the full potential of the 38 Special to be utilized. An optional 10″ barrel with 3x scope in 22 Hornet is in place on the basic T/C frame about as often as the larger caliber barrel. Using factory loads or the home-brewed variety, rifle-type accuracy is possible.

A Ruger Super Blackhawk 44 Magnum revolver with 7½″ barrel compliments the ballistic attributes of the old 44 Special cartridge. Handloading to "soup-up the Special can be done, but this removes the cartridge from the fun gun class. To date, this is the most accurate revolver round I've worked with. It does a splendid job on small game and doesn't do a lot of damage to the meat.

Most of the strongpoints of the 44 Special can also be had with the 45 Colt cartridge. I have found the performance of the two cartridges to be almost identical, with a very slight accuracy edge going to the Special. From my experience, the best accuracy is obtained in either cartridge using heavy lead bullets loaded to approximate factory ballistics (800-900 fps). For the 45 Colt, I favor either the S&W Model 25-5 with six-inch barrel, or a 7½″-barreled Ruger Blackhawk single action. I haven't had the opportunity to test the Winchester Model 94 lever action in 45 Colt, but it definitely should fit in the totin' fun gun category and would make a perfect companion piece for a revolver of the same caliber.

I use several rifles and carbines as fun guns. For those which handle cartridges that interchange with handguns, I use the same load interchangeably to enhance familiarity and to eliminate the confusion of having to keep track several different loadings. The Rossi Model 92 SRC is in my gun cabinet in both 38 and 44 calibers. Magnum ammo is seldom used in either gun. Such a gun is accurate, light and very compact. A Savage 340 bolt action in 22 Hornet has proven to be very useful over the years, particularly with its 4x scope in place. The Hornet has considerably more punch than the 22 rimfire, but when firing the Hornet the difference is hardly noticeable due to the low

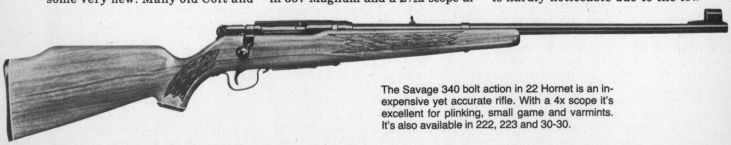

The Savage 340 bolt action in 22 Hornet is an inexpensive yet accurate rifle. With a 4x scope it's excellent for plinking, small game and varmints. It's also available in 222, 223 and 30-30.

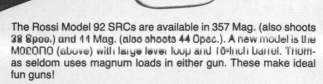

The Rossi Model 92 SRCs are available in 357 Mag. (also shoots 38 Spec.) and 44 Mag. (also shoots 44 Spec.). A new model is the M92ONO (above) with large lever loop and 16-inch barrel. Thomas seldom uses magnum loads in either gun. These make ideal fun guns!

Five cartridges which fit Thomas' requirements for fun gun shooting, from the left: 22 Hornet, 32-20 Win., 38 Spec., 44 Spec. and 45 Colt.

The author has had excellent results with economical lead bullets in his fun guns. From left: 51-gr. 22-cal. gas-check bullet for the 22 Hornet from Lyman #22415 mould, sized to .225″; 115-gr. Lyman #311316 gas-check sized to .312″ for the 32-20; 150-gr. 38 Spec. bullet; 250-gr. Lyman #429244 gas-check, sized to .430″ for the 44s; and a Keith-style 255-gr. Lyman #454424, sized to .454″ for the 45 Colt.

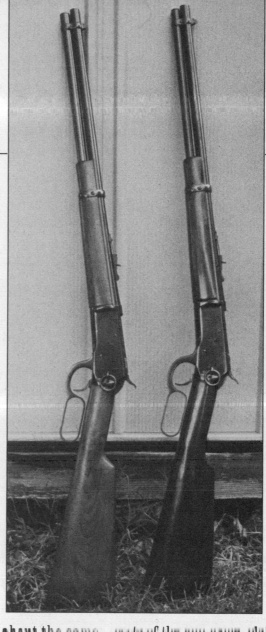

noise level and lack of recoil.

My "ultimate" fun gun is something of an antique. A Winchester 1885 low-wall single shot in 32-20 caliber, it was made in the latter part of the 19th century, and has a heavy 28″ octagon barrel. Two sets of factory sights make the rifle quite versatile. The regular elevator-type semi-buckhorn rear and front post are fine for 50-yard shooting. For increased range, the tang-mounted adjustable peep and globe front allow the shooter to draw a very fine bead. The 32-20 cartridge is a real pipsqueak by modern standards, but fits the fun-gun mould perfectly. Winchester 100-gr., lead-bullet factory ammo chronographs at 1100 fps through my rifle. My handloads are comparable, with a 115 gr. bullet at about the same speed. The low-wall weighs more than a lever action carbine, but is certainly not heavy. There is no discernible recoil. Muzzle blast is very low and accuracy is excellent. A lot of these old guns are still around at fair prices, but I'll admit I had difficulty finding one with a good bore.

Fun guns are the most used as well as the most useful guns in my conglomeration of firearms. I suspect this is the case with many other shooters. For those of us who sometimes become too deeply involved in the very technical (and sometimes frustrating) aspects of the gun game, plain, simple, and inexpensive fun guns provide a welcome escape. When I turn to such "toys" for enjoyment, I rid my mind of such intricacies as sectional densities, ballistic coefficients, wind-drift, and case-head thrust. I don't worry about why a $1500 bench gun won't shoot better than ½-inch groups at 100 yards because I'm too busy toppling tomato cans with a $100 rifle that won't shoot a ½″ group at 10 yards, let alone 100. Fun guns have a calming effect that makes the whole sport seem simple again—just like it ought to be. ●

# The Mediocre MAS:

## A Look At the French Model

## 1936 Service Rifle

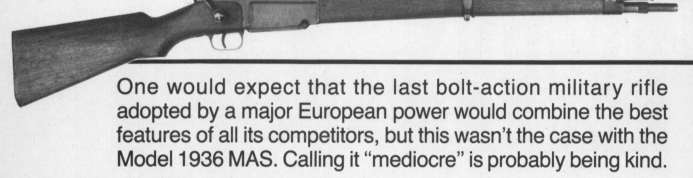

One would expect that the last bolt-action military rifle adopted by a major European power would combine the best features of all its competitors, but this wasn't the case with the Model 1936 MAS. Calling it "mediocre" is probably being kind.

WHAT WOULD YOU expect of the very last bolt-action fighting rifle to be designed—and adopted—by a major European power? Most probably, you'd expect such a rifle to incorporate, as far as possible, all the best turnbolt features that technology had developed. You'd anticipate finding absolutely superb sights, such as those appearing on most U.S. battle rifles. You'd look for a large-capacity magazine, as on Britain's Lee-Enfield. You'd demand superlative accuracy, similar to that of a Swiss K.31. You'd want to see a fine trigger action, as on a peacetime Mauser. You would, of course, expect a workable safety system, as nearly all rifles possess. And, you might even desire a fine appearance, perhaps like an '03 Springfield's.

Well, would you believe that, were you to hold Europe's last bolt rifle in your hands right now, what you'd have is . . . none of the above? The gun you'd have is France's MAS Model of 1936—as thoroughly mediocre a long gun as it is possible to imagine. The MAS, incredible though it may sound, is a five-shot turnbolt, one with no sort of manual safety at all (!), that was designed contemporary with our own Garand semi-auto and Russia's

SVT-38 self-loader. It is thus an anachronism: a bolt-action—and not a particularly advanced one—engineered in an era which had already recognized the self-shucker as the path to the future. So how did so uninspired an arm come to "make it big" in a nation which, popular opinion to the contrary, wasn't really all that inept vis-a-vis weapons design? (The French were, as of 1940, developing a faster prop-driven fighter, the Bloch 157, and a better destroyer, Fantasque-class, than anyone else on Earth, but you don't read much about that in the histories.) We may discover an answer to that question if, prior to our testing of a sample MAS 1936, we investigate the story of the MAS's creation and development.

Interestingly enough, the history of the MAS M1936 rifle begins not during the early '30s when design work on the gun commenced, but rather in the dark year of 1917, when France was still at war with Germany. "Les Allemands" would sue for peace within a year, but on the battlefield this was hardly noticeable: France continued to suffer many more casualties than she could inflict. And thus the French Army high command, in an effort to introduce a "wonder weapon"

which might alleviate matters, pushed into service the 1917 RSC (more commonly termed the "St. Etienne")—the Allies' very first semi-auto combat rifle.

Now the RSC was a fascinating brute: 52 inches long, almost 12 pounds empty, in 8mm Lebel caliber, and fed by a five-shot magazine. And the effort expended on its behalf was no small one: more than 86,000 RSCs were completed at Saint Etienne Arsenal and issued to key units at the Front. But alas, the gun simply didn't work. It was, for one thing, not a totally de-bugged design, for it had been rushed into production with little thought given to such niceties as developmental trials. (As we know today, it's nearly impossible to design a workable auto-rifle around a rimmed cartridge like the 8mm Lebel anyway.) In addition, the mud of the trenches raised absolute hob with the RSCs complex internal workings, and the guns jammed endlessly. Hence, Fusil Mitrailleur RSC Modele 1917 was an abysmal and costly flop—one that caused vocational heads to roll in high places in France. The lessons to be learned from this entire "RSC experience" were not lost upon career-minded French officers.

# by ROBERT T. SHIMEK

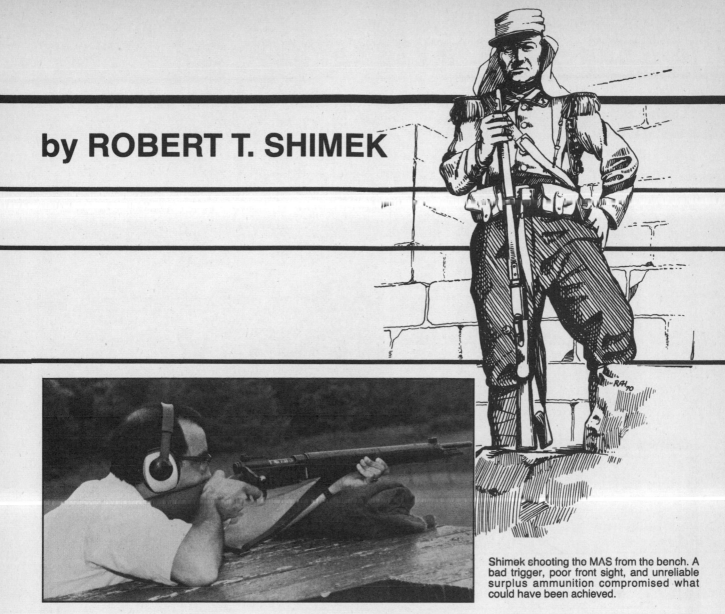

Shimek shooting the MAS from the bench. A bad trigger, poor front sight, and unreliable surplus ammunition compromised what could have been achieved.

It is not surprising, then, that when in 1930 it came time to choose a successor to the long-time-standard Berthier bolt rifle, the *selbstladegewehr* was given wide berth. After all, wasn't the next war likely to be fought in the mud too? And weren't the British—co-victors in La Guerre Mondiale—stolidly staying with the turnbolt? And weren't the Germans—stung, too, by their World War experience with self-loading rifles and saddled with Versailles' research restrictions—unlikely to field anything but a bolt-action? And weren't those designers who *were* trying to build a serviceable auto-rifle still, as of 1930, having one deuce of a time coming up with something that worked under combat conditions? Hence the French decision to stay with the bolt gun.

It may, of course, be asked at this point just why France ever elected to replace the old Berthier anyway: one

five-shot mid-bore turnbolt would seem to offer only limited advantages over another. But the answer here is to standardize cartridges. As of 1929, the military had finally ditched the old 8mm Lebel round in order to adopt a cartridge more suitable to machine gun use. The new cartridge had been the 7.5mm MAS, a modern rimless effort that propelled a 139-grain .308-inch diameter bullet at 2675 fps. This round had soon found an ideal vehicle in the M1929 Chatellerault machine gun, which the Army had quickly taken to its bosom. But it was, of course, unwise to have the service rifle chambered for a round different from the standard machine gun's, added to which the Berthiers in service were becoming decrepit. Hence the call for a new rifle.

Said call was answered some three years later when Manufacture d'Armes de Saint Etienne introduced

its MAS Model of 1932. This gun was basically an MAS 36 sans refinement: it previewed the engineering that would characterize the M1936, but it was not without faults. And thus it was built in trial quantities only; the Army would not accept it until fully four years' worth of improvements had been incorporated into its design. It was this improved M1932 which became known as the Model of 1936, and which went into production almost immediately.

Specifications of the 1936 MAS rifle were unspectacular . . . as, indeed, was the whole design. Length was a middlin'-short 40 inches; the barrel was 22 inches long; weight was 8¼ pounds; feeding was from a five-shot integral mag that one nourished by means of stripper-clip. The action was a modified Mauser with locking lugs in the rear; the rear-mounted lugs lent a short bolt travel while compro-

Below—The MAS rear sight is a 200-1200 meter sliding adjustable ramp with aperture, and it works well. Right—An interesting feature of the sight is that windage is adjusted by swapping apertures. This one is marked "G" for *Gauche* or "Left," and the hole is offset to the left. Those for "Right" windage would be marked "D" for *Droit*. Below right—The front sight is a flattened pyramid that offers quick acquisition, but not precision.

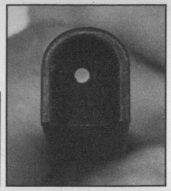

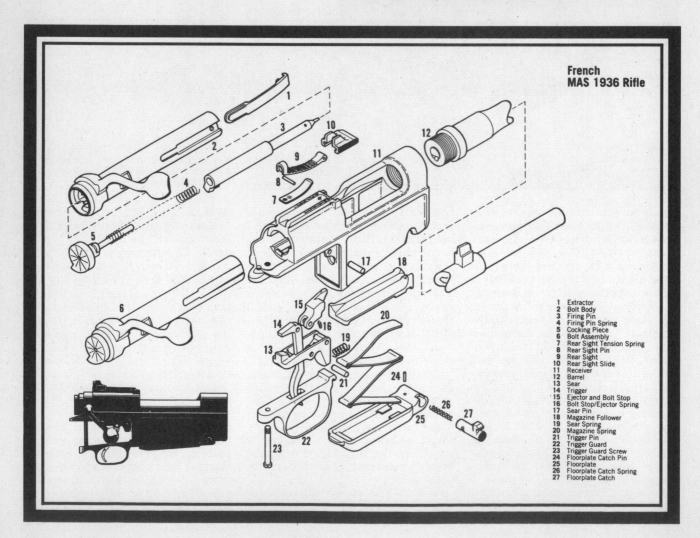

### French MAS 1936 Rifle

1 Extractor
2 Bolt Body
3 Firing Pin
4 Firing Pin Spring
5 Cocking Piece
6 Bolt Assembly
7 Rear Sight Tension Spring
8 Rear Sight Pin
9 Rear Sight
10 Rear Sight Slide
11 Receiver
12 Barrel
13 Sear
14 Trigger
15 Ejector and Bolt Stop
16 Bolt Stop/Ejector Spring
17 Sear Pin
18 Magazine Follower
19 Sear Spring
20 Magazine Spring
21 Trigger Pin
22 Trigger Guard
23 Trigger Guard Screw
24 Floorplate Catch Pin
25 Floorplate
26 Floorplate Catch Spring
27 Floorplate Catch

Above—Standard rifle cartridges of three World War II powers, left to right: 7.5 MAS (France); 8mm Mauser (Germany); 30-06 (USA). The 7.5 MAS was an efficient round, shooting a 139-gr., 30-caliber FMJ bullet at 2675 fps.

The swept-forward bolt handle places the knob directly over the trigger, where it belongs. Without the forward sweep, bolt manipulation would be very clumsy.

mising action strength only minimally. (The MAS is generally regarded as having an "adequately strong" action, thanks to the large-diameter bolt and beefy lugs and receiver.) The bolt handle was bent sharply forward, sacrificing appearance but gaining ergonomically. Sighting was by a range-adjustable aperture and the windage was adjustable by swapping rear sights! Stocking was two-piece, which could cause accuracy troubles, and the fore-end ran to within 5 inches of the muzzle. The quaint, and quite useless, French cruciform bayonet was utilized. And, as stated earlier, the gun had no safety at all; one carried it with the chamber empty—something France's hapless *Poilus* had been doing with their perenially safetyless bolt guns ever since long before the turn of the century.

In any event, it was with such an uninspired turnbolt (and in fact, usually with even less inspired, older guns, for MAS 36 production proceeded slowly) that the Republique faced the onslaught of 1940. And, not surprisingly, France was defeated quickly—certainly not because of her issue rifles, but not in spite of them either. And so the victorious Germans, displaying their usual "packrat" tendencies where captured weapons were concerned, at once pirated every MAS they could find for issue to their own rear-echelon troops. It was in so ignominious a role that M1936s served

until war's end.

With the Liberation though, MAS 36 production was resumed, as was isssue of the gun to the French Army. Indeed, a few interesting MAS variants were even built and/or designed in the post-war period (talk about flagellation of the proverbial dead horse!) to fulfill special roles. Noteworthy among these was the M1936M51, which incorporated a muzzle-mounted grenade-launcher. And the M1936CR39, an aluminum-stocked paratroop version engineered before the war, was put back into production also, to answer French needs in the colonial wars. Finally, as of 1949, time had run out for Europe's last bolt-action fighting rifle, at least insofar as manufacture of the standard version was concerned. The MAS 1949, which looked shockingly similar to the '36 though it was of semi-auto configuration, usurped the bolt gun's place on the assembly lines. At that point most of the M1936s found their way into various French arsenals where they were carefully put into mothballs alongside other obsolete arms dating from as far back as pre-World War I. The French military rarely ever throws out anything, I am told. A few MASs, those sold to the Gendarmerie, rather than stored, would later rematerialize in police hands during the student riots of the late '60s. Ultimately, a semblance of MAS 36 engineering (albeit in much,

A typical five-shot 100-yd. group from the test MAS measured 4 inches or so; center-to-center.

*much* altered form) would reappear as late as the 1970s, when France revealed her "new" — and hyper-expensive—RF-F1 sniper rifle to the world.

All of which brings us to the present. One would, of course, assume that with so many M1936s either in storage or in police lockers, it would be difficult to find a MAS test piece. And to be sure, such is usually the case, for only a few '36s were imported into this country before GCA '68 ended the "Golden Era of Surplus" forever. But in this regard, the author was very fortunate: friend Tony Terrana of T'NT Guns (135 East

6th Ave., Tarentum, PA 15084) just happened, by sheer coincidence, to have a finely-preserved MAS — and several hundred rounds of hard-to-find 7.5 surplus ammo—in stock at the time such was needed! A single phone call was sufficient to effect loan of the rifle and purchase of adequate rounds for testing.

The testing commenced with a series of 100-yard benchrest accuracy efforts, all of which yielded groups of around 4 inches for five shots. This was disappointing performance, to be sure, and indeed, 4 MOA just may represent the maximum consistent groupability for the test rifle. But still, I'd be remiss if I failed to point out that shooter error might well have accounted for at least some of the sparseness in the "patterns" we're discussing here. Simply put, the test MAS, with its surplus fodder, did not make for a sweet-shooting combo.

The ammunition, for one thing, was atrociously unreliable. One cartridge in five failed to ignite; one in seven or so gave a disturbing, flintlock-style, hangfire ignition. This happened despite the fact that my surplus 7.5mm stuff was decidedly minty: it came out of original sealed factory cartons (which were themselves in fine shape); it was post-war issue; and there was not a trace of verdigris or corrosion anywhere. But still, ignition was very much a sometimes thing . . . as it so often seems to be with French surplus ammo, regardless of age or condition. Shoot to the capacity of the gun with such fodder? Well, maybe.

But bad ammo wasn't the sole obstacle one had to surmount in shooting the test MAS. The trigger was something of a pain too: it broke at a challenging 7½ pounds, fully one-half

of which was occasioned by the overpowered trigger return spring. And, though there was virtually no creep, overtravel was substantive. Then there was the front sight: a pyramidal, barleycorn-style affair with the apex of the pyramid flattened somewhat. This was quick to acquire, to be sure, but it was hardly precise, and the fine MAS rear aperture would seem to lend itself to precision otherwise. So, once again, shoot to the capacity of the gun against such obstacles? Perhaps I did just that. But on one occasion, at 200-yards, when the light was just right, and when my trigger finger was rested and fresh, and when by sheer good fortune I got five proper ignitions in a row, well . . . 6½ inches for five shots rewarded my efforts. So you, I fear, must be the judge. Whate'er the case, we can agree, I think, that the gun is neither tackdriver nor clunk, which is in keeping with its mediocre image, I suppose.

Speaking of said "image," mediocrity does imply, usually, that there are some good features to counter the bad.

And since the MAS M1936 does possess a single, absolutely dreadful-class feature—the total absence of any sort of manual safety device—it follows that there should be some MAS boons to help make up for this. To be sure, there are such (though nothing, but nothing, could compensate completely for so glaring a design error as a non-existent safety, in my view).

First among M1936 positives is the quite slick, easily manipulated action. The MAS isn't state-of-the-art in this regard, of course. The Enfield offers a slightly smaller bolt arc, while many Japanese Type 38 and German Mauser actions are slicker—like glass, in fact. But the M1936s bolt travel is super-short; indeed, it's less than 3½ inches. Added to which, the MAS doesn't cock clumsily on the closing stroke, as the Enfield does. All this aids in rapid fire, as does the "adequately slick" feel.

The gun seems handy too. It wields like somewhat less than its 40 inches and it hefts like somewhat less than its 8¼ pounds. It is by no means muz-

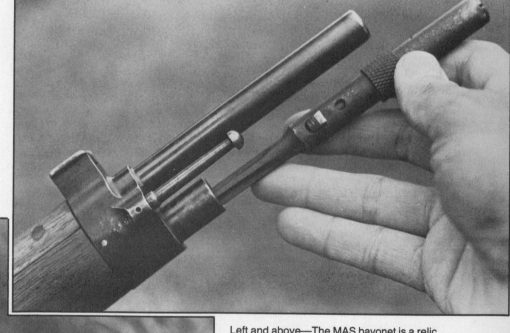

Left and above—The MAS bayonet is a relic, suitable for another (much earlier) time frame. It stores neatly in the fore-end when not in use.

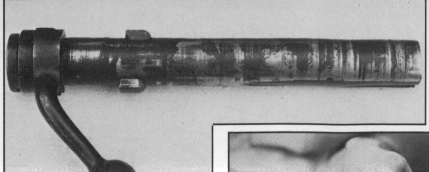

The bolt is of large diameter and has beefy rear-mounted locking lugs. Bolt travel is a short 3½".

Below—Five-round stripper clips for the 1936 MAS work beautifully, quite unlike many other designs. This makes for fast reloading.

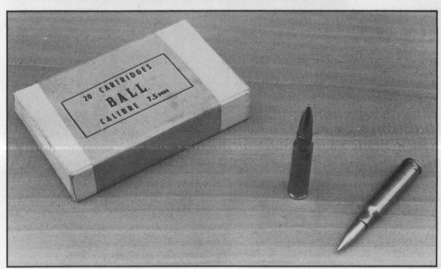

The test ammunition was French surplus in beautiful condition, but was totally unreliable. There is no commercial source for modern, Boxer-primed 7.5mm cartridges.

From 200 yards, with conditions just right, Shimek printed this 6½", five-shot group which represents the best performance achieved in the tests.

zle-heavy. Yet it's adequately robust for heavy service. The '36 also mounts nicely, at least for me, though it's of interest to note that I adapt easily to short buttstocks while many shooters don't.

Another MAS positive concerns reloadability. The stripper clips issued for use with this arm actually work! I know that's a compliment to the clips, not the gun, but I'll make this allusion to the MAS 1936 "system" all the same. Insert the clip in the guide, press down with the thumb and—voila!—cartridges strip into the magazine with no problem at all. The strength of a bear is not required, and yes, there is a lesson here for some manufacturers.

Simplicity is our final MAS strongpoint. The MAS is one of the simplest high-powered repeating rifles ever created. The bolt assembly consists of but five components; the entire gun contains but 36 parts; and field-stripping involves all of three steps. Such simplicity is, of course, a boon under wartime conditions.

As can be seen then, the MAS M1936 is not totally without its plusses. And yet, one cannot help but feel that it says much regarding the '36s indifferent engineering that one is forced to take such phenomena as a reasonably slick action and stripper clips that work and deem them salient virtues. But remember, these relative trivialities must be weighed against such deficiencies as the limited magazine capacity, the lack of an intelligent readiness mode, the bad front sight and trigger, etc. I should also report, as I pen these final lines, that word has just reached me that the French Army, in a rare house-clean-

ing move, is at this very moment putting the torch to those stored surplus MASs we spoke of earlier. Apparently, not even "The Army Which Hoards Everything" sees reason to keep the mediocre MAS so much as one more year. And yet, lest I condemn too easily, I am forced also to reflect upon a news photograph in my possession; said pix illustrates what appears to be an Afghan tribesman lying in wait behind cover, probably to ambush a Soviet foe. Clutched tightly in the Afghan's hand is an MAS M1936.

Who knows, perhaps no rifle which can still serve so admirable a cause under such appalling field conditions should ever be treated too harshly in the sterile world of print. ●

# Colt's
# AIRCREWMAN
## Rarest Horse in the Stable?

by WALTER L. RICKELL

With just over 1,000 of these 12½-oz. Colts produced, they could be the rarest models. If nothing else, these guns are proof that alloys and revolvers can work together.

ALUMINUM AND HANDGUNS are a combination that has always created controversy. Strength and durability have been questioned, with the general concensus being that it won't work. But is that really true? Test and field experience over the past 35 years indicate that it *can* work, with limitations, since the models in question are still with us and very popular.

It all began after World War II when the Air Force was searching for a lightweight sidearm. They had decided on a revolver since it made a practical survival weapon. Now before all you semi-auto fans start rumbling, consider that a double-action revolver can be operated by a pilot with one hand if his other hand or arm is disabled.

Next to consider is weight in a combat aircraft—every ounce must be accounted for. Every gram saved could mean more fuel or spare ammo. The double-action revolver with 2-inch barrel was selected for the weapon and designated the M-13 (Air Force designation), manufactured by both Colt and Smith & Wesson.

Called the "Aircrewman," it was made almost entirely of aluminum, with 2-inch barrel, in 38 Special caliber and based on respective models in each company's lines. Smith & Wesson used their Model 10 "Airweight" (now known as the Model 12) and Colt chose their old standby Detective Special in the Cobra configuration. Characteristic of the Aircrewman models were frames, sideplates and cylinders made of aluminum alloy, with all other parts of conventional ordnance steel.

The rarest of these models is the Colt since only 1,189 revolvers were

manufactured, much less than the total production by Smith & Wesson. The grips were checkered walnut, and had Air Force medallions on both sides on the upper sections, replacing the rampant Colt and intertwined S&W logos. The grip was a major design departure for Colt in that it resembled the Smith & Wesson Magna-style with the wood extending up and over the frame, covering part of the sideplate. Also the Colt had a grip screw entering from the right panel with a blind escutcheon on the left.

First manufactured in 1951 to United States Air Force specifications, the Colt Aircrewman weighed in at 12½ ounces, unloaded. The gun had an anodized finish with the flats of the frame semi-bright, the edges left in a matte finish similar to the Government Model. All other steel parts were blued. Since the gun was on the conventional Cobra frame of the period, it had a long, round butt.

Serial numbers ranged in the standard Cobra and Courier production, numbers 1902-LW through 90470-LW, with most of the production being between 2901-LW and 7775-LW. The Air Force added their own numbering system, 1 through 1,189, these numbers placed on the butt, reading A.F. No. XXXX. On the backstrap, in block letters was stamped "PROPERTY OF

Left side of the Aircrewman shows the name on the barrel. Gun is shown with six rounds of M41 ball ammo that eventually brought about its demise.

All Aircrewman guns were marked like this one on the backstrap. The anodized finish appears to have held up well over the years.

Right view of the little Colt revolver shows conventional barrel markings. Grips had the Air Force medallion on both sides, and came up higher on the frame than regular Colt types.

50 CARTRIDGES

**BALL**

CALIBER .38 M41

LOT WCC **6006**

OLIN MATHIESON CHEMICAL CORPORATION

The M41 ball ammo proved destructive in the alloy cylinders and the guns were recalled by the government. Air Force serial numbers (barely visible here) were stamped into the butt.

U.S. AIR FORCE," and on the left side of the barrel, "AIRCREWMAN" in one line, ".38 SPECIAL CTG." in a second line beneath it. The right side of the barrel is marked in the conventional manner, reading "COLT'S MFG. CO.," and below it, "HART-FORD, CT. U.S.A." Issued with each of these pioneering lightweight revolvers were a black leather holster with U.S.A.F. embossed on the flap and a training manual.

The little revolvers functioned well with standard 38 Special ammo, but the introduction of the M-41 military ball 38 round was to signal the demise of both the Colt and Smith & Wesson AIRCREWMAN models. The M-41's jacketed bullet and uneven pressures, as discovered during tests, caused the aluminum alloy cylinders to split. Thus, the Air Force's opinion was that the revolvers were useless for military service, though none are known to have ever failed in the field.

Sometime in 1959 or 1960, all the Aircrewman revolvers were recalled and destroyed at their respective plants, per Pentagon request, hence the rarity of the guns, especially the Colt. Those that survived (and there were a few) have fates unknown, and bring top dollar on the collector market.

The Aircrewman was an important link in the evolution of the American handgun but was really never given a chance to prove itself. With the newer space-age alloys we now have at hand, maybe a lightweight, easy-to-carry revolver such as this should again be given consideration as a personal defense weapon. ●

# To Up Your Hunting Odds

Jamison fitted this Remington with Gun Chaps for the stock; the barrel and scope have been wrapped with non-stick vinyl tape. Very effective!

# Camouflage That Gun

It may sound like picking nits, but it sure can't hurt to mask those reflections that can spook game. Here's the run-down on a number of methods to cut the glare.

## by RICK JAMISON

THOUGH I HAD ALWAYS worn a complete camouflage outfit when calling coyotes, I had never given much thought to camouflaging my rifle. For many years my favorite coyote hunting gun was a 22-250 Remington Model 788, a now-discontinued rifle that used to come with quite a dull finish on it. Later, I traded the Model 788 for a 22-250 Remington Model 700 BDL with the very glossy DuPont RKW stock finish and the shiny metal work.

I prefer to hunt and call coyotes in open country because, in my area at least, they aren't hunted (by calling) as heavily as in the brush country.

Here, a well-camouflaged hunter is in position (under the bush, foreground), calling for coyotes. By sitting in the shade he is barely visible.

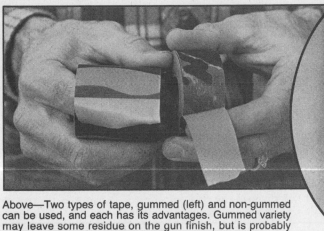

Above—Two types of tape, gummed (left) and non-gummed can be used, and each has its advantages. Gummed variety may leave some residue on the gun finish, but is probably easier to apply. Right—To wrap a barrel, one end of the non-gummed tape is held with masking tape, the barrel wrapped, and the loose end secured with more masking tape.

The peelable-paint camouflage is applied with a brush and comes off easily. A green base coat is applied first, followed by the other colors. This process doesn't alter the lines or handling of the gun.

There aren't generally as many coyotes per square mile in open country but, due to the lack of hunting pressure, the coyotes that are there aren't generally as wary. One of my coyote hunting tactics involves laying down in open country to call. Just because there's no brush or other vegetation to conceal a caller doesn't mean he can't be camouflaged. Coyotes don't expect danger from open country and as long as a hunter is halfway camouflaged, and lying prone, the animals can be called in close.

One of the first calling "stands" I made with the shiny new Remington Model 700 was in open, short-grass country. After five minutes of calling, I saw a coyote far across the prairie, coming closer. The wind direction was in my favor and I had little doubt about nailing that critter; from past experience I knew that it was just a matter of minutes before he would be close enough to shoot.

When I first saw him, he was about 500-600 yards out, and when a coyote is that far away, and running, a hunter that moves slowly to get into position rarely alarms one. I moved my rifle so that it was pointing in the direction of the coyote. However, as soon as I did so, he slammed on the brakes.

He was now about 400 yards out and it didn't appear as if he was coming closer. I tried to coax him in a little more with the call, but he just turned and started trotting away. Then, he stopped broadside. I knew that he probably wasn't going to come closer so I decided to try a long shot. I moved my rifle ever so slightly to get into shooting position and the coyote took off as if he'd been shot at. I hadn't fired and couldn't understand why he was so alarmed, especially at that distance. Then, I realized that the sun was glaring on that shiny RKW stock; it probably revealed my presence like

The purpose of camouflaging a gun is to eliminate reflections and glare and to break up the lines. Camo tape or paint do it very well.

This Remington 788 is camouflaged with tape. Coyote hunter Tony Martinez, also in camo colors, is now ready to begin calling.

a beacon. It was then that I decided there was a need to do something about that flashy rifle.

Predator calling isn't the only hunting sport wherein gun camouflage benefits the sportsman in his quest for wary game. Turkey hunters have long realized the effectiveness of shotgun or rifle camouflage. A dove hunter, sitting on a hill under a dead tree waiting for birds to approach, increases his close-in shooting opportunities with good camouflage. A waterfowl hunter in a cattail blind similarly benefits from camouflage, and, to really be effective, camouflage must be applied to the equipment as well as the shooter.

There are all sorts of ways to camouflage your rifle or shotgun and it doesn't have to be time consuming, expensive, damaging to the gun's finish, or make it awkward to use. Quite the contrary on all counts.

It wasn't all that long ago that riflemen and shotgunners began using the same camouflage tape that bowhunters used to cover their shiny recurves. Another method is to cover it with camouflage-pattern cloth. The first cloth camouflage gun cover I saw was on the rifle of government hunter Jim Nolan. It was a homemade cover that had been fashioned from a discarded camouflage suit.

Since that time, a number of firms have introduced camouflage gun covers with snaps, Velcro fasteners and, in some instances, zippers. You can buy one of these covers for a nominal

fee or you can make your own. To make your own, it's probably easier, and less wasteful of material, if you first make a pattern of paper. The cover can be designed to encompass both the gun and scope if it's a rifle you're working with. Just leave openings, where necessary, for the gun to function. Snaps or Velcro fasteners can be used to attach the cover to the rifle so that it can fit snugly and be removed when desired.

Some "store bought" camo covers encase the entire gun and scope, including the barrel, while others don't cover the scope or the barrel. In the latter instance, an auxiliary camouflage covering will be needed to complete the job.

One method that's used to cover the barrel and scope is to wrap them with strips of vinyl or plastic-looking camouflage material that is available in rolls, much like non-gummed tape. A piece of electrical or masking tape can be used to attach one end of the vinyl strip to the barrel. Then the strip is simply wound tightly around the barrel in an overlapping manner. If wound tightly, the vinyl stretches enough to provide a gapless fit. Continue wrapping until the tube is completely covered. With that done, the strip is cut, and the free end is taped to secure it. The same system can be used to camouflage the riflescope. If you prefer, camo tape can be used instead of vinyl strips. However, the gummed tape is known to leave a residue when it's removed, whereas the

vinyl strips do not. Tape, on the other hand, is generally less bulky and more secure than the heavy vinyl.

In recent years, a peelable paint has been offered to sportsmen for the purpose of camouflaging firearms. The paint is applied in three heavy coats. Generally, a base coat is added first, then stencils are used to paint on a camouflage pattern with two or three other colors. If you prefer, you can design your own pattern by painting it on free-hand rather than using the stencils. The paint dries to a tough rubbery coating, which can be peeled off later, if desired.

Don't apply this paint to a porous surface, like checkering, if you want to remove it later. It will stick to a porous surface and then be difficult to remove. If you do get it in a cut-checkered pattern, a stiff-bristled toothbrush will help remove it.

The paint-on camouflage has the advantage of fitting the gun precisely with no looseness or bulk to alter the gun's trim lines. Its disadvantage is that it is more difficult to remove than a cloth cover.

Cloth or vinyl camouflage covers, or most any camouflage covering material for that matter, also serves the

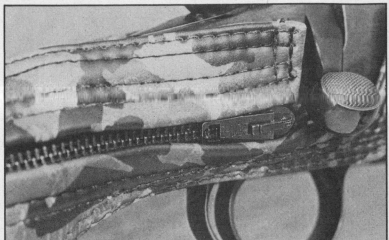

Right and below—Gun chaps is a commercial vinyl camouflage cover that uses a zipper and Velcro fasteners to hold the cover on the rifle. It fits the rifle quite snugly.

This before and after illustrates how camouflage can break up the lines of a rifle and reduce glare. It really does work!

purpose of protecting the gun — both the metal and stock finish — from scratches and abrasions that happen when being carried in the field or in a vehicle.

It's a good idea to periodically check underneath the covering material to see if dirt and moisture have gotten in to cause corrosion.

There is some debate regarding accuracy when it comes to methods of camouflaging rifles. I have seen instances where the hunter has tightly wrapped the rifle barrel and fore-end together. Though I have never camouflaged a rifle in this manner, preferring to allow the barrel to vibrate freely, those who have done it say that this in no way affects the rifle's point of impact or grouping ability. This is very likely a factor of the individual rifle. A gun that is sensitive to slight bedding changes might very well have its point of impact of grouping ability altered by this barrel/forend taping. However, it might also make a finicky rifle shoot even better than it did without the taping. You'll have to experiment a bit.

If you've been thinking about camouflaging your rifle but have resisted because you didn't want to leave the gun gummed up with tape, affect its shooting ability, have it become bulky, or get a flap of cloth in the way that might hamper quick bolt throw, don't hesitate, because all these potential problems can be circumvented. Camouflaging a rifle can be inexpensive and believe me, it is effective in the field.

The camouflage material can be removed after hunting season and the rifle wiped down so that it has all the gloss or sheen you want for it to repose in the gun rack. It might have an even better finish than it would have since it was protected by the camouflage covering during the season! ●

# Wildcatting the 221 Fireball

## for Short-Range Varmints

Big-booming, large-case varmint guns are still desirable but then there are also times when all that powder and blast aren't necessary or ideal. Here's interesting dope on a few experiments based on Remington's little Fireball cartridge.

## by JON LEU

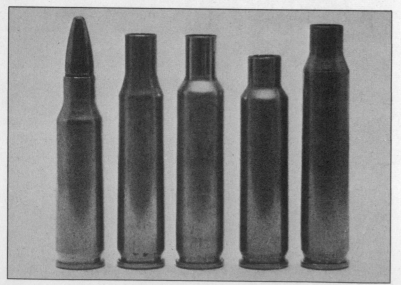

THE TREND IN RECENT years seems to have been toward varmint rifles built around cartridges of ever-increasing size. Winchester introduced their ill-fated 225 cartridge in the mid-60s to replace the aging 220 Swift. The folks at Remington followed suit with a commercialized version of the 22-250, a cartridge which had attained a wide following in over 30 years as a wildcat. Not to be outdone, Ruger offered a limited run of their Model 77 Varmint rifles chambered for the cartridge Winchester had chosen to leave as an orphan, the 220 Swift; and the popularity of this chambering was such that it has been left in their line as a "standard" chambering.

More recently, Jim Carmichael created at least a minor stir among the varmint hunters with the announcement of his 22 Cheetah cartridge for which he claims performance bettering that of the all-time velocity champion — the 220 Swift — and with heavier bullets. It seemed only a matter of months before Rick Jamison, reloading editor for *Shooting Times*, followed suit with an article about his

Several cartridges were scrutinized in the search for the best choice for short-range varmint hunting. Some of them were (left to right) the 221 Fireball, 222 Remington, 222x35, short 222x35 with neck length reduced to that of the 223 Remington, and the 223 Remington.

Where is it carved in stone that effective varmint rifles have to be big, bulky and heavy? This rifle, with 1:15″ twist Hart barrel chambered for the 221 Fireball, weighs well under 7 lbs. fitted with a Leupold 6x scope. Velocities will top the 3400 fps mark with 45-gr. bullets.

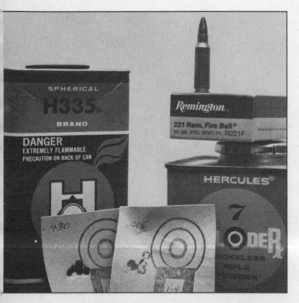

The 221 Firoball in a properly built rifle is capable of excellent accuracy, as shown by these .430″ and .405″ groups fired at 100 yards from benchrest. Hodgdon's H335 and Hercules Reloder 7 proved to be the best powder choices for the 1:15″ twist barrel for both 45- and 50-gr. bullets.

22 C-J cartridge which is, in short, the 6mm Remington case necked down to hold a .224″ bullet.

All of these larger cases, when loaded to their full-throttle potential, share a couple of things in common. First and foremost, they are excellent long range performers. Second, they tend to be hard on barrels, both in terms of barrel life as well as in terms of fouling — two factors which are, or should be, of importance to the varmint hunter. It almost goes wihout saying that varmint hunters pop more caps than their big game hunting brethren and, at the same time, they strive for the finest possible accuracy in light of their relatively small targets. Bore erosion and fouling are *not* the sorts of allies we need in varmint hunting.

In spite of all that has been written on the subject of bore cleaning in recent years, there are still plenty of shooters who scoff at the notion a clean barrel is absolutely necessary for accuracy. The results of some recent experiments with a 1:9-inch twist Hart barrel chambered for the 22-250 Remington cartridge might shed further light on the subject. Loaded with 69-grain Sierra Match King bullets and IMR-4350 powder, this rifle is capable of velocities in the 3,500-3,600 fps range.

Experiments to date have shown that this barrel, when clean, will consistently produce groups in the .2-.3″ range for three shots at 100 yards. However, as the barrel becomes fouled from repeated firing, groups at 100 yards open up to an inch or slightly less. Since accuracy is rarely perfectly linear with increased range, i.e., a .3″ group at 100 yards will not be .6″ group at 200 yards or a .9″ group at 300 yards, the importance of barrel fouling is more readily seen. Clean, it's a terror; dirty, it just uses a lot of powder to make a lot of noise.

Unfortunately, all of the experimenting being done with these large capacity, high velocity cartridges doesn't amount to a hill of beans to what might well be viewed as a growing segment of the varmint hunting population. There's really not much point in having a rifle which is a holy terror at 350 or 400 yards if your shooting is going to be limited to shorter ranges, say 200-250 yards, perhaps less. Like it or not, those of us living east of the Missouri River just don't have all the wide open spaces of the West. And there are other factors to consider.

Some years ago, a friend and I—both clean-cut eastern Iowa high school students—decided an afternoon of varmint hunting, Iowa style, was in order. My shooting buddy was armed, as I recall, with a 257 Roberts loaded with light bullets which were guaranteed to vaporize the wily Iowa ground squirrel on contact. I was carrying a little Marlin-Sako 222.

Our fathers were relatively well known in the community, and it didn't take long for their sons to obtain the permission of a local farmer to attempt to thin his ground squirrel population. Late that afternoon we happened upon a paradise—ground squirrels at ranges which would test both our rifles and our shooting skills.

The plan was simple: I would shoot, and my buddy would spot for me through the telescope on his rifle. Then it was his turn to shoot while I would serve as the spotter. We were having a great time, laying there in the pasture oblivious to everything that wasn't going on in front of our rifles. So oblivious, in fact, we didn't realize our host farmer had arrived until he kicked the daylights out of the bottom of my outstretched foot. As I turned around, he was screaming, "What the *!#% are you guys doing? I'm trying to get my cows up to milk 'em, and your racket's got 'em scattered all over the place!" The remainder of our afternoon of varmint hunting was spent chasing cattle. Lessons learned the hard way are long remembered.

Apparently there are others whose rifles have scared the devil out of ol' Bossy and whose owners are faced with creeping urbanization of the countryside. This, combined with Americans' interest in nostalgia, has seen a rebirth of interest in several of the older—and smaller—varmint cartridges. The 22 Hornet and the 218 Bee, the powerhouse varmint cartridges of a time long since passed, are alive and well and, judging by the

After being fitted with a 221 Fireball rifle barrel, the XP-100 barreled action was conventionally bedded in a McMillan fiberglass stock blank. This particular stock, McMillan's field or hunting blank, is essentially a fiberglass duplicate of the Remington 700 stock, less the cheekpiece. The completed stock, barreled action, and telescope were camouflage painted.

firearms press, enjoying renewed popularity.

The 22 Hornet and the 218 Bee might well be even more popular if their designs were such as to be easily adapted to actions such as the Remington M700 and the post-64 Winchester M70. However, both cases are rimmed designs with head diameters falling just above and just below the more popular 222 Remington (.378") size. Along with rebarreling or rechambering, the man who wants a Hornet or a Bee on, say, a Remington M700 action must pay for a bolt alteration job to accommodate the .350" head (rim) diameter of the 22 Hornet case or the .408" rim diameter of the 218 Bee.

A much simpler solution, and one surprisingly not adopted by any of the major manufacturers, is to chamber a rifle for the 221 Remington Fireball cartridge. Though the capacity of the Fireball is greater than that of either the Hornet or the Bee, it remains the closest in terms of capacity of any commercially-available case which uses a "standard" head diameter.

The 221 Fireball was introduced by Remington in 1963 for their then-new XP-100 pistol. Essentially a shortened version of the 222 Remington cartridge, the 221 Fireball was designed as a short range varmint hunting round. Factory ballistics for the Fireball call for a 50-grain bullet to leave the muzzle of the 10¾-inch XP-100 barrel at 2,650 fps, ballistics very similar to those of the Hornet in a rifle. It is, without much question, a very efficient little cartridge.

The idea of chambering a rifle for the 221 Fireball is certainly not a new one. P.O. Ackley, in his *Pocket Manual For Shooters and Reloaders* (1964), wrote of experimenting with the Fireball chambered in a 22-inch rifle barrel. Similar articles have appeared from time to time in various publications since the Fireball cartridge was introduced.

The alternative, in the eyes of many, is to use reduced powder charges in the readily available rifles chambered for the 222 Remington cartridge. A good idea on the surface, but not without its problems. "Efficiency" has become one of the buzzwords of the '80s, and reducing powder charges in the 222 Remington cartridge to match the ballistics of smaller cases reduces the efficiency of the cartridge. Perhaps more important to the varmint hunter, reduced charges in rifle cartridges rarely result in the best possible accuracy. Benchrest shooters and other experimenters have shown repeatedly that best accuracy generally comes with

Bing, Bang, Boom . . . a trio of varmint hunting cartridges from Remington, the 221 Fireball, 222 Remington, and the 22-250 Remington. In a 1:14" twist barrel, the Fireball has been likened to a modern-day Hornet. Chambered in a 1:15" twist barrel, the little Fireball case will virtually duplicate the performance of the larger 222 Remington, and it will accomplish this task with less powder. The Fireball and the 222 make excellent choices for short-range varmint hunting in settled areas. The 22-250 is an excellent choice for long-range shooting, but it's a bit out of its element when ranges are short and noise is a factor to be considered.

maximum or near-maximum loads. Too, and for reasons that are seemingly not yet completely understood, reduced loads can, at times, result in extremely high pressures which are potentially dangerous to the shooter.

Over the past couple of years we've experimented with several reduced

The search for a cartridge with performance in the Hornet/Bee range has centered around the 221 Fireball and the 222 Remington, primarily due to the wide availability of suitable actions which require no alterations for the cartridge. Some of the cartridges include (left to right) Jim Northum's 221 Shorty, the 221 Remington Fireball with shoulder moved back .125", the commercial 221 Fireball, the 221½, and the 222 Remington. Moving the shoulder of the Fireball back .125" (second cartridge from left) results in a case capacity equal to that of the 22 Jet.

capacity cases which seemed ideally suited to short range varmint hunting needs and corresponded with a number of individuals who share that interest. Having achieved some rather spectacular results—both in terms of accuracy and velocity—with the 223 Remington cartridge in a variety of rifles, we became interested in studying the velocity/accuracy potential of some of the smaller cases.

For the lack of a better name, the first case was simply dubbed the 221½. The name reflected the capacity of the case, which fell about midway between that of the 221 Fireball and the 222 Remington. The idea was to reduce the capacity of the 222 Remington case without resorting to the purchase of an expensive set of case forming dies for the initial experimentation.

Cases were formed by using a floor-mounted arbor press to push 222 cases into a 222 Remington FL sizing die from which the expander unit had been removed. Cases were forced into the die until the head of the case was flush with the mouth of the die. American reloading equipment makers have standardized on a shell holder thickness of .125" (measured from the top of the press ram to the top of the shell holder). Makers of ⅞-14 reloading dies instruct users to thread the die into the press until the mouth of the die contacts the shell holder for correct headspace. As the thickness of the shell holder is .125", pushing the case flush with the mouth of the die will set the shoulder back .125".

After being removed from the die, the cases were run over a .223" expander rod and trimmed .125" to give a neck length equal to that of the parent 222 Remington case. Since a portion of the neck of the 221½ case had originally been the thicker shoulder of the 222 case, the cases were then outside neck turned to a thickness which would allow safe firing in the rifle. For the purposes of the experiment, a factory 222 Remington barrel was shortened and set back .125". Lacking headspace gauges for the cartridge, a formed case was used for a "Go" gauge. By adding a layer of masking tape to the head of this case, it could also be used as a "No Go" gauge.

Since this is *not* the proper way to chamber a barrel, extra care was taken in the fire-forming process. For fire-forming, bullets were seated out to make firm contact with the lands. In this manner, the case head was forced fully into the bolt face when the bolt was closed, and the shoulder, on firing, was blown forward to properly fit the chamber. Had the bullets not been seated out during the fire-forming operation, any excessive headspace could have resulted in the formation of a stretch ring near the head of the case. Given properly reduced loads, this is the best method for all fire-forming operations.

Three different powders and two bullets were tested in the 221½ case. The powders were Hodgdon 4198, Hercules Reloder 7, and Hodgdon H335. Bullets were the Sierra 50-grain Blitz and the Speer 45-grain Hornet (.224"). With both of these bullets, the best accuracy came with the use of Hodgdon H4198. Velocity was considerably higher with Hodgdon H335 powder, but accuracy was not deemed acceptable for varmint hunting.

Using a charge of 18.7 grains of H4198, velocity averaged 2,850 fps from the 18-inch barrel of the rifle; groups hovered around the ½-inch mark with the Sierra 50-grain Blitz bullet. With the 45-grain Speer bullet, velocity averaged 3,045 fps using 20.0 grains of H4198. Three consecutive five-shot groups with this bullet measured .7-inch, .6-inch, and .6-inch.

An interesting pattern developed while working up the load using H4198 powder with the 45-grain Speer bullet. Using a charge of 20.0 grains, initial testing was done with an over-all cartridge length—measured with the aid of a Sinclair bullet comparator—of 2.659-inch. Velocity was 3,057 fps, and the five-shot group measured 1.50 inch. Moving the bullet an additional .009-inch away from the lands shrunk the group to .70-inch and dropped the average velocity for the load to 3,048 fps. The bullet was then moved an additional .005-inch away from the lands, and two five-shot groups were fired. Both of these groups measured .60-inch, and average velocities were 3,046 fps and 3,043 fps. Changing the bullet seating depth by approximately .015-inch had cut the group size in half but had virtually no effect on velocity.

The next experiment used a shortened version of the wildcat 222x35, essentially a sharp-shouldered version of the standard 222 case with

Remington's 222 cartridge (second and third from right) has sired this group of commercial and wildcat cartridges, all the product of the search for cartridges suitable for short-range varmint hunting. Included (from left to right) are the 221 Shorty, the standard 221 Fireball, the 221½ (loaded and fired cases), the 222 Remington (loaded and fired cases), and a shortened 222x35 with neck length shortened to that of the 223 Remington.

body taper reduced. Prior to the coming of the PPC cartridge, the 222x35 was used by many leading benchrest shooters who found it gave superb accuracy, slightly more velocity than the standard 222 Remington, and, due to the sharper shoulder, was somewhat less prone to stretch with repeated firing.

It was found that the shortened 222x35 gave velocities which were nearly identical to those of the standard 222 Remington, and accuracy was no better. Since the performance could be equalled by the standard 222 Remington which required no case forming, the experiment was abandoned.

Both of the previous experiments had been conducted with 1:14-inch twist barrels which are standard for most 22-caliber varmint rifles. The final stage of the experiment was conducted with the standard 221 Fireball cartridge chambered in a 1:15-inch twist Hart barrel. The results of the experiment are shown in the nearby table. These powder charges, suitable in the slow-twist barrel, would be excessive in the 1:12-inch and 1:14-inch twist barrels most commonly used with this cartridge.

In spite of the impressive figures in the table, the 221 Fireball is definitely a short range varmint hunting cartridge. Sighted in for 150 yards with 45-gr. bullets, the bullet will be slightly more than 4½ inches low at 250 yards. While this is something

the average shooter can live with, wind deflection with these lighter bullets is something else again. In a 10 mph crosswind, the bullet will be deflected slightly more than 2½ inches at 150 yards and nearly 5 inches at 200 yards. If the wind picks up to 20 mph, the deflection figures are approximately 5½ inches at 150 yards and nearly 10 inches at 200 yards. The light bullets are accurate and effective, but they are hardly a good choice when the wind is blowing, the targets are small, and the ranges are long.

A recent letter from James L. Northum of Little Rock, Arkansas, outlined experiments he was conducting with a shortened version of the 221 Fireball case:

Thought you might be interested in the enclosed cases even though the little fellow is not a benchrest cartridge. It is a wildcat and accuracy, or the lack of it, was a major factor in its development.

I got into the wildcat game due to a fondness for shooting the 22 Hornet and the 218 Bee. They are low noise, low recoil rounds which do the job I use them for. I have been known to pop a crow once in a while and mainly just shoot for fun. However, the Hornet and Bee rifles I tried just didn't have it in the accuracy department due to poor triggers, two-piece stocks, weak actions, or some combination of these factors.

My first thought was to modify a

good strong bolt action to use the Hornet or Bee, but such an altered action would be unsuited for any future use should the experiment fail. So, modification of the case was the only route open.

I decided to shorten the 221 Fireball case so it would have a capacity in the Hornet/Bee range. After some digging through the books, weighing and calculating, the 221 case was shortened to only .750-inch from base to shoulder and 1.170-inch over-all. The result was a short, fat, strong little case which holds more powder than the Hornet and less than the Bee. Cases formed from military 223 brass were not as uniform as cases from 221 brass. All cases are now formed from 221 brass.

Francis Tool Company made the reamer and Huntington Die Specialties made the case forming dies. A Shilen #4 barrel was fitted to a Remington 600 action. A Canjar trigger and a loading ramp were installed in the action. An old M600 stock had the magazine cutout filled with epoxy when the barreled action was bedded. The result was a rifle with a nice trigger, one-piece stock, and a strong action chambered for a little cartridge in the Hornet/Bee range.

Benchrest techniques are used for case preparation and loading; flash holes and primer pockets uniformed, necks turned, lengths trimmed, and cases sorted by weight. A Neil Jones neck sizer and a Mike Kleiman straight line bullet seater are used for reloading. Powder charges are thrown with a B&M measure. Federal match primers are used for all loads.

What are the results of all this effort? Good 50-52 grain bullets with 13.0 grains of Reloder 7 shoot well enough to make half-inch, five-shot 100-yard groups routine. Quarter-inch groups are not impossible. Had one group of four into about one-eighth inch and, boy, did I think about wasting the last one into the backstop! Number five opened it up to about three-eighths which isn't bad for this type rifle with a 12X scope.

Although Northum hasn't chronographed the loads, he estimates velocities fall within the desired Hornet/Bee range. The exact velocity isn't as important to him as the fact that the rifle performs as expected. All in all, it's not a bad way for the average shooter to judge the performance of any cartridge.

Has all the experimenting been worth the time and effort? The answer would have to be a qualified "yes." The work with the standard 221 Fireball was the most rewarding in that no case forming dies or special reload-

The slow-twist 221 Fireball rifle was built around a Remington XP-100 single shot action, which is extremely rigid and makes an excellent choice for a varmint rifle where a magazine is not needed. The rifle would have been more aesthetically pleasing had the XP-100s "dog leg" bolt handle been replaced with a Remington 700 bolt handle, but it was left for a reason. Fitted with a 23-inch barrel, the action was bedded further to the rear than normal to reduce the over-all length of the rifle. Replacing the bolt handle with a more conventional swept-back style would have brought it too close to the shooter's hand.

ing dies are required, a major savings. Chambered in a standard 1:14-inch twist barrel, the Fireball is essentially a modern version of the Hornet and Bee-class cartridges; and no alterations of the action are required. Given a 1:15-inch twist barrel, the 221 Fireball will duplicate the performance of the larger 222 Remington and do it with less powder. In that more and more varmint rifles are being fitted with custom barrels, the 221 Fireball in either a 1:14 or 1:15-inch twist barrel offers a viable alternative to the hunter looking for a good short-range varmint rifle. Much the same can be said of the little 221½. It's an efficient little case which doesn't require investment in an expensive set of case forming dies—a decided plus for anyone on a limited budget who wants to work with a wildcat cartridge.

The only thing that bothers me about Northum's 221 Shorty is the fact that forming dies are required. On the other hand, pushing a 221 Fireball case into a Fireball FL die until the head is flush with the die mouth will set the shoulder back .125". One of the cases I made in this manner showed the capacity to be nearly identical to that of the 22 Jet.

No alterations of a standard 222 ac-

tion would be required . . . case forming could be done with a standard 221 Fireball die . . . loading dies could be made by shortening Fireball dies .125" . . . there are no immediate pros-

pects for a job in the wide open spaces of the West where a long-range varmint rifle would be an advantage . . . hmm. It just might turn out to be another interesting project. •

### Data
### 221 Fireball with 1:15-inch Twist

| Bullet (grs.) | Primer | Powder/Charge (grs.) | Velocity (fps) | Group (in.) |
|---|---|---|---|---|
| Sierra 50 Blitz | Rem 7½ | Reloder 7/19.2 | 3080 | .80 |
| Sierra 50 Blitz | Rem 7½ | H4227/16.6 | 3002 | 1.30 |
| Sierra 50 Blitz | Rem 7½ | H335/22.2 | 2968 | 1.30 |
| Sierra 50 Blitz | Rem 7½ | H4198/19.0 | 2690 | 1.10 |
| Sierra 40 Hornet | Fed 205M | Reloder 7/19.8 | 3374 | 1.20 |
| Sierra 40 Hornet | Fed 205M | H335/23.0 | 3201 | .50 |
| Sierra 40 Hornet | Fed 205M | H4227/16.8 | 3249 | 1.10 |
| Sierra 40 Hornet | Fed 205M | H4227/17.8 | 3419 | 1.10 |
| Sierra 40 Hornet | Fed 205M | H4198/18.2 | 3073 | 1.20 |
| Sierra 40 Hornet | Rem 7½ | H335/23.0 | 3244 | .75 |
| Sierra 40 Hornet | Rem 7½ | H335/23.0 | 3227 | .75 |
| Sierra 50 Blitz | Rem 7½ | Reloder 7/19.7 | 3189 | .90 |
| Speer 45 Hornet | Fed 205M | Reloder 7/20.2 | 3421 | .50 |
| Speer 45 Hornet | Fed 205M | Reloder 7/20.2 | 3412 | .60 |
| Speer 45 Hornet | Fed 205M | Reloder 7/20.2 | 3417 | 1.00 |
| Speer 45 Hornet | Fed 205M | Reloder 7/20.2 | 3427 | .40 |
| Speer 45 Hornet | Fed 205M | H335/23.0 | 3211 | .60 |
| PCBC 51 (custom) | Fed 205M | Reloder 7/19.9 | 3271 | .75 |

# THE WONDERFULLY VERSATILE
# T/C CONTENDER

## by LAYNE SIMPSON

In the beginning, few shooters thought the Contender would make it to major league status but, over its 20-plus years so far, the design has proved to be incredibly versatile and popular.

AROUND 1960, a fellow who worked for Harrington & Richardson at the time decided to build a single-shot handgun of his very own. He wanted something for shooting varmints. Working in a small shop in the basement of his home in Gardner, Massachusetts, he whittled out a firearm along the lines of rifles with tip up actions, like the old Stevens rifles of the 1890s. This first handgun of his making was chambered for 22 Hornet.

Odd looking though it was, the handgun was amazingly strong and accurate, so much so that everybody who saw it wanted one. In 1965 the handgun designer showed his idea to Ken Thompson, owner of a foundry in Rochester, New Hampshire, called the K.W. Thompson Tool Company. During that same year Thompson/Center Arms Company was formed and two years later the first commercially produced gun left the factory. Introduced in 22 rimfire, 22 WMR, 22 Remington Jet, 22 Hornet and 38 Special, the retail price was $135 with extra barrels going for $36 apiece.

Of course the fellow's name was and is Warren Center and his brainchild is commonly known as the Thompson/Center Contender or simply Contender for short. To simply say that the Contender's success has been phenomenal is rather an understatement. And, anyone who claims to

have predicted such universal acceptance as the big handgun now enjoys is stretching the truth just a tad. Even the first employees at T/C said that it had about as much chance of ever getting off the ground as a lead balloon. After all, who in this world of modern miracles would buy a single-shot handgun of such seemingly antiquated design, and was homely as a fence post to boot?

On the surface the Contender appeared to be no bargain price-wise either. At the time, one could buy a Smith & Wesson Model 53 in 22 Jet, with an extra cylinder for 22 rimfire, for a mere $15 more or a K-38 for $36 less. A K-22 Masterpiece cost $89 while a Model 27 in 357 Magnum would set you back $130. Wow, was everybody (including this writer) wrong! What most of us overlooked was the one feature that, above all others, has led the Contender down the bumpy road to success—its interchangeable barrels. In those days, one could buy a Contender with four extra barrels for $279, which did a lot less

damage to the budget than the purchase of five revolvers. Although Contender prices have escalated quite a bit since its early days, so have the prices of other handguns. Considering what you get for your money it's still a bargain.

Even though nearly every single component part of the Contender has been improved by modification during its 20-odd years of existence, these changes have been made with but little loss of parts interchangeability. In other words, parts being turned out today will fit the first Contenders built. One exception is the original snap-on fore-end; later units are held to the barrel with screws and therefore the two won't interchange. Otherwise, this allows owners of vintage Contenders to keep their guns abreast of the latest developments at minimum cost, if they so desire. Eli Whitney would be most proud of those ingenious folks at T/C. Now let's take a look at a few of these changes.

The very first Contenders had receivers with smooth sides but it

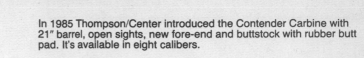

In 1985 Thompson/Center introduced the Contender Carbine with 21″ barrel, open sights, new fore-end and buttstock with rubber butt pad. It's available in eight calibers.

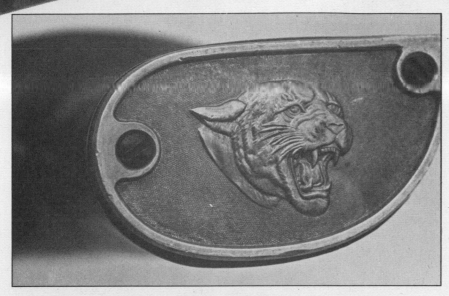

Not many Contenders were built with the silver grip cap with the snarling cougar, and collectors are now very fond of them. The cap is now black plastic.

wasn't long before the now-familiar cougar-on-a-rock appeared. The cougar's head also adorned the silver grip cap but it came later, just before the cap was changed from silver metal to black plastic.

Early Contenders were chambered for relatively mild cartridges so the grip was designed accordingly. However, as more powerful chamberings with their heftier rearward push appeared, shooters found the grip to be most uncomfortable. This prompted T/C to make various modifications to the grip through the years. Actually, today's grip is a result of T/C giving hunters and competitors exactly what they asked for.

Fore-end design has also undergone a few changes; one lost a little wood, the other gained some. T/C, by the way, owns their own sawmill.

The Contender was initially announced with slim 8¾″ and 10″ octagon barrels and various other lengths, including 6″ have been produced. As this is written, six barrel configurations are available: 10″ octagon; 10″ bull; 10″ bull with choke for shooting the Hot-Shot cartridges; 10″ bull in 410/45 Colt; 14″ bull (called the Super-14) and a 10-incher with vent rib and choke. All barrels, of course, fit the same frame.

In 1985, Thompson/Center introduced the Contender Carbine using the same frame, but with a longer fore-end, a buttstock with rubber butt pad and 21″ barrel. Several gunsmiths have been so converting the Contender for a number of years, so I suppose T/C figured it was about time they got in on

Those who aren't familiar with the Contender's potential are always surprised at its accuracy. Bruce Woodson is shooting a Super-14 factory barrel in 30-30 Winchester. Mag-na-porting it or an SSK Industries muzzle brake would make it more comfortable to shoot from the bench.

A big old groundhog is duck soup at 300 yards for Simpson and his Contender. The rubber Pachmayr grip and fore-end help to control the gun and make it less slippery.

Only a few of the over 30 chamberings that have been or are available from T/C, from left: 357 Magnum; 357-44 B&D; 41 Magnum; 44 Magnum; 45 Colt; 454 Magnum; 30 Herrett; 35 Herrett; 30-30; 35 Remington.

The author illustrates his Creedmoor shooting form, most useful when potting away at steel targets some 200 yards away. This 10" factory barrel in 7mm TCU is proven winner in competition.

Here are a few of the Wildcats available for the Contender, from left: 224 JDJ; 6mm JDJ; 25-35 Improved; 6.5 JDJ; 7mm JDJ; 30-30 Ackley Improved; 30-40 Krag Improved; 338 JDJ; 358 JDJ; 375 JDJ; 411 JDJ; 430 JDJ; and the last, not a wildcat, the 45-70.

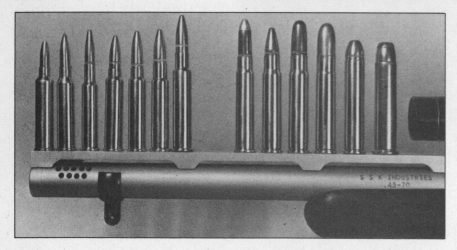

the front sight. For my eyes at least, the blade should be a bit thinner for more daylight on both sides. Although most of my Contender barrels used for hunting wear scopes, I do occasionaly use a 35 Remington tube with factory sights for hunting thick wooded areas. For this kind of activity the rear sight is fine but the front blade really needs a gold bead.

I know of no other firearm on this planet that has been offered in so many different chamberings as the Contender. Over the years well over 30 different calibers have been stamped on its barrel, ranging from 17 to 45. To name a few, both better and lesser known: 17 Bumblebee; 22 rimfire; 22 WMR; 223 Remington; 22 PPC; 6.5 TCU; 25-20 WCF; 7mm TCU; 30-30; 35 Remington; 41 Magnum; 44 Magnum; and 45 Colt. If we add all the wildcats such as the I.H.M.S.A. and SSK Industries series, the tally adds up to well over 100 calibers and probably more.

Such a myriad choice in calibers is why T/C has long enjoyed such brisk barrel sales—it's addictive. Once you buy that first Contender you will, inevitably, buy additional barrels chambered for other calibers. In fact, at least one company, SSK Industries, exists for few purposes other than making custom barrels for the Contender.

Everyone has his own favorite cartridges when it comes to talking about the Contender and I'm certainly no exception. Fact is, I'll even throw the old hat into the ring and describe what I consider to be the ideal Contender battery for shooting everything from paper targets to tin cans and from titmice to moose. First of all, for hunting small game and smallbore metallic silhouette competition, the Contender owner must have a 22 rimfire barrel. When fed ammunition

the act too. I've been shooting one of these little critters, put together by Dennis Bellm (P.O. Ackley Barrels, Inc.) and it's one of the neatest tricks you ever saw, especially for whitetail hunters who hunt from tree stands. Mine is 34¾" long over-all with the 20" bull barrel in 300 Savage, and weighs 6 lbs., 5 ozs. replete with Redfield mounts and Burris 4x Mini scope. I also have a fiberglass buttstock made by Brown Precision and it reduces the weight to exactly 6 lbs. Pretty darned neat.

Since day one, Contender barrels

have been drilled and tapped for scope mounting but the latest open sights are far superior to those of yesteryear. To date, T/C has used five different rear sights and three out front. Now there are but two of each; the 10" octagon, 10" bull and Super-14 barrels share the same sights, while the Hot-Shot barrel wears its own design.

Improvements made in the latest rear sight are, without doubt, a direct result of the input from metallic silhouette shooters and it's a dandy. However, for use in competition I'd like to see yet another change made to

J. D. Jones likes his 6.5 JDJ wildcat, and killed this Springbok at just over 300 paces with one shot. It's an impressive cartridge!

Switching from one barrel to another is simple. Remove the fore-end and push out the hinge pin with a Hornady 375-caliber solid bullet. Shown are an SSK Industries barrel in 6.5 JDJ with Weaver 2x scope. Below is a 44-caliber Hot-Shot barrel.

of its liking, the Contender will rival the best of sporter weight rifles in accuracy.

One of the best buys in Contender barrels, and yet probably the most neglected, is the Hot-Shot barrel. It's available in two styles, regular 10" bull and 10" bull with vent rib, both with removable choke inserts. The former costs $5 more than the regular barrel and the latter a mere $15 more. Both are available in 357 and 44 Remington Magnum and 410-ga./45 Colt which was recently reintroduced. With the choke tube removed, these barrels will handle regular loads just like the other barrels, but with the choke installed, throw devastating shot patterns out to 20 yards or so.

The 44 Magnum Hot-Shot load contains ⅝-oz. of shot and moves out of the 10" barrel at 1200 fps. Ballistically, it is equivalent to 2½", 410-gauge shotshell loads. So, we may as well add a Hot-Shot barrel to the Contender battery, too. These cartridges are available from T/C dealers or you can load your own with shot capsules and data furnished by T/C.

For varmints, I find the 22 Hornet tough to beat out to maybe 150 yards. At farther distances it runs out of steam too fast for quick, humane kills on larger varmints. Without doubt, the best all-round varmint cartridge for the Contender is the 223 Remington. Simply and modestly put, I don't miss many prairie dogs out to 225 yards with this combination; a groundhog munching on a four-leaf clover at 300 yards is also in great danger of having his luck run out

Larry Kelly likes the 375 JDJ wildcat. He killed this nice stone sheep with it, somewhere up in Alaska. Larry has probably taken more big game with a handgun than any other hunter in the world.

The Contender can be a handful of a gun when chambered for a biggie such as the 45-70 shown here. Note the four rings and SSK Industries T'SOB scope mount to keep the scope in place. Pachmayr grips and SSK muzzle brake take the bite out of such a powerful cartridge.

Simpson picks these cartridges for a good Contender battery, from left: 22 LR; 44 Hot-Shot; 22 Hornet; 223 Rem.; 7mm TCU; 30-30; 300 Savage; 6.5 JDJ; 35 Rem.; 375 JDJ; 45-70. Rem.; 375 JDJ; 45-70.

when I launch a Hornady 50-grain SX from my 14″ SSK barrel. If I had to boil it down to one barrel for shooting the wee critters, it would be chambered for the 223 Remington.

For a couple years I shot metallic silhouettes with various handguns and stacked up trophies like cordwood with the Contender. I started out with the 30-30 Winchester and ended up with the 7mm TCU. The 30-30 packs more authority on hard set rams but is slightly edged out in accuracy by the little 7mm. For competition I would still pick these two cartridges because both just plain get the job done.

Although handgun silhouette shooters should be given a lion's share of credit for the Contender's success, big game hunters are the ones who put it on the map and who have kept it there. Name a caliber and you can bet that someone has reamed out a Contender barrel for it and gone out and bumped off some unsuspecting beast. Also, name a big game animal and you can safely bet that at least one of its kind has fallen victim to the Contender.

Larry Kelly of Mag-na-port fame, for example, has taken various and sundry big game with the Contender up to and including Africa's big five. In case you aren't familiar with them, they are elephant, rhino, Cape buffalo, lion and leopard. Larry has taken three jumbo and buffalo with his 375 JDJ loaded with the Hornady 300-grain solid at about 2,000 fps.

My pick of the Contender big game cartridges? Well, let's see. Of the chamberings available from T/C, I'd have to go with the venerable old 35

Remington for woods hunting and the 30-30 loaded with 130- to 150-grain spitzers for open country hunting. However, for most of my hunting with this handgun, I usually tote a couple of wildcats or one of the older factory cartridges. The 6.5 JDJ pushes a 120-grain Speer to 2400 fps and is my pick of the litter for longish shots.

For woods hunting I like the 375 JDJ loaded with Hornady's 220-grain flat nose to 2100 fps, or the 45-70 and Hornady's 300-grain hollow-point at about 1800 fps. Both cartridges hit hard and leave very short blood trails. For all-round use in both open and wooded terrain, a friend of mine swears by an SSK barrel in 300 Savage. He's used it on both North American and African game and says its performance can't be beat. Could be that he has something there.

In order to take advantage of the Contender's performance, one cannot live on iron sights alone. I have quite a number of handgun scopes but only a few see the majority of service on my Contenders. One of my favorites is a stainless steel Weaver in 2x but, sadly enough, that company is no longer with us.

A most rugged and most versatile handgun scope is the Burris 1-4x variable. I've toted this scope through the swamps during summer when chas-

ing feral hogs, through the woods during fall and winter when after deer, and across the mountains and prairies when after varmints. It has yet to let me down. For woods hunting of big game this scope has no peer because of its relatively wide field of view at low power.

For open country hunting of big game and for medium range shooting of varmints, I like the Redfield 4x; but for varmint shooting at all ranges, the Burris 7x is the one I use most. Burris also makes a 10x handgun scope but due to its extremely narrow field of view, I find it better suited for bench-rest shooting. Now let's look at scope mounts.

As off-the-shelf scope mounts go, the Redfield Magnum-proof is a winner, especially on barrels chambered for cartridges in the recoil range of the 30-30 and lower. However, for romping, stomping loads in the more potent wildcats, such as the 375 JDJ, as well as commercial cartridges like the 35 Remington and 45-70, the SSK Industries T'SOB mounting system is tops. It's a bit more expensive than the Redfield but, wow, will it hang on when the recoil gets over on the vicious side.

And, speaking of recoil, the factory wood grips are fine for cartridges of relatively mild voice but, when the big boomers bark, much of their bite

One of the more versatile and best buys in Contender barrels is the Hot-Shot barrel with removable choke. With the choke removed it handles regular 44 magnum loads, but with the choke installed it acts like a 410 shotgun when fed Hot-Shot loads available from T/C. Note the folding rear sight.

is reduced by installing a Pachmayr rubber grip. It's also much easier to hang onto with sweaty hands. Another neat way to reduce muzzle jump and recoil in the Contender is to have its barrel Mag-na-ported. SSK Industries also offers a muzzle brake that works.

It would not be fitting to write about the Contender without at least briefly touching on its safety features. The safety, or hammer block as it is also called, is hidden from view inside the frame. This block engages the external hammer, keeping it from contacting the firing pins under three conditions: when the hammer is pulled back one notch to its safety position; when the hammer is cocked and the trigger guard is accidentally depressed; and even if the thumb should slip off the hammer during cocking.

Early Contenders had no external safety, so to speak, until it was discovered that when the trigger is pulled and the hammer lowered with the thumb, it rested against the firing pin. A sharp blow on the hammer could fire a cartridge in the chamber. Later Contenders have a small transverse bar located in the hammer. Pushing it from right to left cams a pin into protrusion from the hammer face thus keeping the hammer from contacting the firing pins.

Contender frames manufactured after April 1, 1984 don't have the transverse safety bar but, instead, have what T/C calls an external manual firing pin selector. Sitting atop the hammer is a three-position switch with two "hammer noses" inside the hammer face. When the switch is in its center or safe position, both noses are turned out of alignment with the firing pins. Flipping the switch either right or left aligns one of the noses with one of the firing pins, depending on whether you wish to shoot rimfire or centerfire. Pretty darned neat and a very safe system, to say the least.

Probably, one of the more common questions I'm asked about the Contender is, how accurate is it? Accuracy will vary from barrel to barrel, no different from any other mass-produced firearm. Generally, I find that most Contenders will shoot right along with most sporter-weight rifles and, when fitted with a custom barrel, most rifles will have a tough time keeping up with the Contender. It is the rare T/C barrel that can't be made to shoot into 2 MOA with the right handload and some will do it with factory loads. Some barrels will shoot better than others by a considerable margin.

When fed match grade bullets, my 7mm TCU will average right at one MOA. I have several custom barrels made from Shilen blanks that will consistently stay under an inch at 100 yards for five shots. At the moment, the two most accurate barrels I have, both turned out by SSK Industries, are in 223 Remington and 6.5 JDJ. With their favorite handloads, both have shot numerous groups in the ½- to ¾-MOA range and quite a number measuring less than ½-inch.

Why such fine accuracy from a firearm the design of which seems to go against the grain of what we normally consider important in other types of firearms? To be honest, I really don't know. The Contender certainly locks up quite rigidly but not as rigid as a bolt action rifle, and yet several of my

Shown here is the versatility of the Contender. In front is a Contender carbine made up by Dennis Bellm; behind the carbine are four different barrel configurations available from T/C and in the rear are custom barrels in various wildcat chamberings from SSK Industries. Cat at far left is not wild.

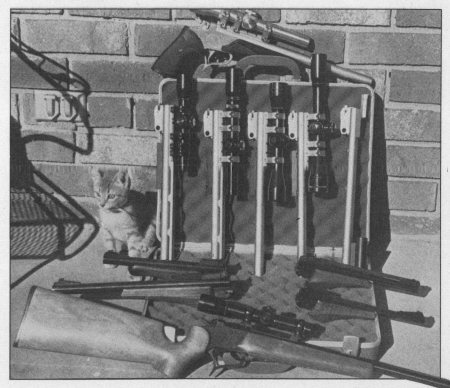

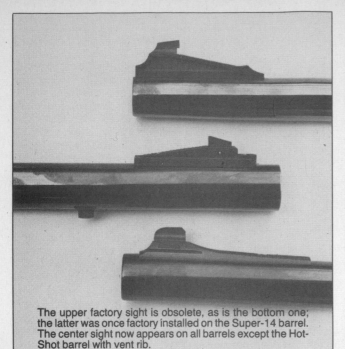

The upper factory sight is obsolete, as is the bottom one; the latter was once factory installed on the Super-14 barrel. The center sight now appears on all barrels except the Hot-Shot barrel with vent rib.

Here are three of the five factory rear sights seen on Contenders through the years. All barrels, with the exception of the Hot-Shot barrel with vent rib, now come with the sight at far right.

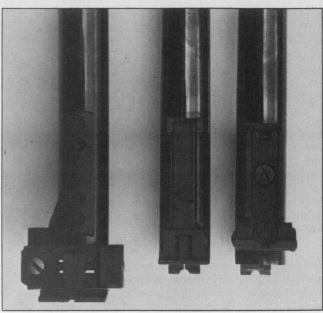

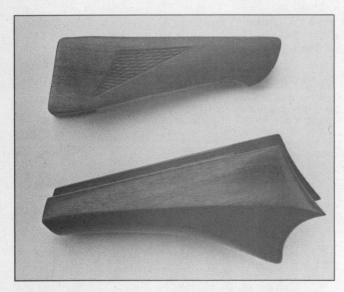

Two types of fore-ends seen on Contenders are the early model (top) and current production (bottom). The evolution of Contender factory grips goes from the earliest (left) to current production (right).

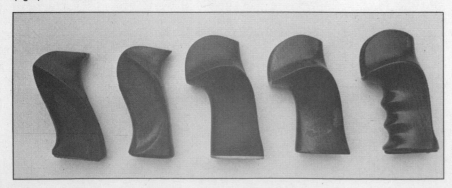

Contender barrels will outshoot a number of my rifles. One factor in the Contender's favor is its barrel—T/C uses very uniform blanks. Another is the Contender's trigger; with a tool no more complex than an Allen wrench, it can be adjusted down to a good clean 1 to 1½ lbs. with no creep or backlash.

The new two-piece locking bolt didn't hurt a thing either. It locks up much tighter than the old one-piece bolt and it is felt by many Contender owners (including me) that those older guns with the solid bolt should be retrofitted with the latest in bolt design. Both the factory and SSK Industries will make this modification.

I've never found the new bolt at all difficult to open but because it locks up much tighter than the old one, it does require a bit harder squeeze on the trigger guard. However, it did create a problem for some shooters so, at serial number 195000, T/C introduced their new easy-open frame. Other than the location of its pivot pin, the frame remains unchanged from the older models.

With the exception of minor trigger adjustment, any gunsmithing of the Contender should be left to those who know exactly what they're doing. The Accuracy Den, 25 Bitterbrush Rd., Reno, NV 89523 is reputed to do an excellent job of tuning Contenders for top accuracy. SSK Industries, Rt. 1, Della Dr., Bloomingdale, OH 43910, offers the T'SOB scope mounting system as well as 10-, 12-, 14- and 21-inch custom barrels made from Shilen blanks in over 50 chamberings—from 17 to 577 caliber. P.O. Ackley Barrels, 2376 S. Redwood Rd., Salt Lake City, UT 84119 also turns out rifle-length barrels for the Contender in just about every caliber. Any of these companies will trade their literature for a 22-cent stamp.

So there you have it, the Thompson/Center Contender. Maligned by some but praised by many others, it's probably safe to say that the Contender is one of the most successful handgun designs introduced during the 20th century. As a good friend of mine is fond of saying, the Contender looks somewhat like a handgun and shoots exactly like a rifle. He's exactly right. ●

Hunter Ken Powell likes to load his 35 Remington Contender with Hornady 200-grain spire point bullets and go after such keen-eyed game as the pronghorn. He dropped this one at about 150 yards with one shot, using a Harris bipod.

## Favorite Contender Loads

| Cartridge | Bullet (grs.) | Primer | Powder (type) | Charge (grs.) | Velocity (fps) | Barrel |
|---|---|---|---|---|---|---|
| 17 Rem. | 25 Hornady HP | Rem. 7½ | IMR-4320 | 25.0 | 3,506 | 14″ SSK |
| 22 Hornet | 40 Speer | Win. 6½ | WW-680 | 12.5 | 2,511 | 10″ Factory |
| 22 Hornet | 45 Hornady | Win. 6½ | WW-680 | 11.5 | 2,435 | 10″ Factory |
| 22 Hornet | 45 Remington Factory Load | | | | 2,359 | 10″ Factory |
| 223 Rem. | 40 Speer | CCI BR-4 | H-335 | 28.5 | 3,115 | 14″ SSK |
| 223 Rem. | 50 Hornady SX | CCI BR-4 | H-335 | 27.0 | 3,006 | 14″ SSK |
| 223 Rem. | 55 HPBT Federal Factory Load | | | | 2,794 | 14″ SSK |
| 6.5mm JDJ | 100 Hornady | CCI BR-2 | IMR-4320 | 36.0 | 2,615 | 14″ SSK |
| 6.5mm JDJ | 120 Speer | CCI BR-2 | IMR-4320 | 34.0 | 2,414 | 14″ SSK |
| 6.5mm JDJ | 120 Speer | CCI BR-2 | IMR-4350 | 38.0 | 2,427 | 14″ SSK |
| 7mm TCU | 120 Hornady | Rem. 7½ | RL-7 | 24.0 | 2,161 | 14″ Factory |
| 7mm TCU | 130 Speer | Rem. 7½ | H-322 | 27.0 | 2,211 | 14″ Factory |
| 7mm TCU | 162 Hornady | Rem. 7½ | IMR-4895 | 26.0 | 1,963 | 14″ Factory |
| 30-30 Win. | 130 Speer | Fed. 210 | IMR-4895 | 34.0 | 2,064 | 10″ Factory |
| 30-30 Win. | 150 Hornady | Fed. 210 | H-4198 | 29.0 | 1,940 | 10″ Factory |
| 30-30 Win. | 200 Speer | Fed. 210 | WW-748 | 32.0 | 1,774 | 10″ Factory |
| 30-30 Win. | 55 Accelerator, Remington Factory Load | | | | 2,722 | 10″ Factory |
| 30-30 Win. | 125 Federal Factory Load | | | | 1,961 | 10″ Factory |
| 30-30 Win. | 150 Winchester Factory Load | | | | 1,917 | 10″ Factory |
| 357 Magnum | 158 Speer | CCI 550 | WW-296 | 16.0 | 1,490 | 10″ Factory |
| 357 Maximum | 180 Speer | CCI 550 | WW-680 | 22.0 | 1,640 | 10″ Factory |
| 35 Rem. | 180 Speer | Rem. 9½ | IMR-3031 | 37.0 | 2,040 | 14″ Factory |
| 35 Rem. | 200 Hornady | Rem. 9½ | IMR-3031 | 36.0 | 1,896 | 14″ Factory |
| 35 Rem. | 200 Remington Factory Load | | | | 1,729 | 14″ Factory |
| 375 JDJ | 220 Hornady | Rem. 9½ | IMR-4895 | 48.0 | 2,159 | 14″ SSK |
| 375 JDJ | 235 Speer | Rem. 9½ | IMR-4895 | 47.0 | 1,934 | 14″ SSK |
| 375 JDJ | 270 Speer | Rem. 9½ | H-322 | 44.0 | 1,915 | 14″ SSK |
| 41 Magnum | 210 Hornady | CCI 350 | WW-296 | 22.0 | 1,571 | 14″ Factory |
| 41 Magnum | 210 Remington Factory Load | | | | 1,558 | 14″ Factory |
| 44 Magnum | 200 Speer | CCI 350 | H-4227 | 26.5 | 1,858 | 14″ Factory |
| 44 Magnum | 265 Hornady | CCI 350 | H-4227 | 24.0 | 1,556 | 14″ Factory |
| 44 Magnum | 240 SJHP Remington Factory Load | | | | 1,592 | 14″ Factory |
| 45-70 | 300 Hornady HP | CCI BR-2 | RL-7 | 46.0 | 1,639 | 14″ SSK |
| 45-70 | 400 Speer | CCI BR-2 | RL-7 | 43.0 | 1,428 | 14″ SSK |
| 45-70 | 300 Federal Factory Load | | | | 1,644 | 14″ SSK |

All loads shown are maximum but safe in the author's guns but may be excessive in other guns. All powder charges must be reduced by ten percent for starting loads in other guns.

# Steyr's Plastic "Vunder Gewehr"

# The AUG

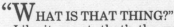

"WHAT IS THAT THING?"

Like it or not, that's the question people ask, and it's one you will get very tired of answering, if you happen to own a Steyr-Daimler-Puch AUG.

The AUG happens to be on the leading edge of manufacturing and small arms technology. If that's not enough to satisfy the curious, tell them that

The AUG is a 223, but that's about all it has in common with the other dozen or so military-style autoloaders on the market. The optics are permanent. The 1.5x scope is intended to gather light in marginal conditions. The trigger guard is a bit more than that, as it will accommodate an entire gloved hand. The rudimentary fixed iron sights (on top of the scope) are not likely to be used unless the optics are damaged.

An advantage of the bullup configuration is easy one-hand use. The plastic magazine is molded in a waffle pattern, a bit like the very early Armalite AR-10 military rifle metal magazines. The AUG magazine survived every test from being run over by a pickup truck, to being used as a hammer to drive a nail into a wood floor.

Though the AUG is radical in appearance, it's very comfortable to shoot. In spite of the breech being close to the shooter's face, the gun is no louder on firing than the AR-15. Gun is shown with the front grip folded down, ready for use.

**The bullpup is here to stay! This radical-appearing battle rifle has lots of plastic and some metal but it has been service tested to prove its worth. Despite its odd design, the AUG is pleasant to shoot, easy to handle ... and accurate.**

# by JOHN LEE

Compared to the Colt AR-15 with collapsible stock extended, the AUG is a few inches shorter, but a bit heavier.

the AUG is a very modern 223-caliber rifle that happens to work better than most. While the AUG is chambered for the 5.56mm NATO (or 223 U.S. service cartridge), few features other than the caliber are likely to be familiar to the other people at the local range.

Steyr-Daimler-Puch, known to some American shooters as simply "Steyr," have built guns of international renown for generations. The Austrian company also builds mopeds, trucks, machine tools and a host of mechanical devices that have nothing whatever to do with shooting.

Gun South, one of the newer American arms importers, would like the AUG to be a familiar rifle to American police agencies, collectors and shooters. At the same time, Steyr-Daimler-Puch would like to capture a share of the growing market for military and police 5.56mm rifles in the Western world.

First impressions of the AUG range from "That's neat," to "What's that thing? Is that *really* a gun?" When the AUG is pulled from its case, there are no middle-ground comments.

The most obvious departure from what we consider "normal" is the use of the permanently mounted optical sights. Intended primarily to gather light in marginal shooting conditions, the low-power scope is rated at 1.5 power. The reticle is a circle, open in the center, with no supporting crosshairs. The circle is such that a car door fits neatly within its confines at 100 meters. Obviously, this scope is intended for military/police purposes, and not for making neat holes in paper. Though it seems silly to point this fact out in test after test, there are still those shooters who are critical of military rifles because they do not perform like target rifles. The low-

magnification sight provides quick target acquisition under the best of conditions, and allows a soldier or police officer to see and shoot at a target in poor light that would make conventional open sights useless. In the event the optics are damaged, there is a very simple set of fixed sights cast into the top of the scope tube. Using them proved a bit difficult, owing to their coarseness and short sight radius.

As a left-handed shooter, the first question I asked was how to keep ejected brass from landing in my mouth when shooting the obviously right-handed AUG. A look at the factory manual showed that a conversion kit, consisting of a left-ejecting bolt, is available to convert the AUG for portside shooting.

To make the switch, it's necessary to field strip the rifle, and swap bolt

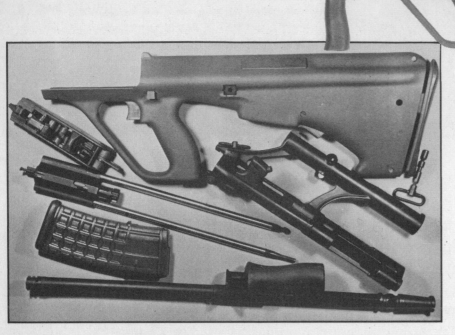

Here's the AUG broken down to major components. The two rods on the bolt carrier combine the functions of gas piston and guides. The left-hand rod functions in conjunction with the operating handle. At the upper left is the firing mechanism, combining the plastic hammer and sear with steel springs. Plastic or not, the trigger pull is the best of any 223 tested.

assemblies. Before putting things together again, the ejection port cover must be moved from one side of the bullpup stock/lower receiver assembly to the other. Conversion amounts to perhaps five minutes work.

Show an American shooter a bullpup rifle and he will wonder aloud about whether or not he really wants that chamber next to his cheek, and to be all that intimate with tens of thousands of pounds of chamber pressure. American impressions aside, the bullpup is not all that new in European military establishments. The French have used a bullpup battle rifle for some years. The British, after tinkering with a succession of designs for more than 30 years, recently adopted a bullpup design with fixed optics, chambered for the 5.56mm NATO round, to replace their British-built variant of the FN FAL rifle. The new British rifle is conceptually similar, but of different appearance than the AUG. The point to be made here is that the bullpup design is becoming more accepted around the world, and modern manufacturing methods, that allow the use of a structural plastic single part to form a lower receiver and stock, are compatible with the bullpup design.

Even though the AUG is readily converted to left-hand use, a real concern remains in terms of what could happen, under stress, if a left-handed cop grabbed a right-handed rifle and yanked the trigger. The same concern would apply to the right-hander who grabbed the lefty's rifle.

Since the result in either case would be severe nasal congestion, consisting of cartridge brass up one's nose, the concern is real. It would be appropriate to clearly mark a rifle converted to left-hand use.

We have discussed some potential concerns of the bullpup concept—so what do we gain? Compared to the standard Colt AR-15, the AUG is just over seven inches shorter, with the same 20-inch barrel length, and a pound heavier than the Colt. (The new M-16 variant weighs about the same as the AUG.) If the comparison is made with Colt's collapsible-stock AR-15 variant, over-all length is virtually the same, with the Colt stock retracted, and the weight advantage more heavily in favor of the Colt product.

So—the question goes—why the bullpup design? Handling qualities in tight quarters lead the list of positive things to justify the bullpup as a general-issue police or G.I. tool. Balance for one-hand use is also enhanced, and using the weapon from inside a vehicle is far easier. Though it doesn't often occur to the average plinker to wonder about such things, it would be vastly simpler to use the AUG from the hatch of an armored vehicle than it would be to wrestle with a full-length rifle under the same handicapped conditions. That sort of situation is not likely to sway buyers away from Remington and Winchester bolt guns, but that's the sort of question that occurs in the minds of people who equip armies and police agencies.

Police agency sales are the obvious goal of the Interarms folk, although that doesn't mean they are not interested in orders from just plain plinkers and collectors. For the just-plain plinker who would like to order an AUG, it's a bit difficult to pin down the price. With the presently strong dollar and changes going on in the international money market, prices quoted for the AUG have ranged from an initial $1,200 to some advertised figures of around $895 or less. Best advice on prices, particularly those of imports, is to go to your dealer and ask "How much?" Suffice it to say that the AUG is not an inexpensive firearm.

While the gas system is reasonably straightforward, no other feature or method of construction is familiar. The gas system involves a piston impinging on an operating rod, which moves a bolt carrier to rotate and unlock a multi-lug bolt. Though the layout is a bit different, the concept isn't all that much changed from the system used in the Armalite AR-180.

Construction is where this piece of machinery is unlike anything else on the gun store shelf. Other than the barrel, bolt, gas system components

The ejection port cover and retainer may be removed and switched to the other side for conversion to left-hand use. Importer can supply a left-ejecting bolt as an option.

The massive action uses a rotating, multi-lug bolt which locks into a steel insert in the alloy upper receiver section. The optics tube and all stressed areas have steel inserts for higher strength and better wear characteristics.

The lockwork is unusually large and is nearly all plastic. The layout is not unlike an AR-15, other than the larger size of the plastic components. Some may deride the use of plastic here, but it works as well as metal.

and upper receiver, most everything else is structural plastic. That includes the hammer, sear, and virtually all the lockwork except springs. The trigger and stock assembly, as well as the magazine, are plastic.

The see-through magazine is numbered at 10, 20 and 30-shot increments, and strips readily for cleaning. Magazines for exotic auto rifles are not cheap, and not always that easy to find, so some questions about the durability of this plastic number crossed my mind.

Tossing the magazine up in the air and letting it crash to the floor produced no damage. Walking on it didn't bother the plastic. A final foolish test, that made me wonder what Interarms would charge me for wrecking the mag, involved driving a nail into a wood floor, using the mag as a hammer. I don't think many carpenters will be carrying AUG magazines in their aprons, but the magazine was not even scratched after sinking the nail! I wouldn't want to repeat that test with a metal AR-15 magazine that I expected to use again.

The buttstock is straight, as has been the practice with battle rifles for some decades. A vertical foregrip folds down from its stowed position beneath the barrel. In the folded position, the foregrip makes a convenient

rest. Folded down, the shape of it resembles a piece of squeezed clay, or to put it more simply, a hand. Nothing tricky—it just works well.

The trigger guard is more than the name implies. An entire gloved hand can be easily slid into place. The wide (.49-inch) trigger breaks at just over three pounds on the test sample. There is an almost imperceptible movement of the trigger before a very crisp break. I wouldn't call it creep or a "first stage," but simply a matter of taking up a small amount of slack in the linkage before things start to happen.

The firing mechanism is a modular plastic unit that slides into the buttstock. The parts look a bit like their counterparts in an AR-15, but they are all plastic, and a good bit larger. The trigger pull was among the best I

have encountered in a 5.56mm military-type rifle, plastic hammer and sear or not.

The upper receiver is an alloy casting, with steel inserts at stress points, including the female lugs into which the quick-detach barrel locks, and against which the bolt achieves lock-up.

That quick-change barrel also has a number of features that are not what we are accustomed to seeing.

The flash hider is threaded to the muzzle, and the threads extend back another five inches along the exposed barrel. The factory literature describes the threads as "cooling fins." The flash hider is open at the front, and resembles the early M-16-type part.

This is one of the very few military weapons smaller than a squad auto-

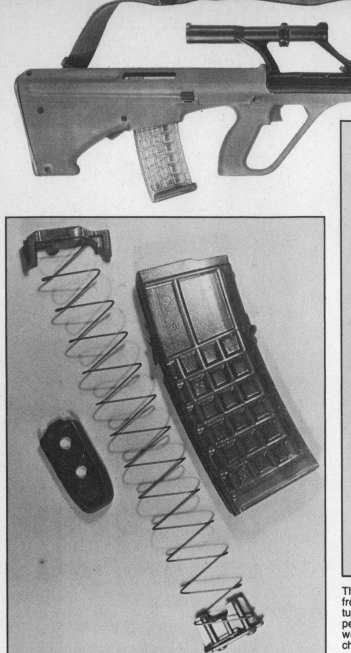

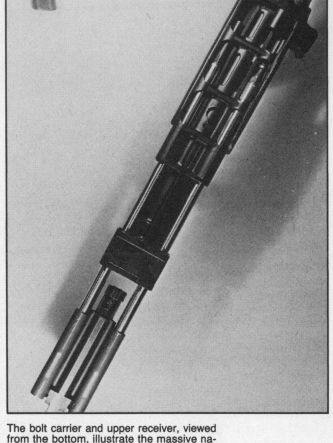

The bolt carrier and upper receiver, viewed from the bottom, illustrate the massive nature of the AUG action. The components appear robust enough to function in a heavier weapon than a personal rifle. The quick-change barrel and modular design of the other components make such a concept distinctly possible.

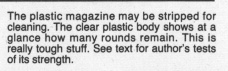

The plastic magazine may be stripped for cleaning. The clear plastic body shows at a glance how many rounds remain. This is really tough stuff. See text for author's tests of its strength.

matic rifle to be equipped with a quick-change barrel. While it simplifies the cleaning task greatly, the advantage is also obvious in a military context. It would also be no great trick to equip the basic weapon with longer, shorter or suppressed barrels for special applications.

As an objective test of the light gathering abilities of the integral optics, I handed the rifle to two local city policemen, who carried it a short distance from town to the county sheriff's range. Despite the 3 a.m. "shots fired"

calls to the sheriff from farmers, and minor chewings-out for the two officers for absenting themselves from town for a short time, their opinions were interesting. The first officer hated the rifle on sight, but shot it anyway. He said the sights worked quite well at the unlighted, rural range. The scope gathered light to the point that otherwise impossible shots could be attempted, and when the general area was illuminated with police car headlights, night was turned into day. (Obviously, the officers were

firing from another spot—not silhouetted by the lights.) The second policeman liked the rifle, but was uncertain about the utility of the sights, until after returning the rifle and recovering from catching heck for shooting near a small town in the middle of the night. It's easy to criticize the iron sights, but it must be remembered that the optics are the AUG's *primary* sights—made to be used in all conditions at all times. Like the plastic hammer, that's a bit foreign to most of us, but it works—and extremely well.

Note the position of the ejection port with the AUG set up for right-hand use. Importer offers a conversion kit to permit left-hand use. The gun handles extremely well despite its unorthodox appearance.

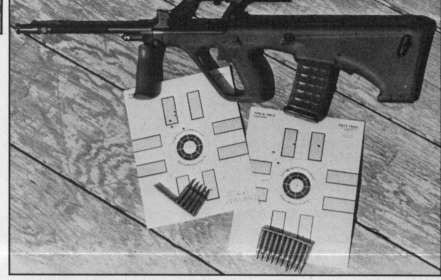

Accuracy from an improvised rest at 100 yards was similar to what might be expected of other good 223 military rifles. Target acquisition was improved, and recovery time shortened by the optics. Ammo used was U.S. military NATO ball.

For a good many years, terms like "different," "plastic" and "light alloy" were equated with cheap unreliable firearms. That day is about at an end. Just as "made in Japan" is now a mark of quality, rather than a pejorative, shooters must realize that plastic works better than milled steel in many applications. "Better" in this context means that soldiers' hands don't freeze to metal triggers or bolt handles in extreme cold. Plastic stocks, as proven by the fiberglass M-14 stocks issued early in the Vietnam War, do not turn green and rot in tropical climates. Plastic firing mechanisms and magazines do not rust and turn to brown, lumpy things when exposed to salt air or rain. Though I'm not likely to get rid of my milled steel and walnut antiques, I will not get into the old foolishness that condemns the use of structural plastics in firearms.

A trip to the local range showed that the AUG shoots as well as other high-quality 5.56mm systems. Shooting from an improvised rest at 50 yards produced 1½-inch groups, and 100-yard efforts yielded 3-inch performance. Ammo used was American G.I., NATO-standard ball. Though I have read of tiny groups printed by out-of-the-box military-type rifles over and over again, I have never shot any of them. After testing just about every 5.56mm system in production, I can say that the AUG shoots as well as the best, and better than many. On the plus side, the trigger is excellent. Plastic parts or not, a better trigger

pull would be difficult to obtain. A factor that opens the groups a bit is the rather coarse scope reticle. Remember, though, that the reticle is not designed for target shooting.

We also used some Korean PMC ammo, and some assorted handloads. Performance was nearly the same, no matter what we fed the AUG. In the course of putting some 400 rounds through the rifle—using only one magazine—no malfunctions were noted.

A few years ago, when military-style auto rifles were very fashionable in some circles, some real turkeys made it to the market place. Some of the guns were simply not developed to the point of sufficient reliability to make it in the American market. Some of the importers were also a bit shaky. The AUG is a sound, fully-developed system that combines innovative engineering and excellent materials in a very modern package. Interarms is also about as solid as a gun importer can be. The AUG may

be different, but it's an interesting piece of equipment that was always fun to pull out at the range or the local gun store. The "What is that thing?" conversations were as much fun as shooting this Austrian import. ●

### Data
### Steyr-Daimler-Puch AUG (Army Universal Gun)

**Caliber:** 5.56mm NATO (223)
**Barrel Length:** 20"; chamber and bore chromed
**Over-all Length:** 31"
**Weight, unloaded, with magazine:** 8.2 lbs.
**Magazine Capacity:** 30 rounds
**Importer:** Gun South, Inc.
P.O. Box 129
108 Morrow Ave. Trussville, AL 35173
**Price:** Check with local dealer
**Comments:** In terms of manufacturing technology, the most modern 5.56mm rifle in production.

# Iron Sights

Venturino, professional hunter Johann von Rooyan, and trackers/
skinners pose with the author's zebra stallion taken with one shot
from the 40-70 Sharps at about 130 yards.

**Thinking of hunting in Africa? Costs compare
with hunting in North America these days.
And, you don't need to take a scope-sighted
"whiz-bang" cannon to bag the plains
animals. Iron sights and a single shot will do
nicely, thank you.**

## by MIKE VENTURINO

IF AN AMERICAN has ever hunted
and enjoyed it he has probably had
dreams of someday hunting in Africa.
This was certainly true in my case.
From the time of my boyhood until
only recently I felt that the cost would
always put an African safari out of
reach. Thankfully, modern air travel
has changed that. Nowadays you can
hunt many non-dangerous species in
Africa for less than you would pay to
hunt Alaska. In fact, in many ways, a
brief African hunt will compare
costwise with hunting elk in our western states. For example, in my own
Yellowstone valley of Montana, elk

# in AFRICA

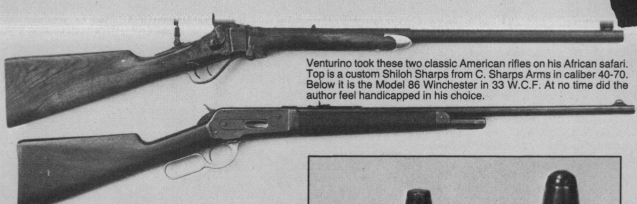

Venturino took these two classic American rifles on his African safari. Top is a custom Shiloh Sharps from C. Sharps Arms in caliber 40-70. Below it is the Model 86 Winchester in 33 W.C.F. At no time did the author feel handicapped in his choice.

Most of Venturino's shots were taken from the kneeling position. Heavy brush such as this made shooting difficult throughout the hunt.

The 33 W.C.F. with 200-gr. Hornady (left) and 40-70 Sharps with 400-gr. Barnes performed extremely well on African plains game. The 33 W.C.F. and '86 Winchester combination proved just to be the ticket for the author's grey duiker.

hunting outfitters charge a daily rate of $260 to $300 for a minimum 10-day hunt. In our first African camp the 10-day rate for both my wife and myself was $270 per day, and accommodations were comfortable stone cabins with indoor bathrooms.

When my friend, single-shot riflesmith, Ed Webber, of Big Timber, Montana, returned from his first African hunt in 1983, he set to work convincing me that I should return with him in 1985. After he explained the economics, I was not all that hard to convince. For 1985 Ed booked with Ventures International, a New Jer-

sey-based safari booking agency. Therefore, I called Ventures International's boss Don "Bucky" Malson and also booked a hunt simultaneously with Ed's.

Once that first step was made and I was committed, the next step was to choose a safari rifle battery. As a full-time gunwriter, it is my work to shoot, reload, and test guns ranging from antique big bore black powder rifles through the most modern high velocity types. I have at least a passing familiarity with most types of hunting rifles.

Initially the choice of rifles posed a

quandry for me. On the one hand I freely admit to a preference for two types of rifles. One of these is the single-shot Sharps, both originals and the new Shilohs. Another rifle type is the lever-action Winchesters in their wide array of obsolete but very interesting calibers.

A troubling thought went through my mind, though: This African trip could possibly be a once-in-a-lifetime adventure. What if the hunting shots were going to be 300-yard-plus situations calling for flat shooting, scoped, modern rifles? Should I not be well armed for those eventualities?

There was, however, one hunting situation I need not worry about. That was dangerous game. My first African hunt was to be only for plains game: kudu, wildebeest, zebra, duiker, etc. I didn't have to worry about bone crunching stopping power, nor fast repeat shots.

After giving the matter some thought I came up with this theory: "If you are going to go on a special hunt, if it might be a once-in-a-lifetime trip, then use rifles that will make the experience unique." Most everyone goes to Africa and shoots scope-sighted, bolt-action repeaters in modern calibers. Therefore, I decided to make my main battery of rifles those that are uniquely American and in American calibers.

My African rifles would be a Sharps and a lever-action Winchester, both carrying iron sights, and both chambered for obsolete calibers.

My favorite hunting Sharps is a custom version from the C. Sharps Arms shop. It has a 26-inch half round/half octagon barrel. Wood is extra fancy French walnut, and it has a straight grip, checkered steel shotgun butt, and German silver "Hartford" fore-end cap. Triggers are the standard Shiloh double-set arrangement which came in extremely handy as I will detail shortly.

Caliber for this rifle is the 40-70 Sharps bottleneck which was first introduced in the late 1860s. Although it was originally a blackpowder cartridge, I have been experimenting of late in souping it up to more modern ballistics. The Shiloh Sharps guns are strong rifles of modern materials and I took this "hot-rodding" upon myself, even though the manufacturer, understandably, doesn't recommend wildcatting antique cartridges. Regardless, using Barnes 300- and 400-grain jacketed bullets and charges of IMR-4064 powder, I have reached 2,200 fps and 1,800 fps respectively. Also, accuracy is exceptional with five-shot, 100-yard groups of less than two inches being the norm.

For a Winchester I chose my Model 1886 in 33 WCF caliber. This particular Winchester is a takedown version which was a convenient asset when traveling.

The load for the 33 WCF consisted of the 200-grain Hornady flat point over 48.0 grains of H4350 powder. Cases were formed from standard Federal 45-70 brass in Pacific dies. The velocity of this load from the Winchester's 24-inch barrel is just over 2,000 fps, and it will group into 2½ inches at 100 yards. The 33 WCF, introduced in 1902, was considered a good elk cartridge in its day. I felt it would suffice for the moderately-sized African antelope.

On the Sharps the rear sight was an old Marble tang-mounted peep originally designed for use on Winchesters. The screw spacing is the same for the Sharps and it required only a new set of screws for mounting. Ed Webber made a custom eyecup with an ⅛-inch aperture so it would be quick for hunting. Up front was the Shiloh globe sight designed to take interchangeable inserts. Only the .05-inch-wide post insert was used on this African adventure.

Sights on the Model '86 Winchester were an ivory bead front with wide, shallow express-type rear. Though not precise for target shooting, these sights are amazingly fast for use in

On the first day of the hunt Venturino's guide pressured him into shooting this blesbok with the 308 Win. Model 70 that was taken along as a backup gun. This was a choice regretted by the author ever since.

It wasn't all a bowl of cherries for Venturino and his single-shot Sharps. He missed an easy shot at a gemsbok when shooting through a hole such as this. Sometimes those things can't be explained!

the game fields.

Shortly before departure date, I lost my nerve in regard to rifles. I was beginning to have nightmares about seeing trophies at 300 yards while carrying my 150-yard guns. At the last minute I decided to take my Winchester Model 70 in 308 Winchester with 2-7x Leupold scope. Loads were 150-grain Nosler bullets over 45.0 grains of IMR-3031. My intention was to use this rig only as a last resort, in case I couldn't get close enough for a shot with the other rifles.

As it turned out, taking the 308 Winchester along was a mistake that I will always regret.

Another item I started to have nightmares about in those last days of preparation was losing my guns in transit. After all, what could be worse than to finally get to Africa only to find that your guns didn't? I need not have worried. Unlike many other airlines, South African Airways is very experienced in transporting firearms, and hunters. We quickly and easily checked in at Houston. There were no hostile stares from the counter personnel, and no one asked us to open the gun cases so they could be inspected. In fact, South African Airways did everything possible to make a very long 19-hour flight comfortable, and when we arrived in Johannesburg everything we had checked in Houston arrived intact.

Our first hunting camp in Africa was in northern Transvaal, very near the Zimbabwe border. Upon arriving in camp we uncased the guns in order to sight in. When I unpacked my Sharps and lever-action Winchester my host's face registered concern. He said, "Didn't you bring anything with a scope on it?" When I said that I did have a scoped rifle he immediately relaxed.

Later that evening he introduced my individual guide, and made the

On the third day of the hunt, this kudu ran into view while the author was stalking zebra. One shot from the 40-70 put him down from about 130 yards.

comment that I would be hunting with iron sights and single shots. The guide merely looked at me dubiously, but showed relief when informed that I also had a scope-sighted bolt-action along.

On the very first day of hunting I began to understand why these professional guides were concerned about my choice of rifles. Some parts of Africa have been experiencing severe drought, and the game herds have been decimated in various regions. This was true where I was hunting. Game was scarce and very spooky. Slight sounds sent most animals running for cover. Also, the guides later informed me, they consider Americans, in general, poor game shots, and never in their experience had they guided a hunter using iron sights. That, coupled with the scarcity of animals, had them worried that my hunt would be a total failure.

Because of the effects of jet lag and general fatigue, I was extremely tired on the first day's hunt. Therefore, when we spotted a small herd of blesbok, medium-sized antelope indigenous to South Africa, I didn't resist too much when the guide shoved the 308 at me and said, "Shoot!"

A larger male had peeled off from the herd and stood directly facing us

at about 150 yards. As I knelt to take aim with the Model 70, I thought to try to slip the bullet in under his chin and into the heart. Intentions are great, but reality was different. Just as my trigger pull was completed, I could see the crosshairs had wavered high, and figured that shot would be a complete miss. But, while still recovering from recoil the guide was pounding my back saying the blesbok had dropped in his tracks. Upon reaching him we could see he had been hit precisely between the eyes. The beaming guide looked at me and said, "Were you aiming there?" I wiped the smile from his face when I replied, "Are you kidding. I was shooting for his chest."

Even though I had my first trophy I was not elated. My shooting was poor, and it had been done with the rifle I intended to use only as a last resort.

The next day as we prepared to walk from the safari car my guide picked up the Model 70 and handed it to me. I set it back in the seat and picked up my 40-70 Sharps. He looked a bit pained but said nothing. Shortly thereafter something spooked a wildebeest toward us at a run. We spotted him and dropped to one knee. The movement alerted him and he stopped at about 80 yards out, turning broadside in the process. When we dropped to one knee I had cocked the Sharps. As I brought it to my shoulder I set the rear trigger. As soon as the post

settled just behind the wildebeest's shoulder I merely touched the front trigger, and we heard the bullet strike home. He ran about 80 yards and we found him dead from a solid lung shot.

Thinking that my guide might relax a bit now, I asked him what he thought of my Sharps. He said it was OK, but now that I had used it how about putting it up and using the scoped rifle?

On the third day we had nearly a repeat performance. During the morning we had hunted hard for kudu in 100-degree heat. A couple of times we got glimpses of animals but no shots. That afternoon we spotted zebra from the safari car and dismounted to stalk them. They saw us and quickly disappeared. This time my guide didn't pay any attention to what rifle I picked up. We followed the zebra tracks only a short distance, then we got quite a surprise. A kudu burst out of the brush about 130 yards ahead and stopped dead when he saw us. Immediately we dropped to one knee and the guide said, "Shoot!"

This was as close as I came to buck fever over there. I had raised the Sharps and set the trigger but the muzzle began wavering great arcs. The guide saw this and later said he figured we were in for a real mess. However, I had the presence of mind to take a deep breath, raise my muzzle and to then lower it slowly. When post front sight showed over kudu shoulder, I touched the pre-set trigger. Of course, this takes much longer to tell than the few seconds it took to happen.

Immediately after the muzzle report we heard the bullet strike and the kudu disappeared in the brush. A short search found him only 100 yards away. The 400-grain Barnes bullet had penetrated diagonally and was under the hide on the off flank.

The next day saw another opportunity to try my iron-sighted, single-shot. This time the target was zebra, extremely alert and wary animals. After an exhausting stalk on our hands and knees through dense brush, we found ourselves behind a tree some 130 yards from a zebra stallion. However, the brush at this point was too dense to shoot from the kneeling position and the tree branches too thick to shoot through standing. My guide came to the rescue. He knelt on one knee and put the other out like a bench. Then he whispered to me, "Sit on my knee." I took position and he eased one last tree limb out of the way. During all of this the zebra was becoming uneasy. Upon taking my rather unusual shooting position I

The author and Ventures International president Don "Bucky" Malson with the trophy-size reedbuck taken with the Sharps rifle.

had cocked the Sharps and set the rear trigger. Just as my front sight settled on the zebra's chest he wheeled to the right to escape. With my set trigger arrangement and fast peep sights I was able to readjust the aiming point to behind his shoulder and touch the front trigger simultaneously. The bullet hit the heart and the zebra died on his feet after running about 30 yards.

All was not success when hunting with the 40-70, however. A few days later we stalked gemsbok for hours, and finally I got a standing, broadside shot on a nice bull at only 80 yards. I stood, took aim, set the triggers, and missed cleanly! There were a few branches that I might have clipped, but we could find no concrete evidence. I made several harder shots but this one had to go down as a plain miss with no excuses. I think my guide would have felt vindicated in his distaste for iron sights except I also must admit to missing an easy shot on another gemsbok bull with the 308 a few days earlier. The gemsbok is a very large, beautiful antelope and I wanted one badly. It just was not in the cards. Oh well, you can't get everything the first time!

From our first hunting camp in the Transvaal we then flew to Zululand in Natal near the Indian Ocean for another brief hunt. This time the guides didn't care what rifle I used, and the reason was quickly evident. This area was not drought plagued and game was plentiful.

Within an hour of starting the hunt I had taken a nice trophy nyala. These beautiful antelope, which range in size between a mule deer and small elk, have twisting horns with small

ivory tips. My shot on the nyala was the longest taken with the Sharps, about 140 yards. The bullet took him a bit too far back but still in the lungs. He merely stood in his tracks. My guide said, "He'll go down, you don't need to shoot again." Those are famous last words as far as I'm concerned. So, I put another 40-caliber bullet through both shoulders and finished the job.

The next afternoon we jumped a large reedbuck out of his bed, and the guide yelled "Shoot!" I promptly pulled the front trigger without setting the rear and flinched badly. At only 50 yards the shot was a complete miss. The reedbuck ran about 25 yards and stopped broadside. By that time I was reloaded and the second shot was placed through both shoulders. He never moved from his tracks.

That finished my African hunting with the Sharps, but not the hunting altogether. Up until this time the '86 Winchester had not been fired at anything. In the first camp the guides didn't want to take it with us at all. They said it was excess baggage, what with all else we were packing every day. In the second camp we did take it along and for that I was grateful.

In the last hour of the last day of hunting we were returning to camp empty-handed. For hours we had been trying unsuccessfully to get in range of a nice impala ram. Finally we gave up and headed back for camp. With about 10 minutes of shooting light left, we spotted a record book sized gray duiker. These small antelope are not impressive in size, but they make desirable trophies because they are so difficult to locate in the dense underbrush of South Africa. This gray

duiker had come out to feed a few minutes too early, and we could see him at about 40 yards under a tall bush. The guide looked with binoculars and said, "He's a very good one. Take him if you want." At this point I was still carrying my Sharps with its peep sight. Three times I aimed at the duiker but in the failing light the front post sight completely faded. I simply could not aim. My wife was behind me with the Winchester '86 which had an ivory bead front sight. Quietly, she passed the gun up to me. When I aimed, the ivory bead showed perfectly on the duiker's shoulder. The shot took him through the heart and he never moved.

When my safari ended, six animals had fallen to my iron-sighted classic rifles—five to the Sharps and one to the Winchester. Both the reedbuck and the gray duiker are large enough to make the Safari Club International record books.

At no point did I feel handicapped by using these guns in obsolete calibers and with their peep and open iron sights. The ranges were always short, and only one time, on the last day, did I turn down a shot because I felt it was too far for my rifles. An impala was standing at 200 yards and the guide urged me to shoot. I declined the shot because up to that point I hadn't wounded anything. Two hundred yards felt just a bit far for the conditions.

As for the Sharps, I never felt hampered because it was a single shot. Never would a faster repeat shot have been possible anyway. The hunting I experienced in Africa was generally in very dense brush. If I missed, the animals would immediately disappear. The only exception was the reedbuck. I reloaded while he ran, and when he made the mistake of stopping again, the rifle was ready to go.

Throughout the trip, when showing my rifles to the various professional hunters, none showed more than a passing interest in the Sharps. Conversely, all wanted to handle the lever-action Winchester. When I asked why, they told me that they had never heard of a Sharps before, but all had seen lots of Winchesters in cowboy movies. This was the first opportunity they ever had to examine one up close.

My African hunting with iron sights and single-shots was a success. If I ever get to go back, and everyone who has hunted Africa wants to return, I will only change one thing in my choice of rifles.

I will leave the scope-sighted gun at home. ●

# Making Sport with the Marlin Model 9 Carbine

**One of the "quiet" companies of the shooting industry, Marlin is now offering a neat little pistol-caliber carbine that's fun and accurate and an excellent companion-piece for the auto pistol buffs.**

## by FRANK PETRINI

MARLIN FIREARMS CO. is a low-keyed, conservative outfit. It seldom makes a splash, just quietly plods along doing what it's been doing so well for the last century: making quality, serviceable, and sturdy rifles and shotguns. Every year the company introduces new products, all of which seem to be well-thought-out and of top quality construction and manufacture. There's little or no fanfair or publicity.

You must watch closely to see what the company's up to on a broader plane to decipher the trend, which, when deciphered, then seems to have been obvious all along. One such trend is the rifle used in conjunction with a handgun—that is, a rifle chambered for the handgun cartridge. Within the industry this is called the rifle/handgun combo phenomenon and it's had surprising popularity.

Back around the turn of the century Marlin rode a similar crest with their popular lever guns of that day, the Models 1888 and 1894, chambered for revolver cartridges of that day, like the 25-20, 32-20, 38-40, and 44-40. In recent times, Marlin, again, has been, quietly and steadily developing a dominance in that end of the shooting business with a line of rifles chambered for a number of today's popular handgun cartridges. Witness today's Model 1894 lever-action chambered in our modern magnum revolver cartridges.

First to receive this treatment was the 44 Magnum back in 1969. Then came the 357 Magnum some years later. What really caught my eye, two years ago, was the introduction of this slick little saddle gun in 41 Magnum, a first to my knowledge. Sadly, I didn't find this chambering listed for the 1894 in this year's Marlin catalog.

In spite of the coarse open sights, the Marlin Model 9 turned in this 25-yd., five-shot group with Federal 125-gr. JHP factory ammo. At the 50-yd. mark, groups opened to over 3 inches.

The standard magazine (left) holds 12 rounds, but a longer, 20-shot unit (right) is also optionally available.

Petrini mounted a Tasco 4x32 scope using Tasco base and rings and it made a nice looking outfit. So equipped, 50-yd. groups averaged 1.9 inches.

Now, with increasing popularity of the 9mm Luger round, and on the heels of the cartridge's acceptance by the U.S. military establishment, Marlin came up with a real first, a semi-automatic *sporting* rifle chambered for the little pistol round.

The Model 9 Camp Carbine hit the market last year and this year it's also chambered for 45 ACP, another popular handgun round. Instead of adding still another pistol-round chambering to the lever-action carbine line, Marlin engineers designed a new firearm, this time a semiautomatic.

At first glance, the Camp Carbine looks like an expansion of Marlin's current line of semi-auto 22 rimfire rifles to include the larger round. And, this is no doubt true to some extent,

although it's fairer to say it shares a stronger family resemblance than just being from the same manufacturer might ordinarily imply.

Having been raised on Marlin firearms, primarily in 22 rimfire persuasion, I see the family resemblance in today's new product that goes back the 30 years of my experience. When I pick up the Camp Carbine and bounce it in my hands, the feel of the wood, the generous, squarish fore-end, the smooth uncheckered hardwood buttstock, the flattened front sight hood, the squared receiver . . ., well you get the message. If being true to yourself counts for something in the gun business, Marlin deserves high marks for the Model 9; it's a chip off the old block.

Like most Marlin products the

Model 9 is a no-frills firearm, meant for general purposes, but primarily for small-game hunting and plinking. Unlike most other Marlin rifles, by virtue of its chambering, it has an additional possible use—personal and home defense. This last point is intriguing and something we'll touch on a little later.

The stock is one piece, of an unidentified, uncheckered, hardwood, finished with walnut stain and sealed. Surprisingly, the stock is fitted with a thin rubber butt pad which must be for appearance sake for, obviously, this 6¾-lb. carbine doesn't generate much in the way of recoil.

The barrel, receiver, and all parts integral to the semi-automatic mechanism are of steel, and of generous proportions. Except for the bolt, all exposed steel is polished and blued. The flat top of the receiver is matte finished to reduce glare and is drilled and tapped for scope mounts.

The Camp Carbine takes the same scope mounts as a number of other Marlin rifles, including the Models 336, 444, and 1894, so finding mounts in the local gunshops shouldn't be a problem.

The short 16½-inch barrel has Marlin's efficient and shallow "Micro-Groove" rifling while the sights are serviceable but coarse "standard" issue found on most rifles these days. They're readily adjustable for elevation but if you've got a windage problem you'd have to tap the rear sight dovetail with a hammer and drift to correct it. The sights are more than adequate for most uses, especially plinking, and even for some target shooting and small-game hunting; however, to take full advantage of this rifle and cartridge in these latter pursuits, a telescopic sight is a good idea. Fortunately, installing one given the proper mounts, takes just a few minutes.

The Carbine's trigger group housing is one piece and includes the trigger guard and connecting magazine well, all made of thick, black plastic. Into the well you insert the detachable magazine, available in 12- and 20-round versions. The 12-round model comes standard with the carbine and, when inserted into the well, is totally covered by the plastic housing. The bottom of it fits flush with that of the well. The 20-round version protrudes 2 inches and gives the carbine a somewhat ominous appearance.

The magazines are staggered column affairs, much like the staggered magazines used in many of today's modern 9mm automatic pistols.

These Marlin magazines are interchangeable with those used in the Smith & Wesson 9mm pistol line. Specifically, the 12-round Marlin magazine works in the Smith & Wesson Models 469 and 669 and vice versa. Also the 14-round magazines from the S&W Models 459 and 659 can be used in the Marlin, although, in this case, the Marlin 12-rounder is too short for a complete switch with these pistols. Also, Marlin's 20-rounder is interchangeable with Smith & Wesson's 20-round magazine sold as an accessory for use with all the above pistols.

Of course, the Marlin carbine uses the exact same ammunition as a score or more semi-automatic 9mm pistols on the market. Interchangeability of magazines with the Smith & Wessons is a nice feature that makes this carbine a totally-compatible companion.

Overall, the Camp Carbine has a pleasant appearance, even if it's a bit plain. Length from muzzle to the edge of the recoil pad is only 35½ inches, making a reasonably compact package. If its 6¾ pounds weight is a bit heavier than what you might expect with such a short, light-caliber carbine, remember that compact dimensions do as much to make a firearm easy to handle as absolute weight alone.

Unfortunately, I have the same

The 20-round magazine protrudes 2 inches below the bottom of the magazine well. Both mags will also fit S&W 9mm pistols.

problem with the Camp Carbine as with so many other similar firearms, like, say, the M-1 Carbine; the protruding magazine hampers a comfortable one-handed carry while walking. The magazine is right at the balance point and a pain in the you-know-what whenever you have to carry it around for extended periods of time. The best solution here, of course, is to simply mount sling swivels on the fore-end and butt and attach a sling adjusted so that the projecting magazine fits comfortably under your armpit. The Camp Carbine doesn't come standard with swivels, but they're easy enough to install.

Other features of the Model 9 include a Garand-type safety located in the forward part of the trigger guard, both manual and automatic bolt-open capabilities, and a loaded-chamber indicator at the rear of the bolt.

The automatic bolt-open feature is activated by the empty magazine. When the last round is chambered the magazine follower pushes up on the bolt stop, which in turn catches the bolt in its rearward position. You can manually get the same result by pressing the bolt handle (called the charging handle in the instruction booklet) inward while, at the same time, pulling the bolt to the rear. This will hold the bolt open even if a loaded magazine is locked in place.

As long as an empty magazine is in place the bolt can't be closed; but with either a loaded magazine, or no magazine at all, the bolt can be closed with a stiff rearward tug on the bolt handle and then lettin'er fly forward.

Finally, the gun has a magazine disconnect feature which makes it impossible to fire when the magazine has been removed from the magazine well. Thus, you can't use the rifle as a single-shot without the magazine in

place as you can on some other semi-automatic designs.

The loaded-chamber indicator is activated by the extractor when it slips over the extraction groove on the cartridge in the chamber. The extractor bar then pivots inward causing the indicator to pivot outward, protruding visibly (with it's red top) from the side and rear of the bolt.

How to disassemble the gun for cleaning is required knowledge for owners. You won't get away with running a couple of patches through the bore and squirting some solvent in the ejection port after each stint at the range, like many do with other firearms.

The instruction booklet recommends the Camp Carbine be thoroughly cleaned after every 250 rounds. Firing 300 or 400 rounds at one sitting will convince you of the soundness of this advice. The action is a simple blow-back design, common with many 22 rimfire semi-autos, and considerable amounts of powder residue are blown back into the mechanism with every shot. Left to accummulate over a large number of rounds, it'll gum the action and cause jams.

I've heard reports of the gun jamming after about 300 rounds but my own experience has shown that you can go as much as 500 or 600 rounds. At that point, believe me, the gun needs a thorough cleaning. The extractor and bolt stop areas of the action were caked with accummulated sludge and residue. The 250-round recommendation may be conservative but I don't think you'd want to go much past 400 rounds, otherwise you may encounter reliability problems.

The disassembly procedure is explained in detail in the instruction manual. First, of course, you must insure the gun is unloaded (chamber

The Camp Carbine has a manual bolt-open feature, activated by pushing in on the bolt handle when it is pulled fully back. Action is a simple blowback.

A variety of ammunition was tested by Petrini in the Model 9. He found that even the JHPs fed reliably. Recoil in the 6¾-lb. gun is almost non-existent.

and magazine), remove the magazine, pull the bolt to the rear and lock it with the manual bolt-open feature. Turning the gun upside down, loosen the front and rear trigger group screws. These screws need only to be loosened, not removed from the stock.

Next, separate the stock from the barreled action and place the stock aside. Then, with a small nail, push out the two take-down pins, one in front, one in the rear, on the receiver. These free the trigger group for removal. At this point the bolt stop will fall free from the receiver. Put this aside also.

Next, lift the front of the bolt from the receiver. With this action the charging handle, or bolt handle, will come free and can easily be removed.

At this point, the bolt, receiver, and trigger group can be thoroughly cleaned using a toothbrush and solvent. The bore, of course, can also be cleaned with rod, patches, brushes, and solvent in the conventional way.

Disassembly to this point is reasonably straightforward, and after doing it once or twice it should take only a few minutes. Reassembly is likewise relatively easy, following the disassembly sequence in reverse order.

To take the firearm down beyond this point is asking for trouble, getting into areas where either special tools, knowledge, or both, are required to put it all back together again. The state of disassembly described is sufficient for all normal cleaning purposes, so there's no reason to take it any further.

The best part of testing the Camp Carbine was working with it at the range, for, you see, this gun is a pleasure to shoot. I'd heard reports that it had an unusually heavy, creepy trigger but this wasn't true with my sample. It was a bit spongy, but that's normal for most production semi-automatic firearms.

The trigger pull measured 5.5 pounds on my gauge, heavy perhaps compared to a fine-tuned varmint or target rifle, but not bad for this type of firearm.

The first ammunition fired was the 115-grain JHP load from Federal. I used the open sights on the 25-yard target and punched my first group of slightly over ½-inch in extreme spread—not bad, and certainly more than adequate for even very serious small-game hunting at that distance. But at the 50-yard point the groups spread out to well over 3 inches. This, I was sure, was more a result of the rather coarse sights than the inherent qualities of the Model 9.

So, I mounted a Tasco scope on the gun using Tasco bases and rings. It took about 8 minutes and I went back to the range.

The Federal groups now came in at 2 inches at 50 yards, with practically every five-shot group fired. Indeed, after six groups the average was 1.9 inches. Velocity over the Oehler Skyscreen III detectors averaged 1201 fps.

Running out of the Federal ammo, I next jumped to some new Norma fodder I had on hand. This was of two types, one the 115-grain JHP, the other 116-grain JSP. These, incidentally, stopped the clock at 1253 and 1297 fps, respectively.

These same loads through my Browning Hi-Power pistol average 1170 fps, so, as you can see, the increase in velocity going from the short pistol barrel to the longer 16½-inch Marlin is barely 100 fps—not much difference. This results from the use of relatively fast-burning powders in this pistol load, no doubt, to provide as high a muzzle velocity as possible out of short 9mm pistols.

There are both good and not so good sides to this situation. First, for the bad. You're carrying a 6¾-pound carbine around and you probably feel you should get considerably more "umph" out of it than what you'd get out of a 4-inch pistol barrel.

For the good side, there are really two points. First, with pistol ammo, which is all you can shoot in this carbine, you're working with bullets designed for use at pistol velocities, in the 1000- to 1200-fps range. If your carbine developed say 1500 fps, a figure you might have expected out of the longer barrel, you'd more than likely experience erratic bullet performance. For example, you might use one of the 115-grain hollowpoints on a cottontail or jackrabbit and literally blow it apart, since the bullet won't hold together at this velocity level. So you'll get more reliable bullet performance out of the carbine at the expense of less than ultra-sonic velocities.

Secondly, while you're not getting

Field-stripping for (frequent) cleaning should go no further than shown. The trigger guard/magazine housing is made of a tough, hard plastic.

Below—Loosening the trigger guard (takedown) screws allow the stock to be separated from the barreled action. Stripping the gun is pretty simple and straightforward.

much in the way of additional velocity with the Marlin, the longer barrel and all that additional weight certainly will beat the average 9mm pistol when it comes to accuracy. I don't know about you, but I can't shoot 2-inch groups at 50 yards with any of my 9mm pistols; indeed, I'm lucky if I can do that well at half the distance. So, for pinpoint shooting, the Marlin has the advantage, and for this kind of firearm it's a big advantage.

Chambering, firing, and ejecting all worked flawlessly with my short Carbine and except for the fact that you should religiously clean this piece frequently, the gun should give you few problems from an ammunition standpoint.

One purpose, no doubt, for the Camp Carbine is for fun use while on extended camping trips. I've always used one or another of my plinking handguns for this purpose, but if you're inclined more to a shoulder arm for such endeavors, the Camp Carbine should meet the need admirably. Certainly it'll supply meat-for-the-pot with more consistency than would, say, a pistol in the hands of a mediocre to average shot.

My first thought when opening the Marlin box was that it would be a great home-defense firearm. Keep it in the closet in the master bedroom with a loaded magazine on the top shelf where the kids can't get at it and you could be loaded up and armed

within a few seconds should an intruder make a midnight call. There are many, I'm sure, who'll buy this gun for just this purpose.

The 9mm round is no showstopper but it's certainly adequate for defense purposes. The U.S. military seems to think so and who are we to disagree with the government? Certainly the additional 10-percent greater velocity out of the Carbine helps it further in this respect. For such uses, I'd recommend one of the jacketed hollowpoint loads.

The gun should also do a bangup job on small game out to as far as, perhaps, 100 yards. A few test groups I fired at that point averaged about 5 inches, pretty much defining the out-

er limit of its range for small game. Under 50 yards, and with the near-1300 fps muzzle velocity, the gun should perform much like a hot-loaded 32 H&R Magnum revolver—which in my experience does a whizbang job on small game and varmints. And, of course, the shooter should be able to pinpoint his shots much more closely than he could with a revolver.

The Camp Carbine is an interesting firearm that just doesn't reach out and hit you with its utility right at the start. But, after working with it awhile, it'll grow on you. If you carry a 9mm pistol often, and the S&W models in particular, you'll certainly find this carbine a suitable companion piece. ●

# Premier Autoloader

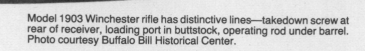

Model 1903 Winchester rifle has distinctive lines—takedown screw at rear of receiver, loading port in buttstock, operating rod under barrel. Photo courtesy Buffalo Bill Historical Center.

# The 1903 Winchester

## by C. RODNEY JAMES

Drafted by one of the lesser known lights of American gun design, the '03 Winchester was nonetheless an excellent rifle. Throughout its production life it was hampered only by its "orphan" cartridge, the 22 Winchester Automatic.

Eleven years after Hugo Borchardt presented his autoloading pistol, and four years after John Browning marketed his autoloading shotgun, the Winchester Repeating Arms Company announced its Model 1903 rifle. Thus, the autoloading rifle arrived a relative late-comer on the shooting scene.

The 03 was the invention of one of the important, though lesser known, lights of American gun design— Thomas Crossly Johnson, whose credits include the Model 12 Winchester shotgun and the series of autoloading rifles based on the 03 action—the 05, 07, and 10.

The 03 rifle was first listed in Winchester's catalog #71 (1904). Over-all length was 36.5 inches with a 20-inch barrel bored with a 1-in-14-inch twist. The rifle weighed 5.5 pounds, held ten cartridges and was available in plain and fancy grades. The latter had checkering on a select walnut stock and a pistol grip. A trigger lock was added in December 1903, at about serial number 5000. In 1906 bronze firing pins were dropped in favor of steel.

The 03 used a simple blow-back system with the force of the discharge counter-balanced by a spring-loaded bolt. The rifle was chambered for a new cartridge—the 22 Winchester Automatic—which remains unique to this day. The stubby rimfire, loaded with smokeless powder and a 45-grain inside lubricated bullet, achieved a muzzle velocity a bit over 900 fps in the original loading. The large (.311") head and (.250") case made it incompatible with the 22 Long Rifle and 22 WRF cartridges. The reasoning behind this was, in part, to ensure only smokeless ammunition would be used in the rifle. At the time of the 03's introduction, both

Thomas Crossly Johnson designed the 1903 Winchester rifle as well as the Model 12 shotgun. Models 05, 07 and 10 also used the 03 action. Photo courtesy Buffalo Bill Historical Center.

Remington brought out their Model 16 to compete with the 03 Winchester in 1914. It was dropped in 1928.

To further counter Winchester's efforts, Remington bought the rights to make this Browning-designed rifle and introduced it as their Model 24 in 1922.

Long Rifle and WRF cartridges were offered in black, semi-smokeless and smokeless loadings. Anticipating that buyers would ignore warnings to use only smokeless ammunition, the 22 Automatic was made *only* as a smokeless cartridge to eliminate fouling which would soon cause a rifle of this type to malfunction.

The *raison d'être* of the cartridge, however, is more complex. The autoloader was a new concept and to insure its acceptance by the public it had to be reliable. Though the 22 Long Rifle would have been the obvious popular choice for a light sporting rifle, at the time of the 03's design there was little standardization of Long Rifle ammunition characteristics in terms of pressure, velocity, powder type, bullet weight or form— the very characteristics that *must* be held constant to make a blow-back action function reliably. To achieve consistency in ammunition, Winchester developed a new, unique cartridge manufactured to the highest standards of reliability possible. Thus was

created the 22 Winchester Automatic rimfire.

Eleven years after the 03's introduction, Remington brought out its competitor, the Model 16. Although using smokeless powder and ballistically identical to the Winchester round, the 22 Remington Autoloading cartridge varied enough in its dimensions to be incompatible with the Winchester. The only advantage the Model 16 offered over the 03 Winchester was a 15-shot capacity. Both used tubular magazines in the stock.

Where the proliferation of new autoloaders and new cartridges might have gone from this point is anybody's guess, but the end came when the Savage Arms Co. introduced its Model 1912 autoloader in 22 Long Rifle. The Savage had a seven-shot, detachable-box magazine. Perhaps Savage felt the advantage of chambering their rifle for a standard caliber outweighed the risk of customer complaints. This move to a popular cartridge proved wise if not inevitable.

Browning, working in Belgium,

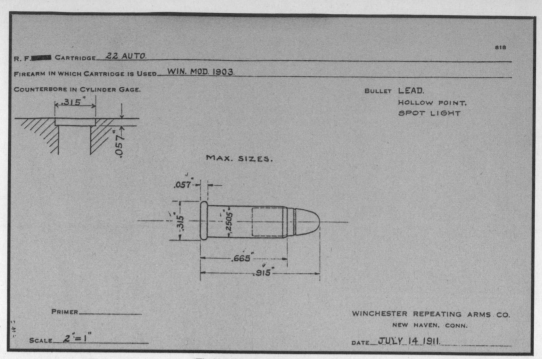

The 03 Winchester's 22 Win. Auto cartridge used a 45-gr. bullet traveling about 980 fps. Penetration on game was good, expansion was lacking.

brought out a 22 Long Rifle autoloader in 1914. Remington soon bought rights to manufacture this rifle in the United States and it appeared as the Model 24 in 1922. Remington dropped the Model 16 in 1928, leaving Winchester the single holdout with its special 22 cartridge. Winchester finally capitulated in 1932 after a production run of about 113,000. The following year it offered a modified 03—the Model 63—chambered for the 22 Long Rifle.

The 03 and its cartridge have acquired an oddly inconsistent reputation for accuracy and killing potential. The original loading, variously listed at 903, 920 and 980 fps was a shade under the Long Rifle velocities of 950 and 1090. The additional five grains of weight in the 22 Automatic bullet undoubtedly gave it more punch than the Long Rifle of that day. By 1911 it was available in hollow point and "Spot Light" (contact explosive) styles.

The excellent pointing qualities, rapid fire and light weight of the 03 made it ideal for trick and fancy shooting, and for this purpose it was employed by Winchester exhibition shooter Adolph Topperwein. Topperwein developed many of the shooting stunts which later became standard in the profession. His early training as a cartoonist led to bullet drawing, a feat requiring 450 slugs delivered at a rate of about 60 per minute to create a profile of an Indian chief in a feathered war bonnet.

Aerial shooting was the meat of marksmanship demonstrations at fairs, expositions, and "wild west" shows popular in late 19th and early 20th century America. Although most shooters relied on shotguns or smoothbored rifles firing fine shot, Topperwein liked to astound the multitudes by shattering glass ball targets with a single rifle bullet. Sending a bullet through the center of a washer tossed in the air invariably caused skeptics to demand the hole be taped, which it was, then neatly punched on the following toss. Topperwein would next turn the autoloader on its side, fire a shot, whip the rifle to his shoulder to shoot down the first ejected cartridge case before it hit the ground.

At the time there were a number of "world's champion" shooters, though few made attempts to prove their claims. The first to do so was Doc Carver who used the 2½-inch glass ball target thrown in the air. Carver, using ten 22 caliber rifles, fired for 12 hours, missing 650 of 60,000. His record of 1900 lasted only a few years until it was broken by B.A. Bartlett who missed 280 of 60,000. Topperwein loaded his 03 Winchester and in December, 1907, prepared to stake his claim to the record.

Perhaps not wishing to be hit by flying glass, Topperwein elected to fire at 2½-inch square wooden blocks. The plan was to shoot 5,000 per day. Topperwein, however, ran ahead of schedule. As one exhausted thrower was replaced by a fresh man, the 03

autoloader popped relentlessly for ten days. When Topperwein, arms and shoulders nearly paralyzed from the effort, laid down the Winchester he did so with a record that stood for more than 50 years—72,500 targets fired at with *nine* misses. He accomplished several runs of 10,000 without a miss and one of 14,540.

Records, of course, are made to be broken, as was Topperwein's, when in 1959 Tom Frye, a former Remington exhibition shooter, fired at 100,020 2½-inch blocks missing *six*; his rifle—a Remington Nylon 66 in 22 Long Rifle.

The 03 Winchester gained a good reputation as a short-range, small game, snap-shooting rifle though many deplored the lack of expansion of the 45-grain bullet on small game—it was definitely an expert's rifle. One thing the solid point bullet *would* do was penetrate and keep on going. In wilderness areas where weight had to be kept to a minimum, brain shots from the 03 in the hands of a skilled stalker-hunter neatly killed beaver and game animals as large as bear and moose. It may be added, these qualities combined with the rifle's quiet report made it a favorite with poachers as well.

As the 22 Long Rifle became the standard by which all other rimfires were judged, the 22 Winchester Automatic gradually fell into disrepute. Somewhere along the way a gun writer looked at some paper ballistics and concluded that the Winchester car-

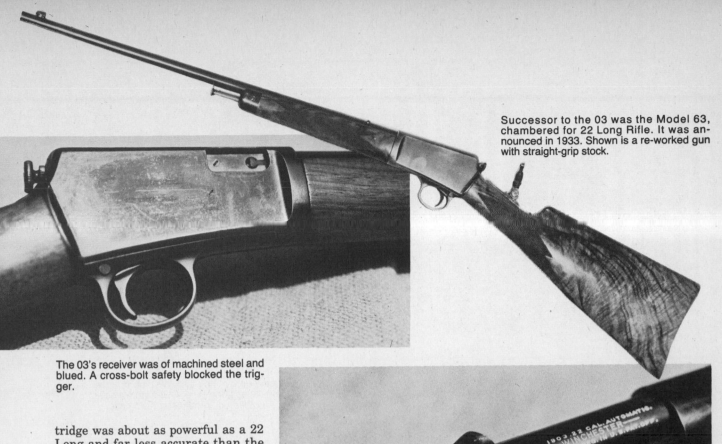

Successor to the 03 was the Model 63, chambered for 22 Long Rifle. It was announced in 1933. Shown is a re-worked gun with straight-grip stock.

The 03's receiver was of machined steel and blued. A cross-bolt safety blocked the trigger.

tridge was about as powerful as a 22 Long and far less accurate than the Long Rifle—a notion passed on and repeated though not verified to this day. How this came about is a moot point, but it is this author's guess that events probably took at least some of the following turns.

The 22 Long Rifle gained its reputation as an accurate small bore cartridge in the 1920s with the advent of the Winchester Model 52—the first precision bolt action rifle made for this cartridge. By the early 1930s, non-corrosive priming had been perfected, resulting in match ammunition equalling the best performance of the corrosive semi-smokeless match cartridges of the 1920s. Tremendous resources were devoted to improving the Long Rifle as both a hunting and target cartridge to deliver maximum killing potential and gilt-edged accuracy. It would seem logical that improvements in priming, powder and lubricants made on behalf of the Long Rifle would be passed on to the poorer relations of the small caliber rimfire family and indeed they were. With the exception of the 22 Extra Long and the 22 Remington Autoloading, all the 22 rimfires received a velocity boost in 1930-31 which, with a few real or imaginary ups and downs, became the standard we recognize today.

In comparing a modern 22 Long to an early 22 Winchester Automatic, the ballistics are about the same. In terms of accuracy, even modern 22

Unlike its successor, the Model 63, the 03 used a rather impractical one-piece rear sight with screw elevation adjustment.

Winchester Automatic ammunition can only be used in the light 03 autoloader, a combination incapable of delivering the degree of accuracy possible with Long Rifle match cartridges in a heavy barreled target rifle.

There is nothing like empirical data to shed light on such matters, so this author, equipped with an 03 Winchester and a box of Remington ammunition of recent manufacture, fired at 35 yards using a sand bag rest. After bobbling out one shot, ten shots went neatly into one ragged hole measuring 9/16-inch. This isn't a bad group under any circumstances. A quick check in John Lachuk's *Gun Digest Book of the .22 Rimfire* gave the following data for *25* yard groups fired with high velocity hunting ammunition in five leading 22 Long Rifle au-

The curved rifle-style butt of the 03 is not as uncomfortable as it appears. The magazine tube withdraws to the rear for loading.

Left to right—22 Long Rifle, 22 Winchester Automatic, 22 Remington Autoloading, 22 WRF, 22 Winchester Magnum.

Little bullet upset was caused by firing into soft pine boards. Left to right—Remington Viper Long Rifle, CCI High Velocity Long Rifle, Remington Autoloading, Winchester Automatic.

toloaders: Browning BAR, $9/_{16}$-inch, Remington 66, $^{11}/_{16}$-inch, Winchester 940, $7/_{16}$-inch, Ruger 10/22, $1^{1}/_{8}$-inch, Weatherby Mark XXII, $7/_{16}$-inch.

The killing potential of the 22 Winchester Auto in comparison to the 22 Long Rifle was more difficult to determine. Paper ballistics give the Automatic 111 foot pounds at the muzzle and 86 at 100 yards, the high speed Long Rifle 158 and 97 which would appear to give the LR the edge. In reality it is a question of penetration versus expansion.

A preliminary study of penetration was conducted using one-inch soft pine boards, placed touching one another, but not clamped together, at a distance of 20 yards. Three-shot groups were fired from a Ruger 10/22 and a 1903 Winchester using round and flat point hunting bullets with the following results:

### Penetration in inches

| Cartridge | Min. | Max. | Avg. |
|---|---|---|---|
| CCI Mini-mag | | | |
| HV RP | 5.4 | 5.9 | 5.7 |
| Rem. Viper | | | |
| HV FP | 4.3 | 4.5 | 4.4 |
| Winchester | | | |
| SV RP | 5.6 | 6.8 | 6.2 |
| Remington | | | |
| SV FP | 5.1 | 5.4 | 5.3 |

A second test at the same distance with blocks of plasticine gave similar results. The major difference was in expansion of the Long Rifle slugs. The flat point Remington-brand 22 Winchester Auto gave slightly better expansion as can be seen by the slightly larger "wound channel" this bullet produced when compared to the round point Winchester bullet.

For hunting, Autoloader shots should be limited to 50 yards to insure a solid hit. The heavy slug at a relatively low velocity performs well in wind and seems less inclined to be sent tumbling by tiny twigs which easily deflect a Long Rifle. Low velocity, greater length and weight than the Long Rifle make the 22 Winchester slug exceedingly prone to ricochets—a factor which should be given careful consideration when taking shots on the ground.

"Wild west" shows, Doc Carver and Ad Topperwein like Buffalo Bill—who could break "onetwothreefourfive pigeonsjustlikethat"—are gone and with them the early autoloaders that thrilled crowds with seemingly impossible feats of marksmanship. When the rifles went out of production, ammunition for them was doomed to follow.

The 45-grain hollow point bullet, which was certainly the most useful for small game in the 03, was discontinued in 1947 and now turns up only occasionally at collector's prices. Shooters planning to hunt with the 03 will do best to stick with flat point style bullets. If improved performance is desired, one can always try his hand at cutting a cross or drilling a hole in the nose to create a hollow point. This must be done with great care or accuracy will suffer.

The end of U.S. manufacture of the 22 Winchester Automatic, the WRF and the 5mm Remington rimfire came in 1982. The 22 Remington Autoloading cartridge disappeared some 20 years ago except as an import from CIL in Canada. The fire which leveled CIL's rimfire plant a few years ago finished this source and, it may be added, the last source of 25 and 32 rimfires. Unless some U.S. company elects to produce "orphan" cartridges as "orphan drugs" are supplied by one or two pharmaceutical houses, those wishing to shoot 03s are in for hard times. Though the long run looks grim, the short run offers a few possibilities. Listed in the back of this volume are sources for foreign and custom ammunition who may have the ammunition. Mail orders, however, must go through dealers and will cost accordingly. Better values may be found by prospecting "old time" hardware and gun stores. Gun shows offer another possibility. Prices as of this writing run from about $2.00 to $6.00 for a box of 50.

At this point a few caveats should be observed. Though a 22 Remington Autoloading round would probably function in an 03 Winchester, the Winchester round will almost certainly *not* chamber in a Remington Model 16 and to force it is to invite trouble. Alteration of the Remington chamber

This 10-shot, 35-yard group fired with the author's M03 printed 9/16", not counting the one low flyer.

Above—When fired into heavy plasticine, the Viper Long Rifle gave good expansion. Left—CCI High Velocity Long Rifle expanded well despite its round nose. Below—The round nose 22 Winchester Auto bullet penetrates deeply with no expansion.

is a job for a competent gunsmith. Do not fire a 22 Long Rifle in either rifle as the case will rupture! In the 03, which has the larger chamber of the two, head separation is a distinct possibility. Even if chamber alterations were made to accommodate the Long Rifle, accuracy would undoubtedly suffer. Long Rifle guns are bored with a groove diameter of from .221" to .223". The 03 and Model 16 bores are about .226" on the average and may in some instances run larger. Finally, beware of old corrosively primed am-

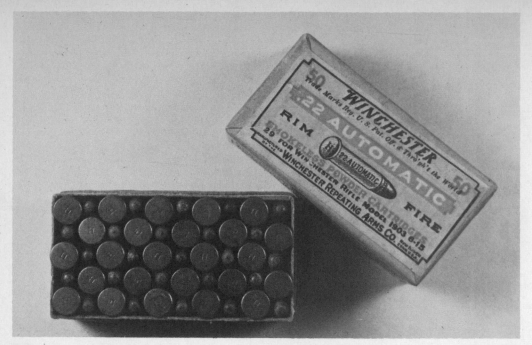

This box of corrosive Winchester ammunition was made around World War I, and has more collector than shooting value.

munition. A full box of these cartridges will probably bring a better price or a better than even trade for modern ammunition from a collector. If shooting a bargain bag of loose ammunition, inspect it carefully. Be sure to clean the rifle with a good solvent immediately afterwards in case some of the cartridges are corrosive. Early cartridges were of copper with unplated bullets. No ammunition showing signs of external corrosion should be fired as they will probably rupture. Inspect boxed cartridges to make sure all within are of the same type and the box is marked "Kleanbore," "Staynless," "Rustless" or "Non Corrosive."

If you have an 03 Winchester and are willing to work a bit for your ammunition, dust it off and enjoy it. This little rifle is still a pleasure to shoot. ●

### Acknowledgements

The author wishes to express his thanks to B.H. Williams of the U.S. Repeating Arms Company and L.K. Goodstal, Supervisor of the Remington Gun Museum for vital information and illustrative material, and to Lew Gray for the macro photos accompanying this article.

Early round of Winchester ammunition. The copper case with heavy crimp was stamped with a "W" near the mouth to distinguish it from the Remington Autoloading cartridge. Corrosion caused the case to split on firing.

## Model 1903 Winchester Production

| Year | Serial # |
|---|---|
| 1903 Est. | 5000 |
| 1904 | 6944 |
| 1905 | 14865 |
| 1906 | 23097 |
| 1907 | 31852 |
| 1908 | 39105 |
| 1909 | 46496 |
| 1910 | 54298 |
| 1911 | 61679 |
| 1912 | 69586 |
| 1913 | 76732 |
| 1914 | 81776 |
| 1915 | 84563 |
| 1916 | 87148 |
| 1917 | 89501 |
| 1918 | 92617 |
| 1919 | 96565 |
| 1920 | N.A. |
| 1921 | 97650 |
| 1922 | 99011 |
| 1923 | 100452 |
| 1924 | 101688 |
| 1925 | 103075 |
| 1926 | 104230 |
| 1927 | 105537 |
| 1928 | 107157 |
| 1929 | 109414 |
| 1930 | 111276 |
| 1931 | 112533 |
| 1932 | 112992 |

Serial numbers were assigned to guns at the end of the calendar year.

Though this model was officially discontinued in 1932 a "clean up" of parts was used for production of approximately 2000 rifles. Total production ended at serial number 114962 in 1936.

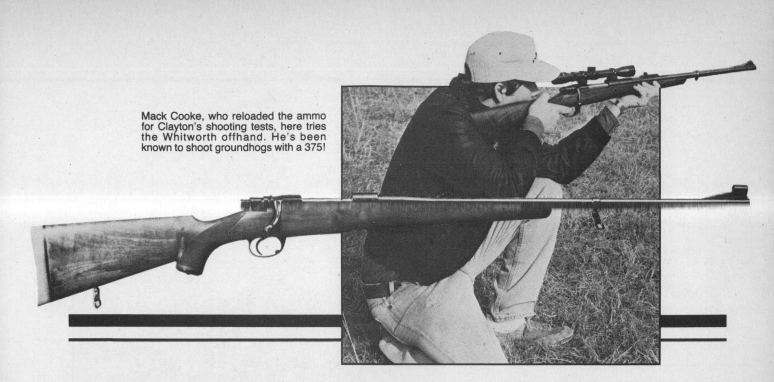

Mack Cooke, who reloaded the ammo for Clayton's shooting tests, here tries the Whitworth offhand. He's been known to shoot groundhogs with a 375!

# Interarms Whitworth 375 Express Rifle
## by ORIS CLAYTON

This shoulder-bruising cousin to the Mark X rifle line has been with us for a decade but it isn't often seen. That's a pity because the Whitworth Express has a lot going for it—Mauser action, good looks and quality—at an attractive price.

BRITISH RIFLE MAKERS have long held positions of esteem among the shooters of the world. Such names as Purdey, Holland & Holland, Vickers, B. S. A., Jeffery, Rigby, Westley Richards, Greener, and Cogswell & Harrison are legendary. The mere mention of their names evokes images of the African veldt, Indian jungles, Canadian snow-topped peaks, pith helmets, and stiff upper lips. Ah, the British.

And Whitworth. Whitworth? Yes. Although not of the same vintage as many of the foregoing list of worthies, Whitworth is a name to reckon with. I have no idea how extensive the Whitworth line is in England, but Interarms, of Alexandria, Virginia, has been importing the Whitworth Express into the United States for more than a decade. (I first saw the Whitworth mentioned in the 1975 *Gun Digest*.) In those early years, the

Whitworth was available in 7mm Remington Magnum, 375 Holland & Holland Magnum, and the 458 Winchester Magnum.

Today the Whitworth is cataloged in the original calibers plus the 22-250 Remington, 243 Winchester, 25-06 Remington, 270 Winchester, 7x57 Mauser, 308 Winchester, 30-06 Springfield, and 300 Winchester Magnum. All but the 375 H&H and the 458 Magnum are labeled the Whitworth "American Field" series; the 375 and 458 are the only ones to carry the "Express" sobriquet.

The Whitworth has outlived several of its siblings, all of which (including the Whitworth) were (and are) based on Yugoslavian-built Mauser actions. Gone by the boards are: the Cavalier, a racy, shiny styling exercise; the Mark X, bread-and-butter member of the line for years; the Con-

The Whitworth Express is an excellent example of the "classic" style rifle. The straight-combed stock is oil finished, and nicely checkered with ample coverage for a good non-slip hold on the gun.

Winchester offers two loads for the 375 H&H: the 270-gr. soft point (shown) and the 300-gr. Silvertip. The latter was the most accurate of all loads tested, factory or handloads.

tinental Mannlicher Mark X, with its butterknife bolt knob; the Marquis Mannlicher Mark X, with its untraditional Monte Carlo comb; the Viscount, loss-leader of the line and a good, non-flossy buy; and the Mark X Alaskan, similar to the standard Mark X but chambered for the 375 and 458 Magnums. Currently only the Whitworth name is cataloged, though in the American Field, Express, and a new Manlicher-style carbine on the same theme.

I have always preferred the Whitworth rifles to the other Mark X permutations, perhaps because I am a traditionalist; I fairly dote on the "classic" stock, of which the Whitworth is a particularly nice example. I take it as a good omen that all the more flashy Mark X iterations have disappeared from the marketplace. Perhaps the American taste is gravitating firmly and finally away from the "California" look as a norm, with more shooters embracing the classic form along with the pragmatic-but-flamboyant Monte Carlo, high-gloss, skip-line styling.

The Whitworth features the following niceties: an all-forged-steel Mauser action, with the controlled-feed, reliable ejector, claw-type extractor for which this action is lauded; hinged floorplate with the release in the forward section of the trigger guard bow;

improved short-fall firing pin; hammer-forged barrel; ramp front sight with British-style three-leaf express open sight ramp; checkered bolt knob (on the underside); high-gloss finish on the metal parts. The European walnut stock boasts the following furniture and attributes: a steel stock throughbolt to prevent stock splitting; a checkered plastic grip cap; black, vertical-joint fore-end tip; rifle-type solid rubber recoil pad; sling swivels, with the forward stud mounted on the underside of the barrel; hand-cut checkering that the catalog says is "sharp 32-line;" dual recoil lugs (on the 375 and 458 Magnums only) bedded in "epoxy/steel resins," with the front lug on the underside of the barrel about halfway up the fore-end. Stock styling is elegant, classic, with an undercut cheekpiece, considerable checkering coverage, a nicely

curved pistol grip, and a mildly pear-shaped fore-end. Nice.

How good is the execution? Good. Not perfect. But quite good. The checkering is excellent in the center of the patterns, well pointed up and tidy, but there are a few runovers and unpointed diamonds at the edge of the patterns. The cheekpiece is nicely sculpted, well done. The pistol grip cap on my gun doesn't fit very well, but the fore-end tip is conjoined nigh-perfectly. Wood-to-metal fit is excellent, far better than the average in this price range (in fact in *any* price range), at least in the upper action area. Beneath, things aren't as impressive; there are gaps in the floorplate/trigger guard area that shouldn't be. The finish of both wood and metal is just fine.

The oil-finished stock is crafted out of one of the most gorgeous hunks of

Interarms uses the Yugoslavian-made Mauser action on the Whitworth Express, a time-tested, proven design. Floorplate release is in the front of the trigger guard. Gun has a steel stock throughbolt to prevent wood splitting.

To further enhance the classic stock lines, the Whitworth Express has a nicely undercut cheekpiece and solid rubber recoil pad. Wood grain is very handsome.

The Whitworth has a silent safety button (just below bolt knob) and Mauser claw-type extractor, probably the most reliable for turnbolt rifles. The Express has a British-style three-leaf rear sight on a small rib.

wood I have ever seen. The color is basically a deep, rich reddish-walnut, with dark, near-black marbling on both sides of the butt (not always the case) and up into the forearm. Beautiful. The dull sheen enhances the wood; the finish doesn't hide it.

The trigger pull on all Whitworth rifles is fully adjustable. I fiddled with it (expertly, of course) and managed a crisp, short, creep-free pull of 3 pounds. In fact, it is one of the best triggers I have used on any rifle. In this day of lousy factory triggers (due to product-liability fears, not poor worksmanship, and serves us right), my sample Whitworth is balm for the afflicted.

The bolt on my test gun is so smooth on the opening stroke, it practically lifts itself. In this time of 60-degree bolt throws and multiple-lug bolts that require both arms to operate, such easy precision astonishes. (It is a little tougher on the downstroke, but certainly no worse than most turnbolts in that respect.) In fact, raising the bolt handle on my test rifle is about as easy when the action is uncocked as it is when it is cocked! Uncanny.

Okay, so the rifle's nice. How does it work? Pretty well, thank you. The Whitworth, like all Mausers I've worked with, feeds slick as oiled spitballs through a soda straw. Believe it or not—and you might not if you've never had experience with a controlled feed turnbolt—the Whitworth will feed empty cases from the magazine without a hitch. Naturally, loaded rounds offer no tendency to bind anything. Extraction is positive; how could it be otherwise? Have you ever known a rifle boasting a side-spring extraction system to balk at pulling a case from the chamber? I haven't either.

Ejection, unfortunately, is another matter. I have never shot an Interarms rifle chambered for a magnum cartridge that had sufficient clearance at the rear end for troublefree expulsion of a fired case. Most of the cases will be kicked clear most of the time. But not always. And there never seems to be *quite* enough room back there.

Ignition is positive, to say the least. Primers are deeply indented, and the firing pin is well centered on my test gun.

Recoil, as you can imagine, is fierce. Not "pretty bad," not "grim," not even "hefty." FIERCE. I borrowed a buckle-on recoil pad, laid a piece of leather across the buttstock where my tender cheek made contact, and settled down to beat myself to death. Anyone who tells you the 375 H&H Magnum is fun to shoot is not the guy to buy a used car from. Don't get me wrong. The 375 is controllable; barely. It shoots very well, if you can stand the punishment. It will not break your bones, but it will abrade your skin severely if you shoot it without benefit of heavy padding. (I have witnesses to the next days' bruising.) Bear in mind that the

375 is designed for large, possibly dangerous game. It's great for lion, death on grizzlies, will do a pachyderm no good at all. No argument. It's a grand old cartridge, respected, revered even. But it is *no* fun to shoot without body armor reminiscent of that worn by a Green Bay lineman. View askance any person who tries to convince you otherwise.

So, you still want a 375? Okay. How accurate is my test rifle, you inquire? Pretty danged accurate. With the 300-grain Winchester Silvertip factory load, my Whitworth managed a 1.50-inch average for three five-shot strings fired from benchrest at 100 yards. I have fired many 30-06 rifles that would not better that with factory ammo, and some that wouldn't even *equal* it with select handloads. The 270-grain Winchester soft point wasn't quite as precise as the heavier slug, going right at 2 inches for the aggregate.

When I received my test gun I got a very short deadline to meet as well. I had no dies, no pet loads for the 375 H&H (which I have in the past successfully avoided at every opportunity), and no time to secure same. In desperation, I called a fellow who is the acknowledged "local expert" on things 375, Mack Cooke.

Mack is a first-rate machinist, an experienced handloader, owns an inquiring mind, and shoots so much heavy artillery that I suspect his wits are slightly addled. Best of all, Mack stables and feeds his own 375 H&H. He knows what makes it perform, what propellants it prefers, and how to coax the best from 375 handloads. I conned Mack into loading me a sizable batch of Whitworth fodder. I tried to con him into doing the bench testing as well, but his brains aren't *that* rattled.

Mack had particularly high expectations for the loads using the 235-grain Speer soft point and the 300-grain Hornady and Sierra bullets. As it worked out, none of the handloads would beat the best factory load, which is par with such limited experimentation.

Most accurate proved to be the 270-grain Hornady soft point over 77.5 grains of IMR 4350. Groups ran just under 1¾ inches for the average, with a muzzle speed of 2440 feet per second. That's a pretty mild load, so far as velocity goes, but the Hornady Handbook doesn't sanction an increase over a 77.7-grain charge. Nonetheless, in my 375, pressure indicators showed low levels.

The runner-up reload consisted of

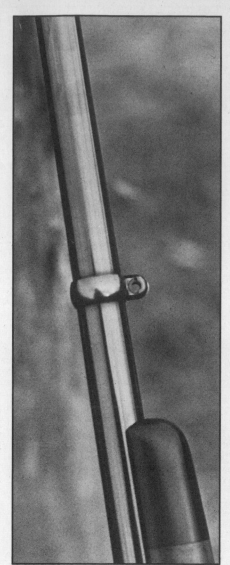

The front sling swivel stud is attached with a barrel band, keeping it from pounding your fingers in recoil. It also looks great on this gun. Steel floorplate and trigger guard (above right) are highly polished and blued.

78.5 grains of Winchester 760 pushing the 300-grain Hornady round-nose soft point, with ignition provided by a Federal 215 magnum cap. Shots clustered into a 1.99-inch average, with one five-shotter going 1⅜ inches. Muzzle speed was a healthy 2499 fps, good for 4159 foot-pounds. That's 109 fps in excess of the 300-grain Winchester factory load, with an attendant increase in muzzle energy of 355 foot-pounds. Good handload, Mack.

The most energy provided by any load came from the great 285-grain Speer Grand Slam, a big-game bullet to reckon with. Decanting 81.0 grains of IMR 4350, Mack produced a recipe that clocked 2610 fps in my Whitworth. That's 60 foot-seconds faster than the 270-grain factory load! Energy rating is a thumping 4310 foot-pounds. If that load wouldn't ruin

a brown bear's day, my grandmother is Tallulah Bankhead. Accuracy is nothing with which to impress your shooting cronies; groups ran over 3 inches.

Fastest load tried was the bitty 235-grain Speer soft point riding 77.0 grains of IMR 4064, with a speed of 2808 fps at the nozzle. Considering that the load carries more than 4100 foot-pounds of energy, that's not the one I would choose for varmints, unless I were being troubled by hippopotamuses in my begonias. Grouping ran to 2 inches or a bit more, not varminting precision. (You think I jest when mentioning varmint hunting with the 375? Wrong. Just yesterday, as I write this, Mr. Cooke went on a woodchuck foray in the North Carolina mountains with his 375 and actually shot at one. You have to watch Mack.)

My Whitworth showed an ability to group five rounds consistently under 2 inches with almost half of the loads tried, and nearly did so with another. In my opinion, that's pretty good. Remember, the 375 moves around on the bags a *lot,* which makes it difficult to reposition exactly the same for each shot.

I was impressed with Editor Murtz's 375 Whitworth Express. And not just because he's my editor. Not even because he owns the handsome rifle and I don't. But because it is a nice gun—well built, good-looking, and it has a terrific trigger. Maybe I won't send it back.　●

These are all good powders to use in the 375 H&H. In the test gun, IMR-4350 gave the best handload accuracy. A can of powder doesn't last long with the big calibers!

The most potent handload tried in the Express used the excellent Speer Grand Slam 285-gr. bullet, 81.0/IMR-4350 for 4310 ft. lbs. of energy.

The Interarms Whitworth Express is just plain handsome and it shoots as good as it looks. Without ample padding at the shoulder, however, it can rattle your brains due to the, well, *stiff* recoil.

## Load Data
### 375 H & H Interarms Whitworth Express

| Bullet Wgt./Make | Powder Wgt. | Type | Primer | Case | Vel. (fps) | Ener. (ft.lbs.) | ES | Group Av. (in.) | Remarks |
|---|---|---|---|---|---|---|---|---|---|
| **Handloads** | | | | | | | | | |
| 235 Speer SP | 77.0 | IMR 4064 | WIN LR | WIN | 2808 | 4114 | 25 | 2.08 | Good load for lighter game or practice |
| 270 Hornady RN | 77.5 | IMR 4350 | WIN LR | WIN | 2440 | 3569 | 59 | 1.73 | Most accurate handload tested |
| 285 Speer GS | 81.0 | IMR 4350 | WIN LR | WIN | 2610 | 4310 | 10 | 3.06 | Erratic accuracy; very consistent |
| 300 Sierra SPBT | 68.0 | IMR 4064 | CCI 250 | WIN | 2412 | 3875 | 33 | 2.64 | Erratic grouping; good energy level |
| 300 Hornady RN | 78.5 | WIN 760 | FED 215 | WIN | 2499 | 4159 | 13 | 1.99 | Third most accurate; high energy level |
| 270 Winchester SP | | Factory Load | | | 2550 | 3897 | 51 | 2.01 | Inconsistent grouping |
| 300 Winchester ST | | Factory Load | | | 2390 | 3804 | 108 | 1.50 | Most accurate load tested |

Group average is for two or three five-shot groups, from benchrest at 100 yards. Loads chronographed with an Oehler M33 Chronotach. SP-Soft Point RN-Round Nose GS-Grand Slam SPBT-Soft Point Boattail ST-Silvertip

# On The Firing Line

## by CLAY HARVEY

Ultra Light Arms Model 20, with 20-oz. short action.

**Some news guns, some variations on existing models, but all are worth comment. Harvey casts his critical eye upon the Ultra Light Arms Model 20, Kimber Model 84, Weatherby Fiberguard, T/C TCR '83 Hunter, and Browning 1885.**

### Ultra Light Arms Model 20

In the summer of 1980, a significant chapter in the saga of ultra-light rifles had its genesis. Melvin Forbes, a prominent gunsmith living in Granville, West Virginia, leaned back, stoked his pipe, and took a long hard look at synthetic-stocked hunting rifles. At that time there were several makers turning out guns, all building their own ideas of the ideal "plastic" stock. These were wed to standard actions such as the Remington 700. Problems abounded.

The tactic resorted to by most makers, and later by Remington with the wood-stocked flyweight Model Seven, was to abbreviate a barrel—usually to 18½ inches—and turn it down to mouse-tail exterior dimensions. This did indeed make a lighter rifle, although not quite as well balanced, aesthetically pleasing, and ballistically efficient as one could hope for. I have tested a lot of these stubby, light-tubed carbines, and most have been sufficiently accurate for any reasonable big-game hunting purpose. How accurate is that? Well, most Remington Model Sevens I've fired (seven or eight at least) would print an average five-shot string around 1½ inches at 100 yards with a pet load. My Ruger International Model 77 in 308 went about 2¼ inches, although a similar gun chambered for 250 Savage grouped well under 1¼ inches. A USRAC 243 Carbine stayed just over 1⅝ inches; my Weatherby Fiberguard 243 printed 1.60 with good handloads. And so on. Note that except for the 250 Savage, and a Model Seven in 222 Remington, most of the superlight carbines did well to group 1½ inches. Now, 1½ MOA is plenty accurate for any big-game hunting I envision, but you haven't heard all the story. Most of the guns aforementioned were tested with quite a number of loads, many of which grouped in the 2½ to 4-inch range! Lightweight rifles are nothing if not picky as to their provender. Or so I concluded. I also concluded that a 6¼-pound rifle was, with rare exceptions, incapable of grouping as well as a typical 7½- to 8-pound sporter. I was wrong. I *should* have concluded that a rifle with a muzzle diameter of only .5-inch wasn't as precise as one of its heavier, stiffer siblings. Rifle weight *of itself* has scant bearing on hunting accuracy.

Back to Melvin Forbes. Our master gunsmith deduced that reducing the heft of a rifle by trimming its barrel to soda-straw contour was putting the bacon before the pig. Not only did it create accuracy-related problems, but it did nothing good for rifle balance, and thus handling characteristics. Melvin decided to build a lighter, better balanced mousetrap and let the world beat a path to his shop.

Criteria for the gun went as follows: use of a Douglas No. 1 (.56-inch) contour Premium barrel; a classic-style

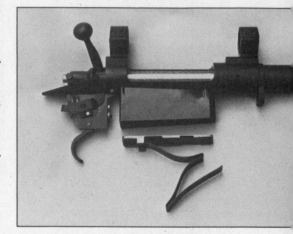

All Ultra Light rifles come with a Timney trigger, ULA's patented two-position, three-function safety, and a blind magazine. The guns are built to close, benchrest tolerances.

synthetic stock; an action of superior quality, materials, and tolerances; reduced weight; a unique safety. And such begat a rifle with a stress-relieved barrel that shoots to the same point of impact, hot or cold; a Kevlar and graphite stock with both light weight and high shear and tensile strength; a strong, modern, recessed-head action weighing only *20* ounces (hence the model designation), complete with a Sako-style extractor and a Model 70-type bolt release; a three-position safety that locks the bolt handle in place when in normal "on safe" position—as when hunting—but enables bolt articulation when depressed, while still blocking the sear.

Although the stock is the most difficult part of the rifle to fabricate, let's leave it for the the moment and look closely at the action. Most manufacturers do at least some machining on their actions prior to heat treatment. Unfortunately, heat treatment can and often does warp the dimensions of the finished part. The Model 20 is therefore heat treated before it's machined, eliminating such warpage. The receiver is machined from 4140 steel, heat treated and stress relieved to Rockwell "C" scale 28 to 32. The bolts are of 4340 steel, hardened and relieved to a Rockwell 38 to 42. First sawed to length then gun drilled and reamed, the action is mandrel-turned to insure concentricity. End facing is done simultaneously, guaranteeing the surfaces to be 90 degrees to the bore. The actions are then chucked into a collet, the barrel-thread diameter bored, and the locking-lug recesses cut, again at precisely 90 degrees to the bore axis. The threads are

no hand bedding required. Barrel harmonics were carefully studied, thus the barrel is bedded its full length. Since the stock is warp-proof, and the mating of action to stock perfect, this is an asset and one of the reasons—in addition to its perfectly concentric action and the Douglas Premium barrel—the Model 20 shoots as well as it does.

The Model 20 wears a Timney trigger, properly adjusted by the factory in all samples I've tried. Melvin's patent-applied-for safety is fitted by Ultra Light gunsmiths at their plant.

So how do all the parts work? Fine thank you. At the risk of an overuse of superlatives, I'll run through my subjective feelings about my test ULA Model 20. The stock design is just right, both in looks and "feel." It fits as if it were tailored expressly for me. The action, though petite, is strong and safe. My sample is also functional; it has not bobbled once, always feeding, extracting, and ejecting on schedule. What's more, it does it with

future rifles. I've just returned from his plant. He did what he said; current production is quite good in the guard area, although still not quite as tight as the incredible inletting.

The Model 20 is fitted with sling swivel studs, affixed to steel inserts imbedded in the stock so they won't pull free, and sealed with Loctite. The gun boasts a blind magazine, which led one scribe to worry about the front guard screw working loose when the "tapped hole in the Kevlar wears out." Not so, friends. Melvin is not obtuse. The front screw is inserted into a steel slug within the stock. (Naturally, the front action screw threads into the bottom of the action itself.)

All Ultra Lights are provided with a solid rubber recoil pad, and the factory will make up most any length of pull you want for no extra tariff. They will also produce most any chambering you want. There are several action lengths; a little bitty one proportioned just right for the 222 family; the Model 24 (at 24 ounces, of course) Long Action for the 30-06 clan; and the Model 28 Magnum Action, long enough for the 300 Winchester but not the H&H pair of cartridges.

At the outset, I mentioned accuracy. My Ultra Light Model 20, a 7mm-08 Remington, weighed just under 5 pounds out of the box with Melvin's dandy 2-ounce scope mounts in place. I mounted a new Redfield 2-7x "Five-Star" variable on the bridge, loaded up a few test loads, and visited the range. At first, accuracy was not anything to paste on the wall. Considering that I was working with an unknown powder, I did not despair. I tried two pet loads, worked up in another 7mm-08.

Using 35.9 grains of IMR 4895 under the 168 Sierra Matchking, I fired two-five-shot strings. The first measured .75-inch, the second .828. I said, "Wow!" Or a word to that effect. Next I grouped five shots with the 115 Speer hollow point over 46.0 grains of IMR 4064: .97-inch. The largest 100-yard five-shot group I've fired since then was a 1.36-incher with this latter load. Does the gun shoot or not?

My pal Layne Simpson, for whom I frequently shoot groundhogs so he can pose with them for his articles, tested a Model 20 in 284 that printed 1.07 inches with its pet recipe, and under 1.2 inches with a pair of others. (See *Gun Digest*, 1986.) Buddy Rick Jamison, *Shooting Times*' resident rifle expert, told me his 6mm Ultra Light averages 1.2 inches, and shot even better before he took it apart. That makes three 5-pound rifles that

ULA Model 24 (long action) with ULA's hardened aircraft aluminum scope mounts. Difficult to see because dark, flat guns don't photograph well, is the near perfect fit of the barreled action in the stock.

cut with a single-point tool to enable perfect concentricity. When the bolts are mated to the receivers, only .002-inch clearance is allowed between the inside receiver dimensions and the exterior of the bolt body.

The foregoing long-winded description was provided to illustrate that the little ULA action is of true benchrest quality. In fact, I predict that when the competitive bench gunners discover Ultra Light Arms, Mr. Forbes may well sell as many actions as rifles.

The graphite-reinforced Kevlar stock is stiff in the extreme, and for all practical purposes the barreled action simply drops into the stock with

style. Bolt manipulation is slick as if on ball bearings. Trigger pull is perfect, the safety silent.

The stock-to-metal fit is, with one exception, perfect. In fact, it appears that my barreled action actually grew out of the stock! I swear. I have *never* seen equal fit on any gun in any price range, custom or factory-produced, so far as the barreled-action is concerned. There is a mild case of gaposis around the trigger guard (a steel unit on my specimen) that I felt was remiss with the rest of the gun. I called Melvin, who explained that the sloppiness was the result of the painting process and that he'd remedy that on

will print under $1\frac{1}{5}$ inches on the average, and in three different chamberings.

The mention of Rick's Model 20 reminds me of one small problem a ULA owner might run into. If the rifle is taken apart, as for cleaning or trigger adjustment, one must be *extremely* careful to insure that the bottom leg of the follower spring doesn't get caught beneath the magazine box. Should this happen in such a tight-toleranced action as the ULA, so much upward pressure results that it can seriously bind the action, creating an accuracy-destroying situation. To avoid this, just rotate the muzzle upward sharply when you slip the action back into place. That should position the follower spring at the rear of the box, where it should be.

The ULA Model 20 is far and away the most accurate *true* lightweight sporter I've ever tested, and among the three or four most precise sporters of *any* weight in a big game caliber. The hunter yields nothing in exchange for this lack of heft. Barrel length is a full 22 inches, to provide excellent ballistics, and the stock proportions are man-sized. No better hunting rifle is available, in my view. At any price. (Which, by the way, is $1,300 at retail.)

---

### Kimber Model 84

When Greg Warne, amiable man-at-the-helm of Kimber of Oregon, introduced the Model 84 to the shooting world, gun writers hither and yon were all ascramble to test one. Which is understandable. Kimber has built a reputation that can be summed in one word: quality. It was assumed that the new rifle, heralded as a mini-Mauser, would not infringe upon that renown. And it didn't. It enhanced it.

As with Kimber's prestige rimfire Model 82, the new centerfire 84 boasted a superbly detailed stock of classic design, proper proportions, quiet elegance. The cut checkering was there, and the checkered steel buttplate, the sling swivel studs, the blued-steel pistol grip cap. Of course, the upgrades were offered: the Custom Classic with its ebony fore-end and Niedner buttplate; the Monte Carlo-stocked Cascade; the Super America, with its extra-fancy claro walnut and undercut cheekpiece. All this was interesting, but not really news.

What was news was the new Model 84 action. It boasted a long side-spring extractor like the '98 Mauser and its imitators, such as the pre-'64 Model 70, the Remington 720 and its forebears, and the Springfield '03. A modified pre-'64 M-70 ejector was included, pivoting at the inside left rear of the action to kick free a case. The bolt release was in the classic Mauser location, at the rear of the left lug race, but didn't resemble the German unit at all. The Kimber 84 is the only American-built controlled-feed bolt action produced currently.

As with the rimfire action, the Model 84 carries the Kimber rotary cam-style safety button at the right rear of the receiver bridge. The trigger unit is fully adjustable, and factory set to about a 2½-pound pull. Quite crisp on most specimens, I might add. The action is compact, light, and machined from solid chrome moly bar stock. Current production rifles are drilled and tapped for scope bases, which are provided with the guns. (Originally the actions were grooved to receive rimfire-style tip-off mounts.) Whereas the rimfire Model 82 is a rear-locking design, the M-84 wears its twin lugs up front.

Weighing a svelte 6¼ pounds, according to Kimber's literature, the Model 84 was designed around the 222 Remington family of cartridges. At first, only the 223 Remington was offered; for 1986, Kimber catalogs the 222, 222 Remington Magnum, 221 Fireball, and the 17 Remington, in addition to the 223. Three wildcat cartridges are available: the 17 Mach IV, 6x45 (6mm-223), and the 6x47 (6mm-222 Magnum.)

I have tested three Model 84 Kimbers, a 223, 221 Fireball, and a 6x45. All are Custom Classic iterations. My 223 averaged .818 inches for three five-shot strings at 100 yards with 25.0 grains of H4895 under Ed Watson's 52-grain match hollow point. Remember, this is a 6¼-pound rifle! Next best handload was the same charge of H4895 pushing the 55 Speer soft point; three groups ran 1.09 inches. The superb Federal 40-grain Blitz hollow point factory number averaged exactly the same for three strings, 1.09. For factory ammo, that is something to write your cousin about! Remington's 55-grain Power-Lokt hollow point showed a 1.22 aggregate. I could go on, but suffice to say that of 16 groups fired with handloads, the largest measured 1.81 inches. Extraordinary from a light-

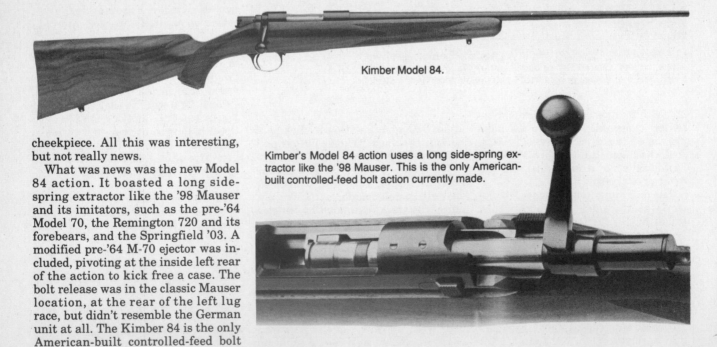

Kimber Model 84.

Kimber's Model 84 action uses a long side-spring extractor like the '98 Mauser. This is the only American-built controlled-feed bolt action currently made.

weight rifle, believe me.

Problems? Yes, a few. At first, my test 223 wouldn't eject its cases. The extractor had insufficient bite to hold the case against the bolt face. I returned the bolt to the factory and got it back the same week. (And I live on the East Coast!) There have been no miscues since.

The only other blemish on my 223 is a floorplate that isn't tight. It moves up and down when you poke it with a finger, a pet peeve of mine. No one else who's handled the rifle has even noticed it.

The wood on my 223 is beautiful, typically honey-blond claro with dark swirls and streaks. Gorgeous! Wood-to-metal fit is fine, excellent in most areas. The checkering is about perfect, with no runovers nor flat-topped diamonds in evidence, and is obviously the product of Kimber's ace lady checkerer, Pat Taylor.

I used my 221 Fireball on a weekend hunt with Greg Warne and his sons Justin and Nick, writer Steve Timm, who handloaded all my ammunition, Kimber's Jim McKinley and his son Greg, and ebullient Mike Hill and his son Jim, from Seattle. I fired 210 rounds of assorted handloads and varied lots of 50-grain Remington factory ammo before running out of provender. I even hit a few ground squirrels. In fact, I show more than one or two out to a full 300 yards, with Steve

as witness. (Unfortunately, whenever I asked Steve to verify a hit, he claimed to have been looking the other way. Nice guy.)

To date, the only paper I've punched with the Fireball was in Oregon, over the hood of a truck, at 75 yards to establish a working zero. Considering that I managed to connect on a squirrel occasionally at ranges I would have considered out of the little Fireball's league, I must rate the gun's accuracy as creditable.

Functioning was another story. Due to the filler plate at the rear of the magazine being a bit forward of the bolt face, I had difficulty loading the rifle with my eyes on game. (Or on Steve, who had the poor manners to keep popping critters whilst I reloaded. And, confound it, he seldom missed.) When in the heat of battle, with Steve blasting away on my right and Greg McKinley cutting loose at my left, I would sometimes have a round or two pop out from under the feed rails and plop at my feet. (I always hollered, "Time out!" but Greg and Steve showed no mercy.) I'm not certain whether my frenzied loading or some minor feeding difficulty contributed to my plight. Later, back at the plant, Jim McKinley tried his best to get my 221 to bobble. Naturally, it functioned without a hiccup.

I've had no such problems with my 6x45. With its barrel twist rate of 1-

in-12 inches, it has been a tad intractable about which loads it likes, but feed it properly and it purrs like a tabby. Best concoction to date is 25.6 grains of H4895 behind the 85 Speer soft-point boattail, for a healthy 2753 feet per second and a .96-inch average of three strings.

I took that gun and load to the Chestnut Hunting Lodge near Taylorsville, North Carolina, a few months ago. With the combo I slew a fine Spanish goat and Barbarossa ram, no fuss, no bother, and came away with much respect for the little Kimber and its wildcat cartridge. Used properly and within a moderate range, they do the job.

I hope Kimber sells a trainload of Model 84 rifles. I suspect they will; the guns have been in a back-order situation since their introduction. If you like Kimber's handsome stock styling, excellent balance and subjective feel, nigh-flawless checkering and inletting, and careful attention to detail on their famous rimfire rifles and the new Model 84 centerfire, wait until 1988. Kimber is resurrecting and actually *improving* the lauded pre-1964 Winchester Model 70, and dubbing it the Kimber Big Game Rifle. When that happens, history will be made. Watch this "little" Oregon-based outfit and its progressive president, Greg Warne. They will soon be legendary.

---

## Weatherby Fiberguard 243

Following up last year's synthetic-stocked Mark V, the Fibermark, Weatherby has introduced a popular-priced glass-handled version of their Vanguard line. Dubbed the Fiberguard, the new gun is made up on both a short and a long action. Calibers are 223 Remington, 243 Winchester (my test chambering), 270 Winchester, 7mm Remington Magnum, 308 Winchester and 30-06 Springfield. That pretty well covers the field.

The Fiberguard sports a 20-inch lightweight barrel, although not so slender as Ruger's Ultra-Light or Remington's Model Seven. The tube is Weatherby's Number One contour. Rifle weight is listed at 6 pounds, 8 ounces in the short action, 2 ounces more for the longer version. My sample rifle tips the beam at 7 pounds, 14 ounces with a 2-7x Weatherby Supreme scope mounted in Buehler all-steel rings and bases. Scoped, loaded,

and with sling my 243 goes 8 pounds, 6 ounces. Not really ultra light, is it?

The synthetic stock is produced for Weatherby by an outside supplier; Weatherby does the painting and baking in house. The color is pea green, and I like it much better than the black pigmentation on the Fibermark. Both rifles have a problem with the finish rubbing off too easily, though this is not limited to Weathrby by any means. Provided with a rough, crinkly exterior, the stock is not slippery to sweaty or rain-soaked hands.

The barreled action is identical to the 6½-pound woodstocked VGL, and has been in use by Weatherby for many years. The two-lug Mauser-type action isn't the smoothest around, nor the most finely finished, but it is strong, boasts a recessed bolt face with typical plunger ejector and shortclaw extractor. All the Vanguards I've tested have fed and extracted without a hitch. Most of them have a tendency to rattle when the

magazine is full of cartridges, so I simply stuff two rounds down the cupboard; that takes care of the noise.

Not so easy to remedy is the trigger pull. It is fully adjustable, but not easily adjustable. When the correct (from the quality of pull standpoint) sear engagement point is arrived at, through trial and error, frequently the safety will not function. When the safety works properly, there is usually to much sear engagement for a crisp pull. Juggling the adjustments doesn't help much. One winds up with: a) an unsafe and unsatisfactory pull, or b) a safe and unsatisfactory pull. Even the ministrations of the best gunsmith I know, Gerry Stover, has not given any of my Vanguards a truly acceptable pull.

The only other problem with my rifle is that it requires a set of ear plugs to *dry fire*. So help me! The buttstock is hollow (or nearly so), and it amplifies the din created by the striker falling, transmitting most of it to your right ear. Dry fire a Fiberguard more

Weatherby Fiberguard with Weatherby 2-7x Supreme scope in Buehler mounts.

than a few times and you'll discover your right ear ringing like a telephone. However, if you never practice with an empty rifle, this needn't concern you.

As mentioned, my 243 worked properly. All the time. You might be surprised how many new rifles don't. Accuracy was acceptable for a lightweight sporter, but not noteworthy. Three five-shot strings with the 80 Remington Power-Lokt varmint load averaged 1.60 inches. Three-shot groups, for those interested, went 1.09

inches with that load. (The test gun nearly always opened up its groups with the last two shots.) The 100 grain Federal Premium boattail soft point printed 1.66 inches for the aggregate. My best handload only equaled Remington's Power-Lokt: 43.0 grains of IMR 4350 and the 100 Hornady round nose grouped 1.60.

Now, for a big-game piece such accuracy is more than sufficient. However, the 243s claim to fame is its application to vermin as well as deer. A 1⅝-moa rifle is a 300-yard chuck

buster, in my view. My sample Weatherby showed more barrel bearing along one side of the barrel channel than the other. I fiddled with it a bit, then shimmed the barrel to regain up-pressure. The accuracy remained about the same.

The Weatherby Fiberguard is a perfectly serviceable big-game rifle, and an ideal way for the first-time synthetic buyer to break into the market. At about $579.95 retail, the Fiberguard is far and away the least expensive synthetic on the market.

## Thompson/Center TCR '83 Hunter Field Model 223

I first encountered the TCR '83 at a SHOT show. I liked its looks immediately, so I strolled over and removed the show sample from its pegs. Tossed it to my shoulder. Put it back on the pegs and walked off with never a rearward glance.

Why? First, the trim little piece had a pistol-grip angle obviously designed by an NBA center. Second, the long reach was exacerbated by double set triggers. I absolutely can not abide a rifle so endowed. I placed the TCR single shot on a mental back burner. Which was a shame, I thought; I love good single-shot rifles.

The quality of the TCR was obvious at a glance. There was excellent checkering (if a bit sparse in coverage) cut into good quality American walnut. Wood-to-metal mating was precise, at least as good as the "big" two single shot producers provide on their guns. Bluing was nice, though perhaps a tad glossy. Stock styling was akin to classic, with no Monte Carlo comb. The action was of top-lever breakopen design, similar to most single-barrel shotguns, and worked like silk. All this was nice, but irrelevant. My right hand and the TCR just couldn't adapt to each other.

And then came the Hunter Field Model. No double set triggers, just an adjustable single-stage unit. Superb.

No fore-end checkering, simply a stylish flute. Looks fine. Matte finish on most of the action, subdued on barrel.

Quietly refined. No cheekpiece. It isn't missed. Best of all, the Hunter Field version retails for 60 bucks less, at $415.

All TCRs have a strong mono-block locking system, which enables them to handle pressures of magnum proportions. Indeed, the guns are chambered for both the 7mm Remington Magnum and the 54,000 c.u.p. 270 Winchester, as well as seven other renderings. Barrel length is 23 inches, which makes for a compact over-all length of only 39½ inches, about like a Marlin lever action. Weight is listed at 6 pounds, 14 ounces.

The first impression you get from the TCR Hunter is solidity. Bankvault tightness. Anvil toughness. The second impression is quality of workmanship, materials. Aside from the angle of the pistol grip, the gun is well thought out. For instance, the opening lever operates in either direction, and is virtually fluid in operation. The gun actually opens itself, from inertia, when the lever is manipulated. Barrels are interchangeable and switching them is a snap. There are no sling swivel studs, which is an unfortunate omission, but easily remedied. A rifle-type solid butt pad is provided, as are open sights.

Ergonomics are laudable. The trigger guard is large enough to admit a gloved hand. The safety button, located in the forward section of the trigger guard, is of the cross-bolt type. Despite its having garnered much criticism, I find no fault with it. As a test, I just asked my wife—who never handled a TCR before—to give the safety a whirl. I instructed her as to its workings, once. I handed her the rifle and told her to push the safety on. SNAP! She did. Told her to poke it to "off." Using the thumb and forefinger of her right hand, she did so. Didn't look at the gun, fiddle around, shuffle her feet. If Barbara can do it (she seldom fires rifles), an experienced rifleman should have no difficulty.

One caveat about the safety: it is *not* silent. Something for big-game seekers to consider.

Functionally, the TCR has little to go amiss. It does not offer an ejector, but simply an extractor that lifts the fired case (or loaded cartridge) about ¼-inch above the chamber face. If rhinos were rooting in my sweet potatoes, the lack of an ejector might give me pause; for the hunting I do with a single shot, the TCR works fine.

About accuracy. I have read of two TCR Aristocrat models (the high-priced spread) that grouped well under an inch. My lanky crony Rick Jamison tested one for *Shooting Times* that printed in the ½-inch neighborhood. Alas, either I or my ri-

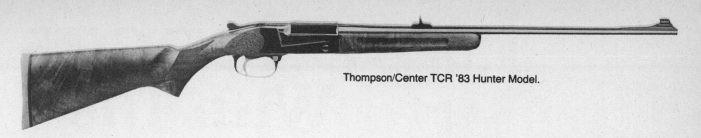

Thompson/Center TCR '83 Hunter Model.

fle can't shoot as well as Rick or his. Of course, I have fired only factory loads in mine to date, which provides some kind of excuse. (Rick resorted to handloading, the cheater.) Federal's surprisingly accurate 40-grain Blitz clustered into a 1.47-inch aggregate of three five-shot strings. The runner-up was the Federal 55-grain hollow-point boattail, at 1.81 inches for six groups.

This level of precision is okay in my book, if not exactly bragworthy. I've shot a fair number of Ruger single shots that would not equal it, and at least two Brownings. I suspect that careful handloading will shrink my groups by 20%, maybe more. Considering that the 223 Remington is a 300-yard varmint load at best, who needs better than that? (If my TCR were a 22-250, my opinion would differ.)

Summing up the TCR '83 Hunter Field, I'll simply state that if Thompson/Center will come up with a re-think on that strange pistol grip, I'll be real happy. So happy, in fact, that I might recommend the Hunter over all other single loaders.

## Browning 1885 Single Shot

Browning Arms has for some years now been making hay with modern versions of revered Winchester (all John Browning designs) classics. First was the Browning B-78, an updated Winchester High-Wall single shot. Then came the B-92, a replica of the 1892 carbine. A couple of years ago, the Utah-based firm replicated the 1895 Winchester levergun, producing both 30-06 and 30-40 Krag iterations. Of these three firearms, only the B-92 is cataloged today.

Last year the B-78 was revived as the Model 1885, replete with an improved adjustable trigger, a 28-inch heavy octagonal barrel only (the B-78 offered a slim octagonal barrel as an option, at 26 inches in length), a satin-finished stock of "classic" styling, in four chamberings. Most reviews of the "new" rifle parroted the Browning literature, claiming that the guns were available in one style only. Not so. The 45-70 permutation comes with open sights, similar to the ones offered on the defunct B-78. My test ri-

fle was so equipped.

The 1885 has a glossy metal finish, ill-advised in a hunting piece, especially considering that the woodwork boasts a non-glare treatment. Likely the problem is that the gun companies are a bit vague on the whys and wherefores of gun finishes; they obviously feel that the public buys this or that style according to taste, not practical considerations like non-reflectability for hunting. Thus such glaring mismarriages as a shiny blue job and a matte stock. This is by no means peculiar to Browning; Ruger does the same thing with their M-77 line.

Aside from the odd choice of externals, the 1885 is a first-rate rifle. The fit of all parts is exemplary, the polishing excellent, metalwork tip-top, fitting of such accouterments as the rubber recoil pad and the Pachmayr sling-swivel receptacles just fine. Trigger pull is heavy but crisp, and the adjustment did nothing to change that assessment. (These suit-happy days, what do you expect?)

In the accuracy department, my test Browning did itself proud. With

its favorite load, the 300-grain Winchester hollow point, four five-shot strings from the bench at 100 yards averaged 1.96 inches. That's the first 45-70 I've ever tested to group under 2 inches for an average. Remington's heavy 405 soft point printed 2.79 inches, still acceptable for a big-bore with factory ammo. One group fired with Federal's 300-grain hollow point went 1.65 inches, but the average wasn't that tight.

Although the big 1885 is scopable, I feel that no 45-70 need be so encumbered unless its user has a vision problem. It does not require a glass sight to deck a buck at 125 yards! I had Gerry Stover, of Randy's Outdoorsmen's Shop, work his magic and mount a Williams receiver sight atop my '85. It was no easy task; no such pairing is suggested by Williams literature. But, as he has proved repeatedly, no gunsmithing task is beyond Gerry's capabilities. The sight looks as if it grew on the rifle.

Over-all, this Browning 1885 rifle suits me just fine, thanks. You really couldn't go wrong with it. ●

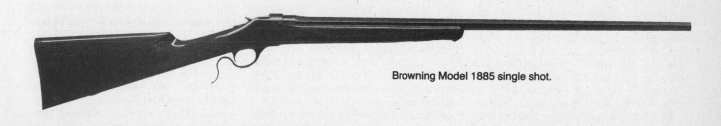

Browning Model 1885 single shot.

# Experiences With The 32-20

**Thinking his "new" Colt SAA in 32-20 would be no more difficult to load for than any other gun in the battery, Venturino embarked on a frustrating, less-than-enjoyable journey that taught him not to take anything for granted.**

## by MIKE VENTURINO

As A WESTERN HISTORY buff and as a shooter I had always wanted a good pre-war Colt Single Action Army revolver. Then, a few years ago at a local gun show, I managed to get one chambered for the 32-20 cartridge. Actually, the 32-20 did not attract me greatly because I already owned loading tools and bullet moulds for most of the big bores, but this gun was the only pre-war Colt SAA that I could make a reasonable deal on. "Besides," I thought, "never owning a 32-caliber handgun, maybe this would be a new experience."

It was a new experience, alright, and a very maddening, frustrating one until I learned the ins and outs of that particular sixgun. For a time after that I must admit to being soured on this fine, small bore cartridge in revolvers.

That particular Colt SAA was holster worn and a little rough looking on the exterior, but mechanically was in very good condition. The bore of the 4¾-inch barrel was perfect as were all of the chambers, and there was no rust or pitting anywhere on the gun. According to a serial number check, it was made in 1907 so it was suitable for smokeless powder loads. All in all, that gun should have been a very fine shooter, but it was not. At least not with just any handload, as I will discuss shortly.

After leaving the gun show with my new treasure, I bought the first box of 32-20 factory loads I could find. Those were Remington-Peters brand and carried 100-grain lead bullets. After firing a few rounds at tin cans and such to familiarize myself with the Colt, the Oehler chronograph and the Lee Pistol Machine Rest were set up. Firing four five-shot groups at 25 yards, I was convinced that I had a winner with my new "jewel." Those groups averaged only 1.69 inches, which I consider fine accuracy from a non-target revolver. Velocity was a low 808 fps, but was still powerful enough for the intended purposes of plinking, informal target shooting, and small game and/or varmint hunting.

I, along with most ardent handloaders, am a bit snobbish towards factory-loaded ammunition and therefore I felt handloads would better my new revolver's already very good performance. On that point I was wrong and at that point I embarked on some of my most frustrating experiences as a handloader.

Firing his new treasure with Remington-Peters factory loads, Venturino was able to get groups into a tight 1.69". Velocity was a low 808 fps, but good enough for plinking and small game hunting.

The very first frustrating thing was the lack of available loading data in various publications and manuals. Lyman's *Reloading Handbook Number 45* was the only manual found that even made mention of the 32-20, and the few loads listed contained a caution not to use them in handguns. Finally, after much searching, I came upon a magazine article written by gun writer Clay Harvey. Along with other information, Clay referred to this cartridge as "contrary." In my ignorance I thought, "Well, he has just gotten a poor gun. I won't have any troubles with this Colt."

With such thoughts in mind a set of Bonanza dies and Lyman mould numbers 311316 and 311316HP were acquired. This particular bullet design looks as if it were made especially for the 32-20. In profile it is nearly identical to the factory loaded bullets. However, these cast bullets are gas checked versions and they were fitted throughout the shooting with Lyman gas checks. When cast from straight wheelweight metal, the solid bullet weighed 116 grains and the hollow-point went 105 grains. Lube was Alox and sizing diameter was .310". That .310" sizing diameter may sound just

a wee bit small as most sources list .311" and .312" as correct for the 32-20, but the bullets in those finely accurate factory loads measured .310", so I assumed it was correct.

However, I must admit that not slugging that Colt's bore at that time was a mistake that cost me in powder, primers, lead, and time. To make a long story short, my initial tests with the gun were sad times. Groups ranged from three to five inches at 25 yards and were very irregular in form. Sometimes in a 10-shot group five of the holes would be touching but the other five were randomly placed. I tried a wide variety of powders and charges but nothing seemed to help. An accurate handload could not be found.

By the time several hundred rounds were fired I wised up and did what should have been done in the beginning: I slugged the bore.

Now, among Colt Single Action

This is the first Colt SAA the author worked with, and which was so troublesome. It was made in 1907 and, except for bore dimensions, is identical to the second gun he shot.

fans it is fairly common knowledge that many older pre-war guns, especially in 32-20, 38-40 and 44-40 calibers, came from the factory with variations in bore diameter. Driving a soft lead slug down the bore and measuring it revealed the answer to all my headaches. The bore was a full .314"! No wonder then that the hard cast .310" bullets were not accurate. The Remington-Peters factory loads were using .310" bullets also, but they were dead soft lead, and were obviously "slugging up" to fill the grooves. The hard cast bullets with copper alloy gas checks on the bases just were not going to obturate so easily. That is why they were not accurate.

So what do you do in a situation like this? Not wanting to invest in more moulds, especially since it wasn't a sure bet if their bullets would be as large as .314" anyway, and not wanting to admit defeat in a loading project, I decided on a compromise.

Sticking with the harder alloy cast bullets, I set out to make that 32-20 into a sort of 32 magnum. By that I mean that the intention was to boost pressures and velocities to the point where the bullets would begin to slug up and give the necessary accuracy.

It worked, too! Not immediately, but eventually. Starting with 7.5 grains of 2400, I worked up in one-half grain steps. Accuracy was poor; there was a lot of unburned powder left in the gun; and not one of the groups went under 2 inches. At 9.0 grains I

could see that the loads were getting a little warm, but since this Colt was a smokeless powder model with very heavy cylinder walls, I thought to proceed to 10.0 grains before stopping altogether.

At 9.5 grains of 2400 the groups did round out and three 10-shot groups averaged only 1.77 inches. Velocity from the 4¾-inch barrel was 1180 fps. So, in the end, I had a 32-20 that was accurate; and one that was just about a "32 magnum."

However, all was not roses. As might be expected, leading was a problem. Shooting a .310" bullet down

Shooting black powder loads in the old Colt was fun, but dirty. With Lyman's #311316 bullet (cast at 116 grains) and 17.5 grains of FFg powder gave 719 fps.

a .314" bore at nearly 1200 fps is a sure recipe for leading. After every 50 rounds or so I had to engage in a very thorough gun cleaning session.

Such a load as I have described above makes the 32-20 a fine varmint handgun and several dozen gophers were taken with it the next spring. But, to my way of thinking there is no pleasure in owning any gun that must

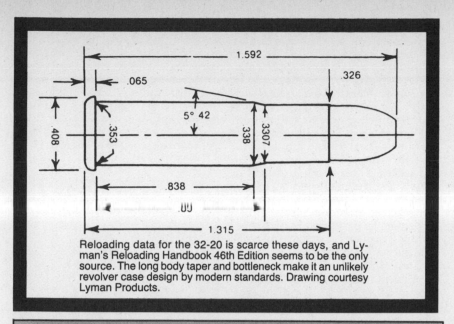

Reloading data for the 32-20 is scarce these days, and Lyman's Reloading Handbook 46th Edition seems to be the only source. The long body taper and bottleneck make it an unlikely revolver case design by modern standards. Drawing courtesy Lyman Products.

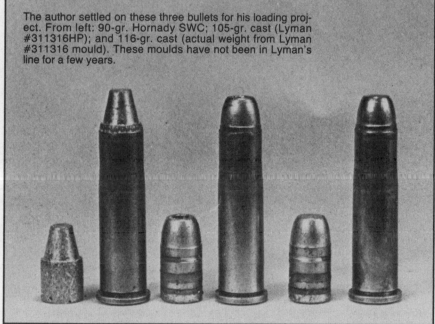

The author settled on these three bullets for his loading project. From left: 90-gr. Hornady SWC; 105-gr. cast (Lyman #311316HP); and 116-gr. cast (actual weight from Lyman #311316 mould). These moulds have not been in Lyman's line for a few years.

be a magnum all of the time. Loaded as it must be to give accuracy, that Colt SAA was no joy to shoot. The muzzle blast was just plain fearsome, and there was no way to accurately load it down for fun shooting. The situation remained the same for about a year and then I did just what any self respecting gun trader would do. I traded off my problem gun to a non-shooting collector and forgot about it.

However, the dies, moulds, and other tools needed for loading the caliber stayed with me, even though at that time I felt that I never wanted to own another 32-20 handgun. Rationally, I realized that the problem had been with the gun itself, and that there was nothing inherently wrong with the cartridge. Still, the whole deal left a

bad taste in my mouth. Since that time I have gone on to own several other Colt SAAs, but every time I was offered a nice 32-20 I told the seller, "Not interested!"

A short while back a good friend showed up at my door cradling a Colt SAA on which he had made a very fine deal. At a glance I could see that the gun was in good shape, and being a Colt SAA fan I felt a bit of excitement until he said it was a 32-20. Then I just said, "Too bad."

But, this buddy knew that I owned all the loading equipment necessary for this caliber and he figured we ought to give it a try. I was cool to the idea at first, but just for the heck of it decided to slug the bore. I must admit to being much more interested when

that slug miked out at an exact .310″. There should be no reason for this gun to be inaccurate at any velocity level and so I entered on my second 32-20 loading project with a Colt SAA.

The 32-20 cartridge was introduced by Winchester in 1882 for their Model 73 lever-action rifle. Original loads carried a 100-grain lead bullet over 20 grains of black powder. Besides the Colt SAAs, the 32-20 has been chambered in such famous firearms as the Winchester Model 92, the Smith & Wesson M&P built on the "K" frame, and a number of lesser known domestic and imported guns. Though all of these different guns are generally available to one degree or another, it has been my experience that those found most often for sale in good shooting condition are the Colt SAAs.

In terms of revolver cartridges the 32-20 case bears no resemblance to anything produced today. Basically, it is a rimmed case 1.315 inches in length, which is long for a handgun case. By comparison the 44 Magnum is only 1.29 inches. However, the 32-20 length is not the oddest thing about its design. What is most notable about the case is that it has a long body taper and a bottleneck. By modern standards a more unlikely revolver case design is hard to imagine. That is reasoning by modern standards, for we modern shooters have been educated to believe that tapered, bottleneck, handgun rounds are not really functional in revolvers. Be that as it may, in all the hundreds of rounds fired through these two Colts I have never had the least problem with cases setting back against the recoil shield and tying up the gun. And, some of the loads have been hot!

Of course the old gents who designed the 32-20 back in the early 1880s didn't intend for it to be souped up to "magnum" velocities. Those fellows were merely trying to put together a case with enough black powder capacity to make for a fairly good small to medium game cartridge. It would seem that they succeeded because with carefully prepared handloads the 32-20 is the very best of all the 32-caliber handgun cartridges. With that statement I include also the 30 Carbine as chambered by Ruger in the Blackhawk revolver.

The 30 Carbine Blackhawk may be able to beat the 32-20 in terms of velocity, but not by much. For instance, my 32-20 loads for a 4¾-inch barreled revolver have given as much as 1200 fps with 115-grain bullets, whereas 30 Carbine loads that I have tried in 7½-inch Ruger Blackhawks gave only 1300 to 1400 fps with 110-grain bullets. Also, the 32-20 has it all over the 30 Carbine as a revolver round because of the latter's rimless design. In the Ruger Blackhawk 30 Carbine the case must headspace on the case mouth, the same as it would in semi-auto guns. This precludes any sort of crimp and makes regular case trimming a manditory chore.

However, to get away from comparisons I will return to the handloading done with the second Colt SAA. For cast bullets I relied on the same solids and hollowpoints. They were also sized and lubed the same as before, and cast from straight wheelweight metal.

Since working with that first 32-20, Hornady has introduced several designs for the new 32 H&R Magnum round. These bullets, incidentally, also work fine in the 32-20. My efforts with factory bullets centered on the Hornady swaged lead 90-grain semi-wadcutter.

Nearly any handgun powder from Bullseye on to IMR-4227 will work in this cartridge, but I restricted myself to Bullseye, HP-38, Unique, and 2400. Of those, Bullseye and HP-38 were used only in light loads. Unique, on the other hand, was used for more powerful loads as would be suitable for small game and varmints. My only purpose in using 2400 powder was to develop more of the "32 Magnum" type loads.

In passing, I would like to say that those hotter, high velocity loads should not be copied directly. They should not be used in older black powder Colts, or lighter frame double actions. They were intended only for my smokeless powder vintage Colt SAAs.

For my own loading in the future, in case another 32-20 comes my way, I will first go with HP-38. That powder, when used for the lighter loads, is capable of giving superb accuracy. In several instances 25 yard groups with it and either the Hornady 90-grain SWC, or the hollowpoint bullet, were of 1½-inch size. Velocity with such loads was from 750 to 800 fps. If a shooter wanted to rely on only one powder for all his 32-20 loading, the old standby Unique would have to be the choice. At no time did Unique give unacceptable grouping.

Speaking of performance, in the beginning I made a big deal of the problems encountered with that first gun. But, with this second gun there were no problems whatsoever. All else being equal, if the bullet diameter matches the bore size then a gun should give accuracy.

For its size and purpose the 32-20 is a very fine number and the old boys who put it together over 100 years ago outdid themselves. The cartridge is generally considered obsolete today, but it is still better than quite a few of our newer cartridges.

Working with this second gun was an education. I learned that one is apt to encounter problems in loading for the 32-20, but that the problems stem not from the cartridge, but from the looser tolerances of the days when most of these guns were made. If you own a good 32-20 then you have a very good gun indeed; if you own one of the "looser" guns you still have quite a gun, but it will require more work at the handloading bench in order to make it a fine shooter. ●

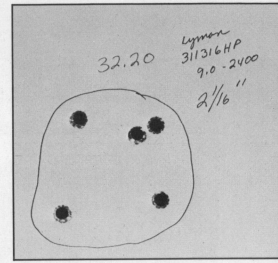

Accuracy with the second Colt was much better than the first gun. Groups such as this were about the norm.

## 32-20 LOAD DATA
## COLT SAA 4¾" BARREL

| Bullet | Grs./Powder | Velocity (fps) | Comments |
|---|---|---|---|
| 90-gr. SWC Hornady swaged | 3.2/Bullseye | 811 | plinking, target |
| 90-gr. SWC Hornady swaged | 3.5/HP 38 | 759 | very accurate |
| 90-gr. SWC Hornady swaged | 5.5/Unique | 1,007 | field load |
| 105-gr. HP Lyman 311316HP | 3.5/HP 38 | 995 | most accurate load |
| 105-gr. HP Lyman 311316HP | 4.5/Unique | 888 | field load |
| 105-gr. HP Lyman 311316HP | 5.0/Unique | 953 | field load |
| 105-gr. HP Lyman 311316HP | 9.0/2400 | 1,024 | accurate |
| 105-gr. HP Lyman 311316HP | 10.0/2400 | 1,192 | highest velocity |
| 116-gr. FN Lyman 311316 | 5.0/Unique | 905 | good all-round load |
| 116-gr. FN Lyman 311316 | 9.5/2400 | 1,113 | max, this bullet |
| 116-gr. FN Lyman 311316 | 17.5/FFg Black | 719 | fun, but dirty |

All loads tested in Colt SAA, vintage 1915
All loads used R-P brass and CCI-500 primers
Chronograph readings taken with start screen at five feet.
Cast bullet weights are actual weights gotten by the author with his metals.

From his testing, Venturino found these four powders worked the best in his 32-20s. The most accurate load used 3.5 grains of HP-38 with the Lyman 105-gr. HP bullet.

# AUSTRALIA:

# Hunting's Last Frontier? by JON R. SUNDRA

**Sure, Africa has a lot of mystique and romance for hunters, but don't overlook the opportunities available on the down-under island continent.**

Y OU WOULD THINK that getting punched in the shoulder to the tune of 45 foot pounds while at the same time having your eardrums assaulted by a deafening dose of decibels is an event you'd remember. But you don't; not when you're shooting at game. At least I don't, and I've shot a head or two over the last quarter-century. Seems like that second or so between the time you decide the sight picture's right, pull the trigger, then recover from the recoil is somehow lost in an irretrievable limbo. Try as you may, you can't quite recall what transpired at the shot, especially when you're not sure it all went according to plan. Like this time.

The buffalo was eyeing me from a broadside position, head turned 90 degrees. At 75 yards he presented a target so big that . . . well, I'd have to work at missing it. Yet, after the inevitable "lost second," I couldn't be

Top—Sundra with his very good buff which scored 94. The best bull taken by the hunting party went 106½. A score of 90 is needed to make the SCI record book.

sure. I heard no "whump" of a bullet striking flesh, and the buff whirled around with the agility of a gazelle as it headed off through the eucalyptus. Now I've shot enough buffalo—and have witnessed the demise of enough more—to know that they just don't go down in their tracks from a chest shot, no matter where in the chest they're hit, and with what. But this one seemed nothing more than irritated at our presence, or maybe at the noise we had made. Doubt swept over me . . . until after 20 yards or so the buff ran smack into a eucalyptus about the size of my forearm and stopped, head pressed against the bare, almost flesh-like trunk.

I was pretty sure the bull was too sick to charge but approached with prudent caution, my professional hunter Simon Yates right beside me. When I got a clear shot from about 10 paces, I slipped a finisher into the massive black neck and the gallant bull slowly and with great dignity, sank to the sandy soil.

It was a fine bull, just the kind of Asian buffalo I was hoping to collect. That's right: an *Asian* not a Cape buffalo. Instead of Africa, it was Australia, though you'd never know it from the looks of the place. Had *Star Trek's* Scotty just beamed me down to the spot, I would have sworn I was in the central highlands of Zimbabwe. Actually, there's a lot about Australia's vast outback that reminds one of Africa, especially the Northern Territory where we were hunting, but the similarity ends with the terrain and flora.

Hunting Australia has always had that exotic, far-off flavor that appeals to me, but the best chance to do something about it came only this past spring when I got a call from my good huntin' buddy, George Daniels. George heads up ISI Sportsmens' Adventures, a complete travel/hunt booking agency holed up at One North Dearborn, Chicago, IL 60602. Since it costs no more to have someone like George do all that running around, calling, writing letters, ticketing, visa-getting and all the other boring but necesary stuff needed to hunt outside the country, I've let George book most of the hunting trips I've made over the past several years. He's also accompanied me on many of them and we've since become good friends.

Anyway, George said he'd just struck a deal with Barry Lees' Nimrod Safaris of Darwin and had put together a 5-day 2x1 (two hunters, one guide), buffalo hunt in the Northern Territory for $2,650. It was the best deal of its kind I'd heard of, roughly comparable to the cost of a cheap elk hunt here in the States.

"I've already got a couple of guys interested in going over in August," said George matter-of-factly. "And I'm going with 'em. You interested?"

Just *getting* to Australia is an adventure; it's 12 time zones from the West Coast and 15 from my home in Pennsylvania. Our group met in Los Angeles where we boarded a Quantas 747 for Sydney via a fuel stop in Tahiti . . . in the middle of the night, dammit. Those 16 or so hours spent airborne were made as pleasant as possible by Quantas, which even in the economy section where we were seated, served us some pretty fine food and unlimited free spirits. It's the only way to fly!

Arriving in Sydney on a Saturday morning, we had two days to unwind and reset our internal timeclocks. Talk about jet lag! Even in Sydney we

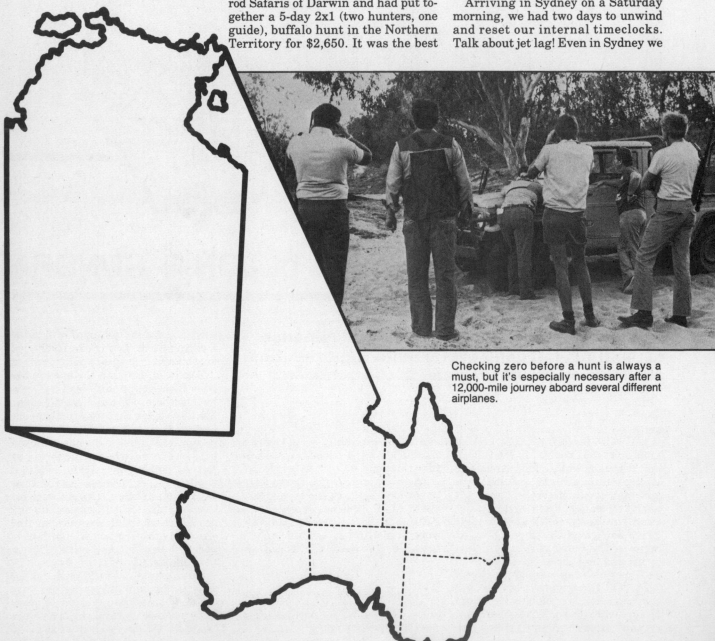

Checking zero before a hunt is always a must, but it's especially necessary after a 12,000-mile journey aboard several different airplanes.

Sundra's 375 JRS is based on a Czech-made Brno 602 action which will hold 5+1 of the big magnum loads. The stock is an all-walnut laminate from Fajen.

Right—At left is a standard 375 H&H case, next to it the 8mm Rem. Mag. By simply pushing the 8 Mag. over a tapered .375" expander, the result is Sundra's 375 JRU (far right).

Professional hunter Simon Yates cautiously approaches a sickly old bull which he subsequently dispatched on humanitarian grounds. Anyone who's been to Africa can relate to the appearance of the terrain.

still had another 3½-hour flight to look forward to Monday morning to get us to Darwin. There, we were met by Barry, Simon and the rest of the Nimrod crew who immediately hustled us off in a waiting charter to take us to our camp at Gimbat Station, some 125 miles southeast of Darwin.

Australia's a big place; its three million square miles puts it about the same size as our own 48 contiguous states, yet its population of 16 million is but seven percent of ours. To put it another way, there's about five Australians per square mile to our 65. And, while the U.S. has a high inland population, the vast majority of this island continent's inhabitants live in the coastal cities of Sydney, Adelaide, Brisbane, Darwin, Perth and Melbourne. That leaves most of those three million square miles virtually uninhabited, even when compared to Africa.

From a hunter's perspective, Australia is an inviting place. Of course, it can't claim the variety of game that Africa offers (but then what place can?), but it takes a back seat to no other. Then, too, Africa is getting smaller and smaller as far as huntable areas go. Recent developments have put Sudan and Ethiopia on the same list as Uganda, Zaire, Angola and Mozambique as places you either can't or wouldn't want to visit. Kenya has been closed to hunting for several years now, and both South Africa and Namibia are showing the kind of unrest that has discouraged many a safari.

So, when you compare Australia's stable political atmosphere and downright friendly folks (they've been accused of actually *liking* Americans), to the handful of African countries still open to hunting, there's some immediate pluses on the "down under" side.

None of Australia's game species are indigenous; indeed, only the marsupials can lay claim to that. Calling the island continent home are weird critters like the wombat, platypus, wallaby, koala and some 230 other species of animals that would have died off millions of years ago had their turf not taken leave of the Asian continent and drifted to the South Pacific. So all the game is "imported," if you will.

Six species of deer have established themselves in the wild here: the Rusa, Red, Fallow, Axis, Sambar and Hog deer. Of those, the Sambar Stag is considered the premier deer trophy. There is no one region where all six are found but the largest concentrations inhabit the eastern states of Queensland, New South Wales and Victoria. There are some commercial sport hunting operations for Sambar out of Melbourne, and for Axis deer (Chital) out of Townsville in northern Queensland, but they're primarily conducted for resident hunters. The only commercial, safari-type hunting operations of international scope are those conducted in the Northern Territory, the only state where all three of Australia's most coveted big game trophies are found: buffalo, Sambar and Banteng.

The Banteng is a wild ox which, along with the Sambar, inhabits the jungles of the Cobourg Peninsula at the very top end of the Northern Territory. Both animals are extremely elusive and the conditions under which they are hunted are very similar to those encountered hunting Bongo in the Sudan. The Cobourg falls under the jurisdiction of an aboriginal tribal council which issues only 20 Banteng permits per year, making this agile forest ox one of the most exclusive trophies found anywhere in the world. And Barry's Nim-

Other than horn conformation, the Asian buffalo is a near "carbon copy" of its African cousin. The Asian's horns are triangular in cross-section, sweep backward and don't have the pronounced "boss."

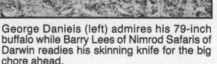

George Daniels (left) admires his 79-inch buffalo while Barry Lees of Nimrod Safaris of Darwin readies his skinning knife for the big chore ahead.

Sundra's hunting partner, Greg James, shot this exceptional Asiatic wild boar sporting tusks nearly 10 inches long. A nice trophy, indeed.

rod Safaris is one of only two companies licensed to hunt the Cobourg.

As much as I would have liked to have at least seen the jungle-like terrain of the Cobourg, to say nothing of actually hunting it, that's a separate trip entirely. A Banteng/Sambar hunt can, of course, be tacked on immediately before or after a buffalo hunt, but it requires a charter flight in the opposite direction—north of Darwin for the Cobourg, south for buffalo country.

This being my first visit to Australia, and my time and money limited, I'd have to content myself with a buffalo-only hunt. That's not as limiting as it sounds though, because Barry had written us that while hunting buffalo we'd also have plenty of opportunities to shoot Asian wild boar,

feral goats, fox, dingo (wild dogs), wallaby (kangaroo) and ducks. There were also fresh and saltwater crocodiles in abundance, as well as feral cattle, camels and donkeys running about in the absolute wild state.

Like I said though, it was buffalo I was after, just as were the other four guys in our group.

The Asian water buffalo got to Australia the same way all other game did: it was brought over as a food source about 150 years ago by early settlers. All it took was the abandonment of one settlement and the release and/or escape of the semi-domesticated stock into the hinterlands

to start the ball rolling. Today, conservative estimates put the buffalo population in the Northern Territory at a quarter-million; others put it at two to three times that. Bear in mind that those numbers exist in spite of decades of market hunting wherein these animals have been shot by the tens of thousands in certain areas and processed for pet food.

Other than its horn conformation, the Asian buffalo is a virtual copy of its African cousin. Instead of the low-slung, vertically-hooked horns of the Cape buffalo, the Asian's horns are triangular in cross-section, sweep backwards in a shallow "U", and are without the pronounced "boss." Other than that, both animals live inside similar, stumpy-legged bodies. In either case, a good-sized bull will tilt a scale to the tune of 1,600-1,700 pounds, has hooves the size of a medium pizza, and enough spare muscle to make a second buffalo. Though the Asian is not quite as ill-tempered as the Cape variety, when wounded he has been known to gore, maim, trample and otherwise inconvenience those responsible.

The 375 H&H is the most popular caliber with visiting hunters and the one Barry recommends to his clients. Actually, I was using an improved 375 of my own design. Called the 375 JRS, it's nothing more than the 8mm Remington Magnum necked up to .375". You can also get the proper brass by fire-forming 375 H&H ammo in the JRS chamber, thus giving the caliber the added advantage of digesting factory ammo in a pinch. In the long action of my Brno magnum Mauser, a 300-grain Hornady bullet seated ⅛-inch shy of the cannelure, atop 85.5 grains of IMR-4350, will produce an honest 2700 fps from a 24-inch barrel (mine's 22½ inches and I get 2685).

As it turned out, I had the smallest gun in camp! My buddy George, as well as the other three hunters who came over with us on this group booking, were all using 458s.

A good trophy buffalo will sport horns 75 inches or more; that's measuring tip to tip following the outside or front curve of the horns across the forehead. Official scoring for the Safari Club International record book, however, is done a different way: Individual horn length is measured (not counting distance across the forehead), then added to the circumference of each base. A bull, then, sporting horns 30 inches in length and measuring 16 inches around the bases

would score 30+30+16+16 or 92 points. To make the SCI record book a score of 90 is required.

Since Barry told us we should all be able to collect a bull in the 75-inch "book" class, no one was anxious to pull the trigger on the first day. I was paired up with Greg James of Chicago, a chap I had met on a previous hunt in Alaska, and together we looked over nearly 40 bulls that first day. A couple of 'em looked quite good to our inexperienced eyes but when Simon told us they wouldn't go 70 inches, we passed.

Using Toyota Land Cruisers in the same manner they do over in Africa, we probably averaged over 100 miles a day. As much country as we saw, however, it was but a fraction of Barry's 2,500-square-mile Gimbat Station concession. And we saw lots of buffalo in five day's time—at least 150 bulls. Most were solitary or in small bachelor groups of one or two others. Some were skittish and ran off at the first sight of the vehicle or of us on foot; others stood their ground defiantly. And why not? Most had never seen or scented a human before and they sure as hell didn't have any natural enemies to fear.

One of our fellows, Bob Peterson, who was hunting with Barry, lucked out early on the first day of the hunt. It was one of those situations wherein they came upon an animal that was so good, there was just no question but to take it, first day or not. As it turned out, Bob's 82-inch bull was easily the best animal taken, scoring 106½. Daniels took second best with a 79-inch buff that scored 102.

My partner, Greg, shot two buffalo

(at $400 trophy fee each, after the first one, you can shoot as many as your pocket book can stand), the best one scoring 93½. Mine scored 94 and I was plenty happy with it. Greg also shot a huge Asiatic boar, its tusks going nearly 10 inches. Being jet black in color, these boars of Australia are quite handsome, as boars go, and a worthwhile addition to anyone's den or trophy room.

Corny as it sounds, I get a real rush when I sense I'm the first white man to have set foot on a certain patch of ground. I got that feeling in Australia's outback more often than any other place I've been. And it's as interesting a country as it is vast. In addition to an incredible amount of bird and animal life, we saw aboriginal caves of early bushmen that were loaded with untouched artifacts, numerous and remarkably well preserved wall paintings, and human skeletal remains. The latter were found neatly stacked like cordwood in a rock fissure about eight feet above the ground. Only the presence of a human skull at the entrance of the fissure—like some grizzly sentry standing guard—prompted us to investigate. We touched nothing.

Like I said: Australia's a neat place, friendly, and one of the last hunting frontiers on earth. I'm going back. ●

This human skull in the fissure marks a burial vault for the bones of several aboriginal skeletons piled behind. Author's hunting party left it undisturbed, of course.

# Franchi's "Project 80" Auto Shotgun

## by WALLACE LABISKY

**A derivitive of Franchi's unique SPAS-12 auto/pump M&P shotgun, the Project 80 system offers good value and handling in two models—the Elite and the Prestige.**

Not long after the end of World War II, an event of historic significance took place within the American firearms industry. A Sears, Roebuck & Co. executive consulted his crystal ball one more time and then struck a deal with High Standard to manufacture a gas-operated shotgun that was to carry the J. C. Higgins brand name.

High Standard, at this time, already had the design down pat, and one cannot help but wonder why the parent company did not forge ahead and introduce the gun under its own banner. Perhaps its negative decision was based on the fact that the gas gun flew so boldly in the face of conventionality. At any rate, the mail-order people grabbed the ball and made a touchdown run. And it was a touchdown that revolutionized autoloading shotgun design.

Today, there are still a few autoloaders being marketed that follow the John Moses Browning design, but

in reality these long-recoil guns are at the threshold of obsolescence. The new kid on the block, with its softer felt recoil and a fixed barrel that kills off the old double-shuffle effect, is now king of the hill—and has been for a long time.

One of the newest offerings comes to us from overseas through F.I.E. (Firearms Import & Export Corp.), which is the U.S. distributor for arms from the well-known Italian maker, Luigi Franchi S.p.A. (Brescia). These "Project 80" autoloaders for sporting use are a direct outgrowth of the unique SPAS-12, a military-and-police shotgun that can be operated as either an autoloader or a pump gun.

A veritable slew of models comprise the Project 80 series. But all are mechanically identical, differing only in such matters as engraving, rib width and styling, stock styling, and wood quality and finish. And all have high-strength, aluminum-alloy receivers with a semi-humpback profile at the rear.

Only two grades are being imported by F.I.E. at the present time, the Elite and the Prestige. The former has a much more "uptown" look, with a better grade of walnut and Renaissance-style engraving (hunting scenes) on the receiver. The Prestige is pretty much plain-Jane, having cut checkering (18 lines per inch) but totally lack-

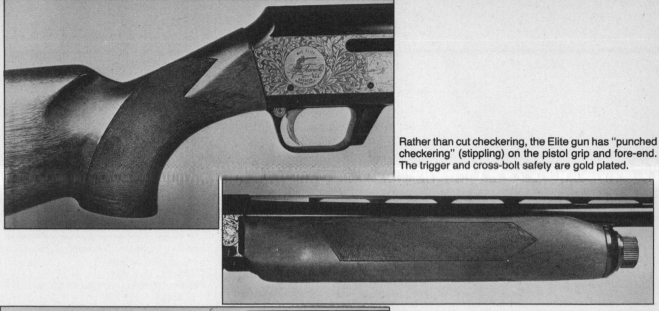

Rather than cut checkering, the Elite gun has "punched checkering" (stippling) on the pistol grip and fore-end. The trigger and cross-bolt safety are gold plated.

The checkering on the Prestige model is deeply cut and runs 18 lines-per-inch. A plastic, shock-absorbing shim is used between the stock and receiver. Fore-end length is the same for all grades of the Project 80 guns. The edges of the 7mm-wide rib are flush with the integral support posts.

ing ornamentation on the receiver panels.

Although both grades have pistol-grip buttstocks (oiled finish), the dimensions differ considerably. The Prestige stock is designed explicitly for field use (14¼" x 1⅝" x 2½"), while that for the Elite is something of a compromise at 14⅝" x 1⅜" x 1⅞", which measurements place it much closer to the target-stock side. Both guns have about a quarter-inch of cast-off.

While the Prestige is adorned with conventional checkering, the Elite has what is described as "punch checkering"—in other words, the wood is impact-stippled to produce a roughened surface. For my money, the cut checkering rates higher in terms of appearance, but from a functional standpoint the two types seem about equal.

Other differences in stocking revolve around pistol-grip styling and comb thickness. The grip on the Pres-tige is a flat oval in cross-section. That for the Elite is diamond-shaped in section, and its minimum circumference of 5⅛ inches is fully ¼-inch greater than for the Prestige because of an anatomical palm swell. The Elite's comb is also noticeably more "beefy."

A ventilated rib of 7mm width is standard on both grades. That for the Elite has a file-cut surface, while the Prestige's rib is machined in a criss-cross arc pattern. Both surfaces are highly effective in eliminating glare. Up front, a red phosphorescent bead offers high visibility under all shooting conditions. Neither grade offers a mid-rib bead.

Only 12-gauge guns with a 2¾-inch chamber are being offered at this time, and it is not likely that this situ-ation will change in the immediate future.

Franchi literature hypes the "dependability, strength and precision" of the Project 80 guns by pointing out that a French shooter, one Michel Pujolle, established a new world record while shooting a pair of standard grade guns—an Elite and a Prestige. Pujolle broke 2,756 clay targets in an hour's time. This feat shattered the former record of 2,264 clays that was set by a New Zealand shooter.

And Franchi is equally proud of the Project 80 gas system itself, stating that if properly lubricated it will require no maintenance for several thousands of rounds. This is due, at least in part, to the fact that the system has few parts, all of them housed outside the magazine tube.

## Pattern Test Results
Franchi 12-Gauge Prestige Auto
28" Modified-Choke Barrel, 2¾" Chamber
Bore Diameter: 0.721" Choke Constriction: 0.016"

**Load:** Winchester Super Pigeon, 3¼-1¼-7½ (432 pellets)
**Distance:** 40 yards.
**Pattern Density** (average for five shots):
  5" annular ring: 128
  20" inner circle: 166
  30" circle: 294 (68.0%)
**Comments:** Pattern efficiency ranged from 66.4% to 71.7% for Imp. Mod. performance. Recoil sensation very mild with this loading.

**Load:** Federal Hi-Power Heavyweight, 3¾-1⅜-4 (194 pellets)
**Distance:** 40 yards
**Pattern Density** (average for five shots):
  5" annular ring: 59
  20" inner circle: 83
  30" circle: 142 (73.2%)
**Comments:** Pattern efficiency ranged from 68.5% to 77.3% for Full-choke performance. Recoil sensation not disturbing with this loading.

## Pattern Test Results
Franchi 12-Gauge Elite Auto
24" Cylinder Barrel, 2¾" Chamber
Bore Diameter: 0.725" Zero Choke Constriction

**Load:** Federal Premium Buckshot (buffered) 34 pellets No. 4 Copper-Plated
**Distance:** 25 yards.
**Pattern Density** (average for five shots):
  5" annular ring: 7
  20" inner circle: 26.4
  30" circle: 33.4 (98.2%)
**Comments:** Pattern efficiency ranged from 94.1% to 100% with three 100% patterns in the five-shot string. Highest count in the 20-inch circle was 30 pellets, lowest 22.

**Load:** Winchester AA Special Skeet, 2¾-1⅛-9 (628 pellets)
**Distance:** 21 Yards
**Pattern Density** (average for five shots):
  5" annular ring: 178
  20" inner circle: 285
  30" circle: 463 (73.7%)
**Comments:** Pattern efficiency ranged from 68.9% to 77%. Effective pattern width ranged from 30" to 32", with the average core count exceeding that of the 5" annular area by 107 pellets.

Here's a quick run-down of the various gas-system parts and how they work: Powder gas is diverted through twin barrel ports located 13 inches forward of the breech. A rather massive barrel ring (hard-chromed on the inside) serves as a gas cylinder, and the gas piston (1.620-inches in length) nests almost entirely inside the barrel ring when the action is in battery position. The piston is made of "inox" steel, which is an extra-hard type similar to stainless. On firing, powder gas rushes into the barrel ring (which is sealed at the front end by a neoprene O-ring) and acts against the piston. Gas vent-off does not begin until the piston has moved rearward a distance of 1.175-inches.

The connecting "links" between the gas piston and the breech-bolt assembly are a rather long transfer sleeve and a pair of action bars. The sleeve has a hard-chromed finish both inside and out, and the blued action bars are made as a single unit in the interest of equalizing the thrust on the bolt slide. The magazine tube is plated, of course, as a matter of reducing friction. Surrounding the magazine tube at the receiver end is a shock-absorbing collar that provides a cushioned stop for the transfer sleeve.

Shortly before the piston has moved far enough to permit gas vent-off to begin, the locking bolt disengages from the hard-chromed barrel exten-

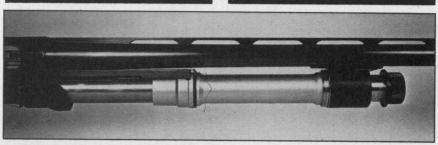

The Project 80 gas system, shown here in battery (closed) position, encircles the magazine tube. The piston nests inside the barrel ring, which serves as a gas cylinder.

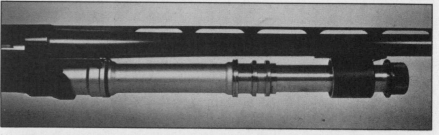

Here, the gas system is shown in its action-open position, with the piston fully visible. Franchi says that several thousand rounds can be fired before maintenance is necessary.

sion and the bolt assembly begins rearward travel. By the time this occurs, the various parts have picked up enough momentum to carry through on their own and bring about extraction and ejection of the fired shell. The cycle is completed when the action spring (housed in the buttstock) drives the breech bolt forward to chamber a fresh round from the magazine.

My test shooting with both a Pres-

tige and an Elite confirms Franchi's claim that the gas system will reliably handle all 2¾-inch loads, no matter how light or how heavy. The two test guns, when fed a diet of Peters 1-ounce target loads, functioned just as flawlessly as when used with 1½-ounce short magnums. I even went one step further and fired 50 rounds of ultra-light ⅞-ounce handloads without any problem—and some of these ultra-lights generated

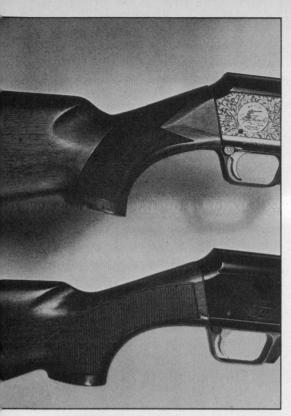

Buttstock styling is one of the differences between the Project 80 guns. The Elite stock (top) has a beefier pistol grip and is more robust all the way through. The Prestige stock (bottom) has better dimensions for field shooting.

less than 7,000 lead units of chamber pressure.

The ejection pattern changes dramatically when switching from heavy to powder-puff loads, of course. With the latter, the empty hulls tend to fall at the shooter's feet, while with a short-magnum loading the empty may go into a low orbit. But the bottom line is that these Project 80 guns will function and keep right on functioning regardless of wide differences in the gas impulse.

Barrel lengths and chokes for the Project 80 autoloaders are as follows: Full (28 and 30 inches); Modified (26 and 28 inches); Improved Cylinder (26 inches); and Cylinder (24 and 26 inches). All lengths and chokes are available as extras, of course, including a 24-inch slug barrel fitted with rifle-type open sights. And all will freely interchange between the various grade guns. Franchi does not, at this time, offer a screw-in choke-tube system, but this is not to say that there isn't one on the drawing board.

All Project 80 barrels undergo a proof test of 1,200 Kg/cm$^2$, which is equal to 17,076 lbs.-per-square-inch. The chambers and bores are chromed, while the barrel exteriors are deeply blued to nearly match the black anodized finish on the receivers. Certainly not to be overlooked are the specially-designed forcing cones which tend to reduce felt recoil.

My Prestige test gun has a 28-inch Modified-choke barrel, the .721-inch bore being constricted .016-inch at the muzzle. In design, the choke is of the conical-parallel type with a total length of 2.50 inches. Since the pattern-test results are detailed elsewhere in these pages, it will suffice to say that the 40-yard performance was well above the 60% level with both loadings that were tried. The patterns centered perfectly on the point of hold when using a dead-level rib picture and covering the small center marker with the front bead.

The bore diameter of the Elite's 25-inch Cylinder barrel is .725-inch, which is in complete agreement with the 18.4mm marking. At a distance of 21 yards, using a Winchester Skeet loading, this choke-free barrel delivered an effective shot cloud that ranged from 30 to 32 inches in width. This barrel shot just a tad higher than the 28-incher, making it necessary to float the small center marker over the front bead in order to center the pattern in the vertical plane. The same sight picture did the trick at 25 yards when using a Federal Premium loading with copper-plated No. 4 buckshot.

On the matter of weight, the Elite grade is slightly more hefty, this being mainly due to the chunkier buttstock. Its empty weight is an even 8 lbs. with a 28-inch barrel. The Prestige, with the same barrel, pulls the scale down to 7 lbs., 10 oz. Featherweights they aren't—that's obvious. But these gun weights, combined with the gas-operated action and the extra-length forcing cone, do a super job of taming buttstock authority. In short, the shooter doesn't take a battering.

Trigger pulls for the two test guns run much the same at 5 lbs. for the Prestige, and 6 lbs. for the Elite. Both pulls have some rough travel preceding let-off, but not enough to be bothersome in actual use.

These Franchi autoloaders offer a six-shot capability—five rounds in the magazine and one in the chamber. A plug is furnished, of course, to reduce the total capacity to three rounds. Franchi offers a magazine extension for the SPAS-12 military shotgun, which will also fit the Project 80 sporting guns. It increases the magazine capacity by two rounds.

One of the design features that was carried over from the SPAS-12 is a magazine cut-off that permits quickly changing the load in the chamber without disturbing the shells in the magazine. The cut-off button is located at the lower front of the receiver on the right side. When this button is pressed down, a small integral flange pivots to make contact with the shell rim on its headface side, and thus the shell is prevented from leaving the magazine when the breech bolt is pulled back to extract the chambered round. The cut-off is designed so that it will lock in place when in the engaged mode. It need not be manually disengaged following load switching; it will disengage automatically when the gun is fired. I should also point out that if the cut-off is manually disengaged when the breech bolt is open, a shell will automatically feed and chamber.

This cut-off certainly rates as a highly practical bit of design. However, I found it to be a bit balky at times, depending on the brand of ammo used, and this was true for both of the test guns. Not once did the cut-off refuse to engage and lock when either ACTIV or Fiocchi ammo was in the magazine; but with Federal, Remington and Winchester brands it was a sometimes yes, sometimes no situation. I eventually discovered that if the bolt-release button (located at the front of the receiver on the left-hand side) was simultaneously actuated (thereby nudging the head of the shell in the direction of the cut-off), there was no problem in getting the cut-off to make positive engagement and lock in place.

Since I am a field shooter first and a claybirder second, I favored the Prestige with its more propitious stock dimensions for the lion's share of the test shooting. All told, about 250 rounds were fired—some at cottontails, some at crows, but mostly at claybirds thrown from a Trius portable trap. This shooting was marred by only one malfunction, this involving a handload that had been sitting on the shelf for years and years. The empty hull extracted, but hung up in a lengthwise position in the ejection port.

As always, when putting a field gun through its paces on clays, I shoot from a low-gun position. This provides a very good indication of how the gun will mount, point and swing under actual hunting conditions. And if the scoresheet can be considered a criterion in evaluating worth as a field gun, then one fact stands out in bold-faced type—the Franchi crew has succeeded in putting together one heck of a sweet package. ●

# LOADING With LEE ... By HAND

Lee Precision is continually expanding its line of low cost but good quality reloading tools, and here's the dope on their latest innovation—the Lee Hand Press.

## by JON LEU

THERE'S AN OLD ADAGE that says, "Build a better mousetrap, and they'll beat a path to your door." Dick Lee's idea of a "better mousetrap" includes quality, innovative thinking, and reasonable prices in reloading equipment; and he's given shooters an entire catalog full of that sort of thinking. His latest innovation, the Lee Hand Press, is but another example of his commitment to shooters and one that's almost certain to become highly popular with reloaders.

A century ago in the early days of fixed cartridge firearms, reloading was a relatively simple process. All the necessary tools and components could be carried in a small bag or box. As shooters became more sophisticated, their needs (or their perceptions of their needs) in reloading tools became more sophisticated. It's not uncommon for the advanced reloader to set aside an entire room in his house for his reloading and attempt to equip that room with all manner of tools to turn out better ammunition.

Truth be known, all that "sophisticated" equipment just isn't needed to turn out quality ammunition. Bench-rest shooters—folks who get their kicks out of accuracy—do virtually all of their loading at the range with a relatively simple set of tools which can be carried in a small tool box. Ammunition is loaded at the range so minor adjustments can be made to attain the best possible accuracy.

The Lee Hand Press answers that same need for a quality, portable reloading press for the average shooter. At $44.98 retail for the kit ($54.98 if ordered with handgun dies which include a carbide sizer), it comes close to the ideal for the reloader who desires the ability to turn out good ammunition anywhere he might be, the shooter just getting started in reloading who just can't afford to spend several hundred dollars for equipment, or for the apartment dweller who simply doesn't have the room to set up a permanent reloading area. The Hand Press alone retails for $29.98.

Those buying the Hand Press in kit form, which is available in all calibers for which Lee manufactures dies, will

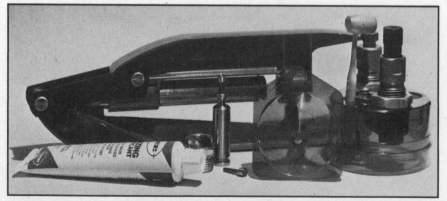

Lee's Hand Press kit provides everything except components to reload ammunition. Included are: the Hand Press, a set of Lee 7/8-14 dies with shell holder and powder dipper, Ram Prime unit with large and small seating stems, powder funnel, and a tube of the excellent Lee resizing lube. Kits are available for all calibers for which Lee makes dies.

receive virtually everything (except the components) needed to load ammunition. Included in the kit is a set of Lee ⅞-14 dies, a Ram Prime unit which will handle both large and small primers, a powder funnel, and case sizing lubricant. Every Lee die set includes a powder dipper which will throw appropriate charges with a variety of powders suitable for the cartridge to be loaded. The die sets also include the proper shell holder, a practice other manufactures might emulate.

Since the kit is designed to provide the shooter with those items needed to get started in metallic cartridge reloading, there are a couple of things that I think might well be added. The first of these would be a chamfering tool, the second would be the appropriate Lee case trimmer. Both are needed by the reloader, and their inclusion in the kit would not significantly hike the price.

The frame of the Lee hand press is cast from a high tensile stength alloy which is fitted with a steel ram and toggles. According to Lee, the alloy used is several times stronger than cast iron; and he backs up that claim with a 2-year guarantee. The overall dimensions of the hand press with the handle closed are 11½ inches high by 3½ inches wide. The small size of the press, which weighs about 1¾ pounds, gives the reloader a go-anywhere tool which will fit just about

anyplace. The press is threaded to handle all standard ⅞-14 reloading dies, and the ram is milled to accept universal shell holders. In spite of its small size and light weight, the Lee Hand Press has a total ram travel of 3¼ inches, suitable—with some caution—for the largest of cases.

The Hand Press kit I received for evaluation contained Lee 30-06 reloading dies. Rumaging around in the closet, I came up with several boxes of Lake City National Match 30-06 cases which had been fired in an M 1 Garand rifle. Although a majority of the cases were visibly swelled in front of the web area, they were given a light coating of Lee sizing lubricant and run through Lee's full length resizing die without so much as a hint of a problem. Though the effort required to size the cases in the Hand Press was greater than would have been required with a bench-mounted press, it certainly was not strenuous.

According to Lee, his resizing lubricant is an industrial deep draw lube used primarily by the automotive industry. Whatever it is, it's good. I've used it for several years both for resizing and for case forming and have never had problems. Best of all, it's as

easy to get off the cases when the sizing or forming operation is completed as it is to put on—hardly the case with most lubricants.

The Lee full length resizing die is a unique design which deserves special mention. Rather than being threaded into the die itself, the decapper/expander unit of the Lee die is held by friction in a collet which is threaded into the top of the die. Should you encounter a case with an off-center flash hole or a severely crimped-in primer, the entire decapper/expander assembly will slide up in the collet rather than breaking the decapping pin. Loosening the collet allows the reloader to readjust the decapping rod to its proper position. Too, should you ever get a case stuck in the die, the collet can be loosened to allow the decapping rod to be used as a stuck case remover by tapping on the end of the rod. All Lee dies are fitted with a unique lock ring. Rather than having a cross-bolt or a cap screw bearing directly against the threads of the die, the bottom of the Lee lock ring is fitted with a rubber O-ring which cre-

The Ram Prime assembly supplied with the Hand Press kit was originally designed for use with Lee's 2001 Challenger bench-mounted press. An aluminum shell holder and a ram extension and priming post is then installed on the ram. It works well, but Leu says it doesn't give the user a high degree of "feel" as the primer is being seated in the case.

Lee reloading dies, available for most popular rifle and handgun cartridges, are packaged in a sturdy, stackable plastic container. Each of the handgun die sets contains a carbide sizer. Much to their credit, Lee supplies the proper shell holder and an appropriate powder dipper with every set of dies. The concentricity of ammunition loaded with the Lee dies while testing the new Hand Press was exceptional, rivalling the quality of the best custom made dies.

The Lee Hand Press isn't a small tool at 11½ inches high, but its size still permits it to be carried to the range for on-site reloading. The author found that sizing 30-06 cases was no great chore with the tool.

ates adequate pressure to lock the die in place when turned up against the press frame. More important, no tools are required to reset the die.

Once the 30-06 cases were primed with the Ram Prime unit, the Lee seating die was installed. Beginning with the first round, it took more pressure to seat bullets than it did to full-length size cases. The problem, as it turns out, was twofold. The Lee sizing die is not the small base variety available for cases which have been fired in semi-automatic rifles. As noted earlier, case heads were visibly swelled after firing in an M-1 service rifle. In discussing the problem with John Lee, I was told their bullet seating dies are reamed somewhat tighter than normal industry standards to give more concentric ammunition. After running the cases through another 30-06 die with a smaller base, no further problems were encountered with the Lee seating die.

Having resolved the problem with the 30-06 die set, the entire process was repeated with a set of Lee 223 Remington dies. The cases used had been fired in my Remington Model 788, and absolutely no problems were encountered with the 223 dies. The problems with the 30-06 seater had been due to a "sloppy" chamber in the rifle rather than any problems with the die.

To learn something of the quality of the Lee reloading dies, a sample of 20 fired 223 Remington cases were mea-

sured before, during, and after being reloaded. Prior to being sized, the average neck runout was calculated at .000825″. After sizing with the Lee full length resizing die, average neck runout was .000922″. After priming, charging the cases with powder, and seating Hornady 55-grain SX bullets, average bullet runout was only .0014″. This is excellent performance for a set of threaded reloading dies and rivals the performance of the best custom benchrest equipment I've used.

In spite of the excellent concentricity of the ammunition loaded with the

The seating stem was the only glitch in an otherwise excellent set of Lee ⅞-14 reloading dies. As can be seen here, the counterbore was not cut deeply enough in the seating stem, allowing the stem to contact the tip of the bullet rather than the ogive. Although the Lee dies produced remarkable ammunition in terms of concentricity, bullet seating depth varied by .011″ in a 20-round sample—too much for best accuracy with a 22-caliber varmint rifle.

Lee dies, all was not beer and skittles. After the 223 ammunition was loaded, over-all length was checked with an ogive comparator which, rather than measuring to the tip of the bullet, measures cartridge length to a plane of constant diameter on the bullet's ogive. This measurement indicated that seating depth varied by a total of .011″ in the 20 rounds—too much for best accuracy, especially with a 22 caliber rifle. When I disassembled the seating die, I found the seating stem contacts the tip of the bullet rather than the ogive as it should. The cone in the seating stem which accepts the nose of the bullet had not been cut deeply enough, a minor problem which Lee officials tell me will be corrected.

My only other complaint—and it is, admittedly, a minor one—is the Ram Prime unit which is supplied with the kit. Priming with the Ram Prime installed on the Hand Press is, at best, a juggling act. Too, because of the design of the press, the reloader does not get a very good "feel" of the primer being seated in the case. Given my druthers, I would rather see the kit supplied with the Lee Improved Priming Tool—a hand-held tool which has long been a favorite with shooters. Substitution of the hand priming tool would improve performance and slightly lower the cost of the kit.

Along with the Hand Press, Lee has introduced two shell holder kits which should be of interest to those who load for a variety of cartridges. Both of the kits retail for $19.98 and each contains 11 shell holders which will fit over 115 different cartridges. The kits, packaged in a sturdy plastic storage box, have a selection chart on the back showing the proper shell holder for each cartridge. One of the kits has a full assortment of universal shell holders which will work with all brands of reloading presses. The second kit contains a selection of the special shell holders designed for the Lee Universal Priming Tool and the Lee Auto Prime. Both of the shell holder kits cover the same range of cartridges, which includes virtually all popular cases with the exception of the PPC and the 45 Auto Rim. Shell holders for those two cases are available from Lee either for the Auto Prime or in a universal model as separate items.

Even though the prices might indicate otherwise, the new tools from Lee aren't just for the beginning handloader. Combining portability, excellent quality, and reasonable pricing, they represent a value which should appeal to a wide range of shooters. ●

Lee's full length resizing die is unique in that the decapper/expander assembly is not threaded into the top of the die, a practice common with other makers. The decapper/expander assembly is held in the die by a collet which is threaded into the top of the die. If excessive pressure is required for decapping, as with a severely crimped-in primer or an off-center flash hole, the assembly will slide up in the collet rather than breaking the decapping pin.

# THE GUNS ILLUSTRATED CATALOG

# GUNDEX®

## A listing of all the guns in the catalog, by name and model, alphabetically and numerically.

This feature of our catalog speeds up the chore of finding the basic facts on a given firearm for the experienced. And it may make the contents of the catalog far more available to the inexperienced.

That is our intention.

To use it, you need the manufacturer's name and model designation. That designation might be a number, as in Winchester Model 94, or it might be a name, as in Colt Python. And you need to know the alphabet.

The manufacturers are listed alphabetically and the entry under each manufacturer is arranged in the quickest way—numbers are in numerical order, names are alphabetical.

It's all very straightforward. It is all pretty voluminous, as well. There are over 1200 entries and at about 230 lines per page, what with headings and all, the GUNDEX® is eight pages long.

We have tried to make it easy to find, too—just look for the black GUNDEX® label along the edge of the page, flip to there, and get your page number in short order.

GUNDE

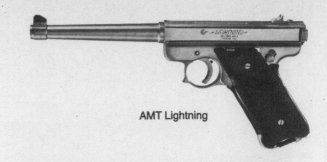

AMT Lightning

### AMT LIGHTNING AUTO PISTOL

**Caliber:** 22 LR, 10-shot magazine.
**Barrel:** Tapered — 6½″, 8½″, 10½″, 12½″; Bull — 5″, 6½″, 8½″, 10½″, 12½″.
**Weight:** 45 oz. (6½″ barrel). **Length:** 10¾″ over-all (6½″ barrel).
**Stocks:** Checkered wrap-around rubber.
**Sights:** Blade front, fixed rear; adjustable rear available at extra cost.
**Features:** Made of stainless steel. Uses Clark trigger with adjustable stops; receiver grooved for scope mounting; trigger guard spur for two-hand hold; interchangeable barrels. Introduced 1984. From AMT.
**Price:** 5″ bull, 6½″ tapered or bull, fixed sight . . . . . . . . . . . . . . . . . . . . . $235.95
**Price:** 8½″, tapered or bull, fixed sight . . . . . . . . . . . . . . . . . . . . . . . . . . $235.95
**Price:** 12½″, tapered or bull, fixed sight . . . . . . . . . . . . . . . . . . . . . . . . . $248.95
**Price:** For adjustable rear sight add . . . . . . . . . . . . . . . . . . . . . . . . . . . . $25.00

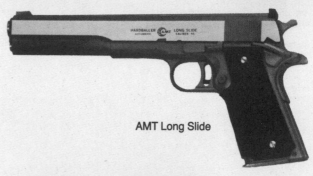

AMT Long Slide

### AMT "BACKUP" AUTO PISTOL

**Caliber:** 22 LR, 8-shot magazine; 380 ACP, 5-shot magazine
**Barrel:** 2½″
**Weight:** 18 oz. **Length:** 4.25″ over-all.
**Stocks:** Checkered Lexon.
**Sights:** Fixed, open, recessed.
**Features:** Concealed hammer, blowback operation; manual and grip safeties. All stainless steel construction. Smallest domestically-produced pistol in 380. From AMT.
**Price:** 22 LR or 380 ACP . . . . . . . . . . . . . . . . . . . . . . . . . . . . . . . . . . . . $249.95

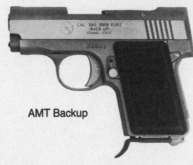

AMT Backup

### AMT 45 ACP HARDBALLER LONG SLIDE

**Caliber:** 45 ACP.
**Barrel:** 7″.
**Length:** 10½″ over-all.
**Stocks:** Wrap-around rubber.
**Sights:** Fully adjustable rear sight.
**Features:** Slide and barrel are 2″ longer than the standard 45, giving less recoil, added velocity, longer sight radius. Has extended combat safety, serrated matte rib, loaded chamber indicator, wide adjustable trigger. From AMT.
**Price:** . . . . . . . . . . . . . . . . . . . . . . . . . . . . . . . . . . . . . . . . . . . . . . . . . $575.00

### AMERICAN ARMS EAGLE 380

**Caliber:** 380 ACP, 6-shot magazine.
**Barrel:** 2½″.
**Weight:** 20 oz. **Length:** 6¼″ over-all.
**Stocks:** Checkered walnut.
**Sights:** Fixed.
**Features:** Double action, stainless steel construction, firing pin lock safety. Comes with fitted carrying case, belt buckle and one magazine. Introduced 1984. From American Arms Corp.
**Price:** . . . . . . . . . . . . . . . . . . . . . . . . . . . . . . . . . . . . . . . . . . . . . . . . . $289.00
**Price:** As above, except with black rubber grips . . . . . . . . . . . . . . . . . . $300.00

### AMT 45 ACP HARDBALLER

**Caliber:** 45 ACP.
**Barrel:** 5″.
**Weight:** 39 oz. **Length:** 8½″ over-all.
**Stocks:** Wrap-around rubber.
**Sights:** Adjustable.
**Features:** Extended combat safety, serrated matte slide rib, loaded chamber indicator, long grip safety, beveled magazine well, adjustable target trigger. All stainless steel. From AMT.
**Price:** . . . . . . . . . . . . . . . . . . . . . . . . . . . . . . . . . . . . . . . . . . . . . . . . . $550.00
**Price:** Government model (as above except no rib, fixed sights) . . . . $440.00

Arminex Trifire

### ARMINEX TRIFIRE AUTO PISTOL

**Caliber:** 9mm. Para. (9-shot), 38 Super. (9-shot), 45 ACP (7-shot).
**Barrel:** 5″, 6″.
**Weight:** 38 oz. **Length:** 8″ over-all.
**Stocks:** Contoured smooth walnut.
**Sights:** Interchangeable post front, rear adjustable for windage and elevation.
**Features:** Single action. Slide mounted firing pin block safety. Specially contoured one-piece backstrap. Convertible by changing barrel, slide, magazine, recoil spring. Introduced 1982. Made in U.S. by Arminex Ltd.
**Price:** Standard Model (5″ bbl.) . . . . . . . . . . . . . . . . . . . . . . . . . . . . . . . $396.00
**Price:** Target Model (6″ bbl.) . . . . . . . . . . . . . . . . . . . . . . . . . . . . . . . . . $448.00
**Price:** Presentation Model (same as Standard but with ambidextrous safety, smooth burl walnut grips, wood presentation case) . . . . . . . . . . . . . $444.00

**CAUTION:** PRICES CHANGE. CHECK AT GUNSHOP.

### ASTRA A-90 DOUBLE-ACTION AUTO PISTOL
**Caliber:** 9mm Para. (15-shot), 45 ACP (9-shot).
**Barrel:** 3.75″.
**Weight:** 40 oz. **Length:** 7″ over-all.
**Stocks:** Checkered black plastic.
**Sights:** Square blade front, square notch rear drift-adjustable for windage.
**Features:** Double or single action; loaded chamber indicator; combat-style trigger guard; optional right-side slide release (for left-handed shooters); automatic internal safety; decocking lever. Introduced 1985. Imported from Spain by Interarms.
**Price:** Blue . . . . . . . . . . . . . . . . . . . . . . . . . . . . . . . . . . . . . . . . . $395.00

Astra A-90 Pistol

### ASTRA CONSTABLE AUTO PISTOL
**Caliber:** 22 LR, 10-shot, 380 ACP, 7-shot.
**Barrel:** 3½″
**Weight:** 26 oz.
**Stocks:** Moulded plastic
**Sights:** Adj. rear.
**Features:** Double action, quick no-tool takedown, non-glare rib on slide. 380 available in blue, stainless steel, or chrome finish. Engraved guns also available—contact the importer. Imported from Spain by Interarms.
**Price:** Blue, 22 . . . . . . . . . . . . . . . . . . . . . . . . . . . . . . . . . . . . . . $265.00
**Price:** Chrome, 22 . . . . . . . . . . . . . . . . . . . . . . . . . . . . . . . . . . . . $285.00
**Price:** Blue, 380 . . . . . . . . . . . . . . . . . . . . . . . . . . . . . . . . . . . . . . $265.00
**Price:** Chrome, 380 . . . . . . . . . . . . . . . . . . . . . . . . . . . . . . . . . . . . $285.00
**Price:** Stainless, 380 . . . . . . . . . . . . . . . . . . . . . . . . . . . . . . . . . . $345.00

### Astra A-60 Double Action Pistol
Similar to the Constable except in 380 only, with 13-shot magazine, slide-mounted ambidextrous safety. Available in blued steel only. Introduced 1980.
**Price:** . . . . . . . . . . . . . . . . . . . . . . . . . . . . . . . . . . . . . . . . . . . . . . $345.00

Auto-Ordnance 1911A1

### AUTO-ORDNANCE 1911A1 AUTOMATIC PISTOL
**Caliber:** 9mm Para., 38 Super, 9-shot, 45 ACP, 7-shot magazine.
**Barrel:** 5″.
**Weight:** 39 oz. **Length:** 8½″ over-all.
**Stocks:** Checkered plastic with medallion.
**Sights:** Blade front, rear adj. for windage.
**Features:** Same specs as 1911A1 military guns—parts interchangeable. Frame and slide blued; each radius has non-glare finish. Made in U.S. by Auto-Ordnance Corp.
**Price:** 45 cal., about . . . . . . . . . . . . . . . . . . . . . . . . . . . . . . . . . . $324.95
**Price:** 9mm, 38 Super, about . . . . . . . . . . . . . . . . . . . . . . . . . . . . $349.95

### BEEMAN SP DELUXE PISTOL
**Caliber:** 22 LR, single shot.
**Barrel:** 8″, 10″, 12″, 15″.
**Weight:** 50 oz. **Length:** 18″ over-all.
**Stocks:** European walnut, anatomically-shaped with adjustable palm rest.
**Sights:** Blade front, notch rear adjustable for windage and elevation.
**Features:** Two-stage trigger; loaded chamber indicator; grooved for scope mount. Detachable fore-end and barrel weight. Standard version available without fore-end and barrel weight. Imported by Beeman. Introduced 1984.
**Price:** Standard, right or left-hand . . . . . . . . . . . . . . . . . . . . . . . . $249.50
**Price:** Deluxe (with fore-end), illus. . . . . . . . . . . . . . . . . . . . . . . . . $299.50

Beeman SP Deluxe

### BERNARDELLI MODEL 80 AUTO PISTOL
**Caliber:** 22 LR (10-shot); 380 ACP (7-shot).
**Barrel:** 3½″.
**Weight:** 26½ oz. **Length:** 6½″ over-all.
**Stocks:** Checkered plastic with thumbrest.
**Sights:** Ramp front, white outline rear adj. for w. & e
**Features:** Hammer block slide safety; loaded chamber indicator; dual recoil buffer springs; serrated trigger; inertia type firing pin. Imported from Italy by Interarms.
**Price:** Model 80, 22 . . . . . . . . . . . . . . . . . . . . . . . . . . . . . . . . . . . . $215.00
**Price:** Model 80, 380 . . . . . . . . . . . . . . . . . . . . . . . . . . . . . . . . . . . $220.00
**Price:** Model 90 (22 or 32, 6″ bbl.) . . . . . . . . . . . . . . . . . . . . . . . . . $245.00

Bernardelli Model 80

## BERETTA MODEL 84/85 DA PISTOLS
**Caliber:** 380 ACP, 13-shot magazine, 22 LR, 8 shot (M87BB).
**Barrel:** 3¾"
**Weight:** About 23 oz. **Length:** 6½" over-all.
**Stocks:** Smooth black plastic (wood optional at extra cost).
**Sights:** Fixed front and rear.
**Features:** Double action, quick take-down, convenient magazine release. Introduced 1977. Imported from Italy by Beretta USA.
**Price:** M-84 (380 ACP) ......................................... $495.00
**Price:** With wood grips ................................................ $510.00
**Price:** M-84, nickel, wood grips .............................. $550.00
**Price:** M-85W, 380 ACP, wood grips, 9-shot mag ..... $460.00
**Price:** M-85, nickel, wood grips .............................. $500.00
**Price:** M-86, 8-shot, walnut grips .......................... $400.00
**Price:** M-87, 22 LR .............................................. $435.00

Beretta Model 84

## BERETTA MODEL 950 BS AUTO PISTOL
**Caliber:** 22 Short, 7 shot, 25 ACP, 9 shot.
**Barrel:** 2½", 4" (22 Short only).
**Weight:** 8 oz. (22 Short, 10 oz.). **Length:** 4½" over-all.
**Stocks:** Checkered black plastic.
**Sights:** Fixed.
**Features:** Thumb safety and half-cock safety; barrel hinged at front to pop up for single loading or cleaning. From Beretta U.S.A.
**Price:** Blue, 25 ........................................ $190.00
**Price:** Blue, 22, 4" ................................... $200.00
**Price:** Nickel, 22 or 25 ............................. $208.00
**Price:** EL model (gold etching) ................ $220.00

Beretta Model 950 BS-4

### Beretta Model 21 Pistol
Similar to the Model 950 BS except chambered for 22 LR, 2.5" barrel, 4.9" over-all length, double-action, 7-round magazine, walnut grips. Introduced 1985.
**Price:** ................................................... $230.00

Beretta Model 92F

## BERETTA MODEL 92F PISTOL
**Caliber:** 9mm Parabellum, 15-shot magazine.
**Barrel:** 4.92"
**Weight:** 33½ oz. **Length:** 8.54" over-all.
**Stocks:** Checkered black plastic; wood optional at extra cost.
**Sights:** Blade front, rear adj. for w.
**Features:** Double-action. Extractor acts as chamber loaded indicator, squared trigger guard, grooved front and back straps, inertia firing pin. Matte finish. Introduced 1977. Imported from Italy by Beretta USA.
**Price:** With plastic grips ...................................... $685.00
**Price:** With wood grips ......................................... $700.00

## BERSA MODEL 224 AUTO PISTOL
**Caliber:** 22 LR, 11-shot.
**Barrel:** 4".
**Weight:** 26 oz.
**Stocks:** Target-type checkered nylon with thumbrest.
**Sights:** Blade front, square notch rear adjustable for windage.
**Features:** Blow-back action; combat-type trigger guard; magazine safety; blue finish. Imported from Argentina by Outdoor Sports Headquarters. Introduced 1984.
**Price:** Model 224 ............................................. $169.00
**Price:** Model 226 (6" barrel) ............................. $159.00
**Price:** Model 223DA (3½" bbl., wood grips) ........ $220.00

Bersa Model 224

## BERSA MODEL 383 AUTO PISTOL
**Caliber:** 380 ACP, 9-shot.
**Barrel:** 3½".
**Weight:** 25 oz.
**Stocks:** Target-type checkered black nylon.
**Sights:** Blade front, square notch rear adjustable for windage.
**Features:** Blow-back action; magazine safety; combat-type trigger guard; blue finish. Imported from Argentina by Outdoor Sports Headquarters. Introduced 1984.
**Price:** Model 383 ............................................. $169.00
**Price:** Model 383DA ......................................... $220.00

Consult our Directory pages for the location of firms mentioned.

**CAUTION:** PRICES CHANGE. CHECK AT GUNSHOP.

Bren Ten Standard

## BREN TEN STANDARD MODEL

**Caliber:** 10mm Auto, 11-shot capacity.
**Barrel:** 5″.
**Weight:** 39 oz. **Length:** 8.37″ over-all.
**Stocks:** Textured black nylon (Hogue Combat).
**Sights:** Adjustable; replaceable, 3-dot combat-type.
**Features:** Full-size combat pistol, with selective double or single action. Has reversible thumb safety and firing pin block. Blued slide, natural stainless frame. Introduced 1983. From Dornaus & Dixon Enterprises, Inc.
**Price:** Standard model ............................................. **$500.00**
**Price:** Military & Police (matte black finish) ..................... **$550.00**
**Price:** Dual-Master (same as standard except comes with extra 45 ACP slide and barrel, better finish, engraving, wood grips, wood case) ...... **$800.00**
**Price:** Jeff Cooper Commemorative (same as Standard except has extra fine finish, 22K gold-filled engraving, details, cartridges, laser engraved Herrett's grips and wood case) ...................................... **$2,000.00**
**Price:** 45 ACP conversion kit (5″ bbl.) .......................... **$150.00**

## Bren Ten Special Forces Model

Similar to the Pocket Model except has standard size grip frame with 11-shot capacity; weight is 33 oz. with 4″ barrel. Available in either all black or natural light finish. Introduced 1984.
**Price:** Black finish ........................................... **$600.00**
**Price:** Light finish .......................................... **$650.00**

## Bren Ten Pocket Model

Similar to the Standard Bren Ten except smaller. Has 4″ barrel giving 7.37″ over-all length, and weighs 28 oz. Fires full load 10mm Auto cartridge with 9 round capacity. Has hard chrome slide, stainless frame.
**Price:** ................................................ **$600.00**

BRNO CZ 75

## BRNO CZ 75 AUTO PISTOL

**Caliber:** 9mm Para., 15-shot magazine.
**Barrel:** 4.7″.
**Weight:** 35 oz. **Length:** 8″ over-all.
**Stocks:** Checkered wood.
**Sights:** Blade front, rear adj. for w.
**Features:** Double action; blued finish. Imported from Czechoslovakia by Bauska Arms Corp.
**Price:** .................................................... **$635.00**

## BRNO CZ 83 DOUBLE ACTION PISTOL

**Caliber:** 32, 15-shot; 380, 13-shot.
**Barrel:** 3.7″.
**Weight:** 26.5 oz. **Length:** 6.7″ over-all.
**Stocks:** Checkered black plastic.
**Sights:** Blade front, rear adj. for w.
**Features:** Double-action; ambidextrous magazine release and safety. Polished or matte blue. Imported from Czechoslovakia by Bauska Arms Corp.
**Price:** .................................................... **$425.00**

BRNO CZ 83

## BRNO CZ-85 Auto Pistol

Same gun as the CZ-75 except has ambidextrous slide release and safety levers, is available in 9mm Para. and 7.65, contoured composition grips, matte finish on top of slide. Introduced 1986.
**Price:** .................................................... **$655.00**

## BROWNING CHALLENGER III SPORTER

**Caliber:** 22 LR, 10-shot magazine.
**Barrel:** 6¾″.
**Weight:** 29 oz. **Length:** 10⅞″ over-all.
**Stocks:** Smooth impregnated hardwood.
**Sights:** ⅛″ blade front on ramp, rear screw adj. for e., drift adj. for w.
**Features:** All steel, blue finish. Wedge locking system prevents action from loosening. Wide gold-plated trigger; action hold-open. Standard grade only. Made in U.S. From Browning.
**Price:** .................................................... **$239.95**

Browning Challenger III Sporter

## Browning Buck Mark 22 Pistol

Similar to the Challenger III except has black moulded composite grips with skip-line checkering, thumb magazine button, sides of barrel are high-polish blue, rest satin finish. New rear sight screw-adjustable for elevation, drift-adjustable for windage. Introduced 1985.
**Price:** .................................................... **$164.95**

Browning Hi-Power

## BROWNING HI-POWER 9mm AUTOMATIC PISTOL
**Caliber:** 9mm Parabellum (Luger), 13-shot magazine.
**Barrel:** 4²¹⁄₃₂″.
**Weight:** 32 oz. **Length:** 7¾″ over-all.
**Stocks:** Walnut, hand checkered, or black Polyamide.
**Sights:** ⅛″ blade front; rear screw-adj. for w. and e. Also available with fixed rear (drift-adj for w.).
**Features:** External hammer with half-cock and thumb safeties. A blow on the hammer cannot discharge a cartridge; cannot be fired with magazine removed. Fixed rear sight model available. Imported from Belgium by Browning.
**Price:** Fixed sight model, walnut grips . . . . . . . . . . . . . . . . . . . . . . . . . . . . **$451.50**
**Price:** Fixed sight model, moulded grips . . . . . . . . . . . . . . . . . . . . . . . . . . **$451.50**
**Price:** 9mm with rear sight adj. for w. and e., walnut grips . . . . . . . . . **$519.50**
**Price:** Standard matte black finish, fixed sight, S/A . . . . . . . . . . . . . . . . **$414.50**

Browning Double Action

## Browning Double Action 9mm
Not a modified Hi-Power, but a new design. Double-action with a firing pin safety block, twin ambidextrous decocking levers that lower the hammer from full cock; squared trigger guard; wrap-around moulded grips; 15-shot capacity; black "Parkerized" finish; rear sight drift adjustable for windage. Introduced 1985.
**Price:** . . . . . . . . . . . . . . . . . . . . . . . . . . . . . . . . . . . . . . . . . . . . . . . . . . . . . . . **$429.50**

## Browning Hi-Power Classic & Gold Classic
Same as standard fixed sight Hi-Power except both editions have game scenes of a bald eagle protecting her young from a lynx on satin grey slide and frame, as well as a profile of John M. Browning. The Gold Classic has the main subjects in contrasting gold inlay. Grips are finely checkered walnut with double border and floral designs. Classic series limited to 5,000, Gold Classic to 500, each with its unique serial number, "1 of 500," and so on. Each gun comes in a velvet lined walnut case.
**Price:** Hi-Power Classic . . . . . . . . . . . . . . . . . . . . . . . . . . . . . . . . . . . . . . . . **$1,000.00**
**Price:** Hi-Power Gold Classic . . . . . . . . . . . . . . . . . . . . . . . . . . . . . . . . . . . **$2,000.00**

Browning BDA-380 Pistol

## BROWNING BDA-380 D/A AUTO PISTOL
**Caliber:** 380 ACP, 13-shot magazine.
**Barrel:** 3¹³⁄₁₆″.
**Weight:** 23 oz. **Length:** 6¾″ over-all.
**Stocks:** Smooth walnut with inset Browning medallion.
**Sights:** Blade front, rear drift-adj. for w.
**Features:** Combination safety and de-cocking lever will automatically lower a cocked hammer to half-cock and can be operated by right or left-hand shooters. Inertia firing pin. Introduced 1978. Imported from Italy by Browning.
**Price:** Blue . . . . . . . . . . . . . . . . . . . . . . . . . . . . . . . . . . . . . . . . . . . . . . . . . . . **$384.50**
**Price:** Nickel . . . . . . . . . . . . . . . . . . . . . . . . . . . . . . . . . . . . . . . . . . . . . . . . . . **$404.50**

## BUSHMASTER AUTO PISTOL
**Caliber:** 223; 30-shot magazine.
**Barrel:** 11½″ (1-10″ twist).
**Weight:** 5¼ lbs. **Length:** 20½″ over-all.
**Stocks:** Synthetic rotating grip swivel assembly.
**Sights:** Post front, adjustable open "y" rear
**Features:** Steel alloy upper receiver with welded barrel assembly, AK-47-type gas system, aluminum lower receiver, one-piece welded steel alloy bolt carrier assembly. From Bushmaster Firearms.
**Price:** . . . . . . . . . . . . . . . . . . . . . . . . . . . . . . . . . . . . . . . . . . . . . . . . . . . . . . . **$339.95**
**Price:** With matte electroless nickel finish . . . . . . . . . . . . . . . . . . . . . . . . **$379.95**

Charter Model 79K

## CHARTER ARMS MODEL 79K DA AUTO PISTOL
**Caliber:** 32 ACP, 380 ACP, 7-shot magazine.
**Barrel:** 3.6″.
**Weight:** 24½ oz. **Length:** 6.5″ over-all.
**Stocks:** Checkered walnut.
**Sights:** Blade front, rear adj. for w. only.
**Features:** Double action with hammer block, firing pin and magazine safeties. Stainless steel finish. Introduced 1984. Imported from West Germany by Charter Arms.
**Price:** 32 or 380 ACP . . . . . . . . . . . . . . . . . . . . . . . . . . . . . . . . . . . . . . . . . **$390.00**

## Charter Arms Model 40 DA Auto Pistol
Similar to the Model 79K except chambered for 22 Long Rifle, 3.3″ barrel, 6.3″ over-all length, and 21½-oz. weight. Stainless steel finish. Introduced 1984. Imported from West Germany by Charter Arms.
**Price:** . . . . . . . . . . . . . . . . . . . . . . . . . . . . . . . . . . . . . . . . . . . . . . . . . . . . . . . **$319.00**

**CAUTION:** PRICES CHANGE. CHECK AT GUNSHOP.

## CHARTER EXPLORER II & SII PISTOL
**Caliber:** 22 LR, 8-shot magazine.
**Barrel:** 8".
**Weight:** 28 oz. **Length:** 15½" over-all.
**Stocks:** Serrated simulated walnut.
**Sights:** Blade front, open rear adj. for elevation.
**Features:** Action adapted from the semi-auto Explorer carbine. Introduced 1980. From Charter Arms.
**Price:** Black or satin finish ..................................... $109.00
**Price:** Extra 6", 8" or 10" barrel ................................. $27.00

Charter Explorer Pistol

## COLT GOV'T MODEL MK IV/SERIES 80
**Caliber:** 9mm, 38 Super, 45 ACP, 7-shot.
**Barrel:** 5".
**Weight:** 38 oz. **Length:** 8½" over-all.
**Stocks:** Checkered walnut.
**Sights:** Ramp front, fixed square notch rear.
**Features:** Grip and thumb safeties, and internal firing pin safety, grooved trigger. Accurizor barrel and bushing.
**Price:** Blue, 45 ACP............................................. $526.50
**Price:** Nickel, 45 ACP ........................................... $562.50
**Price:** 9mm, blue only ........................................... $534.95
**Price:** 38 Super, blue only ...................................... $534.95
**Price:** Stainless steel, 45 ACP.................................. $569.95

Colt Stainless MK IV/Series 80

### Colt Combat Elite MK IV/Series 80
Similar to the Government Model except in 45 ACP only, has stainless frame with ordnance steel slide and internal parts. High profile front, rear sights with three-dot system, extended grip safety, beveled magazine well, Colt checkered rubber grips. Introduced 1986.
**Price:** ....................................................... NA

## COLT 380 GOVERNMENT MODEL
**Caliber:** 380 ACP, 7-shot magazine.
**Barrel:** 3".
**Weight:** 21¾ oz. **Length:** 6" over-all.
**Stocks:** Checkered composition.
**Sights:** Ramp front, square notch rear, fixed.
**Features:** Scaled down version of the 1911A1 Colt G.M. Has thumb and internal firing pin safeties. Introduced 1983.
**Price:** Blue................................................... $340.50
**Price:** Nickel ................................................. $374.50
**Price:** Coltguard .............................................. $361.95

Colt 380 Government

## COLT COMBAT COMMANDER AUTO PISTOL
**Caliber:** 45 ACP, 7-shot; 38 Super Auto, 9mm Luger, 9-shot.
**Barrel:** 4¼".
**Weight:** 36 oz. **Length:** 7¾" over-all.
**Stocks:** Checkered walnut.
**Sights:** Fixed, glare-proofed blade front, square notch rear.
**Features:** Grooved trigger and hammer spur; arched housing; grip and thumb safeties.
**Price:** Blue, 9mm ............................................. $534.95
**Price:** Blue, 45 ............................................... $526.50
**Price:** Blue, 38 super......................................... $534.95
**Price:** Satin nickel, 45, Series 80 ........................... $548.95

### Colt Lightweight Commander Mark IV/Series 80
Same as Commander except high strength aluminum alloy frame, wood panel grips, weight 27 oz. 45 ACP only.
**Price:** Blue.................................................. $526.50

Colt Combat Commander

### Colt Conversion Unit
Permits the 45 and 38 Super Automatic pistols to use the economical 22 LR cartridge. No tools needed. Adjustable rear sight; 10-shot magazine. Designed to give recoil effect of the larger calibers. Not adaptable to Commander models. Blue finish.
**Price:** 22 LR, Series 80........................................ $304.50
**Price:** Fixed sight version, Series 70 .......................... $304.99
**Price:** 9mm Series 80 Conversion Unit ......................... $304.50

---

**CAUTION:** PRICES CHANGE. CHECK AT GUNSHOP.

Colt Officers ACP

## COONAN 357 MAGNUM PISTOL
**Caliber:** 357 Mag., 7-shot magazine.
**Barrel:** 5″.
**Weight:** 38 oz. **Length:** 8.3″ over-all.
**Stocks:** Smooth walnut.
**Sights:** Open, adjustable.
**Features:** Unique barrel hood improves accuracy and reliability. Many parts interchange with Colt autos. Has grip, hammer, half-cock safeties. From Coonan Arms.
**Price:** Model A ............................................. $595.00
**Price:** Model B (linkless barrel, interchangeable ramp front sight, new rear sight) ...................................................... $625.00

## DAVIS P-32 AUTO PISTOL
**Caliber:** 32 ACP, 6-shot magazine.
**Barrel:** 2.8″.
**Weight:** 22 oz. **Length:** 5.4″ over-all.
**Stock:** Laminated wood.
**Sights:** Fixed.
**Features:** Choices of black Teflon or chrome finish. Announced 1986. Made in U.S. by Davis Industries.
**Price:** ........................................................ **NA**

## DETONICS "COMBAT MASTER" MK VI, MK I
**Caliber:** 45 ACP, 6-shot clip; 9mm Para., 38 Super, 7-shot clip.
**Barrel:** 3¼″.
**Weight:** 29 oz. **Length:** 6¾″ over-all, 4½″ high.
**Stocks:** Checkered walnut.
**Sights:** Combat type, fixed and adj. sights avail.
**Features:** Has a self-adjusting cone barrel centering system, beveled magazine inlet, "full clip" indicator in base of magazine; standard 7-shot (or more) clip can be used in the 45. Throated barrel and polished feed ramp. Mark VI, VII available in 9mm and 38 Super. Introduced 1977. From Detonics.
**Price:** MK I, matte finish, fixed sights ........................... $610.95
**Price:** MK VI, polished stainless, adj. sights ...................... $685.95

## DETONICS "POCKET 9" DOUBLE ACTION AUTO
**Caliber:** 9mm Para., 6-shot clip.
**Barrel:** 3″.
**Weight:** 26 oz. **Length:** 5.7″ over-all, 4″ high.
**Stocks:** Black micarta.
**Sights:** Fixed.
**Features:** Stainless steel construction; ambidextrous firing pin safety; trigger guard hook for two-hand shooting; double and single action trigger mechanism; snag-free hammer; captive recoil spring; "Chamber Lok" breech system.
**Price:** About ................................................. $457.95

### Detonics "Pocket 9LS" Double Action Auto
Similar to the Pocket 9 except has 4″ barrel, is 6⅞″ over-all, weighs 28 oz. Other features are the same.
**Price:** ................................................. $457.95
**Price:** "Power 9" model (polished slide flats) ................... $505.95

## COLT OFFICERS ACP MK IV SERIES 80
**Caliber:** 45 ACP, 6-shot magazine.
**Barrel:** 3½″.
**Weight:** 34 oz. **Length:** 7¼″ over-all.
**Stocks:** Checkered walnut.
**Sights:** Ramp blade front with white dot, square notch rear with two white dots.
**Features:** Trigger safety lock (thumb safety), grip safety, firing pin safety; grooved trigger; flat mainspring housing. Also available with lightweight alloy frame and in stainless steel. Introduced 1985.
**Price:** Matte finish ............................................. $516.50
**Price:** Satin nickel ............................................. $569.95
**Price:** L.W., matte finish ....................................... $526.50

Coonan 357 Magnum

Davis P-32

Detonics "Combat Master" MK. I

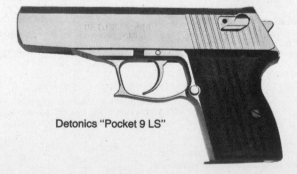

Detonics "Pocket 9 LS"

### DETONICS "POCKET 380" DOUBLE ACTION AUTO
**Caliber:** 380 ACP, 6-shot clip.
**Barrel:** 3".
**Weight:** 23 oz. **Length:** 5¾" over-all.
**Stocks:** Grooved black micarta.
**Sights:** Fixed.
**Features:** Stainless steel construction; ambidextrous firing pin safety; trigger guard hook; snag-free hammer; captive recoil spring.
**Price:** . . . . . . . . . . . . . . . . . . . . . . . . . . . . . . . . . . . . . **$457.95**

Detonics "Pocket 380"

### DETONICS "SERVICEMASTER" AUTO PISTOL
**Caliber:** 45 ACP, 7-shot magazine.
**Barrel:** 4¼".
**Weight:** 32 oz. **Length:** 7⅞" over-all.
**Stocks:** Pachmayr rubber.
**Sights:** Fixed combat.
**Features:** Stainless steel construction; thumb and grip safeties; extended grip safety.
**Price:** Matte finish . . . . . . . . . . . . . . . . . . . . . . . . . . . . . . . **$685.95**
**Price:** "Servicemaster II" (polished slide flats) . . . . . . . . . . . . . . . . . . . **$762.95**

Detonics "Servicemaster"

Desert Eagle 357

### DESERT EAGLE 357 MAGNUM PISTOL
**Caliber:** 357 Magnum, 10-shot clip.
**Barrel:** 6", 14" interchangeable.
**Weight:** 52 oz. (alloy), 60 oz. (steel). **Length:** 10¼" over-all (6" bbl.).
**Stocks:** Wrap-around soft rubber.
**Sights:** Blade on ramp front, combat-style rear. Adjustable avail.
**Features:** Rotating three lug bolt, ambidextrous safety, combat-style trigger guard, adjustable trigger (optional). Military epoxy finish. Contact importer for extra barrel prices. Satin, bright nickel, polished and blued finishes available. Imported from Israel by Magnum Research Inc.
**Price:** 6" barrel, standard pistol . . . . . . . . . . . . . . . . . . . . . . . . . . . **$559.00**
**Price:** 6" barrel, alloy frame . . . . . . . . . . . . . . . . . . . . . . . . . . . . **$579.00**
**Price:** 6" barrel, stainless steel frame. . . . . . . . . . . . . . . . . . . . . . . **$599.00**

Encom MP-45

### ENCOM MP-9, MP-45 ASSAULT PISTOLS
**Caliber:** 9mm, 45 ACP, 10, 30, 40 or 50-shot magazine.
**Barrel:** 4½", 6", 8", 10", 18", 18½".
**Weight:** 6 lbs. (4½" bbl.). **Length:** 11.8" over-all (4½" bbl.).
**Stocks:** Checkered composition.
**Sights:** Post front, fixed Patridge rear.
**Features:** Blowback operation, fires from closed breech with floating firing pin; right or left-hand models available. Made in U.S. From Encom America, Inc.
**Price:** 9mm or 45 ACP, standard pistol . . . . . . . . . . . . . . . . . . . . . . **$275.00**
**Price:** As above, Mini Pistol (3½" bbl.) . . . . . . . . . . . . . . . . . . . . . . **$250.00**
**Price:** Carbine (18½" bbl., retractable wire stock) . . . . . . . . . . . . . . . . **$390.00**

Erma KGP22 Pistol

### ERMA KGP22 AUTO PISTOL
**Caliber:** 22 LR, 8-shot magazine.
**Barrel:** 4".
**Weight:** 29 oz. **Length:** 7¾" over-all.
**Stocks:** Checkered plastic.
**Sights:** Fixed.
**Features:** Has toggle action similar to original "Luger" pistol. Slide stays open after last shot. Imported from West Germany by Excam. Introduced 1978.
**Price:** . . . . . . . . . . . . . . . . . . . . . . . . . . . . . . . . . . . . . . . . **$230.00**

**CAUTION:** PRICES CHANGE. CHECK AT GUNSHOP.

### ERMA KGP38 AUTO PISTOL
**Caliber:** 380 ACP (5-shot).
**Barrel:** 4″.
**Weight:** 22½ oz. **Length:** 7⅜″ over-all.
**Stocks:** Checkered plastic. Wood optional.
**Sights:** Rear adjustable for windage.
**Features:** Toggle action similar to original "Luger" pistol. Slide stays open after last shot. Has magazine and sear disconnect safety systems. Imported from West Germany by Excam. Introduced 1978.
**Price:** Plastic grips . . . . . . . . . . . . . . . . . . . . . . . . . . . . . . . . . . . . . . . . . . . **$230.00**

### F.I.E. "TZ-75" DA AUTO PISTOL
**Caliber:** 9mm Parabellum, 15-shot magazine.
**Barrel:** 4.72″.
**Weight:** 35.33 oz. **Length:** 8.25″ over-all.
**Stocks:** Smooth European walnut.
**Sights:** Undercut blade front, open rear adjustable for windage.
**Features:** Double action trigger system; squared-off trigger guard; rotating slide-mounted safety. Introduced 1983. Imported from Italy by F.I.E. Corp.
**Price:** . . . . . . . . . . . . . . . . . . . . . . . . . . . . . . . . . . . . . . . . . . . **$349.95**
**Price:** Silver chrome with red outline sights. . . . . . . . . . . . . . . . . . . . . . . **$399.95**

### F.I.E. "SUPER TITAN II" PISTOLS
**Caliber:** 32 ACP, 380 ACP.
**Barrel:** 3⅞″.
**Weight:** 28 oz. **Length:** 6¾″ over-all.
**Stocks:** Smooth, polished walnut.
**Sights:** Adjustable.
**Features:** Blue finish only. 12 shot (32 ACP), 11 shot (380 ACP). Introduced 1981. Imported from Italy by F.I.E. Corp.
**Price:** 32 ACP . . . . . . . . . . . . . . . . . . . . . . . . . . . . . . . . . . . . . **$164.95**
**Price:** 380 ACP . . . . . . . . . . . . . . . . . . . . . . . . . . . . . . . . . . . . **$194.95**

F.I.E. "The Best" A27B

### F.I.E. "TITAN II" PISTOLS
**Caliber:** 32 ACP, 380 ACP, 6-shot magazine; 22 LR, 10-shot magazine.
**Barrel:** 3⅞″.
**Weight:** 25¾ oz. **Length:** 6¾″ over-all.
**Stocks:** Checkered nylon, thumbrest-type; walnut optional.
**Sights:** Adjustable.
**Features:** Magazine disconnector, firing pin block. Standard slide safety. Available in blue or chrome. Introduced 1978. Imported from Italy by F.I.E. Corp.
**Price:** 32, blue . . . . . . . . . . . . . . . . . . . . . . . . . . . . . . . . . . . . **$131.95**
**Price:** 32, chrome . . . . . . . . . . . . . . . . . . . . . . . . . . . . . . . . . . **$139.95**
**Price:** 380, blue . . . . . . . . . . . . . . . . . . . . . . . . . . . . . . . . . . . **$164.95**
**Price:** 380, chrome . . . . . . . . . . . . . . . . . . . . . . . . . . . . . . . . . **$174.95**
**Price:** 22 LR, blue . . . . . . . . . . . . . . . . . . . . . . . . . . . . . . . . . . **$119.95**

### F.I.E. "TITAN 25" PISTOL
**Caliber:** 25 ACP, 6-shot magazine.
**Barrel:** 2⁷⁄₁₆″.
**Weight:** 12 oz. **Length:** 4⅝″ over-all.
**Stocks:** Smooth walnut.
**Sights:** Fixed.
**Features:** External hammer; fast simple takedown. Made in U.S.A. by F.I.E. Corp.
**Price:** Blue . . . . . . . . . . . . . . . . . . . . . . . . . . . . . . . . . . . . **$54.95**
**Price:** Dyna-Chrome . . . . . . . . . . . . . . . . . . . . . . . . . . . . . . . . . **$59.95**
**Price:** 24K gold with bright blue frame, smooth walnut grips . . . . . . . . **$79.95**

### ERMA-EXCAM RX 22 AUTO PISTOL
**Caliber:** 22 LR, 8-shot magazine.
**Barrel:** 3¼″.
**Weight:** 21 oz. **Length:** 5.58″ over-all.
**Stocks:** Plastic wrap-around.
**Sights:** Fixed
**Features:** Polished blue finish. Double action. Patented ignition safety system. Thumb safety. Assembled in U.S. Introduced 1980. From Excam.
**Price:** . . . . . . . . . . . . . . . . . . . . . . . . . . . . . . . . . . . . . . . . . . . **$159.00**

F.I.E. "TZ-75"

### F.I.E. "THE BEST" A27B PISTOL
**Caliber:** 25 ACP, 6-shot magazine.
**Barrel:** 2½″.
**Weight:** 13 oz. **Length:** 4⅜″ over-all.
**Stocks:** Checkered walnut.
**Sights:** Fixed.
**Features:** All steel construction. Has thumb and magazine safeties, exposed hammer. Blue finish only. Introduced 1978. Made in U.S. by F.I.E. Corp.
**Price:** . . . . . . . . . . . . . . . . . . . . . . . . . . . . . . . . . . . . . . . . . . . **$114.95**

F.I.E. "Titan II"

F.I.E. "Titan 25"

**CAUTION:** PRICES CHANGE. CHECK AT GUNSHOP.

Falcon Portsider

Fraser Auto

## FALCON PORTSIDER AUTO PISTOL
**Caliber:** 45 ACP, 7-shot magazine.
**Barrel:** 5".
**Weight:** 38 oz. **Length:** 8½" over-all.
**Stocks:** Checkered walnut.
**Sights:** Fixed combat.
**Features:** Made of 17-4 stainless steel. Enlarged left-hand ejection port, extended ejector, long trigger, combat hammer, extended safety, wide grip safety. Introduced 1986. From Falcon Firearms.
**Price:** ....................................................... **$580.00**

## FRASER AUTOMATIC PISTOL
**Caliber:** 25 ACP, 6-shot.
**Barrel:** 2¼".
**Weight:** 10 oz. **Length:** 4" over-all.
**Stocks:** Plastic pearl or checkered walnut.
**Sights:** Recessed, fixed.
**Features:** Stainless steel construction. Has positive manual safety as well as magazine safety. From Fraser Firearms Corp.
**Price:** Satin stainless steel, 25 ACP ............................ **$129.50**
**Price:** Gold plated, with book-type case .......................... **$247.50**
**Price:** With black Q.P.Q. finish ................................. **$149.50**

Glock 17

## GLOCK 17 AUTO PISTOL
**Caliber:** 9mm Para., 17-shot magazine.
**Barrel:** 4.48".
**Weight:** 21.8 oz. (without magazine). **Length:** 7.40" over-all.
**Stocks:** Black polymer.
**Sights:** Dot on front blade, white outline rear adj. for w.
**Features:** Polymer frame, steel slide; trigger safety, mechanical firing pin safety, drop safety; simple take-down without tools; recoil operated action. Adopted by Austrian armed forces 1985. Imported from Austria by Glock, Inc.
**Price:** With extra magazine, magazine loader, cleaning kit ......... **$443.65**

> Consult our Directory pages for the location of firms mentioned.

Goncz High-Tech Pistol

## GONCZ HIGH-TECH LONG PISTOL
**Caliber:** 9mm Para., 30 Mauser, 38 Super, 18- and 32-shot magazine; 45 ACP, 10- and 20-shot magazine.
**Barrel:** 4", 9.5".
**Weight:** 3 lbs., 10 oz. (with 4" barrel). **Length:** 10½" over-all (with 4" barrel).
**Stock:** Alloy grooved pistol grip.
**Sights:** Front adjustable for elevation, rear adjustable for windage.
**Features:** Fires from closed bolt; floating firing pin; safety locks the firing pin. All metal construction. Barrel threaded for accessories. Matte black oxide and anodized finish. Designed by Lajos J. Goncz. Introduced 1985. From Goncz Co.
**Price:** With 9½" barrel ........................................ **$350.00**
**Price:** With 4" barrel .......................................... **$340.00**

## HAMMERLI MODEL 212 HUNTER'S PISTOL
**Caliber:** 22 LR.
**Barrel:** 4.9".
**Weight:** 31 oz. **Length:** 8.5" over-all.
**Stocks:** Checkered walnut.
**Sights:** White dot front adjustable for elevation, rear adjustable for elevation.
**Features:** Semi-automatic based on the Model 208, intended for field use. Uses target trigger system which is fully adjustable. Comes with tool kit. Imported from Switzerland by Osborne's Supplies. Introduced 1984.
**Price:** ....................................................... **$995.00**

Hammerli 212

**CAUTION:** PRICES CHANGE. CHECK AT GUNSHOP.

Heckler & Koch P7-M8

## HECKLER & KOCH P7-M8 AUTO PISTOL

**Caliber:** 9mm Parabellum, 8-shot magazine.
**Barrel:** 4.13".
**Weight:** 29 oz. **Length:** 6.73" over-all.
**Stocks:** Stippled black plastic.
**Sights:** Fixed, combat-type.
**Features:** Unique "squeeze cocker" in front strap cocks the action. Gas-retarded action. Squared combat-type trigger guard. Blue finish. Compact size. Imported from West Germany by Heckler & Koch, Inc.
**Price:** P7-M8 ..................................... $612.00
**Price:** Extra magazine (8-shot) ..................................... $23.00
**Price:** P7-M13 (13-shot capacity, matte black finish, ambidextrous magazine release, forged steel frame) ..................................... $666.00
**Price:** Extra 13-shot magazine ..................................... $39.00

## HECKLER & KOCH P9S DOUBLE ACTION AUTO

**Caliber:** 9mm Para., 9-shot magazine; 45 ACP, 7-shot magazine.
**Barrel:** 4".
**Weight:** 31 oz. **Length:** 7.6" over-all.
**Stocks:** Checkered black plastic.
**Sights:** Open combat type.
**Features:** Double action; polygonal rifling; delayed roller-locked action with stationary barrel. Loaded chamber and cocking indicators; cocking/decocking lever. Imported from West Germany by Heckler & Koch, Inc.
**Price:** P-9S Combat Model, 9mm ............................. $666.00
**Price:** As above, 45 ACP ............................. $732.00
**Price:** P9S Target Model, 9mm ............................. $799.00
**Price:** As above, 45 ACP ............................. $866.00
**Price:** Sports Competition Model with 4" and 5½" barrels, two slides, 9mm only ............................. $1,333.00

Heckler & Koch P9S Combat

## HOLMES MP-83 ASSAULT PISTOL

**Caliber:** 9mm (16 or 32 shot), 45 (10 or 20 shot).
**Barrel:** 6".
**Weight:** 3½ lbs. **Length:** 14½" over-all.
**Stock:** Walnut grip and fore-end.
**Sights:** Post front, open adj. rear.
**Features:** All steel construction, blue finish. Deluxe package includes gun, foam-lined travel case, Zytel stock, black metal vent. barrel shroud, extra magazine and sling. From Holmes Firearms.
**Price:** ..................................... $450.00
**Price:** Deluxe ..................................... $525.00
**Price:** Caliber conversion kit ..................................... $220.00

Holmes MP-83

### Holmes MP-22 Assault Pistol

Similar to the MP-83 except chambered for 22LR, 32-shot capacity. Weighs 2½ lbs., has bolt-notch safety.
**Price:** ..................................... $400.00
**Price:** Deluxe ..................................... $475.00

## IVER JOHNSON 9mm AUTO PISTOL

**Caliber:** 9mm Para., 6-shot magazine.
**Barrel:** 3".
**Weight:** 26 oz. **Length:** 6½" over-all.
**Stocks:** Smooth hardwood.
**Sights:** Blade front, adj. rear.
**Features:** Ambidextrous safety; polished or matte blue finish. Made in U.S.A. Introduced 1986. From Iver Johnson.
**Price:** ..................................... $350.00

## IVER JOHNSON TP22B, TP25B AUTO PISTOL

**Caliber:** 22 LR, 25 ACP, 7-shot magazine.
**Barrel:** 2.85".
**Weight:** 14½ oz. **Length:** 5.39" over-all.
**Stocks:** Black checkered plastic.
**Sights:** Fixed.
**Features:** Double action; 7-shot magazine. Introduced 1981. Made in U.S. From Iver Johnson's.
**Price:** Either caliber, blue ..................................... $137.00

Iver Johnson 9mm

**CAUTION:** PRICES CHANGE. CHECK AT GUNSHOP.

# HANDGUNS—AUTOLOADERS, SERVICE & SPORT

## IVER JOHNSON TRAILSMAN PISTOL
**Caliber:** 22 LR, 10-shot magazine.
**Barrel:** 4½" or 6".
**Weight:** 46 oz. (4½" bbl.) **Length:** 8¾" (4½" bbl.).
**Stocks:** Checkered composition.
**Sights:** Fixed, tagret type.
**Features:** Slide hold-open latch, positive sear block safety, push button magazine release. Made in U.S. Introduced 1984.
**Price:** Blue only .............................................. $170.00
**Price:** Model TM22HB (high-polish blue, wood grips) ............. $190.00

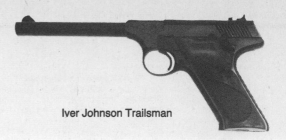

Iver Johnson Trailsman

## IVER JOHNSON MODEL PO380 PONY
**Caliber:** 380 ACP, 6-shot magazine.
**Barrel:** 3".
**Weight:** 20 oz. **Length:** 6" over-all.
**Stocks:** Checkered walnut.
**Sights:** Blade front, rear adj. for w.
**Features:** All steel construction. Inertia firing pin. Thumb safety locks hammer. No magazine safety. Lanyard ring. Made in U.S., available from Iver Johnson's.
**Price:** Blue.................................................. $253.00

Jennings J-22 Pistol

## JENNINGS J-22 AUTO PISTOL
**Caliber:** 22 LR, 6-shot magazine.
**Barrel:** 2½".
**Weight:** 13 oz. **Length:** 4¹⁵⁄₁₆" over-all.
**Stocks:** Walnut on chrome or nickel models; checkered black Cycolac on Teflon model.
**Sights:** Fixed.
**Features:** Choice of bright chrome, satin nickel or black Teflon finish. Introduced 1981. From Jennings Firearms.
**Price:** About ............................................... $69.95

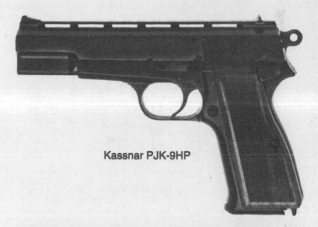

Kassnar PJK-9HP

## KASSNAR PJK-9HP AUTO PISTOL
**Caliber:** 9mm Para., 13-shot magazine.
**Barrel:** 4¾".
**Weight:** 32 oz. **Length:** 8" over-all.
**Stocks:** Checkered European walnut.
**Sights:** Ramp front, rear adj. for w.
**Features:** Single action. Available with or without full length ventilated rib; smooth trigger; lanyard loop on butt; comes with two magazines. Imported from Hungary by Kassnar. Introduced 1986.
**Price:** With or without rib....................................... $299.00

## KORRIPHILA HSP 701 D/A AUTO PISTOL
**Caliber:** 9mm Para., 38 W.C., 38 Super, 45 ACP, 9-shot magazine in 9mm, 7-shot in 45.
**Barrel:** 4" (Type I), 5" (Type II, III).
**Weight:** 35 oz.
**Stocks:** Checkered walnut.
**Sights:** Ramp or target front, adj. rear.
**Features:** Delayed roller lock action with Budichowsky system. Double/single or single action only. Very limited production. Imported from West Germany by Osborne's. Introduced 1986.
**Price:** .................................................. $1,000.00

Korriphila HSP 701

Korth Auto Pistol

## KORTH SEMI-AUTOMATIC PISTOL
**Caliber:** 9mm Parabellum, 13-shot magazine.
**Barrel:** 4½".
**Weight:** 35 oz. **Length:** 10½" over-all.
**Stocks:** Checkered walnut.
**Sights:** Combat-adjustable
**Features:** Double action; 13-shot staggered magazine; forged machined frame and slide. Matte and polished finish. Introduced 1985. Imported from West Germany by Osborne's.
**Price:** .................................................. $2,475.00

**CAUTION:** PRICES CHANGE. CHECK AT GUNSHOP.

## L.A.R. GRIZZLY WIN MAG MK I PISTOL
**Caliber:** 357 Mag., 45 Win. Mag., 7-shot magazine.
**Barrel:** 6½".
**Weight:** 51 oz. **Length:** 10½" over-all.
**Stocks:** Checkered rubber, non-slip combat-type.
**Sights:** Ramped blade front, fully adjustable rear.
**Features:** Uses basic Browning/Colt 1911-A1 design; interchangeable calibers; beveled magazine well; combat-type flat, checkered rubber mainspring housing; lowered and back-chamfered ejection port; polished feed ramp; throated barrel; solid barrel bushings. Announced 1983. From L.A.R. Mfg. Inc.
**Price:** ............................................. **$675.00**
**Price:** Conversion units (9mm Win. Mag., 45 ACP, 357 Mag.) ....... **$149.00**

L.A.R. Grizzly

## L.A.R. Grizzly Win Mag Mk. II Pistol
Similar to the standard Grizzly Win Mag except has fixed rear sight, standard safety, matte Parkerized or blue finish. Other features are the same. Introduced 1986.
**Price:** ............................................. **$550.00**
**Price:** Conversion units (9mm Win. Mag., 45 ACP, 357 Mag.) ...... **$149.00**

## LLAMA OMNI DOUBLE-ACTION AUTO
**Caliber:** 9mm (13-shot), 45 ACP (7-shot).
**Barrel:** 4¼".
**Weight:** 40 oz. **Length:** 9mm—8", 45–7¾" over-all.
**Stocks:** Checkered plastic.
**Sights:** Ramped blade front, rear adjustable for windage and elevation (45), drift-adjustable for windage (9mm).
**Features:** New DA pistol has ball-bearing action, double sear bars, articulated firing pin, buttressed locking lug and low-friction rifling. Introduced 1982. Imported from Spain by Stoeger Industries.
**Price:** 45 ACP ................................................. **$499.95**
**Price:** 9mm ................................................... **$545.95**

Llama Omni D.A. Pistol

Llama Large Frame Auto

## LLAMA LARGE FRAME AUTO PISTOL
**Caliber:** 45 ACP.
**Barrel:** 5".
**Weight:** 40 oz. **Length:** 8½" over-all.
**Stocks:** Checkered walnut.
**Sights:** Fixed.
**Features:** Grip and manual safeties, ventilated rib. Imported from Spain by Stoeger Industries.
**Price:** Blue .................................................... **$284.95**
**Price:** Satin chrome .......................................... **$383.95**

## LLAMA MEDIUM FRAME AUTO PISTOL
**Caliber:** 9mm Para., 9 shot, 45 ACP, 7 shot.
**Barrel:** 4⁵⁄₁₆".
**Weight:** 37 oz.
**Stocks:** Smooth walnut.
**Sights:** Blade front, rear adjustable for windage.
**Features:** Scaled-down version of the Large Frame gun. Locked breech mechanism; manual and grip safeties. Introduced 1985. Imported from Spain by Stoeger Industries.
**Price:** Blue only ............................................. **$284.95**

Llama Medium Frame

Llama Small Frame Auto

## LLAMA SMALL FRAME AUTO PISTOLS
**Caliber:** 22 LR, 380.
**Barrel:** 3¹¹⁄₁₆".
**Weight:** 23 oz. **Length:** 6½" over-all.
**Stocks:** Checkered plastic, thumb rest.
**Sights:** Fixed front, adj. notch rear.
**Features:** Ventilated rib, manual and grip safeties. Model XV is 22 LR, Model IIIA is 380. Both models have loaded indicator; IIIA is locked breech. Imported from Spain by Stoeger Industries.
**Price:** Blue, 22 LR, 380. .................................... **$241.95**
**Price:** Satin chrome, 22 LR or 380 ........................... **$303.95**

**CAUTION:** PRICES CHANGE. CHECK AT GUNSHOP.

## MKE AUTO PISTOL
**Caliber:** 380 ACP; 7-shot magazine.
**Barrel:** 4".
**Weight:** 23 oz. **Length:** 6½" over-all.
**Stocks:** Hard rubber.
**Sights:** Fixed front, rear adjustable for windage.
**Features:** Double action with exposed hammer; chamber loaded indicator. Imported from Turkey by Mandall Shooting Supplies.
**Price:** .......................................................... $350.00

Turkish MKE Pistol

Manurhin PPK/S

## MANURHIN PP AUTO PISTOL
**Caliber:** 22 LR, 10-shot; 32 ACP, 8-shot; 380 ACP, 7-shot.
**Barrel:** 3.87".
**Weight:** 23 oz. (22 LR). **Length:** 6.7" over-all.
**Stocks:** Checkered composition.
**Sights:** White outline front and rear.
**Features:** Double action; hammer drop safety; all steel construction; high-polish blue finish. Each gun supplied with two magazines. Imported from France by Manurhin International.
**Price:** 22 LR ........................................... $429.00
**Price:** 32 and 380 ................................... $419.00

## Manurhin PPK/S Auto Pistol
Similar to the Model PP except has 3.25" barrel and over-all length of 6.12".
**Price:** 22 LR ........................................... $429.00
**Price:** 32 and 380 ................................... $419.00

Navy Arms Standard Luger

## NAVY ARMS LUGER AUTO PISTOL
**Caliber:** 22 LR, 10-shot magazine.
**Barrel:** 4".
**Weight:** 44 ozs. **Length:** 9" over-all.
**Stocks:** Checkered walnut.
**Sights:** Fixed.
**Features:** Blowback toggle action; all-steel construction; made in U.S. From Navy Arms.
**Price:** Standard Model ............................... $165.00
**Price:** War Model (all matte finish) ............... $165.00
**Price:** Naval Model (6" bbl., adj. rear sight) .... $165.00
**Price:** Artillery Model (8" bbl., adj. rear sight on bbl.) ... $165.00

## POCKET PARTNER PISTOL
**Caliber:** 22 LR, 8-shot magazine.
**Barrel:** 2¼", 6-groove rifling.
**Weight:** 10 oz. **Length:** 4¾" over-all.
**Stocks:** Checkered plastic.
**Sights:** Fixed.
**Features:** New design internal hammer. All ordnance steel construction with brushed blue finish. Distributed by Bumble Bee Wholesale, Inc.
**Price:** About ............................................ $99.95

Pocket Partner

## RAVEN MP-25 AUTO PISTOL
**Caliber:** 25 ACP, 6-shot magazine.
**Barrel:** 2⁷⁄₁₆".
**Weight:** 15 oz. **Length:** 4¾" over-all.
**Stocks:** Smooth walnut or ivory-colored plastic.
**Sights:** Ramped front, fixed rear.
**Features:** Available in blue, nickel or chrome finish. Made in U.S. Available from Raven Arms.
**Price:** .................................................... $69.95

Raven MP-25

**CAUTION:** PRICES CHANGE. CHECK AT GUNSHOP.

Ruger Mark II Stainless

## RUGER MARK II STANDARD AUTO PISTOL
**Caliber:** 22 LR, 10-shot magazine.
**Barrel:** 4¾" or 6".
**Weight:** 36 oz. (4¾" bbl.). **Length:** 8⁵⁄₁₆" (4¾" bbl.).
**Stocks:** Checkered hard rubber.
**Sights:** Fixed, wide blade front, square notch rear adj. for w.
**Features:** Updated design of the original Standard Auto. Has new bolt hold-open device, 10-shot magazine, magazine catch, safety, trigger and new receiver contours. Introduced 1982.
**Price:** Blued (MK 4, MK 6) . . . . . . . . . . . . . . . . . . . . . . . . . . . . . . . . . . . . . **$180.00**
**Price:** In stainless steel (KMK 4, KMK 6) . . . . . . . . . . . . . . . . . . . . . . . . **$240.00**

Seecamp LWS 25

## SEECAMP LWS 25, LWS 32 STAINLESS D/A AUTO
**Caliber:** 25 ACP, 8 shot, 32 ACP Win. Silvertip, 6 shot.
**Barrel:** 2", integral with frame.
**Weight:** 25 cal. 12 oz., 32 cal. 10.5 oz. **Length:** 4⅛" over-all.
**Stocks:** Black plastic.
**Sights:** Smooth, no-snag, contoured slide and barrel top.
**Features:** Aircraft quality 17-4 PH stainless steel. Inertia operated firing pin. Hammer fired double action only. Hammer automatically follows slide down to safety rest position after each shot—no manual safety needed. Magazine safety disconnector. LWS 25 is satin stainless, LWS 32 is polished. Introduced 1980. From L.W. Seecamp.
**Price:** . . . . . . . . . . . . . . . . . . . . . . . . . . . . . . . . . . . . . . . . . . . . . . . . . . . . . **$199.95**

## SIG P-210-1 AUTO PISTOL
**Caliber:** 7.65mm or 9mm Para., 8-shot magazine.
**Barrel:** 4¾".
**Weight:** 31¾ oz. (9mm) **Length:** 8½" over-all.
**Stocks:** Checkered walnut, with lacquer finish.
**Sights:** Blade front, rear adjustable for windage.
**Features:** Lanyard loop; polished finish. Conversion unit for 22 LR available. Imported from Switzerland by Osborne's, SIGARMS and Mandall Shooting Supplies.
**Price:** P-210-1 about (Mandall) . . . . . . . . . . . . . . . . . . . . . . . . . . . . . **$1,500.00**
**Price:** P-210-2 Service Pistol (Mandall) . . . . . . . . . . . . . . . . . . . . . . . **$1,600.00**
**Price:** 22 Cal. Conversion unit (Osborne's) . . . . . . . . . . . . . . . . . . . . . **$675.00**
**Price:** P-210-1 (Osborne's) . . . . . . . . . . . . . . . . . . . . . . . . . . . . . . . . . . **$1,450.00**
**Price:** P-210-2 (Osborne's) . . . . . . . . . . . . . . . . . . . . . . . . . . . . . . . . . . **$1,095.00**

SIG P-210-1

## SIG P-210-6 AUTO PISTOL
**Caliber:** 9mm Para., 8-shot magazine.
**Barrel:** 4¾".
**Weight:** 36.2 oz. **Length:** 8½" over-all.
**Stocks:** Checkered black plastic. Walnut optional.
**Sights:** Blade front, micro. adj. rear for w. & e.
**Features:** Adjustable trigger stop; target trigger; ribbed front stap; sandblasted finish. Conversion unit for 22 LR consists of barrel, recoil spring, slide and magazine. Imported from Switzerland by Osborne's and SIGARMS, Inc.
**Price:** P-210-6 (SIGARMS) . . . . . . . . . . . . . . . . . . . . . . . . . . . . . . . . . **$1,526.99**
**Price:** 22 Cal. Conversion unit (Osborne's) . . . . . . . . . . . . . . . . . . . . . **$781.00**
**Price:** As above, from SIGARMS . . . . . . . . . . . . . . . . . . . . . . . . . . . . . . **$719.00**
**Price:** P-210-6 (Osborne's) . . . . . . . . . . . . . . . . . . . . . . . . . . . . . . . . . . **$1,295.00**

SIG P-210-6

SIG-Sauer P-220

## SIG-SAUER P-220 D.A. AUTO PISTOL
**Caliber:** 9mm, 38 Super; 45 ACP. (9-shot in 9mm and 38 Super, 7 in 45).
**Barrel:** 4⅜".
**Weight:** 28¼ oz. (9mm). **Length:** 7¾" over-all.
**Stocks:** Checkered black plastic.
**Sights:** Blade front, drift adj. rear for w.
**Features:** Double action. De-cocking lever permits lowering hammer onto locked firing pin. Squared combat-type trigger guard. Slide stays open after last shot. Imported from West Germany by SIGARMS, Inc.
**Price:** . . . . . . . . . . . . . . . . . . . . . . . . . . . . . . . . . . . . . . . . . . . . . . . . . . . . . **$563.99**

**CAUTION:** PRICES CHANGE. CHECK AT GUNSHOP.

## SIG-SAUER P-225 D.A. AUTO PISTOL

**Caliber:** 9mm Parabellum, 8-shot magazine.
**Barrel:** 3.8".
**Weight:** 26 oz. **Length:** 7³⁄₃₂" over-all.
**Stocks:** Checkered black plastic.
**Sights:** Blade front, rear adjustable for windage.
**Features:** Double action. De-cocking lever permits lowering hammer onto locked firing pin. Squared combat-type trigger guard. Shortened, lightened version of P-220. Imported from West Germany by SIGARMS, Inc.
**Price:** ............................................................... **$601.99**

## SIG-SAUER P-226 D.A. Auto Pistol

Similar to the P-220 pistol except has 15-shot magazine, 4.4" barrel, and weighs 26½ oz. Imported from West Germany by SIGARMS, Inc.
**Price:** ............................................................... **$627.99**

SIG-Sauer P226

## SIG-SAUER P-230 D.A. AUTO PISTOL

**Caliber:** 32 ACP (8 shot), 380 ACP (7 shot).
**Barrel:** 3¾".
**Weight:** 16 oz. **Length:** 6½" over-all.
**Stocks:** Checkered black plastic.
**Sights:** Blade front, rear adj. for w.
**Features:** Double action. Same basic action design as P-220. Blowback operation, stationary barrel. Introduced 1977. Imported from West Germany by SIGARMS, Inc.
**Price:** ............................................................... **$422.99**
**Price:** In stainless steel (P-230 SL) ............................... **$483.99**

SIG-Sauer P-230 D.A. Pistol

## SMITH & WESSON MODEL 439 DOUBLE ACTION

**Caliber:** 9mm Luger, 8-shot clip.
**Barrel:** 4".
**Weight:** 30 oz. **Length:** 7⅝" over-all.
**Stocks:** Checkered walnut.
**Sights:** Serrated ramp front, square notch rear is fully adj. for w. & e. Also available with fixed sights.
**Features:** Rear sight has protective shields on both sides of the sight blade. Frame is aluminum alloy. Firing pin lock in addition to the regular rotating safety. Magazine disconnector. Comes with two magazines. Ambidextrous safety standard. Introduced 1980.
**Price:** Blue, from ............................................. **$422.00**
**Price:** Nickel, from ........................................... **$456.00**
**Price:** Model 639 (stainless), from ........................... **$468.00**

## SMITH & WESSON MODEL 459 DOUBLE ACTION

**Caliber:** 9mm Luger, 14-shot clip.
**Barrel:** 4".
**Weight:** 30 oz. **Length:** 7⅝" over-all.
**Stocks:** Checkered high-impact nylon.
**Sights:** ⅛" square serrated ramp front, square notch rear is fully adj. for w. & e. Also available with fixed sights.
**Features:** Alloy frame. Rear sight has protective shields on both sides of blade. Firing pin lock in addition to the regular safety. Magazine disconnector. Comes with two magazines. Ambidextrous safety standard. Introduced 1980.
**Price:** Blue, from ............................................. **$459.50**
**Price:** Nickel, from ........................................... **$494.00**
**Price:** Model 659 (stainless), from ........................... **$509.00**

## SILE-BENELLI B-76 DA AUTO PISTOL

**Caliber:** 9mm Para., 8-shot magazine.
**Barrel:** 4¼", 6-groove. Chrome-lined bore.
**Weight:** 34 oz. (empty). **Length:** 8¹⁄₁₆" over-all.
**Stocks:** Walnut with cut checkering and high gloss finish.
**Sights:** Blade front with white face, rear adjustable for windage with white bars for increased visibility.
**Features:** Fixed barrel, locked breech. Exposed hammer can be locked in non-firing mode in either single or double action. Stainless steel inertia firing pin and loaded chamber indicator. All external parts blued, internal parts hard-chrome plated. All steel construction. Introduced 1979. From Sile Dist.
**Price:** About ............................................... **$349.95**

Smith & Wesson Model 659

Smith & Wesson Model 469

## Smith & Wesson Model 469 Mini-Gun

Basically a cut-down version of the Model 459 pistol. Gun has a 3½" barrel, 12-round magazine, over-all length of 6¹³⁄₁₆", and weighs 26 oz. Also accepts the 14-shot Model 459 magazine. Cross-hatch knurling on the recurved-front trigger guard and backstrap; magazine has a curved finger extension; bobbed hammer; sandblast blue finish with pebble-grain grips. Ambidextrous safety standard. Introduced 1983.
**Price:** ............................................................... **$432.50**
**Price:** Stainless Model 669 (alloy frame) ..................... **$475.00**

Smith & Wesson Model 645

## SMITH & WESSON MODEL 645 DOUBLE ACTION

**Caliber:** 45 ACP, 8-shot magazine.
**Barrel:** 5″.
**Weight:** 37.5 ozs. **Length:** 8⅝″ over-all.
**Stocks:** Checkered high-impact nylon.
**Sights:** Red ramp front, rear drift-adjustable for windage.
**Features:** Double action. Made of stainless steel. Has manual hammer-drop, magazine disconnect and firing pin safeties. Cross-hatch knurling on the re-curved front trigger guard and backstrap; bevelled magazine well. Introduced 1985.
**Price:** . . . . . . . . . . . . . . . . . . . . . . . . . . . . . . . . . . . . . . . . . . **$550.00**

Springfield Armory 1911-A1

## SPRINGFIELD ARMORY 1911-A1 AUTO PISTOL

**Caliber:** 9mm or 45 ACP, 8-round magazine.
**Barrel:** 5″.
**Weight:** 2¼ lbs. **Length:** 8½″ over-all.
**Stocks:** NA.
**Sights:** Blade front, rear drift-adjustable for windage.
**Features:** All forged parts, including frame, barrel, slide. All new production. Custom slide and parts available. Introduced 1985. From Springfield Armory.
**Price:** Complete pistol, Parkerized . . . . . . . . . . . . . . . . . . . . . . . . . . . . **$362.00**
**Price:** Complete pistol, blued . . . . . . . . . . . . . . . . . . . . . . . . . . . . . **$383.00**
**Price:** Complete parts kit, 45 ACP, Parkerized . . . . . . . . . . . . . . . . . . **$305.00**
**Price:** As above, blued . . . . . . . . . . . . . . . . . . . . . . . . . . . . . . . . **$326.00**
**Price:** 45 to 22 or 9mm conversion kit, Parkerized . . . . . . . . . . . . . . **$181.00**
**Price:** As above, blued . . . . . . . . . . . . . . . . . . . . . . . . . . . . . . . . **$186.00**

## STAR MODEL 30M & 30 PK DOUBLE-ACTION PISTOLS

**Caliber:** 9mm Para., 15-shot magazine.
**Barrel:** 4.33″ (Model M); 3.86″ (Model PK).
**Weight:** 40 oz. (M); 30 oz. (PK). **Length:** 8″ over-all (M); 7.6″ (PK).
**Stocks:** Checkered black plastic.
**Sights:** Square blade front, square notch rear click-adjustable for windage and elevation.
**Features:** Double or single action; grooved front and backstraps and trigger guard face; ambidextrous safety cams firing pin forward; removable back-strap houses the firing mechanism. Model M has steel frame; Model PK is alloy. Introduced 1984. Imported from Spain by Interarms.
**Price:** Model M or PK . . . . . . . . . . . . . . . . . . . . . . . . . . . . . . . . . . **$455.00**

Star Model 30 PK

## STAR MODEL PD AUTO PISTOL

**Caliber:** 45 ACP, 6-shot magazine.
**Barrel:** 3.94″.
**Weight:** 28 oz. **Length:** 7⁷⁄₁₆″ over-all.
**Stocks:** Checkered walnut.
**Sights:** Ramp front, fully adjustable rear.
**Features:** Rear sight milled into slide; thumb safety; grooved non-slip front strap; nylon recoil buffer; inertia firing pin; no grip or magazine safeties. Imported from Spain by Interarms.
**Price:** Blue. . . . . . . . . . . . . . . . . . . . . . . . . . . . . . . . . . . . . . . . . **$333.00**

Star Model PD Pistol

## STAR BM, BKM AUTO PISTOLS

**Caliber:** 9mm Para., 8-shot magazine.
**Barrel:** 3.9″.
**Weight:** 25 oz.
**Stocks:** Checkered walnut.
**Sights:** Fixed.
**Features:** Blue or chrome finish. Magazine and manual safeties, external hammer. Imported from Spain by Interarms.
**Price:** Blue, BM and BKM. . . . . . . . . . . . . . . . . . . . . . . . . . . . . . . . **$305.00**
**Price:** Chrome, BM only . . . . . . . . . . . . . . . . . . . . . . . . . . . . . . . . **$315.00**

## STEEL CITY "DOUBLE DEUCE" PISTOL

**Caliber:** 22 LR (7-shot), 25 ACP (6-shot).
**Barrel:** 2½″.
**Weight:** 18 oz. **Length:** 5½″ over-all.
**Stocks:** Rosewood.
**Sights:** Fixed groove.
**Features:** Double-action; stainless steel construction with matte finish; ambidextrous slide-mounted safety. From Steel City Arms, Inc.
**Price:** 22 or 25 cal. . . . . . . . . . . . . . . . . . . . . . . . . . . . . . . . . . . . **$289.95**

Steel City Double Deuce

**CAUTION:** PRICES CHANGE. CHECK AT GUNSHOP.

Steyr GB

## TARGA MODELS GT32, GT380 AUTO PISTOLS
**Caliber:** 32 ACP or 380 ACP, 6-shot magazine.
**Barrel:** 4⅞".
**Weight:** 26 oz. **Length:** 7⅜" over-all.
**Stocks:** Checkered nylon with thumb rest. Walnut optional.
**Sights:** Fixed blade front; rear drift-adj. for w.
**Features:** Chrome or blue finish; magazine, thumb, and firing pin safeties; external hammer; safety lever take-down. Imported from Italy by Excam, Inc.
**Price:** 32 cal., blue................................. $133.00
**Price:** 32 cal., chrome............................. $143.00
**Price:** 380 cal., blue.............................. $161.00
**Price:** 380 cal., chrome............................ $170.00
**Price:** 380 cal., chrome, engraved, wooden grips ......... $214.00
**Price:** 380 cal., blue, engraved, wooden grips ........... $205.00

## TARGA GT380XE PISTOL
**Caliber:** 380 ACP, 11-shot magazine.
**Barrel:** 3.88".
**Weight:** 26 oz. **Length:** 7.38" over-all.
**Stocks:** Smooth hardwood.
**Sights:** Adj. for windage.
**Features:** Blue or satin nickel. Ordnance steel. Magazine disconnector, firing pin and thumb safeties. Introduced 1980. Imported by Excam.
**Price:** 380 cal., blue................................. $205.00

### Taurus PT-99AF Auto Pistol
Similar to the PT-92 except has fully adjustable rear sight, smooth Brazilian walnut stocks and is available in polished blue or satin nickel. Introduced 1983.
**Price:** Polished blue............................. $392.90
**Price:** Satin nickel.............................. $406.00

> Consult our Directory pages for the location of firms mentioned.

Universal Enforcer Model 3000

## STEEL CITY "WAR EAGLE" PISTOL
**Caliber:** 9mm Para., 13-shot magazine.
**Barrel:** 4".
**Weight:** NA. **Length:** NA.
**Stocks:** Rosewood.
**Sights:** Fixed and adjustable.
**Features:** Double action; matte-finished stainless steel; ambidextrous safety. Announced 1986.
**Price:**............................................. $389.95

## STEYR GB DOUBLE ACTION AUTO PISTOL
**Caliber:** 9mm Parabellum; 18-shot magazine.
**Barrel:** 5.39".
**Weight:** 33 oz. **Length:** 8.4" over-all.
**Stocks:** Checkered walnut.
**Sights:** Post front, fixed rear.
**Features:** Gas-operated, delayed blowback action. Measures 5.7" high, 1.3" wide. Introduced 1981. Imported by Gun South, Inc.
**Price:** About .................................... $595.00

## TARGA MODEL GT27 AUTO PISTOL
**Caliber:** 25 ACP, 6-shot magazine.
**Barrel:** 2⁷/₁₆".
**Weight:** 12 oz. **Length:** 4⅝" over-all.
**Stocks:** Checkered nylon.
**Sights:** Fixed.
**Features:** Safety lever take-down; external hammer with half-cock. Assembled in U.S. by Excam, Inc.
**Price:** Blue..................................... $58.50
**Price:** Chrome.................................. $64.00

## TAURUS MODEL PT-92AF AUTO PISTOL
**Caliber:** 9mm P., 15-shot magazine.
**Barrel:** 4.92".
**Weight:** 34 oz. **Length:** 8.54" over-all.
**Stocks:** Brazilian walnut.
**Sights:** Fixed notch rear.
**Features:** Double action, exposed hammer, chamber loaded indicator. Inertia firing pin. Blue finish. Imported by Taurus International.
**Price:**............................................. $366.90

Taurus PT-99 Pistol

## UNIVERSAL ENFORCER MODEL 3000 AUTO
**Caliber:** 30 M1 Carbine, 5-shot magazine.
**Barrel:** 11¼" with 12-groove rifling.
**Weight:** 4 lbs. **Length:** 19" over-all.
**Stocks:** American walnut with handguard.
**Sights:** Gold bead ramp front. Peep rear.
**Features:** Accepts 15 or 30-shot magazines. 4½-6 lb. trigger pull. From Iver Johnson.
**Price:** Blue finish............................... $225.00

## UZI PISTOL
**Caliber:** 9mm Parabellum.
**Barrel:** 4.5".
**Weight:** 3.8 lbs. **Length:** 9.45" over-all.
**Stocks:** Black plastic.
**Sights:** Post front, open rear adjustable for windage and elevation.
**Features:** Semi-auto blow-back action; fires from closed bolt; floating firing pin. Comes in a molded plastic case with 20-round magazine; 25 and 32-round magazines available. Imported from Israel by Action Arms. Introduced 1984.
**Price:** . . . . . . . . . . . . . . . . . . . . . . . . . . . . . . . . . . . . . **$579.00**

UZI Pistol

## WALTHER PP AUTO PISTOL
**Caliber:** 22 LR, 8-shot; 32 ACP, 380 ACP, 7-shot.
**Barrel:** 3.86".
**Weight:** 23½ oz. **Length:** 6.7" over-all.
**Stocks:** Checkered plastic.
**Sights:** Fixed, white markings.
**Features:** Double action, manual safety blocks firing pin and drops hammer, chamber loaded indicator on 32 and 380, extra finger rest magazine provided. Imported from Germany by Interarms.
**Price:** 22 LR . . . . . . . . . . . . . . . . . . . . . . . . . . . . . . . **$550.00**
**Price:** 32 and 380. . . . . . . . . . . . . . . . . . . . . . . . . . . . . **$530.00**
**Price:** Engraved models . . . . . . . . . . . . . . . . . . . . . . . . **On Request**

### Walther American PPK/S Auto Pistol
Similar to Walther PP except made entirely in the United States. Has 3.27" barrel with 6.1" length over-all. Introduced 1980.
**Price:** 380 ACP only . . . . . . . . . . . . . . . . . . . . . . . . . . . **$475.00**
**Price:** As above, stainless . . . . . . . . . . . . . . . . . . . . . . . **$515.00**

Walther PP Auto Pistol

### Walther American PPK Auto Pistol
Similar to Walther PPK/S except weighs 21 oz., has 6-shot capacity. Made in the U.S. Introduced 1986.
**Price:** Stainless, 380 ACP only . . . . . . . . . . . . . . . . . . . **$515.00**
**Price:** Blue, 380 ACP only . . . . . . . . . . . . . . . . . . . . . . . **$475.00**

## WALTHER P-38 AUTO PISTOL
**Caliber:** 22 LR, 30 Luger or 9mm Luger, 8-shot.
**Barrel:** 4¹⁵/₁₆" (9mm and 30), 5¹/₁₆" (22 LR).
**Weight:** 28 oz. **Length:** 8½" over-all.
**Stocks:** Checkered plastic.
**Sights:** Fixed.
**Features:** Double action, safety blocks firing pin and drops hammer, chamber loaded indicator. Matte finish standard, polished blue, engraving and/or plating available. Imported from Germany by Interarms.
**Price:** 22 LR . . . . . . . . . . . . . . . . . . . . . . . . . . . . . . . . . **$690.00**
**Price:** 9mm or 30 Luger . . . . . . . . . . . . . . . . . . . . . . . . . **$640.00**
**Price:** Engraved models . . . . . . . . . . . . . . . . . . . . . . . . **On Request**

Walther P-38 Auto Pistol

### Walther P-5 Auto Pistol
Latest Walther design that uses the basic P-38 double-action mechanism. Caliber 9mm Luger, barrel length 3½"; weight 28 oz., over-all length 7".
**Price:** . . . . . . . . . . . . . . . . . . . . . . . . . . . . . . . . . . . . . **$750.00**

## WILKINSON "SHERRY" AUTO PISTOL
**Caliber:** 22 LR, 8-shot magazine.
**Barrel:** 2⅛".
**Weight:** 9¼ oz. **Length:** 4⅜" over-all.
**Stocks:** Checkered black plastic.
**Sights:** None.
**Features:** Cross-bolt safety locks the sear into the hammer. Available in all blue finish or blue slide and trigger with gold frame. Introduced 1985.
**Price:** . . . . . . . . . . . . . . . . . . . . . . . . . . . . . . . . . . . . . **$167.95**

Wilkinson "Sherry"

## WILKINSON "LINDA" PISTOL
**Caliber:** 9mm Para., 31-shot magazine.
**Barrel:** 8⁵/₁₆".
**Weight:** 4 lbs., 13 oz. **Length:** 12¼" over-all.
**Stocks:** Checkered black plastic pistol grip, maple fore-end.
**Sights:** Protected blade front, Williams adjustable rear.
**Features:** Fires from closed bolt. Semi-auto only. Straight blowback action. Cross-bolt safety. Removable barrel. From Wilkinson Arms.
**Price:** . . . . . . . . . . . . . . . . . . . . . . . . . . . . . . . . . . . . . **$368.69**

## WILDEY PISTOL
**Caliber:** 475, 44, 41 Wildey Magnum, 45 Win. Mag., 357 Peterbuilt, 44 Auto Mag.; 7-shot.
**Barrel:** 6", 7", 8", 10".
**Weight:** About 58 oz. (6" barrel).
**Stocks:** Black rubber or walnut.
**Sights:** Interchangeable blade front, Eliason-type rear.
**Features:** Right or left-hand ejection (bolts), safety and slide lock stop; ambidextrous magazine catch; interchangeable barrels; drilled and tapped for scope mounting; dual cam-up tilt bolt lock; patented auto. gas system; adjustable trigger. Announced 1985. From Wildey, Inc.
**Price:** . . . . . . . . . . . . . . . . . . . . . . . . . . . . . . . . . . . . . **$799.00**

**CAUTION:** PRICES CHANGE. CHECK AT GUNSHOP.

Air Match 500

## AIR MATCH 500 TARGET PISTOL
**Caliber:** 22 LR, single shot.
**Barrel:** 10.4".
**Weight:** 28 oz.
**Stocks:** Anatomically shaped match grip of stippled hardwood. Right or left hand.
**Sights:** Match post front, fully adjustable match rear.
**Features:** Sight radius adjustable from 14.1" to 16.1"; easy disassembly for cleaning or adjustment. Comes with case, tools, spare front and rear sight blades. Imported from Italy by Kendall International Arms. Introduced 1984.
**Price:** ..................................................... **$718.75**

## ALLEN "PHANTOM" SA SILHOUETTE
**Caliber:** 357 Mag., 44 Mag.
**Barrel:** 10".
**Weight:** NA. **Length:** NA.
**Stocks:** Walnut target-style.
**Sights:** Blade on ramp front, fully adj. rear.
**Features:** Heavier frame than other Allen single actions. Hooked trigger guard. Introduced 1986. Imported by Allen Fire Arms.
**Price:** ................................................. **$369.00**

Beeman/Agner 80

## BEEMAN/AGNER MODEL 80 TARGET PISTOL
**Caliber:** 22 LR, 5-shot magazine.
**Barrel:** 5.9".
**Weight:** 36 oz. **Length:** 9½" overall.
**Stocks:** French walnut briar; anatomically shaped, adjustable.
**Sights:** Fixed blade front, rear adjustable for windage and elevation; 8¾" radius.
**Features:** Security "key" locks trigger, magazine and slide. Design minimizes gun movement; dry-fire button allows trigger practice. Imported from Denmark by Beeman. Introduced 1984.
**Price:** Right-hand ........................................... **$1,295.00**
**Price:** Left-hand ............................................ **$1,395.00**

Beeman/Unique 69

## BEEMAN/UNIQUE D.E.S. 69 TARGET PISTOL
**Caliber:** 22 LR, 5-shot magazine.
**Barrel:** 5.91".
**Weight:** 35.3 oz. **Length:** 10.5" over-all.
**Stocks:** French walnut target style with thumbrest and adjustable shelf; hand checkered panels.
**Sights:** Ramp front, micro. adj. rear mounted on frame; 8.66" sight radius.
**Features:** Meets U.I.T. standards. Comes with 260 gram barrel weight; 100, 150, 350 gram weights available. Fully adjustable match trigger; dry firing safety device. Imported from France by Beeman.
**Price:** Right-hand ........................................... **$599.00**
**Price:** Left-hand ............................................ **$629.00**

## BEEMAN/UNIQUE MODEL 2000-U MATCH PISTOL
**Caliber:** 22 Short, 5-shot magazine.
**Barrel:** 5.9".
**Weight:** 43 oz. **Length:** 11.3" over-all.
**Stocks:** Anatomically shaped, adjustable, stippled French walnut.
**Sights:** Blade front, fully adjustable rear; 9.7" sight radius.
**Features:** Light alloy frame, steel slide and shock absorber; five barrel vents reduce recoil, three of which can be blocked; trigger adjustable for position and pull weight. Comes with 340 gram weight housing, 160 gram available. Imported from France by Beeman. Introduced 1984.
**Price:** Right-hand ........................................... **$799.00**
**Price:** Left-hand ............................................ **$839.00**

Beeman/Unique 2000-U

Bernardelli Model 100

## BERNARDELLI MODEL 100 PISTOL
**Caliber:** 22 LR only, 10-shot magazine.
**Barrel:** 5.9".
**Weight:** 37¾ oz. **Length:** 9" over-all.
**Stocks:** Checkered walnut with thumbrest.
**Sights:** Fixed front, rear adj. for w. and e.
**Features:** Target barrel weight included. Heavy sighting rib with interchangeable front sight. Accessories include cleaning equipment and assembly tools, case. Imported from Italy by Interarms.
**Price:** With case ............................................. **$360.00**

# COMPETITION HANDGUNS

Chipmunk Silhouette

## CHIPMUNK SILHOUETTE PISTOL
**Caliber:** 22 LR.
**Barrel:** 14⅞".
**Weight:** About 2 lbs. **Length:** 20" over-all.
**Stock:** American walnut rear grip.
**Sights:** Post on ramp front, peep rear.
**Features:** Meets IHMSA 22-cal. unlimited category for competition. Introduced 1985.
**Price:** ............................................. **$149.95**

## COLT GOLD CUP NAT'L MATCH MK IV Series 80
**Caliber:** 45 ACP, 7-shot magazine.
**Barrel:** 5", with new design bushing.
**Weight:** 39 oz. **Length:** 8½".
**Stocks:** Blue—Checkered walnut, gold plated medallion; stainless has composition grips.
**Sights:** Ramp-style front, Colt-Elliason rear adj. for w. and e., sight radius 6¾".
**Features:** Arched or flat housing; wide, grooved trigger with adj. stop; ribbed-top slide, hand fitted, with improved ejection port.
**Price:** Blue ............................................. **$687.50**
**Price:** Stainless ....................................... **$744.95**

Colt Gold Cup Series 80

## DETONICS SCOREMASTER TARGET PISTOL
**Caliber:** 45 ACP, 451 Detonics Magnum, 7-shot clip.
**Barrel:** 5" heavy match barrel with recessed muzzle; 6" optional.
**Weight:** 42 oz. **Length:** 8⅜" over-all.
**Stocks:** Pachmayr checkered with matching mainspring housing.
**Sights:** Blade front, Low-Base Bomar rear.
**Features:** Stainless steel; self-centering barrel system; patented Detonics recoil system; combat tuned, ambidextrous safety; extended grip safety; National Match tolerances; extended magazine release. Comes with two spare magazines, three interchangeable front sights, and carrying case. Introduced 1983. From Detonics.
**Price:** 45 ACP or 451 Mag., 6" barrel .......................... **$1,009.95**
**Price:** As above, 5" barrel ...................................... **$992.95**

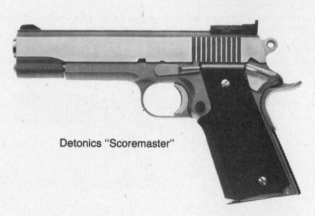

Detonics "Scoremaster"

## FAS 602 MATCH PISTOL
**Caliber:** 22 LR, 5-shot.
**Barrel:** 5.6".
**Weight:** 37 oz. **Length:** 11" over-all.
**Stocks:** Walnut wrap-around; sizes small, medium or large, or adjustable.
**Sights:** Match. Blade front, open notch rear fully adj. for w. and e. Sight radius is 8.66".
**Features:** Line of sight is only ¹¹⁄₃₂" above centerline of bore; magazine is inserted from top; adjustable and removable trigger mechanism; single lever takedown. Full 5 year warranty. Imported from Italy by Beeman Inc. and Osborne's.
**Price:** From Beeman ...................... **$749.00 to $779.00**
**Price:** As above, 32 S&W wadcutter (Beeman) ........ **$754.00 to $784.00**
**Price:** 22LR (Osborne's) ...................................... **$775.00**

## FAS 601 Match Pistol
Similar to SP 602 except has different match stocks with adj. palm, shelf, 22 Short only for rapid fire shooting; weighs 40 oz., 5.6" bbl., has gas ports through top of barrel and slide to reduce recoil, slightly different trigger and sear mechanisms.
**Price:** From Beeman ............................ **$754.00 to $784.00**
**Price:** From Osborne's .................................... **$825.00**
**Price:** FAS 603, 32 S&W wadcutter (Beeman) .................... **$835.00**

## HAMMERLI MODEL 150 FREE PISTOL
**Caliber:** 22 LR. Single shot.
**Barrel:** 11.3"
**Weight:** 43 ozs. **Length:** 15.35" over-all.
**Stocks:** Walnut with adjustable palm shelf.
**Sights:** Sight radius of 14.6". Micro rear sight adj. for w. and e.
**Features:** Single shot Martini action. Cocking lever on left side of action with vertical operation. Set trigger adjustable for length and angle. Trigger pull weight adjustable between 5 and 100 grams. Guaranteed accuracy of .78", 10 shots from machine rest. Imported from Switzerland by Osborne's, Mandall Shooting Supplies and Beeman.
**Price:** About (Mandall) ...................................... **$1,500.00**
**Price:** With electric trigger (Model 152), about (Mandall) ......... **$1,650.00**
**Price:** Model 150 (Osborne's) ................................ **$1,295.00**
**Price:** Model 152 (Osborne's) ................................ **$1,395.00**
**Price:** Model 150 (Beeman) .................................. **$1,195.00**
**Price:** Model 152 (Beeman) .................................. **$1,295.00**

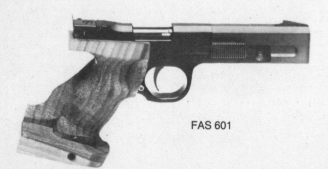

FAS 601

**CAUTION:** PRICES CHANGE. CHECK AT GUNSHOP.

# COMPETITION HANDGUNS

Hammerli 208

## HAMMERLI MODEL 232 RAPID FIRE PISTOL
**Caliber:** 22 Short, 6-shot.
**Barrel:** 5", with six exhaust ports.
**Weight:** 44 oz. **Length:** 10.4" over-all.
**Stocks:** Stippled walnut; wraparound on Model 232-2, adjustable on 232-1.
**Sights:** Interchangeable front and rear blades, fully adjustable micrometer rear.
**Features:** Recoil operated semi-automatic; nearly recoilless design; trigger adjustable from 8.4 to 10.6 oz. with three lengths offered. Wraparound grips available in small, medium and large sizes. Imported from Switzerland by Osborne's, Beeman, Mandall. Introduced 1984.
**Price:** Model 232-1, (Osborne's) . . . . . . . . . . . . . . . . . . . . . . . . . . . . . **$902.00**
**Price:** Model 232-2 (Osborne's) . . . . . . . . . . . . . . . . . . . . . . . . . . . . . **$954.00**
**Price:** Model 232-1 (Beeman) . . . . . . . . . . . . . . . . . . . . . . . . . . . . . . **$829.00**
**Price:** Model 232-2 (Beeman) . . . . . . . . . . . . . . . . . . . . . . . . . . . . . . **$899.00**

## HECKLER & KOCH P9S COMPETITION PISTOL
**Caliber:** 9mm Para.
**Barrel:** 4", 5.5".
**Weight:** 32 oz. **Length:** 9.1" over-all.
**Stocks:** Stippled walnut, target-type.
**Sights:** Blade front, fully adjustable rear.
**Features:** Comes with extra standard 4" barrel, slide and grips, as well as the target gun parts and tools and is fully convertible. Imported from West Germany by Heckler & Koch, Inc.
**Price:** . . . . . . . . . . . . . . . . . . . . . . . . . . . . . . . . . . . . . . . . . . . . . **$1,333.00**

## MANURHIN MR. 32 MATCH REVOLVER
**Caliber:** 32 S&W Long, 6-shot.
**Barrel:** 6".
**Weight:** 42 oz. **Length:** 11¾" over-all.
**Stocks:** Anatomically shaped grip for target shooting; supplied shaped but not finished; small, medium and large sizes.
**Sights:** Interchangeable blade front, adjustable underlying micrometer rear.
**Features:** Target/match 6-shot revolver. Trigger is externally adjustable for weight of pull, and comes with shoe. Imported from France by Manurhin International, Inc. Introduced 1984.
**Price:** . . . . . . . . . . . . . . . . . . . . . . . . . . . . . . . . . . . . . . . . . . . . . **$785.00**
**Price:** Model MR. 38—same as MR. 32 except chambered for 38 Special, 5¾" barrel. . . . . . . . . . . . . . . . . . . . . . . . . . . . . . . . . . . . . . . . . . . . . **$785.00**

## MANURHIN MR 73 LONG RANGE/SILHOUETTE REVOLVER
**Caliber:** 357 Magnum; 6-shot.
**Barrel:** 9" (Long Range), 10¾" (Silhouette).
**Weight:** 45 oz. (9" bbl.); 50 oz. (10¾" bbl.) **Length:** 14" over-all (9"); 16¾" (10¾").
**Stocks:** Checkered walnut.
**Sights:** Interchangeable blade front, adjustable micrometer rear.
**Features:** Trigger externally adjustable for backlash and weight of pull. Single action only. Trigger shoe available. Imported from France by Manurhin International, Inc. Introduced 1984.
**Price:** . . . . . . . . . . . . . . . . . . . . . . . . . . . . . . . . . . . . . . . . . . . . . **$795.00**

Morini Model CM-80

## HAMMERLI STANDARD, MODELS 208 & 211
**Caliber:** 22 LR.
**Barrel:** 5.9", 6-groove.
**Weight:** 37.6 oz. (45 oz. with extra heavy barrel weight). **Length:** 10".
**Stocks:** Walnut. Adj. palm rest (208), 211 has thumbrest grip.
**Sights:** Match sights, fully adj. for w. and e. (click adj.). Interchangeable front and rear blades.
**Features:** Semi-automatic, recoil operated. 8-shot clip. Slide stop. Fully adj. trigger (2¼ lbs. and 3 lbs.). Extra barrel weight available. Imported from Switzerland by Osborne's, Mandall Shooting Supplies, Beeman.
**Price:** Model 208, approx. (Mandall) . . . . . . . . . . . . . . . . . . . . . . . **$1,295.00**
**Price:** Model 211, approx. (Mandall) . . . . . . . . . . . . . . . . . . . . . . . **$1,195.00**
**Price:** Model 215, approx. (Mandall) . . . . . . . . . . . . . . . . . . . . . . . **$1,195.00**
**Price:** Model 208 (Osborne's) . . . . . . . . . . . . . . . . . . . . . . . . . . . . **$1,029.00**
**Price:** Model 211 (Osborne's) . . . . . . . . . . . . . . . . . . . . . . . . . . . . **$1,005.00**
**Price:** Model 215 (Osborne's) . . . . . . . . . . . . . . . . . . . . . . . . . . . . . **$835.00**
**Price:** Model 208 (Beeman) . . . . . . . . . . . . . . . . . . . . . . . . . . . . . . **$950.00**
**Price:** Model 211 (Beeman) . . . . . . . . . . . . . . . . . . . . . . . . . . . . . . **$930.00**
**Price:** Model 215 (Beeman) . . . . . . . . . . . . . . . . . . . . . . . . . . . . . . **$779.00**

Heckler & Koch P9S Competition

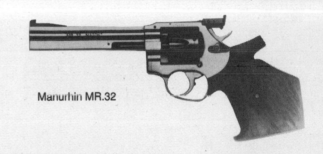

Manurhin MR.32

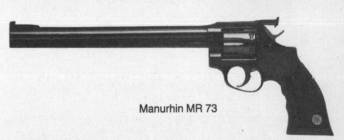

Manurhin MR 73

## MORINI MODEL CM-80 SUPER COMPETITION
**Caliber:** 22 Long Rifle; single shot.
**Barrel:** 10", free floating.
**Weight:** 30 oz., with weights. **Length:** 21.25" over-all.
**Stocks:** Walnut, adjustable or wrap-around in three sizes.
**Sights:** Match; square notch rear adjustable for w. and e.; up to 15.6" radius.
**Features:** Adjustable grip/frame angle, adjustable barrel alignment, adjustable trigger weight (5 to 120 grams), adjustable sight radius. Comes with 20-shot test target (50 meters) and case. Introduced 1985. Imported from Italy by Osborne's.
**Price:** Standard . . . . . . . . . . . . . . . . . . . . . . . . . . . . . . . . . . . . . . . **$810.00**
**Price:** Deluxe . . . . . . . . . . . . . . . . . . . . . . . . . . . . . . . . . . . . . . . . . **$955.00**

**CAUTION:** PRICES CHANGE. CHECK AT GUNSHOP.

# COMPETITION HANDGUNS

Remington XP-100 Silhouette

**REMINGTON XP-100 SILHOUETTE PISTOL**
**Caliber:** 7mm BR Remington, single-shot.
**Barrel:** 14¾".
**Weight:** 4⅛ lbs. **Length:** 21¼" over-all.
**Stocks:** Brown nylon, one piece, checkered grip.
**Sights:** None furnished. Drilled and tapped for scope mounts.
**Features:** Universal grip fits right or left hand; match-type grooved trigger, two-position thumb safety.
**Price:** About . . . . . . . . . . . . . . . . . . . . . . . . . . . . . . . . . . . . . . . . . . . $405.00

**OLYMPIC RAPID FIRE PISTOL**
**Caliber:** 22 Short.
**Barrel:** 5", with exhaust ports.
**Weight:** 43 oz. **Length:** 10.4" over-all.
**Stocks:** Wrap-around walnut; three sizes.
**Sights:** Fully adjustable micrometer rear.
**Features:** Recoil-operated semi-automatic. Trigger adjustable for weight of pull. I.S.U. legal for international competition. Introduced 1985. Imported from Spain by Osborne's.
**Price:** . . . . . . . . . . . . . . . . . . . . . . . . . . . . . . . . . . . . . . . . . . . $895.00

**RUGER MARK II TARGET MODEL AUTO PISTOL**
**Caliber:** 22 LR only, 10-shot magazine.
**Barrel:** 6⅞".
**Weight:** 42 oz. with 6⅞" bbl. **Length:** 11⅛" over-all.
**Stocks:** Checkered hard rubber.
**Sights:** .125" blade front, micro click rear, adjustable for w. and e. Sight radius 9⅜". Introduced 1982.
**Price:** Blued (MK 678) . . . . . . . . . . . . . . . . . . . . . . . . . . . . . . $215.00
**Price:** Stainless, (KMK 678) . . . . . . . . . . . . . . . . . . . . . . . . . . $275.00

Ruger Mark II Target

**Ruger Mark II Bull Barrel**
Same gun as the Target Model except has 5½" or 10" heavy barrel (10" meets all IHMSA regulations). Weight with 5½" barrel is 42 oz., with 10" barrel, 52 oz.
**Price:** Blued (MK-512, MK-10) . . . . . . . . . . . . . . . . . . . . . . . . . $215.00
**Price:** Stainless (KMK-512, KMK-10) . . . . . . . . . . . . . . . . . . . . $275.00

**SIG/HAMMERLI P-240 TARGET PISTOL**
**Caliber:** 32 S&W Long wadcutter, 5-shot.
**Barrel:** 5.9".
**Weight:** 49 oz. **Length:** 10" over-all.
**Stocks:** Walnut, target style with thumbrest. Adjustable palm rest optional.
**Sights:** Match sights; ⅛" undercut front, ⅛" notch micro rear click adj. for w. and e.
**Features:** Semi-automatic, recoil operated; meets I.S.U. and N.R.A. specs for Center Fire Pistol competition; double pull trigger adj. from 2 lbs., 15 ozs. to 3 lbs., 9 ozs.; trigger stop. Comes with cleaning kit, test targets. Imported from Switzerland by Osborne's Supplies and Mandall Shooting Supplies.
**Price:** About (Mandall) . . . . . . . . . . . . . . . . . . . . . . . . . . . . . $1,500.00
**Price:** 22 cal. conversion unit (Osborne's) . . . . . . . . . . . . . . . . $700.00
**Price:** With standard grips (Osborne's) . . . . . . . . . . . . . . . . . $1,195.00
**Price:** With adjustable grips (Osborne's) . . . . . . . . . . . . . . . . $1,250.00

SIG/Hammerli P-240

Smith & Wesson 29 Silhouette

**SMITH & WESSON MODEL 29 SILHOUETTE**
**Caliber:** 44 Magnum, 6-shot.
**Barrel:** 10⅝".
**Weight:** 58 oz. **Length:** 16³⁄₁₆" over-all.
**Stocks:** Over-size target-type, checkered Goncalo Alves.
**Sights:** Four-position front to match the four distances of silhouette targets; micro-click rear adjustable for windage and elevation.
**Features:** Designed specifically for silhouette shooting. Front sight has click stops for the four pre-set ranges. Introduced 1983.
**Price:** . . . . . . . . . . . . . . . . . . . . . . . . . . . . . . . . . . . . . . . . . . $455.50

**SMITH & WESSON 22 AUTO PISTOL Model 41**
**Caliber:** 22 LR, 10-shot clip.
**Barrel:** 7".
**Weight:** 43½ oz. **Length:** 12" over-all.
**Stocks:** Checkered walnut with thumbrest, usable with either hand.
**Sights:** Front, ⅛" Patridge undercut; micro click rear adj. for w. and e.
**Features:** ⅜" wide, grooved trigger with adj. stop.
**Price:** S&W Bright Blue. . . . . . . . . . . . . . . . . . . . . . . . . . . . . . $485.00

Smith & Wesson Model 41

**CAUTION:** PRICES CHANGE. CHECK AT GUNSHOP.

### SMITH & WESSON 22 MATCH HEAVY BARREL M-41
**Caliber:** 22 LR, 10-shot clip.
**Barrel:** 5½" heavy.
**Weight:** 44½ oz. **Length:** 9".
**Stocks:** Checkered walnut with modified thumbrest, usable with either hand.
**Sights:** ⅛" Patridge on ramp base. S&W micro click rear adj. for w. and e.
**Features:** ⅜" wide, grooved trigger; adj. trigger stop.
**Price:** S&W Bright Blue, satin matted top area . . . . . . . . . . . . . . . . . . . . $485.00

### SMITH & WESSON 38 MASTER Model 52 AUTO
**Caliber:** 38 Special (for Mid-range W.C. with flush-seated bullet only). 5-shot magazine.
**Barrel:** 5".
**Weight:** 40.5 oz. with empty magazine. **Length:** 8⅝".
**Stocks:** Checkered walnut.
**Sights:** ⅛" Patridge front, S&W micro click rear adj. for w. and e.
**Features:** Top sighting surfaces matte finished. Locked breech, moving barrel system; checked for 10-ring groups at 50 yards. Coin-adj. sight screws. Dry firing permissible if manual safety on.
**Price:** S&W Bright Blue . . . . . . . . . . . . . . . . . . . . . . . . . . . . . . . . . . . $657.50

Smith & Wesson Model 52

Sokolovsky Automaster

### SOKOLOVSKY 45 AUTOMASTER
**Caliber:** 45 ACP, 6-shot magazine.
**Barrel:** 6".
**Weight:** 3.6 lbs. **Length:** 9½" over-all.
**Stocks:** Smooth walnut.
**Sights:** Ramp front, Millett fully adjustable rear.
**Features:** Intended for target shooting, not combat. Semi-custom built with precise tolerances. Has special "safety trigger" next to regular trigger. Most parts made of stainless steel. Introduced 1985. From Sokolovsky Corp.
**Price:** . . . . . . . . . . . . . . . . . . . . . . . . . . . . . . . . . . . . . . . . . . $3,000.00

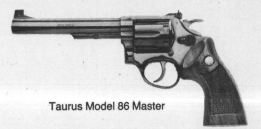

Taurus Model 86 Master

### TAURUS MODEL 86 MASTER REVOLVER
**Caliber:** 38 Spec., 6-shot.
**Barrel:** 6" only.
**Weight:** 34 oz. **Length:** 11¼" over-all.
**Stocks:** Over size target-type, checkered Brazilian walnut.
**Sights:** Patridge front, micro. click rear adj. for w. and e.
**Features:** Blue finish with non-reflective finish on barrel. Imported from Brazil by Taurus International.
**Price:** . . . . . . . . . . . . . . . . . . . . . . . . . . . . . . . . . . . . . . . . . . $245.00
**Price:** Model 96 Scout Master, same except in 22 cal. . . . . . . . . . . . . . $245.00

### THOMPSON-CENTER SUPER 14 CONTENDER
**Caliber:** 22 LR, 222 Rem., 223 Rem., 6mm TCU, 6.5 TCU, 7mm TCU, 30 Herrett, 357 Herrett, 30-30 Win., 35 Rem., 357 Rem. Maximum, 44 Mag. Single shot.
**Barrel:** 14".
**Weight:** 45 oz. **Length:** 17¼" over-all.
**Stocks:** Select walnut grip and fore-end.
**Sights:** Fully adjustable target-type.
**Features:** Break-open action with auto safety. Interchangeable barrels for both rimfire and centerfire calibers. Introduced 1978.
**Price:** . . . . . . . . . . . . . . . . . . . . . . . . . . . . . . . . . . . . . . . . . . $315.00
**Price:** With Armour Alloy II finish. . . . . . . . . . . . . . . . . . . . . . . . . . . $375.00
**Price:** Extra barrels . . . . . . . . . . . . . . . . . . . . . . . . . . . . . . . . . . . $140.00

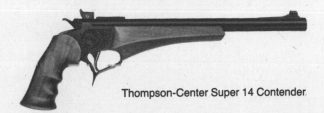

Thompson-Center Super 14 Contender

### VIRGINIAN DRAGOON STAINLESS SILHOUETTE
**Caliber:** 357 Mag., 44 Mag.
**Barrel:** 7½", 8⅜", 10½", heavy.
**Weight:** 51 oz. (7½" bbl.) **Length:** 11½" over-all (7½" bbl.).
**Stocks:** Smooth walnut; also comes with Pachmayr rubber grips.
**Sights:** Undercut blade front, special fully adjustable square notch rear.
**Features:** Designed to comply with IHMSA rules. Made of stainless steel; comes with two sets of stocks. Introduced 1982. Made in the U.S. by Interarms.
**Price:** Either barrel, caliber. . . . . . . . . . . . . . . . . . . . . . . . . . . . . . $425.00

Walther Free Pistol

### WALTHER FREE PISTOL
**Caliber:** 22 LR, single shot.
**Barrel:** 11.7".
**Weight:** 48 ozs. **Length:** 17.2" over-all.
**Stocks:** Walnut, special hand-fitting design.
**Sights:** Fully adjustable match sights.
**Features:** Special electronic trigger. Matte finish blue. Introduced 1980. Imported from Germany by Interarms.
**Price:** . . . . . . . . . . . . . . . . . . . . . . . . . . . . . . . . . . . . . . . . . . $1,295.00

## WALTHER GSP MATCH PISTOL
**Caliber:** 22 LR, 32 S&W wadcutter (GSP-C), 5-shot.
**Barrel:** 5¾".
**Weight:** 44.8 oz. (22 LR), 49.4 oz. (32). **Length:** 11.8" over-all.
**Stocks:** Walnut, special hand-fitting design.
**Sights:** Fixed front, rear adj. for w. & e.
**Features:** Available with either 2.2 lb. (1000 gm) or 3 lb. (1360 gm) trigger. Spare mag., bbl. weight, tools supplied in Match Pistol Kit. Imported from Germany by Interarms.
**Price:** GSP . . . . . . . . . . . . . . . . . . . . . . . . . . . . . . . . . . . . . . . **$955.00**
**Price:** GSP-C . . . . . . . . . . . . . . . . . . . . . . . . . . . . . . . . . . . . **$1,095.00**
**Price:** 22 LR conversion unit for GSP-C . . . . . . . . . . . . . . . . **$595.00**
**Price:** 22 Short conversion unit for GSP-C . . . . . . . . . . . . . . . **$625.00**
**Price:** 32 S&W conversion unit for GSP-C . . . . . . . . . . . . . . . **$725.00**

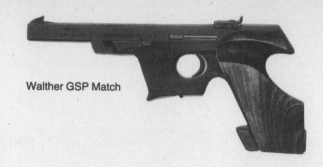

Walther GSP Match

## Walther OSP Rapid-Fire Pistol
Similar to Model GSP except 22 Short only, stock has adj. free-style hand rest.
**Price:** . . . . . . . . . . . . . . . . . . . . . . . . . . . . . . . . . . . . . . . . . . **$975.00**

## DAN WESSON MODEL 40 SILHOUETTE
**Caliber:** 357 Maximum, 6 shot.
**Barrel:** 6", 8", 10".
**Weight:** 64 oz. (8" bbl.) **Length:** 14.3" over-all (8" bbl.).
**Stocks:** Smooth walnut, target-style.
**Sights:** ⅛" serrated front, fully adj. rear.
**Features:** Meets criteria for IHMSA competition with 8" slotted barrel. Blue or stainless steel.
**Price:** Blue, 6" . . . . . . . . . . . . . . . . . . . . . . . . . . . . . . . . . . . **$426.35**
**Price:** Blue, 8" slotted . . . . . . . . . . . . . . . . . . . . . . . . . . . . . . **$450.40**
**Price:** Blue, 10" . . . . . . . . . . . . . . . . . . . . . . . . . . . . . . . . . . . **$456.10**
**Price:** Stainless, 6" . . . . . . . . . . . . . . . . . . . . . . . . . . . . . . . . **$477.30**
**Price:** Stainless, 8" slotted . . . . . . . . . . . . . . . . . . . . . . . . . . **$499.45**
**Price:** Stainless, 10" . . . . . . . . . . . . . . . . . . . . . . . . . . . . . . . **$511.30**

Dan Wesson Model 40

## WICHITA MK-40 SILHOUETTE PISTOL
**Caliber:** 7mm IHMSA, 308 Win. F.L. Other calibers available on special order. Single shot.
**Barrel:** 13", non-glare blue; .700" dia. muzzle.
**Weight:** 4½ lbs. **Length:** 19⅝" over-all.
**Stocks:** Metallic gray fiberthane glass.
**Sights:** Wichita Multi-Range sighting system.
**Features:** Aluminum receiver with steel insert locking lugs, measures 1.360" O.D.; 3 locking lug bolts, 3 gas ports; flat bolt handle; completely adjustable Wichita trigger. Introduced 1981. From Wichita Arms.
**Price:** . . . . . . . . . . . . . . . . . . . . . . . . . . . . . . . . . . . . . . . . . . **$720.00**

Wichita Silhouette

## WICHITA SILHOUETTE PISTOL
**Caliber:** 7mm IHMSA, 308, 7mm x 308. Other calibers available on special order. Single shot.
**Barrel:** 14¹⁵⁄₁₆" or 10¾".
**Weight:** 4½ lbs. **Length:** 21⅜" over-all.
**Stocks:** American walnut with oil finish, or gray fiberglass. Glass bedded.
**Sights:** Wichita Multi-Range sight system.
**Features:** Comes with either right- or left-hand action with right-hand grip. Fluted bolt, flat bolt handle. Action drilled and tapped for Burris scope mounts. Non-glare satin blue finish. Wichita adjustable trigger. Introduced 1979. From Wichita Arms.
**Price:** Center grip stock . . . . . . . . . . . . . . . . . . . . . . . . . . . . . **$825.00**
**Price:** As above except with Rear Position Stock and target-type Lightpull trigger. (Not illus.) . . . . . . . . . . . . . . . . . . . . . . . . . . . . . . . . . . . **$900.00**

Wichita Silhouette/Hunter

## WICHITA CLASSIC PISTOL
**Caliber:** Any, up to and including 308 Win.
**Barrel:** 11¼", octagon.
**Weight:** About 5 lbs.
**Stock:** Exhibition grade American black walnut. Checkered 20 lpi. Other woods available on special order.
**Sights:** Micro open sights standard. Receiver drilled and tapped for scope mount.
**Features:** Receiver and barrel octagonally shaped, finished in non-glare blue. Bolt has three locking lugs and three gas escape ports. Completely adjustable Wichita trigger. Introduced 1980. From Wichita Arms.
**Price:** . . . . . . . . . . . . . . . . . . . . . . . . . . . . . . . . . . . . . . . . . **$1,900.00**
**Price:** Engraved, in walnut presentation case . . . . . . . . . . . . . . **$4,660.00**

## WICHITA HUNTER, INTERNATIONAL PISTOL
**Caliber:** 22 LR, 22 Mag., 7mm INT-R, 30-30 Win., 32 H&R Mag., 357 Mag., 357 Super Mag., single shot.
**Barrel:** 10½".
**Weight:** International — 3 lbs., 13 oz.; Hunter — 3 lbs., 14 oz.
**Stock:** Walnut grip and fore-end.
**Sights:** International — target front, adjustable rear; Hunter has scope mount only.
**Features:** Made of 17-4PH stainless steel. Break-open action. Grip dimensions same as Colt 45 auto. Safety supplied only on Hunter model. Extra barrels are factory fitted. Introduced 1983. Available from Wichita Arms.
**Price:** International . . . . . . . . . . . . . . . . . . . . . . . . . . . . . . . . . . . **$484.95**
**Price:** Hunter . . . . . . . . . . . . . . . . . . . . . . . . . . . . . . . . . . . . . . . **$484.95**
**Price:** Extra barrels . . . . . . . . . . . . . . . . . . . . . . . . . . . . . . . . . **$265.00**

Armscor 38

### Astra Model 44, 45 Double Action Revolver
Similar to the 357 Mag. except chambered for 44 Mag. or 45 Colt. Barrel length of 6" only, giving over-all length of 11⅜". Weight is 2¾ lbs. Introduced 1980.
Price: ............................................. $295.00
Price: 8½" bbl. (44 Mag. only) ..................... $305.00

### CHARTER ARMS BULLDOG
**Caliber:** 44 Special, 5-shot.
**Barrel:** 2½", 3".
**Weight:** 19 oz. **Length:** 7¾" over-all.
**Stocks:** Checkered walnut, Bulldog.
**Sights:** Patridge-type front, square-notch rear.
**Features:** Wide trigger and hammer; beryllium copper firing pin.
Price: Service Blue 3" .......................... $211.00
Price: Stainless steel .......................... $267.00
Price: Service blue, 2½" ........................ $211.00
Price: Stainless steel, 2½" ..................... $270.00
Price: Stainless steel, 3", neoprene grips ...... $267.00

### Charter Arms Bulldog Tracker
Similar to the standard Bulldog except chambered for 357 Mag., has adjustable rear sight, 2½", 4" or 6" bull barrel, ramp front sight, square butt checkered walnut grips on 4" and 6"; Bulldog-style grips on 2½". Available in blue finish only.
Price: ............................................. $214.00

### CHARTER ARMS BULLDOG PUG
**Caliber:** 44 Spec., 5 shot.
**Barrel:** 2½".
**Weight:** 19 oz. **Length:** 7¼" over-all.
**Stocks:** Bulldog walnut or Neoprene.
**Sights:** Ramp front, notch rear.
**Features:** Shrouded ejector rod; wide trigger and hammer spur. Introduced 1986.
Price: ............................................. $234.00

### CHARTER ARMS TARGET BULLDOG
**Caliber:** 357 Mag. or 44 Spec., 5 shot.
**Barrel:** 4".
**Weight:** 21 oz. **Length:** 9" over-all.
**Stocks:** Square butt.
**Sights:** Blade front, rear adj. for w. and e.
**Features:** Shrouded barrel and ejector rod. All-steel frame. Introduced 1986.
Price: 357 Mag. ................................... $232.00
Price: 44 Spec. ................................... $240.00

### CHARTER ARMS POLICE BULLDOG
**Caliber:** 32 H&R Mag., 38 Special, 6-shot.
**Barrel:** 4", 4" straight taper bull.
**Weight:** 21 oz. **Length:** 9" over-all.
**Stocks:** Hand checkered American walnut; square butt.
**Sights:** Patridge-type ramp front, notched rear (adjustable on 32 Mag.).
**Features:** Spring loaded unbreakable beryllium copper firing pin; steel frame; accepts +P ammunition; full length ejection of fired cases.
Price: Blue, 32 Mag. ............................. $208.00
Price: Blue, 38 Spec. ............................ $201.00
Price: Stainless steel, 38 Spec. only ........... $263.00

### ARMSCOR 38 REVOLVER
**Caliber:** 38 Spec.
**Barrel:** 4"
**Weight:** 32 oz.
**Stocks:** Checkered Philippine mahogany.
**Sights:** Ramp front, rear adj. for windage.
**Features:** Ventilated rib; polished blue finish. Introduced 1986. Imported from the Philippines by Pacific International Merchandising Corp.
Price: ............................................. $139.95

### ASTRA 357 MAGNUM REVOLVER
**Caliber:** 357 Magnum, 6-shot.
**Barrel:** 3", 4", 6", 8½".
**Weight:** 40 oz. (6" bbl.). **Length:** 11¼" (6" bbl.).
**Stocks:** Checkered walnut.
**Sights:** Fixed front, rear adj. for w. and e.
**Features:** Swing-out cylinder with countersunk chambers, floating firing pin. Target-type hammer and trigger. Imported from Spain by Interarms.
Price: 3", 4", 6" ................................. $275.00
Price: 8½" ....................................... $285.00
Price: 4", stainless ............................. $305.00

Charter Arms Stainless Bulldog

Charter Bulldog Pug

Charter Target Bulldog

Charter Arms Police Bulldog

## CHARTER ARMS UNDERCOVER REVOLVER

**Caliber:** 38 Special, 5 shot; 32 S & W Long, 6 shot.
**Barrel:** 2″, 3″.
**Weight:** 16 oz. (2″). **Length:** 6¼″ (2″).
**Stocks:** Checkered walnut.
**Sights:** Patridge-type ramp front, notched rear.
**Features:** Wide trigger and hammer spur. Steel frame. Police Undercover, 2″ bbl. (for 38 Spec. + P loads) carry same prices as regular 38 Spec. guns.
**Price:** Polished Blue .......................................... **$195.00**
**Price:** 32 S & W Long, blue, 2″ ................................ **$195.00**
**Price:** Stainless, 38 Spec., 2″.................................. **$252.00**

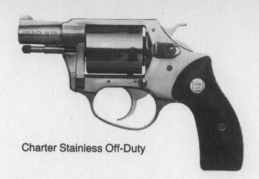

Charter Stainless Off-Duty

### Charter Arms Off-Duty Revolver

Similar to the Undercover except 38 Special only, 2″ barrel, Mat-Black non-glare finish. This all-steel gun comes with Red-Dot front sight and choice of smooth or checkered walnut or neoprene grips. Also available in stainless steel. Introduced 1984.
**Price:** Mat-Black finish .......................................... **$164.00**
**Price:** Stainless steel.......................................... **$219.00**

### Charter Arms Pathfinder

Same as Undercover but in 22 LR or 22 Mag., and has 2″, 3″ or 6″ bbl. Fitted with adjustable rear sight, ramp front. Weight 18½ oz.
**Price:** 22 LR, blue, 3″ ......................................... **$204.00**
**Price:** 22 LR, square butt, 6″ .................................. **$237.00**
**Price:** Stainless, 22 LR, 3″ .................................... **$257.00**
**Price:** 2″, either caliber, blue only .......................... **$204.00**

## COLT AGENT L.W.

**Caliber:** 38 Special, 6-shot.
**Barrel:** 2″.
**Weight:** 16¾ ozs. **Length:** 6¾″ over-all.
**Stocks:** Smooth walnut.
**Sights:** Fixed.
**Features:** A no-frills, lightweight version of the Detective Special. Parkerized-type finish. Name re-introduced 1982.
**Price:** ............................................................ **$259.50**

### Charter Arms Police Undercover

Similar to the standard Undercover except 2″ barrel only, chambered for the 32 H&R Magnum and 38 Spec. (6-shot). Patridge-type front with fixed square notch rear. Blue finish or stainless steel; checkered walnut grips. Also available with Pocket Hammer. Introduced 1984.
**Price:** Standard hammer, 32 Mag., blue ......................... **$198.00**
**Price:** Pocket hammer, 32 Mag., blue .......................... **$202.00**
**Price:** Standard hammer, 38 Spec., blue......................... **$195.00**
**Price:** Pocket hammer, 38 Spec., blue.......................... **$198.00**
**Price:** Standard hammer, 38 Spec., stainless.................... **$252.00**
**Price:** Pocket hammer, 38 Spec., stainless...................... **$256.00**

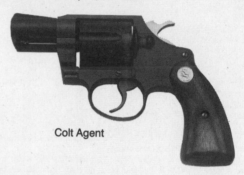

Colt Agent

### Colt Commando Special

Same gun as the Detective Special except comes with rubber grips and matte finish. Introduced 1984.
**Price:** ............................................................ **$299.95**

## COLT DETECTIVE SPECIAL

**Caliber:** 38 Special, 6 shot.
**Barrel:** 2″.
**Weight:** 21½ oz. **Length:** 6¾″ over-all.
**Stocks:** Full, checkered walnut, round butt.
**Sights:** Fixed, ramp front, square notch rear.
**Features:** Glare-proofed sights, smooth trigger. Nickel finish, hammer shroud available as options.
**Price:** Blue................................................... **$428.50**
**Price:** Nickel ................................................ **$481.50**

## COLT KING COBRA REVOLVER

**Caliber:** 357 Magnum, 6 shot.
**Barrel:** 4″, 6″.
**Weight:** 42 oz. (4″ bbl.). **Length:** 9″ over-all (4″ bbl.).
**Stocks:** Checkered rubber.
**Sights:** Red insert ramp front, adj. white outline rear.
**Features:** Stainless steel; full length contoured ejector rod housing, barrel rib; matte finish. Introduced 1986.
**Price:** ............................................................ **$389.95**

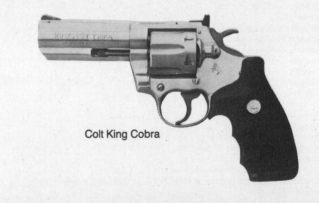

Colt King Cobra

## COLT PYTHON REVOLVER

**Caliber:** 357 Magnum (handles all 38 Spec.), 6 shot.
**Barrel:** 2½″, 4″, 6″ or 8″, with ventilated rib.
**Weight:** 38 oz. (4″ bbl.). **Length:** 9¼″ (4″ bbl.).
**Stocks:** Checkered walnut, target type.
**Sights:** ⅛″ ramp front, adj. notch rear.
**Features:** Ventilated rib; grooved, crisp trigger; swing-out cylinder; target hammer.
**Price:** Blue, 2½″, 4″, 6″, 8″ ................................... **$687.50**
**Price:** Stainless, 4″, 6″....................................... **$775.95**
**Price:** Bright stainless, 2½″, 4″, 6″ .......................... **$786.50**

Colt Python 357

## COLT TROOPER MK V REVOLVER
**Caliber:** 357 Magnum, 6-shot.
**Barrel:** 4″, 6″.
**Weight:** 38 oz. (4″). **Length:** 9″ over-all (4″).
**Stocks:** Checkered walnut target-style.
**Sights:** Orange insert ramp front, adjustable white outline rear.
**Features:** Vent. rib and shrouded ejector rod. Re-designed action results in short hammer throw, lightened trigger pull and faster lock time. Also has re-designed grip frame. Introduced 1982.
**Price:** 4″ blue.............................................. $361.50
**Price:** 4″ nickel,........................................... $395.95
**Price:** 6″, blue............................................. $361.50
**Price:** 6″, nickel.......................................... $398.95

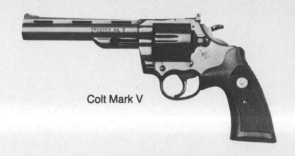

Colt Mark V

## Colt Peacekeeper Revolver
Similar to the Trooper MK V. Available with 4″ or 6″ barrel. Weighs 42 oz. with 6″ barrel; has red insert ramp front sight, white outline fully adjustable rear; rubber "gripper" round bottom combat grips; matte blue finish. Introduced 1985.
**Price:** 4″ or 6″........................................... $320.50

## COLT DIAMONDBACK REVOLVER
**Caliber:** 22 LR or 38 Special, 6 shot.
**Barrel:** 4″ or 6″ with ventilated rib.
**Weight:** 31¾ oz. (4″ bbl.). **Length:** 9″ (4″ bbl.)
**Stocks:** Checkered walnut, target type, square butt.
**Sights:** Ramp front, adj. notch rear.
**Features:** Ventilated rib; grooved, crisp trigger; swing-out cylinder; wide hammer spur.
**Price:** Blue, 4″ or 6″, 22 or 38................................... $460.50
**Price:** Nickel, 4″ or 6″, 22 LR .................................. $513.95

Colt Peacekeeper

## F.I.E. "ARMINIUS REVOLVERS"
**Caliber:** 38 Special, 357 Magnum, 32 S&W, 22 Magnum, 22 LR.
**Barrel:** 2″, 3″, 4″, 6″.
**Weight:** 35 oz. (6″ bbl.). **Length:** 11″ (6″ bbl. 38).
**Stocks:** Checkered plastic; walnut optional.
**Sights:** Ramp front, fixed rear on standard models, w. & e. adj. on target models.
**Features:** Thumb-release, swing-out cylinder. Ventilated rib, solid frame, swing-out cylinder. Interchangeable 22 Mag. cylinder available with 22 cal. versions. Imported from West Germany by F.I.E. Corp.
**Price:** ........................................ $99.95 to $224.95

## F.I.E. "Titan Tiger" REVOLVER
**Caliber:** 38 Special.
**Barrel:** 2″ or 4″.
**Weight:** 27 oz. **Length:** 6¼″ over-all. (2″ bbl.)
**Stocks:** Checkered plastic, Bulldog style. Walnut optional ($15.95).
**Sights:** Fixed.
**Features:** Thumb-release swing-out cylinder, one stroke ejection. Made in U.S.A. by F.I.E. Corp.
**Price:** Blue............................................... $129.95

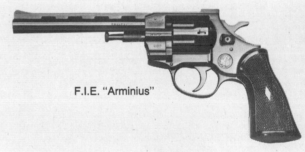

F.I.E. "Arminius"

## KORTH REVOLVER
**Caliber:** 22 LR, 22 Mag., 357 Mag., 9mm Parabellum.
**Barrel:** 3″, 4″, 6″.
**Weight:** 33 to 38 oz. **Length:** 8″ to 11″ over-all.
**Stocks:** Checkered walnut, sport or combat.
**Sights:** Blade front, rear adjustable for windage and elevation.
**Features:** Four interchangeable cylinders available. Major parts machined from hammer-forged steel; cylinder gap of .002″. High polish blue finish. Presentation models have gold trim. Imported from Germany by Osborne's, Beeman.
**Price:** Polished (Osborne's) .................................. $1,200.00
**Price:** Matte finish (Osborne's).............................. $1,100.00
**Price:** From Beeman.......................... $1,046.00 to $2,050.00

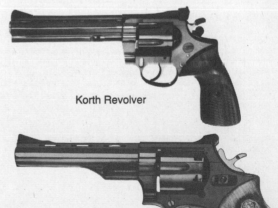

Korth Revolver

## LLAMA COMANCHE III REVOLVERS
**Caliber:** 357 Mag.
**Barrel:** 6″, 4″.
**Weight:** 28 oz. **Length:** 9¼″ (4″ bbl.).
**Stocks:** Checkered walnut.
**Sights:** Fixed blade front, rear adj. for w. & e.
**Features:** Ventilated rib, wide spur hammer. Satin chrome finish available. Imported from Spain by Stoeger Industries.
**Price:** Blue finish ........................................ $271.95
**Price:** Satin chrome........................................ $324.95

## Llama Super Comanche V Revolver
Similar to the Comanche except; large frame, 357 or 44 Mag., 4″, 6″ or 8½″ barrel only; 6-shot cylinder; smooth, extra wide trigger; wide spur hammer; over-size walnut, target-style grips. Weight is 3 lbs., 2 ozs. Blue finish only.
**Price:** 44 Mag. ........................................... $358.95
**Price:** 357 Mag. .......................................... $378.95

Llama Super Comanche

**CAUTION:** PRICES CHANGE. CHECK AT GUNSHOP.

## MANURHIN MR 73 SPORT REVOLVER
**Caliber:** 32 S&W Long, 357 Magnum, 6-shot.
**Barrel:** 5.25".
**Weight:** 37 oz. **Length:** 10.4" over-all.
**Stocks:** Checkered walnut.
**Sights:** Blade front, fully adjustable rear.
**Features:** Double action with adjustable trigger. High-polish blue finish, "Straw" colored hammer and trigger. Comes with sight adjusting tool. Imported from France by Manurhin International, Inc. Introduced 1984.
**Price:** ........................................................ **$750.00**

## ROSSI MODEL 68 REVOLVER
**Caliber:** 38 Spec.
**Barrel:** 2", 3".
**Weight:** 22 oz.
**Stocks:** Checkered wood.
**Sights:** Ramp front, low profile adj. rear.
**Features:** All-steel frame. Thumb latch operated swing-out cylinder. Introduced 1978. Imported from Brazil by Interarms.
**Price:** 38, blue .................................... **$150.00**
**Price:** M68/2 (2" barrel) ........................... **$160.00**

## ROSSI MODEL 88, 89 STAINLESS REVOLVERS
**Caliber:** 32 S&W, 38 Spec., 5-shot.
**Barrel:** 2", 3".
**Weight:** 22 oz. **Length:** 7.5" over-all.
**Stocks:** Checkered wood, service-style.
**Sights:** Ramp front, square notch rear drift adjustable for windage.
**Features:** All metal parts except springs are of 440 stainless steel; matte finish; small frame for concealability. Introduced 1983. Imported from Brazil by Interarms.
**Price:** 3" barrel ..................................... **$175.00**
**Price:** M88/2 (2" barrel) ........................... **$185.00**
**Price:** M89 (32 cal.) ............................... **$160.00**

## ROSSI SPORTSMAN'S 22 REVOLVER
**Caliber:** 22 LR, 6 shot.
**Barrel:** 4".
**Weight:** 30 oz. **Length:** 9" over-all.
**Stocks:** Checkered wood.
**Sights:** Orange-insert ramp front, fully adj. square notch rear.
**Features:** All stainless steel. Shrouded ejector rod; heavy barrel; integral sight rib. Introduced 1986. Imported from Brazil by Interarms.
**Price:** ........................................................ **$205.00**

## RUGER GP-100 REVOLVERS
**Caliber:** 357 Magnum, 6 shot.
**Barrel:** 4" (heavy), 6".
**Weight:** About 40 oz. **Length:** 9.3" over-all (4" bbl.).
**Stocks:** Ruger Cushioned Grip (live rubber with Goncalo Alves inserts).
**Sights:** Interchangeable front blade, fully adj. rear
**Features:** Uses all new action and frame incorporating improvements and features of both the Security-Six and Redhawk revolvers. Full length ejector shroud. Satin and polished blue finish. Introduced 1986.
**Price:** GP-141 (4" bbl.) ........................... **$375.00**
**Price:** GP-160 (6" bbl.) ........................... **$375.00**

## RUGER POLICE SERVICE-SIX 107, 108, 707, 708
**Caliber:** 357 (Model 107, 707), 38 Spec. (Model 108, 708), 6-shot.
**Barrel:** 2¾" or 4".
**Weight:** 33½ oz. (4" bbl.). **Length:** 9¼" (4 bbl.) over-all.
**Stocks:** Checkered rubber or Goncalo Alves.
**Sights:** Fixed, non-adjustable.
**Features:** Solid frame; barrel, rib and ejector rod housing combined in one unit. All steel construction Field strips without tools.
**Price:** Model 107 (357) 2¾" and 4" (SDA 32, SDA 34) ............. **$287.50**
**Price:** Model 108 (38) 4" (SDA 84) ........................... **$287.50**
**Price:** Mod. 707 (357), Stainless, 4", Goncalo Alves or rubber grips (GF 34, GF 34P) ............................................ **$310.00**
**Price:** Mod. 708 (38), Stainless, 4", Goncalo Alves or rubber grips (GF 84, GF 84P) ............................................ **$310.00**

Rossi Model 88 Stainless

Rossi Model 85 Stainless

## ROSSI MODEL 951 REVOLVER
**Caliber:** 38 Special, 6 shot.
**Barrel:** 4", vent. rib.
**Weight:** 30 oz. **Length:** 9" over-all.
**Stocks:** Checkered hardwood, combat-style.
**Sights:** Colored insert front, fully adjustable rear.
**Features:** Polished blue finish, shrouded ejector rod. Medium-size frame. Introduced 1985. Imported from Brazil by Interarms.
**Price:** M951 ....................................... **$200.00**
**Price:** M851 (as above, stainless) .................. **$220.00**
**Price:** M85 (as above, 3" barrel) .................. **$220.00**
**Price:** M941 (as above, solid rib) ................. **$185.00**
**Price:** M841 (as above, stainless steel) ........... **$205.00**
**Price:** M94 (3" barrel, solid rib) ................. **$185.00**

Ruger GP-100

Ruger Model 708

**CAUTION:** PRICES CHANGE. CHECK AT GUNSHOP.

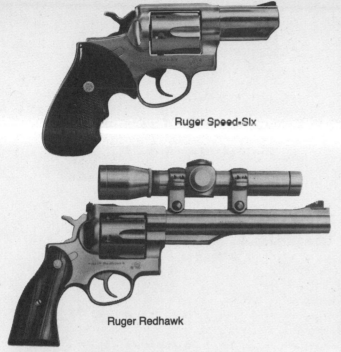

Ruger Speed-Six

Ruger Redhawk

### RUGER SPEED-SIX Models 207, 208, 737, 738
**Caliber:** 357 (Model 207), 38 Spec. (Model 208), 6-shot.
**Barrel:** 2¾" or 4".
**Weight:** 31 oz. (2¾" bbl.). **Length:** 7¾" over-all (2¾" bbl.).
**Stocks:** Goncalo Alves or checkered rubber with finger grooves.
**Sights:** Fixed, non-adjustable.
**Features:** Same basic mechanism as Security-Six. Hammer without spur available on special order. All steel construction. Music wire coil springs used throughout.
**Price:** Model 207, 357 Mag., 2¾", 4", Goncalo Alves or checkered rubber grips (SS 32, SS 32P, SS 34), ........................... $292.00
**Price:** Model 208, 38 Spec. only, 2¾", Goncalo Alves or checkered grips (SS 82)..................................... $292.00
**Price:** Mod. 737, 357 Mag., stainless, 2¾", 4", Goncalo Alves or checkered rubber grips (GS 32, GS 32P, GS 34)...................... $320.00
**Price:** Mod. 738, 38 Spec. only, stainless, 2¾", Goncalo Alves grips (GS 82)..................................... $320.00

### RUGER REDHAWK
**Caliber:** 41 Mag., 44 Rem. Mag., 6-shot.
**Barrel:** 5½", 7½".
**Weight:** About 54 oz. (7½" bbl.). **Length:** 13" over-all (7½" barrel).
**Stocks:** Square butt Goncalo Alves.
**Sights:** Interchangeable Patridge-type front, rear adj. for w. & e.
**Features:** Stainless steel, brushed satin finish, or blued ordnance steel. Has a 9½" sight radius. Introduced 1979.
**Price:** Blued, 41 Mag., 44 Mag., 5½", 7½" ..................... $397.00
**Price:** Blued, 41 Mag., 44 Mag., 7½", with scope mount, rings ...... $430.00
**Price:** Stainless, 41 Mag., 44 Mag., 5½", 7½" ..................... $435.00
**Price:** Stainless, 41 Mag., 44 Mag., 7½", with scope mount, rings ... $470.00

S&W Model 10-H.B.

### SMITH & WESSON M&P Model 10 REVOLVER
**Caliber:** 38 Special, 6 shot.
**Barrel:** 2".
**Weight:** 30½ oz. (4" bbl.). **Length:** 9¼" (4" bbl.).
**Stocks:** Checkered walnut, Service. Round or square butt.
**Sights:** Fixed, ramp front, square notch rear.
**Price:** Blued ..................................... $282.00
**Price:** Nickeled ................................. $303.00

### Smith & Wesson 38 M&P Heavy Barrel Model 10
Same as regular M&P except: 3" or 4" heavy ribbed bbl. with ramp front sight, square rear, square butt, wgt. 33½ oz.
**Price:** Blued ..................................... $282.00
**Price:** Nickeled ................................. $303.00

### SMITH & WESSON 38 M&P AIRWEIGHT Model 12
**Caliber:** 38 Special, 6 shot.
**Barrel:** 2" or 4".
**Weight:** 18 oz. (2" bbl.). **Length:** 6¹⁵⁄₁₆" over-all (2" bbl.).
**Stocks:** Checkered walnut, Magna. Round or square butt.
**Sights:** Fixed, serrated ramp front, square notch rear.
**Price:** Blued ..................................... $320.50

S&W Model 13

### SMITH & WESSON Model 13 H.B. M&P
**Caliber:** 357 and 38 Special, 6 shot.
**Barrel:** 3" or 4".
**Weight:** 34 oz. **Length:** 9⁵⁄₁₆" over-all (4" bbl.).
**Stocks:** Checkered walnut, service.
**Sights:** ⅛" serrated ramp front, fixed square notch rear.
**Features:** Heavy barrel, K-frame, square butt (4"), round butt (3").
**Price:** Blue, M-13............................... $282.00
**Price:** Nickel.................................. $303.00
**Price:** Model 65, as above in stainless steel ................ $305.00

### SMITH & WESSON MODEL 15 COMBAT MASTERPIECE
**Caliber:** 38 Special, 6 shot.
**Barrel:** 2", 4",6", 8⅜".
**Weight:** 32 oz. **Length:** 9⁵⁄₁₆" (4" bbl.).
**Stocks:** Checkered walnut. Grooved tangs.
**Sights:** Front, Baughman Quick Draw on ramp, micro click rear, adjustable for w. and e.
**Price:** Blued, M-15, 2" or 4" ........................ $321.00
**Price:** Nickel M-15, 2" or 4" ........................ $343.50

### SMITH & WESSON MODEL 17 K-22 MASTERPIECE
**Caliber:** 22 LR, 6-shot.
**Barrel:** 4", 6", 8⅜".
**Weight:** 39 oz. (6" bbl.). **Length:** 11⅛" over-all.
**Stocks:** Checkered walnut, service.
**Sights:** Patridge front with 6", 8⅜", serrated on 4", S&W micro. click rear adjustable for windage and elevation.
**Features:** Grooved tang, polished blue finish.
**Price:** 6".................................... $363.50
**Price:** 8¾" bbl. ............................. $376.00
**Price:** Model 48, as above in 22 Mag., 4" or 6" ................. $320.50
**Price:** 8⅜" bbl. ............................. $335.00

**SMITH & WESSON 357 COMBAT MAGNUM Model 19**
**Caliber:** 357 Magnum and 38 Special, 6 shot.
**Barrel:** 2½", 4", 6".
**Weight:** 36 oz. **Length:** 9⁹⁄₁₆" (4" bbl.).
**Stocks:** Checkered Goncalo Alves, target. Grooved tangs.
**Sights:** Front, ⅛" Baughman Quick Draw on 2½" or 4" bbl., Patridge on 6" bbl., micro click rear adjustable for w. and e.
**Price:** S&W Bright Blue or Nickel, adj. sights, from ............... $285.50

S&W Model 19

**SMITH & WESSON MODEL 25 REVOLVER**
**Caliber:** 45 Colt, 6-shot.
**Barrel:** 4", 6", 8⅜".
**Weight:** About 46 oz. **Length:** 11⅜" over-all (6" bbl.).
**Stocks:** Checkered Goncalo Alves, target-type.
**Sights:** S&W red ramp front, S&W micrometer click rear with white outline.
**Features:** Available in Bright Blue or nickel finish; target trigger, target hammer. Contact S&W for complete price list.
**Price:** 4", 6", blue or nickel ..................................... $371.50
**Price:** 8⅜". blue or nickel ...................................... $385.00

S&W Model 25

**SMITH & WESSON 357 MAGNUM M-27 REVOLVER**
**Caliber:** 357 Magnum and 38 Special, 6 shot.
**Barrel:** 4", 6", 8⅜".
**Weight:** 45½ oz. (6" bbl.). **Length:** 11⁵⁄₁₆" (6" bbl.).
**Stocks:** Checkered walnut, Magna. Grooved tangs and trigger.
**Sights:** Serrated ramp front, micro click rear, adjustable for w. and e.
**Price:** S&W Bright Blue or Nickel, 4", 6"......................... $350.00
**Price:** 8⅜" bbl., sq. butt, target hammer, trigger, stocks ............ $375.50

**SMITH & WESSON HIGHWAY PATROLMAN Model 28**
**Caliber:** 357 Magnum and 38 Special, 6 shot.
**Barrel:** 4", 6".
**Weight:** 44 oz. (6" bbl.). **Length:** 11¹⁄₁₆" (6" bbl.).
**Stocks:** Checkered walnut. Grooved tangs and trigger.
**Sights:** Front, Baughman Quick Draw, on ramp, micro click rear, adjustable for w. and e.
**Price:** S&W Satin Blue, sandblasted frame edging and barrel top ... $305.50
**Price:** With target stocks........................................ $327.00

S&W Model 29

**SMITH & WESSON 44 MAGNUM Model 29 REVOLVER**
**Caliber:** 44 Magnum, 44 Special or 44 Russian, 6 shot.
**Barrel:** 4", 6", 8⅜", 10⅝".
**Weight:** 47 oz. (6" bbl.), 44 oz. (4" bbl.). **Length:** 11⅜" (6½" bbl.).
**Stocks:** Oversize target type, checkered Goncalo Alves. Tangs and target trigger grooved, checkered target hammer.
**Sights:** ⅛" red ramp front, micro click rear, adjustable for w. and e.
**Features:** Includes presentation case.
**Price:** S&W Bright Blue or Nickel 4", 6" ......................... $409.00
**Price:** 8⅜" bbl., blue or nickel ................................. $423.50
**Price:** 10⅝", blue only (AF) .................................... $455.50
**Price:** Model 629 (stainless steel), 4", 6") ...................... $472.50
**Price:** Model 629, 8⅜" barrel .................................. $488.50

S&W Model 31

**SMITH & WESSON 32 REGULATION POLICE Model 31**
**Caliber:** 32 S&W Long, 6 shot.
**Barrel:** 2", 3".
**Weight:** 18¾ oz. (3" bbl.). **Length:** 7½" (3" bbl.).
**Stocks:** Checkered walnut, Magna.
**Sights:** Fixed, ¹⁄₁₀" serrated ramp front, square notch rear.
**Features:** Blued
**Price:** .................................................... $313.50

**SMITH & WESSON 1953 Model 34, 22/32 KIT GUN**
**Caliber:** 22 LR, 6 shot.
**Barrel:** 2", 4".
**Weight:** 24 oz. (4" bbl.). **Length:** 8⅜" (4" bbl. and round butt).
**Stocks:** Checkered walnut, round or square butt.
**Sights:** Front, serrated ramp, micro. click rear, adjustable for w. & e.
**Price:** Blued .............................................. $307.50
**Price:** Nickeled........................................... $332.50
**Price:** Model 63, as above in stainless, 4"................... $355.50

**Smith & Wesson Model 650/651 Magnum Kit Gun**
Similar to the Models 34 and 63 except chambered for the 22 WMR. Model 650 has 3" barrel, round butt and fixed sights; Model 651 has 4" barrel, square butt and adjustable sights. Both guns made of stainless steel. Introduced 1983.
**Price:** Model 650 ............................................. $305.00
**Price:** Model 651 ............................................. $345.00

## SMITH & WESSON BODYGUARD MODEL 38
**Caliber:** 38 Special; 5 shot, double action revolver.
**Barrel:** 2″.
**Weight:** 14½ oz. **Length:** 6⁵⁄₁₆″ over-all.
**Stocks:** Checkered walnut.
**Sights:** Fixed serrated ramp front, square notch rear.
**Features:** Alloy frame; internal hammer.
**Price:** Blued . . . . . . . . . . . . . . . . . . . . . . . . . . . . . . . . . . . $327.50
**Price:** Nickeled . . . . . . . . . . . . . . . . . . . . . . . . . . . . . . . . $368.00

## SMITH & WESSON 38 CHIEFS SPECIAL & AIRWEIGHT
**Caliber:** 38 Special, 5 shot.
**Barrel:** 2″, 3″.
**Weight:** 19½ oz. (2″ bbl.); 13½ oz. (AIRWEIGHT). **Length:** 6½″ (2″ bbl. and round butt).
**Stocks:** Checkered walnut, round or square butt.
**Sights:** Fixed, serrated ramp front, square notch rear.
**Price:** Blued, standard Model 36 . . . . . . . . . . . . . . . . . . . . . . $274.00
**Price:** As above, nickel . . . . . . . . . . . . . . . . . . . . . . . . . . . $296.00
**Price:** Blued, Airweight Model 37 . . . . . . . . . . . . . . . . . . . . $294.00
**Price:** As above, nickel . . . . . . . . . . . . . . . . . . . . . . . . . . . $331.00

## Smith & Wesson 60 Chiefs Special Stainless
Same as Model 36 except: 2″ bbl. and round butt only.
**Price:** Stainless steel . . . . . . . . . . . . . . . . . . . . . . . . . . . . $332.00

## Smith & Wesson Bodyguard Model 49, 649 Revolvers
Same as Model 38 except steel construction, weight 20½ oz.
**Price:** Blued, Model 49 . . . . . . . . . . . . . . . . . . . . . . . . . . . $292.00
**Price:** Nickeled, Model 49 . . . . . . . . . . . . . . . . . . . . . . . . . $316.50
**Price:** Stainless Model 649 . . . . . . . . . . . . . . . . . . . . . . . . . $346.00

## SMITH & WESSON 41 MAGNUM Model 57 REVOLVER
**Caliber:** 41 Magnum, 6 shot.
**Barrel:** 4″, 6″ or 8⅜″.
**Weight:** 48 oz. (6″ bbl.). **Length:** 11⅜″ (6″ bbl.).
**Stocks:** Oversize target type checkered Goncalo Alves.
**Sights:** ⅛″ red ramp front, micro. click rear, adj. for w. and e.
**Price:** S&W Bright Blue or Nickel 4″, 6″ . . . . . . . . . . . . . . . . $371.00
**Price:** 8⅜″ bbl. . . . . . . . . . . . . . . . . . . . . . . . . . . . . . . . . . $384.50
**Price:** Stainless, Model 657, 4″, 6″ . . . . . . . . . . . . . . . . . . . $422.50
**Price:** As above, 8⅜″ . . . . . . . . . . . . . . . . . . . . . . . . . . . . . $437.50

## SMITH & WESSON MODEL 64 STAINLESS M&P
**Caliber:** 38 Special, 6-shot.
**Barrel:** 4″.
**Weight:** 34 oz. **Length:** 9⁵⁄₁₆″ over-all.
**Stocks:** Checkered walnut, service style.
**Sights:** Fixed, ⅛″ serrated ramp front, square notch rear.
**Features:** Satin finished stainless steel, square butt.
**Price:** . . . . . . . . . . . . . . . . . . . . . . . . . . . . . . . . . . . . . . . $305.00

## SMITH & WESSON MODEL 66 STAINLESS COMBAT MAGNUM
**Caliber:** 357 Magnum and 38 Special, 6-shot.
**Barrel:** 2½″, 4″, 6″.
**Weight:** 36 oz. **Length:** 9⁹⁄₁₆″ over-all.
**Stocks:** Checkered Goncalo Alves target.
**Sights:** Front, Baughman Quick Draw on ramp, micro clock rear adj. for windage and elevation.
**Features:** Satin finish stainless steel.
**Price:** . . . . . . . . . . . . . . . . . . . . . . . . . . . . . . . . . . . . . . . $329.50

## SMITH & WESSON MODEL 67 K-38 STAINLESS COMBAT MASTERPIECE
**Caliber:** 38 Special, 6-shot.
**Barrel:** 4″.
**Weight:** 32 oz. (loaded). **Length:** 9⁵⁄₁₆″ over-all.
**Stocks:** Checkered walnut, service style.
**Sights:** Front, Baughman Quick Draw on ramp, micro click rear adj. for windage and elevation.
**Features:** Stainless steel. Square butt frame with grooved tangs.
**Price:** . . . . . . . . . . . . . . . . . . . . . . . . . . . . . . . . . . . . . . . $339.00

S&W Model 649

S&W Model 57

> Consult our Directory pages for the location of firms mentioned.

S&W Model 586

## SMITH & WESSON MODEL 586 Distinguished Combat Magnum
**Caliber:** 357 Magnum.
**Barrel:** 4″, 6″, 8⅜″, full shroud.
**Weight:** 46 oz. (6″), 41 oz. (4″).
**Stocks:** Goncalo Alves target-type with speed loader cutaway.
**Sights:** Baughman red ramp front, four-position click-adj. front, S&W microme- ter click rear (or fixed).
**Features:** Uses new L-frame, but takes all K-frame grips. Full length ejector rod shroud. Smooth combat-type trigger, semi-target type hammer. Trigger stop on 6″ models. Also available in stainless as Model 686. Introduced 1981.
**Price:** Model 586 (blue only) . . . . . . . . . . . . . . . . . . . . . . . $340.00
**Price:** Model 586, nickel . . . . . . . . . . . . . . . . . . . . . . . . . . $340.00
**Price:** Model 686 (stainless) . . . . . . . . . . . . . . . . . . . . . . . $374.00
**Price:** Model 581 (fixed sight, blue), 4″ . . . . . . . . . . . . . . . . $313.50
**Price:** Model 581, nickel . . . . . . . . . . . . . . . . . . . . . . . . . . $342.00
**Price:** Model 681 (fixed sight, stainless) . . . . . . . . . . . . . . . $324.00
**Price:** Model 586, 6″, adj. front sight, blue . . . . . . . . . . . . . . $392.00
**Price:** As above, 8⅜″ . . . . . . . . . . . . . . . . . . . . . . . . . . . . . $403.50
**Price:** Model 686, 6″, adj. front sight . . . . . . . . . . . . . . . . . . $413.50
**Price:** As above, 8⅜″ . . . . . . . . . . . . . . . . . . . . . . . . . . . . . $426.50

## SMITH & WESSON MODEL 624 REVOLVER
**Caliber:** 44 Special, 6 shot.
**Barrel:** 4" or 6½".
**Weight:** 41½ oz. (4" bbl.). **Length:** 9½" over-all (4" bbl.)
**Stocks:** Checkered Goncalo Alves, target-type.
**Sights:** Black ramp front, fully adjustable micrometer click rear adj. for w. & e.
**Features:** Limited production of 10,000 guns. Stainless version of the Model 24. The 6½" version has target hammer and trigger. Introduced 1985.
**Price:** 4" barrel ............................................. **$449.50**
**Price:** 6½" barrel ............................................ **$463.50**

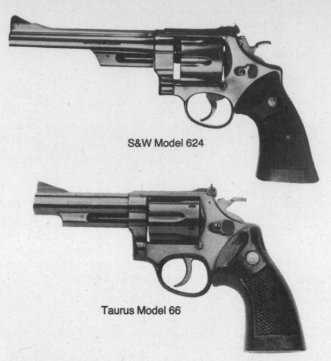

S&W Model 624

## TAURUS MODEL 66 REVOLVER
**Caliber:** 357 Magnum, 6-shot.
**Barrel:** 3", 4", 6".
**Weight:** 35 ozs.
**Stocks:** Checkered walnut, target-type. Standard stocks on 3".
**Sights:** Serrated ramp front, micro click rear adjustable for w. and e.
**Features:** Wide target-type hammer spur, floating firing pin, heavy barrel with shrouded ejector rod. Introduced 1978. From Taurus International.
**Price:** Blue. ................................................. **$220.15**
**Price:** Satin nickel ......................................... **$230.00**
**Price:** Model 65 (similar to M66 except has a fixed rear sight and ramp front), blue. ...................................................... **$204.50**
**Price:** Model 65, satin nickel ................................. **$215.00**

## TAURUS MODEL 73 SPORT REVOLVER
**Caliber:** 32 S&W Long, 6-shot.
**Barrel:** 3", heavy.
**Weight:** 22 oz. **Length:** 8¼" over-all.
**Stocks:** Oversize target-type, checkered Brazilian walnut.
**Sights:** Ramp front, notch rear.
**Features:** Imported from Brazil by Taurus International.
**Price:** Blue. ................................................. **$186.50**
**Price:** Satin nickel ......................................... **$202.80**

Taurus Model 66

Taurus Model 82

## TAURUS MODEL 80 STANDARD REVOLVER
**Caliber:** 38 Spec., 6-shot.
**Barrel:** 3" or 4".
**Weight:** 31 oz. (4" bbl.). **Length:** 9¼" over-all (4" bbl.).
**Stocks:** Checkered Brazilian walnut.
**Sights:** Serrated ramp front, square notch rear.
**Features:** Imported from Brazil by Taurus International.
**Price:** Blue. ................................................. **$180.50**
**Price:** Satin nickel ......................................... **$191.50**

## TAURUS MODEL 82 HEAVY BARREL REVOLVER
**Caliber:** 38 Spec., 6-shot.
**Barrel:** 3" or 4", heavy.
**Weight:** 33 oz. (4" bbl.). **Length:** 9¼" over-all (4" bbl.).
**Stocks:** Checkered Brazilian walnut.
**Sights:** Serrated ramp front, square notch rear.
**Features:** Imported from Brazil by Taurus International.
**Price:** Blue, about ........................................... **$180.50**
**Price:** Satin nickel, about .................................... **$191.5**

Taurus Model 83

## TAURUS MODEL 83 REVOLVER
**Caliber:** 38 Spec., 6-shot.
**Barrel:** 4" only, heavy.
**Weight:** 34½ oz.
**Stocks:** Over-size checkered walnut.
**Sights:** Ramp front, micro. click rear adj. for w. & e.
**Features:** Blue or nickel finish. Introduced 1977. Imported from Brazil by Taurus International.
**Price:** Blue. ................................................. **$190.00**
**Price:** Satin nickel ......................................... **$199.90**

## UBERTI "INSPECTOR" REVOLVER
**Caliber:** 32 S&W Long, 38 Spec., 6 shot.
**Barrel:** 3", 4", 6".
**Weight:** 24 oz. (3" bbl.). **Length:** 8" over-all (3" bbl.).
**Stocks:** Checkered walnut.
**Sights:** Blade on ramp front, fixed or adj. rear.
**Features:** Blue or chrome finish. Introduced 1986. Imported from Italy by Allen Fire Arms.
**Price:** Blue, fixed sights ..................................... **$279.00**
**Price:** Blue, adj. sights ...................................... **$289.00**
**Price:** Chrome, fixed sights ................................... **$289.00**
**Price:** Chrome, adj. sights .................................... **$309.00**

## TAURUS MODEL 85 REVOLVER
**Caliber:** 38 Spec., 5-shot.
**Barrel:** 2", 3".
**Weight:** 21 oz.
**Stocks:** Checkered walnut.
**Sights:** Ramp front, square notch rear.
**Features:** Blue, satin nickel finish or stainless steel. Introduced 1980. Imported from Brazil by Taurus International.
**Price:** Blue. ................................................. **$189.90**
**Price:** Satin nickel ......................................... **$204.00**
**Price:** Stainless steel. ...................................... **$240.90**

**CAUTION:** PRICES CHANGE. CHECK AT GUNSHOP.

## DAN WESSON MODEL 41V & MODEL 44V
**Caliber:** 41 Mag., 44 Mag., six-shot.
**Barrel:** 4″, 6″, 8″, 10″; interchangeable.
**Weight:** 48 oz. (4″). **Length:** 12″ over-all (6″ bbl.).
**Stocks:** Smooth.
**Sights:** ⅛″ serrated front, white outline rear adjustable for windage and elevation.
**Features:** Available in blue or stainless steel. Smooth, wide trigger with adjustable over-travel; wide hammer spur. Available in Pistol Pac set also.

| | |
|---|---|
| **Price:** 41 Mag., 4″, vent. | $373.40 |
| **Price:** As above except in stainless | $416.05 |
| **Price:** 44 Mag., 4″, blue. | $373.40 |
| **Price:** As above except in stainless | $416.05 |

Dan Wesson 44 Magnum

## Dan Wesson 9-2, 15-2 & 32M Revolvers
Same as Models 8-2 and 14-2 except they have adjustable sight. Model 9-2 chambered for 38 Special, Model 15-2 for 357 Magnum. Model 32M is chambered for 32 H&R Mag. Same specs and prices as for 15-2 guns. Available in blue or stainless. Contact Dan Wesson for complete price list.

| | |
|---|---|
| **Price:** Model 9-2 or 15-2, 2½″, blue | $272.50 |
| **Price:** As above except in stainless | $306.55 |
| **Price:** Model 15-2, 8″, blue. | $297.90 |
| **Price:** As above, with 15″ barrel, blue. | $365.25 |

Dan Wesson Model 32M

## DAN WESSON MODEL 22 REVOLVER
**Caliber:** 22 LR, 22 Mag., six-shot.
**Barrel:** 2½″, 4″, 6″, 8″, 10″; interchangeable.
**Weight:** 36 oz. (2½″), 44 oz. (6″). **Length:** 9¼″ over-all (4″ barrel).
**Stocks:** Checkered; undercover, service or over-size target.
**Sights:** ⅛″ serrated, interchangeable front, white outline rear adjustable for windage and elevation.
**Features:** Built on the same frame as the Dan Wesson 357; smooth, wide trigger with over-travel adjustment, wide spur hammer, with short double-action travel. Available in brite blue or stainless steel. Contact Dan Wesson for complete price list.

| | |
|---|---|
| **Price:** 2½″ bbl., blue | $272.50 |
| **Price:** As above, stainless | $306.55 |
| **Price:** With 4″, vent. rib, blue | $300.85 |
| **Price:** As above, stainless | $335.15 |
| **Price:** Stainless Pistol Pac, 22 LR. | $525.95 |

## DAN WESSON MODEL 8-2 & MODEL 14-2
**Caliber:** 38 Special (Model 8-2); 357 (14-2), both 6-shot.
**Barrel:** 2½″, 4″, 6″, 8″; interchangeable.
**Weight:** 30 oz. (2½″). **Length:** 9¼″ over-all (4″ bbl.).
**Stocks:** Checkered, interchangeable.
**Sights:** ⅛″ serrated front, fixed rear.
**Features:** Interchangeable barrels and grips; smooth, wide trigger; wide hammer spur with short double action travel. Available in stainless or brite blue. Contact Dan Wesson for complete price list.

| | |
|---|---|
| **Price:** Model 8-2, 2½″, blue | $220.75 |
| **Price:** As above except in stainless | $253.65 |
| **Price:** Model 14-2, 4″, blue. | $227.15 |
| **Price:** As above except in stainless | $259.20 |
| **Price:** Model 714-2 Pistol Pac, stainless | $430.65 |

# HANDGUNS—SINGLE ACTION REVOLVERS

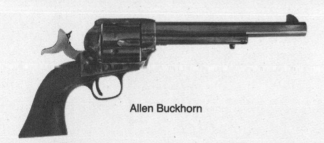

Allen Buckhorn

## ALLEN BUCKHORN SINGLE ACTION REVOLVERS
**Caliber:** 44 Magnum, 44-40, 6 shot.
**Barrel:** 4¾″, 6″, 7½″.
**Weight:** 44 oz. (6″ bbl.). **Length:** 11¾″ over-all (6″ bbl.).
**Stocks:** One-piece smooth walnut.
**Sights:** Blade front, groove rear.
**Features:** Steel or brass backstrap and trigger guard; color case-hardened frame, blued cylinder and barrel. Imported by Allen Fire Arms.

| | |
|---|---|
| **Price:** Fixed sights | $299.00 |
| **Price:** With convertible cylinder | $329.00 |
| **Price:** Target model (ramp front, adj. rear sights, flat-top frame) | $329.00 |
| **Price:** Convertible target model | $349.00 |
| **Price:** Buntline (18″ bbl.) | $349.00 |

## ALLEN CATTLEMAN SINGLE ACTION REVOLVERS
**Caliber:** 22 LR, 22 Mag., 38 Spec., 357 Mag., 44-40, 45 Colt, 6 shot.
**Barrel:** 4¾″, 5½″, 7½″.
**Weight:** 38 oz. (5½″ bbl.). **Length:** 10¾″ over-all (5½″ bbl.).
**Stocks:** One-piece smooth walnut.
**Sights:** Blade front, fixed groove rear.
**Features:** Steel or brass backstrap, trigger guard; color case-hardened frame, blued barrel, cylinder, polished hammer flats. Imported by Allen Fire Arms.

| | |
|---|---|
| **Price:** Fixed sights | $289.00 |
| **Price:** Target (flat-top frame, fully adj. rear sight) | $299.00 |
| **Price:** Buntline (18″ bbl., 357, 44-40, 45 Colt only) | $299.00 |
| **Price:** Sheriff's model (3″ bbl., 44-40) | $289.00 |

Allen Cattleman

**CAUTION:** PRICES CHANGE. CHECK AT GUNSHOP.

## ALLEN 1875 ARMY "OUTLAW" REVOLVER
**Caliber:** 357 Mag., 44-40, 45 Colt, 6 shot.
**Barrel:** 7½".
**Weight:** 44 oz. **Length:** 13¾" over-all.
**Stocks:** Smooth walnut.
**Sights:** Blade front, notch rear.
**Features:** Replica of the 1875 Remington S.A. Army revolver. Brass trigger guard, color case-hardened frame, rest blued. Imported by Allen Fire Arms.
**Price:** . . . . . . . . . . . . . . . . . . . . . . . . . . . . . . . . . . . . . . . . . **$279.00**

Century Model 100

## CENTURY MODEL 100 SINGLE ACTION
**Caliber:** 375 Win., 444 Marlin, 45-70.
**Barrel:** 6½", 8" (standard), 10", 12". Other lengths to order.
**Weight:** 6 lbs. (loaded). **Length:** 15" over-all (8" bbl.).
**Stocks:** Smooth walnut.
**Sights:** Ramp front, Millett adj. square notch rear.
**Features:** Highly polished high tensile strength manganese bronze frame, blue cylinder and barrel; coil spring trigger mechanism. Introduced 1975. Made in U.S. From Century Gun Dist., Inc.
**Price:** 8" barrel . . . . . . . . . . . . . . . . . . . . . . . . . . . . . . . **$600.00**
**Price:** 10", 12" barrel . . . . . . . . . . . . . . . . . . . . . . . . . . . **$665.00**

## COLT SINGLE ACTION ARMY REVOLVER
**Caliber:** 357 Magnum, 44 Spec., 44-40, or 45 Colt, 6 shot.
**Barrel:** 3", 4¾", 5½", 7½", 10", 12".
**Weight:** 37 oz. (5½" bbl.). **Length:** 10⅞" (5½" bbl.)
**Stocks:** Black composite rubber with eagle and shield crest.
**Sights:** Fixed. Grooved top strap, blade front.
**Features:** Blue with color case-hardened frame or all nickel with walnut stocks. Available in limited quantities through the Colt Custom Shop only.
**Price:** From . . . . . . . . . . . . . . . . . . . . . . . . . . . . . . . . . . . **$1,000.00**

## COLT NEW FRONTIER 22
**Caliber:** 22 LR, 6-shot.
**Barrel:** 4¾", 6", 7½".
**Weight:** 29½ oz. (4¾" bbl.). **Length:** 9½" over-all (4¾" bbl.).
**Stocks:** Black composite rubber.
**Sights:** Ramp-style front, fully adjustable rear.
**Features:** Cross-bolt safety. Available in blue only. Re-introduced 1982.
**Price:** 4¾", 6", 7½", blue . . . . . . . . . . . . . . . . . . . . . . . . . . . . . . **$180.95**

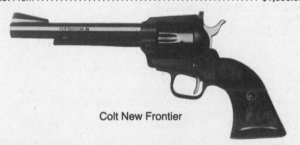
Colt New Frontier

Dakota Bisley

## DAKOTA BISLEY MODEL SINGLE ACTION
**Caliber:** 22 LR, 22 Mag., 32-30, 32 H&R mag., 357, 30 Carbine, 38-40, 44 Spec., 44-40, 45 Colt, 45 ACP.
**Barrel:** 4⅝", 5½", 7½".
**Weight:** 37 oz. **Length:** 10½" over-all with 5½" barrel.
**Stocks:** Smooth walnut.
**Sights:** Blade front, fixed groove rear.
**Features:** Colt-type firing pin in hammer; color case-hardened frame, blue barrel, cylinder, steel backstrap and trigger guard. Also avail. in nickel, factory engraved. Imported by E.M.F.
**Price:** All calibers, bbl. lengths. . . . . . . . . . . . . . . . . . . . . . . . . . **$495.00**
**Price:** Combo models — 22 LR/22 Mag., 32-20/32 H&R, 357/9mm, 44-40/44 Spec., 45 Colt/45 ACP . . . . . . . . . . . . . . . . . . . . . . . . . . . . . . **$560.00**
**Price:** Nickel, all cals. . . . . . . . . . . . . . . . . . . . . . . . . . . . . . . . . . **$540.00**
**Price:** Engraved, all cals., lengths . . . . . . . . . . . . . . . . . . . . . . . . . **$680.00**

## DAKOTA 1875 OUTLAW REVOLVER
**Caliber:** 357, 44-40, 45 Colt.
**Barrel:** 7½".
**Weight:** 46 oz. **Length:** 13½" over-all.
**Stocks:** Smooth walnut.
**Sights:** Blade front, fixed groove rear.
**Features:** Authentic copy of 1875 Remington with firing pin in hammer; color case-hardened frame, blue cylinder, barrel, steel backstrap and brass trigger guard. Also available in nickel, factory engraved. Imported by E.M.F.
**Price:** All calibers . . . . . . . . . . . . . . . . . . . . . . . . . . . . . . . . . . . **$395.00**
**Price:** Nickel . . . . . . . . . . . . . . . . . . . . . . . . . . . . . . . . . . . . . . . **$470.00**
**Price:** Engraved . . . . . . . . . . . . . . . . . . . . . . . . . . . . . . . . . . . . . **$600.00**

Dakota 1890 Police

## DAKOTA SINGLE ACTION REVOLVERS
**Caliber:** 22 LR, 22 Mag., 357 Mag., 30 Carbine, 32-20, 32 H&R Mag., 38-40, 44-40, 44 Spec., 45 Colt, 45 ACP.
**Barrel:** 3½", 4⅝", 5½", 7½", 12", 16¼".
**Weight:** 45 oz. **Length:** 13" over-all (7½" bbl.).
**Stocks:** Smooth walnut.
**Sights:** Blade front, fixed rear.
**Features:** Colt-type hammer with firing pin, color case-hardened frame, blue barrel and cylinder, brass grip frame and trigger guard. Available in blue or nickel plated, plain or engraved. Imported by E.M.F.
**Price:** 22 LR, 30 Car., 357, 44-40, 45 L.C., 4⅝", 5½", 7½" . . . . . . . . **$395.00**
**Price:** 22 LR/22 Mag., 45 Colt/45 ACP, 32-20/32 H&R, 357/9mm, 44-40/44 Spec., 5½", 7½" . . . . . . . . . . . . . . . . . . . . . . . . . . . . . . . . . . **$495.00**
**Price:** 357, 44-40, 45, 12" . . . . . . . . . . . . . . . . . . . . . . . . . . . . . . **$450.00**
**Price:** 357, 44-40, 45, 3½" . . . . . . . . . . . . . . . . . . . . . . . . . . . . . . **$495.00**

## Dakota 1890 Police Revolver
Similar to the 1875 Outlaw except has 5½" barrel, weighs 40 oz., with 12½" over-all length. Has lanyard ring in butt. Calibers 357, 44-40, 45 Colt. Imported by E.M.F.
**Price:** All calibers . . . . . . . . . . . . . . . . . . . . . . . . . . . . . . . . . . . **$425.00**
**Price:** Nickel . . . . . . . . . . . . . . . . . . . . . . . . . . . . . . . . . . . . . . . **$490.00**
**Price:** Engraved . . . . . . . . . . . . . . . . . . . . . . . . . . . . . . . . . . . . . **$625.00**

## F.I.E. "TEXAS RANGER" REVOLVER

**Caliber:** 22 LR, 22 Mag.
**Barrel:** 4¾", 6½", 9",.
**Weight:** 31 oz. (4¾" bbl.). **Length:** 10" over-all.
**Stocks:** American walnut.
**Sights:** Blade front, notch rear.
**Features:** Single-action, blue/black finish. Introduced 1983. Made in the U.S.
  by F.I.E.
**Price:** 22 LR, 4¾" ............................................ $69.95
**Price:** As above, convertible (22 LR/22 Mag.). ................... $86.95
**Price:** 22 LR, 6½" ............................................ $75.95
**Price:** As above, convertible (22 LR/22 Mag.). ................... $92.95
**Price:** 22 LR, 9" .............................................. $84.95
**Price:** As above, convertible (22 LR/22 Mag.) .................... $102.95

F.I.E. "Texas Ranger"

F.I.E. "Little Ranger"

## F.I.E. "Little Ranger" Revolver

Similar to the "Texas Ranger" except has 3¼" barrel, birdshead grips. Introduced 1986. Made in U.S.
**Price:** 22 LR ................................................. $75.95
**Price:** 22 LR/22 Mag. convertible .............................. $94.95

## F.I.E."HOMBRE" SINGLE ACTION REVOLVER

**Caliber:** 357 Mag., 44 Mag., 45 LC.
**Barrel:** 6" or 7½".
**Weight:** 45 oz. (6" bbl.).
**Stocks:** Smooth walnut with medallion.
**Sights:** Blade front, grooved topstrap (fixed) rear.
**Features:** Color case hardened frame. Bright blue finish. Super-smooth action.
  Introduced 1979. Imported from West Germany by F.I.E. Corp.
**Price:** 357, 45 Colt ........................................... $179.95
**Price:** 44 Mag. ............................................... $179.95
**Price:** 357, 45 Colt, brass backstrap and trigger guard ........... $199.95
**Price:** As above, 44 Magnum. ................................... $199.95
**Price:** 357, 45 Colt, 24K gold plated ........................... $229.95
**Price:** As above, 44 Magnum. ................................... $229.95

F.I.E. "Hombre"

F.I.E. "Buffalo Scout"

## F.I.E. "BUFFALO SCOUT" REVOLVER

**Caliber:** 22 LR/22 Mag.
**Barrel:** 4¾".
**Weight:** 32 oz. **Length:** 10" over-all.
**Stocks:** Black checkered nylon, walnut optional.
**Sights:** Blade front, fixed rear.
**Features:** Slide spring ejector. Blue, chrome, gold or blue with gold backstrap
  and trigger guard models available.
**Price:** Blued, 22 LR, 4¾" ...................................... $62.95
**Price:** Blue, 22 convertible, 4¾" ............................... $79.95
**Price:** Chrome or blue/gold, 22 LR, 4¾" ......................... $74.95
**Price:** Chrome or blue/gold, convertible, 4¾" .................... $91.95
**Price:** Gold, 22 convertible, 4¾" ............................... $124.95

Freedom Arms 454 Casull

Freedom Arms Mini Revolver

## FREEDOM ARMS 454 CASULL

**Caliber:** 44 Mag., 45 Colt, 454 Casull, 5-shot.
**Barrel:** 4¾", 6", 7½", 10", 12".
**Weight:** 50 oz. **Length:** 14" over-all (7½" bbl.).
**Stocks:** Impregnated hardwood.
**Sights:** Blade front, notch or adjustable rear.
**Features:** All stainless steel construction; sliding bar safety system. Made in
  U.S.A.
**Price:** Fixed sight ........................................... $795.00
**Price:** Adjustable sight ....................................... $895.00

## FREEDOM ARMS MINI REVOLVER

**Caliber:** 22 Short, Long, Long Rifle, 5-shot, 22 Mag., 4-shot.
**Barrel:** 1",1¾", 3".
**Weight:** 4 oz. **Length:** 4" over-all.
**Stocks:** Black ebonite.
**Sights:** Blade front, notch rear.
**Features:** Made of stainless steel, simple take down; half-cock safety; floating
  firing pin; cartridge rims recessed in cylinder. Comes in gun rug. Lifetime
  warranty. Also available in percussion — see black powder section. From
  Freedom Arms.
**Price:** 22 LR, 1" barrel ....................................... $105.35
**Price:** 22 LR, 1¾" barrel ...................................... $105.35
**Price:** 22 LR, 3" barrel ....................................... $118.70
**Price:** 22 Mag., 1" barrel ..................................... $124.00
**Price:** 22 Mag., 1¾" barrel .................................... $124.00
**Price:** 22 Mag., 3" barrel ..................................... $137.35

### Freedom Arms Boot Gun

Similar to the Mini Revolver except has 3″ barrel, weighs 5 oz. and is 5⅞″ over-all. Has over-size grips, floating firing pin. Made of stainless steel. Lifetime warranty. Comes in rectangular gun rug. Introduced 1982. From Freedom Arms.
**Price:** 22 LR ................................................................ **$118.70**
**Price:** 22 Mag. ............................................................. **$137.35**

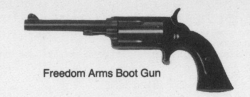

Freedom Arms Boot Gun

### MITCHELL SINGLE ACTION ARMY REVOLVERS

**Caliber:** 22 LR, 357 Mag., 44 Mag., 45 Colt, 6 shot.
**Barrel:** 4¾″, 5½″, 6″, 6½″, 7½″, 10″, 12″, 18″.
**Weight:** NA. **Length:** NA.
**Stocks:** One-piece walnut.
**Sights:** Serrated ramp front, fixed or adjustable rear.
**Features:** Color case-hardened frame, brass backstrap, balance blued; hammer block safety. Stainless steel and dual cylinder models available. Imported by Mitchell Arms.
**Price:** Fixed sight, 22 LR, 4¾″, 5½″, 7½″ ........................ **$259.95**
**Price:** As above, 357, 45 ......................................... **$264.95**
**Price:** As above, 44 Mag. ......................................... **$269.95**
**Price:** Adjustable sight, 22 LR, 4¾″, 5½″, 7½″ ................. **$265.00**
**Price:** As above, 357, 45 ......................................... **$279.95**
**Price:** As above, 44 Mag. ......................................... **$284.95**
**Price:** Stainless steel, 22 LR, 4¾″, 5½″, 7½″ ................. **$299.00**
**Price:** As above, 357 Mag. ....................................... **$319.95**
**Price:** 44 Mag./44-40, dual cylinder, 4¾″, 6″, 7½″ .......... **$319.95**
**Price:** 22 LR/22 Mag., dual cylinder, 4¾″, 5½″, 7½″ ........ **$275.00**
**Price:** Silhouette Model, 44 Mag., 10″, 12″, 18″ ............... **$299.95**

North American Mini

Phelps Heritage I

Ruger N.M. Blackhawk

### NORTH AMERICAN 450 MAGNUM EXPRESS

**Caliber:** 450 Magnum Express, 45 Win. Mag., 5 shot.
**Barrel:** 7½″, 10½″.
**Weight:** 52 oz. (7½″ bbl.). **Length:** 13½″ (7½″ bbl.).
**Stocks:** Smooth walnut.
**Sights:** Blade front, fully adj. rear.
**Features:** All stainless steel construction. Patented hammer safety. Factory 450 Mag. Exp. ammo available. From North American Arms.
**Price:** Either caliber ............................................ **$1,069.40**

### NORTH AMERICAN MINI-REVOLVERS

**Caliber:** 22 S, 22 LR, 22 Mag., 5 shot.
**Barrel:** 1⅛″, 1⅝″, 2½″.
**Weight:** 4 oz.
**Stocks:** Laminated wood.
**Sights:** Blade front, notch fixed rear.
**Features:** All stainless steel construction. Polished satin and matte finish. From North American Arms.
**Price:** 22 Short, 1⅛″ bbl. ....................................... **$119.95**
**Price:** 22 LR, 1⅛″ bbl. ........................................... **$123.95**
**Price:** 22 LR, 1⅝″ bbl. ........................................... **$124.95**
**Price:** 22 Mag., 1⅝″ bbl. ........................................ **$139.95**
**Price:** 22 Mag., 2½″ bbl. ........................................ **$142.95**

### PHELPS HERITAGE I, EAGLE I REVOLVERS

**Caliber:** 444 Marlin, 45-70, 6-shot.
**Barrel:** 8″ or 12″.
**Weight:** 5½ lbs. **Length:** 19½″ over-all (12″ bbl.).
**Stocks:** Smooth walnut.
**Sights:** Ramp front, adjustable rear.
**Features:** Single action; polished blue finish; safety bar. From E. Phelps Mfg. Co.
**Price:** Heritage I (45-70), Eagle I (444 Marlin) 8″ barrel ............ **$650.00**
**Price:** As above, 12″ barrel. ..................................... **$675.00**

### RUGER NEW MODEL SUPER BLACKHAWK

**Caliber:** 44 Magnum, 6-shot. Also fires 44 Spec.
**Barrel:** 7½″ (6-groove, 20″ twist), 10½″.
**Weight:** 48 oz. (7½″ bbl.) 51 oz. (10½″ bbl.). **Length:** 13⅜″ over-all (7½″ bbl.).
**Stocks:** Genuine American walnut.
**Sights:** ⅛″ ramp front, micro click rear adj. for w. and e.
**Features:** New Ruger interlocked mechanism, non-fluted cylinder, steel grip and cylinder frame, square back trigger guard, wide serrated trigger and wide spur hammer.
**Price:** Blue (S-47N, S-411N) ..................................... **$276.00**
**Price:** Stainless (KS-47N, KS-411N) ........................... **$325.00**

### RUGER NEW MODEL BLACKHAWK REVOLVER

**Caliber:** 30 Carbine, 38 Special, 357 or 41 Mag., 45 Colt, 6-shot.
**Barrel:** 4⅝″ or 6½″, either caliber, 7½″ (30 Carbine, 45 Colt only).
**Weight:** 42 oz. (6½″ bbl.). **Length:** 12¼″ over-all (6½″ bbl.).
**Stocks:** American walnut.
**Sights:** ⅛″ ramp front, micro click rear adj. for w. and e.
**Features:** New Ruger interlocked mechanism, independent firing pin, hardened chrome-moly steel frame, music wire springs throughout.
**Price:** Blue, 30 Carbine (7½″), 357 Mag. (4⅝″, 6½″) .............. **$247.75**
**Price:** Blue, 357/9mm (4⅝″, 6½″) ............................... **$260.00**
**Price:** Stainless, 357 (4⅝″, 6½″) ............................... **$307.50**
**Price:** Blue, 41 Mag. (4⅝″, 6½″), 45 Colt (4⅝″, .7½″) .............. **$247.75**

**CAUTION:** PRICES CHANGE. CHECK AT GUNSHOP.

# HANDGUNS—SINGLE ACTION REVOLVERS

Ruger N.M. Bisley Blackhawk

Ruger Super Single-Six

## Ruger Small Frame New Model Bisley Single-Six

Similar to the New Model Single-Six except frame is styled after the classic Bisley "flat-top." Most mechanical parts are unchanged. Hammer is lower and smoothly curved with a deeply checkered spur. Trigger is strongly curved with a wide smooth surface. Longer grip frame designed with a hand-filling shape, and the trigger guard is a large oval. Dovetail rear sight drift-adjustable for windage; front sight base accepts interchangeable square blades of various heights and styles. Weight about 41 oz. Chambered for 22 LR and 32 H&R Mag., 6½" barrel only. Introduced 1985.
**Price:** ........................................ **$258.00**

## Ruger New Model Single-Six Revolver

Similar to the Super Single-Six revolver except chambered for 32 H&R Magnum (also handles 32 S&W and 32 S&W Long). Weight is about 34 oz. with 6½" barrel. Same barrel lengths as Super Single-Six. Introduced 1985.
**Price:** ........................................ **$212.00**

## SEVILLE SUPER MAG SINGLE ACTION

**Caliber:** 357 Maximum, 375 Super Magnum, 6-shot.
**Barrel:** 7½" (standard), 5½", 6½", 10½" optional.
**Weight:** 52 oz. **Length:** 14" over-all.
**Stocks:** Smooth walnut.
**Sights:** Flourescent insert ramp front, micro. adj. rear. Fixed sights available.
**Features:** Made of 17-4 PH stainless steel; coil spring action; floating Beryllium copper firing pin, trigger spring; hand-fitted action; brushed satin finish standard, others available. From United Sporting Arms, Inc.
**Price:** 357 Maximum. ........................... **$546.00**
**Price:** 375 Super Mag. ......................... **$568.00**

## TEXAS LONGHORN RIGHT HAND SINGLE ACTION

**Caliber:** All centerfire pistol calibers.
**Barrel:** 4¾".
**Weight:** NA. **Length:** NA.
**Stocks:** One-piece fancy walnut, or any fancy AAA wood.
**Sights:** Blade front, grooved top-strap rear.
**Features:** Loading gate and ejector housing on left side of gun. Cylinder rotates to the left. All steel construction; color case-hardened frame; high polish blue; music wire coil springs. Lifetime guarantee to original owner. Introduced 1984. From Texas Longhorn Arms.
**Price:** South Texas Army Limited Edition — hand-made, only 1,000 to be produced; "One of One Thousand" engraved on barrel; comes with glass-covered display case ............................... **$1,500.00**

## Texas Longhorn Sesquicentennial Model Revolver

Similar to the South Texas Army Model except has ¾-coverage Nimschke-style engraving, antique golden nickel plate finish, one-piece elephant ivory grips. Comes with hand-made solid walnut presentation case, factory letter to owner. Limited edition of 150 units. Introduced 1986.
**Price:** ........................................ **$2,500.00**

## Ruger New Model Bisley Blackhawk

Similar to standard New Model Blackhawk except the hammer is lower with a smoothly curved, deeply checkered wide spur, the trigger is strongly curved with a wide smooth surface. Longer grip frame has a hand-filling shape. Adjustable rear sight, ramp-style front. Cylinder is unflutted and is roll-marked with a classic foliate engraving pattern and depiction of the old time Bisley marksman and a Bisley trophy. Chambered for 357, 41, 44 Mags. and 45 Colt; 7½" barrel; over-all length of 13". Introduced 1985.
**Price:** ........................................ **$307.00**

## RUGER NEW MODEL SUPER SINGLE-SIX CONVERTIBLE REVOLVER

**Caliber:** 22 LR, 6-shot; 22 Mag. in extra cylinder (stainless model only).
**Barrel:** 4⅝", 5½", 6½" or 9½" (6-groove).
**Weight:** 34½ oz. (6½" bbl.). **Length:** 11¹³⁄₁₆" over-all (6½" bbl.).
**Stocks:** Smooth American walnut.
**Sights:** Improved Patridge front on ramp, fully adj. rear protected by integral frame ribs.
**Features:** New Ruger "interlocked" mechanism, transfer bar ignition, gate-controlled loading, hardened chrome-moly steel frame, wide trigger, music wire springs throughout, independent firing pin.
**Price:** 4⅝", 5½", 6½", 9½" barrel ................. **$207.00**
**Price:** 5½", 6½" bbl. only, stainless steel (convertible) ........... **$278.00**

Ruger Bisley Single-Six

Seville Single Action

## TANARMI S.A. REVOLVER MODEL TA76

**Caliber:** 22 LR, 22 Mag., 6-shot.
**Barrel:** 4¾".
**Weight:** 32 oz. **Length:** 10" over-all.
**Stocks:** Walnut.
**Sights:** Blade front, rear adj. for w. & e.
**Features:** Manual hammer block safety; color hardened steel frame; brass backstrap and trigger guard. Imported from Italy by Excam.
**Price:** 22 LR, blue ............................ **$60.00**
**Price:** Combo, blue ........................... **$79.00**
**Price:** 22 LR, chrome.......................... **$77.00**
**Price:** Combo, chrome ......................... **$92.00**

Texas Longhorn South Texas Army

## Texas Longhorn Arms Texas Border Special
Similar to the South Texas Army Limited Edition except has 3½″ barrel, birds-head style grip. Same special features, display case. Introduced 1984.
**Price:** ...................................................... $1,500.00

Texas Longhorn Flat Top

## Texas Longhorn Arms Cased Set
Set contains one each of the Texas Longhorn Right-Hand Single Actions, all in the same caliber, same serial numbers (100, 200, 300, 400, 500, 600, 700, 800, 900). Ten sets to be made (#1000 donated to NRA museum). Comes in hand-tooled leather case. All other specs same as Limited Edition guns. Introduced 1984.
**Price:** ...................................................... $5,750.00
**Price:** With ¾-coverage "C-style" engraving.................... $7,650.00

## Texas Longhorn Arms West Texas Flat Top Target
Similar to the South Texas Army Limited Edition except choice of barrel length from 7½″ through 15″; flat-top style frame; ⅛″ contoured ramp front sight, old model steel micro-click rear adjustable for w. and e. Same special features, display case. Introduced 1984.
**Price:** ...................................................... $1,500.00

Texas Longhorn Flat Top

Virginian Dragoon

## THE VIRGINIAN DRAGOON REVOLVER
**Caliber:** 44 Mag.
**Barrel:** 6″, 7½″, 8⅜″.
**Weight:** 50 oz. (6″ barrel). **Length:** 10″ over-all (6″ barrel).
**Stocks:** Smooth walnut.
**Sights:** Ramp-type Patridge front blade, micro. adj. target rear.
**Features:** Color case-hardened frame, spring-loaded floating firing pin, coil main spring. Firing pin is lock-fitted with a steel bushing. Introduced 1977. Made in the U.S. by Interarms Industries, Inc.
**Price:** 6″, 7½″, 8⅜″, blue...................................... $295.00
**Price:** 44 Mag., 6″, 7½″, 8⅜″, stainless ......................... $295.00
**Price:** 44 Mag., 7½″, 8⅜″, 10½″ Sil. model .................... $425.00

## Virginian Dragoon Engraved Models
Same gun as the standard Dragoon except offered only in 44 Mag. 6″ or 7½″ barrel; choice of fluted or unfluted cylinder, stainless or blued. Hand-engraved frame, cylinder and barrel. Each gun comes in a felt-lined walnut presentation case. Introduced 1983.
**Price:** ...................................................... $625.00

## Virginian Dragoon "Deputy" Model
Similar to the standard Dragoon except comes with traditional fixed sights, blue or stainless, in 357. (5″ barrel), 44 Mag. (6″ barrel). Introduced 1983.
**Price:** ...................................................... $295.00

## VIRGINIAN 22 CONVERTIBLE REVOLVERS
**Caliber:** 22 LR, 22 Mag.
**Barrel:** 5½″.
**Weight:** 38 oz. **Length:** 10¾″ over-all.
**Stocks:** Smooth walnut.
**Sights:** Ramp-type Patridge front, open fully adjustable rear.
**Features:** Smaller version of the big-bore Dragoon revolvers; comes with both Long Rifle and Magnum cylinders, the latter unfluted; color case-hardened frame, rest blued. Introduced 1983. Made by Uberti; imported from Italy by Interarms.
**Price:** Blue, with two cylinders................................... $219.00
**Price:** Stainless with two cylinders ............................. $239.00

Virginian 22 Convertible

# HANDGUNS—MISCELLANEOUS

## ALLEN ROLLING BLOCK PISTOL
**Caliber:** 22 LR, 22 Mag., 357 Mag., single shot.
**Barrel:** 9⅞″, half round, half octagon.
**Weight:** 44 oz. **Length:** 14″ over-all.
**Stocks:** Walnut grip and fore-end.
**Sights:** Blade front, fully adj. rear.
**Features:** Replica of the 1891 rolling block target pistol. Brass trigger guard, color case-hardened frame, blue barrel. Imported by Allen Fire Arms.
**Price:** ...................................................... $229.00

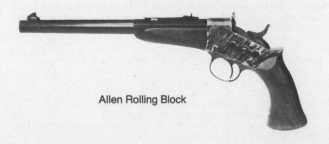

Allen Rolling Block

**CAUTION:** PRICES CHANGE. CHECK AT GUNSHOP.

American Derringer Model 1

## AMERICAN DERRINGER MODEL 3
**Caliber:** 38 Special.
**Barrel:** 2.5".
**Weight:** 8.5 oz. **Length:** 4.9" over-all.
**Stocks:** Rosewood.
**Sights:** Blade front.
**Features:** Made of stainless steel. Single shot with manual hammer block safety. Introduced 1985. From American Derringer Corp.
**Price:** ..................................................... $115.00

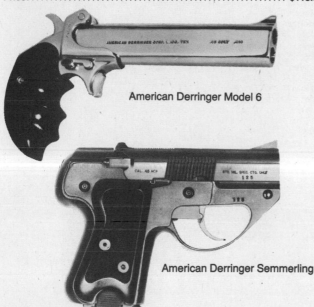

American Derringer Model 6

American Derringer Semmerling

## ARM TECH. DERRINGER
**Caliber:** 22 LR, 22 Mag., 4-shot.
**Barrel:** 2.6".
**Weight:** 19 ozs. **Length:** 4.6" over-all.
**Stocks:** Hard rubber or walnut, checkered or smooth.
**Sights:** Fixed, non-snagging.
**Features:** Four barrels with 90° rotating indexing firing pin system. All stainless steel parts. Double-action only. Blued model available. Introduced 1983. From Armament Technologies Inc.
**Price:** Stainless, 22 LR, rubber grips ......................... $184.50
**Price:** As above, 22 Mag. .................................... $189.00
**Price:** Blued, 22 LR, walnut grips .......................... $174.50
**Price:** As above, 22 Mag. .................................... $179.00

## BAFORD ARMS THUNDER DERRINGER
**Caliber:** 410 2½" and 44 Spec. with insert sleeves for 22 S, LR, 22 Mag., 25 ACP, 32 ACP, 32 H&R Mag., 30 Luger, 380 ACP, 38 Super, 38 Spec., 38 S&W, 9mm.
**Barrel:** Various lengths according to caliber.
**Weight:** 8½ oz. **Length:** 5⅞" over-all.
**Stocks:** Smooth walnut.
**Sights:** None. Scope and mount available.
**Features:** Side-swinging barrel with positive lock and half-cock safety. Blued steel frame, barrel, polished stainless hammer, trigger. Introduced 1986.
**Price:** Base gun in 410, 44 Special ........................... $169.95
**Price:** Extra barrel inserts to change caliber, each ............ $29.95

## AMERICAN DERRINGER MODEL 1
**Caliber:** 22 LR, 22 Mag., 22 Hornet, 223 Rem., 30 Luger, 30-30 Win., 32 ACP, 38 Super, 380 ACP, 38 Spec., 9 × 18, 9mm Para., 357 Mag., 41 Mag., 44-40 Win., 44 Spec., 44 Mag., 45 Colt, 45 ACP, 410-ga. (2½").
**Barrel:** 3".
**Weight:** 15½ oz. (38 Spec.). **Length:** 4.82" over-all.
**Stocks:** Rosewood, Zebra wood.
**Sights:** Blade front.
**Features:** Made of stainless steel with high-polish or satin finish. Two shot capacity. Manual hammer block safety. Introduced 1980. Contact the factory for complete list of available calibers and prices. From American Derringer Corp.
**Price:** 22 LR or Mag. ...................................... $212.00
**Price:** 223 Rem. ........................................... $369.00
**Price:** 38 Spec. ........................................... $187.50
**Price:** 357 Mag. ........................................... $225.00
**Price:** 9mm, 380. .......................................... $172.50
**Price:** 44 Spec. ........................................... $275.00
**Price:** 44-40 Win., 45 Colt ................................. $275.00
**Price:** 41, 44 Mags. ....................................... $369.00
**Price:** Lightweight (7½ oz.) Model 7, 38 Spec., 38 S&W, 380, 22 LR only ................................................ $199.00
**Price:** 45-70 (as above), single shot. ...................... $369.00
**Price:** 45 Colt, 410, 2½" .................................. $312.00
**Price:** 45 ACP. ............................................ $218.00

## American Derringer Model 4
Similar to the Model 1 except has 4.1" barrel, over-all length of 6", and weighs 16½ oz.; chambered for 3" 410-ga. shotshells or 45 Colt. Can be had with 45-70 upper barrel and 3" 410-ga. or 45 Colt bottom barrel. Made of stainless steel. Manual hammer block safety. Introduced 1985.
**Price:** 3" 410/45 Colt (either barrel) ...................... $359.00
**Price:** 3" 410/45 Colt or 45-70 (Alaskan Survival model) ........... $369.00

## American Derringer Model 6
Similar to the Model 1 except has 6" barrels chambered for 3" 410 shotshells or 45 Colt, rosewood stocks, 8.2" o.a.l. and weighs 21 oz. Shoots either round for each barrel. Manual hammer block safety. Introduced 1986.
**Price:** .................................................... $375.00

## American Derringer Model 7
Similar to Model 1 except made of high strength aircraft aluminum. Weighs 7½ oz., 4.82" o.a.l., rosewood stocks. Available in 22 LR, 32 S&W Long, 32 H&R Mag., 380 ACP, 38 S&W, 38 Spec., 44 Spec. Introduced 1986.
**Price:** 22 LR or 38 Spec. .................................. $187.50
**Price:** 38 S&W, 380 ACP, 32 S&W Long ....................... $157.50
**Price:** 32 H&R Mag. ........................................ $172.50
**Price:** 44 Spec. ........................................... $500.00

## AMERICAN DERRINGER SEMMERLING LM-4
**Caliber:** 9mm Para., 7-shot magazine, or 45 ACP, 5-shot magazine.
**Barrel:** 3.625".
**Weight:** 24 oz. **Length:** 5.2" over-all.
**Stocks:** Checkered plastic on blued guns, rosewood on stainless guns.
**Sights:** Open, fixed.
**Features:** Manually-operated repeater. Height is 3.7", width is 1". Comes with manual, leather carrying case, spare stock screws, wrench. From American Derringer Corp.
**Price:** Blued. .............................................. $1,250.00
**Price:** Stainless steel ..................................... $1,650.00

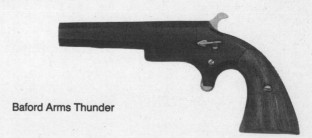

Baford Arms Thunder

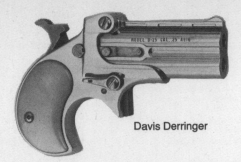

Davis Derringer

F.I.E. Model D-86

## GUNWORKS MODEL 9 DERRINGER
**Caliber:** 38/357 Mag., 9mm/9mm Mag.
**Barrel:** 3"; button rifled, bottom hinged.
**Weight:** 15 oz.
**Stocks:** Smooth wood.
**Sights:** Millett blaze orange bar front, fixed rear.
**Features:** All steel; half-cock, through-frame safety; dual extraction; electroless nickel finish; comes with in-pant holster. Made in U.S. by Gunworks, Ltd.
**Price:** ..................................................... **$148.50**

## LJUTIC LJ II PISTOL
**Caliber:** 22 Magnum.
**Barrel:** 2¾".
**Stocks:** Checkered walnut.
**Sights:** Fixed.
**Features:** Stainless steel; double action; ventilated rib; side-by-side barrels; positive on/off safety. Introduced 1981. From Ljutic Industries.
**Price:** ..................................................... **$799.00**

Ljutic Space Pistol

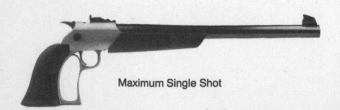

Maximum Single Shot

## C. O. P. 357 MAGNUM
**Caliber:** 38/357 Mag., 4 shots.
**Barrel:** 3¼".
**Weight:** 28 oz. **Length:** 5.5" over-all.
**Stocks:** Checkered composition.
**Sights:** Open, fixed.
**Features:** Double-action, 4 barrels, made of stainless steel. Width is only one inch, height 4.1". From M & N Distributors.
**Price:** About ........................................... **$250.00**
**Price:** In 22 Mag. ...................................... **$250.00**
**Price:** In 22 LR (blued, aluminum frame) ........................ **$229.95**

## DAVIS DERRINGERS
**Caliber:** 22 LR, 22 Mag., 25 ACP, 32 ACP.
**Barrel:** 2.4".
**Weight:** 9.5 oz. **Length:** 4" over-all.
**Stocks:** Laminated wood.
**Sights:** Blade front, fixed notch rear.
**Features:** Choice of black Teflon or chrome finish; spur trigger. Introduced 1986. Made in U.S. by Davis Industries.
**Price:** ..................................................... **$64.90**

## F.I.E. MODEL D-86 DERRINGER
**Caliber:** 38 Special.
**Barrel:** 3".
**Weight:** 14 oz.
**Stocks:** Checkered black nylon, walnut optional.
**Sights:** Fixed.
**Features:** Dyna-Chrome finish. Spur trigger. Tip-up barrel, extractors. Made in U.S. by F.I.E. Corp.
**Price:** With nylon grips ........................................ **$104.95**
**Price:** With walnut grips ...................................... **$124.95**

Gunworks Model 9

## LJUTIC RECOILESS SPACE PISTOL
**Caliber:** 22 Mag., 357 Mag., 44 Mag., 308 Win.; single shot.
**Barrel:** 13½".
**Weight:** 5 lbs. (with scope).
**Stocks:** Walnut grip and fore-end.
**Sights:** Scope mounts extra.
**Features:** Twist-bolt action; button trigger. From Ljutic Industries.
**Price:** ..................................................... **$995.00**

## MAXIMUM SINGLE SHOT PISTOL
**Caliber:** 22 Hornet, 223 Rem., 22-250, 6mm BR, 6mm-223, 243, 250 Savage, 6.5mm-35, 7mm TCU, 7mm BR, 7mm-35, 7mm INT-R, 7mm-08, 30 Herrett, 308 Win., 357 Mag., 358 Win., 44 Mag.
**Barrel:** 10½", 14".
**Weight:** 61 oz. (10½" bbl.), 78 oz. (14" bbl.). **Length:** 15", 18½" over-all (with 10½" and 14" bbl., respectively).
**Stocks:** Smooth walnut stocks and fore-end.
**Sights:** Ramp front, fully adjustable open rear.
**Features:** Falling block action; drilled and tapped for most popular scope mounts; integral grip frame/receiver; adjustable trigger; Douglas barrel (interchangeable); Armoloy finish. Introduced 1983. Made in U.S. by M.O.A. Corp.
**Price:** Either barrel length ................................... **$499.00**
**Price:** Extra barrel ......................................... **$129.00**
**Price:** Scope mount ......................................... **$39.00**

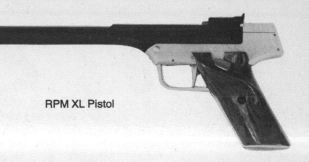

RPM XL Pistol

## RPM XL SINGLE SHOT PISTOL
**Caliber:** 22 LR, 22 Mag., 225 Win., 25 Rocket, 6.5 Rocket, 32 H&R Mag., 357 Max., 357 Mag., 30-30 Win., 30 Herrett, 357 Herrett, 41 Mag., 44 Mag., 375 Win., 7mm Merrill, 30 Merrill, 7mm Rocket, 270 Rocket, 45-70.
**Barrel:** 9″ or 10¾″, 14″; .450″ wide vent. rib, matted to prevent glare.
**Weight:** About 54 oz. **Length:** 12¼″ over-all (10¾″ bbl.)
**Stocks:** Smooth walnut with thumb and heel rest.
**Sights:** Front .125″ blade (.100″ blade optional); rear adj. for w. and e.
**Features:** Polished blue finish, hard chrome optional. Barrel is drilled and tapped for scope mounting. Cocking indicator visible from rear of gun. Has spring-loaded barrel lock, positive thumb safety. Trigger adjustable for weight of pull and over-travel. For complete price list contact RPM.
**Price:** Regular ¾″ frame, right hand action ....................... $585.00
**Price:** As above, left hand action................................. $610.00
**Price:** Wide ⅞″ frame, right hand action only .................... $635.00
**Price:** Extra barrel, 8″-10¾″.................................... $180.00
**Price:** Extra barrel, 12″-14″.................................... $250.00

## REMINGTON XP-100 "VARMINT SPECIAL"
**Caliber:** 223 Rem., single shot.
**Barrel:** 10½″, ventilated rib.
**Weight:** 60 oz. **Length:** 16¾″.
**Stock:** Brown nylon one-piece, checkered grip with white spacers.
**Sights:** Tapped for scope mount.
**Features:** Fits left or right hand, is shaped to fit fingers and heel of hand. Grooved trigger. Rotating thumb safety, cavity in fore-end permits insertion of up to five 38 cal., 130-gr. metal jacketed bullets to adjust weight and balance. Included is a black vinyl, zippered case.
**Price:** Including case, about................................... $396.00

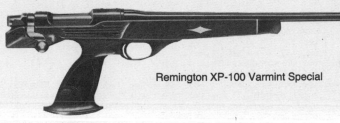

Remington XP-100 Varmint Special

## Remington XP-100 Custom Long Range Pistol
Similar to the XP-100 "Varmint Special" except chambered for 7mm-08 Rem. and 35 Rem., comes with sights—interchangeable blade on ramp front, fully adjustable Bo-Mar rear. Custom Shop 14½″ barrel, Custom Shop English walnut stock. Action tuned in Custom Shop. Weight is under 4½ lbs. Introduced 1986.
**Price:** ...................................................... $887.00

## TEXAS LONGHORN "THE JEZEBEL" PISTOL
**Caliber:** 22 Short, Long, Long Rifle, single shot.
**Barrel:** 6″.
**Weight:** 15 oz. **Length:** 8″ over-all.
**Stocks:** One-piece fancy walnut grip (right or left hand), walnut fore-end.
**Sights:** Bead front, fixed rear.
**Features:** Top-break action; all stainless steel; automatic hammer block safety; music wire coil springs. Barrel is half round, half octagon. Announced 1986. From Texas Longhorn Arms.
**Price:** About ............................................... $185.00

Texas Longhorn "Jezebel"

## TANARMI O/U DERRINGER
**Caliber:** 38 Special.
**Barrel:** 3″.
**Weight:** 14 oz. **Length:** 4¾″ over-all.
**Stocks:** Checkered white nylon.
**Sights:** Fixed.
**Features:** Blue finish; cross bolt safety; tip-up barrel. Assembled in U.S. by Excam, Inc.
**Price:** ..................................................... $80.00

## THOMPSON-CENTER ARMS CONTENDER
**Caliber:** 7mm T.C.U., 30-30 Win., 22 S, L, LR, 22 Mag., 22 Hornet, 6.5 T.C.U., 223 Rem., 30 & 357 Herrett, 32 H&R Mag., 32-20 Win., 357 Mag., 357 Rem. Max., also 222 Rem., 41 Mag., 44 Mag., 45 Colt, single shot.
**Barrel:** 10″, tapered octagon, bull barrel and vent. rib.
**Weight:** 43 oz. (10″ bbl.). **Length:** 13¼″ (10″ bbl.).
**Stocks:** Select walnut grip and fore-end, with thumb rest. Right or left hand.
**Sights:** Under cut blade ramp front, rear adj. for w. & e.
**Features:** Break open action with auto-safety. Single action only. Interchangeable bbls., both caliber (rim & centerfire), and length. Drilled and tapped for scope. Engraved frame. See T/C catalog for exact barrel/caliber availability.
**Price:** Blued (rimfire cals.) ..................................... $305.00
**Price:** Blued (centerfire cals.)................................... $305.00
**Price:** With Armour Alloy II finish............................... $365.00
**Price:** With internal choke...................................... $370.00
**Price:** As above, vent. rib...................................... $380.00
**Price:** Extra bbls. (standard octagon)........................... $130.00
**Price:** Bushnell Phantom scope base............................ $9.95
**Price:** 45/410, vent. rib, internal choke bbl...................... $145.00

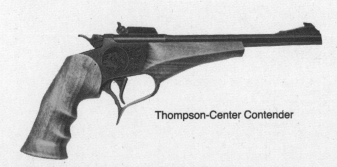

Thompson-Center Contender

Auto Ordnance 27 A-1

**AUTO ORDNANCE MODEL 27 A-1 THOMPSON**
**Caliber:** 45 ACP, 30-shot magazine.
**Barrel:** 16".
**Weight:** 11½ lbs. **Length:** About 42" over-all (Deluxe).
**Stock:** Walnut stock and vertical fore-end.
**Sights:** Blade front, open rear adj. for w.
**Features:** Re-creation of Thompson Model 1927. Semi-auto only. Deluxe model has finned barrel, adj. rear sight and compensator; Standard model has plain barrel and military sight. From Auto-Ordnance Corp.
**Price:** Deluxe .................................................. **$595.00**
**Price:** Standard (horizontal fore-end) ............................ **$575.00**
**Price:** 1927A5 Pistol (M27A1 without stock; wgt. 7 lbs.) ............ **$556.00**
**Price:** Lightweight model ..................................... **$469.95**

**Auto Ordnance Thompson M1**
   Similar to the Model 27 A-1 except is in the M-1 configuration with side cocking knob, horizontal fore-end, smooth un-finned barrel, sling swivels on butt and fore-end. Matte black finish. Introduced 1985.
**Price:** ..................................................... **$565.00**

Barrett Light-Fifty

**BARRETT LIGHT-FIFTY MODEL 82**
**Caliber:** 50 BMG; 11-shot detachable box magazine.
**Barrel:** 33".
**Weight:** 35 lbs. **Length:** 63" over-all.
**Stock:** Uni-body construction.
**Sights:** None furnished.
**Features:** Semi-automatic, recoil operated with recoiling barrel. Three-lug locking bolt; six-port harmonica-type muzzle brake. Bipod legs and M-60 mount standard. Fires same 50-cal. ammunition as the M2HB machine gun. Introduced 1985. From Barrett Firearms.
**Price:** Parkerized ............................................. **$3,180.00**
**Price:** Custom ................................................ **$4,200.00**

**BERETTA AR70 RIFLE**
**Caliber:** 223, 30-shot magazine.
**Barrel:** 17¾".
**Weight:** 8¼ lbs. **Length:** 38" over-all.
**Stock:** Black high-impact plastic.
**Sights:** Blade front, diopter rear adjustable for windage and elevation.
**Features:** Matte black epoxy finish; easy take-down. Imported from Italy by Beretta U.S.A. Corp. Introduced 1984.
**Price:** ..................................................... **$800.00**

**BUSHMASTER AUTO RIFLE**
**Caliber:** 223; 30-shot magazine
**Barrel:** 18½".
**Weight:** 6¼ lbs. **Length:** 37.5" over-all.
**Stock:** Rock maple
**Sights:** Protected post front adj. for elevation, protected quick-flip rear peep adj. for windage; short and long range.
**Features:** Steel alloy upper receiver with welded barrel assembly, AK-47-type gas system, aluminum lower receiver; silent sling and swivels; bayonet lug; one-piece welded steel alloy bolt carrier assembly. From Bushmaster Firearms.
**Price:** With maple stock ........................................ **$384.95**
**Price:** With nylon-coated folding stock ........................... **$394.95**
**Price:** Matte electroless finish, maple stock ..................... **$394.95**
**Price:** As above, folding stock ................................. **$394.95**

Bushmaster Auto Rifle

Colt AR-15A2

**COLT AR-15A2 SPORTER II**
**Caliber:** 223 Rem.
**Barrel:** 20".
**Weight:** 7½ lbs. **Length:** 39" over-all.
**Stock:** High-strength nylon.
**Sights:** Post front, adjustable for elevation, flip-type rear for short, long range, windage.
**Features:** 5-round detachable box magazine, recoil pad, flash suppressor, sling swivels. Forward bolt assist included. Introduced 1985.
**Price:** ..................................................... **$706.50**

**CAUTION:**   PRICES CHANGE. CHECK AT GUNSHOP.

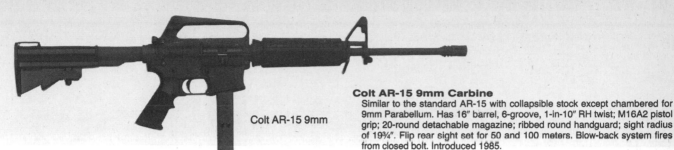

Colt AR-15 9mm

## Colt AR-15 9mm Carbine
Similar to the standard AR-15 with collapsible stock except chambered for 9mm Parabellum. Has 16" barrel, 6-groove, 1-in-10" RH twist; M16A2 pistol grip; 20-round detachable magazine; ribbed round handguard; sight radius of 19¾". Flip rear sight set for 50 and 100 meters. Blow-back system fires from closed bolt. Introduced 1985.
Price: . . . . . . . . . . . . . . . . . . . . . . . . . . . . . . . . . . . . . . . . . . . . . . . . . . . . $695.50

## Colt AR-15A2 H-BAR
Similar to the AR-15A2 Sporter II except has heavy barrel, 800-meter M16A2 rear sight adjustable for windage and elevation, case deflector for left-hand shooters, target-style nylon sling. Introduced 1986.
Price: . . . . . . . . . . . . . . . . . . . . . . . . . . . . . . . . . . . . . . . . . . . $808.50

## Colt AR-15A2 Carbine
Same as standard AR-15A2 except has telescoping nylon-coated aluminum buttstock, and redesigned fore-end. Over-all length collapsed is 32", extended 35". Barrel length is 16", weight is 5.8 lbs. Has 14½" sight radius. Introduced 1985.
Price: . . . . . . . . . . . . . . . . . . . . . . . . . . . . . . . . . . . . . . . . . . . $748.95

Daewoo MAX-2

## DAEWOO MAX-1 AUTO RIFLE
**Caliber:** 5.56mm (223), 30-round magazine.
**Barrel:** 17".
**Weight:** 6.5 lbs. **Length:** 38.4" over-all (butt extended).
**Stock:** Retractable.
**Sights:** Post front, adjustable peep rear.
**Features:** Machine-forged receiver; gas-operated action; uses AR-15/M-16 magazines. Introduced 1985. Imported from Korea by Stoeger Industries.
Price: . . . . . . . . . . . . . . . . . . . . . . . . . . . . . . . . . . . . . . . . . . . $625.00

## COMMANDO AMMO CARBINE
**Caliber:** 45 ACP.
**Barrel:** 16½".
**Weight:** 8 lbs. **Length:** 37" over-all.
**Stock:** Walnut buttstock.
**Sights:** Blade front, peep rear.
**Features:** Semi-auto only. Cocking handle on left side. Choice of magazines—5, 20, 30 or 90 shot. From Commando Arms.
Price: Mark 9 or Mark 45, blue . . . . . . . . . . . . . . . . . . . . . . . . . . . . . $219.00
Price: Nickel plated . . . . . . . . . . . . . . . . . . . . . . . . . . . . . . . . . . . $254.00

## Daewoo MAX-2 Auto Carbine
Similar to the MAX-1 except has a folding buttstock giving over-all length of 38.9" (extended), 28.7" (folded). Weight is 7.5 lbs.; barrel length is 18.3". Has hooded post front sight, adjustable peep rear. Uses AR-15/M-16 magazines. Introduced 1985. Imported from Korea by Stoeger Industries.
Price: . . . . . . . . . . . . . . . . . . . . . . . . . . . . . . . . . . . . . . . . . . . $645.00

FN-LAR Competition

## FN-LAR COMPETITION AUTO
**Caliber:** 308 Win., 20-shot magazine.
**Barrel:** 21" (24" with flash hider).
**Weight:** 9 lbs., 7 oz. **Length:** 44½" over-all.
**Stock:** Black composition butt, fore-end and pistol grip.
**Sights:** Post front, aperture rear adj. for elevation, 200 to 600 meters.
**Features:** Has sling swivels, carrying handle, rubber recoil pad. Consecutively numbered pairs available at additional cost. Imported by Gun South, Inc.
Price: . . . . . . . . . . . . . . . . . . . . . . . . . . . . . . . . . . . . . . . . $1,189.00

## FN 308 Model 50-63
Similar to the FN-LAR except has 18" barrel, skeleton-type folding buttstock, folding cocking handle. Introduced 1982. Imported from Belgium by Gun South, Inc. Distr., Inc.
Price: . . . . . . . . . . . . . . . . . . . . . . . . . . . . . . . . . . . . . . . $1,264.00

## FNC AUTO RIFLE
**Caliber:** 223 Rem.
**Barrel:** 18".
**Weight:** 9.61 lbs.
**Stock:** Synthetic stock.
**Sights:** Post front; flip-over aperture rear adj. for elevation.
**Features:** Updated version of FN-FAL in shortened carbine form. Has 30-shot box magazine, synthetic pistol grip, fore-end. Introduced 1981. Imported by Gun South, Inc.
Price: Standard model . . . . . . . . . . . . . . . . . . . . . . . . . . . . . . . . $683.00
Price: Paratrooper, with folding stock. . . . . . . . . . . . . . . . . . . . . . . $713.00

FNC Auto Rifle

## FN-LAR Heavy Barrel 308 Match
Similar to FN-LAR competition except has wooden stock and fore-end, heavy barrel, folding metal bipod. Imported by Gun South, Inc.
**Price:** With wooden, stock ....................................... $1,636.00
**Price:** With synthetic stock .................................... $1,480.00

## FN-LAR Paratrooper 308 Match 50-64
Similar to FN-LAR competition except with folding skeleton stock, shorter barrel, modified rear sight. Imported by Gun South, Inc.
**Price:** ............................................................... $1,264.00

## GALIL 308 ARM SEMI-AUTO RIFLE
**Caliber:** 308 Win., 20-shot magazine.
**Barrel:** 21″.
**Weight:** 8.7 lbs. **Length:** 41.3″ over-all (stock extended).
**Stock:** Tube-type metal folding stock.
**Sights:** Post-type front, flip-type "L" rear.
**Features:** Gas operated, rotating bolt. Cocking handle, safety and magazine catch can be operated from either side. Folding bipod, carrying handle. Introduced 1982. Imported from Israel by Action Arms Ltd.
**Price:** ................................................................ $940.00
**Price:** As above in 223 (18.1″ bbl., 38.6″ o.a.l.). .................. $875.00

Galil Auto Rifle

## GONCZ HIGH-TECH CARBINE
**Caliber:** 9mm Para., 30 Mauser, 38 Super, 18- and 32-shot magazine; 45 ACP, 10- and 20-shot magazine.
**Barrel:** 16.1″.
**Weight:** 4 lbs., 2 oz. **Length:** 31″ over-all.
**Stock:** Grooved alloy pistol grip, black high-impact plastic butt. Walnut optional at extra cost.
**Sights:** Front adjustable for e., rear adjustable for w.
**Features:** Fires from closed bolt; floating firing pin; safety locks the firing pin; all metal construction; barrel threaded for accessories. Matte black oxide and

Goncz Carbine

anodized finish. Designed by Lajos J. Goncz. Introduced 1985. From Goncz Co.
**Price:** ................................................................ $375.00
**Price:** With laser sight system .................................. $1,495.00

## HECKLER & KOCH HK-91 AUTO RIFLE
**Caliber:** 308 Win., 5- or 20-shot magazine.
**Barrel:** 17.71″.
**Weight:** 9½ lbs. **Length:** 40¼″ over-all.
**Stock:** Black high-impact plastic.
**Sights:** Post front, aperture rear adj. for w. and e.
**Features:** Delayed roller lock action. Sporting version of West German service rifle. Takes special H&K clamp scope mount. Imported from West Germany by Heckler & Koch, Inc.
**Price:** HK-91 A-2 with plastic stock............................ $666.00
**Price:** HK-91 A-3 with retractable metal stock ................... $746.00
**Price:** HK-91 scope mount with 1″ rings......................... $260.00

Heckler & Koch HK-91

## Heckler & Koch HK-93 Auto Rifle
Similar to HK-93 except in 223 cal., 16.13″ barrel, over-all length of 35½″, weighs 7¾ lbs. Same stock, fore-end.
**Price:** HK-93 A-2 with plastic stock.............................. $666.00
**Price:** HK-93 A-3 with retractable metal stock .................... $746.00

## HECKLER & KOCH HK-94 AUTO CARBINE
**Caliber:** 9mm Parabellum, 15-shot magazine.
**Barrel:** 16″.
**Weight:** 6½ lbs. (fixed stock). **Length:** 34¾″ over-all.
**Stock:** High-impact plastic butt and fore-end or retractable metal stock.
**Sights:** Hooded post front, aperture rear adjustable for windage and elevation.
**Features:** Delayed roller-locked action; accepts H&K quick-detachable scope mount. Introduced 1983. Imported from West Germany by Heckler & Koch, Inc..
**Price:** HK94-A2 (fixed stock) .................................... $562.00
**Price:** HK94-A3 (retractable metal stock) ........................ $636.00
**Price:** 30-shot magazine......................................... $24.00
**Price:** Clamp to hold two magazines ............................. $18.00

Heckler & Koch HK-94

**CAUTION:** PRICES CHANGE. CHECK AT GUNSHOP.

# CENTERFIRE RIFLES—MILITARY STYLE AUTOLOADERS

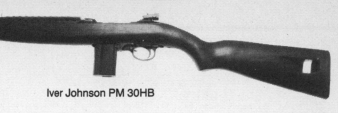

**IVER JOHNSON PM30HB CARBINE**
**Caliber:** 30 U.S. Carbine, 5.7 MMJ.
**Barrel:** 18" four-groove.
**Weight:** 6½ lbs. **Length:** 35½" over-all.
**Stock:** Glossy-finished hardwood or walnut.
**Sights:** Click adj. peep rear.
**Features:** Gas operated semi-auto carbine. 15-shot detachable magazine. Made in U.S.A
**Price:** Blue finish, hardwood stock ............................... $203.50
**Price:** Blue finish, walnut stock .................................. $217.50

Iver Johnson PM 30HB

MAS 223 Auto

**MAS 223 SEMI-AUTO RIFLE**
**Caliber:** 223, 25-shot magazine.
**Barrel:** 19.2".
**Weight:** About 8 lbs. **Length:** 29.8" over-all.
**Stock:** Rubber-covered adjustable check piece converts to left- or right-hand shooters.
**Sights:** Adjustable blade front with luminescent spot for night use, aperture adj. rear.
**Features:** Converts to left- or right-hand ejection. Armored plastic guards vital parts, including sights. Civilian version of the French FAMAS assault rifle. Introduced 1986. Imported from France by Century Arms.
**Price:** With spare parts kit, bipod sling, spare magazine, about.... **$1,495.00**

Mitchell AK-47

**MITCHELL AK-47 SEMI-AUTO RIFLE**
**Caliber:** 223, 308, 7.62 x 39, 30-shot magazine.
**Barrel:** 19.6".
**Weight:** 9.1 lbs. **Length:** 40.6" over-all with wood stock.
**Stock:** Teak.
**Sights:** Hooded post front, open adj. rear.
**Features:** Gas operated semi-automatic. Last-round bolt hold-open. Imported from Yugoslavia by Mitchell Arms.
**Price:** Wood stock ...................................................... $495.00
**Price:** Folding metal stock ....................................... $525.00

Mitchell M-76

**MITCHELL M-76 COUNTER-SNIPER RIFLE**
**Caliber:** 7.9 mm.
**Barrel:** 21.8". Muzzle brake, flash hider.
**Weight:** 10.9 lbs. **Length:** 44.6" over-all.
**Stock:** Teak.
**Features:** Uses AK-47 action. Optional scope, night sight, mounts available. Imported from Yugoslavia by Mitchell Arms.
**Price:** ................................................................... $595.00

**MITCHELL M-59 SEMI-AUTO RIFLE**
**Caliber:** 7.62 x 39, 10-shot magazine.
**Barrel:** 18".
**Weight:** 9 lbs. **Length:** 44" over-all.
**Stock:** Walnut.
**Sights:** Hooded post front, open adj. rear.
**Features:** Gas-operated likeness of the SKS rifle. Imported from Yugoslavia by Mitchell Arms.
**Price:** ................................................................... $539.95

Ruger Mini-14/5R

**Stock:** American hardwood, steel reinforced.
**Sights:** Ramp front, fully adj. rear.
**Features:** Fixed piston gas-operated, positive primary extraction. New buffer system, redesigned ejector system. Ruger S100RH scope rings included. 20-shot magazines available from Ruger dealers, 30-shot magazine available only to police departments and government agencies.
**Price:** Mini-14/5R, blued ........................................ $420.00
**Price:** K Mini-14/5R, stainless ................................ $460.00
**Price:** K Mini-14/5RF, stainless, folding stock .......... $520.00

**RUGER MINI-14/5R RANCH RIFLE**
**Caliber:** 223 Rem., 5-shot detachable box magazine.
**Barrel:** 18½".
**Weight:** 6.4 lbs. **Length:** 37¼" over-all.

# CENTERFIRE RIFLES—MILITARY STYLE AUTOLOADERS

Ruger XGI Auto

## Ruger Mini-14/5F Folding Stock
Same as the Ranch Rifle except available with folding stock, checkered high impact plastic vertical pistol grip. Over-all length with stock open is 37¾", length closed is 27½". Weight is about 7¾ lbs.
**Price:** Blued ordnance steel, standard stock....................... **$390.00**
**Price:** Stainless ............................................. **$430.00**
**Price:** Blued, folding stock .................................... **$465.00**
**Price:** Stainless, folding stock ................................ **$494.50**

## RUGER XGI AUTO RIFLE
**Caliber:** 243 Win., 308 Win., 5-shot detachable box magazine.
**Barrel:** 20".
**Weight:** 7.9 lbs. **Length:** 39⅞" over-all.
**Stock:** American hardwood; rubber butt pad.
**Sights:** Blade front on ramp, folding peep rear adjustable for w. and e.
**Features:** Uses a Garand-type gas system with fixed cylinder and moving piston with a simplified Garand-type rotating bolt. Ruger integral scope mounting system. Patented recoil buffer system; bolt lock mechanism. Introduced 1985.
**Price:** ............................................... **$425.00**

SIG-AMT

## SIG PE-57 AUTO RIFLE
**Caliber:** 7.5mm Swiss, 24-round box magazine.
**Barrel:** 23.8", with flash suppressor.
**Weight:** 12.6 lbs. **Length:** 43.6" over-all.
**Stock:** Black high-impact synthetic butt and pistol grip.
**Sights:** Folding hooded post front, folding click-adjustable aperture rear.
**Features:** Semi-automatic, gas-assisted delayed roller-lock action; bayonet lug, bipod, winter trigger, leather sling, maintenance kit, and 6-round magazine included; quick detachable scope mount optional. Imported from Switzerland by Osborne's. Introduced 1984.
**Price:** About................................................ **$1,995.00**

## SIG-AMT AUTO RIFLE
**Caliber:** 308 Win. (7.62mm NATO), 20-shot magazine.
**Barrel:** 18¾".
**Weight:** 9½ lbs. **Length:** 39" over-all.
**Stock:** Walnut butt and fore-end, black grooved synthetic pistol grip.
**Sights:** Adjustable post front, adjustable aperture rear.
**Features:** Roller-locked breech system with gas-assisted action; right-side cocking lever; loaded chamber indicator. No tools needed for take-down. Comes with bipod and winter trigger. Spare 5- and 10-shot magazines available. Imported from Switzerland by Osborne's. Introduced 1984.
**Price:** About............................................... **$1,995.00**

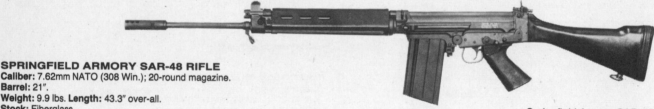

## SPRINGFIELD ARMORY SAR-48 RIFLE
**Caliber:** 7.62mm NATO (308 Win.); 20-round magazine.
**Barrel:** 21".
**Weight:** 9.9 lbs. **Length:** 43.3" over-all.
**Stock:** Fiberglass.
**Sights:** Adjustable front, adjustable peep rear.
**Features:** New production. Introduced 1985. From Springfield Armory.
**Price:** ................................................... **$899.00**

Springfield Armory SAR-48

Springfield Armory M1A

## SPRINGFIELD ARMORY M1A RIFLE
**Caliber:** 7.62mm Nato (308), 243 Win., 5-, 10- or 20-round box magazine.
**Barrel:** 25¹⁄₁₆" with flash suppressor, 22" without suppressor.
**Weight:** 8¾ lbs. **Length:** 44¼" over-all.
**Stock:** American walnut or birch with walnut colored heat-resistant fiberglass handguard. Matching walnut handguard available.
**Sights:** Military, square blade front, full click-adjustable aperture rear.
**Features:** Commercial equivalent of the U.S. M-14 service rifle with no provision for automatic firing. From Springfield Armory. Military accessories available including 3x-9x2 ART scope and mount.
**Price:** Standard M1A Rifle, about ............................. **$782.00**
**Price:** Match Grade, about.................................... **$998.00**
**Price:** Super Match (heavy Premium barrel), about .............. **$1,125.00**
**Price:** M1A-A1 Assault Rifle, walnut stock, about ................ **$790.00**
**Price:** As above, folding stock, about ......................... **$857.00**

---

Consult our Directory pages for the location of firms mentioned.

**CAUTION:** PRICES CHANGE. CHECK AT GUNSHOP.

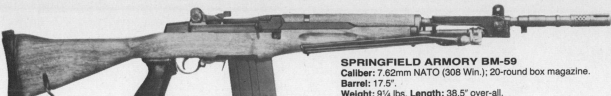

Springfield Armory BM 59

### SPRINGFIELD ARMORY BM-59
**Caliber:** 7.62mm NATO (308 Win.); 20-round box magazine.
**Barrel:** 17.5".
**Weight:** 9¼ lbs. **Length:** 38.5" over-all.
**Stock:** Walnut, with trapped rubber butt pad.
**Sights:** Military square blade front, click adj. peep rear.
**Features:** Full military-dress Italian service rifle. Available in selective fire or semi-auto only. Refined version of the M-1 Garand. Accessories available include: folding alpine stock, muzzle brake/flash suppressor/grenade launcher combo, bipod, winter trigger, grenade launcher sights, bayonet, oiler. Extremely limited quantities. Introduced 1981.
**Price:** Standard Italian model, about ......................... $1,248.00
**Price:** Alpine model, about ............................... $1,435.00
**Price:** Alpine Paratrooper model, about ..................... $1,624.00
**Price:** Nigerian Mark IV model, about ...................... $1,365.00

### SPRINGFIELD ARMORY M1 GARAND RIFLE
**Caliber:** 308, 30-06, 8-shot clip.
**Barrel:** 24".
**Weight:** 9½ lbs. **Length:** 43½" over-all.
**Stock:** Walnut, military.
**Sights:** Military square blade front, click adjustable peep rear.
**Features:** Commercially-made M-1 Garand duplicates the original service rifle. Introduced 1979. From Springfield Armory.
**Price:** Standard, about ................................ $696.00
**Price:** National Match, about ......................... $837.00
**Price:** Ultra Match, about ............................ $944.00
**Price:** Sniper rifle, about ............................ $1,065.00
**Price:** M1-T26 "Tanker," walnut stock, about............ $732.00
**Price:** As above, folding stock, about ................. $774.00
**Price:** Standard M-1 Garand with Beretta-made receiver, about ... $1,510.00

### STEYR A.U.G. AUTOLOADING RIFLE
**Caliber:** 223 Rem.
**Barrel:** 20".
**Weight:** 8½ lbs. **Length:** 31" over-all.
**Stock:** Synthetic, green. One-piece moulding houses receiver group, hammer mechanism and magazine.
**Sights:** 1.5x scope only; scope and mount form the carrying handle.
**Features:** Semi-automatic, gas-operated action; can be converted to suit right or left-handed shooters, including ejection port. Transparent 30- or 40-shot magazines. Folding vertical front grip. Introduced 1983. Imported from Austria by Gun South, Inc.
**Price:** Right or left-hand model ........................ $889.00

Steyr A.U.G. Rifle

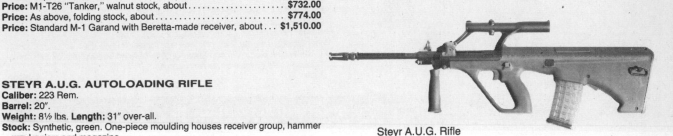

Universal 1006 Carbine

### UNIVERSAL 1003 AUTOLOADING CARBINE
**Caliber:** 30 M1, 5-shot magazine.
**Barrel:** 16", 18".
**Weight:** 5½ lbs. **Length:** 35½" over-all.
**Stock:** American hardwood stock inletted for "issue" sling and oiler, blued metal handguard.
**Sights:** Blade front with protective wings, adj. rear.
**Features:** Gas operated, cross lock safety. Receiver tapped for scope mounts. Made in U.S.A. From Iver Johnson.
**Price:** ................................................ $218.00

### Universal Model 5000PT Carbine
Same as standard Model 1003 except comes with "Schmeisser type paratrooper" folding stock. Barrel length 18". Over-all length open 36"; folded 27". Made in U.S.A.
**Price:** Blue. ......................................... $217.50

### UZI CARBINE
**Caliber:** 9mm Parabellum, 45 ACP, 25-round magazine.
**Barrel:** 16.1".
**Weight:** 8.4 lbs. **Length:** 24.4" (stock folded).
**Stock:** Folding metal stock. Wood stock available as an accessory.
**Sights:** Post-type front, "L" flip-type rear adj. for 100 meters and 200 meters. Both click-adjustable for w. and e.
**Features:** Adapted by Col. Uzi Gal to meet BATF regulations, this semi-auto has the same qualities as the famous submachine gun. Made by Israel Military Industries. Comes in moulded carrying case with sling, magazine, sight adjustment key, and a short "display only" barrel. Exclusively imported from Israel by Action Arms Ltd. 9mm introduced 1980; 45 ACP introduced 1985.
**Price:** ................................................ $679.00

UZI Carbine

# CENTERFIRE RIFLES—MILITARY STYLE AUTOLOADERS

Valmet M-76

## VALMET M-76 STANDARD RIFLE
**Caliber:** 223, 15 or 30-shot magazine, or 7.62 x 39, 30-shot magazine.
**Barrel:** 16¾".
**Weight:** About 8½ lbs. **Length:** 37¾" over-all.
**Stock:** Wood or folding metal type; composition fore-end.
**Sights:** Hooded adjustable post front, peep rear with luminous night sight.
**Features:** Semi-automatic only. Has sling swivels, flash supressor. Bayonet, cleaning kit, 30-shot magazine, scope adaptor cover optional. Imported from Finland by Valmet.
**Price:** Wood stock . . . . . . . . . . . . . . . . . . . . . . . . . . . . . . . . . $649.00
**Price:** Folding stock . . . . . . . . . . . . . . . . . . . . . . . . . . . . . . . . $674.00

## VALMET M78 SEMI-AUTO
Similar to M76 except chambered for 223, 7.62 x 39 or 308 Win., has 24¼" heavy barrel, weighs 11 lbs., 43¼" over-all; 20- or 30-round magazine; bi-pod; machined receiver. Length of pull on wood stock dimensioned for American shooters. Rear sight adjustable for w. and e., open-aperture front sight; folding carrying handle. Imported from Finland by Valmet.
**Price:** . . . . . . . . . . . . . . . . . . . . . . . . . . . . . . . . . . . . . . . . . . $824.00

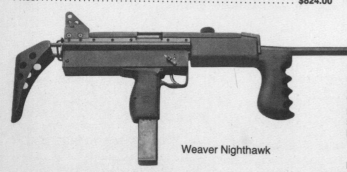

Weaver Nighthawk

## WEAVER ARMS NIGHTHAWK
**Caliber:** 9mm Para., 25-shot magazine.
**Barrel:** 16.1".
**Weight:** 7 lbs. **Length:** 26½" (stock retracted).
**Stock:** Retractable metal frame.
**Sights:** Hooded blade front, adjustable peep V rear.
**Features:** Semi-auto fire only; fires from a closed bolt. Has 21" sight radius. Black nylon pistol grip and finger-groove front grip. Matte black finish. Introduced 1983. From Weaver Arms Corp.
**Price:** . . . . . . . . . . . . . . . . . . . . . . . . . . . . . . . . . . . . . . . . . . $395.00

# CENTERFIRE RIFLES—SPORTING AUTOLOADERS

Browning Auto Rifle

## BROWNING HIGH-POWER AUTO RIFLE
**Caliber:** 243, 270, 30-06, 308.
**Barrel:** 22" round tapered.
**Weight:** 7⅜ lbs. **Length:** 43" over-all.
**Stock:** French walnut p.g. stock (13⅝"x2"x1⅝") and fore-end, hand checkered.
**Sights:** Adj. folding-leaf rear, gold bead on hooded ramp front.
**Features:** Detachable 4-round magazine. Receiver tapped for scope mounts. Trigger pull 3½ lbs. Gold plated trigger on Grade IV. Imported from Belgium by Browning.
**Price:** Grade I . . . . . . . . . . . . . . . . . . . . . . . . . . . . . . . . . . . . . $552.00
**Price:** Grade IV . . . . . . . . . . . . . . . . . . . . . . . . . . . . . . . . . . . $1,670.00

## Browning Commemorative BAR
Similar to the standard BAR except has silver grey receiver with engraved and gold inlaid whitetail deer on the right side, a mule deer on the left; a gold-edged scroll banner frames "One of Six Hundred" on the left side, the numerical edition number replaces "One" on the right. Chambered only in 30-06. Fancy, highly figured walnut stock and fore-end. Introduced 1983.
**Price:** . . . . . . . . . . . . . . . . . . . . . . . . . . . . . . . . . . . . . . . . . $3,550.00

## Browning Magnum Auto Rifle
Same as the standard caliber model, except weighs 8⅜ lbs., 45" over-all, 24" bbl., 3-round mag. Cals. 7mm Mag., 300 Win. Mag.
**Price:** Grade I . . . . . . . . . . . . . . . . . . . . . . . . . . . . . . . . . . . . . $604.00
**Price:** Grade IV . . . . . . . . . . . . . . . . . . . . . . . . . . . . . . . . . . . $1,720.00

Heckler & Koch HK770

## HECKLER & KOCH HK770 AUTO RIFLE
**Caliber:** 308 Win., 3-shot magazine.
**Barrel:** 19.6".
**Weight:** 7½ lbs. **Length:** 42.8" over-all.
**Stock:** European walnut. Checkered p.g. and fore-end.
**Sights:** Vertically adjustable blade front, open, fold-down rear adj. for w.
**Features:** Has the delayed roller-locked system and polygonal rifling. Magazine catch located at front of trigger guard. Receiver top is dovetailed to accept clamp-type scope mount. Imported from West Germany by Heckler & Koch, Inc.
**Price:** . . . . . . . . . . . . . . . . . . . . . . . . . . . . . . . . . . . . . . . . . . $666.00
**Price:** HK630, 223 Rem. . . . . . . . . . . . . . . . . . . . . . . . . . . . . . $666.00
**Price:** HK940, 30-06 . . . . . . . . . . . . . . . . . . . . . . . . . . . . . . . . $706.00
**Price:** Scope mount with 1" rings . . . . . . . . . . . . . . . . . . . . . . . $159.00

**CAUTION:** PRICES CHANGE. CHECK AT GUNSHOP.

Heckler & Koch SL7

## HECKLER & KOCH SL7 AUTO RIFLE
**Caliber:** 308 Win., 3-shot magazine.
**Barrel:** 17".
**Weight:** 8 lbs. **Length:** 39¾" over-all.
**Stock:** European walnut, oil finished.
**Sights:** Hooded post front, adjustable aperture rear.
**Features:** Delayed roller-locked action; polygon rifling; receiver is dovetailed for H&K quick-detachable scope mount. Introduced 1983. Imported from West Germany by Heckler & Koch, Inc.
**Price:** .................................................. $599.00
**Price:** Model SL6 (as above except in 223 Rem.) ................ $599.00
**Price:** Quick-detachable scope mount .......................... $159.00
**Price:** 10-shot magazine ....................................... $27.00

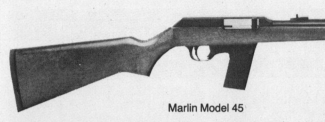

Marlin Model 45

## MARLIN MODEL 9 CAMP CARBINE
**Caliber:** 9mm Parabellum, 12-shot magazine (20-shot available).
**Barrel:** 16½", Micro-Groove® rifling.
**Weight:** 6¾ lbs. **Length:** 35½" over-all.
**Stock:** Walnut-finished hardwood; rubber butt pad; Mar-Shield® finish.
**Sights:** Ramp front with bead with Wide-Scan® hood, adjustable open rear.
**Features:** Manual bolt hold-open; Garand-type safety, magazine safety; loaded chamber indicator; receiver drilled, tapped for scope mounting. Introduced 1985.
**Price:** .................................................. $259.95

## MARLIN MODEL 45 CARBINE
Similar to the Model 9 except chambered for 45 ACP, 7-shot magazine. Introduced 1986.
**Price:** .................................................. $259.95

Remington Model Four

## REMINGTON MODEL FOUR AUTO RIFLE
**Caliber:** 243 Win., 270 Win., 280 Rem., 308 Win. and 30-06.
**Barrel:** 22" round tapered.
**Weight:** 7½ lbs. **Length:** 42" over-all.
**Stock:** Walnut, deluxe cut checkered p.g. and fore-end. Full cheekpiece, Monte Carlo.
**Sights:** Gold bead front sight on ramp; step rear sight with windage adj.
**Features:** Redesigned and improved version of the Model 742. Positive cross-bolt safety. Receiver tapped for scope mount. 4-shot clip mag. Has cartridge head medallion denoting caliber on bottom of receiver. Introduced 1981.
**Price:** About .............................................. $524.00
**Price:** D Grade, about ...................................... $2,291.00
**Price:** F Grade, about ...................................... $4,720.00
**Price:** F Grade with gold inlays, about ..................... $7,079.00

## Remington Model 7400 Auto Rifle
Similar to Model Four except also chambered for 6mm Rem., does not have full cheekpiece Monte Carlo stock, has slightly different fore-end design, impressed checkering, no cartridge head medallion. Introduced 1981.
**Price:** About .............................................. $460.00

## Remington "Sportsman" 74 Auto Rifle
Similar to the Model Four rifle except available only in 30-06, 4-shot magazine, 22" barrel, walnut-finished hardwood stock and fore-end, open adjustable sights. Introduced 1984.
**Price:** About .............................................. $385.00

Valmet Hunter

## VALMET HUNTER AUTO RIFLE
**Caliber:** 223, 15-, 30-shot magazines; 243, 9-shot magazine; 308, 5-, 9- and 20-shot magazines.
**Barrel:** 20½".
**Weight:** 8 lbs. **Length:** 42" over-all.
**Stock:** American walnut butt and fore-end. Checkered palm-swell p.g. and fore-end.
**Sights:** Blade front, open flip-type rear.
**Features:** Uses semi-auto Kalashnikov-type gas-operated action with rotating bolt. Stock is adjustable for length via spacers. Optional cleaning kit, sling, ejection buffer, scope mount. Introduced 1986. Imported from Finland by Valmet.
**Price:** .................................................. $639.00

# CENTERFIRE RIFLES—SPORTING AUTOLOADERS

Voere Model 2185

**VOERE MODEL 2185 AUTO RIFLE**
**Caliber:** 222 Rem. 222 Rem. Mag., 243, 308, 7 x 64, 270, 30-06, 9.3 x 62, 2-shot clip.
**Barrel:** 24″
**Weight:** NA. **Length:** NA.
**Stock:** European walnut.
**Sights:** Hooded bead front, open rear adj. for w. & e.
**Features:** Hand checkered stock; rotary safety; sling swivels. Muzzle stabilizer available. Imported from Austria by L. Jos. Rahn.
**Price:** 222, 222 Mag., 243, 308 ................................. $560.00
**Price:** 7 x 64, 270, 30-06 .................................. $660.00
**Price:** 9.3 x 62 ................................. $700.00

# CENTERFIRE RIFLES—LEVER, SLIDE & MISC.

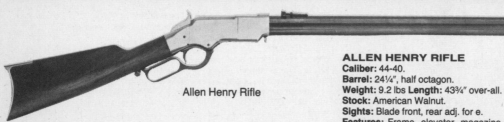

Allen Henry Rifle

**ALLEN HENRY RIFLE**
**Caliber:** 44-40.
**Barrel:** 24¼″, half octagon.
**Weight:** 9.2 lbs **Length:** 43¾″ over-all.
**Stock:** American Walnut.
**Sights:** Blade front, rear adj. for e.
**Features:** Frame, elevator, magazine follower, buttplate are brass, balance polished steel. Imported by Allen Fire Arms.
**Price:** ................................. $569.00
**Price:** Henry Carbine(22¼″ bbl.) ................................. $569.00

Allen 1866 Rifle

**ALLEN MODEL 1866 SPORTING RIFLE**
**Caliber:** 22 LR, 22 Mag., 38 Spec., 44-40.
**Barrel:** 24¼″, octagonal.
**Weight:** 8.1 lbs. **Length:** 43¼″ over-all.

**Stock:** Walnut.
**Sights:** Blade front adj. for w., rear adj. for e.
**Features:** Frame, buttplate, fore-end cap of polished brass, balance blued. Imported by Allen Fire Arms.
**Price:** ................................. $449.00
**Price:** Yellowboy Carbine (19″ round bbl.) ................................. $429.00
**Price:** Yellowboy "Indian" Carbine (engraved receiver, "nails" in wood) ................................. $469.00
**Price:** 1866 "Red Cloud Commemorative" Carbine .............. $469.00
**Price:** 1866 "Trapper's Model" Carbine (16″ bbl., 44-40) .......... $429.00

Allen 1873 Rifle

**ALLEN 1873 SPORTING RIFLE**
**Caliber:** 22 LR, 22 Mag., 357 Mag., 44-40.
**Barrel:** 24¼″, octagonal.
**Weight:** 8.1 lbs. **Length:** 43¼″ over-all.

**Stock:** Walnut.
**Sights:** Blade front adj. for w., open rear adj. for e.
**Features:** Color case-hardened frame, blued barrel, hammer, lever, buttplate, brass elevator. Imported by Allen Fire Arms.
**Price:** ................................. $569.00
**Price:** 1873 Carbine (19″ round bbl.) ................................. $499.00
**Price:** 1873 Carbine, nickel plated ................................. $569.00
**Price:** 1873 "Trapper's Model" Carbine (16″ bbl., 44-40) .......... $499.00

**ALLEN 1875 ARMY TARGET REVOLVING CARBINE**
**Caliber:** 357 Mag., 44-40, 45 Colt, 6 shot.
**Barrel:** 18″.
**Weight:** 4.9 lbs. **Length:** 37″ over-all.
**Stock:** Walnut.
**Sights:** Ramp front, rear adj. for elevation.
**Features:** Polished brass trigger guard and buttplate, color case-hardened frame, rest is blued. Carbine version of the 1875 revolver. Imported by Allen Fire Arms.
**Price:** ................................. $389.00

**ALLEN CATTLEMAN REVOLVING CARBINE**
**Caliber:** 22 LR/22 Mag., 357 Mag., 44-40, 45 Colt, 6 shot.
**Barrel:** 18″.
**Weight:** 4.4 lbs. **Length:** 34″ over-all.
**Stock:** Walnut.
**Sights:** Blade front, groove rear.
**Features:** Carbine version of the single-action revolver. Brass buttplate, color case-hardened frame, blued cylinder and barrel. Imported by Allen Fire Arms.
**Price:** ................................. $339.00
**Price:** Buckhorn (44 Mag.) ................................. $399.00
**Price:** As above, convertible (44 Mag./44-40 cylinders) ........... $409.00

**CAUTION:** PRICES CHANGE. CHECK AT GUNSHOP.

Browning Model 1886

## BROWNING MODEL 1886 LEVER ACTION RIFLE
**Caliber:** 45-70 Govt., 8-round magazine.
**Barrel:** 26" octagonal.
**Weight:** 9 lbs. 5 oz. **Length:** 45".

**Stock:** Straight grip walnut stock and fore-end with matte finish. High grade has Grade III French walnut, fine checkering, high gloss finish.
**Sights:** Gold bead on elevated ramp front, buckhorn rear with elevator.
**Features:** Exact replica of John M. Browning's first lever action repeater design to be manufactured. Full-length tubular magazine, loaded through side port. Half-cock safety, metal crescent buttplate. High Grade model has gold plated American bison and elk scenes engraved on gray receiver. Limited production issue (7,000 in Grade I, 3,000 in High Grade). Introduced 1986. Imported from Japan by Browning.
**Price:** Grade I . . . . . . . . . . . . . . . . . . . . . . . . . . . . . . . . . . . . . . . . **$577.95**
**Price:** High Grade . . . . . . . . . . . . . . . . . . . . . . . . . . . . . . . . . . . . . **$634.95**

Browning B-92

## BROWNING B-92 LEVER ACTION
**Caliber:** 357 Mag., 11-shot magazine.
**Barrel:** 20" round.

**Weight:** 6 lbs., 6 oz. **Length:** 37½" over-all.
**Stock:** Straight grip stock and classic fore-end in French walnut with high gloss finish. Steel, modified crescent buttplate. (12¾" x 2 " x 2⅞").
**Sights:** Post front, classic cloverleaf rear with notched elevation ramp. Sight radius 16⅝".
**Features:** Tubular magazine. Follows design of original Model 92 lever-action. Introduced 1979. Imported from Japan by Browning.
**Price:** . . . . . . . . . . . . . . . . . . . . . . . . . . . . . . . . . . . . . . . . . . . . **$341.50**

Browning BLR

## BROWNING BLR LEVER ACTION RIFLE
**Caliber:** 222, 223, 22-250, 243, 257 Roberts, 7mm-08, 308 Win. or 358 Win. 4-shot detachable mag.
**Barrel:** 20" round tapered.

**Weight:** 6 lbs. 15 oz. **Length:** 39¾" over-all.
**Stock:** Checkered straight grip and fore-end, oil finished walnut.
**Sights:** Gold bead on hooded ramp front; low profile square notch adj. rear.
**Features:** Wide, grooved trigger; half-cock hammer safety. Receiver tapped for scope mount. Recoil pad installed. Imported from Japan by Browning.
**Price:** . . . . . . . . . . . . . . . . . . . . . . . . . . . . . . . . . . . . . . . . . . . . **$402.95**

Dixie Model 1873

## DIXIE ENGRAVED MODEL 1873 RIFLE
**Caliber:** 44-40, 11-shot magazine.
**Barrel:** 20", round.
**Weight:** 7¾ lbs. **Length:** 39" over-all.
**Stock:** Walnut.
**Sights:** Blade front, adj. rear.
**Features:** Engraved and case hardened frame. Duplicate of Winchester 1873. Made in Italy. From Dixie Gun Works.
**Price:** . . . . . . . . . . . . . . . . . . . . . . . . . . . . . . . . . . . . . . . . . . . . **$550.00**
**Price:** Plain, blued carbine . . . . . . . . . . . . . . . . . . . . . . . . . . . . . . **$495.00**

## E.M.F. HENRY CARBINE
**Caliber:** 44-40 or 44 rimfire.
**Barrel:** 21".
**Weight:** About 9 lbs. **Length:** About 39" over-all.
**Stock:** Oil stained American walnut.
**Sights:** Blade front, rear adj. for e.
**Features:** Reproduction of the original Henry carbine with brass frame and buttplate, rest blued. From E.M.F.
**Price:** Standard . . . . . . . . . . . . . . . . . . . . . . . . . . . . . . . . . . . **$600.00**
**Price:** Engraved . . . . . . . . . . . . . . . . . . . . . . . . . . . . . . . . . . . . **$1000.00**

## MARLIN 336CS LEVER ACTION CARBINE
**Caliber:** 30-30 or 35 Rem., 6-shot tubular magazine
**Barrel:** 20" Micro-Groove®.
**Weight:** 7 lbs. **Length:** 38½".
**Stock:** Select American black walnut, capped p.g. with white line spacers. Mar-Shield® finish.
**Sights:** Ramp front with Wide-Scan™ hood, semi-buckhorn folding rear adj. for w. & e.
**Features:** Hammer block safety. Receiver tapped for scope mount, offset hammer spur; top of receiver sand blasted to prevent glare.
**Price:** Less scope . . . . . . . . . . . . . . . . . . . . . . . . . . . . . . . . . **$295.95**

## Marlin Model 336 Extra-Range Carbine
Similar to the standard Model 336CS except chambered for 356 Win.; has new hammer block safety, rubber butt pad, 5-shot magazine. Comes with detachable sling swivels and branded leather sling. Introduced 1983.
**Price:** . . . . . . . . . . . . . . . . . . . . . . . . . . . . . . . . . . . . . . . . . . . . **$323.95**

## Marlin 336TS Lever Action Carbine
Same as the 336CS except: straight stock; cal. 30-30 only. Squared finger lever, 18½" barrel, weight 6½ lbs. Hammer block safety.
**Price:** . . . . . . . . . . . . . . . . . . . . . . . . . . . . . . . . . . . . . . . . . . . . **$295.95**

## Marlin 30AS Lever Action Carbine
Same as the Marlin 336CS except has walnut-finished hardwood p.g. stock, 30-30 only, 6-shot. Hammer block safety.
**Price:** . . . . . . . . . . . . . . . . . . . . . . . . . . . . . . . . . . . . . . . . . . . . **$282.95**

**CAUTION:** PRICES CHANGE. CHECK AT GUNSHOP.

Marlin 1894S

**MARLIN 1894S LEVER ACTION CARBINE**
**Caliber:** 44 Magnum, 10-shot tubular magazine
**Barrel:** 20" Micro-Grove®.
**Weight:** 6 lbs. **Length:** 37½".
**Stock:** American black walnut, straight grip and fore-end. Mar-Shield® finish.
**Sights:** Wide-Scan® hooded ramp front, semi-buckhorn folding rear adj. for w. & e.
**Features:** Hammer block safety. Receiver tapped for scope mount, offset hammer spur, solid top receiver sand blasted to prevent glare.
**Price:** .................................................. $315.95

**Marlin Model 1894CS Carbine**
Similar to the standard Model 1894S except chambered for 38 Special/357 Magnum with 9-shot magazine, 18½" barrel, hammer block safety, brass bead front sight. Introduced 1983.
**Price:** .................................................. $315.95

Marlin 1895SS

**MARLIN 1895SS LEVER ACTION RIFLE**
**Caliber:** 45-70, 4-shot tubular magazine.
**Barrel:** 22" round.
**Weight:** 7½ lbs. **Length:** 40½".
**Stock:** American black walnut, full pistol grip. Mar-Shield® finish; rubber butt-pad; q-d. swivels; leather carrying strap.
**Sights:** Bead front with Wide-Scan hood, semi-buckhorn folding rear adj. for w. and e.
**Features:** Hammer block safety. Solid receiver tapped for scope mounts or receiver sights, offset hammer spur.
**Price:** .................................................. $339.95

**MARLIN 444SS LEVER ACTION SPORTER**
**Caliber:** 444 Marlin, 5-shot tubular magazine
**Barrel:** 22" Micro-Groove®.
**Weight:** 7½ lbs. **Length:** 40½".
**Stock:** American black walnut, capped p.g. with white line spacers, rubber rifle butt pad. Mar-Shield® finish; q.d. swivels, leather carrying strap.
**Sights:** Hooded ramp front, folding semi-buckhorn rear adj. for w. & e.
**Features:** Hammer block safety. Receiver tapped for scope mount, offset hammer spur, leather sling with detachable swivels.
**Price:** .................................................. $339.95

Navy Arms Henry

**NAVY ARMS HENRY CARBINE**
**Caliber:** 44-40 or 44 rimfire.
**Barrel:** 24".
**Weight:** About 8¼ lbs. **Length:** 39" over-all.
**Stock:** Oil stained American walnut.
**Sights:** Blade front, rear adj. for e.
**Features:** Reproduction of the original Henry carbine with brass frame and buttplate, rest blued. Will be produced in limited edition of 1,000 standard models, plus 50 engraved guns. Made in U.S. by Navy Arms.
**Price:** Standard .................................. $595.00
**Price:** Engraved ................................ $1,500.00

**Price:** Iron Frame rifle (similar to Carbine except has blued frame) . **$795.00**
**Price:** Military Rifle (similar to Carbine except has sling swivels, different rear sight) ................................................. **$595.00**
**Price:** Trapper model (16½" bbl., 7¼ lbs., 34½" o.a.l) ............. **$595.00**

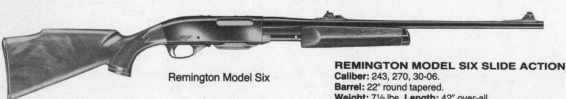

Remington Model Six

**REMINGTON MODEL SIX SLIDE ACTION**
**Caliber:** 243, 270, 30-06.
**Barrel:** 22" round tapered.
**Weight:** 7½ lbs. **Length:** 42" over-all.
**Stock:** Cut-checkered walnut p.g. and fore-end, Monte Carlo with full cheekpiece.
**Sights:** Gold bead front sight on matted ramp, open step adj. sporting rear.
**Features:** Redesigned and improved version of the Model 760. Has cartridge head medallion denoting caliber on bottom of receiver. Detachable 4-shot clip. Cross-bolt safety. Receiver tapped for scope mount. Also available in high grade versions. Introduced 1981.
**Price:** About .................................... $484.00

Consult our Directory pages for the location of firms mentioned.

**Remington Model 7600 Slide Action Rifle**
Similar to Model Six except also chambered for 6mm Rem., does not have Monte Carlo stock or cheekpiece no cartridge head medallion. Slightly different fore-end design. Impressed checkering. Introduced 1981.
**Price:** About ............................................ $417.00

**Remington "Sportsman" 76 Pump Rifle**
Similar to the Model Six except available only in 30-06, 4-shot magazine, 22" barrel, walnut-finished hardwood stock and fore-end, open adjustable sights. Introduced 1984.
**Price:** About ............................................ $348.00

**CAUTION:** PRICES CHANGE. CHECK AT GUNSHOP.

Rossi Carbine

### ROSSI SADDLE-RING CARBINE M92 SRC
**Caliber:** 38 Spec., 357 Mag., 44-40, 44 Mag., 10-shot magazine.
**Barrel:** 20".
**Weight:** 5¾ lbs. **Length:** 37" over-all.
**Stock:** Walnut.
**Sights:** Blade front, buckhorn rear.
**Features:** Re-creation of the famous lever-action carbine. Handles 38 and 357 interchangeably. Has high-relief Puma medallion inlaid in the receiver. Introduced 1978. Imported by Interarms.
**Price:** ............................................ $237.00
**Price:** Blue, engraved .............................. $277.00
**Price:** 44-40 ..................................... $242.00
**Price:** 44 Spec./44 Mag. ............................ $252.00
**Price:** 38/357, 16" bbl. ............................ $232.00

### Rossi Puma M92 SRS Short Carbine
Similar to the standard M92 except has 16" barrel, over-all length of 33", in 38/357 only. Has large lever loop, Puma medallion on side of receiver. Introduced 1986.
**Price:** ............................................ $232.00

Savage Model 99C

### SAVAGE 99C LEVER ACTION RIFLE
**Caliber:** 243 or 308 Win., detachable 4-shot magazine.
**Barrel:** 22", chrome-moly steel.
**Weight:** 8 lbs. **Length:** 41¾" over-all.
**Stock:** Walnut with checkered p.g. and fore-end.
**Sights:** Ramp front, adjustable ramp rear sight. Tapped for scope mounts.
**Features:** Grooved trigger, top tang slide safety locks trigger and lever. Black rubber butt pad.
**Price:** ............................................ $469.00

Winchester Model 94

### WINCHESTER MODEL 94 SIDE EJECT
**Caliber:** 307 Win., 356 Win., 375 Win., 6-shot magazine.
**Barrel:** 20".
**Weight:** 7 lbs. **Length:** 38⅝" over-all.
**Stock:** Monte Carlo-style American walnut. Satin finish.
**Sights:** Hooded ramp front, semi-buckhorn rear adjustable for w. & e.
**Features:** All external metal parts have Winchester's deep blue high polish finish. Rifling twist 1 in 12". Rubber recoil pad fitted to buttstock. Introduced 1983. Made under license by U.S. Repeating Arms Co.
**Price:** About ...................................... $319.75

### WINCHESTER MODEL 94 SIDE EJECT CARBINE
**Caliber:** 30-30, (12" twist), 6-shot tubular magazine.
**Barrel:** 16", 20".
**Weight:** 6½ lbs. (30-30) **Length:** 37¾" over-all.
**Stock:** Straight grip walnut stock and fore-end.
**Sights:** Hooded blade front, semi-buckhorn rear. Drilled and tapped for receiver sight and scope mount.
**Features:** Solid frame, forged steel receiver; side ejection, exposed rebounding hammer with automatic trigger-activated safety transfer bar. Introduced 1984.
**Price:** 30-30, about ............................... $290.00
**Price:** Trapper model (16" bbl., 30-30), about ....... $290.00
**Price:** As above, 45 Colt, 44 Mag./44 Spec., about ... $315.30

### Winchester Model 94 120th Anniversary Edition
Similar to standard Model 94 except chambered for 44-40, has hoop-type finger lever, crescent buttplate, blade front sight. Traditional buttstock and extended fore-end of select walnut with semi-gloss finish, deep-cut checkering. Special 120th Anniversary medallion affixed to left side of receiver which also displays the Horse-and-Rider trademark. Right side has a gold-etched portrait of Oliver F. Winchester with his signature on the tang. Left side of the 20" barrel has the Winchester name in old-style "lightning" lettering; right side has a rendering of the original factory. Magazine cap, front sight are gold plated. Only 1,000 guns to be made. Introduced 1986.
**Price:** About ...................................... $1,136.70

Winchester Model 94XTR

### Winchester Model 94XTR Side Eject Carbine
Same as standard Model 94 except has high-grade finish on stock and fore-end with cut checkering on both. Metal has highly polished deep blue finish.
**Price:** About ...................................... $316.97

### Winchester Model 94XTR Side Eject, 7x30 Waters
Same as Model 94 Side Eject except has 24" barrel, 7-shot magazine, over-all length of 41¾" and weight is 7 lbs. Barrel twist is 1-12". Rubber butt pad instead of plastic. Introduced 1984.
**Price:** About ...................................... $345.55

### Winchester Ranger Side Eject Carbine
Same as Model 94 Side Eject except has 5-shot magazine, American hardwood stock and fore-end, no front sight hood. Introduced 1985.
**Price:** About ...................................... $244.90
**Price:** With 4 x 32 Bushnell scope, mounts, about .... $282.57

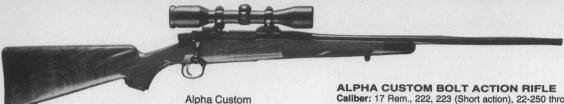

Alpha Custom

## ALPHA CUSTOM BOLT ACTION RIFLE
**Caliber:** 17 Rem., 222, 223 (Short action), 22-250 through 338-284 (Medium action), 25-06 through 35 Whelan (Standard action), 257 Wea. through 338 Win. Mag. (Magnum action).
**Barrel:** 20″—23″ depending on caliber.
**Weight:** 6-7 lbs. **Length:** 40″-43″ over-all.
**Stock:** Classic-style California claro walnut with hand rubbed oil finish, hand checkered 22-24 l.p.i., ebony fore-end tip, custom steel grip cap, Talley inletted swivel studs, solid butt pad.
**Sights:** None furnished. Drilled and tapped for scope mounting. Custom open sights available.
**Features:** Three action lengths with three-lug locking system and 60° bolt rotation; three-position Model 70-type safety, pillar bedding system; steel floorplate/trigger guard; satin finish blue. Right or left-hand models available. Introduced 1984. Made in U.S. by Alpha Arms, Inc.
**Price:** With hard case, Super Sling . . . . . . . . . . . . . . . . . . . . . . . . . . . **$1,735.00**

## Alpha Grand Slam Bolt Action Rifle
Similar to the Custom model except has classic-style stock of Alphawood, Niedner-style grip cap. Weight is about 6½ lbs. Other specs remain the same. Right or left-hand models available. Introduced 1984.
**Price:** With hard case, Super Sling . . . . . . . . . . . . . . . . . . . . . . . . . . . **$1,465.00**

Alpha Alaskan

## Alpha Alaskan Bolt Action Rifle
Similar to the Custom model except has stainless steel barrel and receiver with all other parts coated with Nitex. Has classic-style Alphawood stock, Niedner-style steel grip cap, barrel band swivel stud, inletted swivel stud on butt. Weight is 6¾ to 7¼ lbs. Same chamberings as Custom. Right or left-hand models available. Introduced 1984.
**Price:** With hard case, Super Sling . . . . . . . . . . . . . . . . . . . . . . . . . . . **$1,675.00**

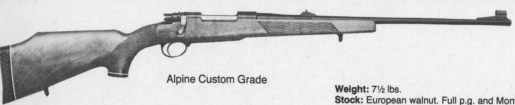

Alpine Custom Grade

## ALPINE BOLT ACTION RIFLE
**Caliber:** 22-250, 243 Win., 264 Win., 270, 30-06, 308, 308 Norma Mag., 7mm Rem Mag., 8mm, 300 Win. Mag., 5-shot magazine (3 for magnum).
**Barrel:** 23″ (std. cals.), 24″ (mag.).

**Weight:** 7½ lbs.
**Stock:** European walnut. Full p.g. and Monte Carlo; checkered p.g. and fore-end; rubber recoil pad; white line spacers; sling swivels.
**Sights:** Ramp front, open rear adj. for w. and e.
**Features:** Made by Firearms Co. Ltd. in England. Imported by Mandall Shooting Supplies.
**Price:** Standard Grade . . . . . . . . . . . . . . . . . . . . . . . . . . . . . . . . . . . . . **$375.00**
**Price:** Custom Grade (illus.) . . . . . . . . . . . . . . . . . . . . . . . . . . . . . . . . . **$395.00**

Anschutz 1432D/1532D

## ANSCHUTZ 1432D/1532D CLASSIC RIFLES
**Caliber:** 22 Hornet (1432D), 5-shot clip, 222 Rem. (1532D), 2-shot clip.
**Barrel:** 23½″; ¹³/₁₆″ dia. heavy.
**Weight:** 7¾ lbs. **Length:** 42½″ over-all.
**Stock:** Select European walnut with checkered pistol grip and fore-end.
**Sights:** None furnished, drilled and tapped for scope mounting.
**Features:** Adjustable single stage trigger. Receiver drilled and tapped for scope mounting. Introduced 1982. Imported from Germany by PSI.
**Price:** 1432D (22 Hornet) . . . . . . . . . . . . . . . . . . . . . . . . . . . . . . . . . . . **$673.75**
**Price:** 1532D (222 Rem.) . . . . . . . . . . . . . . . . . . . . . . . . . . . . . . . . . . . **$673.75**

## ARMSPORT 2801 BOLT ACTION RIFLE
**Caliber:** 243, 308, 30-06, 7mm Rem. Mag., 300 Win. Mag.
**Barrel:** 24″.
**Weight:** 8 lbs.
**Stock:** European walnut with Monte Carlo comb.
**Sights:** Ramp front, open adj. rear.
**Features:** Blue metal finish, glossy wood. Introduced 1986. Imported from Italy by Armsport.
**Price:** . . . . . . . . . . . . . . . . . . . . . . . . . . . . . . . . . . . . . . . . . . . . . . . . . **$575.00**

## ANSCHUTZ 1432D/1532D Custom Rifles
Similar to the Classic models except have roll-over Monte Carlo cheekpiece, slim fore-end with Schnabel tip, Wundhammer palm swell on pistol grip, rosewood grip cap with white diamond insert. Skip-line checkering on grip and fore-end. Introduced 1982. Imported from Germany by PSI.
**Price:** 1432D (22 Hornet) . . . . . . . . . . . . . . . . . . . . . . . . . . . . . . . . . . . **$721.75**
**Price:** 1532D (222 Rem.) . . . . . . . . . . . . . . . . . . . . . . . . . . . . . . . . . . . **$721.75**

**CAUTION:** PRICES CHANGE. CHECK AT GUNSHOP.

Beeman/Krico Model 420

## BEEMAN/KRICO MODEL 600/700L DELUXE BOLT ACTION
**Caliber:** 17 Rem., 222, 223, 22-250, 243, 308, 7x57, 7x64, 270, 30-06, 9.3x62, 8x68S, 7mm Rem. Mag., 300 Win. Mag., 9.3x64.
**Barrel:** 24″ (26″ in magnum calibers).
**Weight:** 7.5 lbs. **Length:** 44″ over-all (24″ barrel).
**Stock:** Traditional European style, select fancy walnut with rosewood Schnable fore-end, Bavarian cheekpiece, 28 lpi checkering.
**Sights:** Hooded front ramp, rear adjustable for windage.
**Features:** Butterknife bolt handle; gold plated single-set trigger; front sling swivel attached to barrel with ring; silent safety. Introduced 1983. Made in West Germany. Imported by Beeman.
**Price:** Model 600, varmint calibers . . . . . . . . . . . . . . . . . . . . . . . . . $1,049.50
**Price:** Model 600, standard calibers . . . . . . . . . . . . . . . . . . . . . . . . $1,049.50
**Price:** Model 700, magnum calibers . . . . . . . . . . . . . . . . . . . . . . . . $1,049.50

Beeman/Krico Model 640 Varmint

## BEEMAN/KRICO MODEL 400 BOLT ACTION RIFLE
**Caliber:** 22 Hornet, 5-shot magazine.
**Barrel:** 23.5″.
**Weight:** 6.8 lbs. **Length:** 43″ over-all.
**Stock:** Select European walnut, curved European comb with cheekpiece; solid rubber butt pad; cut checkered grip and fore-end.
**Sights:** Blade front on ramp, open rear adjustable for windage.
**Features:** Detachable box magazine; action has rear locking lugs, twin extractors. Available with single or optional match and double set trigger. Receiver grooved for scope mounts. Made in West Germany. Imported by Beeman.
**Price:** . . . . . . . . . . . . . . . . . . . . . . . . . . . . . . . . . . . . . . . . . . . . . . . . $649.50
**Price:** Model 420 (as above except 19.5″ bbl., full-length Mannlicher-style stock, double set trigger) . . . . . . . . . . . . . . . . . . . . . . . . . . . . . . $749.50

## Beeman/Krico Model 620/720 Bolt Action Rifle
Similar to the Model 600/700 except has 20.75″ barrel,. weighs 6.8 lbs., and has full-length Mannlicher-style stock with metal Schnabel fore-end tip; double set trigger with optional match trigger available. Receiver drilled and tapped for scope mounting. Imported from West Germany by Beeman.
**Price:** Model 620 (308 Win.) . . . . . . . . . . . . . . . . . . . . . . . . . . . . . . $995.00
**Price:** Model 720 (270 Win.) . . . . . . . . . . . . . . . . . . . . . . . . . . . . . . $995.00
**Price:** Model 720 (30-06) . . . . . . . . . . . . . . . . . . . . . . . . . . . . . . . . $995.00

## BEEMAN/KRICO MODEL 640 VARMINT RIFLE
**Caliber:** 222 Rem., 4-shot magazine.
**Barrel:** 23.75″.
**Weight:** 9.6 lbs. **Length:** 43½″ over-all.
**Stock:** Select European walnut with high Monte Carlo comb, Wundhammer palm swell, rosewood fore-end tip; cut checkered grip and fore-end.
**Sights:** None furnished. Drilled and tapped for scope mounting.
**Features:** Free floating heavy bull barrel; double set trigger with optional match trigger available. Imported from West Germany by Beeman.
**Price:** . . . . . . . . . . . . . . . . . . . . . . . . . . . . . . . . . . . . . . . . . . . . . . . . $995.00

Beretta 500 Series

## BERETTA 500 SERIES BOLT ACTION RIFLE
**Caliber:** 222, 223 (M500); 243, 308 (M501); 270, 7mm Rem. Mag., 30-06, 375 H&H (M502).
**Barrel:** 23.62″ to 24.41″.
**Weight:** 6.4 to 8.4 lbs. **Length:** NA
**Stock:** Walnut, with oil finish, hand checkering.
**Sights:** None furnished; drilled and tapped for scope mounting.
**Features:** Model 500 — short action; 501 — medium action; 502 — long action. All models have rubber butt pad. Imported from Italy by Beretta U.S.A. Corp. Introduced 1984.
**Price:** Model 500, 501, from . . . . . . . . . . . . . . . . . . . . . . **$665.00 to $1,785.00**
**Price:** Model 502, from . . . . . . . . . . . . . . . . . . . . . . . . . . . **$710.00 to $1,785.00**

BRNO ZKK 602

## BRNO ZKK 531 BOLT ACTION RIFLE
**Caliber:** 30-06, 270, 7x57, 7x64, 8x57JS, 8x64S, 8x68S, 300 Win. Mag., 338 Win. Mag., 7mm Rem. Mag., 280 Rem. (internal magazine); 243, 308 (detachable box magazine).
**Barrel:** 23½″.
**Weight:** NA.
**Stock:** European walnut.
**Sights:** Hooded front, open rear adj. for w.
**Features:** Double set triggers, tang safety, spring-type extractor, sling swivels. Drilled and tapped for scope mounts. Imported from Czechoslovakia by Bauska Arms Corp.
**Price:** . . . . . . . . . . . . . . . . . . . . . . . . . . . . . . . . . . . . . . . . . . . . . . . . . . . NA

## BRNO ZKK 600, 601, 602 BOLT ACTION RIFLES
**Caliber:** 30-06, 270, 7x57, 7x64 (M600); 223, 243, 308 (M601); 8x68S, 375 H&H, 458 Win. Mag. (M602), 5-shot magazine.
**Barrel:** 23½″ (M600, 601), 25″ (M602).
**Weight:** 6 lbs., 3 oz. to 9 lbs., 4 oz. **Length:** 43″ over-all (M601).
**Stock:** Walnut.
**Sights:** Hooded ramp front, open folding leaf adj. rear.
**Features:** Adjustable set trigger (standard trigger included); easy-release floorplate; sling swivels. Imported from Czechoslovakia by Bauska Arms Corp.
**Price:** ZKK Standard . . . . . . . . . . . . . . . . . . . . . . . . . . . . . . . . . . . . $479.00
**Price:** As above, Monte Carlo stock . . . . . . . . . . . . . . . . . . . . . . . . . $499.00
**Price:** ZKK 601 Standard . . . . . . . . . . . . . . . . . . . . . . . . . . . . . . . . . $379.00
**Price:** As above, Monte Carlo stock . . . . . . . . . . . . . . . . . . . . . . . . . $399.00
**Price:** ZKK 602, Monte Carlo stock . . . . . . . . . . . . . . . . . . . . . . . . . $599.00

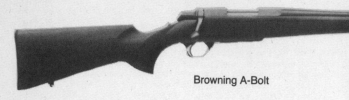

BRNO ZKB 680 FOX

## BRNO ZKB 680 FOX BOLT ACTION RIFLE
**Caliber:** 22 Hornet, 222 Rem., 5-shot magazine.
**Barrel:** 23½".
**Weight:** 5 lbs., 12 oz. **Length:** 42½" over-all.
**Stock:** Turkish walnut, with Monte Carlo.
**Sights:** Hooded front, open adj. rear.
**Features:** Detachable box magazine; adj. double set triggers. Imported from Czechoslovakia by Bauska Arms Corp.
**Price:** ............................................................. $399.00

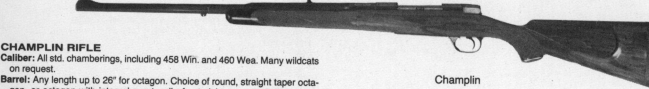

Browning A-Bolt

## BROWNING A-BOLT RIFLE
**Caliber:** 25-06, 270, 30-06, 7mm Rem. Mag., 300 Win. Mag., 338 Win. Mag.
**Barrel:** 22" medium sporter weight with recessed muzzle.
**Weight:** 6½ to 7½ lbs. **Length:** 44¾" over-all. (Magnum and standard), 41¾" (short action).
**Stock:** Classic style American walnut; recoil pad standard on magnum calibers.
**Features:** Short-throw (60°) fluted bolt, 9 locking lugs, plunger-type ejector; adjustable trigger is grooved and gold plated. Hinged floorplate, detachable box magazine (4 rounds std. cals., 3 for magnums). Slide tang safety. Medallion has glossy stock finish, rosewood grip and fore-end caps, high polish blue; Hunter has oil finish stock, matte blue. Introduced 1985. Imported from Japan by Browning.
**Price:** Medallion, no sights ...................................... $446.50
**Price:** Hunter, no sights ......................................... $379.95
**Price:** Hunter, with sights ...................................... $424.95

## Browning Short Action A-Bolt
Similar to the standard A-Bolt except has short action for 22-250, 243, 257 Roberts, 7mm-08, 308 chamberings. Available in Hunter or Medallion grades. Weighs 6½ lbs. Other specs essentially the same. Introduced 1985.
**Price:** Medallion, no sights ...................................... $446.50
**Price:** Hunter, no sights ......................................... $379.95
**Price:** Hunter, with sights ...................................... $424.95

## Browning A-Bolt High Grade Limited Edition
### Big Horn Sheep Issue
Same specifications as standard A-Bolt except 270 Win. only, stock is high grade walnut, and brass spacers highlight the grip caps and recoil pad; high gloss finish. Deep relief engraving on the receiver, barrel, floorplate and trigger guard serve as a setting for the game species, displayed in 24K gold. Stock has cut skipline checkering with a pearl border design. Limited to only 600 units. Introduced 1986.
**Price:** ...................................................... $1,365.00

> Consult our Directory pages for
> the location of firms mentioned.

Champlin

## CHAMPLIN RIFLE
**Caliber:** All std. chamberings, including 458 Win. and 460 Wea. Many wildcats on request.
**Barrel:** Any length up to 26" for octagon. Choice of round, straight taper octagon, or octagon with integral quarter rib, front sight ramp and sling swivel stud.
**Weight:** About 8 lbs. **Length:** 45" over-all.
**Stock:** Hand inletted, shaped and finished. Checkered to customer specs. Select French, Circassian or claro walnut. Steel p.g. cap, trap buttplate or recoil pad.
**Sights:** Bead on ramp front, 3-leaf folding rear.
**Features:** Right-hand Champlin action, tang safety or optional shroud safety, Canjar adj. trigger, hinged floorplate.
**Price:** From ................................................ $5,400.00

Churchill Regent

## CHURCHILL BOLT ACTION RIFLE
**Caliber:** 25-06, 270, 30-06 (4-shot magazine) 7mm Rem. Mag. (3-shot).
**Barrel:** 22" (7mm Rem. Mag. has 24").
**Weight:** 7½-8 lbs. **Length:** 42½" over-all with 22" barrel.
**Stock:** European walnut, checkered p.g. and fore-end. Regent grade has Monte Carlo, Highlander has classic design.
**Sights:** Gold bead on ramp front, fully adj. rear.
**Features:** Positive safety locks trigger; oil-finished wood; swivel posts; recoil pad. Imported by Kassnar Imports, Inc. Introduced 1986.
**Price:** Highlander, without sights, either cal. ...................... $549.00
**Price:** As above, with sights .................................... $584.00
**Price:** Regent, without sights .................................. $759.00
**Price:** As above, with sights .................................... $789.00

**CAUTION:** PRICES CHANGE. CHECK AT GUNSHOP.

Du Biel Modern Classic

Consult our Directory pages for
the location of firms mentioned.

## Du BIEL ARMS BOLT ACTION RIFLES
**Caliber:** Standard calibers 22-250 thru 458 Win. Mag. Selected wildcat calibers available.
**Barrel:** Selected weights and lengths. Douglas Premium
**Weight:** About 7½ lbs.
**Stock:** Five styles. Walnut, maple, laminates. Hand checkered.
**Sights:** None furnished. Receiver has integral milled bases.
**Features:** Basically a custom-made rifle. Left or right-hand models available. Five-lug locking mechanism; 36 degree bolt rotation; adjustable Canjar trigger; oil or epoxy stock finish; Presentation recoil pad; jeweled and chromed bolt body; sling swivel studs; lever latch or button floorplate release. All steel action and parts. Introduced 1978. From Du Biel Arms.
**Price:** Rollover Model, left or right-hand . . . . . . . . . . . . . . . . . . . . . . . $2,500.00
**Price:** Thumbhole, left or right hand . . . . . . . . . . . . . . . . . . . . . . . . . $2,500.00
**Price:** Classic, left or right hand . . . . . . . . . . . . . . . . . . . . . . . . . . . . $2,500.00
**Price:** Modern Classic, left or right hand. . . . . . . . . . . . . . . . . . . . . . . $2,500.00
**Price:** Thumbhole Mannlicher, left or right hand . . . . . . . . . . . . . . . $2,500.00

## DUMOULIN MODEL BAVARIA BOLT ACTION RIFLE
**Caliber:** 222, 222 Rem. Mag., 223, 270, 280 Rem., 30-06, 6.5x57, 7x57, 7x64, 243, 264 Win., 7mm Rem. Mag., 300 Win., 338 Win., 6.5x68, 8x68S, 25-06, 22-250, 6mm, 300 Wea., 308 Norma, 240 Wea., 375 H&H, 9.3x64, 458 Win. Others on request.
**Barrel:** 21″, 24″, 25″, octagon.
**Weight:** About 7 lbs.

**Stock:** Select walnut with oil finish; hand checkered p.g. and fore-end.
**Sights:** Blade on ramp front (hooded), classic 2-leaf rear.
**Features:** Mauser system action; adj. trigger; M70-type safety; Boehler steel barrel, q.d. swivels, front on fore-end or barrel; solid butt pad. Imported from Belgium by Midwest Gun Sport.
**Price:** About. . . . . . . . . . . . . . . . . . . . . . . . . . . . . . . . . . . . . . . . . . $1,940.00
**Price:** Model Diane (as above except with round barrel) . . . . . . . . . $1,750.00

## DUMOULIN AFRICAN SAFARI RIFLE
**Caliber:** 264 Win., 7mm Rem. Mag., 300 Win., 338 Win., 6.5x58, 8x68S, 300 H&H, 375 H&H, 9.3x64, 458 Win., 404 Jeffrey, 416 Rigby, 416 Hoffman, 7mm Wea., 300 Wea., 340 Wea. Others on request.
**Barrel:** 24″ to 26″.
**Weight:** 8½-9 lbs. **Length:** 44″ over-all with 24″ barrel.

**Stock:** Deluxe European walnut in classic English style; oil finish; recoil lug; buffalo horn grip cap; solid rubber butt pad.
**Sights:** Hooded front on banded ramp, quarter-rib with 2-leaf rear.
**Features:** Mauser Oberndorf or modified Sako action; adj. trigger; M70-type or side safety. Custom-built gun. Imported from Belgium by Midwest Gun Sport.
**Price:** About. . . . . . . . . . . . . . . . . . . . . . . . . . . . . . . . . . . . . . . . . . $2,750.00

Heym Model SR-20L

## HEYM MODEL SR-20 BOLT ACTION RIFLES
**Caliber:** 5.6x57, 243, 6.5x55, 6.5x57, 270, 7x57, 7x64, 308, 30-06 (SR-20L); 9.3x62 (SR-20N) plus SR-20L cals.; SR-20G—6.5x68, 7mm Rem. Mag., 300 Win. Mag., 8x68S, 375 H&H.
**Barrel:** 20½″ (SR-20L), 24″ (SR-20N), 26″ (SR-20G).
**Weight:** 7-8 lbs. depending upon model.
**Stock:** Dark European walnut, hand-checkered p.g. and fore-end. Oil finish. Recoil pad, rosewood grip cap. Monte Carlo-style. SR-20L has full Mannlicher-style stock, others have sporter-style with schnabel tip.
**Sights:** Silver bead ramp front, adj. folding leaf rear.
**Features:** Hinged floorplate, 3-position safety,. Receiver drilled and tapped for scope mounts. Adjustable trigger. Options available include double-set triggers, left-hand action and stock, Suhler olaw mounts, deluxe engraving and stock carving. Imported from West Germany by Paul Jaeger, Inc.

## Heym SR-40 Bolt Action Rifle
Same as the SR-20 except has short action, chambered for 222 Rem., 223 Rem., 5.6x50 Mag. Over-all length of 44″, weight about 6¼ lbs., 24″ barrel. Carbine Mannlicher-style stock. Introduced 1984.
**Price:** . . . . . . . . . . . . . . . . . . . . . . . . . . . . . . . . . . . . . . . . . . . . . . . $798.00
**Price:** Single set trigger, add . . . . . . . . . . . . . . . . . . . . . . . . . . . . . . . $70.00

**Price:** SR-20L . . . . . . . . . . . . . . . . . . . . . . . . . . . . . . . . . . . . . . . . . $985.00
**Price:** SR-20N . . . . . . . . . . . . . . . . . . . . . . . . . . . . . . . . . . . . . . . . . $875.00
**Price:** SR-20-G. . . . . . . . . . . . . . . . . . . . . . . . . . . . . . . . . . . . . . . . . $920.00
**Price:** Single set trigger, add . . . . . . . . . . . . . . . . . . . . . . . . . . . . . . . $70.00

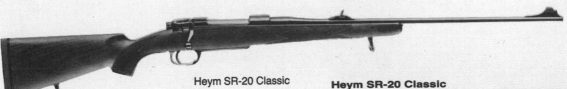

Heym SR-20 Classic

## Heym SR-20 Classic
Similar to the standard SR-20N except chambered for 5.6x57, 6.5x57, 6.5x55 SM, 7x57, 7x64, 9.3x62, 243, 270, 308, 30-06 (standard cals.); 6.5x68, 8x68 S, 7mm Rem. Mag., 300 Win. Mag., 375 H&H (magnum cals.). Has 24″ barrel (std. cals.), 25″ (mag. cals.). Classic-style French walnut stock with cheekpiece, hand checkering, Pachmayr Old English pad, q.d. swivels, oil finish, steel grip cap. Open sights on request. Choice of adjustable, single-set or double-set trigger. Introduced 1985.
**Price:** SR-20 Classic, right-hand . . . . . . . . . . . . . . . . . . . . . . . . . . . . $875.00
**Price:** SR-20 Classic, left-hand . . . . . . . . . . . . . . . . . . . . . . . . . . . . $1,150.00
**Price:** Magnum calibers, right or left-hand add . . . . . . . . . . . . . . . . . . $45.00
**Price:** Single set trigger, add . . . . . . . . . . . . . . . . . . . . . . . . . . . . . . . $70.00
**Price:** Open sights, from. . . . . . . . . . . . . . . . . . . . . . . . . . . . . . . . . . $125.00

## Heym SR-20, SR-40 Left Hand Rifles
All Heym bolt action rifles are available with true left-hand action and stock, in all calibers listed for the right-hand version, for an additional . . . . . $165.00

KDF K-15 Improved

## KDF K-15 Fiberstock "Pro-Hunter" Rifle

Same as K-15 Improved Rifle except standard with Brown Precision fiberglass stock (black, green, gray, brown or camo) wrinkle finish, KDF recoil arrestor installed and choice of parkerized, matte-blue or electroless nickel finish.

**Price:** Standard calibers . . . . . . . . . . . . . . . . . . . . . . . . . . . . . . . . . . . . . **$1,600.00**
**Price:** Magnum calibers . . . . . . . . . . . . . . . . . . . . . . . . . . . . . . . . . . . . . **$1,650.00**

## KDF K-15 "Dangerous Game" Rifle

Same as K-15 Improved Rifle except chambered for 411 KDF Magnum caliber. Standard with KDF Recoil Arrestor, choice of iron sights or scope mounts, hinged floorplate, and choice of high-gloss blue, matte blue, parkerized or electroless nickel metal finish.

**Price:** . . . . . . . . . . . . . . . . . . . . . . . . . . . . . . . . . . . . . . . . . . . . . . . . . **$1,800.00**

## KDF K-15 IMPROVED RIFLE

**Caliber:** 243, 25-06, 270, 7x57, 308, 30-06, 4-shot magazine, (standard); 257 Wea., 270 Wea., 7mm Rem. Mag., 300 Win. Mag., 300 Wea., 308 Norma Mag., 375 H&H, 3-shot magazine. Special chamberings avail.
**Barrel:** 24" (standard), 26" (magnum).
**Weight:** About 8 lbs. **Length:** 44½" over-all (24" bbl.).
**Stock:** Oil finished, hand checkered European walnut; recoil pad, swivel studs. Choice of Featherweight Classic with Schnabel or European Monte Carlo with rosewood grip cap, fore-end tip. High luster finish avail.
**Sights:** None furnished; drilled and tapped for scope mounting. Open sights, rings, bases avail. from KDF.
**Features:** KDF pillar bedding system; ultra-fast lock time. Three year accuracy guarantee from maker — 3-shot ½" group at 100 yds. From KDF, Inc.
**Price:** Standard calibers . . . . . . . . . . . . . . . . . . . . . . . . . . . . . . . . . . . . **$1,100.00**
**Price:** Magnum calibers . . . . . . . . . . . . . . . . . . . . . . . . . . . . . . . . . . . . **$1,150.00**
**Price:** Special chamberings . . . . . . . . . . . . . . . . . . . . . . . . . . . . . . . . . . **P.O.R.**

Kimber Model 82

## KIMBER MODEL 82 SPORTER

**Caliber:** 22 Hornet; 3-shot flush-fitting magazine; 218 Bee, 25-20, single shot.
**Barrel:** 22½", 6 grooves; 1-in-14" twist; 24" heavy.
**Weight:** About 6¼ lbs. **Length:** 42" over-all.
**Stock:** Three styles available. "Classic" is Claro walnut with plain, straight comb; "Cascade" has Monte Carlo comb with cheekpiece. "Custom Classic" is of fancy select grade Claro walnut, ebony fore-end tip, Niedner-style buttplate. All have 18 lpi hand cut, borderless checkering, steel grip cap, checkered steel buttplate.

**Sights:** Hooded ramp front with bead, folding leaf rear (optional).
**Features:** All steel construction; twin rear horizontally opposed locking lugs; fully adjustable trigger; rocker-type safety. Receiver grooved for Kimber scope mounts. Available in true left-hand version in selected models. Introduced 1982.
**Price:** Classic stock, no sights (left hand also avail.) . . . . . . . . . . . . . . **$750.00**
**Price:** Cascade stock, no sights . . . . . . . . . . . . . . . . . . . . . . . . . . . . . . . . **$805.00**
**Price:** Custom Classic, no sights (left hand also avail.) . . . . . . . . . . . . **$995.00**
**Price:** Kimber scope mounts, from . . . . . . . . . . . . . . . . . . . . . . . . . . . . . . **$48.00**
**Price:** Open sights fitted (optional) . . . . . . . . . . . . . . . . . . . . . . . . . . . . . **$55.00**
**Price:** 218 Bee, Custom Classic, plain or heavy barrel . . . . . . . . . . . . . **$995.00**
**Price:** 25-20, Custom Classic, plain barrel . . . . . . . . . . . . . . . . . . . . . . . **$995.00**

Kimber Model 84

## Kimber Model 82,84 Super America

Super-grade version of the Model 82. Has a Classic stock only of specially selected, high-grade, California claro walnut, with Continental beaded cheekpiece and ebony fore-end tip; borderless, full-coverage 20 lpi checkering; Niedner-type checkered steel buttplate; comes with barrel quarter-rib which has a folding leaf sight. Round-top receiver on the 1986 model is drilled and tapped to accept Kimber's screw-on scope mount bases. Available in 22 Long Rifle, 22 Magnum, 22 Hornet, 223 Rem.
**Price:** Model 82, 22 Long Rifle, less 4x scope . . . . . . . . . . . . . . . . . . **$1,150.00**
**Price:** Model 82, 22 Hornet, less scope . . . . . . . . . . . . . . . . . . . . . . . . **$1,150.00**
**Price:** Model 84, 223 Rem. . . . . . . . . . . . . . . . . . . . . . . . . . . . . . . . . . . . **$1,250.00**

## KIMBER MODEL 84 SPORTER

**Caliber:** 17 Rem., 17 Mach IV, 221 Fireball, 222 Rem., 222 Rem. Mag., 223 Rem., 6x45, 6x47; 5-shot magazine.
**Barrel:** 22" (Sporter), 24" (Varmint).
**Weight:** About 6¼ lbs. **Length:** 40½" over-all (Sporter).
**Stock:** Three styles available. "Classic" is Claro walnut with plain, straight comb; "Cascade" has Monte Carlo comb with cheekpiece. "Custom Classic" is of fancy select grade Claro walnut, ebony fore-end tip, Niedner-style buttplate. All have 18 lpi hand cut, borderless checkering, steel grip cap, checkered steel buttplate.
**Sights:** Hooded ramp front with bead, folding leaf rear (optional).
**Features:** All new Mauser-type head locking bolt action; steel trigger guard and hinged floorplate; Mauser-type extractor; fully adjustable trigger; chrome-moly barrel. Round-top receiver drilled and topped for scope mounting. Varmint gun prices same as others. Introduced 1984.
**Price:** Classic stock, no sights . . . . . . . . . . . . . . . . . . . . . . . . . . . . . . . **$850.00**
**Price:** Cascade stock, no sights . . . . . . . . . . . . . . . . . . . . . . . . . . . . . . . **$905.00**
**Price:** Custom Classic stock, no sights . . . . . . . . . . . . . . . . . . . . . . . . . **$1,095.00**
**Price:** Kimber scope mounts, from . . . . . . . . . . . . . . . . . . . . . . . . . . . . . **$48.00**
**Price:** Open sights fitted (optional) . . . . . . . . . . . . . . . . . . . . . . . . . . . . . **$55.00**

Marathon Sportsman

## MARATHON SPORTSMAN BUSH & FIELD RIFLE

**Caliber:** 243, 308, 7x57, 30-06, 270, 7mm Rem. Mag., 300 Win. Mag.
**Barrel:** 24".
**Weight:** 7.9 lbs. **Length:** 45" over-all.
**Stock:** Select walnut with Monte Carlo and rubber recoil pad.
**Sights:** Bead front on ramp, open adjustable rear.
**Features:** Uses the Santa Barbara Mauser action. Triple thumb locking safety blocks trigger, firing pin and bolt. Blue finish. Also available as a kit requiring assembly, wood and metal finishing. Introduced 1984. Imported from Spain by Marathon Products.
**Price:** Finished . . . . . . . . . . . . . . . . . . . . . . . . . . . . . . . . . . . . . . . . . . . . **$339.99**
**Price:** Kit . . . . . . . . . . . . . . . . . . . . . . . . . . . . . . . . . . . . . . . . . . . . . . . . . . **$209.99**

**CAUTION:** PRICES CHANGE. CHECK AT GUNSHOP.

Mossberg Model 1500

## Mossberg Model 1550 Rifle

Similar to the M1500 except has removable box magazine. In cals. 243, 270, 30-06 only. Introduced 1986.

Price: ................................................................ NA

## Mossberg Model 1500 Deluxe Rifle

Similar to Standard model except comes without sights, has engine-turned bolt; floorplate has decorative scroll. Stock has skip-line checkering, pistol grip cap with inset S&W seal, white spacers. Sling, swivels and swivel posts are included. Magnum models have vent, recoil pad.

Price: Deluxe, std. cals. ........................................ $363.00
Price: Deluxe, magnum cals..................................... $386.00

### MOSSBERG M1500 MOUNTAINEER RIFLE

Caliber: 222, 223, 22-250, 243, 25-06, 270, 30-06, 308, 7mm Rem. Mag., 300 Win. Mag., 338 Win. Mag.
Barrel: 22" (24" in magnum calibers.).
Weight: 7½-7¾ lbs. Length: 42" over-all (42½" for 270, 30-06, 7mm).
Stock: American walnut with Monte Carlo comb and cheekpiece; 18-line-per-inch checkering on p.g. and fore-end.
Sights: Hooded ramp gold bead front, open round-notch rear adj. for w. & e. Drilled and tapped for scope mounts.
Features: Trigger guard and magazine box are a single unit with a hinged floorplate. Comes with q.d. swivel studs. Composition non-slip buttplate with white spacer. Magnum models have rubber recoil pad. Introduced 1979.

Price: Standard cals., no sights................................. $341.00
Price: Magnum cals., no sights ................................. $356.00
Price: Standard cals., with sights .............................. $365.00
Price: Magnum cals., with sights................................ $379.00

Mossberg Classic Hunter

## Mossberg Model 1500 Varmint Deluxe Rifle

Similar to the standard 1500 except has a 22" heavy barrel and fully adjustable trigger. Chambered for 222, 22-250 and 223. Weighs 9 lbs. 5 oz. Skip-line checkering, q.d. swivels. Introduced 1982.

Price: Blue................................................... $425.00
Price: Parkerized, oil finished stock ............................ $432.00

### Mossberg Model 1700LS "Classic Hunter"

Similar to the standard Model 1500 except has classic-style stock with tapered fore-end and Schnabel tip, ribbon hand checkering, black rubber butt pad with black spacer; flush mounted sling swivels; removeable 5-shot magazine; jeweled bolt body with knurled bolt knob. Chambered only for 243, 270, 30-06. Introduced 1983.

Price: ............................................................ $454.00

Parker-Hale 81 Classic

## PARKER-HALE MODEL 81 CLASSIC RIFLE

Caliber: 22-250, 243, 6mm Rem., 270, 6.5x55, 7x57, 7x64, 308, 30-06, 300 Win. Mag., 7mm Rem. Mag., 4-shot magazine.
Barrel: 24".
Weight: About 7¾ lbs. Length: 44½" over-all.

Stock: European walnut in classic style with oil finish, hand-cut checkering; palm swell pistol grip, rosewood grip cap.
Sights: None furnished. Drilled and tapped for open sights and scope mounting.
Features: Uses Mauser-style action; one-piece steel, Oberndorf-style trigger guard with hinged floorplate; rubber butt pad; quick-detachable sling swivels. Imported from England by Precision Sports, Inc. Introduced 1984.

Price: ...................................................... $649.95
Price: Optional set trigger..................................... $74.95

Parker-Hale 81 African

### Parker-Hale Model 81 African Rifle

Similar to the Model 81 Classic except chambered only for 300 H&H, 308 Norma Mag., 375 H&H and 9.3x64. Has adjustable trigger, barrel band front swivel, African express rear sight, engraved receiver. Classic-style stock has a solid butt pad, checkered p.g. and fore-end. Introduced 1986.

Price: ...................................................... $789.95

Parker-Hale Model 1100

### Parker-Hale Model 1100 Lightweight Rifle

Similar to the Model 81 Classic except has slim barrel profile, hollow bolt handle, alloy trigger guard/floorplate. The Monte Carlo stock has a Schnabel fore-end hand-cut checkering, swivel studs, palm swell pistol grip. Comes with hooded ramp front sight, open Williams rear adjustable for windage and elevation. Same calibers as Model 81. Over-all length is 43", weight 6½ lbs., with 22" barrel. Imported from England by Precision Sports, Inc. Introduced 1984.

Price: ...................................................... $529.95
Price: Optional set trigger..................................... $74.95
Price: Optional Deluxe fancy wood.............................. $64.95

---

**CAUTION:** PRICES CHANGE. CHECK AT GUNSHOP.

Parker-Hale 1200 Super

## PARKER-HALE MODEL 1200 SUPER BOLT ACTION
**Caliber:** 22-250, 243, 6mm, 25-06, 270, 6.5x55, 7x57, 7x64, 308, 30-06, 8mm.
**Barrel:** 24".
**Weight:** About 7½ lbs. **Length:** 44½" over-all.
**Stock:** European walnut, rosewood grip and fore-end tips, hand-cut checkering; roll-over cheekpiece; palm swell pistol grip; ventilated recoil pad; wraparound checkering.
**Sights:** Hooded post front, open rear.
**Features:** Uses Mauser-style action with claw extractor; gold plated adjustable trigger; silent side safety locks trigger, sear and bolt; aluminum trigger guard. Imported from England by Precision Sports, Inc. Introduced 1984.
**Price:** . . . . . . . . . . . . . . . . . . . . . . . . . . . . . . . . . . . . . . . . . . . **$549.95**
**Price:** Optional set trigger . . . . . . . . . . . . . . . . . . . . . . . . . . . . . . . . **$74.95**

### Parker-Hale Model 1200 Super Clip Rifle
Same as the Model 1200 Super except has a detachable steel box magazine and steel trigger guard. Imported from England by Precision Sports, Inc. Introduced 1984.
**Price:** . . . . . . . . . . . . . . . . . . . . . . . . . . . . . . . . . . . . . . . . . . . **$579.95**
**Price:** Optional set trigger . . . . . . . . . . . . . . . . . . . . . . . . . . . . . . . . **$74.95**

### Parker-Hale Model 1100M African Magnum
Similar to the Model 1000 Standard except has 24" barrel, 46" over-all length, weighs 9½ lbs., and is chambered for 375 H&H Magnum, 404 Jeffery and 458 Win. Magnum. Has hooded post front sight, shallow V-notch rear, 180° flag safety (low 45° scope safety available). Specially lengthened steel magazine has hinged floorplate; heavily reinforced, glass bedded and weighted stock has a ventilated rubber recoil pad. Imported from England by Precision Sports, Inc. Introduced 1984.
**Price:** . . . . . . . . . . . . . . . . . . . . . . . . . . . . . . . . . . . . . . . . . . . **$789.95**

### Parker-Hale Model 1000 Standard Rifle
Similar to the Model 1200 Super except has standard walnut Monte Carlo stock with satin varnish finish, no rosewood grip/fore-end caps; fitted with checkered buttplate, standard sling swivels. Imported from England by Precision Sports, Inc. Introduced 1984.
**Price:** . . . . . . . . . . . . . . . . . . . . . . . . . . . . . . . . . . . . . . . . . . . **$429.95**
**Price:** Optional set trigger . . . . . . . . . . . . . . . . . . . . . . . . . . . . . . . . **$74.95**

## PARKER-HALE MODEL 2100 MIDLAND RIFLE
**Caliber:** 22-250, 243, 6mm, 270, 6.5x55, 7x57, 7x64, 308, 30-06.
**Barrel:** 22".
**Weight:** About 7 lbs. **Length:** 43" over-all.
**Stock:** European walnut, cut-checkered pistol grip and fore-end; sling swivels.
**Sights:** Hooded post front, flip-up open rear.
**Features:** Mauser-type action has twin front locking lugs, rear safety lug, and claw extractor; hinged floorplate; adjustable single stage trigger; silent side safety. Imported from England by Precision Sports, Inc. Introduced 1984.
**Price:** . . . . . . . . . . . . . . . . . . . . . . . . . . . . . . . . . . . . . . . . . . . **$299.00**

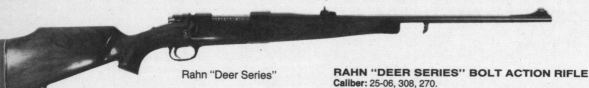

Rahn "Deer Series"

## RAHN "DEER SERIES" BOLT ACTION RIFLE
**Caliber:** 25-06, 308, 270.
**Barrel:** 24".
**Weight:** NA. **Length:** NA.
**Stock:** Circassian walnut with rosewood fore-end and grip caps, Monte Carlo cheekpiece, semi-Schnabel fore-end; hand checkered.
**Sights:** Bead front, open adjustable rear. Drilled and tapped for scope mount.
**Features:** Free floating barrel; rubber recoil pad; one-piece trigger guard with hinged, engraved floorplate; 22 rimfire conversion insert available. Introduced 1986. From Rahn Gun Works, Inc.
**Price:** . . . . . . . . . . . . . . . . . . . . . . . . . . . . . . . . . . . . . . . . . . . **$750.00**
**Price:** With custom stock made to customer specs . . . . . . . . . . . . . . . **$800.00**

### Rahn "Himalayan Series" Rifle
Similar to the "Deer Series" except chambered for 5.6x57 or 6.5x68S, short stock of walnut or fiberglass, and floorplate engravings of a yak with scroll border. Introduced 1986.
**Price:** . . . . . . . . . . . . . . . . . . . . . . . . . . . . . . . . . . . . . . . . . . . **$800.00**
**Price:** With walnut stock made to customer specs . . . . . . . . . . . . . . . . **$850.00**

### Rahn "Safari Series" Rifle
Similar to the "Deer Series" except chambered for 308 Norma Mag., 300 Win. Mag., 8x68S, 9x64. Choice of Cape buffalo, rhino or elephant engraving. Gold oval nameplate with three initials. Introduced 1986.
**Price:** . . . . . . . . . . . . . . . . . . . . . . . . . . . . . . . . . . . . . . . . . . . **$900.00**
**Price:** With stock made to customer specs . . . . . . . . . . . . . . . . . . . . . **$950.00**

### Rahn "Elk Series" Rifle
Similar to the "Deer Series" except chambered for 6mmx56, 30-06, 7mm Rem. Mag. and has elk head engraving on floorplate. Introduced 1986.
**Price:** . . . . . . . . . . . . . . . . . . . . . . . . . . . . . . . . . . . . . . . . . . . **$785.00**
**Price:** With stock made to customer specs . . . . . . . . . . . . . . . . . . . . . **$835.00**

Remington 700 Classic

## REMINGTON 700 "CLASSIC" RIFLE
**Caliber:** 264 Win. Mag. only, 4-shot magazine.
**Barrel:** 24".
**Weight:** About 7¾ lbs. **Length:** 44½" over-all.
**Stock:** American walnut, 20 l.p.i. checkering on p.g. and fore-end. Classic styling. Satin finish.
**Sights:** No sights furnished. Receiver drilled and tapped for scope mounting.
**Features:** A "classic" version of the M700ADL with straight comb stock. Fitted with rubber butt pad on all but magnum caliber, which has a full recoil pad. Sling swivel studs installed. Limited production in 1986 only
**Price:** About . . . . . . . . . . . . . . . . . . . . . . . . . . . . . . . . . . . . . . . . . **$465.00**

**CAUTION:** PRICES CHANGE. CHECK AT GUNSHOP.

Remington 700 BDL

## REMINGTON 700 ADL BOLT ACTION RIFLE
**Caliber:** 22-250, 243, 25-06, 270, 308 and 30-06.
**Barrel:** 22″ or 24″ round tapered.
**Weight:** 7 lbs. **Length:** 41½″ to 43½″.
**Stock:** Walnut, RKW finished p.g. stock with impressed checkering, Monte Carlo (13⅜″x1⅝″x2⅜″).
**Sights:** Gold bead ramp front; removable, step-adj. rear with windage screw.
**Features:** Side safety, receiver tapped for scope mounts.
**Price:** About .................................................. $400.00
**Price:** 7mm Rem. Mag., about............................... $420.00

## Remington 700BDL Left Hand
Same as 700 BDL except: mirror-image left-hand action, stock. Available in 270, 30-06 only.
**Price:** About .................................................. $520.00
**Price:** 7mm Rem. Mag., about............................... $539.00

### Remington 700 BDL Bolt Action Rifle
Same as 700-ADL, except: also available in 222, 223, 6mm, 7mm-08 Rem.; skip-line checkering; black fore-end tip and p.g. cap, white line spacers. Matted receiver top, quick release floorplate. Hooded ramp front sight. Q.D. swivels and 1″ sling.
**Price:** About .................................................. $471.00
Available also in 17 Rem., 7mm Rem. Mag. and 300 Win. Mag. calibers. 44½″ over-all, weight 7½ lbs.
**Price:** About .................................................. $490.00
**Price:** Custom Grade I, about............................... $1,131.00
**Price:** Custom Grade II, about.............................. $2,056.00
**Price:** Custom Grade III, about............................. $3,181.00
**Price:** Custom Grade IV, about.............................. $4,933.00

### Remington 700 BDL Varmint Special
Same as 700 BDL, except: 24″ heavy bbl., 43½″ over-all, wgt. 9 lbs. Cals. 222, 223, 22-250, 243, 6mm Rem., 25-06, 7mm-08 Rem. and 308. No sights.
**Price:** About .................................................. $501.00

### Remington 700 Safari
Same as the 700 BDL except 8mm Rem. Mag., 375 H&H or 458 Win. Magnum calibers only. Hand checkered, oil finished stock in classic or Monte Carlo style with recoil pad installed. Delivery time is about five months.
**Price:** About .................................................. $775.00

Remington 700 Mountain

### Remington Model 700 "Mountain Rifle"
Similar to the 700BDL except weighs 6¾ lbs., has a 22″ tapered barrel. Redesigned pistol grip, straight comb, contoured cheekpiece, satin stock finish, fine checkering, hinged floorplate and magazine follower, 2-position thumb safety. Chambered for 270 Win., 280 Rem., 30-06, 4-shot magazine. Over-all length is 42½″. Introduced 1986.
**Price:** About .................................................. $477.00

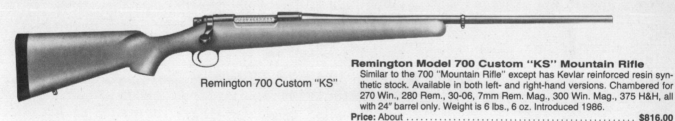

Remington 700 Custom "KS"

### Remington Model 700 Custom "KS" Mountain Rifle
Similar to the 700 "Mountain Rifle" except has Kevlar reinforced resin synthetic stock. Available in both left- and right-hand versions. Chambered for 270 Win., 280 Rem., 30-06, 7mm Rem. Mag., 300 Win. Mag., 375 H&H, all with 24″ barrel only. Weight is 6 lbs., 6 oz. Introduced 1986.
**Price:** About .................................................. $816.00

Remington Sportsman 78

### Remington "Sportsman" 78 Bolt Action Rifle
Similar to the Model 700 except available only in 223, 243, 308, 270 Win. or 30-06, 4-shot magazine, 22″ barrel, straight comb walnut-finished hardwood stock. Open adjustable sights; weight about 7 lbs. Introduced 1984.
**Price:** About .................................................. $327.00

Remington Model Seven

### REMINGTON MODEL SEVEN BOLT ACTION RIFLE
**Caliber:** 223 Rem. (5-shot), 243, 7mm-08, 6mm, 308 (4-shot).
**Barrel:** 18½″.
**Weight:** 6¼ lbs. **Length:** 37½″ over-all.
**Stock:** Walnut, with modified Schnabel fore-end. Cut checkering.
**Sights:** Ramp front, adjustable open rear.
**Features:** New short action design; silent side safety; free-floated barrel except for single pressure point at fore-end tip. Introduced 1983.
**Price:** About .................................................. $467.00

Ruger Model 77R

Ruger Model 77RS

Ruger International 77

Ruger 77 Ultra Light

Ruger 77 Varmint

Sako Hunter

## RUGER 77R BOLT ACTION RIFLE

**Caliber:** 22-250, 6mm, 243, 308, 220 Swift (Short Stroke action); 270, 7x57, 257 Roberts, 280 Rem., 30-06, 25-06, 7mm Rem. Mag., 300 Win. Mag., 338 Win. Mag. (Magnum action).
**Barrel:** 22" round tapered (24" in 220 Swift and magnum action calibers).
**Weight:** 6¾ lbs. **Length:** 42" over-all (22" barrel).
**Stock:** Hand checkered American walnut (13¾"x1⅝"x2⅛"), p.g. cap, sling swivel studs and recoil pad.
**Sights:** None supplied; comes with scope rings.
**Features:** Integral scope mount bases, diagonal bedding system, hinged floor plate, adj. trigger, tang safety.
**Price:** With Ruger steel scope rings, no sights (77R) ............. **$440.00**

## Ruger Model 77RS Tropical Rifle

Similar to the Model 77RS Magnum except chambered only for 458 Win. Mag., 24" barrel, steel trigger guard and floorplate. Weight about 8¾ lbs. Comes with open sights and Ruger 1" scope rings.
**Price:** .................................................... **$600.00**

## Ruger Model 77RS Magnum Rifle

Similar to Ruger 77 except: magnum-size action. Calibers 270, 7x57, 30-06, 243, 308 have 22" barrel, 25-06, 7mm Rem. Mag., 300 Win., Mag., 338 Win. Mag., with 24" barrel. Weight about 7 lbs. Integral-base receiver, Ruger 1" rings and open sights.
**Price:** Model 77 RS ........................................... **$474.00**

## Ruger International Model 77 RSI Rifle

Same as the standard Model 77 except has 18½" barrel, full-length Mannlicher-style stock, with steel fore-end cap, loop-type sling swivel. Integral base receiver, open sights, Ruger 1" steel rings. Improved front sight. Available in 22-250, 250-3000, 243, 308, 270, 30-06. Weighs 7 lbs. Length over-all is 38⅜".
**Price:** .................................................... **$480.00**

## Ruger Model 77RL Ultra Light

Similar to the standard Model 77 except weighs only 6 lbs., chambered for 243, 270, 30-06, 257, 22-250, 250-3000 and 308; barrel tapped for target scope blocks; has 20" Ultra Light barrel. Over-all length 40". Ruger's steel 1" scope rings supplied. Introduced 1983.
**Price:** Model 77 RL ........................................... **$455.00**

## RUGER MODEL 77V VARMINT

**Caliber:** 22-250, 220 Swift, 243, 6mm, 25-06, 308.
**Barrel:** 24" heavy straight tapered, 26" in 220 swift.
**Weight:** Approx. 9 lbs. **Length:** Approx. 44" over-all (24" barrel).
**Stock:** American walnut, similar in style to Magnum Rifle.
**Sights:** Barrel drilled and tapped for target scope blocks. Integral scope mount bases in receiver.
**Features:** Ruger diagonal bedding system, Ruger steel 1" scope rings supplied. Fully adj. trigger. Barreled actions available in any of the standard calibers and barrel lengths.
**Price:** (Model 77V) ........................................... **$440.00**

**Weight:** 5¾ lbs. (short); 6¼ lbs. (med.); 7¼ lbs. (long).
**Stock:** Hand-checkered European walnut.
**Sights:** None furnished. Scope mounts included.
**Features:** Adj. trigger, hinged floorplate. 222 and 223 have short action, 243 and 22-250 have medium action, others are long action. Imported from Finland by Stoeger.

## SAKO HUNTER RIFLE

**Caliber:** 17 Rem., 222, 223 (short action); 22-250, 220 Swift, 243, 6.5x55, 7mm-08, 308 (medium action); 25-06, 270, 30-06, 7mm Rem. Mag., 7x64, 300 Win. Mag., 338 Win. Mag., 375 H&H Mag. (long action).
**Barrel:** 21¼"—22" depending on caliber.
**Price:** Short and medium action ................................. **$816.95**
**Price:** Long action ........................................... **$834.95**
**Price:** Magnum cals. ......................................... **$849.95**
**Price:** 375 H&H ............................................. **$866.95**

**CAUTION:** PRICES CHANGE. CHECK AT GUNSHOP.

Sako Handy Carbine

## Sako Carbine
Same action as the Hunter except has full "Mannlicher" style stock. 18½" barrel, weighs 7½ lbs., chambered for 222 Rem., 243, 270, 308 and 30-06. Introduced 1977. From Stoeger.
**Price:** ........................................ **$927.95**
**Price:** 338, 375 H&H ....................... **$985.00**

## Sako Safari Grade Bolt Action
Similar to the Hunter except available in long action, calibers 300 Win. Mag., 338 Win. Mag. or 375 H&H Mag. only. Stocked in French walnut, checkered 20 l.p.i., solid rubber butt pad; grip cap and fore-end tip; quarter-rib "express" rear sight, hooded ramp front. Front sling swivel band-mounted on barrel.
**Price:** .................................... **$2,245.00**

## Sako Handy Carbine
Same 18½" barreled action and calibers as Sako Carbine but with conventional oil-finished stock of the Hunter model. Introduced 1986.
**Price:** 22-250, 243, 7mm-08, 308 Win. ................... **$816.95**
**Price:** 25-06, 6.5x55, 270, 7x64, 30-06 .................. **$834.95**
**Price:** 7mm Rem. Mag., 300 Win., 338 Win., 375 H&H ...... **$849.95**
**Price:** As Handy/Fiberclass with black fiberglass stock, 25-06, 6.5x55, 7x64, 270, 30-06 ............................................. **$1,190.00**
**Price:** As above, 7mm Rem. Mag., 308 Mag., 338 Win., 375 H&H . **$1,225.00**

## Sako Fiberclass Sporter
Similar to the Hunter except has a black fiberglass stock in the classic style, with wrinkle finish, rubber butt pad. Barrel length is 23", weight 7 lbs., 2 oz. Long action only. Comes with scope mounts. Introduced 1985.
**Price:** 25-06, 270, 30-06 ........................... **$1,190.00**
**Price:** 7mm Rem. Mag., 300, 338 Win. Mag., 375 H&H ......... **$1,225.00**

## Sako Super Deluxe Sporter
Similar to Deluxe Sporter except has select European Walnut with high gloss finish and deep cut oak leaf carving. Metal has super high polish, deep blue finish.
**Price:** .................................... **$2,245.00**

Sako Deluxe Sporter

## Sako Heavy Barrel
Same as std. Super Sporter except has beavertail fore-end; available in 222, 223 (short action), 220 Swift, 22-250, 243, 308 (medium action). Weight from 8¼ to 8½ lbs. 5-shot magazine capacity.
**Price:** 222, 223 (short action) ....................... **$985.00**
**Price:** 22-250, 243, 308 (medium action) ............. **$985.00**

## Sako Deluxe Sporter
Same action as Hunter except has select wood, rosewood p.g. cap and fore-end tip. Fine checkering on top surfaces of integral dovetail bases, bolt sleeve, bolt handle root and bolt knob. Vent. recoil pad, skip-line checkering, mirror finish bluing.
**Price:** 222 or 223 cals. ............................ **$1,120.00**
**Price:** 22-250, 243, 308 ........................... **$1,120.00**
**Price:** 25-06, 270, 30-06 .......................... **$1,120.00**
**Price:** 7mm Rem. Mag., 300 Win. Mag., 338 Mag., 375 H&H ...... **$1,145.00**

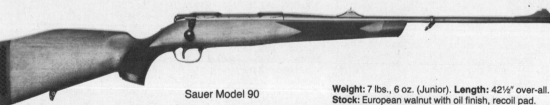

Sauer Model 90

## SAUER 90 RIFLE
**Caliber:** 222, 22-250, 243, 308 (Junior, Stutzen Junior); 6.5x57, 270, 7x64, 30-06, 8x68S (Medium, Stutzen); 6.5x68, 7mm Rem. Mag., 300 Win., 300 Wea., 8x68S, 9.3x64, 375 H&H (Magnum); 458 Win. Mag. (Safari).
**Barrel:** 20" (Stutzens), 24", 26".

**Weight:** 7 lbs., 6 oz. (Junior). **Length:** 42½" over-all.
**Stock:** European walnut with oil finish, recoil pad.
**Sights:** Post front on ramp, open rear adj. for w.
**Features:** Detachable 3-4 round box magazine; rear bolt locking lugs; 65° bolt throw; front sling swivel on barrel band. Introduced 1986. Imported from West Germany by SIGARMS.
**Price:** About ................................... **$1,085.00**
**Price:** Safari, about ............................. **$1,625.00**

Sauer Model 200

## SAUER MODEL 200 RIFLE
**Caliber:** 243, 308, 25-06, 30-06.
**Barrel:** 24".
**Weight:** 6⅔ lbs. (Alloy) to 7¾ lbs. (Steel). **Length:** 44" over-all.
**Stock:** European walnut with recoil pad; checkered p.g. and fore-end.

**Sights:** None furnished. Drilled and tapped for iron sights and scope mount.
**Features:** Easily interchangeable barrels, buttstock and fore-end; removable box magazine; steel and alloy versions; left-hand models available. Introduced 1986. Imported from West Germany by SIGARMS.
**Price:** Steel, 243, 308, about ....................... **$745.00**
**Price:** Steel, 25-06, 30-06, 270, about .............. **$770.00**
**Price:** Alloy, 243, 308, about ....................... **$785.00**
**Price:** Alloy, 25-06, 30-06, 270, about .............. **$815.00**
**Price:** Left-hand, steel, 243, 308, about ............ **$830.00**
**Price:** Left-hand, steel, 25-06, 30-06, 270, about .... **$860.00**
**Price:** Left-hand, alloy, 243, 308, about ............ **$875.00**
**Price:** Left-hand, alloy, 25-06, 30-06, 270, about .... **$895.00**

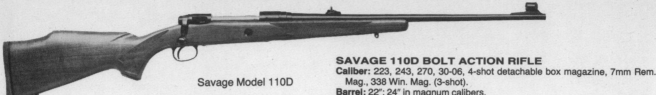

Savage Model 110D

## SAVAGE 110D BOLT ACTION RIFLE
**Caliber:** 223, 243, 270, 30-06, 4-shot detachable box magazine, 7mm Rem. Mag., 338 Win. Mag. (3-shot).
**Barrel:** 22"; 24" in magnum calibers.
**Weight:** 7lbs. **Length:** 43½" over-all.
**Stock:** Select walnut with Monte Carlo, cut checkered p.g. and fore-end. Swivel studs.
**Sights:** Removable ramp front, open rear adj. for w. & e.
**Features:** Tapped for scope mounting, free floating barrel, top tang safety, rubber recoil pad on all calibers.
**Price:** Right hand 110D standard cals.. . . . . . . . . . . . . . . . . . . . . . . . . $369.00
**Price:** As above, magnum cals.. . . . . . . . . . . . . . . . . . . . . . . . . . . . $435.00
**Price:** Left hand 110DL (no 338) . . . . . . . . . . . . . . . . . . . . . . . . . . $419.00

## Savage Model 110K Bolt Action Rifle
Similar to the Model 110D except has laminated camouflage stock, calibers 243, 270, 30-06. Introduced 1986.
**Price:** . . . . . . . . . . . . . . . . . . . . . . . . . . . . . . . . . . . . . . . . . . . . . $337.49

## SAVAGE 110E BOLT ACTION RIFLE
**Caliber:** 270, 308, 30-06, 243, 7mm Rem. Mag., 4-shot.
**Barrel:** 22" round tapered, 24" for magnum.
**Weight:** 6¾ lbs. **Length:** 43" (22"barrel).
**Stock:** Walnut finished hardwood with Monte Carlo; hard rubber buttplate.
**Sights:** Gold bead removable ramp front, removeable step adj. rear.
**Features:** Top tang safety, receiver tapped for scope mount.
**Price:** . . . . . . . . . . . . . . . . . . . . . . . . . . . . . . . . . . . . . . . . . . . $289.00
**Price:** Without sights . . . . . . . . . . . . . . . . . . . . . . . . . . . . . . . . $280.97

## Savage Model 110-V Varmint Rifle
Same as the Model 110D except chambered only for 223 or 22-250, with heavy 26" barrel, special "varmint" stock. Introduced 1983.
**Price:** . . . . . . . . . . . . . . . . . . . . . . . . . . . . . . . . . . . . . . . . . . . $385.00

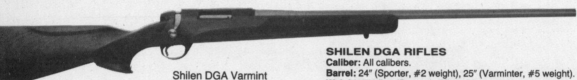

Shilen DGA Varmint

## SHILEN DGA RIFLES
**Caliber:** All calibers.
**Barrel:** 24" (Sporter, #2 weight), 25" (Varminter, #5 weight).
**Weight:** 7½ lbs. (Sporter), 9 lbs., (Varminter).
**Stock:** Selected Claro walnut. Barrel and action hand bedded to stock with free-floated barrel, bedded action. Swivel studs installed.
**Sights:** None furnished. Drilled and tapped for scope mounting.
**Features:** Shilen Model DGA action, fully adjustable trigger with side safety. Stock finish is satin sheen epoxy. Barrel and action non-glare blue-black. From Shilen Rifles, Inc.
**Price:** Sporter or Varminter rifle, from . . . . . . . . . . . . . . . . . . . . . . . . $1,600.00

Steyr-Mannlicher Professional

## STEYR-MANNLICHER MODEL M
**Caliber:** 7x64, 7x57, 25-06, 270, 30-06. Left-hand action cals.—7x64, 25-06, 270, 30-06. Optional cals.—6.5x57, 8x57JS, 9.3x62, 6.5x55, 7.5x55.
**Barrel:** 20" (full stock); 23.6" (half stock).
**Weight:** 6.8 lbs. to 7.5 lbs. **Length:** 39" (full stock); 43" (half stock).
**Stock:** Hand checkered walnut. Full Mannlicher or std. half stock with M.C. and rubber recoil pad.
**Sights:** Ramp front, open U-notch rear.
**Features:** Choice of interchangeable single or double set triggers. Detachable 5-shot rotary magazine. Drilled and tapped for scope mounting. Available as "Professional" model with parkerized finish and synthetic stock (right hand action only). Imported by Gun South, Inc.
**Price:** Full stock (carbine) . . . . . . . . . . . . . . . . . . . . . . . . . . . . . . $1,095.00
**Price:** Half stock (rifle) . . . . . . . . . . . . . . . . . . . . . . . . . . . . . . . $1,016.00
**Price:** For left hand action add about . . . . . . . . . . . . . . . . . . . . . . . . $220.00
**Price:** Professional model with iron sights. . . . . . . . . . . . . . . . . . . . . $915.00

## Steyr-Mannlicher "Luxus"
Similar to Steyr-Mannlicher models L and M except has single-set trigger and detachable 3-shot steel magazine. Same calibers as L and M. Oil finish or high gloss lacquer on stock.
**Price:** Full stock . . . . . . . . . . . . . . . . . . . . . . . . . . . . . . . . . . . . $1,425.00
**Price:** Half stock . . . . . . . . . . . . . . . . . . . . . . . . . . . . . . . . . . . . $1,355.00

Steyr-Mannlicher L

## STEYR-MANNLICHER MODELS SL & L
**Caliber:** SL—222, 222 Rem. Mag., 223; SL Varmint—222; L—22-250, 6mm, 243, 308 Win.; L Varmint—22-250, 243, 308 Win.
**Barrel:** 20" (full stock); 23.6" (half stock).
**Weight:** 6 lbs. (full stock). **Length:** 38¼" (full stock).
**Stock:** Hand checkered walnut. Full Mannlicher or standard half-stock with Monte Carlo.
**Sights:** Ramp front, open U-notch rear.
**Features:** Choice of interchangeable single or double set triggers. Five-shot detachable "Makrolon" rotary magazine, 6 rear locking lugs. Drilled and tapped for scope mounts. Imported by Gun South, Inc.
**Price:** Full Stock . . . . . . . . . . . . . . . . . . . . . . . . . . . . . . . . . . . . $1,095.00
**Price:** Half-stock . . . . . . . . . . . . . . . . . . . . . . . . . . . . . . . . . . . . $1,016.00

## Steyr-Mannlicher Varmint, Models SL and L
Similar to standard SL and L except chambered only for: 222 Rem. (SL), 22-250, 243, 308. Has 26" heavy barrel, no sights (drilled and tapped for scope mounts). Choice of single or double-set triggers. Five-shot detachable magazine.
**Price:** . . . . . . . . . . . . . . . . . . . . . . . . . . . . . . . . . . . . . . . . . . . $1,095.00

**CAUTION:** PRICES CHANGE. CHECK AT GUNSHOP.

# CENTERFIRE RIFLES—BOLT ACTIONS

## STEYR-MANNLICHER MODELS S & S/T

**Caliber:** Model S—300 Win. Mag., 338 Win. Mag., 7mm Rem. Mag., 300 H&H Mag., 375 H&H Mag. (6.5x68, 8x68S, 9.3x64 optional); S/T—375 H&H Mag., 458 Win. Mag. (9.3x64 optional).
**Barrel:** 25.6″.
**Weight:** 8.4 lbs. (Model S). **Length:** 45″ over-all.
**Stock:** Half stock with M.C. and rubber recoil pad. Hand checkered walnut. Available with optional spare magazine inletted in butt.
**Sights:** Ramp front, U-notch rear.
**Features:** Choice of interchangeable single or double set triggers., detachable 4-shot magazine. Drilled and tapped for scope mounts. Imported by Gun South, Inc.
**Price:** Model S.................................. $1,295.00
**Price:** Model ST 375 H&H, 458 Win. Mag.......... $1,375.00

## TIKKA MODEL 55 DELUXE RIFLE

**Caliber:** 17 Rem., 222, 22-250, 6mm Rem., 243, 308
**Barrel:** 23″.
**Weight:** About 6½ lbs. **Length:** 41½″ over-all.
**Stock:** Hand checkered walnut with rosewood fore-end tip and grip cap.
**Sights:** Bead on ramp front, rear adjustable for windage and elevation.
**Features:** Detachable 3-shot magazine with 5- or 10-shot magazines available. Roll-over cheekpiece, palm swell in pistol grip. Adjustable trigger. Receiver dovetailed for scope mounting. Imported from Finland by Mandall.
**Price:**............................................... $650.00
**Price:** QD scope mounts............................. $89.95

Ultra Light Model 20

## Ultra Light Arms Model 20S Rifle

Similar to the Model 20 except uses short action chambered for 17 Rem., 222 Rem., 223 Rem., 22 Hornet. Has 22″ Douglas Premium No. 1 contour barrel, weighs 4¾ lbs., 41″ over-all length.
**Price:**......................................... $1,300.00
**Price:** Model 20S Left Hand (left-hand action and stock) ......... $1,400.00

## Ultra Light Arms Model 28 Rifle

Similar to the Model 20 except in 264, 7mm Rem. Mag., 300 Win. Mag., 338 Win. Mag. (standard). Improved and other calibers on request. Uses 24″ Douglas Premium No. 2 contour barrel. Weighs 5½ lbs., 45″ over-all length. K.D.F. or U.L.A. recoil arrestor built in. Any custom feature available on any U.L.A. product can be incorporated.
**Price:**......................................... $2,150.00

## ULTRA LIGHT ARMS MODEL 20 RIFLE

**Caliber:** 22-250, 243, 6mm Rem., 257 Roberts, 7x57, 7mm-08, 284, 308, standard. Improved and other calibers on request.
**Barrel:** 22″ Douglas Premium No. 1 contour.
**Weight:** 4½ lbs. **Length:** 41½″ over-all.
**Stock:** Composite Kevlar, graphite reinforced. Dupont Imron paint colors — green, black, brown and camo options. Choice of length of pull.
**Sights:** None furnished. Scope mount included.
**Features:** Timney adj. trigger; two-position three-function safety. Benchrest quality action. Matte or bright stock and metal finish. 3″ magazine length. Shipped in a hard case. From Ultra Light Arms, Inc.
**Price:**......................................... $1,300.00
**Price:** Model 20 Left Hand (left-hand action and stock)........... $1,400.00
**Price:** Model 24 (25-06, 270, 280, 30-06, 3⅜″ magazine length)... $1,375.00
**Price:** Model 24 Left Hand (left-hand action and stock).......... $1,475.00

Voere Titan

## VOERE TITAN BOLT ACTION RIFLE

**Caliber:** 243, 25-06, 270, 7x57, 308, 30-06, 4-shot magazine (standard); 257 Wea., 270 Wea., 7mm Rem. Mag., 300 Win. Mag., 300 Wea., 308 Norma Mag., 375 H&H, 3-shot magazine (magnum).
**Barrel:** 24″ (standard), 26″ (magnum).

**Weight:** About 8 lbs. **Length:** 44½″ over-all (24″ bbl.).
**Stock:** Oil finished, hand checkered European walnut with Monte Carlo. Recoil pad and swivel studs standard.
**Sights:** None furnished. Drilled and tapped for scope mounts. Open sights, rings, bases avail. from KDF.
**Features:** Three-lug, front-locking action with ultra-fast lock time. Imported from West Germany by KDF, Inc.
**Price:** Standard calibers......................................... $799.00
**Price:** Magnum calibers ......................................... $849.00

Voere Titan Menor

## VOERE TITAN MENOR RIFLE

**Caliber:** 222 Rem., 223 Rem., 3-shot magazine.
**Barrel:** 23½″.
**Weight:** About 6 lbs. **Length:** 42″ over-all.

**Stock:** Oil finished, hand checkered European walnut with Monte Carlo, rosewood fore-end tip and grip cap.
**Sights:** None furnished. Grooved receiver is drilled and tapped for scope mounting. Open sights, rings, bases avail. from KDF.
**Features:** Rifle carries a three-year guarantee by maker. Competition model available. Introduced 1986. Imported from West Germany by KDF, Inc.
**Price:** Standard model ....................................... $699.00
**Price:** Competition model.................................... $799.00

## VOERE 2155, 2165 BOLT ACTION RIFLE

**Caliber:** 22-250, 270, 308, 243, 30-06, 7x64, 5.6x57, 6.5x55, 8x57 JRS, 7mm Rem. Mag., 300 Win. Mag., 8x68S, 9.3x62, 9.3x64, 6.5x68.
**Stock:** European walnut, hog-back style; checkered pistol grip and fore-end.
**Sights:** Ramp front, open adjustable rear.
**Features:** Mauser-type action with 5-shot detachable box magazine; double set or single trigger; drilled and tapped for scope mounting. Imported from

Austria by L. Joseph Rahn. Introduced 1984.
**Price:** Standard calibers, single trigger ........................ $440.00
**Price:** As above, double set triggers............................ $467.00
**Price:** Magnum calibers, single trigger ........................ $475.00
**Price:** As above, double set triggers............................ $505.00
**Price:** Full-stock, single trigger .............................. $575.00
**Price:** As above, double set triggers............................ $595.00

**CAUTION:** PRICES CHANGE. CHECK AT GUNSHOP.

Weatherby Euromark

## WEATHERBY VANGUARD VGX, VGS RIFLES

**Caliber:** 22-250, 25-06, 243, 270, and 30-06 (5-shot), 7mm Rem. and 300 Win. Mag. (3-shot).
**Barrel:** 24″ hammer forged.
**Weight:** 7⅞ lbs. **Length:** 44½″ over-all.
**Stock:** American walnut, p.g. cap and fore-end tip, hand inletted and checkered. 13½″ pull.
**Sights:** Optional, available at extra cost.
**Features:** Side safety, adj. trigger, hinged floorplate, receiver tapped for scope mounts. Imported from Japan by Weatherby.
**Price:** VGS ........................................... **$399.95**
**Price:** VGX—deluxe wood, different checkering, ventilated recoil pad **$499.95**

## Weatherby Mark V Rifle Left Hand

Available in all Weatherby calibers except 224 and 22-250 (and 26″ No. 2 contour 300WM). Complete left handed action; stock with cheekpiece on right side. Prices are $20 higher than right hand models except the 378 and 460WM are unchanged.

Weatherby Fiberguard

## Weatherby Lazer Mark V Rifle

Same as standard Mark V except stock has extensive laser carving under cheekpiece, on butt, p.g. and fore-end. Introduced 1981.
**Price:** 22-250, 224 Wea., 24″ bbl. ................................ **$914.95**
**Price:** As above, 26″ bbl. ..................................... **$929.95**
**Price:** 240 Wea. thru 300 Wea., 24″ bbl. ........................ **$934.95**
**Price:** As above, 26″ bbl. ..................................... **$954.95**
**Price:** 340 Wea. ............................................. **$954.95**
**Price:** 378 Wea. ............................................ **$1,109.95**
**Price:** 460 Wea. ............................................ **$1,249.95**

Weatherby Mark V

Weatherby Fibermark Rifle

## WEATHERBY EUROMARK BOLT ACTION RIFLE

**Caliber:** All Weatherby calibers except 224, 22-250.
**Barrel:** 24″ or 26″ round tapered.
**Weight:** 6½ — 10½ lbs. **Length:** 44¼″ over-all (24″ bbl.).
**Stock:** Walnut, Monte Carlo with extended tail fine-line hand checkering, satin oil finish, ebony fore-end tip and grip cap with maple diamond, solid butt pad.
**Sights:** Optional (extra).
**Features:** Cocking indicator; adj. trigger; hinged floor plate; thumb safety; q.d. sling swivels. Introduced 1986.
**Price:** With 24″ barrel (240, 257, 270, 7mm, 30-06, 300) .......... **$879.95**
**Price:** 26″ No. 2 Contour barrel ............................. **$899.95**
**Price:** As above, left hand .................................. **$899.95**
**Price:** 340 WM, 26″ ........................................ **$899.95**
**Price:** As above, left hand .................................. **$914.95**
**Price:** 378WM, 26″, right or left hand ....................... **$1,054.95**
**Price:** 460WM, 26″, right or left hand ....................... **$1,194.95**

## Weatherby Vanguard VGL Rifle

Similar to the standard Vanguard except has a short action, chambered for 223, 243, 270, 30-06, 7mm Rem. Mag. with 20″ barrel. Barrel and action have a non-glare blue finish. Guaranteed to shoot a 1½″ 3-shot group at 100 yards. Stock has a non-glare satin finish, hand checkering and a black butt pad with black spacer. Introduced 1984.
**Price:** ................................................ **$399.95**

## Weatherby Vanguard Fiberguard Rifle

Uses the Vanguard barreled action and a forest green wrinkle-finished fiberglass stock. All metal is matte blue. Has a 20″ barrel, weighs 6½ lbs., measures 40″ in 223, 243, and 308; 40½″ in 270, 7mm Rem. Mag., 30-06. Accepts same scope mount bases as Mark V action. Introduced 1985.
**Price:** Right-hand only. ...................................... **$579.95**

## WEATHERBY MARK V BOLT ACTION RIFLE

**Caliber:** All Weatherby cals., 22-250 and 30-06
**Barrel:** 24″ or 26″ round tapered.
**Weight:** 6½-10½ lbs. **Length:** 43¼″-46½″.
**Stock:** Walnut, Monte Carlo with cheekpiece, high luster finish, checkered p.g. and fore-end, recoil pad.
**Sights:** Optional (extra).
**Features:** Cocking indicator, adj. trigger, hinged floorplate, thumb safety, quick detachable sling swivels.
**Price:** Cals. 224 and 22-250, std. bbl. ...................... **$798.95**
**Price:** With 26″ semi-target bbl. ............................ **$814.95**
**Price:** Cals. 240, 257, 270, 7mm, 30-06 and 300 (24″ bbl.) ...... **$819.95**
**Price:** With 26″ No. 2 contour bbl. .......................... **$839.95**
**Price:** Cal. 340 (26″ bbl.). ................................. **$839.95**
**Price:** Cal. 378 (26″ bbl.). ................................. **$994.95**
**Price:** Cal. 460 (26″ bbl.) ................................. **$1,134.95**

## Weatherby Fibermark Rifle

Same as the standard Mark V except the stock is of fiberglass; finished with a non-glare black wrinkle finish and black recoil pad; receiver and floorplate have low luster blue finish; fluted bolt has a satin finish. Currently available in right-hand model only, 24″ or 26″ barrel, 240 Weatherby Mag. through 340 Weatherby Mag. calibers. Introduced 1983.
**Price:** 240 W.M. through 300 W.M., 24″ bbl. .................... **$949.95**
**Price:** 240 W.M. through 340 W.M., 26″ bbl. .................... **$969.95**

# CENTERFIRE RIFLES—BOLT ACTIONS

Whitworth Express Rifle

## WHITWORTH EXPRESS RIFLE
**Caliber:** .22-250, .240, .25-00, .270, 7x57, .000, .00-06, .000 Win. Mag., 7mm Rem. Mag., 375 H&H, 458 Win. Mag.
**Barrel:** 24".
**Weight:** 7½-8 lbs. **Length:** 44".

**Stock:** Classic English Express rifle design of hand checkered, select European Walnut.
**Sights:** Three leaf open sight calibrated for 100, 200, 300 yards on ¼-rib, ramp front with removable hood (375, 458 only); other calibers have standard open sights.
**Features:** Solid rubber recoil pad, barrel mounted sling swivel, adjustable trigger, hinged floor plate, solid steel recoil cross bolt. Imported by Interarms
**Price:** ..................................................... $525.00
**Price:** 375, 458, with express sights ............................. $650.00
**Price:** Mannlicher-style carbine, cals. 243, 270, 308, 7x57, 30-06 only, 20" bbl. ....................................................... $675.00

Wichita Varmint Rifle

## WICHITA CLASSIC RIFLE
**Caliber:** 17 Rem. thru 308 Win., including 22 and 6mm PPC.
**Barrel:** 21⅛".
**Weight:** 8 lbs. **Length:** 41" over-all.
**Stock:** AAA Fancy American walnut. Hand-rubbed and checkered (20 l.p.i). Hand-inletter, glass bedded, steel grip cap. Pachmayr rubber recoil pad.
**Sights:** None. Drilled and tapped for scope mounting.
**Features:** Available as single shot or repeater. Octagonal barrel and Wichita action, right or left-hand. Checkered bolt handle. Bolt is hand-fitted, lapped and jewelled. Adjustable Canjar trigger is set at 2 lbs. Side thumb safety. Firing pin fall is 3/16". Non-glare blue finish. Shipped in hard case. From Wichita Arms.
**Price:** Single shot .................................... $1,900.00
**Price:** With blind box magazine ........................... $2,050.00

## WICHITA VARMINT RIFLE
**Caliber:** 17 Rem. thru 308 Win., including 22 and 6mm PPC.
**Barrel:** 20⅛".
**Weight:** 9 lbs. **Length:** 40⅛" over-all.
**Stock:** AAA Fancy American walnut. Hand-rubbed finish, hand-checkered, 20 l.p.i. pattern. Hand-inletted, glass bedded steel grip cap, Pachmayr rubber recoil pad.
**Sights:** None. Drilled and tapped for scope mounts.
**Features:** Right or left-hand Wichita action with three locking lugs. Available as a single shot or repeater with 3-shot magazine. Checkered bolt handle. Bolt is hand fitted, lapped and jeweled. Side thumb safety. Firing pin fall is 3/16". Non-glare blue finish. Shipped in hard case. From Wichita Arms.
**Price:** Single shot ........................................ $1,185.00
**Price:** With blind box magazine .............................. $1,335.00

Winchester 70 XTR Express

## WINCHESTER MODEL 70 LIGHTWEIGHT CARBINE
**Caliber:** 270, 30-06 (standard action); 250 Savage, 22-250, 223, 243, 308 (short action), both 5-shot magazine, except 6-shot in 223.
**Barrel:** 20".
**Weight:** 6¼ lbs. (std.), 6 lbs. (short). **Length:** 40½" over-all (std.) and 40" (short).
**Stock:** American walnut with satin finish, deep-cut checkering.
**Sights:** None furnished. Drilled and tapped for scope mounting.
**Features:** Three position safety; stainless steel magazine follower; hinged floorplate; sling swivel studs. Introduced 1984.
**Price:** With sights, about .................................... $425.25
**Price:** Without sights, about ................................. $442.25

## WINCHESTER 70 XTR SUPER EXPRESS MAGNUM
**Caliber:** 375 H&H Mag., 458 Win. Mag., 3-shot magazine.
**Barrel:** 24" (375), 22" (458).
**Weight:** 8½ lbs.
**Stock:** American walnut with Monte Carlo cheekpiece. XTR wrap-around checkering and finish.
**Sights:** Hooded ramp front, open rear.
**Features:** Two steel crossbolts in stock for added strength. Front sling swivel mounted on barrel. Contoured rubber butt pad. Made under license by U.S. Repeating Arms Co.
**Price:** About ............................................... $831.63

Winchester 70 Lightweight

## Winchester 70 XTR Sporter Varmint Rifle
Same as 70 XTR Sporter Magnum except: 223, 22-250 and 243 only, no sights, 24" bbl., 44½" over-all, 7¾ lbs. American walnut Monte Carlo stock with cheekpiece, high luster finish.
**Price:** About ............................................... $470.24

## WINCHESTER 70 XTR SPORTER MAGNUM
**Caliber:** 264 Win. Mag., 7mm Rem. Mag., 300 Win. Mag., 338 Win. Mag., 3-shot magazine.
**Barrel:** 24".
**Weight:** 7¾ lbs. **Length:** 44½" over-all.
**Stock:** American walnut with Monte Carlo cheekpiece. XTR checkering and satin finish.
**Sights:** None furnished; optional hooded ramp front, adjustable folding leaf rear.
**Features:** Three-position safety, detachable sling swivels, stainless steel magazine follower, rubber butt pad, epoxy bedded receiver recoil lug. Made under license by U.S. Repeating Arms Co.
**Price:** With sights, about .................................... $470.25
**Price:** Without sights, about ................................. $487.25

# CENTERFIRE RIFLES—BOLT ACTIONS

Winchester 70 Winlite

### Winchester Model 70 Winlite Rifle
Similar to the Model 70XTR Sporter except has brown fiberglass stock. Action bed and fore-end are reinforced Kevlar/Graphite. No sights are furnished but receiver is drilled and tapped for scope mounting. Available in 270, 30-06 (22″ barrel, 4-shot magazine), 7mm Rem. Mag., 338 Win. Mag. (24″ barrel 3-shot magazine). Weight is 6¼-6½ lbs. for 270, 30-06, 6¾-7 lbs. for 7mm Mag., 338. Introduced 1986.
**Price:** About . . . . . . . . . . . . . . . . . . . . . . . . . . . . . . . . . . . . . . . . **$637.25**

Winchester Ranger

### Winchester Ranger Rifle
Similar to Model 70 XTR Sporter except chambered only for 270, 30-06, with 22″ barrel. American hardwood stock, no checkering, composition butt plate. Metal has matte blue finish. Introduced 1985.
**Price:** About . . . . . . . . . . . . . . . . . . . . . . . . . . . . . . . . . . . . . . . . **$360.62**
**Price:** Ranger Youth, 243 only, scaled-down stock . . . . . . . . . . . . . . **$371.50**

Winchester 70 Featherweight

### Winchester Model 70 XTR Featherweight
Available with standard action in 6.5x55, 270 Win., 30-06, short action in 22-250, 223, 243, 308; 22″ tapered Featherweight barrel; classic-style American walnut stock with Schnabel fore-end, wrap-around XTR checkering fashioned after early Model 70 custom rifle patterns. Red rubber butt pad with black spacer; sling swivel studs. Weighs 6¾ lbs. (standard action), 6½ lbs. (short action). Introduced 1984.
**Price:** About . . . . . . . . . . . . . . . . . . . . . . . . . . . . . . . . . . . . . . **$487.25**
**Price:** European Featherweight, 6.5x55, about . . . . . . . . . . . . . . . . . . **$487.25**

### Winchester Model 70 XTR Sporter
Same as the Model 70 XTR Sporter Magnum except available only in 308, 25-06, 270 Win. and 30-06, 5-shot magazine.
**Price:** With sights (except 308), about . . . . . . . . . . . . . . . . . . . . . . . . . **$487.25**
**Price:** Without sights, about . . . . . . . . . . . . . . . . . . . . . . . . . . . . . . . . **$470.25**

# CENTERFIRE RIFLES—SINGLE SHOTS

Allen Rolling Block

### ALLEN ROLLING BLOCK BABY CARBINE
**Caliber:** 22 LR, 22 Mag., 357 Mag., single shot.
**Barrel:** 22″.
**Weight:** 4.8 lbs. **Length:** 35½ over-all.
**Stock:** Walnut stock and fore-end.
**Sights:** Blade front, fully adj. open rear.
**Features:** Resembles Remington New Model No. 4 carbine. Brass trigger guard and buttplate; color case-hardened frame, blued barrel. Imported by Allen Fire Arms
**Price:** . . . . . . . . . . . . . . . . . . . . . . . . . . . . . . . . . . . . . . . . . . . . **$264.00**

### ALLEN SHARPS/GEMMER SPORTING RIFLE
**Caliber:** 45-70.
**Barrel:** 32″, octagonal.
**Weight:** 11 lbs. **Length:** 49″ over-all.
**Stock:** Walnut
**Sights:** Blade front, buckhorn rear.
**Features:** Authentic reproduction of 1870s J.P. Gemmer Hawken-Sharps hybrid. Introduced 1986. Imported by Allen Fire Arms.
**Price:** . . . . . . . . . . . . . . . . . . . . . . . . . . . . . . . . . . . . . . **$599.00**

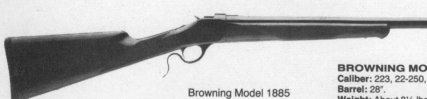

Browning Model 1885

### BROWNING MODEL 1885 SINGLE SHOT RIFLE
**Caliber:** 223, 22-250, 30-06, 270, 7mm Rem. Mag., 45-70.
**Barrel:** 28″.
**Weight:** About 8½ lbs. **Length:** 43½″ over-all.
**Stock:** Walnut with straight grip, Schnabel fore-end.
**Sights:** None furnished; drilled and tapped for scope mounting.
**Features:** Replica of J.M. Browning's high-wall falling-block rifle. Octagon barrel with recessed muzzle. Imported from Japan by Browning. Introduced 1985.
**Price:** . . . . . . . . . . . . . . . . . . . . . . . . . . . . . . . . . . . . . . . . **$551.50**

**CAUTION:** PRICES CHANGE. CHECK AT GUNSHOP.

# CENTERFIRE RIFLES—SINGLE SHOTS

Heym-Ruger HR 30/38

## HEYM-RUGER Model HR 30/38 RIFLE
**Caliber:** 243, 6.5x57R, 7x64, 7x65R, 308, 30-06 (standard); 6.5x68R, 300 Win. Mag., 8x68S, 9.3x74R (magnum).
**Barrel:** 24" (standard cals.), 25" (magnum cals.).
**Weight:** 6½ to 7 lbs.
**Stock:** Dark European walnut, hand checkered p.g. and fore-end. Oil finish, re-coil pad. Full Mannlicher-type or sporter-style with Schnabel fore-end, Bavarian cheekpiece.
**Sights:** Bead on ramp front, leaf rear.
**Features:** Ruger No. 1 action and safety, Canjar single-set trigger, hand-engraved animal motif. Options available include deluxe engraving and stock carving. Imported from West Germany by Paul Jaeger Inc.
**Price:** HR-30N, round bbl., sporter stock, std. cals............ **$1,990.00**
**Price:** HR-30G, as above except in mag. cals................. **$1,990.00**
**Price:** HR-30L, round bbl., full stock, std. cals............... **$2,095.00**
**Price:** For octagon barrel, add................... **$247.00**
**Price:** For sideplates with large hunting scenes, add ............ **$640.00**

## EMF SHARPS "OLD RELIABLE" RIFLE
**Caliber:** 45-70, 45-120-3¼" Sharps
**Barrel:** 28" full octagon, polished blue.
**Weight:** 9½ lbs. **Length:** 45" over-all.
**Stock:** Walnut with deluxe checkering at p.g. and fore-end.
**Sights:** Sporting blade front, folding leaf rear. Globe front, Creedmoor rear optional at extra cost.
**Features:** Falling block, lever action. Color case-hardened hammer, buttplate and action, Seven models of the Sharps are available in M/L configuration. All are available with engraved action for $175.00 extra. From E.M.F.
**Price:** Old Reliable................................... **$377.50**
**Price:** Sporter Rifle ................................. **$362.50**
**Price:** Military Carbine............................... **$345.00**
**Price:** Sporter Carbine .............................. **$362.50**

Ljutic Space Rifle

## LJUTIC RECOILESS SPACE RIFLE
**Caliber:** 22-250, 30-30, 30-06, 308; single-shot.
**Barrel:** 24".
**Weight:** 8¾ lbs. **Length:** 44" over-all.
**Stock:** Walnut stock, fore-end and grip.
**Sights:** Iron sights or scope mounts.
**Features:** Revolutionary design has anti-recoil mechanism. Twist-bolt action uses six moving parts. Scope and mounts extra. Introduced 1981. From Ljutic Industries.
**Price:** ...................................... **$3,695.00**

Ruger No. 1B Rifle

## RUGER NO. 1B SINGLE SHOT
**Caliber:** 220 Swift, 22-250, 223, 243, 6mm Rem., 25-06, 257 Roberts, 270, 280, 30-06, 7mm Rem. Mag., 300 Win. Mag., 338 Win. Mag. 270 Wea., 300 Wea.
**Barrel:** 26" round tapered with quarter-rib; with Ruger 1" rings.
**Weight:** 8 lbs. **Length:** 43⅜" over-all.
**Stock:** Walnut, two-piece, checkered p.g. and semi-beavertail fore-end.
**Sights:** None, 1" scope rings supplied for integral mounts.
**Features:** Under lever, hammerless falling block design has auto ejector, top tang safety. Standard Rifle 1B illus.
**Price:** ...................................... **$575.00**
**Price:** Barreled action ............................ **$389.50**

## Ruger No. 1A Light Sporter
Similar to the No. 1-B Standard Rifle except has lightweight 22" barrel, Alexander Henry style fore-end, adjustable folding leaf rear sight on quarter-rib, dovetailed ramp front with gold bead. Calibers 243, 30-06, 270 and 7x57. Weight about 7¼ lbs.
**Price:** No. 1-A................................... **$575.00**
**Price:** Barrreled action ............................ **$389.50**

Ruger No. 1 International

## Ruger No. 1V Special Varminter
Similar to the No. 1-B Standard Rifle except has 24" heavy barrel. Semi-beavertail fore-end, barrel tapped for target scope block, with 1" Ruger scope rings. Calibers 22-250, 220 Swift, 223, 25-06, 6mm. Weight about 9 lbs.
**Price:** No. 1-V................................... **$575.00**
**Price:** Barreled action ............................ **$389.50**

## Ruger No. 1H Tropical Rifle
Similar to the No. 1-B Standard Rifle except has Alexander Henry fore-end, adjustable folding leaf rear sight on quarter-rib, ramp front with dovetail gold bead front, 24" heavy barrel. Calibers 375 H&H (weight about 8¼ lbs.) and 458 Win. Mag. (weight about 9 lbs.).
**Price:** No. 1-H................................... **$575.00**
**Price:** Barreled action ............................ **$389.50**

## Ruger No. 1 RSI International
Similar to the No. 1-B Standard Rifle except has lightweight 20" barrel, full length Mannlicher-style fore-end with loop sling swivel, adjustable folding leaf rear sight on quarter rib, ramp front with gold bead. Calibers 243, 30-06, 270 and 7x57. Weight is about 7¼ lbs.
**Price:** No. 1-RSI.................................. **$595.00**
**Price:** Barreled action ............................ **$389.50**

## Ruger No. 1S Medium Sporter
Similar to the No. 1B Standard Rifle except has Alexander Henry style fore-end, adjustable folding leaf rear sight on quarter-rib, ramp front sight base and dovetail-type gold bead front sight. Calibers 7mm Rem. Mag., 338 Win. Mag., 300 Win. Mag. with 26" barrel, 45-70 with 22" barrel. Weight about 7½ lbs. in 45-70.
**Price:** No. 1-S................................... **$575.00**
**Price:** Barreled action ............................ **$389.50**

**CAUTION:** PRICES CHANGE. CHECK AT GUNSHOP.

Ruger No. 3 Carbine

### RUGER NO. 3 CARBINE SINGLE SHOT
**Caliber:** 45-70.
**Barrel:** 22" round.
**Weight:** 7¼ lbs. **Length:** 38½".
**Stock:** American walnut, carbine-type.
**Sights:** Gold bead front, adj. folding leaf rear.
**Features:** Same action as No. 1 Rifle except different lever. Has auto ejector, top tang safety, adj. trigger. Drilled and tapped for Ruger bases and Ruger 1" rings.
**Price:** . . . . . . . . . . . . . . . . . . . . . . . . . . . . . . . . . . . . . . . . . . **$284.00**

### NAVY ARMS ROLLING BLOCK RIFLE
**Caliber:** 45-70.
**Barrel:** 30".
**Stock:** Walnut finished.
**Sights:** Fixed front, adj. rear.
**Features:** Reproduction of classic rolling block action. Available in Buffalo Rifle (octagonal bbl.) and Creedmore (half round, half octagonal bbl.) models. Made in U.S. by Navy Arms.
**Price:** 26", 30" full octagon barrel . . . . . . . . . . . . . . . . . . . . . . . . . . **$398.00**
**Price:** Creedmore Model, 30" full octagon . . . . . . . . . . . . . . . . . . . . . **$425.00**
**Price:** 30", half-round . . . . . . . . . . . . . . . . . . . . . . . . . . . . . . . . . . . . **$398.00**
**Price:** 26", half-round . . . . . . . . . . . . . . . . . . . . . . . . . . . . . . . . . . . . **$395.00**
**Price:** Half-round Creedmore . . . . . . . . . . . . . . . . . . . . . . . . . . . . . . . **$425.00**

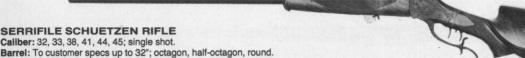

### SERRIFILE SCHUETZEN RIFLE
**Caliber:** 32, 33, 38, 41, 44, 45; single shot.
**Barrel:** To customer specs up to 32"; octagon, half-octagon, round.
**Weight:** To customer specs.
**Stock:** Fancy walnut in early Helm pattern.
**Sights:** None furnished; comes with scope blocks.
**Features:** Based on a replica Winchester Hi-Wall action with flat top receiver ring, thick or thin wall design, blue or case hardened. Hammer action uses Niedner-type firing pin; hammerless model uses a coil spring striker. Many options in finger levers, buttplates available. Introduced 1984. From Serrifile, Inc.
**Price:** Hammer model, from . . . . . . . . . . . . . . . . . . . . . . . . . . . . . . . **$1,853.50**

Serrifile Schuetzen

### C. SHARPS ARMS NEW MODEL 1875 RIFLE
**Caliber:** 22 LR Stevens, 32-40 & 38-55 Ballard, 40-90 3¼", 40-90 2⅝", 40-70 2¹⁄₁₀", 40-70 2¼", 40-70 2½", 40-50 1¹¹⁄₁₆", 40-50 1⅞", 45-90 2⁴⁄₁₀", 45-70 2¹⁄₁₀".
**Barrel:** 22" to 30", round and octagon depending upon model.
**Weight:** 8-12 lbs.
**Stock:** Walnut, straight grip, shotgun butt.
**Sights:** Blade front, improved Lawrence-pattern buckhorn rear.
**Features:** Recreation of the 1875 Sharps rifle. Production guns will have case colored receiver. Available in Custom Sporting and Target versions upon request. Announced 1986. From C. Sharps Arms Co.
**Price:** 1875 Carbine (24" tapered round bbl.) . . . . . . . . . . . . . . . . . . . **$550.00**
**Price:** 1875 Saddle Rifle (26" tapered oct. bbl.) . . . . . . . . . . . . . . . . . **$725.00**
**Price:** 1875 Standard Sporter (30" tapered oct. bbl.) . . . . . . . . . . . . . . **$675.00**
**Price:** 1875 Deluxe Sporter (30" tapered oct. bbl.) . . . . . . . . . . . . . . . **$775.00**

Sharps Model 1875

> Consult our directory pages for the location of firms mentioned.

Thompson/Center TCR '83 Hunter

### THOMPSON/CENTER TCR '83 SINGLE SHOT RIFLE
**Caliber:** 22 Hornet, 222 Rem., 223 Rem., 22-250, 243 Win., 270, 308, 7mm Rem. Mag., 30-06, 12 ga. slug.
**Barrel:** 23".
**Weight:** About 6¾ lbs. **Length:** 39½" over-all.
**Stock:** American black walnut, checkered p.g. and fore-end.
**Sights:** Blade on ramp front, open rear adj. for windage only.
**Features:** Break-open design with interchangeable barrels. Double-set or single-stage trigger function. Cross-bolt safety. Sights removable for scope mounting. Made in U.S. by T/C. Introduced 1983.
**Price:** Aristocrat . . . . . . . . . . . . . . . . . . . . . . . . . . . . . . . . . . . . . . . . . **$475.00**
**Price:** Hunter Field model (single trigger, grooved fore-end, no cheekpiece) . . . . . . . . . . . . . . . . . . . . . . . . . . . . . . . . . . . . . . . . . . **$415.00**
**Price:** Extra barrel . . . . . . . . . . . . . . . . . . . . . . . . . . . . . . . . . . . . . . . . **$175.00**

### THOMPSON-CENTER CONTENDER CARBINE
**Caliber:** 22 LR, 22 Hornet, 222 Rem., 223 Rem., 7mm T.C.U., 7 x 30 Waters, 30-30 Win., 357 Rem. Maximum, single shot.
**Barrel:** 21".
**Weight:** 5 lbs., 2 oz. **Length:** 35" over-all.
**Stock:** Checkered American walnut with rubber butt pad.
**Sights:** Blade front, open adj. rear.
**Features:** Uses the T/C Contender action. Eight interchangeable barrels available, all with sights, drilled and tapped for scope mounting. Introduced 1985. Offered as a complete Carbine only.
**Price:** . . . . . . . . . . . . . . . . . . . . . . . . . . . . . . . . . . . . . . . . . . . . . . . **$345.00**
**Price:** Extra barrels, each . . . . . . . . . . . . . . . . . . . . . . . . . . . . . . . . . . **$145.00**

## ARMSPORT 2783 O-U TURKEY GUN
**Caliber/Gauge:** 12 ga. (3″) over 222 Rem., 270 Win.; 20 ga. over 222, 243, 270.
**Barrel:** 28″ (Full).
**Weight:** 8 lbs.
**Stock:** European walnut.
**Sights:** Blade front, leaf rear.
**Features:** Ventilated top and middle ribs; flip-up rear sight; silvered receiver. Introduced 1986. Imported from Italy by Armsport.
**Price:** ......................................................... $1,095.00

## BERETTA EXPRESS S689 DOUBLE RIFLE
**Caliber:** 30-06, 9.3x74R, 375 H&H, 458 win. Mag.
**Barrel:** 23″.
**Weight:** 7.7 lbs.
**Stock:** European walnut, checkered grip and fore-end.
**Sights:** Blade front on ramp, open V-notch rear.
**Features:** Boxlock action with silvered, engraved receiver; ejectors; double triggers; solid butt pad. Imported from Italy by Beretta U.S.A. Corp. Introduced 1984.
**Price:** S689, 30-06, 9.3x74R ........................... $2,700.00
**Price:** SSO, 375 H&H, 458 Win. Mag. ................... $9,375.00

## BRNO SUPER EXPRESS O/U DOUBLE RIFLE
**Caliber:** 7 x 65R, 9.3 x 74R, 375 H&H, 458 Win. Mag.
**Barrel:** 23½.″
**Weight:** 8½ to 9 lbs. **Length:** 40″ over-all.
**Stock:** European walnut with raised cheek piece, skip-line checkering.
**Sights:** Bead on ramp front, quarter rib with open rear.
**Features:** Sidelock action with engraved side plates; double set triggers; selective automatic ejectors; rubber recoil pad. Barrels regulated for 100 meters. Imported from Czechoslovakia by Bauska Arms Corp.
**Price:** 7x65R .......................................... $2,100.00
**Price:** 9.3x74R ........................................ $2,299.00
**Price:** 375 H&H, 458 Win. Mag. ....................... $2,599.00

## BRNO ZH SERIES 300 COMBINATION GUN
**Caliber/Gauge:** 5.6x52R/12 ga., 5.6x50R Mag./12, 7x57R/12, 7x57R/16.
**Barrel:** 23½″ (Full).
**Weight:** 7.9 lbs. **Length:** 40½″ over-all.
**Stock:** Walnut.
**Sights:** Bead on blade front, folding leaf rear.
**Features:** Boxlock action; 8-barrel set for combination calibers and o/u shotgun barrels in 12 ga. (Field, Trap, Skeet) and 16 ga. (Field). Imported from Czechoslovakia by Bauska Arms Corp.
**Price:** ......................................................... $2,799.00

Browning Continental

## BROWNING SUPERPOSED CONTINENTAL
**Caliber/Gauge:** 20 ga. x 20 ga. with extra 30-06x30-06 o/u barrel set.
**Barrel:** 20 ga.—26½″ (Mod. & Full, 3″ chambers), vent. rib, with medium raised German nickel silver sight bead. 30-06—24″.
**Weight:** 6 lbs. 14 oz. (rifle barrels), 5 lbs. 14 oz. (shotgun barrels)
**Stock:** Select high grade American walnut with oil finish. Straight grip stock and Schnabel fore-end with 26 lpi hand checkering.
**Sights:** Rifle barrels have flat face gold bead front on matted ramp, folding leaf rear.
**Features:** Action is based on a specially engineered Superposed 20-ga. frame. Single selective trigger works on inertia; let-off is about 4½ lbs. Automatic selective ejectors. Manual top tang safety incorporated with barrel selector. Furnished with fitted luggage-type case. Introduced 1979. Imported from Belgium by Browning.
**Price:** ......................................................... $4,375.00

## BROWNING EXPRESS RIFLE
**Caliber:** 270 or 30-06.
**Barrel:** 24″.
**Weight:** About 6 lbs., 14 oz. **Length:** 41″ over-all.
**Stock:** Select walnut with oil finish; straight grip, Schnabel fore-end; hand checkered to 25 lpi.
**Sights:** Gold bead on ramp front, adjustable folding leaf rear.
**Features:** Specially engineered Superposed action with reinforced breech face. Receiver hand engraved. Single selective trigger, auto. selective ejectors, manual safety. Comes in fitted luggage case. Imported from Belgium by Browning.
**Price:** Either caliber ...................................... $3,125.00

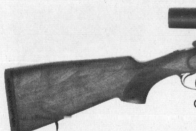

Churchill Regent Combo

## CHURCHILL REGENT COMBINATION GUN
**Caliber/Gauge:** 12 (3″) over 222 Rem.
**Barrel:** 25″ (Imp. Mod.)
**Weight:** 8 lbs. **Length:** 42″ over-all.
**Stock:** Hand checkered European walnut, oil finish, Monte Carlo comb.
**Sights:** Blade on ramp front, open rear.
**Features:** Silvered, engraved receiver; double triggers; dovetail scope mount. Imported by Kassnar Imports, Inc. Introduced 1985.
**Price:** ......................................................... $1,139.00

## DUMOLIN "PIONNIER" EXPRESS DOUBLE RIFLE
**Caliber:** 338 Win., 375 H&H, 458 Win., 470 N.E., 416 Rigby, 416 Hoffman, 500 N.E. Standard calibers also available.
**Barrel:** 24″ to 26″.
**Weight:** About 9½ lbs. **Length:** 45″ over-all with 24″ barrel.
**Stock:** Deluxe European walnut in English style with oil finish, beavertail or classic English fore-end. To customer's specifications.
**Sights:** Bead on ramp front, 2-leaf on quarter-rib.
**Features:** Box-lock triple lock system with Greener cross-bolt; articulated front trigger; Holland & Holland-type ejectors. Imported from Belgium by Midwest Gun Sport.
**Price:** About ............................................... $8,300.00
**Price:** Standard calibers start at about ................. $5,400.00

## Dumoulin "Sidelock Prestige" Double Rifle
Similar to the "Pionnier" except with sidelock action with reinforced 60mm table; internal parts are gold plated to resist corrosion. Choice of traditional chopper lump or "Classic Ernest Dumoulin" barrel system, with quarter-rib, in lengths of 22″ to 24″ according to caliber. Grand Luxe European walnut; Purdey lock system available on fore-end. All calibers available, special on request. Built to customer specs. Ten grades offered, differing in types, styles of engraving.
**Price:** About .......................... $14,500.00 to $18,000.00

Heym Model 33 Drilling

## HEYM MODEL 33 BOXLOCK DRILLING
**Caliber/Gauge:** 5.6x50R Mag., 5.6x57R, 6.5x57R, 7x57R, 7x65R, 8x57JRS, 9.3x74R, 222, 243, 270, 308, 30-06; 16x16 (2¾"), 20x20 (3").
**Barrel:** 25" (Full & Mod.).
**Weight:** About 6½ lbs. **Length:** 42" over-all.
**Stock:** Dark European walnut, checkered p.g. and fore-end; oil finish.
**Sights:** Silver bead front, folding leaf rear. Automatic sight positioner. Available with scope and Suhler claw mounts.
**Features:** Greener-type crossbolt and safety, double under-lugs. Double set triggers. Plastic or steel trigger guard. Engraving coverage varies with model. Imported from West Germany by Paul Jaeger Inc.
**Price:** Model 33, from. . . . . . . . . . . . . . . . . . . . . . . . . . . . . . . . . . **$3,544.00**

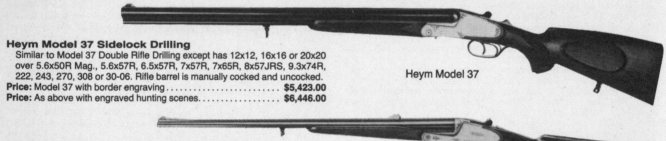

Heym 22S Combo

## HEYM MODEL 22S SAFETY COMBO GUN
**Caliber/Gauge:** 16 or 20 ga. (2¾", 3"), 12 ga. (2¾") over 22 Hornet, 22 WMR, 222 Rem., 222 Rem. Mag., 223, 243 Win., 5.6x50R, 6.5x57R, 7x57R, 8x57 JRS.
**Barrel:** 24", solid rib.
**Weight:** About 5½ lbs.
**Stock:** Dark European walnut, hand-checkered p.g. and fore-end. Oil finish.
**Sights:** Silver bead ramp front, folding leaf rear.
**Features:** Tang mounted cocking slide, separate barrel selector, single set trigger. Base supplied for quick-detachable scope mounts. Patented rocker-weight system automatically uncocks gun if accidentally dropped or bumped hard. Imported from West Germany. Contact Heym for more data.
**Price:** Model 22S . . . . . . . . . . . . . . . . . . . . . . . . . . . . . . . . . . . . **$1,452.00**
**Price:** Model 22SZ takedown . . . . . . . . . . . . . . . . . . . . . . . . . . **$1,650.00**
**Price:** Scope mounts, add . . . . . . . . . . . . . . . . . . . . . . . . . . . . . . **$120.00**

## HEYM MODEL 37B DOUBLE RIFLE DRILLING
**Caliber/Gauge:** 7x65R, 30-06, 8x57JRS, 9.3x74R; 20 ga. (3").
**Barrel:** 25" (shotgun barrel choked Full or Mod.).
**Weight:** About 8½ lbs. **Length:** 42" over-all.
**Stock:** Dark European walnut, hand-checkered p.g. and fore-end. Oil finish.
**Sights:** Silver bead front, folding leaf rear. Available with scope and Suhler claw mounts.
**Features:** Full side-lock construction. Greener-type crossbolt, double under lugs, cocking indicators. Imported from West Germany by Paul Jaeger, Inc.
**Price:** Model 37 double rifle drilling . . . . . . . . . . . . . . . . . . . . . . . **$7,172.00**
**Price:** Model 37 Deluxe (hunting scene engraving) from, . . . . . . . . **$8,195.00**

## Heym Model 37 Sidelock Drilling
Similar to Model 37 Double Rifle Drilling except has 12x12, 16x16 or 20x20 over 5.6x50R Mag., 5.6x57R, 6.5x57R, 7x57R, 7x65R, 8x57JRS, 9.3x74R, 222, 243, 270, 308 or 30-06. Rifle barrel is manually cocked and uncocked.
**Price:** Model 37 with border engraving . . . . . . . . . . . . . . . . . . . . . . **$5,423.00**
**Price:** As above with engraved hunting scenes. . . . . . . . . . . . . . . . . **$6,446.00**

Heym Model 37

## HEYM MODEL 88B SIDE-BY-SIDE DOUBLE RIFLE
**Caliber:** 7x57, 270, 30-06, 8x57JRS, 300 Win. Mag., 9.3x74R, 375 H&H.
**Barrel:** 25".
**Weight:** 7½ lbs. (std. cals), 8½ lbs. (mag.) **Length:** 42" over-all.
**Stock:** Fancy French walnut, classic North American design.
**Sights:** Silver bead post on ramp front, fixed or 3-leaf express rear.
**Features:** Action has complete coverage hunting scene engraving. Available as boxlock or with q.d. sidelocks. Imported from West Germany by Paul Jaeger, Inc.
**Price:** Boxlock, from . . . . . . . . . . . . . . . . . . . . . . . . . . . . . . . . . . **$5,170.00**
**Price:** Sidelock, Model 88B-SS, from . . . . . . . . . . . . . . . . . . . . . . **$7,249.00**
**Price:** Disengageable ejectors, add . . . . . . . . . . . . . . . . . . . . . . . . **$198.00**
**Price:** Interchangeable barrels, add . . . . . . . . . . . . . . . . . . . . . . . **$2,838.00**

Heym Model 88B

Heym 88B Safari

## HEYM MODEL 88B SAFARI DOUBLE RIFLE
**Caliber:** 375 H&H, 458 Win. Mag., 470 Nitro Express.
**Action:** Boxlock with interceptor sear. Automatic ejectors with disengagement sear.
**Barrel:** 25".
**Weight:** About 10 lbs.
**Stock:** Best quality Circassian walnut; classic design with cheekpiece; oil finish, hand-checkering; Presentation butt pad; steel grip cap.
**Sights:** Large silver bead on ramp front, quarter-rib with three-leaf express rear.

**Features:** Double triggers; engraved, silvered frame. Introduced 1985. Imported from West Germany by Paul Jaeger, Inc.
**Price:** 375 and 458 . . . . . . . . . . . . . . . . . . . . . . . . . . . . . . . . . . . . **$6,000.00**
**Price:** 470 Nitro Express . . . . . . . . . . . . . . . . . . . . . . . . . . . . . . . . **$6,800.00**
**Price:** Trap door grip cap . . . . . . . . . . . . . . . . . . . . . . . . . . . . . . . . **$235.00**
**Price:** Best quality leather case . . . . . . . . . . . . . . . . . . . . . . . . . . . **$350.00**

**CAUTION:** PRICES CHANGE. CHECK AT GUNSHOP.

## HEYM MODEL 55B/55SS O/U DOUBLE RIFLE
**Caliber:** 7x65R, 308, 30-06, 8x57JRS, 9.3x74R; 375 H&H.
**Barrel:** 25"
**Weight:** About 8 lbs., depending upon caliber. **Length:** 42" over-all.
**Stock:** Dark European walnut, hand-checkered p.g. and fore-end. Oil finish.
**Sights:** Silver bead ramp front, open V-type rear.
**Features:** Boxlock or full sidelock; Kersten double crossbolt, cocking indicators; hand-engraved hunting scenes. Options available include interchangeable barrels, Zeiss scopes in claw mounts, deluxe engravings and stock carving, etc. Imported from West Germany by Paul Jaeger, Inc.
**Price:** Model 55B boxlock . . . . . . . . . . . . . . . . . . . . . . . . . . . . . . . . . . . . . . $3,839.00
**Price:** Model 55SS sidelock . . . . . . . . . . . . . . . . . . . . . . . . . . . . . . . . . . . . $6,094.00
**Price:** Interchangeable shotgun barrels . . . . . . . . . . . . . . . . . . . . . . . . . $1,793.00
**Price:** Interchangeable rifle barrels . . . . . . . . . . . . . . . . . . . . . . . . . . . . $2,541.00

## PERUGINI-VISINI DOUBLE RIFLE
**Caliber:** 22 Hornet, 30-06, 7mm Rem. Mag., 7x65R, 9.3x74R, 270 Win., 300 H&H., 338 Win., 375 H&H, 458 Win. Mag., 470 Nitro.
**Barrel:** 22"-26".
**Weight:** 7¼ to 8½ lbs., depending upon caliber. **Length:** 39½" over-all (22" bbl.).
**Stock:** Oil-finished walnut; checkered grip and fore-end; cheekpiece.
**Sights:** Bead on ramp front, express rear on ¼-rib.
**Features:** True sidelock action with ejectors; sideplates are hand detachable; comes with leather trunk case. Introduced 1983. Imported from Italy by Wm. Larkin Moore.
**Price:** . . . . . . . . . . . . . . . . . . . . . . . . . . . . . . . . . . . . . . . . . . . . . . . . $10,500.00

## Heym Model 55BF/55BFSS O/U Combo Gun
Similar to Model 55B/77B o/u rifle except chambered for 12, 16 or 20 ga. (2¾" or 3") over 5.6x50R, 222 Rem., 5.6x57R, 243, 6.5x57R, 270, 7x57R, 7x65R, 308, 30-06, 8x57JRS, 9.3x74R, or 375 H&H. Has solid rib barrel. Available as boxlock or sidelock, with interchangeable shotgun and rifle barrels.
**Price:** Model 55BF boxlock . . . . . . . . . . . . . . . . . . . . . . . . . . . . . . . . . . $3,212.00
**Price:** Model 55BFSS sidelock . . . . . . . . . . . . . . . . . . . . . . . . . . . . . . . $5,467.00

## LEBEAU-COURALLY SIDELOCK DOUBLE RIFLE
**Caliber:** 8x57 JRS, 9.3x74R, 375 H&H, 458 Win.
**Barrel:** 23½" to 26".
**Weight:** 7 lbs., 8 oz. to 9 lbs., 8 oz.
**Stock:** Dimensions to customer specs. Best quality French walnut selected for maximum strength, pistol grip with cheekpiece, splinter or beavertail fore-end; steel grip cap.
**Sights:** Bead on ramp front, express rear on ¼-rib.
**Features:** Holland & Holland pattern sidelock with ejectors, chopper lump barrels; reinforced action with classic pattern; choice of numerous engraving patterns; can be furnished with scope in fitted claw mounts. Imported from Belgium by Wm. Larkin Moore.
**Price:** From . . . . . . . . . . . . . . . . . . . . . . . . . . . . . . . . . . . . . . . . . . . $20,500.00

Perugini-Visini O/U Double

## PERUGINI-VISINI O/U DOUBLE RIFLE
**Caliber:** 7mm Rem. Mag., 7x65R, 9.3x74R, 270 Win., 338 Win. Mag., 375 H&H, 458 Win. Mag.
**Barrel:** 24".
**Weight:** 8 lbs. **Length:** 40½" over-all.
**Stock:** Oil-finished walnut, checkered grip and fore-end, cheekpiece, rubber recoil pad.
**Sights:** Bead on ramp front, express rear on ¼-rib; Swarovski scope and claw mounts optional.
**Features:** Boxlock action with ejectors; silvered receiver, rest blued; double triggers. Comes with trunk case. Deluxe engraving, better wood, etc. available. Introduced 1983. Imported from Italy by Wm. Larkin Moore.
**Price:** . . . . . . . . . . . . . . . . . . . . . . . . . . . . . . . . . . . . . . . . . . . . . . . $4,000.00

Perugini-Visini Boxlock Double

## PERUGINI-VISINI BOXLOCK DOUBLE RIFLE
**Caliber:** 7x65R, 7x57, 308, 9.3x74R, 375 H&H, 444 Marlin, 458 Win. Mag.
**Barrel:** 25".
**Weight:** 8 lbs. **Length:** 41½" over-all.
**Stock:** Oil-finished walnut; checkered grip and fore-end; cheekpiece; rubber recoil pad.
**Sights:** Bead on ramp front, express rear on ¼-rib.
**Features:** Boxlock action with ejectors; color case-hardened receiver; double triggers. Also available with scope in claw mounts. Comes with trunk case. Introduced 1983. Imported from Italy by Wm. Larkin Moore.
**Price:** From . . . . . . . . . . . . . . . . . . . . . . . . . . . . . . . . . . . . . . . . . . . . $3,500.00

> Consult our Directory pages for
> the location of firms mentioned.

## SAUER MODEL 3000 DRILLING
**Caliber/Gauge:** 12 ga. over 30-06, 12 ga. over 243.
**Action:** Top lever, cross bolt, box lock.
**Barrel:** 25" (Mod. & Full).
**Weight:** 8 lbs. **Length:** 41¾" over-all.
**Stock:** American walnut, oil finish. Checkered p.g. and fore-end. Black p.g. cap, recoil pad. 14¼"x2"1½".
**Sights:** Blade front with brass bead, folding leaf rear.
**Features:** Cocking indicators, tang barrel selector, automatic sight positioner, set rifle trigger, side safety. Blue finish with bright receiver engraved with animal motifs and European-style scrollwork. Imported from West Germany by SIGARMS.
**Price:** Standard, about . . . . . . . . . . . . . . . . . . . . . . . . . . . . . . . . . . . . . $2,635.00
**Price:** Lux, about . . . . . . . . . . . . . . . . . . . . . . . . . . . . . . . . . . . . . . . . . $2,920.00

## SAUER BBF O/U COMBO GUN
**Caliber/Gauge:** 16 (2¾") over 243 or 30-06.
**Barrel:** 25".
**Weight:** About 6 lbs. **Length:** 42" over-all.
**Stock:** European walnut, with cheekpiece.
**Sights:** Post front, folding leaf rear on solid rib.
**Features:** Double set triggers, sear safety; satin oil finish on wood. Luxus model has better wood with white spacers at p.g. and buttplate, engraving. Introduced in U.S. 1986. Imported from West Germany by SIGARMS.
**Price:** Standard, About . . . . . . . . . . . . . . . . . . . . . . . . . . . . . . . . . . . . . $2,495.00
**Price:** Luxus, about . . . . . . . . . . . . . . . . . . . . . . . . . . . . . . . . . . . . . . . $2,745.00

**CAUTION:** PRICES CHANGE. CHECK AT GUNSHOP.

Savage Model 24-C

## SAVAGE MODEL 24-C O/U
**Caliber/Gauge:** Top bbl. 22 S, L, LR; bottom bbl. 20 gauge cyl. bore.
**Action:** Take-down, low rebounding visible hammer. Single trigger, barrel selector spur on hammer.

**Barrel:** 20″ separated barrels.
**Weight:** 5¾ lbs. **Length:** 35″ (taken down 20″).
**Stock:** Walnut finished hardwood.
**Sights:** Ramp front, rear open adj. for e.
**Features:** Trap door butt holds one shotshell and ten 22 cartridges, comes with special carrying case. Measures 7″x22″ when in case.
**Price:** . . . . . . . . . . . . . . . . . . . . . . . . . . . . . . . . . . . . . . . . . . . . . . . . . . **$208.39**

### Savage Model 24-F.G. O/U
Same as Model 24-C except: color case hardened frame, 24″ barrel, stock is walnut finished hardwood, no checkering.
**Price:** . . . . . . . . . . . . . . . . . . . . . . . . . . . . . . . . . . . . . . **$187.29**

### Savage Model 24-V
Similar to Model 24-C except: 222 Rem., 223 Rem. or 30-30 and 20 ga; 24″ barrel; stronger receiver; color case-hardened frame; folding leaf rear sight; receiver tapped for scope.
**Price:** . . . . . . . . . . . . . . . . . . . . . . . . . . . . . . . . . . . . . . **$272.89**

Springfield Armory M6

## SPRINGFIELD ARMORY M6 SCOUT SURVIVAL RIFLE
**Caliber:** 22 LR, 22 Mag., 22 Hornet over 410 shotgun.
**Barrel:** 18″.
**Weight:** 4 lbs. **Length:** 31½″ over-all.
**Stock:** Steel, folding, with magazine for 15 22 LR, four 410 cartridges.
**Sights:** Blade front, military aperture for 22; V-notch for 410.
**Features:** All metal construction. Designed for quick disassembly and minimum maintenance. Folds for compact storage. Introduced 1982. Made in U.S. by Springfield Armory.
**Price:** About . . . . . . . . . . . . . . . . . . . . . . . . . . . . . . . . . . . . . . . **$115.00**

Tikka Model 07

## TIKKA MODEL 07 COMBINATION GUN
**Caliber/Gauge:** 12 (2¾″) over 222 Rem.
**Barrel:** Shotgun — 25″ (Full), rifle — 22¾″.
**Weight:** About 7 lbs. **Length:** 40⅔″ over-all.
**Stock:** Walnut, Monte Carlo-style with palm-swell p.g.
**Sights:** Blade front, open rear adj. for w.
**Features:** Exposed hammer; receiver dovetailed for scope mounting; rifle barrel has a muzzle brake. Imported by Kassnar Imports, Inc.
**Price:** . . . . . . . . . . . . . . . . . . . . . . . . . . . . . . . . . . . . . . . . . . . **$1,070.00**

Valmet 412S Double

## VALMET 412S DOUBLE RIFLE
**Caliber:** 243, 308, 30-06, 375 Win., 9.3x74R.
**Barrel:** 24″.
**Weight:** 8⅝ lbs.
**Stock:** American walnut with Monte Carlo style.
**Sights:** Ramp front, adjustable open rear.
**Features:** Barrel selector mounted in trigger. Cocking indicators in tang. Recoil pad. Valmet scope mounts available. Interchangeable barrels. Introduced 1980. Imported from Finland by Valmet.
**Price:** Extractors, 243, 308, 30-06 . . . . . . . . . . . . . . . . . . . . . . . . . . . **$999.00**
**Price:** With ejectors, 375 Win., 9.3x74R. . . . . . . . . . . . . . . . . . . . . . **$1,099.00**
**Price:** Extra barrels, from . . . . . . . . . . . . . . . . . . . . . . . . . . . . . . . . . . **$599.00**

## VALMET 412S COMBINATION GUN
**Caliber/Gauge:** 12 over 222, 223, 243, 308, 30-06.
**Barrel:** 24″ (Imp. Mod.).
**Weight:** 7⅝ lbs.
**Stock:** American walnut, with recoil pad. Monte Carlo style. Standard measurements 14″x1⅜″x2″x2⅜″.
**Sights:** Blade front, flip-up-type open rear.
**Features:** Barrel selector on trigger. Hand checkered stock and fore-end. Barrels are screw-adjustable to change bullet point of impact. Barrels are interchangeable. Introduced 1980. Imported from Finland by Valmet.
**Price:** . . . . . . . . . . . . . . . . . . . . . . . . . . . . . . . . . . . . . . . . . . . . . **$899.00**
**Price:** Extra barrels, from . . . . . . . . . . . . . . . . . . . . . . . . . . . . . . . . . . **$499.00**

## A. ZOLI RIFLE-SHOTGUN O/U COMBO
**Caliber/Gauge:** 12 ga./308 Win., 12 ga./222, 12 ga./30-06.
**Barrel:** Combo—24″; shotgun—28″ (Mod. & Full).
**Weight:** About 8 lbs. **Length:** 41″ over-all (24″ bbl.).
**Stock:** European walnut.
**Sights:** Blade front, flip-up rear.
**Features:** Available with German claw scope mounts on rifle/shotgun barrels. Comes with set of 12/12 (Mod. & Full) barrels. Imported from Italy by Mandall Shooting Supplies.
**Price:** With two barrel sets, without claw mounts . . . . . . . . . . . . . . . **$1,495.00**
**Price:** With two barrel sets, scope and claw mounts . . . . . . . . . . . . **$1,895.00**

AMT Lightning 25/22

**AMT LIGHTNING 25/22 RIFLE**
**Caliber:** 22 LR, 25-shot magazine.
**Barrel:** NA.
**Weight:** 6 lbs. **Length:** 26½" (folded).
**Stock:** Folding stainless steel; finger grooved vertical pistol grip.
**Sights:** Ramp front, rear adjustable for windage.
**Features:** Made of stainless steel with matte finish. Receiver dovetailed for scope mounting. Extended magazine release. Standard or "bull" barrel. Introduced 1984. From AMT.
**Price:** ..................................................... $245.00

**AP-74 AUTO RIFLE**
**Caliber:** 22 LR, 32 ACP, 15 shot magazine.
**Barrel:** 20" including flash reducer.
**Weight:** 6½ lbs. **Length:** 38½" over-all.
**Stock:** Black plastic.
**Sights:** Ramp front, adj. peep rear.
**Features:** Pivotal take-down, easy disassembly. AR-15 look-alike. Sling and sling swivels included. Imported by EMF.
**Price:** ................................................ $250.00
**Price:** With walnut stock and fore-end ...................... $280.00
**Price:** 32 ACP ........................................... $255.00
**Price:** With wood stock and fore-end ...................... $260.00

Anschutz Model 520/61

**Weight:** 6½ lbs. **Length:** 43" over-all.
**Stock:** European hardwood; checkered pistol grip, Monte Carlo comb, beaver-tail fore-end.
**Sights:** Hooded ramp front, folding leaf rear.
**Features:** Rotary safety, empty shell deflector, single stage trigger. Receiver grooved for scope mounting. Introduced 1982. Imported from Germany by PSI.
**Price:** ..................................................... $276.50

**ANSCHUTZ DELUXE MODEL 520/61 AUTO**
**Caliber:** 22 LR, 10-shot clip.
**Barrel:** 24".

Auto-Ordnance 1927A-3

**AUTO ORDNANCE MODEL 1927A-3**
**Caliber:** 22 LR, 10, 30 or 50-shot magazine.
**Barrel:** 16", finned.
**Weight:** About 7 lbs.
**Stock:** Walnut stock and fore-end.
**Sights:** Blade front, open rear adjustable for windage and elevation.
**Features:** Re-creation of the Thompson Model 1927, only in 22 Long Rifle. Alloy receiver, finned barrel.
**Price:** ..................................................... $424.75

**BINGHAM PPS-50 CARBINE**
**Caliber:** 22 LR, 50-shot drum.
**Barrel:** 16.1".
**Weight:** 6½ lbs. **Length:** 33¾" over-all.
**Stock:** Beechwood (standard), walnut optional.
**Sights:** Blade front, folding leaf rear.
**Features:** Semi-auto carbine with perforated barrel jacket. Standard model has blue finish with oil-finish wood. From Bingham Ltd.
**Price:** Standard ........................................... $229.95
**Price:** Deluxe (blue with walnut stock) ..................... $249.95
**Price:** Duramil (chrome with walnut stock) ................. $259.95

**BINGHAM AK-22 CARBINE**
**Caliber:** 22 LR, 15-shot magazine.
**Barrel:** 17¾".
**Weight:** 6 lbs., 1 oz. **Length:** 35½" over-all.
**Stock:** Beechwood (standard), walnut optional.
**Sights:** Hooded post front, open adjustable rear.
**Features:** Semi-auto rimfire version of the Soviet assault rifle. A 28-shot "Military Look-Alike" magazine optional. From Bingham Ltd.
**Price:** Standard ........................................... $229.95
**Price:** Deluxe (walnut stock) ............................... $249.95

Browning Auto Rifle

**BROWNING AUTOLOADING RIFLE**
**Caliber:** 22 LR, 11-shot.
**Barrel:** 19¼".
**Weight:** 4¾ lbs. **Length:** 37" over-all.
**Stock:** Checkered select walnut (13¾"x1¹³⁄₁₆"x2⅝") with p.g. and semi-beavertail fore-end.
**Sights:** Gold bead front, folding leaf rear.
**Features:** Engraved receiver is grooved for tip-off scope mount; cross-bolt safety; tubular magazine in buttstock; easy take down for carrying or storage. Imported from Japan by Browning.
**Price:** Grade I ............................................. $295.50

Charter AR-7 Explorer

**CHARTER AR-7 EXPLORER CARBINE**
**Caliber:** 22 LR, 8-shot clip.
**Barrel:** 16″ alloy (steel-lined).
**Weight:** 2½ lbs. **Length:** 34½″/16½″ stowed.
**Stock:** Moulded black Cycloac, snap-on rubber butt pad.
**Sights:** Square blade front, aperture rear adj. for e.
**Features:** Take-down design stores bbl. and action in hollow stock. Light enough to float.
**Price:** Black or Silvertone finish....................................... $115.00
**Price:** Camouflage finish.......................................... $120.00

F.I.E. Black Beauty

**F.I.E. GR-8 BLACK BEAUTY AUTO RIFLE**
**Caliber:** 22 LR, 14-shot tubular magazine.
**Barrel:** 19⅝″.
**Weight:** 4 lbs. **Length:** 38½″ over-all.
**Stock:** Moulded black nylon, checkered pistol grip and fore-end.
**Sights:** Blade on ramp front, adjustable open rear.
**Features:** Made mostly of moulded nylon; tube magazine housed in buttstock; top tang safety; receiver grooved for tip-off scope mounts. Imported from Brazil by F.I.E. Introduced 1984.
**Price:**........................................................ $109.95

**F.I.E./FRANCHI PARA RIMEFIRE RIFLE**
**Caliber:** 22 LR, 11-shot magazine.
**Barrel:** 19″.
**Weight:** 4 lbs., 12 oz. **Length:** 39¼″ over-all.
**Stock:** Metal skeleton buttstock, walnut p.g. and fore-end.
**Sights:** Hooded front, open adj. rear.
**Features:** Take-down rifle comes in its own fitted carrying case. Receiver grooved for scope mounting. Tube magazine feeds through buttplate. Limited production. Introduced 1986. Imported from Italy by F.I.E. Corp.
**Price:**.................................................. $274.95

Heckler & Koch 300

**Stock:** European walnut, Monte Carlo with cheek rest; checkered p.g. and Schnabel fore-end.
**Sights:** Post front adj. for elevation, V-notch rear adj. for windage.
**Features:** Polygonal rifling, comes with sling swivels; straight blow-back inertia bolt action; single-stage trigger (3½-lb. pull). Clamp scope mount with 1″ rings available at extra cost. Limited quantity available. Imported from West Germany by Heckler & Koch, Inc.
**Price:** HK300 ............................................... $346.00
**Price:** Scope mount with 1″ rings ............................... $159.00

**HECKLER & KOCH MODEL 300 AUTO RIFLE**
**Caliber:** 22 Mag., 5-shot box mag.
**Barrel:** 19¾″.
**Weight:** 5¾ lbs. **Length:** 39½″ over-all.

Iver Johnson EW.22HBA

**IVER JOHNSON MODEL EW.22HBA RIFLE**
**Caliber:** 22 Long Rifle (15-shot magazine).
**Barrel:** 18½″.
**Weight:** 5.8 lbs. **Length:** 38″ over-all.
**Stock:** Walnut-finished hardwood.
**Sights:** Blade front, peep rear adjustable for w. and e.
**Features:** Resembles the U.S. 30-cal. M-1 Carbine. Introduced 1985. From Iver Johnson.
**Price:**........................................................ $162.95
**Price:** Model EW.22MHBA (22 Mag., gas operated).............. $267.95

Marlin Model 990

**MARLIN MODEL 990 SEMI-AUTO RIFLE**
**Caliber:** 22 LR, 17-shot tubular magazine.
**Barrel:** 22″ Micro-Groove®.
**Weight:** About 5½ lbs. **Length:** 40¾″ over-all.
**Stock:** American black walnut, Monte Carlo style with fluted comb and full pistol grip; checkered p.g. and fore-end; white buttplate spacer; Mar-Shield® finish.
**Sights:** Ramp bead front with Wide-Scan™ hood, adjustable folding semi-buckhorn rear.
**Features:** Receiver grooved for tip-off mount; manual bolt hold-open device; automatic last-shot bolt hold-open device; cross-bolt safety. Introduced 1979.
**Price:**........................................................ $147.95

**MARLIN MODEL 995 SEMI-AUTO RIFLE**
**Caliber:** 22 LR, 7-shot clip magazine
**Barrel:** 18″ Micro-Grove®.
**Weight:** 5 lbs. **Length:** 36¾″ over-all.
**Stock:** American black walnut, Monte Carlo-style, with full pistol grip. Checkered p.g. and fore-end; white buttplate spacer; Mar-Shield® finish.
**Sights:** Ramp bead front with Wide-Scan hood; adjustable folding semi-buckhorn rear.
**Features:** Receiver grooved for tip-off scope mount; bolt hold-open device; cross-bolt safety. Introduced 1979.
**Price:**...................................................... $137.95

# RIMFIRE RIFLES—AUTOLOADERS

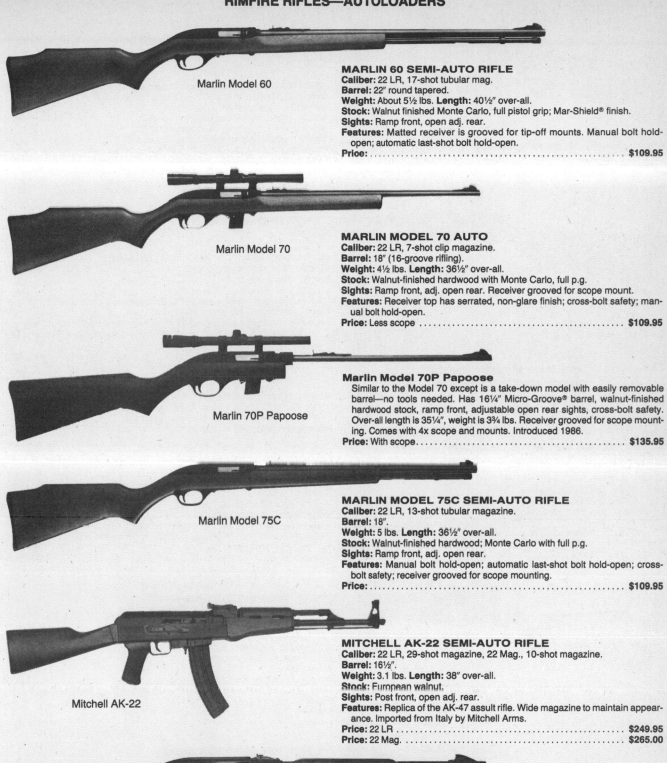

Marlin Model 60

## MARLIN 60 SEMI-AUTO RIFLE
**Caliber:** 22 LR, 17-shot tubular mag.
**Barrel:** 22″ round tapered.
**Weight:** About 5½ lbs. **Length:** 40½″ over-all.
**Stock:** Walnut finished Monte Carlo, full pistol grip; Mar-Shield® finish.
**Sights:** Ramp front, open adj. rear.
**Features:** Matted receiver is grooved for tip-off mounts. Manual bolt hold-open; automatic last-shot bolt hold-open.
**Price:** .................................................... $109.95

Marlin Model 70

## MARLIN MODEL 70 AUTO
**Caliber:** 22 LR, 7-shot clip magazine.
**Barrel:** 18″ (16-groove rifling).
**Weight:** 4½ lbs. **Length:** 36½″ over-all.
**Stock:** Walnut-finished hardwood with Monte Carlo, full p.g.
**Sights:** Ramp front, adj. open rear. Receiver grooved for scope mount.
**Features:** Receiver top has serrated, non-glare finish; cross-bolt safety; manual bolt hold-open.
**Price:** Less scope ................................ $109.95

Marlin 70P Papoose

## Marlin Model 70P Papoose
Similar to the Model 70 except is a take-down model with easily removable barrel—no tools needed. Has 16¼″ Micro-Groove® barrel, walnut-finished hardwood stock, ramp front, adjustable open rear sights, cross-bolt safety. Over-all length is 35¼″, weight is 3¾ lbs. Receiver grooved for scope mounting. Comes with 4x scope and mounts. Introduced 1986.
**Price:** With scope................................ $135.95

Marlin Model 75C

## MARLIN MODEL 75C SEMI-AUTO RIFLE
**Caliber:** 22 LR, 13-shot tubular magazine.
**Barrel:** 18″.
**Weight:** 5 lbs. **Length:** 36½″ over-all.
**Stock:** Walnut-finished hardwood; Monte Carlo with full p.g.
**Sights:** Ramp front, adj. open rear.
**Features:** Manual bolt hold-open; automatic last-shot bolt hold-open; cross-bolt safety; receiver grooved for scope mounting.
**Price:** .................................................... $109.95

Mitchell AK-22

## MITCHELL AK-22 SEMI-AUTO RIFLE
**Caliber:** 22 LR, 29-shot magazine, 22 Mag., 10-shot magazine.
**Barrel:** 16½″.
**Weight:** 3.1 lbs. **Length:** 38″ over-all.
**Stock:** European walnut.
**Sights:** Post front, open adj. rear.
**Features:** Replica of the AK-47 assult rifle. Wide magazine to maintain appearance. Imported from Italy by Mitchell Arms.
**Price:** 22 LR ..................................... $249.95
**Price:** 22 Mag. ................................... $265.00

Remington Nylon 66

## REMINGTON NYLON 66MB AUTO RIFLE
**Caliber:** 22 LR, 14-shot tubular mag.
**Barrel:** 19⅝″ round tapered.
**Weight:** 4 lbs. **Length:** 38½″ over-all.
**Stock:** Moulded Mohawk Brown Nylon, checkered p.g. and fore-end.
**Sights:** Blade ramp front, adj. open rear.
**Features:** Top tang safety, double extractors, receiver grooved for tip-off mounts.
**Price:** About ....................................... $135.00

**Remington Nylon 66BD Auto Rifle**
Same as the Model 66MB except has black stock, barrel, and receiver cover. Black diamond-shape inlay in fore-end. Introduced 1978.
**Price:** About ................................................. $135.00

Remington Model 552A

## Remington Model 552BDL Deluxe Auto Rifle
Same as Model 552A except: Du Pont RKW finished walnut stock, checkered fore-end and capped p.g. stock. Blade ramp front and fully adj. rear sights.
**Price:** About .................................................... **$209.00**

**REMINGTON 552A AUTOLOADING RIFLE**
**Caliber:** 22 S (20), L (17) or LR (15) tubular mag.
**Barrel:** 21" round tapered.
**Weight:** About 5¾ lbs. **Length:** 40" over-all.
**Stock:** Full-size, walnut-finished hardwood.
**Sights:** Bead front, step open rear adj. for w. & e.
**Features:** Positive cross-bolt safety, receiver grooved for tip-off mount.
**Price:** About ........................................... **$183.00**

Ruger 10/22 Sporter

**RUGER 10/22 AUTOLOADING CARBINE**
**Caliber:** 22 LR, 10-shot rotary mag.
**Barrel:** 18½" round tapered.
**Weight:** 5 lbs. **Length:** 37¼" over-all.
**Stock:** American hardwood with p.g. and bbl. band.
**Sights:** Gold bead front, folding leaf rear adj. for e.
**Features:** Detachable rotary magazine fits flush into stock, cross-bolt safety, receiver tapped and grooved for scope blocks or tip-off mount. Scope base adapter furnished with each rifle.
**Price:** Model 10/22 RB ........................................ **$176.00**

**Ruger 10/22 Auto Sporter**
Same as 10/22 Carbine except: Walnut stock with hand checkered p.g. and fore-end with straight buttplate, no bbl. band, has sling swivels.
**Price:** Model 10/22 DSP ...................................... **$222.00**

Consult our Directory pages for the location of firms mentioned.

**SOVEREIGN TOMMY AUTO CARBINE**
**Caliber:** 22 LR, 10-shot clip standard; 30-shot magazine or 50-shot drum optional.
**Barrel:** 18¼".
**Weight:** 6 lbs. **Length:** 35" over-all.
**Stock:** Walnut finished hardwood.
**Sights:** Bead front, open adj. rear.
**Features:** Looks like Soviet PPS carbine. Available in matte blue or satin chrome finish. Introduced 1986. Imported by Southern Gun & Tackle.
**Price:** With 10-shot clip...................................... **$178.95**
**Price:** 50-round drum......................................... **$31.50**

**SOVEREIGN TD.22 AUTO RIFLE**
**Caliber:** 22 LR, 10-shot clip.
**Barrel:** 21".
**Weight:** 6½ lbs. **Length:** 41" over-all.
**Stock:** Walnut finished hardwood.
**Sights:** Hooded ramp front, fully adj. open rear.
**Features:** Take-down rifle for easy storage, carry; blue finish. Introduced 1986. Imported by Southern Gun & Tackle.
**Price:** ..................................................... **$92.95**

Stevens Model 987

**STEVENS MODEL 987 AUTO RIFLE**
**Caliber:** 22 LR, 15-shot magazine.
**Barrel:** 20".
**Weight:** About 6 lbs. **Length:** 40½" over-all.
**Stock:** Walnut finish with Monte Carlo; checkered pistol grip and fore-end.
**Sights:** Bead front, open adjustable rear.
**Features:** Top tang safety; metal parts blued.
**Price:** .................................................... **$106.50**

Tradewinds Model 260-A

**TRADEWINDS MODEL 260-A AUTO RIFLE**
**Caliber:** 22 LR, 5-shot (10-shot mag. avail.).
**Barrel:** 22½".
**Weight:** 5¾ lbs. **Length:** 41½".
**Stock:** Walnut, with hand checkered p.g. and fore-end.
**Sights:** Ramp front with hood, 3-leaf folding rear, receiver grooved for scope mount.
**Features:** Double extractors, sliding safety. Imported by Tradewinds.
**Price:** .................................................... **$250.00**

CAUTION: PRICES CHANGE. CHECK AT GUNSHOP.

# RIMFIRE RIFLES—AUTOLOADERS

Voere Model 2005

**VOERE MODEL 2005 AUTO RIFLE**
**Caliber:** 22 LR, 5- or 8-shot magazine.
**Barrel:** 19½".
**Weight:** 6 lbs. **Length:** 41" over-all.

**Stock:** European hardwood with Monte Carlo. Butt pad and swivel studs standard.
**Sights:** Hooded front, open fully adj. rear.
**Features:** Deluxe model with checkering and raised cheekpiece available. Introduced 1986. Imported from West Germany by KDF, Inc.
**Price:** Standard ................................................. $149.00
**Price:** Deluxe .................................................... $169.00

Voere 2115

**VOERE MODEL 2115 AUTO RIFLE**
**Caliber:** 22 LR, 8 or 15-shot magazine.
**Barrel:** 18.1".
**Weight:** 5.75 lbs. **Length:** 37.7" over-all.

**Stock:** Walnut-finished beechwood with cheekpiece; checkered pistol grip and fore-end.
**Sights:** Post front with hooded ramp, leaf rear.
**Features:** Clip-fed autoloader with single stage trigger, wing-type safety. Imported from Austria by L. Joseph Rahn. Introduced 1984.
**Price:** Model 2115 ............................................. $245.00
**Price:** Model 2114S (as above except no cheekpiece, checkering or white line spacers at grip, buttplate) ............................. $225.00

Weatherby Mark XXII

**WEATHERBY MARK XXII AUTO RIFLE, CLIP MODEL**
**Caliber:** 22 LR only, 5- or 10-shot clip.
**Barrel:** 24" round contoured.
**Weight:** 6 lbs. **Length:** 42¼" over-all.
**Stock:** Walnut, Monte Carlo comb and cheekpiece, rosewood p.g. cap and fore-end tip. Skip-line checkering.
**Sights:** Gold bead ramp front, 3-leaf folding rear.
**Features:** Thumb operated tang safety. Single shot or semi-automatic side lever selector. Receiver grooved for tip-off scope mount. Single pin release for quick takedown.
**Price:** ..................................................... $369.95

**Weatherby Mark XXII Tubular Model**
Same as Mark XXII Clip Model except: 15-shot tubular magazine.
**Price:** ..................................................... $369.95

# RIMFIRE RIFLES—LEVER & SLIDE ACTIONS

Browning BL-22

**BROWNING BL-22 LEVER ACTION RIFLE**
**Caliber:** 22 S(22), L(17) or LR(15). Tubular mag.
**Barrel:** 20" round tapered.
**Weight:** 5 lbs. **Length:** 36¾" over-all.
**Stock:** Walnut, 2-piece straight grip Western style.
**Sights:** Bead post front, folding-leaf rear.
**Features:** Short throw lever, ½-cock safety, receiver grooved for tip-off scope mounts. Imported from Japan by Browning.
**Price:** Grade I ................................................. $264.50
**Price:** Grade II, engraved receiver, checkered grip and fore-end .... $302.50

Iver Johnson EW.22HBL

**IVER JOHNSON EW.22HBL RIFLE**
**Caliber:** 22 Long Rifle (21 Short, 17 Long, 15 Long Rifle), 22 Mag. (12-shot magazine).
**Barrel:** 18½".
**Weight:** 5¾ lbs. **Length:** 36½" over-all.
**Stock:** Walnut-finished hardwood.
**Sights:** Hooded ramp front, open adjustable rear.
**Features:** Polished blue finish. Receiver grooved for scope mounting. Introduced 1985. From Iver Johnson.
**Price:** 22 Long Rifle ........................................... $189.95
**Price:** 22 Magnum .............................................. $204.95

Marlin 1894M

**MARLIN MODEL 1894M CARBINE**
**Caliber:** 22 Mag., 11-shot magazine.
**Barrel:** 20" Micro-Groove®.

**Weight:** 6¼ lbs. **Length:** 37½" over-all.
**Stock:** Straight grip stock of American black walnut, Mar-Shield® finish.
**Sights:** Ramp front with brass bead, adjustable semi-buckhorn folding rear.
**Features:** Has new hammer block safety. Side-ejecting solid-top receiver tapped for scope mount or receiver sight; squared finger lever, reversible off-set hammer spur for scope use. Scope shown is optional. Introduced 1983.
**Price:** ........................................................ **$315.95**

Marlin Golden 39A

**MARLIN GOLDEN 39M CARBINE**
**Caliber:** 22 S(21), L(16), LR(15), tubular magazine.
**Barrel:** 20" Micro-Grove®.
**Weight:** 6 lbs. **Length:** 36" over-all.
**Stock:** American black walnut, straight grip, white line buttplate spacer. Mar-Shield® finish.
**Sights:** "Wide-Scan"™ ramp front with hood, folding rear semi-buckhorn adj. for w. and e.
**Features:** Squared finger lever. Receiver tapped for scope mount (supplied) or receiver sight, offset hammer spur, take-down action; gold plated steel trigger.
**Price:** ........................................................ **$281.95**

**MARLIN GOLDEN 39A LEVER ACTION RIFLE**
**Caliber:** 22 S(26), L(21), LR(19), tubular magazine.
**Barrel:** 24" Micro-Groove®.
**Weight:** 6½ lbs. **Length:** 40" over-all.
**Stock:** American black walnut with white line spacers at p.g. cap and buttplate; Mar-Shield® finish.
**Sights:** Bead ramp front with detachable "Wide-Scan"™ hood, folding rear semi-buckhorn adj. for w. and e.
**Features:** Take-down action, receiver tapped for scope mount (supplied), off-set hammer spur; gold plated steel trigger.
**Price:** ........................................................ **$281.95**

Remington Model 572

**Remington Model 572 BDL Deluxe**
Same as the 572 except: p.g. cap, walnut stock with RKW finish, checkered grip and fore-end, ramp front and fully adj. rear sights.
**Price:** About ............................................. **$221.00**

**REMINGTON 572A FIELDMASTER PUMP RIFLE**
**Caliber:** 22 S(20), L(17) or LR(14). Tubular mag.
**Barrel:** 21" round tapered.
**Weight:** 5½ lbs. **Length:** 42" over-all.
**Stock:** Walnut-finished hardwood with p.g. and grooved slide handle.
**Sights:** Blade ramp front; sliding ramp rear adj. for w. & e.
**Features:** Cross-bolt safety, removing inner mag. tube converts rifle to single shot, receiver grooved for tip-off scope mount.
**Price:** About ............................................. **$192.00**

Rossi 62 SA

**Rossi 62 SAC Carbine**
Same as standard model except has 16¼" barrel. Magazine holds slightly fewer cartridges.
**Price:** Blue ................................................ **$162.00**
**Price:** Nickel ............................................. **$177.00**
**Price:** Stainless steel.................................. **$192.00**

**ROSSI 62 SA PUMP RIFLE**
**Caliber:** 22 S, L or LR, 22 Mag.
**Barrel:** 23", round or octagon.
**Weight:** 5¾ lbs. **Length:** 39¼" over-all.
**Stock:** Walnut, straight grip, grooved fore-end.
**Sights:** Fixed front, adj. rear.
**Features:** Capacity 20 Short, 16 Long or 14 Long Rifle. Quick takedown. Imported from Brazil by Interarms.
**Price:** Stainless steel.................................. **$192.00**
**Price:** Blue................................................. **$162.00**
**Price:** Nickel ............................................. **$177.00**
**Price:** Blue, with octagon barrel....................... **$187.00**
**Price:** 22 Mag., as Model 59 ........................... **$197.00**

Winchester 9422

**Winchester 9422M XTR Lever Action Rifle**
Same as the 9422 except chambered for 22 Mag. cartridge, has 11-round mag. capacity.
**Price:** About ............................................. **$320.27**

**WINCHESTER 9422 XTR LEVER ACTION RIFLE**
**Caliber:** 22 S(21), L(17), LR(15). Tubular mag.
**Barrel:** 20½". (16" twist).
**Weight:** 6¼ lbs. **Length:** 37⅛" over-all.
**Stock:** American walnut, 2-piece, straight grip (no p.g.).
**Sights:** Hooded ramp front, adj. semi-buckhorn rear.
**Features:** Side ejection, receiver grooved for scope mounting, takedown action. Has XTR wood and metal finish. Made under license by U.S. Repeating Arms Co.
**Price:** About ............................................. **$320.27**

**CAUTION:** PRICES CHANGE. CHECK AT GUNSHOP.

# RIMFIRE RIFLES—LEVER & SLIDE ACTIONS

Winchester 9422 Classic

## Winchester 9422 XTR Classic
Similar to 9422 XTR except has uncheckered, satin-finished walnut stock with fluted comb, crescent steel buttplate, curved finger lever, and capped pistol grip. Over-all length is 39⅛", barrel length 22½", weight is 6½ lbs. In 22 Short, Long, Long Rifle and 22 Magnum. Introduced 1985.
**Price:** About . . . . . . . . . . . . . . . . . . . . . . . . . . . . . . . . . . . . . . . . . . . . . **$354.45**

## RIMFIRE RIFLES—BOLT ACTIONS & SINGLE SHOTS

Anschutz 1416/1516

### Anschutz 1418D/1518D Deluxe Rifles
Similar to the 1416D/1516D rifles except has full length Mannlicher-style stock, shorter 19¾" barrel. Weighs 5½ lbs. Stock has buffalo horn Schnabel tip. Double set trigger available on special order. Model 1418D chambered for 22 LR, 1518D for 22 Mag. Imported from Germany by PSI.
**Price: 1418D** . . . . . . . . . . . . . . . . . . . . . . . . . **$528.00**
**Price: 1518D** . . . . . . . . . . . . . . . . . . . . . . . . . **$531.50**

### ANSCHUTZ DELUXE 1416/1516 RIFLES
**Caliber:** 22 LR (1416D), 5-shot clip, 22 Mag. (1516D), 4-shot clip.
**Barrel:** 22½".
**Weight:** 6 lbs. **Length:** 41" over-all.
**Stock:** European walnut; Monte Carlo with cheekpiece, Schnabel fore-end, checkered pistol grip and fore-end.
**Sights:** Hooded ramp front, folding leaf rear.
**Features:** Uses Model 1403 target rifle action. Adjustable single stage trigger. Receiver grooved for scope mounting. Imported from Germany by PSI.
**Price: 1416D, 22 LR** . . . . . . . . . . . . . . . . . . . . . . . . . . . . . . . . **$372.00**
**Price: 1516D, 22 Mag.** . . . . . . . . . . . . . . . . . . . . . . . . . . . . . . . **$377.75**
**Price: 1416D Classic left hand** . . . . . . . . . . . . . . . . . . . . . . . . **$424.75**

Anschutz 1422/1522

### Anschutz 1422D/1522D Custom Rifles
Similar to the Classic models except have roll-over Monte Carlo cheekpiece, slim fore-end with Schnabel tip, Wundhammer palm swell on pistol grip, rosewood grip cap with white diamond insert. Skip-line checkering on grip and fore-end. Introduced 1982. Imported from Germany by PSI.
**Price: 1422D** . . . . . . . . . . . . . . . . . . . . . . . . . **$652.50**
**Price: 1522D** . . . . . . . . . . . . . . . . . . . . . . . . . **$645.75**

### ANSCHUTZ 1422D/1522D CLASSIC RIFLES
**Caliber:** 22 LR (1422D), 5-shot clip, 22 Mag. (1522D), 4-shot clip.
**Barrel:** 24".
**Weight:** 7¼ lbs. **Length:** 43" over-all.
**Stock:** Select European walnut; checkered pistol grip and fore-end.
**Sights:** Hooded ramp front, folding leaf rear.
**Features:** Uses Match 54 action. Adjustable single stage trigger. Receiver drilled and tapped for scope mounting. Introduced 1982. Imported from Germany by PSI.
**Price: 1422D (22 LR)** . . . . . . . . . . . . . . . . . . . . . . . . . . . . . . . **$606.50**
**Price: 1522D (22 Mag.)** . . . . . . . . . . . . . . . . . . . . . . . . . . . . . **$609.75**

Beeman/Krico 320

### BEEMAN/KRICO MODEL 320 BOLT ACTION RIFLE
**Caliber:** 22 LR, 5-shot magazine.
**Barrel:** 19.5".
**Weight:** 6 lbs. **Length:** 38½" over-all.
**Stock:** Select European walnut; full-length Mannlicher-style with curved European comb and cheekpiece; cut checkered grip and fore-end.
**Sights:** Blade front on ramp, open rear adjustable for windage.
**Features:** Single or double set trigger; blued steel fore-end cap; detachable box magazine. Imported from West Germany by Beeman.
**Price:** . . . . . . . . . . . . . . . . . . . . . . . . . . . . . . . . . . . . . . . . . . . . . **$549.50**

### BEEMAN/KRICO MODEL 300 BOLT ACTION RIFLE
**Caliber:** 22 LR, 5-shot magazine.
**Barrel:** 23.5".
**Weight:** 6.5 lbs. **Length:** 43" over-all.
**Stock:** European walnut with straight American-style comb; cut checkered grip and fore-end.
**Sights:** Hooded blade front on ramp, open rear adjustable for windage.
**Features:** Dual extractors; single, match or double set triggers available; detachable box magazine. Imported from West Germany by Beeman.
**Price:** . . . . . . . . . . . . . . . . . . . . . . . . . . . . . . . . . . . . . . . . . . . . . **$495.50**

### BRNO ZKM 452 BOLT ACTION RIFLE
**Caliber:** 22 LR, 5- or 10-shot magazine.
**Barrel:** 25".
**Weight:** 6 lbs., 10 oz. **Length:** 43½" over-all.
**Stock:** Beechwood.
**Sights:** Hooded bead front, open rear adj. for e.
**Features:** Blue finish; oiled stock with checkered p.g. Imported from Czechoslovakia by Bauska Arms Corp.
**Price:** . . . . . . . . . . . . . . . . . . . . . . . . . . . . . . . . . . . . . . . . . . . . . **$239.00**

**CAUTION:** PRICES CHANGE. CHECK AT GUNSHOP.

Browning A-Bolt 22

## BROWNING A-BOLT 22 BOLT ACTION RIFLE
**Caliber:** 22 LR, 5- and 15-shot magazines standard.
**Barrel:** 22″.
**Weight:** 5 lbs., 9 oz. **Length:** 40¼″ over-all.

**Stock:** Laminated walnut.
**Sights:** Offered with or without open sights. Open sight model has ramp front and adjustable folding leaf rear.
**Features:** Short 60-degree bolt throw. Top tang safety. Grooved for 22 scope mount. Drilled and tapped for full size scope mounts. Detachable magazines. Gold-colored trigger preset at about 4 lbs. Imported from Japan by Browning. Introduced 1986.
**Price:** A-Bolt 22, no sights ................................... $299.95
**Price:** A-Bolt 22, with open sights ........................... $309.95

## CABANAS MASTER BOLT ACTION RIFLE
**Caliber:** 177, round ball or pellet; single shot.
**Barrel:** 19½″.
**Weight:** 8 lbs. **Length:** 45½″ over-all.
**Stock:** Walnut target-type with Monte Carlo.
**Sights:** Blade front, fully adjustable rear.
**Features:** Fires round ball or pellet with 22-cal. blank cartridge. Bolt action. Imported from Mexico by Mandall Shooting Supplies. Introduced 1984.
**Price:** ................................................. $149.95
**Price:** Varmint model (21½″ barrel, 4½ lbs., 41″ o.a.l., varmint-type stock) ............................................. $109.95

### Cabanas Espronceda IV Bolt Action Rifle
Similar to the Leyre model except has full sporter stock, 18¾″ barrel, 40″ over-all length, weighs 5½ lbs.
**Price:** ................................................. $119.95

### Cabanas Leyre Bolt Action Rifle
Similar to Master model except 44″ over-all, has sport/target stock.
**Price:** ................................................. $134.95
**Price:** Model R83 (17″ barrel, hardwood stock, 40″ o.a.l.) ........... $79.95
**Price:** Mini 82 Youth (16½″ barrel, 33″ o.a.l., 3½ lbs.) .............. $69.95

Chipmunk Rifle

## F.I.E. MODEL 122 BOLT ACTION RIFLE
**Caliber:** 22 S, L, LR, 6-shot magazine.
**Barrel:** 21″.
**Weight:** 5½ lbs. **Length:** 39″ over-all.
**Stock:** Walnut-finished hardwood.
**Sights:** Blade front, open rear adj. for w. & e.
**Features:** Sliding wing-type safety lever, double extractors, red cocking indicator, receiver grooved for scope mounts. Imported from Brazil by F.I.E. Introduced 1986.
**Price:** ................................................. $114.95

## CHIPMUNK SINGLE SHOT RIFLE
**Caliber:** 22, S, L, LR, or 22 Mag., single shot.
**Barrel:** 16⅛″.
**Weight:** About 2½ lbs. **Length:** 30″ over-all.
**Stock:** American walnut, or camouflage.
**Sights:** Post on ramp front, peep rear adj. for windage and elevation.
**Features:** Drilled and tapped for scope mounting using special Chipmunk base ($9.95). Made in U.S.A. Introduced 1982. From Chipmunk Mfg.
**Price:** ................................................. $119.95
**Price:** Fully engraved Presentation Model with hand checkered fancy stock ..................................................... $500.00

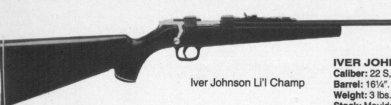

Iver Johnson Li'l Champ

## IVER JOHNSON LI'L CHAMP RIFLE
**Caliber:** 22 S, L, LR, single shot.
**Barrel:** 16¼″.
**Weight:** 3 lbs., 2 oz. **Length:** 32½″ over-all.
**Stock:** Moulded composition.
**Sights:** Blade on ramp front, adj. rear.
**Features:** Sized for junior shooters. Nickel-plated bolt. Made in U.S.A. Introduced 1986. From Iver Johnson.
**Price:** ................................................. $89.00

KDF K-22

## KDF K-22 BOLT ACTION RIFLE
**Caliber:** 22 LR, 22 Mag., 5- or 8-shot magazine.
**Barrel:** 21½″.
**Weight:** 6½ lbs. **Length:** 40″ over-all.
**Stock:** Oil finished, hand checkered European walnut with Monte Carlo.
**Sights:** None furnished. Receiver grooved for scope mounts.
**Features:** Bolt has front-locking lugs; uses KDF pillar bedding system. Introduced 1984. From KDF, Inc.
**Price:** K-22 Standard, 22 LR ................................. $299.00
**Price:** As above, 22 Mag. .................................... $349.00
**Price:** K-22 Deluxe (22 LR) has rosewood fore-end tip, rubber recoil pad, q.d. sling swivels. ........................................... $449.00

> Consult our Directory pages for the location of firms mentioned.

**CAUTION:** PRICES CHANGE. CHECK AT GUNSHOP.

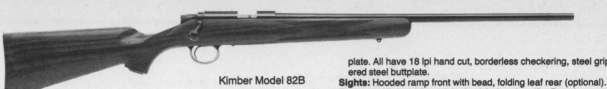

Kimber Model 82B

### KIMBER MODEL 82B BOLT ACTION RIFLE
**Caliber:** 22 LR, 5-shot detachable magazine.
**Barrel:** 22"; 6-grooves; 1-in 16" twist; 24" varmint.
**Weight:** About 6¼ lbs. **Length:** 40½" over-all (Sporter).
**Stock:** Three styles available. "Classic" is Claro walnut with plain, straight comb; "Cascade" has Monte Carlo comb with cheekpiece; "Custom Classic" is of fancy select grade Claro walnut, ebony fore-end tip, Niedner-style butt-plate. All have 18 lpi hand cut, borderless checkering, steel grip cap, checkered steel buttplate.
**Sights:** Hooded ramp front with bead, folding leaf rear (optional).
**Features:** High quality, adult-sized, bolt action rifle. Barrel screwed into receiver; rocker-type silent safety; twin rear locking lugs. All steel construction. Fully adjustable trigger; receiver grooved for Kimber scope mounts. High polish blue. Barreled actions available. Also available in true left-hand version in selected models. Made in U.S.A. Introduced 1979.
**Price:** 22 LR Classic stock, no sights, plain or heavy bbl. (left hand avail.) . . . . . . . . . . . . . . . . . . . . . . . . . . . . . . . . . . . . . . . . . . . **$750.00**
**Price:** As above, Cascade stock (left hand avail.) . . . . . . . . . . . . . . . . **$805.00**
**Price:** As above, Custom Classic, plain or heavy bbl. (left hand avail.) **$995.00**
**Price:** Kimber scope mounts, from . . . . . . . . . . . . . . . . . . . . . . . . . . . . . **$48.00**
**Price:** Optional open sights fitted. . . . . . . . . . . . . . . . . . . . . . . . . . . . . . . **$55.00**

Kimber Super America

### Kimber Model 82, 84 Super America
Super-grade version of the Model 82. Has the Classic stock only of specially selected, high-grade, California claro walnut, with Continental beaded cheekpiece and ebony fore-end tip; borderless, full-coverage 20 lpi checkering; Niedner-type checkered steel buttplate; comes with barrel quarter-rib which has a folding leaf sight. Round-top receiver of the 1986 model is drilled and tapped to accept Kimber's screw-on scope mount bases. Available in 22 Long Rifle, 22 Hornet, 223 Rem.

**Price:** Model 82 22 Long Rifle, less scope . . . . . . . . . . . . . . . . . . . . . **$1,150.00**
**Price:** Model 82 22 Hornet, less scope . . . . . . . . . . . . . . . . . . . . . . . . **$1,150.00**
**Price:** Model 84, 223 . . . . . . . . . . . . . . . . . . . . . . . . . . . . . . . . . . . . . . . **$1,250.00**

### MARATHON SUPER SHOT 22 BOLT ACTION
**Caliber:** 22 LR, single shot.
**Barrel:** 24".
**Weight:** 4.9 lbs. **Length:** 41½" over-all.
**Stock:** Select hardwood.
**Sights:** Bead front, step-adjustable open rear.
**Features:** Blued metal parts; receiver grooved for scope mounting. Also available as a kit, requiring assembly and metal and wood finishing. Introduced 1984. Imported from Spain by Marathon.
**Price:** Finished . . . . . . . . . . . . . . . . . . . . . . . . . . . . . . . . . . . . . . . . . . . . **$74.99**
**Price:** Kit . . . . . . . . . . . . . . . . . . . . . . . . . . . . . . . . . . . . . . . . . . . . . . . . . **$55.99**
**Price:** First Shot (youth model of above with 16½" barrel, 3.8 lbs., 31" o.a.l.), assembled . . . . . . . . . . . . . . . . . . . . . . . . . . . . . . . . . . . . . . . . . . . . **$74.99**
**Price:** As above, kit . . . . . . . . . . . . . . . . . . . . . . . . . . . . . . . . . . . . . . . . . **$55.99**

Marlin Model 780

### MARLIN 780 BOLT ACTION RIFLE
**Caliber:** 22 S, L, or LR; 7-shot clip magazine.
**Barrel:** 22" Micro-Groove.
**Weight:** 5½ lbs. **Length:** 41".
**Stock:** Monte Carlo American black walnut with checkered p.g. and fore-end. White line spacer at buttplate. Mar-Shield® finish.
**Sights:** "Wide-Scan"™ ramp front, folding semi-buckhorn rear adj. for w. & e.
**Features:** Receiver anti-glare serrated and grooved for tip-off scope mount.
**Price:** . . . . . . . . . . . . . . . . . . . . . . . . . . . . . . . . . . . . . . . . . . . . . . . . . . **$141.95**

### Marlin 781 Bolt Action Rifle
Same as the Marlin 780 except: tubular magazine holds 25 Shorts, 19 Longs or 17 Long Rifle cartridges. Weight 6 lbs.
**Price:** . . . . . . . . . . . . . . . . . . . . . . . . . . . . . . . . . . . . . . . . . . . . . **$147.95**

### Marlin 782 Bolt Action Rifle
Same as the Marlin 780 except: 22 Rimfire Magnum cal. only, weight about 6 lbs. Sling and swivels attached
**Price:** . . . . . . . . . . . . . . . . . . . . . . . . . . . . . . . . . . . . . . . . . . . . . **$155.95**

Marlin Model 783

### Marlin 783 Bolt Action Rifle
Same as Marlin 782 except: Tubular magazine holds 12 rounds of 22 Rimfire Magnum ammunition.
**Price:** . . . . . . . . . . . . . . . . . . . . . . . . . . . . . . . . . . . . . . . . . . . . . . . . . . **$161.95**

### Marlin 25 Bolt Action Repeater
Similar to Marlin 780, except: walnut finished p.g. stock, adjustable open rear sight, ramp front.
**Price:** . . . . . . . . . . . . . . . . . . . . . . . . . . . . . . . . . . . . . . . . . . . . . **$108.95**

### Marlin Model 25M Bolt Action Rifle
Similar to the Model 25 except chambered for 22 Mag. Has 7-shot clip magazine, 22" Micro-Groove® barrel, walnut-finished hardwood stock. Introduced 1983.
**Price:** . . . . . . . . . . . . . . . . . . . . . . . . . . . . . . . . . . . . . . . . . . . . . . . . . . **$124.95**

### MARLIN 15Y "LITTLE BUCKAROO"
**Caliber:** 22, S, L, LR, single shot.
**Barrel:** 16¼" Micro-Groove®.
**Weight:** 4¼ lbs. **Length:** 33¼" over-all.
**Stock:** One-piece walnut-finished hardwood with Monte Carlo.

**Sights:** Ramp front, adjustable open rear.
**Features:** Beginner's rifle with thumb safety, easy-load feed throat, red cocking indicator. Receiver grooved for scope mounting. Introduced 1984.
**Price:** Less scope . . . . . . . . . . . . . . . . . . . . . . . . . . . . . . . . . . . . . . . . . . . . . . **$105.95**

Remington Model 541-T

### REMINGTON MODEL 541-T
**Caliber:** 22 S, L, LR, 5-shot clip.
**Barrel:** 24".
**Weight:** 5⅞ lbs. **Length:** 42½" over-all.
**Stock:** Walnut, cut-checkered p.g. and fore-end. Satin finish.
**Sights:** None. Drilled and tapped for scope mounts.
**Features:** Clip repeater. Thumb safety. Re-introduced 1986.
**Price:** About . . . . . . . . . . . . . . . . . . . . . . . . . . . . . . . . . . . . . . . . . . . . . . **$368.00**
**Price:** Extra 10-shot clip, about . . . . . . . . . . . . . . . . . . . . . . . . . . . . . **$7.00**

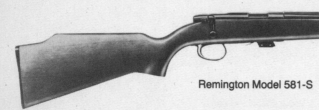

Remington Model 581-S

### REMINGTON MODEL 581-S "SPORTSMAN" RIFLE
**Caliber:** 22 S, L or LR. 5-shot clip mag.
**Barrel:** 24" round.
**Weight:** 4¾ lbs. **Length:** 42⅜" over-all.
**Stock:** Walnut finished hardwood, Monte Carlo with p.g.
**Sights:** Bead post front, screw adj. open rear.
**Features:** Sliding side safety, wide trigger, receiver grooved for tip-off scope mounts. Comes with single-shot adapter. Re-introduced 1986.
**Price:** About . . . . . . . . . . . . . . . . . . . . . . . . . . . . . . . . . . . . . . . . . . . . . . **$200.00**

Ruger 77/22

### SAVAGE-STEVENS MODEL 72 CRACKSHOT
**Caliber:** 22 S, L, LR, single shot.
**Barrel:** 22" octagonal.
**Weight:** 4½ lbs. **Length:** 37" over-all.
**Stock:** Walnut, straight grip stock and fore-end.
**Sights:** Blade front, step adj. rear.
**Features:** Falling block action, color case hardened frame.
**Price:** . . . . . . . . . . . . . . . . . . . . . . . . . . . . . . . . . . . **$144.39**

### RUGER 77/22 RIMFIRE BOLT ACTION RIFLE
**Caliber:** 22 Long Rifle, 10-shot magazine.
**Barrel:** 20".
**Weight:** About 5¾ lbs. **Length:** 39¾" over-all.
**Stock:** Straight-grained American walnut.
**Sights:** Gold bead front, adjustable folding leaf rear, or no sights.
**Features:** Mauser-type action uses Ruger's 10-shot rotary magazine; 3-position safety; simplified bolt stop; patented bolt locking system. Uses the dual-screw barrel attachment system of the 10/22 rifle. Integral scope mounting system with 1" Ruger rings. Announced 1983.
**Price:** 77/22 R (plain barrel, no sights, with Ruger 1" rings) . . . . . . . . **$364.50**
**Price:** 77/22 S (gold bead front sight, folding leaf rear) . . . . . . . . . . . . . **$364.50**
**Price:** 77/22 RS (scope rings and open sights) . . . . . . . . . . . . . . . . . . **$384.50**

Voere Model 1007/1013

### VOERE MODEL 1007/1013 BOLT ACTION RIFLE
**Caliber:** 22 LR (M1007 Biathlon), 22 Mag. (M1013).
**Barrel:** 18".
**Weight:** About 5½ lbs. (M1007)
**Stock:** Oil-finished beechwood.
**Sights:** Hooded front, open adjustable rear.
**Features:** Single-stage trigger (M1013 available with double set). Military-look stock; sling swivels. Convertible to single shot. Imported from Austria by L. Joseph Rahn. Introduced 1984.
**Price:** 1007 Biathlon . . . . . . . . . . . . . . . . . . . . . . . . . . . . . . . . . . . . **$215.00**
**Price:** 1013 22 Mag. . . . . . . . . . . . . . . . . . . . . . . . . . . . . . . . . . . . . . **$315.00**

Voere Model 2107

### VOERE MODEL 2107 BOLT ACTION RIFLE
**Caliber:** 22 LR, 5- or 8-shot magazine.
**Barrel:** 19½".
**Weight:** 6 lbs. **Length:** 41" over-all.
**Stock:** European hardwood with Monte Carlo. Butt pad, swivel studs standard.
**Sights:** Hooded front, open fully adj. rear.
**Features:** Deluxe model with checkered stock and raised cheekpiece available. Introduced 1986. Imported from West Germany by KDF, Inc.
**Price:** Standard . . . . . . . . . . . . . . . . . . . . . . . . . . . . . . . . . . . . . . . . . . **$169.00**
**Price:** Deluxe . . . . . . . . . . . . . . . . . . . . . . . . . . . . . . . . . . . . . . . . . . . . **$189.00**

**CAUTION:** PRICES CHANGE. CHECK AT GUNSHOP.

Anschutz Mark 2000

**ANSCHUTZ MARK 2000 TARGET RIFLE**
**Caliber:** 22 LR, single-shot.
**Barrel:** 26", heavy. 7/8" diameter.
**Weight:** 8 lbs. **Length:** 43" over-all.
**Stock:** Walnut finished hardwood.
**Sights:** Globe front (insert-type), micro-click peep rear.
**Features:** Has 3-lb. single-stage trigger; stock has thumb groove, Wundhammer swell, full length slide rail. Imported from West Germany by PSI.
**Price:** Without sights ........ $265.00
**Price:** Sight set #2 ........ $30.00

**ANSCHUTZ MODEL 64-MS, 64-MS LEFT**
**Caliber:** 22 LR, single shot.
**Barrel:** 21¾", medium heavy, 7/8" diameter.
**Weight:** 8 lbs. 1 oz. **Length:** 39½" over-all.
**Stock:** Walnut-finished hardwood, silhouette-type.
**Sights:** None furnished. Receiver drilled and tapped for scope mounting.
**Features:** Designed for metallic silhouette competition. Stock has stippled checkering, contoured thumb groove with Wundhammer swell. Two-stage #5091 trigger. Slide safety locks sear and bolt. Introducted 1980. Imported from West Germany by PSI.
**Price:** Model 64-MS ........ $450.00
**Price:** Model 64-MS Left ........ $498.00
**Price:** 64-MS FWT (same as 64-MS except weighs about 6¼ lbs, has #5094 trigger. Designed for lightweight-class silhouette shooting) ........ $450.00

**ANSCHUTZ 1811 MATCH RIFLE**
**Caliber:** 22 LR. Single Shot.
**Barrel:** 27¼" round (1" dia.)
**Weight:** 11 lbs. **Length:** 46" over-all.
**Stock:** Walnut-finished European hardwood; American prone style with Monte Carlo, cast-off cheek-piece, checkered p.g., beavertail fore-end with swivel rail and adj. swivel, adj. rubber buttplate.
**Sights:** None. Receiver grooved for Anschutz sights (extra). Scope blocks.
**Features:** Two-stage #5018 trigger adjustable from 2.1 to 8.6 oz. Extremely fast lock time. Imported from West Germany by PSI.
**Price:** Right hand, no sights ........ $963.00
**Price:** M1811-L (true left-hand action and stock) ........ $1,062.00
**Price:** Anschutz Int'l. sight set ........ $173.40

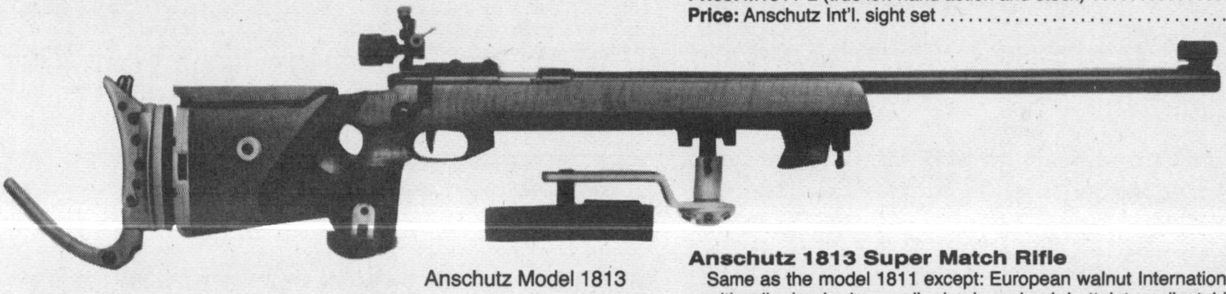

Anschutz Model 1813

**Anschutz 1813 Super Match Rifle**
Same as the model 1811 except: European walnut International-type stock with adj. cheek-piece, adj. aluminum hook buttplate, adjustable hand stop, weight 15½ lbs., 46" over-all. Imported from West Germany by PSI.
**Price:** Right hand, no sights ........ $1,381.00
**Price:** M1813-L (left-hand action and stock) ........ $1,570.00

**Anschutz Model 1810 Super Match II**
Similar to the Super Match 1813 rifle except has a stock of European hardwood with tapered fore-end and deep receiver area. Hand and palm rests not included. Uses Match 54 action. Adjustable hook buttplate and cheekpiece. Sights not included. Introduced 1982. Imported from Germany by PSI.
**Price:** Right-hand ........ $1,232.00
**Price:** Left-hand ........ $1,289.00
**Price:** International sight set ........ $173.40
**Price:** Match sight set ........ $124.75

**Anschutz 1807 Match Rifle**
Same as the model 1811 except: 26" bbl. (7/8" dia.), weight 10 lbs. 44½" over-all to conform to ISU requirements and also suitable for NRA matches.
**Price:** Right hand, no sights ........ $801.00
**Price:** M1807-L (true left-hand action and stock) ........ $890.00
**Price:** Int'l sight set ........ $173.40
**Price:** Match sight set ........ $124.75

Anschutz 54.18 MS

**Anschutz Model 54.18 MS Silhouette Rifle**
Same basic features as Anschutz 1813 Super Match but with special metallic silhouette European hardwood stock and two-stage trigger. Has 22" barrel; receiver drilled and tapped.
**Price:** ........ $998.00
**Price:** Model 54.18 MSL (true left-hand version of above) ........ $834.00

**ANSCHUTZ 1808ED SUPER RUNNING TARGET**
**Caliber:** 22 LR, single shot.
**Barrel:** 23½"; 7/8" diameter.
**Weight:** 9¼ lbs. **Length:** 42" over-all.
**Stock:** European hardwood. Heavy beavertail fore-end, adjustable cheekpiece, buttplate, stippled pistol grip and fore-end.
**Sights:** None furnished. Receiver grooved for scope mounting.
**Features:** Uses Super Match 54 action. Adjustable trigger from 14 oz. to 3.5 lbs. Removable sectioned barrel weights. **Special Order Only.** Introduced 1982. Imported from Germany by PSI.
**Price:** Right-hand ........ $839.00
**Price:** Left-hand, 1808EDL ........ $923.00

**ANSCHUTZ MODEL 1403D MATCH RIFLE**
**Caliber:** 22 LR only. Single shot.
**Barrel:** 26" round (1 1/16" dia.)
**Weight:** 7¾ lbs. **Length:** 44" over-all.
**Stock:** Walnut finished hardwood, cheekpiece, checkered p.g., beavertail fore-end, adj. buttplate.
**Sights:** None furnished.
**Features:** Sliding side safety, adj. #5053 single stage trigger, receiver grooved for Anschutz sights. Imported from West Germany by PSI.
**Price:** Without sights ........ $467.00
**Price:** 1403DL (left hand stock only) ........ $492.00
**Price:** Match sight set #6723 ........ $124.75

Anschutz 1827B Biathlon

**ANSCHUTZ 1827B BIATHLON RIFLE**
**Caliber:** 22 LR, 5-shot magazine.
**Barrel:** 21½″.

**Weight:** 9 lbs. with sights. **Length:** 42½″ over-all.
**Stock:** Walnut-finished hardwood; cheekpiece, stippled pistol grip and fore-end.
**Sights:** Globe front specially designed for Biathlon shooting, micrometer rear with hinged snow cap.
**Features:** Uses Match 54 action and adjustable trigger; adjustable wooden buttplate, Biathlon butt hook, adjustable hand-stop rail. **Special Order Only.** Introduced 1982. Imported from Germany by PSI.
**Price:** Right-hand ............................................. $1.073.00
**Price:** Left-hand ............................................. $1,223.00

BSA Martini Match

**BSA MARTINI ISU MATCH RIFLE**
**Caliber:** 22 LR, single shot.
**Barrel:** 28″.
**Weight:** 10¾ lbs. **Length:** 43-44″ over-all.
**Stock:** Match type French walnut butt and fore-end; flat cheekpiece, full p.g.; spacers are fitted to allow length adjustment to suit each shooting position; adj. buttplate.
**Sights:** Modified PH-1 Parker-Hale tunnel front, PH-25 aperture rear with aperture variations from .080″ to .030″.

**Features:** Fastest lock time of any commercial target rifle; designed to meet I.S.U. specs. for the Standard Rifle. Fully adjustable trigger (less than ½ lb. to 3½ lbs.). Mark V has heavier barrel, weighs 12¼ lbs. Imported from England by Freelands Scope Stands.
**Price:** I.S.U., Standard weight .................................. $950.00
**Price:** Mark V heavy bbl. ...................................... $1,000.00

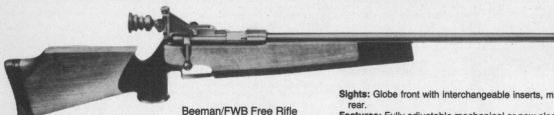

Beeman/FWB Free Rifle

**BEEMAN/FEINWERKBAU ULTRA MATCH 22 FREE RIFLE**
**Caliber:** 22 LR, single shot.
**Barrel:** 26.4″.
**Weight:** 17 lbs. (with accessories).
**Stock:** Anatomically correct thumbhole stock of laminated wood.

**Sights:** Globe front with interchangeable inserts, micrometer match aperture rear.
**Features:** Fully adjustable mechanical or new electronic trigger; accessory rails for moveable weights and adjustable palm rest; adjustable cheekpiece and hooked buttplate. Right or left hand. Introduced 1983. Imported by Beeman.
**Price:** Right hand, electronic trigger ......................... $1,595.00
**Price:** As above, mechanical trigger ......................... $1,295.00
**Price:** Left hand, electronic trigger.......................... $1,730.00
**Price:** As above, mechanical trigger ......................... $1,465.00

**BEEMAN/FEINWERKBAU 2000 TARGET RIFLE**
**Caliber:** 22 LR.
**Barrel:** 26¼″; 22″ for Mini-Match.
**Weight:** 9 lbs. 12 oz. **Length:** 43¾″ over-all (26¼″ bbl.).
**Stock:** Standard match. Walnut with stippled p.g. and fore-end; walnut-stained birch for the Mini-Match.

**Sights:** Globe front with interchangeable inserts; micrometer match aperture rear.
**Features:** Meets ISU standard rifle specifications. Shortest lock time of any small bore rifle. Electronic or mechanical trigger, fully adjustable for weight, release point, length, lateral position, etc. Available in Standard and Mini-Match models. Introduced 1979. Imported from West Germany by Beeman.
**Price:** Model 2000 .................................... $795.00 to $925.00
**Price:** Mini-Match.................................... $770.00 to $839.00

Beeman/FWB 2600

**BEEMAN/FEINWERKBAU 2600 TARGET RIFLE**
**Caliber:** 22 LR, single shot.
**Barrel:** 26.3″.
**Weight:** 10.6 lbs. **Length:** 43.7″ over-all.
**Stock:** Laminated hardwood and hard rubber.
**Sights:** Globe front with interchangeable inserts; micrometer match aperture rear.
**Features:** Identical smallbore companion to the Beeman/FWB 600 air rifle. Free floating barrel. Match trigger has fingertip weight adjustment dial. Introduced 1986. Imported from West Germany by Beeman
**Price:** ............................................... $878.00

**CAUTION:** PRICES CHANGE. CHECK AT GUNSHOP.

# COMPETITION RIFLES—CENTERFIRE & RIMFIRE

Beeman/FWB 2000 M.S.

**BEEMAN/FWB 2000 METALLIC SILHOUETTE RIFLE**
**Caliber:** 22 LR, single shot.
**Barrel:** 21.8".
**Weight:** 6.8 lbs. **Length:** 39" over-all.
**Stock:** Walnut, anatomical grip and fore-end are stippled.
**Sights:** None furnished; grooved for standard mounts.
**Features:** Fully adjustable match trigger from 3.5 to 8.5 ozs. Heavy bull barrel. Introduced 1985. Imported by Beeman.
**Price:** ...................................................... **$795.00**

**BEEMAN/KRICO 640 STANDARD SNIPER**
**Caliber:** 308 Win.
**Barrel:** 20", semi-bull.
**Weight:** 7.5 lbs.
**Stock:** French walnut with ventilated fore-end.
**Sights:** None furnished.
**Features:** Five-shot repeater with detachable box magazine. Available with single or double-set trigger. Imported from West Germany by Beeman.
**Price:** 308 Win. ..................................... **$1,049.00**
**Price:** Model 440S, 22 Hornet ............................. **$795.00**

**BEEMAN/KRICO 340 SILHOUETTE RIFLE**
**Caliber:** 22 Long Rifle, 5-shot clip.
**Barrel:** 21", match quality.
**Weight:** 7.5 lbs. **Length:** 39.5" over-all.
**Stock:** European walnut match-style designed for off-hand shooting. Suitable for right- or left-hand shooters. Stippled grip and fore-end.
**Sights:** None furnished. Receiver grooved for tip-off mounts.
**Features:** Free-floated heavy barrel; fully adjustable two-stage match trigger or double-set trigger. Meets NRA official MS rules. Introduced 1983. Imported by Beeman.
**Price:** ...................................................... **$649.50**

Beeman/KRICOtronic 540

**Beeman/KRICOtronic 540 Silhouette Rifle**
Same basic specs as standard 340 Silhouette rifle except has KRICOtronic electronic ignition system for conventional ammunition. System replaces the firing pin with an electrical mechanism that ignites the primer electrically. Lock time is so fast it is not measureable by present technology. Introduced 1985.
**Price:** ...................................................... **$795.00**

Beeman/Krico 640 Super

**BEEMAN/WEIHRAUCH HW60 TARGET RIFLE**
**Caliber:** 22 LR, single shot.
**Barrel:** 26.8".
**Weight:** 10.8 lbs. **Length:** 45.7" over-all.
**Stock:** Walnut with adjustable buttplate. Stippled p.g. and fore-end. Rail with adjustable swivel.
**Sights:** Hooded ramp front, match-type aperture rear.
**Features:** Adj. match trigger with push-button safety. Left-hand version also available. Introduced 1981. Imported from West Germany by Beeman.
**Price:** Right-hand ............................................ **$495.00**
**Price:** Left-hand ............................................. **$519.00**

**BEEMAN/KRICO 640 SUPER SNIPER**
**Caliber:** 223, 308.
**Barrel:** 26". Specially designed match bull barrel, matte blue finish, with muzzle brake/flash hider.
**Weight:** 9.6 lbs. **Length:** 44¾" over-all.
**Stock:** Select walnut with oil finish. Spring-loaded, adj. cheekpiece, adjustable recoil pad. Standard model (640S) is without adjustable stock.
**Sights:** None furnished. Drilled and tapped for scope mounts.
**Features:** Match trigger with 10mm wide shoe; single standard or double set trigger available. All metal has matte blue finish. Bolt knob has 1¼" diameter. Scope mounts available for special night-sight devices. Imported from West Germany by Beeman.
**Price:** Without scope, mount ........................... **$1,298.50**
**Price:** Model 640S, as above but without moveable cheekpiece . . . **$1,049.50**

Finnish Lion Standard

**FINNISH LION STANDARD TARGET RIFLE**
**Caliber:** 22 LR, single-shot.
**Barrel:** 27⅝".
**Weight:** 10½ lbs. **Length:** 44⁹⁄₁₆" over-all.

**Stock:** French walnut, target style.
**Sights:** None furnished. Globe front, International micrometer rear available.
**Features:** Optional accessories: palm rest, hook buttplate, fore-end stop and swivel assembly, buttplate extension, 5 front sight aperture inserts, 3 rear sight apertures, Allen wrench. Adjustable trigger. Imported from Finland by Mandall Shooting Supplies.
**Price:** ...................................................... **$500.00**
**Price:** Thumbhole stock model ............................. **$695.00**
**Price:** Heavy barrel model (either stock) ..................... **$535.00**
**Price:** Sight set (front and rear) ............................ **$100.00**

**CAUTION:** PRICES CHANGE. CHECK AT GUNSHOP.

Heckler & Koch PSG-1

### HECKLER & KOCH PSG-1 MARKSMAN RIFLE
**Caliber:** 308, 5- and 20-shot magazines.
**Barrel:** 25.6″, heavy.
**Weight:** 17.8 lbs. **Length:** 47.5″ over-all.
**Stock:** Matte black high impact plastic, adj. for length, pivoting butt cap, verti-cally-adj. cheek-piece; target type pistol grip with adj. palm shelf.
**Sights:** Hendsoldt 6 x 42 scope.
**Features:** Uses HK-91 action with low-noise bolt closing device; special fore-end with T-way rail for sling swivel or tripod. Gun comes in special foam-fitted metal transport case with tripod, two 20-shot and two 5-shot magazines, cleaning rod. Imported from West Germany by Heckler & Koch, Inc. Introduced 1986.
**Price:** . . . . . . . . . . . . . . . . . . . . . . . . . . . . . . . . . **$5,980.00**

### HECKLER & KOCH B.A.S.R. BOLT ACTION RIFLE
**Caliber:** 22 PPC, 22-250, 6mm PPC, 308 Win. 30-06, 300 Win. Mag., blind 4-shot magazine for standard calibers, 3-shot for magnums, or single shot. Other calibers available.
**Barrel:** 16″-26″ stainless steel.
**Weight:** To customer specs. **Length:** To customer specs.
**Stock:** Black high density, urethane foam-filled Kevlar; comes with recoil pad, q.d. swivel studs.
**Sights:** None furnished; drilled and tapped for scope mounting.
**Features:** Uses H&K's own action of chrome moly steel with cone breech system, fluted bolt; fully adjustable trigger; 3-position safety. Guaranteed accuracy of ½-m.o.a. A custom-made gun. Comes with H&K hardcase, bore guide, cleaning rod. From Heckler & Koch, Inc.
**Price:** . . . . . . . . . . . . . . . . . . . . . . . . . . . . . . . . . **$2,199.00**

Remington Model 40-XC

### REMINGTON 40-XR RIMFIRE POSITION RIFLE
**Caliber:** 22 LR, single-shot.
**Barrel:** 24″, heavy target.
**Weight:** 10 lbs. **Length:** 43″ over-all.
**Stock:** Position-style with front swivel block on fore-end guide rail.
**Sights:** Drilled and tapped. Furnished with scope blocks.
**Features:** Meets all I.S.U. specifications. Deep fore-end, buttplate vertically adjustable, wide adjustable trigger.
**Price:** About . . . . . . . . . . . . . . . . . . . . . . . . . . . . . **$711.00**

### REMINGTON 40-XC NAT'L MATCH COURSE RIFLE
**Caliber:** 7.62 NATO, 5-shot.
**Barrel:** 23¼″, stainless steel.
**Weight:** 10 lbs. without sights. **Length:** 42½″ over-all.
**Stock:** Walnut, position-style, with palm swell.
**Sights:** None furnished.
**Features:** Designed to meet the needs of competitive shooters firing the national match courses. Position-style stock, top loading clip slot magazine, anti-bind bolt and receiver, bright stainless steel barrel. Meets all I.S.U. Army Rifle specifications. Adjustable buttplate, adjustable trigger.
**Price:** About . . . . . . . . . . . . . . . . . . . . . . . . . . . . **$970.00**

Remington Model 40-XB

### REMINGTON 40-XB RANGEMASTER TARGET Centerfire
**Caliber:** 222 Rem., 22-250, 6mm Rem., 243, 25-06, 7mm Rem. Mag., 30-338 (30-7mm Rem. Mag.), 300 Win. Mag., 7.62 NATO (308 Win.), 30-06. Single shot.
**Barrel:** 27¼″ round (Stand. dia.—¾″, Hvy. dia.—⅞″)
**Weight:** Std.—9¼ lbs., Hvy.—11¼ lbs. **Length:** 47″.
**Stock:** American walnut with high comb and beavertail fore-end stop. Rubber non-slip buttplate.
**Sights:** None. Scope blocks installed.
**Features:** Adjustable trigger pull. Receiver drilled and tapped for sights.
**Price:** Standard s.s., stainless steel barrel, about . . . . . . . . . . . . . . . . . **$896.00**
**Price:** Repeating model, about . . . . . . . . . . . . . . . . . . . . . . . . . **$964.00**
**Price:** Extra for 2 oz. trigger, about . . . . . . . . . . . . . . . . . . . . . . . . **$116.00**

Remington Model 40XB-BR

### REMINGTON MODEL 40XB-BR
**Caliber:** 22 BR Rem., 222 Rem., 223, 6mm x47, 6mm BR Rem., 7.62 NATO (308 Win.).
**Barrel:** 20″ (light varmint class), 26″ (heavy varmint class).
**Weight:** Light varmint class, 7¼ lbs., Heavy varmint class, 12 lbs. **Length:** 38″ (20″ bbl.), 44″ (26″ bbl).
**Stock:** Select walnut.
**Sights:** None. Supplied with scope blocks.
**Features:** Unblued stainless steel barrel, trigger adj. from 1½ lbs. to 3½ lbs. Special 2 oz. trigger at extra cost. Scope and mounts extra.
**Price:** About . . . . . . . . . . . . . . . . . . . . . . . . . . . . . . . . . **$945.00**
**Price:** Extra for 2-oz. trigger, about . . . . . . . . . . . . . . . . . . . . . . **$116.00**

# COMPETITION RIFLES—CENTERFIRE & RIMFIRE

## SHILEN DGA BENCHREST SINGLE SHOT RIFLE
**Caliber:** 22, 22-250, 6x47, 308.
**Barrel:** Select/Match grade stainless. Choice of caliber, twist, chambering, contour or length shown in Shilen's catalog.
**Weight:** To customer specs.
**Stock:** Fiberglass. Choice of Classic or thumbhole pattern.
**Sights:** None furnished. Specify intended scope and mount.
**Features:** Fiberglass stocks are spray painted with acrylic enamel in choice of basic color. Comes with Benchrest trigger. Basically a custom-made rifle. From Shilen Rifles, Inc.
**Price:** From ............................................... $1,600.00

## SIG SAUER SSG 2000 RIFLE
**Caliber:** 223, 308, 7.5 Swiss, 300 Weatherby Magnum; 4-shot detachable box magazine.
**Barrel:** 24" (25.9" in 300 W.M.).
**Weight:** 13.2 lbs. (without scope). **Length:** 47.6" (24" barrel).
**Stock:** Walnut; thumbhole-type with adjustable comb and buttplate; adjustable fore-end rail; stippled grip and fore-end.
**Sights:** None furnished. Comes with scope mounts.
**Features:** Uses the Sauer 80/90 rifle action. Available in right- or left-hand models; flash hider/muzzle brake; double-set triggers; push-button sliding safety; EAW scope mount. Choice of Zeiss ZA 8 x 56 or Schmidt & Bender 1½-6 x 42 scope. Introduced 1985. Imported by SIGARMS, Inc.
**Price:** ............................................... $2,848.99

Steyr SSG Marksman

## Steyr-Mannlicher SSG Match
Same as Model SSG Marksman except has heavy barrel, match bolt, Walther target peep sights and adj. rail in fore-end to adj. sling travel. Weight is 11 lbs.
**Price:** Synthetic half stock........................... $1,462.00
**Price:** Walnut half stock.............................. $1,625.00

## STEYR-MANNLICHER SSG MARKSMAN
**Caliber:** 308 Win.
**Barrel:** 25.6".
**Weight:** 8.6 lbs. **Length:** 44.5" over-all.
**Stock:** Choice of ABS "Cycolac" synthetic half stock or walnut. Removable spacers in butt adjusts length of pull from 12¾" to 14".
**Sights:** Hooded blade front, folding leaf rear.
**Features:** Parkerized finish. Choice of interchangeable single or double set triggers. Detachable 5-shot rotary magazine (10-shot optional). Drilled and tapped for scope mounts. Imported from Austria by Gun South, Inc.
**Price:** Synthetic half stock........................... $1,040.00
**Price:** Walnut half stock.............................. $1,217.00

## STEYR-MANNLICHER MATCH UIT RIFLE
**Caliber:** 243 Win. or 308 Win., 10-shot magazine.
**Barrel:** 25.5".
**Weight:** 10.9 lbs. **Length:** 44.48" over-all.
**Stock:** Walnut with stippled grip and fore-end. Special UIT Match design.
**Sights:** Walther globe front, Walther peep rear.
**Features:** Double-pull trigger adjustable for let-off point, slack, weight of first-stage pull, release force and length; buttplate adjustable for height and length. Meets UIT specifications. Introduced 1984. Imported from Austria by Gun South, Inc.
**Price:** ............................................... $2,142.00

## SWISS K-31 TARGET RIFLE
**Caliber:** 308 Win., 6-shot magazine.
**Barrel:** 26".
**Weight:** 9½ lbs. **Length:** 44" over-all.
**Stock:** Walnut.
**Sights:** Protected blade front, ladder-type adjustable rear.
**Features:** Refined version of the Schmidt-Rubin straight-pull rifle. Comes with sling and muzzle cap. Imported from Switzerland by Mandall Shooting Supplies.
**Price:** ............................................... $1,000.00

Tanner Free Rifle

## TANNER 300 METER FREE RIFLE
**Caliber:** 308 Win., 7.5 Swiss; single shot.
**Barrel:** 28.7".
**Weight:** 15 lbs. **Length:** 45.3" over-all.
**Stock:** Seasoned walnut, thumb-hole style, with accessory rail, palm rest, adjustable hook butt.
**Sights:** Globe front with interchangeable inserts, Tanner-design micrometer-diopter rear with adjustable aperture.
**Features:** Three-lug revolving-lock bolt design; adjustable set trigger; short firing pin travel; supplied with 300-meter test target. Imported from Switzerland by Osborne's Supplies. Introduced 1984.
**Price:** About............................................. $2,695.00

Tanner UIT

## TANNER STANDARD UIT RIFLE
**Caliber:** 308, 7.5mm Swiss, 10-shot.
**Barrel:** 25.8".
**Weight:** 10.5 lbs. **Length:** 40.6" over-all.
**Stock:** Match style of seasoned nutwood with accessory rail; coarsely stippled pistol grip; high cheekpiece; vented fore-end.
**Sights:** Globe front with interchangeable inserts, Tanner micrometer-diopter rear with adjustable aperture.
**Features:** Two locking lug revolving bolt encloses case head. Trigger adjustable from ½ to 6½ lbs.; match trigger optional. Comes with 300-meter test target. Imported from Switzerland by Osborne's. Introduced 1984.
**Price:** About............................................. $2,595.00

**CAUTION:** PRICES CHANGE. CHECK AT GUNSHOP.

## TANNER 50 METER FREE RIFLE
**Caliber:** 22 LR; single shot.
**Barrel:** 27.7″.
**Weight:** 13.9 lbs. **Length:** 43.4″ over-all.
**Stock:** Seasoned nutwood with palm rest, accessory rail, adjustable hook butt-plate.
**Sights:** Globe front with interchangeable inserts, Tanner micrometer-diopter rear with adjustable aperture.
**Features:** Bolt action with externally adjustable set trigger. Supplied with 50-meter test target. Imported from Switzerland by Osborne's Supplies. Introduced 1984.
**Price:** About. . . . . . . . . . . . . . . . . . . . . . . . . . . . . . . . . . . . . . . $2,195.00

## TIKKA MODEL 65 WILD BOAR RIFLE
**Caliber:** 7x64, 308, 30-06, 7mm Rem. Mag., 300 Win. Mag.; 5-shot detachable clip.
**Barrel:** 20½″.
**Weight:** About 7½ lbs. **Length:** 41″ over-all.
**Stock:** Hand checkered walnut; vent. rubber recoil pad.
**Sights:** Bead on post front, special ramp-type open rear.
**Features:** Adjustable trigger; palm swell in pistol grip. Sight system developed for low-light conditions. Imported from Finland by Mandall Shooting Supplies.
**Price:** . . . . . . . . . . . . . . . . . . . . . . . . . . . . . . . . . . . . . . . . . . . . . . $595.00

Walther U.I.T. Special

## WALTHER U.I.T. SPECIAL
**Caliber:** 22 LR, single shot.
**Barrel:** 25½″.
**Weight:** 10 lbs., 3 oz. **Length:** 44¾″.
**Stock:** Walnut, adj. for length and drop; fore-end guide rail for sling or palm rest.
**Sights:** Globe-type front, fully adj. aperture rear.
**Features:** Conforms to both NRA and U.I.T. requirements. Fully adj. trigger. Left hand stock available on special order. Imported from Germany by Interarms.
**Price:** . . . . . . . . . . . . . . . . . . . . . . . . . . . . . . . . . . . . . . . . . . . . . . $845.00

## Walther Model U.I.T.-E Match Rifle
Similar to the U.I.T. Special model except has state-of-the-art electronic trigger. Introduced 1984.
**Price:** . . . . . . . . . . . . . . . . . . . . . . . . . . . . . . . . . . . . . . . . . . . . $1,250.00

## Walther GX-1 Match Rifle
Same general specs as U.I.T. except has 25½″ barrel, over-all length of 44½″, weight of 15½ lbs. Stock is designed to provide every conceivable adjustment for individual preference and anatomical compatibility. Left-hand stock available on special order. Imported from Germany by Interarms.
**Price:** . . . . . . . . . . . . . . . . . . . . . . . . . . . . . . . . . . . . . . . . . . . . $1,350.00

Walther U.I.T. Match

## Walther U.I.T. Match
Same specifications and features as standard U.I.T. Super rifle but has scope mount bases. Fore-end had new tapered profile, fully stippled. Imported from Germany by Interarms.
**Price:** . . . . . . . . . . . . . . . . . . . . . . . . . . . . . . . . . . . . . . . . . . . . . . $925.00

## WALTHER RUNNING BOAR MATCH RIFLE
**Caliber:** 22 LR, single shot.
**Barrel:** 23.6″.
**Weight:** 8 lbs. 5 oz. **Length:** 42″ over-all.
**Stock:** Walnut thumb-hole type. Fore-end and p.g. stippled.
**Features:** Especially designed for running boar competition. Receiver grooved to accept dovetail scope mounts. Adjustable cheekpiece and butt plate. 1.1 lb. trigger pull. Left hand stock available on special order. Imported from Germany by Interarms.
**Price:** . . . . . . . . . . . . . . . . . . . . . . . . . . . . . . . . . . . . . . . . . . . . . . $815.00

> Consult our Directory pages for
> the location of firms mentioned.

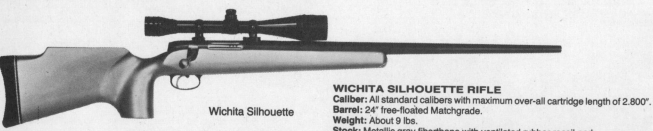

Wichita Silhouette

## WICHITA SILHOUETTE RIFLE
**Caliber:** All standard calibers with maximum over-all cartridge length of 2.800″.
**Barrel:** 24″ free-floated Matchgrade.
**Weight:** About 9 lbs.
**Stock:** Metallic gray fiberthane with ventilated rubber recoil pad.
**Sights:** None furnished. Drilled and tapped for scope mounts.
**Features:** Legal for all NRA competitions. Single shot action. Fluted bolt, 2-oz. Canjar trigger; glass-bedded stock. Comes with hard case. Introduced 1983. From Wichita Arms.
**Price:** . . . . . . . . . . . . . . . . . . . . . . . . . . . . . . . . . . . . . . . . . . . . $1,310.00
**Price:** Left-hand . . . . . . . . . . . . . . . . . . . . . . . . . . . . . . . . . . . . . $1,410.00

**CAUTION:** PRICES CHANGE. CHECK AT GUNSHOP.

Beretta A-302

## ARMSPORT 2751 GAS AUTO SHOTGUN
**Gauge:** 12, 3" chamber.
**Barrel:** 28" (Mod.), 30" (Full).
**Weight:** 7 lbs.
**Stock:** European walnut.
**Features:** Gas-operated action; blued receiver with light engraving. Introduced 1986. Imported from Italy by Armsport.
**Price:** With fixed chokes ............................... $450.00
**Price:** Blue, choke tubes, 28" bbl. .................. $495.00
**Price:** With silvered receiver ........................... $525.00

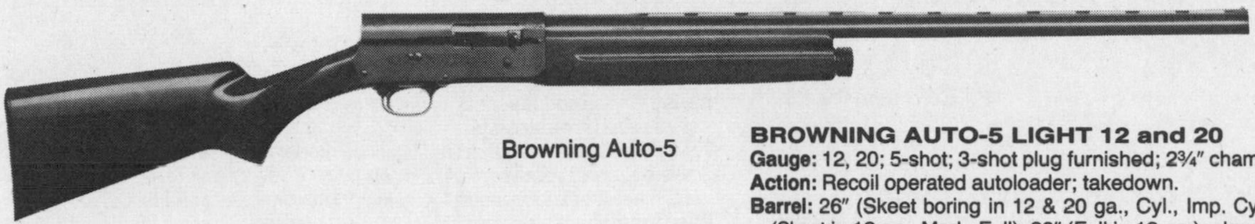

## BERETTA A-302 AUTO SHOTGUN
**Gauge:** 12 or 20, 2¾" or 3".
**Barrel:** 12 ga. — 22" (Slug); 26" (Imp. Cyl., Skeet); 28" (Mod., Full, Multichoke); 30" (Full, Full Trap); 20 ga. — 26" (Imp. Cyl., Skeet); 28" (Mod., Full).
**Weight:** About 6½ lbs. (20 ga.).
**Stock:** European walnut; hand checkered grip and fore-end.
**Features:** Gas-operated action, alloy receiver with scroll engraving; magazine cut-off, push-button safety. Multi-choke models come with four interchangeable screw-in choke tubes. Introduced 1983. Imported from Italy by Beretta U.S.A.
**Price:** 12 or 20 ga., standard chokes ........................... $585.00
**Price:** Multi-choke, 12 ga. or 20 ga. ............................. $614.00
**Price:** 12 ga. trap with Monte Carlo stock (A303) ................ $690.00
**Price:** 12 or 20 ga. Skeet (A303) ................................ $680.00
**Price:** Slug, 12 or 20 ga. .......................................... $599.00
**Price:** Super Lusso (custom gun), 12 or 20 ga. .................. $2,500.00

Browning Auto-5

## Browning Auto-5 Classic & Gold Classic
Same as the standard Auto-5 Light 12 with 28" (Mod.) barrel. Classic edition has hunting and wildlife scenes engraved on the satin grey receiver, including a portrait of John M. Browning, and is limited to 5,000 guns. Also engraved is "Browning Classic. One of Five Thousand." The Gold Classic has a variation of the engraved scenes but with gold animals and portrait. Only 500 will be made, each numbered "1 of Five Hundred," etc. with "Browning Gold Classic."
Both editions have select, figured walnut, special checkering with carved border, and the semi-pistol grip stock. Scheduled for 1984 delivery. Introduced 1984.
**Price:** Auto-5 Classic ......................................... $1,200.00
**Price:** Auto-5 Gold Classic ................................... $6,500.00

## BROWNING AUTO-5 LIGHT 12 and 20
**Gauge:** 12, 20; 5-shot; 3-shot plug furnished; 2¾" chamber.
**Action:** Recoil operated autoloader; takedown.
**Barrel:** 26" (Skeet boring in 12 & 20 ga., Cyl., Imp. Cyl., Mod in 20 ga.); 28" (Skeet in 12 ga., Mod., Full); 30" (Full in 12 ga.); also available with 26", 28", 30" and 32" Invector (choke tube) barrel.
**Weight:** 12 ga. 7¼ lbs., 20 ga. 6⅜ lbs.
**Stock:** French walnut, hand checkered half-p.g. and fore-end. 14¼" x 1⅝" x 2½".
**Features:** Receiver hand engraved with scroll designs and border. Double extractors, extra bbls. interchangeable without factory fitting; mag. cut-off; cross-bolt safety. Buck Special no longer inventoried, but can be ordered as a Buck Special extra barrel, plus an action only. Imported from Japan by Browning.
**Price:** Vent. rib only ......................................... $559.95
**Price:** Extra barrels, vent. rib only ......................... $175.00
**Price:** Invector model ....................................... $589.95
**Price:** Extra Invector barrels, vent. rib only ................ $205.00

## Browning Auto-5 Magnum 12
Same as Std. Auto-5 except: chambered for 3" magnum shells (also handles 2¾" magnum and 2¾" HV loads). 28" Mod., Full; 30" and 32" (Full) bbls. Also available with Invector choke tubes. 14"x1⅝"x2½" stock. Recoil pad. Wgt. 8¾ lbs.
**Price:** Vent. rib only ......................................... $569.95
**Price:** Invector model ....................................... $599.95

## Browning Auto-5 Magnum 20
Same as Magnum 12 except barrels 28" Full or Mod., or 26" Full, Mod., Imp. Cyl. or Invector. With ventilated rib, 7½ lbs.
**Price:** ....................................................... $569.95
**Price:** Invector model ....................................... $599.95

Browning B-80 Upland

## Browning B-80 Upland Special Auto Shotgun
Same as standard B-80 except has 22" Invector barrel in 2¾" chambering. Straight grip stock with 14" length of pull; 12 and 20 gauge. Introduced 1986.
**Price:** ....................................................... $534.50

## BROWNING B-80 AUTO SHOTGUN
**Gauge:** 12 (2¾" & 3"), 20 (2¾" & 3")
**Barrel:** 24" (Slug), 26" (Imp. Cyl., Cyl., Skeet, Full, Mod.), 28" (Full, Mod.), 30" (Full), 32" (Full). Invector barrels in 22", 26", 28", 30", 12 or 20 ga.
**Weight:** 12 ga. about 7 lbs., 20 ga. about 5¾ lbs.
**Stock:** 14¼" x 1⅝" x 2½". Hand checkered French walnut. Solid black recoil pad.
**Features:** Vent. rib barrels have non-reflective rib; alloy receiver; cross-bolt safety; interchangeable barrels. Buck Special no longer inventoried, but can be ordered as a Buck Special extra barrel and action only. Introduced 1981. Imported from Belgium by Browning.
**Price:** Invector, vent. rib, 12 or 20 ga. ........................... $534.50
**Price:** Extra Invector barrels. .................................... $188.50
**Price:** Extra fixed-choke barrels ................................. $105.60
**Price:** Extra Buck Special barrel ................................. $188.50

---

Charles Daly Field

## CHARLES DALY FIELD AUTO SHOTGUN
**Gauge:** 12, 2¾" or 3".
**Barrel:** 27" (Full, Mod., Imp. Cyl., Invector choke tubes), 30" (Extra Full, Full, Mod., Invector choke tubes).
**Weight:** About 7¼ lbs.
**Stock:** Walnut, with checkered pistol grip and fore-end, high gloss finish.
**Features:** Alloy receiver with bright chromed bolt; cross-bolt safety; stainless steel gas piston. Imported from Japan by Outdoor Sports Headquarters. Introduced 1984.
**Price:** ............................................. $386.00
**Price:** Super Field (12 ga., 23", straight stock) .................... $399.50
**Price:** Slug gun (12 ga., 20", rifle sights) ......................... $386.00

## COSMI AUTOMATIC SHOTGUN
**Gauge:** 12 or 20, 2¾" or 3" chamber.
**Barrel:** 22" to 34". Choke (including choke tubes) and length to customer specs. Boehler steel.
**Weight:** About 6¼ lbs. (20 ga.)
**Stock:** Length and style to customer specs. Hand-checkered exhibition grade circassian walnut standard.
**Features:** Hand-made, essentially a custom gun. Recoil-operated auto with tip-up barrel. Made completely of stainless steel (lower receiver polished); magazine tube in buttstock holds 7 rounds. Double ejectors, double safety system. Comes with fitted leather case. Imported from Italy by Incor Inc.
**Price:** From ................................................ $6,200.00

F.I.E/Franchi PG-80

**Stock:** Oil finished European walnut. Prestige model is checkered, Elite is stippled with palm-swell p.g.
**Features:** Gas-operated action. Prestige model has plain blued receiver, Elite has engraved receiver. Both models have 7mm-wide vent. rib. Gas piston is stainless steel. Introduced 1985. Imported from Italy by F.I.E. Corp.
**Price:** Prestige ............................................. $479.95
**Price:** Elite ................................................ $509.95
**Price:** Extra barrels ........................................ $144.95

## F.I.E./FRANCHI PG-80 GAS AUTO SHOTGUNS
**Gauge:** 12, 2¾", 3" chamber.
**Barrel:** 24" (Slug), 26" (Imp. Cyl.), 26", 28" (Mod.), 28" (Full), 30", 32" (3" Full).
**Weight:** 7 lbs., 6 oz. **Length:** 50" over-all.

Franchi Model 48/AL

## F.I.E./FRANCHI 48/AL AUTO SHOTGUN
**Gauge:** 12 or 20, 5-shot. 2¾" or 3" chamber.
**Action:** Recoil-operated automatic.
**Barrel:** 24" (Imp. Cyl. or Cyl.); 26" (Imp. Cyl. or Mod); 28" (Skeet, Mod. or Full); 30", 32" (Full). Interchangeable barrels.
**Weight:** 12 ga. 6¼ lbs., 20 ga. 5 lbs. 2 oz.
**Stock:** Epoxy-finished walnut, with cut-checkered pistol grip and fore-end.
**Features:** Chrome-lined bbl., easy takedown, 3-round plug provided. Ventilated rib barrel. Imported from Italy by F.I.E.
**Price:** Vent. rib 12, 20 .................................... $439.95
**Price:** Hunter model (engraved) ............................ $465.95
**Price:** 12 ga. Magnum ...................................... $465.95
**Price:** Extra barrel ......................................... $144.95

**F.I.E./Franchi Slug Gun**
Same as Standard automatic except 22" Cylinder bored plain barrel, adj. rifle-type sights, sling swivels.
**Price:** 12 or 20 ga., standard ............................... $439.95
**Price:** As above, Hunter grade .............................. $465.95
**Price:** Extra barrel ......................................... $144.95

Ithaca 51A Turkey

## ITHACA MODEL 51A WATERFOWLER
**Gauge:** 12, 3" chamber.
**Barrel:** 30" (Full).
**Weight:** About 7½ lbs.
**Stock:** Checkered walnut.
**Features:** Matte-finish metal; comes with sling and swivels; ventilated rib.
**Price:** ............................................. $625.00
**Price:** As Turkey Gun, 26" bbl., sling and swivels ................. $625.00
**Price:** Camo Vent, 26", 30" (Full) ........................... $700.00

**Ithaca Model 51A Supreme Trap**
Same gun as Model 51A Waterfowler with blued metal, fancy American walnut trap stock, 30" (Full).
**Price:** ............................................. $869.00
**Price:** With Monte Carlo stock ............................... $905.00

**Ithaca Model 51A Supreme Skeet**
Same gun as Model 51 Trap with fancy American walnut stock, 26" (Skeet) barrel, 12 or 20 ga..
**Price:** ............................................. $855.00

# SHOTGUNS—AUTOLOADERS

Ithaca Mag-10 Auto

> Consult our Directory pages for the location of firms mentioned.

**ITHACA MAG-10 GAS OPERATED SHOTGUN**
**Gauge:** 10, 3½" chamber, 3-shot.
**Barrel:** 26", 28" (Full, Mod.), 32".
**Weight:** 11¼ lbs.
**Stock:** American walnut, checkered p.g. and fore-end (14⅛"x2⅜"x1½"), p.g. cap, rubber recoil pad.
**Sights:** White Bradley.
**Features:** "Countercoil" gas system. Piston, cylinder, bolt, charging lever, action release and carrier made of stainless steel. ⅜" vent. rib. Vapor Blast matte finish. Reversible cross bolt safety. Low recoil force. Supreme has full fancy claro American black walnut.
**Price:** Standard, plain barrel, 32" (Full) only .................... $726.00
**Price:** Deluxe, vent. rib, 26", 32" only (Full) ...................... $924.00
**Price:** Standard, vent. rib ......... $781.00
**Price:** Supreme, vent. rib, 32" (Full) only ...................... $1,124.00
**Price:** Camouflage, 26" and 32" (Full), standard vent ............. $857.00

**Ithaca Mag-10 Deerslayer**
Similar to the standard Mag-10 except has 22" barrel, rifle sights.
**Price:** Std., vent. rib, Vapor Blast finish .......................... $781.00

K.F.C. Model 250

**KAWAGUCHIYA K.F.C. M-250 AUTO SHOTGUN**
**Gauge:** 12, 2¾".
**Barrel:** 26" (Imp. Cyl.), 28" (Mod.), 30" (Full); or with Tru-Choke interchangeable choke tube system.

**Weight:** 7 lbs. **Length:** 48" over-all (28" barrel).
**Stock:** 14⅛"x1½"x2½". American walnut, hand checkered p.g. and fore-end.
**Features:** Gas-operated, ventilated barrel rib. Has only 79 parts. Cross-bolt safety is reversible for left-handed shooters. Available with fixed or Tru-Choke interchangeable choke tube system. Introduced 1980. Imported from Japan by La Paloma Marketing.
**Price:** Standard Grade with Tru-Choke ......................... $565.00
**Price:** Deluxe Grade (silvered, etched receiver) with Tru-Choke..... $599.00

Mossberg Model 712

**MOSSBERG 712 AUTO SHOTGUN**
**Gauge:** 12 only, 2¾" or 3" chamber.
**Barrel:** 18½" (Cyl.), 24" (Slugster), 26" (Imp. Cyl.), 28" (Mod.), 30" (Full, 2¾" or 3").

**Weight:** 7½ lbs. **Length:** 48" over-all (with 28" barrel).
**Stock:** 14"x1½"x2½". Walnut-finished hardwood.
**Sights:** Bead front.
**Features:** Safety located on top of receiver. Interchangeable barrels and ACCU-CHOKE choke tubes. Introduced 1983.
**Price:** About ............... $344.95
**Price:** Slug gun, about...... $326.95

Mossberg Model 1000

**MOSSBERG MODEL 1000 AUTO**
**Gauge:** 12, 2¾" or 3" chamber, 4-shot.
**Action:** Gas-operated autoloader.
**Barrel:** 26" (Skeet, Imp. Cyl.), 28" (Mod. Full). Also available with screw-in Multi-Choke tubes.
**Weight:** 7½ lbs. (28" bbl.). **Length:** 48" over-all (28" bbl.).
**Stock:** 14"x1½"x2⅜", American walnut.
**Features:** Interchangeable cross-bolt safety, vent. rib with front and middle beads, engraved alloy receiver, pressure compensator and floating piston for light recoil.
**Price:** ............... $464.00

**Mossberg Model 1000 Trap Shotgun**
Similar to the standard Model 1000 except has Monte Carlo trap stock, medium width stepped rib with white middle bead, Bradley front; integral wire shell catcher; specially tuned trigger; 30" Multi-Choke barrel with Full, Mod. and Imp. Mod. tubes. Steel receiver. Introduced 1983.
**Price:** ................ $560.00

**Mossberg Model 1000 Super 12 Shotgun**
Similar to the standard Model 1000 auto shotgun except has a new gas metering system to allow the gun to handle any shell from 3-inch mags to 1-oz. 2¾-inch field loads without changing the barrel. Super 12 barrels are not interchangeable with other Model 1000 guns, or vice versa. A longer magazine tube gives four-shot capability. In 12-gauge only, the Super 12 has a 3-inch chamber with choice of 26, 28 or 30-inch Multi-Choke barrel; also available in a Parkerized "Waterfowler" version with 28-inch Multi-Choke barrel.
**Price:** Super 12 ..................... $534.00
**Price:** Super Waterfowler .................. $562.00

**Mossberg Model 1000S Super Skeet, 12 & 20**
Similar to Model 1000 except has "recessed-type" Skeet choke with a compensator system to soften recoil and reduce muzzle jump. Stock has right-hand palm swell. Trigger is contoured (rounded) on right side; pull is 2½ to 3 lbs. Vent. rib has double sighting beads with a "Bright Point" fluorescent red front bead. Fore-end cap weights (included) of 1 and 2 oz. can be used to change balance. Select-grade walnut with oil finish. Barrel length is 25", weight 8¼ lbs., over-all length 45.7". Stock measures 14"x1½"x2½" with .08" cast-off at butt, .16" at toe.
**Price:** ............... $657.00

Remington Model 1100

## Remington 1100 Magnum

Same as 1100 except: chambered for 3" magnum loads. Available in 12 ga. (30") or 20 ga. (28") Mod. or Full., or 12 ga. (28") with REM Choke tubes; 14"×1½"×2½" stock with recoil pad, Wgt. 7¾ lbs.

Price: With vent rib, about .................... $551.00
Price: As above, 12 ga., 28" REM Chokes, about ................. $588.00
Price: Left hand model with vent. rib, about ..................... $636.00
Price: As above, 12 ga., 28" REM Chokes, about ................. $673.00

## REMINGTON MODEL 1100 AUTO

Gauge: 12, 3-shot plug furnished.
Barrel: 26" (Imp. Cyl.), 28" (Mod., Full), 30" (Full); 26", 28" with REM Chokes.
Weight: 7½ lbs.
Stock: 14"x1½"x2½" American walnut, checkered p.g. and fore-end.
Features: Quickly interchangeable barrels. Matted receiver top with scroll work on both sides of receiver. Cross-bolt safety.

Price: With vent. rib, about .................... $505.00
Price: As above, with REM Chokes, about ..................... $542.00
Price: Left hand model with vent. rib, about ................... $586.00
Price: As above, with REM Chokes, about ..................... $623.00

## Remington 1100 Small Gauge

Same as 1100 except: 28 ga. 2¾" (5-shot) or 410, 3" (except Skeet, 2½" 4-shot). 45½" over-all. Available in 25" bbl. (Full, Mod., or Imp. Cyl.) only.

Price: With vent. rib, about..................... $550.00
Price: SA Skeet, about ........................ $578.00
Price: Tournament Skeet, about................ $682.00

## Remington 1100D Tournament Auto

Same as 1100 Standard except: vent, rib, better wood, more extensive engraving.

Price: About................................. $2,290.00

---

Consult our Directory pages for the location of firms mentioned.

---

## Remington 1100F Premier Auto

Same as 1100D except: select wood, better engraving
Price: About.................................. $4,720.00
Price: With gold inlay, about.................. $7,079.00

Remington 1100 SP Deer

## Remington 1100 LT-20 Youth Gun

Basically the same design as Model 1100, but with special weight-saving features that retain strength and dependability of the standard Model 1100. Has 21" (Mod., Imp. Cyl.) barrel, weighs 6½ lbs.

Price: About .................................. $505.00
Price: LT-20 Deer Gun (20" bbl.), about ........... $505.00

## Remington Model 1100 "Special Purpose" Deer Gun

Similar to the 1100 "Special Purpose" Magnum except 2¾" chamber, 21" Imp. Cyl. barrel with rifle sights. Over-all length is 41½", weight about 7¾ lbs. Barrel and receiver have non-reflective Parkerized finish, bolt and carrier have dull black oxide finish. Oil-finished stock and fore-end. Comes with recoil pad and padded Cordura nylon sling. Introduced 1986.

Price: About ................................... $505.00

Remington 1100 SP Magnum

## Remington 1100 "Special Purpose" Magnum

Similar to the Model 1100 except chambered for 12-ga., 3" shells, vent. rib, 26" or 30" (both Full) or 26" REM Choke barrels. All exposed metal surfaces are finished in dull, non-reflective black. Wood has an oil finish. Comes with padded Cordura, 2" wide sling, quick-detachable swivels. Chrome-lined bores. Dark recoil pad. Introduced 1985.

Price: About ................................... $551.00
Price: With REM Choke, about ................... $588.00

Remington 1100 TA Trap

## Remington 1100 TA Trap

Same as the standard 1100 except: recoil pad. 14⅜"x1⅜"x1¾" stock. Right- or left-hand models. Wgt. 8¼ lbs. 12 ga. only. 30" (Mod. Trap, Full) vent. rib bbl. Ivory bead front and white metal middle sight.

Price: About .................................. $576.00
Price: With Monte Carlo stock, about............ $586.00
Price: 1100TA Trap, left hand, about............ $608.00
Price: With Monte Carlo stock, about............ $621.00
Price: Tournament Trap, about................... $680.00
Price: Tournament Trap with M.C. stock, better grade wood, different checkering, cut checkering, about................... $690.00

CAUTION: PRICES CHANGE. CHECK AT GUNSHOP.

**Remington 1100 Special Field**

## Remington 1100 SA Skeet
Same as the 1100 except: 26" bbl., special Skeet boring, vent. rib (high rib on LT-20), ivory bead front and metal bead middle sights. 14"x1½"x2½" stock. 12, 20, 28, 410 ga. Wgt. 7½ lbs., cut checkering, walnut, new receiver scroll.
**Price:** 12 ga., Skeet SA, about .................................. $563.00
**Price:** 12 ga. Left hand model with vent. rib, about ................ $598.00
**Price:** 28 & 410 ga., 25" bbl., about ............................. $578.00
**Price:** Tournament Skeet (28, 410), about ........................ $682.00
**Price:** Tournament Skeet (12 or 20), about ....................... $668.00

## Remington 1100 "Special Field"
Similar to standard Model 1100 except comes with 21" barrel only, choked Imp. Cyl., Mod., Full; 12 ga. weighs 7¼ lbs., LT-20 version 6½ lbs.; has straight-grip stock, shorter fore-end, both with cut checkering. Comes with vent rib only; matte finish receiver without engraving. Introduced 1983.
**Price:** 12 ga., 21" REM Choke, about ......................... $569.00
**Price:** 20 ga., fixed choke, about ............................. $532.00

## Remington 1100 Deer Gun
Same as 1100 except: 12 ga. only, 22" bbl. (Imp. Cyl.), rifle sights adjustable for w. and e.; recoil pad with white spacer. Weight 7¼ lbs.
**Price:** about ............................................... $505.00
**Price:** Left-hand Deer Gun, about ........................... $586.00

**Remington Sportsman**

## Remington "Sportsman" 12 Auto Shotgun
Similar to the Model 1100 except in 12 ga. only with 2¾" chamber, 28" (REM Choke), 30" (Full) barrels. Stock and fore-end are checkered, walnut-stained hardwood with satin finish. Weight about 7¾ lbs. Introduced 1985.
**Price:** With fixed choke, vent. rib, about ....................... $409.00
**Price:** With REM Choke, about ................................ $439.00

**Tradewinds Model H-170**

## TRADEWINDS H-170 AUTO SHOTGUN
**Gauge:** 12 only, 2¾" chamber.
**Action:** Recoil-operated automatic.
**Barrel:** 26", 28" (Mod.) and 28" (Full), chrome lined.
**Weight:** 7 lbs.
**Stock:** Select European walnut stock, p.g. and fore-end hand checkered.
**Features:** Light alloy receiver, 5-shot tubular magazine, ventilated rib. Imported from Italy by Tradewinds.
**Price:** ..................................................... $395.00

**Weatherby Eighty-Two Auto**

Consult our Directory pages for the location of firms mentioned.

## WEATHERBY EIGHTY-TWO AUTO
**Gauge:** 12 only, 2¾" and 3" chamber.
**Barrel:** 22" Slug (with sights), 26", 28", 30" with IMC (Integral Multi-Choke) tubes; 26" available with Mod., Imp. Cyl., Skeet, others with Full, Mod., Imp. Cyl.
**Weight:** 7½ lbs. **Length:** 48½" (28" bbl.).
**Stock:** Walnut, hand checkered p.g. and fore-end, rubber recoil pad.
**Features:** Gas operated autoloader with "Floating Piston." Cross-bolt safety, fluted bolt, gold plated trigger. Each gun comes with three flush fitting IMC choke tubes. Imported from Japan by Weatherby. Introduced 1982.
**Price:** ..................................................... $469.95
**Price:** Extra interchangeable barrel ........................... $203.00
**Price:** Extra IMC choke tubes ............................... $15.00

**Winchester Ranger**

## WINCHESTER RANGER AUTO SHOTGUN
**Gauge:** 12 and 20, 2¾" chamber.
**Barrel:** 28" vent. rib with Winchoke tubes (Imp. Cyl., Mod., Full), or 28" plain barrel (Mod.).
**Weight:** 7 to 7¼ lbs. **Length:** 48⅝" over-all.
**Stock:** Walnut-finished hardwood, finger-grooved fore-end with deep cut checkering.
**Sights:** Metal bead front.
**Features:** Cross-bolt safety, front-locking rotating bolt, black serrated buttplate, gas-operated action. Made under license by U.S. Repeating Arms Co.
**Price:** Vent. rib with Winchoke, about ......................... $310.61
**Price:** Deer barrel combo, about .............................. $349.44
**Price:** Deer gun, about .................................... $309.74

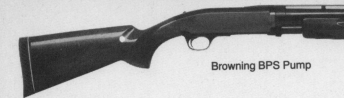

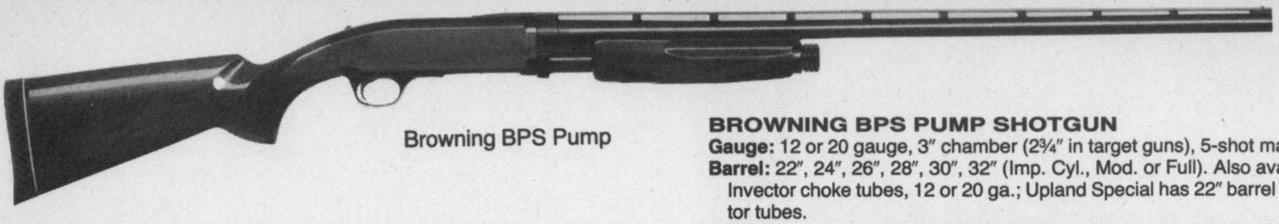

Browning BPS Pump

## Browning BPS Pump Shotgun (Ladies and Youth Model)
Same as BPS Upland Special except 20 ga. only, 22″ Invector barrel, stock has pistol grip with recoil pad. Length of pull is 13¼″. Introduced 1986.
**Price:** .................................................. **$385.95**

## ARMSPORT 2755 PUMP SHOTGUN
**Gauge:** 12, 3″ chamber.
**Barrel:** 28″ (Mod.), 30″ (Full).
**Weight:** 7 lbs.
**Stock:** European walnut.
**Features:** Ventilated rib; rubber recoil pad; polished blue finish. Introduced 1986. Imported from Italy by Armsport.
**Price:** Fixed chokes ............................... **$299.00**
**Price:** 28″, 30″, choke tubes ...................... **$350.00**
**Price:** Police model with 20″ (Imp. Cyl.), black receiver ........... **$275.00**

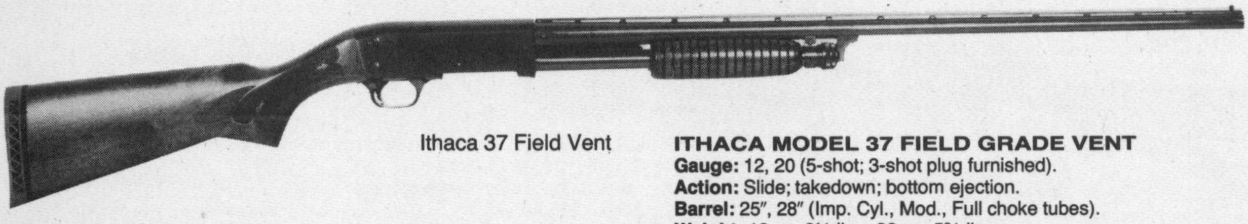

## BROWNING BPS PUMP SHOTGUN
**Gauge:** 12 or 20 gauge, 3″ chamber (2¾″ in target guns), 5-shot magazine.
**Barrel:** 22″, 24″, 26″, 28″, 30″, 32″ (Imp. Cyl., Mod. or Full). Also available with Invector choke tubes, 12 or 20 ga.; Upland Special has 22″ barrel with Invector tubes.
**Weight:** 7 lbs. 8 oz. (28″ barrel). **Length:** 48¾″ over-all (28″ barrel).
**Stock:** 14¼″x1½″x2½″. Select walnut, semi-beavertail fore-end, full p.g. stock.
**Features:** Bottom feeding and ejection, receiver top safety, high post vent. rib. Double action bars eliminate binding. Vent. rib barrels only. Introduced 1977. Imported from Japan by Browning.
**Price:** Grade I Hunting, Upland Special, Invector ................ **$385.95**
**Price:** Extra Invector barrel .............................. **$164.95**
**Price:** Extra fixed-choke barrel ............................ **$98.85**
**Price:** Buck Special barrel with rifle sights ................ **$159.95**

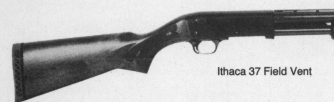

Ithaca 37 Field Vent

## Ithaca Model 37 Ultralite
Weighs five pounds. Same as standard Model 37 except walnut stock, comes only with 25″ vent. rib. Has recoil pad, gold plated trigger, Sid Bell-designed grip cap. Also available as Ultra-Deerslayer with 20″ barrel, 20 ga. only.
**Price:** With choke tubes ....................... **$522.00**
**Price:** Deerslayer model ...................... **$450.00**
**Price:** 20 ga., 20″ (Special Bore) .............. **$480.00**

## Ithaca Model 37 Supreme
Same as Model 37 except: hand checkered fore-end and p.g. stock, Ithaca recoil pad and vent. rib. Model 37 Supreme also with Skeet (14″x1½″x2¼″) or Trap (14½″x1½″x1⅞″) stocks available at no extra charge. Other options available at extra charge.
**Price:** ............................................ **$769.00**

## ITHACA MODEL 37 FIELD GRADE VENT
**Gauge:** 12, 20 (5-shot; 3-shot plug furnished).
**Action:** Slide; takedown; bottom ejection.
**Barrel:** 25″, 28″ (Imp. Cyl., Mod., Full choke tubes).
**Weight:** 12 ga. 6½ lbs., 20 ga. 5¾ lbs.
**Stock:** 14″x1⅝″x2⅝″. Checkered hardwood p.g. stock and ring-tail fore-end.
**Features:** Ithaca Raybar front sight; cross-bolt safety; action release for removing shells.
**Price:** ............................................. **$428.00**
**Price:** Deluxe Vent, 12 or 20, fixed chokes ...................... **$464.00**

## Ithaca Model 37 Magnum D/X
Same as standard Model 37 except chambered for 3″ shells with resulting longer receiver. Stock dimensions are 14″x1⅞″x1½″. Grip cap has a Sid Bell-designed flying mallard on it. Has a recoil pad, vent. rib barrel with Raybar front sight. Available in 12 or 20 ga. with 30″ (Full), 28″ (Mod.) and 26″ (Imp. Cyl.) barrel. Weight about 7¼ lbs. Introduced 1978.
**Price:** ............................................. **$464.00**
**Price:** Camouflage model, 12 ga., 26″ (Full) only ................. **$500.00**

Ithaca 37 English Ultra

## Ithaca Model 37 Deerslayer
Same as Model 37 except: 26″ or 20″ bbl. designed for rifled slugs; sporting rear sight, Raybar front sight: rear sight ramp grooved for Redfield long eye relief scope mount. 12, or 20 gauge. With checkered stock, beavertail fore-end and recoil pad.
**Price:** ............................................ **$450.00**

## Ithaca Model 37 English Ultralite
Similar to the standard Model 37 Ultralite except vent. rib barrel has straight-grip stock with better wood. Introduced 1981.
**Price:** With choke tubes (Full, Mod., Imp. Cyl.) ................... **$522.00**

## LISA MODEL PUMP SLUG SHOTGUN
**Gauge:** 12, 2¾″ chamber, 5 or 8 shot.
**Barrel:** 21″ standard, or to customer specs.
**Weight:** About 7½ lbs.
**Stock:** Walnut or select hardwood.
**Sights:** None furnished. Drilled and tapped for scope mounting.
**Features:** Free floated barrel (heavy or lightweight); thick action bridge; uses special Pennsylvania Arms slug barrel. Introduced 1986. From Pennsylvania Arms.
**Price:** From ............................................... **$499.95**

Mossberg Model 3000

### Mossberg Model 3000 Waterfowler Pump
Similar to the standard Model 3000 except all exterior metal is Parkerized to reduce glare, bolt is black oxidized, stock has a dull oil finish. Comes with q.d. swivels and a padded, camouflaged sling. Available with 30" (Full) barrel with 3" chamber. Introduced 1982.
**Price:** .................................................... **$412.00**

### MOSSBERG MODEL 3000 PUMP
**Gauge:** 12 or 20 ga., 3" chamber.
**Barrel:** 22" (Cyl.) with rifle sights, 26" (Imp. Cyl.), 28" (Mod.), 30" (Full), vent. rib or plain. Also available with Multi-Choke system.
**Weight:** About 7½ lbs. **Length:** 48½" over-all (28" bbl.).
**Stock:** 14"x1⅜"x2¼". American walnut
**Features:** Dual action bars for smooth functioning. Rubber recoil pad, steel receiver, chrome plated bolt. Cross-bolt safety reversible for left-handed shooters. Introduced 1980.
**Price:** .................................................... **$360.00**

Mossberg Model 500

### Mossberg Model 500AHT/AHTD
Same as Model 500 except 12 ga. only with extra-high Simmons Olympic-style free floating rib and built-up Monte Carlo trap-style stock. 30" barrel (Full), 28" ACCU-CHOKE with 3 interchangeable choke tubes (Mod., Imp. Mod., Full).
**Price:** With 30" barrel, fixed choke ........................... **$326.95**
**Price:** With ACCU-CHOKE barrel, 28" or 30" ................... **$346.95**

### Mossberg Model 500ASG Slugster
Same as standard Mossberg Model 500 except has Slugster barrel with ramp front sight, open adj. folding-leaf rear, running deer scene etched on receiver. 12 ga.—18½", 24", 20-ga.—24" bbl.
**Price:** .................................................... **$236.95**

### MOSSBERG MODEL 500
**Gauge:** 12, 20, 410, 3".
**Action:** Takedown.
**Barrel:** 28" ACCU-CHOKE (interchangeable tubes for Imp. Cyl., Mod., Full). Vent. rib only.
**Weight:** 6¾ lbs. (20-ga.), 7¼ lbs. (12-ga.) **Length:** 48" over-all.
**Stock:** Walnut-finished hardwood; checkered p.g. and fore-end; recoil pad. (14"x1½"x2½").
**Features:** Side ejection; top tang safety; trigger disconnector prevents doubles. Easily interchangeable barrels within gauge.
**Price:** Vent rib, ACCU-CHOKE, either gauge, about .............. **$315.00**
**Price:** Extra barrels, from ................................... **$31.50**
**Price:** Youth gun, 20 ga., 13" stock, 24" (ACCU-CHOKE), about .... **$257.95**

### Mossberg Model 500 410 Ga.
Similar to Mossberg Model 500 except: 410 bore only, 26" bbl. (Full); 2½", 3" shells; holds six 2¾" or five 3" shells. Walnut-finished stock with checkered p.g. and fore-end, fluted comb and recoil pad (14"x1¼"x2½"). Weight about 6 lbs., length over-all 45¾".
**Price:** With vent. rib barrel ................................... **$221.00**

Remington Model 870

### Remington Model 870 Brushmaster Deluxe
Carbine version of the M870 with 20" bbl. (Imp. Cyl.) for rifled slugs. 40½" over-all, wgt. 6½ lbs. Recoil pad. Adj. rear, ramp front sights, 12 or 20 ga. Deluxe.
**Price:** Brushmaster, about .................................... **$380.00**
**Price:** Standard, 12 ga. only, about ........................... **$360.00**
**Price:** Left-hand model, about ................................. **$434.00**

### REMINGTON 870 PUMP GUN
**Gauge:** 12, 20, (5-shot; 3-shot wood plug), 3" chamber.
**Action:** Takedown, slide action
**Barrel:** 12, 20, ga., 26" (Imp. Cyl.); 28" (Mod. or Full); 12 ga., 30" (Full); 12 ga., 26", 28" (REM CHOKE).
**Weight:** 7 lbs., 12 ga. (7¾ lbs. with Vari-Weight plug); 6½ lbs., 20 ga.
**Length:** 48½" over-all (28" bbl.).
**Stock:** 14"x1⅝"x2½". Checkered walnut, p.g.; fluted extension fore-end; fitted rubber recoil pad;
**Features:** Double action bars, crossbolt safety. Receiver machined from solid steel. Hand fitted action.
**Price:** With vent. rib, about ................................... **$401.00**
**Price:** Left hand, vent. rib., 12 ga. only, about .................. **$458.00**
**Price:** Youth Gun, 21" vent. rib, Imp. Cyl., Mod., about ........... **$401.00**
**Price:** 12 ga., 26", 28" REM Choke, about ....................... **$438.00**
**Price:** As above with REM Choke, left hand, about ............... **$495.00**

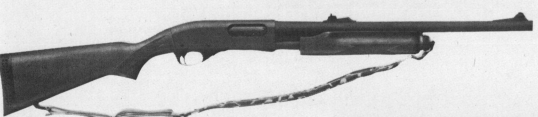

Remington 870 SP Deer

### Remington Model 870 "Special Purpose" Deer Gun
Similar to the 870 "Special Purpose" Magnum except comes only with 20" Imp. Cyl. barrel with rifle sights. Over-all length is 40½", weight about 7 lbs. Barrel and receiver are Parkerized, bolt and carrier have dull black oxide finish. Oil-finished stock and fore-end. Comes wtih recoil pad and padded Cordura nylon sling. Introduced 1986.
**Price:** About ............................................... **$380.00**

Remington 870 "Wingmaster"

## Remington Model 870 "Wingmaster"
Similar to the standard Model 870 except has cut checkered stock and fore-end, ivory Bradley-type bead front and middle bead sights. Available in 12 ga. 3″ only with 26″, 28″ (REM Choke, or 30″ (Full) barrels. Introduced 1986.
**Price:** 26″, 28″ REM Choke, about ............................... **$489.00**
**Price:** 30″ fixed Full choke, about ............................... **$445.00**

Remington 870 Special Field

## Remington Model 870 "Special Field"
Similar to the standard Model 870 except comes with 21″ barrel only, 3″ chamber, choked Imp. Cyl., Mod., Full and REM Choke; 12 ga. weighs 6¾ lbs., Ltwt. 20 weighs 6 lbs.; has straight-grip stock, shorter fore-end, both with cut checkering. Vent. rib barrel only. Introduced 1984.
**Price:** 12 ga. REM Choke, about.............................. **$465.00**
**Price:** 20 ga., fixed choke, about.............................. **$429.00**

## Remington 870 "Special Purpose" Magnum
Similar to the Model 870 except chambered only for 12-ga., 3″ shells, vent. rib. 26″ (REM Choke) or 30″ (Full) barrels. All exposed metal surfaces are finished in dull, non-reflective black. Wood has an oil finish. Comes with padded Cordura, 2″ wide sling, quick-detachable swivels. Chrome-lined bores. Dark recoil pad. Introduced 1985.
**Price:** About .................................................. **$401.00**

## Remington Model 870 Competition Trap
Same as standard 870 except single shot, gas reduction system, select wood. Has 30″ (Full choke) vent. rib barrel
**Price:** About .................................................. **$685.00**

## Remington 870F High Grade
Same as M870, except select walnut, better engraving
**Price:** About................................................. **$4,720.00**
**Price:** With gold inlay, about................................... **$7,079.00**

## Remington 870D High Grade
Same as 870 except: better walnut, hand checkering. Engraved receiver and bbl. Vent. rib. Stock dimensions to order.
**Price:** About.............................................. **$2,290.00**

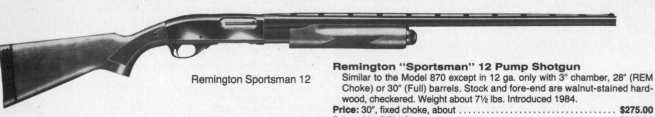

Remington 870 TA Trap

## Remington 870 Small Gauges
Exact copies of the large ga. Model 870, except that guns are offered in 28 and 410 ga. 25″ barrel (Full, Mod., Imp. Cyl.). D and F grade prices same as large ga. M870 prices.
**Price:** With vent. rib barrel, about............................... **$429.00**

## Remington 870 TA Trap
Same as the M870 except: 12 ga. only, 30″ (Mod., Full) vent. rib. bbl., ivory front and white metal middle beads. Special sear, hammer and trigger assy. 14⅜″x1½″x1⅞″ stock with recoil pad. Hand fitted action and parts. Wgt. 8 lbs.
**Price:** Model 870TA Trap, about............................... **$436.00**
**Price:** TA Trap with Monte Carlo stock, about .................... **$447.00**

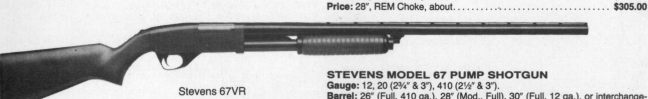

Remington Sportsman 12

## Remington "Sportsman" 12 Pump Shotgun
Similar to the Model 870 except in 12 ga. only with 3″ chamber, 28″ (REM Choke) or 30″ (Full) barrels. Stock and fore-end are walnut-stained hardwood, checkered. Weight about 7½ lbs. Introduced 1984.
**Price:** 30″, fixed choke, about ................................. **$275.00**
**Price:** 28″, REM Choke, about................................. **$305.00**

Stevens 67VR

## STEVENS MODEL 67 PUMP SHOTGUN
**Gauge:** 12, 20 (2¾″ & 3″), 410 (2½″ & 3″).
**Barrel:** 26″ (Full, 410 ga.), 28″ (Mod., Full), 30″ (Full, 12 ga.), or interchangeable choke tubes.
**Weight:** 7 lbs. **Length:** 49½″ over-all (30″ bbl.).
**Stock:** Walnut-finished hardwood; checkered p.g. and slide handle. 14″x1½″x2½″.
**Sights:** Metal bead front.
**Features:** Grooved slide handle, top tang safety, steel receiver. From Savage Arms. Introduced 1981.
**Price:** Model 67 . . . . . . . . . . . . . . . . . . . . . . . . . . . . . . . . **$198.61**
**Price:** Model 67VR (vent. rib). . . . . . . . . . . . . . . . . . . . . . . . **$214.75**
**Price:** Model 67 Slug Gun (21″ barrel, rifle sights) . . . . . . . . . . . . . . . **$202.29**
**Price:** Model 67-VRT (as above with vent. rib) . . . . . . . . . . . . . . . . . **$229.29**
**Price:** Model 67-VRT-Y (youth gun, 20 ga.) . . . . . . . . . . . . . . . . . . . **$229.29**
**Price:** Model 67-VRT-K (12, 20, choke tubes, laminated camo stock) **$250.29**

**CAUTION:** PRICES CHANGE. CHECK AT GUNSHOP.

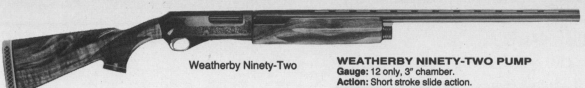

Weatherby Ninety-Two

**WEATHERBY NINETY-TWO PUMP**
**Gauge:** 12 only, 3" chamber.
**Action:** Short stroke slide action.
**Barrel:** 22" Slug (with sights), 26", 28", 30" with IMC (Integral Multi-Choke) tubes; 26" with Mod., Imp. Cyl., Skeet, others with Full, Mod., Imp. Cyl.
**Weight:** About 7½ lbs. **Length:** 48⅛" (28" bbl.)
**Stock:** Walnut, hand checkered p.g. and fore-end, white line spacers at p.g. cap and recoil pad.
**Features:** Short stroke action, cross-bolt safety. Comes with three flush-fitting IMC choke tubes. Introduced 1982. Imported from Japan by Weatherby.
**Price:** ............................................... **$399.95**
**Price:** Extra interchangeable bbls. ............................. **$175.00**
**Price:** Extra IMC choke tubes ................................. **$15.00**

Winchester 1300 XTR

**Winchester Model 1300XTR Featherweight**
Similar to the standard 1300 Featherweight except comes in 12 ga. only with 28" barrel (Winchoke), rubber recoil pad. Weight is 7¼ lbs. with 48⅝" over-all length. Introduced 1986.
**Price:** About ................................................. **$364.00**

**Winchester Model 1300 Turkey**
Similar to the standard Model 1300 Featherweight except 12 ga. only, 30" barrel with Mod., Full and Extra Full Winchoke tubes, matte finish wood and metal, and comes with recoil pad, Cordura sling and swivels.
**Price:** About ................................................. **$364.00**

**WINCHESTER MODEL 1300 FEATHERWEIGHT PUMP**
**Gauge:** 12 and 20, 3" chamber, 5-shot capacity.
**Barrel:** 22", vent. rib, with Full, Mod., Imp. Cyl. Winchoke tubes.
**Weight:** 6⅜ lbs. **Length:** 42⅝" over-all.
**Stock:** American walnut, with deep cut checkering on pistol grip, traditional ribbed fore-end; high luster finish.
**Sights:** Metal bead front.
**Features:** Twin action slide bars; front-locking rotating bolt; roll-engraved receiver; blued, highly polished metal; cross-bolt safety with red indicator. Introduced 1984.
**Price:** About ................................................. **$345.45**

Winchester 1300 Waterfowl

**Winchester 1300 Waterfowl Pump**
Similar to the 1300 Featherweight except in 3" 12 ga. only, 30" vent. rib barrel with Winchoke system; stock and fore-end of walnut with low-luster finish. All metal surfaces have special non-glare matte finish. Introduced 1985.
**Price:** About ................................................. **$364.00**

Winchester Ranger

**Winchester Ranger Pump Gun Combination**
Similar to the standard Ranger except comes with two barrels: 24⅛" (Cyl.) deer barrel with rifle-type sights and an interchangeable 28" vent. rib Winchoke barrel with Full, Mod. and Imp. Cyl. choke tubes. Available in 12 and 20 gauge 3" only, with recoil pad. Introduced 1983.
**Price:** With two barrels, about ................................. **$311.57**

**WINCHESTER RANGER PUMP GUN**
**Gauge:** 12 or 20, 3" chamber, 4-shot magazine.
**Barrel:** 28" vent rib or plain with Full, Mod., Imp. Cyl. Winchoke tubes, or 30" plain.
**Weight:** 7 to 7¼ lbs. **Length:** 48⅝" to 50⅝" over-all.
**Stock:** Walnut finished hardwood with ribbed fore-end.
**Sights:** Metal bead front.
**Features:** Cross-bolt safety, black rubber butt pad, twin action slide bars, front-locking rotating bolt. Made under license by U.S. Repeating Arms Co.
**Price:** Plain barrel, about ..................................... **$231.00**
**Price:** Vent. rib barrel, Winchoke, about ......................... **$269.80**
**Price:** Vent. rib. Mod. choke, about ............................. **$242.86**

**Winchester Ranger Youth Pump Gun**
Similar to the standard Ranger except chambered only for 3" 20 ga., 22" vent. rib barrel with Winchoke tubes (Full, Mod., Imp. Cyl.) or 22" plain barrel with fixed Mod. choke. Weighs 6½ lbs., measures 41⅝" o.a.l. Stock has 13" pull length and gun comes with discount certificate for full-size stock. Introduced 1983. Made under license by U.S. Repeating Arms Co.
**Price:** Vent. rib barrel, Winchoke, about ......................... **$275.48**
**Price:** Plain barrel, Mod. choke, about ........................... **$239.88**

> Consult our Directory pages for
> the location of firms mentioned.

**CAUTION:** PRICES CHANGE. CHECK AT GUNSHOP.

**ARMSPORT MODEL 2700 O/U**
**Gauge:** 12 or 20 ga.
**Barrel:** 26" (Imp. Cyl. & Mod.); 28" (Mod. & Full); vent. rib.
**Weight:** 8 lbs.
**Stock:** European walnut, hand checkered p.g. and fore-end.
**Features:** Single selective trigger, automatic ejectors, engraved receiver. Imported by Armsport.
**Price:** .......... **$495.00**
**Price:** With extractors only .......... **$425.00**
**Price:** With double triggers .......... **$375.00**
**Price:** M2733/2735 (Boss-type action, 12, 20, extractors) .......... **$495.00**
**Price:** M2741/2743 (as above with ejectors) .......... **$550.00**
**Price:** M2730/2731 (as above with single trigger, screw-in chokes) . **$650.00**
**Price:** M2705 (410 ga., 26" Imp. & Mod., double triggers) .......... **$399.95**
**Price:** M2720 (as above with single trigger) .......... **$465.00**

**ARMSPORT 2900 TRI-BARREL SHOTGUN**
**Gauge:** 12, 3" chambers.
**Barrel:** 28" (Imp. Cyl. & Mod. & Full).
**Weight:** 7¾ lbs.
**Stock:** European walnut.
**Features:** Top-tang barrel selector; double triggers; silvered, engraved frame. Introduced 1986. Imported from Italy by Armsport.
**Price:** .......... **$895.00**

**ARMSPORT MODEL 2700 O-U GOOSE GUN**
**Gauge:** 10 ga., 3½" chambers.
**Barrel:** 32" (Full & Full).
**Weight:** About 9 lbs.
**Stock:** European walnut.
**Features:** Boss-type action; double triggers; extractors. Introduced 1986. Imported from Italy by Armsport.
**Price:** .......... **$595.00**

**ARMSPORT 1225/1226 O-U FOLDING SHOTGUN**
**Gauge:** 12, 20, 3" chambers.
**Barrel:** 26", 28" (Mod. & Full)
**Weight:** 6 lbs.
**Stock:** European walnut.
**Features:** Top-break folding action; double triggers; extractors; silvered receiver with light engraving. Introduced 1986. Imported from Italy by Armsport.
**Price:** .......... **$295.00**

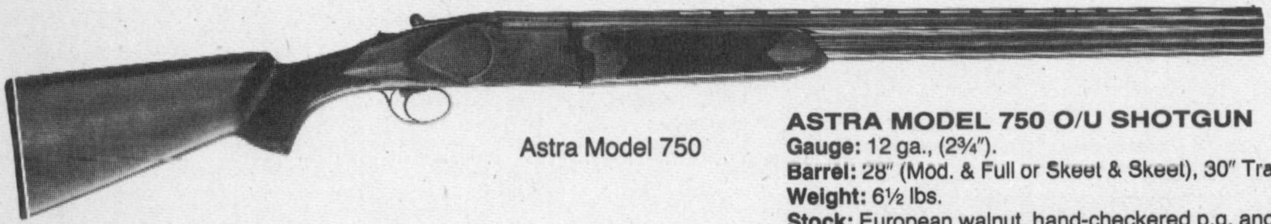

Astra Model 750

**ASTRA MODEL 750 O/U SHOTGUN**
**Gauge:** 12 ga., (2¾").
**Barrel:** 28" (Mod. & Full or Skeet & Skeet), 30" Trap (Mod. & Full).
**Weight:** 6½ lbs.
**Stock:** European walnut, hand-checkered p.g. and fore-end.
**Features:** Single selective trigger, scroll-engraved receiver, selective auto ejectors, vent. rib. Introduced 1980. From L. Joseph Rahn, Inc.
**Price:** .......... **$735.00**
**Price:** With extractors only .......... **$600.00**
**Price:** Trap or Skeet (M.C. stock and recoil pad.) .......... **$850.00**

**Astra Model 650 O/U Shotgun**
Same as Model 750 except has double triggers.
**Price:** With extractors .......... **$495.00**
**Price:** With ejectors .......... **$630.00**

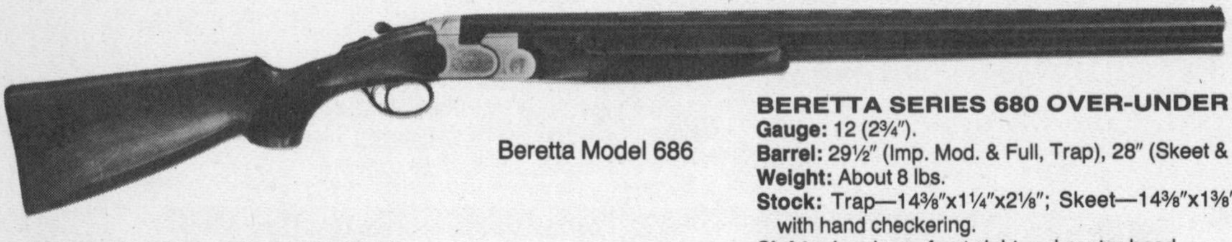

Beretta Model 686

**BERETTA SERIES 680 OVER-UNDER**
**Gauge:** 12 (2¾").
**Barrel:** 29½" (Imp. Mod. & Full, Trap), 28" (Skeet & Skeet).
**Weight:** About 8 lbs.
**Stock:** Trap—14⅜"x1¼"x2⅛"; Skeet—14⅜"x1⅜"x2⁷⁄₁₆". European walnut with hand checkering.
**Sights:** Luminous front sight and center bead.
**Features:** Trap Monte Carlo stock has deluxe trap recoil pad, Skeet has smooth pad. Various grades available—contact Beretta U.S.A. for details. Imported from Italy by Beretta U.S.A. Corp.
**Price:** M682, Trap or Skeet, from .......... **$2,100.00**
**Price:** M682X, Trap or Skeet, from .......... **$2,100.00**
**Price:** M682 Field .......... **$2,175.00**
**Price:** M685 Field .......... **$875.00**
**Price:** M686 Field, from .......... **$1,025.00**
**Price:** M687 Field, from .......... **$1,175.00**

**BERETTA SO-3 O/U SHOTGUN**
**Gauge:** 12 ga. (2¾" chambers).
**Action:** Back-action sidelock.
**Barrel:** 26", 27", 28", 29" or 30", chokes to customer specs.
**Stock:** Standard measurements—14⅛"x1⁷⁄₁₆"x2⅜". Straight "English" or p.g.-style. Hand checkered European walnut.
**Features:** SO-3—"English scroll" floral engraving on action body, sideplates and trigger guard. Stocked in select walnut. SO-3EL—as above, with full engraving coverage. Hand-detachable sideplates. SO-3EELL—as above with deluxe finish and finest full coverage engraving. Internal parts gold plated. Top lever is pierced and carved in relief with gold inlaid crown. Introduced 1977. Imported from Italy by Beretta U.S.A. Corp.
**Price:** SO-3 .......... **$6,850.00**
**Price:** SO-3EELL .......... **$9,750.00**

**Beretta SO-4 Target Shotguns**
Target guns derived from Model SO-3EL. Light engraving coverage. Single trigger. Skeet gun has 28" (Skeet & Skeet) barrels, 10mm rib, p.g. stock (14⅛"x2⁹⁄₁₆"x1⅜"), fluted beavertail fore-end. "Skeet" is inlaid in gold into trigger guard. Weight is about 7 lbs. 10 ozs. Trap guns have 30" (Imp. Mod. & Full or Mod. & Full) barrels, trap stock dimensions, fitted recoil pad, fluted beavertail fore-end. Weight is about 7 lbs. 12 ozs. "Trap" is inlaid in gold into trigger guard. Special dimensions and features, within limits, may be ordered. Introduced 1977.
**Price:** Skeet or trap .......... **$7,400.00**
**Price:** Trap Combo .......... **$9,500.00**

Consult our Directory pages for the location of firms mentioned.



**CAUTION:** PRICES CHANGE. CHECK AT GUNSHOP.

Bettinsoli Model 845

## BETTINSOLI MODEL 845 EM OVER-UNDER
**Gauge:** 12, 2¾" or 3" chambers.
**Barrel:** 27½" Interchoke (five choke tubes—Full, Mod., Imp. Cyl., Imp. Mod., Skeet).
**Weight:** About 7 lbs.
**Stock:** 14½"x1½"x2½". Hand checkered European walnut; rubber "slip pad."
**Features:** Boxlock action, single selective trigger, selective automatic ejectors; silver frame with English rose and scroll engraving. Introduced 1986. Imported from Italy. For further information contact Proofmark, Ltd.
**Price:** . . . . . . . . . . . . . . . . . . . . . . . . . . . . . . . . . . . . . . . . . . . . . . $619.00
**Price:** Model 840 EM (as above but with fixed Full & Mod. chokes) . $529.00

## BETTINSOLI SENIOR LUX OVER-UNDER
**Gauge:** 12, 2¾" chambers.
**Barrel:** 27⅝", 30", choked to customer specs.
**Weight:** About 8 lbs.
**Stock:** 14½"x1⁷⁄₁₆"x1⅜". Hand checkered European walnut; oil finish; Monte Carlo; palm swell; rubber magnum "slip pad." Left or right-hand avail.
**Features:** Blued boxlock action with single selective trigger; automatic selective ejectors. Skeet model available. Comes with fitted Italian luggage-style case. Introduced 1986. Imported from Italy. Contact Proofmark, Ltd. for full information.
**Price:** . . . . . . . . . . . . . . . . . . . . . . . . . . . . . . . . . . . . . . . . . . . . . . $940.00
**Price:** As above except with silvered, engraved frame . . . . . . . . . . $1,800.00

## BERNARDELLI MODEL 190
**Gauge:** 12 only, 3" chamber.
**Barrel:** 28", 29¾", choke tubes.
**Weight:** 7 lbs., 4 oz.
**Stock:** 14⅜"x1⅜"x2⅜"; European walnut with oil or high-gloss finish.
**Features:** Engraved, coin-finished receiver; single selective trigger; vent. rib. Imported from Italy by Quality Arms, Inc.
**Price:** . . . . . . . . . . . . . . . . . . . . . . . . . . . . . . . . . . . . . . . . . . . . . . $950.00

Baby Bretton

## BABY BRETTON OVER-UNDER SHOTGUN
**Gauge:** 12 or 20, 2¾" chambers.
**Barrel:** 27½" (Cyl.,Imp. Cyl., Mod., Full choke tubes).
**Weight:** About 5 lbs.
**Stock:** Walnut, checkered pistol grip and fore-end, oil finish.
**Features:** Receiver slides open on two guide rods, is locked by a large thumb lever on the right side. Extractors only. Light alloy barrels. Imported from France by Mandall Shooting Supplies and Quality Arms (Deluxe only).
**Price:** . . . . . . . . . . . . . . . . . . . . . . . . . . . . . . . . . . . . . . . . . . . . . . $695.00
**Price:** Deluxe (silvered, engraved receiver, double triggers, 12, 16, 20 ga.) . . . . . . . . . . . . . . . . . . . . . . . . . . . . . . . . . . . . . . . . . . $950.00

BRNO Super

## BRNO SUPER OVER-UNDER SHOTGUN
**Gauge:** 12, 2¾" or 3").
**Barrel:** 27½" (Full & Mod.).
**Weight:** 7 lbs., 4 oz. (Field). **Length:** 44" over-all.
**Stock:** Walnut, with raised cheekpiece.
**Features:** Sidelock action with double safety interceptor sears; double triggers on Field model; automatic selective ejectors; engraved sideplates. Trap and Skeet models available. Imported from Czechoslovakia by Bauska Arms Corp.
**Price:** . . . . . . . . . . . . . . . . . . . . . . . . . . . . . . . . . . . . . . . . . . . . . . $999.00

## BRNO 500 OVER-UNDER SHOTGUN
**Gauge:** 12, 2¾".
**Barrel:** 27½" (Full & Mod.).
**Weight:** 7 lbs. **Length:** 44½" over-all.
**Stock:** Walnut, with raised cheekpiece.
**Features:** Boxlock action with ejectors; double triggers; acid-etched engraving. Imported from Czechoslovakia by Bauska Arms Corp.
**Price:** . . . . . . . . . . . . . . . . . . . . . . . . . . . . . . . . . . . . . . . . . . . . . . $579.00

BRNO ZH 301

## BRNO ZH 301 OVER-UNDER SHOTGUN
**Gauge:** 12, 2¾" or 3".
**Barrel:** 27½" (Full & Mod.).
**Weight:** 7 lbs. **Length:** 44½" over-all.
**Stock:** Walnut.
**Features:** Boxlock action with acid-etch engraving; double triggers. Imported from Czechoslovakia by Bauska Arms Corp.
**Price:** . . . . . . . . . . . . . . . . . . . . . . . . . . . . . . . . . . . . . . . . . . . . . . $439.00

## BRNO CZ 581 OVER-UNDER SHOTGUN
**Gauge:** 12, 2¾" or 3".
**Barrel:** 28" (Full & Mod.).
**Weight:** 7 lbs., 6 oz. **Length:** 45½" over-all.
**Stock:** Turkish walnut with raised cheekpiece.
**Features:** Boxlock action; automatic selective ejectors; automatic safety; sling swivels; vent. rib; double triggers. Imported from Czechoslovakia by Bauska Arms Corp.
**Price:** . . . . . . . . . . . . . . . . . . . . . . . . . . . . . . . . . . . . . . . . . . . . . . $599.00

Browning Citori Field

## Browning Citori O/U Skeet Models

Similar to standard Citori except: 26", 28" (Skeet & Skeet) only; stock dimensions of 14⅜"x1½"x2", fitted with Skeet-style recoil pad; conventional target rib and high post target rib.

**Price:** Grade I Invector (high post rib) .......................... $968.50
**Price:** Grade I, 12 & 20 (high post rib) .......................... $937.50
**Price:** Grade I, 28 & 410 (high post rib) ...................... $978.50
**Price:** Grade III, all gauges (high post rib) .................. $1,303.00
**Price:** Grade VI, all gauges, (high post rib) ................ $1,840.00
**Price:** Four barrel Skeet set — 12, 20, 28, 410 barrels, with case, Grade I only ............................................. $3,140.00
**Price:** Grade III, four-barrel set (high post rib) ................ $3,450.00
**Price:** Grade VI, four-barrel set (high post rib) .............. $3,915.00

## BROWNING CITORI O/U SHOTGUN

**Gauge:** 12, 20, 28 and 410.
**Barrel:** 26", 28" (Mod. & Full, Imp. Cyl. & Mod.), in all gauges, 30" (Mod. & Full, Full & Full) in 12 ga. only. Also offered with Invector choke tubes.
**Weight:** 6 lbs. 8 oz. (26" 410) to 7 lbs. 13 oz. (30" 12-ga.).
**Length:** 43" over-all (26" bbl.).
**Stock:** Dense walnut, hand checkered, full p.g., beavertail fore-end. Field-type recoil pad on 12 ga. field guns and trap and Skeet models.
**Sights:** Medium raised beads, German nickel silver.
**Features:** Barrel selector integral with safety, auto ejectors, three-piece takedown. Imported from Japan by Browning.

**Price:** Grade I, Invector........................................ $875.50
**Price:** Grade I, 12 and 20, fixed chokes........................ $836.50
**Price:** Grade III, Invector, 12 and 20........................... $1,185.00
**Price:** Grade VI, Invector, 12 and 20........................... $1,730.00
**Price:** Grade I, 28 and 410, fixed chokes....................... $865.50
**Price:** Grade III, 28 and 410, fixed chokes..................... $1,303.00
**Price:** Grade VI, 28 and 410, high post rib, fixed chokes......... $1,840.00

Browning Citori Superlight

## Browning Citori O/U Trap Models

Similar to standard Citori except: 12 gauge only; 30", 32" (Full & Full, Imp. Mod. & Full, Mod. & Full), 34" single barrel in Combo Set (Full, Imp. Mod., Mod.), or Invector model; Monte Carlo cheekpiece (14⅜"x1⅜"x1⅜"x2"); fitted with trap-style recoil pad; conventional target rib and high post target rib.

**Price:** Grade I, Invector high post target rib. .............. $978.50
**Price:** Grade I, fixed chokes, high post target rib ............. $937.50
**Price:** Grade III, Invector, high post target rib ............... $1,303.00
**Price:** Grade VI, Invector, high post target rib ............... $1,840.00

## Browning Superlight Citori Over-Under

Similar to the standard Citori except availiable in 12, 20, 28 or 410 with 24", 26" barrels choked Imp. Cyl. & Mod. or 28" choked Mod. & Full. Has straight grip stock, Schnabel fore-end tip. Superlight 12 weighs 6 lbs. 9 oz. (26" barrels); Superlight 20, 5 lbs., 12 oz. (26" barrels). Introduced 1982.

**Price:** Grade I only, 12, 20, 28 or 410............................ $865.50
**Price:** Grade III, Invector, 12 or 20 ............................ $1,185.00
**Price:** Grade III, 28 or 410.................................... $1,303.00
**Price:** Grade VI, Invector, 12 or 20 ............................ $1,730.00
**Price:** Grade VI, 28 or 410 .................................... $1,840.00
**Price:** Grade I Invector .................................... $901.50
**Price:** Grade I Invector, Upland Special (24" bbls.) ............... $901.50

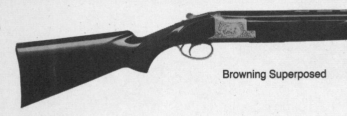

Browning Superposed

## Browning Over-Under Classic & Gold Classic

Same as the standard Superposed 20-ga. with 26" (Imp. Cyl. & Mod.) barrels except has an upland setting of bird dogs, pheasant and quail on the satin grey receiver. Gold Classic has the animals in inlaid gold. Straight grip stock and Schnabel fore-end are of select American walnut. Classic has pearl borders around the checkering and high gloss finish; Gold Classic has fine checkering and decorative carving with oil finish. Delivery scheduled for 1986. Introduced 1984.

**Price:** Over-Under Classic ................................... $2,000.00
**Price:** Over-Under Gold Classic............................... $6,000.00

## BROWNING SUPERPOSED SUPERLIGHT

**Gauge:** 12 & 20, 2¾" chamber.
**Action:** Boxlock, top lever, single selective trigger. Bbl. selector combined with manual tang safety.
**Barrel:** 26½" (Mod. & Full, or Imp. Cyl. & Mod.)
**Weight:** 6⅜ lbs., average
**Stock:** Straight grip (14¼"x1⅝"x2½") hand checkered (fore-end and grip) select walnut.
**Features:** The Superposed is available in four grades. Pigeon, Pointer, Diana grades have silver grayed receivers with hand-engraved game scenes ascending in artistic design with each successive grade. Midas grade has specially blued steel with deeply hand-carved background and 18 carat gold inlaid pheasants and ducks on the 12 ga., smaller game birds on 20 ga. Lightning has full pistol grip stock, Superlight has straight grip. Basically this gives the buyer a wide choice of engraving styles and designs and mechanical options which would place the gun in a "custom" bracket. Options are too numerous to list here and the reader is urged to obtain a copy of the latest Browning catalog for the complete listing. Imported from Belgium by Browning.

**Price:** Pigeon Grade, Lightning and Superlight................. $4,350.00
**Price:** Pointer Grade, Lightning and Superlight................. $5,350,00
**Price:** Diana Grade, Lightning and Superlight................. $6,400.00
**Price:** Midas Grade, Lightning and Superlight................. $7,900.00

## Browning Limited Edition Waterfowl Superposed

Same specs as the Lightning Superposed. Available in 12 ga. only, 28" (Mod. & Full). Limited to 500 guns, the edition number of each gun is inscribed in gold on the bottom of the receiver with "Black Duck" and its scientific name. Sides of receiver have two gold inlayed black ducks, bottom has two, and one on the trigger guard. Receiver is completely engraved and grayed. Stock and fore-end are highly figured dark French walnut with 24 lpi checkering, hand-oiled finish, checkered butt. Comes with form fitted, velvet-lined, black walnut case. Introduced 1983.

**Price:** ................................................. $8,000.00
**Price:** Similar treatment as above except for the Pintail Duck Issue $7,700.00

**CAUTION:** PRICES CHANGE. CHECK AT GUNSHOP.

# SHOTGUNS—OVER-UNDERS

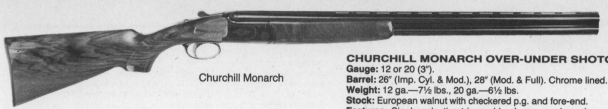

Churchill Monarch

**CHURCHILL MONARCH OVER-UNDER SHOTGUNS**
**Gauge:** 12 or 20 (3").
**Barrel:** 26" (Imp. Cyl. & Mod.), 28" (Mod. & Full). Chrome lined.
**Weight:** 12 ga.—7½ lbs., 20 ga.—6½ lbs.
**Stock:** European walnut with checkered p.g. and fore-end.
**Features:** Single selective trigger; blued, engraved receiver; vent. rib. Introduced 1986. Imported by Kassnar Imports, Inc.
**Price:** ............................................................. **$529.00**

Churchill Windsor Flyweight

**CHURCHILL WINDSOR OVER-UNDER SHOTGUNS**
**Gauge:** 12, 20, 410, 3" chambers.
**Barrel:** 26" (Skeet & Skeet, Imp. Cyl. & Mod.), 28" (Mod. & Full), 30" (Mod. & Full, Full & Full), 12 ga.; 26" (Skeet & Skeet, Imp. Cyl. & Mod.), 28" (Mod. & Full) 20 ga.; 24", 26" (Full & Full), 410 ga.; or 27", 30" ICT choke tubes.
**Stock:** European walnut, checkered pistol grip, oil finish.
**Features:** Boxlock action with silvered, engraved finish; single selective trigger; automatic ejectors on Windsor IV, extractors only on Windsor III. Also available in Flyweight version with 23", 25" barrels, fixed or ICT chokes, straight-grip stock. Imported from Italy by Kassnar. Introduced 1984.
**Price:** Windsor III, fixed chokes ....................... **$665.00 to $745.00**
**Price:** 12 or 20 ga. ICT choke tubes ............................ **$745.00**
**Price:** Windsor IV, fixed chokes ...................... **$784.00 to $864.00**
**Price:** 12 or 20 ga., ICT choke tubes ........................... **$864.00**

## Churchill Regent Over-Under Shotguns
Similar to the Windsor Grade except better wood with oil finish, better engraving; available only in 12 or 20 gauge (2¾" chambers), 27" barrels, with ICT interchangeable choke tubes (Imp. Cyl., Mod., Full). Regent VII has dummy sideplates. Introduced 1984.
**Price:** Regent VII, 12 or 20 ga. ............................... **$1,144.00**
**Price:** Regent VII Flyweight, 23", 25", ICT ..................... **$1,144.00**

## Churchill Regent Trap & Skeet
Similar to the Regent V except Trap has ventilated side rib, Monte Carlo stock, ventilated recoil pad. Oil finished wood, fine checkering, chrome bores. Weight is 8 lbs. Regent Skeet available in 12 or 20 ga., 26" (Skeet & Skeet); oil finished stock measures 14½", 1½" x 2⅜". Both guns have silvered and engraved receivers. Introduced 1984.
**Price:** Regent Trap (30" Imp. Mod. & Full) ...................... **$1,104.00**
**Price:** Regent Skeet, 12 or 20 ga. ............................. **$1,049.00**
**Price:** Regent Trap (30" ICT) ................................. **$1,104.00**

> Consult our Directory pages for the location of firms mentioned.

Daly Field III

**CHARLES DALY FIELD III OVER-UNDER**
**Gauge:** 12 or 20.
**Barrel:** 26" (Imp. Cyl. & Mod.), 28", 30" (Full & Mod.); vent. rib.
**Weight:** About 6¾ lbs.
**Stock:** Select European walnut, checkered pistol grip and fore-end.
**Features:** Single selective trigger; extractors only; blued and engraved frame; chrome lined bores. Imported from Italy by Outdoor Sports Headquarters. Introduced 1984.
**Price:** ............................................................. **$425.00**

## Charles Daly Superior II Over-Under
Similar to the Field II model except single selective trigger, auto ejectors, better wood, silvered receiver, more and better engraving. Same barrel lengths and chokes.
**Price:** ............................................................. **$674.00**
**Price:** 12 ga., 3", 30" (Mod. & Full) ............................ **$710.00**
**Price:** Skeet, 12, 20 ......................................... **$674.00**

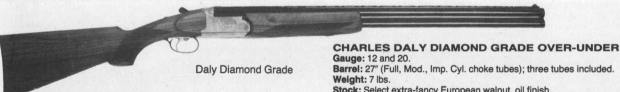

Daly Diamond Grade

**CHARLES DALY DIAMOND GRADE OVER-UNDER**
**Gauge:** 12 and 20.
**Barrel:** 27" (Full, Mod., Imp. Cyl. choke tubes); three tubes included.
**Weight:** 7 lbs.
**Stock:** Select extra-fancy European walnut, oil finish.
**Features:** Boxlock action with single selective competition trigger; silvered and engraved receiver; selective automatic ejectors; 22 lpi checkering on grip and fore-end. Imported from Italy by Outdoor Sports Headquarters. Introduced 1984.
**Price:** ............................................................. **$895.00**

## Charles Daly Presentation Grade Over-Under
Similar to the Diamond Grade except has dummy sideplates, better wood, finish, and extensive game scene engraving on the silvered receiver and sideplates.
**Price:** ............................................................. **$1,165.00**

## Charles Daly Diamond Trap Over-Under
Similar to the Diamond Grade except has competition vent. top and middle ribs, target trigger; oil-finished Monte Carlo stock. Available in 12 gauge, 30" (Full & Imp. Mod.).
**Price:** ............................................................. **$1,030.00**

## Charles Daly Diamond Skeet Over-Under
Similar to the standard Diamond Grade except has oil-finished Skeet stock, competition vent. rib, target trigger. Available in 12 gauge only, 26" (Skeet & Skeet).
**Price:** ............................................................. **$1,030.00**

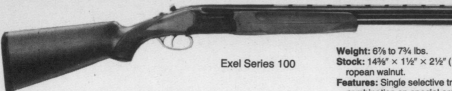

Exel Series 100

## EXEL SERIES 100 OVER-UNDER SHOTGUNS
**Gauge:** 12 only; 2¾", 3" chambers.
**Barrel:** 26" (Imp. Cyl. & Mod., M101), 27⅝" (Imp. Cyl. & Mod., Imp. Cyl. & Imp. Mod., or choke tubes, M102, M104, M105, M106), 29½" (Mod. & Full, choke tubes, M103, M107).

**Weight:** 6⅞ to 7¾ lbs.
**Stock:** 14⅜" × 1½" × 2½" (14½"× 1¼"× 1¾" for Trap M107); checkered European walnut.
**Features:** Single selective trigger, selective auto. ejectors. Virtually any choke combination on special order. M105, 106 come with five choke tubes; M107 Trap has upper barrel Full choke, lower barrel three choke tubes. Made in Spain by Lanber. Imported by Exel Arms.
**Price:** Model 101, 102 . . . . . . . . . . . . . . . . . . . . . . . . . . . . . . . . . . $450.80
**Price:** Model 103 . . . . . . . . . . . . . . . . . . . . . . . . . . . . . . . . . . . . . $466.91
**Price:** Model 104 . . . . . . . . . . . . . . . . . . . . . . . . . . . . . . . . . . . . . $543.29
**Price:** Model 105 . . . . . . . . . . . . . . . . . . . . . . . . . . . . . . . . . . . . . $644.00
**Price:** Model 106, 107 . . . . . . . . . . . . . . . . . . . . . . . . . . . . . . . . . $845.25

Exel Model 305

## EXEL SERIES 300 OVER-UNDER SHOTGUNS
**Gauge:** 12, 20 ga., 2¾" or 3" (20 ga. only) chambers.
**Barrel:** 28" (Full & Mod.), 29" (Full & Mod. or Full & Imp. Mod.).
**Weight:** 6½ to 8 lbs.

**Stock:** 14⅜" x 1⅜" x 2½" (Field), 14⅜" x 1½" x 1⅝" (Monte Carlo). European walnut with checkered grip and fore-end.
**Features:** Boxlock action with silvered and engraved finish; ventilated rib; full pistol grip stock; automatic selective ejectors. Made in Spain by Laurona; imported by Exel Arms of America. Introduced 1984.
**Price:** Model 301, 302 . . . . . . . . . . . . . . . . . . . . . . . . . . . . . . . . . $552.92
**Price:** Model 303, 304 . . . . . . . . . . . . . . . . . . . . . . . . . . . . . . . . . $622.71
**Price:** Model 305, 306, 305A, 306A (choke tubes) . . . . . . . . . . . . . $710.71
**Price:** Model 307, 308 . . . . . . . . . . . . . . . . . . . . . . . . . . . . . . . . . $668.31
**Price:** Model 309, 310 . . . . . . . . . . . . . . . . . . . . . . . . . . . . . . . . . $726.49
**Price:** Model 306T Turkey Gun (matte finish wood, metal, four choke tubes) . . . . . . . . . . . . . . . . . . . . . . . . . . . . . . . . . . . . . . . . . $710.71

## F.I.E./FRANCHI DIAMOND GRADE OVER-UNDER
**Gauge:** 12 ga. only, 2¾" chambers.
**Barrel:** 28" (Mod. & Full).
**Weight:** 6 lbs. 13 oz.
**Stock:** French walnut with cut checkered pistol grip and fore-end.
**Features:** Top tang safety, automatic ejectors, single selective trigger. Chrome plated bores. Decorative scroll on silvered receiver. Introduced 1982. Imported from Italy by F.I.E. Corp.
**Price:** Diamond Grade . . . . . . . . . . . . . . . . . . . . . . . . . . . . . . . $850.00

## F.I.E./Franchi Alcione SL Super Deluxe
Similar to the Falconet Super except has best quality hand engraved, silvered receiver, 24K gold plated trigger, elephant ivory bead front sight. Comes with luggage-type fitted case. Has 14K gold inlay on receiver. Same barrel and chokes as on Falconet Super. Introduced 1982.
**Price:** Alcione Super Deluxe . . . . . . . . . . . . . . . . . . . . . . . . . . . $1,595.00

## F.I.E./MAROCCINI O/U SHOTGUN
**Gauge:** 12 or 20 ga., 3".
**Barrel:** 28" (Mod. & Full); vent. top and middle ribs.
**Weight:** 7¾ lbs.
**Stock:** Walnut, hand checkered.
**Features:** Auto. safety; extractors; double triggers; engraved antique silver receiver. Imported from Italy by F.I.E.
**Price:** . . . . . . . . . . . . . . . . . . . . . . . . . . . . . . . . . . . . . . . . . . $399.95

## ARMI FAMARS FIELD OVER-UNDER
**Gauge:** 12 (2¾"), 20 (3").
**Barrel:** 26", 28", 30" (Mod. & Full).
**Weight:** 6½ to 6¾ lbs.
**Stock:** 14½" x 1½" x 2½". European walnut.
**Sights:** Gold bead front.
**Features:** Boxlock action with single selective trigger; automatic selective trigger. Color case-hardened receiver with engraving. Imported from Italy by Mandall Shooting Supplies.
**Price:** . . . . . . . . . . . . . . . . . . . . . . . . . . . . . . . . . . . . . . . . . . $750.00

## LANBER MODEL 844 OVER-UNDER
**Gauge:** 12, 2¾" or 3".
**Barrel:** 28" (Imp. Cyl. & Imp. Mod.), 30" (Mod. & Full).
**Weight:** About 7 lbs. **Length:** 44⅜" (28" bbl.).
**Stock:** 14¼" x 1⅝" x 2½". European walnut; checkered grip and fore-end.
**Features:** Single non-selective or selective trigger, double triggers on magnum model. Available with or without ejectors. Imported from Spain by Lanber Arms of America, and Exel Arms of America. Introduced 1981.
**Price:** Field, with selective trigger, extractors . . . . . . . . . . . . . . . $450.80
**Price:** As above, 3" Mag., 844 MST . . . . . . . . . . . . . . . . . . . . . . $466.91

## Lanber Model 2004 Over-Under
Same basic specifications as Model 844 except fitted with LanberChoke interchangeable choke tube system. Available in trap, Skeet, pigeon and field models; ejectors only; single selective trigger; no middle rib on target guns (2008, 2009). Imported from Spain by Lanber Arms of America and Exel Arms of America.
**Price:** Model 2004 . . . . . . . . . . . . . . . . . . . . . . . . . . . . . . . . . . $644.00
**Price:** Model 2008 . . . . . . . . . . . . . . . . . . . . . . . . . . . . . . . . . . $845.25
**Price:** Model 2009 (30" bbl.) . . . . . . . . . . . . . . . . . . . . . . . . . . . $845.25

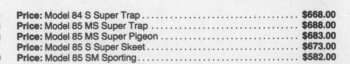

## LAURONA SUPER MODEL OVER-UNDERS
**Gauge:** 12, 20, 2¾" or 3".
**Barrel:** 26" (Multichokes), 28" (Mod. & Full, Imp. Cyl. & Imp. Mod.), 29" (Multichokes or Full).
**Weight:** About 7 lbs.
**Stock:** European walnut. Dimensions vary according to model. Full pistol grip.
**Features:** Boxlock action, silvered with engraving. Automatic selective ejectors; choke tubes available on most models; single selective or twin single triggers; black chrome barrels. Imported from Spain by International Sporting Goods.
**Price:** Model 85 MS Super Game . . . . . . . . . . . . . . . . . . . . . . . . $579.00

Laurona Super Game

**Price:** Model 84 S Super Trap . . . . . . . . . . . . . . . . . . . . . . . . . . . $668.00
**Price:** Model 85 MS Super Trap . . . . . . . . . . . . . . . . . . . . . . . . . . $688.00
**Price:** Model 85 MS Super Pigeon . . . . . . . . . . . . . . . . . . . . . . . . $683.00
**Price:** Model 85 S Super Skeet . . . . . . . . . . . . . . . . . . . . . . . . . . . $673.00
**Price:** Model 85 SM Sporting . . . . . . . . . . . . . . . . . . . . . . . . . . . . $582.00

**CAUTION:** PRICES CHANGE. CHECK AT GUNSHOP.

Ljutic BiGun Super Deluxe

## LJUTIC BIGUN O/U SHOTGUN
**Gauge:** 12 ga only.
**Barrel:** 28″ to 34″; choked to customer specs for live birds, trap, International Trap.
**Weight:** To customers specs.
**Stock:** To customer specs. Oil finish, hand checkered.
**Features:** Custom-made gun. Hollow-milled rib, pull or release trigger, push-button opener in front of trigger guard. From Ljutic Industries.
**Price:** ............................................... $7,995.00
**Price:** BiGun Combo (interchangeable single barrel, two trigger guards, one for single trigger, one for doubles) ........................... $12,995.00
**Price:** Super Deluxe LTD TC BiGun ........................ $9,984.00
**Price:** Extra barrels with screw-in chokes or O/U barrel sets ...... $3,995.00

## Ljutic Four Barrel Skeet Set
Similar to BiGun except comes with matched set of four 28″ barrels in 12, 20, 28 and 410. Ljutic Paternator chokes and barrel are integral. Stock is to customer specs, of American or French walnut with fancy checkering.
**Price:** Four barrel set........................................ $26,995.00

## MAROCCHI AMERICA TARGET SHOTGUN
**Gauge:** 12 or 20, 2¾″ chambers.
**Barrel:** 26″ to 29″ (Skeet), 27″ to 32″ (trap), 32″ (trap mono, choice of top single or high rib under), 30″ (over-under with extra 32″ single).
**Weight:** 7¼ to 8 lbs.
**Stock:** Hand checkered select walnut with left or right-hand palm swell; choice of beavertail or Schnabel fore-end.
**Features:** Designed specifically for American target sports. Frame has medium engraving coverage with choice of three finishes. No extra charge for special stock dimensions or stock finish. Comes with fitted hard shell case. Custom engraving and inlays available. Introduced 1983. Imported from Italy by Marocchi U.S.A.
**Price:** From .................................................. $2,000.00

## MAROCCHI CONTRAST TARGET SHOTGUN
**Gauge:** 12 or 20 ga., 2¾″ chambers.
**Barrel:** 26″ to 29″ (Skeet), 27″ to 32″ trap.
**Weight:** 7¼ to 8 lbs.
**Stock:** Select walnut with hand rubbed wax finish; hand checkered p.g. and fore-end; beavertail or Schnabel fore-end; grip has right or left palm swell.
**Features:** Lightly engraved frame on standard grade, or can be ordered with custom engraving and inlays in choice of three finishes. Optional different buttstock available. Gun comes with fitted hard shell case. Introduced 1983. Imported from Italy by Marocchi U.S.A.
**Price:** From .................................................. $2,000.00

Navy Bird Hunter

## NAVY ARMS MODEL 83/93 BIRD HUNTER O-U
**Gauge:** 12, 20; 3″ chambers.
**Barrel:** 28″ (Imp. Cyl. & Mod., Mod. & Full).

**Weight:** About 7½ lbs.
**Stock:** European walnut, checkered grip and fore-end.
**Sights:** Metal bead front.
**Features:** Boxlock action with double triggers; extractors only; silvered, engraved receiver; vented top and middle ribs. Imported from Italy by Navy Arms. Introduced 1984.
**Price:** Model 83 (extractors).................................... $320.00
**Price:** Model 93 (ejectors) .................................... $389.00

## Navy Arms Model 95/96 Sportsman
Same as the 83/93 Bird Hunter except come with five interchangeable choke tubes. Model 96 has gold-plated single trigger and ejectors.
**Price:** Model 95 (extractors)................................... $415.00
**Price:** Model 96 (ejectors) .................................... $520.00

## NAVY ARMS MODEL 410 O-U SHOTGUN
**Gauge:** 410, 3″ chambers.
**Barrel:** 26″ (Full & Full, Skeet & Skeet).
**Weight:** 6¼ lbs.
**Stock:** European walnut; checkered p.g. and fore-end.
**Features:** Chrome-lined barrels, hard chrome finished receiver with engraving, vent. rib. Single trigger. Imported from Italy by Navy Arms. Introduced 1986.
**Price:** ................................................... $299.00

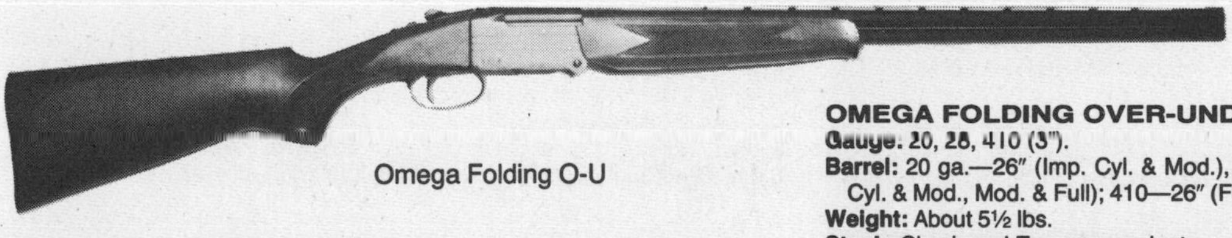

Omega Folding O-U

## OMEGA FOLDING OVER-UNDER SHOTGUNS
**Gauge:** 20, 28, 410 (3″).
**Barrel:** 20 ga.—26″ (Imp. Cyl. & Mod.), 28″ (Mod. & Full); 28 ga.—26″ (Imp. Cyl. & Mod., Mod. & Full); 410—26″ (Full & Full).
**Weight:** About 5½ lbs.
**Stock:** Checkered European walnut.
**Features:** Single trigger; automatic safety; vent rib. Imported from Italy by Kassnar Imports, Inc. Introduced 1986.
**Price:** ........................................ $377.00 to $392.00

## ROTTWEIL OLYMPIA '72 SKEET SHOTGUN
**Gauge:** 12 ga. only.
**Action:** Boxlock.
**Barrel:** 27″ (special Skeet choke), vent. rib. Chromed lined bores, flared chokes.
**Weight:** 7¼ lbs. **Length:** 44½″ over-all.
**Stock:** French walnut, hand checkered, modified beavertail fore-end. Oil finish.
**Sights:** Metal bead front.
**Features:** Inertia-type trigger, interchangeable for any system. Frame and lock milled from steel block. Retracting firing pins are spring mounted. All coil springs. Selective single trigger. Action engraved. Extra barrels are available. Introduced 1976. Imported from West Germany by Dynamit Nobel.
**Price:** ................................................... $2,295.00
**Price:** Trap model (Montreal) is similar to above except has 30″ (Imp. Mod. & Full) bbl., weighs 8 lbs., 48½″ over-all....................... $2,295.00

## ROTTWEIL 72 AMERICAN SKEET
**Gauge:** 12, 2¾″.
**Barrel:** 26¾″ (Skeet & Skeet).
**Weight:** About 7½ lbs.
**Stock:** 14½″ x 1⅜″ x 1⅜″ x ¼″. Select French walnut with satin oil finish; hand checkered grip and fore-end; double ventilated recoil pad.
**Sights:** Plastic front in metal sleeve, center bead.
**Features:** Interchangeable trigger groups with coil springs; interchangeable buttstocks; special .433″ ventilated rib; matte finish silvered receiver with light engraving. Introduced 1978. Imported from West Germany by Dynamit Nobel.
**Price:** ................................................... $2,295.00

# SHOTGUNS—OVER-UNDERS

## ROTTWEIL AMERICAN TRAP COMBO

**Gauge:** 12 ga. only.
**Action:** Boxlock
**Barrel:** Separated o/u, 32" (Imp. Mod. & Full); single is 34" (Full), both with high vent. rib.
**Weight:** 8½ lbs. (o/u and single)
**Stock:** Monte Carlo style, walnut, hand checkered and rubbed. Unfinished stocks available. Double vent. recoil pad. Choice of two dimensions.
**Sights:** Plastic front in metal sleeve, center bead.
**Features:** Interchangeable inertia-type trigger groups. Trigger groups available: single selective; double triggers;, release/pull; release/release selective. Receiver milled from block steel. Chokes are hand honed, test fired and reworked for flawless patterns. All coil springs, engraved action. Introduced 1977. Imported from West Germany by Dynamit Nobel.
**Price:** .................................. **$2,850.00**
**Price:** American Trap O/U (as above except only with o/u bbls.) ... **$2,295.00**

Rottweil American Trap

## ROTTWEIL AAT TRAP GUN

**Gauge:** 12, 2¾".
**Barrel:** 32" (Imp. Mod. & Full).
**Weight:** About 8 lbs.
**Stock:** 14½"x1⅜"x1⅜"x1⅞". Monte Carlo style of selected French walnut with oil finish. Checkered fore-end and p.g.
**Features:** Has infinitely variable point of impact via special muzzle collar. Extra single lower barrels available—32" (Imp. Mod.) or 34" (Full). Special trigger groups—release/release or release/pull—also available. Introduced 1979. From Dynamit Nobel.
**Price:** With single lower barrel .............................. **$2,295.00**
**Price:** Combo (single and o/u barrels) ..................... **$2,295.00**
**Price:** Interchangeable trap trigger group ...................... **$345.00**

Rottweil Field Supreme

## ROTTWEIL FIELD SUPREME O/U SHOTGUN

**Gauge:** 12 only.
**Action:** Boxlock.
**Barrel:** 28" (Mod. & Full, Imp. Cyl. & Imp. Mod.), vent. rib.
**Weight:** 7¼ lbs. **Length:** 47" over-all.
**Stock:** Select French walnut, hand checkered and rubbed. Checkered p.g. and fore-end, plastic buttplate. Unfinished stocks available.
**Sights:** Metal bead front.

**Features:** Removable single trigger assembly with button selector (same trigger options as on American Trap Combo); retracting spring mounted firing pins; engraved action. Extra barrels available. Imported from West Germany by Dynamit Nobol.
**Price:** ......................................................... **$2,295.00**
**Price:** Live Pigeon (28" Mod. & Full) ........................... **$2,295.00**

Royal Model 100

## ROYAL ARMS MODEL 100 OVER-UNDER

**Gauge:** 12 or 20 ga., 2¾" or 3" chambers.
**Action:** Boxlock with Greener cross-bolt.

**Barrel:** 26" (Imp. & Mod.), 28", 30" (Mod. & Full).
**Weight:** 7 lbs.
**Stock:** 14" × 1⅜" × 2¼". European walnut, checkered grip and fore-end.
**Features:** Extractors only; vent. rib; automatic safety; double triggers; silver gray action with arabesque scroll etching. Imported by Royal Arms International. Introduced 1985.
**Price:** ......................................................... **$389.95**
**Price:** Model 100AE (3", 12 ga. only, single trigger, selective auto ejectors) ................................................. **$429.95**

Ruger 12 Ga. Red Label

## RUGER "RED LABEL" O/U SHOTGUN

**Gauge:** 20 and 12, 3" chambers.
**Barrel:** 20 ga.—26", 28" (Skeet & Skeet, Imp. Cyl. & Mod.), 28" (Imp. Cyl. & Mod., Full & Mod.); 12 ga.—26", 28" (Skeet & Skeet, Imp. Cyl. & Mod., Full & Mod.).

**Weight:** About 7 lbs. (20 ga.), 7½ lbs. (12 ga.). **Length:** 43" (26" barrels).
**Stock:** 14"x1½"x2½". Straight grain American walnut. Checkered p.g. and fore-end, rubber recoil pad.
**Features:** Automatic safety/barrel selector, stainless steel trigger. Patented barrel side spacers may be removed if desired. 20 ga. available in blued steel only, 12 ga. available only with stainless receiver. 20 ga. introduced 1977; 12 ga. introduced 1982.
**Price:** 20 ga., blued ........................................... **$798.00**
**Price:** 12 ga., stainless receiver ............................... **$798.00**

## SENATOR FOLDING O/U SHOTGUNS

**Gauge:** 12, 20, 410, 3".
**Barrel:** 26" (410 only), 28" (Full & Mod.).
**Weight:** 7 lbs. (12 ga.)
**Stock:** European walnut.
**Features:** Engraved boxlock action with under-lever cocking/opening lever. Blued barrels with ventilated top and middle ribs. Introduced 1986. Imported from Italy by Excam.
**Price:** 12, 20 or 410 ga. ....................................... **$275.00**

Senator Folding O-U

**CAUTION:** PRICES CHANGE. CHECK AT GUNSHOP.

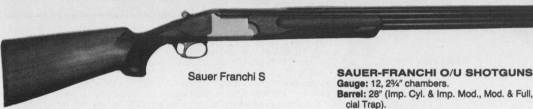

Sauer Franchi S

## SOVEREIGN OVER-UNDER SHOTGUN
**Gauge:** 12 or 20, 2¾" chambers.
**Barrel:** 28" (Mod. & Full).
**Weight:** 7 lbs. (12 ga.), 6¾ lbs. (20 ga.).
**Stock:** 14⅝"x1⅜"x2¼". European walnut with checkered p.g. and fore-end.
**Features:** Chrome action with engraving; ventilated rib; double triggers. Two frame sizes for each gauge. Introduced 1986. Imported from Italy by Southern Gun & Tackle.
**Price:** ........................................... $285.95

## SAUER-FRANCHI O/U SHOTGUNS
**Gauge:** 12, 2¾" chambers.
**Barrel:** 28" (Imp. Cyl. & Imp. Mod., Mod. & Full, Skeet 1 & Skeet 2); 29" (Special Trap).
**Weight:** 7½ lbs. **Length:** 45⅓" over-all.
**Stock:** European walnut.
**Features:** Blued frame on Standard model, others with silvered, engraved frames; single selective trigger; selective auto. ejectors; vent. rib. Introduced in U.S. 1986. Imported from West Germany by SIGARMS.
**Price:** Standard, about .......................... $785.00
**Price:** Regent, about ............................ $825.00
**Price:** Favorit, about ............................ $875.00
**Price:** Diplomat, about .......................... $1,520.00
**Price:** Sporting S, Trap, Skeet models, about ... $1,375.00

IGA Over-Under

## STOEGER/IGA OVER-UNDER SHOTGUN
**Gauge:** 12, 20, 3" chambers.
**Barrel:** 26" (Full & Full, Imp. Cyl. & Mod.), 28" (Mod. & Full).
**Weight:** 6¾ to 7 lbs.
**Stock:** 14½" x 1½" x 2½". Oil finished hardwood with checkered pistol grip and fore-end.
**Features:** Manual safety, double triggers, extractors only, ventilated top rib. Introduced 1983. Imported from Brazil by Stoeger Industries.
**Price:** Double triggers ........................... $296.95
**Price:** Single trigger ............................ $341.95

## TECHNI-MEC MODEL SPL 640 FOLDING O-U
**Gauge:** 12, 16, 20, 28, (2¾") 410 (3").
**Barrel:** 26" (Mod. & Full).
**Weight:** 5½ lbs.
**Stock:** European walnut.
**Features:** Gun folds in half for storage, transportation. Chrome lined barrels; ventilated rib; photo-engraved silvered receiver. Imported from Italy by L. Joseph Rahn. Introduced 1984.
**Price:** Double triggers ........................... $240.00
**Price:** Single trigger ............................ $256.00

## TECHNI-MEC MODEL SR 692 EM OVER-UNDER
**Gauge:** 12, 16, 20, 2¾" or 3".
**Barrel:** 26", 28", 30" (Mod., Full, Imp. Cyl., Cyl.).
**Weight:** 6½ lbs.
**Stock:** 14½" x 1½" x 2½". European walnut with checkered grip and fore-end.
**Features:** Boxlock action with dummy sideplates, fine game scene engraving; single selective trigger; automatic ejectors available. Imported from Italy by L. Joseph Rahn. Introduced 1984.
**Price:** ........................................... $550.00

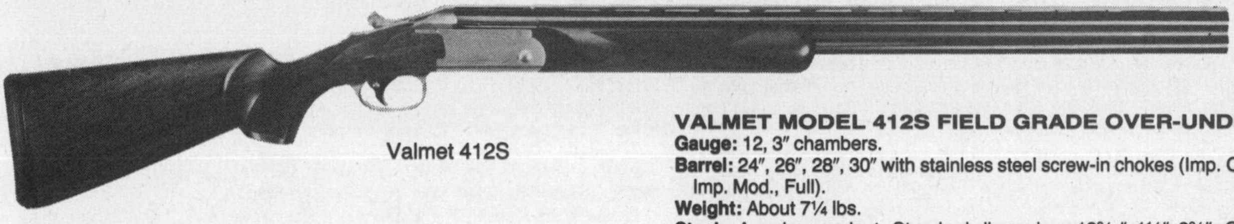

Valmet 412S

## WEATHERBY ORION O/U SHOTGUN
**Gauge:** 12 or 20 ga. (3" chambers; 2¾" on Trap gun).
**Action:** Boxlock (simulated side-lock).
**Barrel:** 12 ga. 30" (Full & Mod.), 28" (Full & Mod., Mod. & Imp. Cyl.), 26" (Mod. & Imp. Cyl., Skeet & Skeet); 20 ga. 28" (Full & Mod., Mod. & Imp. Cyl.), 26" (Mod. & Imp. Cyl., Skeet & Skeet).
**Weight:** 7 lbs., 8 oz. (12 ga. 26").
**Stock:** American walnut, checkered p.g. and fore-end. Rubber recoil pad. Dimensions for field and Skeet models, 20 ga. 14"x1½"x2½".
**Features:** Selective auto ejectors, single selective mechanical trigger. Top tang safety, Greener cross-bolt. Introduced 1982. Imported from Japan by Weatherby.
**Price:** Skeet, fixed choke ......................... $859.95
**Price:** 12 ga. Trap, fixed choke .................. $899.95
**Price:** 12 or 20 ga., IMC Multi-Choke Field ....... $849.95
**Price:** IMC Multi-Choke Trap ...................... $899.95
**Price:** Extra IMC choke tubes ..................... $15.00

## VALMET MODEL 412S FIELD GRADE OVER-UNDER
**Gauge:** 12, 3" chambers.
**Barrel:** 24", 26", 28", 30" with stainless steel screw-in chokes (Imp. Cyl., Mod., Imp. Mod., Full).
**Weight:** About 7¼ lbs.
**Stock:** American walnut. Standard dimensions-13⅞₁₀"x1½"x2⅖". Checkered p.g. and fore-end.
**Features:** Free interchangeability of barrels, stocks and fore-ends into double rifle model, combination gun, etc. Barrel selector in trigger; auto. top tang safety; barrel cocking indicators. Introduced 1980. Imported from Finland by Valmet.
**Price:** Model 412S (ejectors) ..................... $799.00
**Price:** Extra barrels with choke tubes ............ $399.00

## Valmet 412 ST Target Series
Both trap and Skeet versions of the 412S gun. Stocks are drilled for insertion of a recoil reducer; quick-change butt stocks; beavertail fore-end; Monte Carlo stock has wider comb and double palm swell; trap stock has Pachmayr pad; wide trigger; barrel indicators near the tang. High vent rib, stepped and tapered on trap gun. Trap guns have choke tubes, 32", 34" barrel (mono), 30", 32" (o/u); weight 9 lbs. Skeet has 28" barrels (12 ga.); weight 8 lbs. Skeet gun also has choke tubes. Introduced 1985.
**Price:** Trap .................................... $899.00
**Price:** Skeet ................................... $899.00
**Price:** Extra barrels ........................... $449.00

Weatherby Athena

## WEATHERBY ATHENA O/U SHOTGUN
**Gauge:** 12 or 20 ga. (3″ chambers; 2¾″ on Trap gun).
**Action:** Boxlock (simulated side-lock) top lever break-open. Selective auto ejectors, single selective trigger (selector inside trigger guard).
**Barrel:** Fixed choke, 12 or 20 ga. — 26″ (Mod. & Imp. Cyl., Skeet & Skeet), 28″ (Mod. & Imp. Cyl., Full & Mod.), 30″ (Full & Mod., Full & Imp. Mod.), 32″ Trap (Full & Imp. Mod.). IMC Multi-Choke, 12 ga. only — 26″ (Mod., Imp. Cyl., Skeet), 28″ (Full, Mod., Imp. Cyl.), 30″ (Full, Mod., Imp. Mod.).
**Weight:** 12 ga. 7⅜ lbs., 20 ga. 6⅞ lbs.
**Stock:** American walnut, checkered p.g. and fore-end (14¼″x1½″x2½″).
**Features:** Mechanically operated trigger. Top tang safety, Greener cross-bolt, fully engraved receiver, recoil pad installed. IMC models furnished with three interchangeable flush-fitting choke tubes. Imported from Japan by Weatherby. Introduced 1982.
**Price:** Skeet, fixed choke.................................... $1,329.95
**Price:** 12 or 20 ga., IMC Multi-Choke Field ...................... $1,349.95
**Price:** IMC Multi-Choke Trap ................................ $1,369.00
**Price:** Extra IMC Choke tubes .................................... $15.00

Winchester 101 Field

## WINCHESTER 101 WINCHOKE O/U FIELD GUN
**Gauge:** 12, or 20, 3″ chambers.
**Action:** Top lever, break open. Manual safety combined with bbl. selector at top of receiver tang.
**Barrel:** 27″, Winchoke interchangeable choke tubes.
**Weight:** 12 ga. 7 lbs. Others 6½ lbs. **Length:** 44¾″ over-all.
**Stock:** 14″x1½″x2½″. Checkered walnut p.g. and fore-end; fluted comb.
**Features:** Single selective trigger, auto ejectors. Hand engraved satin gray receiver. Comes with hard gun case. Manufactured in and imported from Japan by Winchester Group, Olin Corp.
**Price:** .......................................................... $1,225.00
**Price:** Two Barrel Set (12 and 20) .............................. $2,200.00

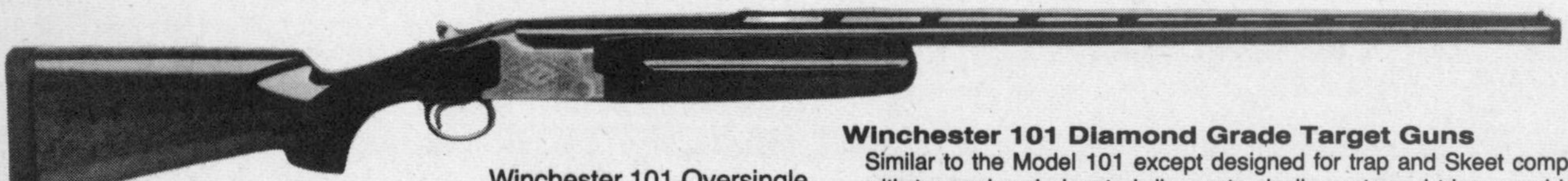

## Winchester Model 101 Waterfowl Winchoke
Same as Model 101 Field Grade except in 12 ga. only, 3″ chambers, 30″ or 32″ barrels. Comes with four Winchoke tubes: Mod., Imp. Mod., Full, Extra-Full. Blued receiver with hand etching and engraving. Introduced 1981. Manufactured in and imported from Japan by Winchester Group, Olin Corp.
**Price:** ......................................................... $1,225.00

Winchester 101 Oversingle

## WINCHESTER MODEL 501 GRAND EUROPEAN O-U
**Gauge:** 12 ga. (Trap), 12 and 20 ga. (Skeet). 2¾″ chambers.
**Barrel:** 27″ (Skeet & Skeet), 30″ (Imp. Mod. & Full), 32″ (Imp. Mod. & Full).
**Weight:** 7½ lbs. (Skeet), 8½ lbs. (Trap) **Length:** 47⅛″ over-all (30″ barrel).
**Stock:** 14⅛″x1½″x2½″ (Skeet). Full fancy walnut, hand-rubbed oil finish.
**Features:** Silvered, engraved receiver; engine-turned breech interior. Slide-button selector/safety, selective auto. ejectors. Chrome bores, tapered vent. rib. Trap gun has Monte Carlo or regular stock, recoil pad; Skeet gun has rosewood buttplate. Introduced 1981. Manufactured in and imported from Japan by Winchester Group, Olin Corp.
**Price:** Trap or Skeet ................................... $1,720.00
**Price:** Grand European Featherweight 20 ga., 25½″ (Imp. Cyl. & Mod.) .................................................. $1,720.00

## Winchester 101 Diamond Grade Target Guns
Similar to the Model 101 except designed for trap and Skeet competition, with tapered and elevated rib, anatomically contoured trigger and internationally-dimensioned stock. Receiver has deep-etched diamond-pattern engraving. Skeet guns available in 12, 20, 28 and 410 with ventilated muzzles to reduce recoil. Trap guns in 12 ga. only; over-under, combination and single-barrel configurations in a variety of barrel lengths with Winchoke system. Straight or Monte Carlo stocks available. Introduced 1982. Manufactured in and imported from Japan by Winchester Group, Olin Corp.
**Price:** Trap, o/u, standard and Monte Carlo, 30″, 32″ ............. $1,720.00
**Price:** Trap, single barrel, 32″ or 34″ .......................... $1,820.00
**Price:** Trap, o/u-single bbl. combo sets ......................... $2,775.00
**Price:** Skeet, 12 and 20 ...................................... $1,720.00
**Price:** Skeet, 28 and 410...................................... $1,720.00
**Price:** Four barrel Skeet set (12, 20, 28, 410) .................. $4,600.00
**Price:** Trap Oversingle, 34″, Monte Carlo or std. stock .......... $1,900.00

## Winchester Model 101 Pigeon Grade
Similar to the Model 101 Field except comes in two styles: Lightweight-Winchoke (12 or 20 ga., six choke tubes for 12 ga., four for 20, 28 ga., 27″, 28″), Featherweight (12 or 20 ga., Imp. Cyl. & Mod., 25½″), all with 3″ chambers. Vent. rib barrel with middle bead, fancy American walnut. Featherweight has English-style stock. Hard case included. Introduced 1983. Manufactured in and imported from Japan by Winchester Group, Olin Corp.
**Price:** Featherweight ......................................... $1,580.00
**Price:** Lightweight-Winchoke ................................. $1,675.00

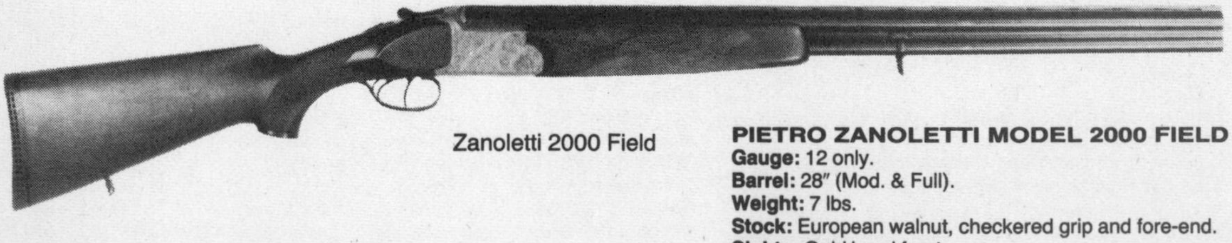

Consult our Directory pages for the location of firms mentioned.

Zanoletti 2000 Field

## PIETRO ZANOLETTI MODEL 2000 FIELD O-U
**Gauge:** 12 only.
**Barrel:** 28″ (Mod. & Full).
**Weight:** 7 lbs.
**Stock:** European walnut, checkered grip and fore-end.
**Sights:** Gold bead front.
**Features:** Boxlock action with auto ejectors, double triggers; engraved receiver. Imported from Italy by Mandall Shooting Supplies. Introduced 1984.
**Price:** ........................................................... $695.00

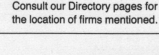

# SHOTGUNS—OVER-UNDERS

Zoli Angel

## A. ZOLI DELFINO S.P. O/U
**Gauge:** 12 or 20 (3" chambers).
**Barrel:** 28" (Mod. & Full); vent. rib.
**Weight:** 5½ lbs.
**Stock:** Walnut. Hand checkered p.g. and fore-end; cheekpiece.
**Features:** Color case hardened receiver with light engraving; chrome lined barrels; automatic sliding safety; double triggers; ejectors. From Mandall Shooting Supplies.
**Price:** . . . . . . . . . . . . . . . . . . . . . . . . . . . . . . . . $795.00

## A. ZOLI MODEL ANGEL FIELD GRADE O-U
**Gauge:** 12, 20.
**Barrel:** 26", 28", 30" (Mod. & Full).
**Weight:** About 7½ lbs.
**Stock:** Straight grained walnut with checkered grip and fore-end.
**Sights:** Gold bead front.
**Features:** Boxlock action with single selective trigger, auto ejectors; extra-wide vent. top rib. Imported from Italy by Mandall Shooting Supplies.
**Price:** . . . . . . . . . . . . . . . . . . . . . . . . . . . . . . . . $895.00
**Price:** Condor model . . . . . . . . . . . . . . . . . . . . . . . . . $895.00

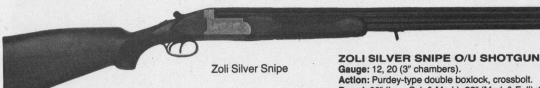

Zoli Silver Snipe

## Zoli Golden Snipe O/U Shotgun
Same as Silver Snipe except selective auto. ejectors.
**Price:** Field . . . . . . . . . . . . . . . . . . . . . . . . . . . . . . . . $895.00

## ZOLI SILVER SNIPE O/U SHOTGUN
**Gauge:** 12, 20 (3" chambers).
**Action:** Purdey-type double boxlock, crossbolt.
**Barrel:** 26" (Imp. Cyl. & Mod.), 28" (Mod. & Full), 30", 12 only (Mod. & Full); 26" Skeet (Skeet & Skeet), 30" Trap (Full & Full).
**Weight:** 6½ lbs. (12 ga.).
**Stock:** Hand checkered p.g. and fore-end, European walnut.
**Features:** Auto. safety (exc. Trap and Skeet), vent rib, single trigger, chrome bores. Imported from Italy by Mandall Shooting Supplies.
**Price:** Field . . . . . . . . . . . . . . . . . . . . . . . . . . . . . . . . $795.00

# SHOTGUNS—SIDE-BY-SIDES

BGJ 10 Gauge

## ARMSPORT 1050 SIDE-BY-SIDE SHOTGUNS
**Gauge:** 12, 20, 410, 3" chambers.
**Barrel:** 12 ga.—28" (Mod. & Full), 20 ga., 410—26" (Imp. Cyl. & Mod.)
**Weight:** 5¾-6 lbs.
**Stock:** European walnut
**Features:** Double triggers; extractors; silvered, engraved receiver. Introduced 1986. Imported from Italy by Armsport.
**Price:** 12, 20 ga . . . . . . . . . . . . . . . . . . . . . . . . . . . . . $399.95
**Price:** 410 . . . . . . . . . . . . . . . . . . . . . . . . . . . . . . . . . $425.00

## BGJ 10 GAUGE MAGNUM SHOTGUN
**Gauge:** 10 ga. (3½" chambers).
**Action:** Boxlock.
**Barrel:** 32" (Full).
**Weight:** 11 lbs.
**Stock:** 14½"x1½"x2⅝". European walnut, checkered at p.g. and fore-end.
**Features:** Double triggers; color hardened action, rest blued. Front and center metal beads on matted rib; ventilated rubber recoil pad. Fore-end release has positive Purdey-type mechanism. Imported from Spain by Mandall Shooting Supplies.
**Price:** . . . . . . . . . . . . . . . . . . . . . . . . . . . . . . . . . . $500.00

## Bernardelli Series Roma Shotguns
Similar to the Series S. Uberto models except with dummy sideplates to simulate sidelock action. Same gauges and specifications apply.

|  | |
|---|---|
| Price: Roma 3 | $1,154.00 to $1,113.92 |
| Price: As above with ejectors | $1,263.00 to $1,243.72 |
| Price: Roma 4 | $1,314.00 to $1,273.22 |
| Price: As above with ejectors | $1,423.00 to $1,401.84 |
| Price: Roma 6 | $1,562.00 to $1,552.88 |
| Price: As above with ejectors | $1,675.00 to $1,682.88 |

## Bernardelli System Holland H. Side-by-Side
Similar to the Las Palomas model with true sidelock action. Available in 12 gauge only, reinforced breech, three round Purdey locks, automatic ejectors, folding right trigger. Model VB Liscio has color case hardened receiver and sideplates with light engraving, VB and VB Tipo Lusso are silvered and engraved.

|  | |
|---|---|
| Price: VB Liscio | $5,700.00 to $5,596.74 |
| Price: VB | $6,400.00 to $6,485.28 |
| Price: VB Tipo Lusso | $7,700.00 to $7,589.76 |

## BERNARDELLI SERIES S. UBERTO DOUBLES
**Gauge:** 12, 16, 20, 28; 2¾", or 3" chambers.
**Barrel:** 25⅝", 26¾", 28", 29⅛" (Mod. & Full).
**Weight:** 6 to 6½ lbs.
**Stock:** 14³⁄₁₆" x 2⅜" x 1⁹⁄₁₆" standard dimensions. Select walnut with hand checkering.
**Features:** Anson & Deeley boxlock action with Purdey locks, choice of extractors or ejectors. Uberto 1 has color case hardened receiver, Uberto 2 and F.S. silvered and differ in amount and quality of engraving. Custom options available. Prices vary with importer and are shown respectively. Imported from Italy by Armes De Chasse and Quality Arms.

|  | |
|---|---|
| Price: S. Uberto 1 | $1,081.00 to $1,014.80 |
| Price: As above with ejectors | $1,190.00 to $1,144.60 |
| Price: S. Uberto 2 | $1,130.00 to $1,063.18 |
| Price: As above with ejectors | $1,239.00 to $1,191.80 |
| Price: S. Uberto F.S. | $1,300.00 to $1,243.72 |
| Price: As above with ejectors | $1,409.00 to $1,372.52 |

# SHOTGUNS—SIDE-BY-SIDES

Beretta Model 627 EL

## BERETTA 625 SERIES SIDE-BY-SIDES
**Gauge:** 12 (2¾″), 20 (3″).
**Action:** Beretta patent boxlock; double underlugs and bolts.
**Barrel:** 12 ga.—26″ (Imp. Cyl. & Mod.), 28″ (Mod. & Full); 20 ga.—26″ (Imp. Cyl. & Mod.), 28″ (Mod. & Full).

**Weight:** 6 lbs. 10 oz. (12 ga.).
**Stock:** 14⅛″x1⁹⁄₁₆″x2⁹⁄₁₆″. "English" straight-type or pistol grip, hand checkered European walnut.
**Features:** Coil springs throughout action; double triggers (front is hinged); automatic safety; extractors. Concave matted barrel rib. Introduced 1985. Imported by Beretta U.S.A. Corp.
**Price:** M625, 12 or 20 ga. .................................... **$935.00**
**Price:** M626, 12 or 20 ga. .................................... **$1,225.00**
**Price:** M627, from .......................................... **$2,300.00**

## BRNO ZP149, ZP349 SIDE-BY-SIDE
**Gauge:** 12, 2¾″ or 3″.
**Barrel:** 28½ (Full & Mod.).
**Weight:** 7 lbs., 3 oz. **Length:** 45″ over-all.
**Stock:** Turkish or Yugoslavian walnut with raised checkpiece.
**Features:** Sidelock action with double triggers, auto ejectors, barrel indicators, auto safety. Imported from Czechoslovakia by Bauska Arms Corp.
**Price:** ZP 149, standard .................................. **$489.00**
**Price:** As above, engraved ............................... **$509.00**
**Price:** ZP 349, extractors, standard ..................... **$519.00**
**Price:** As above, engraved .............................. **$539.00**

BRNO ZP 149

Browning B-SS

## Browning B-SS Sidelock
Similar to the B-SS Sporter except gun is a true sidelock. Receiver, fore-end iron, trigger guard, top lever, and tang are all satin grey with rosettes and scroll work. Straight grip stock with checkered butt of French walnut. Double triggers, automatic safety and cocking indicator. Introduced 1984.
**Price:** 12 or 20 gauge ....................................... **$1,627.50**

## BROWNING B-SS
**Gauge:** 12, 20 (3″).
**Action:** Top lever break-open action, top tang safety, single trigger.
**Barrel:** 26″ (Mod. and Full or Imp. Cyl. and Mod.), 28″ (Mod. and Full), 30″ (Full & Full or Mod. & Full).
**Weight:** 6¾ lbs. (26″ bbl., 20 ga.); 7½ lbs. (30″ bbl., 12 ga.).
**Stock:** 14¼″x1⅝″x2½″. French walnut, hand checkered. Full p.g., full beavertail fore-end.
**Features:** Automatic safety, automatic ejectors. Hand engraved receiver, mechanical single selective trigger with barrel selector in rear of trigger guard. Imported from Japan by Browning.
**Price:** Grade I, 12 or 20 ga. ............................... **$775.00**

Browning B-SS Sporter

## Browning B-SS Sporter
Similar to standard B-SS except has straight-grip stock and full beavertail fore-end with traditional oil finish. Introduced 1977.
**Price:** Grade I, 12 or 20 ga. ............................... **$775.00**

Churchill Windsor I

## Churchill Regent Side-by-Side Shotguns
Similar to the Windsor Grade except fancy walnut, better checkering and engraving; tapered Churchill rib; 25″ (Imp. Cyl. & Mod.) or 28″ (Mod. & Full) barrels only; 12 or 20 ga., 2¾″ only. Regent VI is full sidelock, with double triggers, automatic selective ejectors, straight English-style stock and splinter fore-end. Imported from Spain by Kassnar.Introduced 1984.
**Price:** Regent VI. ........................................... **$945.00**
**Price:** Regent VI, ICT. ..................................... **$1,084.00**

## CHURCHILL WINDSOR SIDE-BY-SIDE SHOTGUNS
**Gauge:** 10 (3½″), 12, 16, 20, 28, 410 (2¾″ 16 ga., 3″ others).
**Barrel:** 24″ (Mod. & Full), 410 and 20 ga.; 26″ (Imp. Cyl. & Mod., Mod. & Full); 28″ (Mod. & Full, Skeet & Skeet — 28 ga.); 30″ (Full & Full, Mod. & Full); 32″ (Full & Full — 10 ga.).
**Weight:** About 7½ lbs. (12 ga.).
**Stock:** Hand checkered European walnut with rubber butt pad.
**Features:** Anson & Deeley boxlock action with silvered and engraved finish; automatic top tang safety; double triggers; beavertail fore-end. Windsor I with extractors only; Windsor II has selective automatic ejectors. Also available in Flyweight versions, 23″, 25″, fixed or ICT chokes, straight stock. ICT choke tubes also available on Windsor. Imported from Spain by Kassnar. Introduced 1984.
**Price:** Windor I, 10 ga. ...................................... **$599.00**
**Price:** Windsor I, 12 through 410 ga. ................. **$449.00** to **$465.00**
**Price:** Windsor II, 12 or 20 ga. only. .......................... **$665.00**
**Price:** Windsor II, ICT ...................................... **$729.00**

**CAUTION:** PRICES CHANGE. CHECK AT GUNSHOP.

Hermanos Model 150

## DUMOULIN "LIEGE" MODEL DOUBLE
**Gauge:** 12, 16, 20, 28, 2¾", or 3" chambers.
**Barrel:** 26" to 32", choked to customer specs
**Weight:** 6 4 lbs
**Stock:** Circassian or French walnut, to customer specs.
**Features:** Anson & Deeley boxlock (or sidelock) action. Essentially a custom gun. Imported from Belgium by Midwest Gun Sport.
**Price:** From . . . . . . . . . . . . . . . . . . . . . . . . . . . . . . . . . . . . . $5,300.00

## CRUCELEGUI HERMANOS MODEL 150 DOUBLE
**Gauge:** 12, 16 or 20 (2¾" chambers).
**Action:** Greener triple crossbolt.
**Barrel:** 20", 26", 28", 30", 32" (Cyl. & Cyl., Full & Full, Mod. & Full, Mod. & Imp. Cyl., Imp. Cyl. & Full, Mod. & Mod.).
**Weight:** 5 to 7¼ lbs.
**Stock:** Hand checkered walnut, beavertail fore-end.
**Features:** Exposed hammers; double triggers; color case hardened receiver; sling swivels; chrome lined bores. Imported from Spain by Mandall Shooting Supplies.
**Price:** . . . . . . . . . . . . . . . . . . . . . . . . . . . . . . . . . . . . . . . . . $399.95
**Price:** Model 225 (hammerless version) . . . . . . . . . . . . . . . . . . . . . . $399.95

Exel Series 200

## Exel Models 207, 208, 209, 210 Doubles
Similar to the Models 201, 202, 203 except full sidelock action. Models 207, 208, 209 in 12 ga., 2¾" chambers; 28" (Mod. & Full) for 207 and 208, 26" (Imp. Cyl. & Mod.) for 209, 20 ga., 3", 27" (Mod. & Full) for 210. Selective ejectors, trigger, stock and frame finish to customer specs.
**Price:** Model 207 . . . . . . . . . . . . . . . . . . . . . . . . . . . . . . . $611.83
**Price:** Model 208, 209, 210 . . . . . . . . . . . . . . . . . . . . . . . . $671.52
**Price:** Models 211, 212, 213 (similar to above but with better wood, engraving) . . . . . . . . . . . . . . . . . . . . . . . . . . . . . . . . . . . . . . . $3,100.00
**Price:** Model 281, 281A (28 ga., 26" Mod. & Full, Imp. Cyl. & Mod.) . $471.79
**Price:** Model 240, 240A (410, 26" Full & Mod., Imp. Cyl. & Mod.) . . . . $471.79

## EXEL MODELS 201, 202, 203 DOUBLES
**Gauge:** 12, 2¾" chambers (M201, 202); 20, 3" chambers (M203, M203A).
**Barrel:** Model 201 — 28" (Full & Mod.); Model 202 — 26" (Imp. Cyl. & Mod.); Model 203 — 27" (Full & Mod.); Model 203A—26" (Imp. Cyl. & Mod.).
**Weight:** 6½-7 lbs.
**Stock:** 14⅜" x 1½" x 2½". Walnut, straight or full pistol grip.
**Sights:** Metal bead front.
**Features:** Boxlock action with color case hardened finish; double triggers; extractors only; high matted rib; hand checkered stock and fore-end. Made in Spain by Ugartechea; imported by Exel Arms of America.
**Price:** . . . . . . . . . . . . . . . . . . . . . . . . . . . . . . . . . . . . . . . . . $428.91

## Exel Models 204, 205, 206 Doubles
Similar to Models 201, 202, 203 except with silvered and engraved receiver, automatic selective ejectors, single or double triggers. Others specs are the same.
**Price:** . . . . . . . . . . . . . . . . . . . . . . . . . . . . . . . . . . . . . . . . . $626.76

Ferlib Model FVII

## FERLIB MODEL F VII DOUBLE SHOTGUN
**Gauge:** 12, 20, 28, 410.
**Barrel:** 25" to 28".
**Weight:** 5½ lbs. (20 ga.).
**Stock:** Oil-finished walnut, checkered straight grip and fore-end.
**Features:** Boxlock action with fine scroll engraved, silvered receiver. Double triggers standard. Introduced 1983. Imported from Italy by Wm. Larkin Moore and Quality Arms, Inc..
**Price:** 12 or 20 ga. . . . . . . . . . . . . . . . . . . . . . . . . . . . . . . . $3,600.00
**Price:** 28 or 410 ga. . . . . . . . . . . . . . . . . . . . . . . . . . . . . . . $3,550.00
**Price:** Extra for single trigger, beavertail fore-end . . . . . . . . . . . . . . $310.00

Garbi Model 51B

## GARBI MODEL 51 SIDE-BY-SIDE
**Gauge:** 12, 16, 20 (2¾" chambers).
**Barrel:** 28" (Mod. & Full)
**Weight:** 5½ to 6½ lbs.
**Stock:** Walnut, to customer specs.
**Features:** Boxlock action; hand-engraved receiver; hand-checkered stock and fore-end; double triggers; extractors. Introduced 1980. Imported from Spain by L. Joseph Rahn, Inc.
**Price:** Model 51A, 12 ga., extractors . . . . . . . . . . . . . . . . . . . . . $540.00
**Price:** Model 51B, 12, 16, 20 ga., ejectors. . . . . . . . . . . . . . . . . . $890.00

Garbi Model 60

## GARBI MODEL 60 SIDE-BY-SIDE
**Gauge:** 12, 16, 20 (2¾" chambers).
**Barrel:** 26", 28", 30"; choked to customers specs.
**Weight:** 5½ to 6½ lbs.
**Stock:** Select walnut. Dimensions to customer specs.
**Features:** Sidelock action. Scroll engraving on receiver. Hand checkered stock. Double triggers. Extractors. Imported from Spain by L. Joseph Rahn, Inc.
**Price:** Model 60A, 12 ga. only . . . . . . . . . . . . . . . . . . . . . . . . . . $820.00
**Price:** With demi-bloc barrels and ejectors, 12, 16, 20 ga. . . . . . . . . $1,195.00

Garbi Model 71

## Garbi Model 62
Similar to Model 60 except choked Mod. & Full, plain receiver with engraved border, demi-bloc barrels, gas exhaust valves, jointed triggers, extractors. Imported from Spain by L. Joseph Rahn.
**Price:** Model 62A, 12 ga., only.................... **$870.00**
**Price:** Model 62B, 12, 16, 20 ga., ejectors .................... **$1,170.00**

## GARBI MODEL 100 DOUBLE
**Gauge:** 12, 16, 20.
**Barrel:** 26″, 28″, choked to customer specs.
**Weight:** 5½ to 7½ lbs.
**Stock:** 14½x2¼″x1½″. European walnut. Straight grip, checkered butt, classic fore-end.
**Features:** Sidelock action, automatic ejectors, double triggers standard. Color case-hardened action, coin finish optional. Single trigger; beavertail fore-end, etc. optional. Five other models are available. Imported from Spain by Wm. Larkin Moore.
**Price:** From .................... **$2,100.00**

## Garbi Model 101 Side-by-Side
Similar to the Garbi Model 100 except is available with optional level, file-cut, Churchill or ventilated top rib, and in a 12-ga. pigeon or wildfowl gun. Has Continental-style floral and scroll engraving, select walnut stock. Better overall quality than the Model 100. Imported from Spain by Wm. Larkin Moore.
**Price:** .................... **$3,500.00**

## Garbi Model 200 Side-by-Side
Similar to the Garbi Model 100 except has barrels of nickel-chrome steel, heavy duty locks, magnum proofed. Very fine continental-style floral and scroll engraving, well figured walnut stock. Other mechanical features remain the same. Imported from Spain by Wm. Larkin Moore.
**Price:** .................... **$4,600.00**

## GOROSABEL MODEL 503 SIDE-BY-SIDE
**Gauge:** 12, 16, 20, 28, 410
**Barrel:** 26″, 27″, 28″, all standard chokes and combinations.
**Stock:** Select European walnut, English or pistol grip, sliver or beavertail fore-end; hand checkered.
**Features:** Anson & Deeley-style boxlock action with scalloped frame and scroll engraving; automatic ejectors. Introduced in U.S. 1986. Imported by Des Moines Imports.
**Price:** About .................... **$959.00**
**Price:** Model 502, as above except less fancy wood, engraving ..... **$875.00**
**Price:** Models 500, 501, as above, standard-grade models, about... **$645.00**

## GOROSABEL MODEL 505 SIDE-BY-SIDE
**Gauge:** 12, 20, 2¾″ or 3″ chambers.
**Barrel:** 26″, 27″, 28″, all standard chokes and combinations
**Stock:** Select European walnut, English or pistol grip, sliver or beavertail fore-end; hand checkered.
**Features:** Holland & Holland-style sidelock action; Purdey-style fine scroll and rose engraving. All "Best" gun options. Introduced in U.S. 1986. Imported by Des Moines Imports.
**Price:** About.................... **$1,335.00**
**Price:** Model 504, as above except less fancy wood, has Holland-style large scroll engraving.................... **$995.00**

## GARBI MODEL 71 DOUBLE
**Gauge:** 12, 16, 20.
**Barrel:** 26″, 28″, choked to customer specs.
**Weight:** 5 lbs., 15 oz. (20 ga.).
**Stock:** 14½x2¼″x1½″. European walnut. Straight grip, checkered butt, classic fore-end.
**Features:** Sidelock action, automatic ejectors, double triggers standard. Color case-hardened action, coin finish optional. Five other models are available. Imported from Spain by L. Joseph Rahn and Wm. Larkin Moore.
**Price:** Model 71, from.................... **$1,600.00**

## GARBI MODEL 102 SHOTGUN
**Gauge:** 12, 16, 20.
**Barrel:** 12 ga.-25″ to 30″; 16 & 20 ga.-25″ to 28″. Chokes as specified.
**Weight:** 20 ga.-5 lbs., 15 oz. to 6 lbs., 4 oz.
**Stock:** 14½″x2¼″x1½″; select walnut.
**Features:** Holland pattern sidelock ejector with chopper lump barrels, Holland-type large scroll engraving. Double triggers (hinged front) std., non-selective single trigger available. Many options available. Imported from Spain by Wm. Larkin Moore.
**Price:** From .................... **$3,500.00**

## Garbi Model 103A, B Side-by-Side
Similar to the Garbi Model 100 except has Purdey-type fine scroll and rosette engraving. Better over-all quality than the Model 101. Model 103B has nickel-chrome steel barrels, H&H-type easy opening mechanism; other mechanical details remain the same. Imported from Spain by Wm. Larkin Moore and L. Joseph Rahn, Inc.
**Price:** Model 103A, from .................... **$2,562.00**
**Price:** Model 103B, from .................... **$3,400.00**

Garbi Model 200

## Garbi Model Special Side-by-Side
Similar to the Garbi Model 100 except has best quality wood and metal work. Special game scene engraving with or without gold inlays, fancy figured walnut stock. Imported from Spain by Wm. Larkin Moore.
**Price:** From .................... **$4,600.00**

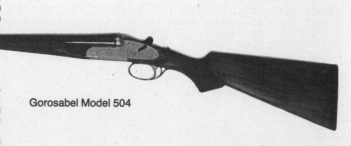

Gorosabel Model 503

Gorosabel Model 504

**CAUTION:** PRICES CHANGE. CHECK AT GUNSHOP.

# SHOTGUNS—SIDE-BY-SIDES

## LEBEAU-COURALLY MODEL 1225 DOUBLE
**Gauge:** 12, 20, 28, 2¾″, or 3″ chambers.
**Barrel:** 26″ to 28″, choked to customer specs.
**Weight:** 6.4 lbs. (12 gauge).
**Stock:** Grand Luxe walnut, straight English-style, to customer specs.
**Features:** Holland & Holland sidelock action; automatic ejectors; double trigger; color case-hardened frame with fine English engraving. Imported from Belgium by Midwest Gun Sport.
**Price:** . . . . . . . . . . . . . . . . . . . . . . . . . . . . . . . . . . . . . . . . . . . . . . . . $9,900.00

## LEBEAU-COURALLY BOXLOCK SHOTGUN
**Gauge:** 12, 16, 20, 28.
**Barrel:** 26″ to 30″, choked to customer specs.
**Weight:** 6 lbs., 6 oz. to 8 lbs., 4 oz. (12 ga.).
**Stock:** Dimensions to customer specs. Select French walnut with hand rubbed oil finish, straight grip (p.g. optional), splinter fore-end (beavertail optional).
**Features:** Anson & Deeley boxlock with ejectors, Purdey-type fastener; choice of rounded action, with or without sideplates; choice of level rib, file cut or smooth; choice of numerous engraving patterns. Imported from Belgium by Wm. Larkin Moore.
**Price:** . . . . . . . . . . . . . . . . . . . . . . . . . . . . . . . . . . . . . . . . . . . . . . . . $9,400.00

Lebeau-Courally Sidelock

## LEBEAU-COURALLY SIDELOCK SHOTGUN
**Gauge:** 12, 16, 20 (standard), 28 (optional).
**Barrel:** 26″ to 30″, choked to customer specs.
**Weight:** 6 lbs., 6 oz. to 8 lbs., 4 oz. (12 ga.)

**Stock:** Dimensions to customer specs. Best quality French walnut with hand rubbed oil finish, straight grip stock and checkered butt (std.), classic splinter fore-end.
**Features:** Holland & Holland pattern sidelock ejector double with chopper lump barrels; choice of classic or rounded action; concave or level rib, file cut or smooth; choice of numerous engraving patterns. Can be furnished with H&H type self-opening mechanism. Imported from Belgium by Wm. Larkin Moore.
**Price:** From . . . . . . . . . . . . . . . . . . . . . . . . . . . . . . . . . . . . . . . . . . $18,700.00

Mercury Magnum

## MERCURY MAGNUM DOUBLE BARREL SHOTGUN
**Gauge:** 10 (3½″).
**Action:** Triple-lock Anson & Deeley type.
**Barrel:** 32″ (Full & Full).
**Weight:** 10⅛ lbs.
**Stock:** 14″x1⅝″x2¼″ walnut, checkered p.g. stock and beavertail fore-end, recoil pad.
**Features:** Double triggers, front hinged, auto safety, extractors; safety gas ports, engraved frame. Imported from Spain by Tradewinds.
**Price:** (10 ga.). . . . . . . . . . . . . . . . . . . . . . . . . . . . . . . . . . . . . . . . . . . $480.00

## OMEGA SIDE-BY-SIDE SHOTGUNS
**Gauge:** 20, 28, 410 (3″).
**Barrel:** 20 ga.—26″(Imp. Cyl. & Mod.); 28 ga.—26″ (Mod. & Full); 410—26″ (Full & Full).
**Weight:** 5½ lbs.
**Stock:** Standard has checkered beechwood, Deluxe has walnut; both have semi-pistol grip.
**Features:** Blued barrels and receiver; top tang safety. Imported from Italy by Kassnar. Introduced 1984.
**Price:** Standard. . . . . . . . . . . . . . . . . . . . . . . . . . . . . . . . . $270.00 to 313.00
**Price:** Deluxe . . . . . . . . . . . . . . . . . . . . . . . . . . . . . . . . . . . . . . . . . . $306.00

Navy Model 100

## NAVY ARMS MODEL 100 FIELD HUNTER
**Gauge:** 12 and 20, 3″ chambers.
**Barrel:** 28″ (Imp. Cyl. & Mod., Mod. & Full).
**Weight:** About 7 lbs.
**Stock:** Checkered walnut.
**Features:** Chrome-lined barrels; engraved hard chrome receiver; gold plated double triggers. Introduced 1985. Imported from Italy by Navy Arms.
**Price:** Model 100 (extractors). . . . . . . . . . . . . . . . . . . . . . . . . . . . . . $389.00
**Price:** Model 150 (ejectors) . . . . . . . . . . . . . . . . . . . . . . . . . . . . . . $464.00

Parker DHE

Consult our Directory pages for the location of firms mentioned.

## PARKER DHE SIDE-BY-SIDE SHOTGUN
**Gauge:** 20, 28, 2¾″ or 3″ chambers.
**Barrel:** 26″ (Imp. Cyl. & Mod., 2¾″ chambers), Skeet & Skeet available, 28″ (Mod. & Full, 3″ chambers only).
**Weight:** About 6½ lbs. (20 ga.), 5½ lbs. (28 ga.).
**Stock:** Fancy American walnut, checkered grip and fore-end. Straight stock or pistol grip, splinter or beavertail fore-end; 28 l.p.i. checkering.
**Features:** Reproduction of the original Parker DHE — most parts interchangeable with original. Double or single selective trigger; checkered skeleton buttplate; selective ejectors; bores hard chromed, excluding choke area. Two-barrel sets available. Hand engraved scroll and scenes on case-hardened frame. Fitted leather trunk included. Introduced 1984. Made by Winchester in Japan. Imported by Parker Div. of Reagent Chemical.
**Price:** . . . . . . . . . . . . . . . . . . . . . . . . . . . . . . . . . . . . . . . . . . . . . . . . $2,800.00

Parker Hale 645E

**Features:** Boxlock action; silvered, engraved action; auto. safety; ejectors or extractors. E-models have double triggers, concave rib (XXV models have Churchill-type rib); A-models have single, non-selective trigger, raised matted rib. Made in Spain by Ugartechea. Imported by Precision Sports. Introduced 1986.
**Price:** 640E (12, 16, 20; 26", 28"), extractors .................... $449.95
**Price:** 640E (28, 410; 27" only), extractors ...................... $499.95
**Price:** 640A (12, 16, 20; 26", 28"), extractors .................... $549.96
**Price:** 645E (12, 16, 20; 26", 28"), with ejectors ................. $559.95
**Price:** 645E (28, 410; 27"), with ejectors ....................... $639.95
**Price:** 645A (12, 16, 20; 26", 28") with ejectors ................. $669.95
**Price:** 645E-XXV (12, 16, 20; 25"), with ejectors ................. $589.95
**Price:** 670E (12, 16, 20, 26", 28") sidelock, with ejectors ........ $2,450.00
**Price:** 670E (28, 410; 27") sidelock, with ejectors................ $2,600.00
**Price:** 680E-XXV (12, 16, 20; 25") sidelock, ejectors, case-color action............................................................ $2,350.00
**Price:** 680E-XXV (28, 410; 25") sidelock, ejectors, case-color action $2,500.00

## PARKER-HALE MODEL "600" SERIES DOUBLES
**Gauge:** 12, 16, 20, (2¾"), 28, 410 (3").
**Barrel:** 25", 26", 27", 28" (Imp. Cyl. & Mod., Mod. & Full).
**Weight:** 12 ga., 6¾-7 lbs.; 20 ga., 5¾-6 lbs.
**Stock:** 14½"x1½"x2½. Hand checkered walnut with oil finish. "E" (English) models have straight grip, splinter fore-end, checkered butt. "A" (American) modes have p.g. stock, beaver-tail fore-end, butt plate.

## PIOTTI MODEL PIUMA SIDE-BY-SIDE
**Gauge:** 12, 16, 20, 28, 410.
**Barrel:** 25" to 30" (12 ga.), 25" to 28" (16, 20, 28, 410).
**Weight:** 5½ to 6¼ lbs. (20 ga.).
**Stock:** Dimensions to customer specs. Straight grip stock with checkered butt, classic splinter fore-end, hand rubbed oil finish are standard; pistol grip, beavertail fore-end, satin luster finish optional.
**Features:** Anson & Deeley boxlock ejector double with chopper lump barrels. Level, file-cut rib, light scroll and rosette engraving, scalloped frame. Double triggers with hinged front standard, single non-selective optional. Coin finish standard, color case hardened optional. Imported from Italy by Wm. Larkin Moore.
**Price:** ..................................................... $4,000.00

**Piotti Model Monte Carlo Side-by-Side**
Similar to the Piotti King No. 1 except has Purdey-style scroll and rosette engraving, no gold inlays, over-all workmanship not as finely detailed. Other mechanical specifications remain the same. Imported from Italy by Wm. Larkin Moore.
**Price:** ..................................................... $8,750.00

**Piotti Model King Extra Side-by-Side**
Similar to the Piotti King No. 1 except highest quality wood and metal work. Choice of either bulino game scene engraving or game scene engraving with gold inlays. Engraved and signed by a master engraver. Exhibition grade wood. Other mechanical specifications remain the same. Imported from Italy by Wm. Larkin Moore.
**Price:** ..................................................... $13,700.00

Piotti King No. 1

## PIOTTI KING NO. 1 SIDE-BY-SIDE
**Gauge:** 12, 16, 20, 28, 410.
**Barrel:** 25" to 30" (12 ga.), 25" to 28" (16, 20, 28, 410). To customer specs. Chokes as specified.
**Weight:** 6½ lbs. to 8 lbs. (12 ga., to customer specs.)

**Stock:** Dimensions to customer specs. Finely figured walnut; straight grip with checkered butt with classic splinter fore-end and hand-rubbed oil finish standard. Pistol grip, beavertail fore-end, satin luster finish optional.
**Features:** Holland & Holland pattern sidelock action, auto. ejectors. Double trigger with front trigger hinged standard; non-selective single trigger optional. Coin finish standard; color case-hardened optional. Top rib: level, file cut standard; concave, ventilated optional. Very fine, full coverage scroll engraving with small floral bouquets, gold crown in top lever, name in gold, and gold crest in fore-end. Imported from Italy by Wm. Larkin Moore.
**Price:** ..................................................... $10,900.00

Piotti Lunik

**Piotti Model Lunik Side-by-Side**
Similar to the Piotti King No. 1 except better over-all quality. Has Renaissance-style large scroll engraving in relief, gold crown in top lever, gold name, and gold crest in fore-end. Best quality Holland & Holland-pattern sidelock ejector double with chopper lump (demi-bloc) barrels. Other mechanical specifications remain the same. Imported from Italy by Wm. Larkin Moore.
**Price:** ..................................................... $11,600.00

Rossi Overland

## ROSSI OVERLAND DOUBLE BARREL
**Gauge:** 12, 20, 410 (3" chambers).
**Action:** Sidelock with external hammers; Greener crossbolt.
**Barrel:** 12 ga., 20" (Imp. Cyl., Mod.) 28" (Mod. & Full), 20 ga., 20", 26" (Imp. Cyl. & Mod.), 410 ga., 26" (Full & Full).
**Weight:** 6½ to 7 lbs.
**Stock:** Walnut p.g. with beavertail fore-end.
**Features:** Solid raised matted rib. Exposed hammers. Imported by Interarms.
**Price:** 12 or 20 ..................................... $267.00
**Price:** 410 ............................................. $272.00

## ROSSI "SQUIRE" DOUBLE BARREL
**Gauge:** 12, 20, 410 (3" chambers).
**Barrel:** 12 — 28" (Mod. & Full); 20 ga.—26" (Imp. Cyl. & Mod.), 28" (Mod. & Full); 410—26" (Full & Full).
**Weight:** About 7½ lbs.
**Stock:** Walnut finished hardwood.
**Features:** Double triggers, raised matted rib, beavertail fore-end. Massive twin underlugs mesh with synchronized sliding bolts. Introduced 1978. Imported by Interarms.
**Price:** 12 or 20 ga. .................................. $292.00
**Price:** 410 ............................................. $297.00

**CAUTION:** PRICES CHANGE. CHECK AT GUNSHOP.

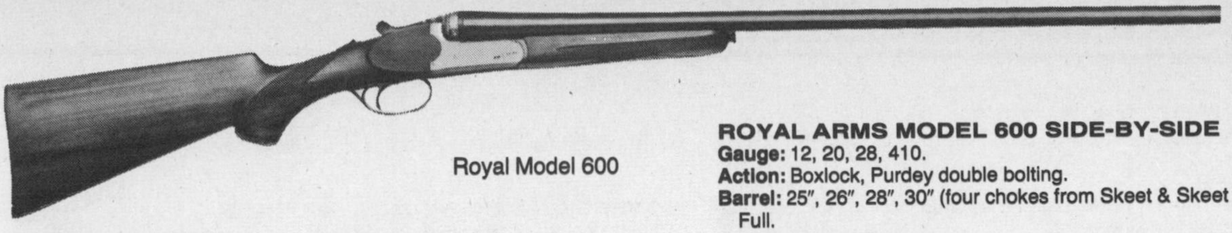

Royal Model 600

## ROYAL ARMS MODEL 800 SIDE-BY-SIDE
**Gauge:** 12, 20, 28, 410.
**Action:** True quick detachable bar spring sidelocks.
**Barrel:** 24", 26", 28" (Mod. & Full, Imp. Cyl. & Mod., Imp. Cyl. & Full).
**Weight:** 7 lbs.
**Stock:** 15" x 2½" x 1½". Fancy select European walnut; straight grip with fine-line checkering, classic fore-end and butt.
**Features:** Holland & Holland auto. selective ejectors; gated and fully scroll engraved grayed action; cocking indicators; articulated front trigger; Churchill rib; vented firing pins; auto safety. Introduced 1985. Imported from Spain by Royal Arms International.
**Price:** All gauges . . . . . . . . . . . . . . . . . . . . . . . . . . . . . . . . . . . . . . . . $899.00

## ROYAL ARMS MODEL 600 SIDE-BY-SIDE
**Gauge:** 12, 20, 28, 410.
**Action:** Boxlock, Purdey double bolting.
**Barrel:** 25", 26", 28", 30" (four chokes from Skeet & Skeet through Imp. Cyl. & Full.
**Weight:** 7 lbs., 12 ozs.
**Stock:** Oil finished European walnut; checkered grip and fore-end.
**Features:** Double triggers; vent rib; automatic safety; chrome lined barrels. Introduced 1985. Imported from Spain by Royal Arms International.
**Price:** . . . . . . . . . . . . . . . . . . . . . . . . . . . . . . . . . . . . . . . . . . . . . . $329.95
**Price:** Model 600AE (3", 12 ga. only, single selective trigger, selective auto ejectors) . . . . . . . . . . . . . . . . . . . . . . . . . . . . . . . . . . . . . . . . . $419.95

Savage-Fox B-SE

## SAVAGE-STEVENS MODEL 311 DOUBLE
**Gauge:** 12, 20, 410 (12, 20 and 410, 3" chambers).
**Action:** Top lever, hammerless; double triggers, auto. top tang safety.
**Barrel:** 12, 20 ga. 26" (Imp. Cyl., Mod.); 12 ga. 28" (Mod., Full); 12 ga. 30" (Mod., Full); 410 ga. 26" (Full, Full).
**Weight:** 7-8 lbs. (30" bbl.). **Length:** 45¾" over-all.
**Stock:** 14"x1½"x2½". Walnut finish, p.g., fluted comb.
**Features:** Box-type blued frame.
**Price:** . . . . . . . . . . . . . . . . . . . . . . . . . . . . . . . . . . . . . . . . . . $278.00

## W&C SCOTT BLENHEIM GAME GUN
**Gauge:** 12, 16, 20.
**Barrel:** 25", 26", 27", 28", 30" (chokes to order); concave rib standard, flat or Churchill optional.
**Weight:** 6½ lbs.
**Stock:** Measurements to order. French walnut with 28 l.p.i. checkering (32 l.p.i. checkering and exhibition grade wood on Deluxe model).
**Features:** Best quality bar action sidelock ejector, finest rose and scroll engraving; gold name plate. Introduced 1985. Imported from England by British Guns.
**Price:** Blenheim Deluxe, 12 or 16 ga. . . . . . . . . . . . . . . . . . . . . . $16,500.00
**Price:** As above, 20 ga. . . . . . . . . . . . . . . . . . . . . . . . . . . . . . . . . $20,500.00

## SAVAGE FOX MODEL B-SE DOUBLE
**Gauge:** 12, 20, 410 (20, 2¾" and 3"; 410, 2½" and 3" shells).
**Action:** Hammerless, takedown; non-selective single trigger; auto. safety. Automatic ejectors.
**Barrel:** 12, 20 ga., 26" (Imp. Cyl., Mod.); 12 ga. (Mod., Full); 410, 26" (Full, Full). Vent. rib on all.
**Weight:** 12 ga. 7 lbs., 16 ga. 6¾ lbs., 20 ga. 6½ lbs., 410 ga. 6¼ lbs.
**Stock:** 14"x1½"x2½". Walnut, checkered p.g. and beavertail fore-end.
**Features:** Decorated, blued frame; white bead front and middle sights.
**Price:** . . . . . . . . . . . . . . . . . . . . . . . . . . . . . . . . . . . . . . . . . $467.06
**Price:** Model B (double triggers) . . . . . . . . . . . . . . . . . . . . . . . $369.00

## W&C Scott Bowood DeLuxe Game Gun
Similar to the Chatsworth Grande Luxe except less ornate metal and wood work; checkered 24 lpi at fore-end and pistol grip. Imported from England by L. Joseph Rahn and British Guns.
**Price:** 12 or 16 ga. . . . . . . . . . . . . . . . . . . . . . . . . . . . . . . . . . $5,900.00
**Price:** 20 or 28 ga. . . . . . . . . . . . . . . . . . . . . . . . . . . . . . . . . . $6,500.00

## W&C Scott Kinmount Game Gun
Similar to the Bowood DeLuxe Game Gun except less ornate engraving and wood work; checkered 20 lpi; other details essentially the same. Imported from England by L. Joseph Rahn and British Guns.
**Price:** 12 or 16 ga. . . . . . . . . . . . . . . . . . . . . . . . . . . . . . . . . . $5,175.00
**Price:** 20 or 28 ga. . . . . . . . . . . . . . . . . . . . . . . . . . . . . . . . . . $5,500.00

W&C Scott Chatsworth

## W&C SCOTT CHATSWORTH GRANDE LUXE DOUBLE
**Gauge:** 12, 16, 20, 28.
**Barrel:** 25", 26", 27", 28", 30" (chokes to order); concave rib standard, Churchill or flat rib optional.
**Weight:** About 6½ lbs. (12 ga.).
**Stock:** 14¾" x 1½" x 2¼", or made to customer specs. French walnut with 32 lpi checkering.

**Features:** Entirely hand fitted; boxlock action (sideplates optional); English scroll engraving; gold name plate shield in stock. Imported from England by L. Joseph Rahn and British Guns.
**Price:** 12 or 16 ga. . . . . . . . . . . . . . . . . . . . . . . . . . . . . . . . . . $7,650.00
**Price:** 20 or 28 ga. . . . . . . . . . . . . . . . . . . . . . . . . . . . . . . . . . $7,800.00

IGA Side-by-Side

## STOEGER/IGA SIDE-BY-SIDE SHOTGUN
**Gauge:** 12, 20, 28 (2¾"), 410 (3").
**Barrel:** 26" (Full & Full, 410 only, Imp. Cyl. & Mod.), 28" (Mod. & Full).
**Weight:** 6¾ to 7 lbs.
**Stock:** 14½" x 1½" x 2½". Oil-finished hardwood. Checkered pistol grip and fore-end.
**Features:** Automatic safety, extractors only, solid matted barrel rib. Double triggers only. Introduced 1983. Imported from Brazil by Stoeger Industries.
**Price:** . . . . . . . . . . . . . . . . . . . . . . . . . . . . . . . . . . . . . . . . . $229.95
**Price:** Coach Gun, 12 or 20 ga., 20" bbls. . . . . . . . . . . . . . . . . . $224.95

## VENTURA REGIS MODEL DOUBLE
**Gauge:** 12 (2¾"), 20 (3"), 28 (2¾"), 410 (3").
**Barrel:** 26", 28".
**Weight:** 6½ lbs. (12 ga.)
**Stock:** Select figured French walnut, hand checkered English straight or p.g. stock with slender beavertail fore-end.
**Features:** H & H sidelock with intercepting safeties and triple locks; single selective or double triggers; automatic ejectors; floral engraving. Options include second barrel set, leather trunk case. Introduced 1986. Imported from Italy by Ventura Imports.
**Price:** .......................................... $1,448.00 to $1,596.00

*Ventura Regis*

## SOVEREIGN SIDE-BY-SIDE SHOTGUN
**Gauge:** 12 or 20, 3" chambers.
**Barrel:** 28" (Mod. or Full).
**Weight:** 6 lbs.
**Stock:** European walnut with checkered p.g. and fore-end.
**Features:** Chrome-lined bores, automatic safety; chromed, engraved action; double triggers. Introduced 1986. Imported from Italy by Southern Gun & Tackle.
**Price:** ................................................ $335.95

## VENTURA VICTRIX MODEL DOUBLE
**Gauge:** 12 (2¾"), 20 (3"), 28 (2¾"), 410 (3").
**Barrel:** 26", 28".
**Weight:** 6½ lbs. (12 ga.).
**Stock:** French walnut with hand-checkered p.g. or straight English stock, slender beavertail fore-end.
**Features:** Anson & Deeley boxlock with triple locks; single selective or double triggers; automatic ejectors. Optional screw-in chokes, leather trunk case. Introduced 1986. Imported from Italy by Ventura Imports.
**Price:** .......................................... $796.00 to $876.00
**Price:** Victrix Extra Lusso (as above with select wood, full floral engraving) ........................................ $1,048.00 to $1,148.00

*Ventura Victrix*

*Winchester Model 23*

## WINCHESTER MODEL 23 PIGEON GRADE LIGHTWEIGHT
**Gauge:** 12, 20, 3" chambers
**Barrel:** 25½" (Imp. Cyl. & Mod.).
**Weight:** 6¾ lbs. (12 ga.).
**Stock:** High grade American walnut with English-style straight grip, semi-beavertail fore-end.
**Features:** Mechanical trigger; tapered ventilated rib; selective ejectors. Receiver, top lever and trigger guard have silver-gray finish with engraved bird scenes. Comes with hard case. Introduced 1981. Manufactured in and imported from Japan by Winchester Group, Olin Corp.
**Price:** ............................................... $1,420.00

*Winchester 23 Winchoke*

## Winchester Model 23 Pigeon Grade Winchoke
Same features as Model 23 Pigeon Grade Lightweight except has 25½" barrels with interchangeable Winchoke tubes, pistol grip stock. Six choke tubes are supplied with 12 ga. (Skeet, Imp. Cyl., Mod., Imp. Mod., Full, Extra Full), four with 20 ga. (Skeet, Imp. Cyl., Mod., Full). Comes with hard case. Introduced 1983.
**Price:** ............................................... $1,460.00

*Winchester 23 Classic*

## Winchester Model 23 Classic
Similar to the Model 23 Pigeon Grade Winchoke except has fancy grade American walnut stock with grip cap, 26" barrel choked Imp. Cyl. & Mod. for 12, 20, 28 gauge, Full & Mod. for 410. Blued receiver with scroll engraving, gold inlay on bottom of receiver: pheasant for 12 and 20 gauge; quail on 28 and 410. Ebony inlay in fore-end, gold-initial plate in stock. Introduced 1986.
**Price:** 12 and 20 gauge ................................... $1,750.00
**Price:** 28 and 410 gauge .................................. $1,850.00

## Winchester Model 23 Light Duck
Same basic features as the standard Model 23 Pigeon Grade except has plain, blued frame, 28" barrels choked Full and Full; 20 ga.; 3" chambers. Comes with hard case. Matching serial numbers to previously issued Heavy Duck. Introduced 1983.
**Price:** ............................................... $1,650.00
**Price:** Golden Quail (12 ga., 25½", Imp. Cyl. & Mod.) ........... $1,790.00
**Price:** Custom Two Barrel Set (20, 28 ga. bbls., full fancy walnut, leather luggage-style case) ........................................ $4,650.00

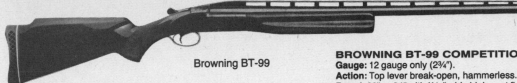

Browning BT-99

FIE Hamilton & Hunter

Ithaca 5E Single

Marlin Model 55

## EXEL MODEL 51 FOLDING SHOTGUN
**Gauge:** 410, 3".
**Barrel:** 26" (Mod. & Full).
**Weight:** 4 lbs.
**Stock:** Folding. Splinter fore-end.
**Features:** Non-ejector; case-hardened frame; exposed hammers. Introduced 1985. Imported from Spain by Exel Arms.
**Price:** .................................................. $217.00

## F.I.E. "S.S.S." SINGLE BARREL
**Gauge:** 12, 20, 410 (3").
**Action:** Button-break on trigger guard.
**Barrel:** 18½" (Cyl.).
**Weight:** 6½ lbs.
**Stock:** Walnut finished hardwood, full beavertail fore-end.
**Features:** Exposed hammer. Automatic ejector. Imported from Brazil by F.I.E. Corp.
**Price:** .................................................. $99.95

## LJUTIC MONO GUN SINGLE BARREL
**Gauge:** 12 ga. only.
**Barrel:** 34", choked to customer specs; hollow-milled rib, 35½" sight plane.
**Weight:** Approx. 9 lbs.
**Stock:** To customer specs. Oil finish, hand checkered.
**Features:** Totally custom made. Pull or release trigger; removable trigger guard contains trigger and hammer mechanism; Ljutic pushbutton opener on front of trigger guard. From Ljutic Industries.
**Price:** ............................................. $3,695.00
**Price:** With Olympic Rib, custom 32" barrel .............. $3,795.00
**Price:** As above with screw-in chokes. ................. $3,995.00

## BROWNING BT-99 COMPETITION TRAP SPECIAL
**Gauge:** 12 gauge only (2¾").
**Action:** Top lever break-open, hammerless.
**Barrel:** 32" or 34" with 11/32" wide high post floating vent. rib. Comes with Invector choke tubes.
**Weight:** 8 lbs. (32" bbl.).
**Stock:** French walnut; hand checkered, full pistol grip, full beavertail fore-end; recoil pad. Trap dimensions with M.C. 14⅜"x1⅜"x1⅜"x2".
**Sights:** Ivory front and middle beads.
**Features:** Gold plated trigger with 3½-lb. pull, deluxe trap-style recoil pad, auto ejector, no safety. Available with either Monte Carlo or standard stock. Imported from Japan by Browning.
**Price:** Grade I Invector ..................................... $876.50

## F.I.E. "HAMILTON & HUNTER" SINGLE BARREL
**Gauge:** 12, 20, 410 (3").
**Barrel:** 12 ga. & 20 ga. 28" (Full); 410 ga. (Full).
**Weight:** 6½ lbs.
**Stock:** Walnut stained hardwood, beavertail fore-end.
**Sights:** Metal bead front.
**Features:** Trigger guard button is pushed to open action. Exposed hammer, auto ejector, three-piece takedown. Imported from Brazil by F.I.E. Corp.
**Price:** ............................................... $89.95
**Price:** Youth model ...................................... $89.95

## ITHACA 5E GRADE SINGLE BARREL TRAP GUN
**Gauge:** 12 only.
**Action:** Top lever break open hammerless, dual locking lugs.
**Barrel:** 32" or 34", rampless vent. rib.
**Stock:** (14½"x1½"x1⅞"). Select walnut, checkered p.g. and beavertail fore-end, p.g. cap, recoil pad, Monte Carlo comb, cheekpiece. Cast-on, cast-off or extreme deviation from standard stock dimensions $100 extra. Reasonable deviation allowed without extra charge.
**Features:** Frame, top lever and trigger guard extensively engraved and gold inlaid. Gold name plate in stock.
**Price:** Custom made ...................................... $7,000.00
**Price:** Dollar Grade. ..................................... $9,700.00

## MARLIN MODEL 55 GOOSE GUN BOLT ACTION
**Gauge:** 12 only, (3" mag. or 2¾").
**Action:** Bolt action, thumb safety, detachable 2-shot clip. Red cocking indicator.
**Barrel:** 36", Full choke.
**Weight:** 8 lbs. **Length:** 56¾" over-all.
**Stock:** Walnut-finished hardwood, p.g., ventilated recoil pad, leather strap & swivels. Mar-Shield® finish.
**Features:** Swivels and leather carrying strap. Brass bead front sight, U-groove rear sight.
**Price:** .................................................. $180.95

# SHOTGUNS—BOLT ACTIONS & SINGLE SHOTS

Ljutic LTX Mono

## Ljutic LTX Super Deluxe Mono Gun
Super Deluxe version of the standard Mono Gun except has exhibition quality wood, extra-fancy checkering pattern in 24 lpi, double recessed choking. Weight is 8¼ lbs., extra light 33" barrel; medium-height Olympic rib. Introduced 1984.
Price: .................................................. $4,995.00
Price: With three screw-in choke tubes ...................... $5,595.00

Ljutic Space Gun

## LJUTIC RECOILLESS SPACE GUN SHOTGUN
Gauge: 12 only, 2¾" chamber.
Barrel: 30" (Full).
Weight: 8½ lbs.
Stock: 14½" to 15" pull length; universal comb; medium or large p.g.
Sights: Choice of front sight or vent. rib model.
Features: Choice of pull or release button trigger; anti-recoil mechanism. Revolutionary new design. Introduced 1981. From Ljutic Industries.
Price: From .................................................. $3,695.00

## NAVY ARMS MODEL 600 FOLDING SHOTGUNS
Gauge: 12, 20, 410
Barrel: 28" (12, 20 ga., Full), 26" (410 ga., Full).
Stock: Beech on Standard, European walnut on Deluxe, both with checkered p.g. and fore-end.
Features: Gun folds for compact carry and storage. Chrome-lined barrel, engraved hard chrome receiver. Imported from Italy by Navy Arms. Introduced 1986.
Price: Standard model .......................................... $158.00
Price: Deluxe model ............................................ $165.00

## OMEGA FOLDING SHOTGUN
Gauge: 12, 16, 20, 28, 410, 2¾", 3" chamber.
Barrel: 410 — 26" (Full); 12, 16, 20, 28 — 28" (Full); 12 — 30" (Full).
Stock: Standard has checkered beechwood, Deluxe has checkered walnut.
Sights: Metal bead front.
Features: Standard model has matte chrome receiver, top opening lever; Deluxe has blued receiver, vent. rib. Both guns fold for storage and transport. Imported from Italy by Kassnar. Introduced 1984.
Price: Standard ............................................... $185.00
Price: Deluxe ................................................. $242.00

Omega Single Barrel

## OMEGA SINGLE BARREL SHOTGUN
Gauge: 12 (2¾"), 20, 410 (3").
Barrel: 12 ga.—26" (Imp.Cyl.), 28" (Mod.), 28", 30" (Full); 20 ga.—26" (Imp. Cyl.), 28" (Mod., Full); 410—26" (Full).
Weight: About 5½ lbs.
Stock: Indonesian walnut.
Features: Rebounding hammer; top lever breaks to either side. Imported by Kassnar Imports, Inc. Introduced 1986.
Price: .................................................. $89.00

## SOVEREIGN FOLDING SINGLE BARREL
Gauge: 12, 16, 20, 410, 3" chamber.
Barrel: 28" (12, 20, Full or Mod.) 28" (16, Full) 26" (410, Full).
Weight: 6 lbs.
Stock: Walnut finished hardwood; cut checkered p.g., fore-end.
Features: Chrome lined barrel, engraved and plated receiver; tang safety; bottom opening lever. Introduced 1986. Imported by Southern Gun & Tackle.
Price: .................................................. $94.95

# SHOTGUNS—MILITARY & POLICE

Benelli Super 90

## BENELLI SUPER 90 SHOTGUN
Gauge: 12, 3" chamber, 7-shot magazine.
Barrel: 19¾" (Cyl.).
Weight: 7 lbs., 4 oz. Length: 39¾" over-all.
Stock: High-impact polymer with sling loop in side of butt; rubberized pistol grip on optional SWAT stock.
Sights: Post front, buckhorn rear adj. for w.
Features: Alloy receiver with rotating locking lug bolt; matte finish; automatic shell release lever. Comes with carrier for speed loading and magazine reducer plug. Optional vent. rib and interchangeable barrels available. Introduced 1986. Imported by Heckler & Koch, Inc.
Price: .................................................. $539.00
Price: Optional pistol grip stock............................... $76.00

CAUTION: PRICES CHANGE. CHECK AT GUNSHOP.

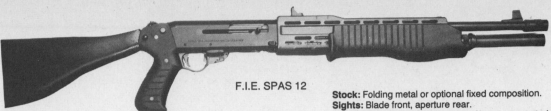

F.I.E. SPAS 12

## F.I.E. SPAS 12 PUMP/AUTO ASSAULT SHOTGUN
**Gauge:** 12, 2¾".
**Barrel:** 21½". Barrel threaded for SPAS choke tubes.
**Weight:** 9.6 lbs. **Length:** 31¾" (stock folded).

**Stock:** Folding metal or optional fixed composition.
**Sights:** Blade front, aperture rear.
**Features:** Functions as pump and/or gas-operated auto. Has 8-shot magazine. Parkerized alloy receiver, chrome lined bore, resin pistol grip and pump handle. Made in Italy by Franchi. Introduced 1983. Imported by FIE Corp.
**Price:** ............................................................ $599.95
**Price:** Mod. or Full choke tube ........................................ $94.95
**Price:** Optional fixed stock ........................................... $64.95

Ithaca 37 M&P

## ITHACA MODEL 37 M & P SHOTGUN
**Gauge:** 12, 2¾" chamber, 5-shot and 8-shot magazine.
**Barrel:** 18½" (Cyl.), 20" (Cyl.).
**Weight:** 6½ lbs.
**Stock:** Oil-finished walnut with grooved walnut pump handle.
**Sights:** Bead front.
**Features:** Metal parts are Parkerized. Available with vertical hand grip instead of full butt.
**Price:** 5-shot, Parkerized, 20" .................................... $380.00
**Price:** 8-shot, Parkerized, 20" only ............................... $400.00
**Price:** Handgrip stock, 5-shot, 18½" ............................. $405.00
**Price:** Handgrip stock, 8-shot, 20" ............................... $425.00
**Price:** M&P II, Handgrip with buttstock ........................... $370.00

## Ithaca Model 37 LAPD
Similar to the Model 37 DSPS except comes with sling, swivels, sling, rubber recoil pad. Parkerized finish. Rifle-type sights, checkered pistol grip stock, 5-shot magazine.
**Price:** ............................................................ $430.00

Ithaca 37 DSPS

## Ithaca Model 37 DSPS Shotgun
Law enforcement version of the Model 37 Deerslayer. Designed primarily for shooting rifled slugs but equally effective with buckshot. Available in either 5- or 8-shot models. Has 20" barrel, oil-finished stock, adjustable rifle-type sights.
**Price:** Parkerized, 5-shot ..................................... $397.00
**Price:** Parkerized 8-shot ........................................ $417.00
**Price:** With Handgrip and buttstock (DSPS II) ................... $407.00

Ithaca Mag-10 Roadblocker

## ITHACA MAG-10 ROADBLOCKER
**Gauge:** 10, 3½" chamber.
**Barrel:** 22" (Cyl.).

**Weight:** 10¾ lbs.
**Stock:** Walnut stock and fore-end, oil finish.
**Sights:** Bead front.
**Features:** Non-glare finish on metal parts. Uses Ithaca's Countercoil gas system. Rubber recoil pad. Vent. rib or plain barrel.
**Price:** Plain barrel ............................................. $741.00
**Price:** Vent rib barrel .......................................... $771.00

Mossberg 500

## MOSSBERG MODEL 500 SECURITY SHOTGUNS
**Gauge:** 12, 20 (2¾"), 410 (3").
**Barrel:** 18½", 20" (Cyl.).
**Weight:** 5½ lbs. (410), 7 lbs. (12 ga.).
**Stock:** Walnut-finished hardwood; synthetic on some models, or folding metal.
**Sights:** Rifle-type front and rear or metal bead front.
**Features:** Available in 6- or 8-shot models. Top-mounted safety, double action slide bars, sling swivels, rubber recoil pad. Blue, Parkerized or electroless nickel finishes. Price list not complete—contact Mossberg for full list.
**Price:** 12 ga., 6-shot, 18½", blue, bead sight, about ............... $178.95
**Price:** As above, Parkerized, about ............................. $215.00
**Price:** As above, nickel, about ................................. $240.00
**Price:** 12 ga., 8-shot, 20" Parkerized, rifle sights, about ......... $218.00
**Price:** 20 ga., 6-shot, 18½", blue, bead sight, about .............. $202.00
**Price:** Model 500 US, Parkerized finish, handguard, about ......... $220.00
**Price:** Model 500 ATP, blued, bayonet lug, sling, about ........... $245.00

## Mossberg Cruiser Persuader Shotgun
Similar to the Model 500 Security guns except fitted with the "Cruiser" pistol grip. Grip and fore-end are solid black. Available in either blue or electroless nickel; 12 gauge only with 18½" (6-shot) or 20" (8-shot) barrel. Folding stock. Muzzle cut with "Muzzle Brake" slots to reduce recoil. Comes with extra long black web sling. Weight is 5¾ lb. (18½"), 6 lb. (20"). Over-all length is 28" with 18½" barrel.
**Price:** 6-shot, 18½", blue, about ............................... $200.00
**Price:** As above, nickel, about ................................. $240.00
**Price:** 8-shot, 20", blue, about ................................ $215.00
**Price:** As above, nickel, about ................................. $240.00

Mossberg 500 Bullpup

## MOSSBERG 500 BULLPUP
**Gauge:** 12, 2¾", 6 or 8 shot.
**Barrel:** 18½", 20".
**Weight:** NA. **Length:** NA.
**Stock:** Bullpup design of high-impact plastics.
**Sights:** Fixed, mounted in carrying handle.
**Features:** Uses the M500 pump shotgun action. Introduced 1986.
**Price:** ........................................................... **NA**

## MOSSBERG 3000 SECURITY SHOTGUN
**Gauge:** 12, 2¾", 5-shot magazine.
**Barrel:** 18", 20".
**Weight:** 6¾ lbs. **Length:** 38¾" over-all (18½" bbl.).
**Stock:** Plastic Speedfeed (black or camo), folding metal, or pistol grip only.

**Sights:** Bead front or rifle sights.
**Features:** Blue/black, Parkerized/camo, Parkerized/black metal and stock finishes.
**Price:** ........................................................... **NA**

Remington 870 Police

## REMINGTON MODEL 870P POLICE SHOTGUN
**Gauge:** 12, 3" chamber.
**Barrel:** 18", 20" (Police Cyl.), 20" (Imp. Cyl.).
**Weight:** About 7 lbs.
**Stock:** Lacquer-finished hardwood or folding stock.
**Sights:** Metal bead front or rifle sights.
**Features:** Solid steel receiver, double-action slide bars.
**Price:** Wood stock, 18" or 20", bead sight, about ................. **$324.00**
**Price:** Wood stock, 20", rifle sights, about ....................... **$349.00**

Savage 69-R/69-RXL

## STEVENS MODEL 311-R GUARD GUN DOUBLE
**Gauge:** 12 ga.
**Barrel:** 18¼" (Cyl. & Cyl.).
**Weight:** 6¾ lbs. **Length:** 35¼" over-all.
**Stock:** Hardwood, tung-oil finish.
**Sights:** Bead front.
**Features:** Top tang safety, double triggers, color case-hardened frame, blue barrels. Ventilated rubber recoil pad. Introduced 1982.
**Price:** ........................................................... **$278.00**

## SAVAGE MODEL 69-RXL PUMP SHOTGUN
**Gauge:** 12 only, 3" chamber.
**Barrel:** 18¼" (Cyl.).
**Weight:** 6½ lbs. **Length:** 39" over-all.
**Stock:** Hardwood, tung-oil finish.
**Sights:** Bead front.
**Features:** Top tang safety, 7-shot magazine. Stock has fluted comb and full pistol grip, ventilated rubber pad. QD swivel studs. Introduced 1982.
**Price:** Either model ............................................. **$208.39**

Striker 12

## STRIKER 12 SPECIAL PURPOSE SHOTGUN
**Gauge:** 12, 2¾", 12-shot capacity.
**Barrel:** 18" rifled or smooth, other lengths on request.
**Weight:** 9 lbs.
**Stock:** Folding metal buttstock, composition p.g. and front grip.
**Features:** Semi-auto action; threaded, free-floated barrel of stainless or ordnance steel; sight base designed for optional Armson or laser sight. Made in U.S. Introduced 1986. From Pennsylvania Arms.
**Price:** ........................................................... **$799.95**

Winchester Defender

## Winchester Pistol Grip Pump Security Shotguns
Same as regular Security Series but with pistol grip and fore-end of high-impact resistant ABS plastic with non-glare black finish. Introduced 1984.
**Price:** Pistol Grip Defender, about ............................. **$242.80**

## Winchester "Stainless Marine" Pump Gun
Same as the Defender except has bright chrome finish, stainless-steel barrel, rifle-type sights only. Has special fore-end cap for easy cleaning and inspection.
**Price:** About ................................................... **$416.60**

## WINCHESTER DEFENDER PUMP GUN
**Gauge:** 12, 3" chamber, 5 or 8-shot capacity.
**Barrel:** 18" (Cyl.).
**Weight:** 6¾ lbs. **Length:** 38⅝" over-all.
**Stock:** Walnut finished hardwood stock and ribbed fore-end.
**Sights:** Metal bead front.
**Features:** Cross-bolt safety, front-locking rotating bolt, twin action slide bars. Black rubber butt pad. Made under license by U.S. Repeating Arms Co.
**Price:** 8-shot, about .............................................. **$242.80**
**Price:** 5-shot, about .............................................. **$236.64**
**Price:** As above with rifle sights, about .......................... **$252.36**

**CAUTION:** PRICES CHANGE. CHECK AT GUNSHOP.

The following pages catalog the black powder arms currently available to U.S. shooters. These range from quite precise replicas of historically significant arms to totally new designs created expressly to give the black powder shooter the benefits of modern technology.

Most of the replicas are imported, and many are available from more than one source. Thus examples of a given model such as the 1860 Army revolver or Zouave rifle purchased from different importers may vary in price, finish and fitting. Most of them bear proof marks, indicating that they have been test fired in the proof house of their country of origin.

A list of the importers and the retail price range are included with the description for each model. Many local dealers handle more than one importer's products, giving the prospective buyer an opportunity to make his own judgment in selecting a black powder gun. Most importers have catalogs available free or at nominal cost, and some

are well worth having for the useful information on black powder shooting they provide in addition to their detailed descriptions and specifications of the guns.

A number of special accessories are also available for the black powder shooter. These include replica powder flasks, bullet moulds, cappers and tools, as well as more modern devices to facilitate black powder cleaning and maintenance. Ornate presentation cases and even detachable shoulder stocks are also available for some black powder pistols from their importers. Again, dealers or the importers will have catalogs.

The black powder guns are arranged in four sections: Single Shot Pistols, Revolvers, Muskets & Rifles, and Shotguns. The guns within each section are arranged roughly by date of the original, with the oldest first. Thus the 1836 Paterson replica leads off the revolver section, and flintlocks precede percussion arms in the other sections.

## BLACK POWDER SINGLE SHOT PISTOLS—FLINT & PERCUSSION

Scottish Black Watch

### BLACK WATCH SCOTCH PISTOL
**Caliber:** 577 (.550″ round ball).
**Barrel:** 7″, smoothbore.
**Weight:** 1½ lbs. **Length:** 12″ over-all.
**Stock:** Brass.
**Sights:** None.
**Features:** Faithful reproduction of this military flintlock. From Dixie.
**Price:** ...................................................... $135.00

Dixie Charleville

### CHARLEVILLE FLINTLOCK PISTOL
**Caliber:** 69, (.680″ round ball).
**Barrel:** 7½″.
**Weight:** 48 oz. **Length:** 13½″ over-all.
**Stock:** Walnut.
**Sights:** None.
**Features:** Brass frame, polished steel barrel, iron belt hook, brass buttcap and backstrap. Replica of original 1777 pistol. Imported by Dixie.
**Price:** ...................................................... $135.00

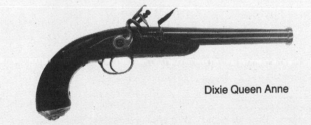

Dixie Queen Anne

### DIXIE QUEEN ANNE FLINTLOCK PISTOL
**Caliber:** 50 (.490″ round ball).
**Barrel:** 7½″, smoothbore.
**Stock:** Walnut.
**Sights:** None.
**Features:** Browned steel barrel, fluted brass trigger guard, brass mask on butt. Lockplate left in the white. Made by Pedersoli in Italy. Introduced 1983. Imported by Dixie Gun Works.
**Price:** ...................................................... $99.95

Lyman Plains Pistol

### LYMAN PLAINS PISTOL
**Caliber:** 50 or 54.
**Barrel:** 8″, 1-in-30″ twist, both calibers.
**Weight:** 50 oz. **Length:** 15″ over-all.
**Stock:** Walnut half-stock.
**Sights:** Blade front, square notch rear adj. for windage.
**Features:** Polished brass trigger guard and ramrod tip, color case-hardened coil spring lock, spring-loaded trigger, stainless steel nipple, blackened iron furniture. Hooked patent breech, detachable belt hook. Introduced 1981. From Lyman Products.
**Price:** Finished ............................................. $139.95
**Price:** Kit .................................................. $109.95

## HARPER'S FERRY 1806 PISTOL
**Caliber:** 58 (.570" round ball).
**Barrel:** 10".
**Weight:** 40 oz. **Length:** 16" over-all.
**Stock:** Walnut.
**Sights:** Fixed.
**Features:** Case hardened lock, brass mounted browned bbl. Replica of the first U.S. Gov't.-made flintlock pistol. Imported by Navy Arms, Dixie.
**Price:** .............................................. $135.00 to $182.00

Dixie Pennsylvania Pistol

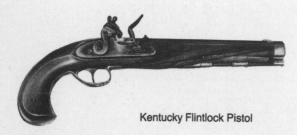

Kentucky Flintlock Pistol

H & A Kentucky Percussion

CVA Hawken Pistol

Dixie Overcoat Pistol

## DIXIE PENNSYLVANIA PISTOL
**Caliber:** 44 (.430" round ball).
**Barrel:** 10" (⅞" octagon).
**Weight:** 2½ lbs.
**Stock:** Walnut-stained hardwood.
**Sights:** Blade front, open rear drift-adj. for windage; brass.
**Features:** Available in flint or percussion. Brass trigger guard, thimbles, nose-cap, wedgeplates; high-lustre blue barrel. Imported from Italy by Dixie Gun Works.
**Price:** Flint, finished............................................. $119.95
**Price:** Percussion, finished...................................... $105.00
**Price:** Flint, kit................................................... $85.00
**Price:** Percussion, kit............................................ $72.50

## KENTUCKY FLINTLOCK PISTOL
**Caliber:** 44, 45.
**Barrel:** 10⅛".
**Weight:** 32 oz. **Length:** 15½" over-all.
**Stock:** Walnut.
**Sights:** Fixed.
**Features:** Specifications, including caliber, weight and length may vary with importer. Case hardened lock, blued bbl.; available also as brass bbl. flint Model 1821 ($136.75, Navy). Imported by Armsport, Navy Arms, The Armoury, Dixie.
**Price:** ................................................ $40.95 to $145.00
**Price:** In kit form, from.............................. $90.00 to $112.00
**Price:** Single cased set (Navy Arms) ........................... $234.00
**Price:** Double cased set (Navy Arms) .......................... $394.00

## Kentucky Percussion Pistol
Similar to flint version but percussion lock. Imported by The Armoury, Dixie, Navy Arms, CVA, Armsport, Hopkins & Allen.
**Price:** About ..................................... $97.50 to $133.00
**Price:** In kit form .............................. $35.95 to $102.00
**Price:** Single cased set (Navy Arms) ........................... $224.00
**Price:** Double cased set (Navy Arms) .......................... $370.00

## CVA HAWKEN PERCUSSION PISTOL
**Caliber:** 50.
**Barrel:** 9¾", octagonal, 1" flats; rifled.
**Weight:** 50 oz. **Length:** 16½" over-all.
**Stock:** Select walnut.
**Sights:** Beaded blade front, fully adjustable rear.
**Features:** Hooked breech, early-style brass trigger. Color case-hardened lock plate; brass wedge plate, nose cap, ramrod thimbles, trigger guard, grip cap; blue barrel and sights.
**Price:** Finished.............................................. $118.95
**Price:** Kit ................................................... $77.95

## CVA COLONIAL PISTOL
**Caliber:** 45.
**Barrel:** 6¾", octagonal, rifled.
**Length:** 12¾" over-all.
**Stocks:** Selected hardwood.
**Features:** Case hardened lock, brass furniture, fixed sights. Steel ramrod. Available in percussion only. Imported by CVA.
**Price:** Finished.............................................. $73.95
**Price:** Kit ................................................... $52.75

## DIXIE OVERCOAT PISTOL
**Caliber:** 39.
**Barrel:** 4", smoothbore.
**Weight:** 13 oz. **Length:** 8" over-all.
**Stock:** Walnut-finished hardwood. Checkered p.g.
**Sights:** Bead front.
**Features:** Shoots .380" balls. Breech plug and engraved lock are burnished steel finish; barrel and trigger guard blued.
**Price:** Engraved model ...................................... $34.50

**CAUTION:** PRICES CHANGE. CHECK AT GUNSHOP.

# BLACK POWDER SINGLE SHOT PISTOLS—FLINT & PERCUSSION

## PHILADELPHIA DERRINGER PERCUSSION PISTOL
**Caliber:** 45.
**Barrel:** 3⅛".
**Weight:** 14 oz. **Length:** 7" over-all.
**Stock:** Walnut, checkered grip.
**Sights:** Fixed.
**Features:** Engraved wedge holder and bbl. Also available in flintlock version. Imported by CVA.
**Price:** .............................................................. $66.95
**Price:** Kit form................................................... $44.95

Dixie Philadelphia

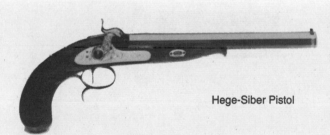
Dixie Brass Frame

Hege-Siber Pistol

Le Page Dueling Pistol

## MOORE & PATRICK FLINT DUELING PISTOL
**Caliber:** 45.
**Barrel:** 10", rifled.
**Weight:** 32 oz. **Length:** 14½" over-all.
**Stock:** European walnut, checkered.
**Sights:** Fixed.
**Features:** Engraved, silvered lock plate, blue barrel. German silver furniture. Imported from Italy by Hopkins & Allen, Dixie and Navy Arms.
**Price:** ............................................ $200.00 to $295.00

## DIXIE LINCOLN DERRINGER
**Caliber:** 41.
**Barrel:** 2", 8 lands, 8 grooves.
**Weight:** 7 oz. **Length:** 5½" over-all.
**Stock:** Walnut finish, checkered.
**Sights:** Fixed.
**Features:** Authentic copy of the "Lincoln Derringer." Shoots .400" patched ball. German silver furniture includes trigger guard with pineapple finial, wedge plates, nose, wrist, side and teardrop inlays. All furniture, lockplate, hammer, and breech plug engraved. Imported from Italy by Dixie Gun Works.
**Price:** With wooden case ........................................ $159.95
**Price:** Kit (not engraved) .................................... $59.95

## DIXIE PHILADELPHIA DERRINGER
**Caliber:** 41.
**Barrel:** 3½", octagon.
**Weight:** 8 oz. **Length:** 5½" over-all.
**Stock:** Walnut, checkered p.g.
**Sights:** Fixed.
**Features:** Barrel and lock are blued; brass furniture. From Dixie Gun Works.
**Price:** .............................................................. $45.00

## DIXIE BRASS FRAME DERRINGER
**Caliber:** 41.
**Barrel:** 2½".
**Weight:** 7 oz. **Length:** 5½" over-all.
**Stocks:** Walnut.
**Features:** Brass frame, color case hardened hammer and trigger. Shoots .395" round ball. Engraved model available. From Dixie Gun Works.
**Price:** Plain model ...................................... $49.95
**Price:** Engraved model ................................. $59.95
**Price:** Kit form, plain model ......................... $37.50

## DIXIE ABILENE DERRINGER
**Caliber:** 41.
**Barrel:** 2½", 6-groove rifling.
**Weight:** 8 oz. **Length:** 6½" over-all.
**Stocks:** Walnut.
**Features:** All steel version of Dixie's brass-framed derringers. Blued barrel, color case hardened frame and hammer. Shoots .395" patched ball. Comes with wood presentation case.
**Price:** .............................................................. $54.95
**Price:** Kit form................................................... $45.00

## HEGE-SIBER PISTOL
**Caliber:** 33, 44.
**Barrel:** 10".
**Weight:** 34 oz. **Length:** 15½" over-all.
**Stock:** French walnut, cut-checkered grip.
**Sights:** Barleycorn front, micro adjustable rear.
**Features:** Reproduction of pistol made by Swiss watchmaker Jean Siber in the 1000s. Precise lock and set trigger give fast lock time. Has engraving, plum browned barrel, trigger guard. Imported by Navy Arms. Introduced 1984.
**Price:** British version ......................................... $865.00

## NAVY ARMS LE PAGE DUELING PISTOL
**Caliber:** 44.
**Barrel:** 9", octagon, rifled.
**Weight:** 34 oz. **Length:** 15" over-all.
**Stock:** European walnut.
**Sights:** Adjustable rear.
**Features:** Single set trigger. Polished metal finish. From Navy Arms.
**Price:** .............................................................. $295.00
**Price:** Single cased set ...................................... $464.00
**Price:** Double cased set ..................................... $785.00
**Price:** Flintlock, rifled ....................................... $387.00
**Price:** Flintlock, smoothbore ............................. $387.00
**Price:** Flintlock, single cased set ....................... $559.00
**Price:** Flintlock, double cased set ...................... $975.00

**CAUTION:** PRICES CHANGE. CHECK AT GUNSHOP.

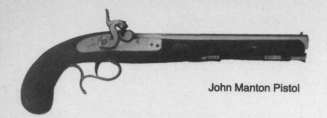

John Manton Pistol

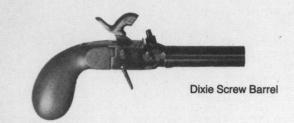

Dixie Screw Barrel

## JOHN MANTON MATCH PISTOL
**Caliber:** 45, uses .440" round ball.
**Barrel:** 10", rifled.
**Weight:** 36 oz. **Length:** 15½" over-all.
**Stock:** European walnut; checkered grip.
**Sights:** Bead front.
**Features:** Highly polished steel barrel and lock, brass furniture. From Hopkins & Allen.
**Price:** Finished gun .............................................. $125.00

## DIXIE SCREW BARREL PISTOL
**Caliber:** .445".
**Barrel:** 2½".
**Weight:** 8 oz. **Length:** 6½" over-all.
**Stocks:** Walnut.
**Features:** Trigger folds down when hammer is cocked. Close copy of the originals once made in Belgium. Uses No. 11 percussion caps.
**Price:** ...................................................... $79.95

## ELGIN CUTLASS PISTOL
**Caliber:** 44 (.440").
**Barrel:** 4¼".
**Weight:** 21 oz. **Length:** 12" over-all.
**Stock:** Walnut.
**Sights:** None.
**Features:** Replica of the pistol used by the U.S. Navy as a boarding weapon. Smoothbore barrel. Available as a kit or finished. Made in U.S. by Navy Arms.
**Price:** Kit .................................................... $78.50
**Price:** Finished ............................................. $104.95

Elgin Cutlass Pistol

## CLASSIC TWISTER O/U
**Caliber:** 36.
**Barrel:** 3⅜".
**Weight:** 24 ozs.
**Stocks:** Pearlite.
**Sights:** None.
**Features:** Over-under barrels rotate on an axis for two separate shots. Spur trigger. From Navy Arms.
**Price:** Complete, blued barrel ................................... $84.95
**Price:** Kit .................................................... $54.00

## NAVY SOUTHERNER DERRINGER
**Caliber:** 44.
**Barrel:** 2½".
**Weight:** 12 ozs. **Length:** 5" over-all.
**Stock:** Pearlite.
**Sights:** None.
**Features:** Blued barrel, brass frame. Uses .440" round ball. From Navy Arms.
**Price:** Finished ............................................... $84.95
**Price:** Kit .................................................... $54.00

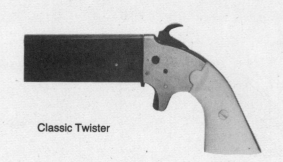

Classic Twister

## NAVY ARMS SNAKE EYES
**Caliber:** 36.
**Barrel:** 2⅝", double barrel.
**Weight:** 24 ozs. **Length:** 6¾" over-all.
**Stock:** Composition pearl.
**Sights:** None.
**Features:** Solid brass barrels and receiver. Also comes in kit form, 90% complete with only 14 pieces. From Navy Arms.
**Price:** Complete ............................................... $74.95
**Price:** Kit .................................................... $54.00

## NAVY ARMS DUCKFOOT
**Caliber:** 36.
**Barrel:** 2⅞", three barrels.
**Weight:** 32 ozs. **Length:** 10½" over-all.
**Stock:** Walnut.
**Sights:** None.
**Features:** Steel barrels and receiver, brass frame. Also comes in kit form, 90% completed, no drilling or tapping. From Navy Arms.
**Price:** Complete ............................................... $69.95
**Price:** Kit .................................................... $48.95

Navy Southerner

## ETHAN ALLEN PEPPERBOX
**Caliber:** 36.
**Barrel:** 3⅛", four smoothbore barrels.
**Weight:** 38 ozs. **Length:** 9" over-all.
**Stock:** Walnut.
**Sights:** None.
**Features:** Steel barrels, brass receiver. Also comes in kit form, 90% completed. From Navy Arms.
**Price:** Complete ............................................... $79.95
**Price:** Kit .................................................... $59.25

CAUTION: PRICES CHANGE. CHECK AT GUNSHOP.

# BLACK POWDER SINGLE SHOT PISTOLS—FLINT & PERCUSSION

## NEW ORLEANS ACE
**Caliber:** 44.
**Barrel:** 3½", rifled or smoothbore.
**Weight:** 16 ozs. **Length:** 9" over-all.
**Stock:** Walnut.
**Sights:** None.
**Features:** Solid brass frame (receiver). Available complete or in kit form. Kit is 90% complete, no drilling or tapping, fully inletted. From Navy Arms.
**Price:** Complete (smoothbore) ................................... $58.50
**Price:** Kit (smoothbore) ......................................... $43.25
**Price:** Complete (rifled bore) .................................... $64.25
**Price:** Kit (rifled bore) ......................................... $45.75

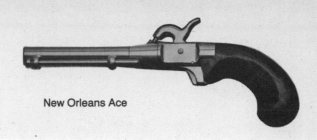
New Orleans Ace

H & A Target Boot

## HOPKINS & ALLEN BOOT PISTOL
**Caliber:** 45.
**Barrel:** 6".
**Weight:** 42 oz. **Length:** 13" over-all.
**Stock:** Walnut.
**Sights:** Silver blade front; rear adj. for e.
**Features:** Under-hammer design. From Hopkins & Allen.
**Price:** ........................................................ $71.50
**Price:** Kit form ................................................ $55.20
**Price:** Target version with wood fore-end, ramrod, hood front sight, elevator rear ........................................................ $89.80

## CVA VEST POCKET DERRINGER
**Caliber:** 44.
**Barrel:** 2½", brass.
**Weight:** 7 oz.
**Stock:** Two-piece walnut.
**Features:** All brass frame with brass ramrod. A muzzle-loading version of the Colt No. 3 derringer.
**Price:** Finished ............................................... $40.95
**Price:** Kit .................................................... $35.95

CVA Prospector

## CVA PROSPECTOR SINGLE SHOT PERCUSSION PISTOL
**Caliber:** 44.
**Barrel:** 8½", octagonal.
**Weight:** 42 oz. **Length:** 12¾" over-all.
**Stocks:** One-piece walnut.
**Sights:** Blade front, hammer notch rear.
**Features:** Brass backstrap and trigger guard, rest blued. Frame engraved with two different scenes. Introduced 1984.
**Price:** Finished ............................................... $83.95
**Price:** Kit .................................................... $63.95

Dixie Tornado Target

## DIXIE TORNADO TARGET PISTOL
**Caliber:** 44 (.430" round ball).
**Barrel:** 10", octagonal, 1-in-22" twist.
**Stock:** Walnut, target-style. Left unfinished for custom fitting. Walnut fore-end.
**Sights:** Blade on ramp front, micro-type open rear adjustable for windage and elevation.
**Features:** Grip frame style of 1860 Colt revolver. Improved model of the Tingle and B.W. Southgate pistol. Trigger adjustable for pull. Frame, barrel, hammer and sights in the white, brass trigger guard. Comes with solid brass, walnut-handled cleaning rod with jag and nylon muzzle protector. Introduced 1983. From Dixie Gun Works.
**Price:** ........................................................ $145.00

Thompson/Center Patriot

## THOMPSON/CENTER PATRIOT PERCUSSION PISTOL
**Caliber:** 36, 45.
**Barrel:** 9¼".
**Weight:** 36 oz. **Length:** 16" over-all.
**Stock:** Walnut.
**Sights:** Patridge-type. Rear adj. for w. and e.
**Features:** Hook breech system; double set triggers; coil mainspring. From Thompson/Center Arms.
**Price:** ........................................................ $215.00

## TINGLE PERCUSSION TARGET PISTOL
**Caliber:** 44.
**Barrel:** 10", octagonal.
**Weight:** 42 oz.
**Stocks:** Smooth walnut.
**Sights:** Bead front, rear adj. for w. & e.
**Features:** Engraved scenes on frame sides; brass backstrap and trigger guard; case-hardened frame and hammer. From E.M.F.
**Price:** ........................................................ $150.00

Texas Paterson 1836

### TEXAS PATERSON 1836 REVOLVER
**Caliber:** 36 (.376″ round ball).
**Barrel:** 7½″.
**Weight:** 42 oz.
**Stocks:** One-piece walnut.
**Sights:** Fixed.
**Features:** Copy of Sam Colt's first commercially-made revolving pistol. Has no loading lever but comes with loading tool. From Dixie Gun Works, Navy Arms.
**Price:** ...................................................... $225.00
**Price:** Engraved (Navy Arms) ................................. $500.00

Walker 1847

### WALKER 1847 PERCUSSION REVOLVER
**Caliber:** 44, 6-shot.
**Barrel:** 9″.
**Weight:** 72 oz. **Length:** 15½″ over-all.
**Stocks:** Walnut.
**Sights:** Fixed.
**Features:** Case hardened frame, loading lever and hammer; iron backstrap; brass trigger guard; engraved cylinder. Imported by CVA, E.M.F., Navy Arms, Dixie, Armsport, Allen Fire Arms.
**Price:** About ......................................... $250.00
**Price:** Single cased set (E.M.F., Navy Arms) ........... $235.00 to $319.00
**Price:** Kit (CVA) ...................................... $165.95

Allen 1st Dragoon

### ALLEN 1st MODEL DRAGOON
**Caliber:** 44.
**Barrel:** 7½″, part round, part octagon.
**Weight:** 66 oz.
**Stocks:** One piece walnut.
**Sights:** German silver blade front, hammer notch rear.
**Features:** First model has oval bolt cuts in cylinder, square-back flared trigger guard, V-type mainspring, short trigger. Ranger and Indian scene on cylinder. Color cased frame, loading lever, plunger and hammer; blue barrel, cylinder, trigger and wedge. Available with old-time charcoal blue or standard blue-black finish. Polished brass backstrap and trigger guard. From Allen Fire Arms.
**Price:** ...................................................... $229.00

### Allen 2nd Model Dragoon Revolver
Similar to the 1st Model except this model is distinguished by its rectangular bolt cuts in the cylinder, straight square-back trigger guard, short trigger and flat mainspring with roller in hammer.
**Price:** ...................................................... $229.00
**Price:** As Confederate Tucker & Sherrard, with 3rd Model loading lever and special cylinder engraving..................................... $229.00

Allen 2nd Dragoon

### Allen 3rd Model Dragoon Revolver
Similar to the 2nd Model except has oval trigger guard, long trigger.
**Price:** ...................................................... $229.00
**Price:** With silver plated guard and backstrap..................... $249.00

### DIXIE THIRD MODEL DRAGOON
**Caliber:** 44 ((.454″ round ball).
**Barrel:** 7⅜″.
**Weight:** 4 lbs., 2½ oz.
**Stocks:** One-piece walnut.
**Sights:** Brass pin front, hammer notch rear, or adjustable folding leaf rear.
**Features:** Cylinder engraved with Indian fight scene. This is the only Dragoon replica with folding leaf sight. Brass backstrap and trigger guard; color case-hardened steel frame, blue-black barrel. Imported by Dixie Gun Works.
**Price:** ...................................................... $140.00

Dixie Third Dragoon

### BABY DRAGOON AND MODEL 1849 REVOLVERS
**Caliber:** 31.
**Barrel:** 3″, 4″, 5″; 7 groove, RH twist.
**Weight:** About 21 oz.
**Stocks:** Varnished walnut.
**Sights:** Brass pin front, hammer notch rear.
**Features:** No loading lever on Allen Baby Dragoon models. Unfluted cylinder with Ranger and Indian scene; cupped cylinder pin; no grease grooves; one safety pin on cylinder and slot in hammer face; straight (flat) mainspring. Silver backstrap and trigger guard. From Allen Fire Arms, Dixie, CVA.
**Price:** ...................................................... $199.00
**Price:** 6″ barrel, with loading lever (Dixie) ...................... $125.00
**Price:** 4″ barrel, brass frame, no loading lever (CVA) .............. $88.95
**Price:** Kit (CVA) ............................................... $74.95

Dixie Baby Dragoon

**CAUTION:** PRICES CHANGE. CHECK AT GUNSHOP.

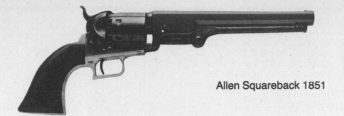

Allen Squareback 1851

Dixie 1851 Navy

## NEW MODEL 1858 ARMY PERCUSSION REVOLVER
**Caliber:** 36 or 44, 6-shot.
**Barrel:** 6½" or 8".
**Weight:** 40 oz. **Length:** 13½" over-all.
**Stocks:** Walnut.
**Sights:** Blade front, groove-in-frame rear.
**Features:** Replica of Remington Model 1858. Also available from some importers as Army Model Belt Revolver in 36 cal., shortened and lightened version of the 44. Target Model (Allen, Navy) has fully adj. target rear sight, target front, 36 or 44. Imported by CVA, (as 1858 Remington Army), Dixie, Navy Arms, Hopkins & Allen, The Armoury, E.M.F., Euroarms of America (engraved, stainless and plain), Armsport, Allen.
**Price:** About .................................................. $229.00
**Price:** Single cased set (Navy Arms) ......................... $235.00
**Price:** Double cased set (Navy Arms) ......................... $390.00
**Price:** Nickel finish (E.M.F.) ................................ $152.75
**Price:** Stainless steel (Euroarms, Navy Arms, Allen)..... $140.00 to $299.00
**Price:** Target model (Euroarms, Navy Arms, E.M.F., Allen) $95.95 to $185.00
**Price:** Brass frame, finished (CVA, Navy Arms) ......... $99.00 to $122.95
**Price:** As above, kit (CVA, Navy Arms) ................. $80.00 to $101.95

## Allen 1861 Navy Percussion Revolver
Similar to 1851 Navy except has round 7½" barrel, rounded trigger guard, German silver blade front sight, "creeping" loading lever.
**Price:** ................................................. $229.00
**Price:** Stainless ..................................... $269.00

## 1851 NAVY-SHERIFF
Same as 1851 Sheriff model except has 4" barrel. Imported by Allen, CVA, E.M.F., Euroarms of America.
**Price:** ........................................ $80.00 to $199.00
**Price:** Kit (CVA) ................................... $83.95
**Price:** Engraved, brass and nickel plated (CVA) ......... $200.00

## ARMY 1851 PERCUSSION REVOLVER
**Caliber:** 44, 6-shot.
**Barrel:** 7½".
**Weight:** 45 oz. **Length:** 13" over-all.
**Stocks:** Walnut finish.
**Sights:** Fixed.
**Features:** 44 caliber version of the 1851 Navy. Imported by The Armoury, E.M.F.
**Price:** ........................................ $65.00 to $138.00

## 1851 SHERIFF MODEL PERCUSSION REVOLVER
**Caliber:** 36, 44, 6-shot.
**Barrel:** 5".
**Weight:** 40 oz. **Length:** 10½" over-all.
**Stocks:** Walnut.
**Sights:** Fixed.
**Features:** Brass back strap and trigger guard; engraved navy scene; case hardened frame, hammer, loading lever. Imported by E.M.F.
**Price:** Steel frame .................................... $85.00
**Price:** Brass frame ................................... $102.00
**Price:** Kit, brass or steel frame....................... $65.00

CVA 1858 Army

Consult our Directory pages for the location of firms mentioned.

## NAVY MODEL 1851 PERCUSSION REVOLVER
**Caliber:** 36, 6-shot.
**Barrel:** 7½".
**Weight:** 44 oz. **Length:** 13" over-all.
**Stocks:** Walnut finish.
**Sights:** Post front, hammer notch rear.
**Features:** Brass backstrap and trigger guard; some have 1st model squareback trigger guard, engraved cylinder with navy battle scene; case hardened frame, hammer, loading lever. Imported by The Armoury, Navy Arms, Allen, E.M.F., Dixie, Euroarms of America, Armsport, Hopkins & Allen, CVA.
**Price:** Brass frame.................................. $60.00 to $199.00
**Price:** Steel frame .................................. $31.50 to $209.00
**Price:** Stainless Squareback (Allen)................... $259.00
**Price:** Kit form .................................... $60.00 to $119.95
**Price:** Engraved model (Dixie)........................ $97.50
**Price:** Also as "Buntline" (Dixie) .................... $166.95
**Price:** Navy-Civilian model (E.M.F., Allen) ........... $229.00
**Price:** Single cased set, steel frame (Navy Arms) ...... $218.00
**Price:** Double cased set, steel frame (Navy Arms) ...... $357.00
**Price:** London Model with iron backstrap (Allen) ....... $229.00

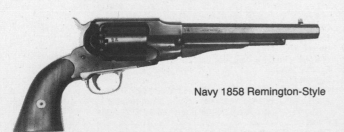

Navy 1858 Remington-Style

## NAVY ARMS 1858 REMINGTON-STYLE REVOLVER
**Caliber:** 44.
**Barrel:** 8".
**Weight:** 2 lbs., 13 ozs.
**Stock:** Smooth walnut.
**Sights:** Dovetailed blade front.
**Features:** First exact reproduction — correct in size and weight to the original, with progressive rifling; highly polished with charcoal blue finish. From Navy Arms.
**Price:** Deluxe model ................................. $250.00
**Price:** As above, single cased set (Navy Arms) .......... $195.00
**Price:** As above, double cased set (Navy Arms) .......... $310.00
**Price:** Steel frame, finished (CVA) ................... $167.95
**Price:** As above, kit (CVA) .......................... $126.95

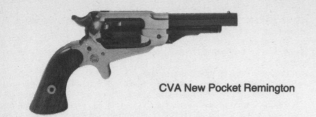

CVA New Pocket Remington

Dixie 1860 Army

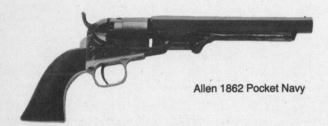

Allen 1862 Pocket Navy

## 1862 LEECH & RIGDON REVOLVER
**Caliber:** 36.
**Barrel:** 7½".
**Weight:** 2 lbs., 10 oz. **Length:** 13½" over-all.
**Stocks:** Smooth walnut.
**Sights:** Fixed.
**Features:** Modern version of the famous Civil War revolver. Brass backstrap and trigger guard. Color case hardened frame. Copy of the Colt Navy but with rounded Dragoon-type barrel. From Allen Fire Arms.
**Price:** .......................................... $199.00

## J.H. DANCE & BROS. REVOLVER
**Caliber:** 36, 6 shot.
**Barrel:** 7½" round.
**Weight:** 44 oz. **Length:** 13" over-all.
**Stocks:** One piece walnut.
**Sights:** Blade front, notch rear.
**Features:** Replica of the J.H. Dance revolver made for the Confederacy in Texas in 1862. Blued barrel and cylinder; color case-hardened frame. Imported by Southwest Muzzle-Loaders Supply
**Price:** .......................................... $275.00

## ROGERS & SPENCER PERCUSSION REVOLVER
**Caliber:** 44.
**Barrel:** 7½".
**Weight:** 47 oz. **Length:** 13¾" over-all.
**Stocks:** Walnut.
**Sights:** Cone front, integral groove in frame for rear.
**Features:** Accurate reproduction of a Civil War design. Solid frame; extra large nipple cut-out on rear of cylinder; loading lever and cylinder easily removed for cleaning. Comes with six spare nipples and wrench/screwdriver. From Euroarms of America (engraved, burnished, target models), Navy Arms, Dixie.
**Price:** ............................. $120.00 to $169.00
**Price:** Nickel plated ........................... $120.00
**Price:** Kit version ............................. $95.00
**Price:** Target version.......................... $200.00

## CVA NEW MODEL POCKET REMINGTON
**Caliber:** 31.
**Barrel:** 4", octagonal.
**Weight:** 15½ oz. **Length:** 7½" over-all.
**Stocks:** Two-piece walnut.
**Sights:** Post front, grooved top-strap rear.
**Features:** Spur trigger, brass frame with blued barrel and cylinder. Available finished or in kit form. Introduced 1984.
**Price:** Finished .............................. $82.95
**Price:** Kit ..................................... $68.95

## 1860 ARMY PERCUSSION REVOLVER
**Caliber:** 44, 6-shot.
**Barrel:** 8".
**Weight:** 40 oz. **Length:** 13⅝" over-all.
**Stocks:** Walnut.
**Sights:** Fixed.
**Features:** Engraved navy scene on cylinder; brass trigger guard; case hardened frame, loading lever and hammer. Some importers supply pistol cut for detachable shoulder stock, have accessory stock available. Imported by E.M.F., CVA, Navy Arms, The Armoury, Dixie (half-fluted cylinder, not roll engraved), Euroarms of America (engraved, stainless steel or burnished steel model), Armsport, Hopkins & Allen, Allen.
**Price:** About ................................ $229.00
**Price:** Single cased set (Navy Arms, E.M.F.) .......... $149.00 to $230.00
**Price:** Double cased set (Navy Arms) ............... $385.00
**Price:** 1861 Navy: Same as Army except 36 cal., 7½" bbl., wt. 41 oz., cut for stock; round cylinder (fluted avail.), from E.M.F., Allen, CVA (brass frame) .......................... $99.95 to $245.00
**Price:** Kit (CVA, E.M.F.) ..................... $90.00 to $124.95
**Price:** Stainless steel (Euroarms, Allen)............... $200.00 to $269.00

## ALLEN 1862 POCKET NAVY PERCUSSION REVOLVER
**Caliber:** 36.
**Barrel:** 4½", 5½", 6½", octagonal, 7 groove, LH twist.
**Weight:** 27 oz. (5½" barrel)
**Stocks:** One piece varnished walnut.
**Sights:** Brass pin front, hammer notch rear.
**Features:** Rebated cylinder, hinged loading lever, brass backstrap and trigger guard, color cased frame, hammer, loading lever, plunger and latch, rest blued. Has original-type markings. From Allen Fire Arms.
**Price:** .......................................... $199.00

## 1862 POCKET POLICE PERCUSSION REVOLVER
**Caliber:** 36, 5-shot.
**Barrel:** 4½", 5½", 7½".
**Weight:** 26 oz. **Length:** 12" (6½" bbl.).
**Stocks:** Walnut.
**Sights:** Fixed.
**Features:** Half-fluted and rebated cylinder; case hardened frame, loading lever and hammer; silver trigger guard and backstrap. Imported by CVA, Navy Arms (5½" only), Euroarms of America (7½" only) Allen (all lengths).
**Price:** ............................. $93.95 to $155.00
**Price:** Cased with accessories (Navy Arms) ............. $225.00
**Price:** Stainless steel (Allen) ................... $259.00

## J.H. Dance & Bros. Commemorative Ltd.
Same gun as the standard model except has charcoal blue finish with special commemorative markings and gold inlays. Comes with lined display case with brass inscription plate, leather covered powder flask, bullet mould, screwdriver, nipple wrench, six spare nipples. Only 500 guns to be issued.
**Price:** .......................................... $1,500.00

## GRISWOLD & GUNNISON PERCUSSION REVOLVER
**Caliber:** 36 or 44, 6-shot.
**Barrel:** 7½".
**Weight:** 44 oz. (36 cal.). **Length:** 13" over-all.
**Stocks:** Walnut.
**Sights:** Fixed.
**Features:** Replica of famous Confederate pistol. Brass frame, backstrap and trigger guard; case hardened loading lever; rebated cylinder (44 cal. only). Rounded Dragoon-type barrel. Imported by Navy Arms, Allen, E.M.F.
**Price:** ............................. $96.00 to $169.00
**Price:** Kit (Navy Arms, E.M.F.)................... $73.50
**Price:** Single cased set (Navy Arms) ............... $192.00
**Price:** Double cased set (Navy Arms) ............... $299.00

**CAUTION:** PRICES CHANGE. CHECK AT GUNSHOP.

# BLACK POWDER REVOLVERS

Dixie Spiller & Burr

## SPILLER & BURR REVOLVER
**Caliber:** 36 (.375″ round ball).
**Barrel:** 7″, octagon.
**Weight:** 2½ lbs. **Length:** 12½″ over-all.
**Stocks:** Two-piece walnut.
**Sights:** Fixed.
**Features:** Reproduction of the C.S.A. revolver. Brass frame and trigger guard. Also available as a kit. From Dixie, Navy Arms.
**Price:** ................................................. $69.95 to $109.00
**Price:** Kit form ........................................ $39.95 to $65.00

## LE MAT CAVALRY MODEL REVOLVER
**Caliber:** 44/65.
**Barrel:** 6¾″ (revolver); 4⅞″ (single shot).
**Weight:** NA.
**Stocks:** Hand-checkered walnut.
**Sights:** Post front, hammer-notch rear.
**Features:** Exact reproduction with all-steel construction; 44-cal. 9-shot cylinder, 65-cal. single barrel; color case-hardened hammer with selector; spur trigger guard; ring at butt; lever-type barrel release. From Navy Arms.
**Price:** ........................................................ $500.00
**Price:** Army model (round trigger guard, pin-type barrel release) .... $500.00
**Price:** Naval-style (thumb selector or hammer) ................... $500.00

Le Mat Cavalry Model

Dixie "Wyatt Earp"

## DIXIE "WYATT EARP" REVOLVER
**Caliber:** 44.
**Barrel:** 12″ octagon.
**Weight:** 46 oz. **Length:** 18″ over-all.
**Stocks:** Two piece walnut.
**Sights:** Fixed.
**Features:** Highly polished brass frame, backstrap and trigger guard; blued barrel and cylinder; case hardened hammer, trigger and loading lever. Navy-size shoulder stock ($45.00) will fit with minor fitting. From Dixie Gun Works.
**Price:** ........................................................ $99.95

## E.M.F. 44 BALLISTER REVOLVER
**Caliber:** 44, 6-shot.
**Barrel:** 12″.
**Weight:** 2¾ lbs.
**Stocks:** Two-piece walnut.
**Sights:** Fixed.
**Features:** Barrel and cylinder blued, frame and trigger guard are brass; hammer and loading lever are color case hardened. From E.M.F.
**Price:** ........................................................ $99.00

Consult our Directory pages for the location of firms mentioned.

Freedom Mini Percussion

## FREEDOM ARMS PERCUSSION MINI REVOLVER
**Caliber:** 22, 5-shot.
**Barrel:** 1″, 1¾″, 3″.
**Weight:** 4¾ oz. (1″ bbl.).
**Stocks:** Simulated ebony, or rosewood (optional).
**Sights:** Fixed.
**Features:** Percussion version of the 22 RF gun. All stainless steel; spur trigger. Gun comes with leather carrying pouch, bullet setting tool, powder measure, 20 29-gr. bullets. Introduced 1983. From Freedom Arms.
**Price:** 1″ barrel ................................................ $130.00
**Price:** 1¾″ barrel .............................................. $130.00
**Price:** 3″ barrel ............................................... $142.70

Ruger Old Army

## RUGER 44 OLD ARMY PERCUSSION REVOLVER
**Caliber:** 44, 6-shot. Uses .457″ dia. lead bullets.
**Barrel:** 7½″ (6-groove, 16″ twist).
**Weight:** 46 oz. **Length:** 13¾″ over-all.
**Stocks:** Smooth walnut.
**Sights:** Ramp front, rear adj. for w. and e.
**Features:** Stainless steel standard size nipples, chrome-moly steel cylinder and frame, same lockwork as in original Super Blackhawk. Also available in stainless steel in very limited quantities. Made in USA. From Sturm, Ruger & Co.
**Price:** Stainless steel (Model KBP-7) ........................... $321.00
**Price:** Blued steel (Model BP-7) ............................... $251.50

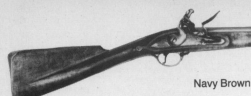

Navy Brown Bess

## NAVY ARMS CHARLEVILLE MUSKET
**Caliber:** 69
**Barrel:** 44⅝".
**Weight:** 8¾ lbs. **Length:** 59⅜" over-all.
**Stock:** Walnut.
**Sights:** Blade front.
**Features:** Replica of Revolutionary War 1763 musket. Bright metal, walnut stock. From Navy Arms.
**Price:** Finished .............................................. $370.00
**Price:** Kit ..................................................... $310.00

## SECOND MODEL BROWN BESS MUSKET
**Caliber:** 75, uses .735" round ball.
**Barrel:** 42", smoothbore.
**Weight:** 9½ lbs. **Length:** 59" over-all.
**Stock:** Walnut (Navy); walnut-stained hardwood (Dixie).
**Sights:** Fixed.
**Features:** Polished barrel and lock with brass trigger guard and buttplate. Bayonet and scabbard available. From Navy Arms, Dixie.
**Price:** Finished ...................................... $290.00 to $450.00
**Price:** Kit ............................................. $265.00 to $345.00

Dixie Indian Gun

## DIXIE INDIAN GUN
**Caliber:** 75.
**Barrel:** 31", round tapered.
**Weight:** About 9 lbs. **Length:** 47" over-all.
**Stock:** Hardwood.
**Sights:** Blade front.
**Features:** Modified Brown Bess musket; brass furniture, browned lock and barrel. Lock is marked "GRICE 1762" with crown over "GR." Serpent-style sideplate. Introduced 1983.
**Price:** Complete ..................................................... $375.00
**Price:** As above, in kit form ................................... $360.00

Dixie Tennessee Rifle

## DIXIE TENNESSEE MOUNTAIN RIFLE
**Caliber:** 32 or 50.
**Barrel:** 41½", 6-groove rifling, brown finish.
**Length:** 56" over-all.
**Stock:** Walnut, oil finish; Kentucky-style.
**Sights:** Silver blade front, open buckhorn rear.
**Features:** Re-creation of the original mountain rifles. Early Schultz lock, interchangeable flint or percussion with vent plug or drum and nipple. Tumbler has fly. Double-set triggers. All metal parts browned. From Dixie.
**Price:** Flint or Percussion, finished rifle, 50 cal. .................... $250.00
**Price:** Kit, 50 cal. ...................................................... $195.00
**Price:** Left-hand model, flint or perc.. .............................. $250.00
**Price:** Left-hand kit, flint or perc., 50 cal. .......................... $225.00
**Price:** Squirrel Rifle (as above except in 32 cal. with ¹³⁄₁₆" barrel), flint or percussion ................................................. $295.00
**Price:** Kit, 32 cal., flint or percussion ............................. $255.00

## KENTUCKY FLINTLOCK RIFLE
**Caliber:** 44 or 45.
**Barrel:** 35".
**Weight:** 7lbs. **Length:** 50" over-all.
**Stock:** Walnut stained, brass fittings.
**Sights:** Fixed.
**Features:** Available in Carbine model also, 28" bbl. Some variations in detail, finish. Kits also available from some importers. Imported by Navy Arms, The Armoury, CVA (45-cal. only), Armsport, Hopkins & Allen.
**Price:** About ....................................................... $273.75
**Price:** Kit form (CVA, Hopkins & Allen) ................. $119.95 to 189.95
**Price:** Deluxe model, flint or percussion, 50-cal. (Navy Arms)....... $275.00

## Kentucky Percussion Rifle
Similar to flintlock except percussion lock. Finish and features vary with importer. Imported by Navy Arms, The Armoury, CVA, Hopkins & Allen, Armsport (rifle-shotgun combo).
**Price:** ........................................................ $54.95 to 250.00
**Price:** Armsport combo......................................... $235.00
**Price:** 50 cal. (Navy Arms) ................................... $259.00

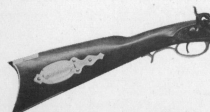

Kentuckian Rifle

## KENTUCKIAN RIFLE & CARBINE
**Caliber:** 44.
**Barrel:** 35" (Rifle), 27½" (Carbine).

**Weight:** 7 lbs. (Rifle), 5½ lbs. (Carbine). **Length:** 51" (Rifle) over-all, Carbine 43".
**Stock:** Walnut stain.
**Sights:** Brass blade front, steel V-Ramp rear.
**Features:** Octagon bbl., case hardened and engraved lock plate. Brass furniture. Imported by Dixie.
**Price:** Rifle or carbine, flint.................................... $185.00
**Price:** As above, percussion ................................. $175.00

# BLACK POWDER MUSKETS & RIFLES

Dixie York County

**Weight:** 7½ lbs. **Length:** 51½" over-all.
**Stock:** Maple, one piece.
**Sights:** Blade front, V-notch rear, brass.
**Features:** Adjustable double-set triggers. Brass trigger guard, patchbox, butt-plate, nosecap and sideplate. Case-hardened lockplate. From Dixie Gun Works.
**Price:** Percussion. . . . . . . . . . . . . . . . . . . . . . . . . . . . . . . . . . . . . . . . . $210.00
**Price:** Flint . . . . . . . . . . . . . . . . . . . . . . . . . . . . . . . . . . . . . . . . . . . . . $215.00
**Price:** Percussion Kit. . . . . . . . . . . . . . . . . . . . . . . . . . . . . . . . . . . . . $149.00
**Price:** Flint Kit . . . . . . . . . . . . . . . . . . . . . . . . . . . . . . . . . . . . . . . . . . $160.00

## YORK COUNTY RIFLE
**Caliber:** 45 (.445" round ball).
**Barrel:** 36", rifled, ⅞" octagon, blue.

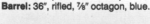

## HATFIELD SQUIRREL RIFLE
**Caliber:** 36, 45, 50
**Barrel:** 39½", octagon, 32" on half-stock.
**Weight:** 8 lbs. (32 cal.).
**Stock:** American fancy maple fullstock.
**Sights:** Silver blade front, buckhorn rear
**Features:** Recreation of the traditional squirrel rifle. Available in flint or percussion with brass trigger guard and buttplate. From Hatfield Rifle Works. Introduced 1983.

Hatfield Squirrel Rifle

**Price:** Full-stock, flint or percussion Grade I . . . . . . . . . . . . . . . . . . . . $295.00
**Price:** As above, Grade II . . . . . . . . . . . . . . . . . . . . . . . . . . . . . . . . . . $395.00
**Price:** As above, Grade III . . . . . . . . . . . . . . . . . . . . . . . . . . . . . . . . . $395.00

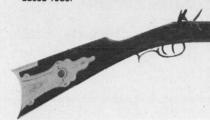

CVA Pennsylvania

## CVA PENNSYLVANIA LONG RIFLE
**Caliber:** 50.
**Barrel:** 40", octagonal; ⅞" flats.
**Weight:** 8 lbs., 3 ozs. **Length:** 55¾" over-all.
**Stock:** Select walnut.
**Sights:** Brass blade front, fixed semi-buckhorn rear.
**Features:** Color case-hardened lock plate, brass buttplate, toe plate, patch-box, trigger guard, thimbles, nosecap; blued barrel, double-set triggers; authentic V-type mainspring. Introduced 1983. From CVA.
**Price:** Finished, percussion . . . . . . . . . . . . . . . . . . . . . . . . . . . . . . . . . $307.95
**Price:** Finished, flintlock . . . . . . . . . . . . . . . . . . . . . . . . . . . . . . . . . . $318.95
**Price:** Kit, percussion . . . . . . . . . . . . . . . . . . . . . . . . . . . . . . . . . . . . . $265.95
**Price:** Kit, flintlock . . . . . . . . . . . . . . . . . . . . . . . . . . . . . . . . . . . . . . . $275.95

## PECOS VALLEY HALF STOCK PENNSYLVANIA RIFLE
**Caliber:** 36, 45.
**Barrel:** 35½"; 1-in-48" twist (36-cal.), 1-in-72" twist (45-cal.).
**Weight:** About 6½ lbs. **Length:** 50½" over-all.
**Stock:** Select grade maple with satin finish, 13½" length of pull.
**Sights:** Silver blade, buckhorn rear.
**Features:** Durs Egg percussion lock by L&R; Davis double set trigger; brass furniture. Made in U.S. by Pecos Valley Armory. Introduced 1984.
**Price:** . . . . . . . . . . . . . . . . . . . . . . . . . . . . . . . . . . . . . . . . . $399.00

Ozark Taney County

## OZARK MOUNTAIN TANEY COUNTY RIFLE
**Caliber:** 32, 36, 40.
**Barrel:** 36".
**Weight:** 7½ lbs. **Length:** 53" over-all.
**Stock:** American maple, fullstock design.
**Sights:** German silver blade front, full buckhorn rear.
**Features:** Available in flint or percussion, right or left hand; double set trigger.
**Price:** From . . . . . . . . . . . . . . . . . . . . . . . . . . . . . . . . . . . . . . . . . . . . $585.00

## Ozark Mountain Muskrat Rifle
Same as the Taney County rifle except has maple half-stock. Available in right or left hand, flint or percussion.
**Price:** From . . . . . . . . . . . . . . . . . . . . . . . . . . . . . . . . . . . . . . . . . . . . $525.00

Oregon Trail Transition

**Sights:** Steel blade front, semi-buckhorn rear.
**Features:** Available as various Leman patterns, right- or left-hand—Early Rifle (1⁵⁄₁₆" or 1" × 39" barrel), Transition Rifle (1" × 34" barrel), Indian Trade Rifle (1" or 1¹⁄₁₆" × 30" barrel), Light Rifle (⅞" × 38" barrel). Full stock or half stock, single trigger, brass furniture. Many options available. From Oregon Trail Riflesmiths.
**Price:** Half stock Leman, percussion, right or left hand. . . . . . . . . . . $715.00
**Price:** Half stock, flintlock, right or left hand . . . . . . . . . . . . . . . . . . $725.00
**Price:** Full stock Indian Trade, Transition, percussion, right or left-hand model . . . . . . . . . . . . . . . . . . . . . . . . . . . . . . . . . . . . . . . . . . . . . $775.00
**Price:** As above, flintlock, right- or left-hand . . . . . . . . . . . . . . . . . . . $785.00

## OREGON TRAIL LEMAN PATTERN RIFLES
**Caliber:** 36, 40, 45, 50, 54, 58.
**Barrel:** 30" to 39", depending upon style of rifle.
**Weight:** NA. **Length:** NA.
**Stock:** Curly maple.

# BLACK POWDER MUSKETS & RIFLES

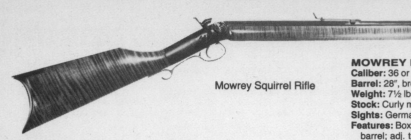

Mowrey Squirrel Rifle

## MOWREY ETHAN ALLEN SQUIRREL RIFLE
**Caliber:** 36 or 45.
**Barrel:** 28″, browned ocatgon, 13/16″ flats, 8-groove gain-twist rifling.
**Weight:** 7½ lbs. **Length:** 43″ over-all.
**Stock:** Curly maple, Premium or Fancy grade.
**Sights:** German silver and brass blade front, open, adj. semi-buckhorn rear.
**Features:** Boxlock action, brass or browned steel frame and furniture; cut-rifled barrel; adj. trigger; hand-rubbed oil finish. Made in U.S. Add $38 for Fancy wood.
**Price:** Complete, brass or steel . . . . . . . . . . . . . . . . . . . . . . . . . . . . . . . . $330.00
**Price:** Kit (amateur) . . . . . . . . . . . . . . . . . . . . . . . . . . . . . . . . . . . . . . . $250.00
**Price:** Kit (expert) . . . . . . . . . . . . . . . . . . . . . . . . . . . . . . . . . . . . . . . . $190.00

## MOWREY GUN WORKS MODEL "1N30"
**Caliber:** 45, 50, 54.
**Barrel:** 45 cal. — 28″, browned octagon, 7/8″ flats; 50, 54 cal. — 28″, browned octagon with 1″ flats.
**Weight:** 45 cal. — 8 lbs.; 50, 54 cal. — 10 lbs. **Length:** 44″ over-all.
**Stock:** Curly maple, Premium or Fancy grade.
**Sights:** White dot blade front, modern fully adj. rear.
**Features:** Rifling and twist specially designed for conical bullets; steel action and furniture; boxlock action; adj. trigger; oil finsh on wood. Made in U.S. Add $38 for fancy wood.
**Price:** Complete . . . . . . . . . . . . . . . . . . . . . . . . . . . . . . . . . . . . . . . . . . $330.00
**Price:** Kit (amateur) . . . . . . . . . . . . . . . . . . . . . . . . . . . . . . . . . . . . . . . $250.00
**Price:** Kit (expert) . . . . . . . . . . . . . . . . . . . . . . . . . . . . . . . . . . . . . . . . $190.00

## Mowrey Ethan Allen Plains Rifle
Similar to the Squirrel Rifle except in 50 or 54 caliber, 32″ browned octagon barrel with 1″ flats, weighs 10 lbs. and has 48″ over-all length. Add $30 for Schuetzen buttplate.
**Price:** Complete, brass or steel . . . . . . . . . . . . . . . . . . . . . . . . . . . . . . . . $330.00
**Price:** Kit (amateur) . . . . . . . . . . . . . . . . . . . . . . . . . . . . . . . . . . . . . . . $250.00
**Price:** Kit (expert) . . . . . . . . . . . . . . . . . . . . . . . . . . . . . . . . . . . . . . . . $190.00

Mowrey Rocky Mountain

## MOWREY ETHAN ALLEN ROCKY MOUNTAIN HUNTER
**Caliber:** 50 or 54.
**Barrel:** 28″, browned octagon, 1″ flats, 8-groove gain-twist rifling.
**Weight:** 8 lbs. **Length:** 44″ over-all.
**Stock:** Curly maple, Premium or Fancy grade.
**Sights:** Blade front with white dot, modern fully adj. rear.
**Features:** Steel box-lock action and furniture; adj. trigger; hand-rubbed oil finish. Made in U.S. Add $38 for Fancy wood.
**Price:** Complete . . . . . . . . . . . . . . . . . . . . . . . . . . . . . . . . . . . . . . . . . . $330.00
**Price:** Kit (amateur) . . . . . . . . . . . . . . . . . . . . . . . . . . . . . . . . . . . . . . . $250.00
**Price:** Kit (expert) . . . . . . . . . . . . . . . . . . . . . . . . . . . . . . . . . . . . . . . . $190.00

## ALLEN SQUIRREL RIFLE
**Caliber:** 32.
**Barrel:** 28″, octagonal.
**Weight:** NA. **Length:** NA.
**Stock:** Walnut.
**Sights:** Blade front, fully adj. rear.
**Features:** Color case-hardened lock, brass trigger guard, balance blued. Imported by Allen Fire Arms.
**Price:** Flintlock . . . . . . . . . . . . . . . . . . . . . . . . . . . . . . . . . . . . . . . . . . $229.00
**Price:** Percussion . . . . . . . . . . . . . . . . . . . . . . . . . . . . . . . . . . . . . . . . . $199.00

H&A Plainsman Rifle

## HOPKINS & ALLEN PLAINSMAN RIFLE
**Caliber:** 45.
**Barrel:** 37″.
**Weight:** 7½ lbs. **Length:** 53″ over-all.
**Stock:** Walnut.
**Sights:** Blade front, rear adjustable for w. & e.
**Features:** Double set triggers, blued barrel has 13/16″ flats, solid brass barrel rib, engraved percussion lockplate. From Hopkins & Allen.
**Price:** . . . . . . . . . . . . . . . . . . . . . . . . . . . . . . . . . . . . . . . . . . . . . . . . $292.60

CVA Squirrel Rifle

## CVA SQUIRREL RIFLE
**Caliber:** 32.
**Barrel:** 25″, octagonal; 11/16″ flats.
**Weight:** 5 lbs., 12 oz. **Length:** 40¾″ over-all.
**Stock:** Hardwood.
**Sights:** Beaded blade front, fully adjustable hunting-style rear.
**Features:** Available in right or left-hand versions. Color case-hardened lock plate, brass buttplate, trigger guard, wedge plates, thimbles; double-set triggers; hooked breech; authentic V-type mainspring. Introduced 1983. From CVA.

**Price:** Finished, percussion, right hand . . . . . . . . . . . . . . . . . . . . . . $201.95
**Price:** Finished, left hand . . . . . . . . . . . . . . . . . . . . . . . . . . . . . . . . . . $212.95
**Price:** Kit, percussion, right hand . . . . . . . . . . . . . . . . . . . . . . . . . . . . $143.95
**Price:** Kit, left hand . . . . . . . . . . . . . . . . . . . . . . . . . . . . . . . . . . . . . . $153.95
**Price:** Kit, flintlock . . . . . . . . . . . . . . . . . . . . . . . . . . . . . . . . . . . . . . . $153.95

**CAUTION:** PRICES CHANGE. CHECK AT GUNSHOP.

# BLACK POWDER MUSKETS & RIFLES

Lyman Great Plains

## LYMAN GREAT PLAINS RIFLE
**Caliber:** 50 or 54 cal.
**Barrel:** 32″, 1-66″ twist.
**Weight:** 9 lbs.
**Stock:** Walnut.
**Sights:** Steel blade front, buckhorn rear adj. for w. & e. and fixed notch primitive sight included.
**Features:** Blued steel furniture. Stainless steel nipple. Coil spring lock, Hawken-style trigger guard and double set triggers. Round thimbles recessed and sweated into rib. Steel wedge plates and toe plate. Introduced 1979. From Lyman.
**Price:** Percussion............................................. $294.95
**Price:** Flintlock.............................................. $304.95
**Price:** Percussion Kit........................................ $209.95

## CVA KENTUCKY RIFLE
**Caliber:** 45 (.451″ bore).
**Barrel:** 33½″, rifled, octagon (⅞″ flats).
**Length:** 48″ over-all.
**Stock:** Select hardwood.
**Sights:** Brass Kentucky blade type front, dovetail open rear.
**Features:** Available in either flint or percussion. Stainless steel nipple included. From CVA.
**Price:** Percussion............................................. $205.95
**Price:** Flint................................................... $217.95
**Price:** Percussion Kit........................................ $119.95
**Price:** Flint Kit.............................................. $133.95

## PENNSYLVANIA FULL STOCK RIFLE
**Caliber:** 45 or 50.
**Barrel:** 32″ rifled, ¹⁵/₁₆″ dia.
**Weight:** 8½ lbs.
**Stock:** Walnut.
**Sights:** Fixed.
**Features:** Available in flint or percussion. Blued lock and barrel, brass furniture. Offered complete or in kit form. From The Armoury.
**Price:** Flint................................................... $235.00
**Price:** Percussion............................................. $210.00

Lyman Trade Rifle

**Weight:** 8¾ lbs. **Length:** 45″ over-all.
**Stock:** European walnut.
**Sights:** Blade front, open rear adj. for w. or optional fixed sights.
**Features:** Fast twist rifling for conical bullets. Polished brass furniture with blue steel parts, stainless steel nipple. Hook breech, single trigger, coil spring percussion lock. Steel barrel rib and ramrod ferrules. Introduced 1980. From Lyman.
**Price:** Percussion............................................. $209.95
**Price:** Kit, percussion........................................ $159.95
**Price:** Flintlock.............................................. $219.95

## LYMAN TRADE RIFLE
**Caliber:** 50 or 54.
**Barrel:** 28″ octagon, 1-48″ twist.

CVA Frontier

## CVA FRONTIER RIFLE
**Caliber:** 45, 50.
**Barrel:** 28″, octagon; ¹⁵/₁₆″ flats, 1-66″ twist.
**Weight:** 6 lbs., 14 oz. **Length:** 44″ over-all.
**Stock:** American hardwood.
**Sights:** Brass blade front, fully adjustable hunting-style rear.
**Features:** Available in flint or percussion. Solid brass nosecap, trigger guard, buttplate, thimbles and wedge plates; blued barrel; color case hardened lock and hammer. Double set triggers, patented breech plug bolster, V-type mainspring. Hooked breech. Introduced 1980.
**Price:** 50 cal., percussion, complete rifle.................... $223.95
**Price:** Finished, left hand.................................... $234.95
**Price:** 50 cal. flint, complete rifle......................... $234.95
**Price:** 45, 50 cal., percussion, kit.......................... $167.95
**Price:** Percussion kit, left hand............................. $170.95
**Price:** 50 cal. flint, kit.................................... $177.95

Oregon Trail "Poor Boy"

Consult our Directory pages for the location of firms mentioned.

## OREGON TRAIL "POOR BOY" RIFLE
**Caliber:** 32, 36, 40, 45, 50, 54, 58.
**Barrel:** Up to 40″; ¹³/₁₆″, ⅞″, ¹⁵/₁₆″ or 1″ flats.
**Weight:** NA. **Length:** NA.
**Stock:** Plain maple; horn heel fitting instead of buttplate.
**Sights:** Steel blade front, semi-buckhorn rear.
**Features:** Classic rifle of North Carolina, eastern Tenn. Steel furniture; long tang, single trigger. Buttplate, double set triggers, fancy wood available. Introduced 1986.
**Price:** Percussion, right- or left-hand....................... $595.00
**Price:** As above, flintlock................................... $635.00
**Price:** As Southern iron-mounted rifle with patch box, buttplate entry thimble, steel nose cap, percussion.......... $785.00
**Price:** As above, flintlock................................... $795.00

# BLACK POWDER MUSKETS & RIFLES

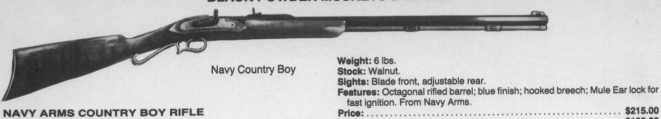

Navy Country Boy

**Weight:** 6 lbs.
**Stock:** Walnut.
**Sights:** Blade front, adjustable rear.
**Features:** Octagonal rifled barrel; blue finish; hooked breech; Mule Ear lock for fast ignition. From Navy Arms.

**NAVY ARMS COUNTRY BOY RIFLE**
**Caliber:** 32, 36, 45, 50.
**Barrel:** 26″.

**Price:** .......................................... $215.00
**Price:** Kit .................................... $165.00

H&A Pa. Hawken

**Weight:** 7½ lbs. **Length:** 44″ over-all.
**Stock:** Walnut.
**Sights:** Blade front, open rear adjustable for elevation.
**Features:** Single trigger, dual barrel wedges. Convertible ignition system. Brass patch box.

**HOPKINS & ALLEN PA. HAWKEN RIFLE**
**Caliber:** 50.
**Barrel:** 29″.

**Price:** With percussion lock .................... $199.50
**Price:** Conversion kit (percussion to flint)....... $39.95

Oregon Trail Hawken

**TENNESSEE VALLEY TENNESSEE RIFLE**
**Caliber:** 32, 36, 40, 45, 50, 54, 58.
**Barrel:** 42″ standard; shorter lengths available.
**Weight:** 7½-8 lbs. **Length:** 56″ (with 42″ barrel).
**Stock:** Maple, walnut or cherry.
**Sights:** Silver blade front, buckhorn rear.
**Features:** Steel mounted, double-set triggers standard. Metal parts browned, oil-finished stock. From Tennessee Valley Mfg.
**Price:** Percussion ............................. $410.00
**Price:** Flintlock ............................... $425.00
**Price:** Left hand, flint or percussion ........... $440.00
**Price:** Brass-mounted early Lancaster rifle ...... $695.00
**Price:** Steel-mounted early Virginia rifle......... $595.00

**OREGON TRAIL HAWKEN FULL STOCK RIFLE**
**Caliber:** 50, 54, 58.
**Barrel:** 35″, 1″ flats. Other lengths and calibers available.
**Weight:** NA. **Length:** NA.
**Stock:** Curly maple.
**Sights:** Steel blade front, semi-buckhorn rear.
**Features:** Steel furniture; double set triggers. Tapered barrel, fancy wood optional. Introduced 1986.
**Price:** Flint or percussion, right- or left-hand ...... $995.00
**Price:** As half-stock Hawken .................... $895.00

**ALLEN SANTA FE HAWKEN RIFLE**
**Caliber:** 54.
**Barrel:** 32″, octagonal.
**Weight:** 9.4 lbs. **Length:** 50″ over-all.
**Stock:** Walnut, with cheekpiece.
**Sights:** German silver blade front, buckhorn rear.
**Features:** Browned finish, color-case-hardened lock, German silver ferrule, wedge plates. Imported by Allen Fire Arms.
**Price:** ..................................... $299.00

**DIXIE DELUX CUB RIFLE**
**Caliber:** 40.
**Barrel:** 28″.
**Weight:** 6½ lbs.
**Stock:** Walnut.
**Sights:** Fixed.
**Features:** Short rifle for small game and beginning shooters. Brass patchbox and furniture. Flint or percussion.
**Price:** Finished ............................... $240.00
**Price:** Kit .................................... $195.00

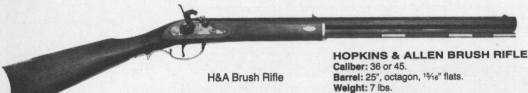

H&A Brush Rifle

**HOPKINS & ALLEN BRUSH RIFLE**
**Caliber:** 36 or 45.
**Barrel:** 25″, octagon, ¹⁵⁄₁₆″ flats.
**Weight:** 7 lbs.
**Stock:** Hardwood.
**Sights:** Silver blade front, notch rear.
**Features:** Convertible ignition system. Brass furniture. Introduced 1983.
**Price:** Percussion.............................. $189.00
**Price:** Flint................................... $200.10
**Price:** Pre-assembled kit, percussion ........... $129.00
**Price:** As above, flint ......................... $140.10
**Price:** Kit, percussion......................... $99.50
**Price:** Kit, flint............................... $110.60

**TRYON RIFLE**
**Caliber:** 50, 54 cal.
**Barrel:** 34″, octagon; 1-63″ twist.
**Weight:** 9 lbs. **Length:** 49″ over-all.
**Stock:** European walnut with steel furniture.
**Sights:** Blade front, fixed rear.
**Features:** Reproduction of an American plains rifle with double set triggers and back-action lock. Imported from Italy by Dixie.
**Price:** ..................................... $299.00
**Price:** Kit .................................... $249.00

**CAUTION:** PRICES CHANGE. CHECK AT GUNSHOP.

# BLACK POWDER MUSKETS & RIFLES

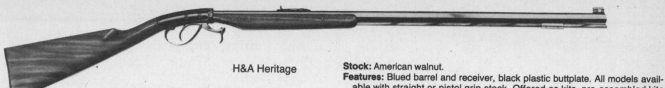

### H&A Heritage

**Stock:** American walnut.
**Features:** Blued barrel and receiver, black plastic buttplate. All models available with straight or pistol grip stock. Offered as kits, pre-assembled kits ("white" barrel, unfinished stock), or factory finished. Prices shown are for factory finished guns.
**Price:** 31, 36, 45, 20" or 25" bbl. × ¹⁵⁄₁₆" ........................... $214.50
**Price:** Heritage, 36, 45, 50-cal. 32" bbl. × ¹⁵⁄₁₆" ................... $226.50
**Price:** Deerstalker, 58-cal., 28" bbl. × 1⅛" ..................... $233.95
**Price:** Target, 45-cal., 42" bbl. × 1⅛" ........................... $245.95

### HOPKINS & ALLEN UNDERHAMMER RIFLES
**Caliber:** 31, 36, 45, 50, 58.
**Barrel:** 20", 25" 32", 42", octagonal.
**Weight:** 6½ lbs. **Length:** 37" over-all.

### Thompson/Center Renegade

**Weight:** 8 lbs.
**Stock:** American walnut.
**Sights:** Open hunting (Patridge) style, fully adjustable for w. and e.
**Features:** Coil spring lock, double set triggers, blued steel trim.
**Price:** Percussion model ..................................... $255.00
**Price:** Flintlock model, 50 cal. only ....................... $270.00
**Price:** Percussion kit ........................................ $195.00
**Price:** Flintlock kit .......................................... $210.00
**Price:** Left-hand precussion, 50 or 54 cal. ................ $255.00

### THOMPSON/CENTER RENEGADE RIFLE
**Caliber:** 50 and 54 plus 56 cal., smoothbore.
**Barrel:** 26", 1" across the flats.

### Thompson/Center Hawken

### THOMPSON/CENTER HAWKEN RIFLE
**Caliber:** 45, 50 or 54.
**Barrel:** 28" octagon, hooked breech.
**Stock:** American walnut.
**Sights:** Blade front, rear adj. for w. & e.
**Features:** Solid brass furniture, double set triggers, button rifled barrel, coil-type main spring. From Thompson/Center Arms.
**Price:** Percussion Model (45, 50 or 54 cal.) ................. $295.00
**Price:** Flintlock model (50 cal.) .............................. $310.00
**Price:** Percussion kit .......................................... $220.00
**Price:** Flintlock kit ........................................... $235.00

### Thompson/Center Hawken Cougar
Similar to the standard T/C Hawken except stock is of highly figured walnut; all furniture—lock plate, hammer, triggers, trigger plate, trigger guard, fore-end cap, thimbles escutcheons, etc. are of stainless steel with matte finish. Replacing the patch box is a stainless steel medallion cast in deep relief depicting a crouching cougar. Internal parts, breech plug, tang, barrel, sights and under rib are ordnance steel. Barrel, sights and under rib are blued. Buttplate is solid brass, hard chromed to match the stainless parts. Limited production. Introduced 1982. From Thompson/Center Arms.
**Price:** ...................................................... $350.00

### Thompson/Center Cherokee

**Stock:** American walnut. Same as Seneca except minus patch box, toe plate, fore-end cap.
**Sights:** Open hunting style; round notch rear fully adjustable for w. and e.
**Features:** Interchangeable barrels. Uses T/C Seneca breech, lock, triggers, sights and stock. Brass buttplate, trigger guard, fore-end escutcheons and lock plate screw bushing. Introduced 1984.
**Price:** 32 or 45 caliber .......................................... $250.00
**Price:** Interchangeable 32 or 45-cal. barrel ................. $115.00
**Price:** Kit, percussion, 32 or 45 ............................. $190.00
**Price:** Kit barrels ............................................. $75.00

### THOMPSON/CENTER CHEROKEE RIFLE
**Caliber:** 32 or 45.
**Barrel:** 24"; 1³⁄₁₆" across flats.
**Weight:** About 6 lbs.

### Thompson/Center Seneca

### THOMPSON/CENTER SENECA RIFLE
**Caliber:** 36, 45.
**Barrel:** 27".
**Weight:** 6½ lbs.
**Stock:** American walnut.
**Sights:** Open hunting style, square notch rear fully adj. for w. and e.
**Features:** Coil spring lock, octagon bbl. measures ¹³⁄₁₆" across flats, brass stock furniture.
**Price:** ...................................................... $300.00

Buffalo Hunter Rifle

## BUFFALO HUNTER PERCUSSION RIFLE
**Caliber:** 58.
**Barrel:** 25½".
**Weight:** 8 lbs. **Length:** 41½" over-all.
**Stock:** Walnut finished, hand checkered, brass furniture.
**Sights:** Fixed.
**Features:** Designed for primitive weapons hunting. 20 ga. shotgun bbl. also available \$90.00. Imported by Dixie.
**Price:** About .................................................... **\$264.00**

Charles Daly Hawken

## CHARLES DALY HAWKEN RIFLE
**Caliber:** 45, 50, 54.
**Barrel:** 28" octagonal, ⅞" flats.
**Weight:** 7½ lbs. **Length:** 45½" over-all.
**Stock:** European hardwood.
**Sights:** Blade front, open fully adjustable rear.
**Features:** Color case-hardened lock uses coil springs; trigger guard, buttplate, fore-end cap, ferrules and ramrod fittings are polished brass. Left-hand model available in 50-cal. only. Imported by Outdoor Sports Headquarters. Introduced 1984.
**Price:** Right-hand, percussion .................................. **\$229.95**
**Price:** Left-hand, percussion (50-cal. only) ...................... **\$257.00**
**Price:** Right-hand, flintlock .................................... **\$255.00**
**Price:** Left-hand, flintlock (50-cal. only) ...................... **\$286.00**
**Price:** Carbine, right hand, 22" bbl., recoil pad ................. **\$229.95**

## ARMOURY R140 HAWKIN RIFLE
**Caliber:** 45, 50 or 54.
**Barrel:** 29".
**Weight:** 8¾ to 9 lbs. **Length:** 45¾" over-all.
**Stock:** Walnut, with cheekpiece.
**Sights:** Dovetail front, fully adjustable rear.
**Features:** Octagon barrel, removable breech plug; double set triggers; blued barrel, brass stock fittings, color case hardened percussion lock. From Armsport, The Armoury.
**Price:** .................................................... **\$199.00**

Ozark Hawken Rifle

## OZARK MOUNTAIN HAWKEN RIFLE
**Caliber:** 50, 52, 54, 58.
**Barrel:** 34".
**Weight:** About 9½ lbs. **Length:** 50¼" over-all.
**Stock:** American maple; full and half-stock designs available.
**Sights:** Blade front, semi-buckhorn rear.
**Features:** Flint or percussion, right or left hand models (except in flintlock — right-hand only); browned steel furniture.
**Price:** From .................................................... **\$675.00**

## ITHACA-NAVY HAWKEN RIFLE
**Caliber:** 50 and 54.
**Barrel:** 32" octagonal, 1-inch dia.
**Weight:** About 9 lbs.
**Stock:** Walnut.
**Sights:** Blade front, rear adj. for w.
**Features:** Hooked breech, 1⅞" throw percussion lock. Attached twin thimbles and under-rib. German silver barrel key inlays, Hawken-style toe and buttplates, lock bolt inlays, barrel wedges, entry thimble, trigger guard, ramrod and cleaning jag, nipple and nipple wrench. Introduced 1977. From Navy Arms.
**Price:** Complete, percussion ................................... **\$375.00**
**Price:** Kit, percussion ......................................... **\$270.00**

## CVA HAWKEN RIFLE
**Caliber:** 50.
**Barrel:** 28", octagon; 1" across flats; 1-66" twist.
**Weight:** 7 lbs. 15 oz. **Length:** 44" over-all.
**Stock:** Select walnut.
**Sights:** Beaded blade front, fully adj. open rear.
**Features:** Fully adj. double set triggers; brass patch box, wedge plates, nose cap, thimbles, trigger guard and buttplate; blued barrel; color case-hardened, engraved lockplate. Percussion or flintlock. Hooked breech. Introduced 1981.
**Price:** Finished rifle, percussion ............................... **\$273.95**
**Price:** Presentation Grade (checkered walnut stock, engraved lock plate) .................................................... **\$650.00**

Kassnar Hawken

## HAWKEN RIFLE
**Caliber:** 45, 50, 54 or 58.
**Barrel:** 28", blued, 6-groove rifling.
**Weight:** 8¾ lbs. **Length:** 44" over-all.
**Stock:** Walnut with cheekpiece.
**Sights:** Blade front, fully adj. rear.
**Features:** Coil mainspring, double set triggers, polished brass furniture. Also available with chrome plated bore or in flintlock model from Sile. Introduced 1977. From Kassnar (flint or percussion, right- or left-hand), Dixie (45 or 50 only, walnut stock), Armsport, Hopkins & Allen, 50-cal. only.
**Price:** ........................................ **\$199.00 to \$219.00**
**Price:** True left-hand rifle, percussion (Kassnar) ................. **\$234.00**
**Price:** As above, flintlock (Kassnar) ........................... **\$254.00**

**CAUTION:** PRICES CHANGE. CHECK AT GUNSHOP.

# BLACK POWDER MUSKETS & RIFLES

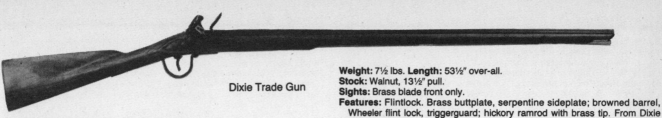

Dixie Trade Gun

**DIXIE NORTHWEST TRADE GUN**
**Caliber/Gauge:** 20 (.600" round ball or 1 oz.#6 shot).
**Barrel:** 36", smoothbore.

**Weight:** 7½ lbs. **Length:** 53½" over-all.
**Stock:** Walnut, 13½" pull.
**Sights:** Brass blade front only.
**Features:** Flintlock. Brass buttplate, serpentine sideplate; browned barrel, Wheeler flint lock, triggerguard; hickory ramrod with brass tip. From Dixie Gun Works.
**Price:** Finished . . . . . . . . . . . . . . . . . . . . . . . . . . . . . . . . . . . . . . . . . **$495.00**
**Price:** Kit . . . . . . . . . . . . . . . . . . . . . . . . . . . . . . . . . . . . . . . . . . . . . . . **$350.00**

Dixie Wesson Rifle

**DIXIE PERCUSSION WESSON RIFLE**
**Caliber:** 50.
**Barrel:** 28"; 1⅛" octagon, with false muzzle.
**Length:** 45" over-all.
**Stock:** Hand checkered walnut.
**Sights:** Blade front, rear adj. for e.
**Features:** Adjustable double set triggers, color case hardened frame. Comes with loading rod and loading accessories. From Dixie Gun Works.
**Price:** With false muzzle . . . . . . . . . . . . . . . . . . . . . . . . . . . . . . . . . **$325.00**

Parker-Hale 1853

**PARKER-HALE ENFIELD 1853 MUSKET**
**Caliber:** .577".
**Barrel:** 39", 3-groove cold-forged rifling.

**Weight:** About 9 lbs. **Length:** 55" over-all.
**Stock:** Seasoned walnut.
**Sights:** Fixed front, rear step adj. for elevation.
**Features:** Three band musket made to original specs from original gauges. Solid brass stock furniture, color hardened lock plate, hammer; blued barrel, trigger. Imported from England by Navy Arms.
**Price:** . . . . . . . . . . . . . . . . . . . . . . . . . . . . . . . . . . . . . . . . . . . . . . . . **$495.00**

London Armory 3-Band Enfield

**LONDON ARMORY 3-BAND 1853 ENFIELD**
**Caliber:** 58 (.577" Minie, .575" round ball, .580" maxi ball).
**Barrel:** 39".
**Weight:** 9½ lbs. **Length:** 54" over-all.
**Stock:** European walnut.
**Sights:** Inverted "V" front, traditional Enfield folding ladder rear.
**Features:** Re-creation of the famed London Armory Company Pattern 1862 Enfield Musket. One-piece walnut stock, brass buttplate, trigger guard and nosecap. Lockplate marked "London Armoury Co." and with a British crown. Blued Baddeley barrel bands. From Dixie, Euroarms of America, Navy Arms.
**Price:** About . . . . . . . . . . . . . . . . . . . . . . . . . . . . . . . . . . . . . . . . . . . **$450.00**

**LONDON ARMORY 2-BAND ENFIELD 1858**
**Caliber:** .577" Minie, .575" round ball.
**Barrel:** 33".
**Weight:** 10 lbs. **Length:** 49" over-all.
**Stock:** Walnut.
**Sights:** Folding leaf rear adjustable for elevation.
**Features:** Blued barrel, color case-hardened lock and hammer, polished brass buttplate, trigger guard, nose cap. From Navy Arms, Euroarms of America, Dixie.
**Price:** . . . . . . . . . . . . . . . . . . . . . . . . . . . . . . . . . . . . . . . . . . . . **$410.00**

**PARKER-HALE ENFIELD PATTERN 1858 NAVAL RIFLE**
**Caliber:** .577".
**Barrel:** 33".
**Weight:** 8½ lbs. **Length:** 48½" over-all.
**Stock:** European walnut.
**Sights:** Blade front, step adj. rear.
**Features:** Two-band Enfield percussion rifle with heavy barrel. 5-groove progressive depth rifling, solid brass furniture. All parts made exactly to original patterns. Imported from England by Navy Arms.
**Price:** . . . . . . . . . . . . . . . . . . . . . . . . . . . . . . . . . . . . . . . . . . . . . . . . **$460.00**

Parker-Hale 1861

**PARKER-HALE ENFIELD 1861 CARBINE**
**Caliber:** .577".
**Barrel:** 24".
**Weight:** 7½ lbs. **Length:** 40¼" over-all.
**Stock:** Walnut.
**Sights:** Fixed front, adj. rear.
**Features:** Percussion muzzle loader, made to original 1861 English patterns. Imported from England by Navy Arms.
**Price:** . . . . . . . . . . . . . . . . . . . . . . . . . . . . . . . . . . . . . . . . . . . . . . . . **$370.00**

# BLACK POWDER MUSKETS & RIFLES

## PARKER-HALE VOLUNTEER RIFLE
**Caliber:** .451″.
**Barrel:** 32″.
**Weight:** 9½ lbs. **Length:** 49″ over-all.
**Stock:** Walnut, checkered wrist and fore-end.
**Sights:** Globe front, adjustable ladder-type rear.
**Features:** Recreation of the type of gun issued to volunteer regiments during the 1860's. Rigby-pattern rifling, patent breech, detented lock. Stock is glass bedded for accuracy. Comes with comprehensive accessory/shooting kit. From Navy Arms.
**Price:** . . . . . . . . . . . . . . . . . . . . . . . . . . . . . . . . . . . . . . . . . . $600.00

## COOK & BROTHER CONFEDERATE CARBINE
**Caliber:** 58.
**Barrel:** 24″.
**Weight:** 7½ lbs. **Length:** 40½″ over-all.
**Stock:** Select walnut.
**Features:** Re-creation of the 1861 New Orleans-made artillery carbine. Color case-hardened lock, browned barrel. Buttplate, trigger guard, barrel bands, sling swivels and nosecap of polished brass. From Euroarms of America.
**Price:** . . . . . . . . . . . . . . . . . . . . . . . . . . . . . . . . . . . . . . . . . . $190.00

Parker-Hale Whitworth

## PARKER-HALE WHITWORTH MILITARY TARGET RIFLE
**Caliber:** 45.
**Barrel:** 36″.
**Weight:** 9¼ lbs. **Length:** 52½″ over-all.
**Stock:** Walnut. Checkered at wrist and fore-end.
**Sights:** Hooded post front, open step-adjustable rear.
**Features:** Faithful reproduction of the Whitworth rifle, only bored for 45-cal. Trigger has a detented lock, capable of being adjusted very finely without risk of the sear nose catching on the half-cock bent and damaging both parts. Introduced 1978. Imported from England by Navy Arms.
**Price:** . . . . . . . . . . . . . . . . . . . . . . . . . . . . . . . . . . . . . . . . . . $600.00

## U.S. M-1862 REMINGTON CONTRACT RIFLE
**Caliber:** 58.
**Barrel:** 33″.
**Weight:** 9½ lbs. **Length:** 48½″ over-all.
**Stock:** Walnut, brass furniture.
**Sights:** Blade front, folding 3-leaf rear.
**Features:** Re-creation of the 1862 military rifle. Each rifle furnished with two stainless steel nipples. From Euroarms of America.
**Price:** About . . . . . . . . . . . . . . . . . . . . . . . . . . . . . . . . . . . . . . $200.00

Dixie 1863 Musket

## DIXIE 1863 SPRINGFIELD MUSKET
**Caliber:** 58 (.570″ patched ball or .575″ Minie).
**Barrel:** 50″, rifled.
**Stock:** Walnut stained.
**Sights:** Blade front, adjustable ladder-type rear.
**Features:** Bright-finish lock, barrel, furniture. Reproduction of the last of the regulation muzzle loaders. Imported from Japan by Dixie Gun Works.
**Price:** Finished . . . . . . . . . . . . . . . . . . . . . . . . . . . . . . . . . . . . $265.00
**Price:** Kit . . . . . . . . . . . . . . . . . . . . . . . . . . . . . . . . . . . . . . . . . . $225.00

Navy 1863 Springfield

**Weight:** 9½ lbs. **Length:** 56″ over-all.
**Stock:** Walnut.
**Sights:** Open rear adj. for elevation.
**Features:** Full-size 3-band musket. Polished bright metal, including lock. From Navy Arms.
**Price:** Finished rifle . . . . . . . . . . . . . . . . . . . . . . . . . . . . . . . . . $450.00
**Price:** Kit . . . . . . . . . . . . . . . . . . . . . . . . . . . . . . . . . . . . . . . . . . $350.00

## NAVY ARMS 1863 SPRINGFIELD
**Caliber:** 58, uses .575″ mini-ball.
**Barrel:** 40″, rifled.

Dixie Zouave Rifle

## ZOUAVE PERCUSSION RIFLE
**Caliber:** 58, 59.
**Barrel:** 32½″.
**Weight:** 9½ lbs. **Length:** 48½″ over-all.
**Stock:** Walnut finish, brass patch box and buttplate.
**Sights:** Fixed front, rear adj. for e.
**Features:** Color case-hardened lock plate, blued barrel. From Dixie.
**Price:** About . . . . . . . . . . . . . . . . . . . . . . . . . . . . . . . . . . . . . . $265.00

## Mississippi Model 1841 Percussion Rifle
Similar to Zouave Rifle but patterned after U.S. Model 1841. Imported by Dixie.
**Price:** . . . . . . . . . . . . . . . . . . . . . . . . . . . . . . . . . . . . . . . . . . . $275.00

## E.M.F. SHARPS MILITARY CARBINE
**Caliber:** 54 Sharps. Black powder breech-loading.
**Barrel:** 22″, round, polished blue.
**Weight:** 7¾ lbs. **Length:** 39″ over-all.
**Stock:** Walnut.
**Sights:** Blade front, rear adj. for w. and e.

**Features:** Faithful reproduction of the original 1863 carbine. Receiver, side-plate, hammer and buttplate are color case hardened. Rifle model has 28″ barrel, checkered p.g. and fore-end. Six different models of the Sharps are now available. From E.M.F.
**Price:** Carbine, about . . . . . . . . . . . . . . . . . . . . . . . . . . . . . . . . $350.00
**Price:** Rifle, about . . . . . . . . . . . . . . . . . . . . . . . . . . . . . . . . . . . $400.00

**CAUTION:** PRICES CHANGE. CHECK AT GUNSHOP.

# BLACK POWDER MUSKETS & RIFLES

C. Sharps 1874

## C. SHARPS ARMS 1874 SPORTING RIFLE
**Caliber:** 40, 45, 50.
**Barrel:** 30", Octagon.
**Weight:** 9½ lbs.
**Stock:** American walnut.
**Sights:** Blade front, Lawrence-style open rear.
**Features:** Color case-hardened receiver, buttplate, and barrel bands, blued barrel. Recreation of the original Sharps rifles. Five other models in many original chamberings available. From C. Sharps Arms Co.
**Price:** 1874 Military Rifle...................................... $685.00
**Price:** 1874 Carbine............................................ $580.00
**Price:** 1874 Business Rifle................................... $620.00
**Price:** 1874 Sporting Rifle No. 1............................. $775.00
**Price:** 1874 Sporting Rifle No. 3............................. $675.00
**Price:** 1874 Long Range Express Sporting Rifle ............... $830.00

## ALLEN ST. LOUIS RIFLE
**Caliber:** 45, 50, 54, 58.
**Barrel:** 30", octagonal.
**Weight:** NA. **Length:** NA.
**Stock:** Walnut.
**Sights:** German silver blade front, adj. rear.
**Features:** Browned barrel, color case-hardened lock. Percussion or flintlock. Imported by Allen Fire Arms.
**Price:** Flintlock, 45, 50.................................... $259.00
**Price:** As above, 54 ....................................... $289.00
**Price:** Percussion, 45, 50.................................. $249.00
**Price:** As above, 54, 58................................... $259.00

Dixie Sharps Rifle

### Dixie Sharps Rifle
Similar to the E.M.F. Sharps Military Carbine except has 28½" barrel, checkered half-stock fore-end and stock wrist, flat lockplate. Carbine-style case hardened buttplate. Imported from Italy by Dixie Gun Works.
**Price:** ................................................... $349.95
**Price:** Military Carbine (22" barrel) ......................... $329.95

MAC Silverwolf

**Stock:** Choice of walnut or maple; soft recoil pad.
**Sights:** Brass-bead front, adjustable folding leaf rear.
**Features:** New design uses straight-line ignition with #209 shotshell primer. Fires from an open bolt; has positive safety notch. Fully adjustable trigger. Introduced 1980. Made in U.S. by Michigan Arms Corp.
**Price:** Blue ordnance steel .................................. $398.00
**Price:** As above except in stainless steel (Silverwolf) ............. $595.00
**Price:** Friendship Special (select barrel, Lyman globe front, Williams target peep rear, adjustable recoil pad, custom stock, special breech block) ................................................... $599.00

## MAC WOLVERINE RIFLE
**Caliber:** 45, 50, 54; 20-ga. shotgun.
**Barrel:** 26", octagon, 1" flats.
**Weight:** 7¾ lbs.

Navy Federal Target

**Weight:** 13¼ lbs. **Length:** 49½" over-all.
**Stock:** European walnut with hook buttplate, Schuetzen-style trigger guard.
**Sights:** Tunnel front, aperture rear adjustable for windage and elevation.
**Features:** Hand-built reproduction of 1800s target rifle; quick detachable, five-lever, double-set trigger, adjustable to 4 oz. Color case-hardened furniture. Imported from Italy by Navy Arms. Introduced 1984.
**Price:** ................................................... $895.00
**Price:** Swiss-style palm rest................................. $35.00

## NAVY SWISS FEDERAL TARGET RIFLE
**Caliber:** 45.
**Barrel:** 32".

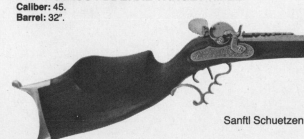

Sanftl Schuetzen

## SANFTL SCHUETZEN PERCUSSION TARGET RIFLE
**Caliber:** 45 (.445" round ball).
**Barrel:** 29", ⅞" octagon.
**Weight:** 9 lbs. **Length:** 43" over-all.
**Stock:** Walnut, Schuetzen-style.
**Sights:** Open tunnel front post, peep rear adjustable for windage & elevation.
**Features:** True back-action lock with "backward" hammer; screw-in breech plug; buttplate, trigger guard and stock inlays are polished brass. Imported from Italy by Dixie Gun Works, Hopkins & Allen.
**Price:** ................................................... $595.00

Rigby-style Target

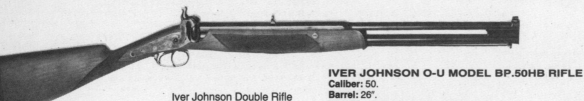

Morse/Navy Rifle

**RIGBY-STYLE TARGET RIFLE**
**Caliber:** .451.
**Barrel:** 32½".
**Weight:** 7¾ lbs.
**Stock:** Walnut; hand-checkered pistol grip, fore-end.
**Sights:** Target front with micrometer adjustment; adjustable vernier peep rear.
**Features:** Comes cased with loading accessories—bullet starter, bullter sizer, special ramrod. Introduced 1985. From Navy Arms.
**Price:** . . . . . . . . . . . . . . . . . . . . . . . . . . . . . . . . . . . . . . . . . . . . . . $500.00

**MORSE/NAVY RIFLE**
**Caliber:** 45, 50 or 58.
**Barrel:** 26", octagonal.
**Weight:** 6 lbs. (45 cal.). **Length:** 41½" over-all.
**Stock:** American walnut, full p.g.
**Sights:** Blade front, open fixed rear.
**Features:** Brass action, trigger guard, ramrod pipes. Made in U.S. by Navy Arms.
**Price:** . . . . . . . . . . . . . . . . . . . . . . . . . . . . . . . . . . . . . $167.00
**Price:** Kit . . . . . . . . . . . . . . . . . . . . . . . . . . . . . . . . . . . . . $100.00

**CVA EXPRESS RIFLE**
**Caliber:** 50 (.490" ball)
**Barrels:** 28", round.
**Weight:** 9 lbs.
**Stock:** Walnut-stained hardwood.
**Sights:** Bead and post front, adjustable rear.
**Features:** Double rifle with twin percussion locks and triggers. Hooked breech. Introduced 1985. From CVA.
**Price:** Finished . . . . . . . . . . . . . . . . . . . . . . . . . . . . . . . $299.95
**Price:** Kit . . . . . . . . . . . . . . . . . . . . . . . . . . . . . . . . . . . $269.95
**Price:** Presentation Express (hand-checkered stock, engraved and polished locks, hammers, tang) . . . . . . . . . . . . . . . . . . . . . . . . . . . $830.00

**CVA Blazer II Rifle**
Similar to the Blazer except has 24½" barrel, over-all length of 38", and weighs 5¾ lbs. Introduced 1986.
**Price:** Finished, 50 cal. . . . . . . . . . . . . . . . . . . . . . . . . . . . $89.95
**Price:** Kit, 50 cal. . . . . . . . . . . . . . . . . . . . . . . . . . . . . . . $69.95

**CVA BLAZER RIFLE**
**Caliber:** 50 (.490" ball)
**Barrel:** 28", octagon.
**Weight:** 6 lbs., 13 oz.
**Stock:** Hardwood.
**Sights:** Brass blade front, fixed semi-buckhorn rear.
**Features:** Straight-line percussion with pistol-grip stock of modern design. Introduced 1985. From CVA.
**Price:** Finished . . . . . . . . . . . . . . . . . . . . . . . . . . . . . . . $99.95
**Price:** Kit . . . . . . . . . . . . . . . . . . . . . . . . . . . . . . . . . . . $79.95

Iver Johnson Double Rifle

**IVER JOHNSON O-U MODEL BP.50HB RIFLE**
**Caliber:** 50.
**Barrel:** 26".
**Weight:** 8½ lbs. **Length:** 41¼" over-all.
**Stock:** Checkered walnut
**Sights:** Blade front with gold bead, folding rear adjustable for w. and e.
**Features:** Two-shot over-under with two hammers, two triggers. Polished blue finish. Introduced 1985. From Iver Johnson.
**Price:** . . . . . . . . . . . . . . . . . . . . . . . . . . . . . . . . . . . . . $364.95

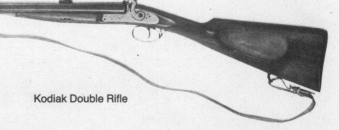

Kodiak Double Rifle

**KODIAK DOUBLE RIFLE**
**Caliber:** 58x58, 50x50 and 58-cal./12 ga. optional.
**Barrel:** 28", 5 grooves, 1-in-48" twist.
**Weight:** 9½ lbs. **Length:** 43¼" over-all.
**Stock:** Czechoslovakian walnut, hand checkered.
**Sights:** Adjustable bead front, adjustable open rear.
**Features:** Hooked breech allows interchangeability of barrels. Comes with sling and swivels, adjustable powder measure, bullet mould and bullet starter. Engraved lock plates, top tang and trigger guard. Locks and top tang polished, rest blued. Imported from Italy by Trail Guns Armory, Inc.
**Price:** 58 cal. SxS . . . . . . . . . . . . . . . . . . . . . . . . . . . . . . $525.00
**Price:** 50 cal. SxS . . . . . . . . . . . . . . . . . . . . . . . . . . . . . . $525.00
**Price:** 50 cal. x 12 ga., 58x12. . . . . . . . . . . . . . . . . . . . . . . $525.00
**Price:** Spare barrels, 58x12 ga. . . . . . . . . . . . . . . . . . . . . . . $294.25
**Price:** Spare barrels, 12 ga. x 12 ga. . . . . . . . . . . . . . . . . . . . $185.00

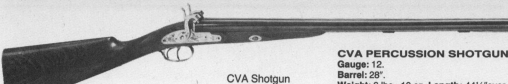

CVA Shotgun

## CVA PERCUSSION SHOTGUN
**Gauge:** 12.
**Barrel:** 28".
**Weight:** 6 lbs., 10 oz. **Length:** 44½"over-all.
**Stock:** Select hardwood; checkered pistol grip and fore-end.
**Sights:** Brass bead front.
**Features:** Hooked breech system. Blued barrels and thimbles, polished steel wedge plates, trigger guard, triggers, tang, lock and hammers; engraved lock, hammers, tang and trigger guard. Introduced 1983. From CVA.
**Price:** Finished . . . . . . . . . . . . . . . . . . . . . . . . . . . . . . . . . . . . . . . . . . . . . . . $274.95
**Price:** Kit . . . . . . . . . . . . . . . . . . . . . . . . . . . . . . . . . . . . . . . . . . . . . . . . . . . $209.95
**Price:** Presentation Grade (checkered European walnut stock, polished and engraved lock plates, hammers, tang) . . . . . . . . . . . . . . . . . . . . . . . $770.00

## CVA 410 PERCUSSION SHOTGUN
**Gauge:** 410.
**Barrel:** 24".
**Weight:** 6 lbs., 4 oz. **Length:** 38" over-all.
**Stock:** Hardwood with pistol grip, M.C. comb.
**Sights:** Brass bead front.
**Features:** Color case-hardened lock plates; double triggers (front is hinged); brass wedge plates; stainless nipple. Introduced 1986. From CVA.
**Price:** Finished . . . . . . . . . . . . . . . . . . . . . . . . . . . . . . . . . . . . . . . . . . . $159.95
**Price:** Kit . . . . . . . . . . . . . . . . . . . . . . . . . . . . . . . . . . . . . . . . . . . . . . . . $114.95

Mowrey Ethan Allen

## MOWREY ETHAN ALLEN SHOTGUN
**Gauge:** 12 or 28.
**Barrel:** 12 ga. — 32", browned octagon, 1" flats; 28 ga. — 28", browned octagon, ¹³⁄₁₆" flats.
**Weight:** 12 ga. — 8 lbs., 28 ga. — 6½ lbs. **Length:** 48" over-all (12 ga.).
**Stock:** Curly maple, Premium or Fancy grade; hand-rubbed oil finish.
**Sights:** ⅛" bead front.
**Features:** Percussion only; steel or brass boxlock action and furniture; flat shotgun-style butt. Uses standard wads. Made in U.S. Add $38 for Fancy wood.
**Price:** Complete, brass or steel . . . . . . . . . . . . . . . . . . . . . . . . . . . . . . . $330.00
**Price:** Kit (amateur) . . . . . . . . . . . . . . . . . . . . . . . . . . . . . . . . . . . . . . . . $250.00
**Price:** Kit (expert) . . . . . . . . . . . . . . . . . . . . . . . . . . . . . . . . . . . . . . . . . $190.00

## E.M.F. CLASSIC DOUBLE BARREL SHOTGUN
**Gauge:** 12.
**Barrel:** 28".
**Weight:** 7 lbs., 12 ozs. **Length:** 45" over-all.
**Stock:** Walnut.
**Features:** Color case-hardened lock plates and hammers; hand checkered stock. Imported by E.M.F.
**Price:** . . . . . . . . . . . . . . . . . . . . . . . . . . . . . . . . . . . . . . . . . . . . . . . . . . $325.00
**Price:** Kit . . . . . . . . . . . . . . . . . . . . . . . . . . . . . . . . . . . . . . . . . . . . . . . . $250.00

## EUROARMS OF AMERICA MAGNUM CAPE GUN
**Gauge:** 12.
**Barrel:** 32" (Cyl.).
**Weight:** 7½ lbs.
**Stock:** Walnut.
**Features:** Single barrel percussion with polished steel lock, blued trigger guard and buttplate; hooked breech for easy takedown. From Euroarms of America.
**Price:** . . . . . . . . . . . . . . . . . . . . . . . . . . . . . . . . . . . . . . . . . . . . . . . . . . $215.00

---

Consult our Directory pages for
the location of firms mentioned.

---

## MAC WOLVERINE FOWLER SHOTGUN
**Gauge:** 20.
**Barrel:** 28".
**Weight:** 7½ lbs. **Length:** 46" over-all.
**Stock:** Choice of walnut or curly maple.
**Features:** Fires from an open bolt, uses #209 shotshell primer for ignition. Modern rifle trigger; O-ring barrel seal; aluminum ramrod drilled and tapped for shotgun and standard blackpowder cleaning accessories. Left-hand model available at no extra charge. Introduced 1985. Made in U.S. by Michigan Arms Corp.
**Price:** . . . . . . . . . . . . . . . . . . . . . . . . . . . . . . . . . . . . . . . . . . . . . . . . . . $395.00

## NAVY ARMS HUNTER SHOTGUN
**Gauge:** 20.
**Barrel:** 28½", interchangeable choke tubes (Full, Mod.).
**Stock:** Walnut, Hawken-style, checkered p.g. and fore-end.
**Sights:** Bead front.
**Features:** Chrome-lined barrel; rubber butt pad; color case-hardened lock; double set triggers; blued furniture. Comes with two flush-mounting choke tubes. Introduced 1986. From Navy Arms.
**Price:** . . . . . . . . . . . . . . . . . . . . . . . . . . . . . . . . . . . . . . . . . . . . . . . . . $245.00

Navy T&T Shotgun

## NAVY ARMS T&T SHOTGUN
**Gauge:** 12.
**Barrel:** 28" (Full & Full).
**Weight:** 7½ lbs.
**Stock:** Walnut.
**Sights:** Bead front.
**Features:** Color case-hardened locks, blued steel furniture. From Navy Arms.
**Price:** . . . . . . . . . . . . . . . . . . . . . . . . . . . . . . . . . . . . . . . . . . . . . . . . . . $334.00

# BLACK POWDER SHOTGUNS

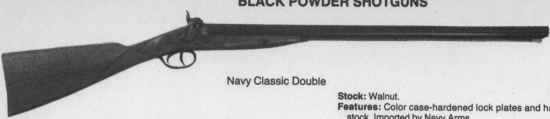

Navy Classic Double

## NAVY CLASSIC DOUBLE BARREL SHOTGUN
**Gauge:** 10, 12.
**Barrel:** 28".
**Weight:** 7 lbs., 12 ozs. **Length:** 45" over-all.

**Stock:** Walnut.
**Features:** Color case-hardened lock plates and hammers; hand checkered stock. Imported by Navy Arms.
**Price:** 12 ga. ................................................. $359.00
**Price:** 10 ga. ................................................. $359.00
**Price:** Kit, 12 ga. ........................................... $265.00
**Price:** Kit, 10 ga. ........................................... $265.00
**Price:** Fowler model, 12 ga. only ........................ $249.00

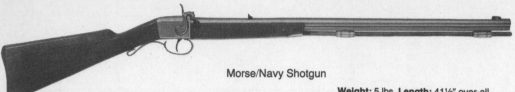

Morse/Navy Shotgun

## MORSE/NAVY SINGLE BARREL SHOTGUN
**Gauge:** 12 ga.
**Barrel:** 26".

**Weight:** 5 lbs. **Length:** 41½" over-all.
**Stock:** American walnut, full p.g.
**Sights:** Front bead
**Features:** Brass receiver, black buttplate. Made in U.S. by Navy Arms.
**Price:** .................................................... $167.00
**Price:** Kit ................................................. $142.00

Dixie Double Barrel

## DIXIE MAGNUM PERCUSSION SHOTGUN
**Gauge:** 10, 12.
**Barrel:** 30" (I.C.&Mod.) in 10 ga.; 28" in 12 ga.

**Weight:** 6¼ lbs. **Length:** 45" over-all.
**Stock:** Hand checkered walnut, 14" pull.
**Features:** Double triggers, light hand engraving. Case hardened locks in 12 ga.; polished steel in 10 ga. with sling swivels. From Dixie.
**Price:** Upland ............................................. $299.85
**Price:** 12 ga. kit ......................................... $235.00
**Price:** 10 ga. ............................................. $335.00
**Price:** 10 ga. kit ......................................... $285.00

T/C "New Englander"

## THOMPSON-CENTER "NEW ENGLANDER" SHOTGUN
**Gauge:** 12.
**Barrel:** 28" (Imp. Cyl.), round.
**Weight:** 5 lbs., 2 oz.
**Stock:** Select American black walnut with straight grip.
**Features:** Percussion lock is color case-hardened, rest blued. Also accepts 26" round 50-cal. rifle barrel. Introduced 1986.
**Price:** .................................................... $240.00
**Price:** Accessory rifle barrel ........................... $110.00

## TRAIL GUNS KODIAK 10 GAUGE DOUBLE
**Gauge:** 10.
**Barrel:** 20", 30¾" (Cyl. bore).
**Weight:** About 9 lbs. **Length:** 47⅛" over-all.
**Stock:** Walnut, with cheek rest. Checkered wrist and fore-end.
**Features:** Chrome plated bores; engraved lockplates, brass bead front and middle sights; sling swivels. Introduced 1980. Imported from Italy by Trail Guns Armory.
**Price:** .................................................... $379.95

# AIR GUNS—HANDGUNS

## AIR MATCH MODEL 600 PISTOL
**Caliber:** 177, single shot.
**Barrel:** 8.8".
**Weight:** 32 oz. **Length:** 13.19" over-all.
**Power:** Single stroke pneumatic.
**Stocks:** Match-style with adjustable palm shelf.
**Sights:** Interchangeable post front, fully adjustable match rear with interchangeable blades.
**Features:** Velocity of 420 fps. Adjustable trigger with dry-fire option. Comes with fitted case. Available with three different grip styles, barrel weight, sight extension. Add $5.00 for left-hand models. Introduced 1984. Imported from Italy by Kendall International Arms.
**Price:** With adjustable or fixed grip ...................... $386.25

Air Match 600

**CAUTION:** PRICES CHANGE. CHECK AT GUNSHOP.

# AIR GUNS—HANDGUNS

**BEEMAN P1 MAGNUM AIR PISTOL**
**Caliber:** 177, single shot.
**Barrel:** 8.4".
**Weight:** 2.5 lbs. **Length:** 11" over-all.
**Power:** Top lever cocking; spring piston.
**Stocks:** Checkered walnut.
**Sights:** Blade front, square notch rear with click micrometer adjustments for w. and e. Grooved for scope mounting.
**Features:** Dual power: low setting gives 350-400 fps; high setting 500-600 fps. Rearward expanding mainspring simulates firearm recoil. All Colt 45 auto grips fit gun. Optional wooden shoulder stock. Introduced 1985. Imported by Beeman.
**Price:** .................................................... $189.95

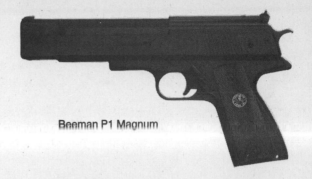
Beeman P1 Magnum

**BEEMAN/FEINWERKBAU MODEL 2 CO² PISTOL**
**Caliber:** 177, single shot
**Barrel:** 10.1".
**Weight:** 2.5 lbs. **Length:** 16¼" over-all.
**Power:** Special CO² cylinder.
**Stocks:** Stippled walnut with adjustable palm shelf.
**Sights:** Blade front with interchangeable inserts; open micro. click rear with adjustable notch width.
**Features:** Power adjustable from 360 fps to 525 fps. Fully adjustable trigger; three weights for balance and weight adjustments. Short-barrel Mini-2 model also available. Introduced 1983. Imported by Beeman.
**Price:** Right hand ............................................. $610.00
**Price:** Left hand .............................................. $650.00
**Price:** Mini-2, right hand ..................................... $635.00
**Price:** Mini-2, left hand ...................................... $675.00

FWB Mini-2

**BEEMAN/WEBLEY HURRICANE PISTOL**
**Caliber:** 177 or 22, single shot.
**Barrel:** 8", rifled.
**Weight:** 2.4 lbs. **Length:** 11½" over-all.
**Power:** Spring piston.
**Stocks:** Thumbrest, checkered high-impact synthetic.
**Sights:** Hooded front, micro-click rear adj. for w. and e.
**Features:** Velocity of 470 fps (177-cal.). Single stroke cocking, adjustable trigger pull, manual safety. Rearward recoil like a firearm pistol. Steel piston and cylinder. Scope base included; 1.5x scope $39.95 extra. Shoulder stock available. Introduced 1977. Imported from England by Beeman.
**Price:** .................................................... $139.50

Beeman/Webley Hurricane

**BEEMAN/WEBLEY TEMPEST AIR PISTOL**
**Caliber:** 177 or 22, single shot.
**Barrel:** 6.75", rifled ordnance steel.
**Weight:** 32 oz. **Length:** 9" over-all.
**Power:** Spring piston.
**Stocks:** Checkered black epoxy with thumbrest.
**Sights:** Post front; rear has sliding leaf adjustable for w. and e.
**Features:** Adjustable trigger pull, manual safety. Velocity 470 fps (177 cal.). Steel piston in steel liner for maximum performance and durability. Unique rearward spring simulates firearm recoil. Shoulder stock available. Introduced 1979. Imported from England by Beeman.
**Price:** .................................................... $109.50

Beeman/Webley Tempest

**BEEMAN/FEINWERKBAU FWB-65 MKII AIR PISTOL**
**Caliber:** 177, single shot.
**Barrel:** 6.1"; fixed bbl. wgt. avail.
**Weight:** 42 oz. **Length:** 14.1" over-all.
**Power:** Spring, sidelever cocking.
**Stocks:** Walnut, stippled thumbrest; adjustable or fixed.
**Sights:** Front, interchangeable post element system, open rear, click adj. for w. & e. and for sighting notch width. Scope mount avail.
**Features:** New shorter barrel for better balance and control. Cocking effort 9 lbs. 2-stage trigger, 4 adjustments. Quiet firing, 525 fps. Programs instantly for recoil or recoilless operation. Permanently lubricated. Steel piston ring. Special switch converts trigger from 17.6 oz. pull to 42 oz. let-off. Imported by Beeman.
**Price:** Right-hand................................... $525.00 to $623.00
**Price:** Left-hand ................................... $560.00 to $633.00
**Price:** Model 65 Mk.I (7.5" bbl.)..................... $515.00 to $610.00

FWB 65 Mk. II

**CAUTION:** PRICES CHANGE. CHECK AT GUNSHOP.

Beeman/Weihrauch HW-70

## BENJAMIN SUPER S. S. TARGET PISTOL SERIES 130
**Caliber:** BB, single shot.
**Barrel:** 8″; BB smoothbore; 22 and 177, rifled.
**Weight:** 2 lbs. **Length:** 11″ over-all.
**Power:** Hand pumped.
**Features:** Bolt action; fingertip safety; adj. power.
**Price:** M130, BB .............................................. **$76.00**

Benjamin 232

## CROSMAN MODEL 357 AIR PISTOL
**Caliber:** 177, 6-shot.
**Barrel:** 4″ (Model 357 Four), 6″ (Model 357 six), 8″ (Model 357 Eight); rifled steel.
**Weight:** 32 oz. (6″) **Length:** 11⅜″ over-all.
**Power:** $CO_2$ Powerlet.
**Stocks:** Checkered wood-grain plastic.
**Sights:** Ramp front, fully adjustable rear.
**Features:** Average 430 fps (Model 357 Six). Break-open barrel for easy loading. Single or double action. Vent rib barrel. Wide, smooth trigger. Two speed loaders come with each gun. Models Four and Six introduced 1983, Model Eight introduced 1984.
**Price:** 4″ or 6″, about ...................................... **$45.00**
**Price:** 8″, about ............................................. **$70.00**

Consult our Directory pages for
the location of firms mentioned.

Crosman 1600

## BEEMAN/WEIHRAUCH HW-70 AIR PISTOL
**Caliber:** 177, single shot.
**Barrel:** 6¼″, rifled.
**Weight:** 38 oz. **Length:** 12¾″ over-all.
**Power:** Spring, barrel cocking.
**Stocks:** Plastic, with thumbrest.
**Sights:** Hooded post front, square notch rear adj. for w. and e.
**Features:** Adj. trigger. 24-lb. cocking effort, 410 f.p.s. M.V.; automatic barrel safety. Imported by Beeman.
**Price:** From Beeman ........................................ **$119.50**

## BEEMAN/FEINWERKBAU MODEL 90 PISTOL
**Caliber:** 177, single shot.
**Barrel:** 7.5″, 12-groove rifling.
**Weight:** 3.0 lbs. **Length:** 16.4″ over-all.
**Power:** Spring piston, single stroke sidelever cocking.
**Stocks:** Stippled walnut with adjustable palm shelf.
**Sights:** Interchangeable blade front, fully adjustable open notch rear.
**Features:** Velocity of 475 to 525 fps. Has new adjustable electronic trigger. Recoilless action, metal piston ring and dual mainsprings. Cocking effort is 12 lbs. Introduced 1983. Imported by Beeman.
**Price:** .............................................. **$685.00 to $715.00**

## BENJAMIN 232/237 SINGLE SHOT PISTOLS
**Caliber:** 177 and 22.
**Weight:** 32 oz. **Length:** 11¾″ over-all.
**Power:** Hand pumped.
**Stocks:** Walnut, with walnut pump handle.
**Sights:** Blade front, open adjustable rear.
**Features:** Bolt action; fingertip safety; adjustable power.
**Price:** Model 232 (22 cal.)..................................... **$84.45**
**Price:** Model 237 (177 cal.) .................................... **$84.45**

Crosman Model 357

## CROSMAN MODEL 1322 AIR PISTOL
**Caliber:** 22, single shot.
**Barrel:** 8″, button rifled.
**Weight:** 37 oz. **Length:** 13⅝″.
**Power:** Hand pumped.
**Sights:** Blade front, rear adj. for w. and e.
**Features:** Moulded plastic grip, hand size pump forearm. Cross bolt safety. Also available in 177 Cal. as **Model 1377** (same price).
**Price:** About .................................................... **$45.00**

## CROSMAN 1600 BB PISTOL
**Caliber:** BB, 17-shot.
**Barrel:** 7¾″.
**Weight:** 29 oz. **Length:** 11⅜″ over-all.
**Power:** Standard $CO_2$.
**Stocks:** Contoured with thumbrest.
**Sights:** Patridge-type front, fully adj. rear.
**Features:** Gives about 80 shots per powerlet, slide-action safety, steel barrel, die-cast receiver. Introduced 1983.
**Price:** About .................................................... **$30.00**

**CAUTION:**   PRICES CHANGE. CHECK AT GUNSHOP.

## CROSMAN MARK II TARGET PISTOL
**Caliber:** 177 or BB.
**Barrel:** 7¼", button rifled.
**Weight:** 44 oz. **Length:** 11⅛" over-all.
**Power:** Crosman Powerlet $CO_2$ cylinder.
**Features:** New system provides same shot-to-shot velocity of 435-485 fps (pellets). Checkered thumbrest grips, right or left. Patridge front sight, rear adj. for w. & e. Adj. trigger.
**Price:** About . . . . . . . . . . . . . . . . . . . . . . . . . . . . . . . . . . $58.00

Crosman Mark II

Daisy Softair 04

## DAISY SOFTAIR 04
**Caliber:** 25-cal. plastic pellets.
**Barrel:** Smoothbore.
**Weight:** 1.1 lbs. **Length:** 10.5" over-all.
**Power:** Spring.
**Stocks:** Woodgrain moulded grip with checkering.
**Sights:** Blade and ramp front, notched rear.
**Features:** Fully detailed replica of a classic 44 Magnum, six-shot revolver with swing-out cylinder for easy loading.
**Price:** About . . . . . . . . . . . . . . . . . . . . . . . . . . . . . . . . . . $44.00

## DAISY MODEL 08 SOFTAIR PISTOL
**Caliber:** 25 (6mm) plastic pellets; 6-shot clip.
**Barrel:** Smoothbore.
**Weight:** NA. **Length:** 9¾" over-all.
**Stocks:** Woodtone, molded with checkering.
**Sights:** Post front, notch rear.
**Features:** Fires 25-cal. plastic pellets loaded into plastic cartridges; semi-auto action ejects spent shells. Introduced 1985.
**Price:** About . . . . . . . . . . . . . . . . . . . . . . . . . . . . . . . . . . $39.00

Daisy Softair 08

Daisy Softair 09

## DAISY SOFTAIR 09
**Caliber:** 25-cal. plastic shot.
**Barrel:** Smoothbore.
**Weight:** 12 oz. **Length:** 9.5" over-all.
**Power:** Slide action, spring air.
**Stocks:** Moulded grip with checkering.
**Sights:** Blade front, notched rear.
**Features:** Detailed replica of the official 9mm sidearm recently adopted by the U.S. Armed Forces, the Beretta 9mm. Takes seven-shot clip, ejects spent shells.
**Price:** About . . . . . . . . . . . . . . . . . . . . . . . . . . . . . . . . . . $44.00

Daisy Softair 13

## DAISY SOFTAIR GUN 13
**Caliber:** 25-cal. plastic shot.
**Barrel:** Smoothbore.
**Weight:** 2.6 lbs. **Length:** 15.5" over-all.
**Power:** Bolt action, spring air.
**Stock:** Molded grip and receiver.
**Sights:** Post front, notched rear.
**Features:** Replica of the world-famous Israeli semi-automatic assault pistol; loads with 22-shot clip.
**Price:** About . . . . . . . . . . . . . . . . . . . . . . . . . . . . . . . . . . $83.00

## DAISY MODEL 38 SOFTAIR PISTOL
**Caliber:** 25 (6mm) plastic pellets; single shot.
**Barrel:** Smoothbore.
**Weight:** NA. **Length:** 10" over-all.
**Stocks:** Molded, grooved plastic.
**Sights:** Post front, notch rear.
**Features:** Fires 25-cal. plastic pellets loaded into a pop-up chamber in barrel. Introduced 1985.
**Price:** About . . . . . . . . . . . . . . . . . . . . . . . . . . . . . . . . . . $39.00

## DAISY SOFTAIR 45
**Caliber:** 25-cal. plastic shot.
**Barrel:** Smoothbore.
**Weight:** 12 oz. **Length:** 8.5" over-all.
**Power:** Slide cocking, spring air.
**Stocks:** Moulded grip with checkering.
**Sights:** Ramp front, notched rear.
**Features:** Detailed replica of the 45 auto pistol. Holds seven-shot clip, ejects spent shells.
**Price:** About . . . . . . . . . . . . . . . . . . . . . . . . . . . . . . . . . . $44.00

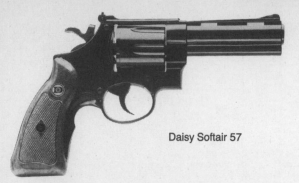

Daisy Softair 57

Daisy Power Line 92

## DAISY MODEL 188 BB PISTOL
**Caliber:** BB.
**Barrel:** 9.9″, steel smoothbore.
**Weight:** 1.67 lbs. **Length:** 11.7″ over-all.
**Stocks:** Die-cast metal; checkered with thumbrest.
**Sights:** Blade and ramp front, open fixed rear.
**Features:** 24-shot repeater. Spring action with under-barrel cocking lever. Grip and receiver of die-cast metal. Introduced 1979.
**Price:** About . . . . . . . . . . . . . . . . . . . . . . . . . . . . . . . . . . . . . . . . $26.00

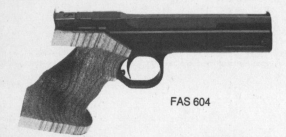

FAS 604

## HAMMERLI "MASTER" CO₂ TARGET PISTOL
**Caliber:** 177, single shot.
**Barrel:** 6.4″, 12-groove.
**Weight:** 38.4 oz. **Length:** 16″ over-all.
**Power:** 12 gram cylinder.
**Stocks:** Plastic with thumbrest and checkering.
**Sights:** Ramp front, micro rear, click adj. Adj. sight radius from 11.1″ to 13.0″.
**Features:** Single shot, manual loading. Residual gas vented automatically. 5-way adj. trigger. Available from Mandall Shooting Supplies.
**Price:** . . . . . . . . . . . . . . . . . . . . . . . . . . . . . . . . . . . . . . . . . . . . $495.00

## MARKSMAN 17 AIR PISTOL
**Caliber:** 177, single shot.
**Barrel:** 7.5″.
**Weight:** 46 oz. **Length:** 14.5″ over-all.
**Power:** Spring air, barrel-cocking.
**Stocks:** Checkered composition with right-hand thumb rest.
**Sights:** Tunnel front, fully adj. rear.
**Features:** Velocity of 330-360 fps. Introduced 1986. Imported from Spain by Marksman Products.
**Price:** . . . . . . . . . . . . . . . . . . . . . . . . . . . . . . . . . . . . . . . . . . . . $75.00

## DAISY MODEL 57 SOFTAIR REVOLVER
**Caliber:** 25 (6mm) plastic pellets; 6-shot.
**Barrel:** Smoothbore.
**Weight:** NA. **Length:** 10½″ over-all.
**Stocks:** Molded woodgrain with checkering.
**Sights:** Blade and ramp front, notch rear.
**Features:** Fires spring-activated 25-cal. plastic pellets loaded into plastic cartridges. Cylinder swings out for loading. Introduced 1985.
**Price:** About . . . . . . . . . . . . . . . . . . . . . . . . . . . . . . . . . . . . . . . . $39.00

## DAISY MODEL 59 SOFTAIR PISTOL
**Caliber:** 25 (6mm) plastic pellets; 10-shot clip.
**Barrel:** Smoothbore.
**Weight:** NA. **Length:** 9″ over-all.
**Stocks:** Molded with checkering.
**Sights:** Blade and ramp front, notch rear.
**Features:** Fires 25-cal. plastic pellets loaded into plastic cartridges. Clip fed, semi-auto action ejects spent bullets. Introduced 1985.
**Price:** About . . . . . . . . . . . . . . . . . . . . . . . . . . . . . . . . . . . . . . . . $39.00

## DAISY POWER LINE MODEL 92 PISTOL
**Caliber:** 177 pellets, 10-shot magazine.
**Barrel:** Rifled steel.
**Weight:** 2.15 lbs. **Length:** 8.5″ over-all.
**Power:** CO₂.
**Stocks:** Cast checkered metal.
**Sights:** Blade front, adjustable V-slot rear.
**Features:** Semi-automatic action; 400 fps. Replica of the official 9mm side arm of the United States armed forces.
**Price:** About . . . . . . . . . . . . . . . . . . . . . . . . . . . . . . . . . . . . . . . . $71.00

Daisy Model 188

## FAS MODEL 604 AIR PISTOL
**Caliber:** 177, single shot.
**Barrel:** 7.4″, 10-groove rifled steel.
**Weight:** 2.3 lbs. **Length:** 11.3″ over-all.
**Power:** Single stroke pneumatic.
**Stocks:** Anatomically shaped stippled walnut; small, medium, large sizes.
**Sights:** Adjustable.
**Features:** Top of receiver is cocking arm, requires 13 lbs. effort. Adjustable trigger may be dry-fired without fully cocking pistol. Imported from Italy by Osborne's, Beeman. Introduced 1984.
**Price:** Beeman . . . . . . . . . . . . . . . . . . . . . . . . . . . . . . . . . $495.00 to $525.00
**Price:** Osborne's . . . . . . . . . . . . . . . . . . . . . . . . . . . . . . . . . . . . . . . . $375.00

Marksman Model 17

**CAUTION:** PRICES CHANGE. CHECK AT GUNSHOP.

# AIR GUNS—HANDGUNS

Marksman Plainsman

**Marksman Model 54 Air Revolver**
Similar to the Orion except is 5-shot revolver with 4" barrel, 9" over-all length, weighs 21 oz. Velocity of 475-525 fps. Uses same Saxby-Palmer pre-primed cartridge system.
**Price:** With portable pump, 5 cartridges . . . . . . . . . . . . . . . . . . . . . . . . $260.00

**MARKSMAN #1010 REPEATER PISTOL**
**Caliber:** 177, 20-shot repeater.
**Barrel:** 2½", smoothbore.
**Weight:** 24 oz. **Length:** 8¼".
**Power:** Spring
**Features:** Thumb safety. Uses BBs, darts or pellets. Repeats with BBs only.
**Price:** Matte black finish . . . . . . . . . . . . . . . . . . . . . . . . . . . . . . . . . . . **$17.00**
**Price:** Model 1020 (as above except fires BBs only) . . . . . . . . . . . . . . **$17.00**

**MAUSER JUMBO AIR PISTOL**
**Caliber:** 177, single shot.
**Barrel:** 6", rifled.
**Weight:** 25 oz. **Length:** 7.25" over-all.
**Power:** Spring air.
**Stocks:** Checkered walnut.
**Sights:** Blade front, fixed rear.
**Features:** Velocity of 300-325 fps; extra pellet storage in grip; thumb safety. Imported from West Germany by Marksman Products.
**Price:** . . . . . . . . . . . . . . . . . . . . . . . . . . . . . . . . . . . . . . . . . . . . . . . . . $74.00

Norica Black Widow

**POWER LINE MATCH 777 PELLET PISTOL**
**Caliber:** 177, single shot.
**Barrel:** 9.61" rifled steel by Lothar Walther.
**Weight:** 32 oz. **Length:** 13½" over-all.
**Power:** Sidelever, single pump pneumatic.
**Stocks:** Smooth hardwood, fully contoured with palm and thumb rest.
**Sights:** Blade and ramp front, match-grade open rear with adj. width notch, micro. click adjustments.
**Features:** Adjustable trigger; manual cross-bolt safety. MV of 385 fps. Comes with cleaning kit, adjustment tool and pellets.
**Price:** About . . . . . . . . . . . . . . . . . . . . . . . . . . . . . . . . . . . . . . . . . . . . . $272.00

**MARKSMAN PLAINSMAN 1049 CO₂ PISTOL**
**Caliber:** BB, 100-shot repeater.
**Barrel:** 5⅞", smooth.
**Weight:** 28 oz. **Length:** 9½" over-all.
**Stocks:** Simulated walnut with thumbrest.
**Power:** 8.5 or 12.5 gram CO₂ cylinders.
**Features:** Velocity of 400 fps. Three-position power switch. Auto. ammunition feed. Positive safety.
**Price:** . . . . . . . . . . . . . . . . . . . . . . . . . . . . . . . . . . . . . . . . . . . . . . . . . $35.00

**MARKSMAN ORION AIR REVOLVER**
**Caliber:** 177, 6-shot.
**Barrel:** 6".
**Weight:** 2 lbs., 3 oz. **Length:** 11" over-all.
**Power:** Compressed air cartridges.
**Stocks:** Composition semi-match style with thumbrest.
**Sights:** Blade front, fully-adj. rear.
**Features:** Velocity of 525-575 fps. Single/double action. Power source from Saxby-Palmer pre-primed cartridges; recoilless; comes with compressor unit, 6 cartridges. Gun made in W. Germany, cartridge system from England. Imported by Marksman Products. Introduced 1986.
**Price:** With table-top pump, 6 cartridges . . . . . . . . . . . . . . . . . . . . . . . . $375.00
**Price:** With portable pump, 6 cartridges . . . . . . . . . . . . . . . . . . . . . . . . $335.00

Marksman 1010

Mauser Jumbo

**NORICA BLACK WIDOW AIR PISTOL**
**Caliber:** 177, single shot.
**Barrel:** 7¾".
**Weight:** 2 lbs. **Length:** 16" over-all.
**Power:** Spring air, barrel cocking.
**Stocks:** Target-style of black high-impact plastic.
**Sights:** Hooded front, open adjustable rear.
**Features:** Velocity 395 fps. Side mounted automatic safety; receiver grooved for scope mounting. Imported from Spain by Kassnar.
**Price:** . . . . . . . . . . . . . . . . . . . . . . . . . . . . . . . . . . . . . . . . . . . . . . . . . $74.00

Power Line 777

## POWER LINE 717 PELLET PISTOL
**Caliber:** 177, single shot.
**Barrel:** 9.61".
**Weight:** 2.8 lbs. **Length:** 13½" over-all.
**Stocks:** Molded wood-grain plastic, with thumbrest.
**Sights:** Blade and ramp front, micro. adjustable notch rear.
**Features:** Single pump pneumatic pistol. Rifled steel barrel. Cross-bolt trigger block. Muzzle velocity 385 fps. From Daisy. Introduced 1979.
**Price:** About .................................................. $64.00

## POWER LINE CO₂ 1200 PISTOL
**Caliber:** BB, 177.
**Barrel:** 10½", smooth.
**Weight:** 1.6 lbs. **Length:** 11.1" over-all.
**Power:** Daisy CO₂ cylinder.
**Stocks:** Contoured, checkered molded wood-grain plastic.
**Sights:** Blade ramp front, fully adj. square notch rear.
**Features:** 60-shot BB reservoir, gravity feed. Cross-bolt safety. Velocity of 420-450 fps for more than 100 shots.
**Price:** About .................................................. $39.00

## RWS MODEL 5G AIR PISTOL
**Caliber:** 177, single shot.
**Barrel:** 7".
**Weight:** 2¾ lbs. **Length:** 16" over-all.
**Power:** Spring air, barrel cocking.
**Stocks:** Plastic, thumbrest design.
**Sights:** Tunnel front, micro click open rear.
**Features:** Velocity of 410 fps. Two-stage trigger with automatic safety. Imported from West Germany by Dynamit Nobel of America.
**Price:** ........................................... $130.00

## RWS MODEL 6M MATCH AIR PISTOL
**Caliber:** 177, single shot.
**Barrel:** 7".
**Weight:** 3 lbs. **Length:** 16" over-all.
**Power:** Spring air, barrel cocking.
**Stocks:** Walnut-finished hardwood with thumbrest.
**Sights:** Adjustable front, micro click open rear.
**Features:** Velocity of 410 fps. Recoilless double piston system, moveable barrel shroud to protect front sight during cocking. Imported from West Germany by Dynamit Nobel of America.
**Price:** ........................................... $260.00

Power Line 717

RWS Model 5G

## RWS MODEL 5GS AIR PISTOL
Same as the Model 5G except comes with 1.5×15 pistol scope with ramp-style mount, muzzle brake/weight. No open sights supplied. Introduced 1983.
**Price:** ........................................... $175.00

## RWS Model 10 Match Air Pistol
Refined version of the Model 6M. Has special adjustable match trigger, oil finished and stippled match grips, barrel weight. Also available in left-hand version, and with fitted case.
**Price:** Model 10 ......................................... $450.00
**Price:** Model 10, left hand .............................. $480.00
**Price:** Model 10, with case ............................... $470.00
**Price:** Model 10, left hand, with case .................... $500.00

## SHERIDAN MODEL HB PNEUMATIC PISTOL
**Caliber:** 5mm; single shot.
**Barrel:** 9⅜", rifled.
**Weight:** 36 oz. **Length:** 12" over-all.
**Power:** Underlever pneumatic pump.
**Stocks:** Checkered simulated walnut; fore-end is walnut.
**Sights:** Blade front, fully adjustable rear.
**Features:** "Controller-Power" feature allows velocity and range control by varying the number of pumps—3 to 10. Maximum velocity of 400 fps. Introduced 1982. From Sheridan Products.
**Price:** ........................................... $86.95

## SHERIDAN MODEL EB CO₂ PISTOL
**Caliber:** 20 (5mm).
**Barrel:** 6½", rifled, rust proof.
**Weight:** 27 oz. **Length:** 9" over-all.
**Power:** 12 gram CO₂ cylinder.
**Stocks:** Checkered simulated walnut. Left- or right-handed.
**Sights:** Blade front, fully adjustable rear.
**Features:** Turn-bolt single-shot action. Gives about 40 shots at 400 fps per CO₂ cylinder.
**Price:** ........................................... $65.25

RWS Model 10

## WALTHER CP CO₂ AIR PISTOL
**Caliber:** 177, single shot.
**Barrel:** 9".
**Weight:** 40 oz. **Length:** 14¾" over-all.
**Power:** CO₂.
**Stocks:** Full target type stippled wood with adjustable hand-shelf.
**Sights:** Target post front, fully adjustable target rear.
**Features:** Velocity of 520 fps. CO₂ powered; target-quality trigger; comes with adaptor for charging with standard CO₂ air tanks, case, and accessories. Introduced 1983. Imported from West Germany by Interarms.
**Price:** ........................................... $565.00
**Price:** Junior model (modified grip, shorter gas cylinder) .......... $565.00

Sheridan Model HB

**CAUTION:** PRICES CHANGE. CHECK AT GUNSHOP.

### BEEMAN/FEINWERKBAU 124/127 MAGNUM
**Caliber:** 177 (FWB-124); 22 (FWB-127); single shot.
**Barrel:** 18.3", 12-groove rifling.
**Weight:** 6.8 lbs. **Length:** 43½" over-all.
**Power:** Spring piston air; single stroke barrel cocking.
**Stock:** Walnut finished hardwood.
**Sights:** Tunnel front; click-adj. rear for w , slide-adj. for e.
**Features:** Velocity 680-820 fps, cocking effort of 18 lbs. Forged steel receiver; nylon non-drying piston and breech seals. Auto. safety, adj. trigger. Standard model has no checkering, cheekpiece. Deluxe has hand-checkerd p.g. and fore-end, high comb cheekpiece, and buttplate with white spacer. Imported by Beeman.
**Price:** Standard model . . . . . . . . . . . . . . . . . . . . . . . . . . . . . . . . . . . . . $319.50
**Price:** Deluxe model (illus.) . . . . . . . . . . . . . . . . . . . . . . . . . . . . . . . . . $339.50

Beeman/FWB 124

### BEEMAN/FEINWERKBAU 300-3 SERIES MATCH RIFLE
**Caliber:** 177, single shot.
**Barrel:** 19.9", fixed solid with receiver.
**Weight:** Approx. 10 lbs. with optional bbl. sleeve. **Length:** 42.8" over-all.
**Power:** Single stroke sidelever, spring piston.
**Stock:** Match model—walnut, deep fore-end, adj. buttplate.
**Sights:** Globe front with interchangeable inserts. Click micro. adj. match aperture rear. Front and rear sights move as a single unit.
**Features:** Recoilless, vibration free. Five-way adjustable match trigger. Grooved for scope mounts. Permanent lubrication, steel piston ring. Cocking effort 9 lbs. Optional 10 oz. bbl. sleeve. Available from Beeman.
**Price:** Right hand . . . . . . . . . . . . . . . . . . . . . . . . . . . . . . . . . . . . . . . . . . $735.00
**Price:** Left hand . . . . . . . . . . . . . . . . . . . . . . . . . . . . . . . . . . . . . . . . . . . $785.00

### BEEMAN/FEINWERKBAU 300-S "UNIVERSAL" MATCH
**Caliber:** 177, single shot.
**Barrel:** 19.9".
**Weight:** 10.2 lbs. (without barrel sleeve). **Length:** 43.3" over-all.
**Power:** Spring piston, single stroke sidelever.
**Stock:** Walnut, stippled p.g. and fore-end. Detachable cheekpieces (one std., high for scope use.) Adjustable buttplate, accessory rail. Buttplate and grip cap spacers included.
**Sights:** Two globe fronts with interchangeable inserts. Rear is match aperture with rubber eyecup and sight viser. Front and rear sights move as a single unit.

FWB 300-S Universal

**Features:** Recoilless, vibration free. Grooved for scope mounts. Steel piston ring. Cocking effort about 9½ lbs. Barrel sleeve optional. Left-hand model available. Introduced 1978. Imported by Beeman.
**Price:** Right-hand . . . . . . . . . . . . . . . . . . . . . . . . . . . . . . . . . . . . . . . . . . $830.00
**Price:** Left-hand . . . . . . . . . . . . . . . . . . . . . . . . . . . . . . . . . . . . . . . . . . . $890.00

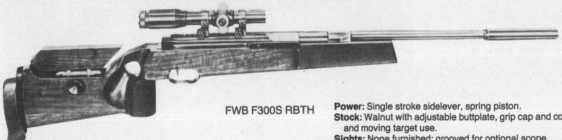

FWB F300S RBTH

### BEEMAN/FEINWERKBAU F300-S RUNNING BOAR (TH)
**Caliber:** 177, single shot.
**Barrel:** 19.9", rifled.
**Weight:** 10.9 lbs. **Length:** 43" over-all.

**Power:** Single stroke sidelever, spring piston.
**Stock:** Walnut with adjustable buttplate, grip cap and comb. Designed for fixed and moving target use.
**Sights:** None furnished; grooved for optional scope.
**Features:** Recoilless, vibration free. Permanent lubrication and seals. Barrel stabilizer weight included. Crisp single-stage trigger. Available from Beeman.
**Price:** Right-hand . . . . . . . . . . . . . . . . . . . . . . . . . . . . . . . . . . . . . . . . . . $735.00
**Price:** Left-hand . . . . . . . . . . . . . . . . . . . . . . . . . . . . . . . . . . . . . . . . . . . $795.00

FWB Mini-Match

### BEEMAN/FEINWERKBAU 300-S MINI-MATCH
**Caliber:** 177, single shot.
**Barrel:** 17⅛".
**Weight:** 8.8 lbs. **Length:** 40" over-all.

**Power:** Spring piston, single stroke sidelever cocking.
**Stock:** Walnut. Stippled grip, adjustable buttplate. Scaled-down for youthful or slightly built shooters.
**Sights:** Globe front with interchangeable inserts, micro. adjustable rear. Front and rear sights move as a single unit.
**Features:** Recoilless, vibration free. Grooved for scope mounts. Steel piston ring. Cocking effort about 9½ lbs. Barrel sleeve optional. Left-hand model available. Introduced 1978. Imported by Beeman.
**Price:** Right-hand . . . . . . . . . . . . . . . . . . . . . . . . . . . . . . . . . . . . . . . . . . $685.00
**Price:** Left-hand . . . . . . . . . . . . . . . . . . . . . . . . . . . . . . . . . . . . . . . . . . . $735.00

Beeman/Feinwerkbau 600

## BEEMAN HW 55 TARGET RIFLES

| Model: | 55SM | 55MM | 55T |
|---|---|---|---|
| Caliber: | 177 | 177 | 177 |
| Barrel: | 18½" | 18½" | 18½" |
| Length: | 43½" | 43½" | 43½" |
| Wgt. lbs.: | 7.8 | 7.8 | 7.8 |
| Rear sight: | All aperture | | |
| Front sight: | All with globe and 4 interchangeable inserts. | | |
| Power: | All spring (barrel cocking). 660-700 fps. | | |
| Price: | $369.50 | $399.50 | $469.50 |

**Features:** Trigger fully adj. and removable. Micrometer rear sight adj. for w. and e. on all. Pistol grip high comb stock with beavertail fore-end, walnut finish stock on 55SM. Walnut stock on 55MM, Tyrolean stock on 55T. Imported by Beeman.

## BEEMAN/FEINWERKBAU MODEL 600 AIR RIFLE
**Caliber:** 177, single shot.
**Barrel:** 16.6".
**Weight:** 10.8. **Length:** 43" over-all.
**Power:** Single stroke pneumatic.
**Stock:** Special laminated hardwoods and hard rubber for stability.
**Sights:** Tunnel front with interchangeable inserts, click micrometer match aperture rear.
**Features:** Recoilless action; double supported barrel; special, short rifled area frees pellet from barrel faster so shooter's motion has minimum effect on accuracy. Fully adjustable match trigger. Trigger and sights blocked when loading latch is open. Imported by Beeman. Introduced 1984.
**Price:** Right hand . . . . . . . . . . . . . . . . . . . . . . . . . . . . . . . . . . . . . . . . . . . . **$875.00**
**Price:** Left hand . . . . . . . . . . . . . . . . . . . . . . . . . . . . . . . . . . . . . . . . . . . . **$899.50**

Beeman HW77

## BEEMAN/HW77 AIR RIFLE & CARBINE
**Caliber:** 177 or 22, single shot.
**Barrel:** 18.5", 12-groove rifling.
**Weight:** 8.9 lbs. **Length:** 43.7" over-all.
**Power:** Spring-piston; underlever cocking.
**Stock:** Walnut-stained beech; rubber buttplate, cut checkering on grip; cheekpiece.
**Sights:** Blade front, open adjustable rear.
**Features:** Velocity 830 fps. Fixed-barrel with fully opening, direct loading breech. Extended underlever gives good cocking leverage. Adjustable trigger. Grooved for scope mounting. Carbine has 14.5" barrel, weighs 8.7 lbs., and is 39.7" over-all. Imported by Beeman.
**Price:** Right-hand, rifle or carbine . . . . . . . . . . . . . . . . . . . . . . . . . . . . . **$359.50**
**Price:** Left-hand, rifle or carbine . . . . . . . . . . . . . . . . . . . . . . . . . . . . . **$389.50**

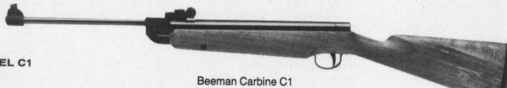

Beeman Carbine C1

## BEEMAN CARBINE MODEL C1
**Caliber:** 177, single shot.
**Barrel:** 14", 12-groove rifling.
**Weight:** 6¼ lbs. **Length:** 38" over-all.
**Power:** Spring-piston, barrel cocking.
**Stock:** Walnut-stained beechwood with rubber butt pad.
**Sights:** Blade front, rear click-adjustable for windage and elevation.
**Features:** Velocity 830 fps. Adjustable trigger. Receiver grooved for scope mounting. Imported by Beeman.
**Price:** . . . . . . . . . . . . . . . . . . . . . . . . . . . . . . . . . . . . . . . . . . . . . . . **$177.50**

Beeman/Webley Omega

## BEEMAN/WEBLEY OMEGA AIR RIFLE
**Caliber:** 177.
**Barrel:** 19¼", rifled.
**Weight:** 7.8 lbs. **Length:** 43½" over-all.
**Power:** Spring-piston air; barrel cocking.
**Stock:** Walnut-stained beech with cut-checkered grip; cheekpiece; rubber butt pad.
**Features:** Special quick-snap barrel latch; self-lubricating piston seal; receiver grooved for scope mounting. Introduced 1985. Imported from England by Beeman.
**Price:** . . . . . . . . . . . . . . . . . . . . . . . . . . . . . . . . . . . . . . . . . . . . . . . **$269.50**

## BEEMAN/WEBLEY VULCAN II DELUXE
**Caliber:** 177 or 22, single shot.
**Barrel:** 17", rifled.
**Weight:** 7.6 lbs. **Length:** 43.7" over-all.
**Power:** Spring piston air, barrel cocking.
**Stock:** Walnut. Cut checkering, rubber butt pad, checkpiece. Standard version has walnut-stained beech.
**Sights:** Hooded front, micrometer rear.
**Features:** Velocity of 830 fps (177), 675 fps (22). Single stage adjustable trigger; receiver grooved for scope mounting. Self-lubricating piston seal. Introduced 1983. Imported by Beeman.
**Price:** Standard . . . . . . . . . . . . . . . . . . . . . . . . . . . . . . . . . . . . . . . . . . **$198.50**
**Price:** Deluxe . . . . . . . . . . . . . . . . . . . . . . . . . . . . . . . . . . . . . . . . . . . . **$245.00**

**CAUTION:** PRICES CHANGE. CHECK AT GUNSHOP.

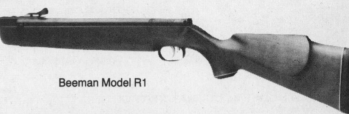

Weihrauch Model 35EB

## BEEMAN HW 35L/35EB SPORTER RIFLES
**Caliber:** 177 (35L), 177 or 22 (35EB), single shot.
**Barrel:** 19½".
**Weight:** 8 lbs. **Length:** 43½" over-all (35L).
**Power:** Spring, barrel cocking.
**Stock:** Walnut finish with high comb, full pistol grip.
**Sights:** Globe front with five inserts, target micrometer rear with rubber eye-cup.
**Features:** Fully adjustable trigger, manual safety. Thumb-release barrel latch. Model 35L has Bavarian cheekpiece stock, 35EB has walnut, American-style stock with cheekpiece, sling swivels, white spacers. Imported by Beeman.
**Price:** Model 35L ............................................. $269.50
**Price:** Model 35EB ............................................ $309.50

Beeman Model R1

## BEEMAN R1 AIR RIFLE
**Caliber:** 177, 20 or 22, single shot.
**Barrel:** 19.6", 12-groove rifling.
**Weight:** 8.5 lbs. **Length:** 45.2" over-all.
**Power:** Spring-piston, barrel cocking.
**Stock:** Walnut-stained beech; cut checkered pistol grip Monte Carlo comb and cheekpiece; rubber butt pad.
**Sights:** Tunnel front with interchangeable inserts, open rear click adjustable for windage and elevation. Grooved for scope mounting.
**Features:** Velocity of 940-1050 fps (177), 860 fps (20), 800 fps (22). Non-drying nylon piston and breech seals. Adjustable metal trigger. Right or left hand stock. Imported by Beeman.
**Price:** Right hand ............................................. $349.50
**Price:** Left hand ............................................. $379.50

## BEEMAN R8 AIR RIFLE
**Caliber:** 177, single shot.
**Barrel:** 18.3".
**Weight:** 7.2 lbs. **Length:** 43.1" over-all.
**Power:** Barrel cocking, spring-piston.
**Stock:** Walnut with Monte Carlo cheekpiece; checkered pistol grip.
**Sights:** Globe front, fully adjustable rear; interchangeable inserts.
**Features:** Velocity of 735 fps. Similar to the R1. Nylon piston and breech seals. Adjustable match-grade, two-stage, grooved metal trigger. Rubber butt pad. Imported by Beeman.
**Price:** ..................................................... $246.50

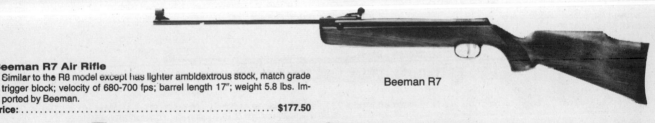

Beeman R7

## Beeman R7 Air Rifle
Similar to the R8 model except has lighter ambidextrous stock, match grade trigger block; velocity of 680-700 fps; barrel length 17"; weight 5.8 lbs. Imported by Beeman.
**Price:** ..................................................... $177.50

Beeman R10 Deluxe

## BEEMAN R10 AIR RIFLES
**Caliber:** 177, 20, 22, single shot.
**Barrel:** 16.1" and 19.7"; 12-groove rifling.
**Weight:** 7.9 lbs. **Length:** 46" over-all.
**Power:** Spring piston, barrel cocking.
**Stock:** Standard—walnut finished hardwood with M.C. comb, rubber buttplate, Deluxe has white spacers at grip cap, buttplate, checkered grip, cheekpiece, rubber buttplate.
**Sights:** Tunnel front with interchangeable inserts, open rear click adj. for w. and e. Receiver grooved for scope mounting.

**Features:** Over 1000 fps. in 177 cal. only; 26 lb. cocking effort; milled steel safety and body tube. Right and left hand models available. Introduced 1986. Imported by Beeman.
**Price:** ..................................................... NA

Benjamin Series 340

## BENJAMIN SERIES 340 AIR RIFLE
**Caliber:** 22 or 177, pellets or BB; single shot.
**Barrel:** 23", rifled and smoothbore.
**Weight:** 6 lbs. **Length:** 35" over-all.
**Power:** Hand pumped.
**Features:** Bolt action, walnut Monte Carlo stock and pump handle. Ramp-type front sight, adj. stepped leaf type rear. Push-pull safety.
**Price:** M340, BB ............................................. $104.05
**Price:** M343, 22 ............................................. $104.05
**Price:** M347, 177 ............................................ $104.05

Crosman Model 66

**CROSMAN MODEL 66 POWERMASTER**
**Caliber:** 177 (single shot) or BB
**Barrel:** 20″, rifled, solid steel.
**Weight:** 3 lbs., 14 oz. **Length:** 38½″ over-all.
**Stock:** Wood-grained plastic; checkered p.g. and fore-end.
**Sights:** Ramp front, fully adjustable open rear.
**Features:** Velocity about 675 fps. Bolt action, cross-bolt safety. Introduced 1983.
**Price:** About . . . . . . . . . . . . . . . . . . . . . . . . . . . . . . . . . . . . . . . . . . . . . . . **$40.00**

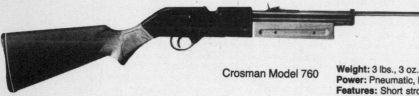

Crosman Model 84

**CROSMAN MODEL 84 CO₂ MATCH RIFLE**
**Caliber:** 177, single shot.
**Barrel:** 20″. Barrel has a chrome shroud to give extra sight radius.
**Weight:** 9 lbs., 9 oz. **Length:** 45.5″ over-all.

**Power:** Refillable CO₂ cylinders.
**Stock:** Walnut; Olympic match design with stippled pistol grip and fore-end, adjustable buttplate and comb.
**Sights:** Match sights — globe front micrometer adjustable rear.
**Features:** A CO₂ pressure regulated rifle with adjustable velocity up to 720 fps. Each CO₂ cylinder has more than enough power to complete a 60-shot Olympic match course. Electric trigger adjustable from ½ oz. to 3 lbs. Each gun can be custom fitted to the shooter. Made in U.S.A. Introduced 1984.
**Price:** About. . . . . . . . . . . . . . . . . . . . . . . . . . . . . . . . . . . . . . . . . **$1,379.00**

Crosman Model 760

**CROSMAN MODEL 760 PUMPMASTER**
**Caliber:** 177 pellets or BB, 200 shot.
**Barrel:** 19½″, rifled steel.

**Weight:** 3 lbs., 3 oz. **Length:** 35″ over-all.
**Power:** Pneumatic, hand pump.
**Features:** Short stroke, power determined by number of strokes. Walnut finished plastic checkered stock and fore-end. Post front sight and adjustable rear sight. Cross-bolt safety. Introduced 1983.
**Price:** About . . . . . . . . . . . . . . . . . . . . . . . . . . . . . . . . . . . . . . . . . . . . . . **$30.00**

Crosman Model 781

**CROSMAN MODEL 781 SINGLE PUMP**
**Caliber:** 177, BB, 4-shot pellet clip, 195-shot BB magazine.
**Barrel:** 19½″.
**Weight:** 2 lbs., 14 oz. **Length:** 35¾″ over-all.
**Power:** Pneumatic, single pump.
**Stock:** Wood-grained plastic; checkered p.g. and fore-end.
**Sights:** Blade front, open adjustable rear.
**Features:** Velocity of 350-400 fps (pellets). Uses only one pump. Hidden BB reservoir holds 195 shots; pellets loaded via 4-shot clip. Introduced 1984.
**Price:** About . . . . . . . . . . . . . . . . . . . . . . . . . . . . . . . . . . . . . . . . . . . . . . **$28.00**

**CROSMAN MODEL 788 BB SCOUT RIFLE**
**Caliber:** 177, BB.
**Barrel:** 14″, steel.
**Weight:** 2 lbs. 7 oz. **Length:** 31″ over-all.
**Stock:** Wood-grained ABS plastic.
**Sights:** Blade on ramp front, open adj. rear.
**Features:** Variable pump power—3 pumps give MV of 330 fps, 6 pumps 437 fps, 10 pumps 500 fps (BBs, average). Steel barrel, cross-bolt safety. Introduced 1978.
**Price:** About . . . . . . . . . . . . . . . . . . . . . . . . . . . . . . . . . . . . . . . . . . . . . . **$26.00**

Crosman 2100 Classic

**CROSMAN MODEL 2200 MAGNUM AIR RIFLE**
**Caliber:** 22, single-shot.
**Barrel:** 19″, rifled steel.
**Weight:** 4 lbs., 13 oz. **Length:** 39″ over-all.
**Stock:** Full-size, wood-grained plastic with checkered p.g. and fore-end.
**Sights:** Ramp front, open step-adjustable rear.
**Features:** Variable pump power—3 pumps give 395 fps, 6 pumps 530 fps, 10 pumps 620 fps (average). Full-size adult air rifle. Has white line spacers at pistol grip and buttplate. Introduced 1978.
**Price:** About . . . . . . . . . . . . . . . . . . . . . . . . . . . . . . . . . . . . . . . . . . . . . . **$54.00**

**CROSMAN MODEL 2100 CLASSIC AIR RIFLE**
**Caliber:** 177 pellets or BBs, 200-shot BB magazine.
**Barrel:** 21″, rifled.
**Weight:** 4 lbs., 13 oz. **Length:** 39¾″ over-all.
**Power:** Pump-up, pneumatic.
**Stock:** Wood-grained checkered ABS plastic.
**Features:** Three pumps gives about 450 fps, 10 pumps about 795 fps. Cross-bolt safety; concealed reservoir holds over 180 BBs.
**Price:** About . . . . . . . . . . . . . . . . . . . . . . . . . . . . . . . . . . . . . . . . . . . . . . **$45.00**

**CAUTION:** PRICES CHANGE. CHECK AT GUNSHOP.

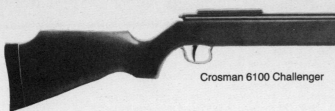

Crosman 6100 Challenger

## CROSMAN MODEL 6100 CHALLENGER RIFLE
**Caliber:** 177, single shot.
**Weight:** 7 lbs., 12 oz. **Length:** 46″ over-all.
**Power:** Spring air, barrel cocking.
**Stock:** Stained hardwood with checkered pistol grip, rubber recoil pad.
**Sights:** Globe front, open fully adjustable rear.
**Features:** Average velocity 820 fps. Automatic safety, two-stage adjustable trigger. Receiver grooved for scope mounting. Introduced 1982. Imported from West Germany by Crosman Air Guns.
**Price:** About . . . . . . . . . . . . . . . . . . . . . . . . . . . . . . . . . . . . . . **$200.00**

## CROSMAN MODEL 6300 CHALLENGER AIR RIFLE
**Caliber:** 177.
**Power:** Spring-air, barrel-cocking.
**Stock:** Stained hardwood.
**Sights:** Hooded front, micrometer adjustable rear.
**Features:** Velocity of 680 to 710 fps. Adjustable trigger; automatic safety; comes with mount base for peep sight or scope. Introduced 1985.
**Price:** About . . . . . . . . . . . . . . . . . . . . . . . . . . . . . . **$126.00**

### Crosman Model 6500 Challenger Air Rifle
Similar to the Model 6300 except has tunnel front sight with interchangeable bead for post or aperture inserts; positive barrel locking mechanism; automatic safety; rubber butt pad. Introduced 1985.
**Price:** About . . . . . . . . . . . . . . . . . . . . . . . . . . . . . . . . . . . . . . **$140.00**

## DAISY MODEL 25 CENTENNIAL
**Caliber:** BB, 46-shot repeater.
**Barrel:** Smoothbore steel with removable shot tube.
**Weight:** 3.25 lbs. **Length:** 37″ over-all.
**Power:** Spring air.
**Stock:** American black walnut with hand-rubbed finish, centennial medallion embedded in left side.
**Sights:** Post front, adjustable v-slot rear.

Daisy Model 25

**Features:** Authentic styling after 1913 Daisy original. Muzzle velocity up to 340 fps; case-hardened finish lever, blued barrel and receiver parts.
**Price:** About . . . . . . . . . . . . . . . . . . . . . . . . . . . . . . . . . . . . . . **$99.00**

Daisy Model 95

## DAISY YOUTHLINE RIFLES

| Model: | 95 | 111 | 105 |
|---|---|---|---|
| Caliber: | BB | BB | BB |
| Barrel: | 18″ | 18″ | 13½″ |
| Length: | 35.2″ | 34.3″ | 29.8″ |
| Power: | Spring | Spring | Spring |
| Capacity: | 700 | 650 | 400 |
| Price: About | $32.00 | $29.00 | $14.09 |

**Features:** Model 95 stock and fore-end are wood; 105 and 111 have plastic stocks.

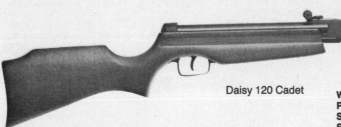

Daisy 120 Cadet

## DAISY/POWER LINE MODEL 120 CADET RIFLE
**Caliber:** 177, single shot.
**Barrel:** 15.7″, rifled.

**Weight:** 5 lbs. **Length:** 36.8″ over-all.
**Power:** Spring air, barrel cocking.
**Stock:** Stained hardwood.
**Sights:** Hooded post front on ramp, open micro-adjustable rear.
**Features:** Velocity of 500 fps. Lever-type automatic safety, blued steel receiver. Imported from Spain by Daisy. Introduced 1981.
**Price:** About . . . . . . . . . . . . . . . . . . . . . . . . . . . . . . . . . . . . . . **$69.00**

Daisy Model 840

## DAISY MODEL 840
**Caliber:** 177 pellet (single-shot) or BB (350-shot).
**Barrel:** 19″, smoothbore, steel.
**Weight:** 2.7 lbs. **Length:** 36.8″ over-all.
**Stock:** Molded wood-grain stock and fore-end.
**Sights:** Ramp front, open, adj. rear.
**Features:** Single pump pneumatic rifle. Muzzle velocity 335 fps (BB), 300 fps (pellet). Steel buttplate; straight pull bolt action; cross-bolt safety. Fore-end forms pump lever. Introduced 1978.
**Price:** About . . . . . . . . . . . . . . . . . . . . . . . . . . . . . . . **$41.00**

## DAISY/POWER LINE 856 PUMP-UP AIR GUN
**Caliber:** 177 (pellets), BB, 100-shot BB magazine.
**Barrel:** Rifled steel with shroud.
**Weight:** 2¾ lbs. **Length:** 37.4″ over-all.
**Power:** Pneumatic pump-up.
**Stock:** Molded woodgrain plastic.
**Sights:** Ramp and blade front, open rear adjustable for e.
**Features:** Velocity from 315 fps (two pumps) to 650 fps (10 pumps). Finger grooved fore-end. Cross-bolt trigger-block safety. Introduced 1985. From Daisy.
**Price:** About . . . . . . . . . . . . . . . . . . . . . . . . . . . . . . . . . . . . . . **$44.00**

Power Line Model 860

## DAISY/POWER LINE 860 PUMP-UP AIR GUN
**Caliber:** 177 (pellets), BB, 100-shot BB magazine.
**Barrel:** Rifled steel with shroud.
**Weight:** 4.18 lbs. **Length:** 37.4″ over-all.
**Power:** Pneumatic pump-up.
**Stock:** Molded woodgrain with Monte Carlo cheekpiece.
**Sights:** Ramp and blade front, open rear adjustble for e.
**Features:** Velocity from 315 fps (two pumps) to 650 fps (10 pumps). Shoots BBs or pellets. Heavy die cast metal receiver. Cross-bolt trigger-block safety. Introduced 1984. From Daisy.
**Price:** About . . . . . . . . . . . . . . . . . . . . . . . . . . . . . . . . . . . . . . . . **$53.00**

## DAISY/POWER LINE 880 PUMP-UP AIR GUN
**Caliber:** 177 pellets, BB.
**Barrel:** Rifled steel with shroud.
**Weight:** 4.5 lbs. **Length:** 37¾″ over-all.
**Power:** Pneumatic pump-up.
**Stock:** Wood grain molded plastic with Monte Carlo cheekpiece.
**Sights:** Ramp front, open rear adj. for e.
**Features:** Crafted by Daisy. Variable power (velocity and range) increase with pump strokes. 10 strokes for maximum power. 100-shot BB magazine. Cross-bolt trigger safety. Positive cocking valve.
**Price:** About . . . . . . . . . . . . . . . . . . . . . . . . . . . . . . . . . . . . . . . . **$62.00**
**Price:** Model 980 (as above with hardwood stock and fore-end), about **$73.00**

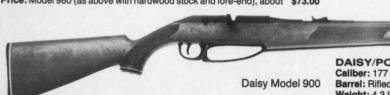

Daisy Model 900

## DAISY/POWER LINE 900 PELLET REPEATER
**Caliber:** 177 pellets, 5-shot clip.
**Barrel:** Rifled steel.
**Weight:** 4.3 lbs. **Length:** 38.4″ over-all.
**Power:** Spring air.
**Stock:** Full length moulded stock with checkering, cheekpiece, white spacers.
**Sights:** Blade and ramp front, V-slot rear fully adjustable for w. & e.
**Features:** Easy loading, automatic indexing five-shot clip. Heavy die-cast metal receiver, dovetail mount for scope, heavy die-cast pump lever. Single pump for 545 fps muzzle velocity.
**Price:** About . . . . . . . . . . . . . . . . . . . . . . . . . . . . . . . . . . . . . . . . **$86.00**

Power Line Model 922

## DAISY/POWER LINE MODEL 922
**Caliber:** 22, 5-shot clip.
**Barrel:** Rifled steel with shroud.
**Weight:** 4.5 lbs. **Length:** 37¾″ over-all.
**Stock:** Molded wood-grained plastic with checkered p.g. and fore-end, Monte Carlo cheekpiece.
**Sights:** Ramp front, full adj. open rear.
**Features:** Muzzle velocity from 270 fps (two pumps) to 530 fps. (10 pumps).

Straight pull bolt action. Separate buttplate and grip cap with white spacers. Introduced 1978.
**Price:** About . . . . . . . . . . . . . . . . . . . . . . . . . . . . . . . . . . . . . . . . **$72.00**
**Price:** Models 970/920 (as above with hardwood stock and fore-end), about . . . . . . . . . . . . . . . . . . . . . . . . . . . . . . . . . . . . . . . . **$85.00**

Daisy Model 953

## DAISY/POWER LINE 953
**Caliber:** 177 pellets.
**Barrel:** 20.9″; 12-groove rifling, high-grade solid steel by Lothar Walther®, precision crowned; bore sized for precision match pellets.

**Weight:** 5.08 lbs. **Length:** 38.9″ over-all.
**Power:** Single-pump pneumatic.
**Stock:** Full length, select American hardwood, stained and finished; black buttplate with white spacers.
**Sights:** Globe front with four aperture inserts; precision micrometer adjustable rear peep sight mounted on a standard ⅜″ dovetail receiver mount.
**Features:** Single-shot.
**Price:** About . . . . . . . . . . . . . . . . . . . . . . . . . . . . . . . . . . . . . . . . **$180.00**

Daisy Red Ryder

## DAISY 1938 RED RYDER COMMEMORATIVE
**Caliber:** BB, 650-shot repeating action.
**Barrel:** Smoothbore steel with shroud.
**Weight:** 2.2 lbs. **Length:** 35.4″ over-all.
**Stock:** Wood stock burned with Red Ryder lariat signature.
**Sights:** Post front, adjustable V-slot rear.
**Features:** Wood fore-end. Saddle ring with leather thong. Lever cocking. Gravity feed. Controlled velocity. Commemorates one of Daisy's most popular guns, the Red Ryder of the 1940s and 1950s.
**Price:** About . . . . . . . . . . . . . . . . . . . . . . . . . . . . . . . . . . . . . . . . **$49.00**

Daisy Model 1894

### DAISY 1894 SPITTIN' IMAGE CARBINE
**Caliber:** BB, 40-shot.
**Barrel:** 17½", smoothbore.
**Weight:** 3 lbs. **Length:** 38" over-all.
**Power:** Spring.
**Stock:** Molded wood-grain stock and fore-end.
**Sights:** Blade and ramp front, open adjustable rear.
**Features:** Cocks halfway on forward stroke of lever, halfway on return.
**Price:** About .................................................... $56.00

Daisy Softair 12

### DAISY SOFTAIR GUN 12
**Caliber:** 25-cal. plastic shot.
**Barrel:** Smoothbore.
**Weight:** 3.25 lbs. **Length:** 18.5" over-all.
**Power:** Pump or bolt action, spring air.
**Stock:** Molded grip.
**Sights:** Blade front, notched rear.
**Features:** Detailed replica of a famous American-made semi-automatic fire-arm; takes 30-shot clip.
**Price:** About .................................................... $79.00

Daisy Softair 14

### DAISY SOFTAIR GUN 14
**Caliber:** 25-cal. plastic shot.
**Barrel:** Smoothbore.
**Weight:** 2.9 lbs. **Length:** 26" over-all.
**Power:** Pump or bolt action, spring air.
**Stock:** Hardwood stock with molded pistol and pump grips.
**Sights:** Blade front, adjustable rear peep sight.
**Features:** Fully-detailed replica of a famous semi-automatic rifle; takes 10-shot clip
**Price:** About .................................................... $118.00

Daisy Softair 15

### DAISY SOFTAIR 15
**Caliber:** 25-cal. plastic shot.
**Barrel:** Smoothbore.
**Weight:** 2.5 lbs. **Length:** 15.5" over-all.
**Power:** Pump action, spring air.
**Stock:** Moulded receiver and grip.
**Sights:** Post front, 4-way adjustable rear.
**Features:** Detailed replica of the famous German-made police weapon. 12-shot banana clip, automatically ejects spent shells.
**Price:** About .................................................... $66.00

Daisy Softair 870

### DAISY SOFTAIR 870
**Caliber:** 25-cal. plastic shot.
**Barrel:** Smoothbore.
**Weight:** 3.6 lbs. **Length:** 40" over-all.
**Power:** Slide action, spring air.
**Stock:** Moulded, with checkering.
**Sights:** Bead front.
**Features:** Detailed replica of Remington 870 Wingmaster; authentic working action, five-shot magazine, ejects spent shells.
**Price:** About .................................................... $89.00

FX-1

### FX-1 AIR RIFLE
**Caliber:** 177, single shot.
**Barrel:** 18", rifled.
**Weight:** 6.6 lbs. **Length:** 43" over-all.
**Power:** Spring-piston, barrel cocking.
**Stock:** Walnut-stained hardwood.
**Sights:** Tunnel front with interchangeable inserts; rear with rotating disc to give four sighting notches.
**Features:** Velocity 680 fps. Match-type adjustable trigger. Receiver grooved for scope mounting. Imported by Beeman.
**Price:** .................................................... $146.50

### FX-2 Air Rifle
Similar to the FX-1 except weighs 5.8 lbs., 41" over-all; front sight is hooded post on ramp, rear sight has two-way click adjustments. Adjustable trigger. Imported by Beeman.
**Price:** .................................................... $116.50

**CAUTION:** PRICES CHANGE. CHECK AT GUNSHOP.

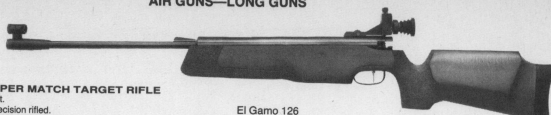

El Gamo 126

## EL GAMO 126 SUPER MATCH TARGET RIFLE
**Caliber:** 177, single shot.
**Barrel:** Match grade, precision rifled.
**Weight:** 10.6 lbs. **Length:** 43.8″ over-all.
**Power:** Single pump pneumatic.
**Stock:** Match-style, hardwood, with stippled grip and fore-end.
**Sights:** Hooded front with interchangeable elements, fully adjustable match rear.
**Features:** Velocity of 590 fps. Adjustable trigger; easy loading pellet port; adjustable butt pad. Introduced 1984. Imported from Spain by Daisy.
**Price:** About . . . . . . . . . . . . . . . . . . . . . . . . . . . . . . . . . . $395.00

Kassnar Model 30-TR

## KASSNAR MODEL 30-TR AIR RIFLE
**Caliber:** 177, single shot.
**Barrel:** 20″.
**Weight:** About 5¾ lbs. **Length:** 36″ over-all.
**Power:** Hand pumped.
**Stock:** Indonesian walnut.
**Sights:** Post front, fully adj. peep rear.
**Features:** Variable muzzle velocity depending upon number of pumps. Imported by Kassnar Imports, Inc. Introduced 1986.
**Price:** . . . . . . . . . . . . . . . . . . . . . . . . . . . . . . . . . . . . . $179.00

## KASSNAR MODEL 427 AIR RIFLE
**Caliber:** 177, single shot.
**Barrel:** 18″.
**Weight:** 4¾ lbs. **Length:** 40″ over-all.
**Power:** Spring piston, barrel cocking.
**Stock:** Stained hardwood.
**Sights:** Tunnel front, open rear adj. for w. & e.
**Features:** Receiver grooved for scope mounting. Imported by Kassnar Imports, Inc. Introduced 1986.
**Price:** . . . . . . . . . . . . . . . . . . . . . . . . . . . . . . . . . . . . . $69.00

Marathon Model 100

## MARATHON MODEL 100 AIR RIFLE
**Caliber:** 177, single shot.
**Barrel:** 17″, rifled.
**Weight:** 5.7 lbs. **Length:** 41″ over-all.
**Stock:** Walnut-stained hardwood with Monte Carlo cheekpiece.
**Sights:** Hooded post front, micro click open rear.
**Features:** Velocity of 525 fps. Automatic safety; receiver grooved for scope mounting. Introduced 1984. Imported from Spain by Marathon Products.
**Price:** . . . . . . . . . . . . . . . . . . . . . . . . . . . . . . . . . . . . . $59.95

### Marathon Model 50 Youth Air Rifle
Similar to the Model 100 rifle except scaled down for small shooters. Over-all length is 36″, barrel length is 15″, length of pull is 12″, and weight is 4.7 lbs. Available in 177-caliber only. Introduced 1985.
**Price:** . . . . . . . . . . . . . . . . . . . . . . . . . . . . . . . . . . . . . $49.99

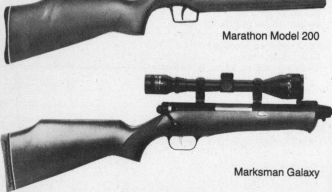

Marathon Model 200

### Marathon Model 200 Air Rifle
Similar to the Model 100 except has adjustable trigger, velocity of 640 fps, tunnel front sight with interchangeable inserts, buttplate with white line spacer, and over-all length of 41¾″. Available in 177 or 22 caliber. Introduced 1984.
**Price:** . . . . . . . . . . . . . . . . . . . . . . . . . . . . . . . . . . . . . $74.99

Marksman Galaxy

## MARKSMAN 306, 308 GALAXY AIR RIFLE
**Caliber:** 177 (M306) or 22 (M308), single shot.
**Barrel:** 17½″.
**Weight:** 6½ lbs. **Length:** 41″ over-all.
**Power:** Compressed air cartridges.
**Stock:** Walnut-stained beechwood.
**Sights:** Open, fully adjustable.
**Features:** Velocity of 1000 fps (177), 800 fps (22). Bolt action, uses pre-primed centerfire cartridges; recoilless action; fully adjustable 2-stage trigger. Comes with a charging unit for the cartridges and 20 cartridges. Introduced 1984. Imported from England.
**Price:** With table-top charger . . . . . . . . . . . . . . . . . . . . . . . . . . . $315.00
**Price:** With portable hand charger . . . . . . . . . . . . . . . . . . . . . . . . $270.00

CAUTION: PRICES CHANGE. CHECK AT GUNSHOP.

Marksman Model 1740

## MARKSMAN 29 AIR RIFLE
**Caliber:** 177 or 22, single shot.
**Barrel:** 10.5".
**Weight:** 8 lbs. **Length:** 41.5" over-all.
**Power:** Spring air, barrel cocking.
**Stock:** Stained hardwood.
**Sights:** Blade front, open adj. rear.
**Features:** Velocity of 790-830 fps (177), 610-640 fps. (22). Introduced 1986. Imported from England by Marksman Products.
**Price:** Either caliber . . . . . . . . . . . . . . . . . . . . . . . . . . . . . . . . . . . . . . . . . $140.00

## MARKSMAN 70 AIR RIFLE
**Caliber:** 177 or 22, single shot.
**Barrel:** 19.75".
**Weight:** 8 lbs. **Length:** 45.5" over-all.
**Power:** Spring air, barrel cocking.
**Stock:** Stained hardwood with M.C. cheekpiece, rubber butt pad, cut checkered p.g.
**Sights:** Hooded front, open fully adj. rear.
**Features:** Velocity of 910-940 fps (177), 740-780 fps (22); two-stage adj. trigger. Introduced 1986. Imported from West Germany by Marksman Products.
**Price:** Either caliber . . . . . . . . . . . . . . . . . . . . . . . . . . . . . . . . . . . . . . . . $215.00

## MARKSMAN 1740 AIR RIFLE
**Caliber:** 177 or 100-shot BB repeater.
**Barrel:** 15½", smoothbore.
**Weight:** 5 lbs., 1 oz. **Length:** 36½" over-all.
**Power:** Spring, barrel cocking.
**Stock:** Moulded high-impact ABS plastic.
**Sights:** Ramp front, open rear adj. for e.
**Features:** Automatic safety; fixed front, adj. rear sight; shoots 177 cal. BB's pellets and darts. Velocity about 475-500 fps.
**Price:** . . . . . . . . . . . . . . . . . . . . . . . . . . . . . . . . . . . . . . . . . . . . . . . . . . $35.00
**Price:** Model 1744 (as above with 4 x 15 scope) . . . . . . . . . . . . . . . . . . $45.80

> Consult our Directory pages for the location of firms mentioned.

## Marksman 55 Air Rifle
Similar to the Model 70 except has uncheckered hardwood stock, no cheekpiece, plastic butt plate. Over-all length is 45.25", weight is 7½ lbs. Available in 177 caliber only.
**Price:** . . . . . . . . . . . . . . . . . . . . . . . . . . . . . . . . . . . . . . . . . . . . . . . . . $185.00

Mauser 300 SL

## MAUSER MODEL 300 SL AIR RIFLE
**Caliber:** 177, single shot.
**Barrel:** 18.9".
**Weight:** 8 lbs., 8 oz. **Length:** 43.7" over-all.
**Power:** Spring air, under-lever cocking.
**Stock:** Match style, hardwood, with stippled p.g., rubber butt pad.
**Sights:** Tunnel front, match aperture rear.
**Features:** Velocity of 550-600 fps. Dovetail mount for diopter or scope. Automatic safety. Imported from West Germany by Marksman Products.
**Price:** . . . . . . . . . . . . . . . . . . . . . . . . . . . . . . . . . . . . . . . . . . . . . . . . . $260.00

Norica Model 73

## NORICA MODEL 73 AIR RIFLE
**Caliber:** 177 or 22, single shot.
**Barrel:** 18".
**Weight:** 6¼ lbs. **Length:** 41¾" over-all.
**Power:** Spring air, barrel cocking.
**Sights:** Hooded front with four interchangeable blades, open adjustable rear.
**Features:** Velocity 610 fps. Adult-size stock with full pistol grip, two-stage trigger; receiver grooved for scope mounting. Imported from Spain by Kassnar. Introduced 1984.
**Price:** . . . . . . . . . . . . . . . . . . . . . . . . . . . . . . . . . . . . . . . . . . . . . . . . . $104.00

Norica Model 80G

## NORICA MODEL 80G AIR RIFLE
**Caliber:** 177 or 22, single shot.
**Barrel:** 18".
**Weight:** 7¼ lbs. **Length:** 43" over-all.
**Power:** Spring air, barrel cocking.
**Stock:** Monte Carlo competition-style.
**Sights:** Hooded front with four interchangeable blades; fully adjustable diopter rear on ramp.
**Features:** Velocity 610 fps. Adjustable trigger; target-type buttplate; blued metal. Imported from Spain by Kassnar. Introduced 1984.
**Price:** . . . . . . . . . . . . . . . . . . . . . . . . . . . . . . . . . . . . . . . . . . . . . . . . . $134.00

Norica Black Widow

## NORICA BLACK WIDOW AIR RIFLE
**Caliber:** 177 or 22, single shot.
**Barrel:** 16½".
**Weight:** 5¼ lbs. **Length:** 37½" over-all.
**Power:** Spring air, barrel cocking.
**Stock:** Black stained hardwood.
**Sights:** Hooded front, open adjustable rear.
**Features:** Velocity 500 fps. Stocked for young shooters. Receiver grooved for scope mounting. Imported from Spain by Kassnar. Introduced 1984.
**Price:** . . . . . . . . . . . . . . . . . . . . . . . . . . . . . . . . . . . . . . . . . . . . . . . . . . . **$83.00**

## RWS MODEL 27 AIR RIFLE
**Caliber:** 177 or 22, single shot.
**Weight:** 6 lbs. **Length:** 42" over-all.
**Power:** Spring air, barrel cocking.
**Stock:** Walnut-finished hardwood.
**Sights:** Globe front, micro click rear with four-way blade.
**Features:** Velocity of 541 fps. Fully adjustable two-stage trigger; dovetail base for peep sight or scope mounting. Small dimensions for young shooters. Imported from West Germany by Dynamit Nobel of America.
**Price:** . . . . . . . . . . . . . . . . . . . . . . . . . . . . . . . . . . . . . . . . . . **$150.00**

RWS Model 27

## RWS MODEL 45 AIR RIFLE
**Caliber:** 177 or 22, single shot.
**Weight:** 7¾ lbs. **Length:** 46" over-all.
**Power:** Spring air, barrel cocking.
**Stock:** Walnut-finished hardwood with rubber recoil pad.
**Sights:** Globe front with interchangeable inserts, micro click open rear with four-way blade.
**Features:** Velocity of 820 fps (177 cal.), 689 fps (22 cal.). Dovetail base for either micrometer peep sight or scope mounting. Automatic safety. Imported from West Germany by Dynamit Nobel of America.
**Price:** 177 or 22 . . . . . . . . . . . . . . . . . . . . . . . . . . . . . . . . . . **$220.00**
**Price:** With deluxe walnut stock. . . . . . . . . . . . . . . . . . . . . . . . . . **$260.00**

## RWS Model 45S Air Rifle
Same as the standard Model 45 except comes without sights and has a 4×20 scope, ramp-type mount, muzzle brake/weight, sling and swivels. Introduced 1983.
**Price:** . . . . . . . . . . . . . . . . . . . . . . . . . . . . . . . . . . . . . . . . . . **$290.00**
**Price:** As above, without scope, mount, sling, swivels . . . . . . . . . . . . **$210.00**

## RWS MODEL 50T 01 AIR RIFLE
**Caliber:** 177, single shot.
**Weight:** 8 lbs. **Length:** 45" over-all.
**Power:** Spring air, under-lever cocking.
**Stock:** Walnut-finished hardwood with cheekpiece, checkered grip, rubber butt pad.
**Sights:** Globe front, micro click open rear.
**Features:** Velocity of 750 fps. Automatic safety. Dovetail base for scope or peep sight mounting. Imported from West Germany by Dynamit Nobel of America.
**Price:** . . . . . . . . . . . . . . . . . . . . . . . . . . . . . . . . . . . . . . . . . . **$310.00**

RWS Model 50

## RWS Model 75KT 01 Running Boar Air Rifle
Similar to the Model 75 Match except has adjustable cheekpiece and buttplate, different stock, sandblasted barrel sleeve, detachable barrel weight, elevated-grip cocking lever, and a 240mm scope mount. Introduced 1983.
**Price:** . . . . . . . . . . . . . . . . . . . . . . . . . . . . . . . . . . . . . . . . . . **$700.00**

## RWS MODEL 75T 01 MATCH AIR RIFLE
**Caliber:** 177, single shot.
**Barrel:** 19".
**Weight:** 11 lbs. **Length:** 43.7" over-all.
**Power:** Spring air, side-lever cocking.
**Stock:** Oil finished walnut with stippled grip, adjustable buttplate, accessory rail, Conforms to I.S.U. rules.
**Sights:** Globe front with 5 inserts, fully adjustable match peep rear.
**Features:** Velocity of 574 fps. Fully adjustable trigger. Model 75 HV has stippled fore-end, adjustable cheekpiece. Uses double opposing piston system for recoilless operation. Imported from West Germany by Dynamit Nobel of America.
**Price:** Model 75T 01 . . . . . . . . . . . . . . . . . . . . . . . . . . . . . . . . . . **$600.00**
**Price:** Model 75 HVT 01 . . . . . . . . . . . . . . . . . . . . . . . . . . . . . . . **$700.00**
**Price:** Model 75T 01 left hand . . . . . . . . . . . . . . . . . . . . . . . . . . . . **$640.00**
**Price:** Model 75 HVT 01 left hand . . . . . . . . . . . . . . . . . . . . . . . . . . **$740.00**
**Price:** Model 75 UT 01 (adj. cheekpiece, buttplate, M82 sight) . . . . . . **$700.00**

## SHARP-INNOVA AIR RIFLE
**Caliber:** 177 and 22, single shot.
**Barrel:** 19.5", rifled.
**Weight:** 4.4 lbs. **Length:** 34.6" over-all.
**Power:** Pneumatic, multi-stroke.
**Stock:** Mahogany.
**Sights:** Hooded front, adjustable aperture rear.
**Features:** Velocity of 960 fps with 8 pumps (177). Adjustable trigger. Receiver grooved for scope mount. Introduced 1983. Imported from Japan by Great Lakes Airguns and Beeman.
**Price:** . . . . . . . . . . . . . . . . . . . . . . . . . . . . . . . . . . . . . . . . . . **$125.00**

## SIG-HAMMERLI MILITARY LOOK 420
**Caliber:** 177 or 22, single shot.
**Barrel:** 19", rifled.
**Weight:** About 7 lbs. **Length:** 44¼" over-all.
**Stock:** Synthetic stock and handguard.
**Sights:** Open, fully adj.
**Features:** Side lever cocking; adjustable trigger; rifled steel barrel. Introduced 1977. Imported by Mandall Shooting Supplies.
**Price:** . . . . . . . . . . . . . . . . . . . . . . . . . . . . . . . . . . . . . . . . . . **$295.00**

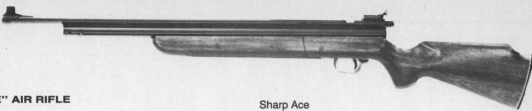

Sharp Ace

## SHARP MODEL "ACE" AIR RIFLE
**Caliber:** 177, 22, single shot.
**Weight:** 6.3 lbs. **Length:** 38.4″ over-all.
**Power:** Pneumatic, multi-stroke.
**Stock:** Stained hardwood.
**Sights:** Hooded ramp front, fully adjustable peep rear.
**Features:** Velocity of 1019 fps (177-cal.), 892 fps (22-cal.). Receiver grooved for scope mounting. Turn-bolt action for loading. Introduced 1984. Imported from Japan by Great Lakes Airguns and Beeman.
**Price:** From Great Lakes ..................................... $216.73
**Price:** From Beeman .......................................... $225.00

### Sharp Model Ace Hunter Deluxe Air Rifle
Similar to the Ace Target model except comes with a 1″ 4x scope, "muzzle brake," sling swivels and leather sling. Has the all metal trigger found on the Target model and the checkered stock. With 12 pumps and RWS Hobby pellets velocity is 1006 fps. Introduced 1985.
**Price:** From Great Lakes ....................... $339.15

### Sharp Model Ace Target Standard Air Rifle
Similar to the Model Ace except the under-barrel pump assembly has been rotated about 120° to the side, new one-piece stock, globe front sight takes interchangeable elements, micro. adjustable peep rear. Checkered p.g. and fore-end, adjustable buttplate. Adjustable trigger. Introduced 1985.
**Price:** From Great Lakes ....................... $293.44

Sheridan CO₂

**Power:** Standard 12.5 gram $CO_2$ cylinder.
**Stock:** Walnut sporter.
**Sights:** Open, adj. for w. and e. Optional Sheridan-Williams 5D-SH receiver sight or Weaver D4 scope.
**Features:** Bolt action single shot, $CO_2$ powered. Velocity approx. 514 fps., manual thumb safety. Blue or Silver finish. Left-hand models avail. at same prices.
**Price:** $CO_2$ Blue Streak .......................................... $96.20
**Price:** $CO_2$ Silver Streak ......................................... $100.55
**Price:** $CO_2$ Blue Streak with receiver sight ..................... $114.40
**Price:** $CO_2$ Blue Streak with scope ............................. $131.90

## SHERIDAN CO₂ AIR RIFLES
**Caliber:** 5mm (20 cal.), single shot.
**Barrel:** 18½″, rifled.
**Weight:** 6 lbs. **Length:** 37″ over-all.

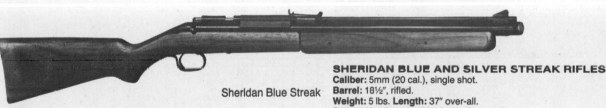

Sheridan Blue Streak

## SHERIDAN BLUE AND SILVER STREAK RIFLES
**Caliber:** 5mm (20 cal.), single shot.
**Barrel:** 18½″, rifled.
**Weight:** 5 lbs. **Length:** 37″ over-all.
**Power:** Hand pumped (swinging fore-end).
**Features:** Rustproof barrel and piston tube. Takedown. Thumb safety. Mannlicher type walnut stock. Left-hand models same price.
**Price:** Blue Streak ........................................... $109.85
**Price:** Silver Streak ......................................... $113.95

Sterling HR-81 Rifle

## STERLING HR-81/HR-83 AIR RIFLE
**Caliber:** 177 or 22, single-shot.
**Barrel:** 18½″.
**Weight:** 8½ lbs. **Length:** 42½″ over-all.
**Power:** Spring air, (barrel cocking).
**Stock:** Stained hardwood, with checkpiece, checkered pistol grip.
**Sights:** Tunnel-type front with four interchangeable elements, open adjustable V-type rear.
**Features:** Velocity of 700 fps (177), 600 fps (22). Bolt action with easily accessible loading port; adjustable single-stage match trigger; rubber recoil pad. Integral scope mount rails. Scope and mount optional. Introduced 1983. Made in U.S.A. by Benjamin Air Rifle Co.
**Price:** HR 81-7 (177 cal., standard walnut stock).................. $235.85
**Price:** HR 81-2 (as above, 22 cal.) ............................. $245.15
**Price:** HR 83-7 (177 cal., deluxe walnut stock).................... $334.75
**Price:** HR 83-2 (as above, 22 cal.) ............................. $338.85
**Price:** For 4x40 wide angle scope, add ......................... $82.35

## WALTHER LGR UNIVERSAL MATCH AIR RIFLE
**Caliber:** 177, single shot.
**Barrel:** 25.5″.
**Weight:** 13 lbs. **Length:** 44¾″ over-all.
**Power:** Spring air, barrel cocking.
**Stock:** Walnut match design with stippled grip and fore-end, adjustable cheekpiece, rubber butt pad.
**Features:** Has the same weight and contours as the Walther U.I.T. rimfire target rifle. Comes complete with sights, accessories and muzzle weight. Imported from West Germany by Interarms.
**Price:** ................................................. $765.00

## Walther LGR Match Air Rifle
Same basic specifications as standard LGR except has a high comb stock, sights are mounted on riser blocks. Introduced 1977.
**Price:** ................................................. $675.00

**CAUTION:** PRICES CHANGE. CHECK AT GUNSHOP.

# AVERAGE CENTERFIRE RIFLE CARTRIDGE BALLISTICS AND PRICES

| Caliber | Bullet Wgt. Grs. | — VELOCITY (fps) — Muzzle | 100 yds. | 200 yds. | 300 yds. | 400 yds. | — ENERGY (ft. lbs.) — Muzzle | 100 yds. | 200 yds. | 300 yds. | 400 yds. | — TRAJ. (in.) — 100 yds. | 200 yds. | 300 yds. | 400 yds. | Approx. Price per box |
|---|---|---|---|---|---|---|---|---|---|---|---|---|---|---|---|---|
| 17 Rem. | 25 | 4040 | 3284 | 2644 | 2086 | 1606 | 906 | 599 | 388 | 242 | 143 | +2.0 | + 1.7 | − 3.7 | −17.4 | $14.08 |
| 22 Hornet | 45 | 2690 | 2042 | 1502 | 1128 | 948 | 723 | 417 | 225 | 127 | 90 | +1.0 | − 5.3 | −27.6 | — | 26.21* |
| 218 Bee | 46 | 2760 | 2102 | 1550 | 1155 | 961 | 778 | 451 | 245 | 136 | 94 | +1.0 | − 5.2 | −26.3 | — | 25.93* |
| 222 Rem. | 50 | 3140 | 2602 | 2123 | 1700 | 1350 | 1094 | 752 | 500 | 321 | 202 | +2.0 | − 0.4 | −10.6 | −33.1 | 11.09 |
| 222 Rem. | 55 | 3020 | 2562 | 2147 | 1773 | 1451 | 1114 | 801 | 563 | 384 | 257 | +2.0 | − 0.4 | −10.5 | −31.8 | 11.09 |
| 222 Rem. Mag. | 55 | 3240 | 2748 | 2305 | 1906 | 1556 | 1282 | 922 | 649 | 444 | 296 | +2.0 | + 0.2 | − 8.2 | −26.3 | 12.60 |
| 223 Rem. | 40 | 3650 | 3010 | 2450 | 1950 | 1530 | 1185 | 805 | 535 | 340 | 205 | +2.0 | + 1.0 | − 5.9 | −22.0 | 12.12 |
| 223 Rem. | 55 | 3240 | 2747 | 2305 | 1906 | 1556 | 1282 | 922 | 649 | 444 | 296 | +2.0 | + 0.2 | − 8.2 | −26.3 | 12.12 |
| 224 Wea. Mag.[2] | 55 | 3650 | 3192 | 2780 | 2403 | 2056 | 1627 | 1244 | 943 | 705 | 516 | +2.0 | + 2.0 | − 2.4 | −12.2 | 23.95 |
| 22-250 Rem. | 40 | 4000 | 3320 | 2720 | 2200 | 1740 | 1420 | 980 | 660 | 430 | 265 | +2.0 | + 1.8 | − 3.2 | −15.5 | 12.12 |
| 22-250 Rem. | 53 | 3710 | 3190 | 2740 | 2250 | 1790 | 1615 | 1200 | 751 | 506 | 377 | +2.0 | + 1.0 | − 3.5 | −16.9 | 12.32 |
| 22-250 Rem. | 55 | 3680 | 3137 | 2656 | 2222 | 1832 | 1654 | 1201 | 861 | 603 | 410 | +2.0 | + 1.3 | − 4.3 | −17.1 | 13.54+ |
| 220 Swift | 50 | 4110 | 3610 | 3135 | 2680 | NA | 1875 | 1450 | 1090 | 800 | NA | +2.0 | + 2.8 | + | − 6.9 | 17.90 |
| 22 Savage Hi-Power | 71 | 2790 | 2295 | 1885 | 1560 | NA | 1225 | 830 | 560 | 383 | NA | +2.0 | − 0.8 | −12.6 | — | 18.85 |
| 243 Win. | 80 | 3350 | 2955 | 2593 | 2259 | 1951 | 1993 | 1551 | 1194 | 906 | 676 | +2.0 | + 0.9 | − 5.4 | −18.6 | 15.13 |
| 243 Win. | 85 | 3320 | 3070 | 2830 | 2600 | 2380 | 2080 | 1770 | 1510 | 1280 | 1070 | +2.0 | + 1.2 | − 4.5 | −14.2 | 16.67+ |
| 243 Win. | 100 | 2960 | 2697 | 2449 | 2215 | 1993 | 1945 | 1615 | 1332 | 1089 | 882 | +2.0 | + 0.2 | − 7.5 | −22.2 | 16.67+ |
| 6mm Rem. | 80 | 3470 | 3064 | 2694 | 2352 | 2036 | 2139 | 1667 | 1289 | 982 | 736 | +2.0 | + 1.1 | − 4.5 | −16.5 | 15.13 |
| 6mm Rem. | 100 | 3100 | 2829 | 2573 | 2332 | 2104 | 2133 | 1777 | 1470 | 1207 | 983 | +2.0 | + 0.6 | − 6.1 | −19.2 | 15.13 |
| 240 Wea. Mag.[2] | 87 | 3500 | 3202 | 2924 | 2663 | 2416 | 2366 | 1980 | 1651 | 1370 | 1127 | +2.0 | + 2.2 | − 1.8 | −10.6 | 23.95 |
| 240 Wea. Mag.[2] | 100 | 3395 | 3106 | 2835 | 2581 | 2339 | 2559 | 2142 | 1785 | 1478 | 1215 | +2.0 | + 1.6 | − 3.0 | −12.8 | 23.95 |
| 25-20 Win. | 86 | 1460 | 1194 | 1030 | 931 | 858 | 407 | 272 | 203 | 165 | 141 | + | − 8.2 | −23.5 | — | 24.57* |
| 256 Win. | 60 | 2760 | 2097 | 1542 | 1149 | 957 | 1015 | 586 | 317 | 176 | 122 | +1.0 | − 5.2 | −28.0 | — | 31.20* |
| 25-35 Win. | 117 | 2230 | 1866 | 1545 | 1282 | 1097 | 1292 | 904 | 620 | 427 | 313 | +2.0 | − 5.3 | −27.4 | — | 16.75 |
| 250-3000 Savage | 87 | 3030 | 2673 | 2342 | 2036 | 1755 | 1773 | 1380 | 1059 | 801 | 595 | +2.0 | + | − 8.4 | −25.2 | 15.35 |
| 250-3000 Savage | 100 | 2820 | 2504 | 2210 | 1936 | 1684 | 1765 | 1392 | 1084 | 832 | 630 | +2.0 | − 0.6 | −10.4 | −29.5 | 15.35 |
| 257 Roberts +P | 100 | 3000 | 2633 | 2295 | 1982 | 1697 | 1998 | 1539 | 1169 | 872 | 639 | +2.0 | − 0.4 | − 9.4 | −27.2 | 16.95 |
| 257 Roberts | 117 | 2650 | 2291 | 1961 | 1663 | 1404 | 1824 | 1363 | 999 | 718 | 512 | +2.0 | − 1.0 | −15.0 | — | 17.37 |
| 25-06 Rem. | 87 | 3440 | 2995 | 2591 | 2222 | 1884 | 2286 | 1733 | 1297 | 954 | 686 | +2.0 | + 1.1 | − 5.1 | −18.4 | 18.08 |
| 25-06 Rem. | 90 | 3440 | 3043 | 2680 | 2340 | 2034 | 2364 | 1850 | 1435 | 1098 | 827 | +2.0 | + 1.2 | − 4.2 | −16.6 | 18.08 |
| 25-06 Rem. | 100 | 3230 | 2893 | 2580 | 2287 | 2014 | 2316 | 1858 | 1478 | 1161 | 901 | +2.0 | + 0.8 | − 5.7 | −18.9 | 18.08 |
| 25-06 Rem. | 120 | 2990 | 2730 | 2484 | 2252 | 2032 | 2382 | 1985 | 1644 | 1351 | 1100 | +2.0 | + | − 7.5 | −22.0 | 18.08 |
| 257 Wea. Mag.[2] | 87 | 3825 | 3456 | 3118 | 2805 | 2513 | 2826 | 2308 | 1878 | 1520 | 1220 | +2.0 | + 2.7 | − 0.3 | − 7.7 | 24.95 |
| 257 Wea. Mag.[2] | 100 | 3555 | 3237 | 2941 | 2665 | 2404 | 2806 | 2326 | 1920 | 1556 | 1283 | +2.0 | + 2.1 | − 1.8 | −10.5 | 24.95 |
| 257 Wea. Mag.[2] | 117 | 3300 | 2882 | 2502 | 2152 | 1830 | 2829 | 2158 | 1626 | 1203 | 870 | +2.0 | + 1.2 | − 5.1 | −18.9 | 24.95 |
| 6.5x50 Jap. | 139 | 2360 | 2185 | 2035 | 1900 | NA | 1720 | 1475 | 1243 | 1083 | NA | +2.0 | − 1.6 | −13.4 | NA | 18.85 |
| 6.5x50 Jap. | 156 | 2065 | 1870 | 1690 | 1530 | NA | 1480 | 1215 | 990 | 810 | NA | +2.0 | − 4.6 | −23.3 | NA | 18.85 |
| 6.5x52 Carcano | 156 | 2430 | 2210 | 2000 | 1800 | NA | 2045 | 1690 | 1385 | 1125 | NA | +2.0 | − 2.0 | −14.7 | NA | 18.85 |
| 6.5x55 Swedish | 140 | 2855 | 2665 | 2500 | 2350 | NA | 2530 | 2210 | 1930 | 1677 | NA | +2.0 | + 0.6 | − 6.7 | NA | 20.30 |
| 6.5x55 Swedish | 156 | 2645 | 2415 | 2205 | 2010 | NA | 2425 | 2015 | 1701 | 1414 | NA | +2.0 | − 1.0 | −12.1 | NA | 18.85 |
| 6.5 Rem. Mag. | 120 | 3210 | 2905 | 2621 | 2353 | 2102 | 2745 | 2248 | 1830 | 1475 | 1177 | +2.0 | + 0.7 | − 5.6 | −19.3 | 26.85 |
| 264 Win. | 100 | 3320 | 2926 | 2565 | 2231 | 1923 | 2447 | 1901 | 1461 | 1105 | 821 | +2.0 | + 0.8 | − 5.8 | −19.4 | 21.23 |
| 264 Win. | 140 | 3030 | 2782 | 2548 | 2326 | 2114 | 2854 | 2406 | 2018 | 1682 | 1389 | +2.0 | + 0.4 | − 6.6 | −18.4 | 21.23 |
| 270 Win. | 100 | 3430 | 3021 | 2649 | 2305 | 1988 | 2612 | 2027 | 1557 | 1179 | 877 | +2.0 | + 1.0 | − 4.9 | −17.5 | 16.44 |
| 270 Win. | 130 | 3060 | 2776 | 2510 | 2259 | 2022 | 2702 | 2225 | 1818 | 1472 | 1180 | +2.0 | + 0.4 | − 6.8 | −20.8 | 18.17+ |
| 270 Win. | 150 | 2850 | 2585 | 2336 | 2100 | 1879 | 2705 | 2226 | 1817 | 1468 | 1175 | +2.0 | − 0.4 | − 9.2 | −25.8 | 22.25+ |
| 270 Wea. Mag.[2] | 100 | 3760 | 3380 | 3033 | 2712 | 2412 | 3139 | 2537 | 2042 | 1633 | 1292 | +2.0 | + 2.4 | − 0.9 | − 8.9 | 24.95 |
| 270 Wea. Mag.[2] | 130 | 3375 | 3100 | 2842 | 2598 | 2366 | 3287 | 2773 | 2330 | 1948 | 1616 | +2.0 | + 1.9 | − 2.4 | −11.6 | 24.95 |
| 270 Wea. Mag.[2] | 150 | 3245 | 3019 | 2803 | 2598 | 2402 | 3507 | 3034 | 2617 | 2248 | 1922 | +2.0 | + 1.8 | − 3.0 | −12.8 | 24.95 |
| 7x30 Waters | 120 | 2700 | 2300 | 1930 | 1600 | 1330 | 1940 | 1405 | 990 | 685 | 470 | +2.0 | − 2.0 | −11.0 | −20.0 | 15.88 |
| 7mm-08 Rem. | 140 | 2860 | 2625 | 2402 | 2189 | 1988 | 2542 | 2142 | 1793 | 1490 | 1228 | +2.0 | − 0.2 | − 8.4 | −23.9 | 16.44 |
| 7mm Mauser | 140 | 2660 | 2435 | 2221 | 2018 | 1827 | 2199 | 1843 | 1533 | 1266 | 1037 | +2.0 | − 1.0 | −11.1 | −29.7 | 16.73 |
| 7mm Mauser | 150 | 2755 | 2540 | 2330 | 2135 | NA | 2530 | 2150 | 1810 | 1515 | NA | +2.0 | + | − 8.4 | NA | 16.90 |
| 7mm Mauser | 175 | 2440 | 2137 | 1857 | 1603 | 1382 | 2313 | 1774 | 1340 | 998 | 742 | +2.0 | − 2.7 | −17.6 | — | 16.73 |
| 7x57R | 150 | 2690 | 2475 | 2285 | 2080 | NA | 2410 | 2040 | 1830 | 1515 | NA | +2.0 | + | − 8.4 | NA | 19.66 |
| 280 Rem. | 140 | 3000 | 2758 | 2528 | 2309 | 2102 | 2797 | 2363 | 1986 | 1657 | 1373 | — | — | — | — | 16.44 |
| 280 Rem. | 150 | 2970 | 2699 | 2444 | 2203 | 1975 | 2937 | 2426 | 1989 | 1616 | 1299 | +2.0 | + 0.2 | − 7.5 | −22.4 | 16.44 |
| 280 Rem. | 165 | 2820 | 2510 | 2220 | 1950 | 1701 | 2913 | 2308 | 1805 | 1393 | 1060 | +2.0 | − 0.6 | −10.3 | −29.3 | 16.44 |
| 7x64 Brenneke | 150 | 2890 | 2600 | 2330 | 2115 | NA | 2780 | 2250 | 1810 | 1490 | NA | +2.0 | + 0.6 | − 8.4 | NA | 19.66 |
| 7x64 Brenneke | 170 | 2500 | 2355 | 2200 | 1915 | NA | 2865 | 2094 | 1694 | 1466 | NA | +2.0 | − 1.6 | −12.4 | NA | 19.66 |
| 284 Win. | 125 | 3140 | 2829 | 2538 | 2265 | 2010 | 2736 | 2221 | 1788 | 1424 | 1121 | +2.0 | + 0.6 | − 6.3 | −18.7 | 19.85 |
| 284 Win. | 150 | 2860 | 2595 | 2344 | 2108 | 1886 | 2724 | 2243 | 1830 | 1480 | 1185 | +2.0 | − 0.2 | − 8.8 | −25.2 | 19.85 |
| 7mm Rem. Mag. | 125 | 3310 | 2976 | 2666 | 2376 | 2105 | 3040 | 2428 | 1972 | 1567 | 1230 | +2.0 | + 1.0 | − 4.9 | −17.0 | 20.37 |
| 7mm Rem. Mag. | 150 | 3110 | 2830 | 2568 | 2320 | 2085 | 3221 | 2667 | 2196 | 1792 | 1448 | +2.0 | + 0.6 | − 6.1 | −19.3 | 22.25+ |
| 7mm Rem. Mag. | 160 | 2950 | 2730 | 2520 | 2320 | 2120 | 3090 | 2650 | 2250 | 1910 | 1600 | +2.0 | + 0.4 | − 7.1 | −21.6 | 26.92+ |
| 7mm Rem. Mag. | 175 | 2860 | 2645 | 2440 | 2244 | 2057 | 3178 | 2718 | 2313 | 1956 | 1644 | +2.0 | + | − 7.9 | −22.7 | 20.37 |
| 7mm Wea. Mag.[2] | 139 | 3400 | 3138 | 2892 | 2659 | 2437 | 3567 | 3039 | 2580 | 2181 | 1832 | +2.0 | + 2.1 | − 2.1 | −11.1 | 24.95 |
| 7mm Wea. Mag.[2] | 160 | 3200 | 3004 | 2816 | 2637 | 2464 | 3637 | 3205 | 2817 | 2469 | 2156 | +2.0 | + 1.7 | − 3.0 | −12.6 | 34.95 |
| 30 Carbine[1] | 110 | 1990 | 1567 | 1236 | 1035 | 923 | 967 | 600 | 373 | 262 | 208 | +1.0 | −11.5 | — | — | 26.40* |
| 30 Rem. | 170 | 2120 | 1822 | 1555 | 1328 | 1153 | 1696 | 1253 | 913 | 666 | 502 | +2.0 | − 5.7 | −27.8 | — | 17.31 |
| 30-30 Win. | 55 | 3400 | 2693 | 2085 | 1570 | 1187 | 1412 | 886 | 521 | 301 | 172 | +2.0 | + | −10.2 | −35.0 | 14.33 |
| 30-30 Win. | 125 | 2570 | 2090 | 1660 | 1320 | 1080 | 1830 | 1210 | 770 | 480 | 320 | +2.0 | − 2.4 | −19.4 | — | 13.41 |
| 30-30 Win. | 150 | 2390 | 1973 | 1605 | 1303 | 1095 | 1902 | 1296 | 858 | 565 | 399 | +2.0 | − 4.2 | −25.6 | — | 13.41 |
| 30-30 Win. | 170 | 2200 | 1895 | 1619 | 1381 | 1191 | 1827 | 1355 | 989 | 720 | 535 | +2.0 | − 4.8 | −25.1 | — | 18.84+ |
| 300 Savage | 150 | 2630 | 2311 | 2015 | 1743 | 1500 | 2303 | 1779 | 1352 | 1012 | 749 | +2.0 | − 1.6 | −13.9 | −36.6 | 16.61 |
| 300 Savage | 180 | 2350 | 2137 | 1935 | 1745 | 1570 | 2207 | 1825 | 1496 | 1217 | 985 | +2.0 | − 2.6 | −19.7 | — | 16.61 |
| 303 Savage | 190 | 1890 | 1612 | 1372 | 1183 | 1055 | 1507 | 1096 | 794 | 591 | 469 | +2.0 | − 8.8 | −38.1 | — | 18.61 |
| 30-40 Krag | 180 | 2430 | 2213 | 2207 | 1813 | 1632 | 2360 | 1957 | 1610 | 1314 | 1064 | +2.0 | − 2.2 | −15.0 | −38.5 | 17.32 |
| 307 Win. | 150 | 2760 | 2321 | 1924 | 1575 | 1289 | 2538 | 1795 | 1233 | 826 | 554 | +2.0 | − 1.4 | −15.4 | — | 16.25 |
| 307 Win. | 180 | 2510 | 2179 | 1874 | 1599 | 1362 | 2519 | 1898 | 1404 | 1022 | 742 | +2.0 | − 2.6 | −17.1 | — | 16.25 |
| 308 Win. | 55 | 3770 | 3215 | 2726 | 2286 | 1888 | 1735 | 1262 | 907 | 638 | 435 | +2.0 | + 1.4 | − 4.2 | −15.8 | 18.24 |
| 308 Win. | 110 | 3180 | 2666 | 2206 | 1795 | 1444 | 2470 | 1736 | 1188 | 787 | 509 | +2.0 | + | − 9.3 | −29.5 | 16.44 |
| 308 Win. | 125 | 3050 | 2697 | 2370 | 2067 | 1788 | 2582 | 2019 | 1659 | 1186 | 887 | +2.0 | + | − 8.2 | −24.6 | 16.44 |
| 308 Win. | 150 | 2820 | 2533 | 2263 | 2009 | 1774 | 2648 | 2137 | 1705 | 1344 | 1048 | +2.0 | − 0.6 | 10.0 | −28.1 | 16.44 |
| 308 Win. | 165 | 2700 | 2520 | 2330 | 2160 | 1990 | 2670 | 2310 | 1990 | 1700 | 1450 | +2.0 | + | − 8.4 | −24.3 | 18.17+ |
| 308 Win. | 180 | 2620 | 2393 | 2178 | 1974 | 1782 | 2743 | 2288 | 1896 | 1557 | 1269 | 2.0 | − 1.2 | −11.7 | −31.3 | 16.44 |
| 308 Win. | 200 | 2450 | 2208 | 1980 | 1767 | 1572 | 2665 | 2165 | 1741 | 1386 | 1097 | +2.0 | − 2.2 | −15.4 | −39.7 | 16.44 |
| 30-06 Spring. | 55 | 4080 | 3485 | 2965 | 2502 | 2083 | 2033 | 1483 | 1074 | 764 | 530 | +2.0 | + 1.9 | − 2.1 | −11.7 | 18.24 |
| 30-06 Spring. | 110 | 3330 | 2799 | 2325 | 1901 | 1532 | 2708 | 1913 | 1321 | 882 | 573 | +2.0 | + 0.4 | − 7.7 | −25.6 | 16.44 |
| 30-06 Spring. | 125 | 3140 | 2780 | 2447 | 2138 | 1853 | 2736 | 2145 | 1662 | 1269 | 953 | +2.0 | + 0.4 | − 7.1 | −22.4 | 16.44 |
| 30-06 Spring. | 130 | 3205 | 2875 | 2506 | 2263 | NA | 2965 | 2390 | 1895 | 1480 | NA | +2.0 | + 1.2 | − 4.9 | NA | 16.57 |
| 30-06 Spring. | 150 | 2910 | 2617 | 2342 | 2083 | 1843 | 2820 | 2281 | 1827 | 1445 | 1131 | +2.0 | − 0.2 | − 8.5 | −24.6 | 18.17+ |
| 30-06 Spring. | 165 | 2800 | 2534 | 2283 | 2047 | 1825 | 2872 | 2352 | 1909 | 1534 | 1220 | +2.0 | − 0.6 | − 9.9 | −27.5 | 18.17+ |
| 30-06 Spring. | 180 | 2700 | 2469 | 2250 | 2042 | 1846 | 2913 | 2436 | 2023 | 1666 | 1362 | +2.0 | − 0.8 | −10.5 | −28.6 | 22.25+ |
| 30-06 Spring. | 200 | 2640 | 2390 | 2220 | 1860 | NA | 3095 | 2535 | 2218 | 1384 | NA | +2.0 | − 1.2 | −11.8 | NA | 16.57 |
| 30-06 Spring. | 220 | 2410 | 2130 | 1870 | 1632 | 1422 | 2837 | 2216 | 1708 | 1301 | 758 | +2.0 | − 2.7 | −20.5 | NA | 16.44 |
| 7.5x55 Swiss | 180 | 2650 | 2460 | 2250 | 2060 | NA | 2800 | 2380 | 2020 | 1690 | NA | +2.0 | − 0.2 | − 9.2 | NA | 19.66 |
| 7.62x54R Russ. | 180 | 2575 | 2360 | 2165 | 1975 | NA | 2650 | 2270 | 1875 | 1560 | NA | +2.0 | − 0.6 | −10.4 | NA | 20.11 |
| 308 Norma Mag. | 180 | 3020 | 2780 | 2580 | 2385 | NA | 3645 | 3095 | 2670 | 2270 | NA | +2.0 | + 1.4 | − 5.9 | NA | 23.30 |
| 300 H&H Mag. | 180 | 2880 | 2640 | 2412 | 2196 | 1990 | 3315 | 2785 | 2325 | 1927 | 1583 | +2.0 | − 0.2 | − 8.3 | −23.7 | 20.96 |
| 300 Win. Mag. | 150 | 3290 | 2951 | 2636 | 2342 | 2068 | 3605 | 2900 | 2314 | 1827 | 1424 | +2.0 | + 0.9 | − 5.3 | −17.8 | 21.51 |
| 300 Win. Mag. | 180 | 2960 | 2745 | 2540 | 2344 | 2157 | 3501 | 3011 | 2578 | 2196 | 1859 | +2.0 | + | − 7.3 | −20.9 | 25.84+ |
| 300 Win. Mag. | 200 | 2830 | 2680 | 2530 | 2380 | 2240 | 3560 | 3180 | 2830 | 2520 | 2230 | +2.0 | + 0.6 | − 6.2 | −19.1 | 23.42+ |
| 300 Win. Mag. | 220 | 2680 | 2448 | 2228 | 2020 | 1823 | 3508 | 2927 | 2424 | 1993 | 1623 | +2.0 | − 1.0 | −11.0 | −29.5 | 21.51 |

# AVERAGE CENTERFIRE RIFLE CARTRIDGE BALLISTICS AND PRICES (continued)

| Caliber | Bullet Wgt. Grs. | VELOCITY (fps) Muzzle | 100 yds. | 200 yds. | 300 yds. | 400 yds. | ENERGY (ft. lbs.) Muzzle | 100 yds. | 200 yds. | 300 yds. | 400 yds. | TRAJ. (in.) 100 yds. | 200 yds. | 300 yds. | 400 yds. | Approx. Price per box |
|---|---|---|---|---|---|---|---|---|---|---|---|---|---|---|---|---|
| 300 Wea. Mag.² | 110 | 3900 | 3441 | 3028 | 2652 | 2305 | 3714 | 2891 | 2239 | 1717 | 1297 | +2.0 | + 2.6 | − 0.6 | − 9.2 | **24.95** |
| 300 Wea. Mag.² | 150 | 3600 | 3297 | 3015 | 2751 | 2502 | 4316 | 3621 | 3028 | 2520 | 1709 | +2.0 | + 2.3 | − 1.2 | − 9.2 | **24.95** |
| 300 Wea. Mag.² | 180 | 3300 | 3077 | 2865 | 2663 | 2470 | 4352 | 3784 | 3280 | 2834 | 2438 | +2.0 | − 2.6 | − 3.0 | −12.4 | **34.95** |
| 300 Wea. Mag.² | 220 | 2905 | 2498 | 2126 | 1787 | 1490 | 4122 | 3047 | 2207 | 1560 | 1085 | +2.0 | − 0.1 | − 9.9 | −22.3 | **24.95** |
| 7.7x58 Jap. | 130 | 2950 | 2635 | 2340 | 2065 | NA | 2513 | 2005 | 1581 | 1230 | NA | +2.0 | + 0.2 | − 7.9 | NA | **20.10** |
| 7.7x58 Jap. | 180 | 2495 | 2290 | 2100 | 1920 | NA | 2485 | 2100 | 1765 | 1475 | NA | +2.0 | + 1.2 | −12.2 | NA | **20.10** |
| 7.65x53 Argen. | 150 | 2660 | 2390 | 2120 | 1870 | NA | 2355 | 1895 | 1573 | 1224 | NA | +2.0 | − 0.2 | − 9.1 | NA | **18.86** |
| 303 British | 180 | 2460 | 2124 | 1817 | 1542 | 1311 | 2418 | 1803 | 1319 | 950 | 687 | +2.0 | − 2.8 | −21.3 | — | **16.92** |
| 8mm Rem. Mag. | 185 | 3080 | 2761 | 2464 | 2186 | 1927 | 3896 | 3131 | 2494 | 1963 | 1525 | +2.0 | + 0.4 | − 7.0 | −21.7 | **25.47** |
| 8mm Rem. Mag. | 220 | 2830 | 2581 | 2346 | 2123 | 1913 | 3912 | 3254 | 2688 | 2201 | 1787 | +2.0 | − 0.4 | − 9.1 | −25.5 | **25.47** |
| 8mm Mauser | 170 | 2360 | 1969 | 1622 | 1333 | 1123 | 2102 | 1463 | 993 | 651 | 476 | +2.0 | − 4.1 | −24.9 | — | **16.95** |
| 8x57 JS Mauser | 165 | 2855 | 2525 | 2225 | 1955 | NA | 2985 | [illegible] | [illegible] | [illegible] | NA | +2.0 | + [illegible] | 0.0 | NA | **[illegible]** |
| 8x57 JS Mauser | 196 | 2525 | 2195 | 1895 | 1625 | NA | 2780 | 2100 | 1560 | 1160 | NA | +2.0 | − 2.0 | −15.7 | NA | **17.22** |
| 32-20 Win. | 100 | 1210 | 1021 | 913 | 834 | 769 | 325 | 231 | 185 | 154 | 131 | + | −32.3 | — | — | **24.79⁺** |
| 32 Win. Spl. | 170 | 2250 | 1921 | 1626 | 1372 | 1175 | 1911 | 1393 | 998 | 710 | 521 | +2.0 | − 4.7 | −24.7 | — | **13.79** |
| 338 Win. Mag. | 200 | 2960 | 2658 | 2375 | 2110 | 1862 | 3890 | 3137 | 2505 | 1977 | 1539 | +2.0 | + | − 8.2 | −24.3 | **25.35** |
| 338 Win. Mag. | 225 | 2780 | 2572 | 2374 | 2184 | 2003 | 3862 | 3306 | 2816 | 2384 | 2005 | +2.0 | − 1.4 | −11.1 | −27.8 | **25.36** |
| 340 Wea. Mag.² | 200 | 3260 | 3011 | 2775 | 2552 | 2339 | 4719 | 4025 | 3420 | 2892 | 2429 | +2.0 | + 1.6 | − 3.3 | −13.5 | **41.95** |
| 340 Wea. Mag.² | 210 | 3250 | 2991 | 2746 | 2515 | 2295 | 4924 | 4170 | 3516 | 2948 | 2455 | +2.0 | + 1.7 | − 3.3 | −13.8 | **41.95** |
| 340 Wea. Mag.² | 250 | 3000 | 2806 | 2621 | 2443 | 2272 | 4995 | 4371 | 3812 | 3311 | 2864 | +2.0 | + 1.0 | − 5.0 | −16.8 | **41.95** |
| 348 Win. | 200 | 2520 | 2215 | 1931 | 1672 | 1443 | 2820 | 2178 | 1656 | 1241 | 925 | +2.0 | − 2.2 | −15.9 | — | **29.85** |
| 351 Win. S.L. | 180 | 1850 | 1556 | 1310 | 1128 | 1012 | 1368 | 968 | 686 | 508 | 409 | + | −13.6 | — | — | **42.35*** |
| 35 Rem. | 150 | 2300 | 1874 | 1506 | 1218 | 1039 | 1762 | 1169 | 755 | 494 | 359 | +2.0 | − 5.1 | −27.8 | — | **15.19** |
| 35 Rem. | 200 | 2080 | 1698 | 1376 | 1140 | 1001 | 1921 | 1280 | 841 | 577 | 445 | +2.0 | − 5.3 | −32.1 | — | **15.19** |
| 356 Win. | 200 | 2460 | 2114 | 1797 | 1517 | 1284 | 2688 | 1985 | 1434 | 1022 | 732 | +2.0 | − 3.0 | −18.9 | — | **22.90** |
| 356 Win. | 250 | 2160 | 1911 | 1682 | 1476 | 1299 | 2591 | 2028 | 1571 | 1210 | 937 | +2.0 | − 4.7 | −23.7 | — | **22.90** |
| 358 Win. | 200 | 2490 | 2171 | 1876 | 1610 | 1379 | 2753 | 2093 | 1563 | 1151 | 844 | +2.0 | − 2.6 | −17.5 | — | **22.90** |
| 357 Magnum | 180 | 1550 | 1160 | 980 | 860 | 770 | 960 | 535 | 383 | 295 | 235 | + | −23.4 | — | — | **25.07*** |
| 350 Rem. Mag. | 200 | 2710 | 2410 | 2130 | 1870 | 1631 | 3261 | 2579 | 2014 | 1553 | 1181 | +2.0 | − 1.2 | −12.1 | −32.9 | **27.09** |
| 9.3x57 Mauser | 286 | 2065 | 1820 | 1580 | 1400 | NA | 2715 | 2100 | 1622 | 1274 | NA | +2.0 | − 2.8 | −25.9 | — | **21.63** |
| 9.3x62 Mauser | 286 | 2360 | 2090 | 1830 | 1580 | NA | 3545 | 2770 | 2177 | 1622 | NA | +2.0 | − 2.0 | −23.2 | — | **21.63** |
| 375 Win. | 200 | 2200 | 1841 | 1526 | 1268 | 1089 | 2150 | 1506 | 1034 | 714 | 527 | +2.0 | − 5.2 | −27.4 | — | **19.75** |
| 375 Win. | 250 | 1900 | 1647 | 1424 | 1239 | 1103 | 2005 | 1506 | 1126 | 852 | 676 | +2.0 | − 7.9 | −34.8 | — | **19.75** |
| 375 H&H Mag. | 270 | 2690 | 2420 | 2166 | 1928 | 1707 | 4337 | 3510 | 2812 | 2228 | 1747 | +2.0 | − 1.0 | −11.5 | −31.4 | **25.20** |
| 375 H&H Mag. | 300 | 2530 | 2171 | 1843 | 1551 | 1307 | 4263 | 3139 | 2262 | 1602 | 1138 | +2.0 | − 2.6 | −17.1 | — | **25.20** |
| 378 Wea. Mag.² | 270 | 3180 | 2976 | 2781 | 2594 | 2415 | 6062 | 5308 | 4635 | 4034 | 3495 | +2.0 | + 1.6 | − 3.4 | −13.2 | **41.95** |
| 378 Wea. Mag.² | 300 | 2925 | 2576 | 2252 | 1952 | 1680 | 5698 | 4419 | 3379 | 2538 | 1881 | +2.0 | + | − 8.7 | −26.9 | **49.95** |
| 38-40 Win. | 180 | 1160 | 999 | 901 | 827 | 764 | 538 | 399 | 324 | 273 | 233 | + | −23.4 | — | — | **31.60*** |
| 38-55 Win. | 255 | 1320 | 1190 | 1091 | 1018 | 963 | 987 | 802 | 674 | 587 | 525 | + | −18.1 | — | — | **18.35** |
| 44-40 Win. | 200 | 1190 | 1006 | 900 | 822 | 756 | 629 | 449 | 360 | 300 | 254 | + | −33.3 | — | — | **32.70*** |
| 44 Rem. Mag. | 240 | 1760 | 1380 | 1114 | 970 | 878 | 1650 | 1015 | 661 | 501 | 411 | + | −17.6 | — | — | **31.15*** |
| 444 Marlin | 240 | 2350 | 1815 | 1377 | 1087 | 941 | 2942 | 1755 | 1010 | 630 | 472 | +2.0 | − 5.8 | −32.7 | — | **18.30** |
| 444 Marlin | 265 | 2120 | 1733 | 1405 | 1160 | 1012 | 2644 | 1768 | 1162 | 791 | 603 | +2.0 | − 6.8 | −33.4 | — | **18.53** |
| 45-70 Gov. | 300 | 1880 | 1650 | 1425 | 1235 | 1105 | 2355 | 1815 | 1355 | 1015 | 810 | + | −12.8 | — | — | **18.45** |
| 45-70 Gov. | 405 | 1330 | 1168 | 1055 | 977 | 918 | 1590 | 1227 | 1001 | 858 | 758 | + | −24.6 | — | — | **18.72** |
| 458 Win. Mag. | 500 | 2040 | 1823 | 1623 | 1442 | 1237 | 4620 | 3689 | 2924 | 1839 | 1469 | +2.0 | − 5.6 | −26.4 | — | **52.00** |
| 458 Win. Mag. | 510 | 2040 | 1770 | 1527 | 1319 | 1157 | 4712 | 3547 | 2540 | 1970 | 1239 | +2.0 | − 6.4 | −27.3 | — | **34.45** |
| 460 Wea. Mag.² | 500 | 2700 | 2404 | 2128 | 1869 | 1635 | 8092 | 6416 | 5026 | 3878 | 2969 | +2.0 | − 0.6 | −10.7 | −31.3 | **49.95** |

From 24" barrel except as noted (1 = 20" bbl.; 2 = 26" bbl.). Energies and velocities based on most commonly used bullet profile. Variations can and will occur with different bullet profiles and/or different lots of ammunition as well as individual barrels. Trajectory based on scope reticle 1.5" above center of bore line. + indicates bullet strikes point of aim.

NOTES: * = 50 cartridges to a box pricing (all others 20 cartridges to a box pricing)
NA = Information not available from the manufacturer.
— = Trajectory falls more than 40 inches below line of sight.
+ = Premium priced ammunition.

Please note that the actual ballistics obtained in your gun can vary considerably from the advertised ballistics. Also, ballistics can vary from lot to lot, even within the same brand. All prices were correct at the time this table was prepared. All prices are subject to change without notice.

# CENTERFIRE HANDGUN CARTRIDGES—BALLISTICS AND PRICES

| Caliber | Bullet Gr. | Style | Velocity (fps) Muzzle | 50 yds. | Energy (ft. lbs.) Muzzle | 50 yds. | Barrel Length in inches | Approx. price/box |
|---|---|---|---|---|---|---|---|---|
| 22 Rem. Jet | 40 | JSP | 2100 | 1790 | 390 | 285 | 8⅜ | **$36.13** |
| 221 Rem. Fireball | 50 | JSP | 2650 | 2380 | 780 | 630 | 10½ | **12.80*** |
| 223 Rem. | 55 | JSP | NA | NA | NA | NA | 14½ | **12.60*** |
| 25 Auto | 45 | LE | 815 | 729 | 66 | 53 | 2 | **16.95** |
| 25 Auto | 50 | FMC | 760 | 707 | 64 | 56 | 2 | **16.04** |
| 30 Luger | 93 | FMC | 1220 | 1110 | 305 | 253 | 4½ | **25.95** |
| 30 Carbine | 110 | JHP, FMC | 1740 | 1552 | 740 | 588 | 10 | **10.97*** |
| 32 S&W | 85, 88 | LRN | 680 | 645 | 90 | 81 | 3 | **15.48** |
| 32 S&W Long | 98 | LRN, LWC | 705 | 670 | 115 | 98 | 4 | **16.04** |
| 32 H&R Mag. | 85 | JHP | 1100 | 1020 | 230 | 195 | 4½ | **21.20** |
| 32 H&R Mag. | 95 | LSWC | 1030 | 940 | 225 | 190 | 4½ | **15.37** |
| 32 Short Colt | 80 | LRN | 745 | 665 | 100 | 79 | 4 | **15.39** |
| 32 Long Colt | 82 | LRN | 755 | 715 | 100 | 93 | 4 | **16.04** |
| 32 Auto | 60 | STHP | 970 | 895 | 125 | 107 | 4 | **20.60** |
| 32 Auto | 71 | FMC | 905 | 855 | 129 | 115 | 4 | **18.38** |
| 380 Auto | 85, 88 | JHP | 1000 | 921 | 189 | 160 | 3¾ | **20.35** |
| 380 Auto | 95 | FMC | 955 | 865 | 190 | 160 | 3¾ | **18.79** |
| 38 Auto | 130 | FMC | 1040 | 980 | 310 | 275 | 4½ | **20.48** |
| 38 Super Auto +P | 115 | JHP | 1300 | 1147 | 431 | 336 | 5 | **23.10** |
| 38 Super Auto +P | 125 | STHP | 1240 | 1130 | 427 | 354 | 5 | **24.56** |
| 38 Super Auto +P | 130 | FMC | 1215 | 1099 | 426 | 348 | 5 | **19.85** |
| 9mm Luger | 95 | JSP | 1350 | 1140 | 385 | 275 | 4 | **23.84** |
| 9mm Luger | 115 | JHP | 1160 | 1060 | 345 | 285 | 4 | **22.81** |
| 9mm Luger | 115 | STHP | 1225 | 1095 | 383 | 306 | 4 | **24.80** |
| 9mm Luger | 123, 124 | FMC | 1110 | 1030 | 339 | 292 | 4 | **22.81** |
| 9mm Win. Mag. | 115 | FMC | 1475 | 1264 | 555 | 408 | 5 | **NA** |
| 38 S&W | 146 | LRN | 685 | 650 | 150 | 135 | 4 | **17.25** |
| 38 Short Colt | 125 | LRN | 730 | 685 | 150 | 130 | 4 | **NA** |
| 38 Special | 148 | LWC | 710 | 634 | 166 | 132 | 4V | **18.05** |
| 38 Special | 110 | STHP | 945 | 894 | 218 | 195 | 4V | **19.51** |
| 38 Special | 158 | LRN, LSWC | 753 | 721 | 200 | 182 | 4V | **17.33** |
| 38 Special | 95 | JHP | 1175 | 1044 | 291 | 230 | 4V | **23.95** |
| 38 Special +P | 110 | JHP | 995 | 926 | 242 | 210 | 4V | **21.99** |
| 38 Special +P | 125 | JSP, JHP | 945 | 898 | 248 | 224 | 4V | **21.92** |
| 38 Special +P | 158 | LSWC, LHP | 890 | 855 | 278 | 257 | 4V | **19.23** |
| 357 Magnum | 110 | JHP | 1295 | 1094 | 410 | 292 | 4V | **24.11** |
| 357 Magnum | 125 | JHP. JSP | 1450 | 1240 | 583 | 427 | 4V | **24.11** |
| 357 Magnum | 145 | STHP | 1290 | 1155 | 535 | 428 | 4V | **26.25** |
| 357 Magnum | 158 | JSP, LSWC, JHP | 1235 | 1104 | 535 | 428 | 4V | **24.11** |
| 357 Magnum | 180 | JHP | 1090 | 980 | 475 | 385 | 4V | **25.07** |
| 357 MAXIMUM | 158 | JHP | 1825 | 1588 | 1168 | 885 | 10½ | **11.57*** |
| 357 MAXIMUM | 180 | JHP | 1555 | 1328 | 966 | 705 | 10½ | **11.57*** |
| 10mm Auto | 165 | JHP | 1400 | NA | 719 | NA | NA | **12.65*** |
| 10mm Auto | 200 | FMC | 1200 | NA | 635 | NA | NA | **12.65*** |
| 41 Rem. Mag. | 175 | STHP | 1250 | 1120 | 607 | 488 | 4V | **34.15** |
| 41 Rem. Mag. | 210 | LSWC | 965 | 898 | 434 | 376 | 4V | **27.07** |
| 41 Rem. Mag. | 210 | JHP, JSP | 1300 | 1162 | 788 | 630 | 4V | **31.71** |
| 44 Special | 200 | LSWC HP, STHP | 900 | 830 | 360 | 305 | 6½ | **25.21** |
| 44 Special | 246 | LRN | 755 | 725 | 310 | 285 | 6½ | **24.27** |
| 44 Rem. Mag. | 180 | JHP | 1610 | 1365 | 1036 | 745 | 4V | **11.49*** |
| 44 Rem. Mag. | 210 | STHP | 1250 | 1106 | 729 | 570 | 4V | **34.25** |
| 44 Rem. Mag. | 220 | FMC | 1390 | 1260 | 945 | 775 | 6½V | **34.89** |
| 44 Rem. Mag. | 240 | LSWC | 1000 | 947 | 533 | 477 | 6½V | **26.28** |
| 44 Rem. Mag. | 240 | LSWC/GC | 1350 | 1186 | 971 | 749 | 4V | **30.80** |
| 44 Rem. Mag. | 240 | JHP, JSP | 1180 | 1081 | 741 | 623 | 4V | **12.60*** |
| 45 Auto | 185 | JWC | 770 | 707 | 244 | 205 | 5 | **26.36** |
| 45 Auto | 185 | JHP | 940 | 890 | 363 | 325 | 5 | **27.35** |
| 45 Auto | 230 | FMC | 810 | 776 | 335 | 308 | 5 | **25.11** |
| 45 Auto Rim. | 230 | LRN | 810 | 770 | 335 | 305 | 5½ | **26.68** |
| 45 Win. Mag. | 230 | FMC | 1400 | 1232 | 1001 | 775 | 5 | **27.05** |
| 45 Colt | 225 | JHP. LHP | 900 | 860 | 405 | 369 | 5½ | **10.75*** |
| 45 Colt | 250, 255 | LRN | 860 | 820 | 420 | 380 | 5½ | **24.64** |

Notes: Blanks are available in 32 S&W, 38 S&W and 38 Special. V after barrel length indicates test barrel was vented and produced results approximating a revolver with its cylinder to barrel gap.

Abbreviations: JSP (jacketed soft point); LE (lead expanding); FMC (full metal case); JHP (jacketed hollow point); LRN (lead round nose); LWC (lead wadcutter); LSWC (lead semi-wadcutter); STHP (silvertip hollow point); LHP (lead hollow point); LSWCHP (lead semi-wadcutter hollow point); LSWC/GC (lead semi-wadcutter with gas check); JWC (jacketed wadcutter)

*20 rounds per box; all others 50 rounds per box

# RIMFIRE AMMUNITION—BALLISTICS AND PRICES

| Cartridge Type | Bullet Wt. Grs. | Bullet Type | Velocity (fps) 22½" Barrel Muzzle | Velocity (fps) 22½" Barrel 50 Yds. | Velocity (fps) 22½" Barrel 100 Yds. | Energy (ft. lbs.) 22½" Barrel Muzzle | Energy (ft. lbs.) 22½" Barrel 50 Yds. | Energy (ft. lbs.) 22½" Barrel 100 Yds. | Velocity (fps) 6" Barrel Muzzle | Velocity (fps) 6" Barrel 50 Yds. | Energy (ft. lbs.) 6" Barrel Muzzle | Energy (ft. lbs.) 6" Barrel 50 Yds. | Approx. Price Per Box 50 Rds. | Approx. Price Per Box 100 Rds. |
|---|---|---|---|---|---|---|---|---|---|---|---|---|---|---|
| 22 CB Short (CCI & Win.) | 29 | solid | 727 | 667 | 610 | 34 | 29 | 24 | 706 | — | 32 | — | **NA** | **13.20(2)** |
| 22 CB Long (CCI only) | 29 | solid | 727 | 667 | 610 | 34 | 29 | 24 | 706 | — | 32 | — | **NA** | **5.10** |
| 22 Short Match (CCI only) | 29 | solid | 830 | 752 | 695 | 44 | 36 | 31 | 786 | — | 39 | — | **NA** | **5.30** |
| 22 Short Std. Vel. (Rem. only) | 29 | solid | 1045 | — | 810 | 70 | — | 42 | 865 | — | 48 | — | **2.49** | **NA** |
| 22 Short H. Vel. (Fed., Rem., Win.) | 29 | solid | 1095 | — | 903 | 77 | — | 53 | — | — | — | — | **2.49** | **NA** |
| 22 Short H. Vel. (CCI only) | 29 | solid | 1132 | 1004 | 920 | 83 | 65 | 55 | 1065 | — | 73 | — | **NA** | **5.00** |
| 22 Short H. Vel. HP (Rem. only) | 27 | HP | 1120 | — | 904 | 75 | — | 49 | — | — | — | — | **2.70** | **NA** |
| 22 Short H. Vel. HP (CCI only) | 27 | HP | 1164 | 1013 | 920 | 81 | 62 | 51 | 1077 | — | 69 | — | **NA** | **5.30** |
| 22 Long Std. Vel. (CCI only) | 29 | solid | 1180 | 1038 | 946 | 90 | 69 | 58 | 1031 | — | 68 | — | **NA** | **5.30** |
| 22 Long H. Vel. (Fed., Rem.) | 29 | solid | 1240 | — | 962 | 99 | — | 60 | — | — | — | — | **2.70** | **NA** |
| 22 LR Pistol Match (Win. only) | 40 | solid | — | — | — | — | — | — | 1060 | 950 | 100 | 80 | **11.55** | **NA** |
| 22 LR Match (Rifle) (CCI only) | 40 | solid | 1138 | 1047 | 975 | 116 | 97 | 84 | 1027 | 925 | 93 | 76 | **NA** | **8.75** |
| 22 LR Std. Vel. | 40 | solid | 1138 | 1046 | 975 | 115 | 97 | 84 | 1027 | 925 | 93 | 76 | **2.85** | **5.70(3)** |
| 22 LR H. Vel. | 40 | solid | 1255 | 1110 | 1017 | 140 | 109 | 92 | 1060 | — | 100 | — | **2.85** | **5.70** |
| 22 LR H. Vel. HP | 36-38 | HP | 1280 | 1126 | 1010 | 131 | 101 | 82 | 1089 | — | 95 | — | **3.16** | **6.32** |
| 22 LR-Hyper Vel. (Fed., Rem., Win.,(4)) | 33-34 | HP | 1500 | 1240 | 1075 | 165 | 110 | 85 | — | — | — | — | **3.19** | **NA** |
| 22 LR-Hyper Vel. | 36 | solid | 1410 | 1187 | 1056 | 159 | 113 | 89 | — | — | — | — | **3.10** | **NA** |
| 22 Stinger (CCI only) | 32 | HP | 1640 | 1277 | 1132 | 191 | 115 | 91 | 1395 | 1060 | 138 | 80 | **3.60** | **NA** |
| 22 Win. Mag. Rimfire | 40 | FMC or HP | 1910 | 1490 | 1326 | 324 | 197 | 156 | 1428 | — | 181 | — | **7.67** | **NA** |
| 22 LR Shot (CCI, Fed., Win.) | — | #11 or #12 shot | 1047 | — | — | — | — | — | 950 | — | — | — | **5.82** | **NA** |
| 22 Win. Mag. Rimfire Shot (CCI only) | — | #11 shot | 1126 | — | — | — | — | — | 1000 | — | — | — | **4.35(1)** | **NA** |

Please Note: The actual ballisctics obtained from your gun can vary considerably from the advertised ballistics. Also, ballistics can vary from lot to lot even within the same brand. All prices were correct at the time this chart was prepared. All prices are subject to change without notice.

(1) 20 per box. (2) per 250 rounds. (3) also packaged 200 rounds per box. (4) also packaged 250 rounds per box.

# SHOTSHELL LOADS AND PRICES

## Winchester-Western, Remington-Peters, Federal

| Dram Equivalent | Shot Ozs. | Load Style | Shot Sizes | Brands | Average Price Per Box | Nominal Velocity (fps) |
|---|---|---|---|---|---|---|
| **10 Gauge 3½" Magnum** | | | | | | |
| 4½ | 2¼ | Premium(1) | BB, 2, 4, 6 | Fed., Win. | $32.32 | 1205 |
| 4¼ | 2 | H.V. | BB, 2, 4, 5, 6 | Fed., Rem. | 29.89 | 1210 |
| Max. | 1¾ | Slug, rifled | Slug | Fed. | 7.22 | 1280 |
| Max. | 54 pellets | Buck, Premium(1) | 00.4 (Buck) | Fed., Win. | 6.84 | 1100 |
| Max. | 1¾ | Steel shot | BB, 2 | Win. | NA | 1260 |
| 4¼ | 1⅝ | Steel shot | BB, 2 | Fed. | 26.61 | 1285 |
| **12 Gauge 3" Magnum** | | | | | | |
| 4 | 1⅞ | Premium(1) | BB, 2, 4, 6 | Fed., Rem., Win. | 21.26 | 1210 |
| 4 | 1⅝ | Premium(1) | 2, 4, 5, 6 | Fed., Rem., Win. | 19.71 | 1280 |
| 4 | 1⅞ | H.V. | BB, 2, 4 | Fed., Rem. | 18.72 | 1210 |
| 4 | 1⅝ | H.V. | 2, 4, 6 | Fed., Rem. | 17.29 | 1280 |
| 4 | Variable | Buck, Premium(1) | 000,00,1,4 | Fed., Rem., Win. | 5.14 | 1210 to 1225 |
| 3½ | 1⅜ | Steel shot | BB, 1, 2, 4 | Fed. | 18.83 | 1245 |
| 3½ | 1¼ | Steel shot | BB, 1, 2, 4 | Rem., Win. | 17.33 | 1375 |
| 4 | 2 | Premium(1) | BB, 2, 4, 6 | Fed. | 22.80 | 1175 |
| **12 Gauge 2¾" Hunting & Target** | | | | | | |
| 3¾ | 1½ | Premium(1), Mag. | BB, 2, 4, 5, 6 | Fed., Rem., Win. | 18.57 | 1260 |
| 3¾ | 1½ | H.V., Mag. | BB, 2, 4, 5, 6 | Fed., Rem. | 15.63 | — |
| 3¾ | 1¼ | H.V., Premium(1) | 2, 4, 6, 7½ | Fed., Rem. | 13.85 | 1330 |
| 3¾ | 1¼ | H.V., Promo. | BB, 2, 4, 5, 6 7½, 8, 9 | Fed., Rem., Win. | 12.50 | 1330 |
| 3¼ | 1¼ | Std. Vel., Premium(1) | 7½, 8 | Fed., Rem. | 12.10 | 1220 |
| 3¼ | 1⅛ | Std. Vel., Premium(1) | 7½, 8 | Fed., Rem. | 11.70 | 1255 |
| 3¼ | 1¼ | Std. Vel. | 6, 7½, 8, 9 | Fed., Rem., Win. | 11.15 | 1220 |
| 3¼ | 1⅛ | Std. Vel. | 4, 5, 6, 7½, 8, 9 | Fed., Rem., Win. | 10.17 | 1255 |
| 3¼ | 1 | Std. Vel., Promo | 6, 7½, 8 | Fed., Rem., Win. | 10.00 | 1290 |
| Max. | 1¼ | Slug, rifled, Mag. | Slug | Fed. | 5.18 | 1490 |
| Max. | 1 | Slug, rifled | Slug | Fed., Rem., Win. | 4.17 | 1560 |
| 4 | Variable | Buck, Mag., Premium(1) | 00, 1, 4 (Buck) | Fed., Rem., Win. | 4.52 | 1075 to 1290 |
| 3¾ | Variable | Buck, Premium(1) | 000, 00, 0, 1, 4 (Buck) | Fed., Rem., Win. | 4.25 | 1250 to 1325 |
| 3¾ | 1⅜ | H.V. | 2, 4, 6 | Fed. | 14.61 | 1295 |
| 3¼ | 1¼ | Pigeon | 6, 7½, 8 | Fed., Win. | 14.00 | 1220 |
| 3 | 1⅛ | Trap & Skeet | 7½, 8, 9 | Fed., Rem., Win. | 7.00 | 1200 |
| 2¾ | 1⅛ | Trap & Skeet | 7½, 8, 8½, 9 | Fed., Rem., Win. | 7.00 | 1145 |
| 2¾ | 1 | Trap & Skeet | 7½, 8, 8½ | Fed., Rem., Win. | 7.00 | 1180 |
| 3¾ | 1¼ | Steel shot | BB, 1, 2, 4, 6 | Fed., Win. | 17.33 | 1275 |
| 3¾ | 1⅛ | Steel shot | 1, 2, 4, 6 | Fed., Rem., Win. | 15.95 | 1365 |

| Dram Equivalent | Shot Ozs. | Load Style | Shot Sizes | Brands | Average Price Per Box | Nominal Velocity (fps) |
|---|---|---|---|---|---|---|
| **16 Gauge 2¾"** | | | | | | |
| 3¼ | 1¼ | H.V., Mag., Premium(1) | 2, 4, 6 | Fed., Rem., Win. | 15.37 | 1260 |
| 3¼ | 1⅛ | H.V., Promo. | 4, 5, 6, 7½, 9 | Fed., Rem., Win. | 12.16 | 1295 |
| 2¾ | 1⅛ | Std. Vel. | 4, 6, 7½, 8, 9 | Fed., Rem., Win. | 10.17 | 1185 |
| 2½ | 1 | Std. Vel., Promo. | 6, 7½, 8 | Fed., Win. | NA | 1165 |
| Max. | ⅘ | Slug, rifled | Slug | Fed., Rem., Win. | 4.17 | 1570 |
| Max. | 12 pellets | Buck | 1 (Buck) | Fed., Rem., Win. | 3.61 | 1225 |
| 3¼ | 1¼ | Premium, Mag. | 2, 4, 6 | Win. | 15.37 | 1260 |
| **20 Gauge 3" Magnum** | | | | | | |
| 3 | 1¼ | Premium(1) | 2, 4, 6 | Fed., Rem., Win. | 14.44 | 1185 |
| 3 | 1¼ | H.V. | 2, 4, 6, 7½ | Fed., Rem. | 12.68 | 1185 |
| Max. | 18 pellets | Buck | 2 (Buck) | Fed. | 4.52 | — |
| Max. | 1 | Steel shot | 4, 6 | Fed., Win. | 15.20 | 1330 |
| **20 Gauge 2¾" Hunting & Target** | | | | | | |
| 2¾ | 1⅛ | Premium(1), Mag. | 4, 6, 7½ | Fed., Rem., Win. | 14.57 | 1175 |
| 2¾ | 1⅛ | H.V., Mag. | 4, 6, 7½ | Fed., Rem. | 12.80 | 1175 |
| 2¾ | 1 | H.V., Premium(1) | 4, 6 | Fed., Rem. | 11.98 | 1220 |
| 2¾ | 1 | H.V., Promo. | 4, 5, 6, 7½, 8, 9 | Fed., Rem., Win. | 11.14 | 1220 |
| 2½ | 1 | Std. Vel., Premium(1) | 7½, 8 | Fed., Rem. | 9.55 | 1165 |
| 2½ | 1 | Std. Vel. | 4, 5, 6, 7½, 8, 9 | Fed., Rem., Win. | 10.59 | 1165 |
| 2½ | ⅞ | Promo. | 6, 7½, 8 | Fed., Win. | NA | 1210 |
| 2¼ | ⅞ | Std. Vel., Promo. | 6, 7½, 8 | Rem., Win. | NA | 1155 |
| Max. | ¾ | Slug, rifled | Slug | Fed., Rem., Win. | 3.81 | 1570 |
| Max. | 20 pellets | Buck | 3 (Buck) | Fed., Rem., Win. | 4.52 | 1200 |
| 2½ | ⅞ | Skeet | 8, 9 | Fed., Rem., Win. | 5.86 | 1200 |
| 2¾ | ¾ | Steel shot | 4, 6 | Fed., Win. | 14.05 | 1425 |
| **28 Gauge 2¾" Hunting & Target** | | | | | | |
| 2¼ | ¾ | H.V. | 6, 7½ | Fed., Rem., Win. | 11.23 | 1295 |
| 2 | ¾ | Skeet | 9 | Fed., Rem., Win. | 6.93 | 1200 |
| **410 Bore Hunting & Target** | | | | | | |
| Max. | 11/16 | 3" H.V. | 4, 5, 6, 7½, 8 | Fed., Rem., Win. | 10.44 | 1135 |
| Max. | ½ | 2½" H.V. | 4, 6, 7½ | Fed., Rem., Win. | 8.86 | 1135 |
| Max. | ½ | 2½" Target | 9 | Fed., Rem., Win. | 5.73 | 1200 |
| Max. | ⅕ | Slug, rifled | Slug | Fed., Rem., Win. | 3.61 | 1815 |

(1)Premium shells usually incorporate high antimony extra hard shot and a granulated polyethelene buffer to increase pattern density at long ranges. In general, prices are per 25-round box. Rifled slugs and buckshot prices are per 5-round pack. Premium buckshot prices per 10-round pack. Not every brand is available in every shot size. Price of Skeet and trap loads may vary widely.

# Chokes & Brakes

## Baker Superior Choke Tubes

Stan Baker's Superior choke tubes can be installed only in single-barrel guns. The external diameter of the barrel is enlarged by swaging, allowing enough for reaming and threading to accept the screw-in WinChoke-style tube. Installation on a single-barrel gun without rib is **$85.00**; with vent rib, cost is **$110.00**. Prices are higher for target guns, so contact Baker for specifics. Price includes honing the bore. Extra choke tubes are **$15.95** each. One tube and wrench are provided. Baker also installs WinChoke tubes.

## Briley Screw-In Chokes

Installation of these choke tubes requires that all traces of the original choking be removed, the barrel threaded internally with square threads and then the tubes are custom fitted to the specific barrel diameter. The tubes are thin and, therefore, made of stainless steel. Cost of installation for single-barrel guns (pumps, autos) runs **$75.00**; un-single target guns run **$150.00**; over-unders and side-by-sides cost **$150.00** per barrel. Prices include one choke tube and a wrench for disassembly. Extra tubes are **$40.00** each.

Briley also makes "Excentrix" choke tubes that allow horizontal or vertical movement of the pattern up to 11″. Add **$35.00** to the prices above. Installation available only from Briley.

## Cellini Recoil Reducer

Designed for handgun and rifle applications, the Cellini Reducer is available as a removable factory-installed accessory. Over-all length is 2½″, weight is 3.5 ounces, and the unit must be installed by the maker. It is said to reduce muzzle jump to zero, even for automatic weapons. Cost starts at $150. Contact Cellini for full details.

## Cutts Compensator

The Cutts compensator is one of the oldest variable choke devices available. Manufactured by Lyman Gunsight Corporation, it is available with a steel body. A series of vents allows gas to escape upward and downward. For the 12-ga. Comp body, six fixed-choke tubes are available: the Spreader—popular with skeet shooters; Improved Cylinder; Modified; Full; Superfull, and Magnum Full. Full, Modified and Spreader tubes are available for 12, or 20, and an Adjustable Tube, giving Full through Improved Cylinder chokes, is offered in 12, or 20 gauges. Cutts Compensator, complete with wrench, adaptor and any single tube **$68.80**; with adjustable tube **$87.80**. All single choke tubes **$18.95** each. No factory installation available.

## Emsco Choke

E.M. Schacht of Waseca, Minn., offers the Emsco, a small diameter choke which features a precision curve rather than a taper behind the 1½″ choking area. 9 settings are available in this 5 oz. attachment. Its removable recoil sleeve can be furnished in dural if desired. Choice of three sight heights. For 12, 16 or 20 gauge. Price installed, **$29.95**. Not installed, **$22.00**.

## Lyman CHOKE

The Lyman CHOKE is similar to the Cutts Comp in that it comes with fixed-choke tubes or an adjustable tube, with or without recoil chamber. The adjustable tube version sells for **$37.95** with recoil chamber, in 12 or 20 gauge. Lyman also offers Single-Choke tubes at **$18.95**. This device may be used with or without a recoil-reduction chamber; cost of the latter is **$8.95** extra. Available in 12 or 20 gauge only. No factory installation offered.

## Mag-Na-Port

Electrical Discharge Machining works on any firearm except those having shrouded barrels. EDM is a metal erosion technique using carbon electrodes that control the area to be processed. The Mag-na-port venting process utilizes small trapezoidal openings to direct powder gases upward and outward to reduce recoil.

No effect is had on bluing or nickeling outside the Mag-na-port area so no refinishing is needed. Cost for the Mag-na-port treatment is **$53.00** for handguns, **$69.00** for rifles, plus transportation both ways, and **$2.50** for handling.

## Poly-Choke

Marble Arms Corp., manufacturers of the Poly-Choke adjustable shotgun choke, now offers two models in 12, 16, 20, and 28 gauge—the Ventilated and Standard style chokes. Each provides nine choke settings including Xtra-Full and Slug. The Ventilated model reduces 20% of a shotgun's recoil, the company claims, and is priced at **$62.50**. The Standard Model is **$56.00**. Postage not included. Contact Marble Arms for more data.

## Pro-Choke

Pro-Choke is a system of interchangeable choke tubes that can be installed in any single or double-barreled shotgun, including over-unders. The existing chokes are bored out, the muzzles over-bored and threaded for the tubes. A choice of three Pro-Choke tubes are supplied—Skeet, Imp. Cyl., Mod., Imp. Mod., or Full. Cost of the installation is **$179.95** for single-barrel guns, **$229.95** for doubles. Extra tubes cost **$40** each. Postage and handling charges are **$8.50**.

## Pro-Port

A compound ellipsoid muzzle venting process similar to Mag-na-porting, only exclusively applied to shotguns. Like Mag-na-porting, this system reduces felt recoil, muzzle jump, and shooter fatigue. Very helpful for Trap doubles shooters. Pro-Port is a patented process and installation is available in both the U.S. and Canada. Cost for the Pro-Port process is **$110.00** for over-unders (both barrels); **$80.00** for only the bottom barrel; and **$69.00** for single barrel shotguns. Prices do not include shipping and handling.

## Walker Choke Tubes

This interchangeable choke tube system uses an adaptor fitted to the barrel without swaging. Therefore, it can be fitted to any single-barreled gun. The choke tubes use the conical-parallel system as used on all factory-choked barrels. These tubes can be used in Winchester, Mossberg, Smith & Wesson, Weatherby, or similar barrels made for the standard screw-in choke system. Available for 10 gauge, 12, 16 and 20. Factory installation (single barrel) with choice of Standard Walker Choke tube is **$105.00**, **$210.00** for double barrels with two choke tubes. A full range of constriction is available. Contact Walker Arms for more data.

## Walker Full Thread Choke Tubes

An interchangeable choke tube system using fully threaded inserts. Designed specifically for over-under or side-by-side shotgun barrels, but can be installed in single barrels, and is nearly invisible. No swaging, adaptor or change in barrel exterior dimensions. Available in 12 or 20 gauge. Factory installation cost: **$105.00**, single barrel with one choke tube; **$210.00** for double barrels with two choke tubes. Contact Walker Arms Co. for more data.

# Micrometer Receiver Sights

**BEEMAN/WEIHRAUCH MATCH APERTURE SIGHT**
Micrometer ¼-minute click adjustment knobs with settings indicated on scales. Price . . . . . . . . . . . . . . . . . . . . . . . . . . . . . . . . . . . . . . . . . . **$69.95**

**BEEMAN/FEINWERKBAU MATCH APERTURE SIGHTS**
Locks into one of four eye-relief positions. Micrometer ¼-minute click adjustments; may be set to zero at any range. Extra windage scale visible beside eyeshade. Primarily for use at 5 to 20 meters. Price. . . . . . . . **$99.95**

**BEEMAN SPORT APERTURE SIGHT**
Positive click micrometer adjustments. Standard units with flush surface screwdriver adjustments. Deluxe version has target knobs.
Price: Standard . . . . . . . . . . . . . . . . . . . . . . . . . . . . . . . **$32.98**
Price: Deluxe . . . . . . . . . . . . . . . . . . . . . . . . . . . . . . . . **$38.98**

**BUEHLER**
"Little Blue Peep" auxiliary rear sight used with Buehler scope mounts.
Price . . . . . . . . . . . . . . . . . . . . . . . . . . . . . . . . . . . . . . . . **$4.75**

**FREELAND TUBE SIGHT**
Uses Unertl 1″ micrometer mounts. For 22-cal. target rifles, inc. 52 Win., 37, 40X Rem. and BSA Martini. Price . . . . . . . . . . . . . . . **$123.00**

**LYMAN No. 57**
¼-min. clicks. Stayset knobs. Quick release slide, adjustable zero scales. Made for almost all modern rifles. Price . . . . . . . . . . . . . . . . **$49.95**

**LYMAN No. 66**
Fits close to the rear of flat-sided receivers, furnished with Stayset knobs. Quick release slide, ¼-min. adj. For most lever or slide action or flat-sided automatic rifles. Price . . . . . . . . . . . . . . . . . . . . . . . . . **$49.95**

**LYMAN No. 66U**
Light-weight, designed for most modern shotguns with a flat-sided, round-top receiver. ¼-minute clicks. Requires drilling, taping. Not for Browning A-5, Rem. M11. Price . . . . . . . . . . . . . . . . . . . . . . **$49.95**

Millett AR-15 sights.

Millett Mini-14.                                 Millett  H&K 91/93.

**MILLETT ASSAULT RIFLE SIGHTS**
Fully adjustable, heat-treated nickel steel peep aperture receiver sights for AR-15, Mini-14, H&K 91/93. AR-15 rear sight has w. & e. adjustments; nonglare replacement ramp-style front also available. Mini-14 sight has fine w. & e. adjustments; replaces original. H&K sight has a large peep disc with .080″ peep; adjustable for w. & e.
Price: Rear sight for above three guns . . . . . . . . . . . . . . . . **$45.95**
Price: Front and rear combo for AR-15 . . . . . . . . . . . . . . . . **$55.95**
Price: Front sight for AR-15. . . . . . . . . . . . . . . . . . . . . . . . **$10.95**

**WILLIAMS FP**
Internal click adjustments. Positive locks. For virtually all rifles, T/C Contender, Heckler & Koch HK-91, Ruger Mini-14, plus Win., Rem. and Ithaca shotguns. Price . . . . . . . . . . . . . . . . . . . . . . . . . . . . . . . . **$38.55**
With Twilight Aperture . . . . . . . . . . . . . . . . . . . . . . . . . . **$39.75**
With Target Knobs . . . . . . . . . . . . . . . . . . . . . . . . . . . . . **$45.85**
With Target Knobs & Twilight Aperture . . . . . . . . . . . . . . . **$47.05**
With Square Notched Blade . . . . . . . . . . . . . . . . . . . . . . . **$40.60**
With Target Knobs & Square Notched Blade . . . . . . . . . . . **$47.90**
FP-GR (for dovetail-grooved receivers, 22s and air guns) . . . . . **$38.55**

**WILLIAMS 5-D SIGHT**
Low cost sight for shotguns, 22's and the more popular big game rifles. Adjustment for w. and e. Fits most guns without drilling or tapping. Also for Br. SMLE. Price . . . . . . . . . . . . . . . . . . . . . . . . . . . . . . **$21.90**
With Twilight Aperture. . . . . . . . . . . . . . . . . . . . . . . . . . **$23.10**
Extra Shotgun Aperture . . . . . . . . . . . . . . . . . . . . . . . . . **$5.15**

**WILLIAMS GUIDE**
Receiver sight for .30 M1 Car., M1903A3 Springfield, Savage 24's, Savage-Anschutz rifles and Wby. XXII. Utilizes military dovetail; no drilling. Double-dovetail W. adj., sliding dovetail adj. for e. Price . . . . . . . . . . **$20.75**
With Twilight Aperture. . . . . . . . . . . . . . . . . . . . . . . . . . **$21.95**
With Open Sight Blade. . . . . . . . . . . . . . . . . . . . . . . . . . **$19.05**

# Sporting Leaf and Open Sights

**BINGHAM SPORTING RIFLE SIGHTS**
All-steel sights are imported from Europe. Many styles of both front and rear sights available; random sampling listed here.
European express gold bead for European express ramp . . . . . . . **$4.25**
European express ramp . . . . . . . . . . . . . . . . . . . . . . . . . **$7.50**
Semi-buckhorn rear, with elevator . . . . . . . . . . . . . . . . . . **$6.50**
Rocky Mountain front, blue or bright . . . . . . . . . . . . . . . . **$3.95**
European 2-leaf folding express rear (V and U notch) . . . . . . . . **$12.50**

**BINGHAM CLASSIC SIGHTS**
All-steel sights for "classic" rifles. Rear sights only. This listing not complete; contact Bingham for full list.
Model 66 folding ladder-type. . . . . . . . . . . . . . . . . . . . . **$19.95**
Model Saddle Ring Carbine (73, 92, 94, etc.) . . . . . . . . . . . **$14.95**
Elevator, Winchester-type, early series (1876-WW II) . . . . . **$4.95**

**BURRIS SPORTING REAR SIGHT**
Made of spring steel, supplied with multi-step elevator for coarse adjustments and notch plate with lock screw for finer adjustments. Price  **$13.95**

**LYMAN No. 16**
Middle sight for barrel dovetail slot mounting. Folds flat when scope or peep sight is used. Sight notch plate adjustable for e. White triangle for quick aiming. 3 heights: A—.400″ to .500″, B—.345″ to .445″, C—.500″ to .600″.
Price . . . . . . . . . . . . . . . . . . . . . . . . . . . . . . . . . . . . . . . **$10.50**

**MARBLE FALSE BASE #72, #73, #74**
New screw-on base for most rifles replaces factory base. ⅜″ dovetail slot permits installation of any Marble rear sight. Can be had in sweat-on models also. Price . . . . . . . . . . . . . . . . . . . . . . . . . . . . . . . . . . . . . **$5.05**

**MARBLE CONTOUR RAMP #14R**
For late model Rem. 725, 740, 760, 742 rear sight mounting. 9/16″ between mounting screws. Price . . . . . . . . . . . . . . . . . . . . . . . . **$11.20**

**MARBLE FOLDING LEAF**
Flat-top or semi-buckhorn style. Folds down when scope or peep sights are used. Reversible plate gives choice of "U" or "V" notch. Adjustable for elevation. Price . . . . . . . . . . . . . . . . . . . . . . . . . . . . . . . . **$10.00**
Also available with both w. and e. adjustment . . . . . . . . . . . . . **$11.70**

**MARBLE SPORTING REAR**
With white enamel diamond, gives choice of two "U" and two "V" notches of different sizes. Adjustment in height by means of double step elevator and sliding notch piece. For all rifles; screw or dovetail installation.
Price: . . . . . . . . . . . . . . . . . . . . . . . . . . . . . . **$10.30-$11.70**

**MILLETT RIFLE SIGHT**
Open, fully adjustable rear sight fits standard ⅜″ dovetail cut in barrel. Choice of white outline or target rear blades, .360″. Front with white or orange bar, .343″, .400″, .430″, .460″, .500″, .540″.
Price: Rear sight . . . . . . . . . . . . . . . . . . . . . . . . . . . . . . **$47.29**
Price: Front sight . . . . . . . . . . . . . . . . . . . . . . . . . . . . . **$10.49**

**MILLETT RUGER 10/22 SIGHT COMBO**
Replacement sight system for the 10/22 rifle has a fully adjustable open rear with deep notch and white outline or target blade. Combo set includes interchangeable white or orange bar front. Also fits Win. 77, 94, Rem. 740-760, 700 old model dovetail rear.
Price: Combo set . . . . . . . . . . . . . . . . . . . . . . . . . . . . . . **$77.69**
Price: Without quick-change front sight feature . . . . . . . . . . . **$56.69**

Millett Scope-Site.

**MILLETT SCOPE-SITE**
Open, adjustable or fixed rear sights dovetail into a base integral with the top scope-mount ring. Blaze orange front ramp sight is integral with the front ring half. Rear sights have white outline aperture. Provides fast, short radius, Patridge-type open sights on top of the scope. Can be used with all Millett rings.
Price: Scope-Site ring set, adjustable . . . . . . . . . . . . . . . . . **$69.95**
Price: As above, fixed . . . . . . . . . . . . . . . . . . . . . . . . . . . **$39.95**
Price: Convertible Top Cap set, adjustable . . . . . . . . . . . . . **$56.95**
Price: As above, fixed . . . . . . . . . . . . . . . . . . . . . . . . . . . **$26.95**

**WICHITA MULTI RANGE SIGHT SYSTEM**
Designed for silhouette shooting. System allows you to adjust the rear sight to four repeatable range settings, once it is pre-set. Sight clicks to any of the settings by turning a serrated wheel. Front sight is adjustable for weather and light conditions with one adjustment. Specify gun when ordering.
Price: Rear sight . . . . . . . . . . . . . . . . . . . . . . . . . . . . . . . . **$77.00**
      Front sight . . . . . . . . . . . . . . . . . . . . . . . . . . . . . . . . . **$44.00**

**WILLIAMS DOVETAIL OPEN SIGHT**
Open rear sight with w. and e. adjustment. Furnished with "U" notch or choice of blades. Slips into dovetail and locks with gib lock. Heights from .281" to .531". Price with blade . . . . . . . . . . . . . . . . . . . . . . . . **$11.60**
Less Blade . . . . . . . . . . . . . . . . . . . . . . . . . . . . . . . . . . . **$7.60**
Extra Blades . . . . . . . . . . . . . . . . . . . . . . . . . . . . . . . . . **$3.70**

**WILLIAMS GUIDE OPEN SIGHT**
Open rear sight with w. and e. adjustment. Bases to fit most military and commercial barrels. Choice of square "U" or "V" notch blade, 3/16", 1/4", 5/16", or 3/8" high. Price with blade. . . . . . . . . . . . . . . . . . . **$14.00**
Extra blades, each . . . . . . . . . . . . . . . . . . . . . . . . . . . . . **$4.00**
Price, less blade . . . . . . . . . . . . . . . . . . . . . . . . . . . . . **$10.00**

# Front Sights

**LYMAN HUNTING SIGHTS**
Made with gold or white beads 1/16" to 3/32" wide and in varying heights for most military and commercial rifles. Dovetail bases. Price . . . **$7.50**

**MARBLE STANDARD**
Ivory, red, or gold bead. For all American made rifles, 1/16" wide bead with semi-flat face which does not reflect light. Specify type of rifle when ordering. Price . . . . . . . . . . . . . . . . . . . . . . . . . . . . . . . . . . . . . . . **$6.15**

**MARBLE-SHEARD "GOLD"**
Shows up well even in darkest timber. Shows same color on different colored objects; sturdily built. Medium bead. Various models for different makes of rifles so specify type of rifle when ordering. Price. . . . . . . **$7.65**

**MARBLE CONTOURED**
Same contour and shape as Marble-Sheard but uses standard 1/16" or 3/32" bead, ivory, red or gold. Specify rifle type. Price . . . . . . . . . . . **$7.05**

**POLY-CHOKE**
Rifle front sights available in six heights and two widths. Model A designed to be inserted into the barrel dovetail; Model B is for use with standard .350 ramp; both have standard 3/8" dovetails. Gold or ivory color 1/16" bead. Price . . . . . . . . . . . . . . . . . . . . . . . . . . . . . . . . . . . . . . **$4.95**

**WILLIAMS GUIDE BEAD SIGHT**
Fits all shotguns, 1/8" ivory, red or gold bead. Screws into existing sight hole. Various thread sizes and shank lengths. Price. . . . . . . . . . . . **$4.05**

# Globe Target Front Sights

**FREELAND SUPERIOR**
Furnished with six 1" plastic apertures. Available in 4½"-6½" lengths. Made for any target rifle. Price . . . . . . . . . . . . . . . . . . . . . . . . **$37.00**
Price with 6 metal insert apertures . . . . . . . . . . . . . . . . . **$39.00**
Price, front base . . . . . . . . . . . . . . . . . . . . . . . . . . . . . . . **$8.00**

**FREELAND TWIN SET**
Two Freeland Superior or Junior Globe Front Sights, long or short, allow switching from 50 yd. to 100 yd. ranges and back again without changing rear sight adjustment. Sight adjustment compensation is built into the set; just interchange and you're "on" at either range. Set includes 6 plastic apertures. Price with 6 metal apertures . . . . . . . . . . . . . . . . . . . **$58.00**

**FREELAND MILITARY**
Short model for use with high-powered rifles where sight must not extend beyond muzzle. Screw-on base; six plastic apertures. Price . . **$35.00**
Price with 6 metal apertures . . . . . . . . . . . . . . . . . . . . . . **$39.00**
Price, front base . . . . . . . . . . . . . . . . . . . . . . . . . . . . . . . **$8.00**

**LYMAN No. 17A TARGET**
Includes 7 interchangeable inserts; 4 apertures, one transparent amber and two posts .50" and .100" in width. Price . . . . . . . . . . . . . . . . **$19.95**

# Ramp Sights

**JAEGER CUSTOM FRONT SIGHT RAMP**
Banded style machined from bar stock. Front sights are interchangeable and slide into the ramp, lock with a set screw. Sights available are Silver Bead ($7.50), Sourdough Bead ($9.00), Silver Bead with Folding Night Sight ($20.00), and Reflective Bead (Raybar-type, $9.00).
Price: Ramp with set screw, wrenches . . . . . . . . . . . . . . . **$45.00**
Price: Sight hood . . . . . . . . . . . . . . . . . . . . . . . . . . . . . . . **$3.90**

**LYMAN SCREW-ON RAMP**
Used with 8-40 screws but may also be brazed on. Heights from .10" to .350". Ramp without sight . . . . . . . . . . . . . . . . . . . . . . . . . . **$13.50**

**MARBLE FRONT RAMPS**
Available in either screw-on or sweat-on style. 5 heights; 3/16", 5/16", 3/8", 7/16", 9/16". Standard 3/8" dovetail slot. Price . . . . . . . . . . . . . . . . . **$12.65**
Hoods for above ramps . . . . . . . . . . . . . . . . . . . . . . . . . . **$2.75**

**WILLIAMS SHORTY RAMP**
Companion to "Streamlined" ramp, about ½" shorter. Screw-on or sweat-on. It is furnished in 1/8", 3/16", 9/32", and 3/8" heights without hood only.
Price . . . . . . . . . . . . . . . . . . . . . . . . . . . . . . . . . . . . . . . . **$10.00**

**WILLIAMS STREAMLINED RAMP**
Hooded style in screw-on or sweat-on models. Furnished in 9/16", 7/16", 3/8", 5/16", 3/16" heights. Price with hood . . . . . . . . . . . . . . . . . . **$15.85**
Price without hood . . . . . . . . . . . . . . . . . . . . . . . . . . . . . **$13.10**

**WILLIAMS SHOTGUN RAMP**
Designed to elevate the front bead for slug shooting or for guns that shoot high. Diameters to fit most 12, 16, 20 ga. guns. Fastens by screwclamp, no drilling required. Price, with Williams gold bead . . . . . . . . **$8.95**
Price, without bead . . . . . . . . . . . . . . . . . . . . . . . . . . . . . **$6.60**
Price, with Guide Bead . . . . . . . . . . . . . . . . . . . . . . . . . . **$10.25**

# Handgun Sights

**BINGHAM PISTOL SIGHTS**
All-steel sights of various designs for Colt Government Model and Browning Hi-Power. Low profile "battle sights" (front and rear) for either Colt G.M. or Browning HP. Price . . . . . . . . . . . . . . . . . . . . . . . . . . . . . . **$16.95**
Combat sight set, low profile, white outline for Colt G.M., front and rear . . . . . . . . . . . . . . . . . . . . . . . . . . . . . . . . . . . . . . . . . **$21.95**
National Match front sight, Colt G.M. . . . . . . . . . . . . . . . . **$3.75**
Camp Perry front sight, Colt G.M. . . . . . . . . . . . . . . . . . . **$4.95**

**BO-MAR DE LUXE BMCS**
Gives 3/8" w. and e. adjustment at 50 yards on Colt Gov't 45, sight radius under 7". For GM and Commander models only. Uses existing dovetail slot. Has shield-type rear blade. Price . . . . . . . . . . . . . . . . . . . . . **$49.50**

**BO-MAR LOW PROFILE RIB & ACCURACY TUNER**
Streamlined rib with front and rear sights; 7⅛" sight radius. Brings sight line closer to the bore than standard or extended sight and ramp. Weighs 5 oz. Made for Colt Gov't 45, Super 38, and Gold Cup 45 and 38. Price **$79.00**

**BO-MAR COMBAT RIB**
For S&W Model 19 revolver with 4" barrel. Sight radius 5¾"; weight 5½ oz. Price . . . . . . . . . . . . . . . . . . . . . . . . . . . . . . . . . . . . . . **$69.00**

**BO-MAR FAST DRAW RIB**
Streamlined full length rib with integral Bo-Mar micrometer sight and serrated fast draw sight. For Browning 9mm, S&W 39, Colt Commander 45, Super Auto and 9mm. Price . . . . . . . . . . . . . . . . . . . . . . . . . . **$69.00**

**BO-MAR WINGED RIB**
For S&W 4" and 6" length barrels—K-38, M10, HB 14 and 19. Weight for the 6" model is about 7¼ oz. Price. . . . . . . . . . . . . . . . . . . . . . . **$79.00**
For 4", 6" Python . . . . . . . . . . . . . . . . . . . . . . . . . . . . . . . **$89.00**

**BO-MAR COVER-UP RIB**
Adj. rear sight, winged front guards. Fits right over revolver's original front sight. For S&W 4" M-10HB, M-13, M-58, M-64 & 65, Ruger 4" models SDA-34, SDA-84, SS-34, SS-84, GF-34, GF-84. Price. . . . . . . . . . . **$75.00**

**C-MORE SIGHTS**
Replacement front sight blades offered in two types and five styles. Made of DuPont Acetal, they come in a set of five high-contrast colors: blue, green, pink, red and yellow. Easy to install. Patridge style for Colt Python (all barrels), Ruger Super Blackhawk (7½"), Ruger Blackhawk (4⅝"); Ramp style for Python (all barrels), Blackhawk (4⅝"), Super Blackhawk (7½" and 10½"). From Mag-num Sales Ltd., Inc. Price, per set . . . . . . . . . . **$14.95**

**MMC MODEL 84 SIGHT SYSTEM**
Replacement sight system for Colt 1911 autos and Browning Hi-Power. Streamlined 1.94" long base covers the dovetail for a custom look. Ideally suited for IPSC, metallic silhouette, bowling pin shooting. Contact MMC for details, full prices.
Complete rear sight . . . . . . . . . . . . . . . . . . . . . . . . . . . . . **$42.99**
Serrated ramp front . . . . . . . . . . . . . . . . . . . . . . . . . . . . . **$8.80**
Dot front . . . . . . . . . . . . . . . . . . . . . . . . . . . . . . . . . . . . . **$13.50**

**MMC COMBAT DESIGN**
Available specifically for Colt M1911 and descendants, High Standard autos, Ruger standard autos. Adaptable to other pistols. Some gunsmithing required. Not necessary to replace front sight. Contact MMC for complete details.
Price, less leaf . . . . . . . . . . . . . . . . . . . . . . . . . . . . . . . . **$28.75**
Plain leaf . . . . . . . . . . . . . . . . . . . . . . . . . . . . . . . . . . . . . **$8.55**
White outline leaf . . . . . . . . . . . . . . . . . . . . . . . . . . . . . . **$12.55**
With reflector beads, add . . . . . . . . . . . . . . . . . . . . . . . . . **$2.50**

### MMC COMBAT FIXED SIGHT SYSTEM
New sculptured design permits snag-free draw. Improved version of the High Visibility Bar Cross system. Available for Colt 1911-style pistols.
Price: Plain .................................................. $14.85
Price: White outline ...................................... $19.05
Price: Dots ................................................. $19.05

### MMC MINI-SIGHT SYSTEM
Miniature-size fully adjustable rear sight. Fits most pocket-size 22, 32 and 380 autos with rear dovetail slot. Sight can also be used on many large-frame autos. Give make and model when ordering.
Price: ...................................................... $49.99

### MILLETT SERIES 100 ADJUSTABLE SIGHTS
Replacement sights for revolvers and auto pistols. Positive click adjustments for windage and elevation. Designed for accuracy and ruggedness. Made to fit S&W, Colt, Beretta, SIG Sauer P220, P225, P226, H&K, Ruger, Dan Wesson, Browning, AMT Hardballer. Rear blades are available in white outline or positive black target. All steel construction and easy to install.
Price ............................................ $41.95 to $67.29

### MILLETT MARK SERIES PISTOL SIGHTS
Mark I and Mark II replacement combat sights for government-type auto pistols. Mark I is high profile, Mark II low profile. Both have horizontal light deflectors.
Mark I, front and rear ................................. $29.39
Mark II, front and rear ................................ $41.95

### MILLETT FRONT SIGHTS
All-steel replacement front sights with either white or orange bar. Easy to install. For Ruger Redhawk, Security-Six, Police-Six, Speed-Six, Colt Python, Dan Wesson 22 and 15-2. Price ............. $11.55 to $13.59

### MILLETT DUAL-CRIMP FRONT SIGHT
Replacement front sight for automatic pistols. Dual-Crimp uses an all-steel two-point hollow rivet system. Available in nine heights and four styles. Has a skirted base that covers the front sight pad. Easily installed with the Millett Installation Tool Set. Available in Blaze Orange Bar, White Bar, Serrated Ramp, Plain Post. Price ................................... $13.59

### MILLETT STAKE-ON FRONT SIGHT
Replacement front sight for automatic pistols. Stake-On sights have skirted base that covers the front sight pad. Easily installed with the Millett Installation Tool Set. Available in seven heights and four styles—Blaze Orange Bar, White Bar, Serrated Ramp, Plain Post. Price .............. $13.59

### OMEGA OUTLINE SIGHT BLADES
Replacement rear sight blades for Colt and Ruger single action guns and the Interarms Virginian Dragoon. Standard Outline available in gold or white notch outline on blue metal. Price ......................... $5.95

### OMEGA MAVERICK SIGHT BLADES
Replacement "peep-sight" blades for Colt, Ruger SAs, Virginian Dragoon. Three models available—No. 1, Plain, No. 2, Single Bar, No. 3 Double Bar Rangefinder. Price, each ............................ $ 6.95

### TRIJICON SELF-LUMINOUS SIGHTS
Three-dot sighting system uses self-luminous inserts in the sight blade and leaf. Tritium "lamps" are mounted in a metal cylinder and protected by a polished crystal sapphire. For most popular handguns, fixed or adjustable sights, and some rifles. From Armson, Inc.
Price: ........................................ $34.95 to $139.90

### THOMPSON/CENTER "ULTIMATE" SIGHTS
Replacement front and rear sights for the T/C Contender. Front sight has four interchangeable blades (.060", .080", .100", .120"), rear sight has four notch widths of the same measurements for a possible 16 combinations. Rear sight can be used with existing soldered front sights.
Price: Front sight ..................................... $25.00
Price: Rear sight ...................................... $55.00

### WICHITA SIGHT SYSTEMS
For 45 auto pistols. Target and Combat styles available. Designed by Ron Power. All-steel construction, click adjustable. Each sight has two traverse pins, a large hinge pin and two elevation return springs. Sight blade is serrated and mounted on an angle to deflect light. Patridge front for target, ramp front for combat. Both are legal for ISPC and NRA competitons.
Rear sight, target or combat ........................ $54.50
Front sight, patridge or ramp ....................... $9.85

### WICHITA GRAND MASTER DELUXE RIBS
Ventilated rib has wings machined into it for better sight acquisition. Made of stainless steel, sights blued. Uses Wichita Multi-Range rear sight, adjustable front sight. Made for revolvers with 6" barrel.
Price: Model 301 (adj. sight K-frames with custom bbl. of 1.000"-1.032" dia., L and N frames with 1.062"-1.100" bbl.) ............... $143.00
Price: Model 302 (fixed-sight K-frames; M10, 65, 13 with 1.000" bbl. N-frame with 1.062" bbl.) ................................ $143.00
Price: Model 303 (Model 29, 629 with factory bbl., adj. sight K, L, N frames) .................................................. $143.00
Price: Extra for white outline rear sight ............ $16.00

### WICHITA COMBAT V RIBS
Designed by Ron Power, the ventilated rib has a lengthwise V-groove that emphasizes the front sight and reduces glare and distortion. Over-size rear

sight blade for the click-adjustable sight. Made for Browning Hi-Power, Colt Commander, Govt. and Gold Cup models, Ruger Mark I, 4" S&W K-frames—models 10HB, 13, 64HB, 65, 58 with 4" barrel. From Wichita Arms Inc. Price: With sights. ..................................... $99.00
Price: Extra for white outline rear sight ............ $16.00

## Sight Attachments

### FREELAND LENS ADAPTER
Fits 1⅛" O.D. presciption ground lens to all standard tube and receiver sights for shooting without glasses. Price without lens .......... $44.00
Clear lens ground to prescription ................... $21.00
Yellow or green prescription lens ................... $21.00

### MERIT ADAPTER FOR GLOBE FRONT SIGHTS
An Iris Shutter Disc with a special adapter for mounting in Lyman or Redfield globe front sights. Price ............................... $46.00

### MERIT IRIS SHUTTER DISC
Eleven clicks gives 12 different apertures. No. 3 and Master, primarily target types, 0.22" to .125"; No. 4, ½" dia. hunting type, .025" to .155". Available for all popular sights. The Master Disc, with flexible rubber light shield, is particularly adapted to extension, scope height, and tang sights. All Merit Deluxe models have internal click springs; are hand fitted to minimum tolerance.
Master Deluxe ........................................ $60.00
No. 4 Hunting Disc ................................... $40.00

### MERIT LENS DISC
Similar to Merit Iris Shutter (Model 3 or Master) but incorporates provision for mounting prescription lens integrally. Lens may be obtained locally from your optician. Sight disc is ⁷⁄₁₆" wide (Mod. 3), or ¾" wide (Master).
Model 3 Deluxe. Price ............................... $63.00
Master Deluxe ........................................ $74.00

### MERIT OPTICAL ATTACHMENT
For revolver and pistol shooters, instantly attached by rubber suction cup to regular or shooting glasses. Any aperture .020" to .156". Price, Deluxe (swings aside) .......................................... $60.00

### WILLIAMS APERTURES
Standard thread, fits most sights. Regular series ⅜" to ½" O.D., .050" to .125" hole. "Twilight" series has white reflector ring. .093" to .125" inner hole. Price, regular series . . . $3.20. Twilight series ...... $4.40
New wide open ⁵⁄₁₆" aperture for shotguns fits 5-D and Foolproof sights.
Price .................................................. $5.75

## Shotgun Sights

### ACCURA-SITE
For shooting shotgun slugs. Three models to fit most shotguns—"A" for vent. rib barrels, "B" for solid ribs, "C" for plain barrels. Rear sight has windage and elevation provisions. Easily removed and replaced. Includes front and rear sights. Price ....................... $25.95 to $27.95

### MARBLE
FOR DOUBLE BARREL SHOTGUNS (PRESS FIT)
Marble 214—Ivory front bead, ¹¹⁄₆₄" . . .$3.40; 215—same with .080" rear bead and reamers . . .$11.15. Marble 220—Bi-color (gold and ivory) front bead, ¹¹⁄₆₄" and .080" rear bead, with reamers . . .$12.85; Marble 221—front bead only . . .$4.90. Marble 223—Ivory rear .080" . . .$3.15. Marble 224—Front sight reamer for 214-221 beads . . .$2.45; Marble 226—Rear sight reamer for 223. Price ................................... $2.45

### MARBLE
FOR SINGLE OR DB SHOTGUNS (SCREW-ON FIT)
Marble 217—Ivory front bead ¹¹⁄₆₄" . . .$3.70; Marble 216 . . .$7.65; Marble 218—Bi-color front, ¹¹⁄₆₄" . . .$5.35; Marble 219 . . .$9.35; Marble 223T—Ivory rear .080" Price .................................. $5.05
Marble Bradley type sights 223BT—⅛", ⁵⁄₆₄" and ¹¹⁄₆₄" long. Gold, Ivory or Red bead. ........................................... $3.00

### MILLETT SHURSHOT SHOTGUN SIGHT
A sight system for shotguns with a ventilated rib. Rear sight attaches to the rib, front sight replaces the front bead. Front has an orange face, rear has two orange bars. For 870, 1100, or other models.
Price: Front and rear ................................ $31.49
Price: Adjustable front and rear .................... $41.95

### POLY-CHOKE
Replacement front sights in four styles—Xpert, Poly Bead, Xpert Mid Rib sights, and Bev-L-Block. Xpert Front available in 3x56, 6x48 thread, ³⁄₃₂" or ⁵⁄₃₂" shank length, gold, ivory ($3.00); or Sun Spot orange bead ($4.00); Poly Bead is standard replacement ⅛" bead, 6x48 ($2.00); Xpert Mid Rib in tapered carrier (ivory only) or 3x56 threaded shank (gold only), $3.00; Hi and Lo Blok sights with 6x48 thread, gold or ivory ($3.00) or Sun Spot Orange ($4.00). From Marble Arms.

### SLUG SITE
A combination V-notch rear and bead front sight made of adhesive-backed formed metal approx. 7" over-all. May be mounted, removed and remounted as necessary, using new adhesive from the pack supplied.
Price .................................................. $10.00

**CAUTION:** PRICES CHANGE. CHECK AT GUNSHOP.

# SCOPES & MOUNTS
## HUNTING, TARGET ■ & VARMINT ■ SCOPES

| Maker and Model | Magn. | Field at 100 Yds (feet) | Relative Brightness | Eye Relief (in.) | Length (in.) | Tube Diam. (in.) | W&E Adjustments | Weight (ozs.) | Price | Other Data |
|---|---|---|---|---|---|---|---|---|---|---|
| **Action Arms** | | | | | | | | | | |
| Mark V | 0 | — | — | — | 5⅛ | 1 | Int. | 5.5 | $183.50 | Variable intensity LED red aiming dot. Average battery life up to 500 hours. Waterproof, nitrogen filled aluminum tube. Fits most standard 1″ rings. |
| **Aimpoint** | | | | | | | | | | |
| Mark III | 0 | — | — | — | 6 | — | Int. | 12 | 219.95 | Illuminates red dot in field of view. No parallax (dot does not need to be centered). Unlimited field of view and eye relief. On/off, adj. intensity. Dot covers 3″ @ 100 yds. Mounts avail. for all sights and scopes. From Aimpoint USA, Inc. |
| Series 2000S | 0 | — | — | — | 5 | 1 | Int. | 5.3 | 188.95 | |
| Series 2000L | 0 | — | — | — | 7.25 | 1 | Int. | 6 | 209.95 | |
| **Apollo** | | | | | | | | | | |
| 4x32 Compact | 4 | 29 | — | 3.3 | 11.7 | 1 | Int. | 10 | 140.95 | Rubber armored, water and fog proof. Come with see through filter caps; ¼-minute click adjustments. [1]Available with matte or gloss finish; multi-coated lenses; duplex reticle; waterproof, shockproof. Limited lifetime warranty. Imported from Japan by Apollo Optics. |
| 3-9x40 Variable | 3-9 | 35.3-13.2 | — | 3.3-3 | 12 | 1 | Int. | 14 | 170.95 | |
| Silver Bullet 4x32[1] | 4 | 36 | — | 3 | — | 1 | Int. | 8.5 | 99.00 | |
| Silver Bullet 3-9x40[1] | 3-9 | 39-15 | — | 3¾ | — | 1 | Int. | 9.9 | 124.00 | |
| Silver Bullet 4-12x4[1] | 4-12 | 32-11 | — | 3¾ | — | 1 | Int. | 10.5 | 135.00 | |
| Western 4x32 | 4 | 28 | — | 3 | 12 | 1 | Int. | 9.5 | 55.10 | |
| Western 3-9x32 | 3-9 | 35-13 | — | 3 | 13 | 1 | Int. | 11.5 | 74.10 | |
| **Armson** | | | | | | | | | | |
| O.E.G. | 0 | — | — | — | 5⅛ | 1 | Int. | 4.3 | 129.90 | Shows red dot aiming point. No batteries needed. Standard model fits 1″ ring mounts (not incl.). Other models available for many popular shotguns, para-military rifles and carbines. Also available is a smaller model for rimfire rifles, with dovetail mount. |
| **Armsport** | | | | | | | | | | |
| 415 | 4 | 19 | 13.7 | 3.5 | 11.5 | ¾ | Int. | 6 | 22.00 | [1]Duplex reticle. Crosshair reticle, $90. 4x20, $79, 4x32, $82 (Duplex). [2]Parallax adjustment. [3]For black powder rifles. Polished brass tube with mounts. 4x32 W.A., 4x40 W.A., 6x40 W.A. also avail. Contact Armsport for full details. |
| 3720 | 3-7 | 22.5-9.5 | 43.5-8.1 | 2.4 | 11 | ¾ | Int. | 8.4 | 56.00 | |
| 2½x32 | 2.5 | 32 | 163.8 | 3.7 | 12 | 1 | Int. | 9.3 | 86.00 | |
| 4x40[1] | 4 | 29 | 100 | 3.5 | 12.5 | 1 | Int. | 9 | 97.00 | |
| 6x32 | 6 | 17.8 | 28 | 3.2 | 12 | 1 | Int. | 9 | 86.00 | |
| 1.5-4.5x32 | 1.5-4.5 | 55.1-20.4 | 707.6-64 | 4-3.1 | 11.8 | 1 | Int. | 14.1 | 124.00 | |
| 2-7x32 | 2-7 | 50-19 | 81-22 | 3.1-2.9 | 12.2 | 1 | Int. | 13.8 | 124.00 | |
| 3-9x40 | 3-9 | 35.8-12.7 | 176.9-19.4 | 3.1-2.9 | 12.8 | 1 | Int. | 15.2 | 131.00 | |
| 4-12x40 WA[2] | 4-12 | 31-11 | 36-10.9 | 2.9-2.8 | 14.7 | 1 | Int. | 16.4 | 245.00 | |
| 4x15 BP-1[3] | 4 | 19 | 13 | 3.5 | 32 | ¾ | Int. | 44 | 110.00 | |
| **Bausch & Lomb** | | | | | | | | | | |
| 3x-9x 40mm | 3.9 | 36-12 | 267 | 3.2 | 13 | 1 | Int. | 16.2 | 357.95 | Contact Bushnell for details. |
| 4x 40 mm | 4 | 28 | 150 | 3.2 | 12¾ | 1 | Int. | 14.5 | 229.95 | |
| 1.5x-6x | 1.5-6 | 75-18 | 294-18.4 | 3.3 | 10.6 | 1 | Int. | 10.5 | 315.95 | |
| ■ 6x-24x | 6-24 | 18-4.5 | 66.1-4.2 | 3.1 | 16.6 | 1 | Int. | 20.1 | 419.95 | |
| **Beeman** | | | | | | | | | | |
| Blue Ring 20[1] | 1.5 | 14 | 150 | 11-16 | 8.3 | ¾ | Int. | 3.6 | 49.95 | All scopes have 5-pt. reticle, all glass, fully coated lenses. [1]Pistol scope; cast mounts included. [2]Pistol scope; silhouette knobs. [3]Rubber armor coating; built-in double adj. mount, parallax-free setting. [4]Objective focus, built-in double-adj. mount; matte finish. [5]Objective focus. [6]Has 8 lenses; objective focus; milled mounts included. [7]Includes cast mounts. [8]Objective focus; silhouette knobs; matte finish. [9]Has 9 lenses; objective focus. Imported by Beeman. |
| Blue Ribbon 25[2] | 2 | 19 | 150 | 10-24 | 9 1/16 | 1 | Int. | 7.4 | 119.50 | |
| SS-1[3] | 2.5 | 30 | 61 | 3.25 | 5½ | 1 | Int. | 7 | 129.50 | |
| SS-2[4] | 3 | 34.5 | 74 | 3.5 | 6.8 | 1.38 | Int. | 13.6 | 189.50 | |
| Blue Ribbon 50R[5] | 2.5 | 33 | 245 | 3.5 | 12 | 1 | Int. | 11.8 | 94.50 | |
| Blue Ring 35R[6] | 3 | 25 | 67 | 2.5 | 11¼ | ¾ | Int. | 5.1 | 44.95 | |
| 30A[7] | 4 | 21 | 21 | 2 | 10.2 | ¾ | Int. | 4.5 | 29.99 | |
| Blue Ribbon 66R[8] | 2-7 | 62-16 | 384-31 | 3 | 11.4 | 1 | Int. | 14.9 | 168.50 | |
| Blue Ring 45R[9] | 3-7 | 26-12 | 67-9 | 2.5 | 10⅝ | ¾ | Int. | 6 | 69.95 | |
| MS-1 | 4 | 23 | 30 | 3.5 | 7.5 | 1 | Int. | 8 | 129.95 | |
| SS-3[4] | 1.5-4 | 44.6-24.6 | 172-24 | 3 | 5.75 | ⅞ | Int. | 8.5 | 169.50 | |
| Blue Ribbon 67R[8] | 3-9 | 435-15 | 265-29 | 3 | 14.4 | 1 | Int. | 15.2 | 229.50 | |
| Blue Ribbon 68R[8] | 4-12 | 30.5-11 | 150-13.5 | 3 | 14.4 | 1 | Int. | 15.2 | 239.50 | |
| Blue Ribbon 54R[5] | 4 | 29 | 96 | 3.5 | 12 | 1 | Int. | 12.3 | 94.50 | |
| SS-2[4] | 4 | 24.6 | 41 | 5 | 7 | 1.38 | Int. | 13.7 | 189.50 | |
| 29 | 4 | 21 | 21 | 2 | 10.2 | ¾ | Int. | 4.5 | 19.98 | |
| **Burris** | | | | | | | | | | |
| 4x Fullfield[1] | 3.8 | 37 | 49 | 3¼ | 11¼ | 1 | Int. | 11 | 182.95 | ½-minute dot $7 extra. LER = Long Eye Relief—ideal for forward mounting on handguns. Plex or cross-hair only. Matte "Satin" finish avail. on 4x, 6x, 2-7x, 3-9x, 4x Mini, 1½-4x LER, 2x LER, 4x LER P.A. at extra cost. [1]3″ dot $6 extra. [2]1″-3″ dot $7 extra. [3]1″-3″ dot $7 extra. [4]With parallax adjustment $152.95. [5]With parallax adjustment $170.95. [6]With parallax adjustment $183.95. Parallax adjustment adds 5 oz. to weight. [7]Available with Fine Plex crosshair. |
| 2x-7x Fullfield[2] HiLume | 2.5-6.8 | 50-19 | 81-22 | 3¼ | 11⅞ | 1 | Int. | 14 | 240.95 | |
| 3x-9x Fullfield[3] HiLume | 3.3-8.6 | 40-15 | 72-17.6 | 3¼ | 12¾ | 1 | Int. | 15 | 254.95 | |
| 2¾ Fullfield | 2.7 | 53 | 49 | 3¼ | 10½ | 1 | Int. | 9 | 165.95 | |
| 6x Fullfield | 5.8 | 24 | 36 | 3¼ | 13 | 1 | Int. | 12 | 195.95 | |
| 1¾-5x Fullfield HiLume | 2.5-6.8 | 70-27 | 121-25 | 3¼ | 10¾ | 1 | Int. | 13 | 213.95 | |
| 4x-12x Fullfield[7] | 4.4-11.8 | 28-10½ | — | 3-3¼ | 15 | 1 | Int. | 18 | 295.95 | |
| ■ 6x-18x Fullfield[7] | 6.5-17.6 | 17-7.5 | — | 3-3¾ | 15.8 | 12 | Int. | 18.5 | 302.95 | |
| ■ 10x Fullfield[7] | 9.8 | 12½ | — | 3¼ | 15 | 1 | Int. | 15 | 238.95 | |
| ■ 12x Fullfield[7] | 11.8 | 11 | — | 3¼ | 15 | 1 | Int. | 15 | 244.95 | |
| 2x LER | 1.7 | 21 | — | 10-24 | 8¾ | 1 | Int. | 6.8 | 135.95 | |
| 3x LER | 2.7 | 17 | — | 10-20 | 8⅞ | 1 | Int. | 6.8 | 145.95 | |
| 4x LER[5] | 3.7 | 11 | — | 10-22 | 9⅝ | 1 | Int. | 8.5 | 152.95 | |
| 5x LER[6] | 4.5 | 8.7 | — | 12-22 | 10⅞ | 1 | Int. | 9.5 | 165.95 | |
| 7x IER[7] | 6.5 | 6.5 | — | 10-16 | 11¼ | 1 | Int. | 10 | 177.95 | |
| 10x IER | 9.5 | 4 | — | 8-12 | 13.6 | 1 | Int. | 14 | 220.95 | |
| 1½x-4x LER | 1.6-3.8 | 16-11 | — | 11-24 | 10½ | 1 | Int. | 11 | 222.95 | |
| 2x-7x Mini | 2.5-6.9 | 32-14 | — | 3¾ | 9⅜ | 1 | Int. | 10.5 | 185.95 | |
| 4x Mini[4,7] | 3.6 | 24 | — | 3¾ | 8¼ | 1 | Int. | 7.8 | 135.95 | |
| 6x Mini | 5.5 | 17 | — | 3¾ | 9 | 1 | Int. | 7.8 | 145.95 | |
| 3x-9x Mini | 3.6-8.8 | 25-11 | — | 3¾ | 9⅞ | 1 | Int. | 11.5 | 188.95 | |
| 4-12x Mini | 4.5-11.6 | 19-8 | — | 3¾ | 11.2 | 1 | Int. | 15 | 254.95 | |

**CAUTION:** PRICES CHANGE. CHECK AT GUNSHOP.

| Maker and Model | Magn. | Field at 100 Yds (feet) | Relative Brightness | Eye Relief (in.) | Length (in.) | Tube Diam. (in.) | W&E Adjustments | Weight (ozs.) | Price | Other Data |
|---|---|---|---|---|---|---|---|---|---|---|
| **Burris** (cont'd.) | | | | | | | | | | |
| 2x Mikro | 1.7 | 15 | — | 7-24 | 9⅛ | ⅝ | Int. | 4 | 140.95 | |
| 3x Mikro | 2.7 | 11 | — | 8-22 | 9⅛ | ⅝ | Int. | 4 | 140.95 | |
| 2¾xXER Scout | 2.7 | 15 | — | 7-14 | 9⅜ | 1 | Int. | 7.5 | 142.95 | |
| **Bushnell** | | | | | | | | | | |
| Scope Chief VI | 4 | 29 | 96 | 3½ | 12 | 1 | Int. | 9.3 | 127.95 | All ScopeChief, Banner and Custom models come with Multi-X reticle, with or without BDC (bullet drop compensator) that eliminates hold-over. Prismatic Rangefinder (PRF) on some models. Contact Bushnell for data on full line. Prices include BDC—deduct $5 if not wanted. Add $30 for PRF. BDC feature available in all Banner models, except 2.5x. [1]Equipped with Wind Drift Compensator and Parallax-free adjustment. [2]Also available with power booster. [3]4-times zoom ratio. [4]Has battery powered lighted reticle. Contact Bushnell for complete details. |
| Scope Chief VI | 3-9 | 35-12.6 | 267-30 | 3.3 | 12.6 | 1 | Int. | 14.3 | 203.95 | |
| Scope Chief VI | 3-9 | 39-13 | 241-26.5 | 3.3 | 12.1 | 1 | Int. | 13 | 258.95 | |
| Scope Chief VI | 2½-8 | 45-14 | 247-96 | 3.3 | 11.2 | 1 | Int. | 12.1 | 179.95 | |
| Scope Chief VI | 1½-4½ | 73.7-24.5 | 267-30 | 3.5-3.5 | 9.6 | 1 | Int. | 9.5 | 175.95 | |
| Scope Chief VI | 4-12 | 29-10 | 150-17 | 3.2 | 13.5 | 1 | Int. | 17 | 249.95 | |
| Centurion Handgun 4x32mm | 4 | 10.2 | 96 | 10-20 | 8¾ | 1 | Int. | 9.3 | 129.95 | |
| Centurion H'gun 1.3x[2] | 1.3 | 17 | — | 7-21 | 7.9 | 1 | Int. | 6.9 | 109.95 | |
| Magnum Phantom 1.3x | 1.3 | 17 | — | 7-21 | 7.8 | 1 | Int. | 5.5 | 79.95 | |
| Magnum Phantom 2.5x | 2.5 | 9 | — | 7-21 | 9.7 | 1 | Int. | 6.5 | 87.95 | |
| Sportview Quad Power 2.5-10x[3] | 2.5-10 | 45-11 | — | 3-2 | 13.5 | 1 | Int. | 14.5 | 109.95 | |
| Sportview Quad Power 5-20x[3] | 5-20 | 22-5.5 | — | 3.1 | 13.5 | 1 | Int. | 15.5 | 139.95 | |
| Sportview Rangemaster 3-9x | 3-9 | 38-12 | — | 3.5 | 11.75 | 1 | Int. | 10 | 89.95 | |
| ■ Sportview Rangemaster 4-12x | 4-12 | 27-9 | — | 3.2 | 13.5 | 1 | Int. | 14 | 119.95 | |
| Sportview Standard 4x | 4 | 28 | — | 4 | 11.75 | 1 | Int. | 9.5 | 55.95 | |
| Sportview Standard 3-9x | 3-9 | 38-12 | — | 3.5 | 11.75 | 1 | Int. | 10 | 75.95 | |
| 22 Rimfire 4x | 4 | 28 | — | 3 | 11.9 | 1 | Int. | 8 | 51.95 | |
| 22 Rimfire 3-7x | 3-7 | 29-13 | — | 2.5 | 10 | ¾ | Int. | 6.5 | 55.95 | |
| Banner Lite-Site 1.5-6x | 1.5-6 | 60-15 | — | 3.2 | 9.8 | 1 | Int. | 12.4 | 229.95 | |
| Banner Lite-Site 3-9x | 3-9 | 36-12 | — | 3.3 | 13.6 | 1 | Int. | 14 | 249.95 | |
| Banner Trophy WA 1.75-5x | 1.75-5 | 68.5-24.5 | — | 3.2 | 10.4 | 1 | Int. | 10.2 | 145.95 | |
| Banner Trophy WA 4x | 4 | 34.2 | — | 3.4 | 12.4 | 1 | Int. | 11.9 | 137.95 | |
| Banner Trophy WA 3-9x | 3-9 | 39-13 | — | 3.3 | 11.8 | 1 | Int. | 12.9 | 153.95 | |
| Banner Standard 2.5x | 2.5 | 45 | — | 3.5 | 10.9 | 1 | Int. | 8 | 87.95 | |
| Banner Standard 4x | 4 | 29 | — | 3.5 | 12 | 1 | Int. | 10 | 101.95 | |
| Banner Standard 6x | 6 | 19.5 | — | 3 | 13.5 | 1 | Int. | 11.5 | 109.95 | |
| Banner Standard 16x | 16 | 7.25 | — | 3.1 | 15.4 | 1 | Int. | 15.3 | 179.95 | |
| Banner Standard 3-9x | 3-9 | 43-14 | — | 3 | 12.1 | 1 | Int. | 14 | 149.95 | |
| Banner Standard 4-12x | 4-12 | 29-10 | — | 3.2 | 13.5 | 1 | Int. | 15.5 | 179.95 | |
| Banner Standard 6-18x | 6-18 | 18-6 | — | 3.1 | 14.5 | 1 | Int. | 16 | 199.95 | |
| **Colt** | | | | | | | | | | |
| AR-15 3x | 3 | 40 | — | — | 6 | — | Int. | — | 206.50 | All Colt scopes come complete with mount and allow use of iron sights. |
| AR-15 4x | 4 | 30 | — | — | 6 | — | Int. | — | 227.50 | |
| **Cougar** | | | | | | | | | | |
| 2.5x32 | 2.5 | 33 | 161 | 3.5 | 11.7 | 1 | Int. | 10.2 | 85.95 | Nitrogen filled, fog proof; ¼-m.o.a. click adjustments; fully coated lenses. Choice of crosshair or four-post crosshair or optional "peep" reticles. [1]Also 4x40 ($105.95) and Full View ($119.95). [2]Also Full View ($136.95). [3]Also Full View ($169.95). [4]Also with "Silver" finish, same price. Imported by Cougar Optics. |
| 4x32[1] | 4 | 29 | 64 | 3.3 | 11.7 | 1 | Int. | 10.2 | 81.95 | |
| 6x40[2] | 6 | 18.5 | 45 | 3.2 | 13 | 1 | Int. | 11.6 | 112.95 | |
| 8x40 | 8 | 13.5 | 25 | 3 | 13 | 1 | Int. | 11.6 | 126.95 | |
| 3-9x40[3] | 3-9 | 35.3-13.2 | 177-20 | 3.3-3.0 | 12 | 1 | Int. | 12.7 | 148.95 | |
| 4-12x40 | 4-12 | 29.5-10.3 | 100-11 | 3.3-3.0 | 13.5 | 1 | Int. | 13.3 | 169.95 | |
| **Pistol Scopes** | | | | | | | | | | |
| P-1.5x20[4] | 1.5 | 20 | 177 | 13.3 | 8.5 | 1 | Int. | 5.8 | 105.95 | |
| P-2.5x20[4] | 2.5 | 15 | 64 | 8 | 8.7 | 1 | Int. | 6.0 | 111.95 | |
| **Davis Optical** | | | | | | | | | | |
| Spot Shot 1½" | 10,12 15,20 25,30 | 10-4 | — | 2 | 25 | .75 | Ext. | — | 116.00 | Focus by moving non-rotating obj. lens unit. Ext. mounts included. Recoil spring $4.50 extra. |
| **Jason** | | | | | | | | | | |
| 860 | 4 | 29 | 64 | 3 | 11.8 | 1 | Int. | 9.2 | 50.00 | Constantly centered reticles, ballbearing click stops, nitrogen filled tubes, coated lenses. 4-Post crosshair about $3.50 extra on models 860, 861, 864, 865. |
| 861 | 3-9 | 35-13 | 112-12 | 3 | 12.7 | 1 | Int. | 10.9 | 76.00 | |
| 862 | 4 | 19 | 14 | 2 | 11 | ¾ | Int. | 5.5 | 13.50 | |
| 863C | 3-7 | 23-10 | 43-8 | 3 | 11 | ¾ | Int. | 8.4 | 44.00 | |
| 865 | 3-9 | 35-13 | 177-19 | 3 | 13 | 1 | Int. | 12.2 | 80.00 | |
| 869 | 4 | 19 | 25 | 2 | 11.4 | ¾ | Int. | 6 | 23.00 | |
| 873 | 4 | 29 | 100 | 3 | 12.7 | 1 | Int. | 11.1 | 75.00 | |
| 875 | 3-9 | 35-13 | 177-19 | 3 | 13 | 1 | Int. | 12.2 | 80.00 | |
| 877 | 4 | 37 | 100 | 3 | 11.6 | 1 | Int. | 11.6 | 85.00 | |
| 878 | 3-9 | 42.5-13.6 | 112-12 | 2.7 | 12.7 | 1 | Int. | 12.7 | 110.00 | |
| **Kahles** | | | | | | | | | | |
| Helia Super 2.5 x 20[1] | 2.5 | 50 | 64 | 3.25 | 9.8 | 1 | Int. | 12.6 | 279.00 | [1]Lightweight model weighs 10.1 oz. [2]Lightweight—11.2 oz. [3]Lightweight—13 oz. [4]Lightweight—16 oz. [5]Lightweight—12.6 oz. [6]Lightweight—15.4 oz. [7]Lightweight—15.7 oz. [8]Lightweight—17.8 oz. [9]Calibrated for 7.62 NATO ammo, 100 to 800 meters. All scopes have constantly centered reticles except ZF84; all come with lens caps. 30mm rings available for Redfield, Burris, Leupold bases. Imported from Austria by Kahles of America. (Del-Sports, Inc.). |
| Helia Super 4 x 32[2] | 4 | 30 | 60 | 3.25 | 11.6 | 1 | Int. | 15 | 319.00 | |
| Helia 6 x 42[3] | 6 | 21.1 | 49 | 3.25 | 12.8 | 1 | Int. | 17.5 | 349.00 | |
| Helia 8 x 56[4] | 8 | 15.6 | 49 | 3.25 | 14.8 | 1 | Int. | 23 | 389.00 | |
| Helia 1.1-4.5 x 20[5] | 1.1-4.5 | 72.2-27 | 328-18 | 3.25 | 10.8 | 30mm | Int. | 15 | 369.00 | |
| Helia 1.5-6 x 20[6] | 1.5-6 | 55.6-19.5 | 784-49 | 3.25 | 12.8 | 30mm | Int. | 20 | 399.00 | |
| Helia 2.2-9 x 42[7] | 2.2-9 | 36.1-13.5 | 364-21 | 3.25 | 13.7 | 30mm | Int. | 20.3 | 449.00 | |
| Helia 3-12 x 56[8] | 3-12 | 27.1-10 | 347-21 | 3.25 | 15.6 | 30mm | Int. | 24.8 | 499.00 | |
| ZF84 Sniper[9] | 6 | 22.5 | 49 | 3.25 | 12.2 | 26mm | Int. | 16.8 | 499.00 | |
| **Kilham** | | | | | | | | | | |
| Hutson Handgunner II | 1.7 | 8 | — | — | 5½ | ⅞ | Int. | 5.1 | 119.95 | Unlimited eye relief; internal click adjustments; crosshair reticle. Fits Thompson/Center rail mounts, for S&W K, N, Ruger Blackhawk, Super, Super Single-Six, Contender |
| Hutson Handgunner | 3 | 8 | — | 10-12 | 6 | ⅞ | Int. | 5.3 | 119.95 | |

**CAUTION:** PRICES CHANGE. CHECK AT GUNSHOP.

| Maker and Model | Magn. | Field at 100 Yds (feet) | Relative Bright-ness | Eye Relief (in.) | Length (in.) | Tube Diam. (in.) | W&E Adjust-ments | Weight (ozs.) | Price | Other Data |
|---|---|---|---|---|---|---|---|---|---|---|
| **Leatherwood** | | | | | | | | | | |
| ART II | 3.0-8.8 | 31-12 | — | 3.5 | 13.9 | 1 | Int. | 42 | 675.00 | |
| ART/MPC | 3.0-8.7 | 31-12 | — | 3.7 | 14.1 | 1 | Int. | 33 | 349.50 | |
| 4x | 4.1 | 27 | — | 4 | 12.25 | 1 | Int. | 12.3 | 125.00 | |
| **Leupold** | | | | | | | | | | |
| M8-2X EER[1] | 1.8 | 22.0 | — | 12-24 | 8.1 | 1 | Int. | 6.8 | 159.65 | Constantly centered reticles, choice of Duplex, tapered CPC, Leupold Dot, Crosshair and Dot. CPC and Dot reticles extra. [1]2x and 4x scope have from 12"-24" of eye relief and are suitable for handguns, top ejection arms and muzzle-loaders. [2]3x9 Compact, 6x Compact, 12x, 3x9, 3.5x10 and 6.5x20 come with Adjustable Objective. [3]Target scopes have 1-min divisions with ¼ min clicks, and Adjustable Objectives. 50-ft. Focus Adaptor available for indoor target ranges, $40.90. Sunshade available for all Adjustable Objective scopes, $11.40. [4]Also available in matte finish for about $20.00 extra. [5]A.O., $237.50. |
| M8-2X EER Silver[1] | 1.8 | 22.0 | — | 12-24 | 8.1 | 1 | Int. | 6.8 | 177.85 | |
| M8-4X EER[1] | 3.5 | 9.5 | — | 12-24 | 8.4 | 1 | Int. | 7.6 | 194.90 | |
| M8-4X EER Silver[1] | 3.5 | 9.5 | — | 12-24 | 8.4 | 1 | Int. | 8.5 | 213.15 | |
| M8-2.5X Compact | 2.3 | 42 | — | 4.3 | 8.5 | 1 | Int. | 7.4 | 175.80 | |
| M8-4X Compact | 3.6 | 26.5 | — | 4.1 | 10.3 | 1 | Int. | 8.6 | 200.00 | |
| 2-7x Compact | 2.5-6.6 | 41.7-16.5 | — | 3.8-3.0 | 9.9 | 1 | Int. | 8.5 | 236.00 | |
| 6x Compact & A.O. | 5.7 | 16 | — | 3.9 | 10.7 | 1 | Int. | 8.5 | 204.90 | |
| 3-9x Compact & A.O. | 3.2-8.5 | 34.5-13.5 | — | 3.8-3.1 | 11 | 1 | Int. | 9.5 | 309.55 | |
| M8-4X[4] | 3.6 | 28 | — | 4.4 | 11.4 | 1 | Int. | 8.8 | 200.80 | |
| M8-6X | 5.9 | 18.0 | — | 4.3 | 11.4 | 1 | Int. | 9.9 | 214.45 | |
| M8-8X[2] | 7.8 | 14.5 | — | 4.0 | 12.5 | 1 | Int. | 13.0 | 285.90 | |
| M8-12X[2] | 11.6 | 9.2 | — | 4.2 | 13.0 | 1 | Int. | 13.5 | 289.65 | |
| 6.5 x 20 Target AO | 6.5-19.2 | 14.8-5.7 | — | 5.3-3.7 | 14.2 | 1 | Int. | 16 | 456.25 | |
| M8-12X Target[3] | 11.6 | 9.2 | — | 4.2 | 13.0 | 1 | Int. | 14.5 | 343.60 | |
| M8-24X[3] | 24.0 | 4.7 | — | 3.2 | 13.6 | 1 | Int. | 14.5 | 456.25 | |
| M8-36X[3] | 36.0 | 3.0 | — | 3.4 | 13.9 | 1 | Int. | 15.5 | 456.25 | |
| Vari-X-II 2X7 | 2.5-6.6 | 44.0-19.0 | — | 4.1-3.7 | 10.7 | 1 | Int. | 10.4 | 268.50 | |
| Vari-X-II 3X9[4] | 3.5-9.0 | 32.0-13.5 | — | 4.1-3.7 | 12.3 | 1 | Int. | 13.1 | 288.40 | |
| Vari-X-II 3X9[2] | 3.5-9.0 | 32.0-13.5 | — | 4.1-3.7 | 12.3 | 1 | Int. | 14.5 | 326.35 | |
| Vari-X-III 1.5X5 | 1.5-4.6 | 66.0-24.0 | — | 4.7-3.5 | 9.4 | 1 | Int. | 9.3 | 294.55 | |
| Vari-X-III 2.5X8[4] | 2.7-7.9 | 38.0-14.0 | — | 4.2-3.4 | 11.3 | 1 | Int. | 11.0 | 332.25 | |
| Vari-X-III 3.5X10 | 3.4-9.9 | 29.5-10.5 | — | 4.6-3.6 | 12.4 | 1 | Int. | 13.0 | 347.50 | |
| Vari-X-III 3.5X10[2] | 3.4-9.9 | 29.5-10.5 | — | 4.6-3.6 | 12.4 | 1 | Int. | 14.4 | 386.50 | |
| Vari-X-III 6.5X20[2] | 6.5-19.2 | 14.8-5.7 | — | 5.3-3.7 | 14.2 | 1 | Int. | 16 | 411.60 | |
| **Nikon** | | | | | | | | | | |
| 4x40 | 4 | 26 | — | 3.4 | 11.6 | 1 | Int. | 13.5 | 275.00 | Multi-coated lenses; ¼-minute windage and elevation adjustments; nitrogen filled; waterproof. From Nikon Inc. |
| 1.5-4.5x20 | 1.5-4.5 | 67.5-22.5 | — | 3.7 | 10 | 1 | Int. | 11.8 | 315.00 | |
| 2-7x32 | 2-7 | 43-12 | — | 4.1 | 11.4 | 1 | Int. | 12.3 | 348.00 | |
| 3-9x40 | 3-9 | 34.5-11.5 | — | 3.5-3.4 | 12.3 | 1 | Int. | 16 | 355.00 | |
| **Pentax** | | | | | | | | | | |
| 4x | 4 | 35 | — | 3¼ | 11.6 | 1 | Int. | 12.2 | 220.00 | Fully coated lenses, fog-proof, water-proof, nitrogen filled. Penta-Plex reticle. Click ¼-m.o.a. adjustments. Imported by Pentax Corp. |
| 6x | 6 | 20 | — | 3¼ | 13.4 | 1 | Int. | 13.5 | 250.00 | |
| 2-7x | 2-7 | 42.5-17 | — | 3-3¼ | 12 | 1 | Int. | 14 | 300.00 | |
| 3-9x | 3-9 | 33-13.5 | — | 3-3¼ | 13 | 1 | Int. | 15 | 320.00 | |
| 3-9x Mini | 3-9 | 26.5-10.5 | — | 3¾ | 10.4 | 1 | Int. | 13 | 270.00 | |
| **RWS** | | | | | | | | | | |
| 100 4x32 | 4 | 20 | — | — | 10⅞ | ¾ | Int. | 6 | 33.00 | Air gun scopes. All have Dyna-Plex reticle. Imported from Japan by Dynamit Nobel of America. |
| 200 3-7x-20 | 3-7 | 24-17 | — | — | 11¼ | ¾ | Int. | 6 | 51.00 | |
| 350 4x32 | 4 | 28 | — | — | 10 | 1 | Int. | 10 | 85.00 | |
| 400 2-7x32 | 2-7 | 50-17 | — | — | 12¾ | 1 | Int. | 12 | 125.00 | |
| 800 1.5x20 | 1.5 | 19 | — | — | 8¾ | 1 | Int. | 6½ | 85.00 | |
| **Redfield** | | | | | | | | | | |
| Illuminator Trad. 3-9x | 2.9-8.7 | 33-11 | — | 3½ | 12¾ | 1 | Int. | 17 | 378.80 | *Accutrac feature avail. on these scopes at extra cost. Traditionals have round lenses. 4-Plex reticle is standard. [1]"Magnum Proof." Specially designed for magnum and auto pistols. Uses "Double Dovetail" mounts. [2]With matte finish $428.95. [3]Also available with matte finish at extra cost. [4]All Golden Five Star scopes come with Butler Creek flip-up lens covers. |
| Illuminator Widefield 3-9x*[2] | 2.9-8.7 | 38-13 | — | 3½ | 12¾ | 1 | Int. | 17 | 420.00 | |
| Tracker 4x[3] | 3.9 | 28.9 | — | 3½ | 11.02 | 1 | Int. | 9.8 | 117.90 | |
| Tracker 2-7x[3] | 2.3-6.9 | 36.6-12.2 | — | 3½ | 12.20 | 1 | Int. | 11.6 | 157.25 | |
| Tracker 3-9x[3] | 3.0-9.0 | 34.4-11.3 | — | 3½ | 14.96 | 1 | Int. | 13.4 | 176.90 | |
| Traditional 4x¾" | 4 | 24½ | 27 | 3½ | 9⅜ | ¾ | Int. | — | 112.50 | |
| Traditional 2½x | 2½ | 43 | 64 | 3½ | 10¼ | 1 | Int. | 8½ | 155.45 | |
| Golden Five Star 4x[4] | 4 | 28.5 | 58 | 3.75 | 11.3 | 1 | Int. | 9.75 | 169.70 | |
| Golden Five Star 6x[4] | 6 | 18 | 40 | 3.75 | 12.2 | 1 | Int. | 11.5 | 187.60 | |
| Golden Five Star 2-7x[4] Royal | 2.4-7.4 | 42-14 | 207-23 | 3-3.75 | 11.25 | 1 | Int. | 12 | 223.40 | |
| Golden Five Star 3-9x[4] | 3.0-9.1 | 34-11 | 163-18 | 3-3.75 | 12.50 | 1 | Int. | 13 | 241.20 | |
| Golden Five Star 4-12xA.O.[4] | 3.9-11.4 | 27-9 | 112-14 | 3-3.75 | 13.8 | 1 | Int. | 16 | 312.70 | |
| Golden Five Star 6-18xA.O.[4] | 6.1-18.1 | 18.6 | 50-6 | 3-3.75 | 14.3 | 1 | Int. | 18 | 330.60 | |
| **Pistol Scopes** | | | | | | | | | | |
| 2½xMP[1] | 2.5 | 9 | 64 | 14-19 | 9.8 | 1 | Int. | 10.5 | 171.50 | |
| 4xMP[1] | 3.6 | 9 | — | 12-22 | 9¹¹⁄₁₆ | 1 | Int. | 11.1 | 183.95 | |
| **Low Profile Scopes** | | | | | | | | | | |
| Widefield 2¾xLP | 2¾ | 55½ | 69 | 3½ | 10½ | 1 | Int. | 8 | 194.75 | |
| Widefield 4xLP | 3.6 | 37½ | 84 | 3½ | 11½ | 1 | Int. | 10 | 217.95 | |
| Widefield 6xLP | 5.5 | 23 | — | 3½ | 12¾ | 1 | Int. | 11 | 237.70 | |
| Widefield 1¾x5xLP | 1¾-5 | 70-27 | 136-21 | 3½ | 10¾ | 1 | Int. | 11½ | 269.85 | |
| Widefield 2x7xLP* | 2-7 | 49-19 | 144-21 | 3½ | 11¾ | 1 | Int. | 13 | 278.80 | |
| Widefield 3x-9xLP* | 3-9 | 39-15 | 112-18 | 3½ | 12½ | 1 | Int. | 14 | 307.40 | |
| **Sanders** | | | | | | | | | | |
| Bisley 2½x20 | 2½ | 42 | 64 | 3 | 10¾ | 1 | Int. | 8¼ | 48.50 | Alum. alloy tubes, ¼" adj. coated lenses. Five other scopes are offered; 6x45 at $68.50, 8x45 at $70.50, 2½x7x at $69.50, 3-9x33 at $72.50 and 3-9x40 at $78.50. Rubber lens covers (clear plastic) are $3.50. Write to Sanders for details. Choice of reticles in CH, PCH, 3-post. |
| Bisley 4x33 | 4 | 28 | 64 | 3 | 12 | 1 | Int. | 9 | 52.50 | |
| Bisley 6x40 | 6 | 19 | 45 | 3 | 12½ | 1 | Int. | 9½ | 56.50 | |
| Bisley 8x40 | 8 | 18 | 25 | 3¼ | 12½ | 1 | Int. | 9½ | 62.50 | |
| Bisley 10x40 | 10 | 12½ | 16 | 2½ | 12½ | 1 | Int. | 10¼ | 64.50 | |
| Bisley 5-13x40 | 5-13 | 29-10 | 64-9 | 3 | 14 | 1 | Int. | 14 | 86.50 | |

**CAUTION:** PRICES CHANGE. CHECK AT GUNSHOP.

| Maker and Model | Magn. | Field at 100 Yds (feet) | Relative Brightness | Eye Relief (in.) | Length (in.) | Tube Diam. (in.) | W&E Adjustments | Weight (ozs.) | Price | Other Data |
|---|---|---|---|---|---|---|---|---|---|---|
| **Schmidt & Bender** | | | | | | | | | | [1]Heavy duty aluminum. [2]Black chrome finish. [3]For silhouette and varmint shooting. Choice of nine reticles. 30-year warranty. All have ⅓-min. click adjustments, centered reticles, nitrogen filling. Most models avail. in aluminum with mounting rail. Imported from West Germany by Paul Jaeger, Inc. |
| Vari-M 1¼-4x20[1] | 1¼-4 | 96-16 | — | 3¼ | 10.4 | 30mm | Int. | 12.3 | 402.00 | |
| Vari-M 1½-6x42 | 1½-6 | 60-19.5 | — | 3¼ | 12.2 | 30mm | Int. | 17.5 | 440.00 | |
| Vari-M 2½-10x56 | 2½-10 | 37.5-12 | — | 3¼ | 14.6 | 30mm | Int. | 21.9 | 512.00 | |
| All Steel 1½x15[2] | 1½ | 90 | — | 3¼ | 10 | 1 | Int. | 11.8 | 297.00 | |
| All Steel 4x36[2] | 4 | 30 | — | 3¼ | 11.4 | 1 | Int. | 14 | 308.00 | |
| All Steel 6x42[2] | 6 | 21 | — | 3¼ | 13.2 | 1 | Int. | 17.3 | 330.00 | |
| All Steel 8x56[2] | 8 | 16.5 | — | 3¼ | 14.8 | 1 | Int. | 21.9 | 385.00 | |
| ■ All Steel 12x42[3] | 12 | 16.5 | — | 3¼ | 13 | 1 | Int. | 17.9 | 368.00 | |
| **Shepherd** | | | | | | | | | | [1]Also avail. in Rimfire version (#1020). [2]Also avail. as Model 1001 Elite for counter sniper, silhouette shooting with extra-fine crosshair. Models 1001, 1002, 1003, 1020 come with reticle pattern set for shooters choice of ballistics. All except 1001 have Dual Reticle System with instant range finder, bullet drop compensator. Waterproof, nitrogen filled, shock-proof. From Shepherd Scope Ltd. |
| 1003 Centerfire[1] | 2.5-7.5 | 42-14 | 164-18 | 2.5-3 | 11⅝ | 1 | Int. | 18 | 231.55 | |
| 1002 Centerfire[2] | 3-10 | 35.3-11.6 | 178-16 | 3-3.75 | 12.8 | 1 | Int. | 16.7 | 280.75 | |
| Deluxe 3-9x | 3-9 | 43.5-15 | 178-20 | 3.3 | 13 | 1 | Int. | 13.5 | 428.00 | |
| **Simmons** | | | | | | | | | | [1]With ring mount. [2]With ring mount. [3]With rings. [4]3-9x32; also avail. 3-9x40. [5]3-9x32; also avail. 3-9x40. [6]4x32; also avail. 4x40 as #1034. [7]3-9x32; also avail. 3-9x40 as #1038. [8]Avail. in brushed aluminum finish as #1052. [9]Avail. with silhouette knobs as #1085, in brushed aluminum as #1088. [10]½-min. dot or Truplex; Truplex reticle also avail. with dot. Sunshade, screw-in lens covers. Parallax adj.; Silhouette knobs; graduated drums. [11]Battery powered, roof prism design. [12]Speed focus, parallax adj., matte finish. [13]"Simcoat" multi-coating on all lenses, 44mm obj. lens, high-gloss finish, parallax adj., polarized and yellow screw-in filters, ¼-min. click adj., leather lens covers incl. Also avail. in wide angle with range finding system. Max-Ilume Mono Tube models have dull finish, speed focus, rubber shock ring, Truplex reticle in all models. All scopes sealed, fog-proof, with constantly centered reticles. Imported from Japan by Simmons Outdoor Corp. **Prices are approximate.** |
| 1002 Rimfire[1] | 4 | 23 | — | 3 | 11.5 | ¾ | Int. | 6 | 11.00 | |
| 1004 Rimfire[2] | 3-7 | 22.5-9.5 | — | 3 | 11 | ¾ | Int. | 8.4 | 27.95 | |
| 1007 Rimfire[3] | 4 | 25 | — | 3 | 10 | 1 | Int. | 9 | 60.00 | |
| 1005 Waterproof | 2½ | 46 | — | 3 | 11.5 | 1 | Int. | 9.3 | 54.00 | |
| 1006 Waterproof | 4 | 29 | — | — | 12 | 1 | Int. | 9.1 | 41.00 | |
| 1010 Waterproof[4] | 3-9 | 37-12.7 | — | 3-3¼ | 12.8 | 1 | Int. | 12.8 | 55.00 | |
| 1014 Waterproof | 4-12 | 30-11 | — | 3-3¼ | 14 | 1 | Int. | 14.9 | 95.00 | |
| 1016 Waterproof | 6-18 | 19-6.7 | — | 3-3¼ | 15.7 | 1 | Int. | 16.2 | 122.00 | |
| 1024 W.A. | 4 | 37 | — | 3 | 11.8 | 1 | Int. | 10.5 | 71.50 | |
| 1025 W.A. | 6 | 24.5 | — | 3 | 12.4 | 1 | Int. | 12 | 90.00 | |
| 1026 W.A. | 1½-4½ | 86-28.9 | — | 3-3¼ | 10.6 | 1 | Int. | 13.2 | 97.00 | |
| 1027 W.A. | 2-7 | 54.6-18.3 | — | 3-3¼ | 12 | 1 | Int. | 12.8 | 97.00 | |
| 1028 W.A.[5] | 3-9 | 42-14 | — | 3-3¼ | 12.9 | 1 | Int. | 12.9 | 90.00 | |
| 1032 Mono Tube[6] | 4 | 37 | — | 3 | 12.2 | 1 | Int. | 11.5 | 100.00 | |
| 1036 Mono Tube[7] | 3-9 | 42-14 | — | 3-3¼ | 13.3 | 1 | Int. | 13 | 130.00 | |
| 1040 Mono Tube | 2-7 | 54-18 | — | 3-3¼ | 13.1 | 1 | Int. | 12.9 | 146.00 | |
| 1049 Compact | 2½ | 37 | — | 3 | 9.3 | 1 | Int. | 9.1 | 106.00 | |
| 1050 Compact[8] | 4 | 22 | — | 3 | 9 | 1 | Int. | 9.1 | 106.00 | |
| 1053 Compact | 1½-4½ | 86-28.9 | — | 3-3¼ | 10.6 | 1 | Int. | 9.1 | 143.00 | |
| 1054 Compact | 3-9 | 40-14 | — | 3-3¼ | 10.5 | 1 | Int. | 10.5 | 136.50 | |
| 1063 Armored | 4 | 37 | — | 3 | 12.4 | 1 | Int. | 14 | 108.00 | |
| 1064 Armored | 3-9 | 42-14 | — | 3-3¼ | 12.3 | 1 | Int. | 17.6 | 120.25 | |
| 1074 | 6½-20 | 18-6 | — | 3 | 15 | 1 | Int. | 16 | 208.00 | |
| 1075 | 6½-10 | 22-12 | — | 3 | 15 | 1 | Int. | 16 | 208.00 | |
| 1076[10] | 15 | 8 | — | 3 | 15 | 1 | Int. | 16 | 169.00 | |
| 1078[10] | 24 | 6 | — | 3 | 15 | 1 | Int. | 16 | 169.00 | |
| 1057 Illum. | 4 | 21 | — | 3 | 8 | 1 | Int. | 11 | 157.00 | |
| 410[11] | 4-10 | 40-15 | — | 3 | 12.75 | 1 | Int. | 15 | 157.00 | |
| 1073 Sil. Airgun | 2-7 | 54.6-18.3 | — | 3-3¼ | 12.1 | 1 | Int. | 15.7 | 128.75 | |
| 1080 Handgun | 2 | 18 | — | 10-20 | 7.1 | 1 | Int. | 8.1 | 83.00 | |
| 1084 Handgun[9] | 4 | 9 | — | 10-20 | 8.7 | 1 | Int. | 9.5 | 122.00 | |
| **Presidential Series** | | | | | | | | | | |
| 1065[13] | 4 | 35 | 121 | 3.5 | 13 | 1 | Int. | 15.5 | 227.50 | |
| 1066[13] | 2-7 | 55.1-18.3 | 484-40 | 3.3-2.9 | 12.6 | 1 | Int. | 16.6 | 260.00 | |
| 1067[13] | 3-9 | 42-14 | 216-54 | 3.3 | 13 | 1 | Int. | 16.2 | 260.00 | |
| 1068[13] | 4-12 | 31-11 | 121-14 | 3.9-3.2 | 14.2 | 1 | Int. | 19.1 | 282.75 | |
| 1069[13] | 6.5-20 | 17.8-6.1 | 46-5 | 3.4-3.2 | 15.4 | 1 | Int. | 19.4 | 302.00 | |
| **Swarovski Habicht** | | | | | | | | | | All models offered in either steel or lightweight alloy tubes except 1.5x20, ZFM 6x42 and Cobras. Weights shown are for lightweight versions. Choice of nine constantly centered reticles. Eyepiece recoil mechanism and rubber ring shield to protect face. Cobra and ZFM also available in NATO Stanag 2324 mounts. Imported by Swarovski America Ltd. |
| Nova 1.5x20 | 1.5 | 61 | — | 3⅛ | 9.6 | 1 | Int. | 12.7 | 330.00 | |
| Nova 4x32 | 4 | 33 | — | 3⅛ | 11.3 | 1 | Int. | 13 | 340.00 | |
| Nova 6x42 | 6 | 23 | — | 3⅛ | 12.6 | 1 | Int. | 14 | 380.00 | |
| Nova 8x56 | 8 | 17 | — | 3⅛ | 14.4 | 1 | Int. | 17 | 455.00 | |
| Nova 1.5 6x42 | 1.5-6 | 61-21 | — | 3⅛ | 12.6 | 1 | Int. | 17 | 470.00 | |
| Nova 2.2-9x42 | 2.2-9 | 39.5-15 | — | 3⅛ | 13.3 | 1 | Int. | 16.5 | 580.00 | |
| Nova 3-12x56 | 3-12 | 30-11 | — | 3⅛ | 15.25 | 1 | Int. | 19 | 640.00 | |
| ZFM 6x42 | 6 | 23 | — | 3⅛ | 12 | 1 | Int. | 18 | 535.00 | |
| Cobra 1.5-14 | 1.5 | 50 | — | 3.9 | 7.87 | 1 | Int. | 10 | 325.00 | |
| Cobra 3x14 | 3 | 21 | — | 3.9 | 8.75 | 1 | Int. | 11 | 340.00 | |
| **Swift** | | | | | | | | | | All Swift Mark I scopes, with the exception of the 4x15, have Quadraplex reticles and are fog-proof and waterproof. The 4x15 has crosshair reticle and is non-waterproof. |
| 600 4x15 | 4 | 16.2 | — | 2.4 | 11 | ¾ | Int. | 4.7 | 19.98 | |
| 650 4x32 | 4 | 29 | — | 3½ | 12 | 1 | Int. | 9 | 68.00 | |
| 651 4x32 WA | 4 | 37 | — | 3½ | 11¾ | 1 | Int. | 10½ | 76.50 | |
| 653 4x40 WA | 4 | 35½ | — | 3¾ | 12¼ | 1 | Int. | 12 | 89.50 | |
| 654 3-9x32 | 3-9 | 35¾-12¾ | — | 3 | 12¾ | 1 | Int. | 13¾ | 92.50 | |
| 656 3-9x40 WA | 3-9 | 42½-13½ | — | 2¾ | 12¾ | 1 | Int. | 14 | 105.00 | |
| 657 6x40 | 6 | 18 | — | 3¾ | 13 | 1 | Int. | 10 | 78.00 | |
| 658 1½-4½x32 | 1½-4½ | 55-22 | — | 3½ | 12 | 1 | Int. | 13 | 98.00 | |
| **Tasco** | | | | | | | | | | [1]MAG-IV gives one-third more power. [2]Supercon®, fully coated lenses; waterproof, shockproof, fogproof; includes haze filter caps, lifetime warranty. [3]Trajectory-Range Finding scopes. |
| WA 1x20 Wide Angle[2,7] | 1 | 98 | — | 3 | 9¾ | 1 | Int. | 9.5 | 194.95 | |
| WA 1-3.5x20 Wide Angle[2,7] | 1-3.5 | 91-31 | — | 3½ | 9¾ | 1 | Int. | 10.5 | 214.95 | |
| WA 4x40 Wide Angle[2,7] | 4 | 36 | 100 | 3¼ | 12⅝ | 1 | Int. | 12½ | 174.95 | |
| WA 3-9x40 Wide Angle[2,7] | 3-9 | 43½-15 | 178-20 | 3¼ | 12⅝ | 1 | Int. | 11½ | 194.95 | |

**CAUTION:** PRICES CHANGE. CHECK AT GUNSHOP.

# HUNTING, TARGET ■ & VARMINT ■ SCOPES

| Maker and Model | Magn. | Field at 100 Yds (feet) | Relative Bright-ness | Eye Relief (in.) | Length (in.) | Tube Diam. (in.) | W&E Adjust-ments | Weight (ozs.) | Price | Other Data |
|---|---|---|---|---|---|---|---|---|---|---|
| **Tasco** (cont'd.) | | | | | | | | | | |
| WA 2.5x32 Wide Angle[2,7] | 2.5 | 52 | 44 | 3¼ | 12 | 1 | Int. | 9½ | 164.95 | [4]30/30 range finding reticle; rubber covered; built-in mounting rings. Also avail. in wide angle models. [5]Waterproof; anodized finish; ¼-min. click stops; R.F. reticle. [6]Adj., built-in mount; adj. rheostat, polarizer; ½-min. clicks. Avail. to fit Rem. 870, 1100, also with side mounts, in wide angle. [7]World Class Wide Angle®. **Contact Tasco for complete list of models offered.** |
| WA 2-7x32 Wide Angle[2,7] | 2-7 | 56-17 | 256-21 | 3¼ | 11½ | 1 | Int. | 11½ | 194.95 | |
| WA 1¾-5x20 Wide Angle[2,7] | 1.75-5 | 72-24 | 131-16 | 3¼ | 10⅝ | 1 | Int. | 10¾ | 184.95 | |
| RC 3-9x40 WA[2,4,7] | 3-9 | 43½-15 | 178-20 | 3¼ | — | 1 | Int. | 12⅝ | 204.95 | |
| TR 3-12x32 TRF[3] | 3-12 | 34-9 | 112-7 | 3 | 12¼ | 1 | Int. | 13¾ | 129.95 | |
| TR 4-16x40 TRF[3] | 4-16 | 25½-7 | 100-6 | 3 | 14¼ | 1 | Int. | 16¾ | 199.95 | |
| W 4x32[5] | 4 | 28 | 64 | 3¼ | 11¾ | 1 | In.t | 9½ | 66.95 | |
| W 3-12x4 MAG-IV[1] | 3-12 | 34-9 | 178-11 | 3 | 12¾ | 1 | Int. | 13¾ | 139.95 | |
| EU 4x44[8] | 4 | 29 | — | 3 | 12⅜ | 30mm | Int. | 16 | 249.95 | |
| EU 6x44[8] | 6 | 31 | [illegible] | [illegible] | 12¾ | 30mm | Int. | 16 | [illegible] | |
| EU 3-9x44[8] | 3-9 | 41-14 | — | 3 | 13½ | 30mm | Int. | 16.5 | 270.00 | |
| EU 3-12x52[8] | 3-12 | 33-8.5 | — | 3 | 12¼ | 30mm | Int. | 18.5 | 299.95 | |
| IR 4x28P[9] | 4 | 65 | — | 16-25 | 9⅜ | 1 | Int. | 13.5 | 229.95 | |
| SW 2.5-10x32[10] | 2.5-10 | 41-10½ | — | 3 | 11¼ | 1 | Int. | 8.5 | 129.95 | |
| BDIXCFV Battery Dot[6] | 1 | — | — | — | 7½ | — | Int. | 10 | 179.95 | |
| **Thompson/Center** | | | | | | | | | | |
| Lobo 1½ x[1] | 1.5 | 16 | 127 | 11-20 | 7¾ | ⅞ | Int. | 5 | 90.00 | [1]May be used on light to medium recoil guns, including muzzleloaders. Coated lenses, nitrogen filled, lifetime warranty. [2]For heavy recoil guns. Nitrogen filled. Duplex reticle only. Target turrets avail. on 1½x, 3x models. Electra Dot illuminated reticle available in RP 2½x ($35 extra) and RP 3x ($40 extra).[3] Rifle scopes have Electra Dot reticle. [4]Rail model for grooved receivers also available—$165. With Electra Dot reticle. |
| Lobo 3x[1] | 3 | 9 | 49 | 11-20 | 9 | ⅞ | Int. | 6.3 | 95.00 | |
| RP 1½ x[2] | 1.5 | 28 | 177 | 11-20 | 7½ | 1 | Int. | 5.1 | 120.00 | |
| RP 2½x[2] | 2.5 | 15 | 64 | 11-20 | 8½ | 1 | Int. | 6.5 | 120.00 | |
| RP 3x[2] | 3 | 13 | 44 | 11-20 | 8¾ | 1 | Int. | 5.4 | 120.00 | |
| RP 4x[2] | 4 | 10 | 71 | 12-20 | 9¼ | 1 | Int. | 10.4 | 140.00 | |
| TC 4x Rifle[3] | 4 | 29 | 64 | 3.3 | 12⅞ | 1 | Int. | 12.3 | 150.00 | |
| TC 3/9V Rifle[3] | 3-9 | 35.3-13.2 | 177-19 | 3.3 | 12⅞ | 1 | Int. | 15.5 | 220.00 | |
| Short Tube 8630[4] | 4 | 29 | 20 | 3 | 7¾ | 1 | Int. | 10.1 | 155.00 | |
| **Trijicon** | | | | | | | | | | |
| 4x40 | 4 | 38 | 100 | 3 | 12.2 | 1 | Int. | 14.8 | 259.00 | Have self-luminous low-light reticle that glow red in poor light, show black in bright light. All have bullet drop compensator. Bar-dot reticle on 4x, 6x, bar-cross on others. From Armson, Inc. |
| 6x56 | 6 | 24 | 87 | 3 | 14 | 1 | Int. | 20.1 | 299.00 | |
| 1.5-5x32 | 1.5-5 | 50-16 | 79 | 4.5-3.5 | 11.9 | 1 | Int. | 14.0 | 329.00 | |
| 2-7x40 | 2-7 | 62-16 | 79 | 3.3-3 | 11.9 | 1 | Int. | 15.8 | 359.00 | |
| 3-9x56 | 3-9 | 35-14 | 82 | 3.3-3 | 14.1 | 1 | Int. | 21.3 | 389.00 | |
| **Unertl** | | | | | | | | | | |
| ■ 1″ Target | 6,8,10 | 16-10 | 17.6-6.25 | 2 | 21½ | ¾ | Ext. | 21 | 154.00 | [1]Dural ¼ MOA click mounts. Hard coated lenses. Non-rotating objective lens focusing. [2]¼ MOA click mounts. [3]With target mounts. [4]With calibrated head. [5]Same as 1″ Target but without objective lens focusing. [6]Price with ¼ MOA click mounts. [7]With new Posa mounts. [8]Range focus until near rear of tube. Price is with Posa mounts. Magnum clamp. With standard mounts and clamp ring **$266.00.** |
| ■ 1¼″ Target[1] | 8,10,12,14 | 12-16 | 15.2-5 | 2 | 25 | ¾ | Ext. | 21 | 206.00 | |
| ■ 1½″ Target | 8,10,12,14 16,18,20 | 11.5-3.2 | — | 2¼ | 25½ | ¾ | Ext. | 31 | 235.00 | |
| ■ 2″ Target[2] | 8,10,12, 14,16,18, 24,30,36 | 8 | 22.6-2.5 | 2¼ | 26¼ | 1 | Ext. | 44 | 322.00 | |
| ■ Varmint, 1¼∞[3] | 6,8,10,12 | 1-7 | 28-7.1 | 2½ | 19½ | ⅞ | Ext. | 26 | 207.00 | |
| ■ Ultra Varmint, 2″[4] | 8,10 12,15 | 12.6-7 | 39.7-11 | 2½ | 24 | 1 | Ext. | 34 | 301.00 | |
| **Unertl** (cont'd.) | | | | | | | | | | |
| ■ Small Game[5] | 4,6 | 25-17 | 19.4-8.4 | 2¼ | 18 | ¾ | Ext. | 16 | 117.00 | |
| ■ Vulture[6] | 8 | 11.2 | 29 | 3-4 | 15⅝ | 1 | Ext. | 15½ | 231.00 | |
| | 10 | 10.9 | 18½ | — | 16⅛ | | | | | |
| ■ Programmer 200[7] | 8,10,12 14,16,18, 20,24,30,36 | 11.3-4 | 39-1.9 | — | 26½ | 1 | Ext. | 45 | 403.00 | |
| ■ BV-20[8] | 20 | 8 | 4.4 | 4.4 | 17⅞ | 1 | Ext. | 21¼ | 287.00 | |
| **Weatherby** | | | | | | | | | | |
| Mark XXII | 4 | 25 | 50 | 2.5-3.5 | 11¾ | ⅞ | Int. | 9.25 | 85.35 | Lumiplex reticle in all models. Blue-black, non-glare finish. |
| Supreme 1¾-5x20 | 1.7-5 | 66.6-21.4 | — | 3.4 | 10.7 | 1 | Int. | 11 | 190.00 | |
| Supreme 4x34 | 4 | 32 | — | 3.1 | 11⅛ | 1 | Int. | 9.6 | 190.00 | |
| Supreme 2-7x34 | 2.1-6.8 | 59-16 | — | 3.4 | 11¼ | 1 | Int. | 10.4 | 240.00 | |
| Supreme 4x44 | 3.9 | 32 | — | 3 | 12½ | 1 | Int. | 11.6 | 240.00 | |
| Supreme 3-9x44 | 3.1-8.9 | 36-13 | — | 3.5 | 12.7 | 1 | Int. | 11.6 | 280.00 | |
| **Williams** | | | | | | | | | | |
| Twilight Crosshair | 2½ | 32 | 64 | 3¾ | 11¼ | 1 | Int. | 8½ | 115.75 | TNT models |
| Twilight Crosshair | 4 | 29 | 64 | 3½ | 11¾ | 1 | Int. | 9½ | 124.75 | |
| Twilight Crosshair | 2-6 | 45-17 | 256-28 | 3 | 11½ | 1 | Int. | 11½ | 164.65 | |
| Twilight Crosshair | 3-9 | 36-13 | 161-18 | 3 | 12¾ | 1 | Int. | 13½ | 178.00 | |
| **Pistol Scopes** | | | | | | | | | | |
| Twilight 1.5x | 1.5 | 19 | 177 | 18-25 | 8.2 | 1 | Int. | 6.4 | 96.95 | |
| Twilight 2x | 2 | 17.5 | 100 | 18-25 | 8.5 | 1 | Int. | 6.4 | 97.95 | |
| **Zeiss** | | | | | | | | | | |
| Diatal C 4x32 | 4 | 30 | — | 3.5 | 10.6 | 1 | Int. | 11.3 | 326.00 | All scopes have ¼-minute click-stop adjustments. Choice of Z-Plex or fine crosshair reticles. Rubber armored objective bell, rubber eyepiece ring. Lenses have T-Star coating for highest light transmission. Z-Series scopes offered in non-rail tubes with duplex reticles only. Imported from West Germany by Zeiss Optical, Inc. |
| Diatal C 6x32 | 6 | 20 | — | 3.5 | 10.6 | 1 | Int. | 11.3 | 364.00 | |
| Diatal C 10x36 | 10 | 12 | — | 3.5 | 12.7 | 1 | Int. | 14.1 | 423.00 | |
| Diatal Z 4x32 | 4 | 34.5 | — | 3.5 | 10.8 | 1.02 (26mm) | Int. | 10.6 | 325.00 | |
| Diatal Z 6x42 | 6 | 22.9 | — | 3.5 | 12.7 | 1.02 (26mm) | Int. | 13.4 | 375.00 | |
| Diatal Z 8x56 | 8 | 18 | — | 3.5 | 13.8 | 1.02 (26mm) | Int. | 17.6 | 425.00 | |
| Diavari 1.5-4.5 | 1.5-4.5 | 72-27 | — | 3.5 | 11.8 | 1 | Int. | 13.4 | 445.00 | |
| Diavari C 3-9x36 | 3-9 | 36-13 | — | 3.5 | 11.2 | 1 | Int. | 15.2 | 578.00 | |
| Diavari Z 1.5-6 | 1.5-6 | 65.5-22.9 | — | 3.5 | 12.4 | 1.18 (30mm) | Int. | 18.5 | 520.00 | |
| Diavari Z 2.5-10 | 2.5-10 | 41-13.7 | — | 3.5 | 14.4 | 1.18 (30mm) | Int. | 22.8 | 610.00 | |

■ Signifies target and/or varmint scope. Hunting scopes in general are furnished with a choice of reticle—crosshairs, post with crosshairs, tapered or blunt post, or dot crosshairs, etc. The great majority of target and varmint scopes have medium or fine crosshairs but post or dot reticles may be ordered. W—Windage E—Elevation MOA—Minute of angle or 1″ (approx.) at 100 yards, etc.

# SCOPE MOUNTS

| Maker, Model, Type | Adjust. | Scopes | Price | Suitable for |
|---|---|---|---|---|
| **Action Arms** | | | | |
| | No | 1″ split rings. | $32.00 | For UZI, Ruger Mk. II, Mini-14, Win. 94, AR-15, Rem. 870, Ithaca 37. From Action Arms. |
| **Aimpoint** | | | | |
| | No | 1″ | 31.95-47.50 | For many popular revolvers, auto pistols, shotguns, military-style rifles/carbines, sporting rifles. Contact Aimpoint for details. |
| **Armson** | | | | |
| AR-15[1] | No | O.E.G. | 28.95 | [1]Fastens with one nut. [2]Models 181, 182, 183, 184, etc. [3]Claw mount. [4]Claw mount, bolt cover still easily removable. From Armson, Inc. |
| Mini-14[2] | No | O.E.G. | 39.95 | |
| H&K[3] | No | O.E.G. | 54.95 | |
| UZI[4] | No | O.E.G. | 54.95 | |
| **Armsport** | | | | |
| 100 Series[1] | No | 1″ rings. | 9.50 | [1]Weaver-type rings. [2]Weaver-type base; most popular rifles. Made in U.S. From Armsport. |
| 104 22-cal. | No | 1″. | 9.50 | |
| 201 See-Thru | No | 1″. | 11.95 | |
| 1-Piece Base[2] | No | | 4.50 | |
| 2-Piece Base[2] | No | | 2.25 | |
| **B-Square** | | | | |
| Pistols | | | | [1]Clamp-on, blue finish. Stainless finish $59.95. [2]For Bushnell Phantom only. [3]Blue finish; stainless finish $59.95. [4]Clamp-on, for Bushnell Phantom only, blue; stainless finish $49.95. [5]Requires drilling & tapping. [6]No gunsmithing, no sight removal; blue; stainless finish $59.95. [7]Clamp-on. [8]Weaver-style rings. Rings not included with Weaver-type bases. Partial listing of mounts shown here. Contact B-Square for more data. |
| Colt Python[1] | E | 1″ | 49.95 | |
| Dan Wesson Clamp-On[3,8] | E | 1″ | 49.95 | |
| Hi-Standard Victor | W&E | 1″ | 49.95 | |
| Ruger 22 Auto Mono-Mount[4] | No | 1″ | 39.95 | |
| Ruger Single-Six[5] | No | 1″ | 39.95 | |
| T-C Contender | W&E | 1″ | 49.95 | |
| Rifles | | | | B-Square also has mounts for Aimpoint scopes to fit many popular military rifles, shotguns and handguns. Write them for a complete listing. |
| Daisy 717/722 Champion[2] | No | 1″ | 19.95 | |
| Mini-14[6] | W&E | 1″ | 49.95 | |
| Mini-14[7] | W&E | 1″ | 49.95 | |
| M-94 Side Mount | W&E | 1″ | 49.95 | |
| Ruger 77 | W&E | 1″ | 49.95 | |
| SMLE Side Mount | E only | 1″ | 49.95 | |
| T-C Single-Shot Rifle | W&E | 1″ | 49.95 | |
| Rem. Model Seven[8] | No | 1″ | 39.95 | |
| Military | | | | |
| M1-A | W&E | 1″ | 59.95 | |
| AR-15/16 | W&E | 1″ | 49.95 | |
| FN-LAR[8] | E only | 1″ | 99.50 | |
| HK-91/93[8] | E only | 1″ | 69.95 | |
| Shotguns | | | | |
| Rem. 870/1100 | No | 1″ | 39.95 | |
| S&W 1000P | No | 1″ | 39.95 | |
| **Beeman** | | | | |
| Double Adjustable | W&E | 1″ | 24.98 | All grooved receivers and scope bases on all known air rifles and 22-cal. rimfire rifles (½″ to ⅝″—6mm to 15mm). [1]Centerfire rifles. Scope detaches easily, returns to zero. [2]Designed specifically for Krico rifles. |
| Deluxe Ring Mounts | No | 1″ | 21.98 | |
| Professional Mounts | W&E | 1″ | 82.50 | |
| Professional Pivot[1] | W | 1″ | 129.50 | |
| Buehler[2] | W | 1″ | 79.00 | |
| **Buehler** | | | | |
| One Piece (T)[1] | W only | 1″ split rings, 3 heights. | Complete—65.75 | [1]Most popular models. [2]Sako dovetail receivers. [3]15 models. [4]No drilling & tapping. [5]Aircraft alloy, dyed blue or to match stainless; for Colt Diamondback, Python, Trooper, Ruger Blackhawk, Single-Six, Security-Six, S&W K-frame, Dan Wesson. |
| | | 1″ split rings | Rings only—91.50 | |
| | | 26mm split rings, 2 heights | Rings only—48.00 | |
| | | 30mm split rings, 1 height | Rings only—57.75 | |
| One Piece Micro Dial (T)[1] | W&E | | Complete—84.25 | |
| Two Piece (T)[1] | W only | 1″ split rings. | Complete—65.75 | |
| Two Piece Dovetail (T)[2] | W only | 1″ split rings. | Complete—81.00 | |
| One Piece Pistol (T)[3] | W only | 1″ split rings. | Complete—65.75 | |
| One Piece Pistol Stainless (T)[1] | W only | 1″ stainless rings. | Complete—86.00 | |
| One Piece Ruger Mini-14 (T)[4] | W only | 1″ split rings. | Complete—81.00 | |
| One Piece Pistol M83 Blue[4,5] | W only | 1″ split rings. | Complete—75.25 | |
| One Piece Pistol M83 Silver[4,5] | W only | 1″ stainless rings. | Complete—88.00 | |
| **Burris** | | | | |
| Supreme One Piece (T)[1] | W only | 1″ split rings, 3 heights. | 1 piece-base—21.95 | [1]Most popular rifles. Universal, rings, mounts fit Burris. Universal, Redfield, Leupold and Browning bases. Comparable prices. [2]Browning Standard 22 Auto rifle. [3]Most popular rifles. [4]Grooved receivers. [5]Universal dovetail; accept Burris, Universal, Redfield, Leupold rings. For Dan Wesson, S&W, Virginian, Ruger Blackhawk, Win. 94. [6]Medium standard front, extension rear, per pair. Low standard front, extension rear, per pair. [7]Mini scopes, scopes with 2″ bell, for M77R. Selected rings and bases available with matte Safari finish. |
| Trumount Two Piece (T) | W only | 1″ split rings, 3 heights. | 2 piece base—19.95 | |
| Browning Auto Mount[2] | No | ¾″, 1″ split rings. | 17.95 | |
| Sight-Thru Mount[3] | No | 1″ Split rings. | 17.95 | |
| Rings Mounts[4] | No | ¾″, 1″ split rings. | 1″ rings—16.95 | |
| L.E.R. Mount Bases[5] | No | | 19.95 | |
| Extension Rings[6] | No | 1″ scopes. | 33.95 | |
| Ruger Ring Mount[7] | W only | 1″ split rings. | 39.95 | |
| **Bushnell** | | | | |
| Detachable (T) mounts only[1] | W only | 1″ split rings, uses Weaver base. | Rings—15.95 | [1]Most popular rifles. Includes windage adj. [2]V-block bottoms lock to chrome-moly studs seated into two 6-48 holes. Rem. XP-100. [3]Heavy loads in Colt, S&W, Ruger revolvers, Ruger Hawkeye. [4]M94 Win., center dovetail. |
| 22 mount | No | 1″ only. | Rings— 7.95 | |
| All Purpose[2] | No | Phantom. | 19.95 | |
| Rigid[3] | No | Phantom. | 19.95 | |
| 94 Win.[4] | No | Phantom. | 19.95 | |
| **Clearview** | | | | |
| Universal Rings (T)[1] | No | 1″ split rings. | 19.95 | [1]All popular rifles including Sav. 99. Uses Weaver bases. [2]Allows use of open sights. [3]For 22 rimfire rifles, with grooved receivers or bases. [4]Fits 13 models. Broadest view area of the type. [5]Side mount for both M94 and M94-375 Big Bore. |
| Mod 101, & 336[2] | No | 1″ split rings. | 19.95 | |
| Broad-View[4] | No | 1″ | 19.95 | |
| Model 22[3] | No | ¾″, ⅞″, 1″ | 11.95 | |
| 94 Winchester[5] | No | 1″ | 19.95 | |

| Maker, Model, Type | Adjust. | Scopes | Price | Suitable for |
|---|---|---|---|---|
| **Conetrol** | | | | |
| Huntur[1] | W only | 1", 26mm, 26.5mm solid or split rings, 3 heights. | 48.93 | [1]All popular rifles, including metric-drilled foreign guns. Price shown for base, two rings. Matte finish. [2]Gunnur grade has mirror-finished, satin-finish base. Price shown for base, two rings. [3]Custum grade has mirror-finished rings and mirror-finished, contoured base. Price shown for base, 2 rings. [4]Win. 94, Krag, older split-bridge Mannlicher-Schoenauer, Mini-14, M-1 Garand, etc. Prices same as above. [5]For all popular guns with integral mounting provision, including Sako, BSA, Ithacagun, Ruger, H&K and many others. Also for grooved-receiver rimfires and air rifles. Prices same as above. [6]For XP-100, T/C Contender, Colt 6⁄XX, Ruger Blackhawk, S&W. [7]Sculptured 2-piece bases as found on fine custom rifles. Price shown is for base alone. Also available unfinished—**$49.98**. [8]Replaces Ruger rib, positions scope farther back. [9]Horizontally split screw connections; 2 heights. |
| Gunnur[2] | W only | 1", 26mm, 26.5mm solid or split rings, 3 heights. | 59.91 | |
| Custum[3] | W only | 1", 26mm, 26.5mm solid or split rings, 3 heights. | 74.91 | |
| One Piece Side Mount Base[4] | W only | 1", 26mm, 26.5mm solid or split rings, 3 heights. | | |
| Pistol Bases, 2 or 3-ring[6] | W only | 1" scopes | | |
| Fluted Bases[7] | W only | Standard Conetrol rings | 74.97 | |
| Ruger No. 1 Base[8] | No | 1", 26mm, 26.5mm solid or split rings. | NA | |
| 30mm Rings[9] | — | 30mm | 74.94 | |
| **EAW** | | | | |
| Quick Detachable Top Mount | W&E | 1"/26mm | 150.00 | Most popular rifles. Elevation adjusted with variable-height sub-bases for rear ring. Imported by Paul Jaeger, Inc., Kahles of America. |
| | W&E | 1"/26mm with front extension ring. | 155.00 | |
| | W&E | 30mm | 160.00 | |
| | W&E | 30mm with front extension ring. | 165.00 | |
| **Griffin & Howe** | | | | |
| Standard Double Lever (S). | No | 1" or 26mm split rings. | 175.00 | All popular models (Garand $295). All rings $65. Top ejection rings available. |
| **Holden** | | | | |
| Wide Ironsighter® | No | 1" Split rings. | 21.36 | [1]Most popular rifles including Ruger Mini-14, H&R M700, and muzzleloaders. Rings have oval holes to permit use of iron sights. [2]For 1" dia. scopes. [3]For ¾" or ⅞" dia. scopes. [4]For 1" dia. extended eye relief scopes. [5]702—Browning A-Bolt; 709—Marlin 39A. [6]732—Ruger 77/22 R&RS, No. 1 Ranch Rifle; 777 fits Ruger 77R, RS. Both 732, 777 fit Ruger integral bases. |
| Ironsighter Center Fire[1] | No | 1" Split rings. | 21.36 | |
| Ironsighter S-94 | No | 1" split rings | 26.46 | |
| Ironsighter 22 cal. rimfire | | | | |
| Model #500[2] | No | 1" Split rings. | 11.71 | |
| Model #600[3] | No | ⅞" Split rings also fits ¾". | 11.71 | |
| Series #700[5] | No | 1", split rings | 21.36 | |
| Model 732, 777[6] | No | 1", split rings | 49.95 | |
| Ironsighter Handguns[4] | No | 1" Split rings. | 23.40 | |
| **Jaeger** | | | | |
| QD, with windage (S) | W only | 1", 3 heights. | 190.00 | All popular models. From Paul Jaeger, Inc. |
| **Kimber** | | | | |
| Standard[1] | No | 1", split rings | 48.90 | [1]High rings; low rings—**$45.00**; both only for Kimber rifles. [2]For Kimber rifles only. Also avail. for Mauser (FN,98) Rem. 700, 721, 722, 725, Win. M70, Mark X. [3]Vertically split rings; for Kimber and other popular CF rifles. |
| Double Lever[2] | No | 1", split rings | 69.00 | |
| Non-Detachable[3] | No | 1", split rings | 48.00 | |
| **Kris Mounts** | | | | |
| Side-Saddle[1] | No | 1", 26mm split rings. | 11.98 | [1]One-piece mount for Win. 94. [2]Most popular rifles and Ruger. [3]Blackhawk revolver. Mounts have oval hole to permit use of iron sights. |
| Two Piece (T)[2] | No | 1", 26mm split rings. | 7.98 | |
| One Piece (T)[3] | No | 1", 26mm split rings. | 11.98 | |
| **KWIK MOUNT** | | | | |
| Shotgun Mount | No | 1" | 49.95 | Wrap-around design; no gunsmithing required. Models for Browning A-5 12 ga., Rem. 870/1100, S&W 916, Savage 67 12 ga., Mossberg 500, Ithaca 37 & 51 12 ga., S&W 1000/3000, Win. 1400. From KenPatable Ent. |
| **Kwik-Site** | | | | |
| KS-See-Thru[1] | No | 1" | 19.95 | [1]Most rifles. Allows use of iron sights. [2]22-cal. rifles with grooved receivers. Allows use of iron sights. [3]Model 94, 94 Big Bore. No drilling or tapping. [4]Most rifles. One-piece solid construction. Use on Weaver bases. 32mm obj. lens or larger. [5]Non-see-through model; for grooved receivers. |
| KS-22 See-Thru[2] | No | 1" | 17.95 | |
| KS-W94[3] | Yes | 1" | 39.95 | |
| KSM Bench Rest[4] | No | 1" | 27.95 | |
| KS-WEV | No | 1" | 19.95 | |
| KS-WEV-HIGH | No | 1" | 19.95 | |
| KS-T22 1"[5] | No | 1" | 17.95 | |
| **Leatherwood** | | | | |
| M-1A, M-14 | W only | ART II, ART/MPC (Weaver rings) | 75.00 | [1]Popular bolt actions. [2]With M-16 adaptor. [3]Adaptor base for H&K rail mounts. |
| AR-15, M-16 | No | As above | 17.95 | |
| FN-FAL | No | As above | 175.00 | |
| SSG | No | As above | 50.00 | |
| One-piece Bridge[1] | No | As above | 9.95 | |
| Night Vision Adaptor[2] | No | Night vision scopes | 37.50 | |
| H&K Adaptor[3] | No | ART II, ART/MPC (Weaver rings) | 59.95 | |
| **Leupold** | | | | |
| STD Bases (T)[1] | W only | One piece base (dovetail front, windage rear) | Base—19.70 | [1]Most popular rifles. Also available in 2-piece version, same price. [2]Ruger revolvers, Thompson/Center Contender, S&W K&N Frame revolvers and Colt .45 "Gold Cup" N.M. Available with silver or blue finish. [3]Reversible extended front; regular rear rings, in two heights. |
| STD Handgun mounts[2] Base and two rings[2] | No | 1" | 50.20 | |
| STD Rings | | 1", 3 ring heights interchangeable with other mounts of similar design. | 1" rings—28.40 | |
| Extension-Ring Sets[3] | | 1" | 39.30 | |
| **Marlin** | | | | |
| One Piece QD (T) | No | 1" split rings. | 12.10 | Most Marlin lever actions. |
| **Millett** | | | | |
| Black Onyx Smooth | | 1" Low, medium, high | 26.95 | Rem. 40X, 700, 722, 725, Ruger 77 (round top) Weatherby, etc. FN Mauser, FN Brownings, Colt 57, Interarms MkX, Parker-Hale, Sako (round receiver), many others. [1]Fits Win. M70, 70XTR, 670, Browning BBR. |
| Chaparral Engraved | | Engraved | 39.95 | |
| Universal Two Piece Bases | | | | |
| 700 Series | W only | Two-piece bases | 20.95 | |
| FN Series | W only | Two-piece bases | 20.95 | |
| 70 Series[1] | W only | 1", two-piece bases | 20.95 | |

# SCOPE MOUNTS

| Maker, Model, Type | Adjust. | Scopes | Price | Suitable for |
|---|---|---|---|---|
| **Redfield** | | | | [1]Low, med. & high, split rings. Reversible extension front rings for 1". 2-piece bases for Sako. Colt Sauer bases $39.85. [2]Split rings for grooved 22's. See-thru mounts $16.15. [3]Used with MP scopes for: S&W K or N frame. XP-100, Colt J or I frame. T/C Contender, Colt autos, black powder rifles. [4]One- and two-piece aluminum base; three ring heights. |
| JR-SR(T)[1] | W only | ¾", 1", 26mm. | JR—19.80-26.95 SR—25.85-39.85 | |
| Ring (T)[2] | No | ¾" and 1". | | |
| Double Dovetail MP[3] | No | 1", split rings. | 58.40 | |
| Midline Base & Rings[4] | No | 1" | 14.25 | |
| See-Thru Rings[4] | No | 1" | 16.15 | |
| **S&K** | | | | [1]1903, A3, M1 Carbine, Lee Enfield #1, MK. III, #4, #5, M1917, M98 Mauser, FN Auto, AR-15, AR-180, M-14, M-1, Ger. K-43, Mini-14, M1-A, Krag, AKM, AK-47, Win. 94. [2]Most popular rifles already drilled and tapped. Horizontally and vertically split rings, matte or high gloss. |
| Insta-Mount (T) base only[1] | W only | Use S&K rings only. | 20.00-99.00 | |
| Conventional rings and bases[2] | W only | 1" split rings. | 50.00 | |
| SKulptured Bases, Rings[2] | W only | 1", 26mm, 30mm | From 50.00 | |
| **SSK Industries** | | | | Custom installation using from two to four rings (included). For T/C Contender, most 22 auto pistols. Ruger and other S.A. revolvers, Ruger, Dan Wesson, S&W, Colt D.A. revolvers. Black or white finish. |
| T'SOB | No | 1" | 45.00-145.00 | |
| **Sako** | | | | Sako, or any rifle using Sako action, 3 heights available, Stoeger, importer. |
| QD Dovetail | W only | 1" only. | 99.95 | |
| **Simmons** | | | | Weaver-type bases. #1401 (low) also in high style (#1403). #1406, 1408 for grooved receiver 22s. Bases avail. for most popular rifles; one- and two-piece styles. Most popular rifles; 1-piece bridge mount. Ring sets—$39.00. [1]For 22 RF rifles. |
| 1401 | No | 1" | 7.00 | |
| 1406 | No | 1" | 7.00 | |
| 1408 | No | 1" | 16.00 | |
| All Steel Tip-Off[1] | No | 1" | 7.00 | |
| **Tasco** | | | | [1]Many popular rifles. [2]For 22s with grooved receivers. [3]Most popular rifles. [4]Most popular rifles. [5]"Quick Peep" 1" ring mount; fits all 22-cal. rifles with grooved receivers. [6]For Ruger Mini-14; also in brushed aluminum. [7]Side mount for Win. 94. [8]Side mount rings and base for Win. 94 in 30-30, 375 Win. [9]Avail. for most rifles. Steel or aluminum rings. |
| 791 and 793 series[1] | No | 1", regular or high. | 9.95 | |
| 797[2] | No | Split rings. | 9.95 | |
| 798 Quick Peep[3] | No | 1" only. | 9.95 | |
| 799[5] | No | 1" only | 9.95 | |
| 885 BK[8] | No | 1" only | 23.95 | |
| 895[7] | No | 1" only | 5.95 | |
| 896[6] | No | 1" only | 39.95 | |
| 800L Series (with base)[4] | No | 1" only. Rings and base. | 13.95 | |
| World Class[9] | Yes | 1", 26mm, 30mm | Bases—29.95 Rings—39.95 | |
| **Thompson/Center** | | | | [1]All Contenders except vent. rib. [2]T/C rail mount scopes; all Contenders except vent. rib. [3]All S&W K and Combat Masterpiece, Hi-Way Patrolman, Outdoorsman, 22 Jet, 45 Target 1955. Requires drilling, tapping. [4]Blackhawk, Super Blackhawk, Super Single-Six. Requires drilling, tapping. [5]45 or 50 cal.; replaces rear sight. [6]Rail mount scopes; 54-cal. Hawken, 50, 54, 56-cal. Renegade. Replaces rear sight. [7]Cherokee 32 or 45 cal., Seneca 36 or 45 cal. Replaces rear sight. |
| Contender 9746[1] | No | T/C Lobo | 9.95 | |
| Contender 9741[2] | No | 2½, 4 RP | 9.95 | |
| Contender 7410 | No | Bushnell Phantom 1.3, 2.5x | 9.95 | |
| S&W 9747[3] | No | Lobo or RP | 9.95 | |
| Ruger 9748[4] | No | Lobo or RP | 9.95 | |
| Hawken 9749[5] | No | Lobo or RP | 9.95 | |
| Hawken/Renegade 9754[6] | No | Lobo or RP | 9.95 | |
| Cherokee/Seneca[7] | No | Lobo or RP | 9.95 | |
| **Unertl** | | | | [1]Unertl target or varmint scopes. [2]Any with regular dovetail scope bases. |
| Posa (T)[1] | Yes | ¾", 1" scopes. | Per set 70.00 | |
| ¼ Click (T)[2] | Yes | ¾", 1" target scopes. | Per set 66.00 | |
| **Weaver** | | | | [1]Nearly all modern rifles. Extension rings, 1" $23.45. [2]Most modern big bore rifles. [3]22s with grooved receivers. [4]Same. Adapter for Lee Enfield—$9.65. [5]⅞"—$13.45. 1" See-Thru extension—$23.45. [6]Colt Officer's Model, Python, Ruger B'hawk, Super B'hawk, Security Six, 22 Autos, Mini-14, Ruger Redhawk, S&W N frames. No drilling or tapping. Also in stainless steel—$58.95. |
| Detachable Mount (T & S)[1] | No | ¾", ⅞", 1" 26mm | 22.00 | |
| Pivot Mount (T)[2] | No | 1" | 29.81 | |
| Tip-Off (T)[3] | No | ¾", ⅞". | 13.31 | |
| Tip-Off (T)[4] | No | 1", two-piece. | 22.44 | |
| See-Thru Mount[5] | No | 1" Split rings ⅞" tip-off Fits all top mounts. | 22.00 15.62 | |
| Mount Base System[6] | No | 1" | 59.51 | |
| **Wideview** | | | | Models for many popular rifles—$18.95. Low ring, high ring and grooved receiver types—$7.95. From Wideview Scope Mount Corp. |
| WSM-22 | No | 1" | 10.95 | |
| WSM-94 | No | 1" | 18.95 | |
| WSM-94AE | No | 1" | 21.86 | |
| **Williams** | | | | [1]Most rifles, Br. S.M.L.E. (round rec) $3.85 extra. [2]Same. [3]Most rifles including Win. 94 Big Bore. [4]Most rifles. [5]Many modern rifles. [6]Most popular rifles. |
| Offset (S)[1] | No | ⅞", 1", 26mm solid, split or extension rings. | 52.95 | |
| QC (T)[2] | No | Same. | 41.60 | |
| QC (S)[3] | No | Same. | 41.60 | |
| Low Sight-Thru[4] | No | 1", ⅞", sleeves $1.80. | 17.75 | |
| Sight-Thru[5] | No | 1", ⅞", sleeves $1.80. | 17.75 | |
| Streamline[6] | No | 1" (bases form rings). | 18.70 | |

(S)—Side Mount  (T)Top Mount  22mm—.866"  25.4mm = 1"1.024"  26.5mm = 1.045"  30mm = 1.81"

Left: S&K is now offering these new vertically split rings on their SKulptured bases; they'll fit most popular rifles. Right: SSK Industries T'SOB handgun mount uses two to four rings to anchor the scope.

**CAUTION:** PRICES CHANGE. CHECK AT GUNSHOP.

# SPOTTING SCOPES

**APOLLO 20 X 50 BOBCAT**—50mm objective lens. Field of view at 1000 yds. is about 100 ft. Length 9.4″, weight 17.5 oz. Tripod socket.
- **Price:** About . . . . . . . . . . . . . . . . . . . . . . . . . . . . . . . . . . . . . . **$154.95**
- Compact tripod, about . . . . . . . . . . . . . . . . . . . . . . . . . . . . . **$20.00**

**BAUSCH & LOMB DISCOVERER**—15X to 60X zoom, 60mm objective. Constant focus throughout range. Field at 1000 yds. 40 ft (60X), 156 ft. (15X). Comes with lens caps. Length 17½″, wgt. 48½ oz.
- **Price:** . . . . . . . . . . . . . . . . . . . . . . . . . . . . . . . . . . . . . . . . . . **$465.95**

**BUSHNELL SPACEMASTER**—60MM objective. Field at 1000 yds., 158′ to 37′. Relative brightness, 5.76. Wgt., 36 oz. Length closed, 11⅝″. prism focusing.
- **Price:** Without eyepiece . . . . . . . . . . . . . . . . . . . . . . . . . . . **$277.95**
- 15X, 20X, 40X and 60X eyepieces, each . . . . . . . . . . . . . . . . . . . **$49.95**
- 22X wide angle eyepiece . . . . . . . . . . . . . . . . . . . . . . . . . **$59.95**

**BUSHNELL SPACEMASTER 45°**—Same as above except: Wgt., 43 oz., length closed 13″. Eyepiece at 45°, without eyepiece.
- **Price:** . . . . . . . . . . . . . . . . . . . . . . . . . . . . . . . . . . . . . . . . . . **$349.95**

**BUSHNELL ZOOM SPACEMASTER**—15X-45X zoom. 60mm objective. Field at 1000 yards 130′-65′. Relative brightness 9-1.7. Wgt. 36 oz., length 11⅝″. Shooter's stand tripod, carrying case.
- **Price:** . . . . . . . . . . . . . . . . . . . . . . . . . . . . . . . . . . . . . . . . . . **$452.95**

**BUSHNELL SENTRY®**—50mm objective. Field at 1000 yards 120′-45′. Relative brightness 6.25. Wgt., 25½ oz., length 12⅝″, without eyepiece.
- **Price:** . . . . . . . . . . . . . . . . . . . . . . . . . . . . . . . . . . . . . . . . . . **$139.95**
- 20X, 32X and 48X eyepieces, each . . . . . . . . . . . . . . . . . . . . . **$49.95**

**BUSHNELL ZOOM SPOTTER**—40mm objective. 9X-30X var. power.
- **Price:** . . . . . . . . . . . . . . . . . . . . . . . . . . . . . . . . . . . . . . . . . . **$99.95**

Bushnell Zoom Spotter

**BUSHNELL COMPETITOR**—40mm objective, 20X. Prismatic. Field at 1000 yards 140′. Minimum focus 33′. Length 9.5″, weight 14.5 oz.
- **Price:** With tripod . . . . . . . . . . . . . . . . . . . . . . . . . . . . . . . . **$99.95**

**BUSHNELL TROPHY**—12X-36X zoom. Rubber armored, prismatic. 50mm objective. Field at 1000 yards 150′ to 80′. Minimum focus 20′. Length with caps 13⅝″, weight 38 oz.
- **Price:** With tripod and carrying case . . . . . . . . . . . . . . . . . . . . . **$391.95**
- Interchangeable eyepieces—20x, 32x, 48x, each . . . . . . . . . . . . **$49.95**
- 12-36X zoom eyepiece . . . . . . . . . . . . . . . . . . . . . . . . . . . . . **$125.95**

**COUGAR MODEL 776**—60mm objective, 20x, 30x, 40x, 50x eyepieces. Rotating head for straight or 45° viewing. Field at 1,000 yds. 131 ft. (20x), 94 ft. (30x), 65 ft. (40x), 52 ft. (50x). Focus by rotating the objective barrel. Length 12¾″, wgt. 4 lbs. From Cougar Optics.
- **Price:** Without eyepiece . . . . . . . . . . . . . . . . . . . . . . . . . . . . . **$241.50**
- **Price:** Eyepiece . . . . . . . . . . . . . . . . . . . . . . . . . . . . . . . . . . **$36.50**

**DICKSON 270**—20x to 60x variable, 60mm objective, achromatic coated objective lens, complete with metal table tripod with 5 vertical and horizontal adjustments. Turret type, 20x, 30x, 40x 60x
- **Price:** . . . . . . . . . . . . . . . . . . . . . . . . . . . . . . . . . . . . . . . . . . **$249.95**

**DICKSON 274A**—20x to 60x variable zoom. 60mm achromatic coated objective lens, complete with adjustable metal table tripod.
- **Price:** . . . . . . . . . . . . . . . . . . . . . . . . . . . . . . . . . . . . . . . . . . **$150.00**

**DICKSON 274B**—As above but with addition of 4 × 16 Finder Scope.
- **Price:** . . . . . . . . . . . . . . . . . . . . . . . . . . . . . . . . . . . . . . . . . . **$161.95**

**KOWA TS-1-45**—Off-set-type. 60mm objective, 25X, fixed and zoom interchangeable eyepieces; field at 1000 yds. 93′; relative brightness 5.8; length 16.5″; wgt. 47.8 oz. Lens shade and caps. Straight-type also available; similar specs **($284.98)**.
- **Price:** . . . . . . . . . . . . . . . . . . . . . . . . . . . . . . . . . . . . . . . . . . **$349.95**
- **Price:** 25X eyepiece . . . . . . . . . . . . . . . . . . . . . . . . . . . . . . . . **$49.95**
- **Price:** 20X eyepiece (wide angle) . . . . . . . . . . . . . . . . . . . . . . **$64.95**
- **Price:** 15X eyepiece . . . . . . . . . . . . . . . . . . . . . . . . . . . . . . . . **$59.95**
- **Price:** 105X eyepiece . . . . . . . . . . . . . . . . . . . . . . . . . . . . . . . **$69.95**

**KOWA TSN-1-45°**—Off-set-type. 77mm objective, 25X, fixed and zoom eyepieces; field at 1000 yds. 94′; relative brightness 9.6; length 15.4″; wgt. 48.8 oz. Lens shade and caps. Straight-type also available with similar specs and prices.
- **Price:** . . . . . . . . . . . . . . . . . . . . . . . . . . . . . . . . . . . . . . . . . . **$499.95**
- **Price:** 20X-60X zoom eyepiece . . . . . . . . . . . . . . . . . . . . . . . **$124.95**
- **Price:** 20X eyepiece (wide angle) . . . . . . . . . . . . . . . . . . . . . **$99.95**
- **Price:** 25X, 40X eyepiece . . . . . . . . . . . . . . . . . . . . . . . . . . . **$74.95**

**KOWA TS-3**—Straight-type. 50mm objective, 20X, standard size, fixed and zoom eyepieces; field at 1000 yds. 120′; relative brightness 6.3; length 13.4″; wgt. 29.4 oz. Lens shade and caps.
- **Price:** . . . . . . . . . . . . . . . . . . . . . . . . . . . . . . . . . . . . . . . . . . **$179.95**
- **Price:** 20X-40X zoom eyepiece . . . . . . . . . . . . . . . . . . . . . . . **$119.95**
- **Price:** 20X eyepiece . . . . . . . . . . . . . . . . . . . . . . . . . . . . . . . . **$49.95**
- **Price:** 16X eyepiece (wide angle) . . . . . . . . . . . . . . . . . . . . . **$64.95**
- **Price:** 12X eyepiece . . . . . . . . . . . . . . . . . . . . . . . . . . . . . . . . **$59.95**
- **Price:** 32X, 48X eyepiece . . . . . . . . . . . . . . . . . . . . . . . . . . . **$54.95**
- **Price:** 84X eyepiece . . . . . . . . . . . . . . . . . . . . . . . . . . . . . . . . **$69.95**

**KOWA TS-4-45**—Off-set-type. 50mm objective, 20X, compact size (measures 12.6″, wgt. 37 oz.). Other specs are same as Model TS-3. Uses TS-3 eyepieces.
- **Price:** . . . . . . . . . . . . . . . . . . . . . . . . . . . . . . . . . . . . . . . . . . **$279.95**

**KOWA TS-8**—Straight-type. 50mm objective, 20X, compact model; fixed power eyepieces; field at 1000 yds. 157′; relative brightness 6.3; length 9.25″; wgt. 23.3 oz. Lens caps.
- **Price:** . . . . . . . . . . . . . . . . . . . . . . . . . . . . . . . . . . . . . . . . . . **$139.95**
- **Price:** 10X, 15X eyepieces, each . . . . . . . . . . . . . . . . . . . . . . . **$34.95**

**KOWA TS-9C**—Straight-type. 50mm objective, 20X compact model; fixed power eyepieces; objective focusing down to 17 ft.; field at 1000 yds. 157′; relative brightness 6.3; length 9.65″; wgt. 22.9 oz. Lens caps.
- **Price:** . . . . . . . . . . . . . . . . . . . . . . . . . . . . . . . . . . . . . . . . . . **$115.95**
- **Price:** 15X, 20X eyepieces, each . . . . . . . . . . . . . . . . . . . . . . . **$24.95**
- **Price:** As above, rubber armored (TS-9R) . . . . . . . . . . . . . . . . **$129.95**

**OPTEX MODEL 420**—15x-60x-60 Zoom; 18″ overall; weighs 4 lbs. with folding tripod (included). From Southern Precision Instrument
- **Price:** . . . . . . . . . . . . . . . . . . . . . . . . . . . . . . . . . . . . . . . . . . **$135.00**

**OPTEX MODEL 421**—15x-45x-50 Zoom; 18″ over-all; weighs 4 lbs. with folding tripod (included). From Southern Precision Instrument
- **Price:** . . . . . . . . . . . . . . . . . . . . . . . . . . . . . . . . . . . . . . . . . . **$110.00**

**OPTEX MODEL 422**—8x-25x-30 Zoom. Armour coated; 18″ over-all; weighs 3 lbs. with tripod (included). From Southern Precision Instrument
- **Price:** . . . . . . . . . . . . . . . . . . . . . . . . . . . . . . . . . . . . . . . . . . **$100.00**

**OPTEX MODEL 423**—Same as Model 422 except 12x-40x-40
- **Price:** . . . . . . . . . . . . . . . . . . . . . . . . . . . . . . . . . . . . . . . . . . **$120.00**

**REDFIELD 30x CAT SPOTTER**—60mm objective, 30x. Field of view 9.5 ft. at 100 yds. Uses catadioptric lens system. Length over-all is 7.5″, weight is 11.5 oz. Eye relief 0.5″. Also comes in camo armor coating.
- **Price:** . . . . . . . . . . . . . . . . . . . . . . . . . . . . . . . . . . . . . . . . . . **$411.05**
- **Price:** With Armor Camouflage . . . . . . . . . . . . . . . . . . . . . . . **$424.95**

**REDFIELD REGAL II & III**—Regal II has 60mm objective, interchangeable 25x and 18x-40x zoom eyepieces. Regal III has 50mm objective, interchangeable 20x and 15x-32x zoom eyepieces, and is shorter and lighter. Field at 1000 yds.—Regal II, 125 ft. @ 25x; Regal III, 157 ft. @ 20x. Both have dual rotation of eyepiece and scope body. With aluminum carrying case, tripod.
- **Price:** Regal II . . . . . . . . . . . . . . . . . . . . . . . . . . . . . . . . . . . . **$521.95**
- **Price:** Regal III . . . . . . . . . . . . . . . . . . . . . . . . . . . . . . . . . . . **$508.95**

**REDFIELD REGAL IV & V**—Conventional straight thru viewing. Regal IV has 60mm objective and interchangeable 25x and 20x-60x zoom eyepieces. Regal V has 50mm objective and 20x and 16x-48x zoom eyepieces and is shorter and lighter. Field at 1000 yds.—Regal IV, 94 ft. @ 25x, Regal V, 118 ft. @ 20x. Both come with tripod and aluminum carrying case.
- **Price:** Regal IV . . . . . . . . . . . . . . . . . . . . . . . . . . . . . . . . . . . **$546.95**
- **Price:** Regal V . . . . . . . . . . . . . . . . . . . . . . . . . . . . . . . . . . . . **$490.95**

**REDFIELD REGAL VI**—60mm objective, 25x fixed and 20x-60x interchangeable eyepieces. Has 45° angled eyepiece, front-mounted focus ring, 180° tube rotation. Field at 1000 yds., 94 ft. @ 25x; length, 12¼″; weight, 40 oz. Comes with tripod, aluminum carrying case.
- **Price:** Regal VI . . . . . . . . . . . . . . . . . . . . . . . . . . . . . . . . . . . **$603.95**

**SIMMONS 1210**—50mm objective, 25x standard, 16, 20, 40, 48, 16-36x zoom eyepieces available. Field at 1000 yds. 22 ft. Length 12.2″, weight 32 oz. Comes with tripod, 3x finder scope with crosshair.
- **Price:** About . . . . . . . . . . . . . . . . . . . . . . . . . . . . . . . . . . . . . . **$150.75**
- **Price:** Fixed eyepieces . . . . . . . . . . . . . . . . . . . . . . . . . . . . . . **$45.50**
- **Price:** Zoom eyepiece . . . . . . . . . . . . . . . . . . . . . . . . . . . . . . **$113.00**

**SIMMONS 1215**—50mm objective, 25x standard, 16, 20, 40, 48, 16-36x zoom eyepieces available. Field at 1000 yds. 22 ft. Length 12.2″, weight 48 oz. Comes with tripod, 3x finder scope with crosshair. Green camo rubber.
- **Price:** About . . . . . . . . . . . . . . . . . . . . . . . . . . . . . . . . . . . . . . **$207.00**
- **Price:** Fixed eyepieces . . . . . . . . . . . . . . . . . . . . . . . . . . . . . . **$45.50**
- **Price:** Zoom eyepiece . . . . . . . . . . . . . . . . . . . . . . . . . . . . . . **$113.00**

**CAUTION:** PRICES CHANGE. CHECK AT GUNSHOP.

**SIMMONS 1220**—60mm objective, 25x standard, 16, 20, 40, 48, 16-36x zoom eyepieces available. Field at 1000 yds. 22 ft. Length 13.8", weight 44 oz. with tripod (included). Has 3x finder scope with crosshairs.

Price: About ............................................. **$253.00**
Price: Fixed eyepieces ................................. **$45.50**
Price: Zoom eyepiece ................................... **$113.00**

**SWAROVSKI HABICHT HAWK 30x75S TELESCOPE**—75mm objective, 30X. Field at 1,000 yds. 90ft. Minimum, focusing distance 90 ft. Length: closed 13 in., extended 20½". Weight: 47 oz. Precise recognition of smallest details even at dusk. Leather or rubber covered, with caps and carrying case.

Price: ................................................. **$895.00**

Same as above with short range supplement. Minimum focusing distance 24 to 30 ft. ...................................... **$935.00**

**SWAROVSKI 25-40X75 TELESCOPE**—75mm objective, variable power from 25x to 40x with a field of 98 ft. (25x) and 72 ft. (40x). Minimum focusing distance 66 ft. (26 ft. with close focus model). Length closed is 11", extended 15.5"; weight 46 oz. Rubber covered.

Price: Standard ....................................... **$880.00**
Price: Close focus model .............................. **910.00**

**SWIFT TELEMASTER M841**—60mm objective. 15X to 60X variable power. Field at 1000 yards 160 feet (15X) to 40 feet (60X). Wgt. 3.4 lbs. 17.6" over-all.

Price: ................................................. **$399.95**
Tripod for above ..................................... **$79.95**
Photo adapter ........................................ **$16.00**
Case for above ....................................... **$57.00**

**TASCO 39T COMPACT SPOTTING SCOPE**—50mm objective, 20X. With BAK-4 prism. Wgt. 3 lbs. With tripod.

Price: ................................................. **$179.95**

**TASCO 34T RUBBER COVERED SPOTTING SCOPE**—50mm objective. 25X. Field at 1000 yds. 136 ft. With tripod and built-in tripod adapter. Weight 29.9 oz. Length 13¾".

Price: ................................................. **$199.95**

**TASCO 21T SPOTTING SCOPE**—40mm objective. 20X. Field at 1000 yds. 136 ft. With Tasco 8P tripod. Weight 18.2 oz. Length 12⅜".

Price: ................................................. **$109.95**

**TASCO 25TPC RUBBER COVERED SPOTTING SCOPE**—60mm objective. 25X. Field at 1000 yds. 94 ft. Prismatic. With Tasco 25P deluxe tripod, olive green to match rubber covering. Weight 38.3 oz. Length 11½".

Price: ................................................. **$499.95**

**TASCO 34TZ RUBBER COVERED**—50mm objective. 18-36X zoom. Comes with tripod and built-in tripod adapter. Weight 29.9 oz., length 13¾".

Price: ................................................. **$239.95**

**UNERTL "FORTY-FIVE"**—54mm objective. 20X (single fixed power). Field at 100 yds. 10'10"; eye relief 1"; focusing range infinity to 33 ft. Wgt. about 32 oz.; over-all length 15¾". With lens covers.

Price: With multi-layer lens coating .................... **$295.00**
Price: With mono-layer magnesium coating ............. **$225.00**

**UNERTL RIGHT ANGLE**—63.5mm objective, 24X. Field at 100 yds., 7 ft. Relative brightness, 6.96. Eye relief, ½". Wgt., 41 oz. Length closed, 19". Push-pull and screw-focus eyepiece. 16X and 32X eyepieces **$38.00** each.

Price: ................................................. **$265.00**

Weatherby Sightmaster 20-60x

Tasco World Class 9000T

Unertl 20x Straight Prismatic

Redfield Regal II

Bushnell Trophy Zoom

**SWIFT M844A COMMANDO PRISMATIC SPOTTING SCOPE/ TELEPHOTO LENS, MK.II**—60mm objective. Comes with 20X eyepiece; 15X, 30X, 40X, 50X, 60X available. Built-in sunshade. Field at 1000 yds. with 20X, 120 ft. Length 13.7", wgt. 2.1 lbs.

Price: ................................................. **$260.00**

**SWIFT M847 SCANNER**—50mm objective. Comes with 25x eyepiece; 20x, 30x, 35x eyepieces available. Field of view at 1000 yds. is 112 ft. (25x). Length 13.6", weight 23 oz.

Price: ................................................. **$139.50**
Each additional eyepiece ............................. **$27.50**
Tubular case ......................................... **$25.00**
Tripod ............................................... **$79.95**

**SWIFT M700 SCOUT**—9X-30X, 30mm spotting scope. Length 15½", weighs 2.1 lbs. Field of 204 ft. (9X), 60 ft. (30X).

Price: ................................................. **$87.00**

**TASCO WORLD CLASS 9000T**—60mm objective, 15-60x zoom. Field at 1,000 yd. 160 ft. (15x), 40 ft. (60x). Has tripod mount socket, sun shade, screw-on lens covers. Comes with case, camera adapter, tripod.

Price: ................................................. **$519.95**
Price: Without tripod ................................. **$459.95**

**UNERTL STRAIGHT PRISMATIC**—Same as Unertl Right Angle except: straight eyepiece and wgt. of 40 oz.

Price: ................................................. **$225.00**

**UNERTL 20X STRAIGHT PRISMATIC**—54mm objective. 20X. Field at 100 yds., 8.5 ft. Relative brightness, 6.1. Eye relief, ½". Wgt. 36 oz. Length closed, 13½". Complete with lens covers.

Price: ................................................. **$190.00**

**UNERTL TEAM SCOPE**—100mm objective. 15X, 24X, 32X eyepieces. Field at 100 yds. 13 to 7.5 ft. Relative brightness, 39.06 to 9.79. Eye relief, 2" to 1½". Weight 13 lbs. 29⅞" overall. Metal tripod, yoke and wood carrying case furnished (total weight, 67 lbs.)

Price: ................................................. **$975.00**

**WEATHERBY**—60mm objective, 20X-60X zoom

Price: Scope only .................................... **$323.95**
Price: Scope and tripod .............................. **$379.95**
Price: Tripod for above .............................. **$69.95**

**CAUTION:** PRICES CHANGE. CHECK AT GUNSHOP.

# Directory of the Arms Trade

## INDEX TO THE DIRECTORY

## AMMUNITION (Commercial)

Activ Industries, Inc., P.O. Box 238, Kearneysville, WV 25430/304-725-0451 (shotshells only)
Alberts Corp., 519 East 19th St., Paterson, NJ 07514/201-684-1676
BBM Corp., 221 Interstate Dr., West Springfield, MA 01089/413-737-3118 (45 ACP shotshell)
Bingham Ltd., 1775-C Wilwat Dr., Norcross, GA 30093
C.W. Cartridge Co., 71 Hackensack St., Wood-Ridge, NJ 07075/201-438-5111 (Sharps combustible cartridges)
Cascade Cartridge Inc., (See Omark)
Dynamit Nobel of America, Inc., 105 Stonehurst Court, Northvale, NJ 07647/201-767-1660(RWS)
Eley-Kynoch, ICI-America, Wilmington, DE 19897/302-575-3000
Estate Cartridge Inc., P.O. Box 3702, Conroe, TX 77305 (shotshell)
Federal Cartridge Co., 2700 Foshay Tower, Minneapolis, MN 55402/612-333-8255
Fisher Enterprises, 655 Main St. #305, Edmonds, WA 98020/206-776-4365 (Prometheus airgun pellets)
Frontier Cartridge Division-Hornady Mfg. Co., Box 1848, Grand Island, NE 68801/308-382-1390

Hansen Cartridge Co., 244 Old Post Rd., Southport, CT 06490/203-259-7337
ICI-America, Wilmington, DE 19897/302-575-3000(Eley-Kynoch)
Midway Arms, Inc., 7450 Old Hwy. 40 West, Columbia, MO 65201/314-445-9521
Nevins Ammunition, Inc., 7614 Lemhi Ave., Suite #1, Boise, ID 83709/208-322-8611 (centerfire handgun)
Omark Industries, P.O. Box 856, Lewiston, ID 83501/208-746-2351
P.P.C. Corp., 625 E. 24th St., Paterson, NJ 07514
Precision Prods. of Wash., Inc., N. 311 Walnut Rd., Spokane, WA 99206/509-928-0604 (Exammo)
Prometheus/Titan Black (See Fisher Enterprises)
RWS (See Dynamit Nobel of America)
Remington Arms Co., 1077 Market St., Wilmington, DE 19898
Service Armament, 689 Bergen Blvd., Ridgefield, NJ 07657
Super Vel, FPC, Inc., Hamilton Rd., Rt. 2, P. O. Box 1398, Fond du Lac, WI 54935/414-921-2652
Ten-X Mfg., 2410 East Foxfarm Rd., Cheynne, WY 82001
3-D Inv., Inc., Box J, Main St., Doniphan, NE 68832/402-845-2285
United States Ammunition Co. (USAC), Inc., 1476 Thorne Rd., Tacoma, WA 98421/206-627-8700
Weatherby's, 2781 E. Firestone Blvd., South Gate, CA 90280
Winchester, Shamrock St., East Alton, IL 62024

## AMMUNITION (Custom)

A Square Co., Inc., Rt. 4, Simmons Rd., Madison, IN 47250/812-273-3633
Accuracy Systems Inc., 15203 N. Cave Creek Rd., Phoenix, AZ 85032/602-971-1991
Beal's Bullets, 170 W. Marshall Rd., Lansdowne, PA 19050/215-259-1220 (Auto Mag Specialists)
Bell's Gun & Sport Shop, 3309-19 Mannheim Rd., Franklin Park, IL 60131
Brass Extrusion Labs. Ltd., 800 W. Maple Lane, Bensenville, IL 60106
C.W. Cartridge Co., 71 Hackensack St., Wood-Ridge, NJ 07075 (201-438-5111)
Russell Campbell Custom Loaded Ammo, 219 Leisure Dr., San Antonio, TX 78201/512-735-1183
Cartridges Unlimited, Rt. 1, Box 50, South Kent, CT 06785/203-927-3053 (British Express; metric; U.S.)
Cumberland Arms, Rt. 1, Shafer Rd., Blantons Chapel, Manchester, TN 37355
Custom Tackle & Ammo, P.O. Box 1886, Farmington, NM 87499/505-632-3539
Eagle Cap Custom Bullets, P.O. Box 659, Enterprise, OR 97828/503-426-4282
E.W. Ellis Sport Shop, RFD 1, Box 315, Corinth, NY 12822
Ellwood Epps Northern Ltd., 210 Worthington St. W., North Bay, Ont. PIB 3B4, Canada
Estate Cartridge Inc., P.O. Box 3702, Conroe, TX 77305/409-539-9144 (shotshell)
Jack First Distributors, Inc., 44633 Sierra Hwy., Lancaster, CA 93534/805-945-6981
Ramon B. Gonzalez, P.O. Box 370, Monticello, NY 12701/914-794-4515
"Gramps" Antique Cartridges, Ellwood Epps, Box 341, Washago, Ont. L0K 2B0 Canada/705-689-5348
Hardin Specialty Distributors, P.O. Box 338, Radcliff, KY 40160/502-351-6649
R.H. Keeler, 817 "N" St., Port Angeles, WA 98362/206-457-4702
K.K. Arms Co., Star Route Box 671, Kerrville, TX 78028/512-257-4718
KTW Inc., 710 Foster Park Rd., Lorain, OH 44053 216/233-6919 (bullets)
Lindsley Arms Cartridge Co., Inc., P.O. Box 5738, Lake Worth, FL 33466/305-968-1678 (inq. S.A.S.E.)
Lomont Precision Bullets, 4236 West 700 South, Poneto, IN 46781/219-694-6792 (custom cast bullets only)
McConnellstown Reloading & Cast Bullets, Inc., R.D. 3, Box 40, Huntingdon, PA 16652/814-627-5402
Mack's Sport Shop, Box 1155, Kodiak, AK 99615/907-486-4276
North American Arms, 1800 North 300 West, Spanish Fork, UT 84660/801-798-9891
Numrich Arms Corp., 203 Broadway, W. Hurley, NY 12491
Olsen Development Lab., 307 Conestoga Way #37, Edgeville, PA 19403/215-631-1716 (Invicta)
Pearl Armory, Revenden Springs, AR 72460
Robert Pomeroy, Morison Ave., Corinth, ME 04427/207-285-7721 (custom shells)
Precision Ammo Co., P.O. Box 63, Garnerville, NY 10923/914-947-2720
Precision Prods. of Wash., Inc., N. 311 Walnut Rd., Spokane, WA 99206/509-928-0604 (Exammo)
Anthony F. Sailer-Ammunition (AFSCO), 731 W. Third St., Owen, WI 54460/715-229-2516
Sanders Cust. Gun Serv., 2358 Tyler Lane, Louisville, KY 40205
Senica Run, Inc., P.O. Box 3032, Greeley, CO 80633
George W. Spence, 115 Locust St., Steele, MO 63877/314-695-4926 (boxer-primed cartridges)
The 3-D Company, Box J, Main St., Doniphan, NE 68832/402-845-2285 (reloaded police ammo)
R. A. Wardrop, P.O. Box 245, Mechanicsburg, PA 17055/717-766-9663
Zero Ammunition Co., Inc., P.O. Box 1188, Cullman, AL 35056/205-739-1606

## AMMUNITION (Foreign)

Action Arms Ltd., P. O. Box 9573, Philadelphia, PA 19124/215-744-0100
Armscor (See Pacific International Merch. Corp.)
Beeman Inc., 47-GDD Paul Drive, San Rafael, CA 94903/415-472-7121
Dan/Arms, 501 Office Center, Suite 128, P.O. Box 5040, Fort Washington, PA 19034/215-646-0720
Dynamit Nobel of America, Inc., 105 Stonehurst Court, Northvale, NJ 07647/210-767-1660(RWS, Geco, Rottweil)
FFV Norma, Inc., 300 S. Jefferson, Suite 301, Springfield, MO 65806/417-865-9314
Fiocchi of America, Inc., 1308 Chase, Springfield, MO 65803/417-864-6970
Hansen Cartridge Co., 244 Old Post Rd., Southport, CT 06490/203-259-7337
Norma, (See Outdoor Sports Headquarters, Inc.)
Hirtenberger Patronen-, Zündhütchen- & Metallwarenfabrik, A.G., Leobersdorfer Str. 33, A2552 Hirtenberg, Austria
Paul Jaeger, Inc., P.O. Box 449, 1 Madison Ave., Grand Junction, TN 38039/901-764-6909 (RWS centerfire ammo)
Kendall International Arms, Inc., 501 East North, Carlisle, KY 40311/606-289-7336 (Lapua)
Lapua (See Kendall International, Inc.)
PMC (See Patton and Morgan Corp.)
Pacific International Merchandising, 2215 "J" St., Sacramento, CA 95816/916-446-2737
Patton and Morgan Corp., 5900 Wilshire Blvd., Suite 1400, Los Angeles, CA 90036/213-938-0143 (PMC ammo)
RWS (Rheinische-Westfälische Sprengstoff) [See Dynamit Nobel of America; Paul Jaeger, Inc.]
Sports Emporium, 1414 Willow Ave., Philadelphia, PA 19126 (Danarms shotshells)

## AMMUNITION COMPONENTS—BULLETS, POWDER, PRIMERS

A Square Co., Inc., Rt. 4, Simmons Rd., Madison, IN 47250/812-273-3633 (cust. bull.; brass)
Accurate Arms Co., Inc., (Propellents Div.), Rt. 1, Box 167, McEwen, TN, 37101/615-729-4207/4208 (powders)
Acme Custom Bullets, 5708 Evers Rd., San Antonio, TX 78238/512-680-4828
Alaska Bullet Works, P.O. Box 54, Douglas, AK 99824 (Alaska copper-bond cust.)
Alberts Corp., 519 E. 19th St., Paterson, NJ 07514/201-684-1676 (swaged bullets)
American Bullets, P.O. Box 15313, Atlanta, GA 30333/404-482-4253
Ammo-O-Mart Ltd., P.O. Box 125, Hawkesbury, Ont., Canada K6A 2R8/613-632-9300 (Nobel powder)
Ballistic Prods., Inc., Box 488, 2105 Shaughnessy Circle, Long Lake, MN 55356
Ballistic Research Industries (BRI), 2825 S. Rodeo Gulch Rd. #8, Soquel, CA 95073/408-476-7981 (12-ga. Sabo shotgun slug)
Barnes Bullets, Inc., P.O. Box 215, American Fork, UT 84003/801-756-4222
Bell's Gun & Sport Shop, 3309-19 Mannheim Rd., Franklin Pk., IL 60131/312-678-1900
Bergman and Williams, 2450 Losee Rd., Las Vegas, NV 89030/702-642-1091 (copper tube 308 cust. bull.; lead wire i. all sizes)
Bitterroot Bullet Co., Box 412, Lewiston, ID 83501/208-743-5635 (Coin or stamps) f.50¢ U.S.; 75¢ Can. & Mex.; intl. $3.00 and #10 SASE for lit.
Black Mountain Bullets, Rte. 3, Box 297, Warrenton, VA 22186/703-347-1199 (custom Fluid King match bullets)
B.E.L.L., Brass Extrusion Laboratories, Ltd., 800 W. Maple Lane, Bensenville, IL 60106
Milton Brynin, 214 E. Third St., Mount Vernon, NY 10550/914-664-1311 (cast bullets)
Buffalo Rock Shooter Supply (See Chevron Bullets)
CCI, (See: Omark Industries)
CheVron Bullets, R.R. 1, Ottawa, IL 61350/815-433-2471
Kenneth E. Clark, 18738 Highway 99, Madera, CA 93637/209-674-6016 (Bullets)
Clete's Custom Bullets, RR 6, Box 1348, Warsaw, IN 46580
Cooper-Woodward, P.O. Box 972, Riverside, CA 92502/714-822-4176
Corbin Mfg. & Supply, Inc., P.O. Box 2659, White City, OR 97503/503-826-5211 (bullets)
Cor-Bon Custom Bullets, P.O. Box 10126, Detroit, MI 48210/313-894-2373 (375, 44, 45 solid brass partition bull.)
Custom Bullets by Hoffman, 2604 Peconic Ave. Seaford, NY 11783 (7mm, 308, 257, 224, 270)
Division Lead, 7742 W. 61 Pl., Summit, IL 60502
DuPont, Explosives Dept., Wilmington, DE 19898
Dynamit Nobel of America, Inc., 105 Stonehurst Court, Northvale, NJ 07647/201-767-1660 (RWS percussion caps)
Eagle Bullet Works, P.O. Box 2104, White City, OR 97503/503-826-7143 (Div-Cor 375, 224, 257 cust. bull.)
Eagle Cap Custom Bullets, P.O. Box 659, Enterprise, OR 97828/503-426-4282
Elk Mountain Shooters Supply Inc., 1719 Marie, Pasco, WA 99301 (Alaskan bullets)
Excalibur Wax, Inc., P.O. Box 432, Kenton, OH 43326/419-673-0512 (wax bullets)
Federal Cartridge Co., 2700 Foshay Tower, Minneapolis, MN 55402/612-333-8255 (nickel cases)
FFV Norma, Inc., 300 S. Jefferson, Suite 301, Springfield, MO 65806/417-865-9314 (powder)
Fisher Enterprises, 655 Main St. #305, Edmonds, WA 98020/206-776-4365
Forty Five Ranch Enterprises, 119 S. Main, Miami, OK 74354/918-542-9307
Fowlers, 3731 McKelvey St., Charlotte, NC 28215/704-568-7661 (benchrest bullets)
Glaser Safety Slug, P.O. Box 8223, Foster City, CA 94404/415-345-7677
Godfrey Reloading Supply, Hi-Way 67-111, Brighton, IL 62012 (cast bullets)
Lynn Godfrey, (See: Elk Mtn. Shooters Supply)
GOEX, Inc., Belin Plant, 1002 Springbrook Ave., Moosic, PA 18507/717-457-6724 (black powder)
Green Bay Bullets, P.O. Box 10446, 1486 Servais St., Green Bay, WI 54307-54304/414-497-2949 (cast lead bullets)
Grills-Hanna Bulletsmith Co., Lt., Box 655, Black Diamond, Alb. TOL OHO Canada/403-652-4393 (38, 9mm, 12-ga.)
GTM Co., George T. Mahaney, 15915B E. Main St., La Puente, CA 91744 (all brass shotshells)
Hansen Custom Bullets, 3221 Shelley St., Mohegan, NY 10547
Hardin Specialty Distr., P. O. Box 338, Radcliff, KY 40160/502-351-6649 (empty, primed cases)
Robert W. Hart & Son, Inc. 401 Montgomery St., Nescopeck, PA 18635/717-752-3655
Hercules Inc., Hercules Plaza, Wilmington, DE 19894 (smokeless powder)
Hodgdon Powder Co. Inc., P.O. Box 2932, Shawnee Mission, KS 66201/913-362-9455
Hoffman New Ideas, Inc., 821 Northmoor Rd., Lake Forest, IL 60045/312-234-4075 (practice sub.vel. bullets)
Hornady Mfg. Co., P.O. Drawer 1848, Grand Island, NE 68802/308-382-1390
N.E. House Co., 195 West High St., E. Hampton, CT 06424/203-267-2133 (zinc bases in 30, 38, 44 and 45-cal. only)
Huntington's, P.O. Box 991, 601 Oro Dam Blvd., Oroville, CA 95965/916-534-1210
Jaro Manuf., P.O. Box 6125, 206 E. Shaw, Pasadena, TX 77506/713-472-0471 (bullets)
J&J Custom Bullet, 1210 El Rey Ave., El Cajon, CA 92021 (Power-Pak)
J&P Enterprises, 2999 Dyke Rd., Northpole, AK 99705/907-488-1534 (Grizzly 4-cal. ogive 32&49 mil. bonded core tubing bull.)
Ka Pu Kapili, P.O. Box 745, Honokaa, HI 96272 (Hawaiian Special cust. bullets)
Kendall International Arms, Inc., 501 East North, Carlisle, KY 40311/606-289-7336 (Lapua bull.)

## AMMUNITION COMPONENTS . . . —cont'd.

Kodiak Custom Bullets, 8261 Henry Circle, Anchorage, AK 99507
L.L.F. Die Shop, 1281 Highway 99 North, Eugene, OR 97402/503-688-5753
Lage Uniwad Co., 1814 21st St., Eldora, IA 50627/515-858-2634
Lapua (See Kendall International Arms)
Ljutic Ind., Inc., Box 2117, Yakima, WA 98902 (Mono-wads)
Lomont Precision Bullets, 4236 West 700 South, Poneto, IN 46781/219-694-6792 (custom cast bullets)
Paul E. Low Jr., R.R. 1, Dunlap, IL 61525/309-685-1392 (jacketed 44- & 45-cal. bullets)
Lyman Products Corp., Rte. 147, Middlefield, CT 06455
McConnellstown Reloading & Cast Bullets, Inc., R.D. 3, Box 40, Huntingdon, PA 16652/814-627-5402
Mack's Sport Shop, Box 1155, Kodiak, AK 99615/907-486-4276 (cust. bull.)
Marshall Enterprises, 792 Canyon Rd., Redwood City, CA 94062/415-356-1230
Michael's Antiques, Box 233, Copiague, L.I., NY 11726 (Ballo Blondeau)
Miller Trading Co., 20 S. Front St., Wilmington, NC 28401/919-762-7107 (bullets)
Morrison Custom Bullet Corp., P.O. Box 5574 Sta. Edmonton, Alb. T6C 3T5 Canada (9mm, 357 handgun)
Muzzleload Magnum Products (MMP), Route 6 Box 383, Harrison, AR 72601/501-741-5019 (sabots f. black powder)
NTC Inc., P.O. Box 4202, Portland, OR 97208
Non-Toxic Components, Inc., P.O. Box 4202, Portland, OR 97208 (steel shot kits)
NORMA (See FFV Norma)
Nosler Bullets Inc., 107 S.W. Columbia, Bend, OR 97702/503-382-5108
Old Western Scrounger, 12924 Hwy A-12, Montague, CA 96064/916-459-5445
Omark Industries, P.O. Box 856, Lewiston, ID 83501/208-746-2351
Oro-Tech Industries, Inc., 1701 W. Charleston Blvd., Suite 510, Las Vegas, NV 89102/702-382-8109 (Golden Powder)
PMC Ammunition, 5400 Wilshire Blvd., Suite 1400, Los Angeles, CA 90036/213-938-3201
Pepperbox Gun Shop, P.O. Box 922, East Moline, IL 61244/309-796-0616 (257, 224 rifle cal. custom swaged bullets)
Pyrodex, See: Hodgdon Powder Co., Inc. (black powder substitute)
Robert Pomeroy, Morison Ave., East Corinth, ME 04427/207-285-7721 (empty cases)
Power Plus Enterprises, 6939 Macon Rd. #15, Columbus, GA 31907/404-561-1717 (12-ga. shotguns slugs; 308, 45 ACP, 357 cust. bull.)
Precision Ammo Co., P.O. Drawer 86, Valley Cottage, NY 10989/914-947-2710
Precision Swaged Bullets, Rte. 1, Box 93H, Ronan, MT 59864/406-676-5135 (silhouette; out-of-prods. Sharps)
Professional Hunter Supplies, P.O. Box 608, Ferndale, CA 95536/707-786-9460 (408, 375, 308, 510 cust. bull.)
Prometheus/Titan Black (See Fisher Enterprises)
Prospect Bullets, D.B.M. Specialty, P.O. Box 58, Holmes, PA 19043/215-586-6240 (9mm, 38 cust.)
Redwood Bullet Works, 3559 Bay Rd., Redwood City, CA 94063 (cust.)
Remington-Peters, 1007 Market St., Wilmington, DE 19898
S&S Precision Bullets, 22963 La Cadena, Laguna Hills, CA 92653/714-768-6836 (linotype cast bull.)
Sansom Bullets, 2506 Rolling Hills, Dr., Greenville, TX 75401 (custom)
Sierra Bullets Inc., 10532 So. Painter Ave., Santa Fe Springs, CA 90670
Speer Products, Box 856, Lewiston, ID 83501
Supreme Products Co., 1830 S. California Ave., Monrovia, CA 91016/800-423-7159/818-357-5395 (rubber bullets)
Swift Bullet Co., Rt. 1, Quinter, KS 67752/913-754-3959 (375 big game, 224 cust.)
Tallon Bullets, 1194 Tidewood Dr., Bethel Park, PA 15102/412-471-4494 (dual. diam. 308 cust.)
Taracorp Industries, 16th & Cleveland Blvd., Granite City, IL 62040/618-451-4400 (Lawrence Brand lead shot)
Traft Gunshop, P.O. Box 1078, Buena Vista, CO 81211/303-395-6034 (cust. bull.)
Trophy Bonded Bullets, P.O. Box 262348, Houston, TX 77207/713-645-4499 (big game 458, 308, 375 bonded cust. bullets only)
Vitt & Boos, 2178 Nichols Ave., Stratford, CT 06497/203-375-6859 (Aerodynamic shotgun slug, 12-ga. only)
Winchester, Shamrock St., East Alton, IL 62024
Worthy Products, Inc., Box 88 Main St., Chippewa Bay, NY 13623/315-324-5450 (slug loads)
Zero Bullet Co. Inc., P.O. Box 1188, Cullman, AL 35056/205-739-1606

## ANTIQUE ARMS DEALERS

AD Hominem, R.R. 3, Orillia, Ont., L3V 6H3, Canada/705-689-5303
Antique Arms Co., David F. Saunders, 1110 Cleveland, Monett, MO 65708/417-235-6501
Antique Gun Parts, Inc., 1118 S. Braddock Ave., Pittsburgh, PA 15218/412-241-1811
Armsport, Inc., 3590 N.W. 49th St., Miami, FL 33142/305-635-7850
Beeman Inc., 47 Paul Dr., San Rafael, CA 94903/415-472-7121 (airguns only)
Wm. Boggs, 1243 Grandview Ave., Columbus, OH 43212
Century Arms, Inc., 5 Federal St., St. Albans, VT 05478/802-524-9541
Dave Chicoine, d/b/a Liberty A.S.P., 19 Key St., Eastport, ME 04631/207-853-2327

Chas. Clements, Handicrafts Unltd., 1741 Dallas St., Aurora, CO 80010/303-364-0403
Continental Kite & Key Co. (CONKKO), P.O. Box 40, Broomall, PA 19008/215-356-0711
Peter Dyson Ltd., 29-31 Church St., Honley, Huddersfield, W. Yorksh. HD7 2AH, England/0484-661062 (acc. f. ant. gun coll.; custom-and machine-made)
Ed's Gun House, Box 62, Rte. 1, Minnesota City, MN 55959/507-689-2925
Ellwood Epps Northern Ltd., 210 Worthington St. W., North Bay, Ont. PIB 3B4 Canada
William Fagan, 126 Belleview, Mount Clemens, MI 48043/313-465-4637
Jack First Distributors, Inc., 44633 Sierra Hwy., Lancaster, CA 93534/805-945-6981
N. Flayderman & Co., Squash Hollow, New Milford, CT 06776/203-354-5567
Chet Fulmer, P.O. Box 792, Rt. 2, Buffalo Lake, Detroit Lakes, MN 56501/218-847-7712
Robert S. Frielich, 396 Broome St., New York, NY 10013/212-254-3045
Garcia National Gun Traders, Inc., 225 S.W. 22nd Ave., Miami, FL 33135
Herb Glass, Bullville, NY 10915/914-361-3021
James Goergen, Rte. 2, Box 182BB, Austin, MN 55912/507-433-9280
Griffin's Guns & Antiques, R.R. 4, Peterboro, Ont., Canada K9J 6X5/705-745-7022
The Gun Shop, 6497 Pearl Rd., Parma Heights (Cleveland), OH 44130/216-884-7476
Hansen & Company, 244 Old Post Rd., Southport, CT 06490/203-259-7337
Kelley's Harold Kelley, Box 125, Woburn, MA 01801/617-935-3389
Lever Arms Serv. Ltd., 572 Howe St., Vancouver, B.C., Canada V6C 2E3/604-685-8945
Log Cabin Sport Shop, 8010 Lafayette Rd., Lodi, OH 44254/216-948-1082
Lone Pine Trading Post, Jct. Highways 61 and 248, Minnesota City, MN 55959/507-689-2925
Charles W. Moore, R.D. #1, Box 276, Schenevus, NY 12155/607-278-5721
Museum of Historical Arms, 1038 Alton Rd., Miami Beach, FL 33139/305-672-7480 (ctlg $5)
Muzzleloaders Etc. Inc., 9901 Lyndale Ave. So., Bloomington, MN 55420/612-884-1161
New Orleans Arms Co., 5001 Treasure St., New Orleans, LA 70186/504-944-3371
Old Western Scrounger, 12924 Hwy A-12, Montague, CA 96064/916-459-5445 (write for list; $2)
Pioneer Guns, 5228 Montgomery, (Cincinnati) Norwood, OH 45212/513-631-4871
Pony Express Sport Shop, Inc., 16606 Schoenborn St., Sepulveda, CA 91343/818-895-1231
Martin B. Retting, Inc., 11029 Washington, Culver City, CA 90232/213-837-6111
Ridge Guncraft, Inc., 125 E. Tyrone Rd., Oak Ridge, TN 37830/615-483-4024
San Francisco Gun Exch., 124 Second St., San Francisco, CA 94105/415-982-6097
Santa Ana Gunroom, P.O. Box 1777, Santa Ana, CA 92701/714-541-3035
Don L. Shrum's Cape Outfitters, 412 So. Kingshighway, Cape Girardeau, MO 63701/314-335-4103
S&S Firearms, 74-11 Myrtle Ave., Glendale, NY 11385/212-497-1100
Steves Gun House, Rte. 1, Minnesota City, MN 55959
James Wayne, 308 Leisure Lane, Victoria, TX 77904/512-578-1258
Ward & Van Valkenburg, 114-32nd Ave. N., Fargo, ND 58102
M.C. Wiest, 125 E. Tyrone Rd., Oak Ridge, TN 37830/615-483-4024
Lewis Yearout, 308 Riverview Dr. E., Great Falls, MT 59404

## APPRAISERS, GUNS, ETC.

Ad Hominem, R.R. 3, Orillia, ON L3V 6H3, Canada/705-689-5303
Antique Gun Parts, Inc., 1118 So. Braddock Ave., Pittsburgh, PA 15218/412-241-1811
Ahlman's, Rt. 1, Box 20, Morristown, MN 55052/507-685-4244
The Armoury Inc., Route 202, New Preston, CT 06777/203-868-0001
Dave Chicoine, dba Liberty Antique Sixgun, 19 Key St., Eastport, ME 04631/207-853-2327
Chas. Clements, Handicrafts Unltd., 1741 Dallas St., Aurora, CO 80010/303-364-0403
Custom Tackle & Ammo, P.O. Box 1886, Farmington, NM 87499/505-632-3539
D.O.C. Specialists (D.A. Ulrich), 2209 So. Central Ave., Cicero, IL 60650/312-652-3606
Ellwood Epps (Orillia) Ltd., R.R. 3, Hwy. 11 No., Orillia, Ont. L3V 6H3, Canada/705-689-5333
N. Flayderman & Co., Inc., RFD 2, Squash Hollow, New Milford, CT 06776/203-354-5567
"Gramps" Antique Cartridges, Ellwood Epps, Box 341, Washago, Ont. L0K 2B0 Canada/705-689-5348
Griffin & Howe, 589 Broadway, New York, NY 10012/212-966-5323
Kelley's Harold Kelley, Box 125, Woburn, MA 01801/617-935-3389
Kenneth Kogan, P.O. Box 130, Lafayette Hills, PA 19444/215-233-4509
Lone Pine Trading Post, Jct. Highways 248 & 61, Minnesota City, MN 55959/507-689-2925
Orvis Co. Inc., Rte. 7A, Manchester, VT 05254/802-362-3622
PM Airservices Ltd., P.O. Box 1573, Costa Mesa, CA 92628/714-968-2689
Pony Express Sport Shop, Inc., 16606 Schoenborn St., Sepulveda, CA 91343/818-895-1231
John Richards, Rte. 2, Bedford, KY 40006/502-255-7222
Lewis Yearout, 308 Riverview Dr. East, Great Falls, MT 59404/406-761-0589

## AUCTIONEERS, GUNS, ETC.

Alberts Corp., 519 East 19th St., Paterson, NJ 07514/201-684-1676
Richard A. Bourne Co. Inc., Corporation St., Hyannis, MA 02647
Christies-East, 219 E. 67th St., New York, NY 10021
Tom Keilman, 12316 Indian Mount, Austin, TX 78758
Kelley's, Harold Kelley, Box 125, Woburn, MA 01801/617-935-3389
"Little John's" Antique Arms, 777 S. Main St., Orange, CA 92668
Wayne Mock, Inc., Box 37, Tamworth, NH 03886/603-323-8749
Parke-Bernet (see Sotheby's)
Sotheby's, 1334 York Ave. at 72nd St., New York, NY 10021
James C. Tillinghast, Box 19GD, Hancock, NH 03449

## BOOKS (ARMS), Publishers and Dealers

Armory Publications, P.O. Box 44372, Tacoma, WA 98444/206-531-4632
Arms & Armour Press, 2-6 Hampstead High Street, London NW3 1QQ, England
Beeman Inc., 47 Paul Dr., San Rafael, CA 94903/415-472-7121 (airguns)
Blacksmith Corp., P.O. Box 424, Southport, CT 06490/203-367-4041
Blacktail Mountain Books, 42 First Ave. West, Kalispell, MT 59901/406-257-5573
Brownlee Books, Box 489, Hooks, TX 75561
DBI Books, Inc., 4092 Commercial Ave., Northbrook IL 60062/312-272-6310
Dove Press, P.O. Box 3882, Enid, OK 73702/405-234-4347
Fortress Publications Inc., P.O. Box 241, Stoney Creek, Ont. L8G 3X9, Canada/416-662-3505
Guncraft Books, Div. of Ridge Guncraft, Inc., 125 E. Tyrone Rd., Oak Ridge, TN 37830/615-483-4024
Gunnerman Books, P.O. Box 4292, Auburn Hills, MI 48057/313-879-2779
Handgun Press, 5832 S. Green, Chicago, IL 60621
Long Survival Publications, P.O. Box 163-GD, Wamego, KS 66547/913-456-7387
Lyman, Route 147, Middlefield, CT 06455
Paladin Press, P.O. Box 1307, Boulder, CO 80306/303-443-7250
Personal Firearms Record Book Co., P.O. Box 2800, Santa Fe, NM 87501/505-983-2381
Petersen Publishing Co., 84990 Sunset Blvd., Los Angeles, CA 99069
Gerald Pettinger Arms Books, Route 2, Russell, IA 50238/515-535-2239
Ray Riling Arms Books Co., 6844 Gorsten St., P.O. Box 18925, Philadelphia, PA 19119/215-438-2456
Rutgers Book Center, Mark Aziz, 127 Raritan Ave., Highland Park, NJ 08904/201-545-4344
Small Arms Press, Box 1316, St. George, UT 84770
Stackpole Books, Cameron & Kelker Sts., Telegraph Press Bldg., Harrisburg, PA 17105
Stoeger Publishing Co., 55 Ruta Court, South Hackensack, NJ 07606
Ken Trotman, 135 Ditton Walk, Unit 11, Cambridge CB5 8QD, England
Winchester Press, 220 Old New Brunswick Rd., Piscataway, NJ 08854/201-981-0820
Wolfe Publishing Co., Inc., 6471 Air Park Dr., Prescott, AZ 86302/602-445-7810

## BULLET & CASE LUBRICANTS

C-H Tool & Die Corp., 106 N. Harding St., Owen, WI 54460/715-229-2146
Chopie Mfg. Inc., 700 Copeland Ave., La Crosse, WI 54601/608-784-0926 (Black-Solve)
Clenzoil Corp., P.O. Box 1226, Sta. C, Canton, OH 44708/216-833-9758
Cooper-Woodward, Box 972, Riverside, CA 92502/714-822-4176 (Perfect Lube)
Corbin Mfg. & Supply Inc., P.O. Box 2659, White City, OR 97503/503-826-5211
Fenwal, Inc., 400 Main St., Ashland, MA 01721/617-881-2000
Green Bay Bullets, 1486 Servais St., Green Bay, WI 54304/414-497-2949 (EZE-Size case lube)
Hodgdon Powder Co., Inc., P.O. Box 2932, Shawnee Mission, KS 66201/913-362-9455
Javelina Products, Box 337, San Bernardino, CA 92402/714-882-5847 (Alox beeswax)
Jet-Aer Corp., 100 Sixth Ave., Paterson, NJ 07524
LeClear Industries, 1126 Donald Ave., P.O. Box 484, Royal Oak, MI 48068/313-588-1025
Lyman Products Corp., Rte. 147, Middlefield, CT. 06455 (Size-Ezy)
Marmel Prods., P.O. Box 97, Utica, MI 48087/313-731-8029 (Marvellube, Marvelux)
Micro-Lube, P.O. Box 117, Mesilla Park, NM 88047/505-524-4215
Mirror Lube, 1305 Simpson Way, Suite K, Escondido, CA 92025/619-480-2518
M&N Bullet Lube, P.O. Box 495, 151 N.E. Jefferson St., Madras, OR 97741/503-475-2992
Northeast Industrial, Inc., P.O. Box 249, 405 N. Canyon Blvd., Canyon City, OR 97820/503-575-2513 (Ten X-Lube; NEI mold prep)
Pacific Tool Co., P.O. Box 2048, Ordnance Plant Rd., Grand Island, NE 68801/308-384-2308
RCBS, Inc., Box 1919, Oroville, CA 95965
Radix Research & Marketing, Box 247, Woodland Park, CO 80863/303-687-3182 (Magnum Dri-Lube)
SAECO Rel, 2207 Border Ave., Torrance, CA 90501/213-320-6973
Shooters Accessory Supply (SAS) (See Corbin Mfg. & Supply)
Tamarack Prods., Inc., P.O. Box 224, Barrington, IL 60010/312-526-9333 (Bullet lube)

## BULLET SWAGE DIES AND TOOLS

C-H Tool & Die Corp., 106 N. Harding St., Owen, WI 54460/715-229-2146
Lester Coats, 416 Simpson Ave., North Bend, OR 97459/503-756-6995 (lead wire core cutter)
Corbin Mfg. & Supply Inc., P.O. Box 2659, White City, OR 97503/503-826-5211
Hollywood, Loading Tools by M&M Engineering, 10642 Arminta St., Sun Valley, CA 91352/818-842-8376
Huntington Die Specialties, P.O. Box 991, Oroville, CA 95965/916-534-1210
Independent Machine & Gun Shop, 1416 N. Hayes, Pocatello, ID 83201/208-232-1264 (TNT bullet dies)
L.L.F. Die Shop, 1281 Highway 99 North, Eugene, OR 97402/503-688-5753
Rorschach Precision Products, P.O. Box 151613, Irving, TX 75015/214-790-3487
SAS Dies, (See Corbin Mfg. & Supply)
Sport Flite Mfg., Inc., 2520 Industrial Row, Troy, MI 48084/313-280-0648
TNT (See Ind. Mach. & Gun Shop)
Whitney Sales, P.O. Box 875, Reseda, CA 91335/818-345-4212 (tungsten carbide rifle dies)

## CARTRIDGES FOR COLLECTORS

AD Hominem, R.R. 3, Orillia, Ont., Canada L3V 6H3/705-689-5303
Ida I. Burgess, Sam's Gun Shop, 25 Squam Rd., Rockport, MA 01966/617-546-6839
Cameron's, 16690 W. 11th Ave., Golden CO 80401/303-279-7365
Chas. E. Duffy, Williams Lane, West Hurley, NY 12419
Tom M. Dunn, 1342 So. Poplar, Casper, WY 82601/307-237-3207
Ellwood Epps (Orillia) Ltd., Hwy. 11 North, Orillia, Ont. L3V 6H3, Canada/705-689-5333
Jack First Distributors, Inc., 44633 Sierra Hwy., Lancaster, CA 93534/805-945-6981
GTM Co., Geo. T. Mahaney, 15915B East Main St., La Puente, CA 91744/818-768-5806
Glaser Safety Slug, Inc., P.O. Box 8223, Foster City, CA 94404/415-345-7677
"Gramps" Antique Cartridges, Box 341, Washago, Ont., Canada L0K 2B0
Griffin's Guns & Antiques, R.R. #4, Peterboro, Ont. K9J 6X5, Canada/705-745-7022
Hansen and Hansen, 244 Old Post Rd., Southport, CT 06490/203-259-7337
Idaho Ammunition Service, 410 21st Ave., Lewiston, ID 83501
Kelley's, Harold Kelley, Box 125, Woburn, MA 01801/617-935-3389
Old Western Scrounger, 12924 Hwy. A-12, Montague, CA 96064/916-459-5445
San Francisco Gun Exchange, 124 Second St., San Francisco, CA 94105/415-982-6097
James C. Tillinghast, Box 405, Hancock, NH 03449/603-525-6615 (list $1)
Lewis Yearout, 308 Riverview Dr. E., Great Falls, MT 59404

## CASES, CABINETS AND RACKS—GUN

Alco Carrying Cases, 601 W. 26th St., New York, NY 10001/212-675-5820 (aluminum)
Bob Allen Sportswear, 214 S.W. Jackson, Des Moines, IA 50315/515-283-1988/800-247-8048 (carrying)
Amacker Products Inc., P.O. Box 1432, Tallulah, LA 71282/318-574-4903
The American Import Co., 1453 Mission St., San Francisco, CA 94103/415-863-1506
Armes de Chasse, P.O. Box 827, Chadsford, PA 19317/215-388-1146
Art Jewel Ltd., 421A Irmen Dr., Addison, IL 60101/312-628-6220
Assault Systems of St. Louis, 869 Horan, St. Louis, MO 63026/314-343-3575 (canvas carrying case)
Beeman Precision Arms, Inc., 47-GDD Paul Dr., San Rafael, CA 94903/415-472-7121
Morton Booth Co., Box 123, Joplin, MO 64801
Boyt Co., Div. of Welsh Sportg. Gds., Box 220, Iowa Falls, IA 50126
Brauer Bros. Mfg. Co., 2020 Delmar Blvd., St. Louis, MO 63103/314-231-2864 (soft gun cases)
Brenik, Inc., 925 W. Chicago Ave., Chicago, IL 60622
Browning, Rt. 4, Box 624-B, Arnold, MO 63010
Cap-Lex Gun Cases, Capitol Plastics of Ohio, Inc., 333 Van Camp Rd., Bowling Green, OH 43402
China IM/EX, P.O. Box 27573, San Francisco, CA 94127/415-661-2212 (soft-type cases)
Chipmunk Mfg. Co., 114 E. Jackson, Medford, OR 97501/503-664-5585 (cases)
Dara-Nes Inc., see: Nesci
Dart Mfg. Co., 4012 Bronze Way, Dallas, TX 75237/214-333-4221
Detroit-Armor Corp., 2233 No. Palmer Dr., Schaumburg, IL 60195/312-397-4070 (Saf-Gard steel gun safe)
Doskocil Mfg. Co., Inc., P.O. Box 1246, Arlington, TX 75010/817-467-5116 (Gun Guard carrying)
East-Tenn Mills, Inc., 3112 Industrial Dr., Skyline Industrial Park, Johnson City, TN 37601/615-928-7186 (gun socks)
Ellwood Epps (Orillia) Ltd., R.R. 3, Hwy, 11 North, Orillia, Ont. L3V 6H3, Canada/705-689-5333 (custom gun cases)
Norbert Ertel, P.O. Box 1150, Des Plaines, IL 60018/312-825-2315 (cust. gun cases)
Flambeau Plastics Corp., 801 Lynn, Baraboo, WI 53913
Fort Knox Security Products, 1051 N. Industrial Park Rd., Orem, UT 84057/801-224-7233 (safes)
Gun-Ho Case Mfg. Co., 110 East 10th St., St. Paul, MN 55101
Hansen and Hansen, 244 Old Post Rd., Southport, CT 06490/203-259-7337
Marvin Huey Gun Cases, P.O. Box 22456, Kansas City, MO 64113/816-444-1637 (handbuilt leather cases)
Jumbo Sports Prods., P.O. Box 280-Airport Rd., Frederick, MD 21701

## CASES, CABINETS AND RACKS—GUN—cont'd.

Kalispel Metal Prods. (KMP), P.O. Box 267, Cusick, WA 99119/509-445-1121 (aluminum boxes)
Kane Products Inc., 5572 Brecksville Rd., Cleveland, OH 44131/216-524-9962
Kolpin Mfg., Inc., Box 231, Berlin, WI 54923/414-361-0400
Marble Arms Corp., 420 Industrial Park, Gladstone, MI 49837/906-428-3710
Bill McGuire, 1600 No. Eastmont Ave., East Wenatchee, WA 98801
Merchandise Brokers, P.O. Box 491, Lilburn, GA 30247/404-923-0015 (GunSlinger portable rack)
Nesci Enterprises, Inc., P.O. Box 119, Summit St., East Hampton, CT 06424/203-267-2588 (firearms security chests)
Nortex Industrial Fan Co., 2821 Main St., Dallas TX 75226/214-748-1157 (automobile gun rack)
Paul-Reed, Inc., P.O. Box 227, Charlevoix, MI 49720
Penguin Industries, Inc., Airport Industrial Mall, Coatesville, PA 19320/215-384-6000
Precise, 3 Chestnut, Suffern, NY 10001
Proofmark, Ltd., P.O. Box 183, Alton, IL 62002/618-463-0120 (Italian Emmebi leather cases)
Protecto Plastics, Div. of Penguin Ind., Airport Industrial Mall, Coatesville, PA 19320/215-384-6000 (carrying cases)
Rahn Gun Works, Inc., P.O. Box 327, 535 Marshall St., Litchfield, MI 49252/517-542-3247 (leather trunk cases)
Red Head Brand Corp., 4949 Joseph Hardin Dr., Dallas, TX 75236/214-333-4141
Richland Arms Co., 321 W. Adrian, Blissfield, MI 49228
Saf-T-Case Mfg. Co., 104 S. Rogers, Irving, TX 75060/214-679-8827
San Angelo Co. 1841 Industrial Ave., San Angelo, TX 76904/915-655-7126
Buddy Schoellkopf, 4949 Joseph Hardin Dr., Dallas, TX 75236/214-333-2121
Schulz Industries, 16247 Minnesota Ave., Paramount, CA 90723/213-636-7718 (carrying cases)
Sealine Enterprises, 821 So. 3rd, Kent, WA 98032/206-852-1784 (vaults)
Security Gun Chest, (See Tread Corp.)
Stearns Mfg. Co., P.O. Box 1498, St. Cloud, MN 56301
Tread Corp., P.O. Box 13207, Roanoke, VA 24032/703-982-6881 (security gun chest)
Weather Shield Sports Equipm. Inc., Rte. #3, Petoskey Rd., Charlevoix, MI 49720
Wilson Case Co., 906 Juniata Ave., Juniata, NE 68955/402-751-2145 (cases)
Woodstream Corp., Box 327, Lititz, PA 17543

## CHOKE DEVICES, RECOIL ABSORBERS & RECOIL PADS

Action Products Inc., 22 N. Mulberry St., Hagerstown, MD 21740/800-228-7763 (rec. shock eliminator)
Bob Allen Companies, 214 S.W. Jackson St., Des Moines, IA 50302/515-283-2191
Arms Ingenuity Co., Box 1; 51 Canal St., Weatogue, CT 06089/203-658-5624 (Jet-Away)
Armsport, Inc., 3590 N.W. 49th St., Miami, FL 33142/305-635-7850 (choke devices)
Baer Custom Guns, 1725 Minesite Rd., Allentown, PA 18103/215-398-2362 (compensator syst. f. 45 autos)
Stan Baker, 5303 Roosevelt Way NE, Seattle, WA 98105/206-522-4575 (shotgun)
Briley Mfg. Co., 1085-A Gessner, Houston, TX 77055/713-932-6995 (choke tubes)
C&H Research, 115 Sunnyside Dr., Lewis, KS 67552/316-324-5445 (Mercury recoil suppressor)
Vito Cellini, Francesca Inc., 3115 Old Ranch Rd., San Antonio, TX 78217/512-826-2584 (recoil reducer; muzzle brake)
Clinton River Gun Serv. Inc., 30016 S. River Rd., Mt. Clemens, MI 48045 (Reed Choke)
Dahl Gun Shop, 6947 King Ave. West, Billings, MT 59106/406-652-3909
Edwards Recoil Reducer, 269 Herbert St., Alton, IL 62002/618-462-3257
Emsco Variable Shotgun Chokes, 101 Second Ave., S.E., Waseca, MN 56093/507-835-1779
Fabian Bros. Sptg. Goods, Inc., 3333 Midway Dr., Suite 104, San Diego, CA 92110/619-223-3955 (DTA Muzzle Mizer rec. abs.; MIL/brake)
Griggs Recreational Prods. Inc., P.O. Box 789, Bountiful, UT 84010/801-295-9696 (recoil director)
William E. Harper, The Great 870 Co., P.O. Box 6309, El Monte, CA 91734/213-579-3077
I.N.C., Inc., 1133 Kresky #4, Centralia, WA 98531/206-339-2042 (Sorbothane Kick-Eez recoil pad)
La Paloma Marketing, 1735 E. Ft. Lowell Rd., Suite 7, Tucson, AZ 85719/602-881-4750 (Action rec. shock eliminator)
Lyman Products Corp., Rte. 147, Middlefield, CT. 06455 (Cutts Comp.)
Mag-na-port International, Inc., 41302 Executive Drive, Mt. Clemens, MI 48045/313-469-6727 (muzzle-brake system)
Mag-Na-Port of Canada, 1861 Burrows Ave., Winnipeg, Manitoba R2X 2V6, Canada
Marble Arms Corp., 420 Industrial Park, Gladstone, MI 49837/906-428-3710 (Poly-Choke)
Multi-Gauge Enterprises, 433 W. Foothill Blvd., Monrovia, CA 91016/818-357-6117/358-4549 (screw-in chokes)
Pachmayr Gun Works, Inc., 1220 So. Grand Ave., Los Angeles, CA 90015/213-748-7271 (recoil pads)
P.A.S.T. Corp., 210 Park Ave., P.O. Box 7372, Columbia, MO 65205/314-449-7278 (recoil reducer shield)
Poly-Choke (See Marble Arms)
Pro-Port Ltd., 41302 Executive Dr., Mt. Clemens, MI 48045/313-469-7323
Purbaugh, see: Multi-Gauge Enterprises
Supreme Products Co., 1830 S. California Ave., Monrovia, CA 91016/800-423-7159/818-357-5395 (recoil pads)

## CHRONOGRAPHS AND PRESSURE TOOLS

B-Square Co., Box 11281, Ft. Worth, TX 76110/800-433-2909
Custom Chronograph Co., Rt. 1, Box 98, Brewster, WA 98812/509-689-2004
D&H Precision Tooling, 7522 Barnard Mill Rd., Ringwood, IL 60072/815-653-9611 (Pressure Testing Receiver)
H-S Precision, Inc., 112 N. Summit St., Prescott, AZ 86302/602-445-0607 (press. barrels)
Paul Jaeger, Inc., P.O. Box 449, 1 Madison Ave., Grand Junction, TN 38039
Oehler Research, Inc., P.O. Box 9135, Austin, TX 78766/512-327-6900
Telepacific Electronics Co., Inc., P.O. Box 1329, San Marcos, CA 92069/714-744-4415
Tepeco, P.O. Box 342, Friendswood, TX 77546/713-482-2702 (Tepeco Speed-Meter)
M. York, 5508 Griffith Rd., Gaithersburg, MD 20760/301-253-4217 (press. tool)

## CLEANING & REFINISHING SUPPLIES

A.C. Enterprises, P.O. Box 448, Edenton, NC 27932/919-482-4992
American Gas & Chemical Co., Ltd., 220 Pegasus Ave., Northvale, NJ 07647/201-767-7300 (TSI gun lube)
Anderson Mfg. Co., P.O. Box 536, 6813 S. 220th St., Kent, WA 98032/206-872-7602 (stock finishes)
Armite Labs., 1845 Randolph St., Los Angeles, CA 90001/213-587-7744 (pen oiler)
Armoloy Co. of Ft. Worth, 204 E. Daggett St., Ft Worth, TX 76104/817-461-0051
Beeman Inc., 47 Paul Dr., San Rafael, CA 94903/415-472-7121
Belltown, Ltd., P.O. Box 74, Route 37, Sherman, CT 06784/203-354-5750 (gun clg. cloth kit)
Birchwood-Casey, 7900 Fuller Rd., Eden Prairie, MN 55344/612-927-7933
Blacksmith Corp., P.O. Box 424, Southport, CT 06490/800-531-2665 (Arctic Friction Free gun clg. equip.)
Blue and Gray Prods., Inc., R.D. #6, Box 362, Wellsboro, PA 16901/717-724-1383
Break-Free, Div. of San/Bar Corp., 1035 So. Linwood Ave., Santa Ana, CA 92705/714-953-1900 (lubricants)
Jim Brobst, 299 Poplar St., Hamburg, PA 19526/215-562-2103 ( J-B Bore Cleaning Compound)
Browning Arms, Rt. 4, Box 624-B, Arnold, MO 63010
J.M. Bucheimer Co., P.O. Box 280, Airport Rd., Frederick, MD 21701/301-662-5101
Burnishine Prod. Co., 8140 N. Ridgeway, Skokie, IL 60076/312-583-1810 (Stock Glaze)
Call 'N, Inc., 1615 Bartlett Rd., Memphis, TN 38134/901-372-1682 (Gunskin)
Chem-Pak, Inc., 11 Oates Ave., P.O. Box 1685, Winchester, VA 22601/703-667-1341 (Gun-Savr.protect. & lubricant)
Chopie Mfg. Inc., 700 Copeland Ave., La Crosse, WI 54601/608-784-0926 (Black-Solve)
Clenzoil Corp., Box 1226, Sta. C, Canton, OH 44708/216-833-9758
Clover Mfg. Co., 139 Woodward Ave., Norwalk, Ct. 06856/800-243-6492 (Clover compound)
Country Cover Co., Inc., P.O. Box 160, Storrs, CT 06268/203-429-3710 (Masking Gun Oil)
J. Dewey Mfg. Co., 186 Skyview Dr., Southbury, CT 06488/203-264-3064 (one-piece gun clg. rod)
Diah Engineering Co., 5177 Haskell St., La Canada, CA 91011/213-625-2184 (barrel lubricant)
Dri-Slide, Inc., 411 N. Darling, Fremont, MI 49412/616-924-3950
The Dutchman's Firearms Inc., 4143 Taylor Blvd., Louisville, KY 40215/502-366-0555
Forster Products, 82 E. Lanark Ave., Lanark, IL 61046/815-493-6360
Fountain Prods., 492 Prospect Ave., W. Springfield, MA 01089/413-781-4551
Forty-Five Ranch Enterpr., 119 S. Main St., Miami, OK 74354/918-542-9307
Heller & Levin Associates, Inc., 88 Marlborough Court, Rockville Center, NY 11570/516-764-9349
Frank C. Hoppe Division, Penguin Ind., Inc., Airport Industrial Mall, Coatesville, PA 19320/215-384-6000
J-B Bore Cleaner, 299 Poplar St., Hamburg, PA 19526/215-562-2103
Ken Jantz Supply, Rt. 1, Sulphur, OK 73086/405-622-3790
Jet-Aer Corp., 100 Sixth Ave., Paterson, NJ 07524 (blues & oils)
Kellog's Professional Prods., Inc., P.O. Box 1201, Sandusky, OH 44870
K.W. Kleinendorst, R.D. #1, Box 113B, Hop Bottom, PA 18824/717-289-4687 (rifle clg. cables)
Terry K. Kopp, Highway 13, Lexington, MO 64067/816-259-2636 (stock rubbing compound; rust preventative grease)
LPS Chemical Prods., Holt Lloyd Corp., 4647 Hugh Howell Rd., Box 3050, Tucker, GA 30084/404-934-7800
LaPaloma Marketing, Inc., 1735 E. Ft. Lowell Rd., Suite 7, Tucson, AZ 85719/602-881-4750 (Amer-Lene solution)
Mark Lee, P.O. Box 20379, Minneapolis, MN 55420/612-884-4060 (rust blue solution)
LEM Gun Spec., Box 31, College Park, GA 30337/404-761-9054 (Lewis Lead Remover)
Liquid Wrench, Box 10628, Charlotte, NC 28201 (pen. oil)
Lynx Line Gun Prods. Div., Protective Coatings, Inc., 20626 Fenkell Ave., Detroit, MI 48223/313-255-6032
MJL Industries, Inc., P.O. Box 122, McHenry, IL 60050/815-344-1040 (Rust Free)
Marble Arms Co., 420 Industrial Park, Gladstone, MI 49837/906-428-3710
Micro Sight Co., 242 Harbor Blvd., Belmont, CA 94002/415-591-0769 (bedding)
Mount Labs, Inc. (See: LaPaloma Marketing, Inc.)
Nesci Enterprises, Inc., P.O. Box 119, Summit St., East Hampton, CT 06424/203-267-2588

New Method Mfg. Co., P.O. Box 175, Bradford, PA 16701/814-362-6611 (gun blue; Minute Man gun care)
Northern Instruments, Inc., 6680 North Highway 49, Lino Lake, MN 55014 (Stor-Safe rust preventer)
Numrich Arms Co., West Hurley, NY 12491 (44-40 gun blue)
Old World Oil Products, 3827 Queen Ave. No., Minneapolis, MN 55412
Omark Industries, P.O. Box 856, Lewiston, ID 83501/208-746-2351
Original Mink Oil, Inc., P.O. Box 20191, 11021 N.E. Beech St., Portland, OR 97220/503-255-2814
Outers Laboratories; see: Omark Industries
Ox-Yoke Originals, Inc., 130 Griffin Rd., West Suffield, CT 06093/203-668-5110 (dry lubrication patches)
Parker-Hale/Precision Sports, P.O. Box 708, Cortland, NY 13045
Bob Pease Accuracy, P.O. Box 787, Zipp Rd., New Braunfels, TX 78131/512-625-1342
A. E. Pennebaker Co., Inc., P.O. Box 1386, Greenville, SC 29602/803-235-8016 (Pyro Dux)
RBS Industries Corp., 1312 Washington Ave., St. Louis, MO 63103/314-241-8564 (Miracle All Purpose polishing cloth)
Reardon Prod., 103 W. Market St., Morrison, IL 61270 (Dry-Lube)
Rice Protective Gun Coatings, 235-30th St., West Palm Beach, FL 33407/305-845-2383
Richards Classic Oil Finish, John Richards, Rt. 2, Box 325, Bedford, KY 40006/502-255-7222 (gunstock oils, wax)
Rig Products, 87 Coney Island Dr., Sparks, NV 89431/703-331-5666
Rusteprufe Labs., Rte. 5, Sparta, WI 54656/608-269-4144
Rust Guardit, see: Schwab Industries
San/Bar Corp., Break-Free Div., 9999 Muirlands Pkwy., Irvine, CA 92718/714-855-9911 (lubricants)
Saunders Sptg. Gds., 338 Somerset, No. Plainfield, NJ 07060 (Sav-Bore)
Schwab Industries, Inc., P.O. Box 1269, Sequim, WA 98382/206-683-2944
Tyler Scott, Inc., P.O. Box 193, Milford, OH 45150/513-831-7603 (ML black solvent; patch lube)
Secoa Technologies, Inc., 3915 U.S. Hwy. 98 So., Lakeland, FL 33801/813-665-1734 (Teflon coatings)
Shooter's Choice (See Venco Industries)
Silver Dollar Guns, P.O. Box 475, 10 Frances St., Franklin, NH 03235/603-934-3292 (Silicone oil)
TDP Industries, Inc., 603 Airport Blvd., Doylestown, PA 18901/215-345-8687
Taylor & Robbins, Box 164, Rixford, PA 16745 (Throat Saver)
Texas Platers Supply Co., 2453 W. Five Mile Parkway, Dallas, TX 75233
Totally Dependable Products; See: TDP
Treso Ltd., P.O. Box 4640, Pagosa Springs, CO 81157/303-264-2295 (mfg. Durango Gun Rod)
C. S. Van Gorden, 1815 Main St., Bloomer, WI 54724/715-568-2612 (Van's Instant Blue)
United States Products Co., 518 Melwood Ave., Pittsburgh, PA 15213/412-621-2130 (Gold Medallion bore cleaner/conditioner)
Venco Industries, Inc., P.O. Box 598, Chesterland, OH 44026/216-719-9392 (Shooter's Choice bore cleaner & conditioner)
WD-40 Co., P.O. Box 80607, San Diego, CA 92138-9021/619-275-1400
Williams Gun Sight, 7389 Lapeer Rd., Davison, MI 48423 (finish kit)
Winslow Arms Inc., P.O. Box 783, Camden, SC 29020 (refinishing kit)
Wisconsin Platers Supply Co., (See Texas Platers Supply Co.)
Woodstream Corp., P.O. Box 327, Lititz, PA 17543 (Mask)
Zip Aerosol Prods., See Rig

## CUSTOM GUNSMITHS

A Square Co., Inc., A. B. Alphin, Rt. 4, Simmons Rd., Madison, IN 47250
Accuracy Systems Inc., 15203 N. Cave Creek Rd., Phoenix, AZ 85032/602-971-1991
Ahlman's Inc., R.R. 1, Box 20, Morristown, MN 55052/507-685-4244
Don Allen Inc., HC55, Box 322, Sturgis, SD 57785/605-347-4686
American Custom Gunmakers Guild, c/o Jan's Secretariat, 220 Division St., Northfield, MN 55057
Amrine's Gun Shop, 937 Luna Ave., Ojai, CA 93023
Antique Arms Co., D. F. Saunders, 1110 Cleveland Ave., Monett, MO 65708/417-235-6501 (Hawken copies)
Armament Gunsmithing Co., Inc., 525 Route 22, Hillside, NJ 07205/201-686-0960
Armament Systems & Procedures, Inc., Box 356, Appleton, WI 54912/414-731-6903
John & Mary Armbrust, John's Gun Shop, 823 S. Union St., Mishawaka, IN 46544/219-255-0973
Armurier Hiptmayer, P.O. Box 136, Eastman, Que. JOE 1P0, Canada/514-297-2492
Armuriers Liegeois-Artisans Reunis "ALAR," rue Masset 27, 4300 Ans, Belgium
Atkinson Gun Co., P.O. Box 512, Prescott, AZ 86301
Ed von Atzigen, The Custom Shop, 890 Cochrane Crescent, Peterborough, Ont., K9H 5N3 Canada/705-742-6693
Creighton Audette, 19 Highland Circle, Springfield, VT 05156/802-885-2331
Richard W. Baber, Hanson's Gun Center, 1440 N. Hancock Ave., Colorado Springs, CO 80903/303-634-4220
Bain and Davis Sptg. Gds., 307 E. Valley Blvd., San Gabriel, CA 91776/213-573-4241
Baer Custom Guns, 1725 Minesite Rd., Allentown, PA 18103/215-398-2362 (rifles)
Stan Baker, 5303 Roosevelt Way NE, Seattle, WA 98105/206-522-4575 (shotgun specialist)
Joe J. Balickie, Rte. 2, Box 56-G, Apex, NC 27502/919-362-5185
Barta's Gunsmithing, 10231 US Hwy., #10, Cato, WI 54206/414-732-4472
Donald Bartlett, 1808 S. 281st Place, Federal Way, WA 98003/206-946-4311

R. J. Beal, Jr., 170 W. Marshall Rd., Lansdowne, PA 19050/215-259-1220
Behlert Custom Guns, Inc., RD 2 Box 36C, Route 611 North, Pipersville, PA 18947/215-766-8681
George Beitzinger, 116-20 Atlantic Ave., Richmond Hill, NY 11419/718-847-7662
Bell's Custom Shop, 3309 Mannheim Rd., Franklin Park, IL 60131/312-678-1900 (handguns)
Bennett Gun Works, 561 Delaware Ave., Delmar, NY 12054/518-439-1862
Gordon Bess, 708 River St., Canon City, CO 81212/303-275-1073
Al Biesen, 5021 Rosewood, Spokane, WA 99208/509-328-9340
Roger Biesen, W. 2039 Sinto Ave., Spokane, WA 99201
Stephen L. Billeb, Box 1176, Big Piney, WY 83113/307-276-5627
E.C. Bishop & Son Inc., 119 Main St., P.O. Box 7, Warsaw, MO 65355/816-438-5121
Bob's Gun & Tackle Shop, 746 Granby St., Norfolk, VA 23510/804-627-8311
Duane Bolden, 1295 Lassen Dr., Hanford, CA 93230/209-582-6937 (rust bluing)
Boone Mountain Trading Post, 118 Sunrise Rd., Saint Marys, PA 15857/814-834-4879
Charles Boswell (Gunmakers), Div. of Saxon Arms Ltd., 615 Jasmine Ave. No., Tarpon Springs, FL 33589/813-938-4882
Art Bourne, (See Guncraft)
Kent Bowerly, H.C.R. Box 1903, Camp Sherman, OR 97730/503-595-6028
Larry D. Brace, 771 Blackfoot Ave., Eugene, OR 97404/503-688-1278
Breckheimers, Rte. 69-A, Parish, NY 13131
A. Briganti, 475 Rt. 32, Highland Mills, NY 10930/914-928-9816
Brown Precision Inc., P.O. Box 270W, 7786 Molinos Ave., Los Molinos, CA 96055 (rifles)
Buckland Gun Shop, Kenny Jarrett, Rt. 1, Box 44, Cowden Plantation, Jackson, SC 29831/803-471-3616 (rifles)
David Budin, Main St., Margaretville, NY 12455/914-568-4103
George Bunch, 7735 Garrison Rd., Hyattsville, MD 20784
Ida I. Burgess, Sam's Gun Shop, 25 Squam Rd., Rockport, MA 01966/617-546-6839 (bluing repairs)
Leo Bustani, P.O. Box 8125, W. Palm Beach, FL 33407/305-622-2710
Cache La Poudre Rifleworks, 168 No. College Ave., Ft. Collins, CO 80524/303-482-6913 (cust. ML)
Cameron's Guns, 16690 W. 11th Ave., Golden, CO 80401
Lou Camilli, 4700 Oahu Dr. N.E., Albuquerque, NM 87111/505-293-5259 (ML)
Dick Campbell, 1198 Finn Ave., Littleton, CO 80124/303-799-0145
Ralph L. Carter, Carter's Gun Shop, 225 G St., Penrose, CO 81240/303-372-6240
Shane Caywood, P.O. Box 321, Hwy. 51 So., Minocqua, WI 54548/715-356-9631
R. MacDonald Champlin, P.O. Box 693, Manchester, NH 03105/603-483-8559 (ML rifles and pistols)
Mark Chanlynn, Rocky Mtn. Rifle Wks. Ltd., 1704-14th St., Boulder, CO 80302/303-443-9189
Dave Chicoine, d/b/a Liberty A.S.P., 19 Key St., Eastport, ME 04631/207-853-2327
F. Bob Chow's Gun Shop, Inc., 3185 Mission St., San Francisco, CA 94110/415-282-8358
Claude Christopher, 1606 Berkley Rd., Greenville, NC 27834/919-756-0872
Classic Arms Corp., P.O. Box 8, Palo Alto, CA 94302/415-321-7243
John Edward Clark, R.R. #4, Tottenham, Ont. L0G 1W0 Canada/416-936-2131 (ML)
Kenneth E. Clark, 18738 Highway 99, Madera, CA 93637/209-674-6016
Clinton River Gun Serv. Inc., 30016 S. River Rd., Mt. Clemens, MI 48045/313-468-1090
Charles H. Coffin, 3719 Scarlet Ave., Odessa, TX 79762/915-366-4729
Jim Coffin, 250 Country Club Lane, Albany, OR 97321/503-928-4391
John Corry, 628 Martin Lane, Deerfield, IL 60015/312-541-6250 (English doubles & repairs)
Crest Carving Co., 14849 Dillow St., Westminster, CA 92683
Crocker, 1510 - 42nd St., Los Alamos, NM 87544 (rifles)
J. Lynn Crook, Rt. 6, Box 295-A, Lebanon, TN 37087/615-449-1930
Cumberland Knife & Gun Works, 5661 Bragg Blvd., Fayetteville, NC 28303/919-867-0009 (ML)
The Custom Gun Guild, 5091-F Buford Hwy., Doraville, GA 30340/404-455-0346
D&D Gun Shop, 363 Elmwood, Troy, MI 48083/313-583-1512
Dahl Gunshop, 6947 King Ave. West, Billings, MT 59106/406-652-3909
Homer L. Dangler, Box 254, Addison, MI 49220/517-547-6745 (Kentucky rifles; brochure $3)
Davis Co., 2793 Del Monte St., West Sacramento, CA 95691/916-372-6789
Jack Dever, 8520 N.W. 90, Oklahoma City, OK 73132/405-721-6393
R. H. Devereaux, D. D. Custom Rifles, 5240 Mule Deer Dr., Colorado Springs, CO 80919/303-548-8468
Ron Dilliott, Rt. 3, Box 340, Scarlett Rd., Dandridge, TN 37725/615-397-9204
Dominic DiStefano, 4303 Friar Lane, Colorado Springs, CO 80907
Dixon Muzzleloading Shop, Inc., RD #1, Box 175, Kempton, PA 19529/215-756-6271 (ML)
William Dixon, Buckhorn Gun Works, Rt. 4 Box 1230, Rapid City, SD 57702/605-787-6289
C. P. Donnelly-Siskiyou Gun Works, 405 Kubli Rd., Grants Pass, OR 97527/503-846-6604
Duncan's Gunworks Inc., 1619 Grand Ave., San Marcos, CA 92069/619-727-0515
David R. Dunlop, Rte. 1, Box 199, Rolla, ND 58367
Jere Eggleston, P.O. Box 50238, Columbia, SC 29250/803-799-3402
Elko Arms, Dr. L. Kortz, 28 rue Ecole Moderne, B-7400 Soignies, H.T., Belgium
William A. Emick, P.O. Box 741, Philipsburg, MT 59858/406-859-3280
Bob Emmons, 238 Robson Rd., Grafton, OH 44044/216-458-5890
Englishtown Sporting Goods, Inc., David J. Maxham, 38 Main St., Englishtown, NJ 07726/201-446-7717
Armas ERBI, S. coop., Avda. Eulogio Estarta, Elgoibar (Guipuzcoa), Spain
Ken Eyster, Heritage Gunsmiths Inc., 6441 Bishop Rd., Centerburg, OH 43011/614-625-6131

Andy Fautheree, P.O. Box 4607, Pagosa Springs, CO 81157/303-731-2502

Ted Fellowes, Beaver Lodge, 9245-16th Ave., S.W., Seattle, WA 98106/206-763-1698 (muzzleloaders)

Fiberpro, Robert Culbertson, 3636 California St., San Diego, CA 92101/619-295-7703 (rifles)

Jack First Distributors Inc., 44633 Sierra Highway, Lancaster, CA 93534/805-945-6981

Marshall F. Fish, Rt. 22 North, RR2 Box 2439, Westport, NY 12993/518-962-4897

Jerry A. Fisher, 1244-4th Ave. West, Kalispell, MT 59901/406-755-7093

Flaig's Inc., 2200 Evergreen Rd., Millvale, PA 15209/412-821-1717

Flynn's Cust. Guns, P.O. Box 7461, Alexandria, LA 71306/318-445-7130

Larry L. Forster, Box 212, 220-1st St. N.E., Gwinner, ND 58040/701-678-2475

Fountain Products, 492 Prospect Ave., West Springfield, MA 01089/413-781-4651

Frank's Custom Rifles, 10430 E. Dusty Spur, Tucson, AZ 85749/602-749-1503

Freeland's Scope Stands, 3737—14th Ave., Rock Island, IL 61201/309-788-7449

Fredrick Gun Shop, 10 Elson Drive, Riverside, RI 02915/401-433-2805

Frontier Arms, Inc., 420 E. Riding Club Rd., Cheyenne, WY 82001

Frontier Shop & Gallery, Depot 1st & Main, Riverton, WY 82501/307-856-4498

Fuller Gunshop, Cooper Landing, AK 99572

Karl J. Furr, 76 East 350 No., Orem, UT 84057/801-225-2603

Gander Mountain, Inc., P.O. Box 128, Wilmot, WI 53192/414-862-2344

Garcia Natl. Gun Traders, Inc., 225 S.W. 22nd Ave., Miami, FL 33135

Jim Garrett, 1413 B. E. Olive Ct., Fort Collins, CO 80524

David Gentry Custom Gunmaker, P.O. Box 1440, Belgrade, MT 59714/406-586-1405 (cust. Montana Mtn. Rifle)

Edwin Gillman, R.R. 6, Box 195, Hanover, PA 17331/717-632-1662

Gilman-Mayfield, 1552 N. 1st, Fresno, CA 93703/209-237-2500

Dale Goens, Box 224, Cedar Crest, NM 87008

Dave Good, 14906 Robinwood St., Lansing, MI 48906/517-321-5392

A. R. Goode, 4125 N.E. 28th Terr., Ocala, FL 32670/904-622-9575

Goodling's Gunsmithing, R.D. #1, Box 1097, Spring Grove, PA 17362/717-225-3350

Gordie's Gun Shop, Gordon Mulholland, 1401 Fulton St., Streator, IL 61364/815-672-7202

Charles E. Grace, 10144 Elk Lake Rd., Williamsburg, MI 49690/616-264-9483

Roger M. Green & J. Earl Bridges, P.O. Box 984, 315 S. 2nd St., Glenrock, WY 82637/307-436-9804

Griffin & Howe, 589 Broadway, New York, NY 10012/212-966-5323

H. L. "Pete" Grisel, 61912 Skyline View Dr., Bend, OR 97701/503-389-2649

Karl Guenther, 165 Granite Springs Rd., Yorktown Heights, NY 10598/914-245-5610

Gun City, 504 Main Ave., Bismarck, ND 58501/701-223-2304

Guncraft, Inc., 117 W. Pipeline, Hurst, TX 76053/817-282-6481

Guncraft (Kamloops) Ltd., 127 Victoria St., Kamloops, B.C. V2C 1Z4, Canada/604-374-2151

The Gun Works, Joe Williams, 236 Main St., Springfield, OR 97477/503-741-4118 (ML)

The Gunworks Inc., 3434 Maple Ave., Brookfield IL 60513/312-387-7888

H-S Precision, Inc., 112 N. Summit, Prescott, AZ 86302/602-445-0607

Hagn Rifles & Actions, Martin Hagn, Cranbrook, B.C. V1C 4H9, Canada/604-426-3334 (s.s. actions & rifles)

Fritz Hallberg, The Outdoorsman, P.O. Box 339, Ontario, OR 97914/503-889-3135

Charles E. Hammans, P.O. Box 788, 2022 McCracken, Stuttgart, AR 72160/501-673-1388

Dick Hanson, Hanson's Gun Center, 521 So. Circle Dr., Colorado Springs, CO 80910/303-634-4220

Harkrader's Cust. Gun Shop, 825 Radford St., Christiansburg, VA 24073

Rob't W. Hart & Son Inc., 401 Montgomery St., Nescopeck, PA 18635/717-752-3655 (actions, stocks)

Hartmann & Weiss KG, Rahlstedter Bahnhofstr. 47, 2000 Hamburg 73, W. Germany

Hubert J. Hecht, Waffen-Hecht, 10112 Fair Oaks Blvd., Fair Oaks, CA 95628/916-966-1020

Edw. O. Hefti, 300 Fairview, College Station, TX 77840/409-696-4959

Stephen Heilmann, P.O. Box 657, Grass Valley, CA 95945/916-272-8758

Iver Henriksen, 1211 So. 2nd St. W, Missoula, MT 59801 (Rifles)

Heppler's Gun Shop, 6000 B Soquel Ave., Santa Cruz, CA 95062/408-475-1235

Wm. Hobaugh, The Rifle Shop, Box M, Philipsburg, MT 59858/406-859-3515

Hoenig and Rodman, 6521 Morton Dr., Boise, ID 83705/208-375-1116

Dick Holland, 422 N.E. 6th St., Newport, OR 97365/503-265-7556

Hollis Gun Shop, 917 Rex St., Carlsbad, NM 88220/505-835-3782

Bill Holmes, Rt. 2, Box 242, Fayetteville, AR 72701/501-521-8958

Steven Dodd Hughes, P.O. Box 11455, Eugene, OR 97440/503-485-8869 (ML; ctlg. $3)

Al Hunkeler, Buckskin Machine Works, 3235 So. 358th St., Auburn, WA 98001/206-927-5412 (ML)

Huntington's, P.O. Box 991, Oroville, CA 95965/916-534-1210

Hyper-Single Precision SS Rifles, 520 E. Beaver, Jenks, OK 74037/918-299-2391

Independent Machine & Gun Shop, 1416 N. Hayes, Pocatello, ID 83201

Paul Jaeger, Inc. P.O. Box 449, 1 Madison Ave., Grand Junction, TN 38039/901-764-6909

R. L. Jamison, Jr., Route 4, Box 200, Moses Lake, WA 98837/509-762-2659

J. J. Jenkins Ent. Inc., 375 Pine Ave. No. 25, Goleta, CA 93017/805-967-1366

Jerry's Gun Shop, 9220 Ogden Ave., Brookfield, IL 60513/312-485-5200

Neal G. Johnson, Gunsmithing Inc., 111 Marvin Dr., Hampton, VA 23666/804-838-8091

Peter S. Johnson, The Orvis Co., Inc., Manchester, VT 05254/802-362-3622

Jos. Jurjevic, Gunshop, 605 Main St., Marble Falls, TX 78654/512-693-3012

Ken's Gun Specialties, K. Hunnell, Rt. 1 Box 147, Lakeview, AR 72642/501-431-5606

Kennedy Gun Shop, Rte. 12, Box 21, Clarksville, TN 37040/615-647-6043

Kennon's Custom Rifles, 5408 Biffle, Stone Mtn., GA 30088/404-469-9339

Stanley Kenvin, 5 Lakeville Lane, Plainview, NY 11803/516-931-0321

Kesselring Gun Shop, 400 Pacific Hiway No., Burlington, WA 98233/206-724-3113

Benjamin Kilham, Kilham & Co., Main St., Box 37, Lyme, NH 03768/603-795-4112

Don Klein Custom Guns, P.O. Box 277, Camp Douglas, WI 54618/608-427-6948

K. W. Kleinendorst, R.D. #1, Box 113B, Hop Bottom, PA 18824/717-289-4687

Terry K. Kopp, Highway 13, Lexington, MO 64067/816-259-2636

J. Korzinek, R.D. #2, Box 73, Canton, PA 17724/717-673-8512 (riflesmith) (broch. $1.50)

Lee Kuhns, 652 Northeast Palson Rd., Paulsbo, WA 98370/206-692-5790

Sam Lair, 520 E. Beaver, Jenks, OK 74037/918-299-2391 (single shots)

Maynard Lambert, Kamas, UT 84036

Harry Lawson Co., 3328 N. Richey Blvd., Tucson, AZ 85716/602-326-1117

John G. Lawson, (The Sight Shop), 1802 E. Columbia, Tacoma, WA 98404/206-474-5465

Mark Lee, P.O. Box 20379, Minneapolis, MN 55420/612-884-4060

Bill Leeper, (See Guncraft)

Frank LeFever & Sons, Inc., R.D. #1, Box 31, Lee Center, NY 13363/315-337-6722

Leland Firearms Co., 13 Mountain Ave., Llewellyn Park, West Orange, NJ 07052/201-964-7500 (shotguns)

Lilja Precision Rifle Barrels, Inc., 245 Compass Creek Rd., P.O. Box 372, Plains, MT 59859/406-826-3084

Al Lind, 7821—76th Ave. S.W., Tacoma, WA 98498/206-584-6363

Robt. L. Lindsay, J & B Enterprises, 9416 Emory Grove Rd., P.O. Box 805, Gaithersburg, MD 20877/301-948-2941 (services only)

Ljutic Ind., Box 2117, Yakima, WA 98904 (shotguns)

Llanerch Gun Shop, 2800 Township Line, Upper Darby, PA 19082/215-789-5462

James W. Lofland, 2275 Larkin Rd., Boothwyn, PA 19061/215-485-0391 (SS rifles)

London Guns, 1528—20th St., Santa Monica, CA 90404/213-828-8486

Longbranch Gun Bluing Co., 2455 Jacaranda Lane, Los Osos, CA 93402/805-528-1792

McCann's Muzzle-Gun Works, Tom McCann, 200 Federal City Rd., Pennington, NJ 08534/609-737-1707 (ML)

McCormick's Gun Bluing Service, 609 N.E. 104th Ave., Vancouver, WA 98664/206-256-0579

Stan McFarland, 2221 Idella Ct., Grand Junction, CO 81506/303-243-4704 (cust. rifles)

Bill McGuire, 1600 N. Eastmont Ave., East Wenatchee, WA 98801

MPI Stocks, P.O. Box 03266, 7011 N. Reno Ave., Portland, OR 97203/503-289-8025 (rifles)

Harold E. MacFarland, Route #4, Box 1249, Cottonwood, AZ 86326/602-634-5320

Nick Makinson, R.R. #3, Komoka, Ont. N0L 1R0 Canada/519-471-5462 (English guns; repairs & renovations)

Monte Mandarino, 136 Fifth Ave. West, Kalispell, MT 59901/406-257-6208 (Penn. rifles)

Lowell Manley, 3684 Pine St., Deckerville, MI 48427/313-376-3665

Mantzoros Cust. Gunsmith, P.O. Box 795, Cooper Landing, AK 99572/907-595-1201

Dale Marfell, 107 N. State St., Litchfield, IL 62056/217-327-3832

Marquart Precision Co., P.O. Box 1740, Prescott, AZ 86302/602-445-5646

Elwyn H. Martin, Martin's Gun Shop, 937 S. Sheridan Blvd., Lakewood, CO 80226/303-922-2184

Mashburn Arms & Sporting Goods Co., Inc., 1218 N. Pennsylvania, Oklahoma City, OK 73107/405-236-5151

Seely Masker, Custom Rifles, 261 Washington Ave., Pleasantville, NY 10570/914-769-2627

E. K. Matsuoka, 2801 Kinohou Place, Honolulu HI 96822/808-988-3008

Geo. E. Matthews & Son Inc., 10224 S. Paramount Blvd., Downey, CA 90241

Maurer Arms, 2154-16th St., Akron, OH 44314/216-745-6864 (muzzleloaders)

John E. Maxson, 3507 Red Oak Lane, Plainview, TX 79072/806-293-9042 (high grade rifles)

R. M. Mercer, 216 S. Whitewater Ave., Jefferson, WI 53549/414-674-3839

Miller Arms, Inc., Dean E. Miller, P.O. Box 260, St. Onge, SD 57779/605-578-1790

Miller Custom Rifles, 655 Dutton Ave., San Leandro, CA 94577/415-568-2447

Miller Gun Works, S. A. Miller, P.O. Box 7326, Tamuning, Guam 96911

David Miller Co., 3131 E. Greenlee Rd., Tucson, AZ 85716/602-326-3117 (classic rifles)

Tom Miller, c/o Huntington, 601 Oro Dam Blvd., Oroville, CA 95965/916-534-8000

Earl Milliron, 1249 N.E. 166th Ave., Portland, OR 97230/503-252-3725

Monell Custom Guns, Red Mill Road, RD #2, Box 96, Pine Bush, NY 12566/914-744-3021

Wm. Larkin Moore & Co., 31360 Via Colinas, Suite 109, Westlake Village, CA 91360/213-889-4160

J. W. Morrison Custom Rifles, 4015 W. Sharon, Phoenix, AZ 85029/602-978-3754

Mitch Moschetti, P.O. Box 27065, Cromwell, CT 06416/203-632-2308

Mountain Bear Rifle Works, Inc., Wm. Scott Bickett, 100-B Ruritan Rd., Sterling, VA 22170/703-430-0420

Larry Mrock, R.F.D. 3, Box 207, Woodhill-Hooksett Rd., Bow, NH 03301/603-224-4096 (broch. $3)

Bruce A. Nettestad, R.R. 1, Box 140, Pelican Rapids, MN 56572/218-863-4301

Newman Gunshop, 119 Miller Rd., Agency, IA 52530/515-937-5775

Paul R. Nickels, P.O. Box 71043, Las Vegas, NV 89170/702-458-7149

Ted Nicklas, 5504 Hegel Rd., Goodrich, MI 48438/313-797-4493

William J. Nittler, 290 More Drive, Boulder Creek, CA 95006/408-338-3376 (shotgun repairs)

Jim Norman, Custom Gunstocks, 11230 Calenda Rd., San Diego, CA 92127/619-487-4173

Nu-Line Guns, 1053 Caulks Hill Rd., Harvester, MO 63303/314-441-4500

Olympic Arms Inc., 624 Old Pacific Hwy. S.E., Olympia, WA 98503/206-456-3471
Vic Olson, 5002 Countryside Dr., Imperial, MO 63052/314-296-8086
Oregon Trail Riflesmiths, Inc., P.O. Box 45212, Boise, ID 83711/208-336-8631
The Orvis Co., Inc., Peter S. Johnson, Rt. 7A, Manchester, VT 05254/802-362-3622
Maurice Ottmar, Box 657, 113 East Fir, Coulee City, WA 99115/509-632-5717
Pachmayr Gun Works, 1220 S. Grand Ave., Los Angeles, CA 90015
Pasadena Gun Center, 206 E. Shaw, Pasadena, TX 77506/713-472-0417
Paterson Gunsmithing, 438 Main St., Paterson, NJ 07501/201-345-4100
John Pell, 410 College Ave., Trinidad, CO 81082/303-846-9406
Penrod Precision, 126 E. Main St., P.O. Box 307, No. Manchester, IN 46962/219-981-8385
A. W. Peterson Gun Shop, 1693 Old Hwy. 441, Mt. Dora, FL 32757 (ML)
Eugene T. Plante, Gene's Custom Guns, 3890 Hill Ave., P.O. Box 10534, White Bear Lake, MN 55110/612-429-5105
Power Custom, Inc., P.O. Box 1604, Independence, MO 64055/816-833-3102
Ridge Guncraft, Inc., 125 E. Tyrone Rd., Oak Ridge, TN 37830/615-483-4024
Rifle Ranch, Jim Wilkinson, Rte. 10, 3301 Willow Creek Rd., Prescott, AZ 86301/602-778-7501
Rifle Shop, Box M, Philipsburg, MT 59858
Rite Bros. Firearms Inc., P.O. Box 2054, Clearbrook, B.C. V2T 1V6, Canada/604-853-5959
J. J. Roberts, 166 Manassas Dr., Manassas Park, VA 22111/703-361-4513
Wm. A. Roberts Jr., Rte. 4, Box 75, Athens, AL 35611/205-232-7027 (ML)
Don Robinson, Pennsylvania Hse., 36 Fairfaix Crescent, Southowram, Halifax, W. Yorkshire HX3 9SQ, England (airifle stocks)
Bob Rogers Guns, P.O. Box 305, Franklin Grove, IL 61031/815-456-2685
Carl Roth, 4728 Pine Ridge Ave., Cheyenne, WY 82001/307-634-3958
Royal Arms, 1210 Bert Acosta, El Cajon, CA 92020/619-448-5466
R.P.S. Gunshop, 11 So. Haskell, Central Point, OR 97502/503-664-5010
Russell's Rifle Shop, Route 5, Box 92, Georgetown, TX 78626/512-778-5338
SSK Industries, Rt. 1, Della Dr., Bloomingdale, OH 43910/614-264-0176
Sanders Custom Gun Serv., 2358 Tyler Lane, Louisville, KY 40205
Sandy's Custom Gunshop, Rte. #1, Box 20, Rockport, IL 62370/217-437-4241
Saratoga Arms Co., 1752 N. Pleasantview Rd., Pottstown, PA 19464/215-323-8326
Roy V. Schaefer, 965 W. Hilliard Lane, Eugene, OR 97404/503-688-4333
SGW, Inc. (formerly Schuetzen Gun Works), see: Olympic Arms
Schumaker's Gun Shop, Rte. 4, Box 500, Colville, WA 99114/509-684-4848
Schwartz Custom Guns, 9621 Coleman Rd., Haslett, MI 48840/517-339-8939
David W. Schwartz Custom Guns, 2505 Waller St., Eau Claire, WI 54701/715-832-1735
Schwarz's Gun Shop, 41-15th St., Wellsburg, WV 26070/304-737-0533
Butch Searcy, 15, Rd. 3804, Farmington, NM 87401/505-327-3419
Shane's Gunsmithing, P.O. Box 321, Hwy. 51 So., Minocqua, WI 54548/715-356-9631
Shaw's, Finest in Guns, 9447 W. Lilac Rd., Escondido, CA 92026/619-728-7070
E. R. Shaw Inc., Small Arms Mfg. Co., Thoms Run Rd., Bridgeville, PA 15017/412-221-4343
George H. Sheldon, P.O. Box 475, Franklin, NH 03235 (45 autos only)
Lynn Shelton Custom Rifles, 1516 Sherry Court, Elk City, OK 73644/405-225-0372
Shell Shack, 113 E. Main, Laurel, MT 59044/406-628-8986 (ML)
Shilen Rifles, Inc., 205 Metro Park Blvd., Ennis, TX 75119/214-875-5318
Harold H. Shockley, 204 E. Farmington Rd., Hanna City, IL 61536/309-565-4524 (hot bluing & plating)
Shootin' Shack, 1065 Silverbeach Rd. #1, Riviera Beach, FL 33403/305-842-0990 ('smithing services)
Walter Shultz, 1752 N. Pleasantview Rd., Pottstown, PA 19464
Silver Dollar Guns, P.O. Box 475, 10 Frances St., Franklin, NH 03235/603-934-3292 (45 autos only)
Simmons Gun Spec., 700 So. Rogers Rd., Olathe, KS 66062/913-782-3131
Simms Hardware Co., 2801 J St., Sacramento, CA 95816/916-442-3800
John R. Skinner, c/o Orvis Co., Manchester, VT 05250
Steve Sklany, 566 Birch Grove Dr., Kalispell, MT 59901/406-755-4527 (Ferguson rifle)
Jerome F. Slezak, 1290 Marlowe, Lakewood (Cleveland), OH 44107/216-221-1668
Art Smith, 4124 Thrushwood Lane, Minnetonka, MN 55345/612-935-7829
John Smith, 912 Lincoln, Carpentersville, IL 60110
Jordan T. Smith, c/o Orvis Co., Manchester, VT 05250
Snapp's Gunshop, 6911 E. Washington Rd., Clare, MI 48617/517-386-9226
Fred D. Speiser, 2229 Dearborn, Missoula, MT 59801/406-549-8133
Spencer Reblue Service, 1820 Tupelo Trail, Holt, MI 48842/517-694-7474 (electroless nickel plating)
Sportsmen's Equip. Co., 915 W. Washington, San Diego, CA 92103/619-296-1501
Sportsmen's Exchange & Western Gun Traders, Inc., P.O. Box 111, 560 S. "C" St., Oxnard, CA 93032/805-483-1917
Jess L. Stark, Stark Mach. Co., 12051 Stroud, Houston, TX 77072/713-498-5882
Ken Starnes, Rt. 1, Box 269, Scroggins, TX 75480/214-365-2312
Steelman's Gun Shop, 10465 Beers Rd., Swartz Creek, MI 48473/313-753-4884
Keith Stegall, Box 696, Gunnison, CO 81230
Date Storey, 1764 S. Wilson, Casper, WY 82601/307-237-2414
Victor W. Strawbridge, 6 Pineview Dr., Dover Point, Dover, NH 03820/603-742-0013
W. C. Strutz, Rifle Barrels, Inc., P.O. Box 611, Eagle River, WI 54521/715-479-4766
Suter's House of Guns, 332 N. Tejon, Colorado Springs, CO 80902/303-635-1475
A. D. Swenson's 45 Shop, P.O. Box 606, Fallbrook, CA 92028
Talmage Ent., 43197 E. Whittier, Hemet, CA 92344/714-927-2397
Target Airgun Supply, P.O. Box 428, South Gate, CA 90280/213-569-3417

Taylor & Robbins, Box 164, Rixford, PA 16745
James A. Tertin, c/o Gander Mountain, P.O. Box 128 - Hwy. W, Wilmot, WI 53192/414-862-2344
Larry R. Thompson, Larry's Gun Shop, 521 E. Lake Ave., Watsonville, CA 95076/408-724-5328
Daniel Titus, 872 Penn St., Bryn Mawr, PA 19010/215-525-8829
Tom's Gunshop, Tom Gillman, 4435 Central, Hot Springs, AR 71913/501-624-3856
Todd Trefts, 217 W. Koch, Bozeman, MT 59715/406-587-3817
Trinko's Gun Serv., 1406 E. Main, Watertown, WI 53094
Dennis A. "Doc" Ulrich, D.O.C. Specialists, Inc., 2209 S. Central Ave., Cicero, IL 60650/312-652-3606
Upper Missouri Trading Co., Inc., Box 181, Crofton, MO 68730
Chas. VanDyke Gunsmith Service, 201 Gatewood Cir. W., Burleson, TX 76028/817-295-7373 (shotgun & recoil pad specialist)
Milton Van Epps, Rt. 69-A, Parish, NY 13131/313-625-7251
Gil Van Horn, P.O. Box 207, Llano, CA 93544
John Vest, P.O. Box 1552, Susanville, CA 96130/916-253-3681
Vic's Gun Refinishing, 6 Pineview Dr., Dover, NH 03820/603-742-0013
Walker Arms Co., Rt. 2, Box 73, Hiwy 80 West, Selma, AL 36701/205-872-6231
Walker Arms Co., 127 N. Main St., Joplin, MO 64801
R. D. Wallace, Star Rt. Box 76, Grandin, MO 63943/314-593-4773
R. A. Wardrop, Box 245, 409 E. Marble St., Mechanicsburg, PA 17055
Weatherby's, 2781 Firestone Blvd., South Gate, CA 90280/213-569-7186
Weaver Arms Co., P.O. Box 8, Dexter, MO 63841/314-568-3800 (ambidextrous bolt action)
J. S. Weeks & Son, 4748 Bailey Rd., Dimondale, MI 48821 (custom rifles)
Terry Werth, 1203 Woodlawn Rd., Lincoln, IL 62656/217-732-3870
Cecil Weems, P.O. Box 657, Mineral Wells, TX 76067/817-325-1462
Wells Sport Store, Fred Wells, 110 N. Summit St., Prescott, AZ 86301/602-445-3655
R. A. Wells Ltd., 3452 N. 1st Ave., Racine, WI 53402/414-639-5223
Terry Werth, 1203 Woodlawn Rd., Lincoln, IL 62656/217-732-9314
Robert G. West, 27211 Huey Lane, Eugene, OR 97402/503-689-6610
Western Gunstocks Mfg. Co., 550 Valencia School Rd., Aptos, CA 95003
Whitefish Sportsman, Pete Forthofer, 711 Spokane Ave., Whitefish, MT 59937/406-862-7252
Duane Wiebe, P.O. Box 497, Lotus, CA 95651/916-626-6240
M. Wiest & Son, 125 E. Tyrone Rd., Oak Ridge, TN 37830/615-483-4024
Dave Wills, 2776 Brevard Ave., Montgomery, AL 36109/205-272-8446
Williams Gun Sight Co., 7389 Lapeer Rd., Davison, MI 48423
Bob Williams, P.O. Box 143, Boonsboro, MD 21713
Williamson-Pate Gunsmith Service, 117 W. Pipeline, Hurst, TX 76053/817-268-2887
Thomas E. Wilson, 644 Spruce St., Boulder, CO 80302 (restorations)
Robert M. Winter, R.R. 2, Box 484, Menno, SD 57045/605-387-5322
Lester Womack, 512 Westwood Dr., Prescott, AZ 86301/602-778-9624
Mike Yee, 29927-56 Pl. S., Auburn, WA 98001/206-839-3991
York County Gun Works, RR 4, Tottenham, Ont., LOG 1WO Canada (muzzleloaders)
Russ Zeeryp, 1601 Foard Dr., Lynn Ross Manor, Morristown, TN 37814

## CUSTOM METALSMITHS

Don Allen, Inc., HC55, Box 322, Sturgis, SD 57785/605-347-4686
Alley Supply Co., P.O. Box 848, Gardnerville, NV 89410/702-782-3800
Baer Custom Guns, 1725 Minesite Rd., Allentown, PA 18103/215-398-2362
Al Biesen & Assoc., West 2039 Sinto Ave., Spokane, WA 99201/509-328-6818
Ross Billingsley & Brownell, Box 25, Dayton, WY 82836/307-655-9344
E.C. Bishop & Son Inc., 119 Main St., P.O. Box 7, Warsaw, MO 65355/816-438-5121
Ted Blackburn, 85 E., 700 South, Springville, UT 84663/801-489-7341 (precision metalwork; steel trigger guard)
Gregg Boeke, Rte. 2, Box 149, Cresco, IA 52136/319-547-3746
Larry D. Brace, 771 Blackfoot Ave., Eugene, OR 97404/503,688-1278
A. Briganti, 475 Rt. 32, Highland Mills, NY 10930/914-928-9816
Leo Bustani, P.O. 8125, W. Palm Beach, FL 33407/305-622-2710
C&G Precision, 10152 Trinidad, El Paso, TX 79925/915-592-5496
Clinton River Gun Serv. Inc., 30016 S. River Rd., Mt. Clemens, MI 48045/313-468-1090
Dave Cook, 5831-26th Lane, Brampton, MI 49837/906-428-1235
Crandall Tool & Machine Co., 1540 N. Mitchell St., Cadillac, MI 49601/616-775-5562
Daniel Cullity Restorations, 209 Old County Rd., East Sandwich, MA 02537/617-888-1147
The Custom Gun Guild, Frank Wood, 5091-F Buford Highway, Doraville, GA 30340/404-455-0346
D&D Gun Shop, 363 Elmwood, Troy, MI 48083/313-583-1512
D&H Precision Tooling, 7522 Barnard Mill Rd., Ringwood, IL 60072/815-653-9611
Jack Dever, 8520 N.W. 90th, Oklahoma City, OK 73132/405-721-6393
Ken Eyster Heritage Gunsmiths Inc., 6441 Bishop Rd., Centerburg, OH 43011/614-625-43031
Flaig's Inc., 2200 Evergreen Rd., Millvale, PA 15209/412-821-1717
Fountain Prods., 492 Prospect Ave., W. Springfield, MA 01089/413-781-4651
Frank's Custom Rifles, 10420 E. Rusty Spur, Tucson, AZ 85749/602-749-4563
Fredrick Gun Shop, 10 Elson Dr., Riverside, RI 02915/401-433-2805 (engine turning)
Geo. M. Fullmer, 2499 Mavis St., Oakland, CA 94601/415-533-4193 (precise chambering—300 cals.)
Roger M. Green & J. Earl Bridges, P.O. Box 984, 315 S. 2nd St., Glenrock, WY 82637/307-436-9804
Gentry's The Bozeman Gunsmith, 2010 N. 7th, Bozeman, MT 59715/406-586-1405
Griffin & Howe, 589 Broadway, New York, NY 10012/212-966-5323
Karl Guenther, 165 Granite Springs Rd., Yorktown Heights, NY 10598/914-245-5610

Harkrader's Custom Gun Shop, 825 Radford St., Christiansburg, VA 24073
Robert W. Hart & Son, Inc., 401 Montgomery St., Nescopeck, PA 18635/717-752-3655
Hubert J. Hecht, Waffen-Hecht, 10122 Fair Oaks Blvd., Fair Oaks, CA 95628/916-966-1020
Stephen Heilmann, P.O. Box 657, Grass Valley, CA 95945/916-272-8758
Heppler's Gun Shop, 6000 B Soquel Ave., Santa Cruz, CA 95062/408-475-1235
Klaus Hiptmayer, P.O. Box 136, R.R. 112 #750, Eastman, Que. JOE1PO, Canada/514-297-2492
Hollis Gun Shop, 917 Rex St., Carlsbad, NM 88220/505-885-3782
Huntington's, P.O. Box 991, Oroville, CA 95965
Paul Jaeger, Inc., P.O. Box 449, 1 Madison St., Grand Junction, TN 38039/901-764-6909
R. L. Jamison, Jr., Rt. 4, Box 200, Moses Lake, WA 98837/509-762-2659
Ken Jantz, Rt. 1, Sulphur, OK 73086/405-622-3790
Neil A. Jones, RD #1, Box 403A, Saegertown, PA 16433/814-763-2769
Kennons Custom Rifles, 5408 Biffle Rd., Stone Mountain, GA 30088/404-469-9339
Benjamin Kilham, Kilham & Co., Main St., Box 37, Lyme, NH 03768/603-795-4112
Terry K. Kopp, Highway 13, Lexington, MO 64067/816-259-2636
Ron Lampert, Rt. 1, Box 61, Guthrie, MN 56461/218-854-7345
Mark Lee, P.O. Box 20379, Minneapolis, MN 55420/612-884-4060
Lilja Precision Rifle Barrels, Inc., 245 Compass Creek Rd., P.O. Box 372, Plains, MT 59859/406-826-3084
McIntyre Tools & Guns, P.O. Box 491, State Rd. #1144, Troy, NC 27371/919-572-2603
Miller Arms, Inc., P.O. Box 260, St. Onge, SD 57779/605-578-1790
J. W. Morrison Custom Rifles, 4015 W. Sharon, Phoenix, AZ 85029/602-978-3754
Bruce A. Nettestad, Rt. 1, Box 140, Pelican Rapids, MN 56572/218-863-4301
Vic Olson, 5002 Countryside Dr., Imperial, MO 63052/314-296-8086
Pasadena Gun Center, 206 E. Shaw, Pasadena, TX 77506/713-472-0417
Penrod Precision, 126 E. Main St., P.O. Box 307, No. Manchester, IN 46962/219-982-8385
Precise Chambering Co., 2499 Mavis St., Oakland, CA 94601/415-533-4193
Dave Talley, Rt. 4, Box 366, Leesville, SC 29070/803-532-2700
J. W. Van Patten, P.O. Box 145, Foster Hill, Milford, PA 18337/717-296-7069
Herman Waldron, Box 475, Pomeroy, WA 99347/509-843-1404
R. D. Wallace, Star Rt. Box 16, Grandin, MO 64943/314-593-4773
Fred Wells, Wells Sport Store, 110 N. Summit St., Prescott, AZ 86301/602-445-3655
Terry Werth, 1203 Woodlawn Rd., Lincoln, IL 62656/217-732-3870
John Westrom, Precise Firearm Finishing, 25 N.W. 44th Ave., Des Moines, IA 50313/515-288-8680

## DECOYS

Carry-Lite, Inc., 5203 W. Clinton Ave., Milwaukee, WI 53223
Deer Me Products Co., Box 34, 1208 Park St., Anoka, MN 55303/612-421-8971 (Anchors)
Ted Devlet's Custom Purveyors, P.O. Box 886, Fort Lee, NJ 07024/201-886-0196
Flambeau Prods. Corp., 15981 Valplast Rd., Middlefield, OH 44062/216-632-1631
G & H Decoy Mfg. Co., P.O. Box 1208, Henryetta, OK 74437/918-652-3314
Penn's Woods Products, Inc., 19 W. Pittsburgh St., Delmont, PA 15626/412-468-8311
Royal Arms, 1210 Bert Acosta, El Cajon, CA 92020/619-448-5466 (wooden, duck)
Ron E. Skaggs, P.O. Box 34, Princeton, IL 61356/815-875-8207
Woodstream Corp., P.O. Box 327, Lititz, PA 17543

## ENGRAVERS, ENGRAVING TOOLS

Abominable Engineering, P.O. Box 1904, Flagstaff, AZ 86002/602-779-3025
John J. Adams, P.O. Box 167, Corinth, VT 05039/802-439-5904
American Derringer Corp., 127 N. Lacy Dr., Waco, TX 76705/817-799-9111
Paolo Barbetti, c/o Stan's Gunshop, 5303 Roosevelt Way N.E., Seattle, WA 98105/206-522-4575
Robert L. Barnard, P.O. Box 93, Fordyce, AR 71742/501-352-5861
Billy R. Bates, 2905 Lynnwood Circle S.W., Decatur, AL 35603/205-355-3690
Joseph C. Bayer, 439 Sunset Ave., Sunset Hill Griggstown, RD 1, Princeton, NJ 08540/201-359-7283
Angelo Bee, 10703 Irondale Ave., Chatsworth, CA 91311/213-882-1567
Sid Bell Originals Inc., R.D. 2, Box 219, Tully, NY 13159/607-842-6431
Jim Bina, 2007 Howard St., Evanston, IL 60202/312-475-6377
Weldon Bledsoe, 6812 Park Place Dr., Fort Worth, TX 76118/817-589-1704
Rudolph V. Bochenski, 1410 Harlem Rd., Cheektowaga, NY 14206/716-896-3619
Carl Bleile, Box 11464, Cincinnati, OH 45211/513-662-0802
C. Roger Bleile, Box 5112, Cincinnati, OH 45205/513-251-0249
Erich Boessler, Gun Engraving Intl., Am Vogeltal 3, 8732 Münnerstadt, W. Germany/9733-9443
Henry "Hank" Bonham, 218 Franklin Ave., Seaside Heights, NJ 08751/201-793-8309
Boone Trading Co., 562 Coyote Rd., Brinnon, WA 98320/206-796-4330 (ivory, scrimshaw tools)
Bryan Bridges, 6350 E. Paseo San Andres, Tucson, AZ 85710
Frank Brgoch, 1580 So. 1500 East, Bountiful, UT 84010/801-295-1885
Dennis B. Brooker, R.R. 1, Box 62, Prole, IA 50229/515-961-8200
Burgess Vibrocrafters (BVI), Rt. 83, Grayslake, IL 60030
Byron Burgess, 710 Bella Vista Dr., Morro Bay, CA 93442/805-772-3974

Brian V. Cannavaro, Gun City U.S.A., 573 Murfreesboro Rd., Nashville, TN 37210/615-256-6127
Winston Churchill, Twenty Mile Stream Rd., RFD Box 29B, Proctorsville, VT 05153/802-226-7772
Clark Engravings, P.O. Box 80746, San Marino, CA 91108/818-287-1652
Frank Clark, 3714-27th St., Lubbock, TX 79410/806-799-3838
Crocker Engraving, 1510 - 42nd St., Los Alamos, NM 87544
Daniel Cullity, 209 Old County Rd., East Sandwich, MA 02537/617-888-1147
Art A. Darakis, RD #2, Box 350, Fredericksburg, OH 44627/216-695-4271
Tim Davis, 230 S. Main St., Eldorado, OH 45321/513-273-4611
Ed Delorge, 2231 Hwy. 308, Thibodaux, LA 70301/504-447-1633
James R. DeMunck, 3012 English Rd., Rochester, NY 14616/716-225-0626 (SASE)
C. Gregory Dixon, RD 1, Box 175, Kempton, PA 19529/215-756-6271
Howard M. Dove, 52 Brook Rd., Enfield, CT 06082/203-749-9403
Mark Drain, S.E. 3211 Kamilche Point Rd., Shelton, WA 98584/206-426-5452
Michael W. Dubber, 3107 E. Mulberry, Evansville, IN 47714/812-476-4036
Henri Dumoulin & Fils, rue du Tilleul 16, B-4411 Milmoret (Herstal), Belgium
Robert Evans, 332 Vine St., Oregon City, OR 97045/503-656-5693
Ken Eyster, Heritage Gunsmiths Inc., 6441 Bishop Rd., Centerburg, OH 43011/614-625-6131
John Fanzoi, P.O. Box 25, Ferlach, Austria 9170
Jacqueline Favre, 3111 So. Valley View Blvd., Suite B-214, Las Vegas, NV 89102/702-876-6278
Armi FERLIB, 46 Via Costa, 25063 Gardone V.T. (Brescia), Italy
Firearms Engravers Guild of America, Robert Evans, Secy., 332 Vine St., Oregon City, OR 97045/503-656-5693
Fountain Prods., 492 Prospect Ave., W. Springfield, MA 01089/413-781-4651
Henry Frank, Box 984, Whitefish, MT 59937/406-862-2681
Leonard Francolini, 56 Morgan Rd., Canton, CT 06019/203-693-2529
GRS Corp., P.O. Box 748, 900 Overland St., Emporia, KS 66801/316-343-1084 (Gravermeister tool)
Donald Glaser, 1520 West St., Emporia, KS 66801
Eric Gold, Box 1904, Flagstaff, AZ 86002
Howard V. Grant, Hiawatha 153, Woodruff, WI 54568/715-356-7146
Griffin & Howe, 589 Broadway, New York, NY 10012/212-966-5323
Gurney Engraving Method, #513-620 View St., Victoria, B.C. V8W 1J6 Canada/604-383-5243
John K. Gwilliam, 218 E. Geneva Dr., Tempe, AZ 85282/602-894-1739
Hand Engravers Supply Co., 4348 Newberry Ct., Dayton, OH 45432/513-426-6762
Jack O. Harwood, 1191 S. Pendlebury Lane, Blackfoot, ID 83221/208-785-5368
Frank E. Hendricks, Master Engravers, Inc., Star Rt. 1A, Box 334, Dripping Springs, TX 78620/512-858-7828
Heidemarie Hiptmayer, R.R. 112, #750, P.O. Box 136, Eastman, Que. J0E 1PO, Canada/514-297-2492
Harvey Hoover, 1263 Nunneley Rd., Paradise, CA 94969/916-872-1154
Ken Hunt, c/o Hunting World, Inc., 16 E. 53rd St., New York, NY 10022/212-755-3400
Jim Hurst, 4537 S. Irvington Ave., Tulsa, OK 74135/918-627-5460
Ken Hurst/Firearm Engraving Co., P.O. Box 249, Route 501, Rustburg, VA 24588/804-332-6440
Ralph W. Ingle, Master Engraver, #4 Missing Link, Rossville, GA 30741/404-866-5589 (color broch. $3)
Paul Jaeger, Inc., P.O. Box 449, 1 Madison Ave., Grand Junction, TN 38039/901-764-6909
Ken Jantz Supply, Rt. 1, Sulphur, OK 73086/405-622-3790 (tools)
Bill Johns, 1113 Nightingale, McAllen, TX 78501/512-682-2971
Steven Kamyk, 9 Grandview Dr., Westfield, MA 01085/413-568-0457
T. J. Kaye, Rocksprings St. Rt., Box 277, Junction, TX 76849/915-446-3091
Lance Kelly, 1824 Royal Palm Dr., Edgewater, FL 32032/904-423-4933
Jim Kelso, Rt. 1, Box 5300, Worcester, VT 05682/802-229-4254
E. J. Koevenig Engraving Service, P.O. Box 55, Rabbit Gulch, Hill City, SD 57745/605-574-2239
John Kudlas, 622-14th St. S.E., Rochester, MN 55901/507-288-5579
Terry Lazette, 142 N. Laurens Dr., Bolivar, OH 44612/216-874-4403
Leonard Leibowitz, 1202 Palto Alto St., Pittsburgh, PA 15212/412-231-5388 (etcher)
Franz Letschnig, Master-Engraver, 620 Cathcart, Rm. 422, Montreal, Queb. H3B 1M1, Canada/514-875-4989
W. Neal Lewis, 9 Bowers Dr., Newnan, GA 30263/404-251-3045
Frank Lindsay, 1326 Tenth Ave., Holdrege, NE 68949/308-995-4623
Steve Lindsay, P.O. Box 1413, Kearney, NE 68847/308-236-7885
London Guns, 1528-20th St., Santa Monica, CA 90404/213-828-8486
Harvey McBurnette, Rt. 4, Box 337, Piedmont, AL 36272
Dennis McDonald, Box 3, Peosta, IA 52068
Lynton S.M. McKenzie, 6940 N. Alvernon Way, Tucson, AZ 85718/602-299-5090
Wm. H. Mains, 3111 S. Valley View Blvd., Suite B-214, Las Vegas, NV 89102/702-876-6278
Robert E. Maki, School of Firearms Engraving, P.O. Box 947, Northbrook, IL 60062/312-724-8238
Laura Mandarino, 136 5th Ave. West, Kalispell, MT 59901/406-257-6208
George Marek, P.O. Box 213, Westfield, MA 01086/413-568-5957
Frank Mele, P.O. Box 361, Somers, NY 10589/914-277-3040
S. A. Miller, Miller Gun Works, P.O. Box 7326, Tamuning, Guam 96911
Cecil J. Mills, 2265 Sepulveda Way, Torrance, Ca 90501/213-328-8088
Frank Mittermeier, 3577 E. Tremont Ave., New York, NY 10465
Mitch Moschetti, P.O. Box 27065, Denver, CO 80227/303-936-1184
Gary N. Nelson, 975 Terrace Dr., Oakdale, CA 95361/209-847-4590
NgraveR Co., 879 Raymond Hill Rd., Oakdale, CT 06370/203-848-8031 (engr. tool)
New Orleans Arms Co., P.O. Box 26087, New Orleans, LA 70186/504-944-3371
New Orleans Jewelers Supply, 206 Chartres St., New Orleans, LA 70130/504-523-3839 (engr. tool)
Hans Obiltschnig, 12. November St. 7, 9170 Ferlach, Austria
Oker's Engraving, 365 Bell Rd., Bellfort Mtn. Hts., P.O. Box 126, Shawnee, CO 80475/303-838-6042

Gale Overbey, 612 Azalea Ave., Richmond, VA 23227
Pachmayr Gun Works, Inc., 1220 S. Grand Ave., Los Angeles, CA 90015/213-748-7271
Rex C. Pedersen, 2717 S. Pere Marquette, Ludington, MI 49431/616-843-2061
Marcello Pedini, 5 No. Jefferson Ave., Catskill, NY 12414/518-943-5257
E. L. Peters, P.O. Box 1927, Gibsons, B.C. VON 1VO, Canada/604-886-9665
Paul R. Piquette, 40 Royalton St., Chicopee, MA 01020/413-592-1057
Eugene T. Plante, Gene's Custom Guns, 3890 Hill Ave., P.O. Box 10534, White Bear Lake, MN 55110/612-429-5105
Jeremy W. Potts, 1680 So. Granby, Aurora, CO 80012/303-752-2528
Wayne E. Potts, 912 Poplar St., Denver, CO 80220/303-355-5462
Ed Pranger, 1414-7th St., Anacortes, WA 98221/206-293-3488
Proofmark, Ltd., P.O. Box 183, Alton, IL 62002/618-463-0120 (Italian Bottega Incisioni)
E. C. Prudhomme, #426 Lane Building, 610 Marshall St., Shreveport, LA 71101/318-425-8421
Leonard Puccinelli Design, P.O. Box 3494, Fairfield, CA 94533/415-457-9911
Martin Rabeno, Spook Hollow Trading Co., Box 37F, RD  #1, Ellenville, NY 12428/914-647-4567
Jim Riggs, 206 Azalea, Boerne, TX 78006/512-249-8567 (handguns)
J. J. Roberts, 166 Manassas Dr., Manassas Park, VA 22111/703-361-4513
John R. and Hans Rohner, Sunshine Canyon, Boulder, CO 80302/303-444-3841
Bob Rosser, 162 Ramsey Dr., Albertville, AL 35950/205-878-5388
Richard D. Roy, 87 Lincoln Way, Windsor, CT 06095/203-688-0304
Joe Rundell, 6198 Frances Rd., Clio, MI 48420/313-687-0559
Robert P. Runge, 94 Grove St., Ilion, NY 13357/315-894-3036
Shaw-Cullen, Inc., 212 - East 47th St., New York, NY 10017/212-759-8460 (etchers)
Shaw's "Finest In Guns," 9447 W. Lilac Rd., Escondido, CA 92026/619-728-7070
George Sherwood, Box 735, Winchester, OR 97495/503-672-3159
Ben Shostle, The Gun Room, 1201 Burlington Dr., Muncie, IN 47302/317-282-9073
W. P. Sinclair, 36 South St., Warminster, Wiltsh. BA12 8DZ, England
Ron Skaggs, P.O. Box 34, Princeton, IL 61356/815-875-8207
Mark A. Smith, 200 N. 9th, Sinclair, WY 82334/307-324-7929
Ron Smith, 3601 West 7th St., Ft. Worth, TX 76107
R. Spinale, 3415 Oakdale Ave., Lorain, OH 44055/216-246-5344
Robt. Swartley, 2800 Pine St., Napa, CA 94559
George W. Thiewes, 1846 Allen Lane, St. Charles, IL 60174/312-584-1383
Denise Thirion, Box 408, Graton, CA 95444/707-829-1876
Robert B. Valade, 931-3rd. Ave., Seaside, OR 97138/503-738-7672
John Vest, P.O. Box 1552, Susanville, CA 96130/916-253-3681
Ray Viramontez, 4348 Newberry Ct., Dayton, OH 45432/513-426-6762
Vernon G. Wagoner, 2325 E. Encanto, Mesa, AZ 85203/602-835-1307
R. D. Wallace, Star Rt. Box 76, Grandin, MO 63943
Terry Wallace, 385 San Marino, Vallejo, CA 94590
Floyd E. Warren, 1273 State Rt. 305 N.E., Cortland, OH 44410/216-638-4219
Kenneth W. Warren, Mountain States Engraving, 8333 E. San Sebastian Dr., Scottsdale, AZ 85258/602-991-5035
David W. Weber, 1421 East 4th, North Platte, NE 69101/308-534-2525
Rachel Wells, 110 N. Summit St., Prescott, AZ 86301/602-445-3655
Sam Welch, CVSR Box 2110, Moab, UT 84532/801-259-7620
Claus Willig, c/o Paul Jaeger, Inc., P.O. Box 449, 1 Madison Ave. Grand Junction, TN 38039
Mel Wood, P.O. Box 1255, Sierra Vista, AZ 85636/602-455-5541

## GAME CALLS

Black Duck, 1737 Davis Ave., Whiting, IN 46394/219-659-2997
Burnham Bros., Box 669, 912 Main St., Marble Falls, TX 78654/512-693-3112
Call'N, Inc., 1615 Bartlett Rd., Memphis, TN 38134/901-372-1682
Faulk's, 616 18th St., Lake Charles, LA 70601
Lohman Mfg. Co., P.O. Box 220, Neosho, MO 64850/417-451-4438
Mallardtone Game Calls, 2901  16th St., Moline, IL 61265/309-762-8089
Phil. S. Olt Co., Box 550, Pekin, IL 61554/309-348-3633
Quaker Boy Inc., 6426 West Quaker St., Orchard Parks, NY 14127/716-662-3979
Penn's Woods Products, Inc., 19 W. Pittsburgh St., Delmont, PA 15626
Scotch Game Call Co., Inc., 6619 Oak Orchard Rd., Elba, NY 14058/716-757-9958
Johnny Stewart Game Calls, Box 7954, Waco, TX 76710/817-772-3261
Sure-Shot Game Calls, Inc., P.O. Box 816, Groves, TX 77619
Thomas Game Calls, P.O. Box 336, Winnsboro, TX 75494
Weems Wild Calls, P.O. Box 7261, Ft. Worth, TX 76111/817-531-1051

## GUN PARTS, U.S. AND FOREIGN

American Derringer Corp., 127 N. Lacy Dr., Waco, TX 76705/817-799-9111
Armes de Chasse, P.O. Box 827, Chadds Ford, PA 19317/215-388-1146
Armsport, Inc., 3590 N.W. 49th St., Miami, FL 33142/305-635-7850
Badger Shooter's Supply, 106 So. Harding, Owen, WI 54460/715-229-2101
Behlert Custom Guns, Inc., RD 2, Box 36C, Route 611 North, Pipersville, PA 18947/215-766-8681 (handgun parts)
Can Am Enterprises, Fruitland, ON L0R 1L0, Canada/416-643-4357
Cherokee Gun Accessories, 4127 Bay St. Suite 226, Fremont, CA 94538/415-471-5770
Dave Chicoine, d/b/a Liberty A.S.P., 19 Key St., Eastport, ME 04631/207-853-2327 (S&W only; ctlg. $5)
Crown City Arms, Inc., P.O. Box 550, Cortland, NY 13045/607-753-8238 (rifle, handgun)
Charles E. Duffy, Williams Lane, West Hurley, NY 12491

Falcon Firearms Mfg. Corp., P.O. Box 3748, Granada Hills, CA 91344/818-885-0900 (barrels; magazines)
Federal Ordnance Inc., 1443 Potrero Ave., So. El Monte, CA 91733/213-350-4161
Jack First Distributors Inc., 44633 Sierra Highway, Lancaster, CA 93534/805-945-6981
Forster Products, 82 E. Lanark Ave., Lanark, IL 61046/815-493-6360
Gun Clinic, 504 Main, Bismarck, ND 58501/701-223-2304 (magazines, gun parts)
Gun-Tec, P.O. Box 8125, W. Palm Beach, FL 33407 (Win. mag. tubing; Win. 92 conversion parts)
Hansen and Hansen, 244 Old Post Rd., Southport, CT 06490/203-259-7337
Hastings, Box 224, 822-6th St., Clay Center, KS 67432/913-632-3169
Heller & Levin Associates, Inc., 88 Marlborough Court, Rockville Center, NY 11570/516-764-9349
Walter H. Lodewick, 2816 N.E. Halsey, Portland, OR 97232/503-284-2554 (Winchester parts)
Morgan Arms Co., Inc., 2999 So. Highland Dr., Las Vegas, NV 89109/702-737-5247 (MK-I kit)
Numrich Arms Co., West Hurley, NY 12491
Pacific Intl. Merch. Corp., 2215 "J" St., Sacramento, CA 95816/916-446-2737 (Vega 45 Colt mag.)
Potomac Arms Corp. (See Hunter's Haven)
Pre-64 Winchester Parts Co., P.O. Box 8125, West Palm Beach, FL 33407 (send stamped env. w. requ. list)
Martin B. Retting, Inc., 11029 Washington Blvd., Culver City, CA 90232/213-837-6111
Rock Island Armory, Inc., 111 E. Exchange St., Geneseo, IL 61254/309-944-2109
Royal Ordnance Works Ltd., P.O. Box 3245, Wilson, NC 27893/919-237-0515
Sarco, Inc., 323 Union St., Stirling, NJ 07980
Sherwood Intl. Export Corp., 18714 Parthenia St., Northridge, CA 91324
Simms, 2801 J St., Sacramento, CA 95816/916-442-3800
Clifford L. Smires, R.D. 1, Box 100, Columbus, NJ 08022/609-298-3158 (Mauser rifle parts)
Springfield Sporters Inc., R.D. 1, Penn Run, PA 15765/412-254-2626
Triple-K Mfg. Co., 568-6th Ave., San Diego, CA 92101/619-232-2066 (magazines, gun parts)

## GUNS (U.S.-made)

AMT (Arcadia Machine & Tool), 536 N. Vincent Ave., Covina, CA 91722/818-915-7803
Accuracy Systems, Inc., 15203 N. Cave Creek Rd., Phoenix, AZ 85032/602-971-1991
Advantage Arms USA, Inc., 840 Hampden Ave., St. Paul, MN 55114/612-644-5197
Alpha Arms, Inc., 12923 Valley Branch, Dallas, TX 75234/214-243-8124
American Arms, Box 1055, Garden Grove, CA 92643/714-636-5191 (American Arms Eagle 380)
American Arms, Inc., P.O. Box 27163, Salt Lake City, UT 84127/801-971-5006
American Derringer Corp., 127 N. Lacy Dr., Waco, TX 76705/817-799-9111
American Industries, 8700 Brookpark Rd., Cleveland, OH 44129/216-398-8300
ArmaLite, 118 E. 16th St., Costa Mesa, CA 92627
Armament Systems and Procedures, Inc., Box 356, Appleton, WI 54912/414-731-8893 (ASP pistol)
Arminex Ltd., 7882 E. Gray Rd., Scottsdale Airpark, Scottsdale, AZ 85260/602-998-0443 (Excalibur s.a. pistol)
Arm Tech, Armament Technologies Inc., 240 Sargent Dr., New Haven, CT 06511/203-562-2543 (22-cal. derringers)
Armes de Chasse, 3000 Valley Forge Circle, King of Prussia, PA 19406/215-783-6133
Arnett Guns (See Gary DelSignore Weaponry)
Artistic Arms, Inc.,Box 23, Hoagland, IN 46745 (Sharps-Borchardt)
Artistic Firearms Corp., John Otteman, 4005 Hecker Pass Hwy., Gilroy, CA 95020/408-842-4278 (A.F.C. Comm. Rifle 1881-1981)
Auto Nine Corp., see: FTL Marketing Corp.
Auto-Ordnance Corp., Box GD, West Hurley, NY 12491/914-679-7225
BJT, 445 Putman Ave., Hamden, CT 06517 (stainless double derringer)
Baford Arms, Inc., 808 E. Cedar St., Bristol TN 37620/615-968-9397
Barrett Firearms Mfg., Inc., 312 S. Church St., Murfreesboro, TN 37130/615-896-2938 (Light Fifty)
Bighorn Rifle Co., P.O. Box 215, American Fork, UT 84003/801-756-4222
Bren Ten (See Dornaus & Dixon Ent.)
Browning (Gen. Offices), Rt. 1, Morgan, UT 84050/801-876-2711
Browning (Parts & Service), Rt. 4, Box 624-B, Arnold, MO 63010/314-287-6800
Bumble Bee Wholesale, Inc., 12521 Oxnard St., North Hollywood, CA 91606/818-985-2939 (Pocket Partner)
Bushmaster Firearms Co., 803 Forest Ave., Portland ME 04103/207-775-3324 (police handgun)
Century Gun Dist., Inc., 1467 Jason Rd., Greenfield, IN 46140/317-462-4524 (Century Model 100 SA rev.)
Challanger Mfg. Corp., 118 Pearl St., Mt. Vernon, NY 10550 (Hopkins & Allen)
Champlin Firearms, Inc., Box 3191, Enid, OK 73702/405-237-7388
Charter Arms Corp., 430 Sniffens Ln., Stratford, CT 06497
Chipmunk Manufacturing Inc., 114 E. Jackson, Medford, OR 97501/503-664-5585 (22 S.S. rifle)
Classic Arms, 815-22nd St., Union City, NJ 08757/201-863-1493
Colt Firearms, P.O. Box 1868, Hartford, CT 06102/203-236-6311
Commando Arms (See Gibbs Guns, Inc.)
Coonan Arms, Inc., 830 Hampden Ave., St. Paul, MN 55114/612-646-6672 (357 Mag. Autom.)
Cumberland Arms, Rt. 1, Shafer Rd., Blanton Chapel, Manchester, TN 37355
The Custom Gun Guild, 5091-F Buford Highway, Doraville, GA 30340/404-455-0346

Davidson Supply, 2703 High Point Rd., Greensboro, NC 27403/800-367-4867

Davis Industries, 13748 Arapahoe Pl., Chino, CA 91710/714-591-4727 (derringer)

Leonard Day & Sons, Inc., P.O. Box 723, East Hampton, MA 01027/413-527-7990 (ML)

Gary DelSignore Weaponry, 3675 Cottonwood, Cedar City, UT 84720/801-586-2505 (Arnett Guns)

Demro Products Inc., 372 Progress Dr., Manchester, CT 06040/203-649-4444 (Wasp, Tac guns)

Detonics Mfg. Corp., 13456 S.E. 27th Pl., Bellevue, WA 98005/206-747-2100 (auto pistol)

Dornaus & Dixon Enterprises, Inc., 15896 Manufacture Lane, Huntingdon Beach, CA 92649/714-891-5090

DuBiel Arms Co., 1724 Baker Rd., Sherman, TX 75090/214-893-7313

Encom America, Inc., P.O. Box 5314, Atlanta, GA 30307/404-525-2811

Excalibur (See Arminex)

F.I.E. Corp. (See Firearms Import & Export Corp.)

FTL Marketing (See Bumble Bee Wholesale, Inc.)

Falcon Firearms Mfg. Corp., P.O. Box 3748, Granada Hills, CA 91344/818-885-0900 (handguns)

Falling Block Works, P.O. Box 3087, Fairfax, VA 22038/703-476-0043

Feather Enterprises, 2500 Central Ave., Boulder, CO 80301/303-442-7021

Federal Eng. Corp., 3161 N. Elston Ave., Chicago, IL 60618/312-267-4151 (XC-220 carbine)

Firearms Imp. & Exp. Corp., P.O. Box 4866, Hialeah Lakes, Hialeah, FL 33014/305-685-5966 (FIE)

Freedom Arms Co., P.O. Box 1776, Freedom, WY 83120 (mini revolver, Casull rev.)

Freedom Arms Marketing (See: L.A.R. Mfg. Co.)

Frontier Shop & Gallery, Depot 1st & Main, Riverton, WY 82501/307-856-4498

Garrett Accur-Light Inc., 1413 B. E. Olive Ct., Fort Collins, CO 80524/303-224-3067

Gibbs Guns, Inc., Rt. 2, Greenback, TN 37742/615-856-2813 (Commando Arms)

Göncz Co., 11526 Burbank Blvd., #18, No. Hollywood, CA 91601/818-505-0408

Golden Age Arms Co., 14 W. Winter St., Delaware, OH 43015

Gunworks Ltd., 10 Aqua Lane, Buffalo, NY 14150/716-877-2565

HJS Industries, Inc., P.O. Box 4351, Brownsville, TX 78520/512-542-3340 (22 4-bbl.; 38 S&W SS derringers)

Harrington & Richardson, Industrial Rowe, Gardner, MA 01440

Hatfield Rifle Works, 2020 Colhoun, St. Joseph, MO 64501/816-279-8688 (squirrel rifle)

A.D. Heller, Inc., Box 268, Grand Ave., Baldwin, NY 11510

Holmes Firearms Corp., Rte. 6, Box 242, Fayetteville, AR 72703

Hopkins & Allen Arms, 3 Ethel Ave., P.O. Box 217, Hawthorne, NJ 07507/201-427-1165 (ML)

Lew Horton Dist. Co. Inc., 175 Boston Rd., Southboro, MA 01772

Hyper-Single Precision SS Rifles, 520 E. Beaver, Jenks, OK 74037/918-299-2391

Ithaca Gun Co., Ithaca, NY 14850

Jennings Firearms Inc., P.O. Box 5416, Stateline, NV 89449/702-588-6884

Jennings-Hawken, 326½-4th St. N.W., Winter Haven, FL 33880 (ML)

Iver Johnson, 2202 Redmond Rd., Jacksonville, AR 72076/501-982-9491

KK Arms Co., Karl Kash, Star Route, Box 671, Kerrville, TX 78028/512-257-4441 (handgun)

Kimber of Oregon, Inc., 9039 S.E. Jannsen Rd., Clackamas, OR 97015/503-656-1704

Kimel Industries, Box 335, Matthews, NC 28105/704-821-7663

L.A.R. Manufacturing Co., 4133 West Farm Rd., West Jordan, UT 84084/801-255-7106 (Grizzly Win Mag pistol)

Law Enforcement Ordnance Corp., Box 649, Middletown, PA 17057/717-944-5500 (Striker-12 shotgun)

Ljutic Ind., Inc., P.O. Box 2117, 732 N 16th Ave., Yakima, WA 98907/509-248-0476 (Mono-Gun)

Loven-Pierson, Inc., 4 W. Main, P.O. Box 377, Apalachin, NY 13732/607-625-2303 (ML)

M & N Distributors, 23535 Telo St., Torrance, CA 90505/213-530-9000 (Budischowsky)

Magnum Sales, Div. of Mag-na-port, 41302 Executive Drive, Mt. Clemens, MI 48045/313-469-7534 (Ltd. editions & customized guns for handgun hunting)

Marlin Firearms Co., 100 Kenna Drive, New Haven, CT 06473

Matteson Firearms Inc., Otsego Rd., Canajoharie, NY 13317/607-264-3744 (SS rifles)

Merrill Pistol, see: Rock Pistol Mfg.

Michigan Arms Corp., 363 Elmwood, Troy, MI 48084/313-583-1518 (ML)

Military Armament Corp., P.O. Drawer 1358, 1481 So. Loop-Suite 4, Stephensville, TX 76401/817-968-7543 (Ingram submach. gun)

Mitchell Arms Inc., 2101 E. 4th St., Suite 201A, Santa Ana, CA 92705/714-964-3678 (AR-50 survival rifle)

M.O.A. Corp., 110 Front St., Dayton, OH 45402/513-223-6401 (Maximum pistol)

O.F. Mossberg & Sons, Inc., 7 Grasso St., No. Haven, CT 06473

Mowrey Gun Works, 1313 Lawson Rd., Saginaw, TX 76179/817-847-1644

Navy Arms Co., 689 Bergen Blvd., Ridgefield, NJ 07657

North American Arms, 1800 North 300 West, Spanish Fork, UT 84660/801-798-9891

North Georgia Armament, 5265 Jimmy Carter Blvd., Suite 1442, Norcross, GA 30093/404-446-3504

Numrich Arms Corp., W. Hurley, NY 12491

Oregon Trail Riflesmiths, Inc., P.O. Box 45212, Boise, ID 83711/208-336-8631 (ML)

Ozark Mountain Arms, Inc., Rt. 1 Box 44A5, Hwy. 32E, Ashdown, AR 71822/501-898-2345 (ML)

Pecos Valley Armory, 1022 So. Canyon, Carlsbad, NM 88220/505-887-6023 (ML)

Pennsylvania Arms Co., Box 128, Duryea, PA 18642/717-457-4014

Phillips & Bailey, Inc., P.O. Box 219253, Houston, TX 77218/713-392-0207 (357/9 Ultra, rev. conv.)

Precision Small Parts, 155 Carlton Rd., Charlottesville, VA 22901/804-293-6124

Provider Arms, Inc., 261 Haglund Dr., Chesterton, IN 46304/219-879-5590 (ML Predator rifle)

Rahn Gun Works, Inc., P.O. Box 327, 535 Marshall St., Litchfield, MI 49252/517-542-3247

Raven Arms, 1300 Bixby Dr., Industry, CA 91745/213-961-2511 (P-25 pistols)

Remington Arms Co., 1007 Market St., Wilmington, DE 19898

Rock Pistol Mfg., Inc., 150 Viking, Brea, CA 92621/714-990-2444 (Merrill pistol)

Ruger (See Sturm, Ruger & Co.)

Savage Industries, Inc., Springdale Rd., Westfield, MA 01085/413-562-2361

B. Searcy Co., 15, Rd. 3804, Farmington, NM 87401/505-327-3419 (mountain rifle)

L.W. Seecamp Co., Inc., P.O. Box 255, New Haven, CT 06502/203-877-3429

Serrifile, Inc., P.O. Box 508, Littlerock, CA 93543/805-945-0713 (derringer; single shot))

C. Sharps Arms Co., Inc., P.O. Box 885, Big Timber, MT 59011/406-932-4353

Shilen Rifles, Inc., 205 Metro Park Blvd., P.O. Box 1300, Ennis, TX 75119/214-875-5318

Shiloh Products, 181 Plauderville Ave., Garfield, NJ 07026 (Sharps)

The Silhouette, 1409 Benton, Box 1509, Idaho Falls, ID 83401/208-524-0880 (Wichita International pistol)

Six Enterprises, 6564 Hidden Creek Dr., Dan Jose, CA 95120/408-268-8296 (Timberliner rifle)

Smith & Wesson, Inc., 2100 Roosevelt Ave., Springfield, MA 01101

Sokolovsky Corp., Box 70113, Sunnyvale, CA 94086/408-245-9268 (45 Automaster pistol)

Sporting Arms, Inc., 12923 Valley Branch, Dallas, TX 75234/214-243-8124 (Snake Charmer II shotgun)

Springfield Armory, Inc., 420 W. Main St., Geneseo, IL 61254/309-944-5138

SSK Industries, Rt. 1, Della Dr., Bloomingdale, OH 43910/614-264-0176

Steel City Arms, Inc., P.O. Box 81926, Pittsburgh, PA 15217/412-461-3100 (d.a. "Double Deuce" pistol)

Sturm, Ruger & Co., Southport, CT 06490

Tennessee Valley Arms, P.O. Box 2022, Union City, TN 38261/901-885-4456

Texas Longhorn Arms, Inc., P.O. Box 703, Richmond, TX 77469/713-341-0775 (S.A. sixgun)

Thompson-Center Arms, P.O. Box 2426, Rochester, NH 03867/603-332-2394

Tippmann Arms Co., 4402 New Haven Ave., Ft. Wayne, IN 46803/219-422-6448

Traders International, Inc., P.O. Box 595, Indian Trail, NC 28105/704-821-7684

Trail Guns Armoury, 1422 E. Main St., League City, TX 77573/713-332-5833 (muzzleloaders)

Trapper Gun, Inc., 18717 E. 14 Mile Rd., Fraser, MI 48026/313-792-0133 (handguns)

The Ultimate Game Inc., P.O. Box 1856, Ormond Beach, FL 32075/904-677-4358

Ultra Light Arms Co., P.O. Box 1270, Granville, WV 26534/304-599-5687

United Sporting Arms, Inc, 610 Ross Point Rd., Post Falls, ID 83854/208-773-9932 (handguns)

U.S. Repeating Arms Co., P.O. Box 30-300, New Haven, CT 06511/203-789-5000

Universal Firearms, 2202 Redmond Rd., Jacksonville, AR 72076/501-982-9491

Weatherby's, 2781 E. Firestone Blvd., South Gate, CA 90280

Weaver Arms Ltd., P.O. Box 3316, Escondido, CA 92025/619-746-2440

Dan Wesson Arms, 293 So. Main St., Monson, MA 01057

Wichita Arms, 444 Ellis, Wichita, KS 67211/316-265-0661

Wildey, 28 Old Route 7, Brookfield, CT 06804/203-775-4261

Wildey Firearms, 299 Washington St., Newburgh, NY 12550/1-800-243-GUNS

Wilkinson Arms, 26884 Pearl Rd., Parma, ID 83660/208-722-5533

Winchester, (See U.S. Repeating Arms)

York Arms Co., 50 W. State St., Hurricane, UT 84737/801-635-4867

## GUNS (Foreign)

Abercrombie & Fitch, 2302 Maxwell Lane, Houston, TX 77023 (Ferlib)

Action Arms, P.O. Box 9573, Philadelphia, PA 19124/215-744-0100

Allen Firearms Co., 2879 All Trades Rd., Santa Fe, NM 87501/505-471-6090 (ML)

American Arms, Inc., 11023 W. 108th Terr., Overland Park, KS 66210

Anschutz (See PSI)

Armoury Inc., Rte. 202, New Preston, CT 06777

Armes de Chasse, P.O. Box 827, Chadds Ford, PA 19317/215-388-1146 (Merkel, Mauser)

Armscor (See Pacific International Merchandising)

Arms Corp. of the Philippines, Pacific Bank Bldg., 6th Fl., #604, Ayala Ave., Makati, Metro Manila, Philippines

Armsport, Inc., 3590 N.W. 49th St., Miami, FL 33142/305-635-7850

Armurier Liegeois-Artisans Reunis (A.L.A.R.), 27, rue Lambert Masset, 4300 Ans, Belgium

Pedro Arrizabalaga, Eibar, Spain

Bauska Arms Corp., P.O. Box 1995, Kalispell, MT 59903/406-752-2072

Beeman, Inc., 47-GDD Paul Dr., San Rafael, CA 94903/415-472-7121 (FWB, Weihrauch, FAS, Unique, Korth, Krico, Agner, Hammerli firearms)

Benelli Armi, S.p.A. (See: Sile Distributors—handguns; Heckler & Koch—Shotguns)

Beretta U.S.A., 17601 Indian Head Highway, Accokeek, MD 20607/301-283-2191

Bingham Ltd., 1775-C Wilwat Dr., Norcross, GA 30093/404-448-1440

Charles Boswell (Gunmakers), Div. of Saxon Arms Ltd., 615 Jasmine Ave. N., Tarpon Springs, FL 33589/813-938-4882

M. Braun, 32, rue Notre-Dame, 2240 Luxemburg, Luxemburg (all types)

Bretton, 21 Rue Clement Forissier, 42-St. Etienne, France

Britarms/Berdan (Gunmakers Ltd.), See: Action Arms

British Guns, P.O. Box 1924, Corvallis, OR 97339/503-752-5886 (Agent for W.&C. Scott)

Browning (Gen. Offices), Rt. 1, Morgan, UT 84050/801-876-2711

Browning, (parts & service), Rt. 4, Box 624-B, Arnold, MO 63010/314-287-6800

Bumble Bee Wholesale, Inc., 12521 Oxnard St., North Hollywood, CA 91606/818-985-2939 (Valmet auto rifle)

Century Arms Co., 5 Federal St., St. Albans, VT 05478/802-524-9541

Ets. Chapuis, rue de la Chatelaine, 42380 St. Bonnet-le-Chateau, France

Conco Arms, P.O. Box 159, Emmaus, PA 18049/215-967-5477 (Larona)

Connecticut Valley Arms Co., 5988 Peachtree Corners East, Norcross, GA 30071/404-449-4687 (CVA)

Walter Craig, Inc., Box 927, Selma, AL 36701/205-875-7989

Davidson Supply, 2703 High Point Rd., Greensboro, NC 27403/800-367-4867

Des Moines Imports, 21 Glenview Dr., Des Moines, IA 50312/515-279-1987 (Spanish Gorosabel shotguns)

Diana Import, 842 Vallejo St., San Francisco, CA 94133

Charles Daly (See Outdoor Sports HQ)

Dikar s. Coop. (See Connecticut Valley Arms Co.)

Dixie Gun Works, Inc., Hwy 51, South, Union City, TN 38261/901-885-0561 ("Kentucky" rifles)

Double M Shooting Sports, 462 S. Loop Pole Rd., Gylford, CT 06473 (Dr. Franco Beretta)

Dynamit Nobel of America, Inc., 105 Stonehurst Court, Northvale, NJ 07647/201-767-1660 (Rottweil)

E.M.F. Co. Inc. (Early & Modern Firearms), 1900 E. Warner Ave. 1-D, Santa Ana, CA 92705/714-966-0202

Ernest Dumoulin-Deleye, see: Midwest Gun Sport

Henri Dumoulin & Fils, rue du Tilleul 16, B-4411 Milmort (Herstal), Belgium

Peter Dyson Ltd., 29-31 Church St., Honley, Huddersfield, Yorkshire HD7 2AH, England (accessories f. antique gun collectors)

Elko Arms, 28 rue Ecole Moderne, 7400 Soignes, Belgium

Euroarms of American, Inc., P.O. Box 3277, 1501 Lenoir Dr., Winchester, VA 22601/703-661-1863 (ML)

Excam Inc., 4480 E. 11 Ave., P.O. Box 3483, Hialeah, FL 33013

Exel Arms of America, 14 Main St., Gardner, MA 01440/617-632-5008

F.I.E. Corp. (See Firearms Import & Export Corp.)

FTL Marketing (See Bumble Bee Wholesale, Inc.)

J. Fanzoj, P.O. Box 25, Ferlach, Austria 9170

Armi FERLIB di Libero Ferraglio, 46 Via Costa, 25063 Gardone V.T. (Brescia), Italy

Fiocchi of America, Inc., 1308 W. Chase, Springfield, MO 65803/417-864-6970

Firearms Imp. & Exp. Corp., (F.I.E.), P.O. Box 4866, Hialeah Lakes, Hialeah, FL 33014/305-685-5966

Flaig's Inc., 2200 Evergreen Rd., Millvale, PA 15209/412-821-1717

Auguste Francotte & Cie, S.A., rue de Trois Juin 109, 4400 Herstal-Liege, Belgium

Frankonia Jagd, Hofmann & Co., Postfach 6780, D-8700 Wurzburg 1, West Germany

Freeland's Scope Stands, Inc., 3737 14th Ave., Rock Island, IL 61201/309-788-7449

Frigon Guns, 627 W. Crawford, Clay Center, KS 67432/913-632-5607

Renato Gamba, S.p.A., Gardone V.T. (Brescia), Italy (See Steyr Daimier Puch of America Corp.)

Armas Garbi, Urki #12, Eibar (Guipuzcoa) Spain (shotguns, See W. L. Moore)

Gilbert Equipment Co., Inc., 3300 Buckeye Rd. N.W., Suite 220, Atlanta, GA 30341/404-451-5558 (USAS-12 shotgun)

George Granger, 66 Cours Fauriel, 42 St. Etienne, France

Griffin & Howe, 589 Broadway, New York, NY 10012/212-966-5323 (Purdey, Holland & Holland)

Gun South, P.O. Box 129, 108 Morrow Ave., Trussville, AL 35173/205-655-8299 (Steyr, FN, Mannlicher)

Heckler & Koch Inc., 14601 Lee Rd., Chantilly, VA 22021/703-631-2800

Heym, Friedr. Wilh., see: Paul Jaeger, Inc.

HOWCO Dist. Inc., 122 Lafayette Ave., Laurel, MD 20707/301-953-3301

Hunting World, 16 E. 53rd St., New York, NY 10022

IGI Domino Corp., 200 Madison Ave., New York, NY 10016/212-889-4889 (Breda)

Incor, Inc., P.O. Box 132, Addison, TX 75001/214-931-3500 (Cosmi auto shotg.)

Interarmco, See Interarms (Walther)

Interarms Ltd., 10 Prince St., Alexandria, VA 22313 (Mauser, Valmet M-62/S)

International Sporting Goods, 919 Imperial Ave., P.O. Box 496, Calexico, CA 92231/619-357-6641 (Laurona shotguns)

Paul Jaeger Inc., P.O. Box 449, 1 Madison Ave., Grand Junction, TN 38039/901-764-6909 (Heym)

Jenkins Imports Corp., 462 Stanford Pl., Santa Barbara, CA 93111/805-967-5092 (Gebrüder Merkel)

John Jovino Co., 5 Centre Market Pl., New York, NY 10013/212-925-4881 (Terminator)

Kassnar Imports, 5480 Linglestown Rd., Harrisburg, PA 17110

Kawaguchiya Firearms, c/o La Paloma Marketing, 4500 E. Speedway Blvd., Suite 93, Tucson, AZ 85712/602-881-4750

Kendall International, Inc., 501 East North, Carlisle, KY 40311/606-289-7336

Kimel Industries, Box 335, Matthews, NC 28105/704-821-7663

KDF Inc., 2485 Hwy 46 No., Seguin, TX 78155/512-379-8141

Robert Kleinguenther Firearms, P.O. Box 2020, Seguin, TX 78155

Knight & Knight, 302 Ponce de Leon Blvd., St. Augustine, FL 32084/904-829-9671 (Bernardelli shotguns)

L. A. Distributors, 4 Centre Market Pl., New York, NY 10013

Lanber Arms of America, Inc., 377 Logan St., Adrian, MI 49221/517-263-7444 (Spanish o-u shotguns)

La Paloma Marketing, 1735 E. Ft. Lowell Rd., Suite 7, Tucson, AZ 85719/602-881-4750 (K.F.C. shotguns)

Morris Lawing, P.O. Box 9494, Charlotte, NC 28299/704-375-1740

Leland Firearms Co., 13 Mountain Ave., Llewellyn Park, West Orange, NJ 07052/201-325-3379 (Spanish shotguns)

Llama (See Stoeger)

MRE Dist. Inc., 19 So. Bayles Ave., Pt. Washington, NY 11050/516-944-8200 (IGI Domino)

Magnum Research, Inc., 7271 Commerce Circle West, Minneapolis, MN 55432/612-574-1868 (Israeli Galil)

Mandall Shtg. Suppl. 3616 N. Scottsdale Rd., Scottsdale, AZ 85252/602-945-2553

Mannlicher (See Steyr Daimler Puch of Amer.)

Manurhin, See: Matra-Manurhin

Marocchi USA Inc., 5939 W. 66th St., Bedford Park, IL 60638

Marathon Products Inc., East Haddam Industrial Park, East Haddam, CT 06423/203-873-1478

Matra-Manurhin International, Inc., 1640 W. Oakland Park Blvd., Suite 402, Ft. Lauderdale, FL 33311/305-486-8800

Mauser-Werke Oberndorf, P. O. Box 1349, 7238 Oberndorf/Neckar, West Germany

Mendi s. coop. (See Connecticut Valley Arms Co.)

Merkuria, FTC, Argentinska 38, 17000 Prague 7, Czechoslovakia (BRNO)

Midwest Gun Sport, Belgian HQ, 1942 OakWood View Dr., Verona, WI 53593/608-845-7447 (E. Dumoulin)

Mitchell Arms Corp., 116 East 16th St., Costa Mesa, CA 92627/714-548-7701 (Uberti pistols)

Wm. Larkin Moore & Co., 31360 Via Colinas, Suite 109, Westlake Village, CA 91360/213-889-4160 (AYA, Garbi, Ferlib, Piotti, Lightwood, Perugini Visini)

Navy Arms Co., 689 Bergen Blvd., Ridgefield, NJ 07657

O&L Guns Inc., P.O. Box 1146, Seminole, TX 79360/915-758-2933 (Wolverine rifle)

Odin International, Ltd., 818 Slaters Lane, Alexandria, VA 22314/703-339-8005 (Valmet/military types; CETME; Zastava)

Osborne's, P.O. Box 408, Cheboygan, MI 49721/616-625-9626 (Hammerli; Tanner rifles)

Outdoor Sports Headquarters, Inc., 967 Watertower Lane, Dayton, OH 45449/513-865-5855 (Charles Daly shotguns)

PM Air Services Ltd., P.O. Box 1573, Costa Mesa, CA 92626/714-968-2689

Pachmayr Gun Works, 1220 S. Grand Ave., Los Angeles, CA 90015

Pacific Intl. Merch. Corp., 2215 "J" St., Sacramento, CA 95816/916-446-2737

The Parker Gun, Div. of Reagent Chemical & Research, Inc., 1201 N. Watson Rd., Suite 224, Arlington, TX 76011/817-649-8781

Parker-Hale, Bisleyworks, Golden Hillock Rd., Sparbrook, Birmingham B11 2PZ, England

Perazzi U.S.A. Inc., 206 S. George St., Rome, NY 13440/315-337-8566

E. F. Phelps Mfg., Inc., 700 W. Franklin, Evansville, IN 47710/812-423-2599 (Heritage 45-70)

Precise, 3 Chestnut, Suffern, NY 10901

Precision Sales Intl. Inc., PSI, P.O. Box 1776, Westfield, MA 01086/413-562-5055 (Anschutz)

Precision Sports, P.O. Box 708, Kellogg Rd., Cortland, NY 13045/607-756-2851 (Parker-Hale)

Proofmark, Ltd., P.O. Box 183, Alton, IL 62002/618-463-0120 (Bettinsoli shotguns)

Leonard Puccinelli Design, P.O. Box 3494, Fairfield, CA 94533/415-457-9911 (I.A.B. Rizzini, Bernardelli shotguns of Italy; consultant to Beretta U.S.A.)

Quality Arms, Inc., Box 19477, Houston, TX 77224/713-870-8377 (Bernardelli; Ferlib; Bretton shotguns)

Quantetics Corp., Imp.-Exp. Div., 582 Somerset St. W., Ottawa, Ont. K1R 5K2 Canada/613-237-0242 (Unique pistols-Can. only)

Rahn Gun Works, Inc., P.O. Box 327, 535 Marshall St., Litchfield, MI 49252/517-542-3247

Ravizza Carlo Caccia Pesca, s.r.l., Via Melegnano 6, 20122 Milano, Italy

Richland Arms Co., 321 W. Adrian St., Blissfield, MI 49228

Rottweil, (See Dynamit Nobel of America)

Royal Arms International, 22458 Ventura Blvd., Suite E, Woodland Hills, CA 91364/818-704-5110

Sarco, Inc., 323 Union St., Stirling, NJ 07980/201-647-3800

Sauer (See Sigarms)

Savage Industries, Inc., Springdale Rd., Westfield, MA 01085/413-562-2361

Thad Scott, P.O. Box 412; Hwy 82 West, Indianola, MS 38751/601-887-5929 (Perugini Visini; Bertuzzi; Mario Beschi shotguns)

Service Armament, 689 Bergen Blvd., Ridgefield, NJ 07657 (Greener Harpoon Gun)

Sherwood Intl. Export Corp., 18714 Parthenia St., Northridge, CA 91324

Don L. Shrum's Cape Outfitters, 412 So. Kingshighway, Cape Girardeau, MO 63701/314-335-4103

Sigarms, Inc., 8330 Old Courthouse Rd., Suite 885, Tysons Corner, VA 22180/703-893-1940

Sile Distributors, 7 Centre Market Pl., New York, NY 10013/212-925-4111

Simmons Gun Specialties, Inc., 700 S. Rogers Rd., Olathe, KS 66062/913-782-3131

Sloan's Sprtg. Goods, Inc., 10 South St., Ridgefield, CT 06877

Franz Sodia Jagdgewehrfabrik, Schulhausgasse 14, 9170 Ferlach, (Kärnten) Austria

Southern Gun & Tackle Distributors, P.O. Box 25, Opa-Locka (Miami), FL 33054

Southwest Muzzle Loaders Supply, 201 E. Myrtle, Suite 112/P.O. Box 921, Angleton, TX 77515/409-849-4086

Spain America Enterprises Inc., 8581 N.W. 54th St., Miami, FL 33166

Springfield Armory, 420 W. Main St., Geneseo, IL 61254/309-944-5139 (Bernardelli)

Steyr-Daimler-Puch, Gun South, Inc., Box 6607, 7605 Eastwood Mall, Birmingham, AL 35210/800-821-3021 (rifles)

Stoeger Industries, 55 Ruta Ct., S. Hackensack, NJ 07606/201-440-2700

Taurus International Mfg. Inc., P.O. Box 558567, Ludlam Br., Miami, FL 33155/305-662-2529

Thomas & Barrett, North Frost Center, 1250 Northeast Loop 410, Suite 200, San Antonio, TX 78209/512-826-0943

Loren Thomas Ltd., P.O. Box 18425, Dallas, TX 75218 (Bruchet)

Tradewinds, Inc., P.O. Box 1191, Tacoma, WA 98401

Uberti, Aldo. See: Allen Firearms Co.

Ignacio Ugartechea, Apartado 21, Eibar, Spain
Valmet Sporting Arms Div., 7 Westchester Plaza, Elmsford, NY 10523/914-347-4440 (sporting types)
Valor of Florida Corp., 5555 N.W. 36th Ave., Miami, FL 33142/305-633-0127
Ventura Imports, P.O. Box 2782, Seal Beach, CA 90740 (European shotguns)
Verney-Carron, B.P. 72, 54 Boulevard Thiers, 42002 St. Etienne Cedex, France
Perugini Visini & Co. s.r.l., Via Camprelle, 126, 25080 Nuvolera (Bs.), Italy
Waffen-Frankonia, see: Frankonia Jagd
Waverly Arms Inc., 108 Olde Springs Rd., Columbia, SC 29223/803-736-2861 (Armurerie Vouzelaud; shotguns only)
Weatherby's, 2781 Firestone Blvd., So. Gate, CA 90280/213-569-7186
Whittington Arms, Box 489, Hooks, TX 75561
Winchester, Olin Corp., 120 Long Ridge Rd., Stamford, CT 06904
Zavodi Crvena Zastava (See Interarms)
Zoli Group U.S.A. Inc., P.O. Box 729, 1051 Clinton St., Buffalo, NY 14240/716-852-1445

## GUNS (Pellet)

Barnett International, Inc., P.O. Box 934, 1967 Gunn Highway, Odessa, FL 33556/920-2241
Beeman Precision Airguns, 47 Paul Dr., San Rafael, CA 94903/415-472-7121
Benjamin Air Rifle Co., 2600 Chicory Rd., Racine, WI 53403/414-554-7900
Collector's Armoury, Inc., 800 Slaters Lane, Alexandria, VA 22314/703-339-8005
Crosman Airguns, 980 Turk Hill Rd., Fairport, NY 14450/716-223-6000
Daisy Mfg. Co., P.O. Box 220, Rogers, AR 72756/501-636-1200 (also Feinwerkbau)
Dynamit Nobel of America, Inc., 105 Stonehurst Ct., Northvale, NJ 07647/201-767-1660 (Dianawerk)
Great Lakes Airguns, 6175 So. Park Ave., Hamburg, NY 14075/716-648-6666
Harrington & Richardson Arms Co., Industrial Rowe, Gardner, MA 01440 (Webley)
Gil Hebard Guns, Box 1, Knoxville, IL 61448
Interarms, 10 Prince, Alexandria, VA 22313 (Walther)
Kendall International Inc., 501 East North, Carlisle, KY 40311/606-289-7336 (Italian Airmatch)
Mandall Shooting Supplies, Inc., 3616 N. Scottsdale Rd., Scottsdale, AZ 85252/602-945-2553 (Cabanas line)
Marathon Products Inc., East Haddam Industrial Park, East Haddam, CT 06423/203-873-1478
Marksman Products, 5622 Engineer Dr., Huntington Beach, CA 92649/714-898-7535
McMurray & Son, 109 E. Arbor Vitae St., Inglewood, CA 90301/213-412-4187 (cust. airguns)
Paragon Sales & Services, Inc., P.O. Box 2022, Joliet, IL 60434/815-725-9212
Phoenix Arms Co., Phoenix House, Churchdale Rd., Eastbourne, East Sussex BN22 8PX, England (Jackal)
Power Line (See Daisy Mfg. Co.)
Sheridan Products, Inc., 3205 Sheridan, Racine, WI 53403
Smith & Wesson, 2100 Roosevelt Ave., Springfield, MA 01104
Target Airgun Supply, P.O. Box 428, South Gate, CA 90280/213-569-3417

## GUNS & GUN PARTS, REPLICA AND ANTIQUE

Antique Arms Co., David E. Saunders, 1110 Cleveland, Monett, MO 65708/417-235-6501
Antique Gun Parts, Inc., 1118 S. Braddock Ave., Pittsburgh, PA 15218/412-241-1811 (ML)
Armoury Inc., Rte. 202, New Preston, CT 06777
Armsport, Inc., 3590 N.W. 49th St., Miami, FL 33142
Artistic Arms, Inc., Box 23, Hoagland, IN 46745 (Sharps-Borchardt replica)
Beeman Precisions Arms, Inc., 47-GDD Paul Dr., San Rafael, CA 94903/415-472-7121
Bob's Place, Box 283J, Clinton, IA 52732 (obsolete Winchester parts only)
Cache La Poudre Rifleworks, 168 No. College Ave., Fort Collins, CO 90521/303-482-6913
Dave Chicoine, d/b/a Liberty A.S.P., 19 Key St., Eastport, ME 04631/207-853-2327(S&W only; ctlg. $5)
Collector's Armoury, Inc., 800 Slaters Lane, Alexandria, VA 22314/703-339-8005
Dixie Gun Works, Inc., Hwy 51, South, Union City, TN 38261/901-885-0561
Federal Ordnance Inc., 1443 Portrero Ave., So. El Monte, CA 91733/213-350-4161
Jack First Distributors, Inc., 44633 Sierra Hwy., Lancaster, CA 93534/805-945-6981
Fred Goodwin, Goodwin's Gun Shop, Silver Ridge, Sherman Mills, ME 04776/207-365-4451 (Winchester rings & studs)
Hansen & Hansen, 244 Old Post Rd., Southport, CT 06490/203-259-7337
Hopkins & Allen Arms, 3 Ethel Ave., P.O. Box 217, Hawthorne, NJ 07507/201-427-1165
Terry K. Kopp, Highway 13, Lexington, MO 64067/816-259-2636 (restoration & pts. 1890 & 1906 Winch.)
The House of Muskets, Inc., P.O. Box 4640, Pagosa Springs, CO 81157/303-731-2295 (ML guns)
Log Cabin Sport Shop, 8010 Lafayette Rd., Lodi, OH 44254/216-948-1082 (ctlg. $30)
Edw. E. Lucas, 32 Garfield Ave., East Brunswick, NJ 08816/201-251-5526 (45/70 Springfield parts; some Sharps, Spencer parts)
Lyman Products Corp., Middlefield, CT 06455

Tommy Munsch Gunsmithing, Rt. 2, Box 248, Little Falls, MN 56345/612-632-5835 (Winchester parts only; list $1.50; oth. inq. SASE)
Numrich Arms Co., West Hurley, NY 12491
Ram Line, Inc., 406 Violet St., Golden, CO 80401/303-279-0886
Replica Models, Inc., 800 Slaters Lane, Alexandria, VA 22314/703-339-8005
S&S Firearms, 88-21 Aubrey Ave., Glendale, NY 11385/212-497-1100
Sarco, Inc., 323 Union St., Stirling, NJ 07980/201-647-3800
C. H. Stoppler, 1426 Walton Ave., New York, NY 10452 (miniature guns)
Upper Missouri Trading Co., Box 191, Crofton, NE 68730/402-388-4844
C. H. Weisz, Box 311, Arlington, VA 22210/703-243-9161
W. H. Wescombe, P.O. Box 488, Glencoe, CA 95232 (Rem. R.B. parts)

## GUNS, SURPLUS—PARTS AND AMMUNITION

Can Am Enterprises, Fruitland, Ont. LOR ILO, Canada/416-643-4357 (Enfield rifles)
Century Arms, Inc., 5 Federal St., St. Albans, VT 05478/802-524-9541
Walter Craig, Inc., Box 927, Selma, AL 36701/205-875-7989
Eastern Firearms Co., 790 S. Arroyo Pkwy., Pasadena, CA 91105
Federal Ordnance, Inc., 1443 Potrero Ave., So. El Monte, CA 91733/818-350-4161
Garcia National Gun Traders, 225 S.W. 22nd, Miami, FL 33135
Hansen and Hansen, 244 Old Post Rd., Southport, CT 06490/203-259-7337
Lever Arms Serv. Ltd., 572 Howe St., Vancouver, B.C., Canada V6C 2E3/604-685-8945
Paragon Sales & Services, Inc., P.O. Box 2022, Joliet, IL 60434 (ammunition)
Raida Intertraders S.A., Raida House, 1-G Ave. de la Coronne, B1050 Brussels, Belgium
Sarco, Inc., 323 Union St., Stirling, NJ 07980/201-647-3800 (military surpl. ammo)
Service Armament Co., 689 Bergen Blvd., Ridgefield, NJ 07657
Sherwood Intl. Export Corp., 18714 Parthenia St., Northridge, CA 91324/818-349-7600
Springfield Sporters Inc., R.D. 1, Penn Run, PA 15765/412-254-2626

## GUNSMITHS, CUSTOM (see Custom Gunsmiths)

## GUNSMITHS, HANDGUN (see Pistolsmiths)

## GUNSMITH SCHOOLS

Colorado School of Trades, 1575 Hoyt, Lakewood, CO 80215/303-233-4697
Lassen Community College, P.O. Box 3000, Hiway 139, Susanville, CA 96130/016 257 6181
Robert E. Maki, School of Engraving, P.O. Box 947, Northbrook, IL 60062/312-724-8238 (firearms engraving ONLY)
Modern Gun Repair School, 2538 No. 8th St., Phoenix, AZ 85006/602-990-8346 (home study)
Montgomery Technical College, P.O. Box 787, Troy, NC 27371/919-572-3691 (also 1-yr. engraving school)
Murray State College, Gunsmithing Program, 100 Faculty Dr., Tishomingo, OK 73460/405-371-2371
North American School of Firearms, Curriculum Development Ctr., 4401 Birch St., Newport Beach, CA 92663/714-546-7360 (correspondence)
North American School of Firearms, Education Service Center, Oak & Pawnee St., Scranton, PA 18515/717-342-7701
Penn. Gunsmith School, 812 Ohio River Blvd., Avalon, Pittsburgh, PA 15202/412-766-1812
Piedmont Technical School, P.O. Box 1197, Roxboro, NC 27575
Pine Technical Institute, 1100 Fourth St., Pine City, MN 55063/612-629-6764
Police Sciences Institute, 4401 Birch St., Newport Beach, CA 92660/714-546-7360 (General Law Enforcement Course)
Shenandoah School of Gunsmithing, P.O. Box 300, Bentonville, VA 22610/703-743-5494
Southeastern Community College, Admissions "TF" Gear Ave., West Burlington, IA 52655/319-752-2731
Trinidad State Junior College, 600 Prospect, Trinidad, CO 81082/303-846-5621
Yavapai College, 1100 East Sheldon St., Prescott, AZ 86301/602-445-7300

## GUNSMITH SUPPLIES, TOOLS, SERVICES

A.C. Enterprises, P.O. Box 448, Edenton, NC 27932/919-482-4992
Albright Prod. Co., P. O. Box 1144, Portola, CA 96122 (trap buttplates)
Don Allen, Inc., HC55, Box 322, Sturgis, SD 57785/605-347-4686 (stock duplicating machine)
Alley Supply Co., Carson Valley Industrial Park, P.O. Box 848, Gardnerville, NV 89410/702-782-3800 (JET line lathes, mills, etc.)
Ametek, Hunter Spring Div., One Spring Ave., Hatfield, PA 19440/215-822-2971 (trigger gauge)
Anderson Mfg. Co., Union Gap Sta., P.O. Box 3120, Yakima, WA 98903/509-453-2349 (tang safe)
Answer Stocking Systems, 113 N. 2nd St., Whitewater, WI 53190/414-473-4848 (urethane hammers, vice jaws, etc.)
Armite Labs., 1845 Randolph St., Los Angeles, CA 90001/213-587-7744 (pen oiler)
B-Square Co., Box 11281, Ft. Worth, TX 76110/800-433-2909
Jim Baiar, 490 Halfmoon Rd., Columbia Falls, MT 59912 (hex screws)
Behlert Custom Guns, Inc., RD 2 Box 36C, Route 611 North, Pipersville, PA 18947/215-766-8680

Dennis M. Bellm Gunsmithing, Inc., dba P.O. Ackley Rifle Barrels, 2376 S. Redwood Rd., Salt Lake City, UT 84119/801-974-0697 (rifles only)

Al Biesen, W. 2039 Sinto Ave., Spokane, WA 99201 (grip caps, buttplates)

Roger Biesen, 5021 W. Rosewood, Spokane, WA 99208/509-328-9340

Billingsley & Brownell, Box 25, Dayton, Wy 82836/307-655-9344

Blue Ridge Machine and Tool, P.O. Box 536, 2806 Putnam Ave., Hurricane, WV 25526/304-562-3538 (machinery, tools, shop suppl.)

Briganti Custom Gun-Smithing, P.O. Box 56, 475-Route 32, Highland Mills, NY 10930/914-928-9816 (cold rust bluing, hand polishing, metal work)

Brownells, Inc., 222 W. Liberty, Montezuma, IA 50171/515-623-5401

W.E. Brownell Checkering Tools, 3356 Moraga Place, San Diego, CA 92117/619-276-6146

Buehler Scope Mounts, 17 Orinda Way, Orinda, CA 94563/415-254-3201

Burgess Vibrocrafters, Inc. (BVI), Rte. 83, Grayslake, IL 60030

M.H. Canjar, 500 E. 45th, Denver, CO 80216/303-295-2638 (triggers, etc.)

Chapman Mfg. Co., P.O. Box 250, Rte. 17 at Saw Mill Rd., Durham, CT 06422/203-349-9228

Chicago Wheel & Mfg. Co., 1101 W. Monroe St., Chicago, IL 60607/312-226-8155 (Handee grinders)

Dave Chicoine, d/b/a Liberty A.S.P., 19 Key St., Eastport, ME 04631/207-853-2327 (spl. S&W tools)

Chopie Mfg., Inc., 700 Copeland Ave., LaCrosse, WI 54603/608-784-0926

Classic Arms Corp., P.O. Box 8, Palo Alto, CA 94302/415-321-7243 (floorplates, grip caps)

Clover Mfg. Co., 139 Woodward Ave., Norwalk, CT 06856/800-243 6492 (Clover compound)

Clymer Mfg. Co., Inc., 1645 W. Hamlin Rd., Rochester Hills, MI 48063/313-541-5533 (reamers)

Dave Cook, 720 Hancock Ave., Hancock, MI 49930 (metalsmithing only)

Dayton-Traister Co., 9322-900th West, P.O. Box 593, Oak Harbor, WA 98277/206-675-5375 (triggers)

Dem-Bart Hand Checkering Tools, Inc., 6807 Hiway #2, Snohomish, WA 98290/206-568-7356

Dremel Mfg. Co., 4915-21st St., Racine, WI 53406 (grinders)

Chas. E. Duffy, Williams Lane, West Hurley, NY 12491

The Dutchman's Firearms Inc., 4143 Taylor Blvd., Louisville, KY 40215/502-366-0555

Peter Dyson Ltd., 29-31 Church St., Honley, Huddersfield, West Yorksh. HD7 2AH, England/0484-661062 (accessories f. antique gun coll.)

Edmund Scientific Co., 101 E. Gloucester Pike, Barrington, NJ 08007/609-547-3488

Emco-Lux, 2050 Fairwood Ave., P.O. Box 07861, Columbus, OH 43207/614-445-8328

Jack First Distributors, Inc., 44633 Sierra Hwy., Lancaster, CA 93534/805-945-6981

Jerry Fisher, 1244 4th Ave. West, Kalispell, MT 59901/406-755-7093

Forster Products, Inc., 82 E. Lanark Ave., Lanark, IL 61046/815-493-6360

Francis Tool Co., (f'ly Keith Francis Inc.), P.O. Box 7861, Eugene, OR 97401/503-345-7457 (reamers)

G. R. S. Corp., P.O. Box 748, 900 Overlander St., Emporia, KS 66801/316-343-1084 (Gravermeister; Grave Max tools)

Gilmore Pattern Works, P.O. Box 50084, Tulsa, OK 74150/918-245-9627 (Wagner safe-T-planer)

Glendo Corp., P.O. Box 1153, Emporia, KS 66801/316-343-1084 (Accu-Finish tool)

Grace Metal Prod., 115 Ames St., Elk Rapids, MI 49629 (screw drivers, drifts)

Gunline Tools, 2970 Saturn St., Brea, CA 92621/714-993-5100

Gun-Tec, P.O. Box 8125, W. Palm Beach, Fl 33407

Half Moon Rifle Shop, 490 Halfmoon Rd., Columbia Falls, MT 59912/406-892-4409 (hex screws)

Henriksen Tool Co., Inc., P.O. Box 668, Phoenix, OR 97535/503-535-2309 (reamers)

Huey Gun Cases (Marvin Huey), P.O. Box 22456, Kansas City, MO 64113/816-444-1637 (high grade English ebony tools)

Ken Jantz Supply, Rt. 1, Sulphur, OK 73086/405-622-3790

Jeffredo Gunsight Co., 1629 Via Monserate, Fallbrook, CA 92028 (trap buttplate)

Kasenit Co., Inc., P.O. Box 726, Mahwah, NJ 07430/201-529-3663 (surface hardening compound)

Terry K. Kopp, Highway 13, Lexington, MO 64067/816-259-2636 (stock rubbing compound; rust preventive grease)

J. Korzinek, RD#2, Box 73, Canton, PA 17724/717-673-8512 (stainl. steel bluing; broch. $1.50)

John G. Lawson, (The Sight Shop) 1802 E. Columbia Ave., Tacoma, WA 98404/206-474-5465

Lea Mfg. Co., 237 E. Aurora St., Waterbury, CT 06720/203-753-5116

Mark Lee Supplies, P.O. Box 20379, Minneapolis, MN 55420/612-884-4060

Lock's Phila. Gun Exch., 6700 Rowland Ave., Philadelphia, PA 19149/215-332-6225

Longbranch Gun Bluing Co., 2455 Jacaranda Lane, Los Osos, CA 93402/805-528-1792

McIntrye Tools, P.O. Box 491/State Road #1144, Troy, NC 27371/919-572-2603 (shotgun bbl. facing tool)

McMillan Rifle Barrels, U.S. International, P.O Box 3427, Bryan, TX 77805/409-846-3990 (services)

Meier Works, Steve Hines, Box 328, 2102-2nd Ave., Canyon, TX 79015/806-655-9256 (European acc.)

Michaels of Oregon Co., P.O. Box 13010, Portland, OR 97213/503-255-6890

Miller Single Trigger Mfg. Co., R.D. 1, Box 99, Millersburg, PA 17061/717-692-3704

Miniature Machine Co. (MMC), 210 E. Poplar St., Deming, NM 88030/505-546-2151 (screwdriver grinding fixtures)

Frank Mittermeier, 3577 E. Tremont, New York, NY 10465

N&J Sales Co., Lime Kiln Rd., Northford, CT 06472/203-484-0247 (screwdrivers)

Karl A. Neise, Inc., 1671 W. McNab Rd., Ft. Lauderdale, FL 33309/305-979-3900

Olympic Arms Inc., dba SGW, 624 Old Pacific Hwy. S.E., Olympia, WA 98503/206-456-3471

Palmgren Steel Prods., Chicago Tool & Engineering Co., 8383 South Chicago Ave., Chicago, IL 60617/312-721-9675 (vises, etc.)

Panavise Prods., Inc., 2850 E. 29th St., Long Beach, CA 90806/213-595-7621

Pilkington Gun Co., P.O. Box 1296, Muskogee, OK 74402/918-683-9418 (Q.D. scope mt.)

Redman's Rifling & Reboring, Route 3, Box 330A, Omak, WA 98841/509-826-5512 (22 RF liners)

Richland Arms Co., 321 W. Adrian St., Blissfield, MI 49228

Riley's Inc., 121 No. Main St., P.O. Box 139, Avilla, IN 46710/219-897-2351 (Niedner buttplates, grip caps)

Roto/Carve, 6509 Indian Hills Rd., Minneapolis, MN 55435/800-533-8988 (tool)

A.G. Russell Co., 1705 Hiway 71 North, Springdale, AR 72764/501-751-7341 (Arkansas oilstones)

Schaffner Mfg. Co., Emsworth, Pittsburgh, PA 15202 (polishing kits)

SGW, Inc. (formerly Schuetzen Gun Works), See: Olympic Arms

Shaw's, 9447 W. Lilac Rd., Escondido, CA 92026/619-728-7070

James R. Spradlin, Jim's Gun Shop, 113 Arthur, Pueblo, CO 81004/303-543-9462 (rust blues; stock fillers)

L.S. Starrett Co., 121 Crescent St., Athol, MA 01331/617-249-3551

Texas Platers Supply Co., 2453 W. Five Mile Parkway, Dallas, TX 75233 (plating kit)

Teyssier Imported French Walnut, P.O. Box 984, 3155 S. 2nd St., Glenrock, WY 82637/307-436-9804 (blanks)

Timney Mfg. Inc., 3106 W. Thomas Rd., Phoenix, AZ 85017/602-269-6937

Stan de Treville, Box 33021, San Diego, CA 92103/619-298-3393 (checkering patterns)

Turner Co., Div. Cleanweld Prods., Inc., 821 Park Ave., Sycamore, IL 60178/815-895-4545

Twin City Steel Treating Co., Inc. 1114 S. 3rd, Minneapolis, MN 55415/612-332-4849 (heat treating)

Walker Arms Co., Rt. 2, Box 73, Hwy. 80 W, Selma, AL 36701/205-872-6231 (tools)

Weaver Arms Co., P.O. Box 8, Dexter, MO 63841/314-568-3800 (action wrenches & transfer punches)

Will-Burt Co., 169 So. Main, Orrville, OH 44667 (vises)

Williams Gun Sight Co., 7389 Lapeer Rd., Davison, MI 48423

Wilson Arms Co., 63 Leetes Island Rd., Branford, CT 06405/203-488-7297

Wisconsin Platers Supply Co. (See Texas Platers)

W.C. Wolff Co., P.O. Box 232, Ardmore, PA 19003/215-647-1880 (springs)

Woodcraft Supply Corp., 313 Montvale, Woburn, MA 01801

## HANDGUN ACCESSORIES

Ajax Custom Grips, Inc., 12229 Cox Lane, Dallas, TX 75244/214-241-6302

Bob Allen Companies, 214 S.W. Jackson St., Des Moines, IA 50302/515-283-2191

American Gas & Chemical Co., Ltd., 220 Pegasus Ave., Northvale, NJ 07647/201-767-7300 (clg. lube)

Armson, Inc., P.O. Box 2130, Farmington Hills, MI 48018/313-478-2577

Armsport, Inc., 3590 N.W. 49th St., Miami, FL 33142/305-635-7850

Assault Accessories, P.O. Box 8994 CRB, Tucson, AZ 85738/602-791-7860 (pistol shoulder stocks)

Baramie Corp., 6250 E. 7 Mile Rd., Detroit, MI 48234 (Hip-Grip)

Bar-Sto Precision Machine, 73377 Sullivan Rd., Twentynine Palms, CA 92277/619-367-2747

Behlert Precision, RD 2 Box 36C, Route 611 North, Pipersville, PA 18947/215-766-8681

Bingham Ltd., 1775-C Wilwat Dr., Norcross, GA 30093 (magazines)

C'Arco, P.O. Box 308, Highland, CA 92346/714-862-8311 (Ransom Rest)

Centaur Systems, Inc., 15127 NE 24th C-3, Redmond, WA 98052/206-392-8472 (Quadra-Lok bbls.)

Central Specialties Co., 200 Lexington Dr., Buffalo Grove, IL 60090/312-537-3300 (trigger locks only)

Dave Chicoine, d/b/a Liberty A.S.P., 19 Key St., Eastport, ME 04631/207-853-2327 (shims f. S&W revs.)

D&E Magazines Mfg., P.O. Box 4876, Sylmar, CA 91342 (clips)

Detonics Firearms Industries, 13456 SE 27th Pl., Bellevue, WA 98005/206-747-2100

Doskocil Mfg. Co., Inc, P.O. Box 1246, Arlington, TX 75010/817-467-5116 (Gun Guard cases)

Essex Arms, Box 345, Island Pond, VT 05846/802-723-4313 (45 Auto frames)

Frielich Police Equipment, 396 Broome St., New York, NY 10013/212-254-3045 (cases)

R. S. Frielich, 211 East 21st St., New York, NY 10010/212-777-4477 (cases)

HKS Products, 7841 Foundation Dr., Florence, KY 41042/606-342-7841 (speedloader)

K&K Ammo Wrist Band, R.D. #1, Box 448-CA18, Lewistown, PA 17044/717-242-2329

Terry K. Kopp, Highway 13, Lexington, MO 64067/816-259-2636

Lee's Red Ramps, 7252 E. Ave. U-3, Littlerock, CA 93543/805-944-4487 (ramp insert kits; spring kits)

Lee Precision Inc., 4275 Hwy. U, Hartford, WI 53027 (pistol rest holders)

Kent Lomont, 4236 West 700 South, Poneto, IN 46781 (Auto Mag only)

Lone Star Gunleather, 1301 Brushy Bend Dr., Round Rock, TX 78664/512-255-1805

Los Gatos Grip & Specialty Co., P.O. Box 1850, Los Gatos, CA 95030 (custommade)

MTM Molded Prods. Co., 3370 Obco Ct., Dayton, OH 45414/513-890-7461

No-Sho Mfg. Co., 10727 Glenfield Ct., Houston, TX 77096/713-723-5332

Harry Owen (See Sport Specialties)

Pachmayr, 1220 S. Grand, Los Angeles, CA 90015 (cases)

Pacific Intl. Mchdsg. Corp., 2215 "J" St., Sacramento, CA 95818/916-446-2737 (Vega 45 Colt comb. mag.)

Poly-Choke Div., Marble Arms Corp., 420 Industrial Park, Gladstone, MI 49837/906-428-3710 (handgun ribs)

Ranch Products, P.O. Box 145, Malinta, OH 43535 (third-moon clips)
Ransom (See C'Arco)
Sile Distributors, 7 Centre Market Pl., New York, NY 10013
Sport Specialties, (Harry Owen), Box 5337, Hacienda Hts., CA 91745/213-968-5806 (.22 rimfire adapters; .22 insert bbls. f. T/C Contender, autom. pistols)
Sportsmen's Equipment Co., 415 W. Washington, San Diego, CA 92103/619-296-1501
Turkey Creek Enterprises, Rt. 1, Box 10, Red Oak, CA 74563/918-754-2884 (wood handgun cases)
Melvin Tyler, 1326 W. Britton, Oklahoma City, OK 73114/800-654-8415 (grip adaptor)
Whitney Sales, P.O. Box 875, Reseda, CA 91335/818-345-4212

## HANDGUN GRIPS

Ajax Custom Grips, Inc., 12229 Cox Lane, Dallas, TX 75244/214-241-6302
Altamount Mfg., 510 N. Commercial St., P.O. Box 309, Thomasboro, IL 61878/217-634-3225
Art Jewel Enterprises Ltd., 421A Irmen Dr., Addison, IL 60101/312-628-6220
Barami Corp., 6250 East 7 Mile Rd., Detroit, MI 48234/313-891-2536
Bear Hug Grips, P.O. Box 25944, Colorado Springs, CO 80936/303-598-5675 (cust.)
Beeman Inc., 47 Paul Dr., San Rafael, CA 94903/415-472-7121 (airguns only)
Bingham Ltd., 1775-C Wilwat Dr., Norcross, GA 30093
Boone's Custom Ivory Grips, Inc., 562 Coyote Rd., Brinnon, WA 98320/206-796-4330
Dave Chicoine, d/b/a Liberty A.S.P., 19 Key St., Eastport, ME 04631/207-853-2327 (orig. S&W 1855-1950)
Fitz Pistol Grip Co., P.O. Box 171, Douglas City, CA 96024/916-778-3136
Gateway Shooters' Supply, Inc., 10145-103rd St., Jacksonville, FL 32210/904-778-2323 (Rogers grips)
Herrett's , Box 741, Twin Falls, ID 83301
Hogue Combat Grips, P.O. Box 2038, Atascadero, CA 93423/805-466-6266 (Monogrip)
Paul Jones Munitions Systems, (See Fitz Co.)
Russ Maloni (See Russwood)
Millett Industries, 16131 Gothard St., Huntington Beach, CA 92647/714-842-5575 (custom)
Monogrip, (See Hogue)
Monte Kristo Pistol Grip Co., Box 171, Douglas City, CA 96024/916-778-3136
Mustang Custom Pistol Grips, see: Supreme Products Co.
Pachmayr Gun Works, Inc., 1220 S. Grand Ave., Los Angeles, CA 90015/213-748-7271
Robert H. Newell, 55 Coyote, Los Alamos, NM 87544/505-662-7135 (custom stocks)
Rogers Grips (See Gateway Shooters' Supply)
A. Jack Rosenberg & Sons, 12229 Cox Lane, Dallas, TX 75234/214-241-6302 (Ajax)
Royal Ordnance Works Ltd., P.O. Box 3254, Wilson, NC 27893/919-237-0515
Russwood Custom Pistol Grips, 40 Sigman Lane, Elma, NY 14059/716-652-7131 (cust. exotic woods)
SDA, P.O. Box 424, Fallbrook, CA 92028/619-584-0577
Jean St. Henri, 6525 Dume Dr., Malibu, CA 90265/213-457-7211 (custom)
Sile Distr., 7 Centre Market Pl., New York, NY 10013/212-925-4111
Sports Inc., P.O. Box 683, Park Ridge, IL 60068/312-825-8952 (Franzite)
Supreme Products Co., 1830 S. California Ave., Monrovia, CA 91016/800-423-7159/818-357-5359
Sergeant Violin, P.O. Box 25808, Tamarac, FL 33320/305-721-7856 (wood pistol stocks)
R. D. Wallace, Star Rte. Box 76, Grandin, MO 63943/314-593-4773
Wayland Prec. Wood Prods., Box 1142, Mill Valley, CA 94942/415-381-3543

## HEARING PROTECTORS

AO Safety Prods., Div. of American Optical Corp., 14 Mechanic St., Southbridge, MA 01550/617-765-9711 (ear valves, ear muffs)
Bausch & Lomb, 635 St. Paul St., Rochester, NY 14602
Bilsom Interntl. Inc., 11800 Sunrise Valley Dr., Reston, VA 22091/703-620-3950 (ear plugs, muffs)
David Clark Co., Inc., 360 Franklin St., Worcester, MA 01604
Marble Arms Corp., 420 Industrial Park, Gladstone, MI 49837/906-428-3710
North Consumer Prods. Div., 16624 Edwards Rd., P.O. Box 7500, Cerritos, CA 90701/213-926-0545 (Lee Sonic ear valves)
Safety Direct, 23 Snider Way, Sparks, NV 89431/702-354-4451 (Silencio)
Smith & Wesson, 2100 Roosevelt Ave., Springfield, MA 01101
Willson Safety Prods. Div., P.O. Box 622, Reading, PA 19603 (Ray-O-Vac)

## HOLSTERS & LEATHER GOODS

Active Leather Corp., 36-29 Vernon Blvd., Long Island City, NY 11106
Alessi Custom Concealment Holsters, 2465 Niagara Falls Blvd., Tonawanda, NY 14150/716-691-5615
Allen Firearms Co., 2879 All Trades Rd., Santa Fe, NM 87501/505-471-6090
Bob Allen Companies, 214 S.W. Jackson, Des Moines, IA 50315/515-283-2191
American Enterprises, 1480 Avocado, El Cajon, CA 92020/619-588-1222
American Sales & Mfg. Co., P.O. Box 677, Laredo, TX 78040/512-723-6893

Andy Anderson, P.O. Box 225, North Hollywood, CA 91603/213-877-2401 (Gunfighter Custom Holsters)
Armament Systems & Procedures, Inc., P.O. Box 356, Appleton, WI 54912/414-731-8893 (ASP)
Rick M. Bachman (see Old West Reproductions)
Barami Corp., 6250 East 7 Mile Rd., Detroit, MI 48234/313-891-2536
Beeman Inc., 47-GDD Paul Dr., San Rafael, CA 94903/415-472-7121
Behlert Precision, RD 2 Box 36C, Route 611 North, Pipersville, PA 18947/215-766-8681
Bianchi International Inc., 100 Calle Cortez, Temecula, CA 92390/714-676-5621
Ted Blocker's Custom Holsters, 409 West Bonita Ave. San Dimas, CA 91773/714-599-4415
Bo-Mar Tool & Mfg. Co., Rt. 12, Box 405, Longview, TX 75605/214-759-4784
Border Guns & Leather, Box 1423, Deming, NM 88031 (Old West cust.)
Eunice Bosselman, P.O. Box 900, Tombstone, AZ 85638
Boyt Co., Div. of Welsh Sptg., P.O. Box 220, Iowa Falls, IA 51026/515-648-4626
Brauer Bros. Mfg. Co., 2020 Delmar, St. Louis, MO 63103/314-231-2864
Browning, Rt. 4, Box 624-B, Arnold, MO 63010
J.M. Bucheimer Co., P.O. Box 280, Airport Rd., Frederick, MD 21701/301-662-5101
Buffalo Leather Goods, Inc., Rt. 4, Box 187, Magnolia, AR 71753/501-234-6367
Cathey Enterprises, Inc., 3423 Milam Dr., P.O. Box 2202, Brownwood, TX 76804/915-643-2553
Cattle Baron Leather Co., Dept. GD, P.O. Box 100724, San Antonio, TX 78201/512-697-8900 (ctlg. $3)
Chace Leather Prods., Longhorn Div., 507 Alden St., Fall River, MA 02722/617-678-7556
Cherokee Gun Accessories, 4127 Bay St., Suite 226, Fremont, CA 94538/415-471-5770
China IM/EX, P.O. Box 27573, San Francisco, CA 94127/415-661-2212
Chas. Clements, Handicrafts Unltd., 1741 Dallas St., Aurora, CO 80010/303-364-0403
Daisy Mfg. Co., P.O. Box 220, Rogers, AR 72756/501-636-1200
Davis Leather Co., G. Wm. Davis, 3930 "F" Valley Blvd., Unit F, Walnut, CA 91789/714-598-5620
Eugene DeMayo & Sons, Inc., 2795 Third Ave., Bronx, NY 10455/212-665-7075
DeSantis Holster Co., 140 Denton Ave., New Hyde Park, NY 11040/516-354-8000
Ellwood Epps Northern Ltd., 210 Worthington St. W., North Bay, Ont. P1B 3B4, Canada (custom made)
Flatbush Country Leather, Box 116, 410 Houghton, Ione, WA 99139/509-442-3448 (made to order only)
GALCO Gun Leather, 4311 W. Van Buren, Phoenix, AZ 85043/602-233-0596
Gunfighter (See Anderson)
Ernie Hill Speed Leather, 3128 S. Extension Rd., Mesa, AZ 85202/602-831-1919
Horsehoe Leather Prods., The Cottage, Sharow, Ripon HG4 5BP, England
Hoyt Holster Co., Inc., P.O. Box 69, Coupeville, WA 98239/206-678-6640
Don Hume, Box 351, Miami, OK 74354/918-542-6604
Hunter Corp., 3300 W. 71st Ave., Westminster, CO 80030/303-427-4626
John's Custom Leather, 525 S. Liberty St., Blairsville, PA 15717/412-459-6802
Jumbo Sports Prods., P.O. Box 280, Airport Rd., Frederick, MD 21701
Kane Products, Inc., 5572 Brecksville Rd., Cleveland, OH 44131/216-524-9962 (GunChaps)
Kirkpatrick Leather Co., Inc., P.O. Box 3150, Laredo, TX 78041/512-723-6631
Kolpin Mfg. Inc., P.O. Box 231, Berlin, WI 54923/414-361-0400
Morris Lawing, P.O. Box 9494, Charlotte, NC 28299/704-375-1740
George Lawrence Co., 1435 N.W. Northrup, Portland, OR 97209/503-228-8244
Lone Star Gunleather, 1301 Brushy Bend Dr., Round Rock, TX 78664/512-255-1805
Michael's of Oregon, Co., P.O. Box 13010, Portland, OR 97213/503-255-6890 (Uncle Mike's)
Mixson Leathercraft Inc., 1950 W. 84th St., Hialeah, FL 33014/305-820-5190 (police leather products)
No-Sho Mfg. Co., 10727 Glenfield Ct., Houston, TX 77096/713-723-5332
Kenneth L. Null-Custom Concealment Holsters, R.D. #5, Box 197, Hanover, PA 17331 (See Seventrees)
Old West Reproductions, R. M. Bachman, 1840 Stag Lane, Kalispell, MT 59901/406-755-6902 (ctlg. $3)
Orient-Western, P.O. Box 27573, San Francisco, CA 94127
Pioneer Prods., P.O. Box G, Magnolia, AR 71750/501-234-1566
Pony Express Sport Shop Inc., 1606 Schoenborn St., Sepulveda, CA 91343/818-895-1231
Red Head Brand Corp., 4949 Joseph Hardin Dr., Dallas, TX 75236/214-333-4141
Red River Outfitters, P.O. Box 241, Tujunga, CA 91042/213-352-0177
Rogers Holsters Co., Inc., 1736 St. Johns Bluff Rd., Jacksonville, FL 32216/904-641-9434
Roy's Custom Leather Goods, Hwy. 1325 & Rawhide Rd., P.O. Box G, Magnolia, AR 71753/501-234-1566
Safariland Leather Products, 1941 So. Walker Ave., Monrovia, CA 91016/818-357-7902
Safety Speed Holster, Inc., 910 So. Vail, Montebello, CA 90640/213-723-4140
Buddy Schoellkopf Products, Inc., 4949 Joseph Hardin Dr., TX 75236/214-333-2121
Schulz Industries, 16247 Minnesota Ave., Paramount, CA 90723/213-636-7718
Sile Distr., 7 Centre Market Pl., New York NY 10013/212-925-4111
Milt Sparks, Box 187, Idaho City, ID 83631/208-392-6695 (broch. $2)
Robert A. Strong Co., 105 Maplewood Ave., Gloucester, MA 01930/617-281-3300
Torel, Inc., 1053 N. South St., P.O. Box 592, Yoakum, TX 77995/512-293-2341 (gun slings)
Triple-K Mfg. Co., 568 Sixth Ave., San Diego, CA 92101/619-232-2066
Uncle Mike's (See Michaels of Oregon)

Viking Leathercraft, Inc., P.O. Box 2030, 2248-2 Main St., Chula Vista, CA 92012/619-429-8050

Walt Whinnery, 1947 Meadow Creek Dr., Louisville, KY 40218/502-458-4361

Wildlife Leather Inc., P.O. Box 339, Merrick, NY 11566/516-378-8588 (lea. gds. w. outdoor themes)

Utica Duxbak Corp., 1745 S. Acoma St., Denver, CO 80223/303-778-0324

Waffen-Frankonia, see: Frankonia Jagd

Walker Shoe Co., P.O. Box 1167, Asheboro, NC 27203-1167/919-625-1380 (boots)

Weinbrenner Shoe Corp., Polk St., Merrill, WI 54452

Wolverine Boots & Shoes Div., Wolverine World Wide, 9341 Courtland Dr., Rockford, MI 49351/616-866-1561 (footwear)

Woodstream Corp., Box 327, Lititz, PA 17543 (Hunter Seat)

Woolrich Woolen Mills, Mill St., Woolrich, PA 17779/717-769-6464

Yankee Mechanics, RFD No. 1, Concord, NH 03301/603-225-3181 (hand winches)

## HUNTING AND CAMP GEAR, CLOTHING, ETC.

Bob Allen Sportswear, P.O. Box 477, Des Moines, IA 50302/800-247-8048

Eddie Bauer, 15010 NE 36th St., Redmond, WA 98052

L. L. Bean, Freeport, ME 04032

Bear Archery, R.R. 4, 4600 Southwest 41st Blvd., Gainesville, FL 32601/904-376-2327 (Himalayan backpack)

Big Beam, Teledyne Co., 290 E. Prairie St., Crystal Lake, IL 60014 (lamp)

Browning, Rte. 1, Morgan, UT 84050

Brush Hunter Sportswear, Inc., NASCO Ind., 3 NE 21st St., Washington, IN 47501/812-254-4962

Camp-Ways, 1140 E. Sandhill Ave., Carson, CA 90746/213-604-1201

Challanger Mfg. Co., Box 550, Jamaica, NY 11431 (glow safe)

Chippewa Shoe Co., P.O. Box 2521, Ft. Worth, TX 76113/817-332-4385 (boots)

Coleman Co., Inc., 250 N. St. Francis, Wichita, KS 67201

Converse Rubber Co., 55 Fordham Rd., Wilmington, MA 01887 (boots)

Danner Shoe Mfg. Co., P.O. Box 22204, Portland, OR 97222/503-653-2920 (boots)

DEER-ME Prod. Co., Box 34, Anoka, MN 55303/612-421-8971 (tree steps)

Dunham Co., P.O. Box 813, Brattleboro, VT 05301/802-254-2316 (boots)

Durango Boot, see: Georgia/Northlake

Frankonia Jagd, Hofmann & Co., Postfach 6780, D-8700 Wurzburg 1, West Germany

Freeman Ind., Inc., 100 Marblehead Rd., Tuckahoe, NY 10707 (Trak-Kit)

French Dressing Inc., 15 Palmer Heights, Burlington, VT 05401/802-658-1434 (boots)

Game-Winner, Inc., 2625 Cumberland Parkway, Suite 270, Atlanta, GA 30339/404-434-9210 (camouflage suits; orange vests)

Gander Mountain, Inc., P.O. Box 128, Hwy. "W", Wilmot, WI 53192/414-862-2344

Georgia Boot Div., U.S. Industry, 1810 Columbia Ave., Franklin, TN 37064/615-794-1556

Georgia/Northlake Boot Co., P.O. Box 10, Franklin, TN 37064/615-794-1556 (Durango)

Gokeys, 84 So. Wabasha, St. Paul, MN 55107/612-292-3933

Gun Club Sportswear, Box 477, Des Moines, IA 50302

Gun-Ho Case Mfg. Co., 110 E. 10th St., St. Paul, MN 55101

Himalayan Industries, Inc., P.O. Box 7465, Pine Bluff, AR 71611/501-534-6411

Bob Hinman Outfitters, 1217 W. Glen, Peoria, IL 61614

Hunter's Specialties, Inc., 5285 Rockwell Dr. N.E., Cedar Rapids, IA 52402/319-395-0321

Hunting World, 16 E. 53rd St., New York, NY 10022

Kap Outdoors, 1704 Locust St., Philadelphia, PA 19103/215-723-3449 (clothing)

Kenko Intl. Inc., 8141 West I-70 Frontage Rd. No., Arvada, CO 80002/303-425-1200 (footwear & socks)

Langenberg Hat Co., P.O. Box 1860, Washington, MO 63090/314-239-1860

Life Knife Inc., P.O. Box 771, Santa Monica, CA 90406/213-821-6192

Peter Limmer & Sons Inc., Box 66, Intervale, NH 03845 (boots)

Marathon Rubber Prods. Co. Inc., 510 Sherman St., Wausau, WI 54401/715-845-6255 (rain gear)

Marble Arms Corp., 420 Industrial Park, Gladstone, MI 49837

Nelson Recreation Prods., Inc., Fuqua Industries, 14760 Santa Fe Trail Dr., Lenexa, KS 66215/800-255-6061

The Orvis Co., Manchester, VT 05254/802-362-3622 (fishing gear; clothing)

PGB Assoc., 310 E. 46th St., Suite 3E, New York, NY 10017/212-867-9560

Quabaug Rubber Co./Vibram U.S.A., 17 School St. N. Brookfield, MA 01535/617-867-7731 (boots)

Quoddy Moccasins, Div. R. G. Barry Corp., 67 Minot Ave., Auburn, ME 04210/207-784-3555

Ranger Mfg. Co., Inc., P.O. Box 3676, Augusta, GA 30904

Ranger Rubber Co., 1100 E. Main St., Endicott, NY 13760/607-757-4260 (boots)

Red Ball, P.O. Box 3200, Manchester, NH 03105/603-669-0708 (boots)

Red Head Brand Corp., 4949 Joseph Hardin Dr., Dallas, TX 75236/214-333-4141

Refrigiwear, Inc., 71 Inip Dr., Inwood, Long Island, NY 11696

Reliance Prod. Ltd., 1830 Dublin Ave., Winnipeg 21, Man. R3H 0H3 Can. (tent peg)

Safariland Hunting Corp., P.O. Box NN, McLean, VA 22101/703-356-0622 (camouflage rain gear)

Safesport Mfg. Co., 1100 West 45th Ave., Denver, CO 80211/303-433-6506

Saf-T-Bak, see: Kap Outdoors

SanLar Co., Rte. 2, Box 123, Sullivan, WI 53178/414-593-8086 (huntg. sweatsuits)

Servus Rubber Co., 1136 2nd St., Rock Island, IL 61201 (footwear)

Spruce Creek Sportswear, see: Kap Outdoors

Stearns Mfg. Co., P.O. Box 1498, St. Cloud, MN 56301

Teledyne Co., Big Beam, 290 E. Prairie St., Crystal Lake, IL 60014

10-X Mfg. Products Group, 2828 Forest Lane, Suite 1107, Dallas, TX 75234/214-243-4016

Thermos Div., KST Co., Norwich, CT 06361 (Pop Tent)

Norm Thompson, 1805 N.W. Thurman St., Portland, OR 97209

Trim Unlimited, 2111 Glen Forest, Plano, TX 75023/214-596-5059 (electric boat)

## KNIVES AND KNIFEMAKER'S SUPPLIES—FACTORY and MAIL ORDER

A.C. Enterprises, P.O. Box 448, Edenton, NC 27932/919-482-4992

Alcas Cutlery Corp., 1116 E. State St., Olean, NY 14760/716-372-3111 (Cutco)

Atlanta Cutlery, Box 839, Conyers, GA 30207/404-922-3700 (mail order, supplies)

Bali-Song, see: Pacific Cutlery Corp.

L. L. Bean, 386 Main St., Freeport, ME 04032/207-865-3111 (mail order)

Benchmark Knives (See Gerber)

Crosman Blades™, The Coleman Co., 250 N. St. Francis, Wichita, KS 67201

Boker, The Cooper Group, 3535 Glenwood Ave., Raleigh, NC 27612/919-781-7200

Bowen Knife Co., P.O. Box 590, Blackshear, GA 31516/912-449-4794

Browning, Rt. 1, Morgan, UT 84050/801-876-2711

Buck Knives, Inc., P.O. Box 1267; 1900 Weld Blvd., El Cajon, CA 92022/619-449-1100 or 800-854-2557

Camillus Cutlery Co., 52-54 W. Genesee St., Camillus, NY 13031/315-672-8111 (Sword Brand)

W. R. Case & Sons Cutlery Co., 20 Russell Blvd., Bradford, PA 16701/814-368-4123

Cattle Baron Leather Co., P.O. Box 100724, Dept. GD, San Antonio, TX 78201/512-697-8900 (ctlg. $3)

Charlton, Ltd., P.O. Box 448, Edenton, NC 27932/919-482-4992

Charter Arms Corp., 430 Sniffens Lane, Stratford, CT 06497/203-377-8080 (Skatchet)

Chicago Cutlery Co., 5420 N. County Rd. 18, Minneapolis, MN 55428/612-533-0472

Chas. Clements, Handicraft Unltd., 1741 Dallas St., Aurora, CO 80010/303-364-0403 (exotic sheaths)

Collins Brothers Div. (belt-buckle knife), See Bowen Knife Co.

Colonial Knife Co., P.O. Box 3327, Providence, RI 02909/401-421-1600 (Master Brand)

Custom Knifemaker's Supply, P.O. Box 308, Emory, TX 75440/214-473-3330

Custom Purveyors, Maureen Devlet's, P.O. Box 886, Fort Lee, NJ 07024/201-886-0196 (mail order)

Dixie Gun Works, Inc., P.O. Box 130, Union City, TN 38261/901-885-0700 (supplies)

Eze-Lap Diamond Prods., Box 2229, 15164 Weststate St., Westminster, CA 92683/714-847-1555 (knife sharpeners)

Gerber Legendary Blades, 14200 S.W. 72nd Ave., Portland, OR 99223/503-639-6161

Golden Age Arms Co., 14 W. Winter St., Delaware, OH 43015/614-369-6513 (supplies)

Gutmann Cutlery Co., Inc., 120 S. Columbus Ave., Mt. Vernon, NY 10553/914-699-4044

H & B Forge Co., Rte. 2 Geisinger Rd., Shiloh, OH 44878/419-895-1856 (throwing knives, tomahawks)

Russell Harrington Cutlery, Inc., Subs. of Hyde Mfg. Co., 44 River St., Southbridge, MA 01550/617-764-4371 (Dexter; Green River Works)

J. A. Henckels Zwillingswerk, Inc., 9 Skyline Dr., Hawthorne, NY 10532/914-592-7370

Imperial Knife Associated Companies, 1776 Broadway, New York, NY 10019/212-757-1814

Indian Ridge Traders, 306 So. Washington, Room 415, Royal Oak, MI 48067/313-399-6034 (mostly blades)

J.A. Blades, Inc., an affiliate of E. Christoper Firearms Co., State 128 & Ferry Street, Miamitown, OH 45041/513-353-1321 (supplies)

Ken Jantz Supply, Rt. 1, Sulphur, OK 73086/405-622-3790 (supplies)

Jet-Aer Corp., 100 Sixth Ave., Paterson, NJ 07524/201-278-8300

KA-BAR Cutlery Inc., 5777 Grant Ave., Cleveland, OH 44105/216-271-4000

KA-BAR Knives, Collectors Division, 434 No. 9th St., Olean, NY 14760/716-372-5611

Keene Corp., Cutting Serv. Div., 1569 Tower Grove Ave., St. Louis, MO 63110/314-771-1550

Kershaw Knives/Kai Cutlery USA Ltd., Stafford Bus. Pk., 25300 SW Parkway, Wilsonville, OR 97070/503-636-0111

Knifeco, P.O. Box 5271, Hialeah Lakes, FL 33014/305-635-2411

Knife and Gun Finishing Supplies, P.O. Box 13522, Arlington, TX 76013/817-274-1282

Koval Knives, 822 Busch Ct. GD, Columbus, OH 43229/614-888-6486 (supplies)

Lamson & Goodnow Mfg. Co., 45 Conway St., Shelburne Falls, MA 03170/413-625-6331

Lansky Sharpeners, P.O. Box 800, Buffalo, NY 14221/716-634-6333 (sharpening devices)

Life Knife Inc., P.O. Box 771, Santa Monica, CA 90406/ 213-821-6192

Al Mar Knives, Inc., P.O. Box 1626, 5755 SW Jean Rd., Suite 101, Lake Oswego, OR 97034/503-635-9229

Matthews Cutlery, P.O. Box 33095, Decatur, GA 30033/404-636-3970 (mail order)

R. Murphy Co., Inc., 13 Groton-Harvard Rd., P.O. Box 376, Ayer, MA 01432/617-772-3481 (StaySharp)

Nordic Knives, 1643-C Copenhagen Dr., Solvang, CA 93463 (mail order)

Normark Corp., 1710 E. 78th St., Minneapolis, MN 55423/612-869-3291
Ontario Knife, Queen Cutlery Co., P.O. Box 500, Franklinville, NY 14737/716-676-5527 (Old Hickory)
Orient-Western, P.O. Box 27573, San Francisco, CA 94127
Pacific Cutlery Corp., 3039 Roswell St., Los Angeles, CA 90085/213-258-7021 (Bali-Song)
Parker Cutlery, 6928 Lee Highway, Chattanooga, TN 37415/615-894-1782
Plaza Cutlery Inc., 3333 Bristol, #161, South Coast Plaza, Costa Mesa, CA 92626/714-549-3932 (mail order)
Queen Cutlery Co., 507 Chestnut St., Titusville, PA 16354/800-222-5233
R & C Knives and Such, P.O. Box 32631, San Jose, CA 95152/408-923-5728 (mail order; ctlg. $2)
Randall-Made Knives, Box 1988, Orlando, FL 32802/305-855-8075 (ctlg. $1)
Rigid Knives, P.O. Box 816, Hwy. 290E, Lake Hamilton, AR 71951/501-525-1377
A. G. Russell Co., 1705 Hiwy. 71 No., Springdale, AR 72764/501 751 7341
Bob Sanders, 2358 Tyler Lane, Louisville, KY 40205 (Bahco steel)
San Diego Knives, P.O. Box 326, Lakeside, CA 92040/619-561-5900
Schrade Cutlery Corp., 1776 Broadway, New York, NY 10019/212-757-1814
Sheffield Knifemakers Supply, P.O. Box 141, Deland, FL 32720/904-734-7884
Smith & Wesson, 2100 Roosevelt Ave., Springfield, MA 01101/413-781-8300
Jesse W. Smith Saddlery, N. 307 Haven St., Spokane, WA 99202/509-534-3229 (sheathmakers)
Swiss Army Knives, Inc., P.O. Box 846, Shelton, CT 06484/203-929-6391
Tekna, 1075 Old County Rd., Belmont, CA 94002/415-592-4070
Thompson/Center, P.O. Box 2426, Rochester, NH 03867/603-332-2394
Tru-Balance Knife Co., 2155 Tremont Blvd., N.W., Grand Rapids, MI 49504/616-453-3679
Utica Cutlery Co., 820 Noyes St., Utica, NY 13503/315-733-4663 (Kutmaster)
Valor Corp., 5555 N.W. 36th Ave., Miami, FL 33142/305-633-0127
Washington Forge, Inc., Englishtown, NJ 07727/201-446-7777 (Carriage House)
Wenoka Cutlery, P.O. Box 8238, West Palm Beach, FL 33407/305-845-6155
Western Cutlery Co., 1800 Pike Rd., Longmont, CO 80501/303-772-5900
Walt Whinnery, Walts Cust. Leather, 1947 Meadow Creek Dr., Louisville, KY 40218/502-458-4351 (sheathmaker)
J. Wolfe's Knife Works, Box 1056, Larkspur, CA 94939 (supplies)
Wyoming Knife Co., 101 Commerce Dr., Ft. Collins, CO 80524/303-224-3454

## LABELS, BOXES, CARTRIDGE HOLDERS

Milton Brynin, 214 E. Third St., Mount Vernon, NY 10550/914-664-1311
Corbin Mfg. & Supply, Inc., P.O. Box 2659, White City, OR 97503/503-826-5211
Del Rey Products, P.O. Box 91561, Los Angeles, CA 90009/213-823-0494
E-Z Loader, Del Rey Products, P.O. Box 91561, Los Angeles, CA 90009
Hunter Co., Inc., 3300 W. 71st Ave., Westminster, Co 80030/303-472-4626
Peterson Label Co., P.O. Box 186, 23 Sullivan Dr., Redding Ridge, CT 06876/203-938-2349 (cartridge box labels; Targ-Dots)

## LOAD TESTING and PRODUCT TESTING, (CHRONOGRAPHING, BALLISTIC STUDIES)

Accuracy Systems Inc., 15203 N. Cave Creek Rd., Phoenix, AZ 85032/602-971-1991
W.W. Blackwell, 9826 Sagedale, Houston, TX 77089/ 713-484-0935 (computer program f. internal ball. f. rifle cartridges)
D&H Precision Tooling, 7522 Barnard Mill Rd., Ringwood IL 60072/815-653-9611 (Pressure testing equipment)
H-S Precision, Inc., 112 N. Summit, Prescott, AZ 86302/602-445-0607
Hutton Rifle Ranch, P.O. Box 45236, Boise, ID 83711/208-343-9841
Kent Lomont, 4236 West 700 South, Poneto, IN 45781/219-694-6792 (handguns, handgun ammunition)
Plum City Ballistics Range, Norman E. Johnson, Rte. 1, Box 29A, Plum City, WI 54761/715-647-2539
Russell's Rifle Shop, Rte. 5, Box 92, Georgetown, TX 78626/512-778-5338 (load testing and chronographing to 300 yds.)
John M. Tovey, 4710 - 104th Lane NE, Circle Pines, MN 55014/612-786-7268
H. P. White Laboratory, Inc., 3114 Scarboro Rd., Street, MD 21154/301-838-6550

## MISCELLANEOUS

Action, Mauser-style only, Crandall Tool & Machine Co., 1540 N. Mitchell St., Cadillac, MI 49601/616-775-5562
Action, Single Shot, Miller Arms, Inc., P.O. Box 260, St. Onge, SD 57779 (de-Haas-Miller)
Activator, B.M.F. Activator, Inc., P.O. Box 262364, Houston, TX 77207/713-477-8442
Adapters, Sage Industries, P.O. Box 2248, Hemet, CA 92342/714-925-1006 (12-ga. shotgun; 38 S&W blank)
Adapters for Subcalibers, Harry Owen, P.O. Box 5337, Hacienda Hts., CA 91745/818-968-5806
Airgun Accessories, Beeman Precision Arms, Inc., 47 Paul Dr., San Rafael, CA 94903/415-472-7121 (Beeman Pell seat, Pell Size, etc.)
Air Gun Combat Game Supplies, The Ultimate Game Inc., P.O. Box 1856, Ormond Beach, FL 32075/904-677-4358 (washable pellets, marking pistols/rifles)
Archery, Bear, R.R. 4, 4600 Southwest 41st Blvd., Gainesville, FL 32601/904-376-2327

Arms Restoration, J. J. Jenkins Ent. Inc., 375 Pine Ave. No. 25, Goleta, CA 93017/805-967-1366
Assault Rifle Accessories, Cherokee Gun Accessories, 4127 Bay St. Suite 226, Fremont, CA 94538/415-471-5770
Assault Rifle Accessories, Choate Machine & Tool Corp., P.O. Box 218, Bald Knob, AR 72010 (folding stocks)
Assault Rifle Accessories, Feather Enterprises, 2500 Central Ave., Boulder, CO 80301/303-442-7021
Assault Rifle Accessories, Ram-Line, Inc., 406 Violet St., Golden, CO 80401/303-279-0886 (folding stock)
Barrel Band Swivels, Phil Judd, 83 E. Park St., Butte, MT 59701
Bedding Kit, Fenwal, Inc., Resins Systems Div., 400 Main St., Ashland, MA 01721
Belt Buckles, Bergamot Brass Works, 820 Wisconsin St., Delavan, WI 53115/414-728-5572
Belt Buckles, Herrett's Stocks, Inc., Box 741, Twin Falls, ID 83303/800-635-9334 (laser engr. hardwood)
Belt Buckles, Just Brass Inc., 121 Henry St., P.O. Box 112, Freeport, NY 11520/516-079-0404 (ctlg. $2)
Belt Buckles, Pilgrim Pewter Inc., R.D. 2, Tully, NY 13159/607-842-6431
Benchrest & Accuracy Shooters Equipment, Bob Pease Accuracy, P.O. Box 787, Zipp Road, New Braunfels, TX 78130/512-625-1342
Benchrest Rifles & Accessories, Robert W. Hart & Son Inc., 401 Montgomery St., Nescopeck, PA 18635/717-752-3655
Blowgun, PAC Outfitters, P.O. Box 56, Mulvane, KS 67110/316-777-4909
Cannons, South Bend Replicas Ind., 61650 Oak Rd., S. Bend, IN 44614/219-289-4500 (ctlg. $5)
Cartridge Adapters, Sport Specialties, Harry Owen, Box 5337, Hacienda Hts., CA 91745/213-968-5806 (ctlg. $3)
Case Gauge, Plum City Ballistics Range, Rte. 1, Box 29A, Plum City, WI 54761/715-647-2539
Cased, high-grade English tools, Marvin Huey Gun Cases, P.O. Box 22456, Kansas City, MO 64113/816-444-1637 (ebony, horn, ivory handles)
Cherry Converter, Amimex Inc., 2660 John Montgomery Dr., Suite #3, San Jose, CA 95148/408-923-1720 (shotguns)
Clips, D&E Magazines Mfg., P.O. Box 4876, Sylmar, CA 91342 (handgun and rifle)
Computer & PSI Calculator, Hutton Rifle Ranch, P.O. Box 45236, Boise, ID 83711/208-343-9841
Crossbows, Barnett International, 1967 Gunn Highway, Odessa, FL 33552/813-920-2241
Deer Drag, D&H Prods. Co., Inc., 465 Denny Rd., Valencia, PA 16059/412-898-2840
Defendor, Ralide, Inc., P.O. Box 131, Athens, TN 37303/615-745-3525
Dehumidifiers, Buenger Enterprises, P.O. Box 5286, Oxnard, CA 93030/805-985-0541
Dryer, Thermo-Electric, Golden-Rod, Buenger Enterprises, Box 5286, Oxnard, CA 93030/805-985-0541
E-Z Loader, Del Rey Prod., P.O. Box 91561, Los Angeles, CA 90009/213-823-04494 (f. 22-cal. rifles)
Ear-Valve, North Consumer Prods. Div., 16624 Edwards Rd., Cerritos, CA 90701/213-926-0545 (Lee-Sonic)
Electronic Wall Thickness Tester f. Cases/Bullets/Jackets, The Accuracy Den, 25 Bitterbrush Rd., Reno, NV 89523/702-345-0225
Embossed Leather Belts, Wallets, Wildlife Leather, Inc., P.O. Box 339, Merrick, NY 11566/516-378-8588 (outdoor themes)
Farrsight, Farr Studio, 1231 Robinhood Rd., Greenville, TN 37743/615-638-8825 (clip on aperture)
Flares, Colt Industries, P.O. Box 1868, Hartford, CT 06102
Flares, Smith & Wesson Chemical Co., 2399 Forman Rd., Rock Creek, OH 44084
Frontier Outfitters, Red River Outfitters, P.O. Box 241, Tujunga, CA 91042/213-352-0177 (frontier, western, military Americana clothing)
Game Hoist, Cam Gear Ind., P.O. Box 1002, Kalispell, MT 59901 (Sportsmaster 500 pocket hoist)
Game Hoist, Precise, 3 Chestnut, Suffern, NY 10901
Game Scent, Buck Stop Lure Co., Inc., 3600 Grow Rd., Box 636, Stanton, MI 48888/517-762-5091
Game Scent, Pete Rickard, Inc., Rte. 1, Box 209B, Cobleskill, NY 12043/518-234-2731 (Indian Buck lure)
Game Scent, Safariland Hunting Corp., P.O. Box NN, McLean, VA 22101/703-356-0622 (buck lure)
Gargoyles, Pro-tec Inc., 11108 Northrup Way, Bellevue, WA 98004/306-828-6595
Gas Pistol, Penguin Ind., Inc., Airport Industrial Mall, Coatesville, PA 19320/215-384-6000
Grip Caps, Classic Arms Corp., P.O. Box 8, Palo Alto, CA 94301/415-321-7243
Gun Bedding Kit, Fenwal, Inc., Resins System Div., 400 Main St., Ashland, MA 01721/617-881-2000
Gun Jewelry, Sid Bell Originals, R.D. 2, Box 219, Tully, NY 13159/607-842-6431
Gun Jewelry, Pilgrim Pewter Inc., R.D. 2, Box 219, Tully, NY 13159/607-842-6431
Gun Jewelry, Al Popper, 614 Turnpike St., Stoughton, MA 02072/617-344-2036
Gun Jewelry, Sports Style Assoc., 148 Hendricks Ave., Lynbrook, NY 11563
Gun photographer, Mustafa Bilal, 3650 Stoneway Ave. No., Seattle, WA 98103/206-782-1456
Gun photographer, Art Carter, 818 Baffin Bay Rd., Columbia, SC 29210/803-772-2148
Gun photographer, John Hanusin, 3306 Commercial, Northbrook, IL 60062/312-564-2706
Gun photographer, Int. Photographic Assoc., Inc., 4500 E. Speedway, Suite 90, Tucson, AZ 85712/602-326-2941
Gun photographer, Charles Semmer, 7885 Cyd Dr., Denver, CO 80221/303-429-6947
Gun photographer, Weyer Photo Services, Ltd., 333-14th St., Toledo, OH 43624/419-241-5454
Gun photographer, Steve White, 1920 Raymond Dr., Northbrook, IL 60062/312-564-2720

Gun Safety, Gun Alert, Master Products, Inc., P.O. Box 8474, Van Nuys, CA 91409/818-365-0864

Gun Sling, La Paloma Marketing, 1735 E. Ft. Lowell Rd., Suite 7, Tucson, AZ 85719/602-881-4750 (Pro-sling system)

Gun Slings, Torel, Inc., 1053 N. South St., Yoakum, TX 77995

Gun Stock Kits, SDS, P.O. Box 424, Fallbrook, CA 92028/619-584-0577

Gun Vise, Gun-Mate, Inc., Box 2704, Huntington Beach, CA 92647

Hand Exerciser, Action Products, Inc., 22 No. Mulberry St., Hagerstown, MD 21740/301-797-1414

Horsepac, Yellowstone Wilderness Supply, P.O. 129, West Yellowstone, MT 59758/406-646-7613

Horsepacking Equipment/Saddle Trees, Ralide West, P.O. Box 998, 299 Firehole Ave., West Yellowstone, WY 59758/406-646-7612

Hugger Hooks, Roman Products, Inc., 4363 Loveland St., Golden, CO 80403/303-279-6959

Insect Repellent, Armor, Div. of Buck Stop, Inc., 3015 Grow Rd., Stanton, MI 48888

Insert Chambers, GTM Co., Geo. T. Mahaney, 15915B E. Main St., La Puente, CA 91744 (shotguns only)

Insert Barrels and Cartridge Adapters, Sport Specialties, Harry Owen, Box 5337, Hacienda Hts., CA 91745/213-968-5806 (ctlg. $3)

Kentucky Rifle Drawings, New England Historic Designs, P.O. Box 171, Concord, NH 03301/603-224-2096

Knife Sharpeners, Lansky Sharpeners, P.O. Box 800, Buffalo, NY 14221/716-634-6333

Light Load, Jacob & Tiffin Inc., P.O. Box 547, Clanton, AL 35045

Locks, Gun, Bor-Lok Prods., 105 5th St., Arbuckle, CA 95912

Locks, Gun, Master Lock Co., 2600 N. 32nd St., Milwaukee, WI 53245

Lugheads, Floorplate Overlays, Sid Bell Originals, Inc., RD 2, Box 219, Tully, NY 13159/607-842-6431

Lug Recess Insert, P.P.C. Corp., 625 E. 24th St. Paterson, NJ 07514

Magazines, San Diego Knives, P.O. Box 326, Lakeside, CA 92040/619-561-5900 (auto pist., rifles)

Magazines, Mitchell Arms Inc., 2101 E. 4th St. Suite 201A, Santa Ana, CA 92705/714-964-3678 (stainless steel)

Magazines, Ram-Line, Inc., 406 Violet St., Golden, CO 80401/303-279-0886

Miniature Cannons, Karl J. Furr, 76 East, 350 North, Orem, UT 84057/801-225-2603 (replicas)

Miniature Guns, Tom Konrad, P.O. Box 118, Shandon, OH 45063/513-738-1379

Miniature Guns, Charles H. Stoppler, 5 Minerva Place, New York, NY 10468

Monte Carlo Pad, Hoppe Division, Penguin Ind., Airport Industrial Mall, Coatesville, PA 19320/215-384-6000

Old Gun Industry Art, Hansen and Hansen, 244 Old Post Rd., Southport, CT 06490/203-259-7337

Pell Remover, A. Edw. Terpening, 838 E. Darlington Rd., Tarpon Springs, FL 33589

Powderhorns, Frontier, 2910 San Bernardo, Laredo, TX 78040/512-723-5409

Powderhorns, Tennessee Valley Mfg., P.O. Box 1125, Corinth, MS 38834

Powderhorns, Thomas F. White, 5801 Westchester Ct., Worthington, OH 43085/614-888-0128

Practice Ammunition, Hoffman New Ideas Inc., 821 Northmoor Rd., Lake Forest, IL 60045/312-234-4075

Pressure Testg. Machine, M. York, 5508 Griffith Rd., Gaithersburg, MD 20760/301-253-4217

Ram Line, Inc., 406 Violet St., Golden, CO 80401/303-279-0886 (accessories)

Ransom Handgun Rests, C'Arco, P.O. Box 308, Highland, CA 92346/714-862-8311

Reloader's Record Book, Reloaders Paper Supply, Don Doerkson, P.O. Box 556, Hines, OR 97738/503-573-7060

Rifle Magazines, Butler Creek Corp., 290 Arden Dr., Belgrade, MT 59714/406-388-1356 (30-rd. Mini-14)

Rifle Magazines, Condor Mfg. Inc., 415 & 418 W. Magnolia Ave., Glendale, CA 91204/818-240-1745 (25-rd. 22-cal.)

Rifle Magazines, Miller Gun Works, P.O. Box 7326, Tamuning, Guam 96911 (30-cal. M1 15&30-round)

Rifle Slings, Bianchi International, 100 Calle Cortez, Temecula, CA 92390/714-676-5621

Rifle Slings, Butler Creek Corp., 290 Arden Dr., Belgrade, MT 59714/406-388-1356

Rifle Slings, Chace Leather Prods., Longhorn Div., 507 Alden St., Fall River, MA 02722/617-678-7556

Rifle Slings, John's Cust. Leather, 525 S. Liberty St., Blairsville, PA 15717/412-459-6802

Rifle Slings, Kirkpatrick Leather Co., P.O. Box 3150, Laredo, TX 78041/512-723-6631

Rifle Slings, Schulz Industr., 16247 Minnesota Ave., Paramount, CA 90723/213-636-7718

RIG, NRA Scoring Plug, Rig Products, 87 Coney Island Dr., Sparks, NV 89431/702-331-5666

Rubber Cheekpiece, W. H. Lodewick, 2816 N.E. Halsey, Portland, OR 97232/503-284-2554

Saddle Rings, Studs, Fred Goodwin, Sherman Mills, ME 04776

Safeties, William E. Harper, The Great 870 Co., P.O. Box 6309. El Monte, CA 91734/213-579-3077 (f. Rem. 870P)

Safeties, Williams Gun Sight Co., 7389 Lapeer Rd., Davison, MI 48423

Safety Slug, Glaser Safety Slug, P.O. Box 8223, Foster City, CA 94404/415-345-7677

Sav-Bore, Saunders Sptg. Gds., 338 Somerset St., N. Plainfield, NJ 07060

Scrimshaw Engraving, C. Milton Barringer, 244 Lakeview Terr., Palm Harbor, FL 33563/813-785-0088

Scrimshaw, G. Marek, P.O. Box 213, Westfield, MA 01086/413-568-9816

Sharpening Stones, A. G. Russell Co., 1705 Hiway 71 North, Springdale, AR 72764/501-751-7341 (Arkansas Oilstones)

Shell Catcher, Condor Mfg. Inc., 415 & 418 W. Magnolia Ave., Glendale, CA 91204/818-240-1745

Shooter's Porta Bench, Centrum Products Co., 443 Century, S.W., Grand Rapids, MI 49503/616-454-9424

Shooting Coats, 10-X Products Group, 2828 Forest Lane, Suite 1107, Dallas, TX 75234/214-243-4016

Shooting Glasses, American Optical Corp., 14 Mechanic St., Southbridge, MA 01550/617-765-9711

Shooting Glasses, Bilsom Intl., Inc., 11800 Sunrise Valley Dr., Reston, VA 22091/703-620-3950

Shooting Glasses, Willson Safety Prods. Division, P.O. Box 622, Reading, PA 19603

Shooting Range Equipment, Caswell Internatl. Corp., 1221 Marshall St. N.E., Minneapolis, MN 55413/612-379-2000

Shotgun Barrel, Pennsylvania Arms Co., Box 128, Duryea, PA 18642/717-457-0845 (rifled)

Shotgun bore, Custom Shootg. Prods., 8505 K St., Omaha, NE 68127

Shotgun Case Accessories, AC Enterprises, P.O. Box 448, Edenton, NC 27932/919-482-4992 (British-made Charlton)

Shotgun Converter, Amimex Inc., 2660 John Montgomery Dr., Suite #3, San Jose, CA 95148/408-923-1720

Shotgun Ribs, Poly-Choke Div., Marble Arms Corp., 420 Industrial Park, Gladstone, MI 49837/906-428-3710

Shotgun Sight, bi-ocular, Trius Prod., Box 25, Cleves, OH 45002

Shotgun Specialist, Moneymaker Guncraft, 1420 Military Ave., Omaha, NE 68131/402-556-0226 (ventilated, free-floating ribs)

Shotshell Adapter, PC Co., 5942 Secor Rd., Toledo, OH 43623/419-472-6222 (Plummer 410 converter)

Shotshell Adapter, Jesse Ramos, P.O. Box 7105, La Puente, CA 91744/818-369-6384 (12 ga./410 converter)

Snap Caps, Edwards Recoil Reducer, 269 Herbert St., Alton, IL 62002/618-462-3257

Sportsman's Chair, Devlet's Custom Purveyors, P.O. Box 886, Fort Lee, NJ 07024/201-886-0196

Springfield Safety Pin, B-Square Co., P.O. Box 11281, Ft. Worth, TX 76110/800-433-2909

Springs, W. C. Wolff Co., Box 232, Ardmore, PA 19003/215-647-1880

Stock Duplicating Machine, Don Allen, Inc., HC55, Box 322, Sturgis, SD 47785/605-347-4686

Supersound, Edmund Scientific Co., 101 E. Gloucester Pike, Barrington, NJ 08007/609-547-3488 (safety device)

Swivels, Michaels, P.O. Box 13010, Portland, OR 97213/503-255-6890

Swivels, Sile Dist., 7 Centre Market Pl., New York, NY 10013/212-925-4111

Swivels, Williams Gun Sight Co., 7389 Lapeer Rd., Davison, MI 48423

Tomahawks, H&B Forge Co., Rt. 2, Shiloh, OH 44878/419-896-2075

Tree Stand, Portable, Advanced Hunting Equipment Inc., P.O. Box 1277, Cumming, GA 30130/404-887-1171 (tree lounge)

Tree Stand, Climbing, Amacker Prods., P.O. Box 1432; 602 Kimbrough Dr., Tallulah, LA 71282/318-574-4903

Tree Steps, Deer Me Products Co., Box 34, 1208 Park St., Anoka, MN 55303/612-421-8971

Trophies, Blackinton & Co., P.O. Box 1300, Attleboro Falls, MA 02763

Trophies, F. H. Noble & Co., 888 Tower Rd., Mundelein, IL 60060

Walking Sticks, Life Knife Inc., P.O. Box 771, Santa Monica, CA 90406/213-821-6192

Warning Signs, Delta Ltd., P.O. Box 777, Mt. Ida, AR 71957

World Hunting Info., Jack Atcheson & Sons, Inc., 3210 Ottawa St., Butte, MT 59701

World Hunting Info., J/B Adventures & Safaris, Inc., 5655 So. Yosemite St., Suite 200, Englewood CO 80111/303-771-0977

World Hunting Info., Wayne Preston, Inc., 3444 Northhaven Rd., Dallas, TX 75229/214-358-4477

## MUZZLE-LOADING GUNS, BARRELS or EQUIPMENT

Luther Adkins, Box 281, Shelbyville, IN 46176/317-392-3795 (breech plugs)

Allen Firearms Co., 2879 All Trades Rd., Santa Fe, NM 87501/505-471-6090

Anderson Mfg. Co., Union Gap Sta. P.O. Box 3120, Yakima, WA 98903/509-453-2349 (Flame-N-Go fusil; Accra-Shot)

Antique Arms Co., David F. Saunders, 1110 Cleveland, Monett, MO 65708/417-235-6501

Antique Gun Parts, Inc., 1118 S. Braddock Ave., Pittsburgh, PA 15218/412-241-1811 (parts)

Armoury, Inc., Rte. 202, New Preston, CT 06777

Armsport, Inc., 3590 N.W. 49th St., Miami, FL 33142/305-635-7850

Arm Tech, Armament Technologies Inc., 240 Sargent Dr., New Haven, CT 06511/203-562-2543 (22-cal. derringers)

Bauska Rifle Barrels, Inc., 105-9th Ave. West, Box 511, Kalispell, MT 59901/406-755-2635

Beaver Lodge, 9245 16th Ave. S.W., Seattle, WA 98106/206-763-1698

Beeman Precision Arms, Inc., 47-GDD Paul Dr., San Rafael, CA 94903/415-472-7121

Blackhawk West, Box 285, Hiawatha, KS 66434 (blck powder)

Blue and Gray Prods., Inc. RD #6, Box 362, Wellsboro, PA 16901/717-724-1383 (equipment)

Jim Brobst, 299 Poplar St., Hamburg, PA 19526/215-562-2103 (ML rifle bbls.)

Butler Creek Corp., 290 Arden Dr., Belgrade, MT 59714/406-388-1356 (poly & maxi patch)

Cache La Poudre Rifleworks, 168 N. College, Ft. Collins, CO 80521/303-482-6913 (custom muzzleloaders)

Challanger Mfg. Co., 118 Pearl St., Mt. Vernon, NY 10550

R. MacDonald Champlin, P.O. Box 693, Manchester, NH 03105/603-483-8557 (custom muzzleloaders)

Chopie Mfg. Inc., 700 Copeland Ave., LaCrosse, WI 54601/608-784-0926 (nipple wrenches)

Connecticut Valley Arms Co. (CVA), 5988 Peachtree East, Norcross, GA 30071/404-449-4687 (kits also)

Earl T. Cureton, Rte. 2, Box 388, Willoughby Rd., Bulls Gap, TN 37711/615-235-2854 (powder horns)

Homer L. Dangler, Box 254, Addison, MI 49220/517-547-6745

Leonard Day & Sons, Inc., P.O. Box 723, East Hampton, MA 01027/413-527-7990

Denver Arms, Ltd., P.O. Box 4640, Pagosa Springs, CO 81157/303-731-2295

Dixie Gun Works, Inc., P.O. Box 130, Union City, TN 38261

Dixon Muzzleloading Shop, Inc., RD #1, Box 175, Kempton, PA 19529/215-756-6271

Peter Dyson Ltd., 29-31 Church St., Honley, Huddersfield, W. Yorksh. HD7 2AH, England/0484-661062 (acc. f. ML shooter replicas)

EMF Co., Inc., 1900 E. Warner Ave. 1-D, Santa Ana, CA 92705/714-966-0202

Euroarms of America, Inc., P.O. Box 3277, 1501 Lenoir Dr., Winchester, VA 22601/703-662-1863

F.P.F. Co., P.O. Box 211, Van Wert, OH 45891 (black powder accessories)

Andy Fautheree, P.O. Box 4607, Pagosa Springs, CO 81157/303-731-2502 (cust. ML)

Ted Fellowes, Beaver Lodge, 9245 16th Ave. S.W., Seattle, WA 98106/206-763-1698

Firearms Imp. & Exp. Corp., (F.I.E.), P.O. Box 4866, Hialeah Lakes, Hialeah, FL 33014/305-685-5966

Marshall F. Fish, Rt. 22 N., RR 2 Box 2439, Westport, NY 12993/518-962-4897 (antique ML repairs)

The Flintlock Muzzle Loading Gun Shop, 1238 "G" So. Beach Blvd., Anaheim, CA 92804/714-821-6655

Forster Prods., 82 E. Lanark Ave., Lanark, IL 61046/815-493-6360

Frontier, 2910 San Bernardo, Laredo, TX 78040/512-723-5409 (powderhorns)

Getz Barrel Co., Box 88, Beavertown, PA 17813/717-658-7263 (barrels)

GOEX, Inc., Belin Plant, Moosic, PA 18507/717-457-6724 (black powder)

Golden Age Arms Co., 14 W. Winter St., Delaware, OH 43015 (ctlg. $2.50)

A. R. Goode, 4125 N.E. 28th Terr., Ocala, FL 32670/904-622-9575 (ML rifle barrels.)

Green Mountain Rifle Barrel Co., Inc., RFD 1, Box 184, Center Ossipee, NH 03814/603-539-7721

Guncraft Inc., 117 W. Pipeline, Hurst, TX 76053/817-282-6481

The Gun Works, 236 Main St., Springfield, OR 97477/503-741-4118 (supplies)

Hatfield Rifle Works, 2020 Colhoun, St. Joseph, MO 64501/816-279-8688 (squirrel rifle)

Hopkins & Allen, 3 Ethel Ave., P.O. Box 217, Hawthorne, NJ 07507/201-427-1165

The House of Muskets, Inc., P.O. Box 4640, Pagosa Springs, CO 81157/303-731-2295 (ML bbls. & supplies)

Steven Dodd Hughes, P.O. Box 11455, Eugene, OR 97440/503-485-8869 (cust. guns; ctlg. $3)

JJJJ Ranch, Rte. 1, State Route 243, Ironton, OH 45638/614-532-5298

Jennings-Hawken, 326½-4th St. N.W., Winter Haven, FL 33880

Jerry's Gun Shop, 9220 Odgen Ave., Brookfield, IL 60513/312-485-5200

LaChute Ltd., Box 48B, Masury, OH 44438/216-448-2236 (powder additive)

Morris Lawing, P.O. Box 9494., Charlotte, NC 28299/704-375-1740

Leding Loader, R.R. #1, Box 645, Ozark, AR 72949 (conical ldg. acc. f. ML)

Les' Gun Shop (Les Bauska), 105-9th West, P.O. Box 511, Kalispell, MT 59901/406-755-2635

Lever Arms Serv. Ltd., 572 Howe St., Vancouver, BC V6C 2E3, Canada

Log Cabin Sport Shop, 8010 Lafayette Rd., Lodi, OH 44254/216-948-1082 (ctlg. $3)

Loven-Pierson Inc., 4 W. Main, P.O. Box 377, Apalachin, NY 13732/607-625-2303

Lyman Products Corp., Rte. 147, Middlefield, CT 06455

McCann's Muzzle-Gun Works, 200 Federal City Rd., Pennington, NJ 08534/609-737-1707

McKeown's Sporting Arms, R.R. 4, Pekin, IL 61554/309-347-3559 (E-Z load rev. stand)

Mike Marsh, 6 Stanford Rd., Dronfield Woodhouse, Nr. Sheffield S18 SQJ, England (accessories)

Maurer Arms, 2154-16th St., Akron, OH 44314/216-745-6864 (cust. muzzleloaders)

Michigan Arms Corp., 363 Elmwood, Troy, MI 48084/313-583-1518

Mountain State Muzzleloading Supplies, Inc., Box 154-1, State Rt. 14 at Boaz, Williamstown, WV 26187/304-375-7842

Mowrey Gun Works, 1313 Lawson Rd. Saginaw, TX 76179/817-847-1644

Muzzleload Magnum Products (MMP), Rt. 6 Box 383, Harrison, AR 72601/501-741-5019 (Premium Universal Powder Solvent)

Muzzleloaders Etc., Inc., Jim Westberg, 9901 Lyndale Ave. S., Bloomington, MN 55420/612-884-1161

Numrich Corp., W. Hurley, NY 12491 (powder flasks)

Olde Pennsylvania, P.O. Box 17419, Penn Hills, PA 15235 (black powder suppl.)

Oregon Trail Riflesmiths, Inc., P.O. Box 45212, Boise, ID 83711

Ox-Yoke Originals, 130 Griffin Rd., West Suffield, CT 06093/203-668-5110 (dry lubr. patches)

Ozark Mountain Arms Inc., Rt. 1 Box 44AS/Hwy. 32, Ashdown, AR 71822/501-898-2345 (rifles)

Pecos Valley Armory, 1022 So. Canyon, Carlsbad, NM 88220/505-887-6023

A. W. Peterson Gun Shop, 1693 Old Hwy. 441 N., Mt. Dora, FL 32757

Phyl-Mac, 609 N.E. 104th Ave., Vancouver, WA 98664/206-256-0579

Provider Arms, Inc., 261 Haglund Rd., Chesterton, IN 46304/219-879-5590 (Predator rifle)

R.V.I., P.O. Box 1439 Stn. A, Vancouver, B.C. V6C 1AO, Canada/604-524-3214 (high grade BP acc.)

Richland Arms, 321 W. Adrian St., Blissfield, MI 49228

H. M. Schoeller, 569 So. Braddock Ave., Pittsburgh, PA 15221

Tyler Scott, Inc. P.O. Box 193, Milford, OH 45150/513-831-7603 (Shooter's choice black solvent; patch lube)

C. Sharps Arms Co., Inc., P.O. Box 885, Big Timber, MT 59011/406-932-4353

Shiloh Products, 181 Plauderville Ave., Garfield, NJ 07026 (4-cavity mould)

Sile Distributors, 7 Centre Market Pl., New York, NY 10013/213-925-4111

C. E. Siler Locks, 7 Acton Woods Rd., Candler, NC 28715/704-667-2376 (flint locks)

South Bend Replicas, Inc., 61650 Oak Rd., South Bend, IN 46614/219-289-4500

Southwest Muzzle Loaders Supply, 201 E. Myrtle, Suite 112, P.O. Box 921, Angleton, TX 77515/409-849-4086

Ken Steggles, see: Mike Marsh

The Swampfire Shop, 1693 Old Hwy. 441 N., Mt. Dora, FL 32757/904-383-0595

Tennessee Valley Arms, P.O. Box 2022, Union City, TN 38261/901-885-4456

Tennessee Valley Mfg., P.O. Box 1125, Corinth, MS 38834 (powderhorns)

Ten-Ring Precision, Inc., 1449 Blue Crest Lane, San Antonio, TX 78232/512-494-3063

Traditions, Inc., Saybrook Rd., Haddam, CT 06438 (guns, kits, accessories)

Upper Missouri Trading Co., Box 191, Crofton, NE 68730/402-388-4844

Warren Muzzle Loading, Hwy. 21, Ozone, AR 72854 (black powder accessories)

J. S. Weeks & Son, 4748 Bailey Rd., Dimondale, MI 48821/517-636-0591 (supplies)

Fred Wells, Wells Sport Store, 110 N. Summit St., Prescott, AZ 86301/802-445-3655

W. H. Wescomb, P.O. Box 488, Glencoe, CA 95232/209-293-7010 (parts)

Thos. F. White, 5801 Westchester Ct., Worthington OH 43085/614-888-0128 (powder horn)

Williamson-Pate Gunsmith Serv., 117 W. Pipeline, Hurst, TX 76053/817-268-2887

Winchester Sutler, Siler Route, Box 393-E, Winchester, VA 22601/703-888-3595 (haversacks)

York County Gun Works, R.R. #4, Tottenham, Ont. LOG 1WO, Canada (locks)

## PISTOLSMITHS

Accuracy Systems, Inc., 15203 N. Cave Creek Rd., Phoenix, AZ 85032/602-971-1991

Ahlman's Inc., R.R. #1 Box 20, Morristown, MN 55052/507-685-4243

Armament Gunsmithing Co., Inc., 525 Route 22, Hillside, NJ 07205/201-686-0960

Armson, Inc., P.O. Box 2130, Farmington Hills, MI 48018/313-478-2577

Baer Custom Guns, 1725 Minesite Rd., Allentown, PA 18103/215-398-2362 (accurizing 45 autos and Comp II Syst.; cust. XP100s, P.P.C. rev.)

Bain and Davis Sptg. Gds., 307 E. Valley Blvd., San Gabriel, CA 91776/213-573-4241

Lee Baker, 7252 East Ave. U-3, Littlerock, CA 93543/805-944-4487 (cust. blue)

Bar-Sto Precision Machine, 73377 Sullivan Rd., Twentynine Palms, CA 92277/619-367-2747(S.S. bbls. f. 45 ACP)

Barta's Gunsmithing, 10231 US Hwy. #10, Cato, WI 54206/414-732-4472

R. J. Beal, Jr., 170 W. Marshall Rd., Lansdowne, PA 19050/215-259-1220 (conversions, SASE f. inquiry)

Behlert Custom Guns, Inc., RD 2 Box 36C, Route 611 North, Pipersville, PA 18947/215-766-8681 (short actions)

Bell's Custom Guns, 3309 Mannheim Rd., Franklin Park, IL 60131/312-678-1900

Bob's Gun & Tackle Shop, 746 Granby St., Norfolk, VA 23510/804-627-8311

Bowen Classic Arms Corp., P.O. Box 67, Louisville, TN 37777/615-984-3583

F. Bob Chow, Gun Shop, Inc., 3185 Mission, San Francisco, CA 94110/415-282-8358

Brown Custom Guns, Inc., Steven N. Brown, 8810 Rocky Ridge Rd., Indianapolis, IN 46217/317-881-2771 aft. 5 PM

Leo Bustani, P.O. Box 8125, W. Palm Beach, FL 33407/305-622-2710

Dick Campbell, 1198 Finn Ave., Littleton, CO 80124/303-799-0145 (PPC guns; custom)

Cellini's, Francesca Inc., 3115 Old Ranch Rd., San Antonio, TX 78217/512-826-2584

D&D Gun Shop, 363 Elmwood, Troy, MI 48083/313-583-1512

Dave Chicoine, d/b/a Liberty A.S.P., 19 Key St., Eastport, ME 04631/207-853-2327 (rep. & rest. of early S&W prods.)

Davis Co., 2793 Del Monte St., West Sacramento, CA 95691/916-372-6789

Day Arms Corp., 2412 S.W. Loop 410, San Antonio, TX 78227/512-674-5220

Dominic DiStefano, 4303 Friar Lane, Colorado Springs, CO 80907/303-599-3366 (accurizing)

Duncan's Gunworks Inc., 1619 Grand Ave., San Marcos, CA 92069/619-727-0515

Dan Dwyer, 915 W. Washington, San Diego, CA 92103/619-296-1501

Englishtown Sptg. Gds. Co., Inc., David J. Maxham, 38 Main St., Englishtown, NJ 07726/201-446-7717

Jack First Distributors, Inc., 11823 Sierra Hwy., Lancaster, CA 93534/005-045-6981

Fountain Prods., 492 Prospect Ave., W. Springfield, MA 01089/413-781-4651

Frielich Police Equipment, 396 Broome St., New York, NY 10013/212-254-3045

Giles' 45 Shop, 8614 Tarpon Springs Rd., Odessa, FL 33556/813-920-5366

Gilman-Mayfield, 1552 N. 1st., Fresno, CA 93703/209-237-2500

The Gunworks Inc., John Hanus, 3434 Maple Ave., Brookfield, IL 60513/312-387-7888

Gil Hebard Guns, Box 1, Knoxville, IL 61448

Paul Jaeger, Inc., P.O. Box 449, 1 Madison Ave., Grand Junction, TN 38039/901-764-6909

J. D. Jones, Rt. 1, Della Dr., Bloomingdale, OH 43910/614-264-0176

L. E. Jurras & Assoc., P.O. Box 680, Washington, IN 47501/812-254-7698

Kart Sptg. Arms Corp., 1190 Old Country Rd., Riverhead, NY 11901/516-727-2719 (handgun conversions)

Ken's Gun Specialties, Rt. 1 Box 147, Lakeview, AR 72642/501-431-5606

Benjamin Kilham, Kilham & Co., Main St., Box 37, Lyme, NH 03768/603-795-4112

Terry K. Kopp, Highway 13, Lexington, MO 64067/816-259-2636 (rebblg., conversions)

John G. Lawson, The Sight Shop, 1802 E. Columbia Ave., Tacoma, WA 98404/206-474-5465

Kent Lomont, 4236 West South, Poneto, IN 46781/219-694-6792 (Auto Mag only)

Mag-na-port International, Inc., 41302 Executive Drive, Mt. Clemens, MI 48045/313-469-6727

Robert A. McGrew, 3315 Michigan Ave., Colorado Springs, CO 80910/303-636-1940

Rudolf Marent, 9711 Tiltree, Houston, TX 77075/713-946-7028 (Hammerli)

Elwyn H. Martin, Martin's Gun Shop, 937 So. Sheridan Blvd., Lakewood, CO 80226/303-922-2184

Conley E. Morris, 2135 Waterlevel Hwy., Cleveland, TN 37311/615-476-3984

Nu-Line Guns, 1053 Caulks Hill Rd., Harvester, MO 63303/314-441-4501

Pachmayr Gun Works, 1220 S. Grand Ave., Los Angeles, CA 90015

Paterson Gunsmithing, 438 Main St., Paterson, NJ 07502/201-345-4100

Power Custom, Inc., P.O. Box 1604, Independence, MO 64055/816-833-3102

RPS Gunshop, 11 So. Haskell St., Central Point, OR 97502/503-664-5010

Bob Rogers Gunsmithing, P.O. Box 305, Franklin Grove, IL 61031/815-456-2685 (custom)

SSK Industries (See: J. D. Jones)

L. W. Seecamp Co., Inc., Box 255, New Haven, CT 06502/203-877-3429

Hank Shows, dba The Best, 1078 Alice Ave., Ukiah, CA 95482/707-462-9060

Silver Dollar Guns, P.O. Box 475, 10 Frances St., Franklin, NH 03235/603-934-3292 (45 ACP)

Spokhandguns Inc., Vern D. Ewer, P.O. Box 370, 1206 Fig St., Benton City, WA 99320/509-588-5255

Sportsmens Equipmt. Co., 915 W. Washington, San Diego, CA 92103/619-296-1501 (specialty limiting trigger motion in autos)

Irving O. Stone, Jr., 73377 Sullivan Rd., Twentynine Palms, CA 92277/619-367-2747

Victor W. Strawbridge, 6 Pineview Dr., Dover Pt., Dover, NH 03820

A. D. Swenson's 45 Shop, P.O. Box 606, Fallbrook, CA 92028

Randall Thompson, Highline Machine Co., 654 Lela Pl., Grand Junction, CO 81504/303-434-4971

Trapper Gun, 18717 East 14 Mile Rd., Fraser, MI 48026/313-792-0134

Dennis A. "Doc" Ulrich, 2209 So. Central Ave., Cicero, IL 60650/312-652-3606

Vic's Gun Refinishing, 6 Pineview Dr., Dover, NH 03820/603-742-0013

Walters Industries, 6226 Park Lane, Dallas, TX 75225/214-691-5150

## REBORING AND RERIFLING

P.O. Ackley (See Dennis M. Bellm Gunsmithing, Inc.)

Atkinson Gun Co., P.O. Box 512, Prescott, AZ 86301

Dennis M. Bellm Gunsmithing Inc., 2376 So. Redwood Rd., Salt Lake City, UT 84119/801-974-0697 (price list $3; rifle only)

Mark Chanlynn, Rocky Mtn. Rifle Works, Ltd., 1707-14th St., Boulder CO 80302/303-443-9189

Dave Chicoine, d/b/a Liberty A.S.P., 19 Key St., Eastport, ME 04631/207-853-2327 (reline handgun bbls.)

A. R. Goode, 4125 N.E. 28th Terr., Ocala, FL 32760/904-622-9575

H-S Precision, Inc., 112 N. Summit, Prescott, AZ 86302/602-445-0607

Terry K. Kopp, Highway 13, Lexington, MO 64067/816-259-2636 (Invis-A-Line bbl.; relining)

Les' Gun Shop, (Les Bauska), 105-9th West, P.O. Box 511, Kalispell, MT 59901/406-755-2635

Matco, Inc., 126 E. Main St., No. Manchester, IN 46962/219-982-8282

Nu-Line Guns, 1053 Caulks Hill Rd., Harvester, MO 63303/314-441-4500

Redman's Reboring & Rerifling, Route 3, Box 330A, Omak, WA 98841/509-826-5512

Siegrist Gun Shop, 8752 Turtle Rd., Whittemore, MI 48770/517-873-3929

Snapp's Gunshop, 6911 E. Washington Rd., Clare, MI 48617

J. W. Van Patten, P.O. Box 145, Foster Hill, Milford, PA 18337/717-296-7069

Fred Wells, Wells Sport Store, 110 N. Summit St., Prescott, AZ 86301/602-445-3655

Robt. G. West, 27211 Huey Lane, Eugene, OR 97402/503-689-6610

## RELOADING TOOLS AND ACCESSORIES

Activ Industries, Inc., P.O. Box 238, Kearneysville, WV 25430/304-725-0451 (plastic hulls, wads)

Advance Car Mover Co., Inc., Rowell Div., P.O. Box 1181, 112 N. Outagamie St., Appleton, WI 54912/414-734-1878 (bottom pour lead casting ladles)

Advanced Precision Prods. Co., 5183 Flintrock Dr., Westerville, OH 43081/614-895-0560 (case super luber)

American Wad Prods. Co., 14729 Spring Valley Rd., Morrison, IL 61270/815-772-3336 (12-ga. shot wad)

Ammo Load Inc., 1560 E. Edinger, Suite G, Santa Ana, CA 92705/714-558-8858

Arcadia Machine & Tool (AMT), 536 No. Vincent Ave. Covina, CA 91722/818-915-7803 (Autoscale)

Benson Ballistics, Box 3796, Mission Viejo, CA 92690

C'Arco, P.O. Box 308, Highland, CA 92346/714-862-8311 (Ransom "Grand Master" progr. loader)

Colorado Sutler Arsenal, 6225 W. 46th Pl., Wheatridge, CO 80033/303-420-6383

Creighton Audette, 19 Highland Circle, Springfield, VT 05156/802-885-2331 (Universal Case Selection gauge)

B-Square Eng. Co., Box 11281, Ft. Worth, TX 76110/800-433-2909

Ballistic Prods., P.O. Box 488, 2105 Shaughnessy Circle, Long Lake, MN 55356/612-473-1550

Ballistic Research Industries (BRI), 2825 S. Rodeo Gulch Rd. #8, Soquel, CA 95073/408-476-7981 (shotgun slug)

Bear Machine Co., 2110 1st Natl. Tower, Akron, OH 44308/216-253-4039

Belding & Mull, Inc., P.O. Box 428, 100 N. 4th St., Philipsburg, PA 16866/814-342-0607

Berdon Machine Co., P.O. Box 9457, Yakima, WA 98909/509-453-0374 (metallic press)

Blackhawk West, R. L. Hough, Box 285, Hiawatha, KS 66434/303-366-3659

Bonanza (See: Forster Products)

Gene Bowlin, Rt. 1, Box 890, Snyder, TX 79549/915-573-2323 (arbor press)

Brown Precision Co., P.O. Box 270W, 7786 Molinos Ave., Los Molinos, CA 96055/916-384-2506 (Little Wiggler)

C-H Tool & Die Corp., 106 N. Harding St., Owen, WI 54460/715-229-2146

Camdex, Inc., 2330 Alger, Troy, MI 48083/313-518-2300

Carbide Die & Mfg. Co., Inc., 15615 E. Arrow Hwy., Irwindale, CA 91706/213-337-2518

Carter Gun Works, 2211 Jefferson Pk. Ave., Charlottesville, VA 22903

Cascade Cartridge, Inc., (See: Omark)

Cascade Shooters, 60916 McMullin Dr., Bend, OR 97702/503-389-5872 (bull. seating depth gauge)

Central Products f. Shooters, 435 Route 18, East Brunswick, NJ 08816 (neck turning tool)

Chevron Case Master, R.R. 1, Ottawa, IL 61350

Lester Coats, 416 Simpson Ave., No. Bend, OR 97459/503-756-6995 (core cutter)

Container Development Corp., 424 Montgomery St., Watertown, WI 53094

Continental Kite & Key Co., (CONKKO) P.O. Box 40, Broomall, PA 19008/215-356-0711 (primer pocket cleaner)

Cooper-Woodward, Box 972, Riverside, CA 92502/714-822-4176 (Perfect Lube)

Corbin Mfg. & Supply Inc., P.O. Box 2659, White City, OR 97503/503-826-5211

Custom Products, RD #1, Box 483A, Saegertown, PA 16443/814-763-2769 (decapping tool, dies, etc.)

J. Dewey Mfg. Co., 186 Skyview Dr., Southbury, CT 06488/203-264-3064

Dillon Precision Prods., Inc., 7442 E. Butherus Dr., Scottsdale, AZ 85260/602-948-8009

Division Lead Co., 7742 W. 61st Pl., Summit, IL 60502

Eagle Products Co., 1520 Adelia Ave., So. El Monte, CA 91733

Edmisten Co. Inc., P.O. Box 1293, Hwy 105, Boone, NC 28607/704-264-1490 (I-Dent-A Handloader's Log)

Efemes Enterprises, P.O. Box 122M, Bay Shore, NY 11706 (Berdan decapper)

Fitz, Box 171, Douglas City, CA 96024 (Fitz Flipper)

Flambeau Prods. Corp., 15981 Valplast Rd., Middlefield, OH 44062/216-632-1631

Forster Products Inc., 82 E. Lanark Ave., Lanark IL 61046/815-493-6360

Francis Tool Co., P.O. Box 7861, Eugene, OR 97401/503-345-7457 (powder measure)

Freechec' (See: Paco)

Geo. M. Fullmer, 2499 Mavis St., Oakland, CA 94601/415-533-4193 (seating die)

Gene's Gun Shop, Rt. 1, Box 890, Snyder, TX 79549/915-573-2323 (arbor press)

Gopher Shooter's Supply, Box 278, Faribault, MN 55021

Hart Products, Rob W. Hart & Son Inc., 401 Montgomery St., Nescopeck, PA 18635/717-752-3655

Hensley & Gibbs, P.O. Box 10, Murphy, OR 97533 (bullet moulds)

Richard Hoch, The Gun Shop, 62778 Spring Creek Rd., Montrose, CO 81401/303-249-3625 (custom Schuetzen bullet moulds)

Hoffman New Ideas Inc., 821 Northmoor Rd., Lake Forest, IL 60045/312-234-4075 (spl. gallery load press)

Hollywood Loading Tools by M&M Engineering, 10642 Arminta St., Sun Valley, CA 91352/818-842-8376

Hornady Mfg. Co., P.O. Drawer 1848, Grand Island, NE 68802/308-382-1390

Hulme see: Marshall Enterprises (Star case feeder)

Huntington, P.O. Box 991, Oroville, CA 95965/916-534-1210 (Compact Press)

Independent Mach. & Gun Shop, 1416 N. Hayes, Pocatello, ID 83201/208-232-1264

Javelina Products, Box 337, San Bernardino, CA 92402 (Alox beeswax)

Neil Jones, RD #1, Box 483A, Saegertown, PA 16433/814-763-2769 (decapping tool, dies)

Paul Jones Munitions Systems (See Fitz Co.)

King & Co., Edw. R. King, Box 1242, Bloomington, IL 61701

Lage Uniwad Co., 1814 21st St., Eldora, IA 50627/515-858-2364 (Universal Shotshell Wad)

Leding Loader, R.R. #1, Box 645, Ozark, AR 72949 (conical loadg. acc. f. ML)

Lee Custom Engineering, Inc. (See Mequon Reloading Corp.)

Lee Precision, Inc., 4275 Hwy. U, Hartford, WI 53027/414-673-3075

L. L. F. Die Shop, 1281 Highway 99 N., Eugene, OR 97402/503-688-5753

Dean Lincoln, Custom Tackle & Ammo, P.O. Box 1886, Farmington, NM 87401 (mould)

Ljutic Industries Inc., P.O. Box 2117, 732 N. 16th Ave., Yakima, WA 98907/509-248-0476 (plastic wads)

Lock's Phila. Gun Exch., 6700 Rowland, Philadelphia, PA 19149/215-332-6225

Lyman Products Corp., Rte. 147, Middlefield, CT 06455

McKillen & Heyer Inc., 37603 Arlington Dr., Box 627, Willoughby, OH 44094/216-942-2491 (case gauge)

Paul McLean, 2670 Lakeshore Blvd., W., Toronto, Ont. M8V 1G8 Canada/416-259-3060 (Universal Cartridge Holder)

M-A Systems, 42417 Third St. East, Lancaster, CA 93535/805-942-6706

MEC, Inc. (See Mayville Eng. Co.)

MTM Molded Products Co., 3370 Obco Ct., P.O. Box 14117, Dayton, OH 45414/513-890-7461

Magma Eng. Co., P.O. Box 161, Queen Creek, AZ 85242

Marmel Prods., P.O. Box 97, Utica, MI 48087/313-731-8029 (Marvelube, Marvelux)

Marquart Precision Co., P.O. Box 1740, Prescott, AZ 86302/602-445-5646 (precision case-neck turning tool)

Marshall Enterprises, 792 Canyon Rd., Redwood City, CA 94062/415-365-1230 (Hulme autom. case feeder f. Star rel.)

Mayville Eng. Co., 715 South St., Mayville, WI 53050/414-387-4500 (shotshell loader)

Mequon Reloading Corp., P.O. Box 253, Mequon, WI 53092/414-673-3060

Merit Gun Slight Co., P.O. Box 995, Sequim, WA 98382/206-683-6127

## RELOADING TOOLS AND ACCESSORIES—cont'd.

Multi-Scale Charge Ltd., 55 Maitland St. Suite 310, Toronto, Ont. M4Y 1C9, Canada/416-276-6292

Muzzleload Magnum Products (MMP), Rte. 6 Box 383, Harrison, AR 72601/501-741-5019 (Tri-Cut Trimmer; Power Powder Trickler)

Normington Co., Box 6, Rathdrum, ID 83858 (powder baffles)

Northeast Industrial Inc., N.E.I., P.O. Box 249, 405 N. Canyon Blvd., Canyon City, OR 97820/503-575-2513 (bullet mould)

Ohaus Scale, (See RCBS)

Old Western Scrounger, 12924 Hwy. A-12, Montague, CA 96064/916-459-5445 (Press f. 50-cal. B.M.G round)

Omark Industries, Box 856, Lewiston, ID 83501/208-746-2351

P&P Tool Co., 125 W. Market St., Morrison, IL 61270/815-772-7618 (12-ga. shot wad)

Pacific Tool Co., P.O. Box 2048, Ordnance Plant Rd., Grand Island, NE 68801/308-384-2308

Paco, Box 17211, Tucson, AZ 85731 ('Freechec' tool for gas checks)

PBK-TOOL, Roberts Products, 25238 S. E. 32nd, Issaquah, WA 90027/206-392-8172

Pitzer Tool Mfg. Co., RR #3, Box 50, Winterset, IA 50273/515-462-4268 (bullet lubricator & sizer)

Plum City Ballistics Range, Norman E. Johnson, Rte. 1, Box 29A, Plum City, WI 54761/715-647-2539

Ponsness-Warren, P.O. Box 8, Rathdrum, ID 83858/208-687-2231

Marian Powley, Petra Lane, R.R.1, Eldridge, IA 52748/319-285-9214

Quinetics Corp., P.O. Box 29007, San Antonio, TX 78229/516-684-8561 (kinetic bullet puller)

RCBS, Inc., Box 1919, Oroville, CA 95965/916-533-5191

Ransom (See C'Arco)

Redding Inc., 1089 Starr Rd., Cortland, NY 13045/607-753-3331

Reloaders Paper Supply, Don Doerksen, P.O. Box 556, Hines, OR 97738/503-573-7060 (reloader's record book)

Rifle Ranch, Rte. 10, 3301 Willow Creek Rd., Prescott, AZ 86301/602-778-7501

Rochester Lead Works, 76 Anderson Ave., Rochester, NY 14607/716-442-8500 (leadwire)

Rorschach Precision Prods., P.O. Box 151613, Irving, TX 75015/214-790-3487 (carboloy bull. dies)

Rotex Mfg. Co. (See Texan)

SAECO Rel. 2207 Border Ave., Torrance, CA 90501/213-320-6973

SSK Industries, Rt. 1, Della Drive, Bloomingdale, OH 43910/614-264-0176 (primer tool)

Sandia Die & Cartridge Co., Rte. 5, Box 5400, Albuquerque, NM 87123/505-298-5729

Shannon Associates, P.O. Box 32737, Oklahoma City, OK 73123

Shooters Accessory Supply, (See Corbin Mfg. & Supply)

Jerry Simmons, 715 Middlebury St., Goshen, IN 46526/219-533-8546 (Pope de- & recapper)

J. A. Somers Co., P.O. Box 49751, Los Angeles, CA 90049 (Jasco)

Sport Flite Mfg., Inc., 2520 Industrial How, Troy, MI 48084/313-280-0648 (swaging dies)

Star Machine Works, 418 10th Ave., San Diego, CA 92101/619-232-3216

Texan Reloaders, Inc., 444 So. Cips St., Watseka, IL 60970/815-432-5065

Trico Plastics, 590 S. Vincent Ave., Azusa, CA 91702

Tru Square Metal Products, P.O. Box 585, Auburn, WA 98002/206-833-2310 (Thumler's tumbler case polishers; Ultra Vibe 18)

WAMADET, Silver Springs, Goodleigh, Barnstaple, Devon, England

Weatherby, Inc., 2781 Firestone Blvd., South Gate, CA 90280/213-569-7186

Weaver Arms Ltd., P.O. Box 3316, Escondido, CA 92025/619-746-2440 (progr. loader)

Webster Scale Mfg. Co., P.O. Box 188, Sebring, FL 33870/813-385-6362

Whits Shooting Stuff, P.O. Box 1340, Cody, WY 82414

L. E. Wilson, Inc. P.O. Box 324, 404 Pioneer Ave., Cashmere, WA 98815/509-782-1328

Zenith Enterprises, 5781 Flagler Rd., Nordland, WA 98358/206-385-2142

## RESTS—BENCH, PORTABLE, ETC.

Amacker Products, Inc., 602 Kimbrough, Tallulah, LA 71282/318-574-4903

B-Square Co., P.O. Box 11281, Ft. Worth, TX 76109/800-433-2909 (handgun)

Jim Brobst, 299 Poplar St., Hamburg, PA 19526/215-562-2103 (bench rest pedestal)

Bullseye Shooting Bench, 6100 - 40th St. Vancouver, WA 98661/206-694-6141 (portable)

C'Arco, P.O. Box 308, Highland, CA 92346/714-862-8311 (handgun rest)

Centrum Products Co., 443 Century S.W., Grand Rapids, MI 49503/616-454-9424 (Porta Bench)

Philip Cooley, 34 Bay Ridge Ave., Brooklyn, NY 11220/212-745-9311

Cravener's Gun Shop, 1627 - 5th Ave., Ford City, PA 16226/412-763-8312

Decker Shooting Products, 1729 Laguna Ave., Schofield, WI 54476/715-359-5873 (rifle rests)

Garbini Loga Systems, St. Galler Str. 72, CH-9325 Roggwill TG, Switzerland

The Gun Case, 11035 Maplefield, El Monte, CA 91733

Joe Hall's Shooting Products, Inc., 443 Wells Rd., Doylestown, PA 18901/215-345-6354 (adj. portable)

Harris Engineering, Inc., Barlow, KY 42024/502-334-3633 (bipods)

Rob. W. Hart & Son, 401 Montgomery St., Nescopeck, PA 18635

Tony Hidalgo, 12701 S.W. 9th Pl., Davie, FL 33325/305-476-7645 (adj. shooting seat)

J. B. Holden Co., 295 W. Pearl, P.O. Box 320, Plymouth, MI 48170/313-455-4850

Hoppe's Div., Penguin Industries, Inc., Airport Industrial Mall, Coatesville, PA 19320/251-384-6000 (bench rests and bags)

North Star Devices, Inc., P.O. Box 2095, North St. Paul, MN 55109

Progressive Prods., Inc., P.O. Box 67, Holmen, WI 54636/608-526-3345 (Sandbagger rifle rest)

Protektor Model Co., Galeton,, PA 16922/814-435-2442 (sandbags)

Ransom (See Arco)

San Angelo Mfg. Co., 1841 Industrial Ave., San Angelo, TX 76904/915-655-7126

Suter's, Inc., House of Guns, 332 N. Tejon, Colorado Springs, CO 80902/303-635-1475

Turkey Creek Enterprises, Rt. 1, Box 65, Red Oak, OK 74563/918-754-2884 (portable shooting rest)

Wichita Arms, 444 Ellis, Wichita, KS 67211/316-265-06612

## RIFLE BARREL MAKERS

P.O. Ackley Rifle Barrels (See Dennis M. Bellm Gunsmithing Inc.)

Atkinson Gun Co., P.O. Box 512, Prescott, AZ 86301

Jim Baiar, 480 Halfmoon Rd., Columbia Falls, MT 59912/406-892-1190

Bauska Rifle Barrels, Inc., 105-9th Ave. West, Kalispell, MT 59901/406-755-2635

Dennis M. Bellm Gunsmithing Inc., 2376 So. Redwood Rd., Salt Lake City, UT 84119/801-974-0697; price list $3 (new rifle bbls., incl. special & obsolete)

Leo Bustani, P.O. Box 8125, West Palm Beach, FL 33407/305-622-2710 (Win.92 take-down; Trapper 357-44 mag. bbls.)

Ralph L. Carter, Carter's Gun Shop, 225 G St., Penrose, CO 81240/303-372-6240

Mark Chanlynn, Rocky Mtn. Rifle Works, Ltd., 1707-14th St., Boulder, CO 80302/303-443-9189

Charles P. Donnelly & Son, Siskiyou Gun Works, 405 Kubli Rd., Grants Pass, OR 97527/503-846-6604

Douglas Barrels, Inc., 5504 Big Tyler Rd., Charleston, WV 25313/304-776-1341

Douglas Jackalope Gun & Sport Shop, Inc., 1048 S. 5th St., Douglas, WY 82633/307-358-3854

Federal Firearms Co., Inc., P.O. Box 145, Thoms Run Rd., Oakdale, PA 15071/412-221-0300

Getz Barrel Co., Box 88, Beavertown, PA 17813/717-658-7263

A. R. Goode, 4125 N.E. 28th Terr., Ocala, FL 32670/904-622-9575

Green Mountain Rifle Barrel Co., Inc., RFD 1 Box 184, Center Ossipee, NH 03814/603-539-7721

H-S Precision, Inc., 112 N. Summit, Prescott, AZ 86302/602-445-0607

Half Moon Rifle Shop, 490 Halfmoon Rd., Columbia Falls, MT 59912/406-892-4409

Hart Rifle Barrels, Inc., RD 2, Lafayette, NY 13084/315-677-9841

Hastings, Box 224, 822-6th St., Clay Center, KS 67432/913-632-3169 (shotguns ONLY)

Wm. H. Hobaugh, The Rifle Shop, Box M, Philipsburg, MT 59858/406-859-3515

Terry K. Kopp, Highway 13, Lexington, MO 64067/816-259-2636 (22-cal. blanks)

Les' Gun Shop, (Les Bauska), 105-9th West, P.O. Box 511, Kalispell, MT 59901/406-755-2635

Lilja Precision Rifle Barrels, Inc., 245 Compass Creek Rd., P.O. Box 372, Plains, MT 59859/406-826-3084

Marquart Precision Co., P.O. Box 1740, Prescott, AZ 86302/602-445-5646

Matco, Inc., Box 349, 126 E. Main St., No. Manchester, IN 46962/219-982-8282

McMillan Rifle Barrels U.S. International, P.O. Box 0427, Bryan, TX 77805/409-846-3990

Nu-Line Guns, 1053 Caulks Hill Rd., Harvester, MO 63303/314-441-4500

Numrich Arms, W. Hurley, NY 12491

Olympic Arms Inc. dba SGW, 624 Old Pacific Hwy. S.E., Olympia, WA 98503/206-456-3471

John T. Pell Octagon Barrels, (KOGOT), 410 College Ave., Trinidad, CO 81082/303-846-9406

Pennsylvania Arms Co., Box 128, Duryea, PA 18642/717-457-0845 (rifled shotgun bbl. only)

Redman's Rifling & Reboring, Rt. 3, Box 330A, Omak, WA 98841/509-826-5512

Sanders Cust. Gun Serv., 2358 Tyler Lane, Louisville, KY 40205

Gary Schneider, 12202 N. 62d Pl., Scottsdale, AZ 85254/602-948-2525

SGW, Inc., D. A. Schuetz, 624 Old Pacific Hwy. S.E., Olympia, WA 98503/206-456-3471

E. R. Shaw, Inc., Prestley & Thoms Run Rd., Bridgeville, PA 15017/412-221-3636

Shilen Rifles, Inc., 205 Metro Park Blvd., Ennis, TX 75119/214-875-5318

W. C. Strutz, Rifle Barrels, Inc., P.O. Box 611, Eagle River, WI 54521/715-479-4766

Fred Wells, Wells Sport Store, 110 N. Summit St., Prescott, AZ 86301/602-445-3655

Bob Williams, P.O. Box 143, Boonsboro, MD 21713

Wilson Arms, 63 Leetes Island Rd., Branford, CT 06405/203-488-7297

## SCOPES, MOUNTS, ACCESSORIES, OPTICAL EQUIPMENT

A.R.M.S., Inc. (Atlantic Research Marketing Systems), 230 W. Center St., West Bridgewater, MA 02379/617-584-7816

Action Arms Ltd., P.O. Box 9573, Philadelphia, PA 19124/215-744-0100

Aimpoint U.S.A., 201 Elden St., Suite 302, Herndon, VA 22070/703-471-6828 (electronic sight)

Alley Suppl. Co., P.O. Box 848, Gardnerville, NV 89410/702-782-3800

American Arms, Inc., P.O. Box 27163, Salt Lake City, UT 84127/801-972-5006

The American Import Co., 1453 Mission, San Francisco, CA 94103/415-863-1506

Anderson Mfg. Co., Union Gap Sta. P.O. Box 3120, Yakima, WA 98903/509-453-2349 (lens cap)

Apollo Optics (See Senno Corp.)

Armsport, Inc., 3590 N.W. 49th St., Miami, FL 33122/305-635-7850
Armson, Inc., P.O. Box 2130, Farmington Hills, MI 48018/313-478-2577 (O.E.G.)
B-Square Co., Box 11281, Ft. Worth, TX 76109/800-433-2909 (Mini-14 mount)
Bausch & Lomb Inc., 1400 Goodman St., Rochester, NY 14602/716-338-6000
Beeman Inc., 47-GDD Paul Dr., San Rafael, CA 94903/415-472-7121
Bennett, 561 Delaware, Delmar, NY 12054/518-439-1862 (mounting wrench)
Billingsley & Brownell,Box 25, Dayton, WY 82836/307-655-9344 (mounts, accessories)
Browning Arms, Rt. 4, Box 624-B, Arnold, MO 63010
Buehler Scope Mounts, 17 Orinda Highway, Orinda, CA 94563/415-254-3201
Burris Co. Inc., 331 E. 8th St., Box 1747, Greeley, CO 80631/303-356-1670
Bushnell Optical Co., 2828 E. Foothill Blvd., Pasadena, CA 91107
Butler Creek Corp., 290 Arden Dr., Belgrade, MT 59714/406-388-1356 (lens caps)
Kenneth Clark, 18738 Highway 99, Madera, CA 93637/209-674-6016
Clear View Mfg. Co., Inc. 20821 Grand River Ave., Detroit, MI 48219/313-535-0033 (mounts)
Colt Firearms, P.O. Box 1868, Hartford CT 06102/203-236-6311
Compass Instr. & Optical Co., Inc., 104 E. 25th St., New York, NY 10010
Conetrol Scope Mounts, Hwy 123 South, Seguin, TX 78155
Cougar Optics, P.O. Box 115, Groton, NY 13071/607-898-5754
D&H Prods. Co., Inc., 465 Denny Rd., Valencia, PA 16059/412-898-2840 (lens covers)
Davis Optical Co., 528 Richmond St., P.O. Box 6, Winchester, IN 47394/317-584-5311
Del-Sports Inc., Main St., Margaretville, NY 12455/914-586-4103 (Kahles scopes; EAW mts.)
Dickson (See American Import Co.)
Flaig's, Babcock Blvd., Millvale, PA 15209
Fontaine Ind., Inc., 11552 Knott St., Suite 1, Garden Grove, CA 92641/714-898-9163
Freeland's Scope Stands, Inc., 3737 14th, Rock Island, IL 61201/309-788-7449
Griffin & Howe, Inc., 589 Broadway, New York, NY 10012/212-966-5323
Heckler & Koch, Inc., 14601 Lee Rd., Chantilly, VA 22021/703-631-2800
H.J. Hermann Leather Co., Rt. 1, P.O. Box 525, Skiatook, OK 74070/918-396-1226 (lens caps)
J.B. Holden Co., 295 W. Pearl, P.O. Box 320, Plymouth, MI 48170/313-455-4850
The Hutson Corp., 105 Century Dr., No., Mansfield, TX 76063/817-477-3421
Import Scope Repair Co., P.O. Box 2633, Durango, CO 81301/303-247-1422
Interarms, 10 Prince St., Alexandria, VA 22313
Paul Jaeger, Inc., P.O. Box 449, 1 Madison Ave., Grand Junction, TN 38039/901-764-6909 (Schmidt & Bender; EAW mts., Noble)
Jason Empire Inc., 9200 Cody, P.O. Box 14930, Overland Park, KS 66214/913-888-0220
Jennison TCS (See Fontaine Ind., Inc.)
Kahles of America, Div. of Del-Sports, Inc., Main St., Margaretville, NY 12455/914-586-4103
Kenko Intl. Inc., 8141 West I-70 Frontage Rd. No., Arvada, CO 80002/303-425-1200
KenPatable Ent. Inc., P.O. Box 19422, Louisville, KY 40219/502-239-5447 (Kwik-Mount)
Kilham & Co., Main St., Box 37, Lyme, NY 03768/603-795-4112 (Hutson handgun scopes)
Kowa Optimed, Inc., 20001 S. Vermont Ave., Torrance, CA 90502/213-327-1913
Kris Mounts, 108 Lehigh St., Johnstown, PA 15905
Kwik-Site, 5555 Treadwell, Wayne, MI 48184/313-326-1500
T.K. Lee, 2830 S. 19th St., Off. #4, Birmingham, AL 35209/205-871-6065
E. Leitz, Inc., 24 Link Dr., Rockleigh, NJ 07647/201-767-1100
Leupold & Stevens Inc., P.O. Box 688, Beaverton, OR 97075/503-646-9171
Jake Levin and Son, Inc., 9200 Cody, Overland Park, KS 66214
W.H. Lodewick, 2816 N.E. Halsey, Portland, OR 97232/503-284-2554 (scope safeties)
Lyman Products Corp., Route 147, Middlefield, CT. 06455
Mandall Shooting Supplies, 7150 E. 4th St., Scottsdale, AZ 85252
Marble Arms Co., 420 Industrial Park, Gladstone, MI 49837/906-428-3710
Marlin Firearms Co., 100 Kenna Dr., New Haven, CO 06473
Millett Industries, 16131 Gothard St., Huntington Beach, CA 92647/714-842-5575 (mounts)
Nikon Inc., 623 Stewart Ave., Garden City, NY 11530/516-222-0200
Numrich Arms, West Hurley, NY 12491
Nydar, (See Swain Nelson Co.)
Optex (See Southern Precision Instrument Co.)
Orchard Park Enterprise, P.O. Box 563, Orchard Park, NY 14127/716-662-2255 (Saddleproof mount)
Oriental Optical Co., 605 E. Walnut St., Pasadena, CA 91101/213-792-1252 (scope & binocular repairs)
Pachmayr Gun Works, 1220 S. Grand Ave., Los Angeles, CA 90015/213-748-7271
Pentax Corp., 35 Inverness Dr. E., Englewood CO 80112/303-799-8000 (riflescopes)
Pilkington Gun Co., P.O. Box 1296, Muskogee, OK 74402/918-693-9418 (Q. D. mt.)
Pioneer Marketing & Research Inc., 216 Haddon Ave. Suite 522, Westmont, NJ 08108/609-854-2424 (German Steiner binoculars; scopes)
Precise, 3 Chestnut, Suffern, NY 10901
Ram Line, Inc., 406 Violet St., Golden, CO 80401/303-279-0886 (see-thru mt. f. Mini-14)
Ranging, Inc., Routes 5 & 20, East Bloomfield, NY 14443/716-657-6161
Ray-O-Vac, Willson Prod. Div., P.O. Box 622, Reading, PA 19603 (shooting glasses)
Redfield Gun Sight Co., 5800 E. Jewell Ave., Denver, CO 80222/303-757-6411
S & K Mfg. Co., Box 247, Pittsfield, PA 16340/814-563-7808 (Insta-Mount)

SSK Industries, Rt. 1, Della Dr., Bloomingdale, OH 43910/614-264-0176 (bases)
Sanders Cust. Gun Serv., 2358 Tyler Lane, Louisville, KY 40205 (MSW)
Schmidt & Bender, see: Paul Jaeger, Inc.
Seattle Binocular & Scope Repair Co., P.O. Box 46094, Seattle, WA 98146
Senno Corp., S. 323 Grant, P.O. Box 3506, Spokane, WA 99220/800-541-5689
Shepherd Scope Ltd., Box 189, Waterloo, NE 69069/402-779-2386
Sherwood Intl. Export Corp., 18714 Parthenia St., Northridge, CA 91324/818-349-7600 (mounts)
Shooters Supply, 1120 Tieton Dr., Yakima, WA 98902/509-452-1181 (mount f. M14/M1A rifles)
W.H. Siebert, 22720 S.E. 56th St., Issaquah, WA 98027
Simmons Outdoor Corp., 14205 S.W. 119 Ave., Miami, FL 33186/305-252-0477
Southern Precision Inst. Co., 3419 E. Commerce St., San Antonio, TX 78219
Spacetron Inc., Box 84, Broadview, IL 60155(bore lamp)
Steiner (See Pioneer Marketing & Research)
Stoeger Industries, 55 Ruta Ct., S. Hackensack, NJ 07606/201-440-2700
Supreme Lens Covers, (See Butler Creek) (lens caps)
Swain Nelson Co., Box 45, 92 Park Dr., Glenview, IL 60025 (shotgun sight)
Swarovski Optik,Div. of Swarovski America Ltd., One Kenny Dr., Cranston, RI 02920/401-463-6400
Swift Instruments, Inc., 952 Dorchester Ave., Boston, MA 02125
Tasco, 7600 N.W. 26th St., Miami, FL 33122/305-591-3670
Tele-Optics, 5514 W. Lawrence Ave., Chicago, IL 60630/312-283-7757 (optical equipment repair services only)
Thompson-Center Arms, P.O. Box 2426, Rochester, NH 03867/603-332-2394 (handgun scope)
Tradewinds, Inc., Box 1191, Tacoma, WA 98401
Trijicon rifle scopes (See Armson, Inc.)
John Unertl Optical Co., 3551-5 East St., Pittsburgh, PA 15214
United Binocular Co., 9043 S. Western Ave., Chicago, IL 60620
Vissing (See Supreme Lens Covers)
Wasp Shooting Systems, Box 241, Lakeview, AR 72642/501-431-5606 (mtg. system f. Ruger Mini-14 only)
Weatherby's, 2781 Firestone, South Gate, CA 90280/213-569-7186
W.R. Weaver, Omark Industries, Box 856, Lewiston, ID 83501 (mounts & bases only)
Weaver Scope Repair Service, 1121 Larry Mahan Dr., Suite B, El Paso, TX 79925/915-593-1005
Wide View Scope Mount Corp., 26110 Michigan Ave., Inkster, MI 48141/313-274-1238
Williams Gun Sight Co., 7389 Lapeer Rd., Davison, MI 48423
Boyd Williams Inc., 8701-14 Mile Rd. (M-57),Cedar Springs, MI 49319 (BR)
Willrich Precision Instrument Co., 95 Cenar Lane, Englewood, NJ 07631/201-567-1411 (borescope)
Carl Zeiss Inc.,Consumer Prods. Div., Box 2010, 1015 Commerce St., Petersburg, VA 23803/804-861-0033

## SIGHTS, METALLIC

Accura-Sites, The Jim J. Tembelis Co., Inc., P.O. Box 114, 216 Loper Ct.,Neenah, WI 54956/414-722-0039
Alley Supply Co., P.O. Box 848, Gardnerville, NV 89410/702-782-3800
Armson, Inc., P.O. Box 2130, Farmington Hills, MI 48018/313-478-2577
B-Square Eng. Co., Box 11281, Ft. Worth, TX 76110/800-433-2909
Beeman Inc., 47 Paul Dr., San Rafael, CA 94903/415-472-7121 (airguns only)
Behlert Custom Sights, Inc., RD 2 Box 36C, Route 611 North, Pipersviflle, PA 18947/215-766-8681
Bingham Ltd., 1775-C Wilwat Dr., Norcross, GA 30093/404-448-1440
Bo-Mar Tool & Mfg. Co., Rt. 12, Box 405, Longview, TX 75605/214-759-4784
Buehler Scope Mounts, 17 Orinda Highway, Orinda, CA 94563/415-254-3201
Burris Co., Inc., 331-8th St., P.O. Box 1747, Greeley, CO 80632/303-356-1670
Farr Studio, 1231 Robinhood Rd., Greeneville, TN 37743/615-638-8825 (sighting aids—clip-on aperture)
Andy Fautheree, P.O. Box 4607, Pagosa Springs, CO 81157/303-731-2502 ("Calif. Sight" f. ML)
Freeland's Scope Stands, Inc., 3734-14th Ave., Rock Island, IL 61201/309-788-7449
Paul Jaeger, Inc., P.O. Box 449, 1 Madison Ave., Grand Junction, TN 38039/901-764-6909
Lee's Red Ramps, 7252 E. Ave. U-3, Littlerock, CA 93543/805-944-4487 (white outline rear sight)
James W. Lofland, 2275 Larkin Rd., Boothwyn, PA 19061/215-485-0391 (single shot replica)
Lyman Products Corp., Rte. 147, Middlefield, CT 06455
Mag-na-port International, Inc., 41302 Executive Drive, Mt. Clemens, MI 48045/313-469-6727
Marble Arms Corp., 420 Industrial Park, Gladstone, MI 49837/906-428-3710
Merit Gunsight Co., P.O. Box 995, Sequim, WA 98382/206-683-6127
Millett Industries, 16131 Gothard St., Huntington Beach, CA 92647/714-842-5575
Miniature Machine Co., 210 E. Poplar, Deming, NM 88030/505-546-2151 (MMC)
Omega Sales, Inc., P.O. Box 1066, Mt. Clemens, MI 48043/313-469-6727
Poly Choke Div., Marble Arms Corp., 420 Industrial Park, Gladstone, MI 49837/906-428-3710
Redfield Gun Sight Co., 5800 E. Jewell St., Denver, CO 80222
S&M Tang Sights, P.O. Box 1338, West Babylon, NY 11704/516-226-4057
Schwarz's Gun Shop, 41-15th St., Wellsburg, WV 26070
Simmons Gun Specialties, Inc., 700 S. Rodgers Rd., Olathe, KS 66062/913-782-3131
Slug Site Co., Ozark Wilds, Versailles, MO 65084/314-378-6430
Tradewinds, Inc., Box 1191, Tacoma, WA 98401
Wichita Arms, 444 Ellis, Wichita, KS 67211/316-265-0661
Williams Gun Sight Co., 7389 Lapeer Rd., Davison, MI 48423

## STOCKS (Commercial and Custom)

Accuracy Products, 9004 Oriole Trail, Wonder Lake, IL 60097

Advanced Stocking Systems, see: Answer Stocking Systems

Ahlman's Inc., R.R. 1, Box 20, Morristown, MN 55052

Don Allen Inc., HC55, Box 322, Sturgis, SD 57785/605-347-4686

Angelo & Little Custom Gun Stock Wood, N 4026 Sargent St. Spokane, WA 99212/509-926-0794 (blanks only)

Answer Stocking Systems, 113 N. 2nd St., Whitewater, WI 53190/414-473-4848 (synthetic f. shotguns)

Anton Custom Gunstocks, Paul D. Hillmer, 7251 Hudson Heights, Hudson, IA/ 319-988-3941

Creighton Audette, 19 Highland Circle, Springfield, VT 05156/802-885-2331

Jim Baiar, 490 Halfmoon Rd., Columbia Falls, MT 599123

Bain & Davis Sporting Goods, Walter H. Little, 307 E. Valley Blvd., San Gabriel, CA 91776/818-573-4241 (cust.)

Joe J. Balickie, Custom Stocks, Rte. 2, Box 56-G, Apex, NC 27502/919-362-5185

Bartas Gunsmithing, 10231 U.S.H.#10, Cato, WI 54206/414-732-4472

Donald Bartlett, 1805 S. 281st. Pl., #115, Federal Way, WA 98003/206-946-4311 (cust.)

Beeman Inc., 47 Paul Dr., San Rafael, CA 94903/415-472-7121 (airguns only)

Dennis M. Bellm Gunsmithing, Inc., 2376 So. Redwood Rd., Salt Lake City, UT 84119/801-974-0697

Al Biesen, West 2039 Sinto Ave., Spokane, WA 99201

Roger Biesen, 5021 W. Rosewood, Spokane, WA 99208/509-328-9340

Stephen L. Billeb, Box 1176, Big Piney, WY 83113/307-276-5627

E.C. Bishop & Son Inc., 119 Main St., Box 7, Warsaw MO 65355/816-438-5121

Gregg Boeke, Rte. 2, Box 149, Cresco, IA 52136/319-547-3746 (cust.)

John M. Boltin, 2008 Havens Dr., North Myrtle Beach, SC 29582/803-272-6581

Kent Bowerly, H.C.R. Box 1903, Camp Sherman, OR 97730/503-595-6028 (custom)

Larry D. Brace, 771 Blackfoot Ave., Eugene, OR 97404/503-688-1278 (custom)

Garnet D. Brawley, P.O. Box 668, Prescott, AZ 86301/602-445-4768 (cust.)

Frank Brgoch, #1580 South 1500 East, Bountiful, UT 84010/801-295-1885 (cust.)

A. Briganti, 475 Rt. 32, Highland Mills, NY 10930/914-928-9816

Brown Precision Co., P.O. Box 270W; 7786 Molinos Ave., Los Molinos, CA 96055/916-384-2506

W. E. Brownell, 3356 Moraga Pl., San Diego, CA 92117/619-276-6146

Jack Burres, 10333 San Fernando Road, Pacoima, CA 91331/818-899-8000 (English, Claro, Bastogne Paradox walnut blanks only)

Calico Hardwoods, Inc., 1648 Airport Blvd., Windsor, CA 95492/707-546-4045 (blanks)

Dick Campbell, 1198 Finn Ave., Littleton, CO 80124/303-799-0145 (custom)

Kevin Campbell, 10152 Trinidad, El Paso, TX 79925/915-592-5496 (cust.)

Shane Caywood, 321 Hwy. 51 So., Minocqua, WI 54548/715-356-9631 (cust.)

Claude Christopher, 1606 Berkley Rd., Greenville, NC 27834/919-756-0872 (rifles)

Winston Churchill, Twenty Mile Stream Rd., RFD, Box 29B, Proctorsville, VT 05153

Clinton River Gun Serv., Inc., 30016 S. River Rd., Mt. Clemens, MI 48045/313-468-1090

Charles H. Coffin, 3719 Scarlet Ave., Odessa, TX 79762/915-366-4729

Jim Coffin, 250 Country Club Lane, Albany, OR 97321/503-928-4391

Reggie Cubriel, 15610 Purple Sage, San Antonio, TX 78255 (cust. stockm.)

The Custom Gun Guild, 5091-F Buford Highway, Doraville, GA 30340/404-455-0346

D&D Gun Shop, 363 Elmwood, Troy, MI 48083/313-583-1512 (cust.)

Dahl's Custom Stocks, Rt. 4, Box 558, Lake Geneva, WI 53147/414-248-2464 (Martin Dahl)

Dahl Gun Shop, 6947 King Ave. West, Billings, MT 59106/406-652-3909

Homer L. Dangler, Box 254, Addison, MI 49220/517-547-6745

Sterling Davenport, 9611 E. Walnut Tree Dr., Tucson, AZ 85715/602-749-5590 (custom)

Jack Dever, 8520 N.W. 90, Oklahoma City, OK 73132/405-721-6393

Charles De Veto, 1087 Irene Rd., Lyndhurst, OH 44124/216-442-3188

William Dixon, Buckhorn Gun Works, Rte. 4 Box 1230, Rapid City, SD 57702/605-787-6289

Duncan's Gunworks Inc., 1619 Grand Ave., San Marcos, CA 92069/619-727-0515 (cust.)

David R. Dunlop, Rte. 1, Box 199, Rolla, ND 58367

Jere Eggleston, P.O. Box 50238, Columbia, SC 29250/803-799-3402 (cust.)

Wm. A. Emick, P.O. Box 741, Philipsburg, MT 59858/406-859-3280 (cust.)

Bob Emmons, 238 Robson Road, Grafton, OH 44044 (custom)

Englishtown Sporting Goods Co., Inc., David J. Maxham, 38 Main St., Englishtown, NJ 07726/201-446-7717 (custom)

Ken Eyster Heritage Gunsmiths Inc., 6441 Bishop Rd., Centerburg, OH 43011/614-625-6131 (cust.)

Reinhart Fajen, Box 338, Warsaw, MO 65355/816-438-5111

Ted Fellowes, Beaver Lodge, 9245 16th Ave. S.W., Seattle WA 98106/206-763-1698

Fiberlite, P.O. Box 1027, Houston, TX 77011/800-752-7005 (synthetic)

Fiberpro, 3636 California St., San Diego, CA 92101/619-295-7703 (blanks; fiberglass; Kevlar)

Jerry A. Fisher, 1244-4th Ave. W., Kalispell, MT 59901/406-755-7093

Flaig's Inc., 2200 Evergreen Rd., Millvale, PA 15209/412-821-1717

Flynn's Cust. Guns, P.O. Box 7461, Alexandria, LA 71301/318-455-7130 (cust.)

Donald E. Folks, 205 W. Lincoln St., Pontiac, IL 61764/815-844-7901 (custom trap, Skeet, livebird stocks)

Larry L. Forster, P.O. Box 212, Gwinner, ND 58040/701-678-2475

Fountain Prods., 492 Prospect Ave., W. Springfield, MA 01089 (cust.)

Frank's Custom Rifles, 10420 E. Rusty Spur, Tucson, AZ 85749/602-749-4563

Freeland's Scope Stands, Inc., 3737 14th Ave., Rock Island, IL 61201/309-788-7449

Game Haven Gunstocks, 13750 Shire Rd., Wolverine, MI 49799/616-525-8238 (Kevlar riflestocks)

Jim Garrett, Garrett Accur-Light Inc., 1413 B. E. Olive Ct., Fort Collins, CO 80524/303-224-3067 (fiberglass)

Dale Goens, Box 224, Cedar Crest, NM 87008

Gordie's Gun Shop, Gordon Mulholland, 1401 Fulton St., Streator, IL 61364/815-672-7202 (cust.)

Gary Goudy, 263 Hedge Rd., Menlo Park, CA 94025/415-322-1338 (cust.)

Charles E. Grace, 10144 Elk Lake Rd., Williamsburg, MI 49690/616-264-9483

Roger M. Green & J. Earl Bridges, 315 S. 2d St., P.O. Box 984, Glenrock, WY 82637/307-436-9804 (Teyssier French walnut blanks)

Greene's Machine Carving, 17200 W. 57th Ave., Golden, CO 80403 (blanks & custom)

Griffin & Howe, 589 Broadway, New York, NY 10012/212-966-5323 (custom)

Karl Guenther, 165 Granite Springs Rd. Yorktown Heights, NY 10598/914-245-5610

Guncraft, Inc., 117 W. Pipeline, Hurst, TX 76053/817-282-6481

The Gunworks Inc., John Smallwood, 3434 Maple Ave., Brookfield, IL 60513/312-387-7888 (cust.)

Half Moon Rifle Shop, 490 Halfmoon Rd., Columbia Falls, MT 59912

Rick J. Halstead, 1100 W. Polk Ave., Lovington, NM 88260/505-396-3746

Harper's Custom Stocks, 928 Lombrano St., San Antonio, TX 78207/512-732-5780

Robert W. Hart & Son, Inc., 401 Montgomery St., Nescopeck, PA 18635/717-752-3655 (cust.)

Hubert J. Hecht, Waffen-Hecht, 10112 Fair Oaks Blvd., Fair Oaks, CA 95628/916-966-1020

Edward O. Hefti, 300 Fairview, College Station, TX 77840/409-696-4959

Heppler's Gun Shop, 6000 B Soquel Ave., Santa Cruz, CA 95062/408-475-1235

Warren Heydenberk, 187 W. Sawmill Rd., Rt. 4, Quakertown PA 18951/215-536-0798 (custom)

Doug Hill, 4518 Skyline Place, Enid, OK 73701/405-242-4455 (cust.)

Klaus Hiptmayer, P.O. Box 136, Eastman, Que., J0E 1P0 Canada/514-297-2492

Hoenig & Rodman, 6521 Morton Dr., Boise, ID 83705/208-375-1116 (stock duplicating machine)

Hollis Gun Shop, 917 Rex St., Carlsbad, NM 88220

Paul Jaeger, Inc., P.O. Box 449, 1 Madison Ave., Grand Junction, TN 38039/901-764-6909

Robert L. Jamison, Rt. 4, Box 200, Moses Lake, WA 98837/509-762-2659 (cust.)

J. J. Jenkins Enterprises, Inc., 375 Pine Ave. #25, Goleta, CA 93117/805-967-1366 (custom)

Johnson Wood Products, I.D. Johnson & Sons, Rte. #1, Strawberry Point, IA 52076/319-933-4930 (blanks)

David Kartak, SRS Box 3042, South Beach, OR 97366/503-867-4951 (custom)

Stanley Kenvin, 5 Lakeville Lane, Plainview, NY 11803/516-931-0321 (custom)

Don Klein, P.O. Box 277, Camp Douglas, WI 54618/608-427-6948

Richard Knippel, 825 Stoddard Ave., Modesto, CA 95350

Harry Lawson Co., 3328 N. Richey Blvd., Tucson, AZ 85716/602-326-1117 (cust.)

Frank LeFever Arms & Sons, Inc., R.D.#1, Box 31, Lee Center, NY 13363/315-337-6722

Al Lind, 7821 76th Ave. S. W., Tacoma, WA 98498/206-584-6361 (cust. stockm.)

Ron Long, 81 Delta St., Denver, CO 80221

MPI Stocks, P.O. Box 03266, 7011 N. Reno Ave., Portland, OR 97203/503-289-8025 (fiberglass)

Monte Mandarino, 136 Fifth Ave. West, Kalispell, MT 59901/406-257-6208 (cust.)

Earl K. Matsuoka, 2801 Kinohou Pl., P.O. Box 61129, Honolulu, HI 96822/808-988-3008 (cust.)

Dennis McDonald, Box 3, Peosta, IA 52068

Bill McGuire, 1600 N. Eastmont Ave., East Wenatchee, WA 98801/509-884-6021

Maurer Arms, Carl R. Maurer, 2154-16th St., Akron, OH 44314/216-745-6864

John E. Maxson, 3507 Red Oak Lane, Plainview, TX 79072/806-293-9042 (custom)

R. M. Mercer, 216 S. Whitewater Ave., Jefferson, WI 53549/414-674-3839 (custom)

Robt. U. Milhoan & Son, Rt. 3, Elizabeth, WV 26143

Miller Arms, Inc., D. E. Miller, P.O. Box 260, St. Onge, SD 57779/605-578-1790

Millet Industries, 16131 Gothard St., Huntington Beach, CA 92647/714-842-5575 (fiber-reinforced rifle stocks)

Earl Milliron Custom Guns & Stocks, 1249 N.E. 166th Ave., Portland, OR 97230/503-252-3725

Monell Custom Guns, Red Mill Road, RD#2, Box 96, Pine Bush, NY 12566/914-744-3021 (custom)

J.W. Morrison Custom Rifles, 4015 W. Sharon, Phoenix, AZ 85029

Ted Nicklas, 5504 Hegel Rd., Goodrich, MI 48438/313-797-4493 (custom)

Paul R. Nickels, P.O. Box 71043, Las Vegas, NV 89170/702-458-7149

Jim Norman, Custom Gunstocks, 11230 Calenda Road, San Diego, CA 92127/619-487-4173

Oakley and Merkley, Box 2446, Sacramento, CA 95811 (blanks)

Vic Olson, 5002 Countryside Dr., Imperial, MO 63052/314-296-8086 (custom)

Maurice Ottmar, Box 657, 113 E. Fir, Coulee City, WA 99115/509-632-5717 (cust.)

Pachmayr Gun Works, 1220 S. Grand Ave., Los Angeles, CA 90015 (blanks and custom jobs)

Pasadena Gun Center, 206 E. Shaw, Pasadena, TX 77506/713-472-0417 (cust.)

Paulsen Gunstocks, Rte. 71, Box 11, Chinook, MT 59523/406-357-3403 (blanks)

Don Robinson, Pennsylvania Hse., 36 Fairfax Crescent, Southowram, Halifax, W. Yorksh. HX3 9SW, England (blanks only)

Carl Roth, Jr., 4728 Pineridge Ave., Cheyenne, WY 82001/309-634-3958

Matt Row, Lock, Stock 'N Barrel, 8972 East Huntington Dr., San Gabriel, CA 91775/818-287-0051

Royal Arms, 1210 Bert Acosta, El Cajon, CA 92020/619-448-5466

SDS, P.O. Box 424, Fallbrook, CA 92028/619-584-0577 (commercial)
Sage International Ltd., 1856 Star Batt Dr., Rochester, MI 48063/313-852-8733 (telescoping shotgun stock)
Sanders Cust. Gun Serv., 2358 Tyler Lane, Louisville, KY 40205 (blanks)
Saratoga Arms Co., 1752 N. Pleasantview RD., Pottstown, PA 19464/215-323-8386
Roy Schaefer, 965 W. Hilliard Lane, Eugene, OR 97404/503-688-43333 (blanks)
Schwartz Custom Guns, 9621 Coleman Rd., Haslett, MI 48840/517-339-8939
David W. Schwartz, 2505 Waller St., Eau Claire, WI 54701/715-832-1735 (custom)
Shaw's, The Finest in Guns, 9447 W. Lilac Rd., Escondido, CA 92026/619-728-7070
Dan A. Sherk, 1311-105th Ave., Dawson Creek, B.C. V1G 2L9, Canada/604-782-3720 (custom)
Hank Shows, The Best,1078 Alice Ave., Ukiah, CA 95482/707-462-9060
Walter Shultz, 1752 N. Pleasantview Rd., Pottstown, PA 19464
Sile Dist., 7 Centre Market Pl., New York, NY 10013/213-925-4111
Six Enterprises, 6564 Hidden Creek Dr., San Jose, CA 95120/408-268-8296 (fiberglass)
Ed Sowers, 8331 DeCelis Pl., Sepulveda, CA 91343/818-893-1233 (custom hydro-coil gunstocks)
Fred D. Speiser, 2229 Dearborn, Missoula, MT 59801/406-549-8133
Sport Service Center, 2364 N. Neva, Chicago, IL 60635/312-889-1114 (custom)
Sportsmen's Equip. Co., 915 W. Washington, San Diego, CA 92103/714-296-1501 (carbine conversions)
Keith Stegall, Box 696, Gunnison, CO 81230
Talmage Enterpr., 43197 E. Whittier, Hemet, CA 92344/714-927-2397
James C. Tucker, 205 Trinity St., Woodland, CA 95695/916-662-3109 (cust.)
Milton van Epps, Rt. 69-A, Parish, NY 13131/315-625-7251
Gil van Horn, P.O. Box 207, Llano, CA 93544
John Vest, P.O. Box 1552, Susanville, CA 96130/916-253-3681 (classic rifles)
R. D. Wallace, Star Rt. Box 76, Grandin, MO 63943/314-593-4773 (cust.)
Weatherby's, 2781 Firestone, South Gate, CA 90280/213-569-7186
Cecil Weems, P.O. Box 657, Mineral Wells, TX 76067/817-325-1462
Frank R. Wells, 10420 E. Rusty Spur, Tucson, AZ 85749/602-749-4563 (custom stocks)
Fred Wells, Wells Sport Store, 110 N. Summit St., Prescott, AZ 86301/602-445-3655
Terry Werth, 1203 Woodlawn Rd., Lincoln, IL 62656/217-732-9314 (cust.)
Western Gunstocks Mfg. Co., 550 Valencia School Rd., Aptos, CA 95003
Duane Wiebe, P.O. Box 497, Lotus, CA 95651
Bob Williams, P.O. Box 143, Boonsboro, MD 21713
Williamson-Pate Gunsmith Service, 117 W. Pipeline, Hurst, TX 76053/817-268-2887
Jim Windish, 2510 Dawn Dr., Alexandria, VA 22306/703-765-1994 (walnut blanks)
Dave Wills, 2776 Brevard Ave., Montgomery, AL 36109/305-272-8446
Robert M. Winter, R.R. 2, Box 484, Menno, SD 57045/605-387-5322
Mike Yee, 29927-56 Pl. S., Auburn, WA 98001/206-839-3991
Russell R. Zeeryp, 1601 Foard Dr., Lynn Ross Manor, Morristown, TN 37814
Dean A. Zollinger, Rt. 2, Box 135-A, Rexburg, ID 83440/208-356-6167

## TARGETS, BULLET & CLAYBIRD TRAPS

Amacker Products Inc., P.O. Box 1432, Tallulah, LA 71282/318-574-4903
Beeman Inc., 47-GDD Paul Dr., San Rafael, CA 94903/415-472-7121 (airgun targets, silhouettes and traps)
Bulletboard Target Systems Laminations Corp., Box 469, Neenah, WI 54956/414-725-8368
Caswell International Corp. Inc., 1221 Marshall St. N.E., Minneapolis, MN 55413/612-379-2000 (target carriers; commercial shooting ranges)
J.G. Dapkus Co., P.O. Box 180, Cromwell, CT 06416/203-632-2308 (live bullseye targets)
Data-Targ, (See Rocky Mountain Target Co.)
Detroit-Armor Corp., Detroit Bullet Trap Div., 2233 N. Palmer Dr., Schaumburg, IL 60195/312-397-4070 (Shooting Ranges)
The Dutchman's Firearms Inc., 4143 Taylor Blvd., Louisville, KY 40215/502-366-0555
Electro Ballistic Lab., 616 Junipero Serva Blvd., Stanford, CA 94305 (Electronic Trap Boy)
Ellwood Epps Northern Ltd., 210 Worthington St., W., North Bay, Ont. P1B 3B4, Canada (hand traps)
Hunterjohn, P.O. Box 477, St. Louis, MO 63166 (shotgun patterning target)
Jaro Manuf., 206 E. Shaw, Pasadena, TX 77506/713-472-0417 (paper targets)
Laminations Corp. ("Bullettrap"), Box 469, Neenah, WI 54956/414-725-8368
Millard F. Lerch, Box 163, 10842 Front St., Mokena, IL 60448 (bullet target)
MCM (Mathalienne de Construction de Mecanique), P.O. Box 18, 17160 Matha, France (claybird traps)
MTM Molded Prods. Co., 3370 Obco Ct., Dayton, OH 45414/513-890-7461
Outers Laboratories, Div. of Omark Industries, Rte. 2, Onalaska, WI 54650/608-783-1515 (claybird traps)
Peterson Label Co., P.O. Box 186, 23 Sullivan Dr., Redding Ridge, CT 06876/203-938-2349 (paste-ons; Targ-Dots)
Remington Arms Co., 1007 Market St., Wilmington, DE 19898 (claybird traps)
Rocky Mountain Target Co., P.O. Box 700, Black Hawk, SD 57718/605-787-5946 (Data-Targ)
Julio Santiago, P.O. Box O, Rosemount, MN 55068/612-890-7631 (targets)
Sheridan Products, Inc., 3205 Sheridan, Racine, WI 54303 (traps)
Trius Prod., Box 25, Cleves, OH 45002/513-914-5682 (claybird, can thrower)
U.S. Repeating Arms Co., P.O. Box 30-300, New Haven, CT 06511/203-789-5000 (claybird traps)
Winchester, Olin Corp., 120 Long Ridge Rd., Stamford, CT 06904

## TAXIDERMY

Jack Atcheson & Sons, Inc., 3210 Ottawa St., Butte, MT. 59701
Dough's Taxidermy Studio, Doug Domedion, 5112 Edwards Rd., Medina, NY 14103/716-798-4022 (deer head specialist)
Jonas Bros., Inc., 1037 Broadway, Denver, CO 80203 (catlg. $2)
Kulis Freeze-Dry Taxidermy, 725 Broadway Ave., Bedford, OH 44146
Mark D. Parker, 1233 Sherman Dr., Longmont, CO 80501/303-772-0214

## TRAP & SKEET SHOOTERS EQUIP.

A.C. Enterprises, P.O. Box 448, Edenton, NC 27932/919-482-4992
Bob Allen Companies, 214 S.W. Jackson, Des Moines, IA 50315/515-283-2191
The American Import Co., 1453 Mission St., San Francisco, CA 94103/415-863-1506 (Targetthrower)
Anton Custom Gunstocks, Paul D. Hillmer, 7251 Hudson Heights, Hudson, IA 50643/319-988-3941
C&H Research, 115 Sunnyside Dr., Lewis, KS 67552/316-324-5445 (Mercury recoil suppressor)
D&H Prods. Co., Inc., 465 Denny Rd., Valencia, PA 16059/412-898-2840 (snap shell)
Frigon Guns, 627 W. Crawford, Clay Center, KS 67432/913-632-5607
Griggs Recreational Prods. Inc., P.O. Box 789, Bountiful, UT 84010/801-295-9696 (recoil redirector)
Ken Eyster Heritage Gunsmiths, Inc., 6441 Bishop Rd., Centerburg, OH 43011/614-625-6131 (shotgun competition choking)
Hoppe Division, Penguin Inds. Inc., Airport Mall, Coatesville, PA 19320/215-384-6000 (Monte Carlo pad)
Hunter Co., Inc., 3300 W. 71st Ave., Westminster, CO 80030/303-427-4626
Ljutic Industries Inc., P.O. Box 2117; 732 N 16th Ave., Yakima, WA 98907/509-248-0476
MCM (Mathalienne de Construction de Mecanique), P.O. Box 18, 17160 Matha, France (claybird traps)
Meadow Industries, P.O. Box 450, Marlton, NJ 08053/609-953-0922 (stock pad, variable; muzzle rest)
Wm. J. Mittler, 290 Moore Dr., Boulder Creek, CA 95006 (shotgun choke specialist)
Moneymaker Guncraft, 1420 Military Ave., Omaha, NE 68131/402-556-0226 (free-floating, ventilated ribs)
Multi-Gauge Enterprises, 433 W. Foothill Blvd., Monrovia, CA 91061/213-358-4549; 357-6117 (shotgun specialists)
William J. Nittler, 290 Moore Dr., Boulder Creek, CA 95006/408-338-3376 (shotgun barrel repairs)
Outers Laboratories, Div. of Omark Industries, Route 2, Onalaska, WI 54650/608-783-1515 (trap, claybird)
Purbaugh & Sons (See Multi-Gauge) (shotgun barrel inserts)
Remington Arms Co., P.O. Box 1939, Bridgeport, Ct. 06601 (trap, claybird)
Daniel Titus, Shooting Specialties, 872 Penn St., Bryn Mawr, PA 19010/215-525-8829 (hullbag)
Trius Products, Box 25, Cleves, OH 45002/513-941-5682 (can thrower; trap, claybird)
Winchester-Western, New Haven, CT 06504 (trap, claybird)

## TRIGGERS, RELATED EQUIP.

Ametek, Hunter Spring Div., One Spring Ave., Hatfield, PA 19440/215-822-2971 (trigger gauge)
NOC, Cadillac Industrial Park, 1610 Corwin St., Cadillac, MI 49601/616-775-3425 (triggers)
M.H. Canjar Co., 500 E. 45th Ave., Denver, CO 80216/303-295-2638 (triggers)
Central Specialties Co., 200 Lexington Dr., Buffalo Grove, IL 60090/312-537-3300 (trigger locks only)
Crown City Arms, Inc., P.O. Box 550, Cortland, NY 13045/607-753-8238
Custom Products, Neil A. Jones, RD #1, Box 483A, Saegertown, PA 16433/814-763-2769 (trigger guard)
Dayton-Traister Co., 9322-900th West, P.O. Box 593, Oak Harbor, WA 98277/206-675-5375 (triggers)
Electronic Trigger Systems, 4124 Thrushwood Lane, Minnetonka, MN 55345/612-935-7829
Flaig's, 2200 Evergreen Rd., Millvale, PA 15209/412-821-1717 (trigger shoes)
Bill Holmes, Rt. 2, Box 242, Fayetteville, AR 72701/501-521-8958 (trigger release)
Neil A. Jones, see: Custom Products
Mad River Metalcraft Inc., 1524 Winding Trail, Springfield, OH 45503/513-399-0948 (bolt shroud safety)
Michaels of Oregon Co., P.O. Box 13010, Portland, OR 97213/503-255-6890 (trigger guards)
Miller Single Trigger Mfg. Co., R.D. 1, Box 99, Millersburg, PA 17061/717-692-3704
Bruce A. Nettestad, Rt. 1, Box 140, Pelican Rapids, MN 56572/218-863-4301 (trigger guards)
Ohaus Corp., 29 Hanover Rd., Florham Park, NJ 07932 (trigger pull gauge)
Pachmayr Gun Works, 1220 S. Grand Ave., Los Angeles, CA 90015 (trigger shoe)
Pacific Tool Co., P.O. Box 2048, Ordnance Plant Rd., Grand Island, NE 68801 (trigger shoe)
Richland Arms Co., 321 W. Adrian St., Blissfield, MI 49228 (trigger pull gauge)
Serrifile Inc., P.O. Box 508, Littlerock, CA 93543/805-945-0713
Timney Mfg. Co., 3106 W. Thomas Rd., Suite 1104, Phoenix, AZ 85017/602-269-6937 (triggers)
Melvin Tyler, 1326 W. Britton Rd., Oklahoma City, OK 73114/800-654-8415 (trigger shoe)
Williams Gun Sight Co., 7389 Lapeer Rd., Davison, MI 48423 (trigger shoe)